Introduction to
Psychology 12e

James W. Kalat

North Carolina State University

CENGAGE

Australia · Brazil · Canada · Mexico · Singapore · United Kingdom · United States

Introduction to Psychology, **Twelfth Edition**
James W. Kalat

SVP, Higher Education & Skills Product: Erin Joyner

VP, Higher Education & Skills Product: Thais Alencar

Product Director: Laura Ross

Product Manager: Colin Grover

Product Assistant: Jessica Witzak

Learning Designer: Natasha Allen

Content Manager: Tangelique Williams-Grayer

Digital Delivery Lead: Allison Marion

Director, Marketing: Neena Bali

Marketing Manager: Tricia Salata

IP Analyst: Deanna Ettinger

IP Project Manager: Kelli Besse

Production Service: MPS Limited

Art Director: Chris Doughman, Bethany Bourgeois

Cover Image Source: iStockPhoto.com/ ChrisHepburn

For product information and technology assistance, contact us at
Cengage Customer & Sales Support, 1-800-354-9706
or **support.cengage.com**.

For permission to use material from this text or product,
submit all requests online at **www.cengage.com/permissions**.

Library of Congress Control Number: 2020913920

Student Edition:
ISBN: 978-0-357-37272-2

Loose-leaf Edition:
ISBN: 978-0-357-37279-1

Cengage
200 Pier 4 Boulevard
Boston, MA 02210
USA

Cengage is a leading provider of customized learning solutions with employees residing in nearly 40 different countries and sales in more than 125 countries around the world. Find your local representative at **www.cengage.com**.

To learn more about Cengage platforms and services, register or access your online learning solution, or purchase materials for your course, visit **www.cengage.com**.

Printed in the United States of America
Print Number: 01   Print Year: 2021

To my wife, Jo Kalat

JAMES W. KALAT (rhymes with ballot) is Professor Emeritus at North Carolina State University, where he taught Introduction to Psychology and Biological Psychology for 35 years. Born in 1946, he received an AB degree summa cum laude from Duke University in 1968 and a PhD in psychology in 1971 from the University of Pennsylvania, under the supervision of Paul Rozin. He is also the author of *Biological Psychology*, 13th edition (Cengage, 2019), and coauthor with Michelle N. Shiota of *Emotion*, 3rd edition (Oxford University Press, 2018). In addition to textbooks, he has written journal articles on taste-aversion learning, the teaching of psychology, and other topics. A remarried widower, he has three children, two stepsons, and five grandchildren. When not working on something related to psychology, his hobby is bird-watching.

brief contents

contents

3 Biological Psychology 53

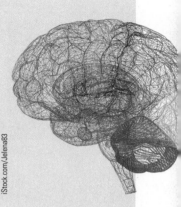

iStock.com/Jelena83

4 Sensation and Perception 95

Christoph Hetzmannseder/Moment/Getty Images

iStock.com/Rich Legg

Nolte Lourens/Shutterstock.com

Chinnapong/Shutterstock.com

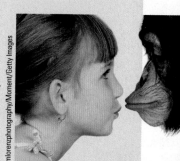

mlorenzphotography/Moment/Getty Images

15 Abnormal Psychology: Disorders and Treatment 477

iStock.com/SDI Productions

Some years ago, I was on a plane that had to turn around shortly after takeoff because one of its two engines had failed. When we were told to get into crash position, the first thing I thought was, "I don't want to die yet! I was looking forward to writing the next edition of my textbook!" True story.

I remember taking my first course in psychology. Frequently, I would describe something I had just learned to my roommate, friends, or relatives. I haven't changed much since then. When I read about interesting new research, I want to tell someone. Psychology is fun. During my 35 years of teaching at North Carolina State University, I would often wake up in the morning and think, "Wow! I get to teach about optical illusions today!" or "Great! Today's topic is emotions!" Do professors in other fields enjoy teaching so much? Does someone in the French department wake up thinking how exciting it will be to teach about adverbs today? I doubt it.

Ideally, a course or textbook in psychology should accomplish two goals. The first is to instill a love of learning so that our graduates will continue to update their education. Even if students permanently remembered everything they learned—and of course they won't—their understanding would gradually go out of date unless they continue to learn about new developments. The second goal is to teach students the skills of evaluating evidence and questioning assertions, so that when they do read about some new research, they will ask the right questions before drawing a conclusion. That skill can carry over to fields other than psychology.

Throughout this text, I have tried to model the habit of critical thinking or evaluating the evidence, particularly in the **What's the Evidence?** features that describe research studies in some detail. I have pointed out the limitations of the evidence and the possibilities for alternative interpretations. The goal is to help students ask their own questions, distinguish between good and weak evidence, and ultimately, appreciate the excitement of psychological inquiry.

Approaches, Features, and Student Aids

Many years ago, I read an educational psychology textbook that said children with learning disabilities and attention problems learn best from specific, concrete examples. I remember thinking, "Wait a minute. I do, too! Don't we *all* learn best from specific, concrete examples?" For this reason, science classes use laboratories to let students see for themselves. Few introductory psychology classes offer laboratories, but we can nevertheless encourage students to try procedures that require little or no equipment. At various points, the text describes **Try It Yourself** exercises, such as negative afterimages, binocular rivalry, encoding specificity, and the Stroop effect. Students who try these activities will understand and remember the concepts far better than if they merely read about them.

Cognitive psychology researchers find that we learn more if we alternate between reading and testing than if we spend the same amount of time reading. The **Concept Checks** pose questions that attentive readers should be able to answer. Students who answer correctly can feel encouraged. Those who miss a question should use the feedback to reread the relevant passages.

Each chapter of this text has two to five modules, each with its own summary, key terms, and review questions. Modules provide flexibility for instructors who wish to take sections in a different order, or who wish to omit a section. Modular format also breaks up the reading assignments so that students read one or two modules for each class. At the end of the text, a combined Subject Index and Glossary define key terms and provide page references.

The technology of education changed only a little from the invention of chalk until the late twentieth century. Today, however, wonderful new technologies are available. MindTap for *Introduction to Psychology* includes an eBook, special Concept Checks for each section, Chapter Quizzes, and more!

What's New in the Twelfth Edition

The most prominent development in psychology over the last decade has been the increased interest in replication and careful research design. The eleventh edition already discussed the replication issue, and this edition increases the emphasis. Also, several studies that the previous edition discussed had to be eliminated because they appear to be non-replicable, and a couple others are mentioned, but described as uncertain because of inconsistent replications. This edition also introduces the methodological problems of HARKing (hypothesizing after results are known) and *p*-hacking (re-analyzing results until one finds a way for *p* to appear significant).

One notable change in the overall organization is that discussion of behaviorism is now in Chapter 6 (learning) instead of Chapter 1 (introduction). Another is the introduction of a new section about conspiracy thinking, in Chapter 8. Chapter 9 has a new section about the relationship between brain size and intelligence. When we compare species, an issue has been why humans are (in our opinion, anyway) the most intelligent, although other species have a larger brain or a larger brain-to-body ratio. We now have an answer: Humans have the largest number of neurons. Chapter 11 raises the difficult, unanswered question about how to rear children who think they might be transgender. Chapter 12 has a new section about ways to facilitate forgetting of a traumatic experience. Chapter 13 introduces "nudges" as a means of persuasion. One more major change: The reference list at the end of the book conforms to the new APA style, including web sites where available, and (by APA's insistence) up to 20 authors per article. Yeah, all those students who care about the names of the 19th and 20th authors of an article will be so pleased.

The content of this text has been brought up to date in many ways. Here are a few of my favorite new studies:

- It was previously shown that acetaminophen can reduce hurt feelings. A new study found that it also reduces pleasure. Evidently it reduces overall emotional responsiveness. (Chapter 4)
- Yes, water does have a taste, not just a texture on the tongue. Water changes the response pattern of sourness receptors. (Chapter 4)
- Adolescents take greater risks in the presence of their peers, and fewer risks if their mothers are watching. (Chapter 5)
- An eyewitness's degree of confidence about an identification correlates with accuracy at the time of initial response, although confidence at the time of a trial does not (because of contamination by feedback from police and others). (Chapter 7)
- When you describe what you remember of some event, you strengthen your memory of the aspects that you describe, but you weaken your memory of aspects you did not mention. This tendency is called retrieval-induced forgetting. (Chapter 7)
- When people regard themselves as highly competent on a topic, they tend to exaggerate that competence. For example, many people who call themselves well informed about

personal finance will rate themselves highly on understanding "pre-rated stocks" and "fixed rate deduction," which are meaningless terms that an experimenter threw in to test them. (Chapter 8)
- Stereotype threat affects old people in a special way. Old people are not worried about defending their group from the stereotype of poor memory. (They generally agree that the stereotype is true.) They are simply worried that they themselves might fit the stereotype. (Chapter 9)
- The famous story about "38 silent witnesses" to the Kitty Genovese story was apparently planted by police to distract attention from their dubious prosecution of an innocent defendant in another case. (Chapter 13)
- Sherif's famous "Robbers Cave" study failed to report several ways in which the "counselors" (experimenters) rigged the procedures to encourage hostility between the two groups. (Chapter 13)
- Ordinarily, romantic couples resemble each other in physical attractiveness, but an exception arises for couples who were friends for years before they started dating. (Chapter 13)
- Most American college students accept the "belief in a just world" for themselves more than for people in general. (Chapter 14)
- Nearly half a century ago, parents reported that children with autism acted more normally when they had a fever. Now, finally, we have an explanation for why this is so. (Chapter 15)

In addition to the throughly updated text, the Test Bank has been revised. Written by the author himself, the test bank for *Introduction to Psychology* consists of more than 3,700 new or reworded items, with an emphasis on clarity. Nearly all items are worded in the form of a question, and none of them include an "all of the above" or "none of the above" choice. The test bank also includes a special file of items that cut across chapters intended for inclusion on a comprehensive final exam. See the Instructor Resources section for more details.

MindTap

MindTap: Empower Your Students

MindTap is a platform that propels students from memorization to mastery. It gives you complete control of your course, so you can provide engaging content, challenge every learner, and build student confidence. Customize interactive syllabi to emphasize priority topics, then add your own material or notes to the eBook as desired. This outcomes-driven application gives you the tools needed to empower students and boost both understanding and performance.

Access Everything You Need in One Place

Cut down on prep with the preloaded and organized MindTap course materials. Teach more efficiently with interactive multimedia, assignments, quizzes, and more. Give your students the power to read, listen, and study on their phones, so they can learn on their terms.

Control Your Course—and Your Content

Get the flexibility to reorder textbook chapters, add your own notes, and embed a variety of content including Open Educational Resources (OER). Personalize course content to your students' needs. They can even read your notes, add their own, and highlight key text to aid their learning.

Get a Dedicated Team, Whenever You Need Them

MindTap isn't just a tool, it's backed by a personalized team eager to support you. We can help set up your course and tailor it to your specific objectives, so you'll be ready to make an impact from day one. Know we'll be standing by to help you and your students until the final day of the term.

Instructor Resources

Additional instructor resources for this product are available online. Instructor assets include an Instructor's Manual, Educator's Guide, PowerPoint® slides, and a test bank powered by Cognero®. Sign up or sign in at **www.cengage.com** to search for and access this product and its online resources.

Acknowledgments

The authorship of this text may have only one name, but a great many people contributed to making it far better than it would have been, beginning with my first editor and long-time friend, Ken King, and continuing with so many others.

For this edition, my acquisitions editor, Colin Grover, has been helpful, supportive, and wise. I have been delighted to work with Tangelique Williams-Grayer, my content manager, who supervised the whole process. Lori Hazzard, my project manager, painstakingly checked every detail. Nisha Bhanu Beegum located new photographs to use throughout the text. I thank them for their tireless help.

Art Directors Bethany Bourgeious and Chris Doughman, who designed the cover and interior, had the patience and artistic judgment to counterbalance this very nonartistic author. Tricia Salata, Marketing Manager, planned and executed the marketing strategies. Kelli Besse and Lumina Datamatics skillfully researched and managed the permissions requests. To each of these, my thanks and congratulations. My wife, Jo Ellen Kalat, not only provided support and encouragement but also listened to my attempts to explain concepts and offered many helpful suggestions and questions.

Many reviewers provided helpful and insightful comments. Each edition builds on contributions from reviewers of previous editions. I would like to thank the following reviewers who contributed their insight to one or more editions:

Jennifer Ackil, Gustavus Adolphus College; Jeffrey Adams, Trent University; Judi Addelston, Valencia College; Mark Affeltranger, University of Pittsburgh; Catherine Sanderson, Amherst College; Susan Anderson, University of South Alabama; Bob Arkin, Ohio State University; Melanie M. Arpaio, Sussex County Community College; Susan Baillet, University of Portland; Cynthia Bane, Denison University; Joe Bean, Shorter University; Mark Bodamer, Gonzaga University; Richard W. Bowen, Loyola University Chicago; Rebecca Brand, Villanova University; Michael Brislawn, Bellevue College; Delbert Brodie, St. Thomas University; John Broida, University of Southern Maine; Thomas Brothen, University of Minnesota; Gordon Brown, Pasadena City College; Gregory Bushman, Beloit College; James Calhoun, University of Georgia; Bernardo Carducci, Indiana University Southeast; Thomas Carskadon, Mississippi State University; Mark Casteel, Pennsylvania State University, York Campus; Liz Coccia, Austin Community College; Carolyn Cohen, Northern Essex Community College; Karen Couture, Keene State College; Alex Czopp, Western Washington University; Deana Davalos, Colorado State University; Patricia Deldin, University of Michigan; Katherine Demitrakis, Central New Mexico Community College; Janet Dizinno, St. Mary University; Alicia M. Doerflinger, Marietta College; Karen Douglas, San Antonio College–Alamo Colleges; Kimberly Duff, Cerritos College; Darlene Earley-Hereford, Southern Union State Community College; David J. Echevarria, University of Southern Mississippi; Vanessa Edkins, University of Kansas; Susan Field, Georgian Court University; Deborah Frisch, University of Oregon; Gabriel Frommer, Indiana University; Rick Fry, Youngstown State University; Robert Gehring, University of Southern Indiana; Judy Gentry, Columbus State Community College; Anna L. Ghee, Xavier University; Bill P. Godsil, Santa Monica College; Kerri Goodwin, Loyola University in Maryland; Joel Grace, Mansfield University; Troianne Grayson, Florida Community

College at Jacksonville; Joe Grisham, Indian River State College; Julie A. Gurner, Quinnipiac University; Alexandria E. Guzmán, University of New Haven; Richard Hanson, Fresno City College; Richard Harris, Kansas State University; Wendy Hart-Stravers, Arizona State University; W. Bruce Haslam, Weber State University; Christopher Hayashi, Southwestern College; Bert Hayslip, University of North Texas; Manda Helzer, Southern Oregon University; W. Elaine Hogan, University of North Carolina Wilmington; Debra Hollister, Valencia College; Susan Horton, Mesa Community College; Charles Huffman, James Madison University; Linda Jackson, Michigan State University; Alisha Janowsky, University of Central Florida; Robert Jensen, California State University, Sacramento; Andrew Johnson, Park University; James Johnson, Illinois State University; Craig Jones, Arkansas State University; Lisa Jordan, University of Maryland; Dale Jorgenson, California State University, Long Beach; Jon Kahane, Springfield College; Peter Kaplan, University of Colorado, Denver; Arthur Kemp, University of Central Missouri; Mark J. Kirschner, Quinnipiac University; Kristina T. Klassen, North Idaho College; Martha Kuehn, Central Lakes College; Cindy J. Lahar, University of Calgary; Chris Layne, University of Toledo; Cynthia Ann Lease, Virginia Polytechnic Institute and State University; Chantal Levesque, University of Rochester; John Lindsay, Georgia College and State University; Mary Livingston, Louisiana Tech University; Linda Lockwood, Metropolitan State College of Denver; Sanford Lopater, Christopher Newport University; Mark Ludorf, Stephen F. Austin State University; Jonathan Lytle, Temple University; Pamelyn M. MacDonald, Washburn University; Steve Madigan, University of Southern California; Don Marzolf, Louisiana State University; Christopher Mayhorn, North Carolina State University; Michael McCall, Ithaca College; David G. McDonald, University of Missouri; Tracy A. McDonough, Mount St. Joseph University; J. Mark McKellop, Juniata College; Mary Meiners, San Diego Miramar College; Diane Mello-Goldner, Pine Manor College; Nancy J. Melucci, Long Beach City College; Michelle Merwin, University of Tennessee at Martin; Rowland Miller, Sam Houston State University; Gloria Mitchell, De Anza College; Paul Moore, Quinnipiac University; Anne Moyer, Stony Brook University; Jeffrey Nagelbush, Ferris State University; Bethany Neal-Beliveau, Indiana University-Purdue University at Indianapolis; Todd Nelson, California State University, Stanislaus; Jan Ochman, Inver Hills Community College; Wendy Palmquist, Plymouth State University; Elizabeth Parks, Kennesaw State University; Gerald Peterson, Saginaw Valley State University; Brady Phelps, South Dakota State University; Shane Pitts, Birmingham-Southern College; William Price, North Country Community College; Thomas Reig, Winona State University; David Reitman, Louisiana State University; Bridget Rivera, Loyola University in Maryland; Robert A. Rosellini, University at Albany; Jeffrey Rudski, Muhlenberg College; Linda Ruehlman, Arizona State University; Richard Russell, Santa Monica College; Mark Samuels, New Mexico Institute of Mining and Technology; Kim Sawrey, University of North Carolina at Wilmington; Troy Schiedenhelm, Rowan-Cabarrus Community College; Michelle N. Shiota, University of California, Berkeley; Eileen Smith, Fairleigh Dickinson University; Noam Shpancer, Otterbein University; James Spencer, West Virginia State University; Jim Stringham, University of Georgia; Robert Stawski, Syracuse University; Whitney Sweeney, Beloit College; Alan Swinkels, St. Edward's University; Natasha Tokowicz, University of Pittsburgh; Patricia Toney, Sandhills Community College; Terry Trepper, Purdue University Calumet; Warren W. Tryon, Fordham University; Katherine Urquhart, Lake Sumter Community College; Stavros Valenti, Hofstra University; Suzanne Valentine-French, College of Lake County; Douglas Wallen, Minnesota State University, Mankato; Michael Walraven, Jackson College; Donald Walter, University of Wisconsin–Parkside; Jeffrey Weatherly, University of North Dakota; Ellen Weissblum, State University of New York Albany; Fred Whitford, Montana State University; Don Wilson, Lane Community College; David Woehr, Texas A&M University; Jay Wright, Washington State University; John W. Wright, Washington State University.

James W. Kalat

Welcome to introductory psychology! I hope you will enjoy reading this text as much as I enjoyed writing it. I have tried to make this book interesting and easy to study.

Features of This Text

Modular Format

Each chapter is divided into two or more modules so that you can study a limited section at a time. Each chapter begins with a table of contents and a list of learning objectives. At the end of each module is a summary of important points, a list of key terms, and a few multiple-choice questions. Although the multiple-choice questions are listed at the end, you may find it a good strategy to try answering them before you read the module. Trying the questions at the start will prime you to pay attention to those topics. Do not assume that the summary points and the review questions include everything you should learn! They are only a sampling.

Key Terms

When an important term first appears in the text, it is highlighted in **boldface** and defined in *italics*. All the boldface terms are listed alphabetically at the end of each module. They appear again with definitions in the combined Subject Index and Glossary at the end of the book. You might want to find the Subject Index and Glossary right now and familiarize yourself with it.

I sometimes meet students who think they have mastered the course because they have memorized the definitions. The title of the course is "psychology," not "vocabulary." You do need to understand the defined words, but don't memorize the definitions word for word. It would be better to try to think of examples of each term. Better yet, when appropriate, think about the evidence relating to the concept.

Questions to Check Your Understanding

People remember material better if they alternate between reading and testing than if they spend the whole time reading. We consider that point again in the chapter on memory. At various points in this text are Concept Checks, questions that ask you to use or apply the information you just read. Try to answer each of them before reading the answer. If your answer is correct, you can feel encouraged. If it is incorrect, you should reread the section.

Try It Yourself Activities

The text includes many items marked "Try It Yourself." Most of these can be done quickly with little or no equipment. The description of a psychological principle will be easier to understand and remember after you have experienced it yourself.

"What's the Evidence?" Features

With the exception of the introductory chapter, every chapter includes a section titled "What's the Evidence?" These features highlight research studies in more detail, specifying the hypothesis (idea being tested), research methods, results, and interpretation. In some cases, the discussion also mentions the limitations of the study. These sections provide examples of how to evaluate evidence.

Indexes and Reference List

A section at the back of the book lists the references cited in the text in case you want to check something for more details. The references include websites where available. The combined Subject Index and Glossary defines key terms and indicates where in the book to find more information. The name index provides the same information for all names mentioned in the text.

Answers to Some Frequently Asked Questions

Do you have any useful suggestions for improving study habits? Whenever students ask me why they did badly on the last test, I ask, "When did you read the assignments?" A common answer is that they read everything the night before the test. If you want to learn the subject matter well, read the assigned material before the lecture, review it after the lecture, and quickly go over it again a few days later. Then reread the textbook assignments and your lecture notes before a test. Memory researchers have established that you will understand and remember something better by studying it several times spread out over days than by studying the same amount of time all at once. Also, of course, the more times you review the material, the better.

When you study, don't just read the text but stop and think about it. The more actively you use the material, the better you will remember it. One way to improve your studying is to read by the SPAR method: **S**urvey, **P**rocess meaningfully, **A**sk questions, **R**eview.

Survey: Know what to expect so that you can focus on the main points. When you start a module, first look over the learning objectives. It also helps if you turn to the end and read the summary and try to answer the review questions.

Process meaningfully: Read the chapter carefully, stopping to think from time to time. Tell someone about something you learned. Think about how you might apply a concept to a real-life situation. Pause when you come to the Concept Checks and try to answer them. Do the Try It Yourself exercises. Try to monitor how well you understand the text and adjust your reading accordingly. Good readers pause frequently to think about what they have read.

Ask questions: When you finish the chapter, try to anticipate what questions your instructor would ask on a test. What questions would you ask if you were the professor? Write out the questions, think about them, and hold them for later.

Review: Pause for at least an hour, and then return to your questions and try to answer them. Check your answers against the text. Reinforcing your memory after you first read the chapter will help you retain the material longer and deepen your understanding. If you study the same material several times at lengthy intervals, you increase your chance of remembering it long after the course is over.

What do those parentheses mean, as in "(Shallice, 2019)"? Am I supposed to remember the names and dates? Psychologists generally cite references in the text in parentheses rather than in footnotes. "(Shallice, 2019)" refers to an article written by Shallice, published in 2019. All the references cited in the text are listed in alphabetical order by the author's last name in the References section at the back of the book. You will also notice a few citations that include two dates separated by a slash, such as "(Wundt, 1862/1961)." This means that Wundt's document was originally published in 1862 and was republished in 1961. No, you should not memorize the parenthetical source citations. They are provided so interested readers can look up the source of a statement and check for further information. The few names that *are* worth remembering, such as B. F. Skinner, Jean Piaget, and Sigmund Freud, are emphasized in the discussion itself.

Can you help me read and understand graphs? You will encounter four kinds of graphs in this text:

pie graphs, bar graphs, line graphs, and scatter plots. Let's look at each kind.

A pie graph shows the components of a whole. Figure 1 shows the proportion of psychologists who work in various settings.

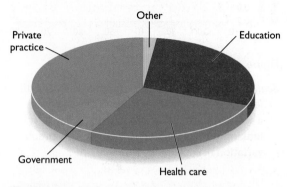

Figure 1

Bar graphs show measurements for two or more groups. Figure 2 shows how much unpleasantness three groups of women reported while they were waiting for a painful shock. The unpleasantness was least if a woman could hold her husband's hand while waiting, intermediate if she held a stranger's hand, and most if she was by herself.

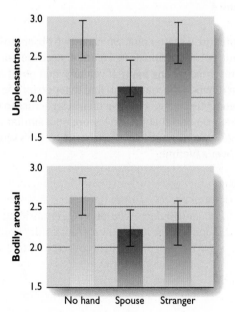

Figure 2

Line graphs show how one variable relates to another variable. Figure 3 shows measurements of conscientiousness in people from age 10 to 80. The upward slope of the line indicates that older people tend to be more conscientious than younger people, on average.

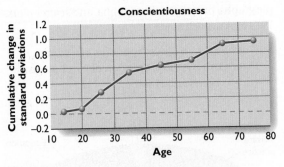

Figure 3

Scatter plots are similar to line graphs, with this difference: A line graph shows averages, whereas a scatter plot shows individual data points. By looking at a scatter plot, we can see how much variation occurs among individuals.

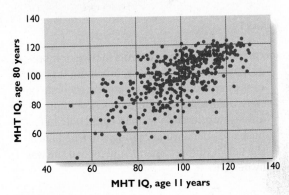

Figure 4

To prepare a scatter plot, we make two observations about each individual. In Figure 4, each person is represented by one point. If you take that point and scan down to the *x*-axis, you find that person's score on an IQ test at age 11. If you then scan across to the *y*-axis, you find that person's score on a similar test at age 80. You can see how consistent people's scores are over a lifetime.

We may have to take multiple-choice tests on this material. How can I do better on those tests?

1. Read each choice carefully. Do not choose the first answer that looks correct because a later answer might be better.
2. If you don't know the correct answer, make an educated guess. An answer that includes absolute words such as "always" or "never" is probably wrong. If you have never heard of something, it is probably not the right answer. Remember, every test question is about something presented either in lecture or in the text.
3. After you finish, don't be afraid to go back and reconsider your answers. Students have been telling each other for decades that "you should stick with your first answer," but research says that most people who change their answers improve their scores. When you examine a question a second time, you sometimes discover that you misunderstood it the first time.

Last Words Before We Start . . .

Most of all, I hope you enjoy the text. I have tried to include the liveliest examples I can find. The goal is not just to teach you some facts but also to teach you a love of learning so that you will continue to read more and educate yourself about psychology long after your course is over.

James W. Kalat

1 | What Is Psychology?

iStock.com/bymraftdeniz

Even when the people we trust seem very confident of their opinions, we should examine their evidence or reasoning.

If you are like most students, you start off assuming that nearly everything you read in your textbooks and everything your professors tell you must be true. What if it isn't? Suppose impostors have replaced your college's faculty. They pretend to know what they are talking about and they all vouch for one another's competence, but in fact, they are all unqualified. They managed to find textbooks that support their prejudices, but those textbooks are full of false information, too. If so, how would you know?

While we are entertaining such skeptical thoughts, why limit ourselves to colleges? When you read books and magazines or listen to political commentators, how do you know who has the right answers?

No one has the right answers all of the time. One professor starts his first day of class by saying, "At least 10 percent of what I tell you will be wrong. But I don't know which 10 percent it is." Sometimes even the best and most conscientious individuals discover to their embarrassment that a confident opinion was wrong. I don't mean to imply that you should disregard everything you read or hear. But you should expect people to tell you the reasons for their conclusions, so that you can decide which ones to follow with confidence and which ones are just a guess.

You have just encountered the theme of this book: Evaluate the evidence. You will hear all sorts of claims concerning psychology, as well as medicine, politics, religion, and other fields. Some are valid, some are wrong, some are hard to evaluate for sure, many are valid under certain conditions, and some are too vague to be either right or wrong. When you finish this book, you will be in a better position to examine evidence and decide which claims to take seriously.

After studying this module, you should be able to:

1. Discuss three major philosophical issues important to psychology.

2. Distinguish psychology from psychiatry and psychoanalysis.

3. Give examples of specializations in psychology, for both research and practice.

Your history text probably doesn't spend much time discussing what the term *history* means, nor does a course on English literature spend the first day defining literature. Psychology is different, because so many people have misconceptions about it. A student once asked me when we would get to the kind of psychology he could "use on" people. Another young man asked me (in my office, not publicly) whether I could teach him tricks to seduce his girlfriend. I told him that (1) psychologists don't try to trick people into doing something against their better judgment, (2) if I did know tricks like that, ethically I couldn't tell him about them, and (3) if I knew powerful tricks to control behavior *and* I had no ethics, I would probably use those powers for profit instead of teaching introduction to psychology!

The term *psychology* derives from the Greek roots *psyche,* meaning "mind" or "soul," and *logos,* meaning "word." Psychology is literally the study of the mind or soul, and people defined it that way until the early 1900s. Around 1920, psychologists became disenchanted with the idea of studying the mind. First, research deals with what we observe, and mind is unobservable. Second, talking about "the mind" implies it is a thing or object. Mental activity is a process. It is not like the river but like the flow of the river, not like the automobile but like the movement of the automobile. Beginning in the early 1900s, psychologists defined their field as the study of behavior.

Behavior is important, but is behavior the only thing we care about? When you look at this optical illusion and say that the horizontal part of the top line looks longer than that of the bottom line (although really they are the same length), we wonder why the line *looks* longer, not why you *said* it looks longer. So let's define psychology as *the systematic study of behavior and experience.* The word *experience* lets us discuss your perceptions without implying that a mind exists independently of your body.

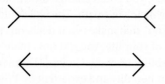

When people think of psychologists, mostly they think of clinical psychologists—those who try to help worried, depressed, or otherwise troubled people. Clinical psychology is part of psychology, but it is only one part. Psychology also includes research on sensation and perception, learning and memory, hunger and thirst, sleep, attention, child development, and more. Perhaps you expect that a course in psychology will teach you to analyze people and decipher hidden aspects of their personality. It will not. You will learn to understand many aspects of behavior, but you will gain no dazzling powers.

Ideally, you will become more skeptical of those who claim to analyze people's personality based on small samples of their behavior.

General Points about Psychology

Let's start with three of the most general statements about psychology. Each of these will arise repeatedly throughout this text.

"It Depends"

Hardly anything is true about the behavior of all people all the time. Almost every aspect of behavior depends on age, genetics, health, past experiences, and whether people are currently awake or asleep. Some aspects of behavior differ between males and females or from one culture to another. Behavior can also vary depending on the time of day, the temperature of the room, or how recently someone ate. How you might answer a question depends on the wording of the question, the wording of the previous question, and who is asking the questions.

If psychology regards "it depends" as a general truth, you may infer that psychology really doesn't know anything. On the contrary, "it depends" is a serious point. The key is to know *what* it depends on. The further you pursue your studies of psychology, the more you will become attuned to the wealth of subtle influences that people easily overlook. Here is an example: Decades ago, two psychology laboratories were conducting similar studies on human learning but reporting contradictory results. Both researchers were highly respected, they were following the same procedures, and they did not understand why their results differed. Eventually, one of them traveled to the other's university to watch the other in action. Almost immediately, he noticed one key difference: the chairs in which the participants sat! His colleague at the other university had obtained chairs from a retired dentist, and therefore his research participants were sitting in *dentist's* chairs, during an era when dental procedures were often painful. The participants were sitting there in a state of heightened anxiety that altered their behavior (Kimble, 1967).

Progress Depends on Good Measurement

Nobel Prize–winning biologist Sydney Brenner was quoted as saying, "Progress in science depends on new techniques, new discoveries, and new ideas, probably in that order" (McElheny, 2004, p. 71). In any field, from astronomy to zoology, new discoveries and ideas depend on good techniques and measurements. Psychologists' understanding has advanced furthest on topics such as sensory processes, learning, and memory, which are easiest to measure. Research progress has been slower in such areas as emotion and personality, where we struggle to find clear definitions and accurate measurements.

Confidence in the Conclusions Should Depend on the Strength of the Evidence

How much television should young children be allowed to watch per day? What should be the limits, if any, on teenagers playing violent video games? To what extent do the behavioral differences between men and women reflect biological influences? What is the best way to deal with the problem of violence in our society? How should parents react if a young child wants to change gender? You probably have opinions on questions like these, and so do many psychologists. However, the opinions are not always based on good evidence. When this text describes research studies in some detail, the reason is to explain how strong the research evidence is (or isn't) behind some conclusion.

Major Philosophical Issues in Psychology

Psychology began in the late 1800s as an attempt to apply scientific methods to questions about the philosophy of mind. Three of the most profound philosophical questions related to psychology are free will versus determinism, the mind–brain problem, and the nature–nurture issue.

Free Will versus Determinism

The scientific approach to anything, including psychology, assumes that we live in a universe of cause and effect. If things just happen for no reason at all, then we have no hope of discovering scientific principles. That is, scientists assume determinism, *the idea that every event has a cause, or determinant,*

Mike Dotta/Shutterstock.com

Behavior is guided by external forces, such as the contour of the environment, and by forces within the individual. According to the determinist view, even those internal forces follow cause-and-effect laws.

that someone could observe or measure. At the level of subatomic particles, certain events apparently occur at random, but for events beyond the subatomic level, determinism seems to apply. Although determinism is an assumption, not a certainty, the success of scientific research attests to its value.

What about human behavior? According to the determinist assumption, everything we do has causes. This view seems to conflict with the impression all of us have that "I make the decisions about my actions. Often when I make a decision, it could have gone either way." *The belief that behavior is caused by a person's independent decisions* is known as free will. Do you think your behavior is predictable? How about other people's behavior? Questionnaires show that most people think their own behavior is less predictable than other people's. That is, you think you have free will, but other people, not so much (Pronin & Kugler, 2010).

Many psychologists maintain that free will is an illusion (Wegner, 2002): What you call a conscious intention is more a prediction than a cause of your behavior. When you have the experience of deciding to move a finger, the behavior has already started to happen, controlled unconsciously.

Other psychologists and philosophers reply that you do make decisions, in the sense that something within you initiates the action (Baumeister, 2008). When a ball bounces down a hill, its motion depends on the shape of the hill. When you run down a hill, you could change direction if you saw a car coming toward you, or a snake lying in your path. The ball could not.

Nevertheless, the "you" that makes your decisions is itself a product of your heredity and the events of your life. You did not create yourself. In a sense, yes, you do have a will, an ability to make choices (Dennett, 2003). However, your will is the product of your heredity and experiences. Whether you have or do not have free will depends on what you mean by "free."

The test of determinism is empirical: If everything you do has a cause, your behavior should be predictable, and psychological researchers should gradually improve their ability to make predictions. However, no one aspires to pinpoint accuracy. Psychologists' predictions are much like predicting the weather. The predictions can become gradually more accurate, but never completely accurate, simply because so many influences are operating.

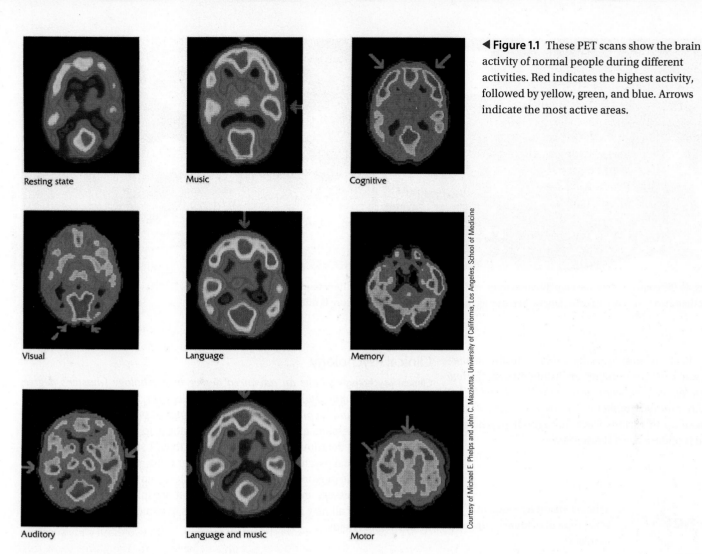

Resting state   Music   Cognitive

Visual   Language   Memory

Auditory   Language and music   Motor

◀ **Figure 1.1** These PET scans show the brain activity of normal people during different activities. Red indicates the highest activity, followed by yellow, green, and blue. Arrows indicate the most active areas.

Courtesy of Michael E. Phelps and John C. Mazziotta, University of California, Los Angeles, School of Medicine

The Mind–Brain Problem

Given that we live in a universe of matter and energy, what, if anything, is the mind? And why does consciousness exist? The *philosophical question of how experience relates to the brain* is the mind–brain problem (or mind–body problem). One view, called dualism, holds that *the mind is separate from the brain but somehow controls the brain and therefore the rest of the body.* However, dualism contradicts the law of conservation of matter and energy, one of the cornerstones of physics. According to that principle, the only way to influence any matter or energy, including the matter and energy that compose your body, is to act on it with other matter or energy. If the mind isn't composed of matter or energy, it cannot *do* anything. For that reason, nearly all brain researchers and philosophers favor monism, *the view that conscious experience is inseparable from the physical brain.* That is, mental activity *is* brain activity. So far as we can tell, consciousness cannot exist without brain activity, and presumably it is also true that certain kinds of brain activity do not exist without consciousness.

The photos in ▲ Figure 1.1 show brain activity while someone participated in nine tasks, as measured by a technique called positron-emission tomography (PET). Red indicates the highest degree of brain activity, followed by yellow, green, and blue. As you can see, the various tasks increased activity in different brain areas, although all areas showed some activity at all times (Phelps & Mazziotta, 1985). You might ask: Did the brain activity cause the thoughts, or did the thoughts cause the brain activity? Brain researchers reply, "Neither," because brain activity and mental activity are the same thing.

Even if we accept this position, we are still far from understanding the mind–brain relationship. What type of brain activity is associated with consciousness? Why does conscious experience exist at all? Research studies are not about to put philosophers out of business, but results do constrain the philosophical answers that we can seriously consider.

The Nature–Nurture Issue

Why do most little boys spend more time than little girls with toy guns and trucks and less time with dolls? Is it because of biological differences or because parents rear their sons and daughters differently? Alcohol abuse is common in some cultures and rare in others. Are these differences entirely a matter of social custom, or do genes influence alcohol use also? Why do people have different interests? Is it because of their genetics or their history of experiences?

Why do different children develop different interests? They had different hereditary tendencies, but they also had different experiences. Separating the roles of nature and nurture is difficult.

Each of these questions relates to the **nature–nurture issue** (or heredity–environment issue): *How do differences in behavior relate to differences in heredity and environment?* The nature–nurture issue shows up in various ways throughout psychology, and it seldom has a simple answer.

1. **What is meant by monism?**
2. **What type of evidence supports monism?**

Answers

2. Every type of mental activity is associated with some type of measurable brain activity. It is also true that any type of brain damage leads to a deficit in some aspect of behavior or experience.

1. Monism is the theoretical statement that mental activity and brain activity are the same thing.

What Psychologists Do

We have considered some philosophical issues related to psychology, but most psychologists deal with smaller, more manageable questions. They work in many occupational settings, as shown in ▶ Figure 1.2. The most common settings are colleges and universities, private practice, hospitals and mental health clinics, and government agencies.

Service Providers to Individuals

It is important to distinguish among types of mental health professionals. The service providers for people with psychological troubles include clinical psychologists, psychiatrists, social workers, and counseling psychologists.

Clinical Psychology

Clinical psychologists *have an advanced degree in psychology (master's degree, doctor of philosophy [PhD], or doctor of psychology [PsyD]), with a specialty in understanding and helping people with psychological problems.* The problems range from depression, anxiety, and substance abuse to marriage conflicts, difficulties making decisions, or even the feeling that "I should be getting more out of life." Clinical psychologists try to understand the reason for the problems and then help the person overcome the difficulties. Some clinical psychologists are college professors and researchers, but most are full-time practitioners. A little over half of all new PhDs are for specialists in clinical psychology or other health-related fields.

Psychiatry

Psychiatry is a *branch of medicine that deals with emotional disturbances.* To become a psychiatrist, you must first earn a medical doctor (MD) degree and then take an additional four years of residency training in psychiatry. Because psychiatrists are medical doctors, they can prescribe drugs, such as antidepressants, whereas most psychologists cannot. In the United States, a few states now permit psychologists with a couple years of additional training to prescribe drugs. Psychiatrists are more likely than clinical psychologists to work in mental hospitals, and to treat clients with severe disorders.

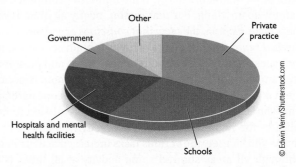

▲ **Figure 1.2** Psychologists work in many settings. (Based on data from https://www.verywellmind.com/employment-of-psychologists-2794920, downloaded September 18, 2019.)

Table 1.1 Mental Health Professionals

Type of Therapist	Education
Clinical psychologist	PhD with clinical emphasis or PsyD plus internship. Ordinarily, 5+ years after undergraduate degree.
Psychiatrist	MD plus psychiatric residency. Total of 8 years after undergraduate degree.
Psychoanalyst	Psychiatry or clinical psychology plus additional training in a psychoanalytic institute. Many others who rely on Freudian methods also call themselves psychoanalysts.
Psychiatric nurse	From 2-year (AA) degree to master's degree plus supervised experience.
Clinical social worker	Master's degree plus 2 years of supervised experience.
Counseling psychologist	PhD, PsyD, or EdD plus supervised experience in counseling.
Forensic psychologist	Doctorate plus additional training in legal issues.

Does psychiatrists' ability to prescribe drugs give them an advantage over clinical psychologists? Not always. Drugs can be useful, but relying on them can be a mistake. Whereas a typical visit to a clinical psychologist includes an extensive discussion of the client's troubles, many visits to a psychiatrist focus almost entirely on checking the effectiveness of a drug and evaluating its side effects. A survey found that over the years, fewer and fewer psychiatrists have been providing talk therapy (Mojtabai & Olfson, 2008).

Other Mental Health Professionals

Several other kinds of professionals also provide help and counsel. Psychoanalysts are *therapy providers who rely heavily on the theories and methods pioneered by the early 20th-century Viennese physician Sigmund Freud and later modified by others.* Freud and his followers attempted to infer the hidden, unconscious, symbolic meaning behind people's words and actions, and psychoanalysts today continue that effort.

There is some dispute about who may rightly call themselves psychoanalysts. Some people apply the term to anyone who attempts to uncover unconscious thoughts and feelings. Others apply the term only to graduates of an institute of psychoanalysis, a program that lasts four years or more. These institutes admit mostly people who are already either psychiatrists or clinical psychologists. Thus, people completing psychoanalytic training will be at least in their mid-30s.

A clinical social worker *does work similar to a clinical psychologist but with different training.* In most cases, a clinical social worker has a master's degree in social work with a specialization in psychological problems. Many health maintenance organizations (HMOs) steer most of their clients with psychological problems toward clinical social workers instead of psychologists or psychiatrists because the social workers, with less formal education, charge less per hour. Some psychiatric nurses (nurses with additional training in psychiatry) provide similar services.

Counseling psychologists *help people make decisions about education, vocation, marriage, health maintenance, and other issues.* A counseling psychologist has a doctorate degree (PhD, PsyD, or EdD) with supervised experience in counseling. Whereas a clinical psychologist deals mainly with anxiety, depression, and other emotional distress, a counseling psychologist deals mostly with life decisions and family or career readjustments. Counseling psychologists work in educational institutions, mental health centers, rehabilitation agencies, businesses, and private practice.

You may also have heard of forensic psychologists, *who provide advice and consultation to police, lawyers, and courts.* Forensic psychologists are clinical or counseling psychologists who have additional training in legal issues. They advise on such decisions as whether a defendant is mentally competent to stand trial or whether someone eligible for parole is dangerous (Otto & Heilbrun, 2002). Several popular films and television series have depicted forensic psychologists helping police investigators develop a psychological profile of a serial killer. That may sound like an exciting, glamorous profession, but few psychologists engage in such activities, and the accuracy of their profiles is uncertain. Most criminal profilers today have training and experience in law enforcement, not psychology.

■ Table 1.1 compares various types of mental health professionals.

3. How does the education of a clinical psychologist differ from that of a psychiatrist?

Answers

3. A clinical psychologist earns an advanced degree in psychology, generally a PhD or PsyD. A psychiatrist earns an MD, like other medical doctors.

Service Providers to Organizations

Psychologists also work in business, industry, and school systems, doing work you might not recognize as psychology. The job prospects in these fields have been good, and you might find them interesting.

Industrial/Organizational Psychology

The psychological study of people at work is known as industrial/organizational (I/O) psychology. It deals with such issues as hiring the right person for a job, training people for jobs, developing work teams, determining salaries and bonuses, providing feedback to workers about their performance, planning an organizational structure, and organizing the workplace so that workers will be productive and satisfied. I/O psychologists attend to both the individual workers and the organization, including the impact of economic conditions and government regulations.

Here's an example of a concern for industrial/organizational psychologists (Campion & Thayer, 1989): A company that manufactures complex electronic equipment needed to publish reference and repair manuals for its products. The engineers who designed the devices did not want to spend their time writing the manuals, and none of them were skilled writers anyway. So the company hired a technical writer to prepare the manuals. After a year, she received an unsatisfactory performance rating because the manuals she wrote contained too many technical errors. She countered that, when she asked various engineers in the company to check her manuals or to explain technical details to her, they were always too busy. She found her job complicated and frustrating. Her office was badly lit, noisy, and overheated, and her chair was uncomfortable. Whenever she mentioned these problems, she was told that she "complained too much."

In a situation like this, an industrial/organizational psychologist helps the company evaluate its options. One solution would be to fire her and hire an expert on electrical engineering who is also an outstanding writer who tolerates a badly lit, noisy, overheated, uncomfortable office. However, if the company cannot find or afford such a person, then it needs to improve the working conditions and provide the current employee with more training and help.

Human Factors

Learning to operate our increasingly complex machinery is one of the struggles of modern life. Mistakes can be serious. Imagine an airplane pilot who intends to lower the landing gear and instead raises the wing flaps, or a worker in a nuclear power plant who fails to notice a warning signal. A type of psychologist known as a **human factors specialist** or **ergonomist** *tries to facilitate the operation of machinery so that people can use it efficiently and safely.* Human factors specialists first worked in military settings, where complex technologies require soldiers to spot nearly invisible targets, understand speech through deafening noise, track objects in three dimensions, and make life-or-death decisions in a split second. The military turned to psychologists to redesign the tasks to fit the skills that their personnel could master.

Human factors specialists soon applied their expertise to the design of everyday devices, such as cameras, computers, microwave ovens, and cell phones. The field combines features of psychology, engineering, and computer science.

Human factors specialists help redesign machines to make them easier and safer to use. This field uses principles of both engineering and psychology.

Military Psychologists

Military psychologists are *specialists who provide services to the military.* Some are similar to industrial/organizational psychologists, conducting intellectual and personality tests to identify people suitable for certain jobs within the military, and then helping to train people for those jobs. Other military psychologists consult with the leadership about strategies, including the challenges of dealing with allies or enemies from a different culture. Still others provide clinical and counseling services to soldiers dealing with stressful experiences. Few experiences in life are more stressful than military combat. Some military psychologists conduct research on how to deal with battlefield stress, sleep deprivation, and other difficulties. Matthews (2014) has argued that military psychologists will become increasingly important, as future conflicts pertain more to influencing people than attacking them.

School Psychology

Many if not most children have school problems at one time or another. Some children have trouble sitting still or paying attention. Others get into trouble for misbehavior. Some have problems with reading or other academic skills. Others master their schoolwork quickly and become bored. They too need special attention.

School psychologists are *specialists in the psychological condition of students,* usually in kindergarten through high school. School psychologists identify children's educational needs, devise a plan to meet those needs, and then either implement the plan themselves or advise teachers how to implement it.

School psychology can be taught in a psychology department, an education department, or a department of educational psychology. In some countries, it is possible to practice school psychology with only a bachelor's degree. In the United States, the minimum education requirement for a school psychologist is usually a master's degree, but a doctorate may become necessary in the future. Most school psychologists work for a school system, but some work for mental health clinics, guidance centers, and other institutions.

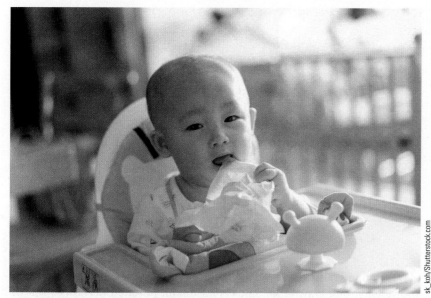
Infants and young children will try to eat almost anything that tastes okay. As they grow older, they begin to avoid foods for reasons other than taste.

Community Psychology

Community psychologists *work as professors, researchers, program directors, or policy developers to promote mental health and well-being for a community, rather than working with one person at a time.* For example, instead of addressing the difficulties of one homeless person, a community psychologist might try to improve government policies about affordable housing. Instead of helping one person get to work, a community psychologist might try to improve public transportation for the neighborhood. The emphasis is on improving the social environment for the betterment of all, especially for people who have had limited opportunities.

Psychologists in Teaching and Research

Many psychologists, especially those who are not clinical psychologists, teach and conduct research in colleges and universities. To some extent, different kinds of psychologists study different topics. For example, developmental psychologists observe children, and biological psychologists examine the effects of brain damage. However, different kinds of psychologists sometimes study the same questions in different ways. To illustrate, let's consider one example: how we select what to eat. Different kinds of psychologists offer different explanations.

Developmental Psychology

Developmental psychologists *study how behavior changes with age,* "from womb to tomb." For example, they might examine language development from age 2 to 4 or memory from age 60 to 80, describing the changes and trying to explain them.

With regard to food selection, some taste preferences are present from birth. Newborns prefer sweet tastes, avoid bitter and sour substances, and appear to be indifferent to salty tastes, as if they could not yet taste them (Beauchamp, Cowart, Mennella, & Marsh, 1994). By about three months, they begin showing a preference for salty tastes (Liem, 2017). Toddlers will try to eat almost anything they can fit into their mouths, unless it tastes sour or bitter. For that reason, parents need to keep dangerous substances like furniture polish out of toddlers' reach. Older children become increasingly selective about the foods they accept, but up to age 7 or 8, usually the only reason children give for refusing something is that they think it would taste bad (Rozin, Fallon, & Augustoni-Ziskind, 1986). As they grow older, they cite more complex reasons for rejecting foods, such as health concerns.

Because children are more sensitive to bitter tastes than adults are, and because most vegetables are at least slightly bitter, most children dislike vegetables, especially unfamiliar ones. Most medicines taste bitter. Adults swallow medicines in pills or capsules that are hard for young children to swallow. Getting young children to swallow a spoonful of bitter medicine is difficult, although adding a sweet taste usually helps (Mennella, Spector, Reed, & Coldwell, 2013).

Learning and Motivation

The research field of **learning and motivation** studies *how behavior depends on the outcomes of past behaviors and current motivations.* How often we engage in any particular behavior depends on the results of that behavior in the past.

We learn our food choices largely by learning what *not* to eat. For example, if you eat something and then feel sick, you form an aversion to the taste of that food, especially if it was unfamiliar. Thus, an important influence on food preferences is familiarity. Most of us like the foods we have eaten since childhood, and we gradually come to accept other foods as they become more familiar.

Cognitive Psychology

Cognition means *thought and knowledge.* A **cognitive psychologist** *studies those processes.* (The root *cogn* also shows up in the word *recognize,* which literally means "to know again.") Typically, cognitive psychologists focus on how people make decisions, solve problems, and convert their thoughts into language. These psychologists study both the best and the worst of human cognition (expert decision making and why people make costly errors).

Cognitive psychologists seldom study anything related to food selection, but cognitions about food do enter into our food decisions. For example, people often refuse an edible food just because of the very idea of it (Rozin & Fallon, 1987; Rozin, Millman, & Nemeroff, 1986). Most people in the United States refuse to eat meat from dogs, cats, or horses. Vegetarians reject all meat, not because they think it would taste bad, but because they dislike the idea of eating animal parts. On average, the longer people have been vegetarians, the more firmly they regard meat eating as wrong (Rozin, Markwith, & Stoess, 1997).

How would you like to try the tasty morsels in ▶ Figure 1.3? You might be repulsed by the idea of eating insects, even if they are guaranteed to be safe and nutritious (Rozin & Fallon, 1987). Would you be willing to drink a glass of apple juice after you watched someone dip a cockroach into it? What if the cockroach was carefully sterilized? Some people not only refuse to drink that particular glass of apple juice but also say they have lost their taste for apple juice in general (Rozin et al., 1986). Would you drink pure water from a brand-new, never-used toilet bowl? Would you eat a piece of chocolate fudge shaped like dog feces? If not, you are guided by the idea of the food, not its taste or safety.

▲ **Figure 1.3** Some cultures consider insects to be good food, whereas others consider them disgusting.

Biological Psychology

A **biopsychologist** or **behavioral neuroscientist** *explains behavior in terms of biological factors, such as activities of the nervous system, the effects of drugs and hormones, genetics, and evolutionary pressures.* How would a biological psychologist approach the question of how people (or animals) select foods?

One factor in taste preferences is that some people have up to three times as many taste buds as others do, mostly for genetic reasons. People with the most taste buds usually have the least tolerance for strong tastes, including black coffee, black breads, hot peppers, grapefruit, radishes, and Brussels sprouts (Bartoshuk, Duffy, Lucchina, Prutkin, & Fast, 1998; Drewnowski, Henderson, Short, & Barratt-Fornell, 1998). Most of them also dislike foods that are too sweet (Yeomans, Tepper, Rietzschel, & Prescott, 2007). However, exceptions occur, especially because of familiarity. Even if you have a high density of taste buds, you may have come to enjoy familiar strong-tasting foods.

If you ate corn dogs and cotton candy and then got sick on a wild ride, something in your brain would blame the food, regardless of what you think consciously. This kind of learning helps us avoid harmful substances.

Hormones also affect taste preferences. Many years ago, one child showed a strong craving for salt. As an infant, he often licked the salt off crackers and bacon without eating the food itself. He put a thick layer of salt on everything he ate. Sometimes he swallowed salt directly from the shaker. At the age of $3\frac{1}{2}$, he had to go to a hospital, and while he was there, he received only the usual hospital fare. He soon died of salt deficiency (Wilkins & Richter, 1940).

The reason was that he had defective adrenal glands, which secrete the hormones that enable the body to retain salt. He craved salt because he had to consume it fast enough to replace what he lost in his urine. (Too much salt is bad for your health, but too little salt is also dangerous.) Later research confirmed that salt-deficient animals immediately show an increased preference for salty tastes (Rozin & Kalat, 1971). Becoming salt deficient causes salty foods to taste especially good (Jacobs, Mark, & Scott, 1988). People often report salt cravings after losing salt by bleeding or sweating, and many women crave salt during menstruation or pregnancy.

Evolutionary Psychology

An **evolutionary psychologist** *tries to explain behavior in terms of the evolutionary history of the species, including why evolution might have favored a tendency to act in particular ways.* For example, why do people and other animals crave sweets and avoid bitter tastes? Here, the answer is easy: Most sweets are nutritious and almost all bitter substances are poisonous (T. R. Scott & Verhagen, 2000). Ancient animals that ate fruits and other sweets survived to become our ancestors.

However, although some evolutionary explanations of behavior are persuasive, others are less certain (de Waal, 2002). The brain is a product of evolution, just as any other organ is, but the research challenge is to separate the evolutionary influences on our behavior from what we have learned during a lifetime.

Social Psychology and Cross-Cultural Psychology

Social psychologists *study how an individual influences other people and how the group influences an individual.* For example, on average, we eat about twice as much when we dine in a large group as we do when eating alone (de Castro, 2000). If you invite guests to your house, you offer them something to eat or drink as a way to strengthen a social relationship.

Cross-cultural psychology *compares the behavior of people from different cultures.* Comparing cultures is central to determining what is characteristic of humans in general and what depends on our background.

Cuisine is one of the most stable and defining features of any culture. In one study, researchers interviewed Japanese students who had spent a year in another country as part of an exchange program. The students' satisfaction with their year abroad had little relationship to the educational system, religion, family life, recreation, or dating customs of the host country. The main determinant of their satisfaction was the food: Students who could sometimes eat Japanese food had a good time. Those who could not became homesick (Furukawa, 1997).

The similarity between the words *culture* and *agriculture* is no coincidence, as cultivating crops was a major step toward civilization. We learn from our culture what to eat and how to prepare it (Rozin, 1996). Consider, for example, cassava, a root vegetable that is poisonous unless someone washes and pounds it for three days to remove the cyanide. Can you imagine discovering that fact? Someone in South America long ago had to say, "So far, everyone who ate this plant died, but I bet that if I wash and pound it for three days, then it will be okay." Once someone made that amazing discovery, culture passed it on to later generations and eventually to other continents.

■ **Table 1.2** summarizes some of the major fields of psychology, including several that have not been discussed.

4. Which type of psychologist helps companies hire the right people for a job and then train them?

5. Why do many menstruating women crave potato chips?

6. Which type of psychologist studies how people influence one another's behavior?

Answers

6. Social psychologist

5. By losing blood, they also lose salt, and a deficiency of salt triggers a craving for salty tastes.

4. Industrial/organizational psychologist

Cassava, a root vegetable native to South America, is now a staple food in much of Africa as well. It grows in climates not suitable for most other crops. However, people must pound and wash it for days to remove the cyanide.

GC Stock/Alamy Stock Photo

Should You Major in Psychology?

On average, students who major in engineering, math, or one of the natural sciences get higher-paying jobs than students who major in other fields (Rajecki & Borden, 2011). What seems an obvious explanation is that the math and science fields teach important information and skills. Yes, but also consider a second explanation: Students who major in math or a natural science must be willing to work hard. No one majors in physics or chemistry expecting it to be easy. Students who work hard in college are also likely to work hard on the job, even if the job has little to do with physics or chemistry. The point is, whatever you choose as your major, get into the habit of working hard at it.

About 25 to 30 percent of students with a bachelor's degree in psychology take jobs related to psychology, such as personnel work or social services. Even for those who take seemingly unrelated jobs, a psychology background is helpful by teaching people to evaluate evidence, organize and write papers, handle statistics, listen carefully to what people say, and respect cultural differences. Those skills are important for almost anything you might do.

Almost half of students majoring in psychology continue with post-graduate education, including medical school, dental school, law school, divinity school, or other professional schools. A psychology major is compatible with preparation for many fields of post-graduate study, although you should check the specific course requirements for your goals.

Suppose you want a career as a psychologist. The educational requirements vary among countries, but in the United States and Canada, nearly all jobs in psychology require education beyond a bachelor's degree. People with a master's degree can get jobs in mental health or educational counseling, but in most states, they must work under the supervision of someone with a doctorate. People with a PhD (doctor of philosophy) in clinical psychology or a PsyD (doctor of psychology) degree can provide mental health services. The main difference between the PhD and PsyD degrees is that the PhD includes an extensive research project, leading to a dissertation, whereas the PsyD degree does not. PsyD programs vary strikingly, including some that are academically strong and others with low standards (Norcross, Kohout, & Wicherski, 2005). A college teaching or research position almost always requires a PhD. An increasing percentage of doctorate-level

Table 1.2 Some Major Specializations in Psychology

Specialization	General Interest	Example of Interest or Research Topic
Biopsychologist	Relationship between brain and behavior	What body signals indicate hunger and satiety?
Clinical psychologist	Emotional difficulties	How can people be helped to overcome severe anxiety?
Cognitive psychologist	Memory, thinking	Do people have several kinds of memory?
Community psychologist	Organizations and social structures	Would improved job opportunities decrease psychological distress?
Counseling psychologist	Helping people make important decisions	Should this person consider changing careers?
Developmental psychologist	Changes in behavior over age	At what age can a child first distinguish between appearance and reality?
Educational psychologist	Improvement of learning in school	What is the best way to test a student's knowledge?
Environmental psychologist	How factors such as noise, heat, and crowding affect behavior	What building design can maximize the productivity of the people who use it?
Evolutionary psychologist	Evolutionary history of behavior	How did people evolve their facial expressions of emotion?
Human factors specialist	Communication between person and machine	How can an airplane cockpit be redesigned to increase safety?
Industrial/organizational psychologist	People at work	Should jobs be made simple and foolproof or interesting and challenging?
Learning and motivation specialist	Learning in humans and other species	What are the effects of reinforcement and punishment?
Personality psychologist	Personality differences	Why are certain people shy and others gregarious?
Psychometrician	Measuring intelligence, personality, interests	How fair are current IQ tests? Can we devise better tests?
School psychologist	Problems that affect schoolchildren	How should the school handle a child who regularly disrupts the classroom?
Social psychologist	Group behavior, social influences	What methods of persuasion are most effective for changing attitudes?

psychologists now work in business, industry, and the military doing research related to practical problems.

For more information about majoring in psychology, prospects for graduate school, and a great variety of jobs for psychology graduates, visit the website of the American Psychological Association.

in closing module 1.1

Types of Psychologists

Psychology researchers, clinical psychologists, human factors specialists, and industrial/organizational psychologists are all psychologists, even though their daily activities have little in common. What unites psychologists is a dedication to progress through research.

The discussion in this module has been simplified in several ways. In particular, biological psychology, cognitive psychology, social psychology, and the other fields overlap significantly. Nearly all psychologists combine insights and information gained from several approaches. Many like to hyphenate their self-description to emphasize the overlap. For example, "I'm a social-developmental-cognitive neuroscientist."

As we proceed through this book, we shall consider one type of behavior at a time and, generally, one approach at a time. That is simply a necessity. No one can talk intelligently about many topics at once. But bear in mind that all these processes do ultimately fit together. What you do at any given moment depends on a great many influences.

Summary

- *What is psychology?* Psychology is the systematic study of behavior and experience. Psychologists deal with both theoretical and practical questions. (page 3)
- *Three general themes.* First, "it depends." That is, almost any aspect of behavior varies as a function of many influences, and a good psychologist becomes attentive to even subtle points that alter how we act and think. Second, research progress depends on good measurement. Third, we need to distinguish between strongly supported and weakly supported conclusions. (page 3)
- *Determinism–free will.* Determinism is the view that everything, including human behavior, has a physical cause. The scientific approach rests on the assumption of determinism. (page 4)
- *Mind–brain.* According to nearly all philosophers and neuroscientists, mental activity and brain activity are inseparable. (page 5)
- *Nature–nurture.* Behavioral differences relate to differences in both heredity and environment. The relative contributions of nature and nurture vary from one instance to another. (page 5)

- *Psychology and psychiatry.* Clinical psychologists have a PhD, PsyD, or master's degree. Psychiatrists are medical doctors. Both clinical psychologists and psychiatrists treat people with emotional problems, but psychiatrists can prescribe drugs and other medical treatments, whereas in most states, psychologists cannot. Counseling psychologists help people deal with difficult decisions, and less often deal with psychological disorders. (page 6)
- *Service providers to organizations.* Nonclinical fields of application include industrial/organizational psychology, human factors, military psychology, school psychology, and community psychology. (page 7)
- *Research fields in psychology.* Subfields of psychological research include biological psychology, learning and motivation, cognitive psychology, developmental psychology, and social psychology. (page 9)
- *Job prospects.* People with a bachelor's degree in psychology enter a wide variety of careers or continue their education in professional schools. Those with an advanced degree in psychology have additional possibilities depending on their area of specialization. (page 11)

Key Terms

biopsychologist (or behavioral neuroscientist) (page 10)

clinical psychologist (page 6)

clinical social worker (page 7)

cognition (page 9)

cognitive psychologist (page 9)

community psychologist (page 9)

counseling psychologist (page 7)

cross-cultural psychology (page 10)

determinism (page 4)

developmental psychologist (page 9)

dualism (page 5)

evolutionary psychologist (page 10)

forensic psychologist (page 7)

free will (page 4)

human factors specialist (or ergonomist) (page 8)

industrial/organizational (I/O) psychology (page 7)

learning and motivation (page 9)

military psychologist (page 8)

mind–brain problem (page 5)

monism (page 5)

nature–nurture issue (page 6)

psychiatry (page 6)

psychoanalyst (page 7)

psychology (page 3)

school psychologist (page 8)

social psychologist (page 10)

Review Questions

1. Scientific research in psychology and other fields relies on which of these assumptions?
   (a) All people are born with an equal probability of success.
   (b) People choose their behaviors by free will.
   (c) We live in a universe of cause and effect.
   (d) Science can solve all of humanity's problems.

2. Mind–body dualism conflicts with which of these physical principles?
   (a) The law of gravity
   (b) The conservation of matter and energy
   (c) Einstein's theory of general relativity
   (d) Quantum mechanics

3. How do clinical psychologists differ from psychiatrists?
   (a) They have different education.
   (b) They follow different theories.
   (c) They have different amounts of experience.
   (d) They do different types of research.

4. What distinguishes psychoanalysts from other types of therapists?
   (a) Psychoanalysts try to explain behavior in terms of brain activity.
   (b) Psychoanalysts follow methods and theories originated by Freud.
   (c) Psychoanalysts work only in mental hospitals.
   (d) Psychoanalysts work only in prisons.

5. Which of these is a major concern for human factors psychologists?
   (a) Explaining why people differ in their food preferences
   (b) Observing behavior changes "from womb to tomb"
   (c) Measuring intelligence and personality differences
   (d) Making machinery easier to use

6. Which of these is a major concern for community psychologists?
   (a) Providing mental health care to everyone in a community
   (b) Helping people move from one place to another.
   (c) Changing the environment to help disadvantaged people
   (d) Making machinery easier to use

7. What type of psychologist is most concerned to understand thinking, knowledge, and problem solving?
   (a) Cognitive psychologists
   (b) Developmental psychologists
   (c) Human factors specialists
   (d) Biopsychologists

Answers: 1c, 2b, 3a, 4b, 5d, 6c, 7a.

module 1.2

Psychology Then and Now

After studying this module, you should be able to:

1. Explain why early psychologists were eager for a "great man" or great theory to revolutionize the field.

2. Describe the research interests of the earliest psychologists.

3. List differences between psychology in its early days and psychology today.

4. Explain why early psychologists avoided the study of conscious experience.

Imagine yourself as a young scholar in 1880. You decide to become a psychologist because you are excited about the field's new scientific approach. Like other early psychologists, you have a background in either biology or philosophy.

So far, so good. But what questions will you address? A good research question is interesting and answerable. How would you choose a research topic? You cannot get research ideas from a psychological journal because the first issue won't be published until the following year (in German). You cannot follow in the tradition of previous researchers because there haven't *been* any. You are on your own. In the next pages, we shall explore changes in what psychologists considered good research topics, including projects that dominated psychology for a while and then faded. ▼ Figure 1.4 outlines some major historical events inside and outside psychology.

The Early Era

Psychological research uses the scientific method, but psychology differs from other sciences in several ways. One of those ways is our history. Astronomy, physics, chemistry, and biology began with centuries of contributions by amateurs who devoted part of their leisure time to observing animals, observing the stars, or conducting simple experiments. By the late 1700s or early 1800s when universities first offered courses in chemistry, physics, and biology, the first professors in those fields already had a substantial amount of information they could teach.

In contrast, psychology began as a deliberate attempt to start a new science. In the late 1800s, several scholars proposed to start a new field of psychology that would apply the methods of the natural sciences to the philosophical questions of mind. Universities supported this optimistic project and before long, many of them hired professors to teach this new science of psychology. However, unlike chemistry or biology, hardly anyone had done amateur research in psychology. What were the early psychology professors going to teach? People today sometimes say that psychology is just common sense. When you finish your study of introduction to psychology, you can form your own judgment about that claim, but back around 1900, it was definitely true. The first English-language textbook of psychological science devoted almost half its pages to what biologists had discovered about vision, hearing, and the other senses (Scripture, 1907). At least that gave psychology professors something to teach.

And so, academic psychology began with an inferiority complex. Early psychology professors eagerly awaited the coming of a great man—yes, "man," as apparently no one imagined that it might be a great woman—who would revolutionize psychology. It was like the prediction of a Messiah.

A review of psychology's early history (Borch-Jacobsen & Shamdasani, 2012) quoted one psychologist who spoke of "a great chance for some future psychologue to make a name greater than Newton's," another one who anticipated that a great psychologist's name will "join those of Copernicus and Darwin," and another who said that "the present psychological situation calls out for a new Darwin of the mind." In their eagerness for that great revolutionary of psychology, early psychologists nominated several of their contemporaries as being that great man. Theodore Flournoy (1903) wrote that if future research confirms the results of Frederic Myers, then Myers would be one of the greats, right up there with Copernicus and Darwin. Unfortunately, future research could not confirm any of Myers's results. That's right, not any of them.

Sigmund Freud immodestly nominated himself as the counterpart to Copernicus and Darwin, largely because he said his ideas were resisted, just as theirs had been (Freud, 1915/1935,[1] p. 252). Most psychologists today reject that analogy. Copernicus and Darwin faced opposition based on religion, whereas the opposition to Freud came mostly from psychologists and psychiatrists—the people in the best position to evaluate his theories.

In any case, early psychology was a highly ambitious field. The hope was to amass knowledge that would quickly become comparable to the impressive accomplishments of chemistry, physics, and biology.

Wilhelm Wundt and the First Psychological Laboratory

A few people had conducted a small amount of psychological research, dating back to the nearly forgotten work of Ferdinand Ueberwasser in 1783 (Schwarz & Pfister, 2016). Nevertheless, the work of Wilhelm Wundt ("Voont") beginning in 1879 in Leipzig, Germany, is recognized as the start of scientific psychology. Wundt's interests were wide-ranging (Zehr, 2000), but one of his goals was to find the elements of experience, comparable to those of chemistry. Psychology's elements were, he maintained, sensations and feelings (Wundt, 1896/1902). At any moment, you might experience the taste of a fine meal, the sound of good music, and a certain degree of pleasure. These elements

[1]A reference citation containing a slash between the years, such as this one, refers to a book originally published in the first year (1915) and reprinted in the second year (1935).

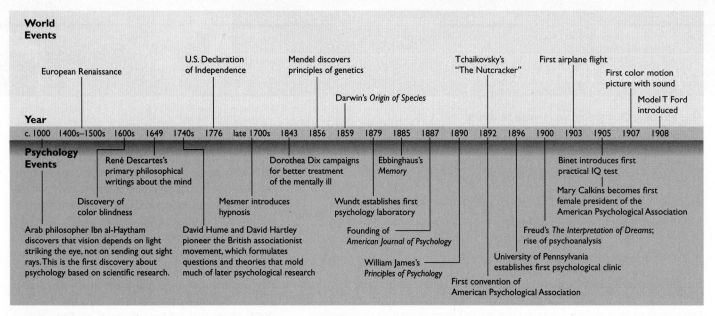

World Events																		

World Events

European Renaissance — c. 1400s–1500s

U.S. Declaration of Independence — 1776

Mendel discovers principles of genetics — 1856

Darwin's *Origin of Species* — 1859

Tchaikovsky's "The Nutcracker" — 1892

First airplane flight — 1903

First color motion picture with sound — 1907

Model T Ford introduced — 1908

Year

c. 1000 1400s–1500s 1600s 1649 1740s 1776 late 1700s 1843 1856 1859 1879 1885 1887 1890 1892 1896 1900 1903 1905 1907 1908

Psychology Events

René Descartes's primary philosophical writings about the mind

Discovery of color blindness

Arab philosopher Ibn al-Haytham discovers that vision depends on light striking the eye, not on sending out sight rays. This is the first discovery about psychology based on scientific research.

David Hume and David Hartley pioneer the British associationist movement, which formulates questions and theories that mold much of later psychological research.

Mesmer introduces hypnosis

Dorothea Dix campaigns for better treatment of the mentally ill

Ebbinghaus's *Memory*

Wundt establishes first psychology laboratory

Founding of *American Journal of Psychology*

William James's *Principles of Psychology*

First convention of American Psychological Association

University of Pennsylvania establishes first psychological clinic

Freud's *The Interpretation of Dreams*; rise of psychoanalysis

Binet introduces first practical IQ test

Mary Calkins becomes first female president of the American Psychological Association

▲ **Figure 1.4** Dates of some important events in psychology and elsewhere. (Based partly on Dewsbury, 2000)

would merge into a compound that was your experience. Furthermore, Wundt maintained, your experience is partly under your voluntary control, because you can shift your attention from one element to another and get a different experience. To test his idea about the components of experience, Wundt presented various kinds of lights, textures, and sounds, and asked subjects to report the intensity and quality of their sensations. That is, he asked them to **introspect**—*to look within themselves.* He recorded the changes in people's reports as he changed the stimuli.

In one of Wundt's earliest studies, he set up a pendulum that struck metal balls and made a sound at two points on its swing. People would watch the pendulum and indicate where it appeared to be when they heard the sound. On average, people reported the pendulum to be about an eighth of a second in front of or behind the ball when they heard the strike (Wundt, 1862/1961). Wundt's interpretation was that a person needs about an eighth of a second to shift attention from one stimulus to another.

Wundt and his students were prolific investigators, and the brief treatment here cannot do him justice. He wrote more than 50,000 pages about his research, but his main impact came from setting the precedent of collecting scientific data to answer psychological questions.

Edward Titchener and Structuralism

At first, most of the world's psychologists received their education from Wundt himself. One of his students, Edward Titchener, came to the United States in 1892 as a psychology professor at Cornell University. Like Wundt, Titchener believed that the main question of psychology was the nature of mental experiences.

Titchener (1910) typically presented a stimulus and asked his subject to analyze it into its separate features—for example, to look at a lemon and describe its yellowness, brightness, shape, and other characteristics. He called his approach **structuralism**, *an attempt to describe the structures that compose the mind,* particularly sensations, feelings, and images. Imagine you are the psychologist: I look at a lemon and try to tell you my experience of its brightness separately from my experience of its yellowness, shape, and other aspects.

Here is the problem. How do you know whether my reports are accurate? After Titchener died in 1927, psychologists abandoned both his questions and his methods. Why? Remember that a good scientific question is both interesting

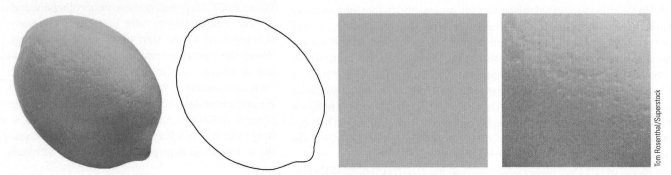

Edward Titchener asked subjects to describe their sensations. For example, they might describe their sensation of shape, their sensation of color, and their sensation of texture while looking at a lemon.

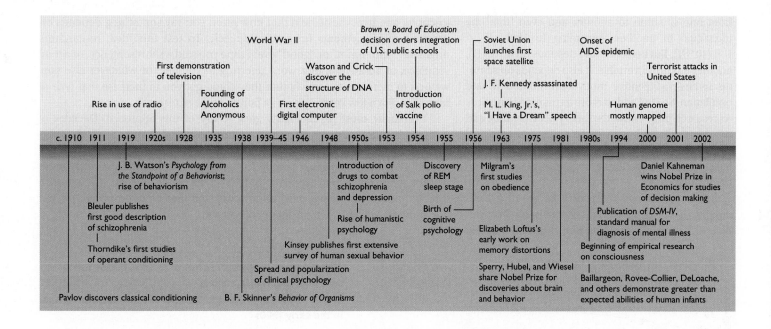

Timeline:

- c. 1910 — Pavlov discovers classical conditioning
- 1911 — Bleuler publishes first good description of schizophrenia
- 1911 — Thorndike's first studies of operant conditioning
- 1919 — J. B. Watson's *Psychology from the Standpoint of a Behaviorist*; rise of behaviorism
- 1920s — Rise in use of radio
- 1928 — First demonstration of television
- 1935 — Founding of Alcoholics Anonymous
- 1938 — B. F. Skinner's *Behavior of Organisms*
- 1938 — Spread and popularization of clinical psychology
- 1939–45 — World War II
- 1946 — First electronic digital computer
- 1948 — Kinsey publishes first extensive survey of human sexual behavior
- 1950s — Rise of humanistic psychology
- 1953 — Watson and Crick discover the structure of DNA
- 1953 — Introduction of drugs to combat schizophrenia and depression
- 1954 — Introduction of Salk polio vaccine
- 1955 — Brown v. Board of Education decision orders integration of U.S. public schools
- 1955 — Birth of cognitive psychology
- 1955 — Discovery of REM sleep stage
- 1956 — Soviet Union launches first space satellite
- 1963 — J. F. Kennedy assassinated
- 1963 — M. L. King, Jr.'s, "I Have a Dream" speech
- 1963 — Milgram's first studies on obedience
- 1975 — Elizabeth Loftus's early work on memory distortions
- 1981 — Sperry, Hubel, and Wiesel share Nobel Prize for discoveries about brain and behavior
- 1980s — Onset of AIDS epidemic
- 1994 — Human genome mostly mapped
- 1994 — Publication of *DSM-IV*, standard manual for diagnosis of mental illness
- 1994 — Beginning of empirical research on consciousness
- 1994 — Baillargeon, Rovee-Collier, DeLoache, and others demonstrate greater than expected abilities of human infants
- 2000 — Human genome mostly mapped
- 2001 — Terrorist attacks in United States
- 2002 — Daniel Kahneman wins Nobel Prize in Economics for studies of decision making

and answerable. Regardless of whether Titchener's questions about the elements of the mind were interesting, they seemed unanswerable.

William James and Functionalism

In the same era as Wundt and Titchener, Harvard University's William James articulated some of the major issues of psychology and earned recognition as the founder of American psychology. James's book *The Principles of Psychology* (1890) defined many of the questions that still dominate psychology today.

James had little patience with searching for the elements of the mind. He focused on what the mind *does* rather than what it *is*. That is, instead of seeking the elements of consciousness, he preferred *to learn how people produce useful behaviors*. For this reason, we call his approach functionalism. He suggested the following examples of good psychological questions (James, 1890):

- How can people strengthen good habits?
- Can someone attend to more than one item at a time?
- How do people recognize that they have seen something before?
- How does an intention lead to action?

James proposed possible answers but did little research of his own. His main contribution was to inspire later researchers to address the questions that he posed.

The Search for the Laws of Learning

Early psychologists eventually lost hope in the arrival of the great man who would revolutionize psychology and instead began to seek simple laws of learning, analogous to the laws of physics. If they could state laws with mathematical precision and use them to predict behavior, then psychology would be as impressive as other sciences.

Many researchers set out to study animal learning. Just as physicists could study gravity by dropping any object in any location, many psychologists in the mid-1900s assumed they could learn all about learning by studying any one example, such as rats in mazes. A highly influential psychologist, Clark Hull, wrote, "One of the most persistently baffling problems which confronts modern psychologists is the finding of an adequate

explanation of the phenomena of maze learning" (1932, p. 25). Another early psychologist, Edward Tolman, wrote, "I believe that everything important in psychology (except perhaps . . . such matters as involve society and words) can be investigated in essence through the continued experimental and theoretical analysis of the determiners of rat behavior at a choice-point in a maze" (1938, p. 34).

Clark Hull offered the most influential attempt at a systematic theory of learning. He started with the hypothesis that learned habit strength linking a stimulus to a response $(_sH_R)$ approaches its maximum (equal to 1) as a function of N, the number of trials, and a, an empirical variable—that is, one that we have to measure because it varies

Early psychological researchers studied rats in mazes. As they discovered that this behavior was more complicated than they supposed, their interest turned to other topics.

from one situation to another and even from one individual to another. According to Hull, $_sH_R = 1 - (10^{-a}N)$. But behavior also depends on drive (D), another empirical variable. It also depends on stimulus intensity, incentive motivation, inhibition, and oscillation. So Hull added more terms to his equation. As research progressed, the theory became more and more complicated, with more and more empirical variables. In fact, it was getting more complicated faster than it was getting more accurate—a bad sign for any theory.

Still, psychological research of the mid-1900s continued trying to explain virtually all behavior in terms of reinforcements and punishments. For example, one hypothesis held that how often you say something depends on previous reinforcements for similar speech. To test this idea, researchers might say "mm hmm" or "good" every time you said a short sentence, or a long sentence, or an adverb, or a word referring to yourself, or whatever else they wanted to increase, to see whether they could get you to increase that type of utterance. For a few years, this was a popular type of research.

Eventually most psychologists grew weary of this approach. Decades of research had gone into an effort with not much payoff. From today's perspective, you might find much research from the mid-1900s to be tedious. Still, we should give those researchers credit for being ambitious. They were trying to develop grand theories to explain as much of behavior as possible. If you browse through today's psychology journals, you will find many interesting studies, but few attempts to build a general theory of behavior.

concept check ✔

7. **Why did psychologists of the mid-1900s spend so much time studying rats in mazes?**

8. **In what way is psychology today less ambitious than it was in the early 1900s?**

Answers

7. They hoped to discover general principles of learning that they could state mathematically.

8. In the early 1900s, psychologists were eager for someone to revolutionize psychology just as Darwin revolutionized biology. Somewhat later researchers tried to develop general laws of learning that would explain as much as possible. After decades of such research, they became discouraged with seeking general, widespread laws.

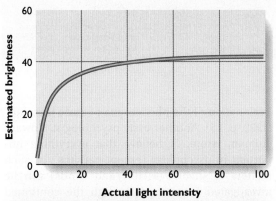

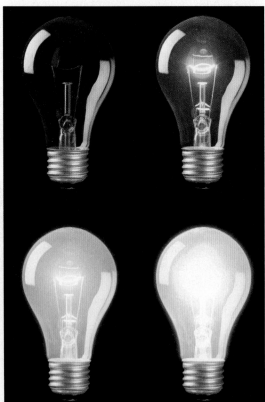

▲ **Figure 1.5** This graph relates the perceived intensity of light to its physical intensity. When a light becomes twice as intense physically, it does not seem twice as bright. (Adapted from Stevens, 1961)

Ultrashock/Shutterstock

Studying Sensation

In the late 1800s and early 1900s, psychologists paid little attention to abnormal behavior, leaving it to psychiatrists. They devoted much of their research to the study of vision and other sensations. Why? One reason was that they wanted to understand mental experience, and experience consists of sensations. Another reason was that it makes sense to start with relatively easy, answerable questions. Sensation was certainly easier to study than, say, personality.

Early psychologists demonstrated differences between physical stimuli and psychological perceptions. For example, a light that is twice as intense as another one does not look twice as bright. ◄ **Figure 1.5** shows the relationship between the intensity of light and its perceived brightness. *The mathematical description of the relationship between the physical stimulus and its perceived properties* is called the **psychophysical function** because it relates psychology to physics. Such research demonstrated the feasibility of scientific research on psychological questions.

Darwin and the Study of Animal Intelligence

Charles Darwin's theory of evolution by natural selection (Darwin, 1859, 1871) had an enormous impact on psychology as well as biology. Darwin argued that humans and other species share a remote common ancestor. If so, then other animals should share features in common with humans, including some degree of intelligence.

Based on this implication, early **comparative psychologists**, *specialists who compare different animal species,* did something that seemed more reasonable then than it does now: They set out to measure animal intelligence. They set various species to such tasks as the delayed-response problem and the detour problem. In the *delayed-response problem,* an animal sees or hears a signal indicating where it can find food. After the signal, the animal is restrained for a delay to see how long the animal remembers the signal (see ▼ Figure 1.6). In the *detour problem,* an animal is separated from food by a barrier to see whether it takes a detour away from the food to reach it (▼ Figure 1.7).

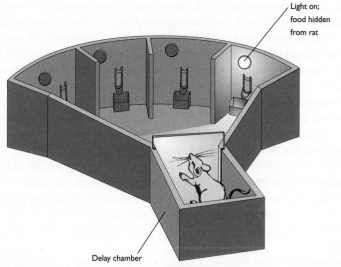

Light on; food hidden from rat

Delay chamber

▲ **Figure 1.6** Early comparative psychologists assessed animal intelligence with the delayed-response problem. Variations on this task are still used today with humans as well as laboratory animals.

Food

▲ **Figure 1.7** In the detour problem, an animal must go away from the food before it can move toward it.

However, measuring animal intelligence turned out to be more difficult than it sounded. A species might seem dull-witted on one task but brilliant on another. For example, zebras are generally slow to learn to approach one pattern instead of another for food, unless the patterns happen to be narrow stripes versus wide stripes, in which case they excel (Giebel, 1958) (see ▼ Figure 1.8). Rats don't learn to find food hidden under the object that looks different from the others, but they easily learn to choose the object that *smells* different from the others (Langworthy & Jennings, 1972). Eventually, psychologists decided that the relative intelligence of nonhuman animals was a pointless question.

Comparative psychologists today continue to study animal learning, but the emphasis has changed. The questions are now, "What can we learn from animal studies about the mechanisms of behavior?" and "How did each species evolve the behavioral tendencies it shows?"

Measuring Human Intelligence

While some psychologists studied animal intelligence, others examined human intelligence. Francis Galton, a cousin of Charles Darwin, was among the first to try to measure intelligence and to try to explain intellectual variations. Galton was fascinated with measurement (Hergenhahn, 1992). For example, he invented the weather map, measured degrees of boredom during lectures, suggested the use of fingerprints to identify individuals, and—in the name of science—attempted to measure the beauty of women in different countries.

In an effort to determine the role of heredity in human achievement, Galton (1869/1978) examined whether the sons of famous and accomplished men tended to become eminent themselves. (Women in 19th-century England had little opportunity for fame.) Galton found that the sons of judges, writers, politicians, and other notable men had a high probability of similar accomplishment themselves. He attributed this edge to heredity. (Do you think he had adequate evidence for his conclusion? If the sons of famous men become famous themselves, is heredity the only explanation?)

Galton tried to measure intelligence using simple sensory and motor tasks, but his measurements were unsatisfactory. In 1905, a French researcher named Alfred Binet devised the first useful intelligence test. Intelligence testing became common in many countries. Psychologists, inspired by the popularity of intelligence tests, developed tests of personality, interests, and other characteristics.

Much research goes into trying to make psychological tests fair and accurate.

From Freud to Modern Clinical Psychology

The Austrian psychiatrist Sigmund Freud revolutionized and popularized psychotherapy with his methods of analyzing patients' dreams and memories. He tried to trace current behavior to early childhood experiences, including children's sexual fantasies. Freud was a persuasive speaker and writer, and his influence was enormous. By the mid-1900s, most psychiatrists in the United States and Europe were following his methods. However, Freud's influence in psychology has faded substantially since then.

Until the mid-1900s, only psychiatrists provided treatment for mental illness. However, the number of returning soldiers needing help after the horrors of World War II overwhelmed the capacities of the limited number of psychiatrists. At that point, clinical psychology as we now know it began to develop. In order to improve therapy, psychologists have conducted extensive research and have developed new, more effective methods.

concept check

9. Why did clinical psychology become more prominent around the middle of the 1900s?

Answer

9. Soldiers returning after World War II needed more help than the limited number of psychiatrists could provide. Clinical psychologists began providing treatment at that time.

▲ **Figure 1.8** Zebras learn rapidly when they have to compare stripe patterns (Giebel, 1958).

Recent Trends

Recall that some of the earliest psychological researchers wanted to study the conscious mind but became discouraged with Titchener's introspective methods. Since the 1960s, cognitive psychology (the study of thought and knowledge) has gained in prominence. Although cognitive psychologists sometimes ask people to describe their thoughts, more often they measure the accuracy and speed of responses to draw inferences about the underlying processes.

Another rapidly growing field is neuroscience. New techniques of brain scanning now enable researchers to examine brain activity without opening the skull. Today, neuroscience influences nearly every aspect of psychology. Evolutionary psychology is another new emphasis. Animals that behaved in certain ways survived, reproduced, and became our ancestors. Those whose behaviors did not lead to reproductive success failed to pass on their genes. In some cases, we can infer the selective pressures that led to our current behaviors.

For many decades, researchers interested in personality concentrated mostly on what can go wrong, such as fear, anger, and sadness. The newer field of **positive psychology** *studies the predispositions and experiences that make people happy, productive, and successful.*

New fields of application have also arisen. Health psychologists study how people's health is influenced by their behaviors, such as smoking, drinking, sexual activities, exercise, diet, and reactions to stress. They also try to help people change their behaviors to promote better health. Sports psychologists apply psychological principles to help athletes set goals, train, and concentrate their efforts.

Psychologists today have also broadened their scope to include more of human diversity. In its early days, around 1900, psychology was more open to women than most other academic disciplines were, but even so, the opportunities for women were limited (Milar, 2000). Mary Calkins, an early memory researcher, regarded as Harvard's best psychology graduate student, was nevertheless denied a PhD because of Harvard's tradition of granting degrees only to men (Scarborough & Furomoto, 1987). She did, however, serve as president of the American Psychological Association, as did Margaret Washburn, another important woman in the early days of psychology.

Today, women receive nearly three-fourths of the new PhDs in psychology and hold many leadership roles in psychological organizations. An increasing percentage of PhDs go to blacks, Hispanics, or other minorities, although much room remains for further progress in seeking diversity (National Science Foundation, 2015).

What will psychology be like in the future? A few likely trends are foreseeable. Because advances in medicine have enabled people to live longer, the psychology of aging is increasingly important. Because of depletion of natural resources and climate change, people will need to change their way of life in many ways. Persuading people to change their behavior is a task for both politicians and psychologists.

in closing | module 1.2

Psychology through the Years

Throughout the early years of psychology, many psychologists devoted enormous efforts to projects that produced disappointing results, such as Titchener's search for the elements of the mind. Not all the efforts of early psychologists were fruitless, and in other chapters, you will encounter many classic studies that we still regard highly. Still, if some past psychologists spent their time on projects we now consider misguided, can we be sure that many of today's psychologists aren't on the wrong track?

We cannot, of course. Of all the theories and research projects that we now respect most dearly, some will stand the test of time and others will not. That is not a reason for despair. Much like a rat in a maze, researchers make progress by trial and error. They advance in a certain direction; sometimes it leads to progress, and sometimes it leads to a dead end. But even exploring a dead end and eliminating it is progress. Even when research doesn't lead to clear answers, at least it leads to better questions.

Summary

- *Origin of psychology.* Psychology began as a deliberate attempt to start a new science that would apply the methods of the natural sciences to the questions of philosophy of mind. (page 15)
- *Psychology's early ambitions.* Many universities appointed psychology professors before psychologists had much to teach. The early days were marked by an impatient eagerness for great theories that would rival those of the natural sciences. (page 15)
- *First research.* In 1879, Wilhelm Wundt established the first laboratory devoted to psychological research. (page 15)
- *Limits of self-observation.* One of Wundt's students, Edward Titchener, attempted to analyze the elements of mental experience, relying on people's own observations. Other psychologists became discouraged with this approach. (page 16)
- *Functionalism.* William James, the founder of American psychology, focused attention on useful behavior rather than on the contents of the mind. He outlined many questions for future researchers. (page 17)
- *The search for laws of learning.* For decades, the search for general laws of learning dominated psychological research.

The hope was to state laws that would apply to as much of behavior as possible. This effort was highly ambitious, but eventually most researchers became discouraged with the enterprise. (page 17)
- *Early sensory research.* In the late 1800s and early 1900s, many researchers concentrated on studies of the senses, partly because sensation is central to mental experience. (page 18)
- *Darwin's influence.* Charles Darwin's theory of evolution by natural selection prompted interest in the intelligence of non-human animals. (page 18)
- *Intelligence testing.* The measurement of human intelligence was a concern of early psychologists that has persisted to the present. (page 19)
- *Freud.* Sigmund Freud's theories heavily influenced the early development of psychotherapy, although other methods are more widespread today. (page 19)
- *Clinical psychology.* At one time, psychiatrists provided nearly all the care for people with psychological disorders. After World War II, clinical psychology began to assume much of this role. (page 19)

Key Terms

comparative psychologist (page 18)

functionalism (page 17)

introspect (page 16)

positive psychology (page 20)

psychophysical function (page 18)

structuralism (page 16)

Review Questions

1. Why did psychology professors of the early 1900s have less information to teach than biology or chemistry professors?
   (a) Textbook publishers at that time concentrated on the natural sciences.
   (b) Structuralists and functionalists were hostile to each other.
   (c) Biology and chemistry had a tradition of amateur research.
   (d) Ethics committees at the time prohibited research on humans.

2. Which of these topics was a major research topic for the earliest psychologists?
   (a) Vision and other sensations
   (b) Mental illness
   (c) Racial prejudice
   (d) Expert problem solving

3. What is the objection to using introspection as a research method?
   (a) Introspection requires complex and expensive equipment.
   (b) Introspection research requires large numbers of participants.
   (c) Ethics committees usually forbid the use of introspection.
   (d) We have no way to check the accuracy of introspection.

4. Why did psychological researchers of the mid-1900s devote so much research to rats in mazes?
   (a) Mazes were the best way to test the theories of structuralism.
   (b) The researchers were trying to help control rat infestations in major cities.
   (c) The researchers sought general laws of behavior.
   (d) The researchers could not get permission to do research on humans.

5. What is a psychophysical function?
   (a) A machine that measures brain activity during a perceptual task
   (b) A mathematical statement relating perception to physical stimuli
   (c) A device that produces a series of increasing or decreasing stimuli
   (d) An explanation of how people make practical use of sensory information

6. What does a comparative psychologist compare?
   (a) Theories
   (b) Animal species
   (c) Parts of the brain
   (d) Languages

7. What historical event led to the rise of clinical psychology?
   (a) World War II
   (b) The Civil Rights protests era
   (c) The translation of Freud's works into English
   (d) The invention and wide use of computers

Answers: 1c, 2a, 3d, 4c, 5b, 6b, 7a.

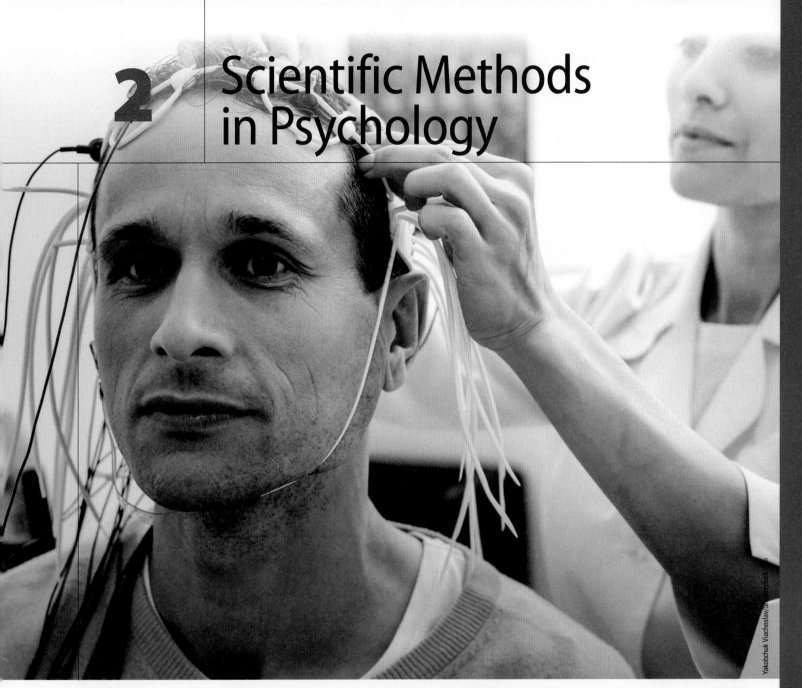

2 Scientific Methods in Psychology

Yakobchuk Viacheslav/Shutterstock

Villiers Steyn/Shutterstock.com

Years ago, I was watching a Discovery Channel documentary about elephants. After the narrator discussed the enormous amount of food they eat, he started on their digestive system. He commented that the average elephant passes enough gas in a day to propel a car for 20 miles (32 km). I thought, "Wow, isn't that amazing!" and I told a couple of people about it.

Later I started to think, "Wait a minute. *Who measured that?* Did someone attach a balloon to an elephant's rear end and collect gas for 24 hours? And then put it into a car and drive it? Was that a full-sized car or an economy car? City traffic or highway? How do they know they measured a typical elephant? Did they determine the mean for a broad sample of elephants?" My doubts quickly grew.

"Oh, well," you might say. "Who cares?" You're right. How far someone could propel a car on elephant gas doesn't matter. However, my point is not to ridicule the makers of this documentary but to ridicule *me.* Remember, I said I told two people about this claim before I started to doubt it. For decades, I had taught students to question assertions and evaluate the evidence, and here I was, uncritically accepting a silly statement and telling other people, who for all I know, may have gone on to tell other people. The point is that all of us yield to the temptation to accept unsupported claims, and we all need to discipline ourselves to question the evidence, especially evidence supporting claims that we would like to believe. This chapter concerns evaluating evidence in psychology.

Yakobchuk Viacheslav/Shutterstock.com

module 2.1

Evaluating Evidence and Thinking Critically

After studying this module, you should be able to:

1. Discuss the importance of replicable results.

2. Contrast falsifiability with burden of proof.

3. Explain why scientists seek the most parsimonious explanation of any result.

4. Explain why most psychologists are skeptical of claims of extrasensory perception.

What constitutes an explanation? Consider the following quote ("The Medals and the Damage Done," 2004, p. 604):

> In 2002, [Michael] Brennan was a British national rowing champion. . . . As the UK Olympic trials loomed, Brennan was feeling confident. But . . . for much of the past 12 months, Brennan's performance has been eroded by constant colds, aching joints and fatigue. . . . When the trials rolled round this April, Brennan . . . finished at the bottom of the heap. "I couldn't believe it," he says. To an experienced sports doctor, the explanation is obvious: Brennan has "unexplained underperformance syndrome" (UPS).

What do you think? Is "unexplained underperformance syndrome" an *explanation?*

Consider other examples: Birds fly south for the winter "because they have an instinct." Certain people get into fights "because they are aggressive." Certain students have trouble paying attention "because they have attention deficit disorder." Are these statements explanations? Or are they no better than unexplained underperformance syndrome? A good explanation goes beyond giving something a name, and finding good explanations requires good research.

Psychological Science

The word *science* derives from a Latin word meaning "knowledge." Science is a way of carefully gaining, testing, and evaluating knowledge. Psychological research follows scientific methods.

Gathering Evidence

Research starts with careful observation. The science of astronomy consists almost entirely of observation and measurement. (It is difficult to conduct experiments on stars and planets!) For a psychological example, Robert Provine (2000) studied laughter by visiting shopping malls and recording who laughed and when.

Good observations and measurements often suggest a pattern that leads to a hypothesis, which is *a clear predictive statement*, often an attempt to explain the observations. A test of a hypothesis goes through the series of steps described in the following four sections and illustrated in ▼ Figure 2.1. Articles in most scientific publications follow this sequence, too. In every chapter of this book other than the introductory chapter, you will find at least one psychological study described in a section entitled "What's the Evidence?" Each of those goes through the sequence from hypothesis to interpretation.

Hypothesis

A hypothesis can start with observations, such as noticing that some children who play violent video games are themselves aggressive. You might then form a hypothesis that imagining violence leads to actual violence. A good hypothesis leads to predictions. For example, "if we let children play violent video games, they will behave more aggressively," or "if we decrease the availability of violent video games, the crime rate will decrease."

Method

Any hypothesis could be tested in many ways. One way to test the effects of violent video games would be to examine whether children who play them more often act more violently themselves. However, that type of research does not tell us about cause and effect: Does playing a violent game lead to violence? Or is it simply that people who are already violent like to play those games?

A better method is to take a set of children, such as those attending a summer camp, randomly assign them to two groups, give them different types of video games (which we hope hold children's attention equally well), and then see whether the group playing more violent games behaves more aggressively. One limitation is that researchers control the

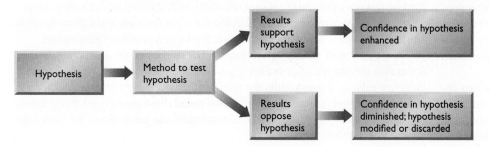

◀ **Figure 2.1** An experiment tests the predictions that follow from a hypothesis. Results either support the hypothesis or indicate a need to revise or abandon it.

children's activities for only a few days. Still another limitation is the ethical restraint against studying anything more than minor acts of aggression.

Because any method has strengths and weaknesses, researchers vary their methods. If studies using different methods all point to the same conclusion, we increase our confidence in the conclusion. A single study is almost never decisive.

Results

Fundamental to any research is measuring the outcome. A phenomenon such as "violent behavior" is tricky to measure. Do threats count? Does verbal abuse? When does a push or shove cross the line between playfulness and violence? It is important for an investigator to set clear rules about measurements. After making the measurements, the investigator determines whether the results are impressive enough to call for an explanation or whether the apparent trends might have been due to chance.

Because we have been using violent video games as the example, you are probably curious about the outcome. Analyses of the many studies of this topic, using many research methods, suggest that playing violent video games leads to a small increase in children's aggressive behaviors, on average (Ferguson, 2015; Furuya-Kanamori & Doi, 2016). However, researchers more easily publish results that support a predicted relationship than those failing to support it, and psychologists are still debating how much of the apparent effect depends on that "publication bias" (Hilgard, Engelhardt, & Rouder, 2017; Kepes, Bushman, & Anderson, 2017).

Interpretation

Researchers' final task is to consider what the results mean. If the results contradict the hypothesis, researchers should abandon or modify the original hypothesis. If the results match the prediction, investigators gain confidence in the hypothesis, but they also should consider other hypotheses that fit the results.

Replicability

Most scientific researchers are scrupulously honest in stating their methods and results. One reason is that anyone who reports a scientific study must include the methods in enough detail for other people to repeat the procedure and, we hope, get similar results. Someone who reports results falsely runs a risk of being caught, and therefore distrusted from then on.

Replicable results are *those that anyone can obtain, at least approximately, by following the same procedures.* Scientists do make certain allowances for small effects. For example, one method of

teaching might work better than another, but only slightly, so the advantage might not appear in all studies. When researchers try to verify a small effect, they use a meta-analysis, *which combines the results of many studies as if they were all one huge study.* A meta-analysis also determines which variations in procedure increase or decrease the effects. However, if no one finds conditions under which the phenomenon occurs fairly consistently, we do not take it seriously. This rule may seem harsh, but it is our best defense against error.

Consider an example of a nonreplicable result. In the 1960s and early 1970s, several researchers trained rats to do something, chopped up the rats' brains, extracted certain chemicals, and injected those chemicals into untrained animals. The recipients then apparently remembered what the first group of rats had learned to do. From what we know of brain functioning, theoretically this procedure shouldn't work, but if it did, imagine the possibilities. Some people proposed, semiseriously, that someday you could get an injection of European history or introduction to calculus instead of going to class. Alas, the results were not replicable. When other researchers repeated the procedures, most of them found no effect from the brain extracts (L. T. Smith, 1974).

Psychological researchers have become increasingly concerned about the replicability of their findings. We shall consider the issue in more detail in the second module of this chapter.

1. **Suppose several studies report some result, whereas several others do not. The studies vary in size, quality, and results. How do we decide whether the results support the hypothesis?**

Answer

1. Someone may conduct a meta-analysis that combines all studies as if they were one large study.

Evaluating Scientific Theories

If replicable data support a hypothesis, eventually researchers propose a theory. In science, a theory is not just a guess. It is *an explanation or model that fits many observations and makes accurate predictions.* A good theory starts with as few assumptions as possible and leads to many correct predictions. In that way, it reduces the amount of information we must remember. The periodic table in chemistry is an excellent example: From the information about the elements, we can predict the properties of an enormous number of compounds.

One important reason for scientific progress is that scientists generally agree on how to evaluate theories. Whereas most people can hardly imagine evidence that would change their religious or political views, scientists can generally imagine evidence that would make them abandon or modify their favorite theories. (Oh, not always, of course. Some people can be stubborn.)

Falsifiability and Burden of Proof

The philosopher Karl Popper emphasized scientists' willingness to disconfirm their theories by saying that the purpose of research is to find which theories are *incorrect.* That is, the point of research is to *falsify* the incorrect theories, and a good theory is one that withstands all attempts to falsify it. It wins by a process of elimination.

A well-formed theory is falsifiable—that is, *stated in such clear, precise terms that we can see what evidence would count against it*—if, of course, such evidence existed. For example, the theory of gravity makes precise predictions about falling objects. Because people have tested these predictions many times, and none of the observations have disconfirmed the predictions, we have high confidence in the theory.

This point is worth restating because "falsifiable" sounds like a bad thing. Falsifiable does not mean we actually have evidence against a theory. (If we did, it would be falsi*fied.*) Falsifiable means we can *imagine* a result that would contradict the theory. If a theory makes no definite prediction, it is not falsifiable. For example, many physicists believe that ours is just one among a huge number, perhaps an infinite number, of other universes. Can you imagine any evidence *against* that view? If not, it is not a good theory (Steinhardt, 2014). For a psychology example, Sigmund Freud claimed that all dreams are motivated by wish fulfillment. If you have a happy dream, it appears to be a wish fulfillment. However, if you have an unhappy dream, then Freud claimed that a censor in your brain disguised the wish. As Domhoff (2003) noted, Freud stated his theory in such a way that any observation counted for it or at least not against it (see ▶ Figure 2.2). If no possible observation could falsify the theory, it is too vague to be useful.

However, when Popper wrote that research is *always* an attempt to falsify a theory, he went too far. "All objects fall" (the law of gravity) is falsifiable. "Some objects fall" is not falsifiable, although it is certainly true—a pitifully weak statement, but nevertheless true. If "some objects fall" *were* false, you could not *demonstrate* it to be false!

Instead of insisting that all research is an effort to falsify a theory, another approach is to discuss **burden of proof**, *the obligation to present evidence to support one's claim.* In a criminal trial, the burden of proof is on the prosecution. If the prosecution does not make a convincing case, the defendant goes free. The reason is that the prosecution should be able to find convincing evidence if someone is guilty, but in many cases innocent defendants could not possibly demonstrate their innocence.

Similarly, in science, the burden of proof is on anyone who makes a claim that should be demonstrable, if it is true. For the claim "some objects fall," the burden of proof is on anyone who supports the claim. (It's easy to fulfill that burden of proof, of course.) For the claim "every object falls," we cannot expect anyone to demonstrate it to be true for every object, and so the burden of proof is on someone who doubts the claim. We continue to believe the statement unless someone shows an exception. For a claim such as "UFOs from outer space have visited Earth" or "some people have psychic powers to perceive things without any sensory information," the burden of proof is on anyone who supports these statements. If they are true, someone should be able to show clear evidence.

Parsimony

What do we do if several theories fit the known facts? Suppose you notice that a picture on your wall is hanging on an angle. You consider four explanations:

- The ground shook when a truck drove by.
- A gust of wind moved the picture.
- One of your friends bumped it without telling you.
- A ghost moved it.

All four explanations fit the observation, but we don't consider them on an equal basis. When given a choice among explanations that seem to fit the facts, we prefer the one whose assumptions are fewer, simpler, or more consistent with what we already know. This is known as the principle of **parsimony** (literally "stinginess") or *Occam's razor* (after the philosopher William of Occam). The principle of parsimony is a conservative idea: We stick with ideas that work and try as hard as we can to avoid new assumptions (e.g., ghosts).

Parsimony and Degrees of Open-Mindedness

The principle of parsimony tells us to adhere to what we already believe, to resist radically new hypotheses. You might protest: "Shouldn't we remain

▲ **Figure 2.2** According to Freud, every dream is based on wish fulfillment. If a dream seems unhappy, it is because a censor in your head disguised the wish. Can you imagine any observation that would contradict this theory?

open-minded to new possibilities?" Yes, if open-mindedness means a willingness to consider proper evidence, but not if it means that "anything has as much chance of being true as anything else." The stronger the reasons behind a current opinion, the more evidence you should need before replacing it.

For example, many people have attempted to build a "perpetual motion machine," one that generates more energy than it uses. ▼ Figure 2.3 shows an example. The U.S. Patent Office is officially closed-minded on this issue, refusing even to consider patent applications for such machines. Physicists are convinced, both for logical reasons and because of consistent observations, that any work wastes energy, and that keeping a machine going always requires energy. If someone shows you what appears to be a perpetual motion machine, look for a hidden battery or other power source. If you don't find one, assume that you overlooked it. A claim as extraordinary as a perpetual motion machine requires extraordinary evidence.

Let's consider a couple of examples from psychology in which people have claimed very surprising results. Although it is fair to examine the evidence, it is also important to maintain a skeptical attitude and look as closely as possible for a simple, parsimonious explanation.

Applying Parsimony: Clever Hans, the Amazing Horse

Early in the 20th century, Wilhelm von Osten, a German mathematics teacher, set out to demonstrate the intellectual ability of his horse, Hans. To teach Hans arithmetic, he first showed him an object, said "one," and lifted Hans's foot. He raised Hans's foot twice for two objects and so on. With practice, Hans learned to look at a set of objects and tap the correct number of times. Soon it was no longer necessary for Hans to see the objects. Von Osten would just call out a number, and Hans would tap the appropriate number.

Mr. von Osten moved on to addition and then to subtraction, multiplication, and division. Hans caught on quickly, soon responding with 90 to 95 percent accuracy. Then von Osten and Hans began touring Germany, giving public demonstrations. Hans's abilities grew until he could add fractions, convert fractions to decimals or decimals to fractions, do algebra, tell time to the minute, and give the values of German coins. Using a letter-to-number code, he could spell the names of objects and identify musical notes such as B-flat. (Evidently, he had perfect pitch.) He was usually correct even when questions were put to him by people other than von Osten, with von Osten out of sight.

Given this evidence, many people were ready to believe that Hans had great intellectual powers. But others sought a more parsimonious explanation. Oskar Pfungst (1911) observed that Hans could answer a question correctly only if the questioner knew the answer. Apparently, the questioner was giving away the answer. Also, Hans was accurate only when the questioner stood in plain sight.

Eventually, Pfungst observed that anyone who asked Hans a question would lean forward to watch Hans's foot. Hans had learned to start tapping whenever someone stood next to his forefoot and leaned forward. After Hans reached the correct number of taps, the questioner would give a slight upward jerk of the head and a change in facial expression, anticipating that this might be the last tap. Even skeptical scientists who tested Hans did this involuntarily. After all, they thought, wouldn't it be exciting if Hans got it right? Hans simply continued tapping until he saw that cue.

In short, Hans was indeed a clever horse, but we do not believe that he understood mathematics. Pfungst demonstrated that he could explain Hans's behavior in the parsimonious terms of responses to facial expressions, and therefore, no one needed to assume anything more complex.

Applying Parsimony: Extrasensory Perception

The possibility of extrasensory perception (ESP) has long been controversial in psychology. Supporters of extrasensory perception claim that *some people sometimes acquire information without receiving any energy through any sense organ.* Supporters claim that people with ESP can identify someone else's thoughts (telepathy) even from a great distance and despite barriers that would block any known form of energy. Supporters also claim that certain people can perceive objects that are hidden

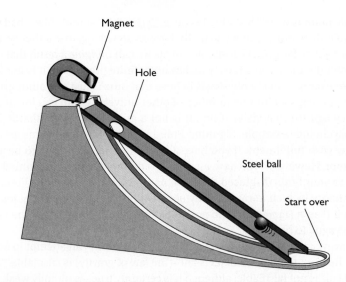

▲ **Figure 2.3** A proposed perpetual motion machine: The magnet pulls the metal ball up the inclined plane. When the ball reaches the top, it falls through the hole and returns to its starting point, from which the magnet will again pull the ball up. Can you see why this device is sure to fail? (See answer A on page 32.)

from sight (clairvoyance), predict the future (precognition), and influence such physical events as a roll of dice by mental concentration (psychokinesis).

Accepting any of these claims would require us not only to overhaul major concepts in psychology but also to discard the most fundamental tenets of physics. What evidence is there for ESP?

Anecdotes

Anecdotes are people's reports of isolated events, such as a dream or hunch that comes true. Such experiences often seem impressive, but they are not scientific evidence. Sooner or later, amazing coincidences are sure to occur, and people tend to remember them. On February 29, 1964, two North Carolina high school basketball teams played a game that lasted 13 overtimes, the

Clever Hans and his owner, Mr. von Osten, demonstrated that the horse could answer complex mathematical questions with great accuracy. The question was, "How?" (After Pfungst, 1911, in Fernald, 1984.)

1. The great man will be struck down in the day by a thunderbolt. An evil deed, foretold by the bearer of a petition. According to the prediction another falls at night time. Conflict at Reims, London, and pestilence in Tuscany.

2. When the fish that travels over both land and sea is cast up on to the shore by a great wave, its shape foreign, smooth, and frightful. From the sea the enemies soon reach the walls.

3. The bird of prey flying to the left, before battle is joined with the French, he makes preparations. Some will regard him as good, others bad or uncertain. The weaker party will regard him as a good omen.

4. Shortly afterwards, not a very long interval, a great tumult will be raised by land and sea. The naval battles will be greater than ever. Fires, creatures which will make more tumult.

◀ **Figure 2.4** According to the followers of Nostradamus, each of these statements is a specific prophecy of a 20th-century event (Cheetham, 1973). What do you think the prophecies mean? Compare your answers to answer B on page 32.

longest high-school game ever. Meanwhile on the same night, two Tennessee high school basketball teams played a game that lasted 9 overtimes, tied for the third longest ever. Wow, what are the odds against that? Well, this is the wrong question. The odds against that particular coincidence may be high, but this was just one of an incalculably huge number of coincidences that could have occurred, somewhere, sometime. In fact, we should expect unlikely coincidences to happen fairly often.

Furthermore, we tend to remember, discuss, and exaggerate the hunches and dreams that come true, while we forget the ones that don't. We could evaluate anecdotal evidence only if people recorded their hunches and dreams *before* the possible events.

You may have heard of the "prophet Nostradamus," a 16th-century French writer who allegedly predicted many events of later centuries. ▲ **Figure 2.4** presents four samples of his writings. All of his predictions are at this level of vagueness. After something happens, people imaginatively reinterpret his writings to fit the event. (If we don't know what a prediction means until *after* it occurs, is it really a prediction?)

Professional Psychics

Various stage performers claim to read other people's minds and perform other amazing feats. The Amazing Kreskin prefers to talk of his "extremely sensitive" rather than "extrasensory" perception (Kreskin, 1991). Still, part of his success as a performer comes from allowing people to believe he has uncanny mental powers.

After carefully observing Kreskin and others, David Marks and Richard Kammann (1980) concluded that they used the same kinds of deception commonly employed in magic acts. For example, Kreskin sometimes begins his act by asking the audience to read his mind. Let's try to duplicate this trick right now: Try to read my mind. I am thinking of a number between 1 and 50. Both digits are odd numbers, but they are not the same. For example, it could be 15 but it could not be 11. (These are the instructions Kreskin gives.) Have you chosen a number? Please do.

Dum, dum, da, dum. . . I am waiting for you to think of a number.

All right, my number was 37. Did you think of 37? If not, how about 35? You see, I started to think 35 and then changed my mind, so you might have got 35.

If you successfully "read my mind," are you impressed? Don't be. At first, it seemed that you had many numbers to choose from (1 to 50), but by the end of the instructions, you had only a few. The first digit had to be 1 or 3, and the second had to be 1, 3, 5, 7, or 9. You eliminated 11 and 33 because both digits are the same, and you probably eliminated 15 because I cited it as a possible example. That leaves only seven possibilities. Most people stay far away from the example given and tend to avoid the highest and lowest possible choices. That leaves 37 as the most likely choice and 35 as the second most likely.

Magician Lance Burton can make people and animals seem to suddenly appear, disappear, float in the air, or do other things that we know are impossible. Even if we don't know how he accomplishes these feats, we take it for granted that they are based on methods of misleading the audience.

Second act: Kreskin asks the audience to write down something they are thinking about while he walks along the aisles talking. Then, back on stage, he "reads people's minds." He might say something like, "Someone is thinking about his mother. . . ." In any large crowd, someone is bound to shout, "Yes, that's me. You read my mind!" On occasion he describes in great detail something that someone has written. Generally, that person was sitting along the aisle where Kreskin was walking.

After a variety of other tricks (see Marks & Kammann, 1980), Kreskin goes backstage while the mayor or some other dignitary hides Kreskin's paycheck somewhere in the audience. Then Kreskin comes back, walks up and down the aisles, across the rows, and eventually shouts, "The check is here!" The rule is that if he guesses wrong, then he does not get paid. (He hardly ever misses.)

How does he do it? It is a Clever Hans trick. Kreskin studies people's faces. Most people want him to find the check, so they get more excited as he gets close to it and more disappointed or distressed if he moves away. In effect they are saying, "Now you're getting closer" and "Now you're moving away." Gradually he closes in on the check.

Experiments

Because anecdotes and stage performances occur under uncontrolled conditions, they are nearly worthless as scientific evidence. Laboratory experiments provide the only evidence about ESP worth serious consideration.

Over the years, researchers have tried many procedures, including guessing the order of a deck of cards, guessing numbers generated by a random-number generator, and describing a remote setting that someone else is viewing. In each case, initial studies generated excitement that subsided after other researchers failed to replicate the findings. For example, in the *ganzfeld* procedure (from German words meaning "entire field"), a "sender" views a photo or film, selected at random from four possibilities, and a "receiver" in another room is asked to describe the sender's thoughts and images. Typically, the receiver wears half Ping-Pong balls over the eyes and listens to static noise through earphones to minimize normal stimuli that might overpower the presumably weak extrasensory stimuli (see ▼ Figure 2.5). Later, a judge examines a transcript of what the receiver said and compares it to the four photos or films, determining which one it matches most closely. On average, it should match the target about one in four times. If a receiver "hits" more often than one in four, we can calculate the probability of accidentally doing that well. One review reported that 6 of the 10 laboratories using this method found positive results (Bem & Honorton, 1994). However, 14 later studies from 7 laboratories failed to find evidence that differed from chance (Milton & Wiseman, 1999).

In 2011, a prestigious journal published a series of studies claiming to show that people can foresee the future (Bem, 2011). In one study, college students clicked on the left or right side of the screen to predict which side would show a picture. After the guess, the computer randomly chose one side or the other. If it matched the student's guess, it displayed an erotic photograph of a couple engaged in a sex act. The experimenter reported that students' guesses matched the computer's choice 53 percent of the time, suggesting an ability to predict the future. In another of the studies, students read a list of words, tried to recall them, and then studied half of the list again. The report was that the students remembered more of the words that they studied again after the recall test. That is, you could improve your score on a test by studying the material after the test was over! (If you believe this can work, you are welcome to try it.)

Radivoke Lajic holds six rocks that he claims are meteorites that struck his house.

Europics/Newscom

Before you revise your study habits, however, you should know that other psychologists have noted many problems and oddities in both the research procedures and the statistical analysis of results (Alcock, 2011; Rouder & Morey, 2011). Also, researchers at seven universities repeated the procedures exactly, using thousands of participants, and failed to find any hint of an effect (Galak, LeBoeuf, & Nelson, 2012; Ritchie, Wiseman, & French, 2012). Another lab tried a modified procedure and also failed to find any benefit from studying again after the test (Traxler, Foss, Polali, & Zirnstein, 2012). Given the long history of promising but unreplicable results, most psychologists remain skeptical of all ESP claims.

The lack of replicability is one major reason to be skeptical of ESP, but another reason is parsimony. If someone claims that a horse does mathematics or a person foresees random events, we should search thoroughly for a simple explanation.

◀ **Figure 2.5** In the ganzfeld procedure, a "receiver," who is deprived of most normal sensory information, tries to describe the photo or film that a "sender" is examining.

Fortean/TopFoto/The Image Works

---

in closing | module 2.1

Scientific Thinking in Psychology

What have we learned about science in general? Science does not deal with proof or certainty. All scientific conclusions are tentative and are subject to revision. Nevertheless, this tentativeness does not imply that it is okay to abandon well-established theories without excellent reasons.

Scientists always prefer the most parsimonious theory. Before they accept any claim that requires a major new assumption, they insist that it be supported by replicable experiments that rule out simpler explanations and by a new theory that is clearly superior to the theory it replaces.

Summary

- *Steps in a scientific study.* A scientific study goes through the following sequence of steps: hypothesis, method, results, and interpretation. Because almost any study is subject to more than one possible interpretation, we base our conclusions on a pattern of results from many studies. (page 25)
- *Replicability.* The results of a given study are taken seriously only if other investigators following the same method obtain similar results. (page 26)
- *Falsifiability and burden of proof.* A good theory should be stated in a way that makes it falsifiable. That is, we should be able to imagine an observation that would contradict it. In any

dispute, the side that should be capable of presenting clear evidence has the obligation to do so. (page 26)
- *Parsimony.* All else being equal, scientists prefer the theory that relies on simpler assumptions, or assumptions consistent with other theories that are already accepted. (page 27)
- *Skepticism about extrasensory perception.* Psychologists carefully scrutinize any claims of extrasensory perception, because the evidence reported so far has been unreplicable, and because the scientific approach includes a search for parsimonious explanations. (page 28)

Key Terms

burden of proof (page 27)

extrasensory perception (ESP) (page 28)

falsifiable (page 26)

hypothesis (page 25)

meta-analysis (page 26)

parsimony (page 27)

replicable result (page 26)

theory (page 26)

Answers to Other Questions in the Module

A. Any magnet strong enough to pull the metal ball up the inclined plane would not release the ball when it reached the hole at the top. It would pull the ball across the hole. (page 28)

B. The prophecies of Nostradamus (see page 29), as interpreted by Cheetham (1973), refer to the following: (1) the assassinations of John F. Kennedy and Robert F. Kennedy, (2) Polaris ballistic missiles shot from submarines, (3) Hitler's invasion of France, and (4) World War II.

Review Questions

1. The term "replicable" applies to which step in a research study?
   (a) The hypothesis
   (b) The results
   (c) The interpretation
   (d) The researcher

2. What does a meta-analysis do?
   (a) It reexamines the results of a disputed study.
   (b) It looks for deeper, hidden meanings.
   (c) It considers the possible conclusions from data not yet collected.
   (d) It combines the results from many studies.

3. Are Nostradamus's predictions falsifiable? Why or why not?
   (a) Yes, they are falsifiable, because many have not come true.
   (b) Yes, they are falsifiable, because they have not been studied scientifically.
   (c) Yes, they are falsifiable, because some of the predictions contradict one another.
   (d) No, they are not falsifiable, because they make no unambiguous predictions.

4. A search for parsimony is a search for what?
   (a) Falsifiability
   (b) Simplicity
   (c) Replicability
   (d) Deep meaning

5. The claims for ESP lack two essential aspects. What are they?
   (a) Hypotheses and data
   (b) Egocentrism and perspicacity
   (c) Replicability and parsimony
   (d) Structuralism and functionalism

Answer: 1b, 2d, 3d, 4b, 5c.

Thought Question

For the statement, "Ours is just one of an infinite number of universes," who has the burden of proof—those who support the statement or those who deny it? How should we handle a statement when it may be impossible to get firm evidence either for it or against it?

Yakobchuk Viacheslav/Shutterstock.com

After studying this module, you should be able to:

1. Give examples of operational definitions.

2. Distinguish between convenience samples, representative samples, random samples, and cross-cultural samples.

3. Explain why experiments can lead to cause-and-effect conclusions, whereas correlational studies do not.

4. Cite pitfalls that might compromise the effectiveness of a survey or an experiment.

5. Describe how researchers use descriptive and inferential statistics to evaluate the results of a study.

6. Discuss reasons why a study's results might not be replicable.

7. Discuss how psychological researchers deal with ethical issues.

Psychology, like any other field, makes progress only when its practitioners distinguish between strong evidence and weak evidence. The goal of this module is not necessarily to prepare you to conduct your own psychological research, but to help you interpret research results intelligently. When you hear about a new study, you should be able to ask pertinent questions to decide how good the evidence is, what conclusion follows, and how confidently you should accept that conclusion.

General Research Principles

Research falls into two major categories, basic and applied. **Basic research** seeks theoretical knowledge, such as understanding the processes of learning and memory. **Applied research** deals with practical problems, such as how to help children with learning disabilities or how to improve study habits. The two kinds of research are mutually supportive. Understanding the basic processes helps applied researchers develop effective interventions. Those working toward practical solutions sometimes discover principles that are theoretically important.

Psychological researchers use scientific methods, but they face problems that chemists and physicists do not. One problem is sampling. A psychologist who studies a group of people has to worry about whether they might be unusual in some way. A chemist studying, say, methane molecules doesn't have that worry. One sample of methane molecules is the same as another. Another problem is that people who know they are in a research study behave self-consciously, because they know someone is watching. Chemists don't have that worry about a jar of chemicals. In this module, we explore some of the special ways that psychologists adapt scientific principles.

concept check

4. **Is a study of cultural differences in social behavior an example of basic or applied research?**

Answer

4. It is basic research, an attempt to understand something. However, it could lead to practical applications.

Operational Definitions

Suppose a physicist asks you to measure the effect of temperature on the length of an iron bar. You reply, "What do we *really mean* by temperature?" The physicist sighs, "Don't worry about it. Here is a thermometer and a ruler. Go measure them."

Psychological researchers use the same strategy. If we want to measure the effect of anger on behavior, we could debate forever about what anger really is, or we could choose a way to measure it. We might ask people to tell us how angry they are, or we might count frowns per minute or swear words per minute, or we might find some other way to measure anger. In doing so, we are using an **operational definition**, *a definition that specifies the operations (or procedures) used to produce or measure something, if possible giving it a numerical value.* You might object that "frowns per minute" is not what anger really is. Of course not, but the reading on a thermometer is also not what temperature really is. An operational definition just says how to measure something. It lets us get on with research.

Suppose we want to investigate friendliness. We would need an operational definition of friendliness. We might define your friendliness as the number of people you smile at during an hour or the number of people you list as close friends. We might operationally define *love* as "how long you remain with someone who asks you to stay nearby."

concept check

5. **Which of the following is an operational definition of forgetting?**

a. The process whereby a memory trace decays in the brain

b. An inability to remember something that you once knew

c. What happens when you don't study hard enough

d. The difference between scores on memory tests at two times

6. **In a study of nonhuman animals, what would you propose as an operational definition of "good mothering"?**

Answers

6. An effective operational definition would be the number of offspring that survive to maturity. Other definitions are possible if they include a method of measurement.

5. (d) The difference between two scores is an operational definition, because it specifies a way to measure.

Population Samples

In a chemistry lab, if you find the properties of some compound, your results apply to that same compound anywhere. Psychology is different. The results of a study on one group of people may or may not apply to other groups of people.

For some purposes, the worry is small. For example, research on certain aspects of vision and hearing can use anyone who is available, and in some cases laboratory animals. Researchers who expect the results to be about the same for almost everyone can use a convenience sample, *a group chosen because of its ease of study.* Unfortunately, many researchers overuse research on college students, a convenience sample that is satisfactory for some purposes but not all.

When comparing two populations, researchers need similar samples of those populations. Consider this example: Every fall, the newspapers report the average SAT scores for each American state, and certain states do consistently better than others. At least part of the explanation relates to sampling. In certain states, nearly all college-bound students take the SAT, whereas in others the in-state colleges require the ACT instead, and the only students taking the SAT are those applying to an out-of-state college (maybe one of the Ivy League colleges, for example). We cannot meaningfully compare the results if we test the average students in one state and the best students in another.

A big improvement over a convenience sample is a representative sample, *one that resembles the population* in its percentage of males and females, various ethnic groups, young and old, or whatever other characteristics seem likely to affect the results. To get a representative sample of the people in a region, an investigator first determines what percentage of the residents belong to each category and then selects people to match those percentages. Of course, a sample that is representative in one way might be unrepresentative in another.

Best of all is a random sample, *one in which every individual in the population has an equal chance of being studied.* To produce a random sample of Toronto residents, an investigator might start with a map of Toronto and select a certain number of city blocks at random, randomly select one house from each of those blocks, and then randomly choose one person from each of those households. *Random* here has a special meaning. If you simply say, "Okay, I'll pick this block, this block, and this block," the results are not random, because you may be following a pattern unintentionally. A better procedure is to draw cards out of a hat or some similar procedure that gives every block an equal chance of being chosen. A random sample has this advantage: The larger a random sample, the smaller the probability that its results differ substantially from the

College students are often used as convenience samples.

whole population. However, although a random sample is theoretically the best, it is difficult to achieve. For example, some of the people you randomly choose might refuse to participate!

A psychologist who wants to talk about humans in general, and not just one culture, needs a cross-cultural sample, *groups of people from at least two cultures.* Most people in the United States have been described as Western, Educated, Industrial, Rich (compared to the rest of the world), and Democratic—abbreviated WEIRD (Henrich, Heine, & Norenzayan, 2010). You might or might not like the abbreviation, but the point is that we need to take cultural differences seriously.

We know to expect cultural differences in matters of diet and leisure activities (Kobayashi, 2011), religion, politics, and sexual behavior. Differences also emerge where we might not have expected them. Here are two examples: First, in the United States, expressions of anger are more common among people of lower social status, presumably because they experience more frustration. In Japan, people of higher status show more anger, because anger is associated with authority (Park et al., 2013). Second, if you were asked to arrange a series of pictures in order from the first event to the last to tell a story, you would probably arrange the pictures from left to right. Australian aborigines arrange the pictures from east to west, regardless of which direction the people themselves are facing (Boroditsky & Gaby, 2010). Doing so, of course, requires them always to know which direction is east. For them, the arrow of time goes east to west, just as Americans think of it as going from left to right.

■ Table 2.1 reviews the major types of samples.

concept
check

7. **Suppose at a shopping mall you interview every person who walks by. What kind of sample is this—convenience, representative, or random?**

8. **In the United States, people who express much anger are more likely than average to suffer heart attacks or other health problems. However, in Japan, expressing anger is associated with good health. What is a reasonable explanation?**

Answers

8. In Japan, only the wealthy or powerful are expected to express anger. Higher socioeconomic status is associated with better health.

7. This is a convenience sample. You did not get a sample that matches the total population in age or anything else, so it is not a representative sample. Everyone in the total population did not have an equal chance of participating, because not all kinds of people are equally likely to be in the mall at that time.

Table 2.1 Types of Samples

Sample	Individuals Included	Advantages and Disadvantages
Convenience sample	Anyone who is available	Easiest to get, but results may not generalize to the whole population
Representative sample	Same percentage of male/female, white/black, etc., as the whole population	Results probably similar to whole population, although sample may be representative in some ways but not others
Random sample	Everyone in population has same chance of being chosen	Difficult to get this kind of sample, but it is the best suited for generalizing to the whole population
Cross-cultural	People from different cultures	Difficulties include language barriers, cooperation problems, etc., but essential for studying many issues

Observational Research Designs

Most research starts with description: What happens and when? Let's first examine several kinds of observational studies. Later we consider experiments, which are designed to explore cause-and-effect relationships.

Naturalistic Observations

A **naturalistic observation** is *a careful examination of what happens under more or less natural conditions.* For example, biologist Jane Goodall (1971) spent years observing chimpanzees in the wild, recording their food habits, social interactions, gestures, and way of life (see ▼ Figure 2.6).

▲ **Figure 2.6** In a naturalistic study, observers record the behavior in a natural setting. Here noted biologist Jane Goodall records her observations on chimpanzees. By patiently staying with the chimps, Goodall gradually won their trust and learned to recognize individual animals.

Similarly, psychologists sometimes try to observe and describe human behavior. A psychologist might observe how many strangers smile at each other when they pass on a street. How much does the behavior differ between small towns and crowded cities? Who smiles more, women or men? Young people or old people?

Case Histories

Some fascinating conditions are rare. For example, some people are almost completely insensitive to pain. People with Capgras syndrome believe that some of their relatives have been replaced with impostors, who look, sound, and act like the real people. People with Cotard's syndrome insist that they are dead or do not exist. A psychologist who encounters someone with a rare condition like these may report a **case history**, *a thorough description of someone's abilities and disabilities, medical condition, life history, unusual experiences, and whatever else seems relevant.* A case history is a kind of naturalistic observation, but we distinguish it because it focuses on a single individual.

A case history has limitations. It includes only those aspects that the researcher recorded, and any researcher overlooks some facts and possibly misinterprets others. Some of the facts that the researcher emphasizes might be irrelevant. Nevertheless, case reports have made important contributions in psychology. Observations of several brain-damaged patients revolutionized our understanding of memory (Shallice, 2019), and studies of other brain-damaged patients added to our understanding of emotion. Case histories are especially useful if researchers locate several individuals with similar conditions.

Surveys

A **survey** is *a study of the prevalence of certain beliefs, attitudes, or behaviors based on people's responses to questions.* No matter what your occupation, at some time you will probably conduct a survey of your employees, your customers, your neighbors, or fellow members of an organization. You will also frequently read and hear about survey results. You should be aware of the ways in which survey results can be useful or misleading.

Sampling

Getting a random or representative sample is important in any research, but especially with surveys. In 1936, the *Literary Digest* mailed 10 million postcards, asking people their choice for president of the United States. Of the 2 million responses, 57 percent preferred the Republican candidate, Alfred Landon.

A psychological researcher tests generalizations about human behavior by comparing people from different cultures.

Later that year, the Democratic candidate, Franklin Roosevelt, defeated Landon by a wide margin. Why was the survey so wrong? The problem was that the *Literary Digest* had selected names from the telephone book and automobile registration lists. In 1936, during the Great Depression, few poor people (who were mostly Democrats) owned telephones or cars.

The Seriousness of Those Responding

When taking a survey, how carefully do you consider your answers? In one survey, only 45 percent of the respondents said they believed in the existence of intelligent life on other planets. However, a few questions later on the survey, 82 percent said they believed the U.S. government was "hiding evidence of intelligent life in space" (Emery, 1997). Did 37 percent of the people *really* think that the U.S. government is hiding evidence of something that doesn't exist? Or did they answer impulsively without much thought? Another survey asked whether you believe the government is hiding what it knows about the North Dakota crash. Many people said yes, in spite of the fact that there had been no North Dakota crash.

Try It Yourself Here's another example: Which of the following programs would you most like to see on television reruns? Rate your choices from highest (1) to lowest (10). (Please fill in your answers, either in the text or on a separate sheet of paper, before continuing to the next paragraph.)

___South Park   ___Game of Thrones

___Star Trek   ___Big Bang Theory

___Cheers   ___The Good Place

___Seinfeld   ___Space Doctor

___I Love Lucy   ___M*A*S*H*

When I conducted a similar survey with my own students at North Carolina State University, nearly all did exactly what I asked—they gave every program a rating, including *Space Doctor,* a program that never existed. More than 10 percent rated it in the top five, and a few ranked it as their top choice. (This survey was inspired by an old *Candid Camera* episode in which interviewers asked people their opinions of the nonexistent program *Space Doctor* and received many confident replies.)

Students who rated *Space Doctor* did nothing wrong, of course. I asked them to rank programs, and they did. The fault lies with anyone who interprets such survey results as if they represented informed opinions.

The Wording of the Questions

Try It Yourself Let's start with a little demonstration. Please answer these two questions:

1. I oppose raising taxes. (Circle one.)

    1   2   3   4   5   6   7

    Strongly agree   Strongly disagree

2. I make it a practice to never lie. (Circle one.)

    1   2   3   4   5   6   7

    Strongly agree   Strongly disagree

Now cover up those answers and reply to these similar questions:

3. I would be willing to pay a few extra dollars in taxes to provide high-quality education to all children. (Circle one.)

    1   2   3   4   5   6   7

    Strongly agree   Strongly disagree

4. Like all human beings, I occasionally tell a white lie. (Circle one.)

    1   2   3   4   5   6   7

    Strongly agree   Strongly disagree

Most students in one study indicated agreement to all four items (Madson, 2005). Note that item 1 contradicts 3, and 2 contradicts 4. You cannot be opposed to raising taxes and in favor of raising taxes. You cannot be honest all the time and occasionally lie. However, the wording of a question changes its connotation. Question 3 talks about raising taxes "a few extra dollars" for a worthy cause. That differs from raising taxes by an unknown amount for unknown reasons. Similarly, depending on what you mean by a "white lie," you might tell one occasionally while still insisting that you "make it a practice to never lie"—at least not much. The point is that someone can bias your answers one way or the other by rewording a question.

"I'm an honest person but when I take an online survey, I'm a big liar."

Some odd survey results merely reflect the fact that people did not take the questions seriously or did not understand the questions.

Bacall, Aaron/Cartoonstock

Here is another example. Women were asked, "How much sexual interest does your friend have in the man she is currently dating?" Also, they were asked, "How much sexual interest would your friend *say* she has in the man she is currently dating?" Asking both questions implies that we expect different answers, and biases women to report a difference (Murray, Murphy, von Hippel, Trivers, & Haselton, 2017). In short, the next time you hear the results of some survey, ask how the question was worded and what choices were offered. A different wording could yield a different percentage.

Surveyor Biases

Sometimes, an organization words the questions of a survey to encourage the answers they hope to receive. According to a 1993 survey, 92 percent of high school boys and 98 percent of high school girls said they were victims of sexual harassment (Shogren, 1993). Shocking, isn't it? However, perhaps the designers of the survey *wanted* to show that sexual harassment is rampant. The survey defined sexual harassment by a long list of acts ranging from major offenses (e.g., having someone rip your clothes off in public) to minor annoyances. For example, if you didn't like some of the sexual graffiti on the restroom wall, you could consider yourself sexually harassed. If you tried to make yourself look sexually attractive (as most teenagers do, right?) and then attracted a suggestive look from someone you *didn't* want to attract, that stare would count as sexual harassment. (I worry about those who said they *weren't* sexually harassed. They liked *all* the graffiti on the restroom walls? How is that even possible? Maybe they can't read.) Sexual harassment is, of course, a serious problem, but a survey that combines major and minor offenses is likely to mislead.

▼ Figure 2.7 shows the results for two surveys conducted on similar populations at about the same time. The issue is whether stem cells derived from aborted fetuses can be used in medical research. Note how the different wording led to different answers (Public Agenda, 2001).

Correlational Studies

Another type of research is a correlational study. A **correlation** is *a measure of the relationship between two variables.* A variable is anything measurable that differs among individuals, such as age, years of education, or reading speed. In a correlational study, investigators

Stem cells are the basic cells from which all of a person's tissues and organs develop. Congress is considering whether to provide federal funding for experiments using stem cells from human embryos. The live embryos would be destroyed in their first week of development to obtain these cells. Do you support or oppose using your federal tax dollars for such experiments?

Sometimes fertility clinics produce extra fertilized eggs, also known as embryos, that are not implanted in a woman's womb. These extra embryos either are discarded, or couples can donate them for use in medical research called stem cell research. Some people support stem cell research, saying it's an important way to find treatments for many diseases. Other people oppose stem cell research, saying it's wrong to use any human embryos for research purposes. What about you—do you support or oppose stem cell research?

◀ **Figure 2.7** The question on the left led most people to express opposition. The question on the right, worded differently, led most people to express support.

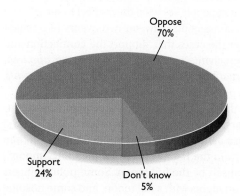

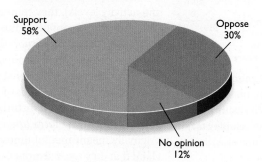

measure the relation between variables that they do not control. For example, someone might measure the correlation between people's height and weight, or the correlation between scores on an extraversion questionnaire and how many friends someone has.

The Correlation Coefficient

Some pairs of variables are related more strongly than others. To measure the strength of a correlation, researchers use a correlation coefficient, *a mathematical estimate of the relationship between two variables*. A correlation coefficient of zero indicates no consistent relationship. A coefficient of +1 or −1 indicates a perfect relationship. That is, if you know the value of one variable, you can predict the other with perfect accuracy. In psychology you probably will never see a perfect +1 or −1 correlation coefficient. A positive coefficient means that as one variable increases, the other usually increases also. A negative coefficient means that as one variable increases, the other usually decreases. A negative correlation is just as useful as a positive correlation. For example, the more often people practice golf, the lower their golf scores, so golf practice is negatively correlated with scores. In nations where people eat more seafood, depression is less common, so seafood consumption is negatively correlated with depression, as shown in ▼ Figure 2.8 (Gómez-Pinilla, 2008).

A 0 correlation indicates that as one variable goes up, the other does not consistently go up or down. A correlation near 0 can mean that two variables really are unrelated, or that one or both of them were poorly measured. For example, if you

ask students how eager they are to do well in school, their answers correlate almost zero with academic success (Dompnier, Darnon, & Butera, 2009). Does that mean that motivation is unimportant for school success? Hardly. How motivated students *say* they are isn't the same as how motivated they *actually* are. If a measurement is poor, we can hardly expect it to correlate with anything else.

▼ Figure 2.9 shows scatter plots for three correlations (real data). In a scatter plot, *each dot represents a given individual, with one measurement for that individual on the x-axis (horizontal) and another measurement on the y-axis (vertical)*. In Figure 2.9, each dot represents one student in an introductory psychology class. The value for that student along the y-axis represents percentage correct on the final exam. In the first graph, values along the x-axis represent scores on the first test in the course. Here the correlation is +0.72, indicating that most of the students who did well on the first test also did well on the final, and most who did poorly on the first test also did poorly on the final. In the second graph, the x-axis represents times absent out of 38 class meetings. Here you see a correlation of −0.44. This negative correlation indicates that, in general, those with more absences had lower exam scores. The third graph shows how the final exam scores related to the last three digits of each student's Social Security number. As you would expect, the correlation is close to 0. If we examined the data for a larger population of students, the correlation would no doubt come closer and closer to 0.

concept check

9. **Which indicates a stronger relationship between two variables, a +0.50 correlation or a −0.75 correlation?**

10. **What does it mean if a correlation is near zero?**

Answers

10. Either the two variables are not related to each other, or at least one of them was measured inaccurately.

9. The −0.75 correlation indicates a stronger relationship—that is, a greater accuracy of predicting one variable based on measurements of the other. A negative correlation is just as useful as a positive one.

Illusory Correlations

Sometimes we think we see a correlation that doesn't really exist. For example, many people believe that consuming sugar makes children hyperactive. However, extensive research found little effect of sugar on activity levels, and some studies found that sugar *calms* behavior (Milich, Wolraich, & Lindgren, 1986; Wolraich et al., 1994). Why, then, do many people believe that sugar makes children hyperactive? Researchers watched two sets of mothers with their 5- to 7-year-old sons after telling one group that they had given the sons sugar and the other that they had given the sons a placebo, *a pill with no known pharmacological effects*. In fact, they had given both a placebo. The mothers who *thought* their sons had been given sugar rated their sons hyperactive during the observation period, whereas the other mothers did not (Hoover & Milich, 1994). That is, people see what they expect to see.

When people expect to see a connection between two events (e.g., sugar and activity levels), they remember the cases that support the connection and disregard the exceptions, thus perceiving an illusory correlation, *an apparent relationship based on casual observations of unrelated or weakly related events*. Many stereotypes about groups of people are illusory correlations.

As another example, consider the common belief that a full moon affects human behavior. For hundreds of years, many people have believed that crime and various kinds of mental disturbance are more common under a full moon than at other times. The term *lunacy* (from the Latin word *luna,* meaning "moon") originally meant mental illness caused by the full moon. Some police officers claim that they receive more calls on nights with a full moon, and some hospital

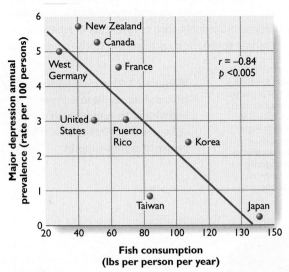

▲ **Figure 2.8** Each dot represents one country. The value along the *x*-axis indicates the amount of seafood that an average person eats in a year. The value along the *y*-axis indicates the probability of developing major depression. As seafood consumption increases, the probability of depression decreases.

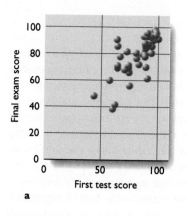
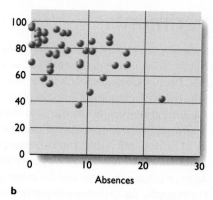
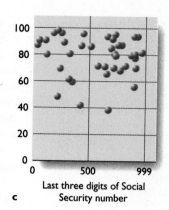

a   b   c

◀ **Figure 2.9** In these scatter plots, each dot represents measurements of two variables for one person. **(a)** Scores on first test and scores on final exam (correlation = +0.72). **(b)** Times absent and scores on final exam (correlation = −0.44). **(c)** Last three digits of Social Security number and scores on final exam (correlation = −0.08).

workers say they have more emergency cases on such nights. However, careful reviews of the data have found no relationship between the moon's phases and either crime or mental illness (Raison, Klein, & Steckler, 1999; Rotton & Kelly, 1985). Why, then, does the belief persist? People remember events that fit the belief and disregard those that do not.

Correlation ≠ Causation

"Correlation does not mean causation." You will hear that statement again and again in psychology and other fields. A correlation indicates how strongly two variables are related to each other, but it does not tell us *why* they are related. If two variables—let's call them A and B—are positively correlated, it could be that A causes B, B causes A, or some third variable, C, causes both of them.

For example, how much sunscreen people use is positively correlated with their chance of getting skin cancer. Does that mean that sunscreen causes cancer? It is more likely that people who are at risk of skin cancer, because they spend much time in the sun, are the ones who use more sunscreen.

There is also a positive correlation between how often parents spank their children and how often the children misbehave. Does this correlation indicate that spankings lead to misbehavior? (Probably true.) Or does misbehavior lead to spankings? (Again, probably true.) Yet another possibility is that parents who had genes promoting aggressive behavior are likely to spank, and their children inherited genes that led to misbehaviors. Because all three of these explanations are possible, the correlation does not tell us about causation.

"Then what good is a correlation?" you might ask. First, correlations help us make predictions. Second, correlational studies pave the way for later experimentation that might lead to a conclusion. For example, if we could persuade half the parents to stop spanking, we might see whether their children's behavior improves.

Here are more examples of why we cannot draw conclusions regarding cause and effect from correlational data (see also ▼ Figure 2.10):

- *Political conservativeness correlates with happiness.* Political conservatives rate themselves as happier than liberals (Napier & Jost, 2008), although these self-reports may not be fully accurate (Wojcik, Hovasapian, Graham, Motyl, & Ditto, 2015). Does a positive correlation mean that being conservative makes you happier? Or that being happy makes you more conservative? Maybe it's neither. Maybe financially secure people are more likely than poor people to be political conservatives, and more likely to be happy.

- *According to one study, people who sleep about seven hours a night are less likely to die within the next few years than those who sleep either more or less* (Kripke, Garfinkel, Wingard, Klauber, & Marler, 2002). Should we conclude (as some people did) that sleeping too much impairs your health? Here is

an alternative: People who have life-threatening illnesses tend to sleep more than healthy people. So perhaps illness causes extra sleep rather than extra sleep causing illness. Or perhaps advancing age increases the probability of both illness and extra sleep. The study included people ranging from young adulthood through age 101!

Now, let me tell you a dirty little secret: In rare circumstances, correlational results *do* imply cause and effect. It is a "dirty little secret" because professors want students to avoid cause-and-effect conclusions from correlations, and mentioning the exceptions is risky. Still, consider the fact that people are generally

Gary yim./Shutterstock.com

People's expectations and faulty memories produce illusory correlations, such as that between the full moon and abnormal behavior.

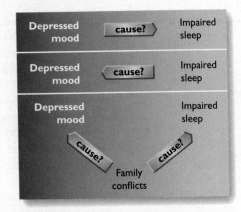

▲ **Figure 2.10** A strong correlation between depression and impaired sleep does not tell us whether depression interferes with sleep, poor sleep leads to depression, or whether another problem leads to both depression and sleep problems.

in a better mood when the weather improves (Keller et al., 2005). A likely explanation is that the weather changes your mood. What other possibility is there? Your mood changes the weather? Surely not. Might something else control both the weather and your mood? If so, what? In the absence of any other hypothesis, we conclude that the weather changes your mood. Also, consider that how often a U.S. congressional representative votes a pro-feminist position, as defined by the National Organization for Women, correlates with how many daughters the representative has (Washington, 2006). It is implausible that someone's voting record would influence the sex of his or her children. It is highly likely that having daughters could influence political views. Again, the results suggest cause and effect. Nevertheless, the point remains: We should almost always be skeptical of causal conclusions that anyone draws from a correlational study.

11. **Suppose we find a 0.9 correlation between students' class attendance and their grade on the final exam. What conclusion can we draw?**

12. **On average, the more medicines people take, the more likely they are to die young. Propose alternative explanations for this correlation.**

Answers

11. We can conclude only that we could use class attendance to predict the final grade. We cannot conclude that class attendance caused better performance. Perhaps the highly motivated students who attend class regularly would have done well without good attendance. In general, correlation does not mean causation.
12. Perhaps people get sick from complications caused by taking too many pills. Or maybe the people who take many medicines are those who already had serious illnesses.

Experiments

To determine causation, an investigator uses an **experiment**, *a study in which the investigator manipulates at least one variable while measuring at least one other variable.* The **independent variable** is *the item that an experimenter controls*—for example, the type of training that people receive. The **dependent variable** is *the item that an experimenter measures to determine the outcome*—for example, how many questions people answer correctly. If the procedure causes different groups to behave differently, you can think of the independent variable as the cause and the dependent variable as the effect.

An **experimental group** *receives the treatment that an experiment is designed to test.* For example, the experimental group might receive some special experience that we think will influence later behavior. The **control group** is *a set of individuals treated in the same way as the experimental group except for the procedure that the experiment is designed to test.* If the people in the experimental group received a special experience, those in the control group do something else during the same time. If those in the experimental group receive a medication, those in the control group receive a placebo. ■ Table 2.2 contrasts experiments with observational studies.

A key procedure for any experiment is **random assignment** of participants to groups: *The experimenter uses a chance procedure, such as drawing names out of a hat, to make sure that all participants have the same probability of being assigned to a given group.* Why is this so important? Consider a couple of examples.

Women at menopause have decreased release of estrogens and related hormones. For years physicians recommended hormone replacement therapy, and the women receiving that therapy tended to be healthier than other women their age. However, women who follow their physicians' advice tend to be more health-conscious in other ways, such as diet and exercise, so they could be healthy for reasons other than the hormones. In an experiment, more than 160,000 women agreed to receive either the hormones or a placebo. The result: Women taking the hormones had decreased risk of hip fractures and colon cancer, but increased risk of heart disease, stroke, and breast cancer (Writing Group for the Women's Health Initiative Investigators, 2002). Overall, the harms seemed at least as great as the benefits.

Another example: Several studies have found that moderate alcohol drinkers (about one glass of beer or wine per day) tend in the long run to be

Table 2.2 Comparison of Five Methods of Research	
Observational Studies	
Naturalistic Observation	Description of behavior under natural conditions
Case Study	Detailed description of single individual; suitable for studying rare conditions
Survey	Study of attitudes, beliefs, or behaviors based on answers to questions
Correlation	Description of the relationship between two variables that the investigator measures but does not control. A correlation determines whether two variables are closely related but does not address questions of cause and effect
Experiment	
	Determination of the effect of a variable controlled by the investigator on some other variable that is measured. An experiment is the only method that demonstrates cause and effect

healthier than heavy drinkers or nondrinkers. It's clear that heavy drinking would be bad, but if you are a nondrinker, should you take up beer or wine? We cannot be sure. First, this is a small effect. In one study, nondrinkers constituted 22 percent of the healthier old people, compared to 25 percent of the less healthy old people (Sun et al., 2011). Second, nondrinkers could differ from moderate drinkers in other ways. Maybe healthy people are more likely to drink than are people who are prone to illness. We cannot be sure, unless someone does a study with random assignment to drinking and not drinking. Yeah, good luck on doing that experiment.

13. **A basketball coach makes the freshman players practice two hours a week longer than the older players and finds that the freshmen improve more than the upper-class players. What is the independent variable in this experiment, and what is the main flaw in the experiment?**

Answer

13. The independent variable is the number of hours of practice. The main flaw is that players were not randomly assigned to the experimental and control groups. Freshmen might improve more just because they have more room for improvement.

Reducing the Influence of Expectations

Experiments can go wrong in many ways, if we're not careful. Let's consider several possible problems and how researchers overcome them.

Experimenter Bias and Blind Studies

Experimenter bias is *the tendency of an observer (either intentionally or unintentionally) to misperceive the results in a way that favors a hypothesis.* For example, of research studies comparing one antipsychotic drug to another, in 90 percent of cases, the results favored the drug company that paid for the research (Heres et al., 2006). Researchers can bias a study like this in many ways without actually lying, such as by including only the type of people believed most likely to respond to a particular drug. A similar bias shows up in the outside world, too. Imagine you are a forensic psychologist, asked to testify in court about how dangerous a particular offender is, and therefore what punishment is appropriate. You interview the offender and examine all the relevant evidence. Would you alter your testimony depending on whether the prosecution or the defense had hired you? Studies show that you probably would (Murrie, Boccaccini, Guarnera, & Rufino, 2013). Even when you try to be objective and fair, you cannot easily ignore your desires and expectations.

To minimize the influence of expectations, it is best to use a **blind observer**—*someone who records data without knowing the researcher's predictions.* Ideally, the experimenter conceals the procedure from the participants

also. Suppose experimenters give children a treatment that is supposed to increase their ability to pay attention. If the children know the prediction, their expectations may influence their behavior. In a **single-blind study**, *either the observer or the participants are unaware of which participants received which treatment* (see ■ Table 2.3). In a **double-blind study**, *both the observer and the participants are unaware of which participants received which treatment.* Of course, the experimenter who organized the study would need to keep records of which participants received which procedure. (If *everyone* loses track of the procedure, it is known jokingly as "triple blind.")

Double-blind studies are sometimes difficult. For example, in an experiment testing a new drug, people who experience side effects can correctly guess that they are in the experimental group, not the placebo group. In a study to determine the effects of psychotherapy, it is not possible to conceal from participants whether they did or did not receive therapy. In a study of the effects of playing violent video games, researchers might ask some people to play violent games and others to play peaceful games (like *The Sims*), but the peaceful game is not exactly a placebo, because the players might have different expectations of effects (Boot, Simons, Stothart, & Stutts, 2013).

Demand Characteristics

People in a psychological experiment know they are in an experiment. Ethically, the researcher is required to tell them and to obtain their consent. If you know you are in a study and someone is watching you, might that influence your behavior? Furthermore, suppose you know or guess what the experimenter hopes to see. Might that expectation alter your behavior?

Here is an example: Experimenters told one group of men that there was reason to believe that seeing the color pink decreases one's strength. They told another group that seeing the color pink increases one's strength. Then they tested the men's grip strength while looking at a pink panel. Those who expected pink to increase their strength showed a 10 percent stronger grip (Smith, Bell, & Fusco, 1986; see ▼ Figure 2.11).

Here is another example: Many years ago, a British television program about the chemical senses concluded by saying (falsely) that smells depend on the rate of vibration of molecules, and the announcer offered to demonstrate. Viewers saw electrodes leading from a cone to an array of electronic equipment. The announcer explained that the electrodes would detect the vibration of molecules in the container, and then relay it to equipment that would produce a sound of the same frequency. Viewers were asked to listen to that frequency and then call or write to the

Table 2.3 Single-Blind and Double-Blind Studies

Who is aware of which participants are in which group?

	Experimenter Who Organized the Study	Observer	Participants
Single-blind	aware	unaware	aware
Single-blind	aware	aware	unaware
Double-blind	aware	unaware	unaware

station to say what, if anything, they had smelled. (The next day, the program explained that this had been an experiment, and smell doesn't really work that way.) Of 179 people who called or wrote, 155 claimed to have smelled something, including 6 who complained that the smell had provoked an attack of hay fever, sneezing, or other distress (O'Mahony, 1978).

Even when researchers don't tell people what they expect, people's guesses influence their behavior. Martin Orne (1969) defined demand characteristics as *cues that tell participants what is expected of them and what the experimenter hopes to find.* To minimize demand characteristics, experimenters often try to conceal the purpose of the experiment. A double-blind study also serves the purpose: If two groups share the same expectations but behave differently because of a treatment, then the differences are not due to their expectations.

Problems related to demand characteristics show up in many contexts, not just in experiments. Often an interviewer unintentionally suggests an answer, or poses a question in a way that lets the interviewee guess what answer is expected. Psychotherapists sometimes suggest, intentionally or otherwise, that they are looking for certain kinds of memories or thoughts. Suggestions are powerful, and difficult to avoid.

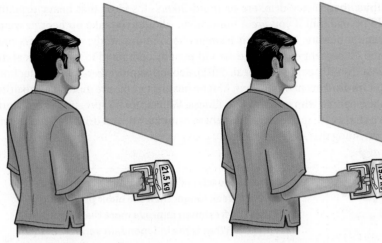

Told that pink increases strength   Told that pink decreases strength

▲ **Figure 2.11** Men who expected to feel stronger while looking at pink were in fact stronger than those who expected to feel weaker while looking at pink.

In any of these cases, can we conclude cause and effect? No, because it is likely that some degree of improvement would have occurred with or without treatment.

Instead of a before-and-after study, a better design is to compare two groups: An investigator provides the treatment for one group (the *experimental group*) and not the other (the *control group*), with participants randomly assigned to the two groups. Any difference that emerges indicates the treatment's effect. Even then, we should beware of generalizing the results too far. Maybe the procedure works only under certain circumstances.

14. Which of the following would an experimenter try to minimize or avoid? Falsifiability, independent variables, dependent variables, blind observers, or demand characteristics.

Answer

14. Of these, only demand characteristics are to be avoided. If you did not remember that falsifiability is a good feature of a theory, check page 26. Every experiment must have at least one independent variable (that the experimenter controls) and at least one dependent variable (that the experimenter measures). Blind observers help avoid experimenter bias.

Problems with a Before-and-After Study

Imagine a chemist adding one clear liquid to another. Suddenly the mixture turns green and explodes. We would conclude cause and effect, as we have no reason to expect that the first liquid was about to turn green and explode on its own. Now imagine procedures in psychology: Researchers give children language training and find that their language skills improve over the next few months. They provide therapy for patients with depression and find that many become gradually less depressed. They provide special training to reduce violence and find that many people become less violent.

what's the evidence?

Inheritance of Acquired Characteristics? Problems in a Before-and-After Study

Let's examine a specific study that illustrates the limitations of a before-and-after study. It pertains to evolution, but the point here is not so much evolution itself as possible pitfalls of research.

According to Darwin's theory of evolution by natural selection, if individuals with one kind of genes reproduce more than those with other genes, then the first set of genes will become more common from one generation to the next. Prior to Darwin, Jean-Baptiste Lamarck had offered a different theory, evolution by inheritance of acquired characteristics. According to that theory, if you exercise your muscles, your children will be born with larger muscles. If you fail to use your little toe, your children will be born with a smaller little toe than you had. The evidence never supported that theory, and by the early 1900s, nearly all biologists abandoned it in favor of Darwin's theory. However, a few holdouts continued defending Lamarckian evolution.

First Study (McDougall, 1938)

Hypothesis If rats learn to swim through a maze, their offspring will learn the maze more quickly.

Method Rats had to learn to swim a particular route to get out of a tank of water. The experimenter trained them until each rat was consistently swimming the correct route. Then he let them breed. He did not select the best learners for breeding, but simply chose rats at random. When rats of the next generation were old enough, he trained them and then let them reproduce. This procedure continued for one generation after another.

Results The average performance improved from one generation to the next for the first few generations. That is, the second generation learned faster than the first, the third faster than the second, and so on for a few generations. Later, the results fluctuated.

Interpretation These results are consistent with the hypothesis, but we should consider other hypotheses, too. If these results really indicate inheritance of acquired characteristics, we would have to imagine that the experience of learning the maze somehow directed the genes to mutate in the right way to help the next generation learn the same maze. It is difficult to imagine how this could happen.

When results conflict so strongly with what we think we know, scientists ask these questions: Are the results replicable? Can we find a more parsimonious explanation? Does the design of the study have any flaws?

Do you, in fact, see anything wrong with the procedure? One group of researchers noticed that this is a before-and-after study with no control group. What would happen, they wondered, if they repeated the study using a control group that was not trained in the maze? Would their offspring also improve from generation to generation?

Second Study (Agar, Drummond, Tiegs, & Gunson, 1954)

Hypothesis If it is possible to replicate McDougall's results, the improvement will also occur in a control group that receives no training in the maze.

Method Rats in the trained group were treated the same as those in McDougall's study: Rats learned the maze and then mated. Rats of the next generation also learned the maze and then mated and so forth.

In the control group, the rats used for training were not used for breeding. Young, healthy rats typically have a litter of about 12 babies. In each generation, a few rats were trained in the maze but not used for breeding. Other rats from the same litter, not trained, were permitted to breed. So in each generation, the researchers obtained a measure of maze learning, but because only untrained rats mated, all the rats in the control group were descended from untrained rats. Any improvement over generations could not be due to the training. The experiment continued for 18 years, with a few generations of rats per year. (Rats reach sexual maturity at about age 60 days.)

Results ▼ Figure 2.12 shows the results. For the first few years, on average, both the trained group and the control group improved from one generation to the next. In later years, the results fluctuated. The two groups performed similarly throughout the study.

Interpretation To most people's surprise, McDougall's results were replicable. However, because the trained group did not differ from the control group, training had nothing to do with the improvement over generations. That is, the results showed no evidence for inheritance of acquired characteristics.

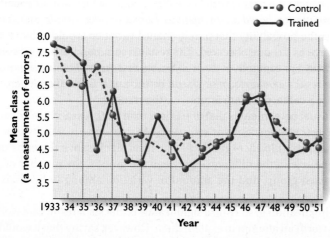

▲ **Figure 2.12** Rats in the experimental group and the control group improved at equal rates from one generation to the next. (From Agar, W. E., Drummond, F. H., Tiegs, O. W., & Gunson, M. M. (1954). Fourth (final) report on a test of McDougall's Lamarckian experiment on the training of rats. *Journal of Experimental Biology, 31,* 307–321.)

How, then, can we explain the improvement over generations? One possibility is that rats of the first generation were stressed. They had just been shipped in by train, in crowded boxes, from rat-breeding facilities to McDougall's laboratory. (Yes, there are companies that specialize in breeding and selling rats.) The second generation grew up in the laboratory, but they were the offspring of highly stressed parents. Conceivably, those effects could persist for several generations.

Another possibility is that the experimenters gradually got better at taking care of rats and running the experiment. We might be seeing a change in the experimenters, not a change in the rats.

A third possibility is that because the experimenters always mated brother with sister, later generations may have become less vigorous. Ordinarily, we expect inbreeding to be a disadvantage, but perhaps less vigorous rats swam more slowly and therefore had more time to consider which direction to turn in the maze. This idea sounds a little far-fetched but not impossible.

We don't know which explanation is correct. The question isn't important enough for anyone to do the additional research to find out. The main conclusion is that we can account for the results without assuming inheritance of acquired characteristics.

This episode illustrates several points about research: (1) If the results seem unlikely, look for a more parsimonious explanation. (2) Beware of before-and-after studies in psychology, biology, or medicine. Without a control group, we don't know what the results mean. (3) If behavior changes from one generation to the next, the explanation doesn't have to be genetic. It might reflect a change in the environment.

Evaluating the Results

Suppose you conduct a well-designed experiment and now you get the results. Suppose that most of the people in the experimental group acted one way and most of those in the control group acted another, but neither group was 100 percent consistent. We need guidelines on how to decide whether the difference is worth taking seriously.

Descriptive Statistics

First, an investigator summarizes the results with **descriptive statistics**, which are *mathematical summaries of results*. We care about the central score—that is, the middle or average. Three ways of representing the central score are the mean, median, and mode. The **mean** is *the sum of the scores divided by the number of scores*. When people say "average," they generally refer to the mean. For example, the mean of 2, 10, and 3 is 5 (15/3). The mean is especially useful if the scores approximate the **normal distribution**

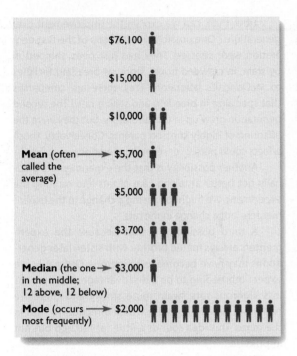

▲ **Figure 2.13** The monthly salaries of the 25 employees of company X, showing the mean, median, and mode. (After Huff, 1954)

(or **normal curve**), *a symmetrical frequency of scores clustered around the mean.*

The mean can be misleading, however. For example, girls have two X chromosomes and boys have one X and one Y, so the "average" (mean) child has one and a half X chromosomes and half a Y chromosome. But no child has that average. Here is another example: A survey asked people how many sex partners they hoped to have, ideally, over the next 30 years. The mean for women was 2.8 and the mean for men was 64.3 (L. C. Miller & Fishkin, 1997). However, almost two-thirds of women and about half of men replied "1." Most of the others said they hoped for a few partners, but a small number of men said they hoped for hundreds or thousands. The result was a mean of 64.3, a misleading figure.

Another example: One university reported the mean starting salary for students who majored in various departments for one year. The highest was for geography majors, who had a mean starting salary of more than 3 million dollars a year! Wait, come back here instead of rushing off to change your major to geography: Only three students that year had majored in geography, and one of them was a star in the National Basketball Association, with a salary of about 9 million dollars per year.

When the population distribution is far from symmetrical, we can better represent the typical scores by the median instead of the mean. To determine the **median**, *arrange the scores in order from the highest to the lowest. The middle score is the median.* For example, for the set of scores 2, 10, and 3, the

median is 3. For the set of scores 3, 2, and 950, the median is 3. Extreme scores greatly affect the mean but not the median.

The median can be misleading also. Suppose over the last 7 months your business posted profits of $9,000, $10,000, $12,000, and $11,000, plus losses of $20,000, $30,000, and $40,000. Your median outcome was a profit of $9,000, even though your overall performance was a huge loss. Frequently, it is better to see both the mean and the median than either one alone.

The third way to represent the central score is the **mode**, *the score that occurs most frequently.* For example, in the distribution of scores 1, 1, 1, 4, 7, 9, and 10, the mode is 1. The mean and median are more useful for most purposes, but the mode calls attention to a common score. In the case of sex chromosomes, the human population has a *bimodal* distribution, with one mode at two X chromosomes and the other mode at one X and one Y.

To summarize: The mean is what most people intend when they say "average." It is the sum of the scores divided by the number of scores. The median is the middle score after the scores are ranked from highest to lowest. The mode is the most common score (see ◄ Figure 2.13).

concept check ✓

15. **For the following distribution of scores, determine the mean, the median, and the mode: 4, 3, 8, 3, 9, 1, 3, 5, 4, 10.**

Answer

15. mean = 5; median = 4; mode = 3.

Inferential Statistics

Suppose researchers randomly assign people to two groups to help them quit smoking cigarettes. One group receives punishments for smoking, and the other group gets rewards for not smoking. Before treatment, both groups average 10 cigarettes per day. At the end of therapy, those in the punishment group average 7.5 cigarettes per day, whereas those in the reward group average 6.5 cigarettes per day. How seriously should we take this difference?

To answer this question, we need to know more than just the numbers 7.5 and 6.5. How many smokers were in the study? (Just a few? Hundreds? Thousands?) Also, are most people's behaviors close to the group means, or did a few extreme scores distort the means?

We evaluate the results with **inferential statistics**, which are *statements about a larger population based on an inference from a smaller sample.* Statistical tests determine the probability that purely chance variation would achieve a difference as large as the one observed. The result is summarized by a *p* (as in *probability)* value. For example, $p < 0.05$ indicates that *the probability that randomly generated results would resemble the observed results is less than 5 percent.* The smaller the *p* value, the more impressive the results.

The usual agreement is that, if *p* is less than 0.05, researchers consider the results **statistically significant** or **statistically reliable**—that is, *results that chance alone would be unlikely to produce.* Statistical significance depends on three factors: the size of the difference between the groups, the number of participants in each group, and the amount of variation among individuals within each group.

The implication of statistical significance is that such results are worth considering, worth an attempt to explain them. However, saying that it would be unlikely for chance alone to produce such results does not mean it is unlikely that chance alone *did* produce these results. It sounds as if those statements might mean the same thing, but they do not. For example, suppose you flip a coin 6 times and you get 6 heads in a row. Pure chance produces a string like that less

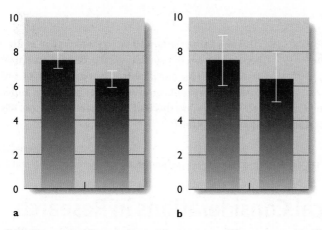

▲ **Figure 2.14** The vertical lines indicate 95 percent confidence intervals. The pair of graphs in part **a** indicate that the true mean has a 95 percent chance of falling within a very narrow range. The graphs in part **b** indicate a wider range.

than 5 percent of the time, but in this case we know that chance *did* produce the result (presuming that it's a normal coin).

Although statistical tests yielding a *p* value have been common through most of psychology's history, objections have been growing (Cumming, 2014). One objection is that it falsely implies an all-or-nothing judgment: Either something is significant, or it is not. More realistically, results range along a continuum from convincing to unimpressive. A second objection is that we should care about the size of the effect, not just whether or not it was statistically significant. If you test a medical procedure on a huge enough sample of patients, you might find a statistically significant effect, even if it produced only a slight improvement for a small percentage of people.

For these and other reasons, an alternative is for researchers to show the means and 95 percent confidence intervals for each group, as shown in ▲ Figure 2.14 (Cumming, 2008). The 95 percent confidence interval is *the range within which the true mean lies, with 95 percent certainty.*

"Wait a minute," you protest. "We already know the means: 7.5 and 6.5. Aren't *those* the 'true' means?" No, those are the means for particular samples of the population. Someone who studies another group may not get the same results. What we care about is the mean for everyone. It is impractical to measure that mean, but if we know the sample mean, the size of the sample, and the amount of variation among individuals (measured by a term called the *standard deviation*), we can estimate how close the sample mean is, probably, to the population mean.

In Figure 2.14a, the 95 percent confidence intervals are small. In other words, the samples were large, the individual variation was small, and the sample means are probably close to the true population means. In Figure 2.14b, the confidence intervals are larger, so the sample means are just approximations of the true population means. Presenting data with confidence intervals enables readers to judge for themselves how large and impressive the difference is between groups (Hunter, 1997; Loftus, 1996).

16. Should we be more impressed with results when the 95 percent confidence intervals are large or small? Should we be more impressed if the *p* value is large or small?

Answer

16. In both cases, smaller. A small 95 percent confidence interval indicates high confidence in the results. A small *p* value indicates a low probability of getting such a large difference merely by chance.

Replicability Issues

Here is a hypothetical study. Let's hope no one ever did anything quite this silly, but it illustrates an important point. Dr. Hopeful measures how long 100 college students can balance on one foot with their eyes closed. Then he tests whether the men differed from the women. No, he finds, on average they did not. How about freshmen versus advanced students? Tall people versus short people? Left-handers versus right-handers? Science majors versus humanities majors? He tries one hypothesis after another, finding little or no difference. Then he runs another comparison and finds that people with last names near the end of the alphabet balance longer than those near the start of the alphabet, with *p* <0.05 and 95 percent confidence intervals that don't overlap. Aha! Maybe people near the end of the alphabet are used to standing in lines for a long time when they line up alphabetically, so they developed this skill. It's a new finding! Calls for a celebration!

Ah, but wait. If you test enough hypotheses, you increase your chance of confirming one or more of them just by accident. Dr. Hopeful has committed the research misconduct known as **HARKing**, *Hypothesizing After the Results are Known.* HARKing is pretending that you predicted something, when you already know that it happened. A related type of research misconduct is *p*-hacking, *analyzing the data one way after another to find a way that is statistically significant.* For example, you might see that the results would be statistically significant except for the data of one participant, who was older than the rest. You then discard that participant's results, even though you would have kept them if they had fit your hypothesis. Or you might start with a certain number of participants, or a certain duration of procedure, and then add participants or extend the procedure just until the results become significant.

The problems of HARKing and *p*-hacking are not limited to psychology. Researchers in neuroscience, medicine, and other fields are also concerned about how many published results might be accidents, or at least overstatements of small effects (Tsilidis et al., 2013).

Back to Dr. Hopeful who found a difference between people at the beginning and end of the alphabet: What if he had tested *only* this one hypothesis? The results would still run a risk of being just a random fluctuation. Researchers throughout the world conduct huge numbers of studies, some of which produce apparently impressive results. But random results will appear to be significant (*p* <0.05) about 5 percent of the time. So, of all the published results, probably a fair number are accidental findings. We should be skeptical of any result until it has been replicated, especially if we had no good theoretical reason for expecting it.

In spite of the agreed importance of replication, most researchers would prefer to make their own new findings than to try to replicate someone else's (Pashler & Harris, 2012). The custom has been changing, however. More and more scientists have been calling for attempts at replication, using the same procedure as the original study, and several journals have agreed to publish the results, whatever they may be. The result has been, not surprisingly, that some published findings are easy to replicate and some are not. As a rule, those that had the strongest effect when first published are the most likely to be successfully replicated later (Klein et al., 2014; Open Science Collaboration, 2015; Schweinsberg et al., 2016; Van Bavel, Mende-Siedlecki, Brady, & Reinero, 2016). However, many well-known results have failed to be replicated, and many psychologists talk about a "replication crisis."

What does it mean when researchers cannot replicate a result? The answer depends on how hard they tried. One or two failures to replicate a finding might mean nothing, especially if the new studies had a small number of participants or imprecise measurements (Lakens & Evers, 2014; Stanley & Spence, 2014). The situation is more serious if the replication attempt had more participants or more careful measurements than the first. Uri Simonsohn (2015) suggests this analogy to astronomy: Suppose someone with a small telescope reports seeing a new asteroid. Then someone with a larger telescope carefully examines the same part of the sky and does not see the reported object. We cannot conclude that the asteroid doesn't exist, but we do conclude that if it does exist, the first telescope wasn't strong enough to see it, and so the report must be in error.

In some cases, a failure to replicate might mean that the result depends on special circumstances. A study might get different results from a similar study of many years ago, just because our culture has changed (Greenfield, 2017). In certain experiments with rats, female researchers get different results from male researchers. The reason is that rats have a stress response to the smell of males, including human males (Sorge et al., 2014). Results can vary for many reasons, but we need to find out why. If we cannot find conditions in which a result occurs consistently, we should disregard it.

17. **Doctors Larry, Curly, and Mo try a new type of therapy for eight types of psychological problems and find that it works well for one problem, but only for men and not women. They report the results for men only, and only for the one type of problem, claiming this had been their prediction. What misconduct have they committed?**

Answer

17. Claiming that this had been their prediction is HARKing. Discarding the results for women is p-hacking.

Ethical Considerations in Research

Ethical concerns are more significant in psychology than in most other scientific fields. Chemists can do whatever they want with a jar of chemicals, as long as they don't blow up the building or pour hazardous chemicals down the drain. Psychologists have ethical limits on what they can do with people, based on both law and conscience.

Ethical Concerns with Humans

Suppose you have a hypothesis about what causes people to commit murder. Will you conduct an experiment to test your hypothesis? I hope not. Or suppose you have a hypothesis about how people react to extreme fear. Will you subject people to extreme fear? If so, will you tell them what is about to happen before they sign up for the experiment?

Researchers were limited only by their own conscience, until some horrendous experiments, especially in medicine, led to legislation in 1974 that required research on humans in the United States to be approved in advance by an Institutional Review Board (IRB) that reviews the ethics of the procedure. One of the most important aspects is informed consent, *a statement by each participant that he or she has been told what to expect and now agrees to continue.* Most procedures in psychology are innocuous, such as tests of perception, memory, or attention. Occasionally, however, the procedure includes something that people might not wish to do, such as examining disgusting photographs or receiving electrical shocks. Participants are told they have the right to quit if they find the procedure too disagreeable. In some cases, an experimenter needs to conceal the purpose of the experiment, because knowing the experimenter's predictions will produce demand characteristics that contaminate the results. In such cases, the IRB decides whether temporary deception is acceptable. In all cases, the participants receive a full explanation at the end of the experiment.

Informed consent is not enough. An IRB probably would reject a proposal to offer cocaine, even if people were eager to give their informed consent. A committee would also ban procedures likely to produce severe embarrassment or other distress. It also insists that the researcher protect each participant's confidentiality. The data should be collected in a way that does not enable anyone to identify individual participants or reveal anything about them personally.

Special problems arise in research with children, people with cognitive impairments, or others who might not understand the instructions well enough to provide informed consent (Bonnie, 1997). In such cases, researchers seek permission from a parent or guardian. In some such cases, IRBs are especially hesitant to grant permission.

The American Psychological Association (APA) published a book discussing the proper ethical treatment of volunteers in experiments

▲ **Figure 2.15** Some animal research consists of observations under natural or nearly natural conditions. Other research raises ethical controversies.

(Sales & Folkman, 2000). The APA censures or expels any member who disregards these principles.

Ethical Concerns with Nonhumans

Much psychological research deals with nonhuman animals, especially research on basic processes such as brain mechanisms, sensation, hunger, and learning (see ▲ Figure 2.15). Researchers use nonhumans if they want to control aspects of life that people will not let them control (e.g., who mates with whom), if they want to study behavior continuously over weeks or months (longer than people are willing to participate), or if the research poses health risks. Animal research has long been essential for preliminary testing of most new drugs, surgical procedures, and methods of relieving pain. People with untreatable illnesses argue that they have the right to hope for cures that might result from animal research (Feeney, 1987). Much of our knowledge in psychology, biology, and medicine made use of animal studies at some point.

Nevertheless, some people oppose much or all animal research. Animals, after all, cannot give informed consent. Some animal rights supporters insist that animals should have the same rights as humans, that keeping animals (even pets) in cages is slavery, and that killing any animal is murder. Others oppose certain types of research but are willing to compromise about others.

Psychologists vary in their attitudes. Most support animal research in general but draw a line somewhere separating acceptable from unacceptable research (Plous, 1996). Naturally, disagreement arises about where to draw that line.

In this debate, as in many other political controversies, a common tactic is for each side to criticize the most extreme actions of its opponents. For example, animal rights advocates point to studies that exposed monkeys or puppies to painful procedures that seem difficult to justify. Researchers point to protesters who have vandalized laboratories, planted bombs, banged on a researcher's children's windows at night, and inserted a garden hose through a window to flood a house (G. Miller, 2007a). When both sides concentrate on criticizing their most extreme opponents, they make points of agreement harder to find.

A careful study by a relatively unbiased outsider concluded that the truth is messy: Some research is painful to the animals *and* nevertheless valuable for scientific and medical progress (Blum, 1994). We must, most people conclude, seek compromises.

Professional organizations such as the Society for Neuroscience and the American Psychological Association publish guidelines for the proper use of animals in research. Colleges and other research institutions maintain laboratory animal care committees to ensure that laboratory animals are treated humanely, that their pain and discomfort are kept to a minimum, and that experimenters consider alternatives before imposing potentially painful procedures.

How can we determine in advance whether the value of the expected experimental results (which is hard to predict) will outweigh the pain the animals will endure (which is hard to measure)? As is common with ethical decisions, reasonable arguments can be raised on both sides of the question, and no compromise is fully satisfactory.

in closing | module 2.2

Psychological Research

Most scientists avoid the word *prove*, because it sounds too final. The most complex and most interesting aspects of human behavior are products of genetics, a lifetime of experiences, and countless current influences. Given the practical and ethical limitations for untangling all these factors, it might seem that psychological researchers would become discouraged. However, the difficulties have inspired researchers to design clever and complex methods. A single study rarely answers a question decisively, but many studies converge to increase our total understanding.

Summary

- *Operational definitions.* For many purposes, psychologists use operational definitions, which state how to measure a phenomenon or how to produce it. (page 33)

- *Sampling.* For some purposes, a convenience sample is adequate. When possible, it is better to use a representative or random sample. A cross-cultural sample tests whether the results are specific to a particular way of life. (page 34)

- *Naturalistic observations.* Naturalistic observations provide descriptions of behavior under natural conditions. (page 35)

- *Case histories.* A case history is a detailed research study of a single individual with unusual characteristics. (page 35)

- *Surveys.* It is easy to conduct a survey and also easy to get misleading results. (page 35)

- *Correlations.* A correlational study examines the relationship between variables that the investigator did not control. The strength of relationship is measured by a correlation coefficient that ranges from 0 (no relationship) to plus or minus 1 (a perfect relationship). (page 37)

- *Inferring causation.* A correlational study cannot uncover cause-and-effect relationships, but an experiment can. (page 39)

- *Experiments.* In an experiment, an investigator manipulates an independent variable to determine its effect on the dependent variable. A before-and-after study often leads to results that are hard to interpret. It is better to compare the results for different groups. (page 40)

- *Random assignment.* All participants should have an equal probability of being assigned to the experimental or the control group. (page 40)

- *Overcoming experimenter bias.* To ensure objectivity, investigators use blind observers who do not know what results are expected. In a double-blind study, neither the observer nor the participants know the researcher's predictions. (page 41)

- *Demand characteristics.* Researchers try to minimize the effects of demand characteristics, which are cues that tell participants what the experimenter expects them to do. (page 41)

- *Mean, median, and mode.* The mean is determined by adding all the scores and dividing by the number of individuals. The median is the middle score after all the scores have been arranged from highest to lowest. The mode is the score that occurs most frequently. (page 43)

- *Inferential statistics.* Inferential statistics are attempts to deduce the properties of a large population based on the results from a small sample of that population. (page 44)

- *Probability of chance results.* Psychologists use inferential statistics to calculate the probability that chance alone could produce results like the ones observed. That probability is low if the difference between the two groups is large, if the variability within each group is small, and if the number of individuals in each group is large. (page 44)

- *Replicability.* Impressive results sometimes arise by accident, especially if an investigator resorts to HARKing or p-hacking. The defense against misleading results is to attempt to replicate them. (page 45)

- *Ethics of experimentation.* Research on human participants should not proceed until the participants have given their informed consent. Psychologists try to minimize risk to their participants, but they sometimes face difficult ethical decisions. (page 46)

Key Terms

95 percent confidence interval (page 45)

applied research (page 33)

basic research (page 33)

blind observer (page 41)

case history (page 35)

control group (page 40)

convenience sample (page 34)

correlation (page 37)

correlation coefficient (page 38)

cross-cultural sample (page 34)

demand characteristics (page 42)

dependent variable (page 40)

descriptive statistics (page 43)

double-blind study (page 41)

experiment (page 40)

experimental group (page 40)

experimenter bias (page 41)

HARKing (page 45)

illusory correlation (page 38)

independent variable (page 40)

inferential statistics (page 44)

informed consent (page 46)

Institutional Review Board (IRB) (page 46)

mean (page 43)

median (page 44)

mode (page 44)

naturalistic observation (page 35)

normal distribution (or normal curve) (page 43)

operational definition (page 33)

$p < 0.05$ (page 44)

p-hacking (45)

placebo (page 38)

random assignment (page 40)

random sample (page 34)

representative sample (page 34)

scatter plot (page 38)

single-blind study (page 41)

statistically significant (or statistically reliable) results (page 44)

survey (page 35)

Review Questions

1. Which of the following is an operational definition of grouchiness?
   - (a) The opposite of happiness
   - (b) The opposite of friendliness
   - (c) A persistent sensation of feeling displeased with one's life
   - (d) The percentage of time someone is frowning

2. Why is a random sample preferable to a representative sample?
   - (a) It is easier to achieve.
   - (b) Everyone has an equal chance of being selected.
   - (c) The sample matches the population in percentage of men and women, old and young.
   - (d) The size of the sample becomes unimportant.

3. What does it mean if scores on some test are negatively correlated with performance in school?
   - (a) The test is useless or worse for predicting performance.
   - (b) Scores on this test have been declining over time.
   - (c) Students with low scores on the test tend to do well in school.
   - (d) Younger students get lower scores than older students.

4. If a researcher finds a low correlation between happiness and honesty, one explanation is that the two variables are unrelated. What is another possible explanation?
   - (a) The researcher studied a random sample of people.
   - (b) The measurements of happiness or honesty were inaccurate.
   - (c) Honesty leads to a decrease in happiness.
   - (d) Happiness leads to a decrease in honesty.

5. Suppose researchers find a negative correlation between time playing sports and grades in school. Which conclusion, if any, can we draw from this result?
   - (a) Playing sports decreases school performance.
   - (b) Students who concentrate on studies do not have time for sports.
   - (c) One of the variables was poorly measured.
   - (d) We can draw none of these conclusions.

6. A researcher has one group watch horror movies while another group watches a comedy, and measures changes in their attention over the next few hours. What is the independent variable?
   - (a) The varying types of people in the two groups
   - (b) The level of attention
   - (c) The type of movie
   - (d) The number of hours before measuring attention

7. Which of the following reduces the influence of experimenter bias?
   - (a) Demand characteristics
   - (b) Independent variables
   - (c) A double-blind study
   - (d) Representative samples

8. A psychologist measures people's mood before the start of therapy and finds an improvement after a few weeks of therapy. What is lacking from this study?
   - (a) A hypothesis
   - (b) A control group
   - (c) A dependent variable
   - (d) Descriptive statistics

9. An experimenter tests 15 vitamin supplements, finds that one of them produces improved attention, and publishes only that finding. What error was committed?
   - (a) HARKing
   - (b) *p*-hacking
   - (c) Demand characteristics
   - (d) Lack of informed consent

10. A researcher provides different diets to prisoners at several institutions, without telling them, and tests changes in behavior. What error was committed?
    - (a) HARKing
    - (b) *p*-hacking
    - (c) Demand characteristics
    - (d) Lack of informed consent

Answers: 1d, 2b, 3c, 4b, 5d, 6c, 7c, 8b, 9a, 10d.

appendix to chapter 2

Statistical Calculations

This appendix provides a little more detail about certain statistics and how to calculate them. It is intended primarily to satisfy your curiosity. Ask your instructor whether you should use this appendix for any other purpose.

Measures of Variation

▼ Figure 2.16 shows two distributions of scores, which might be the results for two tests in an introductory psychology class. Both tests have the same mean, 70, but different distributions. If you had a score of 80, you would beat only 75 percent of the other students on the first test, but with the same score, you would beat 95 percent of the other students on the second test.

To describe the difference between the graphs in Figure 2.16a and b, we need a measurement of the variation (or spread) around the mean. The simplest such measurement is the range of a distribution, *a statement of the highest and lowest scores.* The range in Figure 2.16a is 38 to 100, and in Figure 2.16b, it is 56 to 94.

The range is simple but not the most useful calculation because it reflects only the extremes. A better measure is the standard deviation (SD), *a measurement of the amount of variation among scores in a normal distribution.* When the scores are closely clustered near the mean, the standard deviation is small. When

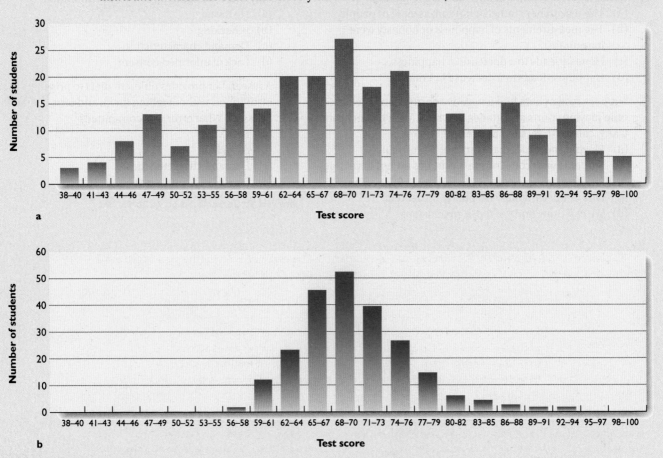

▲ **Figure 2.16** These distributions of test scores have the same mean but different variances and different standard deviations.

the scores are more widely scattered, the standard deviation is large. So, Figure 2.16a has a larger standard deviation, and Figure 2.16b has a smaller one.

As ▶ Figure 2.17 shows, the Scholastic Assessment Test (SAT) was designed to produce a mean of 500 and a standard deviation of 100. Of all people taking the test, 68 percent should score within 1 standard deviation above or below the mean (400 to 600), and 95 percent score within 2 standard deviations (300 to 700). Only 2.5 percent score above 700. Another 2.5 percent score below 300. That was the original intention, anyway. In fact, the results do not quite match the intended distribution.

Standard deviations enable us to compare scores on different tests. For example, if you scored 1 standard deviation above the mean on the SAT, you tested about as well, relatively speaking, as someone who scored 1 standard deviation above the mean on a different test, such as the American College Test.

To calculate the standard deviation (SD):
1. Determine the mean of the scores.
2. Subtract the mean from each of the individual scores.
3. Square each of those results, add the squares together, and divide by the total number of scores.

The result is called the *variance.* The standard deviation is the square root of the variance. Here is an example:

Individual scores	Each score minus the mean	Difference squared
12.5	−2.5	6.25
17.0	+2.0	4.00
11.0	−4.0	16.00
14.5	−0.5	0.25
16.0	+1.0	1.00
16.5	+1.5	2.25
17.5	+2.5	6.25
105		36.00

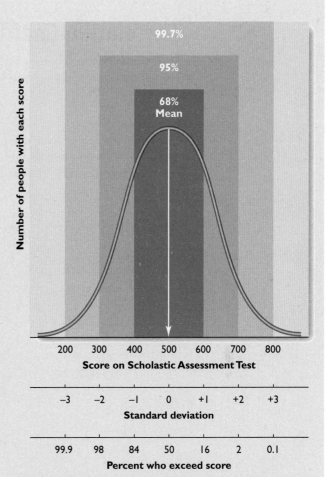

▲ **Figure 2.17** In a normal distribution of scores, the amount of variation from the mean can be measured in standard deviations. In this example, scores between 400 and 600 are said to be within 1 standard deviation from the mean; scores between 300 and 700 are within 2 standard deviations from the mean.

The mean is 15.0 (the sum of the first column, divided by 7). The variance is 5.143 (the sum of the third column, divided by 7). The standard deviation is 2.268 (the square root of 5.143).

concept check

18. **Suppose that you score 80 on your first psychology test. The mean for the class is 70, and the standard deviation is 5. On the second test, you receive a score of 90. This time the mean for the class is also 70, but the standard deviation is 20. Compared to the other students in your class, did your performance improve, deteriorate, or stay the same?**

Answer

18. Even though your score rose from 80 on the first test to 90 on the second, your performance actually deteriorated in comparison to other students' scores. A score of 80 on the first test was 2 standard deviations above the mean, better than 98 percent of all other students. A 90 on the second test was only 1 standard deviation above the mean, a score that beats only 84 percent of the other students.

Correlation Coefficients

To determine a correlation coefficient, we designate one of the variables x and the other one y. We obtain pairs of measures, x_i and y_i. Then we use the following formula:

$$r = \frac{[(\sum x_i y_i)] - n \cdot \bar{x} \cdot \bar{y}}{n \cdot sx \cdot sy}$$

In this formula, $(\sum x_i y_i)$ is the sum of the products of x and y. For each pair of observations (x, y), we multiply x times y and then we add all the products. The term $n \cdot \bar{x} \cdot \bar{y}$ means n (the number of pairs) times the mean of x times the mean of y. The denominator, $n \cdot sx \cdot sy$, means n times the standard deviation of x times the standard deviation of y.

Key Terms

range (page 50)

standard deviation (SD) (page 50)

3 Biological Psychology

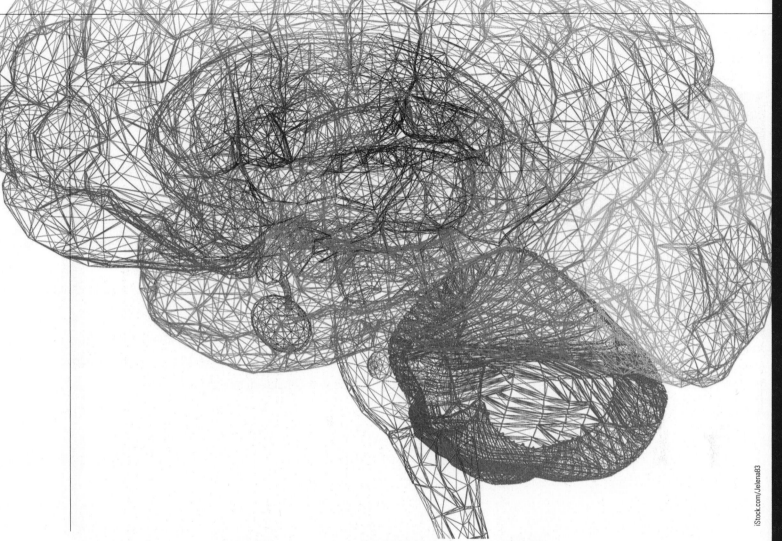

iStock.com/Jelena83

A bee has amazingly complex behavior, but we have no way to get inside the bee's experience to know what (if anything) it feels like to be a bee.

Townsend Dickinson/The Image Works

A human brain weighs only 1.2 to 1.4 kg (2.5 to 3 lbs), and a bee's brain weighs only a milligram. A dollar bill weighs about a gram, so if you imagine a bill chopped into a thousand pieces, one of those pieces weighs about as much as a bee's brain. With that tiny brain, a bee locates food, evades predators, finds its way back to the hive, and then does a dance that directs other bees to the food. It also takes care of the queen bee and protects the hive against intruders.

Everything you perceive or do is a product of brain activity. How does the brain do all that? We would like to know for both practical and theoretical reasons. Some of the practical issues relate to abnormal behavior. Are psychological disorders biological in origin? Can we treat them effectively with drugs or other biological interventions? Can we prevent deterioration in old age? Theoretical issues relate to what makes us tick. How does brain activity relate to consciousness? Do people differ in personality because of differences in their brains? The fascination of such questions impels researchers to tireless efforts.

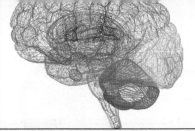

After studying this module, you should be able to:

1. Identify the main structures of a neuron.

2. Describe the action potential.

3. State the all-or-none law of the action potential.

4. Describe communication at synapses.

iStock.com/Jelena83

concept check

1. **Which part of a neuron receives input from other neurons (ordinarily)? Which part sends messages to other neurons?**

Answer

1. Dendrites receive input from other neurons. Axons send messages.

How do you differ from a machine? We usually think of a machine as something made of metal, but really a machine is anything that converts one type of energy into another, such as converting gasoline into the operation of a car. In that sense, you don't differ from a machine at all, because you are a machine. Your body converts the energy in your food into the actions of your body. Your brain is part of that machine, and one way to understand your experiences and actions is to analyze your brain activity.

We start with the individual cells that compose the nervous system. Studying a single cell doesn't take us far toward understanding your behavior, any more than studying a single silicon chip explains a computer. Still, it's a place to start.

Nervous System Cells

Although you experience your "self" as a single entity, your brain consists of separate cells called neurons (NOO-rons). ▼ Figure 3.1 shows estimates of the numbers of neurons in parts of the human nervous system, although the actual numbers vary from one person to another (Reardon et al., 2018; R. W. Williams & Herrup, 1988). The nervous system also contains cells called glia (GLEE-uh) *that insulate neurons, synchronize activity among neighboring neurons, remove waste products, and assist in information processing.* Neurons outnumber glia in some brain areas, but glia are more numerous in others. Contrary to what we once thought, overall the brain has more neurons than glia (von Bartheld, Bahney, & Herculano-Houzel, 2016).

Neurons are similar to other body cells in most ways. The most distinctive feature of neurons is their extreme variety of shapes (see ▼ Figure 3.2). In fact, biologists of the late 1800s were puzzled by what they saw in microscopes, because those odd things did not look at all like the cells of the rest of the body. A neuron consists of three parts: a cell body, dendrites, and an axon (see ▼ Figure 3.3). The cell body *contains the nucleus of the cell.* The dendrites (from a Greek word meaning "tree") are *widely branching structures that receive input from other neurons.* The axon is a *single, long, thin, straight fiber with branches near its tip.* Some vertebrate axons are covered with myelin, *an insulating sheath that speeds up the transmission of impulses along an axon.* As a rule, an axon transmits information to other cells, and the dendrites or cell body receives that information. (Almost any statement about the nervous system has exceptions. In some cases, cell bodies or dendrites pass information to other cells.) The information can be either excitatory or inhibitory. That is, it can increase or decrease the probability that the next cell will send a message of its own.

The Action Potential

The function of an axon is to convey information over long distances, such as from the skin to the spinal cord, from one brain area to another, or from the spinal cord to a muscle. Electrical conduction would convey information almost instantaneously, but your body is a relatively poor conductor of electricity. If axons conducted electrically, impulses would get weaker and weaker as they traveled. Short people would feel a pinch on their toes more intensely than tall people would—if either felt their toes at all.

Instead, axons convey information by a process called an action potential, *an excitation that travels along an axon at a constant strength, no matter how far it travels.* For analogy, imagine a line of people holding hands. The first person squeezes the second person's hand, who squeezes the third person's hand, and so on until the end. The transmission takes a while, but the message is as strong at the end as it was at the beginning. An action potential is a yes–no or on–off message, like flicking a light switch. *The fact that an axon varies the frequency, but not the strength or velocity of its action potentials,* is the all-or-none law of the action potential.

The advantage of an action potential over simple electrical conduction is that action potentials reach your brain at full strength. The disadvantage is that action potentials take time. Your knowledge of what is happening to your toes is at least a 20th of a second out of date. Pain and itch sensations are even slower. A 20th of a second delay will seldom inconvenience you, but that delay is theoretically interesting. When researchers first demonstrated that your touch perceptions are delayed until the message reaches the brain, their result showed that perceptions occur in your head, not in your fingers. When you touch something, it *seems* that the sensation is in your finger, but no, it is in your head. Other evidence for this conclusion is that direct stimulation of certain brain areas

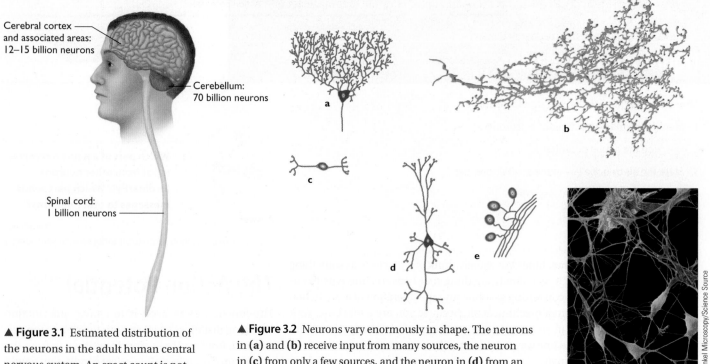

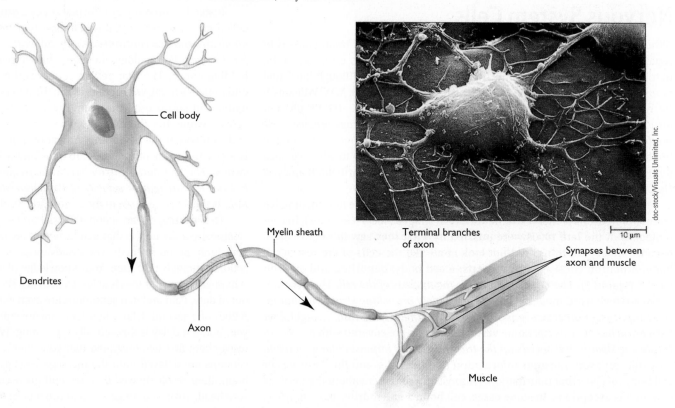

▲ **Figure 3.1** Estimated distribution of the neurons in the adult human central nervous system. An exact count is not feasible, and the number varies from one person to another. (Based on data of R. W. Williams & Herrup, 1988)

▲ **Figure 3.2** Neurons vary enormously in shape. The neurons in (**a**) and (**b**) receive input from many sources, the neuron in (**c**) from only a few sources, and the neuron in (**d**) from an intermediate number of sources. The sensory neurons (**e**) carry messages from sensory receptors to the brain or spinal cord. Inset: Electron micrograph showing cell bodies in orange and axons and dendrites in red. The color was added artificially; electron micrographs are made with electron beams, not light, and therefore, they show no color.

▲ **Figure 3.3** The generalized structure of a motor neuron shows the dendrites, the branching structures that receive transmissions from other neurons, and the axon, a long fiber with branches near its tip. Inset: A photomicrograph of a neuron.

produces touch sensation, even if a finger was amputated, and touching the finger produces no sensation if the relevant brain area is damaged.

Here is how the action potential works:

1. When the axon is not stimulated, its membrane has a **resting potential**, *an electrical polarization across the membrane of an axon.* Typically, the inside has a charge of about −70 millivolts relative to the outside. Because of a mechanism called the sodium-potassium pump, positively charged sodium ions are more concentrated outside the axon, and positively charged potassium ions are more concentrated inside. The negative charge comes from negatively charged proteins inside the cell.

2. If excitation reaches the *threshold* of the axon (typically about −55 millivolts), it briefly opens *gates* in the axon through which sodium and potassium ions can flow. Sodium ions, which are highly concentrated outside the membrane, rush into the cell, attracted by the negative charge inside. That influx is the action potential. The positive charge entering the axon excites the next point along the axon, which then opens sodium channels and repeats the process, as shown in ▶ Figure 3.4.

3. After a few milliseconds, the sodium gates snap shut, but the potassium gates remain open a little longer. Because the sodium ions have brought positive charges into the cell, the inside of the cell no longer attracts potassium ions, and because they are more concentrated inside the cell, they flow out of the cell, carrying positive charges with them. Their exit drives the inside of the axon back to its resting potential (see ▶ Figure 3.5b).

4. Gradually, the sodium-potassium pump removes the extra sodium ions and recaptures the escaped potassium ions.

Remember the highlights: Sodium enters the cell (excitation). Then potassium leaves (return to the resting potential).

Conduction along an axon is analogous to a fire burning along a string: The fire at each point ignites the next point, which in turn ignites the next point. In an axon, after sodium ions enter the membrane, some of them diffuse to the neighboring portion of the axon, exciting it enough to open its own sodium gates. The action potential spreads to this next area and so on down the axon, as shown in ▶ Figure 3.5. In this manner, the action potential remains equally strong all the way to the end of the axon.

How does this information relate to psychology? First, it explains why sensations from your fingers and toes do not fade away by the time they reach your brain. Second, an understanding of action potentials is one step toward understanding the communication between neurons. Third, anesthetic drugs (e.g., Novocain) operate by clogging sodium gates and therefore silencing neurons. When your dentist drills a tooth, the receptors in your tooth send out the message "Pain! Pain! Pain!" But that message does not reach your brain when the sodium gates are blocked.

2. **If you simultaneously received a touch sensation on your left foot and a painful sensation on your right foot, which would you feel first? Why?**
3. **If some drug blocked all sodium gates throughout your brain, what would happen?**
4. **If some drug blocked all potassium gates throughout your brain, what would happen?**

Answers

2. You would feel the touch sensation first, because the action potentials for pain sensation travel more slowly.
3. All action potentials would stop, including those that control breathing. You would die. Do not take that drug.
4. After an action potential, the neuron could not return to its resting potential. Therefore, a stimulus could not cause sodium to enter the cell and produce an action potential. Again, you would die. Do not take that drug.

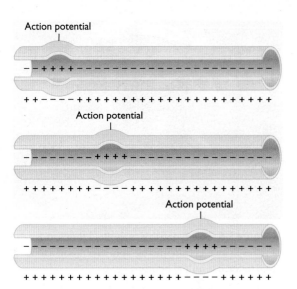

▲ **Figure 3.4** Ion movements conduct an action potential along an axon. At each point along the membrane, sodium ions enter the axon. As each point along the membrane returns to its original state, the action potential flows to the next point.

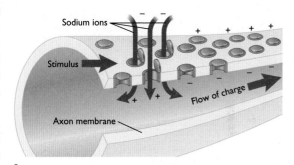

a

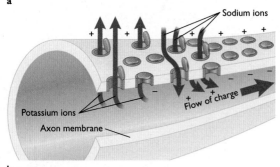

b

▲ **Figure 3.5** (a) During an action potential, sodium gates open, and sodium ions enter the axon, bearing a positive charge. (b) After an action potential occurs, the sodium gates close at that point and open at the next point along the axon. As the sodium gates close, potassium gates open, and potassium ions flow out of the axon. (Modified from Starr & Taggart, 1992)

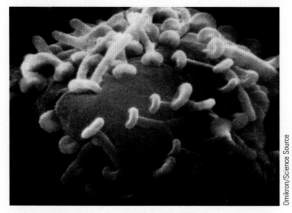

▲ **Figure 3.6** This synapse is magnified thousands of times in an electron micrograph. The tips of axons swell to form terminal boutons.

Omikron/Science Source

Synapses

How do separate neurons combine forces to produce your stream of experience? The answer is communication. Communication between one neuron and the next is not like transmission along an axon. At a **synapse** (SIN-aps), *the specialized junction between one neuron and another* (see ◄ **Figure 3.6**), *a neuron releases a chemical that either excites or inhibits the next neuron.*

A typical axon has branches, each ending with a little bulge called a *presynaptic ending,* or **terminal bouton,** as shown in ▼ **Figure 3.7.** (*Bouton* is French for "button.") When an action potential reaches the terminal bouton, it releases a **neurotransmitter,** *a chemical that activates receptors on another cell* (see Figure 3.7). Neurons use dozens of chemicals as neurotransmitters, but a given neuron releases no more than a few of them. The neurotransmitter molecules diffuse across a narrow gap to receptors on the **postsynaptic neuron,** *the neuron on the receiving end of the synapse.* A neurotransmitter fits into

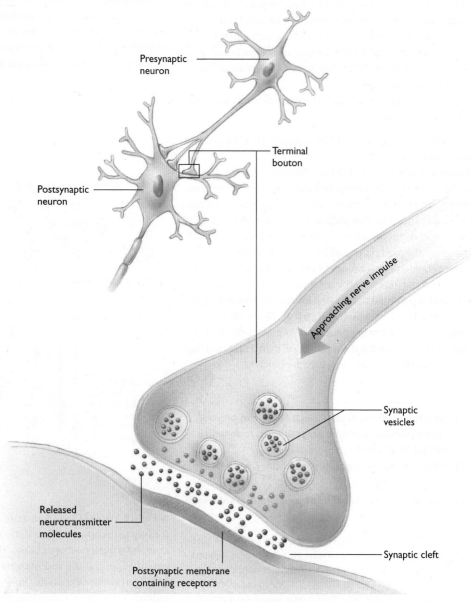

▲ **Figure 3.7** A synapse is a junction of a presynaptic (message-sending) cell and a postsynaptic (message-receiving) cell. The terminal bouton at the tip of the presynaptic axon contains the neurotransmitter.

its receptor as a key fits into a lock, and it either excites or inhibits the postsynaptic neuron.

The messages in a computer are simply on/off (represented as 1 or 0), and scientists used to assume that synaptic messages were like that, too. We now know that synaptic messages are more variable. Depending on the transmitter and its receptor, the effect might have a sudden onset and last only milliseconds, or it might develop gradually and last for seconds. *Peptide* transmitters diffuse to a wider brain area and produce effects that last minutes. A quick, sudden message is important for vision and hearing. Slower, longer-lasting messages are more appropriate for taste and smell. Very slow, minutes-long messages are useful for hunger, thirst, and sex drive. ▼ Figure 3.8 summarizes synaptic transmission.

Inhibitory messages are essential for many purposes. For example, if you step on a tack and reflexively raise your foot, inhibitory synapses prevent you from trying to raise your other foot at the same time. When you see something, your perception depends on which cells in the visual system are excited and which ones are inhibited. The inhibition is just as important as the excitation.

5. Why is it useful to have synapses that vary in their speed and duration of effects?

Answer

5. For vision and hearing, the brain needs instantaneous updates of information. Hunger, thirst, sleepiness, and many other behaviors are gradual or long-term processes.

After a neurotransmitter excites or inhibits a receptor, it separates from it. From that point on, the receptor molecule might bounce back to reexcite

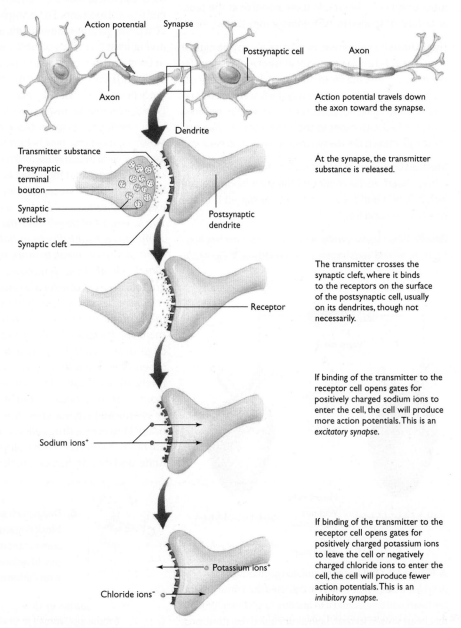

Action potential travels down the axon toward the synapse.

At the synapse, the transmitter substance is released.

The transmitter crosses the synaptic cleft, where it binds to the receptors on the surface of the postsynaptic cell, usually on its dendrites, though not necessarily.

If binding of the transmitter to the receptor cell opens gates for positively charged sodium ions to enter the cell, the cell will produce more action potentials. This is an *excitatory synapse*.

If binding of the transmitter to the receptor cell opens gates for positively charged potassium ions to leave the cell or negatively charged chloride ions to enter the cell, the cell will produce fewer action potentials. This is an *inhibitory synapse*.

▲ **Figure 3.8** The complex process of neural communication takes only 1 to 2 milliseconds.

the postsynaptic receptor, it might diffuse away from the synapse, or it might be reabsorbed by the axon that released it (through a process called *reuptake*). Several drugs block reuptake, thus prolonging a transmitter's effects. Examples include cocaine, Ritalin, and most antidepressant drugs.

what's the evidence?

Neurons Communicate Chemically

You have just learned that neurons communicate by releasing chemicals at synapses. What evidence led to this conclusion?

Today, neuroscientists have a wealth of evidence that neurons release chemicals at synapses. In 1920, Otto Loewi demonstrated that point by a clever experiment using only the simple tools available at the time, as he later described in his autobiography (Loewi, 1960).

Hypothesis If a neuron releases chemicals, an investigator should be able to collect some of those chemicals, transfer them to the same site on another animal, and thereby get the second animal to react the way the first animal was reacting. Loewi could not collect chemicals within the brain, so he worked with axons to the heart muscles. (A nerve-muscle junction is like the synapse between two neurons.)

Method Loewi electrically stimulated axons that slowed a frog's heart. As he continued the stimulation, he collected fluid around that heart and transferred it to the heart of a second frog.

Results When Loewi transferred the fluid from the first frog's heart, the second frog's heart rate also slowed (see ▼ Figure 3.9).

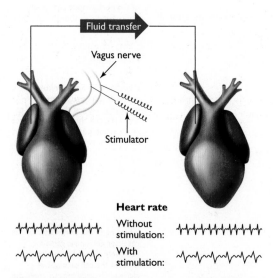

Heart rate

Without stimulation:

With stimulation:

▲ **Figure 3.9** Otto Loewi stimulated axons known to decrease a frog's heart rate. He collected fluid from around the heart and transferred it to another frog's heart. When that heart slowed its beat, Loewi concluded that the axons in the first heart released a chemical that slows heart rate.

Interpretation Evidently, the stimulated axons had released a chemical that slows heart rate. At least in this case, neurons send messages by releasing chemicals.

Loewi won a Nobel Prize in physiology for this and related research. Even outstanding experiments have limitations, however. Loewi's results did not indicate whether axons release chemicals at all synapses, most, or only a few. Answering that question required technologies not available until several decades later. The answer is that the great majority of synapses use chemicals, although a few communicate electrically.

Neurotransmitters and Behavior

The brain has dozens of neurotransmitters, some of them listed in ■ Table 3.1, and many of them activate several types of receptors. For example, the brain has at least 26 types of gamma aminobutyric acid (GABA) receptors and at least 7 families of serotonin receptors, differing in their structure and their response to drugs (C. Wang et al., 2013). Each receptor type controls somewhat different aspects of behavior. For example, because serotonin type 3 receptors are responsible for nausea, researchers have developed drugs to block nausea (Perez, 1995). However, most complex behaviors rely on a combination of several transmitters and receptor types.

A disorder that increases or decreases a particular transmitter or receptor can alter behavior. One example is **Parkinson's disease**, *a condition that affects 1 to 2 percent of people over the age of 65. The main symptoms are difficulty in initiating voluntary movement, slow movement, tremors, rigidity, and depressed mood.* All of these symptoms can be traced to a gradual decay of one set of axons that release *the neurotransmitter* **dopamine** (DOPE-uh-meen). Unlike so many medications discovered by accident, the treatment for Parkinson's disease emerged from knowledge of the underlying mechanism of the disease. Researchers knew they needed to increase dopamine levels in the brain. Dopamine pills or injections would not work because dopamine (like many other chemicals) cannot cross from the blood into the brain. However, a drug called L-dopa does cross into the brain. Neurons absorb L-dopa, convert it to dopamine, and thereby increase their supply of dopamine.

concept check

6. **Drugs such as haloperidol that block dopamine synapses alleviate some cases of schizophrenia. How would haloperidol affect someone with Parkinson's disease?**

Answer

6. Haloperidol would increase the severity of Parkinson's disease. In fact, large doses of haloperidol induce symptoms of Parkinson's disease in anyone.

Table 3.1 Some Important Neurotransmitters

Neurotransmitter	Functions	Comment
Glutamate	The brain's main excitatory transmitter, present at most synapses; essential for almost all brain activities, including learning.	Strokes kill neurons mostly by releasing extra glutamate that overstimulates them.
GABA (gamma- amino- butyric acid)	The brain's main inhibitory transmitter.	Anti-anxiety drugs and anti-epileptic drugs increase activity at GABA synapses.
Acetylcholine	Increases brain arousal.	Acetylcholine is also released by motor neurons to stimulate skeletal muscles.
Dopamine	One path is important for movement (damaged in Parkinson's disease). Another path is important for memory and cognition.	Most antipsychotic drugs decrease activity at dopamine synapses. L-dopa, used for Parkinson's disease, increases availability of dopamine.
Serotonin	Modifies many types of motivated and emotional behavior.	Most antidepressant drugs prolong activity at serotonin synapses.
Norepinephrine	Enhances storage of memory of emotional or otherwise meaningful events.	All or nearly all axons releasing norepinephrine originate from one small brain area, called the locus coeruleus.
Histamine	Increases arousal and alertness.	Antihistamines (for allergies) block histamine and therefore lead to drowsiness.
Endorphins	Decrease pain and increase pleasure.	Morphine and heroin stimulate the same receptors as endorphins.
Nitric oxide	Dilates blood vessels in the most active brain areas.	This is the only known transmitter that is a gas.
Anandamide, 2AG, and others	Sent by the postsynaptic neuron back to the presynaptic neuron to decrease further release of transmitters.	THC, the active chemical in marijuana, stimulates these same presynaptic receptors.

in closing | module 3.1

Neurons, Synapses, and Behavior

Even what seems a simple behavior, such as saying a few words, corresponds to a complicated sequence of well-timed movements. Those complex behaviors emerge from synapses. Complex behavior is possible because of the connections among huge numbers of neurons. No one neuron or synapse does much by itself. Your experience results from dozens of types of neurotransmitters, billions of neurons, and trillions of synapses, each contributing in a small way.

Summary

- *Neuron structure.* A neuron, or nerve cell, consists of a cell body, dendrites, and an axon. The axon conveys information to other neurons. (page 55)
- *The action potential.* Information is conveyed along an axon by an action potential, which is regenerated without loss of strength at each point along the axon. (page 55)
- *All-or-none law.* An axon can alter how often it sends an action potential, but it cannot change the amplitude or velocity of an action potential. (page 55)
- *Mechanism of the action potential.* Sodium enters a neuron, bringing a positive charge. Milliseconds later, potassium leaves the neuron, bringing it back to its resting potential. (page 57)
- *How neurons communicate.* A neuron communicates with another neuron by releasing a chemical called a neurotransmitter at a specialized junction called a synapse. A neurotransmitter can either excite or inhibit the next neuron, with varying rates of onset and duration. (page 58)

- *Neurotransmitters and behavioral disorders.* An excess or deficit of a neurotransmitter can lead to abnormal behavior, such as that exhibited by people with Parkinson's disease. (page 60)

Key Terms

action potential (page 55)

all-or-none law (page 55)

axon (page 55)

cell body (page 55)

dendrite (page 55)

dopamine (page 60)

glia (page 55)

myelin (page 55)

neuron (page 55)

neurotransmitter (page 58)

Parkinson's disease (page 60)

postsynaptic neuron (page 58)

resting potential (page 57)

synapse (page 58)

terminal bouton (page 58)

Review Questions

1. What about a neuron is most unusual, compared to other body cells?
   (a) Size
   (b) Color
   (c) Shape
   (d) Mitochondria

2. For an axon to signal increased or decreased strength of a stimulus, which of the following could it change?
   (a) Frequency of firing action potentials
   (b) Velocity of action potentials
   (c) Amplitude (size) of action potentials
   (d) Neurotransmitters released

3. During an action potential, what is the movement of ions?
   (a) Potassium into the cell, then sodium out
   (b) Sodium into the cell, then potassium out
   (c) Both potassium and sodium into the cell, then both out
   (d) Both potassium and sodium out of the cell, then both in

4. In most cases, which part of a neuron releases a neurotransmitter?
   (a) The cell body
   (b) The dendrites
   (c) The axon
   (d) All parts equally

5. When a neurotransmitter excites the postsynaptic neuron, how long do the effects last?
   (a) Just milliseconds
   (b) About a tenth of a second
   (c) Several seconds or longer
   (d) The results vary from one synapse to another.

6. Because neurons have more than one type of receptor for each neurotransmitter, which of the following is a consequence?
   (a) An excitatory neuron quickly shifts to become inhibitory.
   (b) Certain drugs can alter a behavior or experience.
   (c) Prolonged brain activity can damage neurons.
   (d) Action potentials grow weaker as people age.

Answers: 1c, 2a, 3b, 4c, 5d, 6b.

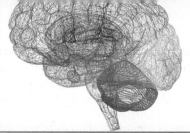

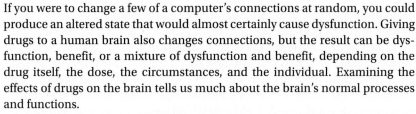

module 3.2
Drugs and Their Effects

iStock.com/Jelena83

After studying this module, you should be able to:

1. Describe how drugs affect behavior by changing actions at synapses.

2. Distinguish among classes of drugs such as stimulants, hallucinogens, anxiolytics, and opiates.

3. Explain why a drug may have one effect immediately and a different effect hours later.

If you were to change a few of a computer's connections at random, you could produce an altered state that would almost certainly cause dysfunction. Giving drugs to a human brain also changes connections, but the result can be dysfunction, benefit, or a mixture of dysfunction and benefit, depending on the drug itself, the dose, the circumstances, and the individual. Examining the effects of drugs on the brain tells us much about the brain's normal processes and functions.

Psychoactive drugs affect synapses in many ways. Some attach to receptors and activate them. Some attach imperfectly, like an almost-fitting key that gets stuck in a lock and prevents the lock from opening. Some increase or decrease the release of transmitters or decrease reuptake (the return of released transmitters to the neuron that released them). A drug that increases activity at a synapse is called an *agonist*, based on the Greek word for a "contestant" or "fighter." A drug that decreases activity at a synapse is an *antagonist*, from the Greek word for an "enemy."

Stimulants

Stimulants are *drugs that increase energy, alertness, and activity.* Amphetamine, methamphetamine, and cocaine block the protein that the presynaptic neuron uses to reabsorb dopamine or serotonin molecules after releasing them,

iStock.com/nazar_ab

Ritalin, a drug given to calm hyperactive children, has the same synaptic effects as cocaine. The difference is quantitative. A Ritalin pill slowly and slightly increases dopamine activity in the brain, whereas cocaine produces a sudden rush of effects.

or reverse that protein so that it releases dopamine instead of reabsorbing it (Beuming et al., 2008; Calipari & Ferris, 2013). As a result, stimulant drugs increase the effects of those transmitters, including dopamine. Dopamine synapses are active during heightened motivations, ranging from sex and food to music, gambling, and video games (Koepp et al., 1998; Maldonado et al., 1997; Salimpoor et al., 2013).

Cocaine has long been available in the powdery form of cocaine hydrochloride, which can be sniffed. Before 1985, the only way to get a more intense effect from cocaine hydrochloride was to transform it into *freebase cocaine*—cocaine with the hydrochloride removed. Freebase cocaine enters the brain rapidly, and fast entry intensifies the experience. *Crack cocaine*, which first became available in 1985, is cocaine that has already been converted into freebase rocks, ready to be smoked (Brower & Anglin, 1987; Kozel & Adams, 1986). It is called "crack" because it makes popping noises when smoked. Crack produces a rush of potent effects within a few seconds.

The behavioral effects of stimulant drugs depend on the dose. Low levels enhance attention. In fact, amphetamine is often prescribed for attention deficit disorder, under the trade name Adderall. At higher doses, amphetamine and cocaine lead to confusion, impaired attention, and impulsiveness (Simon, Mendez, & Setlow, 2007; Stalnaker et al., 2007). Physical effects include higher heart rate, blood pressure, and body temperature, and a risk of convulsions, lung damage, and heart attack.

As amphetamine or cocaine enters the brain, it increases arousal and produces mostly pleasant effects. However, because these drugs inhibit the reuptake of dopamine, it washes away from synapses faster than the presynaptic neurons can replace it. Over the next few hours, the presynaptic neurons' supply of transmitters dwindles and users begin to experience mild lethargy and depression that last until the neurons rebuild their supply.

Methylphenidate (Ritalin), a drug often prescribed for attention deficit disorder, works the same way as cocaine, at the same synapses (Volkow, Wang, & Fowler, 1997; Volkow et al., 1998). The difference is that methylphenidate, taken as a pill, reaches the brain gradually over an hour or more and declines slowly over hours. Therefore, it does not produce the sudden rush that makes crack cocaine so addictive.

Does taking stimulant drugs for attention deficit disorder increase the risk of later substance abuse? Many people with attention deficit disorder do develop substance abuse, but apparently a history of taking stimulant medication does not add to that risk (Groenman, Janssen, & Oosterlaan, 2017; Quinn et al., 2017).

Tobacco delivers nicotine, which stimulates synapses responsive to the neurotransmitter *acetylcholine*, and indirectly enhances dopamine and other neurotransmitters. The increased acetylcholine activity enhances attention and some aspects of cognition, especially for people initially low in cognitive abilities (Valentine & Sofuoglu, 2018). Although nicotine acts as a stimulant, most smokers say it relaxes them. The reason is that abstaining from cigarettes increases tension, and smoking another cigarette relieves the tension (Parrott, 1999). Cigarette smoking is a health risk not because of nicotine, but because of the tars present in tobacco smoke. Electronic cigarettes ("vaping") is a health risk, again not because of nicotine, but because of other chemicals and contaminants in the devices.

Hallucinogens

Drugs that induce sensory distortions are called **hallucinogens** or *psychedelics*. An example is LSD (lysergic acid diethylamide). Many such drugs are derived from mushrooms or plants, and others are manufactured. The sensory distortions are not hallucinations in the usual sense, because the person recognizes that the strange sensory experience is not real. Hallucinogens also sometimes produce emotional changes, a dreamlike state, or an intense mystical experience. Although LSD is considered a high-risk drug, it has sometimes been used under controlled conditions as an adjunct to psychotherapy or for relief of severe anxiety (Smith, Raswyck, & Davidson, 2014). Peyote, a hallucinogen derived from a cactus plant, has a long history of use in Native American religious ceremonies (see ▼ Figure 3.10).

LSD binds to receptors for the neurotransmitter serotonin (Jacobs, 1987). It stimulates those receptors at irregular times and prevents neurotransmitters from stimulating them at the normal times. One result is a decrease in communication among brain areas, such that sensory and emotional experiences occur without the usual guidance and restraint that the frontal cortex would provide.

The drug MDMA (methylenedioxymethamphetamine), popularly known as "ecstasy" (although ecstasy tablets almost always contain a mixture of MDMA and other chemicals), produces both stimulant effects and decreased anxiety. Many young adults use MDMA at parties to increase their energy. Risks include nausea, increased body temperature, sleeplessness, and memory impairments. However, some studies report that in small doses in controlled conditions, MDMA might aid therapy for post-traumatic stress disorder (Thal & Lommen, 2018).

Manu Sassoonian/Art Resource, NY

▲ **Figure 3.10** Tablas, or yarn paintings, created by members of the Huichol tribe (Mexico) evoke the beautiful lights, vivid colors, and "peculiar creatures" experienced after the people eat the hallucinogenic peyote cactus in ritualized ceremonies.

concept check

7. The drug AMPT (alpha-methyl-para-tyrosine) prevents the body from making dopamine. How would a large dose of AMPT affect someone's later responsiveness to cocaine, amphetamine, or methylphenidate?

8. Some people with attention deficit disorder experience benefits for the first few hours after taking methylphenidate pills but become less attentive in the late afternoon and evening. Why?

Answers

7. Someone who took AMPT would become less responsive than usual to amphetamine, cocaine, or methylphenidate. These drugs prolong the effects of dopamine, but if the neurons cannot make dopamine, they cannot release it.
8. Remember what happens after taking cocaine: Neurons release dopamine and other transmitters faster than they resynthesize them. Because cocaine blocks reuptake, the supply of transmitters dwindles, and the result is lethargy and mild depression. The same process occurs to some extent with methylphenidate.

Depressants

Depressants are *drugs that decrease arousal,* such as alcohol and *anxiolytics* (anxiety-reducing drugs). People have been using alcohol since prehistoric times. When archeologists unearthed a Neolithic village in Iran's Zagros Mountains, they found a jar that had been constructed about 5500 to 5400 B.C., one of the oldest human-made crafts ever found (see ▼ **Figure 3.11**). Inside the jar, especially at the bottom, the archeologists found a yellowish residue. They were curious to know what the jar had held, so they sent the residue for chemical analysis. The unambiguous answer came back: It was wine. The jar had been a wine vessel (McGovern, Glusker, Exner, & Voigt, 1996).

Alcohol is a *class of molecules that includes methanol, ethanol, propyl alcohol (rubbing alcohol), and others. Ethanol is the type that people drink.* At moderate doses, alcohol relaxes people by facilitating activity at inhibitory synapses. In greater amounts, it increases risk-taking behaviors, including aggression, by suppressing the fears and inhibitions that ordinarily limit such behaviors. In still greater amounts, as in binge drinking, alcohol suppresses breathing and heart rate to a dangerous degree. Prolonged excessive use damages the liver and other organs, aggravates medical conditions, and impairs memory and motor control. A woman who drinks alcohol during pregnancy risks damage to her baby's brain, health, and appearance.

Anxiolytic drugs or **tranquilizers** *help people relax.* The most widely used anxiolytics are *benzodiazepines*, including diazepam (Valium) and alprazolam (Xanax). Benzodiazepines calm people by facilitating transmission at inhibitory synapses. Taking these drugs at the same time as alcohol can produce dangerous suppression of breathing and heart rate.

One benzodiazepine drug, flunitrazepam (Rohypnol), has attracted attention as a "date rape drug." The drug dissolves quickly in water and has no color, odor, or taste to warn the person who is consuming it. As with other anxiolytics, it induces drowsiness, clumsiness, and memory impairment (Anglin, Spears, & Hutson, 1997; Woods & Winger, 1997). Someone under the influence of the drug does not have the strength to fight off an attacker and may not remember the event clearly. A hospital that suspects someone has been given this drug can detect its presence with a urine test up to three days later. If the drink itself is still available, the drug can be detected weeks later (Gautam, Sharratt, & Cole, 2014). This drug is no longer available legally in the United States.

Another date rape drug, GHB (gamma hydroxybutyrate), has become widespread because it can be made easily (though impurely) with household ingredients. Like flunitrazepam, it relaxes the body and impairs muscle coordination. Large doses induce vomiting, tremors, coma, and death.

Courtesy of Penn Museum, image #151075

▲ **Figure 3.11** This wine jar, dated about 5500 to 5400 B.C., is one of the oldest human crafts ever found.

✓ concept check

9. What do alcohol and anxiolytic drugs have in common?

Answer

9. They increase relaxation by facilitating inhibitory synapses.

Narcotics

Narcotics are *drugs that produce drowsiness, insensitivity to pain, and decreased responsiveness.* **Opiates** are *either natural drugs derived from the opium poppy or synthetic drugs with a chemical structure resembling natural opiates.* Opiates make people feel happy, warm, and content, with little anxiety or pain. Morphine (named after Morpheus, the Greek god of dreams) is often used as a painkiller with controlled doses under medical supervision. Larger doses produce euphoria, but as the drug leaves the brain, elation gives way to anxiety, pain, and exaggerated responsiveness to sounds and other stimuli. These withdrawal symptoms become especially strong after habitual use.

Opiate drugs such as morphine, heroin, methadone, and codeine bind to specific receptors in the brain (Pert & Snyder, 1973). The discovery of neurotransmitter receptors demonstrated that opiates block pain in the brain, not in the skin. Neuroscientists then found that the brain produces its own chemicals, called **endorphins,** that *bind to the opiate receptors* (Hughes et al., 1975). Endorphins inhibit chronic pain. The brain also releases endorphins during eating (Tuulari et al., 2017), sexual activity, and other motivated behaviors.

Following some reports that opiates taken for pain relief seldom become addictive, the U.S. government loosened restrictions on prescription opiates in the 1990s. In many places, especially the eastern half of the United States, prescriptions became more common, many people began taking far more than they needed for pain relief, abuse and addiction became increasingly common, and fatal drug overdoses became so common that we speak of an "opiate epidemic." Since 2010, the rate of opiate prescriptions has decreased (while remaining high), but the use of illegally obtained opiates has increased (Ostling et al., 2018).

Marijuana

Marijuana (*cannabis*) is difficult to classify. It softens pain but not as powerfully as opiates. It produces an illusion that time is passing more slowly than usual, but it does not produce sensory distortions similar to those of LSD. It has a calming effect but not like that of alcohol or tranquilizers.

Marijuana use correlates with memory problems for two reasons. First, students who are doing poorly in school are more likely than others to start using marijuana, and to use it often (Hooper, Woolley, & De Bellis, 2014). Second, using marijuana or its main component, THC (tetrahydrocannabinol), impairs attention and memory, whereas abstaining from its use leads to recovery, generally within three days (Bloomfield et al., 2019). Marijuana use also correlates with increased risk of schizophrenia. The main reason is that many people developing schizophrenia start using marijuana, as well as other drugs. Also, heavy use of marijuana during adolescence, while much brain development is still occurring, probably increases the risk of psychiatric problems.

THC has potential medical uses. It reduces nausea, suppresses tremors, reduces pressure in the eyes, and decreases cell loss in the brain after a stroke (Glass, 2001; Panikashvili et al., 2001). However, animal research shows that marijuana protects the brain from stroke damage only if it is administered quickly after the stroke, or better yet *before* the stroke (Schomacher, Müller, Sommer, Schwab, & Schäbitz, 2008). (It's impractical to recommend that everyone at risk for stroke should remain permanently stoned.) In addition to THC, marijuana contains related chemicals, including cannabidiol, which may be helpful in treating schizophrenia or other conditions (Szkudlarek et al., 2019).

THC attaches to receptors that are abundant throughout the brain (Herkenham, Lynn, deCosta, & Richfield, 1991). The brain produces large amounts of its own chemicals, anandamide and 2-AG, that attach to those receptors (Devane et al., 1992; Stella, Schweitzer, & Piomelli, 1997). These receptors are abundant in brain areas that control memory and movement, but they are nearly absent from the medulla, which controls heart rate and breathing (Herkenham et al., 1990). In contrast, the medulla has many opiate receptors.

Unlike most other neurotransmitter receptors, those for anandamide and 2-AG (and therefore THC) are located on the *pre*synaptic neuron. When the presynaptic neuron releases the transmitters glutamate or GABA, the postsynaptic (receiving) cell releases anandamide or 2-AG, which returns to the presynaptic cell to inhibit further release (Kreitzer & Regehr, 2001; Oliet, Baimoukhametova, Piet, & Bains, 2007; R. I. Wilson & Nicoll, 2002). In effect it says, "I received your signal. You can slow down on sending any more of it." THC, by resembling these natural reverse transmitters, has the same effect, except that it slows the signal before it has been sent. It is as if the presynaptic cell "thinks" it has sent a signal when in fact it has not.

Gary C. Caskey/United Press International (UPI)/Denver/CO/United States

A store owner smiles while selling marijuana legally for the first time in Colorado.

Marijuana has many behavioral effects that researchers need to explain. It decreases nausea by blocking the type of serotonin receptor responsible for nausea (Fan, 1995). It increases activity in brain areas responsible for feeding and appetite (DiMarzo et al., 2001). How it produces the illusion that time is passing slowly is hard to explain, but the same phenomenon occurs in laboratory animals. Under the influence of marijuana smoke, rats show impairments when they have to respond at certain time intervals. They respond too quickly, as if 10 seconds felt like 20 seconds (Han & Robinson, 2001).

concept check

10. An overdose of opiates produces a life-threatening decrease in breathing and heart rate. Marijuana does not ordinarily produce those effects. Why not?

Answer

10. Opiate receptors are abundant in the medulla, which controls heart rate and breathing. The medulla has few receptors sensitive to marijuana.

▼ Figure 3.12 diagrams the effects of several drugs. ■ Table 3.2 summarizes the drugs we have been considering. The list of risks is incomplete because of space. Large or repeated doses of any drug can be dangerous.

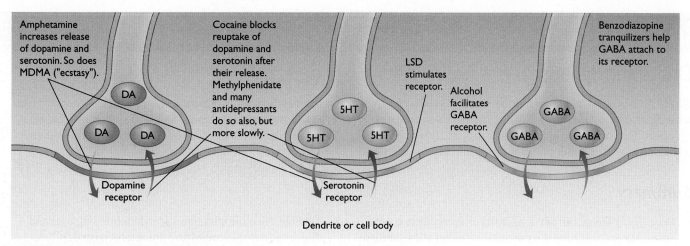

▲ Figure 3.12 Both legal and illegal drugs operate at the synapses. Drugs can increase the release of neurotransmitters, block their reuptake, or directly stimulate or block their receptors.

Table 3.2 Commonly Abused Drugs and Their Effects

Drug Category	Effects on the Nervous System	Short-Term Effects	Risks (Partial List)
Stimulants			
Amphetamine	Increases release of dopamine and decreases reuptake, prolonging effects	Increases energy and alertness	Psychotic reaction, agitation, heart problems, sleeplessness, stroke
Cocaine	Decreases reuptake of dopamine, prolonging effects	Increases energy and alertness	Psychotic reaction, heart problems
Methylphenidate (Ritalin)	Decreases reuptake of dopamine but with slower onset and offset than cocaine	Increases alertness; much milder withdrawal effects than cocaine	Increased blood pressure
Nicotine	Stimulates some acetylcholine synapses; stimulates some neurons that release dopamine	Increases arousal; abstention by a habitual smoker produces tension and depression	Lung cancer from the tars in cigarettes
Depressants			
Alcohol	Facilitates effects of GABA, an inhibitory neurotransmitter	Relaxation, reduced inhibitions, impaired memory and judgment	Automobile accidents, loss of job
Benzodiazepines	Facilitate effects of GABA, an inhibitory neurotransmitter	Relaxation, decreased anxiety, sleepiness	Dependence. Life-threatening if combined with alcohol or opiates
Narcotics			
Morphine, heroin, other opiates	Stimulate endorphin synapses	Decrease pain; withdrawal from interest in real world; unpleasant withdrawal effects during abstention	Heart stoppage
Marijuana			
Marijuana	Excites negative feedback receptors of both excitatory and inhibitory synapses	Decreases pain and nausea; distorted sense of time	Impaired memory
Hallucinogens			
LSD	Stimulates serotonin receptors	Hallucinations, sensory distortions	Psychotic reaction, accidents, panic attacks, flashbacks
MDMA ("ecstasy")	Stimulates neurons that release dopamine; at higher doses also stimulates neurons that release serotonin	At low doses increases arousal; at higher doses, hallucinations	Dehydration, fever
Rohypnol and GHB	Facilitate action at GABA synapses (which are inhibitory)	Relaxation, decreased inhibitions	Impaired muscle coordination and memory

Drugs and Synapses

Except for Novocain and related drugs that block action potentials, drugs produce their psychological effects by acting at synapses. That statement includes the drugs that this module has discussed as well as antidepressant drugs, antianxiety drugs, and drugs to combat schizophrenia. Many drugs have medical uses as well as potential for abuse. Much of the difference between "good" psychiatric drugs and "bad" abused drugs is a matter of how much someone uses, and when, and why.

Summary

- *Drug effects.* Drugs can act as agonists or antagonists at synapses. Many drugs have the potential for either abuse or medical benefits, depending on the individual, the dose, and the circumstances. (page 63)
- *Stimulants.* Stimulant drugs such as amphetamines and cocaine increase activity levels and pleasure by increasing the presence of dopamine and other neurotransmitters at their receptors. Compared to other forms of cocaine, crack enters the brain faster and therefore produces more intense effects. (page 63)
- *Effects of timing.* Stimulant drugs initially increase arousal, but because neurons release dopamine faster than they can replace it, the later result is a swing in the opposite direction. (page 63)

- *Nicotine.* Nicotine stimulates acetylcholine synapses and thereby increases arousal and attention. (page 64)
- *Hallucinogens.* Hallucinogens induce sensory distortions, largely by actions at serotonin synapses. (page 64)
- *Alcohol and anxiolytics.* Both alcohol and anxiolytic drugs (mainly benzodiazepines) produce relaxation and decreased anxiety by facilitating inhibitory synapses. (page 65)
- *Opiates.* Opiate drugs bind to endorphin receptors in the nervous system. The immediate effect of opiates is pleasure and relief from pain. (page 65)
- *Marijuana.* Marijuana's active compound, THC, acts on abundant receptors. Marijuana acts on receptors on the presynaptic neuron, putting the brakes on release of both excitatory and inhibitory transmitters. (page 65)

Key Terms

alcohol (page 65)

anxiolytic drugs (tranquilizers) (page 65)

depressant (page 65)

endorphins (page 65)

hallucinogens (page 64)

narcotics (page 65)

opiates (page 65)

stimulants (page 63)

Review Questions

1. Why do methylphenidate (Ritalin) pills produce milder behavioral effects than cocaine does?
    (a) Methylphenidate acts on acetylcholine synapses, whereas cocaine acts on dopamine synapses.
    (b) Methylphenidate acts on dopamine synapses, whereas cocaine acts on acetylcholine synapses.
    (c) Methylphenidate inhibits dopamine synapses, whereas cocaine stimulates them.
    (d) Methylphenidate enters the brain more slowly and leaves more slowly.

2. For whom, if anyone, is nicotine most likely to facilitate cognition?
    (a) It is most helpful for children.
    (b) It is most helpful for people who already have good cognitive abilities.
    (c) It is most helpful for people with weaker cognitive abilities.
    (d) It is not helpful for anyone.

3. What is meant by the term "anxiolytic"?
    (a) Increases anxiety
    (b) Decreases anxiety

    (c) Increases cognition
    (d) Impairs cognition

4. THC, the active component of marijuana smoke, produces its behavioral effects by what action on neurons?
    (a) It blocks the reuptake of dopamine and serotonin.
    (b) It decreases release of glutamate or GABA.
    (c) It attaches to serotonin receptors.
    (d) It facilitates transmission at inhibitory synapses.

5. What is the main reason why marijuana use correlates with schizophrenia?
    (a) Marijuana blocks dopamine synapses and leads to cognitive impairment.
    (b) Marijuana stimulates serotonin synapses and produces emotional swings.
    (c) Marijuana damages connections between the sense organs and the brain.
    (d) People with schizophrenia increase use of marijuana and other drugs.

Answers: 1d, 2c, 3b, 4b, 5d.

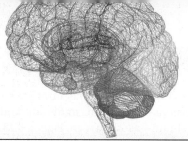

module 3.3

Brain and Behavior

After studying this module, you should be able to:

1. Explain why scientists favor the position called monism.

2. Cite examples of how brain damage affects behavior.

3. Describe methods of measuring brain activity.

4. Cite examples of brain plasticity.

5. Discuss the binding problem.

When studying the brain, you can easily get bogged down in memorizing the names and functions of brain areas. Before we get into all those facts, let's start with two points that are important to remember.

The first is that you use all of your brain. You may have heard that "they say" we use only 10 percent of our brains. No one is sure where this idea originated, but people have been telling it to one another for at least a century. What does it mean? Does anyone believe you could lose 90 percent of your brain and still do as well as you are doing now? Presumably not. Some people say, "Surely we could do so much more with our brains!" Well, yes, but that has nothing to do with using 10 percent. A poor athlete uses all of his or her muscles, just not very skillfully. Similarly, some people use their whole brain but not very skillfully. Perhaps the statement means that at any moment only some of your neurons are firing action potentials. That's true, but do not assume that you would be smarter if you activated all of your neurons at once. Simultaneous contraction of every muscle in your body would give you spasms, not great athletic performance. Similarly, simultaneous activation of every neuron would give you convulsions, not brilliant thoughts. Useful brain activity requires a pattern of activating some neurons while inhibiting others. For analogy, a pianist plays only a few piano keys at a time. Playing them all at once would not produce great music.

The second point to remember is the concept of monism, the idea that mental activity and brain activity are inseparable. I (your author) remember as a young college student taking for granted the idea of dualism—the idea that my mind and brain were separate. And then I learned that nearly all scientists and philosophers reject that idea. You should at least know not to take dualism for granted, and this module will discuss evidence against dualism: If you lose part of your brain, you lose part of your mind. So far as we can tell, you cannot have mental activity without brain activity, and you cannot have certain kinds of brain activity without mental activity. According to monism, mental activity *is* brain activity.

The central nervous system, consisting of *the brain and the spinal cord,* communicates with the rest of the body by the peripheral nervous system, consisting of *nerves connecting the spinal cord with the rest of the body.* One part of the peripheral nervous system is the *somatic nervous system*, which connects to the skin and muscles. Sensory nerves bring information from other body areas to the spinal cord, and motor nerves take information from the spinal cord to the muscles, where they cause contractions. Another part of the peripheral nervous system is the *autonomic nervous system*, which connects to the heart and other organs. Within that system, sympathetic nerves prepare the body for increased activity and parasympathetic nerves prepare it to conserve energy. A special subdivision of the autonomic nervous system is the *enteric nervous system* that controls the gastrointestinal system. If the enteric system is disconnected from the rest of the nervous system, it is capable of continuing its activities. ▼ Figure 3.13 summarizes the major divisions of the nervous system.

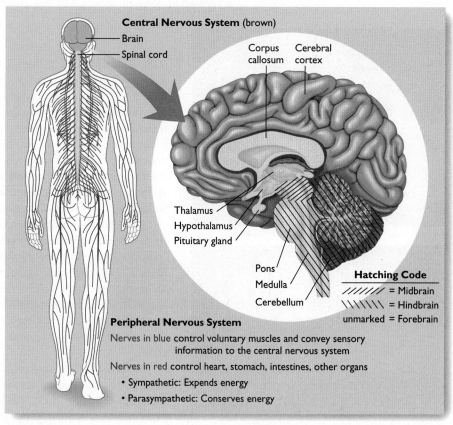

▲ **Figure 3.13** The major components of the nervous system are the central nervous system and the peripheral nervous system, which includes the somatic nervous system and the autonomic nervous system.

The Cerebral Cortex

The vertebrate brain has three major divisions—hindbrain, midbrain, and forebrain—as shown in Figure 3.13. In mammals including humans, the forebrain is by far the largest area. It consists of **hemispheres**, *the left and right halves of the forebrain* (see ▼ Figure 3.14). Each hemisphere controls sensation and movement on the opposite side of the body. (Why does it control the opposite side instead of its own side? No one knows, but the same is true for all vertebrates and some invertebrates.) We consider the differences between the left and right hemispheres later in this module. The *outer covering of the forebrain*, known as the **cerebral cortex**, is especially prominent in humans.

The Occipital Lobe of the Cortex

Researchers describe the cerebral cortex in terms of four *lobes*: occipital,

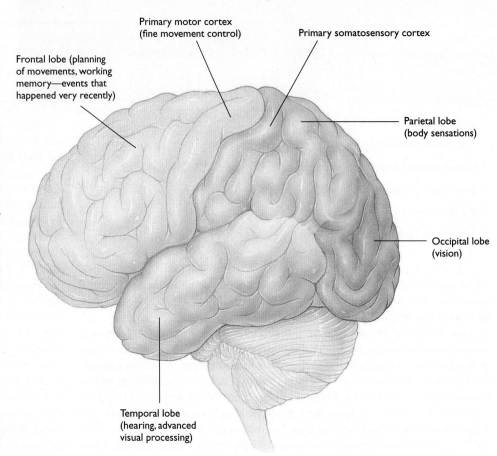

Primary motor cortex (fine movement control)

Primary somatosensory cortex

Frontal lobe (planning of movements, working memory—events that happened very recently)

Parietal lobe (body sensations)

Occipital lobe (vision)

Temporal lobe (hearing, advanced visual processing)

▲ **Figure 3.15** The four lobes of the human forebrain, with some of their functions.

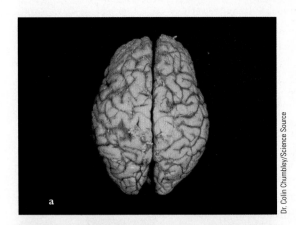

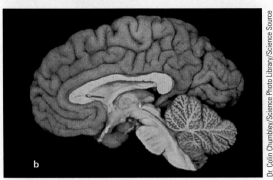

▲ **Figure 3.14** The human cerebral cortex: **(a)** left and right hemispheres; **(b)** a view from inside. The folds greatly extend the brain's surface area.

Dr. Colin Chumbley/Science Source

Dr. Colin Chumbley/Science Photo Library/Science Source

parietal, temporal, and frontal, as shown in ▲ Figure 3.15. The **occipital lobe**, *at the rear of the head, is specialized for vision*. People with damage in this area have *cortical blindness*. Cortical blindness differs from the usual kind of blindness resulting from eye damage. Someone who used to have normal vision and then suffered eye damage can imagine visual scenes and continues (for years, if not necessarily forever) to have visual dreams. People with cortical blindness have no visual imagery, even in dreams. However, the intact eyes continue sending messages to other brain areas, including one that controls wakefulness and sleep. Therefore, someone with cortical blindness continues to synchronize waking and sleeping to daytime and night time.

Some (not all) people with cortical blindness experience **blindsight**, *the ability to point to or otherwise indicate the direction to a visual stimulus, without conscious perception of seeing anything at all* (Weiskrantz, Warrington, Sanders, & Marshall, 1974; Striemer, Chapman, & Goodale, 2009). Some can correctly state an object's color, direction of movement, or approximate shape, again insisting that they are just guessing (Radoeva, Prasad, Brainard, & Aguirre, 2008). Some respond to the emotional expression of a face that they do not see consciously (Andino, de Peralta Menendez, Khateb, Landis, & Pegna, 2009; Tamietto et al., 2009).

What is the explanation? People with blindsight have strong connections that reach visual areas outside the occipital cortex (Ajina, Pestilli Rokem, Kennard, & Bridge, 2015). These areas receive enough visual information for certain functions, but not enough for conscious perception (Schmid et al., 2010). Blindsight demonstrates how much can occur without consciousness. It also provides an example of one of the many possible ways that brain damage can alter experience.

11. What does blindsight tell us about consciousness?

The Temporal Lobe of the Cortex

The temporal lobe of each hemisphere, *located toward the sides of the head, is the main area for hearing and certain aspects of vision.* People with damage in the auditory parts of the temporal lobe do not become deaf, but they are impaired at recognizing patterns of music. They also have difficulty with language comprehension. Their own speech is grammatical but lacking in most nouns, and therefore hard to understand.

Damage to certain parts of the temporal lobe produces visual deficits. One area in the temporal lobe, called the *fusiform gyrus,* responds mainly to the sight of faces (Kanwisher & Yovel, 2006). People with damage in that area no longer recognize faces, although they see well in other regards and recognize people by their voices (Tarr & Gauthier, 2000). They can describe facial features, such as this is a person with a rounded face, short brown hair, and so forth, but they don't easily recognize the individual. You experience the same difficulty if you look at faces just briefly and upside-down.

People vary in their ability to recognize faces. Most people fall in the range from recognizing one thousand to ten thousand faces, but that is a wide range (Jenkins, Dowsett, & Burton, 2018). People also vary in the number of connections to and from the fusiform gyrus. Those with the largest numbers of connections may recognize someone they met just once, years ago. People with far fewer than average connections have difficulty recognizing even familiar people (Grueter et al., 2007; C. Thomas et al., 2009). Oliver Sacks, a famous neurologist, had this problem himself. He had trouble recognizing even his relatives and closest friends, and sometimes looked at himself in the mirror and thought he was looking at some other bearded man (Sacks, 2010). So, if you have difficulty recognizing faces, it's probably not that you aren't trying hard enough. The explanation relates to your brain anatomy.

People with damage to another part of the temporal lobe become motion blind: Although they see the size, shape, and color of objects, they do not track speed or direction of movement (Zihl, von Cramon, & Mai, 1983). They eventually notice that someone who used to be one place is now in another, and therefore must have moved, but they don't see the movement moment by moment. Crossing a street is hazardous for such a person, because the cars seem stationary. Pouring coffee is difficult, as the person cannot monitor the rising level.

It is hard to imagine vision without motion perception, but here is how to demonstrate a small sample of the experience. Look at yourself in the mirror and focus on your left eye. Then move your focus to the right eye. Do you see your eyes moving in the mirror? (Go ahead; try it.) People agree that they do not see their eyes move.

"Oh, but wait," you say. "That movement in the mirror was simply too quick and too small to see." Wrong. Get someone else to look at your left eye and then shift gaze to your right eye. You *do* see the other person's eye movement. You see someone else's eyes move, but you do not see your own eyes move in the mirror.

Why not? During voluntary eye movements, called *saccades,* and in fact beginning 75 milliseconds before such movements, your brain suppresses activity in the part of the temporal cortex responsible for motion perception (Bremmer, Kubischik, Hoffmann, & Krekelberg, 2009; Burr, Morrone, & Ross, 1994; Paus, Marrett, Worsley, & Evans, 1995; Vallines & Greenlee, 2006). That is, you become temporarily motion blind. Now, try to imagine what it would be like to have this condition all the time.

Another part of the temporal lobe, the amygdala (see ▼ Figure 3.16), *responds strongly to emotional information.* People with damage to the amygdala are slow to process emotional information, such as facial expressions and descriptions of emotional situations (Baxter & Murray, 2002). In contrast, people with an easily aroused amygdala tend to be shy and fearful (Hariri et al., 2002; Rhodes et al., 2007).

A simple way to gauge amygdala arousal is to make a sudden, loud sound and measure the startle response. All people except the deaf show some startle response, but some respond more than others, and some *habituate* (decline in response) faster than others. People with a highly reactive amygdala

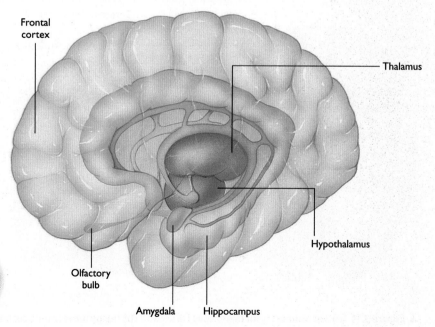

▲ **Figure 3.16** A view of the forebrain, showing internal structures as though the outer structures were transparent.

respond strongly and habituate slowly to a loud noise, indicating anxiety. That response correlates with political attitudes: People who favor vigorous military and police action to protect against potentially dangerous people tend to show strong amygdala responses, whereas those who are more relaxed about such dangers show weaker amygdala responses (Oxley et al., 2008). This research indicates that even our political leanings relate to measurable brain activities.

concept check

12. Why can't you see your own eye movements when looking in a mirror?

Answer

12. During and slightly before a voluntary eye movement, the part of your visual cortex responsible for motion perception becomes unresponsive. You are temporarily motion blind.

The Parietal Lobe of the Cortex

The **parietal lobe**, just anterior (forward) from the occipital lobe, is specialized for the body senses, including touch, pain, temperature, and awareness of the location of body parts in space. The **primary somatosensory** (so-ma-toh-SEN-so-ree, meaning body-sensory) **cortex**, a strip in the anterior portion of the parietal lobe, has cells sensitive to touch in various body areas, as shown in ▼ **Figure 3.17**. In

that figure, note that the largest areas are devoted to touch in the most sensitive areas, such as the lips and hands. Damage to any part of the somatosensory cortex impairs sensation from the corresponding body part.

Although the somatosensory cortex is the primary site for touch sensations, touch also activates other areas that are important for emotional responses. Consider someone who has lost input to the somatosensory cortex. You gently stroke her arm, and she smiles without knowing why. She has the pleasant emotional experience despite no conscious touch sensation (Olausson et al., 2002). We see again that brain damage produces surprisingly specialized changes in behavior and experience.

Parietal lobe damage also interferes with spatial attention. People with such damage see what an object is but not where it is. They have trouble reaching toward it, walking around it, or shifting attention from one object to another. When walking, they can describe what they see, but they bump into objects instead of walking around them. They can describe their furniture from memory but not how it is arranged in the house. Sometimes they have trouble finding various parts of their body (Schenk, 2006).

concept check

13. Parietal lobe damage interferes with which aspect of vision?

Answer

13. It interferes with identifying the object's location.

The Frontal Lobe of the Cortex

The **frontal lobe**, *at the anterior (forward) pole of the brain,* includes the **primary motor cortex**, *important for controlling fine movements,* such as moving a finger or wiggling a toe. Each area of the primary motor cortex controls a different part of the body, and larger areas are devoted to the areas we control with precision,

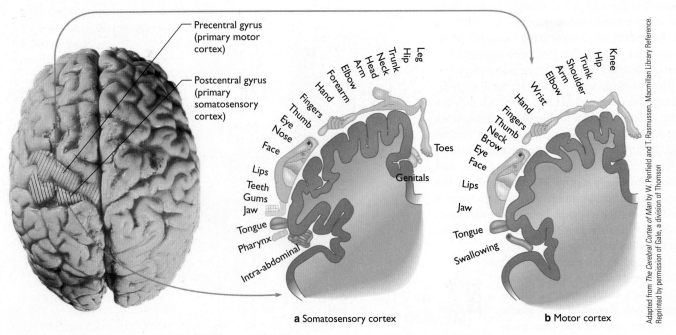

a Somatosensory cortex   b Motor cortex

Adapted from *The Cerebral Cortex of Man* by W. Penfield and T. Rasmussen, Macmillan Library Reference. Reprinted by permission of Gale, a division of Thomson

▲ **Figure 3.17** (a) The primary somatosensory cortex and (b) the primary motor cortex, illustrating which part of the body each brain area controls. Larger areas of the cortex are devoted to body parts that need to be controlled with great precision, such as the face and hands. (parts a and b after Penfield & Rasmussen, 1950)

such as the tongue and fingers, than others such as the shoulder and elbow muscles. The *anterior sections of the frontal lobe,* called the prefrontal cortex, are important for memory of what has just happened and what you are planning to do next. The prefrontal cortex is also critical for directing attention. Suppose you look at pictures of a house superimposed on pictures of a face. Sometimes you are told to pay attention to the house and sometimes you are to attend to the face. The prefrontal cortex facilitates activity in either the part of the temporal cortex that attends to faces or the part that attends to houses (Baldauf & Desimone, 2014).

The prefrontal cortex is also important for making decisions, and damage to the prefrontal cortex often leads to impulsive, poorly considered decisions. We are starting to understand the role of this area in decision making. Which would you prefer for dinner tonight, shrimp or the slightly more expensive salmon? According to research with monkeys, cells in one part of the prefrontal cortex respond most strongly to whichever choice an individual prefers. That is, those cells might respond strongly to the shrimp if that was your preferred item on the menu, but respond less strongly to the shrimp after you found something still better (Xie & Padoa-Schioppa, 2016). If you are debating between two choices of nearly equal value, neurons alternate between two patterns of activity, corresponding to the fact that you waver between favoring one choice and favoring the other (Rich & Wallis, 2016).

Since the late 1990s, many psychologists have become excited about mirror neurons, found in several brain areas but especially in the frontal cortex. Mirror neurons *are active when you make a movement and also when you watch someone else make a similar movement* (Dinstein, Hasson, Rubin, & Heeger, 2007). For example, certain neurons in the frontal cortex become active when you smile or when you see someone else smile (Montgomery, Seeherman, & Haxby, 2009). Do mirror neurons enable you to copy other people's actions? Do they enable you to identify with other people and understand them better? You can see how psychologists might speculate that mirror neurons are the basis for human civilization.

However, before we speculate too far, researchers need to address some important questions. In particular, were you born with mirror neurons that helped you learn to copy other people? Or did you learn to copy other people, and in the process develop mirror neurons? That is, perhaps after you have learned the parallels between what you see and what you can do, seeing someone do something reminds you of your own ability to do the same thing and therefore activates neurons responsible for those actions.

What once appeared to be evidence for built-in mirror neurons came from a study of infants' facial movements. Researchers reported that infants frequently protrude their tongue when they see an adult protruding the tongue, and sometimes match other facial expressions ▼ Figure 3.18 (Meltzoff & Moore, 1977). If infants imitate expressions from the start, they must have some sort of built-in mirror neurons. However, a later study found that infants protrude the tongue about equally in response to seeing other facial expressions. (Many infants stick out their tongue quite frequently.) Similarly, the other facial expressions failed to show clear specificity to what the infants were seeing (Oostenbroek et al., 2016). In short, the evidence for infant imitation is not convincing.

Furthermore, we can see that some mirror neurons developed their properties by learning. If you consistently watch someone else move the little finger every time you move your index finger, certain cells in your frontal cortex come to respond whenever you move your *index* finger or see someone else move the *little* finger (Catmur, Walsh, & Heyes, 2007). In other words, at least some—probably many—neurons develop their mirror quality (or in this case an anti-mirror quality) by learning.

concept check

14. **What evidence suggests that imitation produces mirror neurons as opposed to the idea that mirror neurons produce imitation?**

Answer

14. It is possible to train neurons to respond to one kind of movement when the person produces and a different movement the person watches. If people can learn to develop these "anti-mirror" neurons, then presumably, they could also learn to develop mirror neurons.

The Two Hemispheres and Their Connections

Let's focus on a type of brain damage that produces highly interesting results. Each hemisphere of the brain gets sensory input mostly from the opposite side of the body and controls muscles on the opposite side. The hemispheres differ in other ways, too. For almost all right-handed people and more than 60 percent of left-handed people, parts of the left hemisphere control speech. For most other

Sally and Richard Greenhill/Alamy Stock Photo

▲ **Figure 3.18** Newborns sometimes appear to be imitating facial expressions, but later evidence suggests that what appears to be imitation may be coincidence. (From Meltzoff & Moore, 1977)

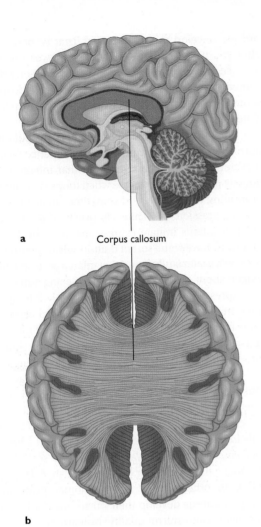

▲ **Figure 3.19** The corpus callosum is a large set of fibers that convey information between the two hemispheres of the cerebral cortex. **(a)** A midline view showing the location of the corpus callosum. **(b)** A horizontal section showing how each axon of the corpus callosum links one spot in the left hemisphere to a corresponding spot in the right hemisphere.

left-handers, both hemispheres control speech. Few people have complete right-hemisphere control of speech. The right hemisphere is more important for certain other functions, including the ability to imagine what an object would look like after it rotates and the ability to understand the emotional connotations of facial expressions, gestures, and tone of voice (Adolphs, Damasio, & Tranel, 2002; Stone, Nisenson, Eliassen, & Gazzaniga, 1996).

In one study, people watched videotapes of 10 people speaking the truth half the time and lying half the time. Do you think you could tell the difference between truth and lies? The average for MIT undergraduates was 47 percent correct, slightly less than they should have done by random guessing. One group that did better than chance was a set

of people with left-hemisphere brain damage! They understood little of what people were saying, so they relied on gestures and facial expressions, which the right hemisphere interprets quite well (Etcoff, Ekman, Magee, & Frank, 2000).

The two hemispheres constantly exchange information. If you feel something with the left hand and something else with the right hand, you can tell whether they are made of the same material because the hemispheres pass information back and forth through the corpus callosum, *a set of axons that connect the left and right hemispheres of the cerebral cortex* (see ◄ Figure 3.19). What would happen if the corpus callosum were cut?

In certain cases, brain surgeons have cut the corpus callosum to relieve epilepsy, *a condition in which cells somewhere in the brain emit abnormal rhythmic, spontaneous impulses.* Most people with epilepsy respond well to antiepileptic drugs and live normal lives, but a few continue having frequent major seizures. When all else failed, surgeons have sometimes severed the corpus callosum. The original idea was that this surgery would limit epileptic seizures to one hemisphere and therefore make the epilepsy less incapacitating. Because other methods have arisen, this surgery is seldom if ever performed today.

The operation was more successful than expected. Not only did it limit seizures to one side of the body, but also it decreased their frequency. The operation interrupts a feedback loop that lets an epileptic seizure echo back and forth between the hemispheres. However, although these split-brain patients resume a normal life, they show some fascinating behavioral effects.

If you, like most people, have left-hemisphere control of speech, the information that enters your right hemisphere passes quickly across the corpus callosum to your left (speaking) hemisphere, enabling you to describe what you see or feel. However, when a split-brain patient feels something with the left hand, the information stays in the right (nonspeaking) hemisphere (Nebes, 1974; Sperry, 1967). If asked to point to the object, the person points correctly with the left hand (controlled by the right hemisphere) while saying (with the left hemisphere), "I don't know what it was. I didn't feel anything."

Now consider what happens when a split-brain patient sees something (see ▼ Figure 3.20). The person in Figure 3.20 focuses on a point in the middle of the screen. The investigator flashes a word such as *hatband* on the screen for a split second, too briefly for an eye movement, and asks for the word. The person replies, "band," which is what the left hemisphere saw. (The left hemisphere sees the right side of the world.) To the question of what *kind* of band, the reply might be, "I don't know. Jazz band? Rubber band?" However, the left hand (controlled by the right hemisphere) points to a hat (which the right hemisphere saw).

A split-brain person reports feeling the same as before the operation and still reports just one consciousness. Of course, it is the left hemisphere that is talking, and it doesn't know about the experiences of the right hemisphere! The left hemisphere continues trying to make sense of everything the body does, as if it were completely in control. Consider this study: While the person stares straight ahead, two pictures flash briefly on a screen so that the left hemisphere sees one and the right hemisphere sees the other. Then, from a set of pictures on cards, each hemisphere uses the hand it controls to select an item related to what it saw. In one case, the left hemisphere saw a chicken claw and pointed with the right hand to a chicken. The right hemisphere saw a snow scene and pointed to a snow shovel (see ▼ Figure 3.21). When asked to explain the choices, the left (talking) hemisphere said the chicken claw goes with the chicken, and you need a shovel to clean out the chicken shed. Gazzaniga (2000) infers that the left hemisphere has a function that he calls the interpreter. It makes up a story to explain what it sees the body doing, even if the behaviors actually happened for a different reason. This is a general point: When we don't know the reasons for our own behavior, we make up explanations that may or may not be correct.

When split-brain patients have been studied many years after the operation, a certain degree of behavioral recovery has occurred (Pinto et al., 2017).

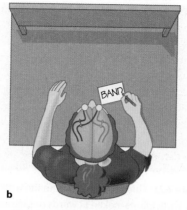

▲ **Figure 3.20** (a) When the word *hatband* flashes on a screen, a split-brain patient reports only what the left hemisphere saw, *band*, and (b) writes *band* with the right hand. However, (c) the left hand (controlled by the right hemisphere) points to a hat, which is what the right hemisphere saw.

For example, when a circle flashes briefly on either the left or right side, the person can point to a circle fairly accurately with either hand, although still unable to say whether something seen on the left side is the same or different from something on the right side. Several explanations are possible, including the likely role of cross-cuing (Volz, Hillyard, Miller, & Gazzaniga, 2018). That is, when the right hemisphere knows something, it can produce subtle movements of the eyes and facial muscles to communicate with the left hemisphere. Over time, the left hemisphere becomes increasingly sensitive to these subtle cues. In effect, the hemispheres act like two people who are nudging each other or winking at each other to pass signals back and forth.

Split-brain surgery is rare. We study such patients not because you are likely to meet one but because they teach us something about brain organization, and raise important questions about what it means to be conscious.

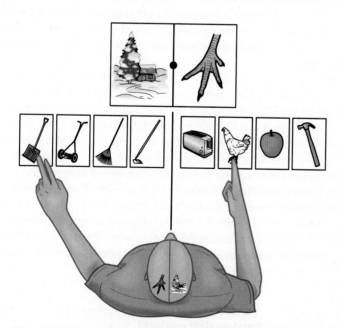

▲ **Figure 3.21** After the two hemispheres see a snow scene and a chicken claw, the two hands point to a chicken and a shovel as the related items. However, the left (talking) hemisphere tries to explain both choices in terms of what it saw, the chicken claw. (From Gazzaniga, M. S., "Cerebral specialization and interhemispheric communication: Does the corpus callosum enable the human condition?" *Brain, 123*, pp. 1293–1326 (Fig. 19a, p. 1318). Copyright © 2000 Oxford University Press. Reprinted by permission.)

concept check

15. **If a split-brain person sees an object in the left half of the world and an object in the right half, can he/she say whether they are the same? Why or why not?**

Answer

15. No, he/she could not say whether they are the same. The left hemisphere sees the right half of the world, the right hemisphere sees the left half, and the two cannot compare images.

Measuring Brain Activity

How did researchers discover the functions of various brain areas? In earlier times, nearly all research concerned patients with brain damage, and much of it still does. However, researchers now also have techniques to examine brain activity in healthy people.

An electroencephalograph (EEG) *uses electrodes on the scalp to record rapid changes in brain electrical activity.* A similar method is a magnetoencephalograph (MEG), *which records magnetic changes.* Both methods provide data on a millisecond-by-millisecond basis, measuring the brain's reactions to lights, sounds, and other events. However, because they record from the surface of the scalp, they provide little precision about the location of the activity.

Another method offers better anatomical localization but less information about timing: Positron-emission tomography (PET) *records radioactivity of various brain areas emitted from injected chemicals* (Phelps & Mazziotta, 1985). First, someone receives an injection of a radioactively labeled compound such as glucose. The most active brain areas rapidly absorb glucose, a sugar that is the brain's main fuel. Therefore, the labeled glucose emits radioactivity primarily from the most active areas. Detectors around the head record the radioactivity and send results to a computer that generates an image such as the one in ▼ Figure 3.22. Red indicates areas of greatest activity, followed by yellow, green, and blue. However, PET scans require exposing the brain to radioactivity.

Another technique, **functional magnetic resonance imaging (fMRI)**, *records the relative activities of brain areas without exposing them to radiation*, as shown in ▶ Figure 3.23. When a brain area increases its activity, more blood flows to that area, and the blood's hemoglobin releases more of its oxygen to the cells. Because hemoglobin's response to a magnetic field changes when it releases oxygen, detectors around the head can use this information to localize brain activity.

If we want to use a PET or fMRI scan to measure the brain activity during some task, the data tell us nothing except by comparison to the activity that occurs otherwise. Suppose we want to find the brain areas important for memory. We record activity while someone is engaged in a memory task and compare that activity to times when the person is doing . . . what? Doing nothing? That comparison wouldn't work; the memory task presumably includes sensory stimuli, motor responses, attention,

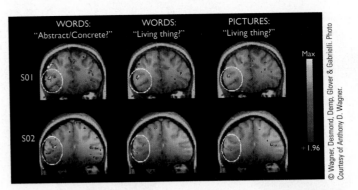

▲ **Figure 3.23** This brain scan was made with functional magnetic resonance imaging (fMRI). Participants looked at words or pictures and judged whether each item was abstract or concrete, living or nonliving. Yellow shows the areas most activated by this decision; red shows areas less strongly activated. (From Wagner, Desmond, Demb, Glover, & Gabrieli, 1997. Photo courtesy of Anthony D. Wagner)

and other processes. Besides that, "doing nothing" (mind wandering) activates certain brain areas, too (Mason et al., 2007). Researchers must design a comparison task that requires attention to the same sensory stimuli, the same hand movements, and so forth as the memory task. Then they set a computer to subtract the activity in the comparison task from the activity in the memory task. The areas with the largest difference between the tasks are presumably important for some aspect of memory.

Brain scans sometimes lead to important insights about behavior. For example, an fMRI study showed that when people taking a placebo say that they feel less pain, the brain areas responsible for pain actually show decreased responses (Wager & Atlas, 2013). However, people sometimes give such research more credit than it deserves. For example, educators have sometimes claimed that neuroscience data taught us that people can continue to learn throughout life, that emotions can interfere with learning, that sleep and exercise help learning, and that second-language learning should start early in life. All those statements are true, and neuroscience does confirm them, but as Bowers (2016) has argued, let's not give neuroscience too much credit for telling us something that we already knew.

Another issue: Suppose a particular brain area becomes more active when you are angry. Later, when that area becomes active again, does that mean that you are angry again? No, unless research shows that the area is active *only* when you are angry. A good test of our understanding is this: Can we take fMRI measures at one time, while we know what you are doing, and then use measures at a later time to infer what you are seeing, hearing, or planning to do? Occasionally the answer is yes. Researchers awakened sleepers and compared fMRI data to the visual images that the people reported having dreamt. After repeating this procedure many times—and this sounds like a tedious experience for those oft-awakened sleepers—the experimenters became able to use the fMRI to predict the dream images that people were about to report (Horikawa, Tamaki, Miyawaki, & Kamitani, 2013). Still, the message is that we should beware of over-interpreting fMRI results.

16. What does fMRI measure?

Answer

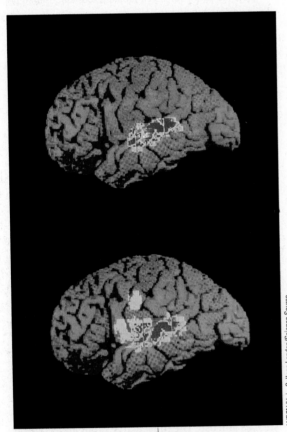

▲ **Figure 3.22** A PET scan of the human brain. Red shows areas of most increased activity during some task; yellow shows areas of next most increased activity.

16. It measures the response of the blood's hemoglobin's response differs depending on whether it is bound to oxygen, and therefore fMRI indicates how much oxygen a brain area is using, and therefore how active that area is.

Subcortical Areas

Figure 3.16 shows some of the structures in the interior of the forebrain. At the center is the *thalamus*, the last stop for almost all sensory information on the way to the cerebral cortex. Surrounding the thalamus are areas called the *limbic system*. (A limbus is a margin or border.) The hippocampus is important for memory and for finding your way around. The hypothalamus, *located just below the thalamus, is important for hunger, thirst, temperature regulation, sex, and other motivated behaviors.*

The cerebral cortex does not directly control the muscles. It sends output to the pons and medulla, *which control the muscles of the head* (e.g., for chewing, swallowing, breathing, and talking), and to the spinal cord, *which controls the muscles from the neck down* (see ▼ Figures 3.13 and ▼ 3.24). The spinal cord also controls many reflexes, such as the knee-jerk reflex. A reflex is a *rapid, automatic response to a stimulus,* such as unconscious adjustments of your legs while you are walking or quickly jerking your hand away from something hot.

The cerebellum (Latin for "little brain"), *part of the hindbrain,* has many functions that have long been underestimated. We have long known its importance for coordinated movement. People with damage to the cerebellum show motor problems like those of alcoholic intoxication, including slurred speech, staggering, and inaccurate eye movements. The reason for the similarity is that alcohol suppresses activity in the cerebellum. In addition, the cerebellum is important for any behavior that requires aim or timing, such as tapping out a rhythm, judging which of two visual stimuli is moving faster, and judging whether one musical tempo is faster or slower than another (Ivry & Diener, 1991; Keele & Ivry, 1990). It is essential for controlling voluntary eye movements, and for learned responses that require a timed response, such as quickly responding to a warning signal (Krupa, Thompson, & Thompson, 1993). It even contributes to recognition of emotional expressions (Ferrari, Oldrati, Gallucci, Vecchi, & Cattaneo, 2018).

17. People with autistic spectrum disorder typically show impairments of voluntary eye movements and difficulty interpreting other people's emotional expressions. Based on material you just read, what brain area is probably not functioning adequately?

Answer

17. The cerebellum

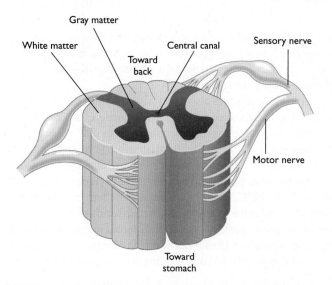

▲ **Figure 3.24** The spinal cord receives sensory information from all body parts except the head. Motor nerves in the spinal cord control the muscles and glands.

The Autonomic Nervous System and Endocrine System

The autonomic nervous system, closely associated with the spinal cord, *controls the heart, digestive system, and other organs.* The term *autonomic* means involuntary, or automatic. You cannot decide to increase your heart rate in the same way that you could decide to wave your hand. Brain activity does, however, influence the autonomic nervous system. For example, your autonomic nervous system reacts more strongly when you are nervous than when you are relaxed.

The autonomic nervous system has two parts: (a) The *sympathetic nervous system,* controlled by a chain of cells lying just outside the spinal cord, increases heart rate, breathing rate, sweating, and other processes that are important for vigorous fight-or-flight activities. It inhibits digestion and sexual arousal, which can wait until the emergency is over. (b) The *parasympathetic nervous system,* controlled by cells at the top and bottom levels of the spinal cord, decreases heart rate, increases digestive activities, and promotes "vegetative" activities that take place during rest (see ▼ Figure 3.25). If you are driving and you see a police car wailing its siren behind you, your sympathetic nervous system arouses. Your heart starts racing, you breathe heavily, and you start sweating. When the police car passes and you see that it is chasing someone else, your parasympathetic nervous system kicks in, and you relax.

Over-the-counter cold remedies act by decreasing parasympathetic actions, such as sinus flow. The side effects come from increased sympathetic actions, such as heart rate, blood pressure, and arousal.

The autonomic nervous system influences the endocrine system, *glands that produce hormones and release them into the blood.* Hormones controlled by the hypothalamus and *pituitary gland* regulate the other endocrine organs. ▼ Figure 3.26 shows some of the endocrine glands. Hormones are *chemicals released by glands and conveyed by the blood to alter activity in organs throughout the body.* Some hormonal effects are brief, such as changes in heart rate or blood pressure. Other hormonal effects prepare an animal for pregnancy, migration, hibernation, or other long-lasting activities. Within the brain, hormones produce temporary changes in the excitability of cells, and they also influence the survival, growth, and connections of cells. The sex hormones (*androgens* and *estrogens*) have strong effects during early development, when they produce differences between male and female anatomies, including certain brain areas (Cahill, 2006).

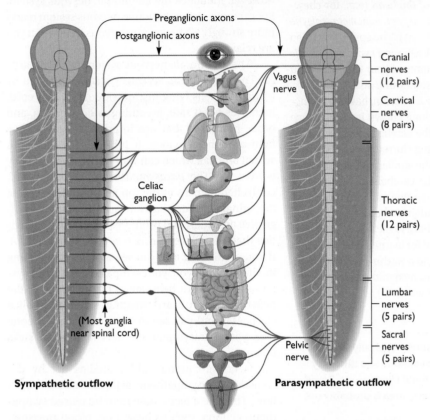

Sympathetic system	Parasympathetic system
Preparation for vigorous activity	**Body at rest**
• Pupils open	• Pupils constrict
• Saliva decreases	• Saliva flows
• Pulse quickens	• Pulse slows
• Sweat increases	• Stomach churns
• Stomach less active	
• Epinephrine (adrenaline) secreted	

▲ **Figure 3.25** The sympathetic nervous system prepares the organs for a brief bout of vigorous activity. The parasympathetic nervous system puts the brakes on vigorous activity and prepares the body for rest and digestion.

concept check

18. While someone is trying to escape danger, the heart rate and breathing rate increase. After the danger passes, heart rate and breathing rate fall below normal. Which part of the autonomic nervous system is more active during the danger, and which is more active after it?

Answer

18. The sympathetic nervous system predominates during the danger, and the parasympathetic system predominates afterward.

Experience and Brain Plasticity

When we talk about brain anatomy, it is easy to get the impression that the structures are fixed. In fact, brain structure shows considerable plasticity—that is, *change as a result of experience*.

Early researchers believed that the nervous system produced no new neurons after early infancy. Later research with rodents found that *undifferentiated cells* called stem cells develop into new neurons in certain brain areas, such as the hippocampus (Gage, 2000; Graziadei & deHan, 1973; Song, Stevens, & Gage, 2002). The first studies indicated that new neurons also form in the human hippocampus and the *basal ganglia*, both of which are important for certain types of learning (Ernst et al., 2014; Kee, Teixeira, Wang, & Frankland, 2007). In later studies, this conclusion became less certain. One research team dissected the brains of people who died at various ages and found new neurons forming in the hippocampus up to age 7, and possibly up to age 13, but none at any later ages (Sorrells et al., 2018). Two other research teams, using different methods, found production of new neurons throughout life, with a rate that declines in old age (Boldrini et al., 2018; Moreno-Jiménez et al., 2019). The issue is important, because some prominent theories about major depression and its treatment rely on the assumption that humans can produce new hippocampal neurons throughout life.

Regardless of whether the adult human brain can form new neurons, experiences do stimulate axons and dendrites to expand and withdraw their branches. These changes, which occur more rapidly in young people but continue throughout life, enable the brain to adapt to changing circumstances (Boyke, Driemeyer, Gaser, Büchel, & May, 2008). For example, one man lost his hand in an accident at age 19. Thirty-five years later, surgeons grafted a new hand onto his arm. Within a few months, axons connected the new hand to his brain, and he regained partial sensation from the hand (Frey, Bogdanov, Smith, Watrous, & Breidenbach, 2008).

Observable brain changes also occur when people learn to read, even if they learn in adulthood (Carreiras et al., 2009; Dehaene et al., 2010). Many studies have examined what happens after people learn to play music. One brain area devoted to hearing is 30 percent larger than average in professional musicians (Schneider et al., 2002), and an area responsive to finger sensations is larger than average in people who play stringed instruments (Elbert, Pantev, Wienbruch, Rockstroh, & Taub, 1995). We might wonder whether musical training caused those changes, or whether people with certain kinds of brains are more likely than others to become musicians. One study found measurable changes in children's brains as a result of 15 months of music training, as compared to similar children who did not undergo such training (Hyde et al., 2009). The implication

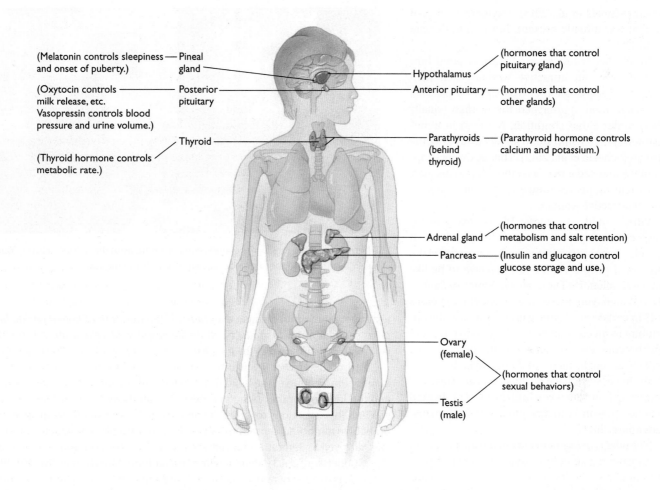

▲ **Figure 3.26** Glands in the endocrine system produce hormones and release them into the bloodstream.

Labels in figure:
(Melatonin controls sleepiness and onset of puberty.) — Pineal gland

(Oxytocin controls milk release, etc. Vasopressin controls blood pressure and urine volume.) — Posterior pituitary

Thyroid

(Thyroid hormone controls metabolic rate.)

Hypothalamus — (hormones that control pituitary gland)

Anterior pituitary — (hormones that control other glands)

Parathyroids (behind thyroid) — (Parathyroid hormone controls calcium and potassium.)

Adrenal gland — (hormones that control metabolism and salt retention)

Pancreas — (Insulin and glucagon control glucose storage and use.)

Ovary (female)

(hormones that control sexual behaviors)

Testis (male)

---

is that music training alters the brain. A follow-up study found that musical training beginning in childhood alters brain anatomy more than does the same amount of training later in life (Steele, Bailey, Zatorre, & Penhune, 2013).

19. In the study showing changes in children's brains as they learn to play music, why was it necessary to have a control group of untrained children?

Answer

19. It was important to separate the effects of music from the effects of growing 15 months older.

Social Neuroscience

Social neuroscience, the study of the biological bases of social behavior, is a new, exciting area of research. For example, an fMRI study of monkeys found a network of neurons in the prefrontal cortex that respond strongly when a monkey sees other monkeys interacting socially, but respond more weakly to any other sight (Sliwa & Freiwald, 2017). A corresponding area of the human brain responds strongly when people are trying to understand what other people know, or why they are acting the way they are.

The hormone oxytocin, released by women when nursing a baby and by both men and women during sexual activity, has received much publicity as the "love hormone." "Love-magnifying" hormone would be a more accurate term. One study examined men who reported being deeply in love. They rated the attractiveness of their female partner and other women, while viewing photos of each. When under the influence of extra oxytocin, each man increased his ratings of the woman he loved, compared to ratings under a placebo, but he did not significantly change ratings of the other women (Scheele et al., 2013). Oxytocin increased love that was already present, but it didn't create new love.

In another study, researchers measured how far away from an attractive woman each man stood, after receiving either oxytocin or a placebo. Unattached men approached the woman equally closely under either condition, but men in a monogamous relationship stood *farther* away after the oxytocin (Scheele et al., 2012). That is, oxytocin apparently enhanced a man's relationship to his partner, increasing his resistance to the temptation of another attractive woman.

What would you guess: Would oxytocin increase conformity to other people's opinions? It depends. Oxytocin increases conformity only to the opinions of people whom you perceive to be like yourself (Stallen, De Dreu, Shalvi, Smidt, & Sanfey, 2012). Would you guess that oxytocin increases trust? In certain economic games, you have the opportunity to invest money in a cooperative venture with someone else, trusting that the other person won't cheat you. In such situations, oxytocin can increase, decrease, or have no effect on your trust, depending on how much you initially liked or disliked the other person (van Ijzendoorn & Bakermans-Kranenburg, 2012).

The effects of oxytocin are not always prosocial. In a threatening situation, oxytocin increases people's attention to possible dangers and heightens their avoidance of strangers (Olff et al., 2013; Poulin, Holman, & Buffone, 2012). People tending to be distrustful in general become even more distrustful under the influence of oxytocin (Bartz et al., 2011).

The apparent pattern is that oxytocin increases attention to social information (Olff et al., 2013). It strengthens positive responses to people whom you love or trust, but only to those people. Unfortunately, many of the studies on oxytocin have used small samples and have reported small effects. We must await further research and attempts to replicate (Nave, Camerer, & McCullough, 2015).

The Binding Problem

We end this module with a theoretical problem that researchers first began to notice around 1990: Vision takes place in one part of your brain, hearing in another, and touch in still another. Those areas do not share much information with one another, nor do they send information to a central location. That is, no "little person in the head" puts it all together. So, when you play a piano, how do you know that the piano you see is also what you hear and feel? When you eat something, how do the taste, smell, and

When you watch a movie, the sound seems to come from the actors' mouths. You bind the sound and the action because they are simultaneous.

texture combine into a single experience? *The question of how separate brain areas combine forces to produce a unified perception of a single object* is the binding problem, also known as the *long-range integration problem* (Treisman, 1999).

Part of the answer lies with spatial perception. Consider the piano: If you identify the location of the hand that you feel, the location of the piano you see, and the location of the sound you hear, and all those locations are the same, you link the sensations together. If you cannot locate something in space, you probably won't bind sensations correctly into a single experience. You might look at a yellow lemon and a red tomato and report seeing a yellow tomato (L. C. Robertson, 2003). People with parietal lobe damage have trouble binding aspects of an experience, because they do not perceive locations accurately (Treisman, 1999; Wheeler & Treisman, 2002).

We also know that binding occurs only for simultaneous events. Have you ever watched a film or television show in which the soundtrack is noticeably ahead of or behind the picture? If so, you knew that the sound wasn't coming from the performers on screen. You get the same experience watching a poorly dubbed foreign-language film. However, when you watch a ventriloquist, the motion of the dummy's mouth simultaneous with the sound lets you perceive the sound as coming from the dummy.

You can experience a demonstration of binding by trying the following (I. H. Robertson, 2005): Stand or sit by a large mirror as in ▼ **Figure 3.27**, watching both your right hand and its reflection in the mirror. Hold your left hand out of sight. Then repeatedly clench and unclench both hands, and touch each thumb to your fingers and palm, in unison. You will feel your left hand doing the same thing that you see the hand in the mirror doing. After a couple of minutes, you may start to experience the hand in the mirror as your own left hand. You are binding your touch and visual experiences because they occur at the same time, apparently in the same location.

try it your self

concept check

20. **What two elements are necessary for binding?**

Answer

20. For binding to occur, the brain must be able to identify that different aspects of the stimulus come from the same location. Also, the different aspects must occur simultaneously.

◄ **Figure 3.27** Move your left and right hands in synchrony while watching the image of one hand in a mirror. Within minutes, you may experience the one in the mirror as being your own hand. This demonstration illustrates how binding occurs.

<h2>in closing | module 3.3</h2>

Brain and Behavior

The main point of this module is that mind and brain activity are tightly linked—indeed, apparently synonymous. If you lose part of your brain, you lose part of your mind. If you have some mental experience, you simultaneously alter activity in some brain area. If two people's behaviors differ, their brains differ too, in some way.

Another major point is that although different brain areas handle different functions without feeding into a central processor, they still manage to function as an organized whole. We could compare the brain to a flock of birds or a school of fish: It has no leader, but the individuals coordinate their actions to work as a unit anyway. Similarly, brain areas act individually and nevertheless produce a single experience.

Research on brain functioning is challenging because the brain itself is so complex. Just think about all that goes on within this 1.3 kg mass of tissue composed mostly of water. It is an amazing structure.

Summary

- *Two key points.* You use all of your brain, not some percentage of it. Although most people take for granted that their mind is separate from the brain, the evidence points to the contrary: Mind activity and brain activity are the same thing. (page 69)
- *The cerebral cortex.* The cerebral cortex has four lobes: occipital lobe (vision), temporal lobe (hearing and some aspects of vision), parietal lobe (body sensations), and the frontal lobe (preparation for movement). (page 70)
- *Cortical damage.* Damage to a part of the cerebral cortex can produce specialized deficits, such as inability to recognize faces, inability to perceive visual motion, and ability to guess certain aspects of a visual stimulus without conscious perception of it. (page 70)
- *Hemispheres of the brain.* Each brain hemisphere controls the opposite side of the body. The left hemisphere of the human brain is specialized for language in most people. The right hemisphere is important for understanding spatial relationships and interpreting emotional expressions. (page 73)
- *Corpus callosum and split-brain patients.* The corpus callosum enables the left and right hemispheres of the cortex to communicate with each other. After damage to the corpus callosum, people can verbally describe information only if it enters the left hemisphere. (page 74)
- *Learning about brain functions.* Modern technology enables researchers to develop images showing the structure and activity of various brain areas in living, waking people. Such methods are powerful, but the results should be interpreted with caution. (page 75)
- *Communication between the cerebral cortex and the rest of the body.* Information from the cerebral cortex passes to the

medulla and then into the spinal cord. The medulla and spinal cord receive sensory input from the periphery and send output to the muscles and glands. (page 77)
- *Autonomic nervous system and endocrine system.* The autonomic nervous system controls the body's organs, preparing them for emergency activities or for relaxed activities. The endocrine system consists of organs that release hormones into the blood. (page 77)
- *Brain plasticity.* Experiences alter brain anatomy, sometimes enough to be visible. (page 78)
- *Social neuroscience.* Biological mechanisms of social behavior have received increasing attention. The hormone oxytocin enhances love and trust toward people that you already regarded highly. (page 79)
- *The binding problem.* Theoretically, it is problematic to understand how brain areas responsible for different sensations combine to yield a unified perception. Binding requires perceiving the various aspects as occurring in the same place at the same time. (page 80)

Key Terms

amygdala (page 71)

autonomic nervous system (page 77)

binding problem (page 80)

blindsight (page 70)

central nervous system (page 69)

cerebellum (page 77)

cerebral cortex (page 70)

corpus callosum (page 74)

electroencephalograph (EEG) (page 75)

endocrine system (page 77)

epilepsy (page 74)

frontal lobe (page 72)

functional magnetic resonance imaging (fMRI) (page 76)

hemisphere (page 70)

hormone (page 77)

hypothalamus (page 77)

interpreter (page 74)

magnetoencephalograph (MEG) (page 75)

medulla (page 77)

mirror neurons (page 73)

monism (page 69)

occipital lobe (page 70)

oxytocin (page 79)

parietal lobe (page 72)

peripheral nervous system (page 69)

plasticity (page 78)

pons (page 77)

positron-emission tomography (PET) (page 75)

prefrontal cortex (page 73)

primary motor cortex (page 72)

primary somatosensory (page 72)

reflex (page 77)

social neuroscience (page 79)

spinal cord (page 77)

stem cells (page 78)

temporal lobe (page 71)

Review Questions

1. What is true about people who lose vision because of massive damage to the primary visual cortex?
   (a) They continue to have vision in their dreams.
   (b) They still synchronize waking and sleeping to daytime and night time.
   (c) They typically pretend that they can still see.
   (d) They can perceive color with their hands.

2. What is meant by "blindsight"?
   (a) The ability of blind people to find their way around by using other senses
   (b) The ability to perceive objects without using any sensory information
   (c) The tendency to see optical illusions, such as thinking one line is longer than another when both are really the same
   (d) The ability to respond to visual stimuli without conscious awareness of those stimuli

3. What is a likely explanation for why some people recognize faces better than other people do, despite being similar in other ways?
   (a) They differ in the number of connections to and from the fusiform gyrus.
   (b) They differ in the ratio of cones to rods in the retina.
   (c) They differ in their language and memory abilities.
   (d) Some of them have damage to the corpus callosum.

4. What evidence led Gazzaniga to infer what he called the "interpreter"?
   (a) Children often respond emotionally to sentences that they do not understand.
   (b) Friends often unintentionally copy each other's gestures and movements.
   (c) Split-brain people sometimes imagine reasons for what the left hand does.
   (d) The left hand often does the opposite of what the right hand is doing.

5. When people moved one finger while they saw someone else move a different finger, certain neurons began responding to both of these events. What does this finding imply about mirror neurons?
   (a) Some mirror neurons develop their properties by learning.
   (b) Mirror neurons make it possible for us to imitate.
   (c) Each mirror neuron corresponds to a different movement.
   (d) Each mirror neuron has a corresponding neuron with similar properties on the opposite side of the brain.

6. What is the advantage of using fMRI instead of PET to measure people's brain activity?
   (a) fMRI does not require expensive equipment.
   (b) fMRI measures brain activity with far greater accuracy.
   (c) fMRI can be used without obtaining informed consent.
   (d) fMRI does not expose the brain to radiation.

7. The cerebellum is important for behaviors that require which of the following?
   (a) Prolonged exertion
   (b) Accurate timing
   (c) Reflexive action
   (d) Coordinating vision with hearing

8. What type of change in the brain, if any, is likely when adults have new experiences?
   (a) Axons increase the velocity and amplitude of their action potentials.
   (b) New neurons form in the cerebral cortex.
   (c) Axons and dendrites expand some branches and withdraw others.
   (d) No change is evident in the structure of the brain.

9. What appears to be the best description of what oxytocin does?
   (a) It increases friendly or loving responses to almost anyone.
   (b) It increases attention to social information.
   (c) It improves memory and problem solving.
   (d) It alters the brain's ratio of excitation to inhibition.

10. Which of the following states the binding problem?
   (a) How does the brain respond to sensory information with motor output?
   (b) How does the brain unite sensations into a unified experience?
   (c) How do people combine information from the left and right hands?
   (d) How do people respond to stimuli when they report no conscious awareness of them?

Answers: 1b, 2d, 3a, 4c, 5a, 6d, 7b, 8c, 9b, 10b.

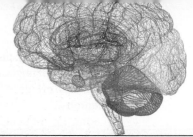

iStock.com/Jelena83

After studying this module, you should be able to:

1. Outline the basic principles of genetics.

2. Discuss epigenetics as a mechanism influencing development.

3. Explain how researchers estimate heritability.

4. Describe the assumptions and goals of evolutionary psychology.

It makes no sense to ask whether some aspect of your behavior depends mainly on heredity or environment. Every behavior depends on both, because without them you could not exist. However, if your behavior differs from someone else's, we can ask whether that *difference* depends more on differences in heredity or environment.

The study of genetics has become increasingly important for citizens of the 21st century. Let's first review some basic points about genetics and then explore their application to human behavior.

Genetic Principles

Except for your red blood cells, all of your cells contain a nucleus that includes *strands of hereditary material* called **chromosomes** (see ▼ Figure 3.28). A human nucleus has 23 pairs of chromosomes,

except that egg and sperm cells have 23 single, unpaired chromosomes. During fertilization, the 23 chromosomes from an egg cell combine with the 23 of a sperm cell to form 23 pairs for the new person (see ▼ Figure 3.29).

Sections along each chromosome, known as **genes**, *control the chemical reactions that direct development*—for example, those that influence height or hair color. Genes are composed of the chemical DNA, which controls the production of another chemical called RNA, which among other functions controls the production of proteins. The proteins either become part of the body's structure or control the rates of chemical reactions in the body. To explain the concept of genes, educators often use an example such as eye color. If you have either one or two genes for brown eyes, you will have brown eyes because the brown-eye gene is **dominant**—*that is, a single copy of the gene is sufficient to produce its effect*. The gene for blue eyes is **recessive**—*its effects appear only if the dominant gene is absent*. You have blue eyes only if you have two genes for blue eyes.

Sex-Linked and Sex-Limited Genes

Because chromosomes come in pairs (one from the mother and one from the father), you have two of almost all genes. The exceptions are those on the chromosomes that determine development as a male or female. Mammals' sex

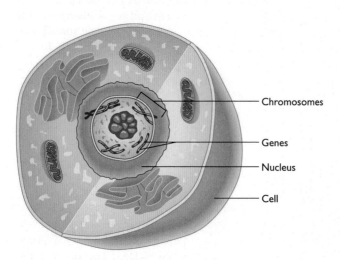

▲ **Figure 3.28** Genes are sections of chromosomes in the nuclei of cells. (Scale is exaggerated for illustration purposes.)

Labels: Chromosomes, Genes, Nucleus, Cell

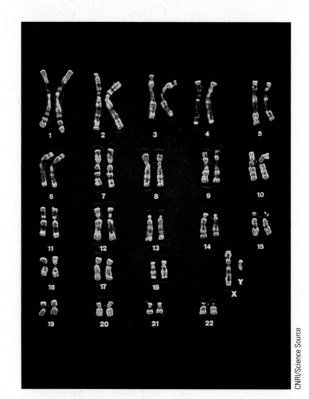

CNRI/Science Source

▲ **Figure 3.29** The nucleus of each human cell contains 46 chromosomes, 23 from the sperm and 23 from the ovum, united in pairs.

Albinos occur in many species, always because of a recessive gene. **(a)** Striped skunk. **(b)** American alligator. **(c)** Mockingbird.

chromosomes are known as X and Y (see ▼ Figure 3.30). *A female has two* X *chromosomes* in each cell. *A male has one X chromosome and one* Y *chromosome*. The mother contributes an X chromosome to each child, and the father contributes either an X or a Y. Because men have one X chromosome and one Y chromosome, they have unpaired genes on these chromosomes. In each of a woman's cells, parts of one of the X chromosomes are activated. In most cases, the corresponding part of the other X chromosome is silenced, but not always.

Genes located on the X or Y chromosome are known as sex-linked genes. A recessive gene on the X chromosome shows its effects more in men than in women. For example, red-green color deficiency depends on an X-linked recessive gene. A man with that gene on his X chromosome will be red-green deficient because he has no other X chromosome. A woman with that gene probably has a gene for normal color vision on her other X chromosome. Consequently, far more men than women have red-green deficiency (see ▼ Figure 3.31).

A sex-limited gene *occurs equally in both sexes but exerts its effects mainly or entirely in one or the other*. For example, both men and women have the genes controlling breast development, but women's hormones activate those genes.

concept check

21. **Suppose a father is red-green deficient and a mother has two genes for normal color vision. What sort of color vision will their children have?**

22. **When boys reach puberty, their increased testosterone activates a gene that controls facial hair. Is that a sex-linked gene or a sex-limited gene?**

Answers

22. It is a sex-limited gene. Even though it is present in both sexes, hormones that are more abundant in males activate it.

21. The sons receive a gene for normal color vision from the mother, and a Y chromosome (irrelevant to color vision) from the father. They will have normal color vision. The daughters receive a gene for normal color vision from the mother and a gene for red-green color deficiency from the father. They will also have normal color vision, but they will be carriers who can pass the red-green deficiency gene to some of their children.

▶ **Figure 3.30** An electron micrograph shows that the X chromosome is longer than the Y chromosome. (From Ruch, 1984)

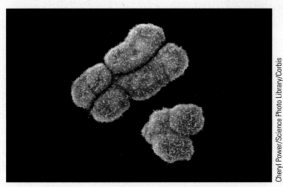

Cheryl Power/Science Photo Library/Corbis

A More Complex View of Genes

To talk about "the gene for" something is convenient at times, but misleading. Even for the supposedly simple case of eye color, researchers have found at least 10 genes with a significant influence (Liu et al., 2010). Variations in height depend on at least 700 genes as well as the effects of diet, health, and other environmental influences (Marouli et al., 2017). Furthermore, almost every gene affects many outcomes, not just eye color, height, or whatever else we happen to have measured.

The field of epigenetics *deals with changes in gene expression without modification of the DNA sequence* (Tsankova, Renthal, Kumar, & Nestler, 2007). For example, when one cell differentiates as a kidney cell and another becomes a liver cell or a brain cell, some of the genes that become active in one cell are silenced in another. Also, within a given cell, a gene can be more active at one time than another. For an obvious example, puberty stimulates certain genes to greater activity. Learning is a less obvious example: When you learn something, you increase activity of certain genes in certain neurons, while decreasing their activity in others (Yamada et al., 2019). Drug addiction produces epigenetic changes in the brain, and so does the feeling of being socially isolated (Sadri-Vakili et al, 2010; Slavich & Cole, 2013).

How does an experience modify genetic activity? Proteins called *histones* wrap the DNA of a chromosome into little balls, as shown in ▼ **Figure 3.32**. When certain chemicals called *acetyl* groups attach to a histone, they loosen the ball and increase the expression of genes in that ball. Other chemicals (called *methyl* groups) can attach to a gene and inactivate it. In this way, an experience can alter the way you react to future events.

In some cases, epigenetic changes extend to later generations. We have long known that changes in the mother's experience can affect her offspring, but the explanation was unclear, because it might relate to either epigenetics or prenatal environment. Studies with laboratory animals have now shown

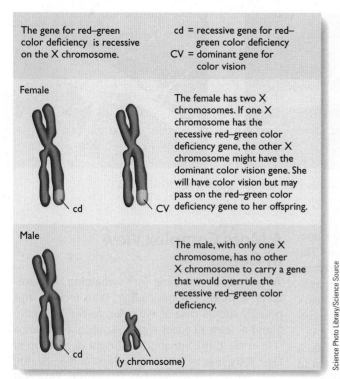

The gene for red–green color deficiency is recessive on the X chromosome.

cd = recessive gene for red–green color deficiency
CV = dominant gene for color vision

Female

The female has two X chromosomes. If one X chromosome has the recessive red–green color deficiency gene, the other X chromosome might have the dominant color vision gene. She will have color vision but may pass on the red–green color deficiency gene to her offspring.

cd

CV

Male

The male, with only one X chromosome, has no other X chromosome to carry a gene that would overrule the recessive red–green color deficiency.

cd

(y chromosome)

Science Photo Library/Science Source

▲ **Figure 3.31** Why males are more likely than females to be red-green color deficient.

that the father's experience can also affect the offspring, confirming the role of epigenetic changes. For example, exposing male mice to extreme stress alters their own behavior, alters the pattern of RNA in their sperm, and alters the behavior of their offspring (Gapp et al., 2014). Also, after male mice have been fed a high-fat diet, they gain weight, they increase the number of methyl groups on certain genes in their sperm, and their offspring show low sensitivity to insulin and a predisposition to diabetes (Ng et al., 2010; Wei et al., 2014). Human studies have also suggested that a man's nutrition can affect the health and life expectancy of his children and grandchildren (Pembrey et al., 2006).

How does an experience "know" which genes to affect epigenetically? For that question, we need to await further research. In any case, epigenetic effects are an important contributor to individual differences.

concept check

23. Why is it misleading to talk about "the gene" for some behavior or ability?

Answer

23. Almost every aspect of behavior depends on the combined influence of many genes and environmental influences. Also, any gene affects more than one outcome.

Estimating Heritability in Humans

Suppose we wonder how much of the variation in a behavior depends on differences in genes. The answer is summarized by the term **heritability**, *an estimate of the variance within a population that is due to heredity*. Heritability ranges from 1, indicating that heredity controls all the variance, to 0, indicating that it controls none of it. For example, red-green color vision deficiency has a heritability of almost 1, whereas which language you speak (such as English or Chinese) has a heritability of 0.

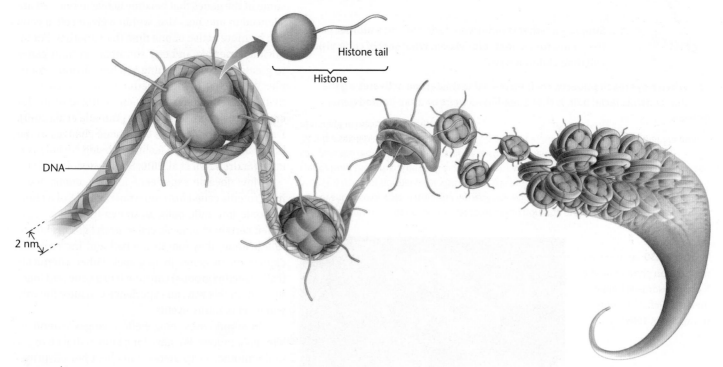

DNA

2 nm

Histone tail

Histone

▲ **Figure 3.32** DNA is wrapped into little balls. Attaching or removing certain chemicals from a histone tail can loosen or tighten the ball, thereby increasing or decreasing the expression of genes in that ball.

Note that the definition of heritability includes the phrase "within a population." The results for one population might differ from those of another, depending on how much genetic variation each population has, and how much environmental variation. Note another point about heritability: What do you suppose is the heritability of how many legs a person has? The answer is, almost zero! We know that genes are responsible having two legs, but the *variation* in genes has almost nothing to do with the *variation* in how many legs someone has. Nearly all of the variation depends on the fact that some people have lost a leg by amputation.

24. If our society changed so that it provided an equally good environment for all children, would the heritability of behaviors increase or decrease?

Answer

24. If all children had equally supportive environments, the total amount of variation in behavior would decrease, but whatever variation remained would have to depend largely on heredity (because differences in the environment have been minimized). Therefore, heritability would increase.

Twin Studies

To estimate the heritability of a behavior, researchers have traditionally relied on evidence from twins and adopted children. **Monozygotic** (mon-oh-zie-GOT-ik) twins *develop from a single fertilized egg (zygote) and therefore have identical genes*. Most people call them "identical" twins, but that term is misleading. Some monozygotic twins are mirror images—one right-handed and the other left-handed. It is also possible for a gene to be activated in one twin and suppressed in the other. **Dizygotic** (DIE-zie-GOT-ik) twins *develop from two eggs and share*

only half their genes (see ▼ Figure 3.33). They are often called "fraternal" twins because they are only as closely related as brother and sister. If dizygotic twins resemble each other almost as much as monozygotic twins do in some trait, then the heritability of that trait is low, indicating that genetic differences had little influence. If monozygotic twins resemble each other more strongly than dizygotic twins do, then the heritability is probably high. An alternative explanation, worth considering in some cases, is that monozygotic twins resemble each other so strongly because people treat them the same way.

Researchers also examine pairs of monozygotic twins who grew up in separate environments. Today's adoption agencies place twins in the same family, but in previous times, many twins were adopted separately (see ▼ Figure 3.34). One pair of monozygotic twins, reunited in adulthood after being reared separately, quickly discovered that they had much in common. Both had been named Jim by their adoptive parents. Each liked carpentry and drafting, had built a bench around a tree in his yard, and worked as a deputy sheriff. Both chewed their fingernails, gained weight at the same age, smoked the same brand of cigarettes, drove Chevrolets, and took their vacations in western Florida. Each married a woman named Linda, divorced her, and married a woman named Betty. One had a son named James Alan and the other had a son named James Allen, and each had a pet dog named

▶ **Figure 3.33** Monozygotic twins develop from the same fertilized egg. Dizygotic twins grow from two eggs fertilized by different sperm.

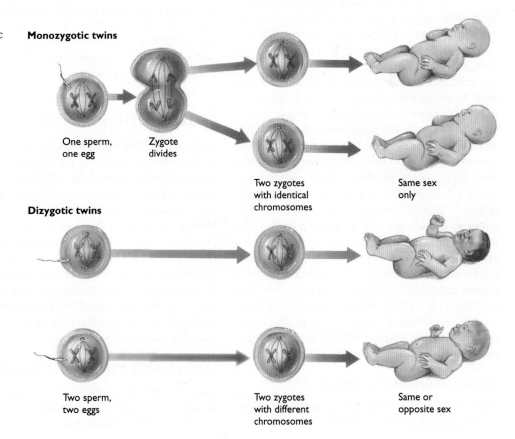

Monozygotic twins

One sperm, one egg

Zygote divides

Two zygotes with identical chromosomes

Same sex only

Dizygotic twins

Two sperm, two eggs

Two zygotes with different chromosomes

Same or opposite sex

▲ **Figure 3.34** Anaïs Bordier and Samantha Futerman were born in Korea and adopted in infancy, one in France and the other in the United States. When one spotted the other on a YouTube video, they connected and discovered many detailed similarities.

Toy. It is, of course, difficult to know how many of these similarities are mere coincidences. However, many other sets of twins reunited in adulthood also reported detailed similarities (Lykken, McGue, Tellegen, & Bouchard, 1992).

Researchers examined about 100 pairs of twins, some monozygotic and others dizygotic, who were reared separately and reunited as adults. On the average, the monozygotic twins resembled each other more strongly with regard to hobbies, vocational interests, answers on personality tests, tendency to trust other people, political beliefs, probability of voting, job satisfaction, life satisfaction, probability of mental illness, consumption of coffee and fruit juices, and preference for awakening early in the morning or staying up late at night (Bouchard & McGue, 2003; Cesarini et al., 2008; DiLalla, Carey, Gottesman, & Bouchard, 1996; Fowler, Baker, & Dawes, 2008; Hur, Bouchard, & Eckert, 1998; Hur, Bouchard, & Lykken, 1998; Lykken, Bouchard, McGue, & Tellegen, 1993; McCourt, Bouchard, Lykken, Tellegen, & Keyes, 1999). The implication is that genes influence a wide variety of behaviors.

Studies of Adopted Children

Another kind of evidence for heritability comes from studies of adopted children. Resemblance to their adopting parents implies an environmental influence. Resemblance to their biological parents implies a genetic influence.

In some cases, the results are sometimes hard to interpret. For example, consider the evidence that many adopted children with an arrest record had biological mothers with a criminal history (Mason & Frick, 1994). The resemblance could indicate a genetic influence, but the mothers also provided the prenatal environment. Chances are, many of the mothers with a criminal record smoked, drank alcohol, perhaps used other drugs, or in other ways endangered the fetus's brain development. Prenatal environment is an important influence on development.

concept check

25. Suppose someone studies adopted children who developed severe depression and finds that many of their biological parents had depression, whereas few of their adopting parents did. A possible interpretation is that genetic factors strongly influence depression. What is another interpretation?

Answer

25. Perhaps biological mothers who are becoming depressed eat less healthy foods, drink more alcohol, or in some other way impair the prenatal environment of their babies.

Examination of Chromosomes

A third type of evidence: Now that biologists have mapped the human genome (the set of all genes on our chromosomes), it is possible to examine the chromosomes and identify genes that are linked to a particular condition. One gene is strongly linked to Huntington's disease. Several genes are linked to increased risk of certain types of cancer.

Researchers have devoted great efforts to identify individual genes that might predispose people to psychological disorders. They did identify one gene that measurably alters the risk of alcohol abuse, but research on other psychological disorders has found no common gene with a large effect (Dick et al., 2015). How can behavior have substantial heritability if we cannot locate a gene with a large effect? One possibility is the influence of epigenetics and another is the influence of rare genes.

How Genes Influence Behavior

Based on studies of twins and adopted children, researchers have found at least moderate heritability for almost every behavior they have examined, including loneliness (McGuire & Clifford, 2000), neuroticism (Lake, Eaves, Maes, Heath, & Martin, 2000), verbal fluency (T. Lee et al., 2018), time spent watching television (Plomin, Corley, DeFries, & Fulker, 1990), skill at drawing pictures (Arden, Trzaskowski, Garfield, & Plomin, 2014), probability of getting divorced (Salvatore, Lönn, Sundquist, Sundquist, & Kendler, 2018), and religious devoutness (Waller, Kojetin, Bouchard, Lykken, & Tellegen, 1990). About the only behavior for which researchers have reported zero heritability is choice of religious denomination (Eaves, Martin, & Heath, 1990). That is, genes apparently influence how often you attend religious services, but your family background is the main influence on *which* services you attend (or don't). How could genes influence this range of behaviors?

Direct and Indirect Influences

In some cases, genes influence behavior by altering development of the brain or sensory receptors. For example, one influence on people's food preferences is the number of taste buds they have on the tongue, largely influenced by

Dustin Finkelstein/Getty Images Entertainment/Getty Images

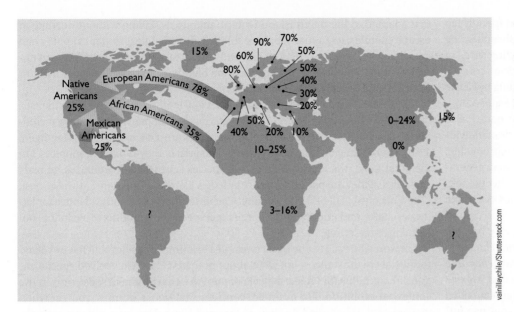

▶ **Figure 3.35** Adult humans vary in their ability to digest lactose, the main sugar in milk. The numbers refer to the percentage of each population's adults that can easily digest lactose. (Based on Flatz, 1987; Rozin & Pelchat, 1988)

genetics. In many cases, however, genes influence behavior by altering something outside the nervous system. Consider dietary choices: Almost all infants can digest *lactose*, the sugar in milk. Within a few years, most Asian children and many others lose the ability to digest it. (The loss depends on genes, not on how often people drink milk.) People who cannot digest lactose can enjoy a little milk and more readily enjoy cheese and yogurt, which are easier to digest, but they get gas and cramps if they consume much milk or ice cream (Flatz, 1987; Rozin & Pelchat, 1988). ▲ **Figure 3.35** shows how the ability to digest dairy products varies among ethnic groups. The point is that a gene can affect behavior—in this case, preference for dairy products—by altering chemical reactions outside the brain.

Genes also influence behaviors by altering body anatomy. Consider genes that make you unusually good-looking. Because many people smile at you, invite you to parties, and try to become your friend, you develop increased self-confidence and social skills. The genes changed your behavior by changing how other people treated you.

The Multiplier Effect

Imagine you have genes that make you tall, and other genes that help you develop fast running skills. At first you have a slight natural advantage at playing basketball, compared to others your age. Therefore, you get to be on teams, you receive coaching, and your skills improve. As your skills improve, you experience more success and receive further encouragement. What started as a small natural advantage becomes greater and greater as a result of environmental influences. Researchers call this tendency a multiplier effect—*A small initial advantage in some behavior, possibly genetic in origin, alters the environment and magnifies that advantage* (Dickens & Flynn, 2001). The same could occur for almost any aspect of behavior. For example, someone who is inclined to be active and vigorous tends to choose outgoing friends and stimulating social situations. Someone with a more reserved temperament gravitates toward quiet activities and smaller social groups. The initial behavioral tendency increases by altering the environment. Thus, it is often difficult to separate the contributions of heredity and environment.

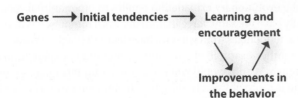

26. Because of the multiplier effect, should we expect estimates of heritability to be higher for children or for adults?

Answer

26. In most cases, heritability estimates should be higher for adults. As people grow older, their behavior tendencies alter their environment in ways that increase or exaggerate the initial differences that genes produced.

Environmental Modification of Genetic Effects

Some people assume that if a gene has a strong influence on some behavior, then we can do nothing about it, short of genetic modification. An example that refutes this assumption is phenylketonuria (PKU), *an inherited condition that, if untreated, impairs brain development.* About 2 percent of people with European or Asian ancestry, and almost no Africans, have the recessive gene that leads to PKU, but because the gene is recessive, one copy is nearly harmless. People with copies from both parents cannot metabolize *phenylalanine*, a common constituent of proteins. On an ordinary diet, an affected child accumulates phenylalanine in the brain and develops intellectual disabilities. However, a diet low in phenylalanine protects the brain. Thus, a diet prevents a disorder that would otherwise show high heritability.

Evolutionary Psychology

Since ancient times, people have practiced selective breeding. Farmers use the best egg-laying chickens and best milk-producing cows to breed the next generation. People have selectively bred friendly lap dogs, reliable guard dogs, and dutiful sheepherding dogs. We have improved crops by selecting seeds of the best-yielding plants. Maize (American corn) is the product of prolonged selective breeding by Native Americans (Gallavotti et al., 2004; see ▼ Figure 3.36).

Charles Darwin's insight was that nature also acts as a selective breeder. If certain kinds of individuals are more successful than others at reproducing, then they pass on their genes, and the next generation resembles them more than it does the less successful individuals. Over time, the species as a whole can change. Darwin's preferred term was *descent with modification*, but the concept quickly became known as evolution, defined as *a gradual change in the frequency of various genes from one generation to the next*. Why do you have the genes that you do? Simply, your parents had those genes and survived long enough to reproduce, and so did your parents' parents. Any gene that is common in a large population presumably had benefits in the past, though not necessarily today.

Natural selection acts on brain and behavior, just as it does on the rest of the body. For example, the dodo was a large bird in the pigeon/dove family

▲ **Figure 3.36** Many centuries ago, Native Americans selectively bred *teosinte*, a plant with barely edible hard kernels, until they developed what we now know as maize (American corn).

that adapted to life on an island with no mammals. Living without needing to escape enemies, it gradually lost the ability to fly. (Flightless dodos evidently had an advantage by saving energy.) The dodo also lost all fear. When humans eventually came to the island, they hunted the flightless, fearless dodos for meat or for sport, and quickly exterminated them.

Kittiwakes, unlike other members of the gull family, usually breed on the narrow ledges of steep cliffs. Many of their behaviors are adapted to this setting, including the fact that their chicks stay in place until they are old enough to fly (Tinbergen, 1958). Even if they are placed on a safe, flat surface, they remain motionless. On the other hand, the chicks of other gull species start walking around at an early age—even if they are placed on a narrow ledge, like the ones where kittiwakes nest. (They, of course, fall off.) The stationary behavior that is so clearly adaptive for kittiwake chicks, and unnecessary for other gull species, is a product of evolution, not learning or reasoning.

It would be easy to cite other examples of animal behavior that have evolved to special circumstances, but what about humans? Have we evolved specializations in our behavior? A few aspects of human behavior make sense only in the context of evolution. For example, consider the "goose bumps" you get when you are cold. What good do they do for you? None. However, other mammals, with hairier skin, gain an advantage by erecting their hairs when they are cold. Their raised hairs provide extra insulation. Hair erection in a cold environment was useful to your ancient ancestors, and you continue to show that reaction, even though your body hairs are short, usually covered with clothing, and generally useless.

Also consider a human infant's grasp reflex: An infant's hand tightly grasps anything placed into the palm, such as a finger. This behavior serves no function today, but for our ancient ancestors, it helped an infant hold onto the mother as she traveled (see ▼ Figure 3.37). Again, in humans this behavior makes sense only as an evolutionary carryover.

Evolutionary psychologists try to infer the benefits that favored certain genes and behaviors. Some of the most controversial interpretations pertain to human sexual behavior. For example, in many species throughout the animal kingdom, males seek mating opportunities with multiple partners more vigorously than females seek multiple partners. When we see this tendency in frogs, birds, or lions, an evolutionary explanation seems clear: A male can spread his genes by mating with many females, whereas a female cannot produce more babies by mating with more males. (She might gain some advantage by additional partners, especially if the first male is infertile, but her potential gain is less than a male's.) In humans, too, as shown in ▼ Figure 3.38, more men than women are eager for multiple sexual partners (Schmitt et al., 2003). The proposed evolutionary explanation parallels that for other species (Bjorklund & Shackelford, 1999; Buss, 2000; Gangestad, 2000; Geary, 2000): A man can spread his genes by either of two strategies: He can devote full efforts to helping one woman rear his children, or have sex with many women and hope they can rear the children without his help (Gangestad & Simpson, 2000). Women can gain possible advantages from multiple partners (Hrdy, 2000), but they cannot multiply their number of children by multiplying their number of sex partners.

This interpretation has been controversial. One objection is that it seems to give men an excuse for sexual infidelity. Evolutionary psychologists respond that explaining what *is* does not equal saying what *ought to be*. Pain is also a product of evolution, for example, but we are quite happy to restrain it. Another objection is that even if the evolutionary explanation applies to other animal species, it does not necessarily have the same force in humans. With humans, it is harder to separate our innate tendencies from what we have learned (Eagly & Wood, 1999).

Here is another example of a possible evolutionary explanation of a male-female difference: Whom would you prefer for a long-term mating relationship, someone who is more physically attractive, or someone who is more financially

▲ **Figure 3.37** Human infants tightly grasp anything in the palm of their hands. In our remote monkey-like ancestors, this reflex helped infants hold onto their mothers.

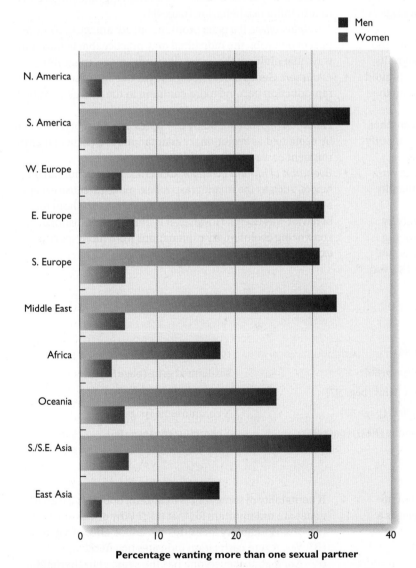

■ Men
■ Women

Percentage wanting more than one sexual partner

▲ **Figure 3.38** In all 52 countries that were surveyed, more men than women hoped for more than one sexual partner within the next month. (Source: Based on data of Schmitt et al., 2003)

successful? Women are more likely than men to prefer the financially successful partner (Buss, 2000). An evolutionary interpretation is that a woman needs a good provider during her time of pregnancy and infant care, when she is limited in her ability to find food and supplies. Therefore, perhaps women evolved to prefer a mate who has this ability. Although this explanation is plausible, it is not convincing. First, the amount of women's preference for a good provider varies considerably among cultures. In countries where women have no economic resources of their own, they prefer a wealthy husband, but where women can get good jobs, they choose a husband for other reasons (Zentner & Mitura, 2012). Second, this tendency is far from universal even among other mammals. In many mammalian species, the male separates from the female after mating and contributes nothing to caring for her or her babies. If women have an evolved tendency to seek a good provider, the gene had to evolve specifically in humans.

In short, it is important to distinguish between the most convincing evolutionary explanations (such as for goose bumps and infant grasp reflex) and the more speculative interpretations (de Waal, 2002). In many cases, it is easy to propose an evolutionary explanation and more difficult to test it.

27. What explanation do evolutionary psychologists offer for the human infant's grasp reflex?

Answer

27. Although the reflex is useless for humans, it was important to ancestral species in which infants had to cling to their mothers while the mothers were walking.

Genes and Experience

Physicists say that the development of the universe depended on its "initial conditions"—the array of matter and energy a fraction of a second after the big bang. The outcome of any experiment in physics or chemistry depends on the initial conditions—the type of matter, its temperature and pressure, and so forth. You had initial conditions, too—your genes. Understanding your genes is important for understanding why you developed differently from someone else, but it would not be enough. Your genes influence how you react to your environment, and your environment activates certain genes and inactivates others. In this module we have explored just a little of the complex ways in which genes interact with experiences.

Summary

- *Genes.* Genes control heredity. A recessive gene exerts its effects only in someone with two copies of the gene per cell. A dominant gene exerts its effects even if one has only a single copy per cell. (page 84)
- *Sex-linked and sex-limited genes.* Genes on the X or Y chromosome are sex linked. An X-linked recessive gene will show its effects more frequently in males than in females. A sex-limited gene is present in both sexes, but it affects one more than the other. (page 84)
- *Epigenetics.* A gene can be more active in one cell than another, and more active at one time than another. Experiences modify the expression of genes. (page 85)
- *Heritability.* Heritability is an estimate of how much the variation in some trait depends on variation in genes. Heritability can vary from one population to another. (page 86)
- *Estimating heritability.* Researchers estimate heritability by comparing monozygotic and dizygotic twins, by examining how adopted children resemble their biological parents, and by finding associations between particular genes and observed outcomes. (page 87)

- *How genes affect behavior.* Genes affect behaviors by altering the chemistry of the brain, or by influencing other organs that in turn influence behavior. (page 88)
- *Multiplier effect.* If a gene promotes an advantage in some aspect of behavior, the individual may practice that behavior in ways that multiply the initial slight advantage. (page 89)
- *Evolution.* Genes that increase the probability of survival and reproduction become more common in the next generation. (page 90)
- *Evolution of behavior.* Many examples of animal behavior can be explained as evolutionary adaptations to a particular environment or way of life. (page 90)
- *Evolution of human behavior.* Certain aspects of human behavior, such as the infant grasp reflex, make no sense except as an evolutionary carryover from ancestors for whom the behavior was useful. However, it is important to distinguish convincing evolutionary explanations from more speculative explanations. (page 90)

Key Terms

chromosome (page 84)	gene (page 84)	recessive (page 84)
dizygotic twins (page 87)	heritability (page 86)	sex-limited gene (page 85)
dominant (page 84)	monozygotic twins (page 87)	sex-linked gene (page 85)
epigenetics (page 85)	multiplier effect (page 89)	X chromosome (page 85)
evolution (page 90)	phenylketonuria (PKU) (page 89)	Y chromosome (page 85)

Review Questions

1. If evidence shows strong heritability for a behavior, but no common gene correlates with it, which of the following is a plausible explanation?
   (a) A sex-limited gene
   (b) A recessive gene
   (c) Epigenetics
   (d) Lamarkian evolution

2. If heritability of some trait is near zero, does that mean that genes are unimportant for that trait? Why or why not?
   (a) Yes. Heritability measures the importance of a gene.
   (b) Yes. A zero correlation indicates no effect.
   (c) No. If almost everyone has the same gene, heritability is low.
   (d) No. Heritability of zero indicates that genes and environment are equally important.

3. Which of these is true of dizygotic twins?
   (a) Either both are male or both are female.
   (b) One is male and the other is female.
   (c) They developed from two fertilized eggs.
   (d) They developed from one fertilized egg that split.

4. Researchers estimate heritability of a behavior by examining three types of evidence. Which of the following is NOT one of those types?
   (a) Differences among cultures
   (b) Examination of chromosomes
   (c) Comparisons between monozygotic and dizygotic twins
   (d) Comparisons of adopted children to their biological and adopting parents

5. What is meant by the "multiplier effect"?
   (a) Genetic factors are more important for twins than for single births.
   (b) The influence of a gene on the X chromosome is twice as great in females as it is in males.
   (c) Heritability times environmental influence equals one.
   (d) The environment can increase the effect of a genetic difference.

6. Observations about phenylketonuria provide evidence *against* which of the following statements?
   (a) A single gene can have a major effect on behavior.
   (b) Behaviors depend on both genetic and environmental influences.
   (c) Most children's temperament is consistent over long periods of time.
   (d) If something is under genetic control, it is fixed and unchangeable.

7. What explanation do evolutionary psychologists offer for the "goose bumps" we get when we are cold?
   (a) Activity of the sympathetic nervous system erects the skin's hairs.
   (b) For our ancient ancestors, hair erection increased insulation.
   (c) Goose bumps increase our probability of attracting a mate.
   (d) Goose bumps may be useful at some time in the future.

Answers: 1c, 2c, 3c, 4a, 5d, 6d, 7b.

4 Sensation and Perception

Christoph Hetzmannseder/Moment/Getty Images

When my son Sam was 8 years old, he asked me, "If we went to some other planet, would we see different colors?" He meant colors that were as different from familiar colors as yellow is from red or blue. I told him that would be impossible, and I tried to explain why. No matter where we go in outer space, we could never experience a color, sound, or other sensation that would be fundamentally different from what we experience on Earth. Different combinations, perhaps, but not fundamentally different sensory experiences.

Three years later, Sam told me he wondered whether people who look at the same thing are all having the same experience: When different people look at something and call it "green," how can we know whether they are having the same experience? I agreed that there is no way to be sure.

Why am I certain that colors on a different planet would look the same as on Earth but uncertain that colors look the same to different people here? If the answer isn't clear to you, perhaps it will be, after you read this chapter.

Sensation is the *conversion of energy from the environment into a pattern of response by the nervous system.* It is the registration of information. **Perception** is *the interpretation of that information.* For example, light rays striking your eyes produce sensation. Your experience of recognizing your roommate is a perception. In practice, the distinction between sensation and perception is often difficult to make.

No matter how exotic some other planet might be, it could not have colors we do not have here. The reason is that our eyes can see only certain wavelengths of light, and color is the experience our brains create from those wavelengths.

A. Gragera/Latin Stock/Science Source

Christoph Hetzmannseder/Moment/Getty Images

After studying this module, you should be able to:

1. Remember that vision occurs because light strikes the retina.

2. Identify the structures of the eye.

3. Explain why the route from the receptors to the brain produces a blind spot.

4. Describe how and why vision in the fovea differs from that in the periphery.

5. Outline the processes necessary for dark adaptation.

6. Compare and contrast three theories of color vision.

Around 1990, someone at the University of Michigan asked every academic department to offer one question that they thought every student should be able to answer before graduation. That is, it was so important that if you cannot answer it, you shouldn't get your diploma, regardless of your major.

The most impressive question came from the chemistry department: Suppose in the middle of a well-insulated, airtight room, you plug in a refrigerator with its door wide open. Will the result be to cool the room, heat the room, or have no effect on room temperature? (Think about it and answer before you read further.)

To answer, you have to know that a refrigerator doesn't create coldness. It moves heat from its inside to the outside. Then compare the heat added on the outside to the heat removed from the inside. For the two to break even, the refrigerator would have to operate at 100 percent efficiency, and to cool the room, it would have to operate at more than 100 percent efficiency. A basic principle in physics is that every machine wastes some energy. Therefore, the refrigerator will heat the room. Another way to think about it: The refrigerator uses electricity. Using electricity always generates some heat. The question requires you to understand and apply the principle of entropy, or the second law of thermodynamics, and it is more important to understand it and apply it than to name it or define it.

By contrast to chemistry's clever question, the psychology department asked, "What is the current definition of psychology?" How embarrassing. After all the research we have done, we have nothing better to offer the world than a definition of ourselves?

Here is a better question. It doesn't represent all of psychology, and it may seem simple-minded, but it's a question that certainly every educated person should be able to answer: Do you see because light enters your eyes, or do you send out sight rays?

The correct answer is that light enters your eyes. When you see a tree, your perception of the tree is in your head, not in the tree. Even if you *did* send sight rays that struck an object, you wouldn't know about it, unless those rays bounced back into your eyes. Nevertheless, a survey found that one-third of college students believed they sent out sight rays (Winer & Cottrell, 1996; Winer, Cottrell, Gregg, Fournier, & Bica, 2002).

The discovery of how vision works was the first research discovery in psychology (Steffens, 2007). About a thousand years ago, the Islamic scholar Ibn al-Haytham reasoned that people see the stars as soon as they open their eyes, and it is implausible that sight rays would travel that fast to something so distant. Further, he demonstrated that when light strikes an object, a viewer sees only the light rays that reflect directly to the viewer's eyes.

In addition to the idea of sight rays, people have other misconceptions about vision. We are often led astray because we imagine that what we see is a copy of the outside world. It is not. Just as a computer translates a sight or sound into a series of 1s and 0s, your brain translates physical stimuli into representations it can use.

1. **Some people say that hawks can see farther than humans can. Is that statement plausible?**

Answer

1. No. How *far* anyone can see depends only on how far the light traveled. On a clear night, humans can see galaxies that are billions of light years away, and presumably hawks cannot see beyond the edge of the universe. It may be that hawks can detect details at greater distances than humans, but that is different from seeing *farther*.

Detecting Light

Sensation is the detection of **stimuli**—*energies from the world around us that affect us in some way.* Our eyes, ears, and other sensory organs are packed with **receptors**—*specialized cells that convert environmental energies into activities of the nervous system.*

What we call *light* is part of the **electromagnetic spectrum,** *the continuum of all frequencies of radiated energy,* from gamma rays and X-rays with very short wavelengths, through ultraviolet, visible light, and infrared, to radio and TV transmissions with very long wavelengths (see ▼ **Figure 4.1**). What we call "visible light" is visible only because we have receptors that respond to those wavelengths—400 to 700 nanometers (nm). With different receptors, we would see a different range of wavelengths. Many insects and birds, in fact, see ultraviolet wavelengths that we do not.

The Structures of the Eye

When we see something, light reflected from the object passes through the **pupil,** an *adjustable opening* that widens and narrows to control the amount of light entering the eye. The **iris,** the *colored structure on the surface of the eye surrounding the pupil,* is what we describe when we say someone has brown, green, or blue eyes.

Light passing through the pupil travels through the *vitreous humor* (a clear jellylike substance) to strike the retina, *a layer of visual receptors covering the back surface of the eyeball.* The cornea and the lens focus the light on the retina, as shown in ▼ Figure 4.2. The cornea, *a rigid transparent structure on the surface of the eyeball,* always focuses light in the same way. The lens, *a flexible structure that varies its thickness,* enables accommodation—that is, *adjusting the focus for objects at different distances.* When you focus on a distant object, your eye muscles relax and let the lens become thinner and flatter, as shown in ▼ Figure 4.3a. When you focus on a close object, your eye muscles tighten and make the lens thicker and rounder (see ▼ Figure 4.3b).

The fovea (FOE-vee-uh), *the central area of the retina,* is adapted for detailed vision (see Figure 4.2). Of all retinal areas, the fovea has the greatest density of receptors. Input from the fovea occupies more of the human visual cortex than input from all the rest of the retinas combined.

Hawks, owls, and other predatory birds have a greater density of receptors on the top of the retina (for looking down) than on the bottom of the retina (for looking up). When they fly, this arrangement lets them see the ground beneath them in detail. When on the ground, however, they have trouble seeing above themselves (see ▼ Figure 4.4).

Some common disorders of vision are listed in ■ Table 4.1.

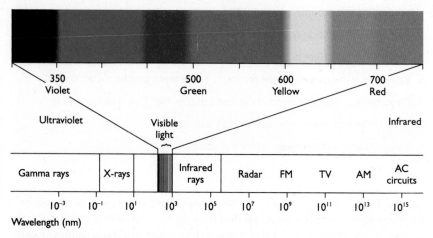

▲ **Figure 4.1** Visible light is a small part of the electromagnetic spectrum. We see these wavelengths because our receptors respond to them.

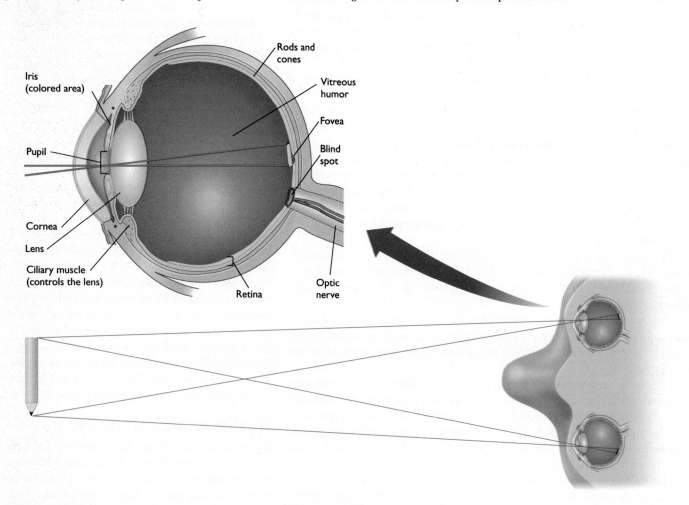

▲ **Figure 4.2** The lens gets its name from the Latin word *lens*, meaning "lentil." This reference to its shape is an appropriate choice, as this cross-section of the eye shows. The names of other parts of the eye also refer to their appearance.

a

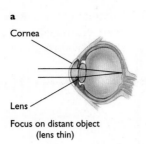

Cornea

Lens

Focus on distant object
(lens thin)

b

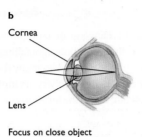

Cornea

Lens

Focus on close object
(lens thick)

▲ **Figure 4.3** The flexible, transparent lens changes shape so that objects (a) far and (b) near can come into focus. The lens bends entering light rays so that they fall on the retina.

concept check

2. **As people grow older, the lens becomes more rigid. How would that rigidity affect vision?**

Answer

2. Because the lens is more rigid, older people are less able to change their focus for objects at different distances. In particular, they find it more difficult to focus on nearby objects.

The Visual Receptors

The retina's two types of visual receptors, cones and rods, differ in function and appearance, as ▼ Figure 4.5 shows. The cones are *adapted for perceiving color and detail in bright light.* The rods are *adapted for vision in dim light.*

Of the visual receptors in the human retina, about 5 percent are cones. Although 5 percent may not sound like much, the cone-rich parts of the retina

▲ **Figure 4.4** Birds of prey, such as these owls, can see down much more clearly than up. In flight that arrangement is helpful. On the ground, they have to turn their heads almost upside down to look up.

send more axons to the brain than do the rod-rich areas, and cone responses dominate the human visual cortex. Nearly all birds also have many cones and good color vision. Species that are active at night—rats and mice, for example—have mostly rods.

The fovea consists entirely of cones (see Figure 4.2). The percentage of rods increases toward the periphery, where color vision becomes weaker.

Try this experiment: Hold several pens or pencils of different colors behind your back. Any objects will work if they are similar in size, shape, and brightness. Pick one without looking at it. Hold it behind your head and bring it slowly into your field of vision, while focusing your eyes straight ahead. When you begin to see the object, you will probably not see its color.

Rods are more effective than cones for detecting dim light for two reasons: First, a rod responds

Table 4.1 Common Disorders of Vision	
Disorder	
Presbyopia	Impaired ability to focus on nearby objects because of decreased flexibility of the lens
Myopia	Nearsightedness—impaired ability to focus on distant objects because of the shape of the eyeball
Hyperopia	Farsightedness—impaired ability to focus on close objects because of the shape of the eyeball
Glaucoma	Damage to the optic nerve, usually caused by increased pressure in the eyeball
Cataract	A disorder in which the lens becomes cloudy

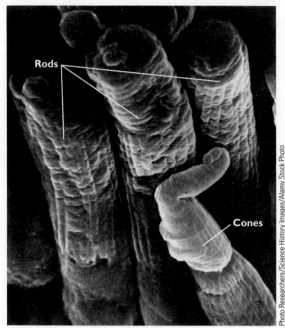

▲ **Figure 4.5** Rods and cones seen through a scanning electron micrograph. The rods, numbering more than 120 million in humans, enable vision in dim light. The 6 million cones in the retina distinguish gradations of color in bright light. (Reprinted from "Scanning electron microscopy of vertebrate visual receptors," by E. R. Lewis, F. S. Werb, & Y. Y. Zeevi, 1969. *Brain Research, 15,* pp. 559–562. Copyright 1969, with permission from Elsevier.)

to faint stimulation more than a cone does. Second and more importantly, the rods pool their resources. Only one or a few cones converge messages onto the next cell, called a *bipolar cell,* whereas many rods converge their messages. In the far periphery of the retina, more than 100 rods send messages to a bipolar cell (see ▲ **Figure 4.6**). ■ Table 4.2 summarizes differences between rods and cones.

3. **Why do you have better color vision in your fovea than in the periphery?**

Answer

3. The center of the retina has only cones, and the periphery has mostly rods, which do not enable color vision.

Dark Adaptation

Suppose you go into a basement at night looking for a flashlight. The only light bulb is burned out. Just a little moonlight comes through a basement window. At first, you see hardly anything, but as time

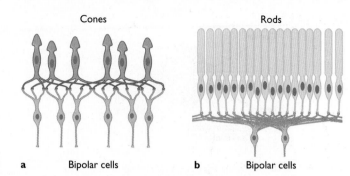

Cones   Rods

a   Bipolar cells   b   Bipolar cells

▲ **Figure 4.6** Because so many rods converge their output to the next layer of the visual system, known as bipolar cells, even a little light falling on the rods stimulates a bipolar cell. Thus, the periphery of the retina, with many rods, readily detects faint light. However, because bipolar cells in the periphery get input from so many receptors, they have only imprecise information about the location and shape of objects.

passes, your vision gradually improves. *Gradual improvement in the ability to see in dim light* is called dark adaptation.

Here is the mechanism: Exposure to light chemically alters molecules called *retinaldehydes,* thereby stimulating the visual receptors. (Retinaldehydes are derived from vitamin A.) Under moderate light the receptors *regenerate* (rebuild) the molecules about as fast as the light keeps breaking them down. In dim light, receptors regenerate their molecules without competition, improving your detection of faint light.

Cones and rods adapt at different rates. When you enter a dark place, your cones regenerate their retinaldehydes first, but by the time the rods finish, the rods gain much greater sensitivity to faint light. At that point, you see mostly with rods.

Here is how a psychologist demonstrates dark adaptation (E. B. Goldstein, 2007): Imagine yourself in a room that is completely dark except for a tiny flashing light. You use a knob to adjust the light so that you barely see it. Over 3 or 4 minutes, you gradually decrease the intensity of the light, as shown in ▼ **Figure 4.7a**. Note that a decrease in the intensity of the light indicates increased sensitivity of your eyes. If you stare straight at the point of light, your results demonstrate the adaptation of your cones to the dim light. (You are focusing the light on your fovea, which has no rods.)

Now the researcher repeats the study with a change in procedure: You stare at a faint light while another light flashes to the side, where it stimulates rods as well

Table 4.2 Differences between Rods and Cones		
	Rods	**Cones**
Shape	Nearly cylindrical	Tapered at one end
Prevalence in human retina	95 percent	5 percent
Abundant in	All vertebrate species	Species active during the day
Area of the retina	Toward the periphery	Toward the fovea
Important for color vision?	No	Yes
Important for detail?	No	Yes
Important in dim light?	Yes	No
Number of types	Just one	Three (in humans)

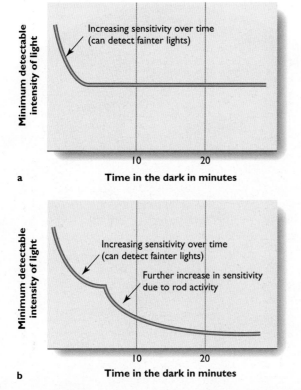

a

Time in the dark in minutes

b

Time in the dark in minutes

▲ **Figure 4.7** These graphs show dark adaptation to (a) a light you stare at directly, using only cones, and (b) a light in your peripheral vision, which you see with both cones and rods. (Based on E. B. Goldstein, 1989)

as cones. You adjust a knob until the flashing light in the periphery is barely visible. (▲ Figure 4.7b.) During the first 7 to 10 minutes, the results are the same as before. But then your rods become more sensitive than your cones, and you begin to see even fainter lights. Your rods continue to adapt over the next 20 minutes or so.

To demonstrate dark adaptation without any apparatus, try this: At night, turn on one light. Close one eye and cover it tightly with your hand for a minute or more. Your covered eye will adapt to the dark while your open eye remains adapted to the light. Then turn off the light and open both eyes. You will see better with your dark-adapted eye than with the light-adapted eye. (This instruction assumes you still have some faint light coming through a window. In a *completely* dark room, of course, you see nothing.)

concept check

4. **When you are well adapted to the dark, you might see something in your peripheral vision, but it disappears when you look straight at it. Why?**

Answer

4. Your peripheral vision has mostly rods, which adapt more strongly than the cones in your fovea.

The Visual Pathway

If you or I were designing an eye, we would probably run connections from the receptors directly back to the brain. Although that route sounds logical, it is not how your eyes actually work. The visual receptors send their impulses *away from* the brain, toward the center of the eye, where they contact neurons called bipolar cells. *The bipolar cells contact still other neurons within the eye,* the ganglion cells. The *axons from the ganglion cells join to form* the optic nerve, *which turns around and exits the eye,* as ▼ Figures 4.2 and 4.8 show. Half of each optic nerve crosses to the opposite side of the brain at the optic chiasm (KI-az-m). Most of the optic nerve goes to the thalamus, which sends information to the primary visual cortex in the occipital lobe. Some people have up to three times as many axons in their optic nerve as others have. Those with larger numbers are better at detecting faint lights and slight movements (Andrews, Halpern, & Purves, 1997; Halpern, Andrews, & Purves, 1999). This type of enhanced visual processing is common among people who excel at sports requiring precise aim, such as badminton, baseball, or basketball (Muraskin, Sherwin, & Sajda, 2015; Wang et al., 2015).

The *area where the optic nerve exits the retina* is called the blind spot. That part of the retina has no receptors because the exiting axons take up all the space. Also, blood vessels enter the eye at this point.

To illustrate, close your left eye and stare at the center of ▼ Figure 4.9; then slowly move the page forward and backward. When your eye is about 25 to 30 cm (10 to 12 inches) away from

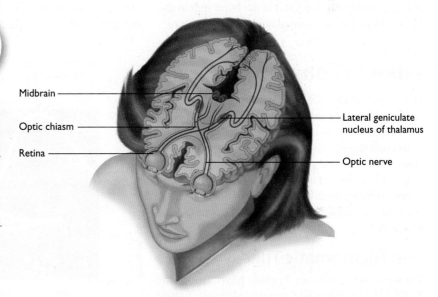

▲ **Figure 4.8** Axons from ganglion cells in the retina depart the eye at the blind spot and form the optic nerve. In humans, about half the axons in the optic nerve cross to the opposite side of the brain at the optic chiasm.

▶ **Figure 4.9** Close your left eye and focus your right eye on the animal trainer. Move the page toward your eyes and away from them until the lion on the right disappears. At that point, the lion is focused on the blind spot of your retina, where you have no receptors.

the page, the lion disappears because it falls into your blind spot. In its place you perceive a continuation of the circle. Ordinarily, you are unaware of your blind spot, partly because your brain "fills in" the missing part, but also because what is in the blind spot of one eye is within the active visual field of the other eye.

Color Vision

How does the visual system convert wavelengths of light into a perception of color? The process begins with three kinds of cones. Later, cells in the visual path code the information in terms of pairs of opposites—red versus green, yellow versus blue, and white versus black. Finally, the cerebral cortex compares the input from various parts of the visual field to synthesize a color experience. Let's examine these stages in turn.

The Trichromatic Theory

Thomas Young was an English physician of the 1700s who, among other accomplishments, helped to decode the Rosetta stone (making it possible to understand Egyptian hieroglyphics), introduced the modern concept of energy, revived and popularized

the wave theory of light, showed how to calculate annuities for insurance, and offered the first theory about how people perceive color (Martindale, 2001). His theory, elaborated and modified by Hermann von Helmholtz in the 1800s, came to be known as the Young-Helmholtz theory, or the trichromatic theory. (*Trichromatic* means "three colors.") Phrased in modern terms, it says that *color vision depends on the relative responses of three types of cones* (see ▼ Figure 4.10).

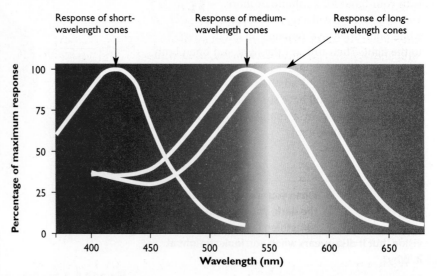

▲ **Figure 4.10** Sensitivity of three types of cones to different wavelengths of light. (Based on data of Bowmaker & Dartnall, 1980)

One type is most sensitive to short wavelengths (which we generally see as blue), another to medium wavelengths (green), and another to long wavelengths (red). Every wavelength of light produces its own distinct ratio of responses by the three kinds of cones. White light excites all three kinds equally. From the ratio among the three types of cones, the brain determines color.

Young and Helmholtz proposed their theory long before anatomists confirmed the existence of three types of cones (Wald, 1968). Helmholtz found that observers could mix various amounts of three wavelengths of light to match all other colors. (Mixing lights is different from mixing paints. Mixing yellow and blue *paints* produces green; mixing yellow and blue *lights* produces white.)

The short-wavelength cones, which respond most strongly to blue, are the least numerous. For the retina to detect blueness, the blue must extend over a somewhat larger area than other colors. ▼ Figure 4.11 illustrates this effect.

5. When you perceive yellow, which cones are most active?

Answer

5. The medium- and long-wavelength cones are about equally active, while the short-wavelength cone is much less active. Check Figure 4.10.

The Opponent-Process Theory

Young and Helmholtz were right about how many cones we have, but the trichromatic theory does not easily explain all aspects of color perception. For example, if you stare for a minute or so at something red and look away, you see a green afterimage. If you stare at something green, yellow, or blue, you see a red, blue, or yellow afterimage. To account for these afterimages, the 19th-century scientist Ewald Hering proposed the **opponent-process theory** of color vision: *We perceive color in terms of paired opposites—red versus green, yellow versus blue, and white versus black.* To illustrate, please follow the instructions in ▼ Figure 4.12.

When you looked away, you saw the logo in its normal coloration. After staring at an image, you replace blue with yellow, yellow with blue, red with green, green with red, white with black, and black with white.

▲ **Figure 4.11** Blue dots look black unless they cover enough area. Count the red dots; then count the blue dots. Try again while standing farther from the page. You will probably count as many red dots as before but fewer blue dots.

Experiences of one color after the removal of another are called **negative afterimages**.

Presumably, the explanation depends on cells somewhere in the nervous system that increase their activity in the presence of, say, blue, and decrease it in the presence of yellow. Then after you have stared at something blue, these cells become fatigued and decrease their response. Your brain then interprets the decrease as the color yellow. We could imagine such cells in the retina itself, but here is an observation that argues against that interpretation: Stare at the center of ▼ Figure 4.13 for a minute or more under bright light, and then look at a white surface. The afterimage you see is red on the outside, as expected. But you see *green*, not gray or black, for the inside circle. Your perception of the inside depends on the surrounding context. That result strongly implies that the negative afterimage, and indeed color perception in general, depends on the cerebral cortex, not just interactions within the retina.

6. The negative afterimage that you created by staring at Figure 4.12 may seem to move against the background. Why doesn't it stay in one place?

Answer

6. The afterimage is on your eye, not on the background. When you try to focus on a different part of the afterimage, you move your eyes and the afterimage moves with them.

▲ **Figure 4.12** Stare at any one point that you choose under a bright light for a minute. Don't move your eyes. Then look at a white page and you will see the golden arches.

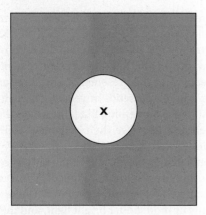

▲ **Figure 4.13** Stare at the center for a minute or more and then look at a white surface. What color do you see at the center?

The Retinex Theory

What you see at any point in space depends on more than the object itself. It depends on contrast with the objects around it. **Brightness contrast** *is the increase or decrease in an object's apparent brightness by comparison to objects around it.* In ▼ Figure 4.14, the pink bars on the right probably look darker than those on the left, but in fact, they are the same. The brain uses its past experience to calculate how that pattern of light probably was generated, taking into account all the contextual information (Purves, Williams, Nundy, & Lotto, 2004). In Figure 4.14, you see what appears to be a partly clear white bar covering the center of the left half of the grid, and the pink bars look light. In the corresponding section to the right, the pink bars appear to be under the red bars and on top of a white background. Here the pink looks darker because you contrast the pink against the white background above and below it.

try it your self

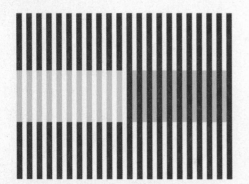

▲ **Figure 4.14** The pink bars in the left center area are in fact the same as the pink bars in the right center area, but those on the left seem lighter.

▲ **Figure 4.15** **(a)** When the block is under yellow light (left) or blue light (right), you still recognize the colors of individual squares. Parts **b** and **c** show what happens if we remove the context: The "blue" squares in the left half of part **a** and the "yellow" squares in the right half are actually the same as each other, and gray. (From *Why we see what we do,* by D. Purves and R. B. Lotto, Figure 6.10, p. 134. Copyright 2003 Sinauer Associates, Inc. Reprinted by permission.)

Color perception also depends on contrast. Suppose you look at a white screen illuminated with green light in an otherwise dark room. How would you know whether this is a white screen illuminated with green light or a green screen illuminated with white light? Or a blue screen illuminated with yellow light? You wouldn't know. Now someone wearing a brown shirt and blue jeans stands in front of the screen. Suddenly, you see the shirt as brown, the jeans as blue, and the screen as white, even though all the objects are reflecting mostly green light. You perceive color by comparing the light one object reflects to the light that other objects reflect. That is, the apparent color of an object depends on the objects surrounding it.

Suppose you take a complex array of objects and shine yellow or blue light on them. Even though everything is now yellowish or bluish, you have no difficulty perceiving which objects are red, green, yellow, blue, black, or white. This *tendency of an object to appear nearly the same color under a variety of lighting conditions* is called **color constancy** (see ▲ Figure 4.15).

In response to such observations, Edwin Land, the inventor of the Polaroid Land camera, proposed the **retinex theory**. According to this theory, *the cerebral cortex compares the patterns of light coming from different parts of the retina and synthesizes a color perception for each area* (Land, Hubel, Livingstone, Perry, & Burns, 1983; Land & McCann, 1971). (*Retinex* is a combination of the words *retina* and *cortex*.)

As Figure 4.15 emphasizes, we should not call short-wavelength light "blue" or long-wavelength light "red." A gray square can look blue in one context and yellow in another (Lotto & Purves, 2002; Purves & Lotto, 2003). Color is something our brain constructs, not a property of the light itself.

Each of the trichromatic, opponent-process, and retinex theories is correct with regard to certain aspects of vision. The trichromatic states that human color vision starts with three kinds of cones. The opponent-process theory explains how later cells organize color information. The retinex theory notes that the cerebral cortex compares color information from various parts of the visual field.

Color Vision Deficiency

Centuries ago, people assumed that anyone who was not blind could see colors (Fletcher & Voke, 1985). Then during the 1600s, the phenomenon of color vision deficiency was unambiguously recognized. Here was the first indication that color vision is a function of our eyes and brains and not just of light itself.

The older term color-*blindness* is misleading because very few people are totally unable to distinguish colors. About 8 percent of men and less than 1 percent of women have difficulty distinguishing red from green (Bowmaker, 1998). The cause is a recessive gene on the X chromosome. Because men have only one X chromosome, they need just one such gene to become red-green color deficient. Women, with two X chromosomes, need two such genes to develop the condition. Red-green color-deficient people have the short-wavelength cone and either the long-wavelength or the medium-wavelength cone (Fletcher & Voke, 1985).

▶ Figure 4.16 gives a crude but usually satisfactory test for red-green color vision deficiency. What do you see in each part of the figure?

How does the world look to people with color vision deficiency? They describe the world with the usual color words: Roses are red, bananas are yellow, and grass is green. But their answers do not mean that they perceive colors the same as other people do. Certain rare individuals are red-green color deficient in one eye but have normal vision in the other eye. Because they know what the color words really mean (from experience with their normal eye), they can describe what their deficient eye sees. They say that objects that look red or green to the normal eye look yellow or yellow-gray to the other eye (Marriott, 1976).

If you have normal color vision, ▼ Figure 4.17 will show you what it is like to be color deficient. First, cover part b, a typical item from a color deficiency test, and stare at part a under a bright light for about a minute. (The brighter the light and the longer you stare, the greater the effect will be.) Then look at part b. Staring at the red field fatigued your long-wavelength cones, weakening your red sensation.

Now stare at part c for about a minute and look at part b again. Because you have fatigued your green cones, the figure in b will stand out even more strongly

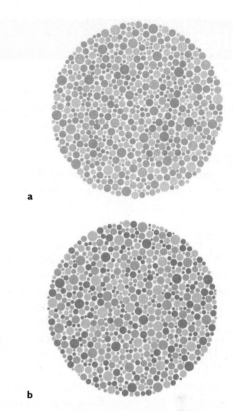

a

b

▲ **Figure 4.16** These items provide an informal test for red-green color vision deficiency. What do you see? Compare your answers to answer A on page 106.

than usual. In fact, certain people with red-green color deficiency may be able to see the number in b after staring at c.

Color vision deficiency illustrates a more general point. Before people knew about color vision deficiency, they easily assumed that the world looked the same to everyone. Still today it is easy to assume that everything tastes the same and smells the same to other people as it does to you. As you will learn in the next module, that assumption is untrue.

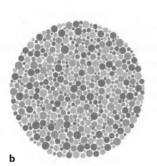

a   b   c

◀ **Figure 4.17** First, stare at pattern **(a)** under bright light for about a minute and then look at **(b)**. What do you see? Next stare at **(c)** for a minute and look at **(b)** again. Now what do you see? See answer B on page 106.

Vision as an Active Process

Before the existence of people or other color-sighted animals on Earth, was there any color? *No.* Light was present, and different objects reflected different wavelengths of light, but color exists only in brains.

Your brain does an enormous amount of processing to determine what you are seeing. Imagine building a robot with

vision. Light strikes the robot's visual sensors, and then . . . what? How will the robot know what objects it sees or what to do about them? Just receiving a pattern of light is only a small step toward understanding what one sees.

Summary

- *How vision works.* Vision occurs when light rays strike the retina at the back of the eye, causing cells to send messages to the brain. We do not send sight rays out of the eyes. (page 97)
- *Light.* Light is the part of the electromagnetic spectrum that excites receptors in the eyes. If we had different types of receptors, we would define other wavelengths as light. (page 97)
- *Focus.* The cornea and lens focus light onto the retina. (page 98)
- *Cones and rods.* Cones, found mainly in and near the fovea, are essential for color vision. Rods, more numerous toward the periphery, detect dim light. (page 99)
- *Blind spot.* The blind spot is the area of the retina through which the optic nerve exits. (page 101)

- *Color vision.* Color vision depends on three types of cones, each sensitive to a particular range of light wavelengths. Cones transmit messages so that later cells in the visual system indicate one color (e.g., blue) by an increase in activity and another color (e.g., yellow) by a decrease. The cerebral cortex compares responses from different parts of the retina to determine color experiences. (page 102)
- *Color vision deficiency.* People with a certain gene on the X chromosome have difficulty distinguishing reds from greens. (page 105)

Key Terms

accommodation (of the lens) (page 98)

blind spot (page 101)

brightness contrast (page 104)

color constancy (page 104)

cone (page 99)

cornea (page 98)

dark adaptation (page 100)

electromagnetic spectrum (page 97)

fovea (page 98)

ganglion cells (page 101)

iris (page 97)

lens (page 98)

negative afterimage (page 103)

opponent-process theory (page 103)

optic nerve (page 101)

perception (page 96)

pupil (page 97)

receptor (page 97)

retina (page 98)

retinex theory (page 104)

rod (page 99)

sensation (page 96)

stimulus (page 97)

trichromatic theory (or Young-Helmholtz theory) (page 102)

Answers to Other Questions in the Module

A. In Figure 4.16a, a person with normal color vision sees the numeral 74; in Figure 4.16b, the numeral 8.

B. In Figure 4.17b, you should see the numeral 29. After you have stared at the red circle in part a, the 29 in part b may look less distinct than usual, as though you were red-green color

deficient. After staring at the green circle, the 29 may be even more distinct than usual. If you do not see either of these effects at once, try again, but this time stare at part a or c longer *and* continue staring at part b a little longer. The effect does not appear immediately.

Review Questions

1. How far some animal can see depends on which of the following?
   (a) The ratio of cones to rods
   (b) The density of cones in the fovea
   (c) The flexibility of the lens
   (d) How far the light traveled

2. Why do we have our most detailed vision in the fovea?
   (a) The lens and cornea focus light most clearly on the fovea.
   (b) The fovea is the point most distant from the blind spot.
   (c) The fovea has the largest percentage of rods.
   (d) The fovea has the greatest ratio of receptors to ganglion cells.

3. Mice can see objects above them better than objects below them. What can we infer about their retina?
   (a) Their retina has more cones than rods.
   (b) Their receptors are more abundant on the bottom of the retina.
   (c) Their blind spot is near the bottom of the retina.
   (d) Their retina is near the center of the head.

4. Why do we see dim light better in the periphery than in the fovea?
   (a) The periphery has a higher percentage of cones.
   (b) Many peripheral receptors converge their input onto each bipolar cell.
   (c) The cornea and lens focus more light to the periphery.
   (d) The fovea is closer to the blind spot.

5. What causes dark adaptation?
   (a) Increased flexibility of the lens
   (b) Regeneration of receptor molecules
   (c) Increased speed of action potentials
   (d) A shift in the ratio of rods to cones

6. According to the trichromatic theory, how does our nervous system tell the difference between bright yellow-green and dim yellow-green light?
   (a) By the relative rates of response by medium-wavelength and long-wavelength cones
   (b) By the relative rates of response by medium-wavelength and short-wavelength cones
   (c) By the relative rates of response by all three types of cones
   (d) By the total amount of activity by all three types of cones

7. Which theory, if any, best explains color constancy?
   (a) The trichromatic theory
   (b) The opponent-process theory
   (c) The retinex theory
   (d) No theory

Answers: 1d, 2d, 3b, 4b, 5b, 6d, 7c.

Christoph Hetzmannseder/Moment/Getty Images

After studying this module, you should be able to:

1. Outline the mechanisms of hearing, touch, pain, taste, and smell.

2. Distinguish between two types of deafness.

3. Describe the mechanisms of pitch perception.

4. Explain how we localize sounds.

5. List factors that increase or decrease perception of pain.

6. Describe the basis for phantom limbs.

Consider these common expressions:

- I *see* what you mean.
- I *feel* your pain.
- I am deeply *touched* by everyone's support and concern.
- She is a person of fine *taste*.
- He was *dizzy* with success.
- The policies of this company *stink*.
- That *sounds* like a good job offer.

The metaphorical use of sensation terms is no accident. As Aristotle and several philosophers after him emphasized, "nothing is in the mind that was not first in the senses." Perhaps you doubt that assertion and object, "Sometimes, I think about numbers, time, love, justice, and all sorts of other nonsensory concepts." Yes, but how did you learn those concepts? Didn't you learn numbers by counting objects you could see or touch? Didn't you learn about time by observing changes in sensations? Didn't you learn about love and justice from events that you saw, heard, and felt? Many people have tried to find exceptions, ideas that do not come from a sensory experience, and maybe they do occur, but if so, they are hard to document. In this module we consider sensations from sounds, head tilt, skin stimulation, and chemicals.

Hearing

What we familiarly call the "ear" is a fleshy structure technically known as the *pinna*. It funnels sounds to the inner ear, where the receptors lie. The mammalian ear converts sound waves into mechanical displacements along a row of receptor cells. **Sound waves** are *vibrations of the air, water, or other medium*. They vary in frequency and amplitude

(see ▼ Figure 4.18). The frequency of a sound wave is the number of *cycles (vibrations) per second,* designated hertz (Hz). **Pitch** is a *perception closely related to frequency.* We perceive a high-frequency sound wave as high pitched and a low-frequency sound as low pitched.

Loudness is a *perception of the intensity of sound waves.* Other things being equal, the greater the amplitude of a sound, the louder it sounds. Because loudness is a psychological experience, other factors influence it also. For example, someone who speaks rapidly seems louder than someone speaking slowly at the same amplitude.

In addition to amplitude and pitch, sounds vary in **timbre** (TAM-ber), which refers to tone complexity. Any instrument playing a note at 128 Hz will simultaneously produce some sound at 256 Hz, 512 Hz, and other multiples, known as the harmonics of the principal note. Because all instruments and voices have a different ratio of harmonics, they sound different, even when they are playing the same note. That difference is due to timbre.

Variations in pitch, loudness, and timbre can convey emotion in many ways. An emphatic "I'm ready" indicates eagerness. A slower "I'm ready" with a different accent means you are sadly resigned to doing something unpleasant but necessary. Strong emphasis on the first word says you are ready but why isn't everyone else? Conveying information by tone of voice is known as *prosody.*

The ear converts relatively weak sound waves into more intense waves of pressure in the *fluid-filled canals of the snail-shaped organ* called the **cochlea** (KOCK-lee-uh), *which contains the receptors for hearing* (see ▼ Figure 4.19).

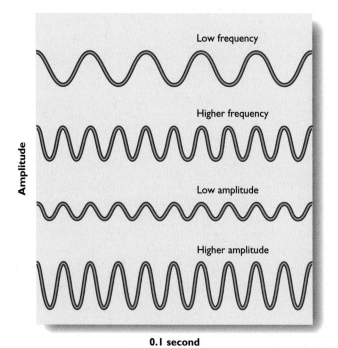

▲ **Figure 4.18** The time between the peaks of a sound wave determines the frequency of a sound. We experience frequencies as different pitches. The vertical range, or amplitude, of a wave determines the sound's intensity.

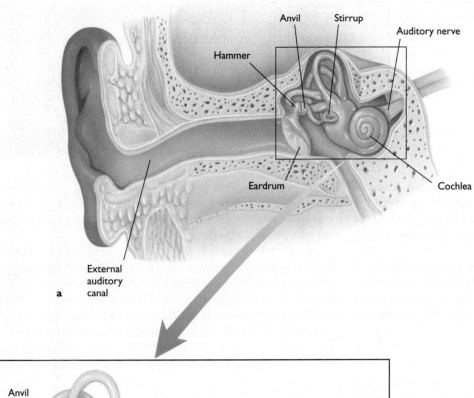

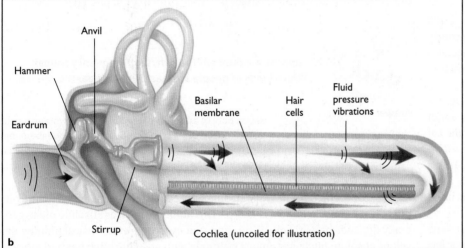

◀**Figure 4.19** Sound waves vibrate the eardrum **(a)**. Three tiny bones convert the eardrum's vibrations into vibrations in the fluid-filled cochlea **(b)**. These vibrations displace hair cells along the basilar membrane in the cochlea, aptly named after the Greek word for "snail." Here, the dimensions of the cochlea have been changed to make the principles clear.

When sound waves strike the eardrum, they cause it to vibrate. The eardrum connects to three tiny bones—the hammer, anvil, and stirrup (also known by their Latin names *malleus, incus,* and *stapes*). As the weak vibrations of the large eardrum travel through these bones, they transform into stronger vibrations of the much smaller stirrup, which transmits the vibrations to the fluid-filled cochlea, where the vibrations displace hair cells along the basilar (BASS-uh-ler) membrane. These hair cells, which act like touch receptors, connect to neurons whose axons form the auditory nerve. The auditory nerve transmits impulses to the brain areas responsible for hearing.

Understanding the mechanisms of hearing helps us explain hearing loss. One kind of hearing loss is conduction deafness, which *occurs when the bones connected to the eardrum cannot transmit sound waves to the cochlea.* Surgery can correct conduction deafness by removing whatever is obstructing the bones' movement. People with conduction deafness still hear their own voice because it is conducted through the skull bones to the cochlea, bypassing the eardrum altogether. The other type of hearing loss is nerve deafness, *resulting from damage*

to the cochlea, hair cells, or auditory nerve. Disease, heredity, and exposure to loud noises are common causes of nerve deafness.

Hearing aids compensate for hearing loss, except in cases of severe nerve deafness. People with damage to parts of the cochlea have trouble hearing only certain frequencies. Modern hearing aids can be adjusted to amplify just those frequencies. However, despite hearing aids, many older people continue to have hearing difficulties, especially in noisy surroundings. One reason is that before they got their hearing aids, their brain areas for language comprehension started deteriorating due to inadequate input (Peelle, Troiani, Grossman, & Wingfield, 2011). A second reason is impaired attention due to difficulty filtering out the irrelevant

sounds (Anderson, Parbery-Clark, White-Schwoch, & Kraus, 2012). Understanding improves when the listener watches the speaker's face, combining the sound with a bit of lip-reading (Golumbic, Cogan, Schroeder, & Poeppel, 2013; see ▲ **Figure 4.20**). Familiarity also helps. Older people are better at understanding their spouse's voice than someone else's voice. They are also better at *ignoring* the spouse's voice when they need to listen to someone else (Johnsrude et al., 2013).

Pitch Perception

Adult humans hear sound waves from about 15–20 hertz to about 15,000–20,000 Hz (cycles per second). The upper limit of hearing declines with age and also after exposure to loud noises. Thus, children hear higher frequencies than adults do.

We hear pitch by different mechanisms at different frequencies. At low frequencies (up to about 100 Hz), *a sound wave through the fluid of the cochlea vibrates all the hair cells, which produce action potentials in synchrony with the sound waves.* This is the **frequency principle**. For example, a sound at a frequency of 50 Hz makes each hair cell send the brain 50 impulses per second.

Beyond about 100 Hz, hair cells cannot keep pace. Still, each sound wave excites at least a few hair cells, and *"volleys" (groups) of them respond to each vibration with an action potential* (Rose, Brugge, Anderson, & Hind, 1967). This is known as

the **volley principle**. Thus, a tone at 1000 Hz might produce 1000 impulses per second, even though no neuron fires that rapidly. Volleys keep pace with sounds up to about 4000 Hz, good enough for almost all speech and music. (The highest note on a piano is 4224 Hz.)

However, beginning at about 100 Hz, we also use a different mechanism. *The highest frequency sounds vibrate hair cells near the stirrup end, and lower frequency sounds (down to about 100 to 200 Hz) vibrate hair cells at points farther along the membrane* (Warren, 1999). This is the **place principle**. Tones less than 100 Hz excite all hair cells equally, and we hear them by the frequency principle. We identify tones from 100 to 4000 Hz by a combination of the volley principle and the place principle. Beyond 4000 Hz, we identify tones only by the place principle. ▼ **Figure 4.21** summarizes the three principles of pitch perception.

7. Suppose a mouse emits a soft, high-frequency squeak. Which kinds of people are least likely to hear the squeak?

Answer

7. Obviously, the people farthest from the mouse are least likely to hear it. In addition, older people would be less likely to hear the squeak because of declining ability to hear high frequencies. Another group unlikely to hear the squeak are those who had damaged their hearing, such as by repeated exposure to loud noises.

Probably you have heard of people who can listen to a note and identify its pitch by name: "Oh, that's a C-sharp." This ability, known as absolute pitch, generally depends on early music training. Not everyone with musical training develops absolute pitch, but almost everyone with absolute pitch has had musical training (Athos et al., 2007). Many musicians have the ability in part. A violinist might show absolute pitch for notes played on a violin but not for notes on other instruments (Wong & Wong, 2014).

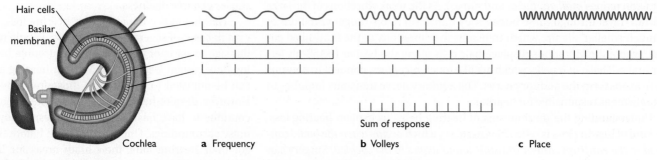

▲ **Figure 4.21** **(a)** At low frequencies, hair cells along the basilar membrane produce impulses in synchrony with the sound waves. **(b)** At medium frequencies, different cells produce impulses in synchrony with different sound waves, but a volley (group) produces one or more impulses for each wave. **(c)** At high frequencies, only one point along the basilar membrane vibrates.

Absolute pitch is more widespread among people who speak tonal languages, such as Vietnamese and Mandarin Chinese, in which children learn from the start to pay close attention to the pitch of a word (Deutsch, Henthorn, Marvin, & Xu, 2006). For example, in Mandarin Chinese, dá (with a rising tone) means dozen, and dà (with a falling tone) means big.

If you are amazed by people with absolute pitch, your own ability to recognize (though not name) a specific pitch might surprise you. In one study, 48 college students with no special talent or training listened to 5-second segments from television theme songs, played in their normal key or a slightly higher or lower key. The students usually chose the correct version, but only of programs they had watched (Schellenberg & Trehub, 2003). That is, they remembered the familiar pitches. Children as young as four years old show this ability (Jakubowski, Müllensiefen, & Stewart, 2017).

People who are said to be "tone-deaf" are not completely tone-deaf, and if they were, they could not understand speech. However, they do not detect a wrong note in a melody, and they have trouble inferring someone's mood from tone of voice (Thompson, Marin, & Stewart, 2012). The problem is not impaired pitch hearing, but impaired pitch memory, because of weaker than average connections between the auditory cortex and the frontal cortex (Norman-Haignere et al., 2016; Tillmann, Leveque, Fornoni, Abouy, & Caclin, 2016). If you do an Internet search for "amusia test," you can find a quick way to test yourself or your friends for tone-deafness.

Localizing Sounds

What you hear is in your ear, but you experience the sound as "out there," and you can generally estimate its place of origin. Many blind people make clicks or other sounds and find their way around by localizing the echoes. With practice, sighted people can do the same (Flanagin et al., 2017). What cues are available for localizing sounds?

The auditory system determines the direction of a sound source by comparing the messages from the two ears. When a sound comes from the front, the messages reach the two ears simultaneously at equal intensity. When it comes from the side, it reaches one ear sooner and more intensely than the other (see ▶ Figure 4.22). The timing is important for localizing low-frequency sounds. Intensity helps us localize high-frequency sounds.

You also detect the approximate distance of sound sources. If a sound grows louder, you interpret it as coming closer. If two sounds differ in pitch, you assume the higher frequency tone is closer. (Low-frequency tones carry better over distance, so if you hear a high-frequency tone, its source is probably close.) However, loudness and frequency tell you only the *relative* distances, not *absolute* distances. The only cue for absolute distance is the amount of reverberation (Mershon & King, 1975). In a closed room, you first hear the sound waves coming directly from the source and then the waves that reflected off the walls, floor, ceiling, or other objects. If you hear many echoes, you judge the source of the sound to be far away. It is hard to localize sound sources in a noisy room where echoes are hard to hear (McMurtry & Mershon, 1985).

You also make inferences about a sound's location based on visual information. When it appears that a ventriloquist's dummy is talking, you localize the sound source as the dummy, and your auditory cortex also responds as if the sound came from there (Callan, Callan, & Ando, 2015).

▲ **Figure 4.22** The ear located closest to the sound receives the sound waves first. That cue is important for localizing low-frequency sounds.

Answer

8. Sounds will be louder in the left ear than in the right, and therefore, they may seem to be coming from the left side even when they aren't. However, a sound from the right will still strike the right ear before the left, so time of arrival at the two ears will compete against the relative loudness. Accuracy will probably be better for low-frequency sounds that we localize by timing.

The Vestibular Sense

Imagine yourself riding a roller coaster. The up and down, and back and forth sensations you feel come from structures called *vestibules* in the inner ear on each side of your head. The **vestibular sense** detects *the tilt and acceleration of the head, and the orientation of the head with respect to gravity*. It plays a key role in posture and balance. Intense vestibular sensations are responsible for motion sickness.

The vestibular sense also enables you to keep your eyes fixated on a target as your head moves. When you walk down the street, you can keep your eyes fixated on a street sign, even though your head is bobbing up and down. The vestibular sense detects your head movements and compensates with eye movements.

8. If someone who ordinarily uses hearing aids in both ears currently wears one in only the left ear, what will be the effect on sound localization?

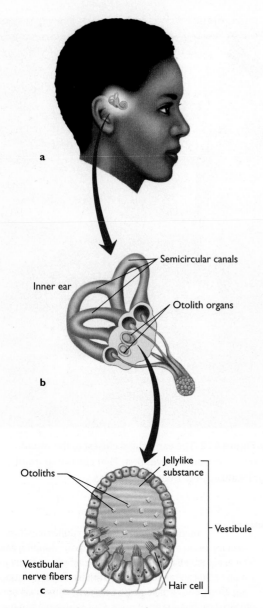

vestibular sense, people report blurry vision while they are walking. To read street signs, they must come to a stop.

The vestibular system consists of three semicircular canals oriented in different directions, and two otolith organs (see ◄ **Figure 4.23b**). The *semicircular canals* are lined with hair cells and filled with a jellylike substance. When the body accelerates in any direction, the jellylike substance in the corresponding semicircular canal pushes against the hair cells, which send messages to the brain. The *otolith organs* shown in ◄ **Figure 4.23b** also contain hair cells (see ◄ **Figure 4.23c**), which lie next to the *otoliths* (calcium carbonate particles). Depending on which way the head tilts, the particles excite different sets of hair cells. The otolith organs report the direction of gravity and therefore which way is up.

For astronauts in the zero-gravity environment of outer space, the vestibular sense cannot identify up or down. Instead, astronauts learn to rely on visual signals, such as the walls of the ship (Lackner, 1993).

The Cutaneous Senses

What we commonly think of as touch consists of several partly independent senses: pressure on the skin, warmth, cold, pain, itch, vibration, movement across the skin, and stretch of the skin. These sensations depend on several kinds of receptors, as ▼ **Figure 4.24** shows (Iggo & Andres, 1982). A pinprick on the skin feels different from a light touch, and both feel different from a burn because each excites different receptors. Collectively, these sensations are known as the **cutaneous senses**, meaning the *skin senses.* They are also known as the *somatosensory system,* meaning *body-sensory system.*

Have you ever wondered about the sensation of itch? Is it a kind of touch, pain, or what? Itch depends on a special type of receptor that sends messages through a special path in the spinal cord (Y.-G. Sun et al., 2009). Itch is unlike pain. In fact, pain inhibits itch (Andrew & Craig, 2001). If a dentist anesthetizes your mouth for dental surgery, the itch receptors recover from the anesthesia before the pain and touch receptors do. If you scratch the itchy spot at that time, you don't feel the scratch and you don't relieve the itch.

Tickle is another kind of cutaneous sensation. Most people cannot tickle themselves, at least not much, because tickle requires surprise. When you are about to touch yourself, your brain makes an anticipation response similar to the actual stimulation (Carlsson, Petrovic, Skare, Petersson, & Ingvar, 2000). The few people who do respond to tickling themselves tend to be those who often perceive their own actions as being controlled by mysterious outside forces (Lemaitre, Luyat, & Lafargue, 2016).

▲ **Figure 4.23** **(a)** Location of and **(b)** structures of the vestibule. **(c)** Moving your head or body displaces hair cells that report the tilt of your head and the direction and acceleration of movement.

To illustrate, try to read this page while you jiggle the book up and down or side to side, keeping your head steady. Then hold the book steady and move your head up and down and from side to side. You probably find it much easier to read when you are moving your head than when you are jiggling the book. The reason is that your vestibular sense keeps your eyes fixated on the print during head movements, but it cannot compensate for movements of the book. After damage to the

try it your self

Pain

The experience of pain mixes body sensation and emotional reaction, which depend on different brain areas (Corder et al., 2019; Fernandez & Turk, 1992). An area in the parietal cortex responds to the sensation itself. The brain area responsive to the emotional aspect—the *anterior cingulate cortex*—also responds to the emotional pain of watching someone else get hurt (Singer et al., 2004). How much it responds depends on who is getting hurt. Your brain shows less emotional impact from watching pain delivered to someone you regard as one of your competitors (Richins, Barreto, Karl, & Lawrence, 2019).

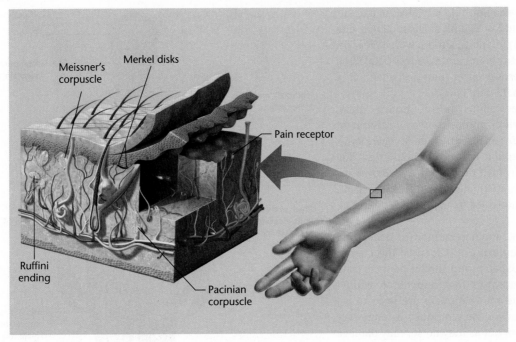

▲ Figure 4.24 Cutaneous sensation is the product of many kinds of receptors, each sensitive to a particular kind of information.

People often talk of "hurt feelings." Is that just a saying, or is social distress really like pain? It is like pain in two ways. First, when someone feels rejected by others, activity increases in the anterior cingulate gyrus, the area responsive to the emotional aspect of pain (Eisenberger, Lieberman, & Williams, 2003). More intense emotional distress, such as that from a difficult romantic breakup, activates that emotional area and also the area associated with the sensation of pain itself (Kross, Berman, Mischel, Smith, & Wager, 2011). Second, you can relieve hurt feelings by taking acetaminophen (Tylenol®)! College students kept a daily log of hurt feelings while taking either acetaminophen or a placebo. Those taking acetaminophen reported fewer hurt feelings, and the frequency declined as they continued taking the drug (De Wall et al., 2010). (So, the next time you hurt people's feelings, don't apologize. Just hand them a pill.) Unfortunately, taking acetaminophen also decreases reports of pleasant experiences (Durso, Luttrell, & Way, 2015). Apparently, it decreases overall emotional reactivity.

The Gate Theory of Pain

If you visit a physician because of pain and the physician tells you the problem is nothing to worry about, suddenly the pain starts to subside. Have you ever had such an experience?

Recall the term *placebo*: A placebo is a drug or other procedure with no important effects beyond those that result from people's expectations. Placebos have little effect on most medical conditions, with two exceptions—pain and depression (Hróbjartsson & Gøtzsche, 2001; Wager et al., 2007). In one experiment, college students had a smelly brownish liquid rubbed onto one finger. It was in fact a placebo, but they were told it was a painkiller. Then they were painfully pinched on that finger and a finger of the other hand. They consistently reported less pain on the finger with the placebo (Montgomery & Kirsch, 1996). How placebos work is unclear, but these results eliminate mere relaxation as an explanation, because relaxation would affect both hands equally. Oddly, many people experience pain relief from placebos even when they know they are receiving placebos (Rosenzweig, 2016).

Because of observations such as these, Ronald Melzack and P. D. Wall (1965) proposed the gate theory of pain, the idea that *pain messages must pass through a gate, presumably in the spinal cord, that can block the messages.* That is, other kinds of input can close the gate, preventing pain messages from reaching the brain. If you injure yourself, rubbing the surrounding skin sends inhibitory messages to the spinal cord, closing the pain gates. Pleasant or distracting events also send inhibitory messages. In contrast, a barrage of painful stimuli not only cause pain at the time, but they also increase responses to similar stimuli in the future (Walters, 2009); (see **▼ Figure 4.25**).

Ways to Decrease Pain

Some people are completely insensitive to pain. Before you start to envy them, consider this: They often burn themselves by picking up hot objects, scald their tongues on hot coffee, cut themselves without realizing it, or bite off the tip of the tongue. Many of them die young (Cox et al., 2006).

Although we shouldn't rid ourselves of pain altogether, we would like to limit it. Distraction is one way. Postsurgical patients in a room with a pleasant view complain less about pain, take less painkilling medicine, and recover faster than do patients in a windowless room (Ulrich, 1984).

Several medications also reduce pain. **Endorphins** are *neurotransmitters that weaken pain sensations* (Pert & Snyder, 1973; see ▼ Figure 4.26). The term *endorphin* is a combination of the terms *endogenous* (self-produced) and *morphine*. Morphine, which stimulates endorphin synapses, has long been known for its ability to inhibit dull, lingering pains.

Paradoxically, another method of decreasing pain begins by inducing it. **Capsaicin**, the chemical that makes jalapeños and similar peppers taste hot, *stimulates receptors that respond to painful heat*. Skin creams with capsaicin are used to relieve aching muscles. They produce a temporary burning sensation, but as they do so, they damage some of the receptors responsible for heat and pain. Application of capsaicin patches for a few hours can decrease pain for days, with results that vary among individuals (Lo Vecchio, Andersen, & Arendt-Nielsen, 2018).

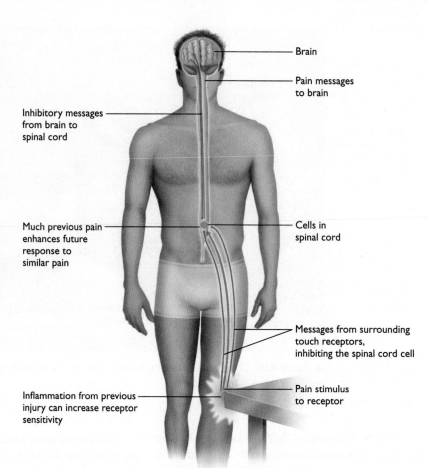

▲ Figure 4.25 Pain messages from the skin are relayed from the spinal cord to the brain. According to the gate theory of pain, spinal cord cells can block or enhance the signal. Green lines indicate axons with excitatory inputs; red lines indicate axons with inhibitory inputs.

9. A hypnotic suggestion to feel no pain decreases the emotional response to pain more than the sensation. What can we infer about how it affects the brain?

Answer

9. Hypnosis affects the anterior cingulate gyrus, which responds to emotional information, more than it affects the somatosensory cortex.

Phantom Limbs

Some people report *continuing pain or other sensations in a limb after it has been amputated*. This phenomenon, known as a **phantom limb**, might last days, weeks, or years after the amputation (Ramachandran & Hirstein, 1998). Physicians and psychologists long wondered about the cause, until research in the 1990s found how an amputation can change the brain.

Figure 3.17 showed the input from various body areas to the somatosensory cortex. ▼ Figure 4.27a repeats part of that illustration. Part b shows what happens immediately after a hand amputation: The hand

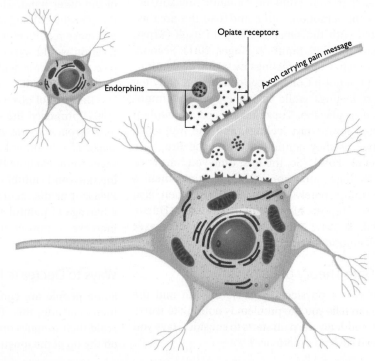

▲ Figure 4.26 Endorphins block the release of a transmitter conveying pain sensations. Opiates imitate the effects of endorphins.

area of the cortex becomes inactive because the axons from the hand are inactive. As time passes, axons from the face, which ordinarily excite only the face area of the cortex, strengthen connections to the nearby hand area of the cortex (see ▼ Figure 4.27c). From then on, stimulation of the face continues to excite the face area but now also excites the hand area. When the axons from the face area stimulate the hand area, they produce a hand experience—that is, a phantom limb (Flor et al., 1995; Ramachandran & Blakeslee, 1998).

It is possible to relieve phantom sensations: People who learn to use an artificial hand or limb lose their phantoms (Lotze et al., 1999). The relevant areas of the cortex start reacting to the artificial limb, and this sensation displaces the abnormal sensations (Di Pino, Guglielmelli, & Rossini, 2009).

vgajic/E+/Getty Images

After someone with an amputation gains experience using an artificial limb, phantom limb sensations fade or disappear.

concept check

10. A phantom hand sensation would be strongest after touch to what body part?

Answer

10. The phantom hand sensation would be strongest when something touches the face.

The Chemical Senses

Humans' heavy reliance on vision and hearing is unusual in the animal kingdom. Most animals depend mainly on taste and smell to find food and mates. We humans often overlook the importance of these sensations.

Taste

The sense of **taste**, which *detects chemicals on the tongue,* serves just one function: It governs eating and drinking. The *taste receptors are* in the **taste buds,** *located in the folds on the surface of the tongue,* mainly along the edge of the tongue in adults (see ▼ Figure 4.28). Children's taste buds are more widely distributed.

Try this demonstration (based on Bartoshuk, 1991): Soak something small (the tip of a cotton swab will do) in sugar water, salt water, or vinegar. Touch it to the center of your tongue, not too far back. You will feel it but taste nothing. Slowly move the soaked substance toward the side or front of your tongue. Suddenly, you taste it. If you go in the other direction (first touching the side of the tongue and then moving toward the center), you will continue to taste

try it yourself

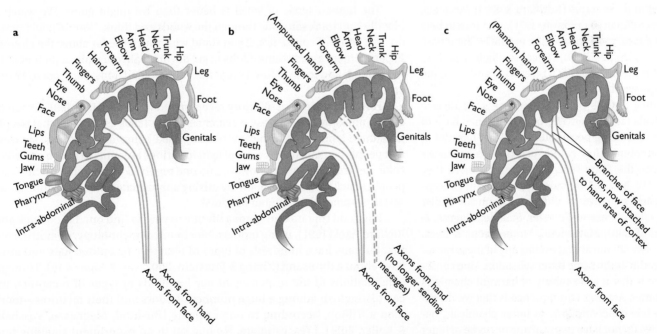

▲ **Figure 4.27** **(a)** Each area of the somatosensory cortex gets input from a different body area. **(b)** If one body part, such as the hand, is amputated, its area of the cortex no longer gets its normal input. **(c)** Axons from a neighboring area branch out to excite the vacated area. Now, stimulation of the face excites both the face area and the hand area, producing both a facial sensation and a phantom hand sensation.

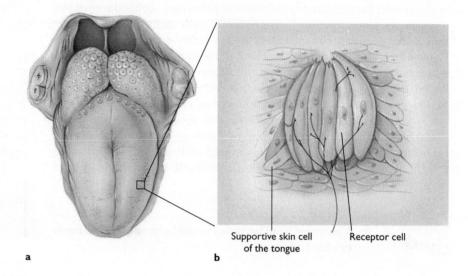

▶ **Figure 4.28** (a) Taste buds, which react to chemicals dissolved in saliva, are located along the edge of the tongue in adult humans. (b) A cross section through part of the surface of the tongue showing taste buds.

Supportive skin cell of the tongue   Receptor cell

a   b

the substance even at the center of your tongue. The explanation is that your taste buds do not tell you *where* you taste something. When you stimulate touch receptors on your tongue, your brain interprets the taste perception as coming from wherever it feels touch.

Types of Taste Receptors

Traditionally, Western cultures have talked about four primary tastes: sweet, sour, salty, and bitter. However, the taste of monosodium glutamate (MSG), common in Asian cuisines and similar to the taste of unsalted chicken soup, cannot be described in these terms (Kurihara & Kashiwayanagi, 1998; Schiffman & Erickson, 1971), and researchers found a taste receptor specific to MSG (Chaudhari, Landin, & Roper, 2000). Because English had no word for the taste of MSG, researchers adopted the Japanese word *umami.*

Bitter taste is puzzling because such diverse chemicals taste bitter. The only thing they have in common is being poisonous or at least harmful in large amounts. How could such diverse chemicals all excite the same receptor? The answer is, they don't. We have 25 or more types of bitter receptors, each sensitive to different chemicals (Adler et al., 2000; Behrens, Foerster, Staehler, Raguse, & Meyerhof, 2007; Matsunami, Montmayeur, & Buck, 2000). Any chemical that excites any of these receptors produces the same bitter sensation. One consequence is that a wide variety of harmful chemicals taste bitter. Another consequence is that we do not detect low concentrations of bitter chemicals, because we do not have many of any one type of bitter receptor.

How do we account for the taste of water? It is not just a texture, because the sensation of water on the tongue differs from the sensation of water on the skin, where the texture is the same. Water produces a special pattern of response in the sourness receptors. Animals that lack sourness receptors (for genetic or other reasons) fail to distinguish between water and any oil with a similar texture (Zocchi, Wennemuth, & Oka, 2017).

Smell

The *sense of smell* is known as **olfaction**. The olfactory receptors, located on the mucous membrane in the rear air passages of the nose (see ▼ **Figure 4.29**), detect airborne molecules. The axons of the olfactory receptors form the olfactory tract, which extends to the olfactory bulbs at the base of the brain.

The human sense of smell is better than we might guess. We watch a bloodhound track someone through the woods and think, "Wow, I could never do that." Well, of course not, if you stand with your nose far above the ground! Experimenters asked young adults to get down on all fours, touch their nose to the ground, and try to follow a scent trail, blindfolded. Most succeeded (Porter et al., 2007).

How many kinds of olfactory receptors do we have? Until 1991, researchers did not know. In contrast, researchers in the 1800s established that people have three kinds of color receptors. They used behavioral methods, showing that people can mix three colors of light in various amounts to match any other color. Regarding olfaction, however, no one reported comparable studies. Can people match all possible odors by mixing appropriate amounts of three, four, seven, or some other number of odors?

It is good that no one spent a lifetime trying to find out. Linda Buck and Richard Axel (1991), using modern biochemical technology, demonstrated that humans have hundreds of types of olfactory receptors. Rats and mice have about a thousand (Zhang & Firestein, 2002; see ▼ **Figure 4.30**). Through combinations of the responses of our hundreds of types of receptors, we can distinguish among a huge number of odors and their mixtures—more than a trillion, according to one estimate (Bushdid, Magnasco, Vosshall, & Keller, 2014). (Yes, estimate. No one sat in an experiment smelling that many odors.)

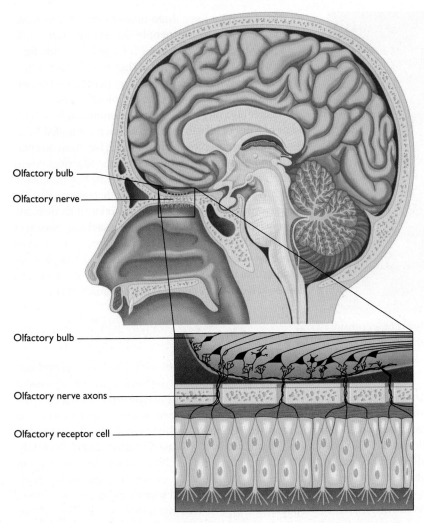

▲ **Figure 4.29** The olfactory receptor cells lining the nasal cavity send information to the olfactory bulb in the brain.

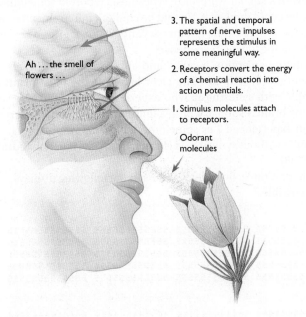

3. The spatial and temporal pattern of nerve impulses represents the stimulus in some meaningful way.

2. Receptors convert the energy of a chemical reaction into action potentials.

1. Stimulus molecules attach to receptors.

Ah ... the smell of flowers ...

Odorant molecules

▲ **Figure 4.30** Olfaction, like any other sensory system, converts physical energy into a complex pattern of brain activity.

Many odors produce strong emotional responses. People who lose the sense of smell lose much of their joy in life and often become depressed (Herz, 2007). Our emotional reactions to odors are not built-in, however. Americans experience wintergreen odor in association with candy. In Britain, wintergreen is often included in rub-on pain medications. Guess what: Most Americans like the odor, and British people do not. One woman reported hating the smell of roses because she first smelled them at her mother's funeral. Another woman reported liking the smell of skunk (from a distance) because it reminded her of a joyful trip through the country when she was a child (Herz, 2007).

Suppose I ask you to smell something labeled "odor of Parmesan cheese." You say you like it. Then I say, "Oops, I'm sorry, I think it was mislabeled. Maybe it was the smell of vomit." Oh, no! Now you hate the smell—the same smell! "Wait, my mistake. I was right the first time. It really is Parmesan." Now do you like it or not? Your emotional reaction to an odor depends on what you think it is (Herz & von Clef, 2001).

Olfaction serves important social functions in most nonhuman mammals. In many species, individuals use olfaction to recognize one another and to identify when a female is sexually receptive. Most humans prefer *not* to recognize one another by smell. The deodorant and perfume industries exist for the sole purpose of removing and covering up human odors. But olfaction is more important to our social behavior than we generally acknowledge. Although results vary among individuals, many can identify whether a body odor has come from a young or old person, male or female, healthy or sick, frightened or calm (de Groot, Semin, & Smeets, 2017). The smell of a sweaty woman—especially a woman near her time of ovulation—causes a heterosexual man to increase his testosterone secretion (Miller & Maner, 2010; Savic, Berglund, & Lindström, 2005). Something in his brain says, "Ooh. I smell a sweaty woman. I bet she is *hot*!" The smell of a sweaty man does not have a comparable effect on women (Wyart et al., 2007). In fact, it causes a woman to increase her secretion of stress hormones! Something in her brain says, "I smell a sweaty man. Uh, oh."

Imagine you are exposed to just the smells of several people, and you are to rate each one's desirability as a potential romantic partner. You can make certain surmises from body odor, including a person's health, because people smell better when they are healthy than when ill (Olsson et al., 2014). Also, most people give a low rating to anyone who smells too much like their own relatives (Havlicek & Roberts, 2009). Women show this tendency more strongly if they are capable of

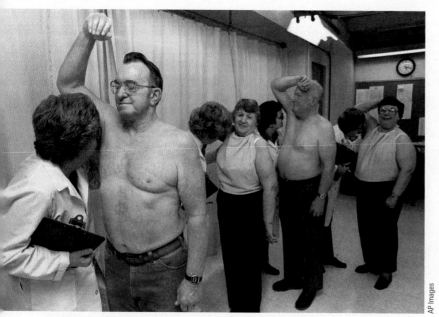

Professional deodorant tester: That's a career option you probably never considered. U.S. industries spend millions of dollars to eliminate the kinds of personal odors that are essential to other mammalian species.

Some people have three times as many taste buds on the tongue as other people do (Hayes, Bartoshuk, Kidd, & Duffy, 2008). Those with more taste buds have more intense taste experiences. They tend to have stronger food likes and dislikes than other people, and generally dislike strong-tasting or highly spiced foods.

People also vary in olfaction. Remember, we have hundreds of types of olfactory receptors, each controlled by its own gene. Many of these genes differ slightly from one person to another, and as a result, a particular odor might seem stronger or weaker to you than to someone else (Mainland et al., 2014). People vary in olfaction for other reasons also. On average, women are more sensitive to odors than men are, in every culture that researchers have tested (e.g., Saxton et al., 2014). Odor sensitivity declines in old age, for some odors more than others (Seow, Ong, & Huang, 2016). Sharply deteriorating olfaction is often an early symptom of Alzheimer's disease or Parkinson's disease (Doty & Kamath, 2014).

becoming pregnant, and less if they are taking contraceptive pills (Roberts, Gosling, Carter, & Petrie, 2008). Avoiding a potential mate who smells like your relatives is a good way to avoid inbreeding, and to provide your child with a variety of genes for immunities.

Synesthesia

We end our tour of the senses with synesthesia, a *condition in which a stimulus of one type, such as sound, also elicits another experience, such as color*. The most common type is perceiving each letter or number as a color, such as seeing E as green or red. One man who was red-green color deficient reported seeing synesthetic colors that he never saw in real life. He called them "Martian colors" (Ramachandran, 2003). Evidently, although his retina could not send messages for those colors, the brain was organized to perceive them. Other types of synesthesia are less common but fascinating. One woman experiences most words and sounds as mouth sensations. As she listens, reads, or speaks, she experiences one taste or smell after another, and occasionally other mouth sensations such as feeling her mouth as full of marbles or feeling as if she just swallowed a button (Colizoli, Murre, & Rouw, 2013). A man with a similar word-taste synesthesia reported sometimes tasting a word before he could think of it. He said he couldn't quite remember what the word was, but it tasted like tuna (Simner & Ward, 2006). It gives a new meaning to the term "tip of the tongue" experience!

A synesthetic perception is quick and automatic. In one study, people listened to sentences such as, "The clear lake was the most beautiful hue of 7." For people with synesthesia who experienced 7 as blue, this sentence evoked a strong brain response within a tenth of a second after hearing the 7. For those who experienced 7 as some other color, the response was weaker, as it is for people without synesthesia (Brang, Edwards, Ramachandran, & Coulson, 2008).

For another example, find the 2s and As in the following displays as quickly as possible.

concept check

11. **Is it possible for someone to taste all types of bitter chemicals except one? Why or why not?**

12. **What accounts for people's emotional responses to smells?**

Answers

11. Yes… well, more likely the person would fail to taste a family of similar chemicals, rather than precisely one chemical. Because we have 25 or more bitter receptors, a mutation could delete one of them without affecting the others. 12. Emotional responses to smells are mostly learned by association with other events.

Individual Differences in Taste and Smell

Suppose we ask many people to rate how strong something tastes or smells, and they all give it about the same rating. We might assume that they all had the same experience, but this conclusion would be wrong. When you rate a taste as "very strong," you mean it is strong compared to your other experiences. You cannot compare it to someone else's experiences.

try it yourself

```
555555555555  555555555555  555555555555  5555555525555
555555555555  555555555525  555555555555  5555555555555
555555555555  555555555555  555255555555  5555555555555
552555555555  555555555555  555555555555  5555555555555
555555555555  555555555555  555555555555  5555555555555

44444444444  44444444444  44444444444  444444444444
44444444444  44A444444444  44444444444  444444444444
44444A444444  44444444444  44444444444  4444444A44444
44444444444  44444444444  44444444444  444444444444
44444444444  44444444444  444444444A44  444444444444
```

One person with synesthesia found it just as hard as anyone else to find the As among 4s because both of them looked red to her. However, because 2s look violet and 5s look yellow to her, she was quicker than average to find the 2s, almost as if—but not quite as if—the displays had been printed like this (Laeng, Svartdal, & Oelmann, 2004):

```
555555555555  555555555555  555555555555  5555555255555
555555555555  5555555555552  555555555555  555555555555
555555555555  555555555555  5552555555555  555555555555
5525555555555  555555555555  5555555555555  555555555555
555555555555  555555555555  555555555555  555555555555
```

These results are surprising. The colors helped her find the 2s, but somehow her brain had to know the 2s from the 5s *before* it could produce the color experiences.

In most cases synesthesia develops gradually during childhood. Many 6- and 7-year-old children show some degree of synesthesia. By the time they are a few years older, some have lost it, whereas others have developed a stronger, more consistent experience (Simner & Bain, 2013). Synesthesia tends to run in families (Barnett et al., 2008), and curiously it often occurs in the same families as people with absolute pitch (Gregerson et al., 2013). In a few families, synesthesia has been linked to genes that control the growth of axons (Tilot et al., 2018).

In some cases we can identify a link to a relevant experience. Ten people are known to have developed letter-color synesthesia in which the colors matched the refrigerator magnets they had played with as children, such as red A, yellow C, and green D (Witthoft & Winawer, 2013). Why these particular children developed synesthesia and others did not, we do not know.

11. **What evidence shows that synesthesia is not just pretended or imagined?**

Answer

13. People who see 2 as one color and 5 as a different color can find 2s among a group of 5s more easily than other people do.

Sensory Systems

The world as experienced by a bat (which hears frequencies up to 100,000 Hz) or a mouse (which depends on its whiskers to explore the world) is in many ways a different world from the one that you experience. The function of the senses is not to tell you about everything in the world but to alert you to the information you are most likely to use, given your human way of life.

Summary

- *Hearing.* Sounds vary in pitch, loudness, and timbre. (page 108)
- *Pitch.* For sounds up to about 100 Hz, we identify pitch by the frequency of vibrations of hair cells in the ears. At higher frequencies, we identify pitch by volleys of responses and by the location where the hair cells vibrate. (page 110)
- *Localizing sounds.* We localize a sound source by detecting differences in the time and loudness of the sounds in the two ears. (page 111)
- *Vestibular system.* The vestibular system detects the tilt, acceleration, and orientation of the head. It enables us to keep our eyes fixated on an object while the head moves. (page 111)
- *Cutaneous receptors.* We experience many types of sensation on the skin, each dependent on different receptors. (page 112)
- *Pain.* The experience of pain has both sensory and emotional components, which occupy different brain areas. According to the gate theory, other experiences can modify or block pain input. Hurt feelings resemble physical pain, especially in their emotional aspect. (page 112)
- *Phantom limbs.* After an amputation, the corresponding portion of the somatosensory cortex stops receiving its normal input. Axons from neighboring cortical areas form branches that excite the silenced areas of cortex. When these cortical areas receive the new input, they produce a phantom sensation. (page 114)
- *Taste receptors.* People have receptors sensitive to sweet, sour, salty, bitter, and umami (MSG) tastes. We have many kinds of bitter receptors, but not many of any one kind. (page 115)
- *Olfactory receptors.* The olfactory system—the sense of smell—depends on hundreds of types of receptors. Olfaction influences our emotions and social responses more than most people realize. (page 116)
- *Individual differences.* Some people have three times as many taste buds as others do, giving them greater sensitivity to taste. People vary in their genes for olfactory receptors, influencing which odors seem stronger. (page 118)
- *Synesthesia.* Some people have consistent experiences of one sensation evoked by another. For example, they might experience particular letters or numbers as having a color. (page 118)

Key Terms

capsaicin (page 114)

cochlea (page 108)

conduction deafness (page 109)

cutaneous senses (page 112)

endorphin (page 114)

frequency principle (page 110)

gate theory (page 113)

hertz (Hz) (page 108)

loudness (page 108)

nerve deafness (page 109)

olfaction (page 116)

phantom limb (page 114)

pitch (page 108)

place principle (page 110)

sound waves (page 108)

synesthesia (page 118)

taste (page 115)

taste bud (page 115)

timbre (page 108)

vestibular sense (page 111)

volley principle (page 110)

Review Questions

1. When hair cells at one point along the basilar membrane become active, we hear a tone at 5000 Hz. What do we hear when the same hair cells double their rate of activity?
   (a) A pitch one octave higher
   (b) The same pitch as before, but louder

2. Suppose you are listening to a monaural (nonstereo) radio. Can it play sounds that you localize as coming from different directions or distances?
   (a) Yes. It can play sounds that you localize as coming from different directions (left/right) and different distances.
   (b) It can play sounds that you localize as coming from different directions (left/right), but not from different distances.
   (c) It can play sounds that you localize as coming from different distances, but not from different directions (left/right).
   (d) No. It cannot play sounds that you localize as coming from either different directions or different distances.

3. What type of deafness can surgery correct?
   (a) Conduction deafness
   (b) Nerve deafness
   (c) Either conduction deafness or nerve deafness
   (d) Neither type

4. Why is vestibular sense useless for astronauts in space?
   (a) The vestibular sense requires the head to remain motionless.
   (b) The vestibular sense depends on a difference between the two ears.
   (c) The vestibular uses gravity to detect head tilt and direction.
   (d) Astronauts have no need for the information vestibular sense would provide.

5. Are hurt feelings similar to real pain? What is the evidence?
   (a) No. Medications that reduce pain have no effect on hurt feelings.
   (b) No. Only English-speaking people use "hurt" to talk about feelings.
   (c) No. Hurt feelings are more temporary than physical pain.
   (d) Yes. Hurt feeling stimulate the same brain areas that pain does.

6. Psychologist Linda Bartoshuk recommends candies containing moderate amounts of jalapeño peppers as a treatment for pain in the mouth. Why?
   (a) Jalapeños excite pleasure centers in the brain.
   (b) Jalapeños decrease overall brain activity.
   (c) After the immediate heat experience, pain receptors become less responsive.
   (d) Jalapeños distract attention from other pain.

7. Which of the following is responsible for the phantom limb experience?
   (a) Crossed connections from the normal limb on the other side of the body
   (b) Anxiety and other psychological reactions to the amputation
   (c) Irritation at the stump where the amputation took place
   (d) Reorganization of connections in the brain

8. What is responsible for the taste of water?
   (a) The texture of the sensation
   (b) A lack of response by all taste receptors
   (c) A pattern of response in the sourness receptors
   (d) A pattern of response in the sweetness receptors

9. Why do so many chemicals taste bitter?
   (a) All bitter chemicals have a similar chemical structure.
   (b) We have many types of bitter receptors.
   (c) Bitter chemicals produce a special texture on the mouth.
   (d) Enzymes in the mouth convert all bitter chemicals into the same metabolite.

10. Of people with letter-color synesthesia, why do many see red as A, yellow as C, and green as D?
    (a) Red uses the same neurotransmitter as A, yellow as C, and so forth.
    (b) They learned to copy one child who started with those associations.
    (c) The brain areas for those colors are near the brain areas for those letters.
    (d) As children, they played with refrigerator magnets of those colors.

Answers: 1b, 2c, 3a, 4c, 5d, 6c, 7d, 8c, 9b, 10d.

Christoph Hetzmannseder/Moment/Getty Images

After studying this module, you should be able to:

1. Explain why it is difficult to specify the minimum detectable stimulus.

2. List what subliminal perception can and cannot do.

3. Discuss the evidence for feature detectors.

4. Discuss the evidence Gestalt psychologists present to show limitations of the feature detector approach.

5. List factors that enable us to perceive depth.

6. Give an example of an optical illusion and explain it.

According to a popular expression, "a picture is worth a thousand words." If so, what is a thousandth of a picture worth? One word? Perhaps not even that.

Printed photographs, such as the one on page 118, are composed of a great many dots, which you can see if you magnify the photo, as in ▼ Figure 4.31. Although one dot by itself tells us nothing, the pattern of many dots becomes a meaningful picture.

Our vision is like this all the time. Your retina includes more than a hundred million rods and cones, each of which sees one dot, but instead of dots, you perceive lines, curves, and objects. Your nervous system starts with a vast amount of information and extracts the important patterns.

Perceiving Minimal Stimuli

Some of the earliest psychological researchers tried to determine the weakest sounds, lights, and touches that people could detect, described as the *absolute threshold*. They also measured the *smallest difference that people could detect*

between one stimulus and another—the just noticeable difference (JND), the *difference threshold*. One of the first research discoveries in psychology is known as Weber's law, also known as the Weber-Fechner law: The JND or difference threshold is a constant fraction of the original stimulus. For example, if you feel two weights and you can just barely tell that 102 grams feels heavier than 100 grams, then you can also just barely tell that 204 grams is heavier than 200 grams, 306 grams is heavier than 300 grams, and so forth. You might not think this result is very exciting—I don't know, maybe you get excited easily—but it was a big deal for psychologists of the early 1900s, because it was one of the first examples of psychological discoveries through research.

However, problems arose, especially with regard to finding absolute thresholds. First, your absolute threshold depends on what you had been doing just before the test. If you had spent the last hour on the beach on a sunny day, you will be poor at detecting faint lights. If you spent the last hour listening to loud music, you will be poor at hearing soft sounds. But even if you spent the last hour in a quiet, dark room, your responses might be hard to interpret.

Sensory Thresholds and Signal Detection

Imagine a typical experiment to determine your threshold of hearing—that is, the minimum intensity that you can hear: On each trial, the experimenter presents either no tone or a faint tone, and you report hearing or not hearing something. ▼ Figure 4.32

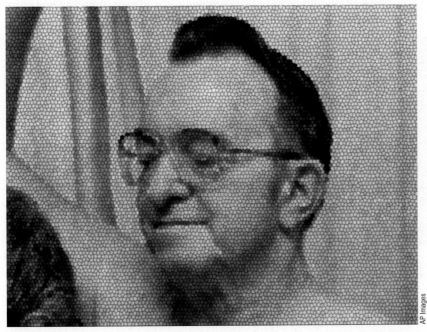

AP Images

▲ **Figure 4.31** From a photograph composed of dots, we see objects and patterns.

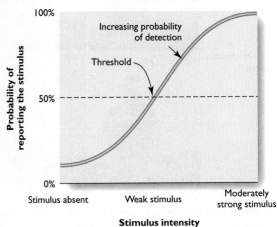

▲ **Figure 4.32** Typical results of an experiment to measure an absolute sensory threshold. No sharp boundary separates stimuli that you perceive from those you do not.

presents typical results. Notice that no sharp line separates what you can hear from what you cannot. Researchers therefore define your **absolute sensory threshold** as the *intensity at which you detect a stimulus 50 percent of the time.* However, you might sometimes report hearing a tone when none was present. We should not be surprised. Throughout the study, you have been listening to faint tones and saying "yes" when you heard almost nothing. The difference between nothing and almost nothing is slim. Still, if you report a tone when none was present, we have to be cautious in interpreting your other responses. How often were you really hearing something, and how often were you just guessing?

When you try to detect weak stimuli, you can be correct in two ways: reporting the presence of a stimulus (a "hit") and reporting its absence (a "correct rejection"). You can also be wrong in two ways: failing to detect a stimulus (a "miss") and reporting it present when it was absent (a "false alarm"). ▼ Figure 4.33 outlines these possibilities.

Signal-detection theory is the *study of people's tendencies to make hits, correct rejections, misses, and false alarms* (D. M. Green & Swets, 1966). The theory originated in engineering, where it applies to such matters as detecting radio signals in the presence of noise. Suppose you report a stimulus present on 80 percent of the trials when the stimulus is

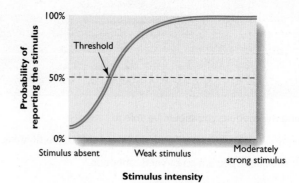

Instructions: You will receive a 10-cent reward for correctly reporting that a light is present. You will be penalized 1 cent for reporting that a light is present when it is not.

a

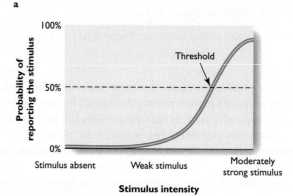

Instructions: You will receive a 1-cent reward for correctly reporting that a light is present. You will be penalized 10 cents *and* subjected to an electric shock for reporting that a light is present when it is not.

b

▲ **Figure 4.34** Results of measuring a sensory threshold with different instructions

present. That statistic is meaningless unless we also know how often you said it was present when it was not. If you also reported the stimulus present on 80 percent of trials when it was absent, then you were just guessing. If you reported it present on 70 percent of trials when it was absent, you were mostly guessing.

In a signal-detection experiment, people's responses depend on their willingness to risk misses or false alarms. When in doubt, you have to risk one or the other. Suppose you are told that you will receive a 10-cent reward whenever you correctly report that a light is present, but you will be fined 1 cent if you say "yes" when it is absent. When you are in doubt, you will guess "yes," with results like those in ▲ Figure 4.34a. Then the rules change: You receive a 1-cent reward for correctly reporting the presence of a light, but you suffer a 10-cent penalty and an electrical shock if you report a light when it was absent. Now you say "yes" only when you are more certain, with results like those in ▲ Figure 4.34b.

People become cautious about false alarms for other reasons, too. In one experiment, participants were asked to read words that flashed briefly on a screen. They performed well with ordinary words such as *river* or *peach.* For emotionally loaded words such as *penis* or *bitch,* however, they generally said they were not sure what they saw. Several explanations are possible (e.g., G. S. Blum & Barbour, 1979). One is that participants hesitate to blurt out an emotionally charged word unless they are certain they are right.

▲ **Figure 4.33** People make two kinds of correct judgments (green backgrounds) and two kinds of errors (yellow backgrounds). If you tend to say the stimulus is present when you are in doubt, you will get many hits but also many false alarms.

The signal-detection approach is important in many settings remote from the laboratory. For example, the legal system is also a signal-detection situation. A jury can be right in two ways and wrong in two ways:

	Defendant is guilty	Defendant is innocent
Jury votes "guilty"	Hit	False alarm
Jury votes "not guilty"	Miss	Correct rejection

Judges instruct juries to vote "not guilty" when in doubt. A miss, setting a guilty person free, is more acceptable than a false alarm that convicts an innocent person.

Another example is screening baggage at an airport. Screeners can err by thinking they see a weapon that is not present, or by missing one that is there. A special problem is that extremely few air travelers actually pack weapons. If you haven't seen a weapon in weeks, you expect not to see one, and you might overlook a weapon even if you do see it (Mitroff & Biggs, 2014; Wolfe, Horowitz, & Kenner, 2005). Forcing inspectors to slow down doesn't help much (Kunar, Rich, & Wolfe, 2010). It just slows down the line at airport security.

Radiologists encounter a related problem. A radiologist might scan through hundreds of X-ray scans, looking for small nodules that might indicate illness. With increasing expertise, they do find most of them, but they sometimes overlook something they hadn't expected to see. In one study, 24 expert radiologists examined chest scans of five people, looking for nodules. In the fifth one, researchers had added a drawing of a gorilla (see ▼ Figure 4.35). Although they found most of the nodules, only 4 of the 24 noticed the gorilla (Drew, Võ, & Wolfe, 2013).

14. **In what situation would the JND be the same as the absolute threshold?**

15. **Suppose that 80 percent of people with depression say they have bad dreams. What, if anything, can we conclude? Think about this problem in terms of signal detection.**

Answers

14. Sorry for the tricky question. If the original stimulus was zero, the absolute threshold would be the same as the JND.

15. We cannot conclude anything. The 80 percent figure means nothing unless we know how many people without depression also have bad dreams.

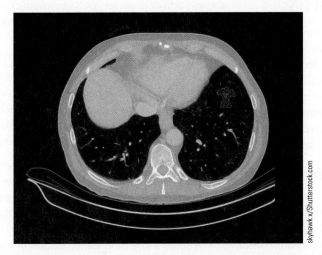

▲ **Figure 4.35** Most radiologists who were looking for lung nodules overlooked the much larger gorilla in this chest X-ray. From "The invisible gorilla strikes again: Sustained inattentional blindness in expert observers," by Drew, T., Võ, M. L.-H., & Wolfe, J. M., 2013. *Psychological Science, 24*, pp. 1848–1853.

Subliminal Perception

If you look at a brief, weak stimulus that you cannot identify consciously, might it affect you anyway? **Subliminal perception** is the phenomenon of *influence by a stimulus that it is presented so faintly or briefly that the observer does not consciously perceive it.* (*Limen* is Latin for "threshold." Thus, subliminal means "below the threshold.")

What Subliminal Perception Doesn't Do

Decades ago, claims were made that subliminal messages could control people's buying habits. For example, a theater owner might insert a single frame, "EAT POPCORN," in the middle of a film. Viewers, unaware of the message, supposedly would flock to the concession stand to buy popcorn. Many tests of this hypothesis found little or no effect (Cooper & Cooper, 2002), and the advertiser eventually admitted he had no evidence (Pratkanis, 1992).

Another claim is that certain rock-'n'-roll recordings contain "satanic" messages that were recorded backward and superimposed on the songs. Some people alleged that listeners unconsciously perceive these messages and then follow the evil advice. If you spend hours listening to rock music played backward—and I hope you have something better to do with your time—with some imagination you can think that you hear a variety of messages, regardless of whether the artists intended any such thing. However, for practical purposes it doesn't matter, because repeated studies have found that when you listen to music played forward, you cannot decipher any backward message, and backward messages have no effect on your behavior (Kreiner, Altis, & Voss, 2003; Vokey & Read, 1985).

A third unsupported claim is that "subliminal audiotapes" with faint, inaudible messages can help you improve your memory, quit smoking, lose weight, or raise your self-esteem. In one study, psychologists asked more than 200 volunteers to listen to a popular brand of audiotape. However, they intentionally mislabeled some of the self-esteem tapes as "memory tapes" and others as "self-esteem tapes." After a month of listening, most people who *thought* they were listening to self-esteem tapes said they had improved their self-esteem, and those who *thought* they were listening to memory tapes said they had improved their memory. The actual content made no difference. The improvement depended on people's expectations, not the tapes (Greenwald, Spangenberg, Pratkanis, & Eskanazi, 1991).

What Subliminal Perception Can Do

Research on subliminal perception has long been controversial, because it is difficult to be certain that participants were unaware of the supposedly subliminal stimulus. When researchers take strong precautions to be sure that participants do not detect the stimulus consciously, the subliminal effects are weak (Kouider & Dehaene, 2007).

Here are a couple examples of reported subliminal effects: If people view a face with an expression subliminally and shortly thereafter see the same face longer, with a neutral expression, they are more likely to evaluate the face favorably if the subliminal face had a pleasant expression, or to evaluate it unfavorably if the subliminal face had an unpleasant expression (Prochnow et al., 2013). In another study, young men viewed pictures for a tiny fraction of a second, followed by interfering pictures, and reported no conscious response to any of the pictures. However, some of the pictures showed naked loving couples. After those pictures, the men's brains showed increased activity in reward-related areas (Oei, Both, van Heemst, & van der Grond, 2014).

Subliminal perception effects emerge only as small changes in average performance, ordinarily in measurements taken shortly after the subliminal stimulus. The fact that such effects occur at all demonstrates unconscious influences, but we should not overestimate the strength of the effect.

16. **Suppose a popular morning television program plays a subliminal message, "Drive carefully." How could someone test the possible effectiveness?**

Answer

16. Play that message on half of all days, chosen randomly. See whether traffic accidents are less common on those mornings than on other mornings.

Perceiving and Recognizing Patterns

People become amazingly good at recognizing objects and patterns. Someday you may attend a high school reunion and see people you haven't seen in many years. Some have grown fat, bald, or changed in other ways, but you will still recognize many of them (Bruck, Cavanagh, & Ceci, 1991). Although we recognize people mostly by facial features, we attend to the hair also. Can you identify the person in ▶ Figure 4.36?

The Feature-Detector Approach

How do we recognize people or anything else? According to one explanation, we begin by breaking a stimulus into its parts. For example, when we look at a letter of the alphabet, *neurons in the visual cortex* called **feature detectors** *respond to the presence of simple features, such as lines and angles.* One neuron might detect a horizontal line, while another detects a vertical line, and so forth.

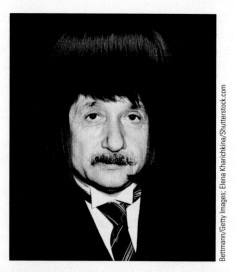

▲ **Figure 4.36** Who is this? We recognize people by hair as well as facial features. If you're not sure who it is, check answer C on page 136.

what's the evidence?

Feature Detectors

What evidence do we have for feature detectors in the brain? The evidence includes studies of laboratory animals and humans.

First Study

Hypothesis Neurons in the visual cortex of cats and monkeys respond only when light strikes the retina in a particular pattern.

Method Two pioneers in the study of the visual cortex, David Hubel and Torsten Wiesel (1981 Nobel Prize winners in physiology and medicine), inserted thin electrodes into cells of the occipital cortex of cats and monkeys and recorded the cells' activity as various light patterns struck the animals' retinas. At first, they used mere points of light that produced little response. Later they tried lines (see ▼ Figure 4.37).

Results They found that each cell responds best in the presence of a particular stimulus (Hubel & Wiesel, 1968). Some cells become active only at the sight of a vertical bar of light, others become active only for a horizontal bar or a diagonal bar, and still others react to additional patterns. In other words, the cells appear to be feature detectors.

Interpretation Hubel and Wiesel reported feature-detector neurons in cats and monkeys. If the organization of the visual cortex is similar in species as distantly related as cats and monkeys, it is likely (though not certain) to be similar in humans as well.

A second line of evidence follows this reasoning: If the human cortex has feature-detector cells, then overstimulation of certain cells should fatigue them. Afterward, someone should see an aftereffect because those cells are less active than usual. (Recall negative

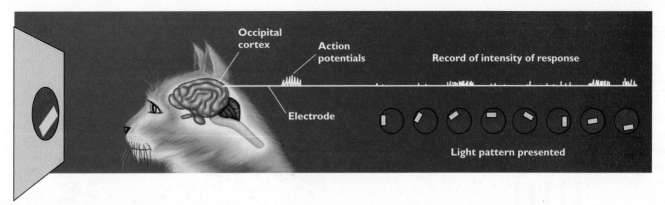

▲ **Figure 4.37** Hubel and Wiesel recorded the activity of neurons in the visual cortex. Most neurons responded vigorously only when a portion of the retina saw a bar of light oriented at a particular angle.

color afterimages, as in Figure 4.12.) An example is the **waterfall illusion:** *If you stare at a waterfall for a minute or more and then turn your eyes to nearby cliffs, the cliffs appear to flow upward.* Staring at the waterfall fatigues neurons that respond to downward motion. When they fatigue, they become inactive, while neurons responding to upward motion remain active. The result is an illusion of upward motion.

A similar effect occurs if you watch a pinwheel like the one shown below rotate clockwise for a minute or so. Spinning it gives the impression of movement toward the center. If you then look away, any object you see appears to be expanding. In fact, this illusion is so effective that it enables you to read letters in tiny print that you would otherwise be unable to read! The illusion makes them actually appear larger (Lages, Boyle, & Jenkins, 2017).

Here is another demonstration:

Second Study

Hypothesis After you stare at vertical lines, you fatigue feature detectors responding to lines of that width. If you then look at wider or narrower lines, they will appear to be even wider or narrower than they really are.

Method Cover the right half of ▶ Figure 4.38 and stare at the little rectangle in the middle of the left half for a minute or more. Do not stare at one point, but move

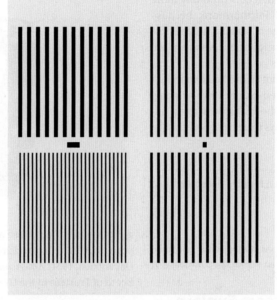

▲ **Figure 4.38** To fatigue your feature detectors and create an afterimage, follow the directions for the second study. (From Blakemore & Sutton, 1969)

your focus around within the rectangle. Then look at the square in the center of the right part of the figure and compare the spacing between the lines of the top and bottom gratings (Blakemore & Sutton, 1969).

Results What did you perceive in the right half? People generally report that the top lines look narrower and the bottom lines look wider.

Interpretation Staring at the left part of the figure fatigues neurons sensitive to wide lines in the top part of the figure and neurons sensitive to narrow lines in the bottom part. Then, when you look at lines of medium width, the fatigued cells are inactive. Cells sensitive to narrower lines dominate your perception in the top part, and those sensitive to wider lines dominate in the bottom part.

To summarize, two types of evidence support the existence of visual feature detectors: (a) The brains of other species contain cells with the properties of feature detectors, and (b) after staring at certain patterns, we see aftereffects that imply fatigue of feature-detector cells in the brain.

The research on feature detectors started an enormous amount of activity by laboratories throughout the world. Later results revised our views of what the earlier results meant. For example, even though certain neurons respond well to a single vertical line,

most respond even more strongly to a sine-wave grating of lines:

Thus, the feature that cells detect is probably more complex than just a line. Furthermore, because each cell responds to a range of stimuli, no cell provides an unambiguous message about what you see at any moment.

An important point about scientific advances: A single line of evidence—even Nobel Prize–winning evidence—seldom provides the final answer to a question. We look for multiple ways to test a hypothesis.

17. What is a feature detector?

Answer

17. A feature detector is a neuron that responds mostly to a particular visual feature, such as a straight horizontal line.

Do Feature Detectors Explain Perception?

The neurons just described are active in the early stages of visual processing. Do we simply add up the responses from various feature detectors to perceive a face?

▲ **Figure 4.39** Context determines our perception. In **(a)** you see the same item as A or H depending on context. In **(b)** the central character can appear as B or the number 13 depending on whether you read horizontally or vertically. (Part b from Kim, 1989)

▲ **Figure 4.40** Do you see an animal in each picture? If not, check answer D on page 136. (From "A puzzle picture with a new principle of concealment," by K. M. Dallenbach, 1951. *American Journal of Psychology, 54,* pp. 431–433. Copyright by the Board of Trustees of the University of Illinois.)

No, feature detectors cannot completely explain how we perceive letters, much less faces. For example, we perceive the words in ◀ **Figure 4.39a** as CAT and HAT, even though the H and A symbols are identical. Likewise, the character in the center of ◀ **Figure 4.39b** can be read as either B or 13. Perceiving a pattern depends on context, not just adding up feature detectors.

Gestalt Psychology

Your ability to perceive something in more than one way, as in Figure 4.39, is the basis of Gestalt psychology, *a field that emphasizes perception of overall patterns. Gestalt* (geh-SHTALT) is a German word that means pattern or configuration. The founders of Gestalt psychology rejected the idea of breaking down a perception into its component parts. A melody broken into individual notes is no longer a melody. Their slogan was, "The whole is different from the sum of its parts."

Gestalt psychology does not deny the importance of feature detectors. It merely insists that feature detectors are not enough. Feature detectors represent a bottom-up process, *in which tiny elements combine to produce larger items.* However, perception also includes a top-down process, *in which you apply your experience and expectations to interpret each item in context.* Here are some examples.

In either the top or bottom part of ▲ Figure 4.40, you might see only meaningless black and white patches for a while and then suddenly you

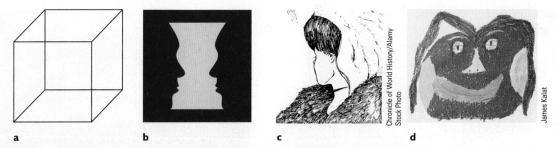

▲ Figure 4.41 Reversible figures: **(a)** The Necker cube. Which is the front face? **(b)** Faces or a vase? **(c)** An old woman or a young woman? **(d)** A face or what?

might see an animal. To perceive the animals, you separate figure and ground—that is, you distinguish the *object from the background.* Ordinarily, you make that distinction almost instantly. You become aware of the process only when it is difficult, as it is here.

▲ Figure 4.41 shows four reversible figures *that can be perceived in more than one way.* In effect, we test hypotheses: "Is this the front of the object or is that the front? Is this section the foreground or the background?" If you continue to look at a reversible figure, you start to alternate between one perception and another (Long & Toppine, 2004). Part a is called the *Necker cube,* after the psychologist who first called attention to it. Which is the front face of the cube? You can see it either way. Part b is either a vase or two profiles. Does part c show an old woman or a young woman? Almost everyone sees one or the other immediately, but many people lock into one perception so tightly that they do not see the other one. The 8-year-old girl who drew part d intended it as a face. Can you find another possibility? If you have trouble with parts c or d, check answers E, F, and G on page 136. The point of the reversible figures is that we perceive by imposing order (top-down), not just by adding up lines and points (bottom-up).

The Gestalt psychologists described principles of how we organize perceptions into meaningful wholes, as illustrated in ◄ Figure 4.42. Proximity is the *tendency to perceive objects that are close together as belonging to a group.* The objects in part a form two groups because of their proximity. The *tendency to perceive similar objects as being a group* is, quite reasonably, called similarity. In part b, we group the Xs together and the •'s together because of similarity.

When lines are interrupted, as in part c, we perceive continuation, *a filling in of the gaps.* You probably perceive this illustration as a rectangle covering the center of a very long hot dog.

When a familiar figure is interrupted, as in part d, we perceive a closure of the figure; that is, *we imagine the rest of the figure* to see something that is simple, symmetrical, or consistent with our past experience (Shimaya, 1997). For example, you probably see the following as an orange rectangle overlapping a blue diamond, although you don't really know what, if anything, is behind the rectangle:

Magicians sometimes apply the principle of closure. A magician might hold the front end of a bent spoon and the back end of another spoon in such a way that you perceive it as one straight spoon. When the back spoon drops behind a curtain, the magician reveals the front spoon, which appears to have bent by the magician's amazing powers (Ekroll, Sayim, & Wagemans, 2017).

The principle of closure resembles continuation. With a complicated pattern, however, closure deals with more information. For example, the white ovals in the first of the pictures on the next page lead you to "fill in the blanks" and think the people are naked, whereas removing the ovals shows they are not.

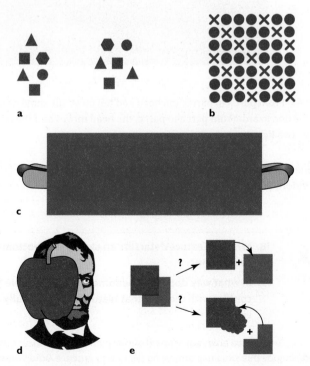

▲ Figure 4.42 Gestalt principles of **(a)** proximity, **(b)** similarity, **(c)** continuation, **(d)** closure, and **(e)** good figure.

On the left, the principle of closure suggests that this couple is naked.

Another Gestalt principle is **common fate:** *We perceive objects as part of the same group if they change or move in similar ways at the same time.* If you see two objects move in the same direction and speed, you see them as parts of the same thing, as in ▶ Figure 4.43. Also, if they grow brighter or darker together, you see them as related (Sekuler & Bennett, 2001).

Finally, when possible, we tend to perceive a **good figure**—*a simple, familiar, symmetrical figure.* Many familiar objects are geometrically simple or close to it: The sun and moon are round, tree trunks meet the ground at almost a right angle, faces and animals are nearly symmetrical, and so forth. If we can interpret something as a circle, square, or straight line, we do. In ▲ Figure 4.42e, the part on the left could represent a red square overlapping a green one or a green backward L overlapping a red object of almost any shape. We are powerfully drawn to the first interpretation because it includes "good," regular, symmetrical objects.

In ▼ Figure 4.44a, we perceive a white triangle overlapping three ovals (Singh, Hoffman, & Albert, 1999). However, if we tilt the blue objects, as in ▼ Figure 4.44b, the illusion of something on top of them disappears. We see the illusion of an overlapping object only if it is a symmetrical, good figure.

Does the principle of good figure apply only in Westernized societies, where people become familiar with squares, triangles, and so forth from an early age? Apparently not. Researchers studied the Himba, a southwest African culture with no manufactured products and few words for shapes. They noticed the difference between squares and

a

b

c

▲ **Figure 4.43** From part a to part b, the head and tail move the same way, and it appears to be one lizard. From part a to part c, the head moves and the tail doesn't, so it must be two lizards.

almost-square shapes, about as well as U.S. college students did (Biederman, Yue, & Davidoff, 2009).

18. **Why are feature detectors an example of bottom-up processing?**

19. **In what way does the phenomenon of reversible figures conflict with the idea that feature detectors fully explain vision?**

Answers

19. If vision were simply a matter of stimulating feature detectors and adding up their responses, then a given display would always produce the same perception.

18. Feature detectors start with input from the receptors, whereas top-down processing starts with expectations mediated by the prefrontal cortex.

a   b

▲ **Figure 4.44** In **(a)** we see a triangle overlapping three irregular ovals. We see it because triangles are "good figures" and symmetrical. If we tilt the ovals, as in **(b)**, the illusory triangle disappears. (From Singh, Hoffman, & Albert, 1999)

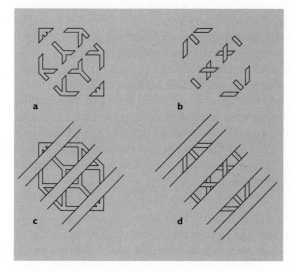

▲ **Figure 4.45** **(a)** and **(b)** appear to be arrays of flat objects. Introducing a context of overlapping lines causes a cube to emerge in **(c)** and **(d)**. (From Kanizsa, 1979)

Similarities between Vision and Hearing

The perceptual organization principles of Gestalt psychology apply to hearing also. Like reversible figures, some sounds can be heard in more than one way. You can hear a clock going "tick, tock, tick, tock" or "tock, tick, tock, tick." You can hear your windshield wipers going "dunga, dunga" or "gadung, gadung."

The Gestalt principles of continuation and closure work best when one item interrupts something else. In ▲ Figure 4.45, the context in parts c and d suggests objects partly blocking our view of a three-dimensional cube. In parts a and b, we are much less likely to see a cube. Similarly, in ▶ Figure 4.46a, we see a series of meaningless patches. In ▶ Figure 4.46b, the addition of some black glop helps us see these patches as the word *psychology* (Bregman, 1981).

a

b

▲ **Figure 4.46** Why is the word *psychology* easier to read in (b) than in (a)? (After Bregman, 1981)

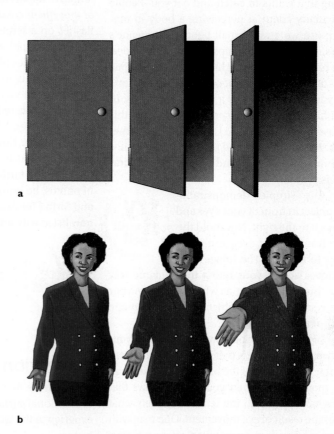

a

b

▲ **Figure 4.47** **(a)** Shape constancy: We perceive all three doors as rectangles. **(b)** Size constancy: We perceive all three hands as equal in size.

The same is true in hearing. If a speech or song is broken up by periods of silence, we do not fill in the gaps and we find the utterance hard to understand. However, if the same gaps are filled with noise, we "hear" what probably occurred during the gaps. That is, we apply continuation and closure (C. T. Miller, Dibble, & Hauser, 2001; Warren, 1970).

Perceiving Movement and Depth

As an automobile moves away from us, its image on the retina grows smaller, but we perceive it as moving, not shrinking. That perception illustrates **visual constancy**—our *tendency to perceive objects as keeping their shape, size, and color, despite distortions in the pattern reaching the retina.* ▲ Figure 4.47 shows examples of shape constancy and size constancy. Constancies depend on our familiarity with objects and on our ability to estimate distances and angles of view.

For example, we know that a door is still rectangular even when we view it from an odd angle. But to recognize that an object keeps its shape and size, we have to perceive movement or changes in distance. How do we do so?

Perception of Movement

Moving objects capture attention for a good reason. Throughout our evolutionary history, moving objects have been more likely than stationary objects to require action. A moving object might be another person, something you could catch and eat, or something that wants to catch and eat you. People are particularly adept at perceiving a body in motion. Suppose we attach small lights to someone's shoulders, elbows, hands, hips, knees, and ankles. Then we turn out all other lights so that you see just the lights on this person. As soon as the person starts to walk, you see the lights as a person in motion. In fact, you have a brain area specialized for just this task (Grossman & Blake, 2001). If you do an Internet search for Biomotion lab, and then click on "Demos and Experiments," you can find a marvelous illustration of this process.

Try this simple demonstration: Hold an object in front of your eyes and then move it to the right. Now hold the object in front of your eyes and move your eyes to the left. The image of the object moves across your retina in the same way when you move the object as when you move your eyes. Yet you perceive the object as moving in one case but not in the other. Why?

The object looks stationary when you move your eyes for two reasons. One is that the vestibular system informs the visual areas of the brain about your head and eye movements. When your brain knows that your eyes have moved to the left, it interprets what you see as the result of eye movement. One man with a rare kind of brain damage could not connect his eye movements with his perceptions. Whenever he moved his head or eyes, the world appeared to be moving. Frequently, he became dizzy and nauseated (Haarmeier, Thier, Repnow, & Petersen, 1997).

The other reason is that you perceive motion when an object moves *relative to the background* (Gibson, 1968). When you move your eyes, stationary objects move across your retina but do not change position relative to the background.

What do you perceive when an object is stationary and the background moves? In that unusual case, you *incorrectly perceive the object as moving,* a phenomenon called induced movement. When you watch clouds moving across the moon, you might perceive the clouds as stationary and the moon as moving. Induced movement is *apparent movement,* as opposed to *real movement.*

You have already read about the waterfall illusion (page 125), another example of apparent movement. Yet another is stroboscopic movement, an *illusion of movement created by a rapid succession of stationary images.* When a scene flashes on a screen, followed a split second later by a slightly different scene, you perceive objects as moving smoothly (see ◀ Figure 4.48). Motion pictures are actually a series of still photos flashed on the screen.

The ability to detect visual movement played an interesting role in the history of astronomy. In 1930, Clyde Tombaugh was searching the skies for a possible undiscovered planet beyond Neptune. He photographed each region of the sky twice, several days apart. A planet, unlike a star, moves from one photo to the next. However, how would he find a small dot that moved among all the countless unmoving dots in the sky? He put each pair of photos on a machine that would flip back and forth between one photo and the other. When he came to one pair of photos, he immediately noticed one dot moving as the machine flipped back and forth (Tombaugh, 1980). He identified that dot as Pluto, which astronomers now list as a dwarf planet (see ▼ Figure 4.49).

concept check

20. **If someone pushed your eyes to the left or right, so that they moved without your intention, what would you perceive?**

Answer

20. It would appear as if objects in the world had moved.

Perception of Depth

Although we live in a world of three dimensions, our retinas are in effect two-dimensional surfaces. Depth perception, the *perception of distance,* enables us to experience the world in three dimensions. This perception depends on several factors.

▲ **Figure 4.48** A movie consists of a series of still photographs flickering at 86,400 per hour. Here you see a series of stills spread out in space instead of time.

 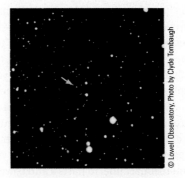

▲ **Figure 4.49** Clyde Tombaugh photographed each area of the sky twice, several days apart. Then he used a machine to flip back and forth between the two photos of each pair. When he came to one part of the sky, he noticed a dot moving between the two photos. That dot was Pluto.

One factor is retinal disparity—*the difference in the apparent position of an object as seen by the left and right retinas.* Try this: Hold a finger at arm's length. Focus on it with one eye and then the other. Note that the apparent position of your finger shifts with respect to the background. Now hold your finger closer to your face and repeat. The apparent position of your finger shifts even more. The amount of discrepancy between the two eyes is one way to gauge distance.

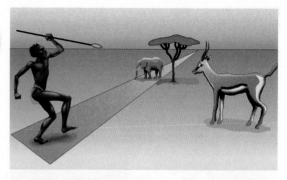

try it yourself

A second cue for depth perception is the convergence of the eyes—that is, *the degree to which they turn in to focus on a close object.* When you focus on something close, your eyes turn in, and you sense the tension of your eye muscles. The more the muscles pull, the closer the object must be.

Retinal disparity and convergence are called binocular cues because they *depend on both eyes.* Monocular cues enable you to *judge depth and distance with just one eye* or when both eyes see the same image, such as the photo in ▼ Figure 4.50. The ability to interpret depth in a picture depends on experience. For example, in ▶ Figure 4.51, does it appear to you that the hunter is aiming his spear at the antelope? When this drawing was shown to African people who had seldom or never seen drawings, many said the hunter was aiming at a baby elephant (Hudson, 1960).

Let's consider some of the monocular cues we use to perceive depth:

Object size: Other things being equal, a nearby object produces a larger image than a distant one. This cue helps only for objects of known size. For example, the backpacker in Figure 4.50 produces a larger image than do the mountains, which we know are larger. So we see the person as closer. However, the mountains in the background differ in actual as well as apparent size, so we cannot assume the ones that look bigger are closer.

Linear perspective: As parallel lines stretch out toward the horizon, they come closer together. Examine the road in Figure 4.50. At the bottom of the photo (close to the viewer), the edges of the road are far apart. At greater distances they come together.

Detail: We see nearby objects, such as the backpacker, in more detail than distant objects.

Brent Winebrenner/Lonely Planet Images/Getty Images

▲ **Figure 4.50** We judge depth and distance in a photograph using monocular cues (those that would work even with just one eye). Closer objects occupy more space on the retina (or in the photograph) than do distant objects of the same type. Nearer objects show more detail. Closer objects overlap distant objects. Objects in the foreground look sharper than objects do on the horizon.

▲ **Figure 4.51** Which animal is the hunter attacking? Many people unfamiliar with drawings and photographs said he was attacking a baby elephant. (From Hudson, 1960)

Interposition: A nearby object interrupts our view of a more distant object. For example, the tree on the right interrupts our view of the mountains, so we see that the tree is closer than the mountains.

Texture gradient: The bushes and leaves on the left of the photo are more clearly separated, whereas those toward the center look less distinct from one another. The "packed together" appearance of objects gives us another cue to their approximate distance.

Shadows: Shadows help us gauge sizes as well as locations of objects.

Accommodation: The lens of the eye *accommodates*— that is, it changes shape—to focus on nearby objects, and your brain detects that change and thereby infers the distance to an object. Accommodation could help tell you how far away the photograph itself is, although it provides no information about the relative distances of objects in the photograph.

Motion parallax: Another monocular cue helps us perceive depth while we are moving, although it does not help with a photograph. If you are walking or riding in a car and fixating at the horizon, nearby objects move rapidly across the retina, while those farther away move less. The *difference in speed of movement of images across the retina as you travel* is the principle of motion parallax. Television and film crews use this principle. If the camera moves slowly, you see closer objects move more than distant ones and you get a sense of depth.

concept check

21. Which monocular cues to depth are available in Figure 4.51?

Answer

21. Object size and linear perspective are cues that the elephant must be far away.

Optical Illusions

Vision is well adapted to understanding what we see, but special situations can fool it. An optical illusion is a *misinterpretation of a visual stimulus.* ▼ Figure 4.52 shows a few examples. If you do an Internet search for optical illusions, you can find a treasure trove of amusing and instructive examples.

Psychologists would like to explain the optical illusions as simply and parsimoniously as possible. One approach that applies to many but not all illusions pertains to mistakes of depth perception.

Depth Perception and Size Perception

As you see in ▼ Figure 4.53, an image on the retina may represent either a small, close object or a large, distant object. If you know the size or the distance, you can estimate the other one. However, if you misjudge size or distance, you will be wrong about the other also.

Watch what happens when you take a single image and change its apparent distance: Stare at Figure 4.12 again to form a negative afterimage. Examine the afterimage while looking at a sheet of paper. As you move the paper backward and forward, you can change the apparent size.

The world provides many cues about the size and distance of objects, but not always for objects in the sky. If you see an unfamiliar object in the sky, you might misjudge its distance, and if so, you will also misjudge its size and speed. For example, if you see an odd-looking small object floating by in the sky but you interpret it as far away, you could easily think you are seeing a large UFO traveling at an impossible speed.

Many optical illusions occur based on misjudging distance. ▼ Figure 4.54a shows people in the Ames room (named for its designer, Adelbert Ames). The room looks like a normal rectangular room, but one corner is actually much closer than the other. If we eliminated all the background cues, we would correctly

If you were a passenger on this train looking toward the horizon, the ground beside the tracks would appear to pass by more quickly than more distant parts of the landscape. In this photo's version of motion parallax, the ground is blurred and more distant objects are crisp.

© Steve McCurry/Magnum Photos

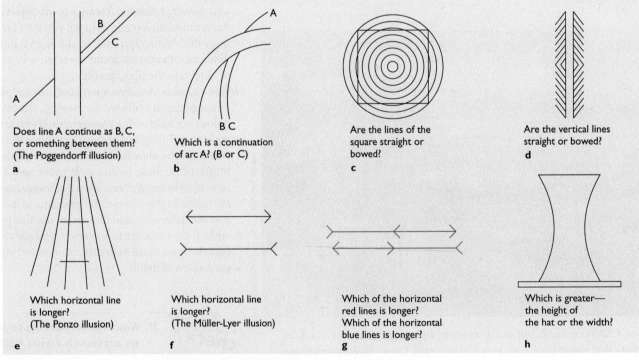

Does line A continue as B, C, or something between them? (The Poggendorff illusion)
a

Which is a continuation of arc A? (B or C)
b

Are the lines of the square straight or bowed?
c

Are the vertical lines straight or bowed?
d

Which horizontal line is longer? (The Ponzo illusion)
e

Which horizontal line is longer? (The Müller-Lyer illusion)
f

Which of the horizontal red lines is longer? Which of the horizontal blue lines is longer?
g

Which is greater— the height of the hat or the width?
h

▲ **Figure 4.52** These geometric figures illustrate optical illusions. Answers (which you are invited to check with ruler and compass): **(a)** B, **(b)** B, **(c)** straight, **(d)** straight, **(e)** equal, **(f)** equal, **(g)** equal, **(h)** equal.

▲ **Figure 4.53** No, it's not a bird on steroids. This night heron was close to the camera. If you misjudge the distance to something, you misjudge its size.

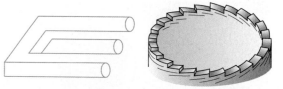

▲ **Figure 4.55** These two-dimensional drawings puzzle us because we try to interpret them as three-dimensional objects.

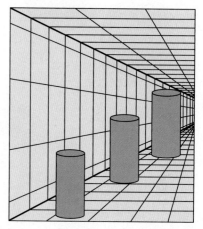

▲ **Figure 4.56** The cylinder on the right seems larger because the context makes it appear farther away.

perceive the woman as being about the same size as the man, and farther away. However, the apparently rectangular room provides such misleading cues to distance that the man appears to be unrealistically tall.

Many two-dimensional drawings offer misleading depth cues. Because of your long experience with photos and drawings, you interpret most drawings as representations of three-dimensional scenes. ▶ **Figure 4.55** shows a bewildering two-prong/three-prong device and a round staircase that seems to run uphill all the way clockwise or downhill all the way counterclockwise. Both drawings puzzle us when we try to see them as three-dimensional objects.

In ▶ **Figure 4.56**, linear perspective suggests that the right of the picture is farther away than the left. We therefore see the cylinder on the right as being the farthest away. If it is that far away and still produces the same size image on the retina as the other two, then it would have to be the largest. When we are misled by the cues that ordinarily ensure constancy in size and shape, we experience an optical illusion (Day, 1972).

▼ **Figure 4.57** shows the tabletop illusion (Shepard, 1990). Here, almost unbelievably, the vertical dimension of the blue table equals the horizontal dimension of the yellow table, and the horizontal dimension of the blue table equals the vertical dimension of the yellow table. Go ahead, get out a ruler and measure them. The yellow table appears long and thin compared to the blue one because we interpret it in depth. In effect, your brain constructs what each table would have to really *be* to look this way (Purves & Lotto, 2003).

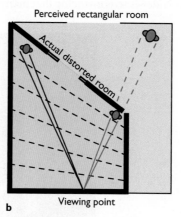

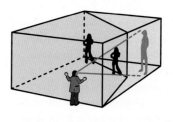

▲ **Figure 4.54** The Ames room is designed to view through a peephole with one eye. **(a)** The man on the right appears much larger than the woman to the left. **(b)** This diagram shows how the shape of the room distorts the viewer's perception of distance. (Part b from J. R. Wilson et al., 1964)

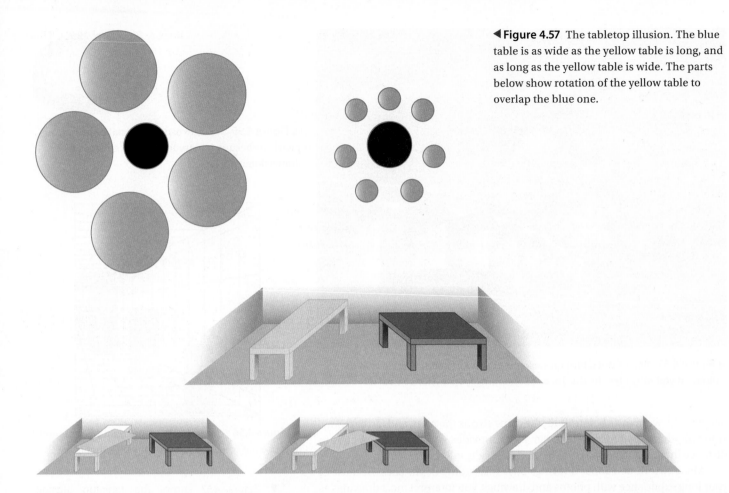

◀ **Figure 4.57** The tabletop illusion. The blue table is as wide as the yellow table is long, and as long as the yellow table is wide. The parts below show rotation of the yellow table to overlap the blue one.

Here is an application of optical illusions: In the display below, the central circles are equal, but most people see the one on the right as larger. Researchers set up putting greens and let golfers try to sink putts, sometimes with large circles surrounding the hole (as on the left) and sometimes with small circles surrounding it (as on the right). People sank almost twice as many putts for the version on the right, where the hole *looked* bigger (Witt, Linkenauger, & Proffitt, 2012). I don't know whether they will let you put circles on the ground during your next golf tournament.

The Moon Illusion

To most people, the *moon at the horizon appears about 30 percent larger than when it is higher in the sky.* This **moon illusion** is so convincing that many people

have tried to explain it by referring to the bending of light rays by the atmosphere or other physical phenomena. However, if you photograph the moon and measure its image, you will find that it is the same size in both locations. ▼ **Figure 4.58** shows the moon at two positions. The atmosphere's bending of light rays makes the moon look orange near the horizon, but it does not increase the size of the image. However, photographs do not capture the strength of the moon illusion as we see it in real life. In Figure 4.58 or any similar pair of photos, the moon looks almost the same at each position. In

▶ **Figure 4.58** Ordinarily, the moon looks much larger at the horizon than it does overhead. In photographs, this illusion disappears almost completely, but the photographs demonstrate that the physical image of the moon is the same in both cases. The moon illusion requires a psychological explanation, not a physical one.

Mark Antman/The Image Works

Mark Antman/The Image Works

the actual night sky, the moon looks enormous at the horizon.

One explanation is size comparison. When you see the moon low in the sky, it seems large compared to the tiny buildings or trees you see at the horizon. When you see the moon high in the sky, it appears small compared to the vast, featureless sky (Baird, 1982; Restle, 1970).

A second explanation is that the terrain between the viewer and the horizon gives an impression of great distance. When the moon is high in the sky, we have no basis to judge distance, and we unconsciously see the overhead moon as closer. Because we see the horizon moon as more distant,

we perceive it as larger (Kaufman & Rock, 1989; Rock & Kaufman, 1962). This explanation is appealing because it relates the moon illusion to perception of distance, a factor already accepted as important for other illusions.

Some psychologists are not satisfied with this explanation, however, because if we ask which looks farther away, many people say they are not sure. If we insist on an answer, most say the horizon moon looks *closer*, contradicting the theory. The reply is complicated: We unconsciously perceive the horizon as farther away. Consequently, we perceive the horizon moon as large. Then, because of the perceived large size of the horizon moon, we consciously say it looks closer, while continuing unconsciously to perceive it as farther (Rock & Kaufman, 1962).

Studies of optical illusions confirm what other phenomena already indicated: What we perceive is not the same as what is "out there." Our visual system does an amazing job of providing us with useful information, but under unusual circumstances, we have distorted perceptions.

in closing | module 4.3

Making Sense of Sensory Information

You have probably heard the expression, "Seeing is believing." The reverse is true also: What you believe or expect influences what you see. Perception is not just a matter of adding up the events striking the retina. We impose order on patterns, we see

three dimensions in two-dimensional drawings, and we see optical illusions. The brain tries to make sense of what the sensory systems are reporting.

Summary

- *Weber's law.* One of the first discoveries from psychological research was that the just-noticeable difference between two stimuli is a constant fraction of the strength of the original stimulus. (page 121)
- *Perception of minimal stimuli.* No sharp dividing line distinguishes sensory stimuli that can be perceived from sensory stimuli that cannot be perceived. (page 121)
- *Signal detection.* To determine how accurately someone detects a signal, we need to consider not only the ratio of hits to misses when the stimulus is present but also the ratio of false alarms to correct rejections when the stimulus is absent. (page 122)
- *Detecting rare stimuli.* When people are trying to detect an item, they are likely to overlook it if it occurs rarely. (page 123)
- *Subliminal perception.* Stimuli too brief or weak for conscious perception can produce brief effects on behavior, but no evidence demonstrates strong or lasting effects. (page 123)
- *Feature detectors.* In the first stages of the process of perception, feature-detector neurons identify lines, points, and simple movement. Visual aftereffects can be interpreted in terms of fatiguing certain feature detectors. (page 124)

- *Perception of organized wholes.* According to Gestalt psychologists, we perceive an organized whole by identifying patterns in a top-down manner. (page 126)
- *Visual constancies.* We ordinarily perceive the shape, size, and color of objects as constant, even when the pattern of light striking the retina varies. (page 129)
- *Motion perception.* We perceive an object as moving if it moves relative to its background. We distinguish between objects that are actually moving and similar patterns of retinal stimulation that result from eye movements. (page 130)
- *Depth perception.* To perceive depth, we use the accommodation of the eye muscles and retinal disparity between the views that our two eyes see. We also use cues that are just as effective with one eye as with two, including object size, linear perspective, detail, interposition, texture gradient, shadows, accommodation, and motion parallax. (page 130)
- *Optical illusions.* Many optical illusions occur because we misperceive the relative distances of objects. (page 132)

Key Terms

absolute sensory threshold (page 122)

binocular cues (page 131)

bottom-up process (page 126)

closure (page 127)

common fate (page 128)

continuation (page 127)

convergence (page 131)

depth perception (page 130)

feature detector (page 124)

Answers to Other Questions in the Module

C.

Bettmann/Getty Images

E.

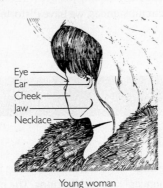

Eye
Ear
Cheek
Jaw
Necklace

Young woman

G.

D.

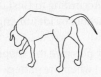

F.

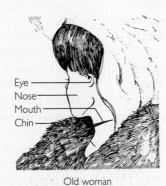

Eye
Nose
Mouth
Chin

Old woman

Review Questions

1. Why is it difficult to determine the absolute threshold for seeing or hearing something?
   (a) The weakest stimuli are too small to measure.
   (b) Most participants report fatigue after a few trials.
   (c) Most IRBs consider the procedure unethical.
   (d) Results vary depending on instructions and other variables.

2. According to signal-detection theory, what happens if a participant adjusts his/her responses to increase the number of hits?
   (a) The number of correct rejections will increase.
   (b) The overall accuracy percentage will increase.
   (c) The number of false alarms will increase.
   (d) The number of misses will increase.

3. Subliminal perception has been demonstrated to produce which of these effects?
   (a) A subliminal message to "buy popcorn" greatly increases popcorn sales.
   (b) Messages recorded backward on rock music turn teenagers to evil deeds.
   (c) Listening to subliminal messages on a recording improves memory or self-esteem.
   (d) Subliminally seeing an emotional expression alters perception of a neutral expression.

4. What evidence indicates that people have feature detectors?
   (a) Recordings from human brains have found cells responding to particular features.
   (b) Prolonged staring at a stimulus can alter perception of another stimulus.
   (c) People can interpret reversible figures in more than one way.
   (d) People can easily recognize an object even after it has changed in color, shape, or direction.

5. What is the emphasis of Gestalt psychology with regard to vision?
   (a) Researchers should emphasize cultural differences.
   (b) Researchers should emphasize species differences.
   (c) Top-down processes control perception.
   (d) Bottom-up processes control perception.

6. With three-dimensional photography, cameras take two views of the same scene from different locations through lenses with different color filters or with different polarized-light filters. The two views are then superimposed. The viewer looks at the composite view through special glasses so that one eye sees the view taken with one camera and the other eye sees the view taken with the other camera. Which depth cue is at work here?
   (a) Motion parallax
   (b) Interposition
   (c) Retinal disparity
   (d) Convergence

7. Which cues to distance are binocular cues?
   (a) Object size and linear perspective
   (b) Accommodation and motion parallax
   (c) Interposition and texture gradient
   (d) Retinal disparity and convergence

8. Which of the following is due to an optical illusion?
   (a) As an object moves away from us, we perceive it as remaining the same size.
   (b) The moon looks larger at the horizon than when higher in the sky.
   (c) Proximity and similarity cause us to see objects as belonging together.
   (d) Convergence of the eyes enables us to estimate distance.

Answers: 1d, 2c, 3d, 4b, 5c, 6c, 7d, 8b.

Liderina/Shutterstock.com

5 Development

Suppose you buy a robot. When you get home, you discover that it does nothing useful. It cannot even maintain its balance. It makes irritating, high-pitched noises, moves its limbs haphazardly, and leaks. The store you bought it from refuses to take it back, and it is illegal to disconnect or discard this robot. So you are stuck with it.

A few years later, your robot walks and talks, reads and writes, draws pictures, and does arithmetic. It follows your directions (usually) and sometimes does useful things without being told. It beats you at memory games.

How did all this happen? After all, you know nothing about how to program a robot. Did your robot have some sort of built-in programming that simply took a long time to phase in? Or was it programmed to learn all these skills?

Children are like that robot. Parents wonder, "How did my children get to be the way they are? And why did my two children turn out so different?" Developmental psychology seeks to understand how nature and nurture combine to produce human behavior "from womb to tomb."

As we grow older, our behavior changes in many ways. Developmental psychologists seek to describe and understand these changes.

David Gifford/Science Photo Library/Science Source

After studying this module, you should be able to:

1. Contrast cross-sectional designs and longitudinal designs.

2. Give examples of cohort effects.

3. Explain how psychologists infer the cognitive abilities of infants.

4. List and describe Piaget's stages of cognitive development.

5. Contrast two methods of inferring the concept of object permanence.

6. Give examples of how infants develop cognitive abilities gradually.

Liderina/Shutterstock.com

Research Designs for Studying Development

When studying psychological development, should a researcher compare younger and older people at the same time, or study one set of people repeatedly as they grow older? Each method has strengths and limitations.

Cross-Sectional and Longitudinal Designs

A **cross-sectional study** *compares groups of individuals of different ages at the same time.* For example, we could compare drawings by 6-year-olds, 8-year-olds, and 10-year-olds. Cross-sectional studies are acceptable for many purposes, but not always. For example, if you compared a random sample of 55-year-olds with a random sample of 85-year-olds, you would find that the 85-year-olds have less interest in sports. You would also find that, on average, 85-year-olds are shorter and have smaller heads. Why? On average, women live longer than men. Women tend to be shorter with smaller heads and less interest in sports. The sample of 55-year-olds you studied was not comparable to the 85-year-olds.

A **longitudinal study** *follows a single group of individuals as they develop.* For example, we could study the same children at ages 6, 8, and 10. ■ Table 5.1 contrasts the two kinds of studies. A longitudinal study necessarily takes years to complete. Also, not everyone who participates the first time is willing and available later. **Selective attrition** is *the tendency for certain kinds of people to drop out of a study* for many reasons, including health, moving away, or loss of interest. The kind of people who stay in the study may differ from those who quit. Psychologists can compensate for selective attrition by discarding the earlier data for people who left the study. However, if they have to discard a substantial amount of data, the results could be misleading.

Certain questions logically require a longitudinal study. For example, to study the effects of divorce on children, researchers compare how each child reacts at first with how that same child reacts later. To study whether happy children become

Young children's artwork is inventive and revealing. One toddler, 1½ years old, proudly showed off a drawing that consisted only of dots. Adults were puzzled. It is a rabbit, the child explained, while making more dots: "Look: hop, hop, hop . . . " (Winner, 1986). When my daughter, Robin, was 6 years old, she drew a picture of a boy and a girl wearing Halloween costumes and drawing pictures (see ▼ Figure 5.1). For the little girl's drawing, she pasted on some wildlife photos that, she insisted, were the little girl's drawings. The little boy's drawing was just a scribble. When I asked why the little girl's drawing was so much better than the little boy's, Robin replied, "Don't make fun of him, Daddy. He's doing the best he can."

Often, as in this case, a drawing expresses the child's worldview. As children grow older, their art becomes more skillful, but often less expressive. As we grow older, we gain many new abilities and skills, but we lose something, too.

Studying the abilities of young children is challenging. They misunderstand our questions and we misunderstand their answers. One theme you will encounter repeatedly in this module is that we reach different conclusions about children depending on how we measure their abilities.

© Robin Kalat

▲ **Figure 5.1** A drawing of two children drawing pictures, courtesy of 6-year-old Robin Kalat.

Table 5.1 Cross-Sectional and Longitudinal Studies

	Description	Advantages	Disadvantages	Example
Cross-sectional	Several groups of subjects of various ages studied at one time	1. Quick 2. No risk of confusing age effects with effects of changes in society	1. Risk of sampling error by getting different kinds of people at different ages 2. Risk of cohort effects	Compare memory abilities of 3-, 5-, and 7-year-olds
Longitudinal	One group of subjects studied repeatedly as the members grow older	1. No risk of sampling differences 2. Can study effects of one experience on later development 3. Can study consistency within individuals over time	1. Takes a long time 2. Some participants quit 3. Sometimes hard to separate effects of age from changes in society	Study memory abilities of 3-year-olds, and of the same children again 2 and 4 years later

happy adults, researchers follow a single group over time.

A sequential (or cross-sequential) design combines cross-sectional and longitudinal designs. In a **sequential design**, a researcher starts with people of different ages and studies them again at later times. For example, one might study 6-year-olds and 8-year-olds and then examine the same children 2 years later:

First study	2 years later
Group A, age 6 years	Group A, now 8 years old
Group B, age 8 years	Group B, now 10 years old

Cohort Effects

If you had been born in 1900, you would have spent your childhood in a world with no telephones or electrical appliances, including radio and television. You would have traveled by foot or by horse, unless yours was one of the few families with a car. You would have been lucky if you got to finish high school before starting work on a farm or in a factory. If you were a woman or a minority, your job opportunities were limited. If you had lived then, how would you have been different?

People of different generations differ in many ways, as a result of *cohort effects* (see ▼ Figure 5.2). A **cohort** is *a group of people born at a particular time or a group of people who enter an organization at a*

concept check

1. **Is selective attrition a problem for cross-sectional studies, longitudinal studies, or both?**

2. **At Santa Enigma College, the average first-year student has a C-minus average, and the average senior has a B-plus average. An observer concludes that, as students progress through college, they improve their study habits. Based on the idea of selective attrition, propose another possible explanation.**

Answers

1. It is a problem for both. In a longitudinal study, some of the people who participated at the first time may be unavailable later. In a cross-sectional study, the type of people who are available (including alive) at a greater age may be different from those available at a younger age.

2. The first-year students with the lowest grades (who lower the grade average for first-year students) do not stay in school long enough to become seniors. This is an example of selective attrition in a cross-sectional study.

particular time. (We could talk about the cohort of students entering a college in a given year, or the cohort of workers that a corporation hires in a given year.)

The era in which you grew up is a powerful influence. For example, Americans whose youth spanned the Great Depression and World War II learned to save money and to sacrifice for the needs of the country. Even after the war was over and prosperity reigned, most remained thrifty and cautious (Rogler, 2002). In contrast, many young people today have more leisure time, more opportunity for recreation, and less urgency about saving.

In the United States long ago, as in many countries today, it was customary for most people to spend their lives near where they were born. Today, many people move frequently in search of better jobs. The results include less identification with their community, fewer lasting friendships, and less feeling of obligation to help their neighbors (Oishi, 2010). Cohort effects can be so powerful that Jean Twenge (2006) has compared them to cultural differences. Much new technology is so unfamiliar to older people that they feel like immigrants to this culture.

▲ **Figure 5.2** People born at different times grow up with different experiences. In an earlier era, bathing suit inspectors prohibited "overly revealing" outfits that would seem modest today.

3. **Suppose you find in a longitudinal study that as people grow older, they go dancing less often. In a cross-sectional study, you find that older people prefer different music from younger people. Which of those differences is likely to represent a cohort effect?**

Answer

3. The difference in music tastes is probably a cohort effect, indicating that people who grew up in different eras listen to different music. The change in dancing behavior cannot be a cohort effect, because you studied the same cohort at both times.

The Fetus and the Newborn

Let's begin at the beginning. You began your life as a *fertilized egg cell,* or zygote, that developed through its first few stages until it became a fetus *about 8 weeks after conception.* As soon as 6 weeks after conception, the nervous system begins producing a few movements. The first movements are spontaneous—that is, not elicited by any stimulus. Contrary to what we might have guessed, the muscles and the nerves controlling these movements mature before the sense organs. Those spontaneous movements are essential, and without them the spinal cord would not develop properly. Later, but still before birth, the sense organs appear, the head and eyes begin to turn toward sounds, and the brain alternates between waking and sleeping (Joseph, 2000). The fetus does a good bit of yawning and hiccupping. The function of these behaviors is unclear (Provine, 2012).

A risk arises if the mother uses alcohol or other drugs, because drugs in her blood reach the fetus as well. *If the mother drinks alcohol during pregnancy,* the infant may develop fetal alcohol syndrome, *a condition marked by malformations of the face, heart, and ears; and nervous system damage, including seizures, hyperactivity, and impairments of learning, memory, problem solving, attention, and motor coordination* (Mattson, Crocker, & Nguyen, 2011). The severity varies from severe to barely noticeable, depending on the amount and timing of the mother's drinking (see ▼ Figure 5.3). Binge drinking is particularly dangerous, and prolonged drinking is worse than brief drinking, but researchers are not sure what level, if any, is safe (May et al., 2013).

The reason for the nervous system damage is now understood: Neurons have a self-destruct program that weeds out the less useful neurons. Neurons receiving less than normal input become "less useful." Because alcohol interferes with the brain's main excitatory neurotransmitter (glutamate) and facilitates the main inhibitory neurotransmitter (GABA), it decreases the input to many neurons and makes them self-destruct (Ikonomidou et al., 2000). Other drugs that interfere with excitatory transmission may be dangerous also, possibly including repeated

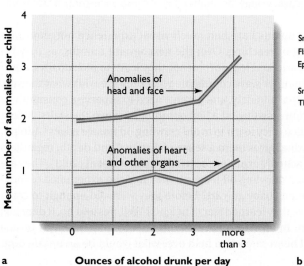

a   **Ounces of alcohol drunk per day**

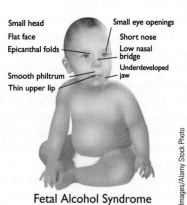

b

Fetal Alcohol Syndrome

◀ **Figure 5.3** **(a)** The more alcohol a woman drinks during pregnancy, the more likely her baby is to have anomalies of the head, face, and organs. (Based on data of Ernhart et al., 1987) **(b)** A child with fetal alcohol syndrome: Note the wide separation between the eyes, a common feature of this syndrome.

exposure to anesthetic drugs (Gleich, Nemergut, & Flick, 2013).

Still, it is remarkable that an occasional "high-risk" child—small at birth, exposed to alcohol or other drugs before birth, from a disadvantaged family, a victim of prejudice, and so forth—overcomes obstacles to become healthy and successful. Resilience (the ability to overcome obstacles) relates partly to genetic influences, education, and supportive relatives and friends (Bonanno & Mancini, 2008).

4. By what mechanism does alcohol harm the brain of a fetus?

Answer

4. Alcohol decreases the excitatory input to neurons. Neurons that do not get enough excitation during early development execute a self-destruct program.

Infancy

Research progress depends on good measurement. How can we measure psychological processes in infants, who can barely control a few muscles? A researcher monitors the few actions available to infants, drawing inferences about their growing understanding of the world.

Infants' Vision

William James, the founder of American psychology, said that as far as an infant can tell, the world is a "buzzing confusion," full of meaningless sights and sounds. Since James's time, psychologists have substantially elevated their estimates of infants' vision.

We can start by recording an infant's eye movements. Even 2-day-old infants spend more time looking at drawings of human faces than at other patterns with similar areas of light and dark (Fantz, 1963; see ▶ **Figure 5.4**). They also pay special attention to people or animals in motion, especially to their eyes and mouth (Constantino et al., 2017). However, infants do not have the same concept of "face" that adults do. As shown in ▼ **Figure 5.5**, newborns gaze equally at distorted and normal faces. However, they gaze longer at right-side-up faces than upside-down faces, regardless of distortion. Evidently, the newborn's concept of face is just an oval with the eyes toward the top (Cassia, Turati, & Simion, 2004).

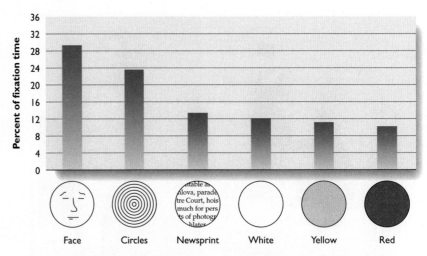

▲ **Figure 5.4** Infants pay more attention to faces than to other patterns. These results suggest that infants are born with certain visual preferences. (Based on Fantz, 1963)

The ability to recognize faces continues developing for years. Parents in one study repeatedly read a storybook with photographs of two children's faces from many angles and with many expressions. After 2 weeks, 4-year-old children easily recognized pictures of the children. However, when they had to choose between a normal picture and one with altered spacing among the features, they guessed randomly (Mondloch, Leis, & Maurer, 2006). By age 6, a child easily notices the difference between the photos in ▼ **Figure 5.6**, but 4-year-olds evidently do not.

The gradual improvement of face recognition depends on experience, and infants, like all of us, become best at recognizing the kinds of faces they frequently see. At first, infants respond equally to faces of all races. Over the first year, they become better at recognizing faces of their own race, and actually decline in their ability to recognize faces of other races (Sugden & Marquis, 2017). To measure face recognition, researchers show a picture of one face, and later that one plus another. Infants who recognize a face tend to look more at the new face. Looking at both equally implies non-recognition.

Adults also tend to recognize faces of their own race better. For some adults it is a small difference, but for others it can be huge (Wan et al., 2017). We need to be aware of this tendency. For example, if an eyewitness to a crime identifies someone, the accuracy may be higher for a same-race than a different-race person.

By age 5 months, infants have had much visual experience but almost no experience at crawling or reaching. Over the next several months, as they increase their control of arm and leg movements, they learn to pick up toys, crawl around objects, and in other ways coordinate what they see with what they do. At first, they crawl indiscriminately, and parents need to supervise constantly to prevent the infants from crawling off a bed or tumbling down the stairs. After a couple weeks of practice, they learn to avoid crawling off unsafe edges (Adolph, 2000). The act of crawling gives them a sense of distance and depth, regardless of whether they have actually experienced a fall (Anderson et al., 2013). They are earlier to learn to avoid crawling off ledges if they had the experience of moving around in a powered "baby go-cart" before they were old enough to crawl (Dahl et al., 2013). Have they learned fear of heights? Well, yes and no. It depends on how we test them. Infants who have learned not to crawl over an unsafe ledge show increased heart rate when held over what would be an unsafe drop

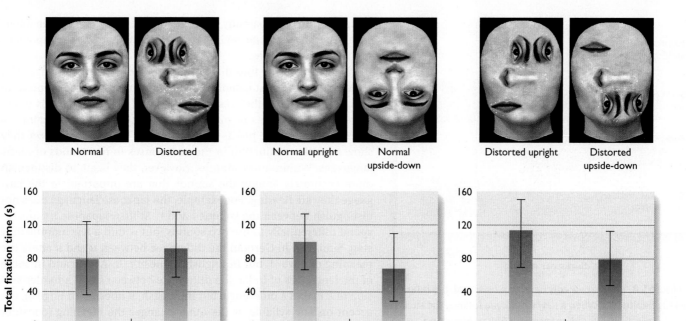

| | Normal | Distorted | | Normal upright | Normal upside-down | | Distorted upright | Distorted upside-down |

▲ **Figure 5.5** Infants gaze about equally at normal and distorted faces, but they stare longer at upright than upside-down faces. (Source: Cassia, Turati, & Simion, 2004)

▲ **Figure 5.6** These faces differ only in the positions of the eyes, nose, and mouth. Four-year-olds do not recognize which face is familiar. (Source: Mondloch, Leis, & Maurer, 2006)

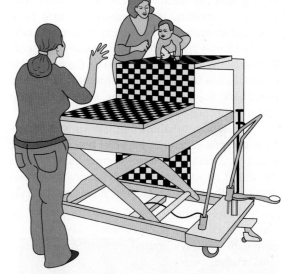

▲ **Figure 5.7** Infants who are starting to crawl learn not to go over deep edges. A few months later when they are starting to walk, they have to learn again what is safe and what is unsafe.

(Dahl et al., 2013). However, when the same infants start to walk a few months later, they again step indiscriminately, and parents need to supervise them until they learn what is and is not a safe step-off distance (Kretch & Adolph, 2013; see also ▶ Figure 5.7). Evidently, for any kind of locomotion, young children gradually learn what they can and cannot do.

concept check

5. In what way are newborns prepared to learn about faces?

Answer

5. Newborns focus their attention on an oval with the eyes on the top side. At first, they are equally attuned to any face, but over time they recognize mostly faces similar to those they have been seeing.

Infants' Hearing

Infants don't do much, but one thing they do is suck. Researchers use that response to measure hearing, because infants suck more vigorously when sounds arouse them.

In one study, the experimenters played a brief sound and noted how it affected infants' sucking rate (see ▼ Figure 5.8). On the first few

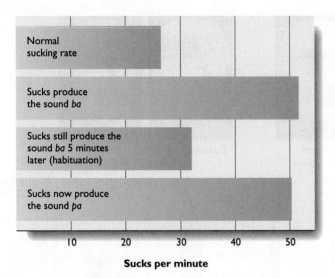

▲ **Figure 5.8** After repeatedly hearing a *ba* sound, the infant's sucking habituates. When a new sound, *pa*, follows, the sucking rate increases. (Based on results of Eimas, Siqueland, Jusczyk, & Vigorito, 1971)

occasions, the sound increased the sucking rate. A repeated sound produced less and less effect. We say that the infant became *habituated* to the sound. Habituation is *decreased response to a repeated stimulus.* When the experimenters substituted a new sound, the sucking rate increased. Evidently, the infant was aroused by the unfamiliar sound. *When a change in a stimulus increases a previously habituated response*, we say that the stimulus produced dishabituation.

Monitoring dishabituation tells us whether infants detect a difference between two sounds. For example, infants who have become habituated to the sound *ba* will increase their sucking rate when they hear the sound *pa* (Eimas, Siqueland, Jusczyk,

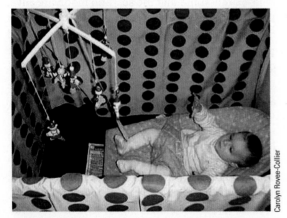

▲ **Figure 5.9** Two-month-old infants rapidly learn to kick to activate a mobile attached to their ankles with a ribbon. They remember how to activate the mobile when tested days later. (From Hildreth, Sweeney, & Rovee-Collier, 2003)

& Vigorito, 1971). Apparently, even month-old infants notice the difference between *ba* and *pa*, an important distinction for later comprehension in many languages.

Newborns come into the world prepared to learn language. The same brain areas that respond to language in adults also respond to it in newborns, and they respond to natural language sounds much more than to whistles or other sounds (May, Gervain, Carreiras, & Werker, 2018). At first, just as they distinguish between *ba* and *pa*, they show a similar distinction in their responses to the sounds of many languages. Within a few months, however, they begin to distinguish more accurately among the sounds that are important in the language they are hearing. For example, the Japanese language does not distinguish between the sounds *l* and *r*. At first, Japanese infants respond differentially to the two sounds, but within a few months they stop. Similarly, in German the difference between *u* and *ü* alters the meaning of a word, but in English it doesn't. In Arabic and in some of the languages of India, the difference between *k* and a harder version of *k* makes a difference, but in English, it doesn't. In English, the accent on one syllable or the other changes the meaning (consider *decade* vs. *decayed* and *weakened* vs. *weekend*), but in French, accent doesn't matter. At first, infants distinguish among all of these sound differences, but within a few months, they get better at distinguishing among sounds important in their community's language, and worse at distinguishing sound differences that do not matter in that language (Choi, Black, & Werker, 2018). All this takes place before they understand what any of those words mean.

One more point about infants' hearing: If 5-month-old infants hear a parent sing a song over and over, they learn to recognize that song, as they indicate by staring at anyone else who sings that melody. If instead they had heard a toy or an unfamiliar person repeatedly sing that song, they would not show the same reaction when they hear it later (Mehr, Song, & Spelke, 2016). In short, infants attend to their parents and learn more from them than from anyone else.

concept check

6. **How could we determine whether an infant hears a difference between "fuh" and "vuh"?**

7. **What is the similarity between development of face recognition and development of language?**

Answers

6. Present one of the sounds until the infant habituates to it. Then present the other sound and see whether sucking rate increases.

7. An infant gradually learns to recognize most accurately the type of faces he/she has been seeing, generally of the same race. An infant also gradually learns to distinguish among sounds that he/she has been hearing, those of the local language.

Infants' Learning and Memory

How could we measure learning and memory in infants who can do so little? Many studies have used the fact that infants learn to suck harder on a nipple if their sucking turns on a sound. Investigators determined whether infants suck harder for some sounds than for others. In one study, babies younger than 3 days old could turn on a tape recording of a woman's voice by sucking on a nipple. The results: They sucked more frequently to turn on recordings of their own mother's voice than another woman's voice (DeCasper & Fifer, 1980). Apparently, they preferred their own mother's voice. Because they showed this preference as early as the day of birth, psychologists believe that the infants learned the sound of the mother's voice before birth.

In a follow-up study, pregnant women read a nursery rhyme three times in a row, twice a day. By age 38 weeks postconception (shortly before birth), fetuses showed a heart rate response to the familiar rhyme, and not to a different rhyme (Krueger & Garvan, 2014). In another study, researchers played a simple piano melody for fetuses to hear twice daily for the last three weeks before birth. Six weeks later, those infants (and not other infants) showed a larger heart rate response to the familiar melody than to a different melody (Granier-Deferre, Bassereau, Ribeiro, Jacquet, & deCasper, 2011). This study shows memory of prenatal experiences lasting at least six weeks.

Carolyn Rovee-Collier (1997, 1999) attached a ribbon to an ankle so that an infant could activate a mobile by kicking with one leg (see ▲ Figure 5.9). Two-month-old infants quickly learned this response and generally kept the mobile going nonstop for a full 45-minute session. (Infants have limited control over their leg muscles, but they don't need much accuracy to keep the mobile going.) They remembered what to do when the ribbon was reattached several days later, to the infants' evident delight. Six-month-old infants remembered the response for 2 weeks. Even after they forgot it, they quickly relearned it (Hildreth, Sweeney, & Rovee-Collier, 2003).

8. Suppose a newborn sucks to turn on a tape recording of its father's voice. Eventually, the baby habituates and the sucking frequency decreases. Now the experimenters substitute the recording of a different man's voice. What would you conclude if the sucking frequency increased? What if it remained the same? What if it decreased?

Answer

8. If the frequency increased, we would conclude that the infant recognizes the difference between the father's voice and the other voice. If the frequency remained the same, we would conclude that the infant did not notice a difference. If the sucking frequency decreased, we would conclude that the infant recognizes a difference and that the infant preferred the sound of the father's voice.

Jean Piaget demonstrated that children with different levels of maturity react differently to the same experience.

Jean Piaget's View of Cognitive Development

Somewhat older children are easier to test, and one quickly discovers that their thinking differs from that of adults. The theorist who made this point most influentially was Jean Piaget (pee-ah-ZHAY; 1896–1980).

Early in his career, while administering IQ tests to children in Switzerland, Piaget was fascinated that so many children of a given age gave the same incorrect answer to certain questions. He concluded that children have qualitatively different thought processes from adults. According to Piaget, as children develop, they do more than accumulate facts. They construct new mental processes.

In Piaget's terminology, behavior is based on schemata (the plural of *schema*). A **schema** is *an organized way of interacting with objects.* For instance, infants have a grasping schema and a sucking schema. Older infants gradually add new schemata and adapt their old ones through the processes of assimilation and accommodation. **Assimilation** means *applying an old schema to new objects or problems.* For example, when a child sees animals move and then sees the sun and moon move, the child may assume that the sun and moon are alive, like animals. **Accommodation** means *modifying an old schema to fit a new object or problem.* A child may learn that "only living things move on their own" is a rule with exceptions, and that the sun and moon are not alive.

Infants shift back and forth between assimilation and accommodation. **Equilibration** is *the establishment of harmony or balance between the two.* Suppose a discrepancy occurs between the child's current understanding and some evidence to the contrary. The child accommodates to that discrepancy and achieves an equilibration at a higher level. Similar processes occur in adults. When you see a new mathematical problem, you try several familiar methods until you find one that works. That is, you assimilate the new problem to an old schema. However, if the new problem is sufficiently different, you modify (accommodate) your schema to find a solution. In this way, said Piaget, intellectual growth occurs.

Piaget contended that children progress through four major stages of intellectual development:

1. *The sensorimotor stage* (from birth to almost 2 years)
2. *The preoperational stage* (from almost 2 to 7 years)
3. *The concrete operations stage* (from about 7 to 11 years)
4. *The formal operations stage* (from about 11 years onward)

The ages vary, and not everyone reaches the formal operations stage. However, all people progress through the stages in the same order. Let's consider each of Piaget's stages.

Piaget's Sensorimotor Stage

Piaget called the first stage of intellectual development the sensorimotor stage because *at this early age (the first 1½ to 2 years) behavior is mostly simple motor responses to sensory stimuli.* According to Piaget, infants respond only to what they see and hear at the moment. What evidence could he have for this view? And might there be evidence to the contrary?

what's the evidence?

The Infant's Concept of Object Permanence

Piaget argued that infants in the first few months of life lack the concept of **object permanence**, *the idea that objects continue to exist even when we do not see or hear them.* That is, for an infant, "Out of sight, out of existence."

Piaget drew his inference from observations like this: Place a toy in front of a 6-month-old infant, who reaches out for it. Later, place a toy in the same place, but before the infant has a chance to grab it, cover it with a clear glass. The infant removes the glass and takes the toy. Now repeat that procedure but use an opaque (nonclear) glass. The infant, who watched you place the glass over the toy, makes no effort to remove the glass and obtain the toy. Next, place a thin barrier between the infant and the toy. An infant who cannot see the toy does not reach for it (Piaget, 1937/1954) (see ▼ Figure 5.10).

According to Piaget, the infant does not know that the hidden toy continues to exist. However, a study by Renee Baillargeon (1986) suggests that infants show signs of understanding object permanence when they are tested differently.

Hypothesis Show an infant an event that would be impossible if objects are permanent. The infant will be surprised and therefore will stare longer than will an infant who sees a possible event.

Method Infants aged 6 or 8 months watched the experimenter raise a screen to show a track and then watched a toy car go down a slope and emerge on the other side of the screen, as shown here. This was called a "possible" event.

The researchers measured how long the child stared after the car passed by. They repeated the procedure until the child's staring time decreased for three trials in a row (showing habituation). Then the experimenters presented a series of "possible" events, as just described, and "impossible" events like this:

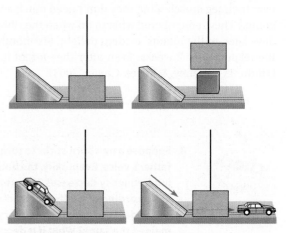

Possible event. The box is behind the track, and the car passes by the box.

In an impossible event, the raised screen showed a box on the track where the car would pass. After the screen lowered, the car went down the slope and emerged on the other side. (The experimenters pulled the box off the track after lowering the screen.) The experimenters measured each child's staring times after both kinds of events. They repeated both events two more times, randomizing the order of events.

Results As shown in ▼ Figure 5.11, infants stared longer after seeing an impossible event. They also stared longer after the first pair of events than after the second and third pairs (Baillargeon, 1986).

Interpretation Why did the infants stare longer at the impossible event? The inference—admittedly only an inference—is that the infants found the impossible event surprising. To be surprised, infants had to expect that the box would continue to exist, and would block the path of the car. If so, even 6-month-old infants have some understanding of object permanence and elementary physics.

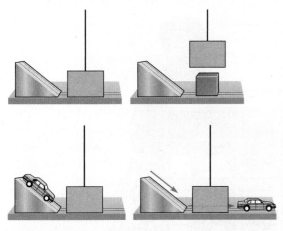

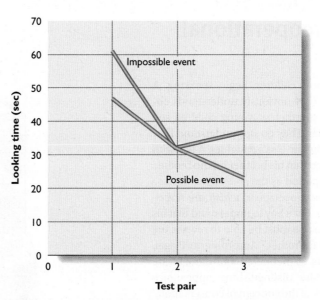

Impossible event. The raised screen shows a box on the track where the car would pass. After the screen lowers, the car goes down the slope and emerges on the other side.

Still, remember that 9-month-olds failed Piaget's object permanence task of reaching out to pick up a hidden object. Do infants understand object permanence

▲ **Figure 5.11** Infants stared longer after watching impossible events than after watching possible events. (From Baillargeon, 1986)

or not? Evidently, this is not a yes-or-no question. Infants use a concept in some situations and not others. The same is true for all of us. Did you ever learn a grammatical rule in English class and then violate it in your own speech? Did you ever learn a math formula and then fail to apply it to a new situation?

Other psychologists modified this procedure to test other infant concepts. Researchers put five objects behind a screen, added five more, and removed the screen. Nine-month-olds stared longer when they saw just five objects than when they saw ten, suggesting that they understand addition (McCrink & Wynn, 2004). Researchers showed 11-month-old infants a display in which a toy car seemed to be floating in mid-air. When the infants had a chance to play with the car, most of them immediately dropped it, apparently to see whether it would fall (Stahl & Feigenson, 2015). When infants watched an animated display in which a larger figure and a smaller figure crossed paths, 10-month-olds stared longer if the larger one bowed and stepped aside to let the smaller one pass (Thomsen, Frankenhuis, Ingold-Smith, & Carey, 2011). If we assume that staring means surprise, then infants apparently understand something about social dominance. However, infants as old as 12 months show no surprise if you place a toy into a container and then pull out a toy of different shape or color (Baillargeon, Li, Ng, & Yuan, 2009). Perhaps infants imagine that objects can magically change shape or color.

Here are two conclusions: First, we should be cautious about inferring what infants can or cannot do, because the results vary with the procedures. Second, concepts develop gradually. An infant may show a concept in one situation and not another.

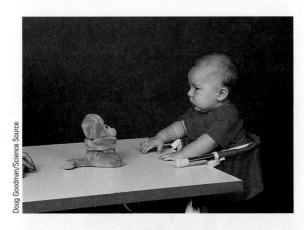

▲ **Figure 5.10 (a)** A 6- to 9-month-old child reaches for a visible toy but not one that is hidden behind a barrier **(b)** even if the child sees someone hide the toy. According to Piaget, this observation indicates that the child hasn't yet grasped the concept of object permanence.

Piaget's Preoperational Stage

By age 1½ to 2, most children begin speaking. A child who asks for a toy obviously understands object permanence. Nevertheless, young children still misunderstand much. They do not understand how a mother can be someone else's daughter. A boy with one brother will assert that his brother has no brother. Piaget refers to this period as the **preoperational stage** because *the child lacks* **operations**, *which are reversible mental processes.* For a boy to understand that his brother has a brother, he must be able to reverse the concept of "having a brother." According to Piaget, three typical aspects of preoperational thought are egocentrism, difficulty distinguishing appearance from reality, and lack of the concept of conservation.

Egocentrism: Failing to Understand Other People's Perspective

According to Piaget, young children's thought is **egocentric.** Piaget did *not* mean selfish. Instead, he meant that *a child sees the world as centered around himself or herself and cannot easily take another person's perspective.* The child can describe how the blocks on the table look from his or her own side but not how they would look to someone in a different position.

However, young children do sometimes understand another person's perspective. In one study, 5- and 6-year-old children had to tell an adult to pick up a particular glass. If a child saw that the adult could see two glasses, the child usually said to pick up the "big" or "little" glass to identify the right one. If the child saw that the adult could see only one glass, the child often said just "the glass" (Nadig & Sedivy, 2002; ▶ Figure 5.12).

Sense of Self

Do children in the preoperational stage have a concept of "self"? How would we know? Here is the evidence: Someone puts a spot of unscented rouge on an infant's nose and then puts the infant in front of a mirror. Infants younger than 1½ years old either ignore the spot on the baby in the mirror or reach out to touch the mirror. At some point after age 1½ years, infants instead touch themselves on the nose, indicating that they recognize themselves in the mirror (see ▶ Figure 5.13). Infants show this sign of self-recognition at varying ages; the age when they first show self-recognition is about the same as when they begin to act embarrassed (M. Lewis, Sullivan, Stanger, & Weiss, 1991). They show a sense of self in both ways or in neither. Chimpanzees and several

▲ **Figure 5.12** Sometimes, a child saw that the adult could see two glasses. At other times, it was clear that the adult could see only one. If two glasses were visible, the child usually told the adult which glass to pick up, instead of saying, "pick up the glass." (From Nadig & Sedivy, 2002)

Thierry Berrod, Mona Lisa Production/Science Source

▲ **Figure 5.13** If someone places a bit of unscented rouge on a child's nose, a 2-year-old looking at a mirror shows self-recognition by touching his or her own nose.

other species also respond to a mirror in a way that implies self-recognition.

Before age 1½, do infants fail to distinguish between self and other? Perhaps, but we cannot be sure. Before then we see no evidence for a sense of self, but absence of evidence is not evidence of absence. Perhaps younger infants would show a sense of self in a test that we have not yet devised.

9. **Which of the following is the clearest example of egocentric thinking?**

a. A writer uses someone else's words without giving credit.
b. A manager blames the employees for everything that goes wrong.
c. A professor gives a lecture without defining some key terms.

Answers

9. c is a case of egocentric thought, a failure to recognize another person's point of view.

Theory of Mind: Understanding That Different People Know Different Things

To say that a child is egocentric implies that he or she does not understand what other people know or don't know. Psychologists say that a young child lacks, but gradually develops **theory of mind**, which is *an understanding that other people have a mind, too, and that each person knows some things that other people don't know.* How can we know whether a child has this understanding? In one study, children hear a story about Lucy, who wants her old pair of red shoes. Lucy's brother Linus enters the room, and she asks him to bring her red shoes. He goes and brings back her new red shoes, and she is angry because she wanted the old red shoes. Young children hearing the story are surprised that he brought the wrong shoes, because *they* knew which shoes she wanted (Keysar, Barr, & Horton, 1998). If they knew, why didn't Linus know?

Here is a more elaborate example:

what's the evidence?

Children's Understanding of Other People's Knowledge and Beliefs

Hypothesis A child who understands that other people have minds knows that someone could have a false belief. This understanding will begin at some age, to be determined.

Method A child watches and listens as an adult acts out this story: Maxi sees his mother put chocolate into the blue cupboard. He plans to return later and get some. However, while he is absent, his mother moves the chocolate to the green cupboard. The questions are: Where will Maxi look for the chocolate? If his grandfather is available to help, where will Maxi tell him to look? If an older brother wants to take the chocolate, and Maxi wants to prevent the brother from finding the chocolate, where will he point? (See ▼ Figure 5.14.)

Results Older children answer correctly: Maxi looks in the blue cupboard and tells his grandfather to get chocolate from the blue cupboard, but tells his brother to look in the green cupboard. Younger children answer incorrectly, as if they thought Maxi had all the correct information that the observers themselves had. The percentage of children answering correctly increases from age 3 to age 6, and most children beyond about 4½ answer correctly (Wellman, Cross, & Watson, 2001; Wimmer & Penner, 1983).

Interpretation Evidently, children gradually develop in their ability to understand other people's thoughts, beliefs, and knowledge.

10. **If the chocolate is now in the green cupboard, what does it mean if a child says Maxi will look in the blue cupboard?**

Answer

10. It means that the child has "theory of mind." The child understands that Maxi, who was absent while the mother moved the chocolate, will have a false belief.

We might be tempted to the simple interpretation that young children lack theory of mind, and at some point they suddenly gain it. However, development is seldom a sudden, all-or-nothing process. In the "Maxi" situation, it is likely that many 3-year-olds don't fully understand the questions. In a later study, 3-year-olds watched as a Lego figure representing a girl put bananas (which she liked to eat) in one of two refrigerators. Then the girl moved forward, with her back to the refrigerators, while the experimenter moved the bananas from one refrigerator to the other. When the experimenter invited the child to play with the girl figure and asked, "What is she going to do now?" in most cases the child moved the figure to the refrigerator that *previously* had the bananas, indicating theory of mind. However, if the experimenter asked where the girl would look for the bananas, the child answered with the wrong refrigerator (Rubio-Fernández & Geurts, 2013). That is, a nonverbal response showed

▲ **Figure 5.14** Maxi watches his mother place chocolate in one place. While he is absent, she moves it. Where will Maxi look for it? Younger children point to the new location, suggesting they do not understand that Maxi will have an incorrect belief.

that the child understood what the girl would know, but answering in words caused confusion. In short, gaining theory of mind—or any other concept—is not a sudden transition. A child can show indications of understanding in some ways or situations and not in others.

Distinguishing Appearance from Reality

During Piaget's preoperational stage, children sometimes seem not to distinguish between appearance and reality. For example, a child who sees you put a white ball behind a blue filter will say that the ball is blue. When you ask, "Yes, I know the ball *looks* blue, but what color is it *really*?" the child replies that it really *is* blue (Flavell, 1986). Similarly, a 3-year-old who encounters a sponge that looks like a rock will say either that it looks like a rock and really is a rock, or that it looks like a sponge and really *is* a sponge.

However, the results depend on how we ask the question. Psychologists showed 3-year-olds a sponge that looked like a rock and let them touch it. When the investigators asked what it looked like and what it was *really,* most of the children said "rock" both times or "sponge" both times. However, if the investigators asked, "Bring me something so I can wipe up some spilled water," the children brought the sponge. And when the investigators asked, "Bring me something so I can take a picture of a teddy bear with something that looks like a rock," they brought the same object. So evidently, the children did understand that something could be a sponge and look like a rock, even if they didn't say so (Sapp, Lee, & Muir, 2000). Again, we see this pattern: A child can show a concept in one way and not another.

Also consider this experiment: A psychologist shows a child a playhouse room that is a scale model of a full-size room. The psychologist hides a tiny toy in the small room and explains that a bigger toy just like it is "in the same place" in the bigger room. Then the psychologist asks the child to find the big toy in the big room. Most 3-year-olds go to the correct place at once (DeLoache, 1989). Most 2½-year-old children, however, search haphazardly (see ▼ Figure 5.15a).

Ah, but the results depend on how we ask the question. As before, a psychologist hides a toy in the small room while the child watches. Then the psychologist shows the child a "machine that can make things bigger." The psychologist aims a beam from the machine at the room and takes the child out of the way. They hear some chunkata-chunkata sounds, and then the psychologist shows the full-size "blown-up" room and asks the child to find the hidden toy. Even 2½-year-olds go immediately to the correct location (DeLoache, Miller, & Rosengren, 1997; see ▼ Figure 5.15b). (Incidentally, the children had no doubt that the machine had expanded the room. Many continued to believe it even after the psychologist explained what happened!)

Developing the Concept of Conservation

According to Piaget, preoperational children lack the concept of **conservation**. They fail to *understand that objects conserve such properties as number, length, volume, area, and mass after changes in the shape or arrangement of the objects.* They cannot perform the mental operations necessary to understand the transformations. ■ Table 5.2 shows typical conservation tasks. For example, if we show two equal glasses with the same amount of water and then pour the contents of one glass into a third glass that is taller and thinner, preoperational children say that the third glass contains more water (see ▼ Figure 5.16).

I once thought perhaps the phrasing of the questions tricks children into saying something they do not believe. If you have the same doubts, find a 5- or 6-year-old child and try it yourself with your own wording. Here's my experience: Once when I was discussing Piaget in my introductory psychology class, I invited my son Sam, then 5½ years old, to take part in a class demonstration. I started with two glasses of water, which he agreed contained equal amounts of water. Then I poured the water from one glass into a wider glass, lowering the water level. When I asked which glass contained more water, Sam confidently pointed to the tall, thin one. After class he complained, "Daddy, why did you ask me such an easy question? Everyone could see that there was more water in that glass! You should have asked me something harder to show how smart I am!" The following year, I brought Sam, now 6½ years old, to class for the same

a A 2½-year-old is shown a small room where a stuffed animal is hidden.

Child is unable to find the stuffed animal in the larger room.

Child is told that the machine expands the room. Child stands out of the way during some noises and then returns.

b Child is shown a small room where a stuffed animal is hidden.

Child is able to find the stuffed animal in the "blown-up" room.

▲ **Figure 5.15** If an experimenter hides a small toy in a small room and asks a child to find a larger toy "in the same place" in the larger room, most 2½-year-olds search haphazardly **(a).** However, the same children know where to look if the experimenter says this is the same room as before, but a machine has expanded it **(b).**

Table 5.2 Typical Tasks Used to Measure Conservation

	Conservation of number Preoperational children say that these two rows contain the same number of pennies. Preoperational children say that the second row has more pennies.
 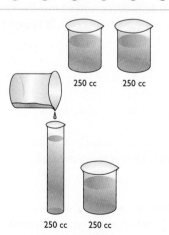	**Conservation of volume** Preoperational children say that the two same-size containers have the same amount of water. Preoperational children say that the taller, thinner container has more water.
	Conservation of mass Preoperational children say that the two same-size balls of clay have the same amount of clay. Preoperational children say that a squashed ball of clay contains a different amount of clay than the same-size round ball of clay.

▲ **Figure 5.16** Preoperational children don't understand that the volume of water remains constant despite changes in its appearance. During the transition to concrete operations, a child finds conservation tasks difficult and confusing.

demonstration. I poured the water from one of the tall glasses into a wider one and asked him which glass contained more water. He looked and paused. His face turned red. Finally, he whispered, "Daddy, I don't know!" After class he complained, "Why did you ask me such a hard question? I'm never coming back to any of your classes again!" The question that used to be embarrassingly easy had become embarrassingly difficult.

The next year, when he was 7½, I tried again (at home). This time he answered confidently, "Both glasses have the same amount of water, of course. Why? Is this some sort of trick question?"

Piaget's Stages of Concrete Operations and Formal Operations

At about age 7, children enter the stage of concrete operations and begin to understand the conservation of physical properties. The transition is gradual, however. A 6-year-old may understand that squashing a ball of clay does not change its weight but still think that squashing it changes how much water it displaces when dropped into a glass.

According to Piaget, during the stage of concrete operations, *children perform mental operations on concrete objects but still have trouble with abstract or hypothetical ideas.* For example, ask this question: "How could you move a mountain of whipped cream from one side of the city to the other?" Older children enjoy devising imaginative answers, but children in the concrete operations stage complain that the question is silly.

Or ask, "If you could have a third eye anywhere on your body, where would you put it?" Children in

the concrete operations stage generally respond immediately that they would put it right between the other two, on their foreheads. Older children suggest more imaginative ideas such as on the back of their head, in the stomach (so they could watch food digesting), or on the tip of a finger (so they could peek around corners).

Finally, in Piaget's stage of formal operations, adolescents develop *logical, deductive reasoning and systematic planning.* According to Piaget, children reach the stage of formal operations at about age 11. Later researchers found that many people reach this stage later or not at all. Thinking with formal operations demonstrates planning. For example, we set up five bottles of clear liquid and explain that it is possible to mix some combination to produce a yellow liquid. The task is to find that combination. Children in the concrete operations stage plunge right in with no plan. They try combining bottles A and B, then C and D, then perhaps A, C, and E. Soon they have forgotten which combinations they've already tried. Adolescents in the formal operations stage approach the problem more systematically. They may first try all the two-bottle combinations: AB, AC, AD, AE, BC, and so forth. If those fail, they try three-bottle combinations: ABC, ABD, ABE, ACD, and so on. By trying every possible combination only once, they are sure to succeed. ■ Table 5.3 summarizes Piaget's four stages.

11. In which of Piaget's stages is each of these children?

a. Child plans responses systematically and easily deals with hypothetical situations.

b. Child responds to the present situation but seems not to understand object permanence.

c. Child does well on conservation tasks but does not plan ahead.

d. Child understands object permanence but does not understand conservation of mass, number, and so forth.

Answer

11. a. formal operations stage; b. sensorimotor stage; c. concrete operations stage; d. preoperational stage

Table 5.3 Summary of Piaget's Stages of Cognitive Development

Stage and Approximate Age	Achievements and Activities	Limitations
Sensorimotor (birth to 1½ years)	Reacts to sensory stimuli through reflexes and other responses	Little use of language; seems not to understand object permanence in the early part of this stage
Preoperational (1½ to 7 years)	Develops language; can represent objects mentally by words and other symbols; can respond to objects that are remembered but not present	Lacks operations (reversible mental processes); lacks concept of conservation; focuses on one property at a time (such as length or width), not on both at once; still has trouble distinguishing appearance from reality
Concrete operations (7 to 11 years)	Understands conservation of mass, number, and volume; can reason logically with regard to concrete objects that can be seen or touched	Has trouble reasoning about abstract concepts and hypothetical situations
Formal operations (11 years onward)	Can reason logically about abstract and hypothetical concepts; develops strategies; plans actions in advance	None beyond the occasional irrationalities of all human thought

Are Piaget's Stages Distinct?

Piaget regarded the four stages of intellectual development as distinct. He believed a transition from one stage to the next required a major reorganization of thinking, like a caterpillar metamorphosing into a chrysalis or a chrysalis metamorphosing into a butterfly. That is, intellectual growth has periods of revolutionary reorganization.

Later research casts doubt on this conclusion. If it were true, then a child in a given stage of development—say, the preoperational stage—should perform consistently at that level. In fact, children's performance fluctuates as a task is made more or less difficult. For example, consider the conservation-of-number task, in which an investigator presents two rows of seven or more objects, spreads out one row, and asks which row has more. Preoperational children reply that the spread-out row has more. However, when Rochel Gelman (1982) presented two rows of only three objects each (see ▼ Figure 5.17) and then spread out one of the rows, even 3- and 4-year-old children usually answered that the rows had the same number of items.

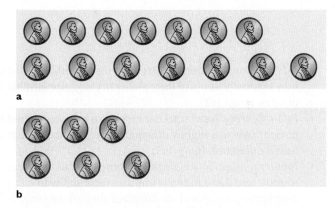

a

b

▲ **Figure 5.17** (a) With the standard conservation-of-number task, preoperational children answer that the spread-out row has more items. (b) With a simplified task, the same children say that both rows have the same number of items.

Whereas Piaget believed children made distinct jumps from one stage to another, most psychologists today see development as gradual and continuous (Courage & Howe, 2002). That is, the difference between older children and younger children is not so much a matter of gaining a new ability. It is a matter of using their abilities more consistently and in more situations.

Differing Views: Piaget and Vygotsky

One implication of Piaget's view is that children must discover certain concepts, such as the concept of conservation, mainly on their own. Teaching a concept means directing children's attention to the key aspects and letting them discover the concept. In contrast, Russian psychologist Lev Vygotsky (1978) argued that educators should not wait for children to rediscover the principles of physics and mathematics. Indeed, the value of language is that it lets us profit from the experience of previous generations.

Vygotsky certainly did not mean that adults should ignore a child's developmental level. Rather, every child has a zone of proximal development, *the distance between what a child can do alone and what is possible with help.* Instruction should remain within that zone. For example, one should not try to teach a typical 4-year-old the concept of conservation of volume. However, a 6-year-old who does not yet understand the concept might learn it with help and guidance. Similarly, children improve their recall of lists or stories if adults help them understand and organize the information (Larkina, Güler, Kleinknecht, & Bauer,

2008). Vygotsky compared this help to *scaffolding,* the temporary supports that builders use during construction: After a building is complete, the scaffolding is removed. Good advice for educators is to be sensitive to a child's zone of proximal development and pursue how much further they can push a child. You see the same in your own experience: In math, science, or a foreign language, you profit from instruction that moves you a little beyond what you can do already, but not from something far beyond your current understanding.

concept check

12. What would Piaget and Vygotsky think about the feasibility of teaching the concept of conservation?

Answer

12. Piaget recommended waiting for a child to discover the concept by himself or herself. For Vygotsky, the answer depends on the child's zone of proximal development. An adult can help a child at the right age.

The zone of proximal development is the gap between what a child does alone and what the child can do with help.

in closing | module 5.1

How Grown Up Are We?

Both Piaget and Vygotsky implied that we advance from infant cognition and to adult thinking, and remain mature from then on. Are they right, or do we sometimes slip into childish ways of thought?

Consider egocentric thinking. Young children seem to assume that whatever they know or understand, other people will know or understand also. Do you ever start talking about "him" or "her" and assume that everyone knows whom you are talking about? Suppose you say, "The daughter of the man and the woman arrived." You know that you meant the man's daughter plus some other woman, but your listener might think you meant that one person arrived, who was the daughter of "the man and the woman." We easily slip into assuming that other people understand everything that we ourselves do (Keysar & Henly, 2002).

In short, as we grow older, we suppress our childlike ways of thinking, but we don't lose them completely. You still have a child's mind hidden inside you. Development is not a matter of suddenly gaining cognitive skills. It is a matter of applying skills more consistently and under a wider variety of conditions.

Summary

- *Cross-sectional and longitudinal studies.* Cross-sectional studies examine people of different ages at the same time. Longitudinal studies monitor people as they grow older. A sequential design combines both methods. (page 141)
- *Cohort effects.* Many differences between young people and old people are due to the era in which they grew up. (page 142)
- *Prenatal development.* The brain begins to mature long before birth. The developing brain is vulnerable to damage by alcohol or other drugs. (page 143)

- *Infant vision.* Newborns focus on items resembling a face, and they gradually improve their ability to recognize familiar types of faces. (page 144)
- *Infant hearing.* Newborns habituate to a repeated sound but dishabituate to a slightly different sound, indicating that they hear a difference. (page 145)
- *Infant responses to language.* Newborns attend to speech sounds, and they gradually improve their ability to discriminate sounds of the language they are hearing. (page 146)

- *Infant memory.* Newborns suck more vigorously to turn on a recording of their own mother's voice than some other woman's voice, indicating that they recognize the sound of the mother's voice. Infants just 2 months old learn to kick and move a mobile, and they remember how to do it several days later. (page 146)
- *Piaget's stages of development.* Jean Piaget described cognitive development as a series of four stages. (page 147)
- *Object permanence.* In Piaget's first stage, the sensorimotor stage, infants may or may not understand the concept of object permanence, depending on how we test them. (page 148)
- *Thinking during Piaget's preoperational stage.* Clever rocedures enable psychologists to infer when young children develop a sense of self, and when they begin to understand that people differ in what they do or do not know. (page 150)
- *Appearance and reality.* Young children sometimes seem not to distinguish between appearance and reality. However, with a simpler task, they do distinguish. Children often show a concept under some conditions and not others. (page 152)
- *Vygotsky.* Lev Vygotsky emphasized how children learn new abilities from adults or older children, but only within a zone of proximal development. (page 155)

Key Terms

accommodation (page 147)

assimilation (page 147)

cohort (page 142)

conservation (page 152)

cross-sectional study (page 141)

dishabituation (page 146)

egocentric (page 150)

equilibration (page 147)

fetal alcohol syndrome (page 143)

fetus (page 143)

habituation (page 146)

longitudinal study (page 141)

object permanence (page 148)

operation (page 150)

preoperational stage (page 150)

schema (pl. schemata) (page 147)

selective attrition (page 141)

sensorimotor stage (page 148)

sequential design (page 142)

stage of concrete operations (page 154)

stage of formal operations (page 154)

theory of mind (page 151)

zone of proximal development (page 155)

zygote (page 143)

Review Questions

1. When would a difference among cohorts be likely to influence a study's results?
   (a) In a longitudinal study
   (b) In a cross-sectional study
   (c) In either a longitudinal or a cross-sectional study, equally
   (d) In neither a longitudinal nor a cross-sectional study

2. What is selective attrition?
   (a) The cues that tell participants what results a researcher expects
   (b) The research misconduct of discarding data that do not fit expectations
   (c) The difference in results by people born in different eras
   (d) The tendency of certain types of person to drop out of a study

3. Which property of neurons is responsible for fetal alcohol syndrome?
   (a) Developing neurons that get too little input will self-destruct.
   (b) Axons vary the frequency of impulses, but not their amplitude or velocity.
   (c) Neurons can have many dendrites, but only one axon.
   (d) The neurons with the greatest activity use the most oxygen.

4. Suppose an infant habituates to the sound *ba*, but when we substitute the sound *boo*, the infant fails to increase the sucking rate. What interpretation would be likely?
   (a) The infant hears a difference between the two sounds.
   (b) The infant does not hear a difference between the two sounds.
   (c) The infant prefers the sound *ba*.
   (d) The infant prefers the sound *boo*.

5. What has enabled researchers to improve their estimates of the vision, hearing, and learning abilities of newborns and other infants?
   (a) Improved behavioral measurements
   (b) Increased access to children in institutions
   (c) Brain scans such as fMRI
   (d) Increased use of virtual reality

6. Why is it difficult to say when a child first shows fear of heights?
   (a) Brain scans necessary for measuring fear are hard to use with children.
   (b) A child who shows fear when crawling might not show it when walking.
   (c) Most young children seem to be afraid almost always.
   (d) The only way to measure fear is by verbal responses.

7. What evidence suggests that even 6- to 8-month-old infants understand object permanence?
   (a) They reach around an opaque barrier to grasp an unseen toy.
   (b) They ask for toys that they do not currently see.
   (c) They stare longer at events that would be impossible if unseen objects continue to exist.
   (d) After they have repeatedly seen one toy and habituated to it, they dishabituate when they see a new toy.

8. To demonstrate "theory of mind," what must a child understand?
   (a) That someone can have a false belief
   (b) That human mental abilities are more advanced than those of other species
   (c) That mental activity is inseparable from brain activity
   (d) That all mental activity requires sensory input

9. One year ago, Sarah did not seem to understand conservation of number, volume, or mass. Today she does. According to Piaget, Sarah has progressed from which stage to which other stage?
   (a) Preoperational stage to concrete operations stage
   (b) Sensorimotor stage to preoperational stage
   (c) Concrete operations stage to formal operations stage
   (d) Formal operations stage to concrete operations stage

Answers: 1b, 2d, 3a, 4b, 5a, 6b, 7c, 8a, 9a.

module 5.2

Social and Emotional Development

After studying this module, you should be able to:

1. Characterize Erikson's stages of social and emotional development.

2. Explain how psychologists measure attachment in young children.

3. Discuss the social and emotional issues people face during adolescence, adulthood, and old age.

You are a contestant on a new TV game show, *What's My Worry?* Behind the curtain is someone you cannot see, who has an overriding concern. You are to identify that concern by questioning a psychologist who knows this person well, asking only questions that can be answered with a single word or a short phrase. Here's the catch: The more questions you ask, the smaller the prize. If you guess correctly after the first question, you win $64,000. After two questions, you win $32,000 and so on. Your best strategy is to ask as few questions as possible and then make an educated guess.

What would your first question be? A good one would be: "How old is this person?" The worries of teenagers differ from those of 20-year-olds, which differ from those of older adults. Each age has its own concerns, opportunities, and pleasures.

Erikson's Description of Human Development

Erik Erikson divided the human life span into eight periods that he called ages or stages. At each stage, he said, people have specific tasks to master, and each stage has its own social and emotional conflicts. ■ Table 5.4 summarizes Erikson's stages.

According to Erikson, failure to master the task of any stage leaves unfortunate consequences that carry over to later stages. For example, an infant deals with basic trust versus mistrust. An infant with a supportive environment forms strong attachments that facilitate future relationships (Erikson, 1963). An infant who is mistreated fails to form a trusting relationship and has trouble developing close ties with people later.

In adolescence, the key issue is identity. Most adolescents in Western societies consider many options of how they will spend the rest of their lives. They entertain alternative identities and consider many possible futures.

According to Erikson, the key decision of young adulthood is intimacy or isolation—that is, sharing your life with someone else or living alone. The quality of an intimate relationship has enormous impact throughout adult life.

If you live a full life span, you will spend about half your life in middle adulthood, where the issue is generativity (producing something important, such as children or work) versus stagnation (not producing). If all goes well, you take pride in your success. If not, then your difficulties and disappointments continue into old age, where the issue is integrity versus despair.

You might describe the main concerns of certain ages differently from what Erikson said. Nevertheless, his general argument seems valid: Each stage has its own special difficulties, and an unsatisfactory

Table 5.4 Erikson's Stages of Human Development		
Stages	**Main Conflict**	**Typical Question**
Infant	Basic trust versus mistrust	Is my social world predictable and supportive?
Toddler (ages 1–3)	Autonomy versus shame and doubt	Can I do things by myself or must I always rely on others?
Preschool child (ages 3–6)	Initiative versus guilt	Am I good or bad?
Preadolescent (ages 6–12)	Industry versus inferiority	Am I successful or worthless?
Adolescent (early teens)	Identity versus role confusion	Who am I?
Young adult (late teens and early 20s)	Intimacy versus isolation	Shall I share my life with another person or live alone?
Middle adult (late 20s to retirement)	Generativity versus stagnation	Will I succeed in my life, both as a parent and as a worker?
Older adult (after retirement)	Ego integrity versus despair	Have I lived a full life or have I failed?

Erik Erikson emphasized that each age has special conflicts.

resolution to the problems of one age produces extra difficulty in later life. Let's examine in more detail some of these social and emotional issues.

Infancy and Childhood

An important aspect of human life is attachment—*a feeling of closeness toward another person.* Attachments begin in infancy. John Bowlby (1973) proposed that infants who develop good attachments have a sense of security and safety, and those without strong attachments have trouble developing close relations later as well. Later research confirms this idea. A longitudinal study found that toddlers who received lower-quality care developed into young adults who had trouble forming strong romantic attachments (Oriña et al., 2011). An even longer study found that children from a nurturing family environment were more likely than average to control their emotions well in middle age and to have good marriages throughout life (Waldinger & Schulz, 2016). Because these are correlational studies, we do not know to what extent parental behavior caused the later emotional stability, and to what extent the effect is the result of shared genetics.

Most research on attachment has measured it in the Strange Situation (usually capitalized), pioneered

Children learn social skills by interacting with brothers, sisters, and friends close to their own age.

by Mary Ainsworth (1979). In this procedure, *a mother and her infant* (typically 12 to 18 months old) *come into a room with many toys. Then a stranger enters the room. The mother leaves and then returns. A few minutes later, both the stranger and the mother leave. Then the stranger returns, and finally, the mother returns.* Through a one-way mirror, a psychologist observes the infant's reactions to each coming and going. Observers classify infants' responses in the following categories:

- *Securely attached.* The infant uses the mother as a base of exploration, cooing at her, showing her toys, and making eye contact with her. The infant shows only mild distress when the mother leaves. When she returns, the infant goes to her with apparent delight, cuddles for a while, and then returns to the toys. Children with a secure attachment have advantages in many ways, including better than average self-control (Pallini et al., 2018).
- *Anxious (or resistant).* Responses toward the mother fluctuate between happy and angry. The infant clings to the mother and cries profusely when she leaves, as if worried that she might not return. When she does return, the infant clings to her again but does not use her as a base to explore the toys. A child with an anxious attachment shows many fears, including a fear of strangers.
- *Avoidant.* While the mother is present, the infant does not stay near her and seldom interacts with her. The infant may or may not cry when she leaves and does not go to her when she returns. An avoidant attachment becomes more common if a child is separated from the parents during a time of crisis. For example, many Australian children were in school when their parents had to flee from a wildfire, and therefore endured a long, difficult period of separation in a time of need (Bryant et al., 2017).
- *Disorganized.* The infant alternates between approach and avoidance and shows more fear than affection. A disorganized attachment is associated with increased risk of later psychopathology. It occurs mostly in cases of maltreatment or neglect by the mother, but genetic influences probably play a role also (Graffi et al., 2018).

The prevalence of the various attachment styles differs from one country to another, but the secure pattern is usually the most common (Ainsworth, Blehar, Waters, & Wall, 1978). Of course, many children do not fit neatly into one category or another. An attachment style is usually stable from one time to another, but not always (Moss, Cyr, Bureau, Tarabulsy, & Dubois-Comtois, 2005). To some extent, psychologists can predict later attachment behavior from observations on infants as young as 3 months. In the Still-Face Paradigm, a parent plays with a child and then suddenly shifts to an unresponsive, expressionless face. Infants who continue looking at the parent with little sign of distress are likely to show a strong, secure attachment at a year old and beyond (Braungart-Rieker et al., 2014).

The Strange Situation is also used to evaluate the relationship between child and father (Belsky, 1996), child and grandparent, or other relationships. As a rule, the quality of one relationship correlates with the quality of others. For example, most children who have a secure relationship with the mother also have a secure relationship with the father, and chances are the parents are happy with each other as well (Elicker, Englund, & Sroufe, 1992; Erel & Burman, 1995). Most infants who have a secure relationship with their parents at age 12 months continue to have a close relationship with them decades later (Waters, Merrick, Treboux, Crowell, & Albersheim, 2000). Those who show a secure attachment in infancy are more likely than others to form high-quality romantic attachments in adulthood (Roisman, Collins, Sroufe, & Egeland, 2005). They are quick to resolve conflicts with romantic partners and other people (Salvatore, Kuo, Steele, Simpson, & Collins, 2011).

Why do some children develop more secure attachments than others? One reason is that children differ in their temperament—*their tendency to be active or inactive, and to respond vigorously or quietly to new stimuli* (Bouchard, Lykken, McGue, Segal, & Tellegen, 1990; Planalp, Van Hulle, Lemery-Chalfant, & Goldsmith, 2017). Children's temperaments differ from the start. As developmental psychologists say, "Any parent who thinks parents have complete control over how their children turn out can be assumed to have no more than one child." Temperament is moderately stable as children grow older (Kopala-Sibley, Olino, Durbin, Dyston, & Klein, 2018). Those with a "difficult" temperament are frightened more easily than others from infancy through adulthood (Kagan, Reznick, & Snidman, 1988; Kagan & Snidman, 1991; Schwartz, Wright, Shin, Kagan, & Rauch, 2003).

Attachment style also relates strongly to how responsive the parents are to the infants' needs, including holding, touching, facial expressions, and so forth. Gentle touch can be very reassuring (Hertenstein, 2002). Developing a secure attachment takes time and effort. One study examined children who were reared in an orphanage in Africa, Asia, Eastern Europe, or Latin America for one to three years before adoption by a U.S. family. By three months after adoption, about half of the children showed an attachment to their adopting parents, and by nine months, about two-thirds showed a secure attachment (Carlson, Hostinar, Mliner, & Gunnar, 2014).

Patterns of attachment are mostly similar across cultures. Sometimes what appears to be a difference in attachment reflects difficulties in measurement. In one study, Western psychologists observing black children in South Africa found low consistency between measurements of attachment in one situation and another. When they enlisted local people as co-investigators, the local observers, who understood the local customs, reported data with greater consistency (Minde, Minde, & Vogel, 2006). Another study reported an unusually high prevalence of "anxious attachment" among Japanese infants. However, Japanese mothers customarily stay with their babies almost constantly, including bathing with them and sleeping in the same bed. When the Japanese mothers were persuaded to leave their infants alone with a stranger, it was in many cases a new experience for the infant, who reacted with horror. The same reaction by a U.S. child would have a different meaning (Rothbaum, Weisz, Pott, Miyake, & Morelli, 2000).

13. What is the similarity between the Strange Situation and the Still-Face Paradigm?

Answer

13. Both are methods of measuring the strength of an attachment. They are used at different ages.

Social Development in Childhood and Adolescence

Whereas attachment to parents or other caregivers is critical for infants, relationships with age-mates become increasingly important during childhood and adolescence. Around puberty, sexual interest begins to enter into peer relationships.

The status of adolescents varies among cultures and eras. If you had been born in the 1800s or early 1900s, or in many parts of the world today, your education probably would have ended in your early teens, if not before, and you would have begun working full-time or taking care of your own children. As ▼ Figure 5.18a shows, the age of menarche (the onset of puberty in girls) has been steadily decreasing over the last century and a half in many countries, because of improved health and nutrition. Meanwhile, as ▼ Figure 5.18b shows, young people have been spending more years in school (Worthman & Trang, 2018). The result is that young people are physically adults for many years before being treated as adults.

Adolescence is sometimes described as a time of "storm and stress," a term that is misleading in most cases. Some degree of conflict with parents is normal as an adolescent is becoming more independent, but the emotional outcome depends on how the adolescent and parents handle the conflict. The best result occurs if they approach it as an opportunity for problem solving. Less favorable

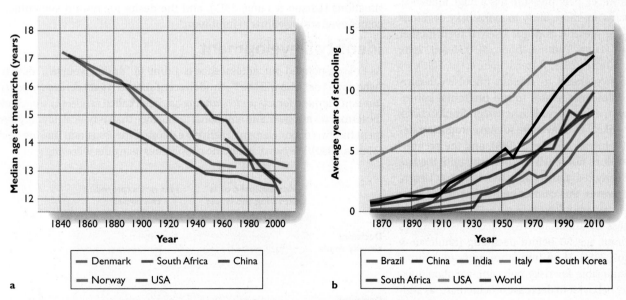

▲ **Figure 5.18** The mean age of menarche (female puberty) has been steadily decreasing **(a)** while the mean age of finishing school has been increasing **(b)**. The result is a long period of physical adulthood without independence. (From Worthman & Trang, 2017)

(a) American teenagers are financially dependent on their parents but have the opportunity to spend much time in whatever way they choose. (b) In many nontechnological societies, teenagers are expected to do adult work and accept adult responsibilities.

approaches are for the adolescent simply to give in, or to withdraw from the parents, or to react with hostility (Missotten, Luyckx, Branje, Hale, & Meeus, 2017).

Adolescence is also a time of risk-taking behaviors. Adolescents are certainly aware of dangers. If asked about the advisability of drunk driving, unprotected sex, and so forth, they describe the dangers as fully as adults do. Why, then, don't they behave like adults? Well, most of the time they do, especially when they take time to consider their decisions. However, peer pressure has a huge influence. Adolescents are more likely to make risky decisions if peers are present, and less likely if their mother is present (Luna, Padmanabhan, & O'Hearn, 2010; Moreira & Telzer, 2018; Telzer, Ichien, & Qu, 2015).

One hypothesis to explain impulsive behavior in adolescents relates to the prefrontal cortex. People with a thinner or less active prefrontal cortex are more likely than average to make impulsive decisions (Pehlivanova et al.., 2018), and the prefrontal cortex does not reach full maturity until the late teens or early 20s (Luna, Padmanabhan, & O'Hearn, 2010). However, this cannot be the full explanation for adolescent impulsiveness. As ▶ Figure 5.19 shows, willingness to undertake risky activities increases up to about age 20 before declining (Shulman & Cauffman, 2014). If an immature prefrontal cortex were responsible for risky behavior, we should expect risky behavior to decrease, not increase, as adolescents grow older. The increased risk taking relates to an increased urge for excitement. The adolescent brain shows powerful responses to reward in many

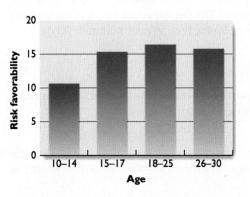

◀ **Figure 5.19** On average, people around age 20 gave higher acceptability ratings to risky activities than did those who were either younger or older. (Based on data from Shulman 2014)

situations (Larsen & Luna, 2015), and the desire for reward sometimes overcomes even strong efforts at inhibition.

Identity Development

As Erikson pointed out, adolescence is a time of "finding yourself," determining "who am I?" or "who will I be?" An adolescent's *concern with decisions about the future and the quest for self-understanding* has been called an identity crisis. However, the term *crisis* implies more emotional turbulence than is typical. Identity development has two major elements: actively exploring the issue and making decisions (Marcia, 1980). We can diagram the possibilities using the following grid:

	Has explored or is exploring the issues	Has not explored the issues
Decisions already made	Identity achievement	Identity foreclosure
Decisions not yet made	Identity moratorium	Identity diffusion

Those who have not yet given any serious thought to making decisions and who have no clear sense of identity are said to have identity diffusion. They are not actively concerned with their identity at the moment. Identity diffusion is more common among people with low self-esteem and a pessimistic attitude toward life (Phillips & Pittman, 2007). If you think you have little chance of achieving anything, there is no reason to decide on any goals. People in identity moratorium are *considering the issues but not yet making decisions.* They experiment with various possibilities and imagine themselves in different roles, but postpone any choices.

Identity foreclosure is a state of *accepting decisions without much thought.* For example, a young man might be told that he is expected to go into the family business with his father, or a young woman might be told that she is expected to marry and raise children. Decrees of that sort were once common in North America and Europe, and they are still common in many societies today. Someone living in such circumstances has little reason to consider alternative possibilities.

Finally, identity achievement is *the outcome of having explored various possible identities and then making one's own decisions.* Identity achievement does not come all at once. For example, you might decide about your career but not about marriage. You might also decide about a career and then reconsider the decision later.

The "Personal Fable" of Teenagers

Answer the following items true or false:

- Other people may fail to realize their life ambitions, but I will realize mine.
- I understand love and sex in a way that my parents never did.
- Tragedy may strike other people but probably not me.
- Almost everyone notices how I look and how I dress.

According to David Elkind, one reason for risky behavior is the "personal fable," which includes the secret belief that "nothing bad can happen to me."

According to David Elkind (1984), teenagers are particularly likely to harbor such beliefs. Taken together, he calls them the personal fable, *the conviction that "I am special—what is true for everyone else is not true for me."* Up to a point, this fable supports an optimistic outlook on life, but it becomes dangerous if it leads to foolish risks.

This attitude is hardly unique to teenagers, however. Most middle-aged adults regard themselves as more likely than other people to succeed on the job and less likely than average to have a serious illness (Quadrel, Fischhoff, & Davis, 1993). People's tendency to be overconfident in their opinions is approximately constant from adolescence through old age (Prims & Moore, 2017). That is, the personal fable seems to be part of human nature.

Adulthood

From early adulthood until retirement, the main concern of most adults is, as Erikson noted, "What will I achieve and contribute to society and my family? Will I be successful?"

Adulthood extends from one's first full-time job until retirement. We lump so many years together because it seems that little is changing. During your childhood and adolescence, you grew taller each year, and each new age brought new privileges, such as permission to stay out late, your first driver's license, the right to vote, and the opportunity to go to college. After early adulthood, one year blends into the next. Important changes occur, but instead of depending on age, they depend on decisions, such as getting married, having children, changing jobs, or moving to a new location.

Daniel Levinson (1986) describes adult development in terms of a series of overlapping eras. After the transition into adulthood at about age 20, give or take a couple of years, comes early adulthood, which lasts until about age 40. During early adulthood, people devote great energy to pursuing their goals. Young adulthood is an exciting time, but also a stressful time. Starting a career, buying a house, and raising a family are difficult.

During middle adulthood, extending from about age 40 to 65, physical strength begins to decline, on average, but not enough to be a problem, except for pro athletes and others with physically demanding jobs. At this point, people have already achieved success at work or have come to accept whatever status they have. For most people, vocational interests are fairly stable over time (Schultz, Connolly, Garrison, Leveille, & Jackson, 2017). That is, if you like your career choice at first and feel highly motivated, you will probably feel the same way years from now.

In middle adulthood, according to Levinson (1986), people go through a midlife transition, *a period of reassessing goals, setting new ones, and preparing for the rest of life.* This transition may occur simply in response to age ("Wow, I'm 40!"), or in response to a divorce, illness, death in the family, career change, or any event that raises questions about past decisions and current goals (Wethington, Kessler, & Pixley, 2004). Just as the adolescent identity crisis is a bigger issue in cultures that offer many choices, the same is true for the midlife transition. If you lived in a society that offered no choices, you would not worry about the paths not taken! In Western society, however, young adults start with high hopes. When my son Sam was getting ready for college, I asked him what his goal was. He replied, "world domination." I thought about that for a while and then asked what he was going to *be*. He replied that he was going to be "awesome." I hope you have similarly high ambitions. However, by middle age you begin to see which of your early goals are achievable, which ones are not, and which ones might still be achievable but only if you start soon. At that point you have your midlife transition and reconsider your goals.

People deal with their midlife transitions in many ways. Most people abandon unrealistic goals and set new goals consistent with the direction their lives have taken. Others decide that they have been ignoring dreams that they are not willing to abandon. They go back to school, set up a new business, or try something else they have always wanted to do. The least satisfactory outcome is to decide, "I can't abandon my dreams, but I can't do anything about them either. I can't take the risk of changing my life, even though I am dissatisfied with it." People with that attitude become discouraged and depressed.

The advice is clear: To increase your chances of feeling good in middle age and beyond, make good decisions when you are young. If you care about some goal, don't wait for a midlife transition. Get started on it now.

14. How does a midlife transition resemble an adolescent identity crisis?

Answer

14. In both cases, people examine their lives, goals, and possible directions for the future.

Old Age

Finally, people reach late adulthood, generally defined as around age 65. According to Erikson, people who feel satisfied with their lives experience "ego integrity," and those who are not satisfied feel "despair." Some older people say, "I hope to live many more years, but even if I don't, I have lived my life well. I did everything that I really cared about." Others say, "I wanted to do so much that I never did." Your satisfaction in old age will depend on how you live while younger.

People age in different ways. Some deteriorate in intellect, coordination, and ability to care for themselves, while others remain alert and active. The best established way to improve older people's memory and cognition is daily physical exercise (Colcombe & Kramer, 2003; Mattson & Magnus, 2006). Just taking a long walk is good, but some evidence suggests even better results by having cognitive activity along with the physical, such as by learning dance steps or martial arts (Gheysen et al., 2018).

Psychologists have long noticed a conflict between test results that show older people declining intellectually, and observations of older people doing well in everyday life. Much of the explanation is that averages are misleading. Some people decline considerably while others do not. Another part of the explanation is that older people concentrate their efforts on tasks that seem more relevant, familiar, or important. As a result, they do well in everyday life and on their jobs, but not so well when their motivation sags, as it might when taking psychological tests (Hess, 2014). Furthermore, older people can call upon their extensive experience instead of solving each problem anew (Umanath & Marsh, 2014).

Several kinds of evidence indicate that healthy older people are, on average, happier and more satisfied with life than younger people are. That result may seem surprising. However, young people face pressures from work and raising children, whereas older people have more leisure. Furthermore, older people deliberately focus their attention on family, friends, and other events that bring them pleasure (Carstensen, Mikels, & Mather, 2006).

Loss of control is a serious issue when health begins to fail. Consider someone who spent half a century running a business who now lives in a nursing

In Tibet, Africa, and many other cultures, children are taught to treat old people with respect and honor.

home where staff members make all the decisions. Leaving even a few of the choices and responsibilities to the residents improves their self-respect, health, alertness, and memory (Rodin, 1986; Rowe & Kahn, 1987).

The Psychology of Facing Death

This is perhaps the greatest lesson we learned from our patients: LIVE, so you do not have to look back and say, "God, how I have wasted my life!"

—Elisabeth Kübler-Ross (1975, p. xix)

The worst thing about death is the fact that when a man is dead it's impossible any longer to undo the harm you have done him, or to do the good you haven't done him. They say: live in such a way as to be always ready to die. I would say: live in such a way that anyone can die without you having anything to regret.

—Leo Tolstoy (1865/1978, p. 192)

Have you ever heard the advice, "Live each day as if it were going to be your last"? The point is to appreciate every moment, but if you really believed you would die today, you wouldn't plan for the future. You wouldn't save money or worry about the long-term health consequences of your actions. You probably wouldn't study this textbook. If we lived each day as if we expected to live forever, maybe we would be more careful about protecting the environment.

Just thinking about the fact of eventual death evokes distress. To go on with life effectively, we try to shield ourselves from thinking too much about dying. According to **terror-management theory**, *we cope with our fear of death by avoiding thoughts about death and by affirming a worldview that provides self-esteem, hope, and value in life* (Pyszczynski, Greenberg, & Solomon, 2000). When something reminds you of your mortality, you do what you can to reduce the anxiety. You reassure yourself that you still have many years to live. "My health is good, I don't smoke, I don't drink too much, and I'm not overweight." If that isn't true, you tell yourself that you plan to quit smoking, you are going to cut down on your drinking, and any day now you are going to start losing weight. You also think about what you expect to accomplish and all the exciting things you will do during the rest of your life (Kasser & Sheldon, 2000).

Still, even excellent health merely postpones death, so a reminder of death redoubles your efforts to defend a belief that life is important. You reaffirm your religious beliefs, your patriotism, or other views that help you find meaning in life, and you behave morally and honestly (Greenberg et al., 2003; Schindler et al., 2019). You vow to repair damaged relationships with relatives or friends (Anglin, 2014). If you are a parent, you think about your children, who will survive after you are gone (Yaakobi, Mikulincer, & Shaver, 2014). You do whatever you can to increase your feeling of control over your future (Zaleskiewicz, Gasiorowska, & Kesebir, 2013). You take pride in how you have contributed to your profession or anything else that will continue after you are gone (Pyszczynski et al., 2000).

How people react to awareness of death varies somewhat as a function of culture. In Western cultures, people primed to think about death distance themselves from victims of violence or other misfortune, saying, "I'm not like that, so it won't happen to me." In Eastern cultures, people become more likely to identify with others, even the unfortunate, saying, "the welfare of the collective society is what matters" (Ma-Kellams & Blascovich, 2011).

Advances in modern medicine raise new ethical issues with regard to dying. We can now keep people alive even though their physical and mental capacities deteriorate. Should we? If someone is bedridden, in pain, and mentally deteriorated, with little hope of recovery, is it acceptable to help the person hasten death? A growing number of people have to face these difficult decisions for themselves and family members.

in closing | module 5.2

Social and Emotional Issues through the Life Span

Let's close by reemphasizing a key point of Erik Erikson's theory: Each age or stage builds on the previous ones. The quality of your early attachments to parents and others correlates with your ability to form close, trusting relationships later. How well you handle the identity issues of adolescence affects your adult life. Your productivity as an adult determines how satisfied you will feel in old age. Life is a continuum, and the choices you make at any age link with those you make before and after.

Summary

- *Erikson's view of development.* Erik Erikson emphasized that each period of human life has its own conflicts. How well you handle each conflict influences your life at later stages. (page 159)
- *Infant attachment.* Infants who form strong early attachments are likely to develop good social and romantic attachments as adults. (page 160)
- *Measuring attachment.* The Strange Situation is a common way to evaluate attachments for ages 12 to 18 months. The

Still-Face Paradigm is appropriate for younger infants. (page 160)
- *Temperament.* Beginning in infancy, people differ in their temperament, how strongly they react to new stimuli. (page 160)
- *Adolescent impulsiveness.* Adolescents are prone to risky behaviors, especially in the presence of peers. (page 162)
- *Identity.* Identity development raises problems in a society that offers many options. (page 162)

- *Adults' concerns.* A major concern of adults is productivity in family and career. Many adults undergo a midlife transition when they reevaluate their goals. (page 163)
- *Old age.* Dignity and independence are key concerns of old age. (page 164)
- *Facing death.* People at all ages face the anxieties associated with the inevitability of death. A reminder of death influences people to defend their worldviews. (page 165)

Key Terms

attachment (page 160)

identity achievement (page 163)

identity crisis (page 162)

identity diffusion (page 163)

identity foreclosure (page 163)

identity moratorium (page 163)

midlife transition (page 163)

personal fable (page 163)

Still-Face Paradigm (page 160)

Strange Situation (page 160)

temperament (page 160)

terror-management theory (page 165)

Review Questions

1. If an infant shows great distress when the mother leaves in the Strange Situation, why would the interpretation differ for Japanese versus American infants?
   (a) Japanese and American infants differ genetically in their reaction to situations.
   (b) It might be the first time the Japanese mother left the infant with a stranger.
   (c) Japanese and American infants have been exposed to different television shows.
   (d) Experimenters show different expectations for Japanese and American infants.

2. What is considered the main explanation for high risk taking in adolescents?
   (a) Adolescents have an increasing tendency to seek excitement and reward.
   (b) The prefrontal cortex shows little development before age 20.
   (c) Adolescents strongly rebel against their parents.
   (d) Adolescents do not understand the dangers of a risky behavior.

3. In a society where almost everyone becomes a farmer, which of the following would be most common?
   (a) Identity diffusion
   (b) Identity moratorium
   (c) Identity foreclosure
   (d) Identity achievement

4. What is meant by "the personal fable"?
   (a) The belief that what is true for others is not true for me
   (b) The explanation that people give for their failures
   (c) The way that people imagine they lived in early childhood
   (d) The story that a person finds to be the most inspiring

5. According to terror-management theory, how do people react to reminders of mortality?
   (a) They pretend that they did not hear the reminder.
   (b) They strengthen beliefs that provide meaning in life.
   (c) They have frightening dreams.
   (d) They seek opportunities to talk about death and dying.

Answers: 1b, 2a, 3c, 4a, 5b.

Liderina/Shutterstock.com

module 5.3

Diversity: Gender, Culture, and Family

After studying this module, you should be able to:

1. Discuss possible explanations for differences between men and women.

2. Discuss the influences of culture on behavior.

3. Evaluate the evidence regarding the influence of birth order and family size.

4. Evaluate the evidence about the contributions of parenting styles, nontraditional families, and divorce on children's development.

Suppose we changed your gender, your ethnicity, and your culture. While we are at it, let's trade you at birth to a different family. How would you be different? With such drastic changes, it is not clear that it would still be *you!* Gender, culture, and family are integral parts of anyone's development and identity.

Gender Influences

Males and females differ biologically in many ways that influence behavior. On average, several brain areas are proportionately larger in men and others are proportionately larger in women (Cahill, 2006), and certain genes are more active in one or the other (Reinius et al., 2008). However, note the term "on average." The distributions for men and those for women overlap enormously. Every aspect of brain anatomy and gene expression varies from one person to another, and few people are male-typical or female-typical in all aspects (Joel et al., 2015).

Regardless of the brain differences, most aspects of behavior and personality differ only slightly on average (Zell, Krizan, & Teeter, 2015). A few differences are reasonably consistent. On average, boys are more active, whereas girls have better self-control (Else-Quest, Hyde, Goldsmith, & Van Hulle, 2006). Men throw harder and get into fights more often (Hyde, 2005). Men are more likely to help a stranger change a flat tire, but women are more likely to provide long-term nurturing support (Eagly & Crowley, 1986). The more pairs of shoes you own, the higher is the probability that you are female. Men and women tend to carry books in different ways, as shown in ▶ Figure 5.20.

On average, females are better than males at recognizing faces and detecting emotional signals (Chen & Haviland-Jones, 2000; Hall & Matsumoto, 2004; Heisz, Pottruff, & Shore, 2013). People have long noted how often men misinterpret a woman's smile, mistaking friendliness for sexual interest. Psychologists used to interpret this trend as wishful thinking until they discovered that the opposite is also true: When a woman is trying to signal sexual interest, many men misinterpret her expression as mere friendliness (Farris, Treat, Viken, & McFall, 2008). Evidently, men are on average less accurate at recognizing almost any emotional expression.

When giving directions, men are more likely to use directions and distances—such as "go four blocks east . . ."—whereas women are more likely to use landmarks—such as "go until you see the library . . ." (Saucier et al., 2002). ▼ Figure 5.21 compares men's and women's ways of giving directions (Rahman, Andersson, & Govier, 2005). Similarly, in monkeys, mice, and several other species, males perform better than females in mazes without landmarks, whereas females remember the landmarks better (Jones, Braithwaite, & Healy, 2003; Williams, Barnett, & Meck, 1990). However, if required to rely on either landmarks or distances, both men and women get along fine (Spelke, 2005).

Another difference: Women apologize more than men do. Why? In one study, men and women kept a diary of how often they did something for which they should have apologized, how often they did apologize, how often they thought someone else should have apologized, and how often that person did. Men reported fewer occasions when they should apologize, and fewer occasions when someone else should apologize (Schumann & Ross, 2010). That is, men often shrug something off as unimportant, when women expect to say or hear, "I'm sorry." You see how

Andersen Ross Photography Inc./DigitalVision/Getty Images

▲ **Figure 5.20** Men usually carry books and similar objects at their sides. Women beyond the age of puberty usually carry them at their chest. Of course, this generalization does not apply to people wearing backpacks.

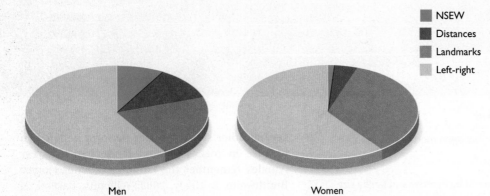

◀ **Figure 5.21** When giving directions, men refer to distances and north, south, east, and west more often than women do. Women describe more landmarks. (Based on data of Rahman, Andersson, & Govier, 2005)

Men   Women

this difference can be a source of friction between men and women. However, this type of behavior is likely to vary among cultures, and we should await cross-cultural studies before drawing a broad conclusion. (P.S. A great quote from a man: "If I have done anything for which I should apologize, I am ready to be forgiven.")

On average, males and females differ in their interests, from childhood through adulthood. Also, males are more likely than females to devote almost all their energies to a single interest, whereas females are more likely to develop a variety of interests (Valla & Ceci, 2014; Wang, Eccles, & Kenny, 2013).

The way people rear children certainly contributes to the development of different interests. For example, children who watch a television commercial showing just boys playing with a particular toy say that this is a toy "just for boys" (Pike & Jennings, 2005). However, biological tendencies may contribute also. Researchers consistently find that boys and girls tend to prefer different toys from age 1 onward, regardless of whether parents are present or not (Todd et al., 2018). Girls 3 to 8 months old (too young to do much besides look) look more at dolls than at toy trucks, whereas boys look at both about equally (Alexander, Wilcox, & Woods, 2009). Even male monkeys prefer to play with "boys' toys," such as a ball and a toy car, whereas female monkeys prefer to play with "girls' toys," such as a soft doll (Alexander & Hines, 2002; Hassett, Siebert, & Wallen, 2008).

More convincingly, researchers have found that girls who were exposed to higher than average levels of the male hormone testosterone during prenatal development tend to play with boys' toys more than the average for other girls (Berenbaum, Duck, & Bryk, 2000; Nordenström, Servin, Bohlin, Larsson, & Wedell, 2002; Pasterski et al., 2005). (Mothers vary in how much testosterone they produce, and some of it enters the developing fetus.) Another study found that girls who had higher than average testosterone levels in the first months of life spent more than average time playing with toy trains at age 14 months (Lamminmäki et al., 2012). Conversely, when pregnant women are exposed to chemicals that interfere with testosterone, their sons show less than average interest in boys' toys at ages 3 to 6 (Swan et al., 2010). These results suggest that males' and females' interests differ for biological as well as socially acquired reasons.

In contrast to interests, men and women are equal in intellectual abilities (Halpern et al., 2007; Hyde, 2005; Levine, Vasilyeva, Lourenco, Newcombe, & Huttenlocher, 2005; Spelke, 2005). Many people believe that men are better in mathematics. Males outperform females in math in countries where men have greater economic and political status than women, but in countries that provide more equal opportunities, the difference in average math performance disappears (Breda, Jouini, & Napp, 2018; Guiso, Monte, Sapienza, & Zingales, 2008). Test scores for 8th graders in science and mathematics show boys doing better than girls in some countries, and girls doing better than boys in other countries, relating largely to cultural influences (Reilly, Neumann, & Andrews, 2019). In the United States, on average, females do as well as or better than males on standardized math test scores and grades in nearly all math courses from elementary school through college (Hyde, Lindberg, Linn, Ellis, & Williams, 2008; Spelke, 2005).

Men often fail to read other people's emotions.

Vastly more men than women become grand masters in chess. However, a study found that boys and girls start at an equal level in chess and progress at equal rates. The main reason more men than women reached the highest level was that vastly more boys than girls *started* playing chess, and a higher percentage continued (Chabris & Glickman, 2006). The difference is in interests, not abilities.

A reasonable expectation would be that in countries that provide better opportunities for women, more would enter the STEM fields (science, technology, engineering, and math). However, the surprising finding is that in countries with greater opportunities for women, a *smaller* percentage enter the STEM fields (Stoet & Geary, 2018). A proposed explanation is that a STEM career offers one of the few ways a woman can achieve financial independence in a country with restricted opportunities. When a wider variety of opportunities are open, women gravitate toward fields they regard as more interesting or enjoyable.

Males and females also show small but consistent differences, on average, in these regards: Females do better at certain aspects of verbal fluency, and males do better on certain geometrical tasks, such as those in ▼ Figure 5.22. With much simpler geometrical tasks, we see a hint of a male advantage even among infants (Constantinescu, Moore, Johnson, & Hines, 2018; Moore & Johnson, 2008; Quinn & Liben, 2008). However, part of this difference reflects a difference in interests. Boys usually spend more time on activities that require attention to angles and directions, providing the opportunity to learn relevant skills. Young women who spent 10 hours playing action video games significantly narrowed the male–female gap on visuospatial tasks (Feng, Spence, & Pratt, 2007).

Gender Roles

People's behaviors depend partly on gender roles (also known as sex roles), *the different activities that society expects of males and females.* Gender roles sometimes constrain people's choices. For example, traditional gender roles discourage some women from pursuing interests or career opportunities that are considered too masculine. Gender roles can be a problem for men, too. In many cultures, young men are required to kill a large animal or withstand great pain to prove their manhood. In the United States, some men feel a need to win fights or engage in other risky behaviors to prove their manhood (Vandello, Bosson, Cohen, Burnaford, & Weaver, 2008).

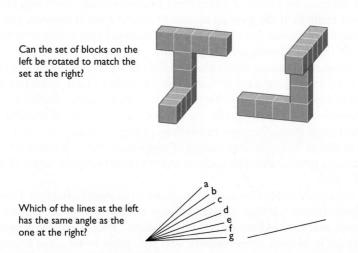

Can the set of blocks on the left be rotated to match the set at the right?

Which of the lines at the left has the same angle as the one at the right?

▲ **Figure 5.22** On average, men perform slightly better than women on tasks like these. (The answers are given below.)

Answer

No, the set on the left cannot be rotated to match the one on the right. For the second question, line e matches the model to its right.

Biology influences a few aspects of gender roles: For example, only women can nurse babies, and men generally have an edge in physical strength. However, most gender roles are customs set by society. Is building a fire mostly men's work or women's? What about basket weaving? Planting crops? Milking cows? The answers vary from one society to another (Wood & Eagly, 2002). (See ▼ **Figure 5.23**.) Cultures also determine the relative status of men and women. As a rule, if a culture lives in conditions that require hunting, fighting, or other use of physical strength, men have greater status than women. When food is abundant and enemies are few, men and women have more equal status.

Over the years, gender roles have changed in many ways in many countries. In the United States, Canada, and Europe, women have become far more likely than before to get a college education, pursue a career, and become financially independent. Women in politics or other positions of leadership, once a rarity, are now common. Dating customs have been more resistant to change, however. Although exceptions occur, most people still expect that a man asks a woman for a date, picks her up, pays for most expenses, drives her home, and takes the initiative for kissing or other sexual contact (Eaton & Rose, 2011).

Reasons for Gender Differences

Gender differences reflect both biological and social influences. Biological influences include the greater size and strength of males, on average, as well as the apparent influence of prenatal hormones on a child's later interests. Social influences include the expectations that parents convey to their children. Even with 6- and 9-month-old infants, mothers talk to their daughters in a more conversational way and give more instructions to their sons, such as "come here" (Clearfield & Nelson, 2006). At this age, the infants themselves are neither walking nor talking, so the difference demonstrates the mother's behavior, not her reaction to the infants' behavior.

In one study, researchers set up cameras and microphones to eavesdrop on families in a science museum. Boys and girls spent about equal time looking at each exhibit, and the parents spent about equal time telling boys and girls how to use each exhibit, but on the average, the parents provided about three times as much scientific explanation to the boys as to the girls, regardless of how many questions the children themselves asked (Crowley, Callanen, Tenenbaum, & Allen, 2001). In another study, college students were told to explain certain scientific concepts to an 8-year-old child, using the Internet. They provided more information when they thought they were talking to a boy than when they thought they were talking to a girl (Newall et al., 2018).

▲ **Figure 5.23** Gender roles vary greatly among cultures and even from one time period to another for a single culture. Here, a Palestinian man (**a**) and a Vietnamese woman (**b**) plow the fields. Men in Bangladesh (**c**) and women in Thailand (**d**) do the wash.

15. What does the evidence say about male–female differences in mathematics and science?

Answer

15. On average, females do at least as well as males in almost all math and science classes, when given the opportunity. Girls are sometimes given less instruction because people expect them to have less interest.

Culture and Ethnicity

Some behaviors are remarkably similar across cultures. Did you know that the average nonromantic hug lasts 3 seconds? The duration is the same in all parts of the world (Nagy, 2011). Many other customs vary enormously. In Europe and North America, parents put their newborn in a crib, encouraging independence from the start. In Asia, infants sleep in the parents' bed. Europeans and Americans consider the Asian custom strange, and Asians consider the European/American custom cruel. In India and China, people seldom say "thank you" when a close relative helps them, because they take it for granted

that relatives help one another. Americans do expect a thank-you (Zhang, Ji, Bai, & Li, 2018).

If you grew up in the United States or a similar country, you spent most of your playtime with other children close to your own age, including few if any of your relatives. If you grew up in parts of Africa or South America, you played in mixed-age groups that almost certainly included your brothers, sisters, and cousins (Rogoff, Morelli, & Chavajay, 2010).

When complaining about some product or service, would you express anger to try to get your way? In Europe or the United States, moderate expressions of anger are generally effective. In Asia, they usually backfire, unless the circumstances obviously justify the anger (Adam, Shirako, & Maddux, 2010). In the United States, frequent expressions of anger correlate with an increased risk of illness. In Japan, expressions of anger correlate with better health, because only people with high social status are likely to express anger (Kitayama et al., 2015).

Descriptions of culture are often prone to overgeneralization. One popular generalization is that Western culture, such as that of the United States, Canada, and most of Europe, is "individualistic." People value independence, strive for individual achievements, and take pride in personal accomplishments. In "collectivist" cultures such as China, people emphasize dependence on one another, strive for group advancement, and take pride in their family's or group's accomplishments more than their own. This generalization is useful in some ways, but overstated (Brewer & Chen, 2007). Furthermore, many "collectivist" countries have been tending toward increased individualism, probably as a result of increased urban life and increased prosperity (Santos, Varnum, & Grossman, 2017).

To the extent that the generalization holds, *why* is Chinese culture generally more collectivist than Western culture? Historically, it may relate to rice farming. Rice farms, common in much of China, require elaborate irrigation systems that require neighbors to cooperate so that everyone gets enough water. Farmers need to stagger their planting times so that each one can help the others harvest their crops. Unless everyone works for the common good, no one profits. In contrast, wheat farming, common in northern China, requires less cooperation. Psychologists have found that people in northern China show a more independent attitude, even though they share the same religion, government, and ethnic background as the southern Chinese (Talhelm et al., 2014).

Ethnic Minorities

Growing up as a member of an ethnic minority poses special issues. Achieving ethnic identity is comparable to the process adolescents go through in finding an individual identity. The result of strong ethnic identity depends on the group's status. In Miami, Florida, researchers found that Cuban Americans with a strong ethnic identification had high self-esteem, but Nicaraguan Americans with a strong ethnic identification had low self-esteem (Cislo, 2008). Cuban Americans dominate Miami politics and culture, so it is easy to see how ethnic identification would work differently for Cuban and Nicaraguan Americans.

Acculturation

Ethnic identity is especially salient for immigrants to a country. Immigrants need to learn new customs and probably a new language. Immigrants, their children, and sometimes further generations experience biculturalism, *partial identification with two cultures.* For example, Mexican immigrants to the United States speak Spanish and follow Mexican customs at home but switch to the English language and U.S. customs in other places. Most immigrants with this type of bicultural attachment are well adjusted, but bicultural identification is difficult if the minority group is widely distrusted. Many Turkish and Russian immigrants to Germany feel ostracized and therefore unable to identify with German culture (Simon, Reichert, & Grabow, 2013). Similarly, Muslim Americans became targets of distrust after the terrorist attacks in September 2001, and consequently found it more difficult to identify as both American and Muslim (Sirin & Fine, 2007). Often, immigrants who live in a neighborhood with others of their own background show better physical and mental health than those in a more mixed neighborhood, perhaps because they face fewer expressions of prejudice (Boyer, Firat, & van Leeuwen, 2015).

Bicultural youth in the United States tend to have low rates of substance use, delinquency, and depression (Coatsworth, Maldonado-Molina, Pantin, & Szapocznik, 2005). One reason is that their parents maintain close supervision (Fuligni, 1998). Another reason is that by not feeling fully part of U.S. youth culture, bicultural adolescents are less subject to its peer pressures.

Just as people master a foreign language better if they start young, people who immigrate at a younger age tend to accept the new culture more readily (Cheung, Chudek, & Heine, 2011). People maintain some parts of their original culture longer than others. For example, most immigrants to the United States maintain their ethnic food preferences long after they have switched to American

Frank Lukassek/Terra/Corbis

Rice farming requires much cooperation among neighbors, leading to a collectivist culture.

customs of dress and entertainment (Ying, Han, & Wong, 2008).

Analogous to biculturalism is biracialism. A growing percentage of people in the United States have parents of different origins, such as African and European, European and Hispanic, or Asian and Native American. People of mixed ancestry are especially common in Hawaii, California, and Puerto Rico. Decades ago, psychologists believed

Christian Science Monitor/Getty Images

Many immigrants are bicultural, being familiar with two sets of customs. These immigrant children attend middle school in Michigan.

Many biracial people have achieved great success. President Barack Obama is a prominent example.

that biracial children and adolescents were at a disadvantage, rejected by both groups. Today, however, racially mixed couples are more common, and most (but not all) biracial youth say they feel reasonably well accepted by both groups. A problem they often mention is how to label themselves. If a form asks for a racial/ethnic identity, they don't want to check just one identity (Shih & Sanchez, 2005). The U.S. Census form now permits people to indicate mixed ancestry.

16. In what way is biracialism similar to biculturalism?

Answer

16. A bicultural person identifies to some extent with two cultures. A biracial person identifies to some extent with two ethnic origins.

The Family

In your early childhood, your parents and other relatives were the most important people in your life. How do early family experiences mold personality and social behavior?

Birth Order and Family Size

You may have heard people say that firstborn children are more successful and ambitious than later-born children. Later-born children are said to be more popular, more independent, less conforming, less neurotic, and possibly more creative.

Many of the studies supporting these generalizations used flawed research methods (Ernst & Angst, 1983; Schooler, 1972). A common way to do the research is this: Ask people to tell you their birth order and something else about themselves, such as their grade point average in school. Then measure the correlation between the measurements. Do you see a possible problem here?

The problem is that many firstborns come from families with only one child, whereas later-born children necessarily come from larger families. Many highly educated and ambitious parents have only one child, who then has many advantages. What appears to be a difference between first- and later-born children could be a difference between small and large families (Rodgers, 2001).

A better method is to compare first- and second-born children in families with at least two children, first- and third-born children in families with at least three children, and so forth. ▼ Figure 5.24 shows the results of one study. The average IQ was higher in small families than in large families. However, within a family of a given size, birth order made little difference (Rodgers, Cleveland, van den Oord, & Rowe, 2000). However, several other studies found that firstborn children did score slightly higher on IQ tests than later-born children, even within the same family (Bjerkedal, Kristensen, Skjeret, & Brevik, 2007; Rohrer, Egloff, & Schmukle, 2015). Well-designed studies of personality show no consistent difference between first-born and later-born children (Boccio & Beaver, 2019; Rohrer, Egloff, & Schmukle, 2017). The general points to remember are that the effect of birth order is small, and research must carefully separate the effects of birth order from those of family size.

17. Why is it improper to compare all the firstborns in your class to all the later-borns?

Answer

17. Many firstborns come from one-child families. Small families differ from large families in various ways.

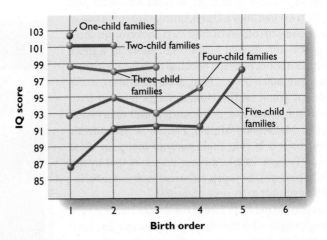

▲ Figure 5.24 Children from small families tend to score higher on IQ tests than children from large families. However, within a family of a given size, birth order is not related to IQ in this study. (Adapted from Rodgers, Cleveland, van den Oord, & Rowe, 2000)

Effects of Parenting Styles

If you have children of your own, will you be loving and kind, or strict and distant? Will you give your children everything they want or make them work for rewards? Will you encourage their independence or enforce restrictions? Moreover, how much does your behavior matter?

Psychologists have done a great deal of research comparing parenting styles to the behavior and personality of the children. Much of this research is based on four parenting styles described by Diana Baumrind (1971):

Authoritative parents: These parents *set high standards and impose controls, but they are also warm and responsive to the child's communications.* They set limits but adjust them when appropriate. They encourage their children to strive toward their own goals.

Authoritarian parents: Like the authoritative parents, authoritarian parents set firm controls, but they tend to be *emotionally more distant from the child. They set rules without explaining the reasons behind them.*

Permissive parents: Permissive parents are *warm and loving but undemanding.*

Indifferent or uninvolved parents: These parents *spend little time with their children and do little more than provide them with food and shelter.*

Of course, not everyone fits neatly into one pattern or another, but most parents are reasonably consistent. The research has found links between parenting style and children's behavior, on average. For example, most children of authoritative parents are self-reliant, cooperative, and successful in school. Children of authoritarian parents tend to be law-abiding but distrustful and not very independent. Children of permissive parents are often socially irresponsible. Children of indifferent parents tend to be impulsive and undisciplined.

However, the meaning of these results is not as clear as it may appear. For years, psychologists assumed that parental indifference *leads to* impulsive, out-of-control children. However, all the results come from correlation studies, which do not justify cause-and-effect conclusions. As Judith Rich Harris (1998) pointed out, other explanations are possible. Maybe impulsive, hard-to-control children cause their parents to withdraw into indifference. Or maybe the parents and children share genes that lead to uncooperative behaviors (Klahr & Burt, 2014). Similarly, the kindly behaviors of authoritative parents could encourage well-mannered behaviors in their children, but it is also likely that children who are well behaved from the start elicit kindly, understanding behaviors in their parents.

A better approach to evaluating parenting styles is to study adopted children, who are genetically unrelated to the parents rearing them. One study of adult twins who had been adopted by separate families found that the parenting style described by one twin correlated significantly with the parenting style described by the other twin, especially for monozygotic twins (Krueger, Markon, & Bouchard, 2003). That is, if one twin reported being reared by kindly, understanding adoptive parents, the other usually did also, even though they were reared in separate families. The twins' temperaments had either affected their adopting parents, or affected how the twins perceived their environments (or both).

If we examine long-term personality traits of adopted children and their adopting parents, the results surprise most people: Children's personalities correlate almost zero with the parents' personalities (Heath, Neale, Kessler, Eaves, & Kendler, 1992; Loehlin, 1992; Viken, Rose, Kaprio, & Koskenvuo, 1994). For this reason, Harris (1995, 1998) argued that parenting style has little influence on most aspects of personality. Much personality variation depends on genetic differences, and the rest of the variation, she argued, depends mostly on the influence of other children.

As you can imagine, not everyone happily accepted Harris's conclusion. Psychologists who had spent a career studying parenting styles were not pleased to be told that their results were inconclusive. Parents were not pleased to be told that they had little influence on their children's personalities. Harris (2000), however, chose her words carefully. She did not say that it makes no difference how you treat your children. For one thing, obviously, if you treat your children badly, they won't like you!

Psychologists have improved their research methods. For example, some studies compare children born to one twin versus their cousins born to the other twin. If genetic factors control the outcome completely, then if the twin parents were monozygotic, the cousins' behavior should correlate just as well with the aunt or uncle's rearing style as with that of their own parents. And if the twin parents were dizygotic, the correlation with the aunt or uncle's style should be weaker. It is a complex argument, but the result is to estimate how strongly rearing style actually impacts children—which turns out to be more strongly for some aspects of behavior than for others (Hannigan et al., 2018).

18. **Why is a correlation between parents' behavior and children's behavior inconclusive concerning how parents influence their children? Why does a correlation between adoptive parents' behavior and that of their adopted children provide more useful information?**

Answer

18. Children can resemble their parents' behavior because of either genetics or social influences. Adoptive children do not necessarily resemble their adopted parents genetically, so any similarity in behavior would reflect environmental influences. Of course, the question would remain as to whether the parents influenced the children or the children influenced the parents.

Nontraditional Families

Western society has considered a traditional family to be a mother, a father, and their children. A nontraditional family is, therefore, anything else. In general, two parents are better than one, partly for financial reasons. We might guess that a child whose mother dies early would be more harmed than one whose father died, simply because on average mothers spend more time with their children. However, children whose father died seem to be at more risk, at least as measured by the probability of eventually becoming depressed (Jacobs & Bovasso, 2009). The apparent explanation is that death of a father has been a greater financial setback in most cases. Children reared by a single mother generally do about as well as children in two-parent homes if the single mother has a good income (MacCallum & Golombok, 2004; Weissman, Leaf, & Bruce, 1987).

Children reared by gay and lesbian parents develop about the same as those reared by heterosexuals in terms of social and emotional development, mental health, romantic relationships, and sexual orientation (Bos, van Balen, & van den Boom, 2007; Farr, 2017; Gartrell, Bos, & Goldberg, 2011; Golombok et al., 2003; Wainright, Russell, & Patterson, 2004). The children's main difficulties relate to the prejudices that their classmates may have against single-sex couples (Bos & Gartrell, 2010).

However, we should be cautious about our conclusions. Many studies comparing traditional and nontraditional families examined only small samples or a limited range of behaviors (Redding, 2001; Schumm, 2008). We can say that being reared by a single parent or by gays or lesbians does not produce a big effect, but the data don't eliminate the possibility of any effect at all.

Parental Conflict and Divorce

In an earlier era, people in the United States considered divorce shameful. Political commentators attributed Adlai Stevenson's defeat in the presidential campaign of 1952 to the fact that he was divorced. Americans would never vote for a divorced candidate, the commentators said. "Never" didn't last very long. By 1980, when Ronald Reagan was elected president, voters hardly noticed his divorce and remarriage.

The effects of divorce on children are highly variable. On average, the children show at least temporary setbacks in academic performance and social relationships. Many pout and seek extra attention, especially in the first year after a divorce (Hetherington, 1989). In the long term, many children reared by a divorced mother have difficulties, partly because of the emotional trauma of the divorce and partly because of financial difficulties. A study across 14 countries found that divorce decreased a child's probability of graduating from college by 7 percent (Bernardi & Radl, 2014). Some

Many children today are reared by a single parent or by gay parents. The research indicates that who rears the child has less influence than whether the caregivers are loving and dependable.

children remain distressed for years, whereas others recover quickly. A few seem to do well at first but become more distressed later. Others are resilient throughout their parents' divorce and afterward. They keep their friends, do all right in school, and maintain good relationships with both parents (Hetherington, Stanley-Hagan, & Anderson, 1989).

Research results show that divorce's effects vary somewhat among cultures and ethnic groups. Divorce is more common in black families, but in most regards, divorced black women adjust better than white women do (McKelvey & McKenry, 2000). Many black families ease the burden of single parenthood by having a grandmother or other relative help with child care.

None of the research implies that parents must stay together for their children's benefit. Children do not fare well if their parents are constantly fighting. Children who observe much conflict between their parents tend to be nervous, unable to sleep through the night (El-Sheikh, Buckhalt, Mize, & Acebo, 2006), and prone to violent and disruptive behaviors (Sternberg, Baradaran, Abbott, Lamb, & Guterman, 2006).

19. You may hear someone say that the right way to rear children is with both a mother and a father. Based on the research evidence, what would be a good reply?

Answer

19. According to the evidence so far, children reared by a single parent, gay or lesbian couple, or divorced parents develop normally, if they are financially secure.

Many Ways of Life

Children grow up in a great variety of environments. Some of the factors exert less influence than we might expect. For example, adopted children's personalities show surprisingly little correlation with that of their adopting parents, and being reared by a gay or lesbian couple produces little effect on children's personality development. However, other factors are clearly important. Culture has a powerful influence on certain aspects of behavior. Overall, it is often difficult to isolate the effects of any one influence on behavior, simply because so many influences are present.

Summary

- *Gender differences.* Males and females differ on average in many regards, but the distributions overlap greatly. Almost no one's brain or behavior is male-typical or female-typical in all regards. (page 167)
- *Interests.* Males and females differ in interests, on average, and part of that difference can be traced to the effects of testosterone, including prenatal exposure to it. (page 168)
- *Math and science.* Females do at least as well as males in math and science courses, when given the opportunity. However, females are often offered less instruction. (page 168)
- *Gender roles.* Gender roles vary among cultures. Female status also varies, largely as a function of whether life conditions require physical strength. (page 169)
- *Cultural differences.* One dimension of culture is collectivist vs. individualistic. Collectivist attitudes are prevalent when neighborhood cooperation is essential, such as in rice farming. (page 170)
- *Birth order.* Many studies comparing firstborn versus later-born children have failed to separate the effects of birth order from the effects of family size. Birth order apparently correlates with a small difference in intelligence, but no consistent differences in personality. (page 172)
- *Parenting styles.* Parental style correlates with children's behavior, but most research does not justify a cause-and-effect conclusion. Parental personality correlates almost zero with the personality of adopted children. (page 173)
- *Nontraditional child care.* Being raised by a single parent or a same-sex couple has no strong effect on personality development. (page 173)

Key Terms

authoritarian parents (page 173)

authoritative parents (page 173)

biculturalism (page 171)

gender roles (page 169)

indifferent or uninvolved parents (page 173)

permissive parents (page 173)

Review Questions

1. Why is it that nearly all the best chess players are men?
   (a) Males have greater mathematical abilities, on average.
   (b) Males are more likely to develop a strong interest in chess, on average.
   (c) Males have larger brains, on average.
   (d) Males have better detailed vision, on average.

2. What evidence suggests a biological influence on a girl's interest in boys' toys?
   (a) Girls with more prenatal exposure to testosterone show greater interest in boys' toys.
   (b) Brain areas related to aggression are larger in girls who show greater interest in boys' toys.
   (c) Girls who are heavier at birth show greater interest in boys' toys.
   (d) Girls who have a brother show greater interest in boys' toys.

3. A collectivist attitude is more common in places that do what?
   (a) Compulsory education of all children
   (b) Competitive sports
   (c) Democratic elections
   (d) Rice farming

4. Suppose someone compares first-born children to third-born children, using anyone available for the study. If a difference emerges, one explanation could be a birth-order effect, but what is another likely explanation?
   (a) All first-born children are older than all third-born children.
   (b) Results were distorted by demand characteristics.
   (c) First-born children are more likely to be males.
   (d) Small families differ from larger families.

5. What evidence suggests that parental behavior has little influence on their children's personality?
   (a) Certain genes have been identified that control most personality differences.
   (b) The personality of first-born children differs significantly from that of later-born children.
   (c) Children's personalities tend to resemble that of the mother more than the father.
   (d) Parents' personality correlates poorly with that of their adopted children.

6. According to the evidence so far, what can be expected of children who are reared by a same-sex couple?
   (a) Most have psychological adjustment problems in childhood, although they are normal in adulthood.
   (b) Most seem normal during childhood, but they develop problems during adulthood.
   (c) Most have psychological adjustment problems during both childhood and adulthood.
   (d) Most develop about about the same as those reared by a heterosexual couple.

Answers: 1b, 2a, 3d, 4d, 5d, 6d.

6 | Learning

Koji Aoki/Getty Images

Andrea Chu/Stone/Getty Images

Newborn humans have almost no control of their muscles, except for their eyes and mouth. Imagine a baby born with complete control of all muscles, including arms, hands, legs, and feet. Would that be a good thing?

After the parents stopped bragging about their precocious youngster, they would discover what a nightmare they had. An infant with extreme mobility but no experience would get into every imaginable danger. From the start, we need to learn what is safe to touch and what isn't, where we can go and where we shouldn't. Almost everything we do requires learning and relearning.

Psychologists have devoted an enormous amount of research to learning, and in the process, they developed and refined research methods that they now routinely apply to other topics. This chapter is about procedures that change behavior—why you lick your lips at the sight of tasty food, why you turn away from a food that once made you sick, why you handle sharp knives cautiously, and why you shudder if you see someone charging toward you with a knife.

module 6.1

Behaviorism and Classical Conditioning

Koji Aoki/Getty Images

After studying this module, you should be able to:

1. Discuss the assumptions and goals of behaviorism.

2. Define classical conditioning and describe the procedures for producing and measuring it.

3. State the procedures for extinction in classical conditioning.

4. Describe how Pavlov tried to explain classical conditioning, and cite later evidence that contradicts his explanation.

5. Explain how classical conditioning pertains to drug tolerance.

In the middle of the 20th century, most of the leading researchers in experimental psychology focused on animal learning, including a huge number of studies of rats in simple mazes and pigeons pecking a disk on the side of the cage. To understand researchers' fixation on these topics, we have to understand something of the history.

Behaviorism

Some of the earliest psychologists, the structuralists, explored mental events by asking people to describe their sensations and experiences. Other psychologists rebelled against that approach because statements about mental states explain nothing:

Q: Why did she yell at him?
A: She yelled because she was angry.
Q: How do you know she was angry?
A: We know she was angry because she was yelling.

Those who objected to discussions of mental states advocated behaviorism, *the position that psychology should concern itself only with what people and other animals do, and the circumstances in which they do it*, without reference to thoughts, emotions, or other internal states. As B. F. Skinner (1990) argued, when you say, "I *intend* to . . . ," what you really mean is "I am about to . . . " or "In situations like this, I usually . . . " or "This behavior is in the preliminary stages of happening." Any statement about mental experiences can be converted into a description of behavior. To the question, "Why did she yell at him?" a behaviorist's reply would identify the circumstances that provoked the outburst.

The same insistence on description is central to the British and American legal systems: A witness is asked, "What did you see and hear?" An acceptable answer might be, "The defendant was sweating and trembling, and his voice was wavering." A witness should not say, "The defendant was nervous and worried," because that statement requires an inference that the witness is not entitled to make.

You might be tempted to dismiss behaviorism because, at least at first glance, it seems so ridiculous: "What do you *mean*, my thoughts and beliefs and emotions don't cause my behavior?!" The behaviorists' reply is, "Exactly right. Your thoughts and other internal states do not cause your behavior because events in your environment caused your thoughts. Those events are the causes of your behavior." Contemplate this: If you believe that your thoughts cause behaviors *independently* of your previous experiences, what evidence could you provide to support your claim?

Jacques Loeb was one of the earliest, most extreme advocates of behaviorism. In Loeb's words, "Motions caused by light or other agencies appear to the layman as expressions of will and purpose on the part of the animal, whereas in reality the animal is forced to go where carried by its legs" (Loeb, 1918/1973, p. 14). Why do certain caterpillars approach light? It is not, according to Loeb, because they are fond of light. It is because light in front of them increases their rate of locomotion. If light strikes mainly from the left or right side, the caterpillar turns toward the light, not because it "wants to," but because light from the side causes greater muscle tension on one side of the body and therefore causes the animal to move one set of legs more than the other. Loeb applied similar explanations to why certain animals tend to move toward heat or cold, toward or away from water, up (away from gravity) or down, and so forth (see ▼ Figure 6.1). Built-in mechanisms caused animals to move in adaptive ways, without the animals necessarily having any desires or intentions. Loeb's view was an example of stimulus–response psychology, *the attempt to explain behavior in terms of how each stimulus triggers a response.*

ChinKC/Shutterstock.com

▲ **Figure 6.1** Jacques Loeb, an early student of animal behavior, argued that much or all of invertebrate behavior could be described as responses to simple stimuli, such as approaching light or moving opposite to the direction of gravity.

Another influential figure, John B. Watson, systematized the approach and popularized behaviorism (Watson, 1919, 1925). Here are two quotes from Watson:

> Psychology as the behaviorist views it is a purely objective experimental branch of natural science. Its theoretical goal is the prediction and control of behavior. (1913, p. 158)
>
> The goal of psychological study is the ascertaining of such data and laws that, given the stimulus, psychology can predict what the response will be; or, on the other hand, given the response, it can specify the nature of the effective stimulus. (1919, p. 10)

The challenge for behaviorism was (and is) to explain as much of behavior as possible, not just the movements of caterpillars and similar invertebrates. The greatest challenge was to explain learning in the simplest possible terms, with no reference to understanding, knowledge, or other mental-sounding terms.

1. **Why do behaviorists reject explanations in terms of thoughts?**

2. **How did Loeb explain why certain animals turn toward the light?**

Answers

1. Previous events and current stimuli are responsible for thoughts, and therefore the events and stimuli are the real causes of behavior.
2. According to Loeb, light from the side caused greater muscle tension on one side of the body. Therefore, muscles on one side or the other moved more vigorously than those on the other side. This imbalance of movement continued until the light stimulation on both sides was equal.

Pavlov and Classical Conditioning

In the early 1900s, Ivan Petrovich Pavlov, a Russian physiologist who had won a Nobel Prize in physiology for his research on digestion, stumbled upon an observation that offered a simple explanation for learning. Given the rise of behaviorism, the mood of the time was ripe for Pavlov's ideas.

One day as Pavlov was pursuing his digestion research, he noticed that a dog secreted digestive juices as soon as it saw the lab worker who customarily fed the dogs. Because this secretion clearly depended on the dog's previous experiences, Pavlov called it a "psychological" secretion. He enlisted the help of other specialists, who discovered that "teasing" a dog with the sight of food produced salivation that was as predictable and automatic as any reflex. Pavlov called it a *conditioned reflex* because it depended on conditions.

Pavlov's Procedures

Pavlov assumed that animals are born with *automatic connections*—called unconditioned reflexes—*between a stimulus such as food and a response such as secreting digestive juices.* He conjectured that animals acquire new reflexes by transferring a response from one stimulus to another. For example, if a particular sound always precedes food, an animal would salivate to the sound as if it were food.

The *process by which an organism learns a new association between two stimuli—a neutral stimulus and one that already evokes a reflexive response—*is known as classical conditioning, or Pavlovian conditioning. It is called classical because it has been known and studied for a long time.

Pavlov selected dogs with a moderate degree of arousal. Highly excitable dogs would not hold still long enough because of what he called their "freedom reflex." Highly inhibited dogs would fall asleep. He attached a tube to one of the salivary ducts in a dog's mouth to measure salivation, as shown in ▼ Figure 6.2. He could have measured stomach secretions, but salivation was easier to measure.

Whenever Pavlov gave a dog food, the dog salivated. The food → salivation connection was automatic, requiring no training. Pavlov called food the unconditioned stimulus, and he called salivation the unconditioned response. The unconditioned stimulus (UCS) is *an event that automatically elicits an unconditioned response.* The unconditioned response (UCR) is *the action that the unconditioned stimulus elicits.*

Next Pavlov introduced a new stimulus, such as a metronome or other sound. Upon hearing the metronome, the dog lifted its ears and looked around but did not salivate, so the metronome was a neutral stimulus with regard to salivation. Pavlov sounded the metronome shortly before giving food to the dog. After a few pairings of the metronome with food, the dog began to salivate as soon as it heard the metronome (Pavlov, 1927/1960).

We call the metronome the conditioned stimulus (CS) because a dog's *response to it depends on the preceding conditions*—that is, pairing the CS with the UCS. The salivation that follows the metronome is

SPUTNIK/Alamy Stock Photo

Ivan P. Pavlov devised simple principles to describe learned changes in a dog's behavior.

At first,

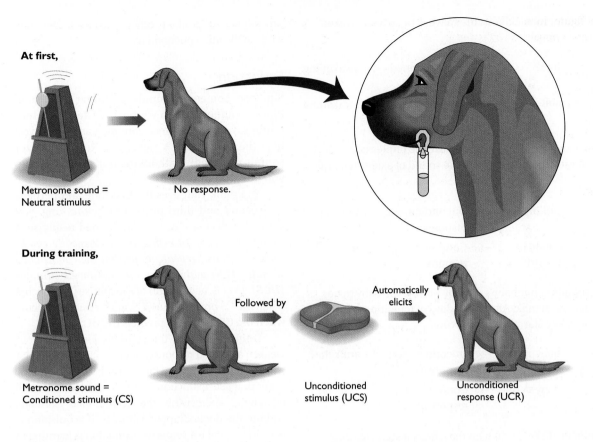

Metronome sound =
Neutral stimulus

No response.

During training,

Metronome sound =
Conditioned stimulus (CS)

Followed by

Unconditioned
stimulus (UCS)

Automatically
elicits

Unconditioned
response (UCR)

After some number of repetitions,

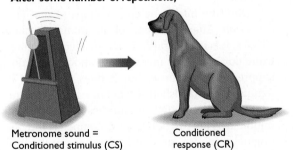

Metronome sound =
Conditioned stimulus (CS)

Conditioned
response (CR)

◀ **Figure 6.2** A conditioned stimulus precedes an unconditioned stimulus. At first, the conditioned stimulus elicits no response, and the unconditioned stimulus elicits the unconditioned response. After sufficient pairings, the conditioned stimulus elicits the conditioned response, which can resemble the unconditioned response.

the conditioned response (CR). The conditioned response is *whatever response the conditioned stimulus elicits as a result of the conditioning (training) procedure.* At the start, the conditioned stimulus elicits no significant response. After conditioning, it elicits a conditioned response. Any detectable event can serve as a conditioned stimulus. For example, a sudden sound works, but so does an interval of silence interrupting otherwise constant noise (Campolattaro, Savage, & Lipatova, 2017).

To review, the *unconditioned stimulus* (UCS), such as food, automatically elicits the *unconditioned response* (UCR), such as salivating. A neutral stimulus, such as a sound, that is paired with the UCS becomes a *conditioned stimulus* (CS). At first, it elicits no response or an irrelevant response, such as looking around. After some number of pairings of the CS with the UCS, the conditioned stimulus elicits the *conditioned response* (CR), which usually resembles the UCR. Figure 6.2 diagrams these relationships.

Conditioning occurs more rapidly if the conditioned stimulus is unfamiliar. If you have heard a tone many times (followed by nothing) and now

start hearing the tone followed by a strong stimulus, you will be slow to show signs of conditioning. Similarly, imagine two people who are bitten by a snake. One has never been near a snake before, and the other has spent years tending snakes at the zoo. You can guess which one will learn a greater fear.

More Examples of Classical Conditioning

Here are more examples of classical conditioning:

- You have programmed a device to awaken you with a few moments of soft music followed by louder music. At first, soft music does not awaken you, but the louder music does. After a week or so, you awaken when you hear the softer music.

| Unconditioned stimulus | = | loud | → | Unconditioned response | = | awakening |
| Conditioned stimulus | = | soft | → | Conditioned response | = | awakening |

- You hear the sound of a dentist's drill shortly before the unpleasant experience of the drill on your teeth. From then on, the sound of a dentist's drill arouses anxiety.

| Unconditioned stimulus | = | drilling | → | Unconditioned response | = | tension |
| Conditioned stimulus | = | sound of the drill | → | Conditioned response | = | tension |

- A nursing mother responds to her baby's cries by putting the baby to her breast, stimulating the flow of milk. After a few days of repetitions, the sound of the baby's cry is enough to start the milk flowing.

| Unconditioned stimulus | = | baby sucking | → | Unconditioned response | = | milk flow |
| Conditioned stimulus | = | baby's cry | → | Conditioned response | = | milk flow |

- Whenever your roommate flicks a switch on the stereo, it starts blasting sounds at a deafening level. You flinch as soon as you hear the flick of the switch.

| Unconditioned stimulus | = | very loud music | → | Unconditioned response | = | flinching |
| Conditioned stimulus | = | flick of the switch | → | Conditioned response | = | flinching |

Note the usefulness of classical conditioning. It prepares an individual for likely events.

One more example: Form an image of a lemon, a nice fresh juicy one. You cut it into slices and then suck on a slice. Imagine that sour taste. As you imagine the lemon, do you notice yourself salivating? If so, your imagination produced enough resemblance to the actual sight and taste of a lemon to serve as a conditioned stimulus.

try it yourself

concept check

3. Someone shows you many photos on several colors of background. Whenever the background is green, the photo is disgusting. After many repetitions you see a neutral photo on a green background, but you react with disgust anyway. In this example, identify the CS, UCS, UCR, and CR.

Answer

3. The CS is the green background. The UCS is the series of disturbing photos. Both the UCR and the CR are your reactions of disgust.

Additional Phenomena of Classical Conditioning

The *process that establishes or strengthens a conditioned response* is known as **acquisition**. After discovering classical conditioning, Pavlov and others varied the procedures to produce other outcomes. Here are some of the main phenomena.

Extinction

Suppose someone sounds a buzzer and then blows a puff of air into your eyes. After a few repetitions, you start to close your eyes as soon as you hear the buzzer (see ▼ **Figure 6.3**). Now the buzzer sounds repeatedly without the puff of air. What do you do?

You blink your eyes the first time and perhaps the second and third times, but before long, you stop. This decrease of the conditioned response is called **extinction**. *To extinguish a classically conditioned response, repeatedly present the conditioned stimulus (CS) without the unconditioned stimulus (UCS).* That is, acquisition of a response (CR) occurs when the CS predicts the UCS, and extinction occurs when the CS no longer predicts the UCS.

Extinction is not the same as forgetting. Both weaken a learned response, but they arise in different ways. You forget during a long period without reminders or practice. Extinction occurs because of a specific experience—perceiving the conditioned stimulus without the unconditioned stimulus. If acquisition is learning to make a response, extinction is learning to inhibit it.

Don't be misled by connotations of the term *extinction*. After extinction of an animal or plant species, it is gone forever. In classical conditioning, extinction does *not* mean obliteration. Extinction suppresses a response, but it does not erase it. Acquisition established a tendency to make a response, and extinction establishes a tendency to inhibit it. The two tendencies compete, and the original response can return, as we see in the next paragraph.

Spontaneous Recovery

Suppose you are in a classical-conditioning experiment. At first, you repeatedly hear a buzzer (CS) that precedes a puff of air to your eyes (UCS). Then the buzzer stops predicting an air puff. After a few trials, your response to the buzzer extinguishes. Next you wait a while with nothing happening until suddenly you hear the buzzer again. What will you do? Chances are, you blink your eyes at least slightly. **Spontaneous recovery** is *a temporary return of an extinguished response after a delay* (see ▼ **Figure 6.4**).

Why does spontaneous recovery occur? Think of it this way: At first, the buzzer predicted a puff of air to your eyes, and then it didn't. You behaved in accordance with the more recent experiences. Hours later, neither experience is much more recent than the other, and the effects of acquisition and extinction are about equally strong.

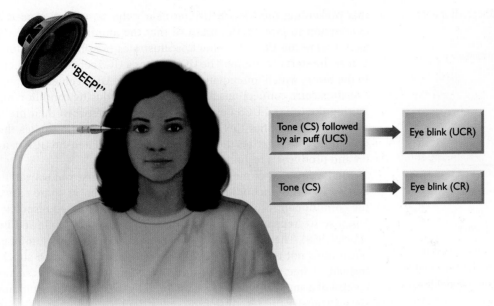

Tone (CS) followed by air puff (UCS) → Eye blink (UCR)

Tone (CS) → Eye blink (CR)

Spontaneous recovery is an important concept to remember in the context of psychotherapy. Many therapies for anxiety disorders attempt to extinguish learned fears. They succeed—at least temporarily—but the learned fears may return later.

concept check

4. **In Pavlov's experiment on conditioned salivation in response to a metronome, what procedure produces extinction? What procedure produces spontaneous recovery?**

5. **In what way might the term "extinction" be misleading?**

Answers

4. To bring about extinction, present the metronome repeatedly without presenting food. To bring about spontaneous recovery, first bring about extinction. Then wait and present the metronome again.
5. The extinction of a species means that it is gone forever. Extinction of a classically conditioned response suppresses it but does not erase it.

Stimulus Generalization

Suppose a bee stings you, and you learn to fear bees. Now you see a wasp or hornet. Will you fear that, too?

You probably will, but you probably will not fear butterflies or other insects that don't resemble bees. The more similar a new stimulus is to the conditioned stimulus, the more likely you are to show a similar response (see ▼ Figure 6.5). Stimulus generalization is the *extension of a conditioned response from the training stimulus to similar stimuli*. Conditioning generalizes more broadly after a strong unconditioned stimulus. For example, if a sound predicts a mild shock, you generalize to similar sounds. After an intense shock, you might generalize to almost any sudden sound (Dunsmoor, Kroes, Braren, &

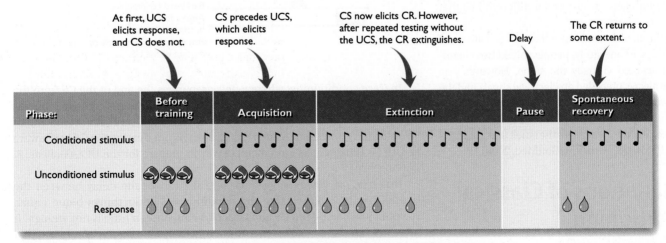

At first, UCS elicits response, and CS does not.

CS precedes UCS, which elicits response.

CS now elicits CR. However, after repeated testing without the UCS, the CR extinguishes.

Delay

The CR returns to some extent.

Phase:	Before training	Acquisition	Extinction	Pause	Spontaneous recovery
Conditioned stimulus					
Unconditioned stimulus					
Response					

▲ **Figure 6.4** If the conditioned stimulus regularly precedes the unconditioned stimulus, acquisition occurs. If the conditioned stimulus is presented by itself, extinction occurs. A pause after extinction yields a brief spontaneous recovery.

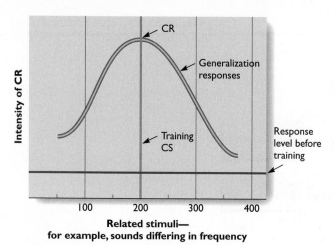

▲ **Figure 6.5** Stimulus generalization is the process of extending a learned response to new stimuli that resemble the one used in training. A less similar stimulus elicits a weaker response.

Phelps, 2017). You can see the relevance to experiences such as post-traumatic stress disorder.

When we speak about generalizing to similar stimuli, it is difficult to specify what we mean by "similar" (Pearce, 1994). For example, after a bee stings you, you might fear the sound of buzzing bees when you are walking through a forest but not when you hear the same sounds in a nature documentary on television. Also, items that seem similar to you might not seem similar to someone else.

Discrimination

You are walking through a wilderness area carrying a baby. When the baby shakes a rattle, you hear the sound and smile. A minute later when you hear the rattle of a rattlesnake, you react differently because you have learned to **discriminate**—*to respond differently to stimuli that predict different outcomes.* Similarly, you discriminate between a bell that signals time for class to start and a different bell that signals a fire alarm.

Discrimination training enhances sensitivity to sensory cues. In one study, people sniffed two chemicals that seemed virtually the same. However, one chemical always preceded an electrical shock, and the other always preceded a safe interval without shock. As training proceeded, people got better at detecting the difference, and they reacted to the smell that predicted shock (Li, Howard, Parrish, & Gottfried, 2008).

Explanations of Classical Conditioning

What is classical conditioning, really? As is often the case, later investigation found it to be more complex than it appeared at first. Pavlov surmised that presenting the CS and UCS at nearly the same time caused a connection to grow in the brain so that the animal treated the CS as if it were the UCS. ▼ Figure 6.6a illustrates possible connections before the start of training: The UCS excites a UCS center somewhere in the brain, which immediately stimulates the UCR center. ▼ Figure 6.6b illustrates connections that might develop during conditioning: Pairing the CS and UCS develops a connection between their brain representations. After this connection develops, the CS excites the CS center, which excites the UCS center, which excites the UCR center and produces a response.

In Pavlov's experiment, the conditioned response was salivation and so was the unconditioned response. However, in some cases, the conditioned response differs from the unconditioned response. Suppose we repeatedly present a rat with a tone (CS) followed by shock (UCS). The rat responds to shock with shrieking and jumping, but it does not respond to the tone as if it were receiving a shock. Instead, it freezes in place and tenses its muscles, a common response of a small animal to a signal for danger. Conditioning did not simply transfer the response from one stimulus to another. The rats reacted to the conditioned stimulus as a danger signal, not as if they felt a shock.

Also consider the effects of timing. Pavlov noted that conditioning depended on the timing between CS and UCS, as shown in the displays below, reading time from left to right:

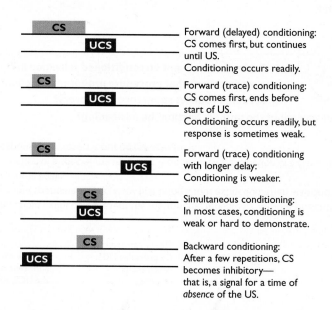

In trace conditioning, where a delay separates the end of the CS from the start of the UCS, the animal does not make a conditioned response immediately after the conditioned stimulus, but instead waits until almost the end of the usual delay between CS and UCS. Again, it is not treating the CS as if it were the UCS; it is using it as a predictor, a way to prepare for the UCS (Gallistel & Gibbon, 2000).

It is true, as Pavlov suggested, that the longer the delay between the CS and the UCS, the weaker the conditioning, other things being equal. However, just having the CS and UCS close together in time is not enough. It is essential that they occur more often together than they occur apart. That is, the CS must be a good predictor of the UCS. Consider this experiment: For rats in both Group 1 and Group 2, every presentation of a CS is followed by a UCS, as shown in ▼ Figure 6.7. For Group 2, the UCS also appears at many

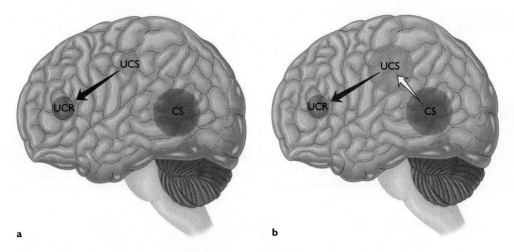

▲ **Figure 6.6** According to Pavlov, **(a)** at the start of conditioning, activity in a UCS center automatically activates the UCR center. **(b)** After sufficient pairings of the CS and UCS, a connection develops between the CS and UCS centers. Afterward, activity in the CS center flows to the UCS center and therefore excites the UCR center.

other times without the CS. For this group, the UCS happens no more often with the CS than without it. Group 1 learns a strong response to the CS, and Group 2 does not (Rescorla, 1968, 1988).

6. If classical conditioning depended entirely on presenting the CS and UCS at nearly the same time, what result should the experimenters have expected for Group 2?

Answer

6. If classical conditioning depended entirely on presenting the CS and UCS at nearly the same time, the rats in Group 2 would have developed a strong conditioned response.

Now consider this more complicated experiment: Rats are shown a light (CS) followed by shock (UCS) until they show a conditioned response to the light—a response of freezing in place. Then they get a series of trials with both a light and a tone, again followed by shock. Will the rats now show a conditioned response to the tone? No, or at least not much. The same pattern occurs with the reverse

order: First, rats learn a response to the tone, and then they get light–tone combinations before the shock. They show a conditioned response to the tone but not to the light (Kamin, 1969; see ▼ Figure 6.8). These results demonstrate the blocking effect: *The previously established association to one stimulus blocks the formation of an association to the added stimulus.* Two explanations are possible: First, if the first stimulus predicts the outcome, the second stimulus adds no new information. Second, the rat attends strongly to the stimulus that already predicts the outcome and therefore pays less attention to the new stimulus. However, although the blocking effect is theoretically significant, it occurs in some circumstances and not in others (Maes et al., 2016).

A principle like the blocking effect holds in human reasoning. Suppose you have several experiences when you eat something with hot peppers and have an upset stomach. Then you have several

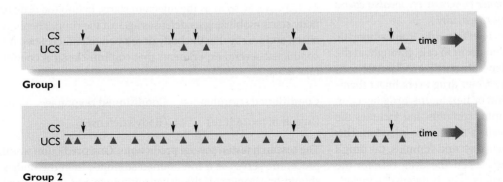

▲ **Figure 6.7** In Rescorla's experiment, the CS always preceded the UCS in both groups, but Group 2 received the UCS frequently at other times also. Group 1 developed a strong conditioned response to the CS, and Group 2 did not.

Group 1

Group 2

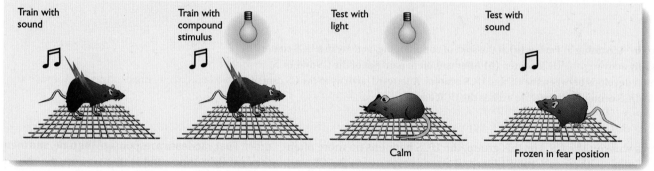

▲ **Figure 6.8** Each rat first learned to associate either light or sound with shock. Then it received a compound of both light and sound followed by shock. Each rat continued to show a strong response to the old stimulus (which already predicted shock) but little to the new stimulus.

experiences when you eat hot peppers and nuts and have the same reaction. You have already decided you should avoid peppers. Do you now avoid nuts also? Probably not (Melchers, Ungor, & Lachnit, 2005).

Drug Tolerance as an Example of Classical Conditioning

Classical conditioning shows up in ways you might not expect. One example is drug tolerance: *Users of certain drugs experience progressively weaker effects after taking the drugs repeatedly.*

Drug tolerance results partly from automatic chemical changes that occur in cells throughout the body, but it also depends partly on classical conditioning. Consider: When drug users inject themselves with morphine or heroin, the drug injection procedure is a complex stimulus that includes the time and place as well as the needle injection. This total stimulus predicts a second stimulus, the drug's entry into the brain. When the drug reaches the brain, it triggers a variety of body defenses—including changes in hormone secretions, heart rate, and breathing rate—that counteract the effects of the drug itself.

First stimulus	→	Second stimulus	→	Automatic response
(Injection procedure)		(Drug enters brain)		(Body's defenses)

Whenever one stimulus predicts a second stimulus that produces an automatic response, classical conditioning can occur. The first stimulus is the CS, the second is the UCS, and the response is the UCR. Let's relabel as follows:

Conditioned stimulus	→	Unconditioned stimulus	→	Unconditioned response
(Injection procedure)		(Drug enters brain)		(Body's defenses)

If conditioning occurs here, what would happen? Suppose the CS (drug injection) produces a CR that resembles the UCR (the body's defenses against the drug). In that case, as soon as the injection starts, before the drug enters the body, the body starts mobilizing its defenses against the drug. Therefore, the drug has less effect, and we say that the body developed tolerance. Shepard Siegel (1977, 1983) conducted several experiments that confirm classical conditioning during drug injections.

Conditioned stimulus	→	Conditioned response
(Injection procedure)		(Body's defenses)

The research tested several predictions. One prediction was this: If the injection procedure serves as a conditioned stimulus, then the body's defense reactions should be strongest if the drug is administered in the usual way, in the usual location, with as many familiar stimuli as possible. The entire experience constitutes the conditioned stimulus. Therefore, the behavioral effects of the drug would be weaker in the familiar setting than in a new one.

The evidence supports this prediction for a variety of drugs (Siegel & Ramos, 2002). For example, rats or mice that have taken heroin or other drugs repeatedly in one location and then take it in a new setting have a stronger, sometimes even a fatal reaction (Siegel, 2016). Observations of people yield a similar conclusion. People drinking alcohol in a familiar setting experience less cognitive impairment than those drinking it in an unfamiliar setting (Birak, Higgs, & Terry, 2011).

A second prediction: If tolerance is classically conditioned, researchers should be able to extinguish it. The procedure for extinction is to present the CS without the UCS. Given the difficulties of working with human drug users, researchers studied rats. Many drug effects are difficult to measure in nonhumans, but one is easy—the ability of morphine to decrease pain. Researchers first measured the smallest pain necessary to make rats flinch. Then they gave the rats morphine and ran the test again, finding that the drug decreased the pain response. The next step was to produce tolerance by daily drug injections, testing the pain response each time. When the rats showed increased pain response, indicating tolerance to the morphine, researchers went to the final step. They gave the rats daily injections of salt water. If we think of the injection procedure as the CS and morphine as the UCS, then injecting salt water is presenting the CS without the UCS. After a few repetitions, tolerance partly extinguished. Now an injection of morphine substantially decreased the pain response (Siegel, 1977). In short, drug tolerance shows the properties we would expect it to have if tolerance depends on classical conditioning. ▼ Figure 6.9 summarizes this experiment.

Research on the classical conditioning of drug tolerance eventually led to applications to help people quit their addictions. People who are trying to abstain from alcohol often experience cravings in the presence of sights, sounds, and smells that remind them of their drug experiences. When psychologists present those stimuli under conditions where the person is able to resist the temptation, the result is partial extinction of the cravings (Loeber, Croissant, Heinz, Mann, & Flor, 2006).

concept check

7. When someone develops tolerance to the effects of a drug injection, what are the conditioned stimulus, the unconditioned stimulus, the conditioned response, and the unconditioned response?

8. How did researchers measure drug tolerance in rats?

Answers

7. The conditioned stimulus is the injection procedure. The unconditioned stimulus is the entry of the drug into the brain. Both the conditioned response and the unconditioned response are the body's defenses against the drug. 8. Drug tolerance was demonstrated when a morphine injection produced less relief from pain than before.

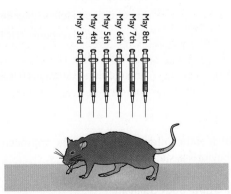

1. Initial response to painful heat: Rat licks its paw.

2. First test under morphine: No response unless heat is turned up much higher.

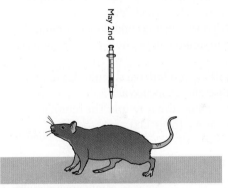

3. After six morphine injections: Rat has tolerance and shows response to pain despite morphine.

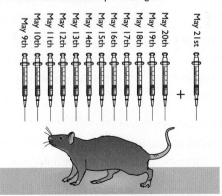

4. After 12 saltwater injections, another morphine injection reduces pain. Tolerance is partly extinguished.

▲ **Figure 6.9** Morphine decreases pain, but after a few repetitions, a rat develops tolerance to this effect. Repeated injections of salt water produce extinction of the learned tolerance.

Classical Conditioning Is More Than Drooling Dogs

If someone had asked you to describe what you hoped to learn from a psychology course, you probably would not have replied, "I want to learn how to make dogs salivate!" I hope you see that the research on conditioned salivation is just a way to explore fundamental mechanisms, much as genetics researchers have studied the fruit fly *Drosophila* or neurophysiologists have studied the nerves of squid. Classical conditioning is important for many important behaviors, ranging from emotional responses to drug tolerance.

Although the behaviorist movement no longer dominates experimental psychology to the extent that it did in the mid-1900s, behaviorism has had a powerful influence on psychological research. Behaviorism's fundamental feature is the insistence that researchers base their results and theories on observable behaviors, not on people's descriptions of their mental events.

Summary

- *Behaviorism.* Behaviorists insist that psychologists should study behaviors and its causes without reference to unobservable mental states. (page 179)
- *Behaviorists' interest in learning.* Much of invertebrate behavior can be described in stimulus-response terms, but the greater challenge for behaviorists was to explain learning. (page 180)
- *Classical conditioning.* Ivan Pavlov discovered that pairing a neutral stimulus (CS) with some stimulus (UCS) that evokes an automatic response such as salivation (UCR) causes the CS to evoke a new response (the CR). (page 180)
- *Extinction.* Repeatedly presenting the conditioned stimulus by itself causes a learned inhibition of the conditioned response. (page 182)
- *Spontaneous recovery.* If the conditioned stimulus is not presented at all for some time after extinction and is then presented again, the conditioned response may return. The return is called spontaneous recovery. (page 182)

- *Stimulus generalization and discrimination.* A conditioned response to a stimulus will extend to other stimuli to the extent that they resemble the trained stimulus. However, the animal (or human) can learn to respond differently to stimuli that predict different outcomes. (page 183–184)
- *Basis of classical conditioning.* Pavlov believed that presenting two stimuli close to each other in time developed a connection between their brain representations. However, animals do not treat the conditioned stimulus as if it were the unconditioned stimulus. Also, being close in time is not enough. Learning occurs if the first stimulus predicts the second stimulus. (page 184)
- *Drug tolerance.* The procedure of injecting a drug predicts the entry of the drug into the blood, a stimulus that evokes the body's defenses. Repeating this sequence produces a classically conditioned increase in the body's defenses, and therefore drug tolerance. (page 186)

Key Terms

acquisition (page 182)

behaviorism (page 179)

blocking effect (page 185)

classical conditioning (or Pavlovian conditioning) (page 180)

conditioned response (CR) (page 181)

conditioned stimulus (CS) (page 180)

discrimination (page 184)

drug tolerance (page 186)

extinction (page 182)

spontaneous recovery (page 182)

stimulus generalization (page 183)

stimulus–response psychology (page 179)

unconditioned reflex (page 180)

unconditioned response (UCR) (page 180)

unconditioned stimulus (UCS) (page 180)

Review Questions

1. Why did behaviorists reject the study of thoughts?
   (a) Behaviorists were interested only in the behavior of invertebrates.
   (b) Thoughts vary too much from one person to another.
   (c) Behaviorists believed in mind–body dualism.
   (d) Events that led to the thoughts are the real cause of behavior.

2. Which of the following describes the approach of the earliest behaviorists, such as Loeb?
   (a) Stimulus-response psychology
   (b) Mind–body dualism
   (c) Psychoanalysis
   (d) Structuralism

3. On the first trial of classical conditioning, the CS, UCS, and UCR are present, but the CR is not. Why not?
   (a) The CR emerges only after pairing the CS with the UCS.
   (b) The CR emerges only after pairing the UCS with the UCR.
   (c) The experimenter begins presenting the CR on the second trial.
   (d) The CR emerges only during the extinction process.

4. How does extinction differ from forgetting?
   (a) Extinction is more complete and more permanent.
   (b) Forgetting depends on changes in brain activity. Extinction does not.
   (c) Extinction depends on changes in brain activity. Forgetting does not.
   (d) Forgetting depends on passage of time. Extinction depends on a specific experience.

5. What produces spontaneous recovery?
   (a) Generalization training followed by discrimination training
   (b) An electrical shock in a new situation
   (c) Extinction followed by a delay
   (d) Additional pairings of the CS with the UCS

6. In some cases, a conditioned response does not resemble the unconditioned response. What does this finding imply about classical conditioning?
   (a) Conditioning occurs only if the CS predicts the UCS.
   (b) Conditioning is not a matter of transferring a response from the UCS to the CS.
   (c) Conditioning is independent of the connections in the brain.
   (d) Conditioning depends on having the CS and UCS close together in time.

7. When classical conditioning produces drug tolerance, what is the CS?
   (a) The injection procedure
   (b) The entry of the drug into the blood
   (c) The "high" that the drug produces
   (d) The body's defense against the drug

8. When classical conditioning produces drug tolerance, what is the CR?
   (a) The injection procedure
   (b) The entry of the drug into the blood
   (c) The "high" that the drug produces
   (d) The body's defense against the drug

Answers: 1d, 2a, 3a, 4d, 5c, 6b, 7a, 8d.

Koji Aoki/Getty Images

After studying this module, you should be able to:

1. Explain how operant conditioning differs from classical conditioning.

2. Define reinforcement and contrast it with punishment.

3. Explain how the procedures for extinction differ between operant and classical conditioning.

4. Explain how shaping, chaining, and schedules of reinforcement alter behaviors.

5. Cite an example of a practical application of operant conditioning.

Suppose a family in another country adopted you at birth. You lived in a land with different language, customs, food, and religious practices. Would that alternative "you" have much in common with the current "you"? Or does your culture and environment mold your behavior completely? The most extreme statement of environmental determinism came from John B. Watson, one of the founders of behaviorism, who said,

> Give me a dozen healthy infants, well-formed, and my own specified world to bring them up in and I'll guarantee to take any one at random and train him to become any type of specialist I might

select—doctor, lawyer, artist, merchant-chief, and yes, even beggar-man thief—regardless of his talents, penchants, tendencies, abilities, vocations, and race of his ancestors. I am going beyond my facts and I admit it, but so have the advocates of the contrary. (1925, p. 82)

Needless to say, Watson never had a chance to demonstrate his point. No one gave him a child and his own specified world. If anyone really did have complete control of the environment, would it be possible to control a child's eventual fate? We may never know, ethics being what they are, after all. Still, one of the goals of behaviorists is to explore all the ways that environment changes behavior.

Thorndike and Operant Conditioning

Shortly before Pavlov's research, Edward L. Thorndike (1911/1970), a Harvard graduate student, began training cats in a basement. Saying that earlier experiments had dealt only with animal intelligence, not animal stupidity, he sought a simple behaviorist explanation of learning. He put cats into puzzle boxes (see ▼ **Figure 6.10**) from which they could escape by pressing a lever, pulling a string, tilting a pole, or other means. Sometimes he placed food outside the box, but usually cats worked just to escape from the box. The cats learned to make whatever response opened the box.

They learned by trial and error. When a cat had to tilt a pole to escape from the box, it might at first paw or gnaw at the door, scratch the walls, or pace back and forth. Eventually, it bumped against the pole and the door opened. The next time, the cat went through a similar repertoire of behaviors but might bump against the pole a little sooner. Over many trials, the cat gradually but inconsistently improved its speed of escape. ▼ **Figure 6.11** shows a learning curve to represent this behavior. A **learning curve** is *a graph of the changes in behavior that occur over the course of learning.*

Did the cat understand the connection between bumping against the pole and opening the door? No, said Thorndike. If the cat gained a new insight at some point, its escape should have been quick from that point on. The graph of the cat's escape times shows no sharp break that could identify the time of an insight.

Thorndike concluded that learning occurs because certain behaviors are strengthened at the expense of others. An animal starts with a repertoire of responses such as pawing the door, scratching the walls, and pacing, labeled R_1, R_2, R_3, etc., in ▼ **Figure 6.12**. If nothing special happens after its first response (R1), it proceeds to other responses, eventually reaching one that opens the door—for example, bumping against the pole (R_7 in this example). Opening the door reinforces that behavior.

Reinforcement is *the process of increasing the future probability of a response that is followed by a positive consequence.* Thorndike said that reinforcement "stamps in," or strengthens, the response. The next time the cat is in the puzzle box, it has a slightly higher probability of the effective response. If it receives reinforcement again, the probability goes up another notch (see Figure 6.12). You see how this view fit with behaviorists' hope for an explanation that did not rely on thoughts, understanding, or other mental processes.

AP Images/Jerome Delay

Growing up in a different environment would change your behavior, but would it completely determine your behavioral development? How much can the environment control, and how much can it not control?

▲ **Figure 6.10** Each of Thorndike's puzzle boxes had a device that could open it. Here, tilting the pole will open the door. (Based on Thorndike, 1911/1970)

▲ **Figure 6.11** As the data from one of Thorndike's experiments show, a cat's time to escape from a box decreases gradually but sporadically. Thorndike concluded that the cat did not at any point "get an idea." Instead, reinforcement gradually increased the probability of the successful behavior.

Thorndike summarized his views in the law of effect (Thorndike, 1911/1970, p. 244):

> Of several responses made to the same situation, those which are accompanied or closely followed by satisfaction to the animal will, other things being equal, be more firmly connected with the situation, so that, when it recurs, they will be more likely to recur.

Hence, the animal becomes more likely to repeat the responses that led to favorable consequences even if it does not understand why. Similarly, a machine could be programmed to produce random responses and repeat the ones that led to reinforcement.

Was Thorndike's interpretation correct? Another way of putting this question: When an animal learns to make a response that produces some outcome, does it "expect" that outcome, or does it simply register, "Make this response in this situation"? In general, it is difficult to answer this question (Burke, Franz, Miller, & Schoenbaum, 2008). However, animals learn more than just muscle movements. An animal with brain damage that impairs walking will stagger or roll through a maze to reach the target (Lashley & McCarthy, 1926). An animal that learned to turn left, but now has a muscle impairment that prevents turning left, will instead rotate 270° to the right, accomplishing the same outcome (Seligman, Railton, Baumeister, & Sripada, 2013).

Thorndike revolutionized the study of animal learning, substituting experimentation for collections of anecdotes. He also demonstrated the possibility of simple explanations for apparently complex behaviors (Dewsbury, 1998). On the negative side, his example of studying animals in contrived laboratory situations led researchers to ignore much about how animals learn in nature (Galef, 1998).

The kind of learning that Thorndike studied is called operant conditioning (because the subject *operates* on the environment to produce an outcome) or instrumental conditioning (because the subject's behavior is *instrumental* in producing the outcome). Operant or instrumental conditioning is *the process of changing behavior by providing a reinforcer or a punishment after a response.* The defining difference between operant conditioning and classical conditioning is the procedure: *In operant conditioning, the subject's behavior produces an outcome that affects future behavior. In classical conditioning, the subject's behavior has no effect on the outcome (the presentation of the UCS).* For example,

in classical conditioning, the experimenter (or the world) presents two stimuli at particular times, regardless of what the subject does or doesn't do. Those stimuli change future behaviors, but the behaviors do not control the events. In operant conditioning, the subject has to make a response to produce an outcome.

In general, the two kinds of conditioning affect different behaviors. Classical conditioning applies mainly to visceral responses (i.e., *responses of the internal organs*), such as salivation and digestion, whereas operant conditioning applies mainly to skeletal responses (i.e., *movements of leg muscles, arm muscles*). However, this distinction sometimes breaks down. For example, if a tone predicts an electric shock (a classical-conditioning procedure), the tone makes the animal freeze in position (a skeletal response) as well as increase its heart rate (a visceral response).

9. **When a bell rings, an animal sits up on its hind legs and drools. Then it receives food. Is the animal's behavior an example of classical conditioning or operant conditioning? So far, you do not have enough information to answer the question. What else do you need to know before you can answer?**

Answer

9. You need to know whether the bell always predicts food (classical conditioning) or whether the animal receives food only when it sits up (operant conditioning).

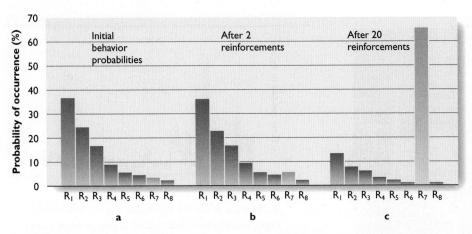

▲ **Figure 6.12** According to Thorndike, a cat starts with many potential behaviors in a given situation. When one of the behaviors leads to reinforcement, the future probability of that behavior increases. We need not assume that the cat understands what it is doing or why.

Of course, some activities are more insistent than others. If you have been deprived of oxygen, even briefly, the opportunity to breathe is extremely reinforcing. If you have been deprived of reading time or piano time, the reinforcement value is less.

10. According to the disequilibrium principle, how could you determine what would be reinforcing for someone?

Answer

10. First find how the person spends time when free from obligations, such as on vacation. Then find which activities have been deprived recently. Those activities should be reinforcing.

Reinforcement and Punishment

Some events work well as reinforcers for some individuals and not others. Consider how many hours someone might play a video game just for a high score. In one quirky experiment, mother rats could press a lever to deliver extra baby rats into their cage. They kept on pressing and pressing, adding more and more babies (Lee, Clancy, & Fleming, 1999). Is there any pattern as to what is a good reinforcer and what isn't?

We might guess that reinforcers are biologically useful to the individual, but many are not. For example, saccharin, a sweet but biologically useless chemical, can be a reinforcer. For many people, alcohol and tobacco are stronger reinforcers than vitamin-rich vegetables. So biological usefulness doesn't define reinforcement.

A useful way of defining reinforcement relies on the concept of equilibrium. If you could spend your day any way you wanted, how would you divide your time, on average? Let's suppose you might spend 30 percent of your day sleeping, 10 percent eating, 8 percent exercising, 11 percent reading, 9 percent talking with friends, 2 percent grooming, 2 percent playing the piano, and so forth. Now suppose something kept you away from one of these activities for a day or two. An opportunity to do that activity would get you back toward equilibrium. According to the **disequilibrium principle** of reinforcement, *anything that prevents an activity produces disequilibrium, and an opportunity to return to equilibrium is reinforcing* (Farmer-Dougan, 1998; Timberlake & Farmer-Dougan, 1991).

Primary and Secondary Reinforcers

Psychologists distinguish between **primary reinforcers** (or *unconditioned reinforcers*) *that are reinforcing because of their own properties,* and **secondary reinforcers** (or *conditioned reinforcers*) *that became reinforcing by association with something else.* Food and water are primary reinforcers. Money (a secondary reinforcer) becomes reinforcing because we can exchange it for food or other primary reinforcers. A student learns that a good grade wins approval, and an employee learns that increased productivity wins the employer's praise. In these cases, *secondary* means "learned," not unimportant. Most of our work is for secondary reinforcers.

Punishment

In contrast to a *reinforcer,* a **punishment** *decreases the probability of a response.* A reinforcer can be either a presentation of something (e.g., receiving food) or a removal (e.g., stopping pain). Similarly, punishment can be either a presentation of something (e.g., receiving pain) or a removal (e.g., withholding food). Punishment is most effective when it is quick and predictable. An uncertain or delayed punishment is less effective. For example, the burn you feel from touching a hot stove is highly effective in teaching you something to avoid. The threat that overeating, inactivity, or cigarettes might give you health problems at some time in the future is less effective.

B. F. Skinner (1938) tested punishment in a famous laboratory study. He first trained food-deprived rats to press a bar to get food and then he stopped reinforcing their presses. For the first 10 minutes, some rats not only failed to get food, but also received a slap on their paws every time they pressed the bar. (The bar slapped their paws.) The punished rats temporarily suppressed their pressing, but in the long run, they pressed as many times as did the unpunished rats. Skinner concluded that punishment produces no long-term effects.

That conclusion, however, is an overstatement (Staddon, 1993). A better conclusion would be that punishment does not greatly weaken a response when no other response is available. Skinner's food-deprived rats had no other way to seek food. (If someone punished you for breathing, you would continue breathing.)

Still, alternatives to punishment are often more effective. How could we get drivers to obey school-zone speed limits? Warning them of fines is not as effective as we would like. A surprisingly effective procedure is to post a driver-feedback

What serves as a reinforcer for one person might not for another. Lucy Pearson (left) has collected more than 110,000 hubcaps. Jim Hambrick (right) collects Superman items.

sign that posts the speed limit and an announcement of "your speed" based on a radar sensor (Goetz, 2011). Just getting individual feedback heightens a driver's likelihood of obeying the law.

Is physical punishment of children, such as spanking, a good or bad idea? Spanking is illegal in many countries, mostly in Europe (Zolotor & Puzia, 2010). Most psychologists strongly discourage spanking, recommending that parents simply reason with the child or use nonphysical methods of discipline, such as time out or loss of television or other privileges. What evidence backs this recommendation?

Many studies show a positive correlation between physical punishment and behavioral problems. Children who are frequently spanked tend to be ill behaved. You can see the problem in interpreting this result: It might mean that spanking causes misbehavior, it might mean that ill-behaved children provoke their parents to spank them, or it might mean a combination of both. It could also mean that spanking is more common for families in stressful conditions, families with much parental conflict, or families with other factors that might lead to misbehaviors (Morris & Gibson, 2011). Better evidence is that physical punishment predicts an increase in later misbehaviors (Gershoff et al., 2018). However, alternative treatments such as psychotherapy or time-out punishment also predict increases in later misbehaviors (Larzelere, Gunnoe, Ferguson, & Roberts, 2019), and no one argues that psychotherapy or time-out causes misbehavior. In any case, the research is clearer that severe physical punishment leads to antisocial behavior, low self-esteem, and hostility toward the parents (Larzelere & Kuhn, 2005), as well as increased risk for a lifetime of health problems (Hyland, Alkhalaf, & Whalley, 2013).

Categories of Reinforcement and Punishment

As mentioned, a reinforcer can be either presenting something like food or avoiding something like pain. Possible punishments include presenting pain or avoiding food. Psychologists use different terms to distinguish these possibilities, as shown in ■ Table 6.1.

The upper left and lower right of the table both show reinforcement. Reinforcement *increases* the probability of a behavior. Reinforcement can be either positive reinforcement—*presenting something such as food,* or negative reinforcement—*avoiding something such as pain.* Many people find the term *negative reinforcement* confusing or misleading (Baron & Galizio, 2005; Kimble, 1993), and most researchers prefer the terms *escape*

learning or *avoidance learning.* The individual is reinforced by an opportunity to escape or avoid a danger.

Punishment *decreases* the probability of a behavior. In Table 6.1, the upper right and lower left

Many secondary reinforcers are surprisingly powerful. Consider how hard children work for a little gold star that the teacher pastes on an assignment.

Table 6.1 Four Categories of Operant Conditioning

	Event Such as Food		Event Such as Pain	
Behavior leads to the event	**Positive Reinforcement** *Result:* Increase in the behavior. *Example:* "If you clean your room, I'll get you a pizza tonight."		**Punishment** *Result:* Decrease in the behavior. *Example:* "If you insult me, I'll slap you."	
Behavior avoids the event	**Punishment (Negative Punishment)** *Result:* Decrease in the behavior. *Example:* "If you hit your little brother again, you'll get no dessert."		**Negative Reinforcement = Escape or Avoidance Learning** *Result:* Increase in the behavior. *Example:* "If you go into the office over there, the doctor will remove the thorn from your leg."	

items show two types of punishment. Punishment can be either presenting something such as pain, or omitting something such as food or privileges. Punishment by omitting something can be known as negative punishment, although that term is seldom used.

To classify some procedure, attend to the wording. If the procedure increases a behavior, it is reinforcement. If it decreases a behavior, it is punishment. If the reinforcer or punishment is the presence of something, it is positive. If the reinforcer or punishment is the absence of something, it is negative. In many cases, you can dispense with the terms positive and negative and just refer to reinforcement or punishment.

11. Identify each of the following examples using the terms in Table 6.1:

a. You pay a bill on time to avoid penalties.
b. Your friends smile at you when they see you coming.
c. You trip and fall because you were texting instead of watching where you were walking.
d. Because you did not get ready on time, you miss the start of the basketball game.

Answer

11. a. avoidance learning (negative reinforcement);
b. positive reinforcement;
c. punishment; d. punishment (negative punishment).

Additional Phenomena of Operant Conditioning

Recall the concepts of extinction, generalization, and discrimination in classical conditioning. The same concepts apply to operant conditioning, with different procedures.

Extinction

No doubt you have heard the saying, "If at first you don't succeed, try, try again." The comedian W. C. Fields said, "If at first you don't succeed, try, try again. Then quit. There's no point in being a damn fool about it."

In operant conditioning, extinction *occurs if responses stop producing reinforcements.* For example, you were once in the habit of asking your roommate to join you for supper. The last few times you asked, your roommate said no, so you stop asking. You used to enjoy a certain television show, but the last few times it seemed boring, so you stop watching. In classical conditioning, extinction is achieved by presenting the CS without the UCS. In operant conditioning, the procedure is response without reinforcement. ■ Table 6.2 compares classical and operant conditioning.

Generalization

Someone who receives reinforcement for a response in the presence of one stimulus will probably make the same response in the presence of a similar stimulus. *The more similar a new stimulus is to the original reinforced stimulus, the more likely is the same response.* This phenomenon is known as stimulus generalization. For example, you might reach for the turn signal of a rented car in the same place you would find it in your own car.

Many animals have evolved an appearance that takes advantage of their predators' stimulus generalization (Darst & Cummings, 2006). A predatory bird that learns to avoid a venomous snake also avoids a harmless look-alike snake. A bird that learns to avoid a bad-tasting butterfly will avoid other butterflies of similar appearance. ▼ Figure 6.13 shows an example.

Table 6.2 Classical Conditioning and Operant Conditioning

	Classical Conditioning	**Operant Conditioning**
Terminology	CS, UCS, CR, UCR	Response, reinforcement
Behavior	Reacts to CS–UCS pairings	Controls reinforcement
Paired during acquisition	CS and UCS	Response and reinforcement (in the presence of certain stimuli)
Responses	Mostly visceral (internal organs)	Mostly skeletal muscles
Extinction procedure	CS without UCS	Response without reinforcement

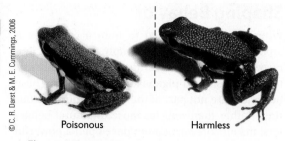

Poisonous   Harmless

▲ **Figure 6.13** The harmless frog evolved an appearance that resembles a poisonous species, taking advantage of the way birds generalize their learned avoidance responses.

Does that definition make sense? Skinner's reply was that it did, because it led to consistent results. When deciding how to define a behavior—any behavior—the best definition is the one that produces the clearest results.

Discrimination and Discriminative Stimuli

If reinforcement occurs for responding to one stimulus and not another, the result is **discrimination** between them, yielding *a response to one stimulus and not the other.* For example, you smile and greet someone you think you know, but then you realize it is someone else. Soon you learn to recognize the difference between the two people. Mushroom hunters learn to pick the edible types and leave the poisonous ones.

A *stimulus that indicates which response is appropriate* is called a **discriminative stimulus.** Much of our behavior depends on discriminative stimuli. For example, you learn to be quiet during a lecture, but you talk when the professor invites discussion. You learn that you can talk to your sister when she just walked into the room, but not when she is busy with a math assignment. You learn to drive fast on certain streets and slowly on others. Throughout your day, one stimulus after another signals which behaviors will yield reinforcement, punishment, or neither. *The ability of a stimulus to encourage some responses and discourage others* is known as **stimulus control.**

B. F. Skinner and the Shaping of Responses

One of the most famous psychological researchers, B. F. Skinner (1904–1990), demonstrated many uses of operant conditioning. Skinner was a devoted behaviorist who sought simple explanations in terms of reinforcement histories rather than mental processes.

One problem confronting any behavior researcher is how to define a response. Skinner simplified the measurement by simplifying the situation (Zuriff, 1995): He set up a box, called an *operant-conditioning chamber* (or *Skinner box,* a term that Skinner himself never used), in which a rat presses a lever or a pigeon pecks an illuminated "key" to receive food (see ▶ **Figure 6.14**). He operationally defined the response as anything that the animal did to depress the lever or key. So, if the rat pressed the lever with its snout instead of its paw, the response still counted. If the pigeon batted the key with its wing instead of pecking it with its beak, it still counted. The behavior was defined by its outcome, not by muscle movements.

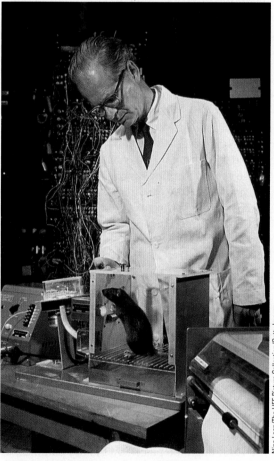

▲ **Figure 6.14** B. F. Skinner examines a rat in an operant-conditioning chamber. When the light above the bar is on, pressing the bar is reinforced. A food pellet rolls out of the storage device (left) and down the tube into the cage.

Shaping Behavior

When Thorndike wanted to train a cat to push a pole or pull a string, he simply put the cat in a puzzle box and waited. Skinner wanted to train rats to push levers and pigeons to peck at keys. These behaviors are not part of the animals' normal routine. Rather than wait for those unnatural behaviors, maybe forever, Skinner developed a powerful technique, called shaping, for *establishing a new response by reinforcing successive approximations to it.*

To shape a rat to press a lever, you might begin by reinforcing the rat for standing up, a common behavior in rats. After a few reinforcements, the rat stands up more frequently. Now you change the rules, giving food only when the rat stands up while facing the lever. Soon it spends more time standing up and facing the lever. It extinguishes its behavior of standing and facing in other directions because those responses are not reinforced. The rat is also showing discrimination, responding to the direction of the lever and not to other directions.

Next you provide reinforcement only when the rat stands facing the correct direction while in the half of the cage nearer the lever. You gradually move the boundary, and the rat moves closer to the lever. Then the rat must touch the lever and, finally, apply weight to it. Through a series of easy steps, you shape the rat to press a lever.

Shaping works with humans, too, of course. Consider education: First, your parents or teachers praise you for counting your fingers. Later, you must add and subtract to earn their congratulations. Step by step, your tasks become more complex until you are doing advanced mathematics.

Chaining Behavior

Taking a trip, getting ready for bed, or writing a paper is not one action but a sequence of actions. To produce a learned sequence, psychologists use a procedure called chaining. Assume you want to train a show horse to go through a sequence of actions. You could *chain* the behaviors, *reinforcing each one with the opportunity to engage in the next one.* The animal starts by learning the final behavior. Then it learns the next to last behavior, which is reinforced by the opportunity to perform the final behavior. And so on.

A rat might be placed on the top platform, as in ▶ Figure 6.15f, where it eats. Then it is put on the intermediate platform with a ladder leading to the top platform. The rat learns to climb the ladder. Then it is placed again on the intermediate platform but without the ladder. It must learn to pull

a string to raise the ladder so that it can climb to the top platform. Then the rat is placed on the bottom platform (▼ Figure 6.15a). It now learns to climb the ladder to the intermediate platform, pull a string to raise the ladder, and then climb the ladder again. A chain like this can go on and on. Each behavior is reinforced with the opportunity for the next behavior, until the final behavior is reinforced with food.

People learn chains of responses, too. As a child, you learned to eat with a fork and spoon. Then you learned to put your own food on the plate. Eventually, you learned to plan a menu, go to the store, buy the ingredients, cook the meal, put it on the plate, and then eat. Each behavior is reinforced by the opportunity to engage in the next behavior.

To show the effectiveness of shaping and chaining, Skinner performed a demonstration: First, he trained a rat to go to the center of a cage. Then he trained it to do so only when he played a certain piece of music. Next he trained it to wait for the music, go to the center of the cage, and sit up on its hind legs. Step by step, he eventually trained the rat to wait for the music (the "Star-Spangled Banner"), move to the center of the cage, sit up on its hind legs, put its claws on a string next to a pole, pull the string to hoist the U.S. flag, and then stand back and salute. Only then did the rat get its reinforcement.

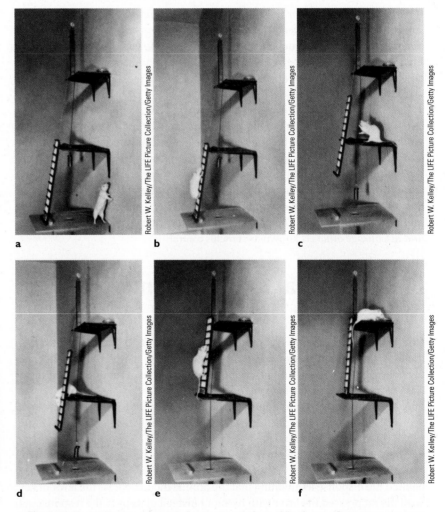

a   b   c

d   e   f

▲ **Figure 6.15** In chaining, each behavior is reinforced by the opportunity to engage in the next behavior. To reach food on the top platform, this rat must climb a ladder and pull a string to raise the ladder so that it can climb again.

Table 6.3 Some Schedules of Reinforcement

Type	Description
Continuous	Reinforcement for every response of the correct type
Fixed ratio	Reinforcement following completion of a specific number of responses
Variable ratio	Reinforcement for an unpredictable number of responses that varies around a mean value
Fixed interval	Reinforcement for the first response that follows a given delay since the previous reinforcement
Variable interval	Reinforcement for the first response that follows an unpredictable delay (varying around a mean value) since the previous reinforcement

Needless to say, patriotism is not part of a rat's usual repertoire. The point is, chaining can produce complex behaviors.

Schedules of Reinforcement

The simplest procedure in operant conditioning is to *provide reinforcement for every correct response*, a procedure known as continuous reinforcement. However, in the real world, continuous reinforcement is not common.

Reinforcement for some responses and not for others is known as intermittent reinforcement or partial reinforcement. Psychologists have investigated the effects of schedules of reinforcement, which are *rules for the delivery of reinforcement*. In addition to continuous reinforcement, four other schedules for the delivery of reinforcement are fixed ratio, fixed interval, variable ratio, and variable interval (see ■ Table 6.3). A ratio schedule provides reinforcements depending on the number of responses. An interval schedule provides reinforcements depending on the timing of responses.

Fixed-Ratio Schedule

A fixed-ratio schedule *provides reinforcement only after a certain (fixed) number of correct responses*—after every sixth response, for example. Examples include factory workers who are paid for every ten pieces they turn out or fruit pickers who get paid by the bushel.

A fixed-ratio schedule requiring a small number of responses, such as two or three, produces a steady rate of response. However, if the schedule requires many responses before reinforcement, the typical result is a pause after each reinforcement, and then resumption of steady responding. Researchers sometimes graph the results with a *cumulative record:* The line is flat when the individual does not respond, and it moves up with each response. For a fixed-ratio schedule requiring ten responses, a typical result would look as shown below. Note that the number of responses per reinforcement is constant, but the time between one reinforcement and another can vary. On average, pauses are longer in schedules requiring greater numbers of responses. For example, if you have just completed 10 math problems, you pause briefly before starting your next assignment. If you had to complete 100 problems, you pause longer.

Variable-Ratio Schedule

A variable-ratio schedule is similar to a fixed-ratio schedule, except that *reinforcement occurs after a variable number of correct responses.* For example, reinforcement might sometimes occur after one or two responses, sometimes after five, sometimes after ten, and so on. Variable-ratio schedules generate steady response rates.

Variable-ratio schedules, or approximations of them, occur whenever each response has a nearly equal probability of success. When you apply for a job, you might or might not be hired. The more applications you submit, the better your chances, but you cannot predict how many applications you need to submit before receiving a job offer. Gambling pays off on a variable ratio. If you enter a lottery, each time you enter you have some chance of winning, but you cannot predict how many times you must enter before winning (if ever).

Fixed-Interval Schedule

A fixed-interval schedule *provides reinforcement for the first response after a specific time interval.* For instance, an animal might get food for its first response after a 15-second interval. Then it would have to wait another 15 seconds before another response is effective. Animals (including humans) on such a schedule learn to pause after reinforcement and begin to respond again toward the end of the time interval. As the time of the next reinforcement approaches, the rate of responding accelerates. The cumulative record is as shown above and to the right. Note that the delay between one reinforcement and the next is constant, but the number of responses will vary.

Checking your mailbox is an example of behavior on a fixed-interval schedule. If your mail is delivered at about 3 p.m. and you are eagerly

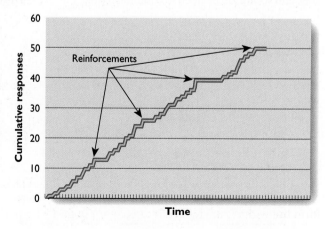

awaiting an important package, you might begin to check around 2:30 and continue checking every few minutes until it arrives. Showing up on time for class is another example of a fixed-interval schedule.

Variable-Interval Schedule

With a **variable-interval schedule**, *reinforcement is available after a variable amount of time.* For example, reinforcement may come for the first response after 2 minutes, then for the first response after the next 7 seconds, then after 3 minutes 20 seconds, and so forth. You cannot know how long before your next response is reinforced. Consequently, responses on a variable-interval schedule are slow but steady. Checking your email or your Facebook account is an example: A new message could appear at any time, so you check occasionally.

Stargazing and birdwatching are also reinforced on a variable-interval schedule. The opportunity to see something unusual appears at unpredictable intervals.

Extinction of Responses Reinforced on Different Schedules

Suppose some animal received continuous reinforcement for response A, but only intermittent reinforcement for response B. It should learn a stronger habit for response A, right? Therefore, behaviorists were surprised to discover that response B would extinguish more slowly.

Several explanations are possible, and one is that the change is more noticeable after continuous reinforcement. Let's imagine it in human terms. Suppose your neighborhood has two restaurants, Yummy's and Gulpy's. In the past, Yummy's has been open every day, but Gulpy's was open only about one-fourth of the time. For the last few days, both were closed. If you want to go to a restaurant tonight, which one would you try? Probably Gulpy's. You are accustomed to seeing it open after being closed several times in a row, and so you are inclined to continue trying.

Another example: You and a friend go to a casino and bet on the roulette wheel. Amazingly, at the start you win every time. Your friend wins only occasionally. Then both of you go into a prolonged losing streak. Presuming both of you have the same amount of money, which of you will probably continue betting longer?

Your friend will, even though you had the favorable early experience. You notice that the payoffs have changed, but your friend will take longer to notice. Responses extinguish more slowly after intermittent reinforcement (either a ratio schedule or an interval schedule) than after continuous reinforcement.

12. Identify which schedule of reinforcement applies to each of the following examples:

a. Your boss gives you a bonus for every fifth customer who submits a favorable review.

b. You find that sometimes when you go fishing you catch a good fish, but other times you do not, on an unpredictable basis.

c. You are expecting an important email, but you don't know when, so you check whenever you think of it.

Answers

12. a. fixed ratio; b. variable ratio; c. variable interval. (Checking will be effective after some interval of time, but the length of that time is unpredictable.)

Applications of Operant Conditioning

Although operant conditioning arose from theoretical interests, it has a long history of applications. Here are two examples.

Persuasion

How could you persuade someone to do something objectionable? For an extreme example, could a captor convince a prisoner of war to cooperate?

An application of shaping is to start by reinforcing a slight degree of cooperation and then working up to the goal little by little. This principle was applied by people who probably never heard of B. F. Skinner or positive reinforcement. During the Korean War, the Chinese Communists forwarded some of the letters written home by American prisoners but intercepted others. (The prisoners could tell from the replies which letters had been forwarded.) The prisoners suspected that they could get their letters through if they wrote something mildly favorable about their captors. They began including occasional remarks that the Communists were not really so bad, that certain aspects of the Chinese system seemed to work pretty well, or that they hoped the war would end soon.

After a while, the Chinese started essay contests, offering extra food or other privileges to the soldier who wrote the best essay in the captors' opinion. Most of the winning essays contained a statement or two that offered a minor compliment to the Communists or a minor criticism of the United States. Gradually, more and more soldiers started including such statements. Then the Chinese might ask, "You said the United States is not perfect. Could you tell us some of the ways in which it is not perfect, so that we can better understand your system?" As time passed, without torture and with only modest reinforcements, the Chinese induced prisoners to denounce the United States, make false confessions, inform on fellow prisoners, and reveal military secrets (Cialdini, 1993).

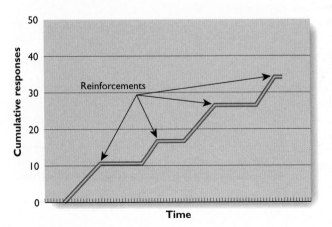

The point is clear: Whether we want to get rats to salute the flag or soldiers to denounce it, the most effective training technique is to start with easy behaviors, reinforce those behaviors, and then gradually shape more complex behaviors.

Applied Behavior Analysis/Behavior Modification

In one way or another, people almost constantly try to influence other people's behavior. Psychologists have applied operant conditioning to enhance that influence.

In applied behavior analysis, also known as behavior modification, a *psychologist removes reinforcement for unwanted behaviors and provides reinforcement for more acceptable behaviors.* For example, school psychologists instituted a program to encourage children with attention-deficit disorder to complete more school assignments. In addition to verbal praise, children received points for each assignment completed and additional points for completing it accurately. They lost points for rule violations, such as being out of the seat. At the end of each week, those who had accumulated enough points could go to a party or take a field trip. The result was increased completion of assignments and better in-class behavior (Fabiano et al., 2007).

Another example: People with a painful injury avoid using the injured arm or leg and receive much sympathy. In some cases, the sympathy and

the excuse for not working become powerful reinforcers, and people continue acting injured even after the injury has healed. To overcome this maladaptive behavior, families and friends can praise or otherwise reinforce attempts at increased mobility, and stop providing sympathy for the complaints (Jensen & Turk, 2014). This policy, of course, requires distinguishing between real pain and exaggerated pain.

13. How might someone use applied behavior analysis to help someone overcome a drug habit?

Answer

13. Periodically test the person for drugs. Whenever he/she shows to be free of drugs, provide a voucher for a free meal or other desirable outcome. This procedure is in fact often successful in treating drug abuse.

---

in closing | module 6.2

Operant Conditioning and Human Behavior

Suppose one of your instructors announces that everyone in the class will receive the same grade at the end of the course, regardless of performance on tests and papers. Will you study hard in that course? Probably not. Or suppose your employer said that all raises and promotions would be made at random, with no regard

to how well you do your job. Would you work as hard as possible? Not likely. Our behavior depends on its consequences, just like that of a rat or pigeon. That is the main point of operant conditioning.

Summary

- *Behaviorism.* Behaviorists emphasize how environmental contingencies mold behavior. (page 190)
- *Reinforcement.* Edward Thorndike defined reinforcement as the process of increasing the future probability of the preceding response. (page 190)
- *Operant conditioning.* Operant conditioning is the process of controlling the rate of a behavior through its consequences. It contrasts with classical conditioning, in which the individual's responses do not alter the probability of the outcome. (page 191)
- *Disequilibrium principle.* If someone has been deprived of the opportunity to engage in a behavior, then the opportunity to return to that behavior is reinforcing. (page 192)
- *Primary and secondary reinforcers.* Primary reinforcers such as food are reinforcing because of their own properties. Secondary reinforcers such as money become reinforcing because of their association with primary reinforcers. (page 192)
- *Reinforcement and punishment.* In most cases positive reinforcement is a more reliable way of influencing behavior than punishment is. (page 192)

- *Extinction.* In operant conditioning, a response is extinguished if it is no longer followed by reinforcement. (page 194)
- *Shaping and chaining.* Shaping trains a behavior by reinforcing successive approximations to it. Chaining trains a sequence of behaviors by making each step an opportunity to perform the next step. (page 195)
- *Schedules of reinforcement.* The frequency and timing of a response depend on the schedule of reinforcement. In a ratio schedule of reinforcement, an individual is given reinforcement after a fixed or variable number of responses. In an interval schedule of reinforcement, an individual is given reinforcement after a fixed or variable period of time. Extinction is slower after intermittent reinforcement than after continuous reinforcement. (page 197)
- *Applications.* People have applied operant conditioning to persuasion and applied behavior analysis. (page 198)

Key Terms

applied behavior analysis (or behavior modification) (page 199)

chaining (page 196)

continuous reinforcement (page 197)

discrimination (page 195)

discriminative stimulus (page 195)

disequilibrium principle (page 192)

extinction (page 194)

fixed-interval schedule (page 197)

fixed-ratio schedule (page 197)

intermittent reinforcement (page 197)

law of effect (page 191)

learning curve (page 190)

negative reinforcement (page 193)

operant conditioning (or instrumental conditioning) (page 191)

partial reinforcement (page 197)

positive reinforcement (page 193)

primary reinforcer (page 192)

punishment (page 192)

reinforcement (page 190)

schedule of reinforcement (page 197)

secondary reinforcer (page 192)

shaping (page 196)

skeletal responses (page 191)

stimulus control (page 195)

stimulus generalization (page 194)

variable-interval schedule (page 198)

variable-ratio schedule (page 197)

visceral responses (page 191)

Review Questions

1. What did Thorndike mean by reinforcement?
   (a) A connection between CS and UCS
   (b) Something that the animal desires or enjoys
   (c) An understanding of the relationship between response and outcome
   (d) An event that stamps in the previous response

2. How does operant conditioning differ from classical conditioning?
   (a) Classical conditioning changes brain connections, and operant conditioning does not.
   (b) Classical conditioning provides rewards, and operant conditioning provides punishments.
   (c) Operant conditioning applies to visceral responses, and classical conditioning applies to skeletal responses.
   (d) In operant conditioning, a response controls the probability of the outcome.

3. According to the disequilibrium principle, what is a reinforcer?
   (a) Any stimulus that attracts attention
   (b) A stimulus that increases activity in the brain's pleasure areas
   (c) An opportunity to do an activity that is biologically useful
   (d) An opportunity to do an activity from which you have been deprived

4. What is meant by a "secondary" reinforcer?
   (a) Something that is reinforcing only when primary reinforcers are unavailable
   (b) Something that became reinforcing by association with primary reinforcers
   (c) Something that reinforces only the simplest responses
   (d) Something that reinforces relatively complex responses

5. What procedure produces extinction in operant conditioning?
   (a) Present the conditioned stimulus without the unconditioned stimulus.
   (b) Present the conditioned stimulus without the conditioned response.
   (c) Present a punishment after a new response.
   (d) Present no reinforcer after the previously reinforced response.

6. Shaping a behavior for an experiment in operant conditioning begins with which of the following?
   (a) Placing an animal into the proper position to make the response
   (b) Reinforcing a simple approximation to the desired behavior
   (c) Demonstrating a response for the individual to imitate
   (d) Punishing all inappropriate responses

7. Which schedule of reinforcement describes the following: Whenever you buy ten pizzas, you get the next one free.
   (a) Fixed interval
   (b) Fixed ratio
   (c) Variable interval
   (d) Variable ratio

8. Which of the following is an example of a variable-interval schedule?
   (a) Checking stores in your neighborhood in hope of seeing a "help wanted" notice
   (b) Opening oysters in hopes of finding a pearl
   (c) Buying ice cream cones at a place that offers a free one after every 10 purchases
   (d) Taking a test that is given in class once a week

9. Behavior modification is LEAST likely to use which of these procedures?
   (a) Positive reinforcement
   (b) Shaping
   (c) Chaining
   (d) Brain stimulation

Answers: 1d, 2d, 3d, 4b, 5d, 6b, 7b, 8a, 9d.

module 6.3

Variations of Learning

After studying this module, you should be able to:

1. Explain how conditioned taste aversions and birdsong learning differ from the types of learning that Pavlov and Skinner studied.

2. Describe research that supports the idea of predispositions to learn some connections more easily than others.

3. Discuss the importance of social learning.

Thorndike, Pavlov, and the other pioneers of research on learning assumed that learning was the same wherever and whenever it occurred. If so, researchers who studied any convenient example, such as salivary conditioning or the responses of pigeons in a Skinner box, could discover all the laws of learning.

However, even the earliest researchers found that some things are easier to learn than others. Thorndike's cats learned to push and pull various devices in their efforts to escape from his puzzle boxes, but when he tried to teach them to scratch or lick themselves for the same reinforcement, they learned slowly and performed inconsistently (Thorndike, 1911/1970). Why?

One explanation is what Thorndike called "belongingness" and later psychologists called **preparedness**, the *concept that evolution has prepared any species to learn some associations more easily than others* (Seligman, 1970). Presumably, cats and their ancestors since ancient times encountered many situations in which pushing or pulling something produced a useful outcome. But when in nature would licking or scratching yourself move an obstacle or get you out of confinement? From an evolutionary standpoint, we should expect cats to be prepared to learn some connections more easily than others.

Similarly, dogs readily learn that a sound from one direction means "raise your left leg" and a sound from another direction means "raise your right leg." They are slow to learn that a ticking metronome means raise the left leg and a buzzer means raise the right leg (Dobrzecka, Szwejkowska, & Konorski, 1966). Again: When in nature would one sound mean "turn to the left" (regardless of where the sound came from) and a different sound mean "turn to the right"?

The idea of preparedness has practical applications. People learn easily to turn a wheel clockwise to move something to the right and counterclockwise to move it to the left (as when turning the steering wheel of a car). If the controls work the opposite way, people often get confused. Many engineers who design machines consult with human-factors psychologists about how to set up the controls so that people can easily learn to use them.

Conditioned Taste Aversions

If a sound (CS) predicts food (UCS), learning proceeds most quickly if the CS precedes the UCS by about half a second. If a rat receives food after pressing a bar, learning is fastest if the reinforcement occurs within a second or two after the response. Based on research of this type, psychologists were at one time convinced that learning occurs only between events happening within seconds of each other (Kimble, 1961).

That generalization fails in certain situations. Consider what happens if you eat something and get sick to your stomach. If learning occurred only for events separated by a few seconds, you would never learn to avoid bad foods. In fact, even if you get sick an hour or more after eating something, you learn an aversion to that food, especially if it was an unfamiliar food. If you try eating it again, you find it repulsive. *Associating a food with illness* is **conditioned taste aversion**, first documented by John Garcia and his colleagues (Garcia, Ervin, & Koelling, 1966). One of its special features is that it occurs reliably after a single pairing of food with illness, even with a long delay between them. In a typical experiment, an animal drinks something such as sweetened water and receives a treatment to produce nausea minutes or hours later. The experimenter waits days for the animal to recover and offers it a choice between sweetened and unflavored water. The animal strongly prefers the unflavored water (Garcia et al., 1966).

If you get sick after eating something, you will learn an aversion even if you know you got sick from something else, such as riding a roller coaster. Some part of your brain reacts, "I feel sick, and I'm not taking any chances. From now on, that food is taboo."

You can learn taste aversions to a familiar food, but you acquire much stronger aversions if you had no previous safe experience with the food. If you eat several foods before becoming ill, you learn aversions mainly to the unfamiliar ones, even if you ate familiar foods closer in time to the illness. A further specialization is that you associate illness with something you ate, and not with other types of events. Let's consider the evidence.

what's the evidence?

Predisposition in Learning

In nature, the food you eat predicts whether you will feel full or hungry, healthy or sick. It doesn't predict pain on your skin. In contrast, what you see or hear might predict pain, but it seldom has anything to do with nausea.

Hypothesis Rats that experience foot shock will learn to avoid visual or auditory signals associated with the shock. Rats that experience nausea will learn to avoid foods that they recently ate.

When rats drink, they taste the saccharin-flavored water and turn on a bright light and a clicking sound. Some rats receive electric shock to their feet 2 seconds after they start drinking. Other rats receive X-rays that produce nausea.

Days later: Rats are given a choice between a tube of saccharin-flavored water and a tube of unflavored water hooked up to the light and the buzzer.

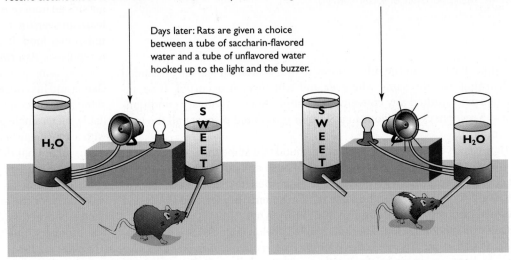

Rats that had been shocked avoid the tube with the lights and noises.

Rats that had been nauseated by X-rays avoid the saccharin-flavored water.

▲ **Figure 6.16** An experiment by Garcia and Koelling (1966): Rats associate illness with what they ate. They associate pain with what they saw or heard.

Method Water-deprived rats were offered a tube of saccharin-flavored water. The tube was set up such that when a rat licked the spout of the tube, it turned on a bright light and a clicking sound, as shown in ▲ Figure 6.16. Thus, each rat experienced the taste, light, and noise simultaneously. Half the rats received a mild foot shock 2 seconds after they started licking the tube. The other half received X-rays, which produce mild nausea. After 2 days to allow rats to recover, the procedure was repeated, and after another 2 days it was repeated again. In the final test, rats could drink from a tube containing saccharin-flavored water, or from a separate tube containing unflavored water but connected to the light and the clicking sound.

Results Rats that had received shock avoided the tube connected to lights and sounds, but they drank normally from the tube with saccharin-flavored water. Rats that had received X-rays avoided the saccharin water but drank normally from the tube connected to lights and sounds.

Interpretation When a rat (or other animal) receives shock to its feet, it learns to avoid the lights or sounds that it detects at the time. When it becomes nauseated,

it learns to avoid something that it ate. Animals evidently come with predispositions to learn some connections more than others. This tendency is an excellent example of preparedness.

Conditioned taste aversions have practical applications. Ranchers have taught coyotes to avoid sheep by giving the coyotes sheep meat laced with chemicals that cause nausea (see ▼ Figure 6.17). This procedure saves the ranchers' sheep without killing the coyotes (Gustavson, Kelly, Sweeney, & Garcia, 1976). One way of treating alcoholism is to let people drink alcohol and then administer a drug that causes nausea. This treatment is not widely used, but when it has been used, it has been quicker and more effective than other treatments for alcoholism (Revusky, 2009). Most pregnant women experience nausea ("morning sickness") during the early weeks of pregnancy. Many of them also experience food aversions, mainly to meats and eggs. Apparently they eat something, feel nausea for reasons unrelated to the food, and develop an aversion to the food. Women with the most nausea during pregnancy tend to be those

▲ **Figure 6.17** This coyote previously fell ill after eating sheep meat containing lithium salts. Now it reacts with revulsion toward both live and dead sheep.

with the strongest food aversions (Bayley, Dye, & Hill, 2009). Similarly, many cancer patients learn aversions to foods they ate just prior to chemotherapy or radiation therapy (Bernstein, 1991; Scalera & Bavieri, 2009). With one treatment after another, they come to dislike more and more foods. A good strategy is to pick a "scapegoat" food and eat it prior to each treatment. In that way, patients learn an aversion to just that food while retaining their enjoyment of others.

14. How does conditioned taste aversion differ from other kinds of learning?

Answer

14. Conditioned taste aversion occurs over long delays, and animals are predisposed to associate a taste (especially an unfamiliar taste) with illness, and not much with other outcomes.

Birdsong Learning

Birdsongs brighten the day for people who hear them, but they are earnest business for the birds themselves. For most songbirds outside the tropics, songs are mostly by males during the mating season. A song says, "Here I am. I am a male of species ___. If you're a female of my species, please come closer. If you're a male of my species, go away." Some species have a built-in song, but others have to learn it. In species that depend on learning, *the learning occurs most readily during a* sensitive period *early in the first year of life* (Marler, 1997). Similarly, human children learn language most easily when they are young.

Song learning is unlike standard examples of classical and operant conditioning. During the sensitive period, the infant bird only listens. At that point, it makes no response and receives no reinforcement, and nevertheless learning occurs. The following spring, when the bird starts to sing, we see a trial-and-error process. At first, the song is a mixture of sounds, like a babbling human infant. As time passes, the bird eliminates some sounds and rearranges others until the song matches what was heard the previous summer (Marler & Peters, 1981, 1982). But the only reinforcer is recognizing that the song is correct.

Later in life, the bird may modify the song depending on competing noises. Many birds now live in suburban neighborhoods with cars, trucks, other machinery, children at play, and so forth. Humans are a noisy species. How is a little bird to make itself heard? Compared to birds away from people,

those near people spend more time singing (Diaz, Parra, & Gallardo, 2011). They shift some of their singing to night, when the neighborhood tends to be quieter (Fuller, Warren, & Gaston, 2007). Also, they sing higher-pitched songs, omitting the low-pitched sounds that car and truck sounds would mask (Slabbekoorn & den Boer-Visser, 2006). Individual birds adjust their calls depending on the noise levels, so the results indicate learning, not changes in their genetics. The point is that the principles of learning vary among situations in a way that makes sense based on the animal's way of life (Rozin & Kalat, 1971).

15. How does birdsong learning differ from classical and operant conditioning?

Answer

15. The most distinctive feature is that birdsong learning occurs when the learner makes no apparent response and receives no apparent reinforcement. Also, birdsong learning occurs most readily during a sensitive period early in life.

A male white-crowned sparrow learns his song in the first months of life but does not begin to sing it until the next year.

Social Learning

Just as many birds learn their song from other birds, humans obviously learn much from each other. Just think of all the things you did *not* learn by trial and error. You don't throw on clothes at random and wait to see which clothes bring the best reinforcements. Instead, you copy the styles that other people are wearing. If you are cooking, you don't make up recipes at random. You start with what other people have recommended. If you are dancing, you don't randomly try every possible muscle movement. Well, I guess you might, but people would laugh at you. More likely, you copy what other people do.

According to the **social-learning approach** (Bandura, 1977, 1986), *we learn about many behaviors by observing the behaviors of others.* Social learning begins in childhood. In one study, 3-year-old children watched an adult perform a task, such as pushing an object from behind. Then they watched a puppet perform the task in a different way, such as pulling it. Many of the children "corrected" the puppet, saying that is the wrong way to do it (Schmidt, Butler, Heinz, & Tomasello, 2016). Another example: Toddlers watched an adult perform two tasks easily, or watched an adult struggle

According to the social-learning approach, we learn by imitating behaviors that are reinforced and avoiding behaviors that are punished. This girl is being blessed by the temple elephant. Others who are watching may later imitate her example.

repeatedly before finally accomplishing the same tasks. Then the toddlers were given a new, difficult task. Those who had watched the adult struggle to accomplish something persisted longer in their own efforts (Leonard, Lee, & Schulz, 2017).

Social learning is a type of operant conditioning, and the underlying mechanisms are similar. However, using social information is usually quicker and more efficient than trying to learn something from scratch on your own.

Modeling and Imitation

If you visit another country with customs unlike your own, you find much that seems bewildering. Even the way to order food in a restaurant may be unfamiliar.

A hand gesture such as ⟨🤏⟩ is considered friendly in some countries but rude and vulgar in others. Many visitors to Japan find the toilets confusing. With effort, you learn foreign customs either because someone explains them to you or because you watch and copy. You *model* your behavior after others or *imitate* others.

In high school, what made certain students popular? No doubt you could cite many reasons, but once they became popular, simply being the center of attention increased their popularity. If a friend showed interest in some boy or girl, you started to notice that person, too. You modeled or imitated your friend's interest. The same is true in nonhumans. If one female shows an interest in mating with a particular male, other females increase their interest in him also (Dubois, 2007).

Why do we imitate? Other people's behavior often provides information. Did you ever have this experience? You tell your parents you want to do something because "everyone else" is doing it. They scream, "If everyone else were jumping off a cliff, would you do it, too?" Well, let's think about it. If literally *everyone* were jumping off a cliff, maybe they have a reason! Maybe you're in great danger where you are. Maybe if you jump, you'll land on something soft. If everyone is jumping off a cliff, you should consider the possibility that they know something you don't.

A Japanese toilet is a hole in the ground with no seat. Western visitors usually have to ask how to use it. (You squat.)

Maciej Wlodarzyk/Shutterstock.com

▲ **Figure 6.18** Does looking at this photo make you want to yawn?

Another reason for imitation is that other people's behavior establishes a norm or rule. For example, you wear casual clothing where others dress casually and formal wear where others dress formally. You drive on the right side of the road in the United States or on the left side in Britain. Doing the same as other people is often helpful.

You also imitate automatically in some cases. If someone yawns, you become more likely to yawn yourself. Even seeing a photo of an animal yawning may have the same result (see ▲ **Figure 6.18**). You are not intentionally copying, and you haven't received any new information. You imitate because seeing a yawn suggested the idea of yawning.

You automatically imitate many other actions that you see, often with no apparent motivation (Dijksterhuis & Bargh, 2001). If you see someone smile or frown, you briefly start to smile or frown. Your expression may be a quick, involuntary twitch that is hard to notice, but it does occur. Spectators at an athletic event sometimes slightly move their arms or legs in synchrony with what some athlete is doing. When expert pianists listen to a composition they have practiced, they start involuntarily tapping their fingers as if they were playing the music (Haueisen & Knösche, 2001). People also copy other people's hand gestures, even while preoccupied with a task requiring careful attention (Ramsey, Darda, & Downing, 2019). You can demonstrate by telling someone, "Please wave your hands" while you clap your hands. Many people copy your actions instead of following your instructions.

try it yourself

Albert Bandura, Dorothea Ross, and Sheila Ross (1963) studied the role of imitation for learning aggressive behavior. They asked two groups of children to watch films in which an adult or a cartoon character violently attacked an inflated "Bobo" doll. Another group watched a different film. They then left the children in a room with a Bobo doll. Only the children who had watched films with attacks on the doll attacked the doll themselves, using many of the same movements they had just seen (see ▶ **Figure 6.19**). A clear implication is that children copy the aggressive behavior they have seen in others.

concept check ✓

16. **What do these results suggest about the effects of media coverage of mass shootings?**

Answer

16. Widespread publicity about mass shootings risks the possibility of "copycat" shootings. Not only children, but also adults imitate the aggressive acts they see in others.

Vicarious Reinforcement and Punishment

A few months ago, your best friend opened a new restaurant. Now you are considering quitting your job and opening your own restaurant. How do you decide what to do?

You probably start by asking how successful your friend has been. You imitate behavior that has been reinforcing to someone else, especially someone that you like (Mobbs et al., 2009). That is, you learn by **vicarious reinforcement** or **vicarious punishment**—by *substituting someone else's experience for your own*. In one study, observers watched someone in a classical conditioning experiment in which a colored square was paired with a shock that was described as painful. Later the observers showed a fear response to that colored square, even though they had not received shocks themselves (Olsson et al., 2016).

Whenever a new business venture succeeds, other companies copy it. When a sports team wins consistently, other teams copy its style of play. When a television program wins high ratings, other producers present similar shows the following year. Politicians imitate the campaign tactics of candidates who previously succeeded.

Advertisers use vicarious reinforcement by showing happy, successful people using their product, suggesting that if you use their product, you too will be happy and successful. Advertisers promoting state lotteries show the ecstatic winners, and never the losers.

© Dr. Albert Bandura, Department of Psychology, Stanford University

▲ **Figure 6.19** This girl attacks a doll after seeing a film of a woman hitting it. Witnessing violence increases the probability of violent behavior.

Vicarious punishment is usually less effective, largely because people do not identify with the person receiving punishment. Children ages 3 to 7 had an opportunity to cheat on a task while the experimenter was supposedly not looking. Then the experimenter read stories in which a child was punished for lying or a story in which a child was rewarded for telling the truth. Finally, the experimenter asked the children whether they had cheated while the experimenter wasn't looking. Those who heard a story about reward for telling the truth were likely to tell the truth, but those who heard the stories about punishment for lying were not (Lee et al., 2014).

We tend to imitate the actions of successful people but only if we feel self-efficacy, a belief that we could perform the task well.

Self-Efficacy

When you watch an Olympic diver win a gold medal, why do you (presumably) *not* try to imitate those dives? You imitate someone else's behavior only if you have a sense of self-efficacy—*the belief of being able to perform the task successfully*. You consider your strengths and weaknesses, compare yourself to the successful person, and estimate your chance of success. If the chance of competing successfully looks slim, people get discouraged. In one case students submitted a writing assignment and then read the papers written by three other students. Those who happened to read very high-quality papers were more likely than average to quit the course (Rogers & Feller, 2016). However, if you see someone similar to yourself achieving success, you persist in your own efforts. In 1993, India passed a law that guaranteed leadership roles for women in certain randomly selected villages. Before long, young girls in those villages expressed higher aspirations for their own accomplishments (Beaman, Duflo, Pande, & Topalova, 2012).

Self-Reinforcement and Self-Punishment

When people set a goal, sometimes they decide to reinforce or punish themselves, just as if they were training someone else. They say, "If I finish this math assignment on time, I'll treat myself to a movie and a new magazine. If I don't finish on time, I'll make myself clean the sink and the toilets." (Nice threat, but people usually forgive themselves without imposing the punishment.)

Some therapists teach clients to use self-reinforcement. One 10-year-old boy had a habit of biting his fingernails, sometimes down to the skin and even drawing blood. He learned to keep records of how much nail biting he did at various times of day, and then he set goals for himself. If he met the goals of reducing his nail biting, he wrote compliments such as "I'm great! I did wonderful!" The penalty for doing worse was that he would return his weekly allowance to his parents. An additional reinforcement was that his father promised that if the son made enough progress, he would let the son be the "therapist" to help the father quit smoking. Over several weeks, the boy quit nail biting altogether (Ronen & Rosenbaum, 2001).

One amusing anecdote shows the limits of self-reinforcement and self-punishment: To try to quit smoking cigarettes, psychologist Ron Ash (1986) vowed to smoke only while he was reading *Psychological Bulletin* and other highly respected but tedious journals. He hoped to associate smoking with boredom. Two months later, he was smoking as much as ever, but he was starting to *enjoy* reading *Psychological Bulletin*!

All Learning Is Not the Same

The biological mechanisms of learning are similar in many animal species and many situations. Nevertheless, we also find variations. Learning is adapted to the demands of particular situations, such as food choice and birdsong. We use social mechanisms to facilitate and hasten learning. The outcome of these specializations increases the efficiency of learning.

Summary

- *Preparedness.* Evolution has prepared us and other animals to learn some associations more readily than others. (page 201)
- *Conditioned taste aversions.* Animals, including people, learn to avoid foods, especially unfamiliar ones, if they become ill afterward. This type of learning occurs reliably after a single pairing, even with a long delay between the food and the illness. Illness is associated much more strongly with foods than with other stimuli. (page 201)
- *Birdsong learning.* Infant birds of some species learn their song during a sensitive period early in life, but they begin to perform it only after reaching maturity a year later. Their only reinforcement is recognizing the match between what they sing and what they remember hearing. (page 203)
- *Social learning.* We learn much by observing other people's actions and their consequences. (page 204)
- *Vicarious reinforcement and punishment.* Because we identify with successful people more than failures, vicarious reinforcement is more effective than vicarious punishment. (page 205)
- *Self-efficacy.* Whether we imitate a behavior depends on whether we believe we are capable of duplicating it. (page 206)
- *Self-reinforcement and self-punishment.* People sometimes plan to reinforce or punish themselves depending on how well they work toward their goals. (page 206)

Key Terms

conditioned taste aversion (page 201)

preparedness (page 201)

self-efficacy (page 206)

sensitive period (page 203)

social-learning approach (page 204)

vicarious reinforcement (or vicarious punishment) (page 205)

Review Questions

1. What is special about conditioned taste aversions?
   (a) Learning requires many repetitions and extinguishes easily.
   (b) Learning readily occurs despite a long delay between two events.
   (c) Learning fails to generalize from one taste to a similar taste.
   (d) Learning occurs only during a sensitive period early in life.

2. Which of the following is most effective in establishing a conditioned taste aversion?
   (a) Illness
   (b) Electric shock
   (c) Imitation
   (d) Verbal explanation

3. What is special about birdsong learning?
   (a) The conditioned stimulus must closely resemble the unconditioned stimulus.
   (b) The ability to learn continues to increase throughout life.
   (c) A bird learns to sing without any external reinforcer.
   (d) The bird must learn from its mother.

4. What is meant by the social-learning approach?
   (a) Positive reinforcement for social behaviors
   (b) Learning by imitation
   (c) Using a social stimulus as a reinforcer for some other behavior
   (d) Teaching a large group of students at one time

5. Why are you unlikely to copy an act that looks too difficult for yourself?
   (a) Vicarious punishment
   (b) Lack of self-efficacy
   (c) Improper CS–UCS interval
   (d) Improper schedule of reinforcement

Answers: 1b, 2a, 3c, 4b, 5b.

7 Memory

iStock.com/Rich Legg

With a suitable reminder, you remember some events distinctly, even after a long delay. Other memories are lost or distorted.

Ariel Skelley/The Image Bank/Getty Images

Suppose I offer you, for a price, an opportunity to do absolutely anything you want for a day. You will not be limited by the usual physical constraints. You can travel in a flash and visit as many places as you wish, even outer space. You can travel forward and backward through time, finding out what the future holds and witnessing the great events of the past. (You will not be able to alter history.) Anything you want to do—just name it and it is yours. Furthermore, I guarantee your safety: No matter where you choose to go or what you choose to do, you will not get hurt.

How much would you pay for this amazing opportunity? Oh, yes, I should mention, there is one catch. When the day is over, you will completely forget everything that happened. Any notes or photos will vanish. And anyone else who takes part in your special day will forget it, too.

Now how much would you be willing to pay? Much less, no doubt, and perhaps nothing. Living without remembering is hardly living at all: Our memories are almost the same as our selves.

iStock.com/Rich Legg

After studying this module, you should be able to:

1. Describe Ebbinghaus's early research on memory.

2. Differentiate among ways of testing memory.

3. Explain ways to minimize errors in eyewitness testimony and suspect lineups.

4. Distinguish types of memory and describe their main features.

5. Characterize the main features of working memory.

Every year, people compete in the World Memory Championships. (You can read about it at **www.worldmemorychampionships.com.**) One event is speed of memorizing a shuffled deck of 52 cards. The all-time record is 13.96 seconds. Another is memorizing a list of numbers after hearing them once, at one word per second. The record is 456 numbers. People also compete at memorizing dates of fictional events, names of unfamiliar faces in photos, and so forth. Dominic O'Brien, eight-time world champion, gives speeches and writes books about how to train your memory. However, he admits that one time while he was practicing card memorization, an irate friend called from an airport to complain that O'Brien had forgotten to pick him up. O'Brien apologized and drove to London's Gatwick Airport, practicing card memorization along the way. When he arrived, he remembered that his friend was at Heathrow, London's other major airport (Johnstone, 1994).

Anyone—you, me, or Dominic O'Brien—remembers some information and forgets the rest. **Memory** is *the retention of information.* It includes skills such as riding a bicycle or tying your shoelaces. It also includes facts that never change (your birthday), facts that seldom change (your mailing address), and facts that frequently change (where you left your cell phone). You remember your most important experiences and some of your unimportant ones, many useful facts and much trivia that you cannot imagine using.

Advice: This chapter includes many Try It Yourself activities. You will gain much more from this chapter if you take the time to try them.

© Rupert Watts

Ebbinghaus's Pioneering Studies of Memory

Suppose you wanted to study memory, but no one had ever done memory research before. Where would you

Dominic O'Brien, eight-time winner of the World Memory Championships and author of several books on training your memory, admits he sometimes forgets practical information, such as promising to meet a friend at Heathrow Airport.

start? You might ask people to describe their memories, but you would not know when the memories formed, how often people had rehearsed them, or even whether the memories were correct. German psychologist Hermann Ebbinghaus (1850–1909) avoided these problems by an approach that we now take for granted: He taught new material so that he knew exactly what someone had learned and when. Then he measured memory after delays. To be sure the material was new, he used lists of nonsense syllables, such as *GAK* or *JEK*. He wrote out 2,300 syllables, assembled them randomly into lists (see ▼ Figure 7.1), and then set out to study memory. He had no cooperative introductory psychology students to enlist in his study, and (as you can imagine) no friends eager to memorize lists of nonsense syllables, so he ran all the tests on himself. For 6 years, he memorized thousands of lists of nonsense syllables and tested himself. He was either very dedicated to his science or uncommonly tolerant of boredom.

Many of his findings were hardly surprising. For example, as shown in ▼ Figure 7.2, he took longer to memorize longer lists than shorter lists. "Of course!" you might scoff. But Ebbinghaus was not just demonstrating the obvious. He measured *how much* longer it took to memorize a longer list. You might similarly object to the law of gravity: "Of course the farther something falls, the longer it takes to hit the ground!" However, measuring the acceleration of gravity was essential to progress in physics, and measuring how long it takes to learn a list enables psychologists to compare conditions: Do we learn some kinds of lists faster than other lists? Does listening to music at the same time interfere with

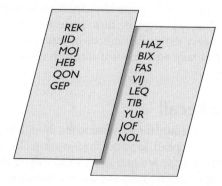

REK	HAZ
JID	BIX
MOJ	FAS
HEB	VIJ
QON	LEQ
GEP	TIB
	YUR
	JOF
	NOL

▲ **Figure 7.1** Hermann Ebbinghaus pioneered the scientific study of memory by observing his own capacity for memorizing lists of nonsense syllables.

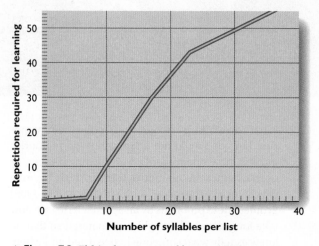

▲ Figure 7.2 Ebbinghaus counted how many times he had to read a list of nonsense syllables before he could recite it once correctly. For a list of seven or fewer, one reading was usually enough. Beyond seven, the longer the list, the more repetitions he needed. (From Ebbinghaus, 1885/1913)

memorizing? Ebbinghaus's approach led to all the later research on memory.

Methods of Testing Memory

Nearly everyone occasionally has a tip-of-the-tongue experience (Brown & McNeill, 1966). You want to remember a word or a name, and all you can think of is something that you know isn't right. Once I was trying to remember the name of a particular researcher, and all I could think of was *Bhagavad Gita* (the Hindu holy writings). Eventually I remembered the name: Paul Bach-y-Rita. In a tip-of-the-tongue experience, you might know the first letter, the number of syllables, and much else, even if you cannot generate the word itself.

In other words, memory is not an all-or-none thing. You might or might not remember something depending on when or how someone tests you. Let's survey the main methods of testing memory. Along the way, we begin to distinguish among types of memory.

Free Recall

A simple method for the researcher, though not for the person tested, is to ask for **free recall**. To recall something is *to produce a response, as you do on essay tests or short-answer tests*. For instance, "Tell me what you did today." Most people will respond with a brief synopsis, although they could elaborate in detail to follow-up questions. Free recall

almost always understates the actual amount you know. If you try to name all the children who were in your second-grade class, you might not do well, but your low recall does not mean that you have completely forgotten them.

Cued Recall

Your accuracy improves with **cued recall**, in which you *receive significant hints about the material*. For example, a photograph of the children in your second-grade class (see ▼ Figure 7.3) or a list of their initials will help you remember. Try this: Cover the right side of ■ Table 7.1 and try to identify the authors of each book on the left. Then uncover the right side, revealing each author's initials, and try again. (This method is cued recall.) Note how much better you do with these hints.

Recognition

With **recognition**, someone *chooses the correct item among several options*. People usually recognize more items than they recall. For example, someone might give you a list of 60 names and ask you to check off the correct names of children in your second-grade class. Multiple-choice tests use the recognition method.

Savings

A fourth method, the **savings method** (also known as the **relearning method**), detects weak memories *by comparing the speed of original learning to the speed of relearning*. Suppose you cannot name the children in your second-grade class and cannot even pick out their names from a list of choices. You would nevertheless learn a correct list of names faster than a list of people you had never met. That is, you save time when you relearn something. The amount of time saved (time needed for original learning minus the time for relearning) is a measure of memory.

Implicit Memory

Free recall, cued recall, recognition, and savings are tests of **explicit** (or **direct**) **memory**. That is, *someone who states an answer regards it as a product of memory*. In **implicit memory** (or **indirect memory**), *an experience influences what you say or*

▲ Figure 7.3 Can you recall the names of the students in your second-grade class? Trying to remember without any hints is *free recall*. Using a photo or a list of initials is *cued recall*.

Table 7.1 Cued Recall

Book	Author

Instructions: First try to identify the author of each book listed in the left column while covering the right column. Then expose the right column, which gives each author's initials, and try again (cued recall).

Book	Author
Moby Dick	H. M.
Emma and *Pride and Prejudice*	J. A.
Hercule Poirot stories	A. C.
Sherlock Holmes stories	A. C. D.
I Know Why the Caged Bird Sings	M. A.
War and Peace	L. T.
To Kill a Mockingbird	H. L.
The Canterbury Tales	G. C.
Great Expectations	C. D.
Of Mice and Men	J. S.
Les Miserables	V. H.

(For answers, see page 220, answer A.)

do even though you might not be aware of the influence. Defining something in terms of a vague concept like "awareness" is not a good practice. This definition is tentative until we develop a better one.

The best way to explain implicit memory is by examples: Suppose you are in a conversation while other people nearby are discussing something else. You ignore the other discussion, but a few words from that background conversation probably creep into your own. Here is a demonstration. For each of the following three-letter combinations, fill in additional letters to make any English word:

CON___
SUP___
DIS___
PRO___

You could have thought of any number of words—the dictionary lists well over 100 familiar CON___ words alone. Did you happen to write any of the following: *conversation, suppose, discussion,* or *probably?* Each of these words appeared in the preceding paragraph. *Reading or hearing a word temporarily* results in priming *that word and increasing the chance that you will use it yourself,* even if you are not aware of the influence (Graf & Mandler, 1984; Schacter, 1987). This demonstration works better if you listen to spoken words than if you read them.
■ Table 7.2 contrasts some memory tests.

Table 7.2 Ways to Test Memory

Title	Description	Example
Recall	You are asked to say what you remember.	Name the Seven Dwarfs.
Cued recall	You are given significant hints to help you remember.	Name the Seven Dwarfs. Hint: One was always smiling, one was smart, one never talked, one always seemed to have a cold . . .
Recognition	You are asked to choose the correct item from among several items.	Which of the following were among the Seven Dwarfs: Sneezy, Sleazy, Dopey, Dippy, Hippy, Happy?
Savings (relearning)	You are asked to relearn something: If it takes you less time than when you first learned that material, some memory has persisted.	Try memorizing this list: Sleepy, Sneezy, Doc, Dopey, Grumpy, Happy, Bashful. Can you memorize it faster than this list: Sleazy, Snoopy, Duke, Dippy, Gripey, Hippy, Blushy?
Implicit memory	You are asked to generate words, without necessarily regarding them as memories.	You hear the story "Snow White and the Seven Dwarfs." Later you are asked to fill in these blanks to make any words that come to mind: _ L _ _ P _ _ N _ _ Z _ _ _ C _ O _ EY _ R _ _ P _ _ _ P P _ _ A _ H _ U _

Procedural Memories and Probabilistic Learning

Procedural memories, *memories of how to do something,* such as juggling balls, riding a bicycle, or eating with chopsticks, are a special kind of memory. Psychologists distinguish procedural memories from **declarative memories,** *memories we can readily state in words.* For example, if you type, you know the locations of the letters well enough to press the right key at the right time (a procedural memory), but can you state that knowledge explicitly? For example, which letter is directly to the right of C? Which is directly to the left of P?

Procedural memory, or habit learning, differs from declarative memory in several ways. First, the two types of memory depend on different brain areas, and brain damage can impair one without impairing the other. Second, procedural memory or habit learning develops gradually, whereas you often form a declarative memory all at once. You need much practice to develop the procedural memories of how to play a piano, but you might very quickly form the declarative memory, "Don't swim here because of the alligators." Habit learning is also well suited for learning something that is usually true or true only under certain circumstances (Shohamy, Myers, Kalanithi, & Gluck, 2008). For example, you might notice that a particular pattern of wind, clouds, and barometric pressure predicts rain, although no one of these cues is reliable by itself.

1. For each of these examples, identify the type of memory test—free recall, cued recall, recognition, savings, or implicit.

a. You watch a horror movie about spiders in the basement of a house. Later, you feel hesitant about going into your own basement, although you don't know why.

b. You scan a list of famous books to count how many you have read.

c. You tell your parents about your favorite experiences this semester.

d. You look at a map of the United States and try to name as many states as you can.

e. Although you thought you had forgotten everything you learned in high school chemistry, you learn college chemistry faster than you had expected.

2. If you remember how to change a flat tire on a car, what type of memory is that?

Answers

2. procedural

e. savings.

1. a. implicit; b. recognition; c. free recall; d. cued recall;

Application: Suspect Lineups as Recognition Memory

Suppose you witness a crime, and now the police want you to look at suspects in a lineup or a book of photos and identify the guilty person. Your task is recognition memory, as you try to identify the correct item among distracters.

The task raises a problem, familiar from your own experience. When you take a multiple-choice test, which is also recognition memory, you select the best one available. What happens if you do the same with a book of photos? You look through the choices and pick the one who looks most like the perpetrator of the crime. You tell the police you think suspect #4 is the guilty person. "Think?" the police ask. "Your testimony won't be worth much in court unless you're sure." You look again, eager to cooperate. Finally, you say you're sure. The police say, "Good, that's the person we thought did it." Given that reassurance, you become more confident. Now that the police have an eyewitness, they stop investigating other possible suspects, and they ignore any evidence that they might be wrong. You testify in court, and the suspect is convicted. But is justice done? Many people who were convicted because of eyewitness testimony were later exonerated by DNA evidence.

Psychologists have proposed ways to improve suspect lineups:

1. Interview witnesses as quickly as possible, before they talk to other people whose comments or reactions might distort the memories.
2. Instruct the witness that the guilty person may or may not be in the lineup. The witness doesn't have to identify someone.
3. The officer supervising the lineup should be a "blind" observer—that is, someone who doesn't know which person the investigators suspect. Otherwise the officer might unintentionally bias the witness.
4. If the witness said that the culprit had some distinctive feature, such as a scar above the left eye, all the suspects in the lineup should have that feature (Zarkadi, Wade, & Stewart, 2009). Otherwise the witness would just

Cotton   **Poole**

© Burlington Police Department

In 1985, Ronald Cotton (left) was convicted of rape, based on a victim's identification from a set of photos. Ten years later, DNA evidence demonstrated that Cotton was innocent and that the real culprit was Bobby Poole (right). Eyewitness testimony has in many cases led to the conviction of innocent people.

pick the one with a scar, who may or may not be guilty. A good way to test the fairness of a lineup is to ask non-witnesses to make a guess. If people unfamiliar with the event tend to pick the person the police suspect, then the lineup is biased (Wixted, Mickes, Dunn, Clark, & Wells, 2016).

5. Postpone as long as possible any feedback about whether the witness chose someone whom the police suspected (Wells, Olson, & Charman, 2003; Zaragoza, Payment, Ackil, Drivdahl, & Beck, 2001). Any sign of agreement adds to a witness's confidence, even if the witness was wrong (Hasel & Kassin, 2009; Semmler, Brewer, & Wells, 2004).

6. Instead of asking for a yes/no decision, ask for each person in the lineup, "How confident are you that this person committed the crime?" A witness could say "90 percent," "75 percent," or any other number, and might give non-zero replies to more than one suspect (Brewer, Weber, Wootton, & Lindsay, 2012). A witness's report of confidence (or lack of it) during the lineup is a better indicator of accuracy than a later estimate that could have been influenced by the police or others (Wixted et al., 2016).

A properly conducted lineup lowers the chance of a false identification (Wixted & Wells, 2017). Many police departments have adopted some or all of these recommendations. One of the most common problems is a failure to interview witnesses before they have talked with other people who might bias their memory (Berkowitz & Frenda, 2018).

3. **Why is it important to ask the witness immediately about his/her level of confidence?**

Answer

3. At a later time, the witness may feel more confident based on other information, and inaccurately report that the eyewitness identification itself was highly confident.

Children as Eyewitnesses

How much should we trust children's reports if they are witnesses or victims of a crime? When researchers ask children to recall events in which the facts are known, such as a medical or dental examination, children as young as 3 years old report with reasonable accuracy even 6 weeks later (Baker-Ward, Gordon, Ornstein, Larus, & Clubb, 1993). One study asked adults to recall a childhood event (known to have occurred) when physicians had inspected their genitals and anus as part of an investigation of possible sexual abuse. Almost half remembered this distinctive event from 20 years ago, including one who had been only 4 years old at the time (Goldfarb, Goodman, Larson, Eisen, & Qin, 2019). Children's reports are most accurate if questioners follow the following rules (Lamb, 2016):

- **Interview soon after the incident.** A child's memory is best at first and becomes less accurate later. The same is true for people at any age, of course.
- **Ask open-ended questions.** To an open-ended question such as, "Tell me what happened," a young child's answer is usually short but accurate. After a suggestive question such as, "Did he touch you under your clothing?" children sometimes say what they think an adult expects them to say (Lamb, Orbach, Hershkowitz, Horowitz, & Abbott, 2007).
- **Emphasize that "I don't know" is an acceptable answer.**
- **Be cautious about repeating a question.** If you ask a child a question, and then shortly thereafter ask the same question again, the child sometimes changes the answer (Krähenbühl & Blades, 2006; Poole & White, 1993). Apparently, the child thinks, "Why is she asking me again? My first

answer must have been wrong!" However, if you ask the same question after enough delay, or if someone else repeats the question, the child is likely to be consistent, and may even add extra details the second time (Baugerud, Magnussen, & Melinder, 2014; Waterhouse, Ridley, Bull, La Rooy, & Wilcock, 2016).

- **Minimize influence from other reports.** A child who hears other children reporting something is likely to say the same thing, even if it is wrong (Principe, Kanaya, Ceci, & Singh, 2006).
- **Beware of using physical representations.** To investigate suspicions of sexual abuse, interviewers sometimes ask a child to act out an event with an anatomically detailed doll. However, children often act out fantasies instead of memories (Greenhoot, Ornstein, Gordon, & Baker-Ward, 1999). Allowing a child to draw pictures of an event might or might not help, but children sometimes add a hippopotamus or other implausible details (Macleod, Gross, & Hayne, 2016).
- **Be sure the child understands the question.** Have you ever seen someone imbosk a lecythus? You probably answer either "I don't know," or "What do you mean?" A 3-year-old child who doesn't understand a question usually answers "yes" (Imhoff & Baker-Ward, 1999).

Adults easily overestimate how well a child understands something. A couple taking their 3-year-old daughter on a trip said they would stop at a barbecue restaurant. She was so excited that she could hardly wait. She spent most of the trip asking, "Now how long till barbecue?" As they finally approached the restaurant, she asked, "Will other children be there too, with their Barbies?" Suddenly it dawned on the parents, "Ah, that's what she thought 'barbie-cue' meant!"

The Information-Processing View of Memory

Over the years, psychologists have repeatedly tried to explain behavior by analogy to the technologies of their time. In the 1600s, René Descartes compared animal behavior to the actions of a hydraulic pump. Psychologists of the early 1900s suggested that learning worked like a telephone switchboard. In the early days of radio, some researchers compared the nervous system to a radio. Today's information-processing model compares human memory to that of a computer: *Information that enters the system is processed, coded, and stored.* Just as a computer has a temporary store for something you have just typed and a more lasting store for something on the hard

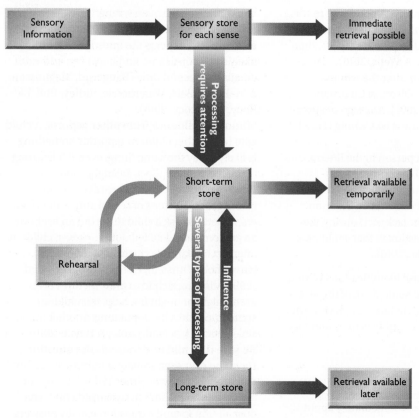

▲ Figure 7.4 The information-processing model of memory resembles a computer's memory system, including temporary and permanent memory.

drive, your memory can store a memory temporarily or permanently. The most influential statement of this process is summarized in **▲ Figure 7.4**, based on a theory by Atkinson and Shiffrin (1968). Although later researchers have amended the theory, the original version still serves as a good approximation. Much of its appeal comes from emphasizing that memory is an active process. You rehearse a memory, code it, process it, and eventually search for it. Let's examine this model.

The Sensory Store

Fluorescent light bulbs flicker at 120 cycles per second, but you do not see them flicker, because the nervous system prolongs each visual sensation for a fraction of a second (Yeonan-Kim & Francis, 2019). Auditory, touch, and other information also linger for varying times. Your memory of what you see also lingers briefly, as you can demonstrate for yourself: Close your eyes, turn yourself around to face something, blink your eyes open and shut, and then describe what you saw. You will be able to describe at least a little of the scene.

How much information did you actually see during that blink of the eyes? You can describe only a little of it, but you know that you saw more than you described. During the time you needed to describe a few items, you lost

the rest of them. George Sperling (1960) conducted a famous experiment to demonstrate this point. He flashed displays like this for a fraction of a second:

A	J	D	O
F	M	E	S
B	W	L	K

If he asked participants to name as many letters as they could, most could name four or five of them. However, in some cases, shortly after flashing the display, he presented a high, middle, or low tone to indicate whether to report the top, middle, or bottom row. Under that condition, people could almost always report the indicated row if they heard the tone just 0.15 seconds after the display, as if they still saw it then. If the tone came half a second after the display, their accuracy was less, and if it came a full second after the display, it did not help at all. The conclusion was that you have a sensory store that maintains an image—an *iconic image*—that lasts for only a fraction of a second. Is the sensory store a prolonged sensation or a very brief memory? We could argue it either way, depending on how we define memory.

Short-Term and Long-Term Memory

As soon as you attend to any information it enters your short-term memory, *temporary storage of recent events*, which is distinct from long-term memory, *a more permanent store*. For example, while you are having a conversation, the last sentence you heard is in your short-term memory, and your knowledge of the topic is in your long-term memory. One type of evidence for the distinction between the two is that certain brain-damaged patients have impairments of short-term memory whereas others have impairments of long-term memory (Malmberg, Raaijmakers, & Shiffrin, 2019).

Psychologists distinguish two categories of long-term memory, semantic and episodic. Semantic memory is *memory of principles and facts*, like what you are taught in school. Episodic memory is *memory for specific events in your life* (Tulving, 1989), almost like reliving those events. Your memory of the law of gravity is a semantic memory, whereas remembering the time you dropped your grandmother's vase is an episodic memory. Remembering who is the mayor of your city is a semantic memory, and remembering the time you met the mayor is an episodic memory. The philosopher and theologian Augustine compared episodic memory to food that you hold in your belly and burp up later to experience again.

Episodic memories are more fragile than semantic memories. If you don't play tennis for a few years, you will still remember the rules, but your memory of a particular tennis game will fade. When you try to recall an event from long ago, you remember the gist but forget many of the details.

4. Classify each of these as semantic memory or episodic memory: (a) Naming the planets of our solar system. (b) Describing what you wore to class yesterday. (c) Remembering your most recent illness. (d) Describing the periodic table in chemistry.

Answer

4. a. semantic b. episodic c. episodic d. semantic.

People sometimes remember a semantic memory, but forget the episodic memory of when or where they learned it (Friedman, Reese, & Dai, 2011). *Forgetting when, where, or how you learned something* is **source amnesia**. Here is the danger: You read a story containing material that might or might not be true. Or you hear a rumor from an unreliable source. If you remember the information but forget that it came from an unreliable source, you might believe it more than you should (Johnson, Hashtroudi, & Lindsay, 1993; Riccio, 1994).

In one study, students read fictional stories that included statements such as "a sextant is a tool used at sea to navigate by the stars." Later, they were asked such questions as, "what tool is used at sea to navigate by the stars?" People who had just read that fact were more likely than other people to answer correctly. Most remembered seeing it in the story, and many said they had already known it before reading the story. Another group of students read stories with misinformation such as "a compass is a tool used at sea to navigate by the stars." Many of these students insisted that they too had "already" known this incorrect information before reading the story! This example illustrates source amnesia (Marsh, Meade, & Roediger, 2003).

How far could we push this tendency? Researchers took students who had correctly answered certain questions (such as "Who invented the lightbulb?" Answer: "Edison"), and had them read stories with misinformation, such as that Franklin invented the lightbulb. Afterward, 20 percent of them incorporated the misinformation, replying that Franklin invented the lightbulb (Fazio, Barber, Rajaram, Ornstein, & Marsh, 2013). Another study had college students read stories with plausible misinformation (listing St. Petersburg as the capital of Russia instead of Moscow, or listing the Gobi as the world's largest desert instead of the Sahara), or stories with implausible information (such as the Pilgrims sailed to the new world on the *Titanic*, or Detroit is the capital of Finland). Many students accepted the plausible misinformation, and a few accepted even the implausible, ridiculous misinformation (Hinze, Slaten, Horton, Jenkins, & Rapp, 2014). Modern technology accentuates the problem. Researchers found that, on average, false information on Twitter spreads faster and to more people than correct information (Vosoughi, Roy, & Aral, 2018). When people see or hear the same thing repeatedly, they generally believe it, even if the sources were unreliable.

Capacity of Short-Term and Long-Term Memory

Psychologists have traditionally drawn distinctions between short-term and long-term memory. One difference is capacity. Long-term memory has a vast, hard-to-measure capacity. Asking how much information long-term memory can store is like asking how many books a library can hold. Asking about short-term memory is more like asking how many books you could hold in one hand. In either case, the answer depends on the size of the books and how you arrange them, but you will run out of room in your hand long before a library runs out of room. Read each of the following letter sequences and then try to repeat them from memory. Or read each aloud and ask a friend to repeat it.

E H G P H
J R O Z N Q
S R B W R C N
M P D I W F B S
Z Y B P I A F M O

Most healthy, educated adults can repeat a list of about seven letters, numbers, or words. Some remember eight or nine; others, only five or six. George Miller (1956) referred to short-term memory capacity as "the magical number seven, plus or minus two." When people try to repeat a longer list, they may fail to remember even the first few items. It is like trying to hold objects in one hand: If you try to hold too many, you drop them all. However, don't take this analogy too seriously. When you store a memory, you do not put it in a single place in your brain.

You can store more information in short-term memory by **chunking**—*grouping items into meaningful sequences or clusters.* For example, the sequence "ventysi" has seven letters, at the limit of most people's capacity. However, "seventysix" with three additional letters can be easily remembered as "76," a two-digit number. "Seventeenseventysix" is even longer, but if you think of it as 1776, an important date in U.S. history, it is a single item to store.

One college student in a lengthy experiment initially could repeat about seven digits at a time. Over a year and a half, working 3 to 5 hours per week, he gradually improved until he could repeat 80 digits, as shown in ▼ Figure 7.5, by chunking. He was a competitive runner, so he might store the sequence "3492 . . ." as "3 minutes, 49.2 seconds, a near world-record time for running a mile." He might store the next set of numbers as a good time for running a kilometer, a mediocre marathon time, or a date in history. With practice, he started recognizing larger and larger chunks of numbers. However, when he was tested on his ability to remember a list of letters, his performance was only average, because he had not developed any chunking strategies for letters (Ericsson, Chase, & Faloon, 1980). People who compete at memorization contests learn to chunk huge sequences of information (Ericsson et al., 2017).

Sometimes we forget where we heard or read something, and believe it more than we should.

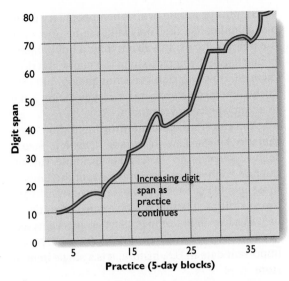

▲ **Figure 7.5** A college student gradually increased his ability to repeat a list of numbers. However, his short-term memory for letters or words did not increase. (From Ericsson, Chase, & Faloon, 1980)

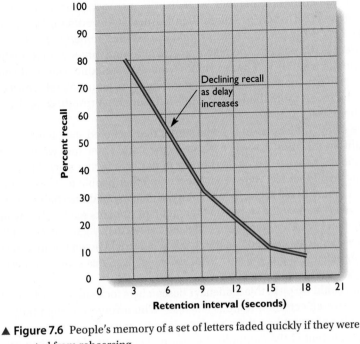

▲ **Figure 7.6** People's memory of a set of letters faded quickly if they were prevented from rehearsing.

Because people are so good at chunking, psychologists have come to doubt that short-term memory really does hold seven items. When you remembered S R B W R C N, did you really remember it as seven items? Or did you group them, such as SR . . . B . . . WR . . . CN? Later research indicates that the limit of adult short-term memory might be four chunks rather than seven items (Cowan, 2010; Mandler, 2013). In any case, the limit depends on familiarity. You could remember a list of meaningful words much more easily than an equally long list of nonsense syllables.

Decay of Memories over Time

A short-term memory, by definition, lasts only briefly unless you rehearse it. Here is the classic demonstration: Lloyd Peterson and Margaret Peterson (1959) presented meaningless sequences of letters, like HOXDF, and then tested people's memory after various delays. If you were in this study, knowing that the experimenter was going to ask you to repeat the letters, you would spend the delay rehearsing, "HOXDF, HOXDF, . . ." To prevent rehearsal, the experimenters added a second task. When they presented the letters, they also presented a number, such as 231. You were supposed to start with that number and count backward by 3s, such as "231, 228, 225, 222, 219, . . ." until the experimenter signaled the end of the delay. At that point, you should say the letters.

▲ Figure 7.6 shows the results. On average, only about 10 percent of the participants could recall the letters after 18 seconds. In other words, short-term memory really is short-term.

Peterson and Peterson dealt with nonsense information, such as HOXDF. With more meaningful material, people quickly form long-term memories. If someone told you to leave the building by the west exit instead of the east exit because a venomous snake is lurking at the east exit, you need not worry that you will forget this advice in the next 18 seconds.

Short-term memories fade for two reasons (Sadeh, Ozubko, Winocur, & Moscovitch, 2016). One reason is that the brain representation decays over time, sometimes suddenly (Pratte, 2018). The other reason is that one memory interferes with another. Suppose you try a Peterson-type experiment: You see or hear a set of five letters and then you count backward by 3s for some period of time. On the first trial you will probably remember the letters, even with a fairly long delay. On later trials, the task gets more difficult, largely because memory of the old items interferes with the new items. Similar results occur for visual memories: You view 100 pictures, 4 per second, and then see another set of pictures and try to remember which ones you also saw in the first set. On average, you would identify about 30 of them correctly. But then you have to do it again and again, and some of the pictures from the first set reappear, but you have to remember which pictures were in the new set. Under these conditions, the interference mounts, until you struggle to get even 3 or 4 correct (Endress & Potter, 2014).

How long do long-term memories last? Some last a lifetime. Harry Bahrick (1984) found that people who had studied Spanish 1 or 2 years ago remembered more than those who had studied it 3 to 6 years ago, but beyond 6 years, the retention appeared to be stable (see ▼ Figure 7.7). However, not all long-term memories are permanent. If you are staying at a motel, you remember your room number as long as you are staying there, but you probably won't remember it a few weeks later.

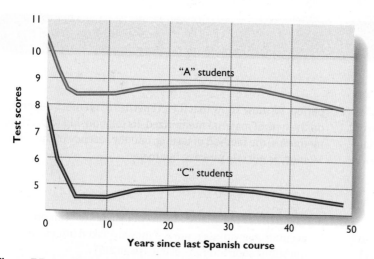

▲ **Figure 7.7** Spanish vocabulary as measured by a recognition test declines in the first few years but then becomes stable. The students who received an "A" performed better, but each group showed similar rates of forgetting. (From Bahrick, 1984)

5. **How does short-term memory differ from long-term memory?**

6. **Is interference important for forgetting in short-term memory, long-term memory, or both?**

Answers

5. Short-term memory has a small capacity, whereas long-term memory has a huge capacity. Also, short-term memory fades within seconds unless you rehearse it.
6. It is important for both.

Working Memory

"Clarence Birdseye patented a method for selling frozen fish." You probably didn't know that. It is now in your short-term memory, and it may or may not become a long-term memory. "Read the first three paragraphs on page 42 and summarize the main points." That instruction is also in short-term memory, but it is of a different kind. Although you might want to remember the fact about Clarence Birdseye, you have no reason to remember the instruction about page 42 after you complete it.

Originally, most psychologists thought of short-term memory as the way to store something while your brain moves it into long-term storage. That is, you gradually consolidate your memory. However, not all short-term memories become long-term memories, even after rehearsal. When you are studying a foreign language, you might repeatedly read list of words and their translations, but you might forget them all a few minutes later. In contrast, if your parents tell you, "Your sister just had a baby," you form a lasting memory quickly.

For many purposes, instead of the term *short-term memory*, many researchers prefer to speak of **working memory**, *a system for working with current information*. Working memory is almost synonymous with your current sphere of attention (Baddeley, 2001; Baddeley & Hitch, 1994; Repovš & Baddeley, 2006). It includes information you use and then forget, like "read the first three paragraphs on page 42." It also includes **executive functioning** that *governs shifts of attention*. The hallmark of good working memory is the ability to shift attention as needed. For example, a hospital nurse has to keep track of the needs of several patients, sometimes interrupting the treatment of one patient to take care of an emergency and then returning to complete work with the first patient.

Here is a simple way to measure how long it takes your central executive to shift attention: Recite aloud a poem, song, or other passage that you know well. If you cannot think of a more interesting example, recite the alphabet. Time how long it takes. Then measure how long it takes you to say the same thing silently. Finally, time how long it takes you to alternate—the first word aloud, the second silent, the third aloud, and so forth. Alternating takes longer because you keep shifting attention.

Another way to measure executive processes is the *n*-back task: You hear a list of letters or numbers such as 2 5 7 5 6 2 3 6 3 4 9 8 4 . . . In the 2-back version, you are to press a key (or make some other signal) whenever an item is the same as what you heard two back. For example, in the list above, you would press the key for the second 5 and the second 3, because each of them matches what came two items previously. In the 3-back version, you press when an item matches what came three before it. In the list above, you would press for the second 6 and the second 4. If you do well enough on that version, the test would proceed to 4-back, and then to 5-back.

People who do well on working memory tasks like these generally do well on other tasks, including school performance (Rose, Feldman, & Jankowitz, 2011), understanding other people's point of view (Barrett, Tugade, & Engle, 2004), learning a second language (Linck, Osthus, Koeth, & Bunting, 2013), and resisting impulses to heavy drinking (Houben, Wiers, & Jansen, 2011). Working memory capacity strongly correlates with intelligence in general (Shipstead, Harrison, & Engle, 2016).

Given that working memory correlates with so many favorable outcomes, educators have sought to train working memory, in hopes that improved working memory would lead to improved overall intelligence and so forth. However, research has found that practice at the *n*-back task or any other working memory task improves performance on that task itself, but fails to benefit anything else (De Simoni & von Bastian, 2018; Gillam, Holbrook, Mecham, & Weller, 2018; Talanow & Ettinger, 2018).

7. **Given that practice on a working memory task does not transfer to other tasks, what can we conclude about the correlation between that task and intelligence?**

Answer

7. We can conclude that good performance on that task may be an indicator of intelligence, but it does not cause intelligence. We can also surmise that raising overall intelligence is not easy.

Varieties of Memory

Researchers agree about what memory is *not:* It is not a single store into which we simply dump things and later take them out. When Ebbinghaus conducted his studies of memory in the late 1800s, he thought he was measuring the properties of memory, period. We now know that the properties of memory depend on the type of material memorized, its relationship to previous memories, the method of testing, and the recency of the event. Memory is not one process, but many.

Summary

- *Ebbinghaus.* Hermann Ebbinghaus pioneered the experimental study of memory by testing his own ability to memorize and retain lists of nonsense syllables. (page 211)
- *Methods of testing memory.* People remember different amounts of information depending on how they are tested. (page 212)
- *Implicit memory.* Implicit memories are changes in behavior based on recent experiences that the person may not be able to describe in words. (page 212)
- *Procedural memory.* Procedural memory, or habit learning, develops gradually, unlike declarative memory, and it depends on different brain areas. (page 214)
- *Suspect lineups.* Suspect lineups are an example of the recognition memory. Witnesses sometimes choose the best available choice, which may not be correct. Psychologists have recommended ways to improve accuracy. (page 214)

- *Children as eyewitnesses.* Even young children can provide accurate eyewitness reports if they are asked unbiased questions soon after the event. (page 215)
- *Sensory store.* Immediately after viewing something, you have an image that will fade rapidly, except for the limited part to which you pay attention. (page 216)
- *Short-term and long-term memory.* Short-term memory has a capacity of only a few items, although chunking can enable us to store much information in each item. Long-term memory has a huge capacity. Short-term memories fade over seconds if not rehearsed. (page 216)
- *Working memory.* Working memory is a system for dealing with current information, including the ability to shift attention back and forth among tasks. (page 219)

Key Terms

chunking (page 217)

cued recall (page 212)

declarative memory (page 214)

episodic memory (page 216)

executive functioning (page 219)

explicit memory (or direct memory) (page 212)

free recall (page 212)

implicit memory (or indirect memory) (page 212)

information-processing model (page 215)

long-term memory (page 216)

memory (page 211)

n-back task (page 219)

priming (page 213)

procedural memory (page 214)

recognition (page 212)

savings method (or relearning method) (page 212)

semantic memory (page 216)

sensory store (page 216)

short-term memory (page 216)

source amnesia (page 217)

working memory (page 219)

Answer to Other Question in the Module

Herman Melville, Jane Austen, Agatha Christie, Arthur Conan Doyle, Maya Angelou, Leo Tolstoy, Harper Lee, Geoffrey Chaucer, Charles Dickens, John Steinbeck, Victor Hugo. (page 213)

Review Questions

1. Which method of testing memory can detect the weakest memories?
   - (a) Free recall
   - (b) Cued recall
   - (c) Recognition
   - (d) Savings

2. How does procedural memory differ from declarative memory?
   - (a) It extinguishes rapidly.
   - (b) It develops despite long CS–UCS intervals.
   - (c) It forms mainly during an early sensitive period.
   - (d) It develops gradually.

3. Without realizing it, you start using some of the same words that you read recently. What type of memory is this?
   (a) Procedural
   (b) Semantic
   (c) Episodic
   (d) Implicit

4. When police ask a witness to identify a suspect from a lineup, what do psychologists recommend?
   (a) Use an array of suspects varying widely in their appearance.
   (b) Offer encouragement if someone identifies the person that the police suspect.
   (c) Ask for percent confidence answers instead of yes/no answers.
   (d) Encourage the witness to identify someone, even if none seem exactly right.

5. If you see a display of numbers for a split second, why can you name only about 4 or 5 of them?
   (a) In that time, you see only that much.
   (b) Short-term memory has a limited capacity.
   (c) Your sensory store fades within a second.
   (d) Your attention wanders.

6. Which of the following is an example of a semantic memory?
   (a) "The numbers I just saw on the screen were 4, 9, 7, and 1."
   (b) "Yesterday morning was hot and dry."
   (c) "Wilhelm Wundt founded the first psychological laboratory."
   (d) "The last novel I read was *Left Hand of Darkness.*"

7. What is a possible explanation for believing false reports you read several times on the Internet?
   (a) Source amnesia
   (b) Sensory store
   (c) Procedural memory
   (d) Executive functioning

8. On average, how long does information remain in short-term memory?
   (a) Less than 1 second
   (b) Whatever time is necessary to consolidate it into long-term memory
   (c) Less than 20 seconds unless it is rehearsed
   (d) Seven seconds, plus or minus two

Answers: 1d, 2d, 3d, 4c, 5c, 6c, 7a, 8c.

After studying this module, you should be able to:

1. Explain why you remember some things better than others.

2. Discuss ways to organize and improve studying.

3. Give examples of mnemonic devices.

4. Discuss memory as a process of reconstruction.

5. Cite examples of hindsight bias.

Have you ever felt distressed because you cannot remember some experience? One woman feels distressed because she cannot stop remembering! When she sees or hears a date—such as April 27, 1994—a flood of episodic memories descends on her. "That was Wednesday. . . . I was down in Florida. I was summoned to come down and to say goodbye to my grandmother who they all thought was dying but she ended up living. My Dad and my Mom went to New York for a wedding. Then my Mom went to Baltimore to see her family. I went to Florida on the 25th, which was a Monday. This was also the weekend that Nixon died. And then I flew to Florida and my Dad flew to Florida the next day. Then I flew home and my Dad flew to Baltimore to be with my Mom" (Parker, Cahill, & McGaugh, 2006, p. 40). Tell her another date, and she describes a similar flood of memories from that time. Researchers checked her reports against her diaries and a book of news events. She was almost always correct for any date since she was 11 years old. They asked her to give the date (e.g., April 7) for every Easter between 1980 and 2003. She was right on all but one and later corrected

herself on that one. What makes this feat even more impressive is that she is Jewish and therefore doesn't celebrate Easter (Parker, Cahill, & McGaugh, 2006).

You might not want to have the detailed episodic memory of this woman, who says her memories so occupy her that she can hardly focus on the present. Still, you might like to improve memories that you do want to remember. Memory consists of three aspects—encoding, storage, and retrieval. The main point of this module is that to improve your memory, improve the way you study.

Encoding

Encoding is the process of forming a memory. What do you do when you want to remember something, such as a textbook definition? If you just repeat it without giving it much thought, you do not guarantee a strong memory. To illustrate, examine ▼ Figure 7.8, which shows a U.S. penny and 14 fakes. If you live in the United States, you have seen pennies countless times, but can you now identify the real one? Most U.S. citizens guess wrong (Nickerson & Adams, 1979). If you do not have a penny in your pocket, check answer B on page 231. If you are not from the United States, try drawing the front or back of a common coin in your own country. If repeated exposure does not produce strong encoding, what does?

try it yourself

Factors That Influence Encoding

One influence on memory formation is simply trying to remember! (You probably never tried to memorize the pattern on a penny.) If you don't expect to need the information, or if you know you could easily find it on the Internet, you put little effort into remembering it (Sparrow, Liu, & Wegner, 2011). In one study, students were told they would play a *Concentration* game in which they needed to remember the locations of various items in an array. Half the students saw all the items and tried to memorize their locations. The other half saw the

Paul Doyle/Alamy Stock Photo

Most actors preparing for a play spend much time thinking about the meaning of what they will say (a deep level of processing) instead of just repeating the words.

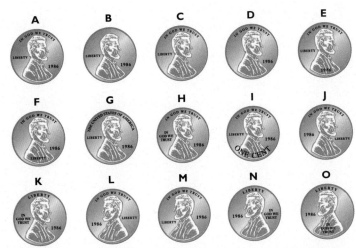

▲ **Figure 7.8** Can you spot the genuine penny among 14 fakes? (Based on Nickerson & Adams, 1979)

items and took notes, but then to their surprise the experimenters took the notes away. The first group remembered better than the second group. Evidently, those taking notes expected to rely on the notes, and they didn't bother trying to remember (Eskritt & Ma, 2014). The harm from taking notes is an old idea. In Plato's Dialogue *Phaedrus*, written in about 370 BC, Socrates opposed writing, saying that it "will create forgetfulness in the learners' souls, because they will not use their memories. They will trust to the external characters." This advice is overstated. Taking notes in class is more often helpful than harmful. However, the point remains that when people think they can rely on notes or other media, they feel less need to remember.

Emotional arousal enhances memory encoding. Chances are, you vividly remember your first day of college, your first kiss, the time your team won the big game, and times you were frightened. Panic interferes with memory, but moderate emotion helps by releasing dopamine and norepinephrine in the brain (Takeuchi et al., 2016) and by releasing cortisol and epinephrine (adrenaline) from the adrenal gland. All those chemicals stimulate brain areas that enhance memory storage (Andreano & Cahill, 2006).

The effects of arousal on memory have been known for centuries. In England in the early 1600s, when people sold land, they did not yet have the custom of recording the sale on paper. Few people could read anyway. Instead, local residents would gather while someone announced the sale and instructed everyone to remember it. Of all those present, whose memory of the sale was most important? It was the children, because they would live the longest. And of all those present, who were least interested? Right, again, it's the children. To increase the chances that the children would remember, the adults would kick them while telling them about the business deal. The same idea persisted in the custom, still common in the early 1900s, of slapping schoolchildren's hands with a stick to make them pay attention. However, no one did controlled experiments to test the effectiveness of this intervention!

Many people report detailed "flashbulb" memories from when they heard highly emotional news (Brown & Kulik, 1977). They remember who told them, where they were, what they were doing, often even the weather and other irrelevant details. When researchers interviewed people both at the time and years later, they found that people's reports sometimes change, while remaining confident and vivid. One person originally reported hearing about the terrorist attacks of September 11, 2001, on a car radio, but 2 years later reported having heard about it while standing in line at an airport (Kvavilashvili, Mirani, Schlagman, Foley, & Kornbrot, 2009). Confident, vivid memories aren't always correct.

People recall emotionally arousing events in great detail, although not always accurately.

8. Most people with post-traumatic stress disorder have lower than normal levels of cortisol. What would you predict about their memory?

Answer

8. Because of the lower cortisol levels, they should have trouble storing memories.

In addition to attention and emotion, many other factors influence how well you store your memories. To illustrate, read the following list, look away from the book, and write as many of the words as you can. For best results, cover the list with a sheet of paper and pull it down one word at a time.

LEMON
GRAPE
POTATO
COCONUT
CUCUMBER
TOMATO
BROCCOLI
APPLE
SPINACH
TOMATO
ORANGE
LETTUCE
CARROT
STRAWBERRY
BANANA
TOMATO
PEACH
NAKED
LIME
PINEAPPLE
TURNIP
MANGO
TOMATO
BLUEBERRY
TOMATO
APRICOT
WATERMELON

I hope you tried the demonstration. If so, *TOMATO* was probably one of the words you remembered, because it occurred five times instead of just once. Repetition is not a strong influence by itself, but it does help somewhat, especially if the repetitions are spread out. You probably also remembered *LEMON* and *WATERMELON* because they were the first and last items on the list. The primacy effect is *the tendency to remember the first items*. The recency effect is *the tendency to remember the final items*.

The primacy and recency effects are robust for almost any type of memory. If you try to list all the vacations you have ever taken or all the sporting events you have ever watched, you will probably include the earliest ones and the most recent. When students try to remember all the presidents of the United States, they generally remember the first few and the most recent few, but forget most of those in the middle, other than Lincoln (Roediger & DeSoto, 2014).

You probably also remembered *CARROT* and *NAKED*. The word *CARROT* was distinctive because of its size, color, and font. *NAKED* stood out as the only item on the list that was neither a fruit nor a vegetable. In a list of items, the unusual ones are easier to remember. We also tend to remember unusual people. If you meet several women of average appearance and similar names, like Jennifer Stevens, Stephanie Jensen, and Jenny Stevenson, you will have trouble remembering their names. You will more quickly remember a tall, redheaded woman named Bimbo Sue Budweiser.

You might not have remembered *MANGO* if you didn't grow up eating mangoes in childhood. People find it easier to remember words they learned in early childhood than words they learned later (Juhasz, 2005). Similarly, if you grew up watching *Sesame Street,* you can probably name Bert, Ernie, and Oscar the Grouch more quickly than many of the characters you have watched on television more recently.

Did you remember the word *LIME?* Probably not because it came right after the word *NAKED.* When people see an unexpected sex-related word, it grabs attention so strongly that they miss the next word (Arnell, Killman, & Fijavz, 2007). The effect would be even stronger if you were watching slides, and one of them had a photo of naked people.

One more determinant: Other things being equal, you would probably remember a list of people or animals better than almost any other list. People and animals grab our attention and interest (Nairne, VanArsdall, & Cogdill, 2017).

Let's try another demonstration. Below are two lists. As you read through one of the lists—it doesn't matter which one—repeat each word for a couple of seconds. So, if the word were *insect,* you would say, "Insect, insect, insect . . ." and then proceed to the next word. For the other list, imagine yourself stranded in the middle of a vast grassland in some foreign country, where you need to find food and water and protect yourself from snakes, lions, and other dangers. As you go through the list, again spend a couple of seconds on each word, thinking about how useful this item would be for survival under these conditions. Give it a rating from 1 (useless) to 5 (highly valuable). You choose whether to do the repetition list first or the rating-for-survival list first. At the end of each list, pause for a minute or more and then try to recall the items you read.

List A	List B
toothbrush	firecracker
thermometer	rollerblades
marionette	umbrella
jewelry	hammock
tuxedo	binoculars
washcloth	encyclopedia
bandage	saxophone
trampoline	camera
metronome	mirror
flashlight	scissors
chain	string
knife	bottle
balloon	radio
carpet	envelope
overcoat	candy
matches	pencil

Most people remember far more words from the survival list than from the repetition list (Nairne, Pandeirada, & Thompson, 2008; Nairne, Thompson, & Pandeirada, 2007). If, instead of rating the words for survival relevance, you rated them for pleasantness, that procedure would help, too, but not as much as rating them for survival. Thinking about survival engages attention and memory better than anything else does. It makes sense for our brains to have evolved this way. In a follow-up study, people read words while rating their value for a hunting contest, or for hunting food for your tribe. Even though it was the same act in both cases— hunting—people remembered more words if they thought of hunting in terms of survival instead of a contest (Nairne, Pandeirada, Gregory, & VanArsdall, 2009).

Simply repeating the words is an ineffective way to study, if you want long-term retention. Actors spend little time simply repeating their lines when rehearsing for a play. Rather, they think about how each statement develops the character and the story (Noice & Noice, 2006). According to the **depth-of-processing principle** (Craik & Lockhart, 1972), *how easily you retrieve a memory depends on the associations you form.* Simply reading a list of words or a chapter in a book is shallow processing, which produces only fleeting memories. You will remember better if you consider various points as you read them, relate them to your own experiences, and think of your own examples to illustrate each principle. The more ways you think about the material, especially as you relate it to yourself, the deeper your processing and the more easily you will remember later. The difference isn't apparent at once. Immediately after you read something, you

9. If you are studying a vocabulary list for a foreign-language course, which words will you probably learn fastest?

Answer

9. Among the first you learn will be the first and last words on the list, any emotionally arousing words, and names of animals. If many of the words on the list are similar to one another, then an unusual word on the list will be easier to remember.

may remember it just as well after shallow processing as after deep processing. But after a longer delay, the value of deep processing emerges (Rose, Myerson, Roediger, & Hale, 2010). How well you remember something immediately after studying it does not predict how well you will remember it later.

10. Many of the students who read the assigned text chapters more slowly than average get the best grades in a course. Why?

Answer

10. Students who pause to think about the meaning are engaging in deep processing. They will remember the material better than those who read a chapter quickly.

Encoding Specificity

When you encode (store) a memory, you form associations. If you form many associations, you develop many possible **retrieval cues** that *can serve as reminders to prompt your memory later*. According to the **encoding specificity principle** (Tulving & Thomson, 1973), *the associations you form at the time of learning will be the most effective retrieval cues later* (see ▶ Figure 7.9). For example, read the pairs of words (which psychologists call *paired associates*) in ■ Table 7.3a. Then move to ■ Table 7.3b below. For each of the words on that list, try to recall a related word on the list you just read. *Please do this now.* (The answers are on page 231, answer B.)

Table 7.3a

Bird—Cardinal	Geometry—Plane
Trinket—Charm	Time of year—Season
Parking ticket—Fine	Music—Rock
Vegetable—Squash	Magic—Spell
Tree—Palm	Envelope—Seal
Computer—Apple	Graduation—Degree

Table 7.3b

Instructions: For each of these words, write one of the second of the paired terms from the list in Table 7.3a.

Animal—	Stone—
Body part—	Personality—
Transportation—	Write—
Temperature—	Clergyman—
Flavoring—	Good—
Sport—	Fruit—

▲ **Figure 7.9** If you think of the word *queen* as *queen bee,* then the cue *playing card* will not remind you of the word later. If you think of the *queen of England,* then *chess piece* will not be a good reminder.

Most people find this task difficult. If they initially coded the word *cardinal* as a type of clergyman, the retrieval cue *bird* doesn't remind them of it. If they thought of it as a bird, then *clergyman* is not a good reminder.

Some police interviewers use encoding specificity when questioning crime witnesses. They ask the witnesses to imagine the original conditions in detail—the location, the weather, the time of day, how they were feeling at the time. Getting back to the original event, at least in imagination, helps people remember more details (Fisher, Geiselman, & Amador, 1989; Launay & Py, 2017).

The encoding specificity principle has this implication: If you want to remember something at a particular time and place, study under the same conditions where you will try to remember. However, if you want to remember something always, you should vary your study habits so that your memory does *not* become specific to one setting.

11. Suppose someone cannot remember what happened at a party last night. What steps might help improve the memory?

Answer

11. Presuming the person wants to remember, it might help to return to the place of the party with the same people present, perhaps even at the same time of day. The more similar the conditions of original learning and later recall, the better the probability of remembering.

Organize Your Studying

Did you ever have this experience? You have studied something and you are sure that you know it well, but when you take the test, you don't remember it as well as you had expected. What went wrong? Much of the problem is that something that seems easy when you study it can be easy to forget (Soderstrom & Bjork, 2015).

Studying All at Once or Spread Out

Should you study a little at a time, or wait and do it all shortly before the test? You know that waiting until just before the test is risky. An unexpected interruption might prevent you from studying at all. Let's change the question to make the answer less obvious: You don't wait until just before the test, but you nevertheless study all at once. Will your result be better, worse, or the same as if you studied a little at a time over several days?

Studying all at once is okay if you need to remember it immediately and never again. However, if you care about long-term memory, studying all at once is worse for almost any type of learning (Cepeda, Pashler, Vul, Wixted, & Rohrer, 2006; Kornell & Bjork, 2008; Küpper-Tetzel, 2014; McDaniel, Fadler, & Pashler, 2013). Suppose you are trying to learn a foreign language. You study a list of words until you know their meanings, and then continue for another 10 minutes. The extra 10 minutes is almost completely wasted (Rohrer & Pashler, 2007). You should do something else now and review the vocabulary list later.

When you wait to study again, how long should you wait? It depends. To remember something next week, you get the best results if you review tomorrow. To remember something next month, you should wait a week and a half before you review. To remember next year, wait about 3 weeks. In each case, it is better to wait a little longer than a little less (Cepeda, Vul, Rohrer, Wixted, & Pashler, 2008). Better yet, of course, review several times.

When you study something all at once, it *seems* that you are learning well because the material is so fresh in your memory. However, people almost always underestimate how much they are going to forget (Koriat, Bjork, Sheffer, & Bar, 2004). To remember something well, you need to practice retrieving the memory, and you cannot get that practice by repeated study within a short time. If you go away and come back later, you need effort to refresh the ideas, and that effort strengthens the memory.

Advantages of Varied Study

Within a study session, you gain by adding variety, although it won't seem that way at the time.

Suppose you are trying to learn the artistic styles of painters so that you can identify new paintings by the same artists. Would you learn better by seeing many paintings by artist A, then many by artist B, many by C, and so forth? Or would it be better to see one by each, and then another by each, and so forth? Most people prefer the first way, but the results show that intermingling painting styles works better (Kornell, Castel, Eich, & Bjork, 2010). Suppose you are trying to learn to solve four types of math problems. It seems easier to solve several examples of one type, then several examples of the next type, and so forth. Nearly all math textbooks are organized that way. But if you want to remember the skills for long, your best strategy is to mix up one type with another until you can solve each of them, then wait a week or so and try again, again mixing up one type with another (Rohrer & Taylor, 2007). When you are reading a textbook like this one, you should occasionally go back to previous chapters and try to answer the review questions and concept checks (Dunlosky, Rawson, Marsh, Nathan, & Willingham, 2013).

Taking Notes During Class

Taking notes in class focuses attention at the time, and it provides material for review later. However, students seldom get much training on how to take notes. Extremely brief notes do little good, but trying to record too much is problematical also. Excessive note-taking is tiring, and your notes will be so long that you will be intimidated about reviewing them later. The best strategy is to record the main ideas in an organized fashion.

Is it a good idea to bring a laptop computer to class to type notes? If you use it just for notes, it can be an advantage, but most students who bring laptops, tablets, or cell phones to class use them for email, games, social media, and other non-academic purposes, and the result is lower course grades (Fried, 2008; Ravizza, Uitvlugt, & Fenn, 2017).

Learning During Testing

Most people assume that they learn while reading but not while recalling. In fact, to strengthen a memory, you need to practice recalling it. In now hundreds of studies, one group of students spends a certain amount of time reading and rereading, while another group alternates between reading and answering questions. Consistently, the group that answers questions remembers the material better later, maintains it better, and applies it to more applications (Pan & Rickard, 2018; Roediger & Karpicke, 2006; Smith, Floerke, & Thomas, 2016). Even an unsuccessful attempt to answer a question is helpful, because it increases your attention when you hear the answer (Kornell, Hays, & Bjork, 2009). If you answer the concept checks and review questions in this text, you will remember the material better.

Although psychologists are not fully agreed on the best way to explain the testing effect, a key element is that a test forces you to generate the material when it is not in your short-term or working memory (Karpicke & Roediger, 2008; Rickard & Pan, 2018). In general, you tend to remember what you say more than what you hear, and you remember what you write more than what you read. Trying to speak a foreign language improves comprehension more than listening does (Hopman & MacDonald, 2018). Of all the events you will remember, most are events that you talked about soon after they happened (Hirst & Echterhoff, 2012). One way to apply this idea is to study something and then tell someone else the key points. I hope your roommate is a patient listener.

Conclusions: (1) You will overestimate how well you have learned something if you haven't waited long enough to see how much you forget. (2) You remember best if you study, wait, and review later instead of studying all at once. (3) Varying the conditions of studying improves long-term memory. (4) You remember better if you test yourself or talk about what you have studied.

12. Why do instructors call upon students to answer questions about what they have just learned?

13. Is the advice to spread out your study consistent with the encoding specificity principle?

Answers

13. The ideas are compatible. If you study all at once, you encode the memory to what you are thinking about at that time. If you study at several times, the memory attaches to a greater variety of retrieval cues.

12. Practicing the retrieval of a memory strengthens it.

A parachute lets you coast down slowly, like the parasympathetic nervous system.

If the symphony excites you, it arouses your sympathetic nervous system.

▲ **Figure 7.10** One mnemonic device is to think of an image that will remind you of what you need to remember.

Mnemonic Devices

If you need to memorize a long, unexciting list, how would you do it? One effective strategy is to attach systematic retrieval cues to each term so that you can remind yourself of the terms when you need them. A **mnemonic device** is *any memory aid based on encoding items in a special way.* The word *mnemonic* (nee-MAHN-ik) comes from a Greek root meaning "memory." The same root appears in the word *amnesia,* "lack of memory." Some mnemonic devices are simple, such as "Every Good Boy Does Fine" to remember the notes EGBDF on the treble clef in music. To remember the functions of the sympathetic and parasympathetic nervous systems, you might try making connections like those shown in ▶ Figure 7.10 (Carney & Levin, 1998).

Suppose you have to memorize a list of Nobel Peace Prize winners (see ▶ Figure 7.11). You might make up a little story: "Dun (Dunant) passed (Passy) the Duke (Ducommun) of Gob (Gobat) some cream (Cremer). That made him ILL (Institute of International Law). He suited (von Suttner) up with some roses (Roosevelt) and spent some money (Moneta) on a Renault (Renault) . . ." You still have to study the names, but your story helps.

Another mnemonic device is the **method of loci** (method of places). *First, you memorize a series of places, and then you use a vivid image to associate each location with something you want to remember.* For example, you might start by memorizing every location along the route from your dormitory room to your psychology classroom. Then you link the locations, in order, to the names.

Suppose the first three locations you pass are the desk in your room, the door to your room, and the corridor. To link the first Nobel Peace Prize winners, Dunant and Passy, to your desk, you might imagine a Monopoly game board on your desk with a big sign "DO NOT (Dunant) PASS (Passy) GO." Then you link the second pair of names to the second location, your door: A DUKE student (as in Ducommun) is standing at the door, giving confusing signals. He says "DO COME IN (Ducommun)" and

Nobel Peace Prize Winners	
1901	H. Dunant and F. Passy
1902	E. Ducommun and A. Gobat
1903	Sir W. R. Cremer
1904	Institute of International Law
1905	Baroness von Suttner
1906	T. Roosevelt
1907	E. T. Moneta and L. Renault
1908	K. P. Arnoldson and F. Bajer
1909	A. M. F. Beernaert and Baron d'Estournelles de Constant

2007	Al Gore and the Intergovernmental Panel on Climate Change
2008	Martti Ahtisaari
2009	Barack Obama
2010	Liu Xiaobo
2011	Ellen Johnson Sirleaf, Leymah Gbowee, and Tawakkol Karman
2012	European Union
2013	Organisation for the Prohibition of Chemical Weapons

▲ **Figure 7.11** A list of Nobel Peace Prize winners: Mnemonic devices can be useful when people try to memorize long lists like this one.

"GO BACK (Gobat)." Then you link the corridor to Cremer, perhaps by imagining someone has spilled CREAM (Cremer) all over the floor (see ▼ Figure 7.12). You continue in this manner until you have linked every name to a location. Now, if you can remember all those locations in order and

▲ **Figure 7.12** With the method of loci, you first learn a list of places, such as "my desk, the door of my room, the corridor, . . ." Then you link each place to an item on a list.

if you have good visual images for each one, you can recite the list of Nobel Peace Prize winners.

Simpler mnemonic devices often help, such as when remembering people's names. You might remember someone named Harry Moore by picturing him as "more hairy." To memorize a traditional wedding vow, you might remember "BRISTLE" to remind you of "**B**etter or worse, **R**icher or poorer, **I**n **S**ickness and health, **T**o **L**ove and to cherish."

Storage

Storing or maintaining a memory sounds like a passive process, but important things happen here, too. As time passes after initial learning, some memories change in ways that increase their later availability. This process is called consolidation—*converting a short-term memory into a long-term memory.* Consolidation strengthens a memory, but it also changes it. When you recall something you did yesterday, your memory is rich in details, including who, what, where, and when. As time passes, your memory changes. You remember the gist of what happened but fewer details (Winocur, Moscovitch, & Sekeres, 2007).

Decades ago, psychologists imagined consolidation as a chemical process that took a fixed

amount of time. However, some memories consolidate faster or more easily than others. When you hear, "Jakarta is the capital of Indonesia," you might struggle to form a lasting memory. If someone says, "Yes, I will go with you to the dance on Friday," you store the memory almost immediately.

If you want to enhance consolidation after learning something, mild exercise helps (Suwabe et al., 2017). So does taking some caffeine (Borota et al., 2014). Exercise and caffeine both increase heart rate and blood flow. You can also improve consolidation by sleeping or resting quietly shortly after learning (Craig & Dewar, 2018; Dewar, Alber, Butler, Cowan, & Della Salla, 2012). Yes, either increased arousal or decreased arousal enhances consolidation, but by different mechanisms.

If you learned something some time ago and now you have a reminder or a similar experience, you *reconsolidate* the memory. Reconsolidation can strengthen a memory or update it in light of new information. Reconsolidation offers an opportunity to modify a painful memory. The procedure is to provide a reminder, pause, and then during the time when reconsolidation should take place, offer modified experiences. In some cases, the result has been to weaken a fearful memory, or at least the fear in response to the memory. However, the results vary greatly, depending on the timing and other details of the procedure (Phelps & Hofmann, 2019).

concept check

14. **Suppose you tested a group of people for their memory of some event 1, 5, 10, 15, and 20 days later to measure consolidation. What would be a better way to design the study?**

Answer

14. Ideally, you should use randomly assigned groups who were tested only once—one group after 1 day, another after 5, and so forth. If you tested a single group at each time, you cannot separate the effects of consolidation from those of repeated testing.

Retrieval

Memory differs from playing back a recording in many ways. Here is one: Suppose you try to list all the cities you have ever visited. You describe all you can, and then you come back a day or two later and try again. On your second try, you will probably recall *more* than you did the first time (Erdelyi, 2010). Whereas loss of memory is called amnesia, this *gain of memory over time* is called hypermnesia. Before the second try, something may have reminded you of items you left out the first time. For this reason, police sometimes interview a witness several times. It is possible to omit something once and remember it later.

Here is another difference between memory and a recording: Suppose someone asks you to describe part of an experience—perhaps, "Tell me about the meals you had on your beach trip." Then someone else asks you to describe the beach trip in general. Answering the first question strengthens your memory of the meals but weakens your memory of everything else about the trip (Bäuml & Samenieh, 2010). This phenomenon is called *retrieval-induced forgetting.*

Furthermore, someone who accompanied you on the beach trip and heard you describe certain aspects will also remember those aspects better than other details (Coman & Hirst, 2015).

Here is a third, highly important difference between memory and a recording: When you try to remember an experience, you start with the details you remember clearly and fill in the gaps with reconstruction: *During an experience, you construct a memory. When you try to retrieve that memory, you reconstruct an account based partly on distinct memories and partly by inferring what else must have happened.* Suppose you try to recall studying in the library last night. With a little effort, you might remember where you sat, what you were reading, who sat next to you, and where you went for a snack afterward. If you try to remember that episode weeks later, you will forget most of the details and rely on reasonable guesses, based on what you usually do in the library (Schmolck, Buffalo, & Squire, 2000).

Reconstruction and Inference in List Memory

Please try this demonstration: Read the words in list A once; then turn away from the list, pause for a few seconds, and write as many of the words as you can remember. Repeat the same procedure for list B. *Please do this now, before reading the following paragraph.*

List A	List B
bed	candy
rest	sour
weep	sugar
tired	dessert
dream	salty
wake	taste
snooze	flavor
keep	bitter
doze	cookies
steep	fruits
snore	chocolate
nap	yummy

After you have written your lists, check how many of the words you got right, but the main point is not how many you got right but whether you included *sleep* on the first list or *sweet* on the second. Many people include these words, which are not on the lists, often with confidence (Deese, 1959; Roediger & McDermott, 1995; Watson, Balota, & Roediger, 2003). In list B, *sweet* is related to the other words in meaning. In list A, *sleep* is related to most of the words in meaning, and the list also includes three words that rhyme with sleep (*weep, keep,* and *steep*). This combined influence produces false recall in a higher percentage of people. Apparently, while learning the individual words, people also learn the gist of what they are all about. When they try to retrieve the list later, they reconstruct a memory of what "must have" been on the list (Seamon et al., 2002).

This effect occurs mainly if you have a memory of intermediate strength. If you learn a list well, you probably won't add an extra word that is not on the list. If you remember few or none of the words on the list, you cannot use them to infer another word (Schacter, Verfaellie, Anes, & Racine, 1998).

15. Sometimes two people who shared the same experience months or years ago remember it differently. Why?

Answer

15. After a delay, the details are hard to remember, so you fill in the gaps with inferences. You and the other person probably reconstruct the missing details differently.

Reconstructing Stories

Suppose you listen to a story about a teenager's day, including normal events (watching television) and oddities (parking a bicycle in the kitchen). Which would you remember better—the normal events or the oddities? It depends. If you are tested immediately while your memory is still strong, you remember the unusual events best. However, as you start forgetting the details, you begin reconstructing a typical day for the teenager, omitting the improbable events and including items that the story omitted, such as "the teenager went to school in the morning." In short, the less certain your memory is, the more you rely on your expectations (Heit, 1993; Maki, 1990). If you tell something repeatedly—either a story you heard or an event from your own experience—the retellings gradually become more coherent (Ackil, Van Abbema, & Bauer, 2003; Bartlett, 1932). They make more sense because you rely more on the gist, keeping the details that fit the overall theme and omitting or modifying the others.

In a study that highlights the role of expectations, U.S. and Mexican adults tried to recall three stories. Some heard U.S. versions of the stories, and others heard Mexican versions. For example, in the "going on a date" story, the Mexican version had the man's sister go along as a chaperone. On average, U.S. participants remembered the U.S. versions better, whereas Mexicans remembered the Mexican versions better (Harris, Schoen, & Hensley, 1992).

16 In history books, it seems that one event led to another in a logical order, but in everyday life, events seem illogical, unconnected, and unpredictable. Why?

Answer

16. Long after the fact, a historian puts together a coherent story based on the gist of events, emphasizing details that fit the pattern. In your everyday life, you are aware of details that do not fit any pattern.

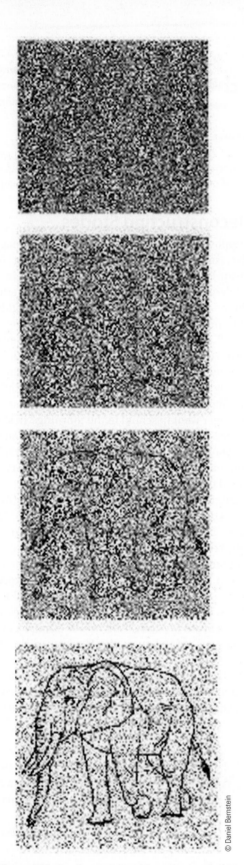

Hindsight Bias

Three weeks before the impeachment trial of U.S. President Clinton in 1999, college students were asked to predict the outcome. On average, they estimated the probability of a conviction at 50.5 percent. A week and a half after Clinton was not convicted, they were asked, "What would you have said 4½ weeks ago was the chance [of a conviction]?" On the average, they reported a 42.8 percent estimate (Bryant & Guilbault, 2002). Their behavior illustrates **hindsight bias**, *the tendency to mold a recollection of the past to fit how events later turned out.* Something happens and we then say, "I *knew* that was going to happen!" Hindsight bias occurs for several reasons. We would like to think the world is an orderly place and that we are smart enough to predict what will happen. We confuse the facts we know now with those we knew earlier. We focus on the facts we knew earlier that fit with the later outcome, and disregard those that didn't fit. Then we put together a meaningful story in which the earlier events seem to lead inevitably to the outcome (Roese & Vohs, 2012).

Another example: As you can see in ◄ Figure 7.13, an image gradually morphs from a blur to an elephant. At what point do you think the average person would identify it as an elephant? After you have seen the elephant, it is hard to imagine not seeing it. On this and similar sequences, most people overestimate how soon people will recognize the image (Bernstein, Atance, Loftus, & Meltzoff, 2004).

Hindsight bias affects judgments in many cases. Suppose a physician makes a diagnosis that turns out to be wrong. After we learn the correct diagnosis, it seems that the physician should have known it also, and a malpractice suit is the result (Arkes, 2013). After people had read about an accident at a nuclear power plant in Japan, most thought the accident was inevitable and predictable, although few people had in fact seen the danger before the accident (von der Beck, Oeberst, Cress, & Nestler, 2017). Hindsight bias also sometimes leads people to blame victims of certain crimes, on the assumption that "they should have known that was a dangerous place" or "the way they were acting was asking for trouble" (Felson & Palmore, 2018).

▲ **Figure 7.13** At what point in this sequence do you think the average person would recognize it as an elephant? (Source: From Bernstein, Atance, Loftus, & Meltzoff, 2004)

Improving Your Memory

If you want to improve your memory for something that happened years ago, what can you do? Not much. You might try returning to where the event happened or finding some other reminder. If you remember little at first, you might try again a few days later. Still, your prospects for finding a long-faded memory are limited. To improve your memory, improve your storage. Think carefully about anything you want to remember, study it under a variety of conditions, and review it frequently.

Summary

- *Encoding.* Encoding is best when you deliberately try to remember. (page 222)
- *Influences on encoding.* Arousal enhances encoding. Of the items you see or hear, you are most likely to remember the first and last, anything unusual, items familiar since childhood, and animals or people. You are especially likely to remember something if you imagine how you could use it for survival. (page 222)
- *Depth of processing.* A memory becomes stronger if you think about the meaning of the material and relate it to other material. (page 224)
- *Encoding specificity.* When you try to recall the memory, a cue is most effective if it resembles the links you formed at the time of storage. (page 225)

- *Methods of study.* Studying is most effective with spaced sessions, varied procedures, and periodic testing. (page 226)
- *Mnemonics.* Specialized techniques for using systematic retrieval cues help people remember lists of items. (page 227)
- *Storage and consolidation.* Whereas some memories are lost, others gradually strengthen over time. As we consolidate an episodic memory, we lose some of the details but remember the gist of the event. (page 228)
- *Retrieval.* Memory is unlike a recording. You reconstruct, combining actual memories with inferences that fill in the gaps. (page 228)
- *Hindsight bias.* People often revise their memories, saying that how an event turned out was what they expected all along. (page 230)

Key Terms

consolidation (page 228)

depth-of-processing principle (page 224)

encoding specificity principle (page 225)

hindsight bias (page 230)

hypermnesia (page 228)

method of loci (page 227)

mnemonic device (page 227)

primacy effect (page 223)

recency effect (page 223)

reconstruction (page 229)

retrieval cue (page 225)

Answers to Other Questions in the Module

A. The correct coin is A. (page 222)

B. Animal—Seal; Body part—Palm; Transportation—Plane; Temperature—Degree; Flavoring—Season; Sport—Squash; Stone—Rock; Personality—Charm; Write—Spell; Clergyman—Cardinal; Good—Fine; Fruit—Apple. (page 225)

Review Questions

1. How does emotional arousal affect memory, if at all?
   - (a) It improves storage.
   - (b) It interferes with storage.
   - (c) It interferes with consolidation.
   - (d) It has no effect.

2. You remember words best if you think about them in what way?
   - (a) How you could use the items in a survival situation
   - (b) What stores sell each item
   - (c) What was the first time you saw each item
   - (d) What was the most recent time you saw each item

3. What is meant by "depth of processing" in memory?
   - (a) How strongly it affects the unconscious mind
   - (b) The number of times you have repeated something
   - (c) The location of synaptic connections in the brain
   - (d) The number and variety of associations

4. Of the following, which is the best strategy for studying?
   - (a) Do all your studying in the same location, such as one place in the library.
   - (b) Study at separated times, in varying situations, and often test yourself.
   - (c) Make a recording and listen to it while you sleep.
   - (d) Repeat each word or concept until you can repeat it.

5. What is the result of testing yourself on what you are trying to learn?
   (a) It wastes time that you could better spend by repeated reading.
   (b) By increasing frustration, it impairs learning and memory.
   (c) On average, it has no effect on strength of memory.
   (d) By forcing you to recall something, testing improves memory.

6. What happens when you try to describe something that you do not remember perfectly?
   (a) You fill in the gaps with reasonable guesses.
   (b) Your account becomes more confusing and less coherent.
   (c) You describe mainly the most unusual or unlikely details.
   (d) You describe only what you saw and not what you heard.

7. Children who fail to display "theory of mind" seem to assume that if they know something, everyone else would know it too. Which of the following phenomena is similar to that assumption?
   (a) Encoding specificity principle
   (b) Hypermnesia
   (c) Hindsight bias
   (d) Depth-of-processing principle

Answers: 1a, 2a, 3d, 4b, 5d, 6a, 7c.

iStock.com/Rich Legg

After studying this module, you should be able to:

1. Explain how interference increases forgetting.

2. Describe evidence that suggestions can lead to false memory reports.

3. Discuss what amnesia tells us about memory.

4. State a possible explanation for infant amnesia.

He: We met at nine.
She: We met at eight.
He: I was on time.
She: No, you were late.
He: Ah, yes! I remember it well. We dined with friends.
She: We dined alone.
He: A tenor sang.
She: A baritone.
He: Ah, yes! I remember it well. That dazzling April moon!
She: There was none that night. And the month was June.
He: That's right! That's right!
She: It warms my heart to know that you remember still the way you do.
He: Ah, yes! I remember it well.
—"I Remember It Well" from the musical *Gigi* by Alan Jay Lerner and Frederick Loewe

We are not surprised when we forget, but we are surprised when we find that a seemingly clear memory was wrong. Here we explore ways of forgetting or distorting memories.

Retrieval and Interference

When you try to remember something, you might confuse it with something else you have learned. Hermann Ebbinghaus, who pioneered memory research, measured how long he could remember lists of nonsense syllables. The results appear as the green line on ▼ Figure 7.14. On average, he forgot more than

half of each list within the first hour (Ebbinghaus, 1885/1913). What a discouraging graph! If people typically forgot that fast, then education would be pointless. However, most college students remember nearly 90 percent of a list of nonsense syllables 24 hours later, as shown in the purple line of Figure 7.14 (Koppenaal, 1963).

Why do you suppose college students remember a list so much better than Ebbinghaus did? You may be tempted to say that college students are very intelligent. Well, yes, but Ebbinghaus was too. Or you might suggest that college students "have had so much practice at memorizing nonsense." (Sorry if you think so.) The correct explanation is the opposite: Ebbinghaus had memorized *too much* nonsense— thousands of lists of syllables. After you memorize many similar lists, your memory is like a cluttered room: The clutter doesn't prevent you from bringing in still more clutter, but it interferes with finding what you want. Ebbinghaus quickly forgot new lists because of interference from older lists.

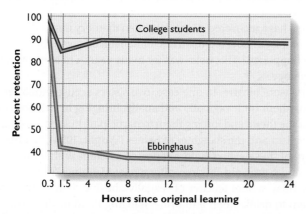

▲ **Figure 7.14** Recall of lists of syllables by Ebbinghaus (1885/1913) and by college students after delays of various lengths (based on Koppenaal, 1963). Ebbinghaus learned as fast as other people but forgot faster.

Bettmann/Getty Images

Ebbinghaus quickly forgot new lists of nonsense syllables because of interference from the previous lists he had learned.

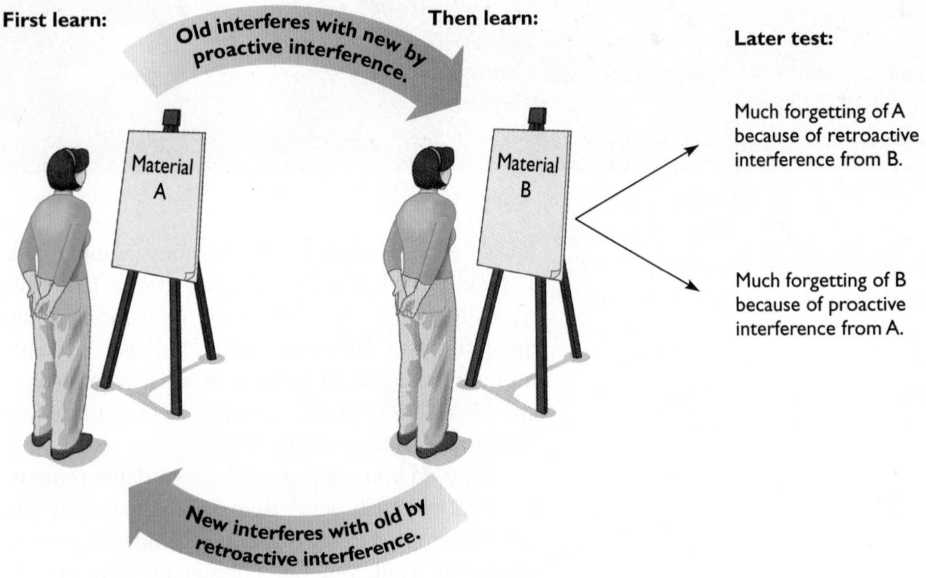

First learn:

Material
A

Old interferes with new by proactive interference.

Then learn:

Material
B

New interferes with old by retroactive interference.

Later test:

Much forgetting of A because of retroactive interference from B.

Much forgetting of B because of proactive interference from A.

◀ **Figure 7.15** If you learn similar materials, each interferes with retrieval of the other.

If you learn several sets of related materials, they interfere with each other. The *old materials increase forgetting of new materials* by proactive interference (acting forward in time). The *new materials increase forgetting of old materials* by retroactive interference (acting backward). ▲ Figure 7.15 contrasts the two kinds of interference.

Interference does not block new learning, but it increases the rate of forgetting. You forget where you parked your car today because of proactive interference from the previous times you parked your car. You forget last week's French vocabulary list because of retroactive interference from this week's list.

concept check

17. Every year, you try to learn the names of all the other students in your class. Over the years, you find that you forget them faster than you used to. Is the forgetting due to retroactive or proactive interference?

18. Remember the concept of spontaneous recovery in learning? Can you explain it in terms of proactive interference? (Hint: Original learning comes first and extinction comes second. What would happen if the first interfered with the second?)

Answers

18. If the original learning interferes proactively with the extinction (that comes later), the result is spontaneous recovery.

17. It is due to proactive interference—interference from memories learned earlier.

A Controversy: "Recovered Memories" or "False Memories"?

Occasionally something reminds you of something you hadn't thought about in years, perhaps something you thought you had forgotten. In most such cases, you describe that memory with little detail and little confidence (Chiu, 2018). In a sense, you have recovered a lost memory, except that it was not really lost, just ignored. With effort, you might also recall a memory of a traumatic experience that you have avoided thinking about. If so, several procedures are available to help you control the distress that accompanies that recall (Engelhard, McNally, & van Schie, 2019).

But could someone help you recover a memory that you lost? Let's imagine that a therapist asks you whether you had some experience, such as childhood sexual abuse, and you say no. The therapist persists: "The fact that you don't remember it doesn't mean that it didn't happen. Perhaps it was so painful that you repressed the memory." The therapist recommends hypnosis, repeated attempts to remember, or trying to imagine how it would have happened if it did. A few sessions later, you say, "It's starting to come back. . . . I think I do remember. . . ." *Reports of long-lost memories, prompted by clinical techniques,* are known as recovered memories.

If you claim to have recovered a long-forgotten memory under these conditions, has the therapist uncovered the truth, or convinced you to believe something that never happened? This issue was for many years a heated, even bitter, dispute in psychology.

Some reports were bizarre. In one case, two sisters accused their father of repeatedly raping them both vaginally and anally, bringing his friends over on Friday nights to rape them, and forcing them to participate in satanic rituals that included cannibalism and the slaughter of babies (Wright, 1994). Neither sister had any memory of these events before repeated sessions with a therapist. In another case, 3- and 4-year-old children, after repeated urgings from a therapist, accused their Sunday school teacher of sexually abusing them with a curling iron, forcing them to drink blood and urine, hanging them upside down from a chandelier, dunking them in toilets, and killing an elephant and a giraffe during Sunday school class (Gardner, 1994). No one found any physical evidence to support the claims, such as scarred tissues or giraffe bones.

Even when claims of recovered memories are less bizarre, their accuracy is doubtful. Researchers compared memories that people spontaneously recovered by themselves after many years, and reports that emerged only after prolonged therapeutic efforts. For people who spontaneously reported a memory of sexual abuse, investigators were usually able to find supporting evidence, such as other people who reported being abused by the same perpetrator. However, for people who reported recovering a memory only as a result of therapy, investigators found no supporting evidence in any of the cases (Geraerts et al., 2007).

When people have abusive experiences, are they likely to forget them for years? Can repeated suggestions get someone to recall an event that never happened?

Memory for Traumatic Events

Sigmund Freud introduced the term **repression** as *the process of moving an unacceptable memory or impulse from the conscious mind to the unconscious mind*. Many clinicians now prefer the term **dissociation**, referring to *memory that one has stored but cannot retrieve* (Alpert, Brown, & Courtois, 1998). The status of these ideas is controversial, and depends on exactly what someone means by them. One interpretation is that repression or dissociation refers to a deliberate effort to avoid thinking about an unpleasant memory. Deliberate avoidance does occur, of course (Brewin & Andrews, 2014). However, repression and dissociation are often presented as unconscious processes that block conscious access to a memory. Although many clinicians and much of the general public believe in this concept, researchers have never found any clear evidence for it (Holmes, 1990).

How often do people forget traumatic events? One study examined 16 children who had witnessed the murder of one of their parents, about as traumatic an event as one could imagine. All had recurring nightmares and haunting thoughts of the experience, and none had forgotten (Malmquist, 1986). Other studies examined prisoners of war who had been severely mistreated (Merckelbach, Dekkers, Wessel, & Roefs, 2003), children who had been kidnapped or forced to participate in pornographic movies (Terr, 1988), and people with other horrible experiences. People either remembered the events, or forgot only about as much as one might expect if the events happened in very early childhood. People avoid thinking about their most painful memories, but they do not forget.

Whether or not someone remembers a traumatic childhood experience depends on the age at the time of the event, its severity, and the reaction of other family members. Several studies examined young adult women who had been victims of childhood sexual abuse, documented by either hospital records or criminal proceedings. In each study, those who were older at the time of the offense remembered it better than those who were younger. Memory was better among those who had more severe or repeated abuse and those who received more family support and encouragement (Alexander et al., 2005; Goodman et al., 2003; Williams, 1994). In these regards, traumatic memories are similar to other memories.

Is recovered memory therapy good for mental health? Sigmund Freud and his followers have long focused on recovering repressed memories as essential to therapy, but dwelling on painful memories, regardless of whether they are accurate or not, often does more harm than good. Studies of people (mostly women) who reported recovering long-lost memories of early childhood abuse found a disturbing pattern: Most remained in therapy for years. All became estranged from their families. Most became suicidal, although few had already been before therapy. Most lost their jobs, about half became divorced or separated, and many started self-mutilation (Loftus, 1997).

<table>
<tr><td>19.</td><td>Based on material earlier in this chapter, why should we expect traumatic events to be remembered better than most other events?</td></tr>
</table>

Answer

19. Emotionally arousing memories are usually more memorable than other events. Also, highly unusual events tend to be memorable.

Influence of Suggestion

For psychologists who doubt that therapy recovers long-forgotten memories, what is the alternative? Memory recall is a process of reconstruction. Perhaps repeated suggestions to recall a memory of childhood abuse (or anything else) can implant a **false memory** (or false report), *an inaccurate report that someone believes to be a memory* (Lindsay & Read, 1994; Loftus, 1993). Early research found that asking misleading questions about a video, such as "Did you see the children getting on the school bus?" caused many people falsely to report having seen a school bus (Loftus, 1975). Could an experimenter also mislead people into reporting false memories about their own lives? Let's examine two experiments.

what's the evidence?

Suggestions and False Memories

First Study

Hypothesis Some people who are told about a childhood event will come to believe it happened, even if in fact it did not.

Method Young adults were told that the study concerned their childhood memories. Each participant was given paragraphs describing four events. Three of the events had actually happened. (The experimenters had contacted parents to get descriptions of childhood events.) A fourth event was a plausible but false story about getting lost. An example for one Vietnamese woman: "You, your Mom, Tien, and Tuan, all went to the Bremerton Kmart. You must have been 5 years old at the time. Your Mom gave each of you some money to get a blueberry ICEE. You ran ahead to get into the line first, and somehow lost your way in the store. Tien found you crying to an elderly Chinese woman. You three then went together to get an ICEE." After reading the four paragraphs, each participant was asked to write whatever additional details he or she could remember of the event. Participants were asked to try again a week later and then again after another week (Loftus, Feldman, & Dashiell, 1995).

Results Of 24 participants, 6 reported remembering the suggested false event, and some elaborated with additional details. The woman in the foregoing example said, "I vaguely remember walking around Kmart crying and looking for Tien and Tuan. I thought I was lost forever. I went to the shoe department, because we always spent a lot of time there. I went to the handkerchief place because we were there last. I circled all over the store it seemed 10 times. I just remember walking around crying. I do not remember the Chinese woman, or the ICEE (but it would be raspberry ICEE if I was getting an ICEE) part. I don't even remember being found."

Interpretation A suggestion can sometimes provoke a memory report of an event that never happened. Granted, this suggestion influenced only a quarter of the people tested, and most of them reported only vague memories. Still, the researchers achieved the effect after just a single brief suggestion. In a similar study, researchers repeatedly asked 60 students to recall two events from their early teenage years. The researchers had previously verified with the students' parents that one of the events was real and the other was not. At first, all denied the false event. However, the researchers urged them to try to remember it and visualize it, because "many people can't recall certain events at first because they haven't thought about them for such a long time." By the third interview, 44 of the 60 "recalled" the false event in some detail, including unlikely events such as being arrested by the police for assault with a weapon (Shaw & Porter, 2015). In short, suggestions can lead people to report memories of events that never happened.

Second Study

Some therapists ask their clients to examine childhood photographs to help evoke old memories. They are certainly right that photographs bring back memories. However, might old photographs also facilitate false memories?

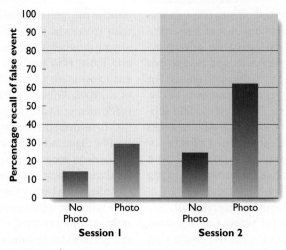

▲ **Figure 7.16** More students who saw a first-grade class photograph reported remembering the suggested (false) event. (From "True photographs and false memories," by D. S. Lindsay, L. Hagen, J. D. Read, K. A. Wada, and M. Garry, 2004. *Psychological Science* 15, pp. 149–154. Copyright 2004 Blackwell Publishing. Reprinted with permission.)

Hypothesis A false suggestion about a childhood event will evoke more memory reports if people have examined photographs from that time period.

Method Researchers asked the parents of 45 college students to describe an event that happened while these students were in third or fourth grade and another that happened in fifth or sixth grade. Both were supposed to be events that the student might or might not remember rather than events the family had repeatedly discussed. The researchers also asked the parents to confirm that the following event—the one they planned to suggest—had *not* happened: In the first grade, the child took a "Slime" toy to school, and then she and another child slid it into the teacher's desk and received a mild punishment later. The researchers also asked the parents for copies of class photographs from first grade, third or fourth grade, and fifth or sixth grade.

After these preparations, they brought in the students and briefly described for each student the two events provided by the parents and the one false event. They asked the students to provide whatever additional information they remembered about each event. Half of them (randomly selected) were shown their class photographs and half were not. At the end of the session, they were asked to think about the first-grade event for the next week and try to remember more about it. Those in the photograph group took the photo with them. A week later, the students returned and again reported whatever they thought they remembered (Lindsay, Hagen, Read, Wade, & Garry, 2004).

Results Most students reported clear memories of the two real events. For the false event of first grade, ▲ Figure 7.16 shows the percentage of students who

▲ **Figure 7.17** If you saw a photo of this train wreck and later saw an altered photo with people added to it, you might report remembering that you had seen the people at first also.

reported the event in the first and second sessions. Memories increased from the first to the second session, and students who saw the photographs reported more memories than those who did not see photographs. By the second session, almost two-thirds of the students who saw a class photograph reported some memory of the false event.

At the end of the study, the researchers explained that the first-grade event did not really happen. Many of the students expressed surprise, such as, "No way! I remember it! That is so weird!" (Lindsay et al., 2004, p. 153).

Interpretation Examining an old photograph increases suggestibility for false memories. Why? When you are trying to decide whether you remember something, you try to call up related thoughts and images. If you can recall extra details, it is probably a real memory. A photo makes it easier for you to recall details and think the event is real (Henkel, 2011; Strange, Garry, Bernstein, & Lindsay, 2011). If you are trying to remember when you and a friend pulled a prank on the teacher, the visual image makes the memory more vivid and more convincing.

In related studies, researchers manipulated photos by computers, showing childhood pictures of people having tea with Prince Charles of England or riding with their families in a hot-air balloon—false events in each case. Many of the participants claimed to remember the events and provided additional details (Strange, Sutherland, & Garry, 2004; Wade, Garry, Read, & Lindsay, 2002). People who viewed doctored photos of historical events misremembered the events to match the photos (Sacchi, Agnoli, & Loftus, 2007; ▲ Figure 7.17.)

concept check

20. **Explain how source amnesia may explain the effect of photos on memory.**

21. **In what way is hindsight bias similar to a false memory?**

Answers

20. Source amnesia occurs if you remember something but don't remember where you learned it. After you see something in the photo, you might think you remember it from an experience long ago.

21. In a case of hindsight bias, something that you learn later operates like a suggestion, so that when you try to remember what you previously thought, you are influenced by that suggestion and change your reported memory to fit it.

Areas of Agreement and Disagreement

What was once an angry dispute between clinical psychologists and psychological researchers is less intense than before, but not entirely settled. Everyone agrees it is possible to have a painful experience, not think about it for years, and remember it later (McNally & Geraerts, 2009). The question is how often (if ever) therapeutic techniques such as suggestion and hypnosis increase the accurate recall of forgotten events, and how often they implant false memories. Over the years, most psychotherapists have become less confident that therapy can recover old memories, and more accepting of the idea that suggestions can implant false memories. Still, on average, therapists are more likely to believe in repression than researchers are, and more likely to believe they can restore repressed memories (Patihis, Ho, Tingen, Lilienfeld, & Loftus, 2014). Fewer therapists try to recover repressed memories today than did so in the 1990s, but some still do (Patihis & Pendergrast, 2019). Researchers do not insist on rejecting every report of a recovered memory, but they strongly recommend treating those reports as uncertain, unless independent evidence supports them.

Amnesia

Imagine you passed your computer through a powerful magnetic field, but instead of erasing all the memories you erased only the text files and not the graphics files. Or suppose the old memories were intact but you could no longer store new ones. From the damage, you would gain hints about how your computer's memory works.

The same is true of human memory. Various kinds of brain damage impair one kind of memory but not another, helping us infer how memory is organized.

Amnesia after Damage to the Hippocampus

Amnesia is *loss of memory*. Even in the most severe cases of amnesia, people don't forget everything. They don't forget how to walk, talk, or eat. (If they did, we would call it *dementia*, not amnesia.) Amnesia results from many kinds of brain damage, and the memory impairment varies depending on the location of damage.

In 1953 Henry Molaison, known in the research literature by his initials H.M., was suffering from many small daily epileptic seizures and about one major seizure per week. He did not respond to any antiepileptic drugs. William Scoville, a surgeon, had heard about two cases in which removal of parts of the temporal lobe of the cortex had relieved epilepsy. He undertook the risky procedure of removing H.M.'s **hippocampus**, *a large forebrain structure in the interior of the temporal lobe* (see ▶ Figure 7.18). At the time, researchers knew little about what to expect after damage to the hippocampus. Since then, animal research has established that the hippocampus is important for encoding and retrieving memories, among other functions.

The surgery greatly decreased the frequency and severity of H.M.'s seizures. His personality remained the same, except that he became more passive (Eichenbaum, 2002). His IQ score increased slightly, presumably because he had fewer epileptic seizures. However, he suffered severe memory problems (Corkin, 1984; Milner, 1959). H.M. suffered massive **anterograde** (ANT-eh-ro-grade) **amnesia**,

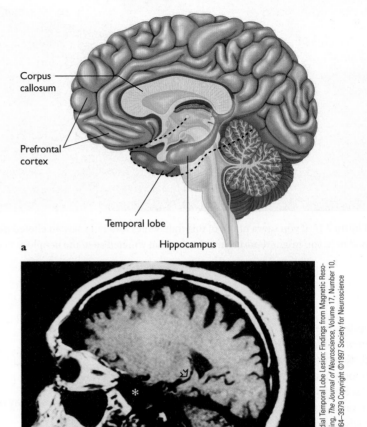

H. M.'s Medial Temporal Lobe Lesion: Findings from Magnetic Resonance Imaging, *The Journal of Neuroscience*, Volume 17, Number 10, 1997 pp. 3964–3979 Copyright ©1997 Society for Neuroscience

▲ **Figure 7.18 (a)** The hippocampus is a large subcortical brain structure. **(b)** The photo shows an MRI scan of H.M.'s brain. The asterisk indicates the area from which the hippocampus is missing. The arrow indicates a portion of the hippocampus that is preserved. (Photo courtesy of Suzanne Corkin and David Amaral)

inability to store new long-term memories. For years after the operation, he cited the year as 1953 and his own age as 27. Later, he took wild guesses (Corkin, 1984). He would read the same issue of a magazine repeatedly without recognizing it. He also suffered **retrograde amnesia**, *loss of memory for events that occurred shortly before the brain damage* (see ▼ Figure 7.19). Initial reports said that H.M.'s retrograde amnesia was limited to the last couple of years before the surgery. Later reports said it extended much further, especially for episodic memories. Another person with amnesia following diffuse brain damage suffered a complete loss of his episodic memory. When he looked at old family photos, he named the people, but he could not describe the event in the photo (Rosenbaum et al., 2005).

▲ **Figure 7.19** Brain damage induces retrograde amnesia (loss of old memories) and anterograde amnesia (difficulty storing new memories).

H.M. had normal short-term memory, as do most other patients with amnesia (Shrager, Levy, Hopkins, & Squire, 2008). If someone told him to remember a number, he could recall it minutes later, if nothing distracted him. However, after any distraction he not only forgot the number, but also forgot that he had tried to remember a number. He often told the same person the same story several times within a few minutes, forgetting that he had told it before (Eichenbaum, 2002).

Like Rip van Winkle, the story character who slept for 20 years and awakened to a vastly changed world, H.M. became more and more out of date with each passing year (Gabrieli, Cohen, & Corkin, 1988; Smith, 1988). He did not recognize people who became famous after the mid-1950s, although when given a famous person's name, he sometimes provided a bit of correct information (O'Kane, Kensinger, & Corkin, 2004). He did not understand the words and phrases that entered the English language after his surgery, such as *Jacuzzi* and *granola* (Corkin, 2002). He guessed that *soul food* meant "forgiveness" and that a *closet queen* might be "a moth" (Gabrieli, Cohen, & Corkin, 1988).

In spite of H.M.'s massive memory difficulties, he could still acquire and retain new procedural memories (skills and habits). For example, he learned to read material written in mirror fashion (Cohen & Squire, 1980), such as shown below. However, he did not remember having learned this or any other new skill and always expressed surprise at his success.

.siht ekil ,sdrawkcab nettirw secnetnes daer dluoc eH

The results for H.M. led researchers to study both people and laboratory animals with similar damage. The following points have emerged:

- The hippocampus is important for declarative memories, especially for episodic memories. Procedural memories depend on a different brain area, the basal ganglia. Many cases of classical conditioning depend on the cerebellum.
- The hippocampus is more important for explicit memory than for implicit memory.
- The hippocampus is especially important for spatial memories—remembering where something is or how to get from one place to another (Jacobs et al., 2013). The hippocampus and the nearby entorhinal cortex have neurons that respond strongly to locations or to the speed or direction of movement (Kropff, Carmichael, Moser, & Moser, 2015; O'Keefe & Burgess, 1996; Sargolini et al., 2006; Stensola et al., 2012). Spatial memory and episodic memory are linked, because most of our episodic memories are tied to a specific location (Robin, Buchsbaum, & Moscovitch, 2018). Any episodic memory necessarily includes remembering a scene in time and place (Rubin & Umanath, 2015).
- Patients with hippocampal damage have trouble imagining the future, just as they have trouble recalling the past. When you imagine a future event, such as a visit to a museum, you build upon what you remember of similar experiences. If you cannot remember your past, you cannot put much detail into your imagined future (Hassabis, Kumaran, Vann, & Maguire, 2007). When your "mind wanders," what do you think about? People with damage to the hippocampus rarely daydream about the past or future. Their mind wandering concerns only the present (McCormick, Rosenthal, Miller, & Maguire, 2018). A patient with amnesia truly lives in the present moment, without a past or a future.

Exactly what is the role of the hippocampus in memory? One view is that the cerebral cortex stores traces of a memory in many places, and the hippocampus provides an index for finding those traces (Tonegawa, Morrissey, & Kitamura, 2018). The hippocampus synchronizes activity in cortical areas,

enabling them to combine their information in recalling an event (Watrous, Tandon, Conner, Pieters, & Ekstrom, 2013).

22. What did the studies of H.M. teach us about memory?

Answer

22. It is possible to hold something for a long time in short-term memory without forming a long-term memory. Procedural memory is different from declarative memory, especially episodic memory. It is possible to retain old memories, especially semantic memories, without being able to store new memories.

Amnesia after Damage to the Prefrontal Cortex

Damage to the prefrontal cortex also produces amnesia (see Figure 7.18). Because the prefrontal cortex receives extensive input from the hippocampus, the symptoms of prefrontal cortex damage overlap those of hippocampal damage, but they also differ in several ways.

Prefrontal cortex damage can be the result of a stroke, head trauma, or Korsakoff's syndrome, *a condition caused by a prolonged deficiency of vitamin B$_1$ (thiamine), usually as a result of chronic alcoholism.* This deficiency leads to widespread loss or shrinkage of neurons, especially in the prefrontal cortex. Patients suffer apathy, confusion, and amnesia (Squire, Haist, & Shimamura, 1989).

Many patients with prefrontal cortex damage answer questions with confabulations, *which are attempts to fill in the gaps in their memory.* Most often they answer a question about what's happening today by describing something from their past (Borsutzky, Fujiwara, Brand, & Markowitsch, 2008; Schnider, 2003). For example, an aged hospitalized woman insisted that she had to go home to feed her baby. A hospitalized former psychiatrist repeatedly insisted that she was one of the staff psychiatrists, not one of the patients. Sometimes patients act out their confabulations, trying to leave the hospital to go home or go to work (Schnider, Nahum, & Ptak, 2017). That is, a confabulation is a belief, not just a verbal answer. Confabulations are not just attempts to hide an inability to answer a question, as Korsakoff's patients almost never confabulate on a question such as "Where is Premola?" or "Who is Princess Lolita?" (Schnider, 2003). If they never knew the answer, they freely admit not knowing. The following interview is a typical example (Moscovitch, 1989, pp. 135–136). Note the mixture of correct information, confabulations that were correct at some time in the past, and imaginative attempts to explain the discrepancies between one answer and another:

Psychologist: How old are you?
Patient: I'm 40, 42, pardon me, 62.
Psychologist: Are you married or single?
Patient: Married.
Psychologist: How long have you been married?
Patient: About 4 months.
Psychologist: What's your wife's name?
Patient: Martha.
Psychologist: How many children do you have?
Patient: Four. (He laughs.) Not bad for 4 months.
Psychologist: How old are your children?
Patient: The eldest is 32; his name is Bob. And the youngest is 22; his name is Joe.
Psychologist: How did you get these children in 4 months?
Patient: They're adopted.
Psychologist: Who adopted them?
Patient: Martha and I.
Psychologist: Immediately after you got married you wanted to adopt these older children?
Patient: Before we were married we adopted one of them, two of them. The eldest girl Brenda and Bob, and Joe and Dina since we were married.
Psychologist: Does it all sound a little strange to you, what you are saying?
Patient: I think it is a little strange.
Psychologist: I think when I looked at your record it said that you've been married for over 30 years. Does that sound more reasonable to you if I told you that?
Patient: No.
Psychologist: Do you really believe that you have been married for 4 months?
Patient: Yes.

Patients with prefrontal cortex damage confidently defend their confabulations and often maintain the same confabulation from one time to the next. This persistence relates to a general inability to update responses. If you were repeatedly rewarded for choosing, for example, the yellow card instead of the blue card, you would start choosing the yellow card. But if that response stopped being correct, you would switch to the blue one. Patients who confabulate tend to stick with a response that used to be correct, instead of switching (Schnider, Nahum, & Ptak, 2017).

Despite their impoverished explicit memory, people with amnesia show relatively normal implicit memory. For example, after hearing a list of words, a patient may not be able to say any of the words on the list. However, when given a set of three-letter stems such as CON—, the patient completes them to make words that were on the list, without remembering that there had been a list (Hamann & Squire, 1997).

Another example: After patients repeatedly practiced playing the video game *Tetris,* they said they did not remember playing the game, although they improved from one session to the next. When they closed their eyes to go to sleep at night, they said they saw little images of blocks and wondered what they were (Stickgold, Malia, Maguire, Roddenberry, & O'Connor, 2000).

One important conclusion emerges from all the studies of brain damage and amnesia: We have several different types of memory. It is possible to impair one type without equally damaging another.

23. **Although confabulation is a kind of false memory, how does it differ from the false memories discussed earlier in this module?**

Answer

23. Most confabulated statements were true at one time, though not now. Also, they are self-generated, not responses to someone's suggestions.

Memory Impairments in Alzheimer's Disease

A more common disorder is Alzheimer's (AHLTZ-hime-ers) disease, *a condition occurring mostly in old age, characterized by increasingly severe memory loss, confusion, depression, disordered thinking, and impaired attention.* Although several genes have been linked to a high risk of Alzheimer's disease before age 60, genetic variation accounts for only a small amount of the risk for the more common late-onset condition. The incidence of Alzheimer's among the Yoruba people of Nigeria is less than half that of Americans. A possible explanation is that high blood pressure is less common among the Yoruba (Ogunniyi et al., 2006).

Alzheimer's disease is marked by accumulation of harmful proteins in the brain and deterioration of brain cells, impairing arousal and attention. The memory problems include both anterograde and retrograde amnesia. Performance varies from one time to another, depending on alertness (Palop, Chin, & Mucke, 2006). Sometimes a cup of coffee or a brisk walk helps by increasing blood flow.

Because the areas of damage include the hippocampus and the prefrontal cortex, memory deficits of people with Alzheimer's disease overlap those of H.M. and patients with Korsakoff's syndrome. Their mixture of memory problems is hardly surprising, given the overall decrease of arousal and attention. However, most can learn new procedural memories, such as how to use a cell phone (Lekeu, Wojtasik, Van der Linden, & Salmon, 2002).

Early Childhood Amnesia

How much do you remember from when you were 5 years old? How about age 4? Age 3? Most adults report at most a few fragmentary memories of early childhood. The *scarcity of early episodic memories* is known as early childhood amnesia or infantile amnesia.

Sigmund Freud called attention to this phenomenon by his provocative suggestion that we *repress* (that is, ban from consciousness) all memories from early childhood because so many of them were sexual in nature and highly disturbing. Few psychologists today take that theory seriously.

Later psychologists proposed theories for why young children fail to form long-term memories. One proposal is that long-term episodic memories require a "sense of self" that develops between ages 3 and 4 (Howe & Courage, 1993). Another idea is that the hippocampus, known to be important for episodic memory, is slow to mature (Moscovitch, 1985). However, these proposals attempt to explain why young children don't form long-term memories. Young children *do* form long-term memories. Four- and five-year-old children remember birthday parties, visits to grandparents, and other events from months ago, sometimes even

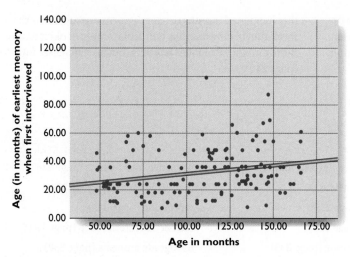

▲ Figure 7.20 Children from ages 4 to 14 reported their oldest episodic memory. In general, the older children's memories went less far back into early childhood. (From Peterson, Warren, & Short, 2011. Used by permission.)

years ago. Perhaps their long-term memories are weaker than those of adults, but they do form. Freud's explanation may seem preposterous, but he was asking the right question: Why do we *forget* the memories we formed in early childhood?

Researchers asked 4- to 13-year-old children to report their earliest memories. ▲ Figure 7.20 shows that as children grow older, they become less likely to recall events from their earliest years (Peterson, Warren, & Short, 2011). In another study, 4- and 6-year-old children described events from months ago. A year later, they had forgotten most of those events (Morris, Baker-Ward, & Bauer, 2010).

Infantile amnesia occurs not only in humans, but in rats, mice, and many other species also. That is, infant animals learn much, but unless they continue to practice what they learn, they forget within days. Studies in several rodent species offer an explanation for infantile amnesia: Early in life, the hippocampus

rapidly forms new neurons that facilitate new learning. However, as an infant rodent continues replacing many of the old neurons with new ones, the result interferes with older memories. Whatever increases the formation of new neurons improves learning, but also increases forgetting. Guinea pigs are born more mature than most other animals, capable of walking around and eating solid food on the day of birth. They have relatively low rates of neuron formation in the hippocampus, and they do not show the tendency to forget their early memories. Overall, it appears that we have a plausible explanation for childhood/infantile amnesia: The turnover of neurons that helps infants learn so fast also facilitates forgetting (Akers et al., 2014).

24. Why is a demonstration of infantile amnesia in rodents important for understanding humans?

Answer

24. The demonstration casts doubt on several explanations of human infantile amnesia. If rodents forget early memories, presumably the reason is not that they are repressing early sexual fantasies. If they remember better later, we might not want to attribute their memory to a "sense of self." Also, demonstrating infantile amnesia in rodents makes it easier to explore the brain changes that might be responsible.

Memory Loss and Distortion

When we try to recall something from long ago, we usually find that the details have faded. Is our tendency to forget a "bug" or a "feature"? Computers can store every detail that we give them, but our brains don't need to. The older some experience is, the less likely we are to need all the details.

Summary

- *Interference.* Much of forgetting is due to interference from similar memories. (page 233)
- *Traumatic memories.* Contrary to the concept of repression, research finds that people almost never forget traumatic memories, except for the forgetting that occurs for almost all memories of early childhood. People may, however, avoid thinking about their traumatic memories. (page 235)
- *"Recovered memory" or "false memory"?* Suggestions, especially repeated suggestions, can induce people to

report remembering events that never happened. (page 235)
- *Amnesia after damage to the hippocampus.* Damage to the hippocampus impairs episodic memory and the ability to form new long-term memories, but it spares short-term memory and procedural memory. People with damage to the hippocampus also have trouble imagining the future. (page 238)
- *Role of the hippocampus.* The hippocampus indexes and links long-term memory traces stored in the cerebral cortex. (page 239)

- *Damage to the prefrontal cortex.* Many people with damage to the prefrontal cortex give confident wrong answers, known as confabulations. Most confabulations were correct information earlier in the person's life. (page 239)
- *Infant amnesia.* Most people remember little from early childhood, even though preschoolers remember experiences that happened months or years ago. An explanation is that the formation of new neurons and replacement of older neurons during infancy facilitates learning, but also increases forgetting. (page 240)

Key Terms

Alzheimer's disease (page 240)

amnesia (page 238)

anterograde amnesia (page 238)

confabulations (page 239)

dissociation (page 235)

early childhood amnesia or infantile amnesia (page 240)

false memory (page 235)

hippocampus (page 238)

Korsakoff's syndrome (page 239)

proactive interference (page 234)

recovered memory (page 234)

repression (page 235)

retroactive interference (page 234)

retrograde amnesia (page 238)

Review Questions

1. How does proactive interference differ from retroactive interference?
   - (a) Proactive interference accelerates forgetting of only short-term memory.
   - (b) Proactive interference accelerates forgetting of only implicit memory.
   - (c) Proactive interference accelerates forgetting of what you learned earlier.
   - (d) Proactive interference accelerates forgetting of what you learn later.

2. Which of the following is an explanation for the recency effect in list learning?
   - (a) The formation of new neurons consolidates the final item on a list.
   - (b) Hindsight bias does not impair the last item on a list.
   - (c) Proactive interference does not impair the last item on a list.
   - (d) Retroactive interference does not impair the last item on a list.

3. What is true of most memories that people spontaneously recall after not remembering them in years?
   - (a) These memories evoke intense emotions.
   - (b) These memories include little detail.
   - (c) These memories are almost always fantasies.
   - (d) These memories show up first in the person's dreams.

4. Which of the following has been a heated controversy among psychologists?
   - (a) Is it better to study all at once, or to spread out the study sessions?
   - (b) How reliably can clinicians get someone to recover a lost memory?
   - (c) How important is interference as a basis of forgetting?
   - (d) Which types of memory does hippocampal damage impair?

5. Which of these was least impaired in H.M. and similar patients?
   - (a) Formation of new long-term memories
   - (b) Episodic memory
   - (c) Procedural memory
   - (d) Ability to imagine future events

6. Which of the following is most characteristic of people with Korsakoff's syndrome?
   - (a) Retrograde amnesia without anterograde amnesia
   - (b) Loss of implicit memory
   - (c) Confabulations
   - (d) Inability to recognize faces

7. Immaturity of the hippocampus could impair memory formation. Why is this fact, at best, an incomplete explanation for infant amnesia?
   - (a) The rate of hippocampal maturation varies among species of animals.
   - (b) The rate of hippocampal maturation varies among children.
   - (c) Preschool children do form long-term memories.
   - (d) Infant amnesia applies mostly to procedural memories.

8. Studies on mice support which explanation for this infantile amnesia?
   - (a) Early memories are emotionally traumatic.
   - (b) Hearing and vision develop gradually after birth.
   - (c) Infants have not yet formed a sense of self.
   - (d) New neurons facilitate new learning but also facilitate forgetting.

Answers: 1d, 2d, 3b, 4b, 5c, 6c, 7c, 8d.

Nolte Lourens/Shutterstock.com

module 8.1

Attention and Categorization

After studying this module, you should be able to:

1. Distinguish between attentive and preattentive processes.

2. Give examples of phenomena related to attention, such as change blindness.

3. Discuss what is known about attention deficit disorder.

4. Discuss how categorization affects thinking.

Cognition means *thinking and using knowledge.* Cognitive psychologists also deal with how people organize their thoughts into language. Since about 1970, psychologists have developed many ways to infer cognitive processes, generally by measuring the speed and accuracy of responses.

Research in Cognitive Psychology

You might think cognitive psychology should be simple. "If you want to find out what people think or know, why not ask them?" Sometimes, psychologists do ask, but people don't always know their own thought processes. Consider this experiment: The experimenter presents two cards at a time, each showing a female face, and asks a participant which one looks more attractive. Sometimes the experimenter surreptitiously switches the cards and shows the face *not*

chosen before asking "Why did you choose this one," as shown in ▼ Figure 8.1. People often do not notice the switch, and give a long, specific, confident explanation for why they chose the switched card (Johansson, Hall, Sikström, & Olsson, 2005). Psychologists call this phenomenon **choice blindness** because people act as if they don't know what they had chosen. Clearly, when people "explain" a choice they hadn't actually made, they must be stating reasons that they made up afterward. Therefore, we suspect that in many other cases, people decide without knowing a reason and then make up an explanation afterward. Choice blindness occurs in many situations. Suppose an eyewitness to a crime describes the event, and a month later an interrogator misquotes what the witness said. In many cases the witness fails to recognize the change, and defends the altered statement (Cochran, Greenspan, Bogart, & Loftus, 2016; Sagana, Sauerland, & Merckelbach, 2017; Stille, Norin, & Sikstrom, 2017).

If we cannot find out people's thought processes just by asking, then what? Let's consider one of the first experiments that measured a mental process.

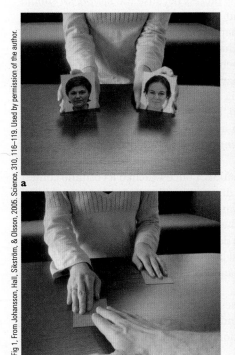

Fig 1, From Johansson, Hall, Sikström, & Olsson, 2005. Science, 310, 116–119. Used by permission of the author.

▲ **Figure 8.1** The participant identified the face considered more attractive. Then the experimenter switched cards and asked why this face seemed more attractive. (From Johansson, Hall, Sikström, & Olsson, 2005)

what's the evidence?

Mental Imagery

If you look at something and try to describe how it would look from a different angle, you would probably say you imagined rotating the object. Roger Shepard and Jacqueline Metzler (1971) reasoned that if people do rotate mental images, then the time it takes to rotate a mental image should be similar to the time needed to rotate a real object.

Hypothesis When people have to rotate a mental image to answer a question, the farther they have to rotate it, the longer it will take to answer the question.

Method Participants examined pairs of drawings of three-dimensional objects, like those in ▼ Figure 8.2, and indicated whether it would be possible to rotate one object to match the other. Try to answer this question yourself before reading further.

try it your self

People pulled one lever to indicate *same* and another lever to indicate *different.* When the

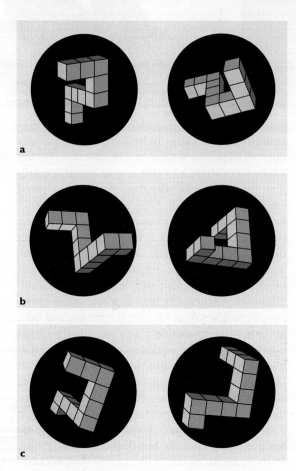

▲ **Figure 8.2** Examples of pairs of drawings used in an experiment by Shepard and Metzler (1971). Do the drawings for each pair represent the same object being rotated, or are they different objects? (See answer A on page 254.) (From "Mental rotation of three-dimensional objects" by R. N. Shepard and J. N. Metzler, 1971. *Science,* 171, pp. 701–703. Copyright 1971. Reprinted with permission from AAAS.)

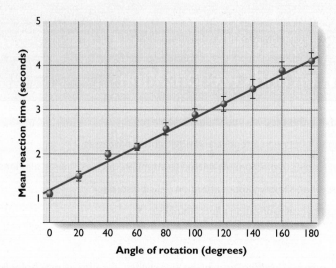

▲ **Figure 8.3** Mean times for correctly saying "same" depending on the required degree of rotation. (From "Mental rotation of three-dimensional objects" by R. N. Shepard and J. N. Metzler, 1971. *Science,* 171, pp. 701–703. Copyright 1971. Reprinted with permission from AAAS.)

correct answer was *same*, someone might determine that answer by rotating a mental image of the first picture until it matched the second. If so, the delay should depend on how far the image had to be rotated.

Results Participants answered nearly all items correctly. As predicted, their reaction time when they responded *same* depended on the angular difference in orientation between the two views, as ▲ Figure 8.3 shows. For every additional 20 degrees of rotation, the time to respond increased by about a third of a second. That is, people reacted as if they were watching an object rotate at a constant speed.

Interpretation Viewing a mental image is partly like vision. In this case, common sense appears to be correct. However, the main point is that researchers can infer thought processes from people's delay in answering a question.

Attention

You are constantly bombarded with more sights, sounds, smells, and other stimuli than you can process. **Attention** is *the tendency to respond to and remember some stimuli more than others.*

Sometimes, something such as a noise or flashing light grabs your attention. Psychologists call this a **bottom-up process** because the *peripheral stimuli control it.* Although almost any sound attracts some attention, hearing your name attracts it even more strongly (Shapiro, Caldwell, & Sorensen, 1997). If you glance at a written page, emotionally charged words get your attention, such as those referring to moral or immoral behavior (Gantman & Van Bavel, 2014). A moving object in an otherwise stationary scene grabs attention, especially if it is moving irregularly, like a meandering animal, or moving directly toward you, posing possible threat (Lin, Franconeri, & Enns, 2008; Pratt, Radulescu, Guo, & Abrams, 2010). However, if everything in the scene is moving or changing except one thing, then the one *unchanging* item grabs attention (Hilchey, Taylor, & Pratt, 2016).

Anything unusual grabs your attention. I once watched a costume contest in which people were told to dress so distinctively that their friends could find them quickly in a crowd. The winner was a young man who came onto the stage naked. Although he certainly earned the prize, the contest had a problem: The most distinctive clothing (or lack of it) depends on what everyone else is wearing. A naked man is easy to spot in most places, but at a nudist beach, you would more quickly notice a man in a coat and tie. The context determines what is unusual.

Magicians use bottom-up processes to control your attention. A magician pulls a rabbit or a dove out of a hat, and the rabbit or dove automatically captures your attention. While your attention is occupied, the magician sets up the next trick (Macknik et al., 2008).

In contrast to a bottom-up process, you can *deliberately control your attention* in a **top-down process**. To illustrate, fixate your eyes on the x in the center and then, without moving your eyes, read the letters in the circle around it clockwise:

try it your self

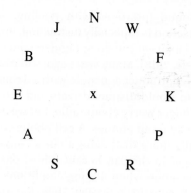

As you see, you can shift your attention without moving your eyes. When you increase your attention to something in your visual field, the part of your visual cortex sensitive to that area becomes more active and receives more blood flow (Müller, Malinowski, Gruber, & Hillyard, 2003). If you focus on a word, such as THIS, and attend to the letters, you increase activity in the language areas of the brain, but if you attend to the color, you shift activity to the color-detecting areas (Polk, Drake, Jonides, Smith, & Smith, 2008).

To illustrate the difference between bottom-up and top-down processes, find the one whooping crane in ▲ Figure 8.4 within the flock of sandhill cranes. That was easy, wasn't it? When anything differs drastically from items around it in size, shape, color, or movement, we find it by a bottom-up process, also known as a **preattentive process**, meaning that it *stands out immediately*. You would find that whooping crane just as fast in a larger flock or smaller flock.

Contrast that task with ▶ Figure 8.5. Here, all the birds are the same species. Your task is to find the one that faces to the right, and you have to check each bird separately. The more birds present, the longer you will need to find the unusual one. (You might find it quickly if you luckily start your search in the correct corner of the photograph.) You had to rely on a top-down process, also known as an **attentive process**—*one that requires searching through the items in series* (Enns & Rensink, 1990; Treisman & Souther, 1985). The *Where's Waldo* books are an excellent example of a task requiring an attentive process.

The distinction between attentive and preattentive processes has practical applications. Imagine yourself as a human-factors psychologist designing a machine with many gauges. Suppose that when the machine is running well, the first gauge should read about 70, the second 40, the third 30, and the fourth 10. If you arrange the gauges as in the top row of ▼ Figure 8.6, then people must check each gauge separately to find anything dangerous. In the bottom row, the gauges are arranged so that all the safe ranges are on the right. Now someone glances at the display and quickly (preattentively) notices anything out of position.

1. **When you search your bookshelf for a particular book, are you using an attentive or preattentive process? When you suddenly notice that one of the book covers is torn, are you using an attentive or preattentive process?**

Answer

1. Searching for a particular book is an attentive process (or top-down). Suddenly noticing a torn cover is a preattentive process (or bottom-up).

▲ **Figure 8.4** Demonstration of preattentive processes: You find the one whooping crane immediately, regardless of how many sandhill cranes are present.

The Attention Bottleneck

Attention is limited, as if various items were trying to get through a bottleneck that permits only a little to pass through at a time. Can you do two things at once? Yes, if the activities are simple and compatible, like walking and chewing gum, or listening to someone and taking notes (Srna, Schrift, & Zauberman, 2018). However, in most cases when you think you are multitasking, you are really alternating between one task and the other. Any attention you give to one task subtracts from what you have available for the other (Redick et al., 2016). Consider this example: Would you notice a

▲ **Figure 8.5** Demonstration of attentive processes: Find the marbled godwit that is facing to the right. In this case, you need to check the birds one at a time.

▲ **Figure 8.6** Each gauge measures something a machine does. The green area of the dial is the safe zone. In the top row, an operator must check gauges one at a time. In the bottom row, all the safe ranges are in the same place, and an unsafe reading stands out.

strong odor of coffee that suddenly breezed into the room? Ordinarily, yes, but not if you were paying close attention to a difficult task (Forster & Spence, 2018).

Even when you are doing only one task, your attention level varies. When your mind wanders, you think about something unrelated to the task, and your ability to process the relevant information decreases (Barron, Riley, Greer, & Smallwood, 2011). As with almost any other variable, some people do more mind-wandering than others do (Forster & Lavie, 2016; Kane et al., 2017).

But *why* does your mind wander? One hypothesis has been that your attention drifts because a task is monotonous and boring. However, mind-wandering occurs sooner on difficult tasks than on easier tasks. A better explanation is that mind-wandering is your default state. Paying attention to a task requires effort, and that effort gradually tires you, prompting you to relax and let your mind wander (Thomson, Besner, & Smilek, 2015). An implication is that people with critical jobs that require constant attention, such as air-traffic controllers, need frequent rest breaks.

Any distraction interferes with performance. One study found that children learned better in a sparsely decorated classroom than in one with many items on the walls, because the children often looked at the walls instead of attending to the lesson (Fisher, Godwin, & Seltman, 2014).

Almost any sound interferes with reading. A background conversation is especially distracting, unless the words are in a language you do not understand (Vasilev. Kirkby, & Angele, 2018). Many years ago, when automobile radios were introduced, people worried that listening to the radio would distract drivers and cause accidents. We no longer worry about radio, but we do worry about drivers using cell phones. A cell phone conversation is generally more distracting than a conversation with a passenger in the car, because most passengers pause a conversation when driving conditions are difficult (Drews, Pasupathi, & Strayer, 2008; Kunar, Carter, Cohen, & Horowitz, 2008).

What if a passenger in the car is talking on a cell phone to someone else? In that case, the driver hears half of a conversation—a "half-alogue"—which is more distracting than a full conversation (Emberson, Lupyan, Goldstein, & Spivey, 2010). A half-conversation has unpredictable starts and stops. Also, a nonparticipant who overhears it tends to fill in the blanks with imagined content, and doing so takes mental effort.

The Stroop Effect

In ▼ Figure 8.7, examine the blocks of color at the top of the figure. Scanning from left to right, name each color as fast as you can. Then examine the nonsense syllables in the center of the figure. Again, say the color of each one as fast as possible. Then turn to the real words at the bottom. Instead of reading them, quickly state each one's color.

Most people read the colors quickly for the first two parts, but they slow down greatly for the colored words (which happen to be the names of colors). After years of reading, you can hardly bring yourself to look at **RED** and

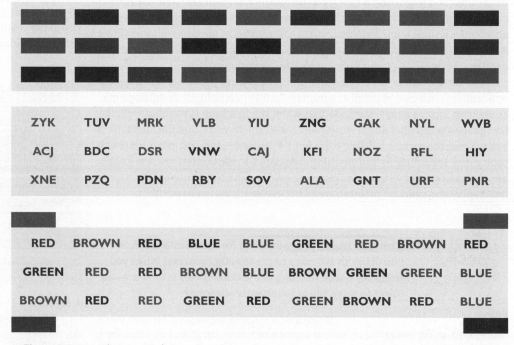

▲ **Figure 8.7** Read (left to right) the color of the ink in each part. Try to ignore the words themselves.

say "green." Reading the words distracts from your attention to the colors. *The tendency to read the words instead of saying the color of ink* is known as the **Stroop effect**, after the psychologist who discovered it. People do better on this task if they blur their vision, say the colors in a different language, or manage to regard the color words as meaningless (Raz, Kirsch, Pollard, & Nitkin-Kaner, 2006).

Do words always take priority over colors? Not necessarily. Try the following: Go back to the bottom portion of Figure 8.7 and notice the colored patches at the four corners. This time, instead of saying anything, point to the correct color patch. When you come to **RED**, point to the blue patch in the lower left. Then try this demonstration again but point to the color corresponding to the *meaning* of the word. That is, when you come to **RED**, point to the red patch in the upper left. Try it now.

You probably found it easy to point to the patch that matches the color of the ink and harder to point to the color matching the word meaning (Durgin, 2000). When you are speaking, you are primed to read the words you see, but when you are pointing, you are more primed to attend to nonverbal cues, such as ink color. In either case, the Stroop effect illustrates the difficulty of shifting your attention to whichever dimension is less salient at the time.

Change Blindness

Movie directors discovered long ago that if they shot different parts of a scene on different days, few viewers noticed changes in the cloud pattern, the background props, or the actors' clothes (Simons & Levin, 2003).

a Change in marginal interest (MI)

b Change in central interest (CI)

▲ **Figure 8.8** How quickly can you find the difference in each pair of pictures? If you need help, check answer B, page 254.

When you look at a complex scene, your eyes dart around from one fixation point to another, fixating about three times per second (Henderson, 2007). During each fixation you pay attention to only a few details (Franconeri, Alvarez, & Enns, 2007). If one of those details changed while you were fixating on it, you would notice, of course. A big, sudden change somewhere else would also grab your attention. But you overlook changes that occur gradually or between one view and a slightly later view (Cohen, Alvarez, & Nakayama, 2011; Henderson & Hollingworth, 2003).

Psychologists call this phenomenon **change blindness**—*the failure to detect changes in parts of a scene.* ◄ Figure 8.8 shows two pairs of photos. In each pair, one differs from the other in a single regard. How quickly can you find those differences? Most people need longer for the top pair (Rensink, O'Regan, & Clark, 1997).

The conclusion is that when you see or hear something, you hold a few details, but not everything. Magicians exploit change blindness (Macknik et al., 2008). A magician throws a ball into the air and catches it a few times and then pretends to throw it again, "watching" it go up. Many viewers do not immediately notice the change. They "see" the ball going up . . . and then disappearing!

concept check

2. Did you find the changes in Figure 8.8 by a preattentive or an attentive mechanism?

Answer

2. The changes did not jump out by a preattentive mechanism. You had to use an attentive process to check each part of the scene one at a time.

Attention Deficit Disorder

People vary in their ability to maintain attention, as in anything else. **Attention deficit disorder (ADD)** is characterized by *easy distraction, impulsiveness, moodiness, and failure to follow through on plans.* **Attention-deficit hyperactivity disorder (ADHD)** is *the same with the addition of excessive activity and "fidgetiness."* People can have problems with attention, impulsivity, or both. Over the years, more and more children have been diagnosed with ADD or ADHD, probably because of an increased tendency to apply the diagnosis to less serious problems. So far as we can tell, the symptoms themselves have remained about equally prevalent (Polanczyk et al., 2014; Rydell, Lundström, Gillberg, Lichtenstein, & Larsson, 2018). As children mature into adulthood, more than half improve to varying degrees (Sudre, Mangalmurti, & Shaw, 2018).

In some cases, ADHD results from fetal alcohol exposure, lead poisoning, epilepsy, or emotional stress (Pearl, Weiss, & Stein, 2001). Researchers have also found evidence for a considerable degree of heritability. Several risk genes have been identified, although none of them by itself accounts for much of the variance (Bidwell et al., 2017; Grimm, Kittel-Schneider, & Reif, 2018). A strong possibility is epigenetics—that is, changes in the expression of genes, rather than changes in the genes themselves. Researchers studied 14 pairs of monozygotic twins in which only one showed ADHD symptoms. The twins with symptoms differed from those without symptoms with regard to the expression of genes affecting development of the cerebellum and other subcortical areas (Chen et al., 2018).

Just as the symptoms of ADHD vary, so does the brain activity. In one study, ADHD was linked to greater than average brain activity (Wang, Jiao, Tang, Wang, & Lu, 2013), and in another it was linked to less than average brain arousal (Strauss et al., 2018). An interesting study found one pattern of brain connections that correlated with inattention, and a different pattern that correlated with impulsivity (Wang, Jiao, & Li, 2017). In any case, the brain abnormalities are not consistent enough to contribute to a diagnosis.

What exactly do we mean by "attention deficit"? People with ADHD pay attention to anything they care about, but they often have trouble maintaining attention to an uninteresting assigned task, or shifting attention from one task to another. One study found that when ADHD children stopped paying attention to an assigned task, they were usually not day-dreaming about something else. Rather, "their mind had gone blank" (Van den Driessche et al., 2017).

Here are two tasks sensitive to attention deficit disorder:

- **Choice-Delay Task** Would you prefer a small reward now or a bigger reward later? Obviously, it depends on how much bigger and how much later. Still, on average, people with ADHD are more likely than other people their age to opt for the immediate reward, especially with longer delays (Yu, Sonuga-Barke, & Liu, 2018).

- **Stop-Signal Task** Suppose your task is to press the X key when you see an X on the screen and the O key when you see an O, as quickly as possible. However, if you hear a beep shortly after either letter, then you should not press. If the letter and beep occur simultaneously, you easily inhibit your urge to press the button. If the beep occurs after you have already started to press, it's too late. The interesting results are with short delays: After how long a delay could you still manage

to stop your finger from pressing the button? Most people with ADD or ADHD have trouble inhibiting their response after short delays (Lipszyc & Schachar, 2010).

The choice-delay task and stop-signal task measure different attentional problems. Some children show impairments on one task but not the other (Solanto et al., 2001; Sonuga-Barke, 2005). However, neither of these tasks has results that would be dependable enough to help with a diagnosis (Minder, Zuberer, Brandeis, & Drechsler, 2018).

The most common treatment for ADD or ADHD is stimulant drugs such as methylphenidate (Ritalin) or amphetamines (Adderall). Stimulant drugs reduce the impulsivity and attention deficit problems, but most research studies have examined results for less than a year. Longer-term studies show less clear benefits, especially for academic performance (Langberg & Becker, 2012; Molina et al., 2009; Parker, Wales, Chalhoub, & Harpin, 2013).

Behavioral therapy methods include classroom rewards for good behavior and time-outs for inappropriate behavior. The research finds that a combination of stimulant drugs and behavior therapy is more effective than either one alone (Catalá-Lopez et al., 2017). Behavior therapy is especially helpful for improving social skills, improving academic performance, and decreasing conduct problems (Daley et al., 2014; Sibley, Kuriyan, Evans, Waxmonsky, & Smith, 2014).

A fair number of healthy people take stimulant drugs to try to enhance their already normal abilities. That practice raises the ethical question of whether it is fair for students to use drugs to get better grades, or for professionals in a competitive field to gain an advantage by using drugs. Regardless of the ethics, research suggests that stimulant drugs produce slightly prolonged attention but no other benefit for people who were already performing well (Ilieva, Boland, & Farah, 2013; MacQueen et al., 2018). Students who *think* they are taking amphetamines, even if really they are taking a placebo, *think* they are doing better (Cropsey, Schiavon, Hendricks, Froelich, Lentowicz, & Ferguson, 2017; Winkler & Hermann, 2019).

Studies in the United States and in Iceland found that stimulant drugs are prescribed more often for children who are young for their grade than those older for their grade. That is, if the cutoff for entering first grade is 6 years old, those who are just barely 6 are more likely to get an ADHD diagnosis, and to be treated with stimulant drugs, than those who are almost 7 (Elder, 2010; Zoëga, Valdimarsdóttir, & Hernández-Díaz, 2012).

3. Given that children young for their grade are more likely to be diagnosed with ADHD, what can we infer about the diagnoses?

Answer

3. Many teachers and psychiatrists are treating immaturity as if it were a medical problem.

Categorizing

Putting things into categories makes our thinking more efficient. What you learn about amphibians tells you what to expect of all amphibians, including a species you meet for the first time. What you learn about cars tells you what to expect of cars in general. And so forth. How do we form categories?

Ways to Describe a Concept

Many animals can learn to respond to concepts such as larger/smaller or same/different. Language, however, is necessary for some concepts (Gentner, 2016). For example, without language, you could never learn the concept "twenty-six."

Some words have simple, unambiguous definitions. For example, a *line* is the shortest distance between two points. Other concepts are hard to define, however. You can probably recognize country music, but can you define it? How should we define "bald"? Is a man who loses one hair bald? Of course not. Then he loses one more hair, then another, and another. Eventually, he *is* bald. At what point did losing one more hair make him bald?

Eleanor Rosch (1978; Rosch & Mervis, 1975) argued that many categories are best described by *familiar or typical examples* called **prototypes**. After we identify good prototypes of country music or a bald person, we compare other items to them. Depending on how closely something matches, we call it a member of the category, a nonmember, or a borderline case. For example, cars and trucks are prototypical members of the category *vehicle*. Flowers are nonmembers. Escalators and water skis are borderline cases. Defining something as abstract as freedom, love, or time poses special problems (Borghi et al., 2017). The philosopher George Berkeley became so frustrated with trying to define abstract concepts that he recommended doing away with them altogether.

A further complication is that we expand or contract our concept of a category depending on how common it is. For example, suppose you are looking through photos searching for "blue things." If the photos have hardly any blue items, you might start counting some of the purplish or bluish-green things as blue. Similarly, if you are looking for "dangerous or threatening expressions" but almost everyone is smiling, you might identify a neutral expression as threatening. This tendency has social and political consequences. Imagine someone who is dedicated to combatting racism, sexism, or other prejudices, but who lives in an enlightened place with few examples of injustice. The tendency would be to expand the category, to start attacking ever-smaller types of offense (Levari et al., 2018).

Conceptual Networks and Priming

Try to think about one word and nothing else. You will soon discover the difficulty. If you don't relate that word to something else, you're just repeating it, not thinking about it. For example, when you think about *bird*, you link it to more specific examples, such as *sparrow*, more general categories, such as *animals*, and related terms, such as *flight* and *eggs*.

We organize items into hierarchies, such as animal as a high-level category, bird as intermediate, and sparrow as a lower-level category. Researchers demonstrate the reality of this kind of hierarchy by measuring the delay for people to answer various questions (Collins & Quillian, 1969, 1970). Answer the following true–false questions as quickly as possible:

- Canaries are yellow.
- Canaries sing.
- Canaries lay eggs.
- Canaries have feathers.
- Canaries have skin.

All five items are true, but most people answer fastest on the *yellow* and *sing* items, slightly slower on the *eggs* and *feathers* items, and still slower on the *skin* item. Why? Yellowness and singing are distinctive of canaries. For eggs or feathers, you reason, "Canaries are birds, and birds lay eggs. So canaries must lay eggs." For skin, you have to reason, "Canaries are birds and birds are animals. Animals have skin, so canaries must have skin."

concept check

4 Which would people answer faster: does Yellowstone Park have geysers, or does Yellowstone Park have grass? Why?

Answer

4. People will answer faster about geysers, because geysers such as Old Faithful are a famous part of Yellowstone. To answer about grass, someone must reason that Yellowstone is a natural area, and most natural areas have grass.

We also link a word or concept to related concepts. ▼ **Figure 8.9** shows a possible network of conceptual links that someone might have at a particular moment (Collins & Loftus, 1975). Suppose this network describes your own concepts. *Thinking about one of the concepts shown in this figure will activate, or prime, the concepts linked to it* through a process called **spreading activation** (Collins & Loftus, 1975). For example, if you hear *flower*, you are primed to think of *rose*, *violet*, and other flowers. If you also hear *red*, the combination of *flower* and *red* primes you to think of *rose*.

When you hear something described metaphorically, the choice of words controls how the activation spreads. For example, if someone

Things

Living things · Nonliving things

Plants · Animals

Mammals · Birds · Reptiles · Insects · etc.

Sparrows · Robins · Hawks · Canaries · etc.

The robin I saw this morning · My aunt's pet canary

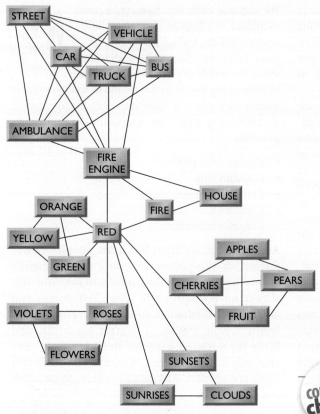

▲ **Figure 8.9** We link each concept to a variety of other related concepts. Any stimulus that activates one of these concepts will also partly activate (or prime) the ones that are linked to it. (From Collins & Loftus, 1975)

describes crime as a "virus," people become more likely to support social reforms, because a virus implies a need for a medical-type treatment. If someone describes crime as a "beast," people tend to favor stronger law enforcement, because a beast requires violent defense (Thibodeau, Hendricks, & Boroditsky, 2017).

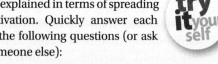

Here is an illustration that can be explained in terms of spreading activation. Quickly answer each of the following questions (or ask someone else):

1. How many animals of each kind did Moses take on the ark?
2. What was the famous saying uttered by Louis Armstrong when he first set foot on the moon?
3. Some people pronounce St. Louis "saint loo-iss" and some pronounce it "saint loo-ee." How would you pronounce the capital city of Kentucky?

You can check answer C at the end of this module, page 254. Why do so many people miss these questions? ▼ **Figure 8.10** offers an explanation in terms of spreading activation (Shafto & MacKay, 2000): The question about Louis Armstrong activates a series of sounds and concepts. The sound *Armstrong* and the ideas *first astronaut on the moon* and *famous sayings* are all linked to "One small step for a man . . ." The name *Louis Armstrong* is loosely linked to *Neil Armstrong* because both are famous people. The combined effect of all these influences automatically triggers the answer, "One small step for a man . . ."

An essential aspect of spreading activation is priming. The idea of priming a concept is analogous to priming a pump: If you put some water in the pump to get it started, you can continue using the pump to draw water from a well. Similarly, priming *a concept gets it started.* Reading or hearing one word makes it easier to think of or recognize a related word. Seeing something makes it easier to recognize a related object. If you are trying to find something, forming a mental image of it helps you notice it (Reinhart, McClenahan, & Woodman, 2015).

Priming occurs in many situations. For example, if you look at pictures and try to identify the people or objects in the foreground, you will find the task easier if the background primes the same answer as the object in the foreground (Davenport & Potter, 2004) (see ▼ **Figure 8.11**).

concept check

5 Why do you understand the word "racket" differently in a sentence about tennis and a sentence about noise?

Answer

5. A sentence about tennis and a sentence about noise activate different sets of meanings by spreading activation. You adopt the meaning of "racket" that fits the set that was activated.

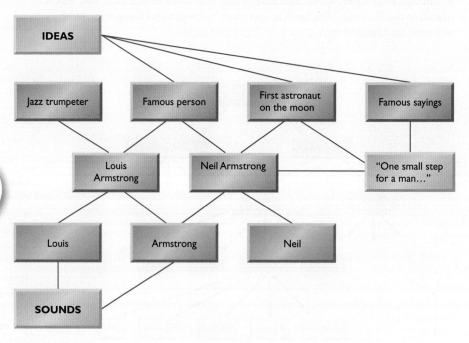

▲ **Figure 8.10** According to one explanation, the word *Armstrong* and the ideas *astronaut, first person on the moon,* and *famous sayings* all activate the linked saying "One small step for a man. . . ."

◄ **Figure 8.11** A bullfight setting primes recognition of a matador, and a library setting primes recognition of a librarian. When people are placed in the opposite settings, we take longer to identify them.

Pisaphotography/Shutterstock.com, Filipe B. Varela/Shutterstock.com

<table>
<tr><td>**in closing**</td><td>module 8.1</td></tr>
</table>

Thinking about Attention and Concepts

Behaviorists traditionally avoided the topic of cognition because thinking and knowledge are unobservable. Although this module has demonstrated the possibilities for research on cognition, you should also see that the behaviorists' objections were not frivolous. Research on cognition requires cautious inferences from masses of data. Nevertheless, the research is important, for practical as well as theoretical reasons. For example, the better we can understand "attention," the better we can help people with attention deficits.

Summary

- *Choice blindness.* People sometimes act as if they do not remember what choice they made. They "explain the choice they made" even when asked about the choice they did not make. (page 245)

- *Inferring cognitive processes.* Early experiments demonstrated how to use speed and accuracy to infer cognitive processes. (page 245)

- *Top-down and bottom-up processes.* Some stimuli grab our attention automatically. We also control our attention, deliberately shifting it from one item to another. (page 246)

- *Attentive and preattentive processes.* We quickly notice items that are unusual in certain ways, regardless of potential distracters. Noticing less distinct items requires attention to one target after another. (page 247)

- *Attention bottleneck.* Attention is limited, and items compete for it. (page 247)

- *Lapses of attention.* Mind wandering occurs faster when someone is engaged in a difficult task. (page 248)

- *The Stroop effect.* When we are speaking, written words grab attention, making it difficult to attend to the color of the letters. (page 248)

- *Change blindness.* We often fail to detect changes in a scene if they occur slowly or between one view and a slightly later one. (page 249)

- *Attention deficit disorder.* Attention deficit disorder or attention deficit hyperactivity disorder are heterogeneous conditions in which someone has trouble attending to assigned tasks or trouble shifting attention. (page 249)

- *Categorization.* We can specify a category by a definition or by prototypes. We tend to broaden a category if we find few examples of it. (page 250)

- *Conceptual networks and priming.* We represent words or concepts with links to related concepts. Thinking about a concept primes thinking about related concepts. (page 251)

Key Terms

attention (page 246)

attention deficit disorder (ADD) (page 249)

attention-deficit hyperactivity disorder (ADHD) (page 249)

attentive process (page 247)

bottom-up process (page 246)

change blindness (page 249)

choice blindness (page 245)

choice-delay task (page 250)

cognition (page 245)

preattentive process (page 247)

priming (page 252)

prototype (page 251)

spreading activation (page 251)

stop-signal task (page 250)

Stroop effect (page 249)

top-down process (page 246)

Answers to Other Questions in the Module

A. The objects in pair a are the same; in b they are the same; and in c they are different. (page 246)

B. In the top scene, one item on the green scoreboard has disappeared in the right side version. In the bottom scene, the position of mama bear has moved. (page 249)

C. 1. None. Noah had an ark, not Moses. 2. Neil Armstrong, not Louis Armstrong, set foot on the moon. 3. The correct pronunciation of Kentucky's capital is "frank-furt." (Not "loo-ee-ville"!) (page 252)

Review Questions

1. The phenomenon of choice blindness led to which of these conclusions?
   (a) People usually choose the option that seems to be the most popular.
   (b) After people have made a decision, they ignore evidence against it.
   (c) The reasons people give for their actions are often made up afterward.
   (d) People make most of their decisions at random.

2. Preattentive or bottom-up processes lead you to pay attention to what?
   (a) Objects in the periphery of a display
   (b) The prototypes of a concept
   (c) Inanimate objects
   (d) Anything that is unusual

3. When is mind-wandering most likely?
   (a) When someone is bored
   (b) At the start of a long, simple project
   (c) After some time on a demanding project
   (d) About every 15 minutes

4. What does the Stroop effect demonstrate?

   (a) Most of our decisions are based on unconscious motives.
   (b) Any unusual item captures attention automatically.
   (c) It is hard to suppress a habitual way of responding.
   (d) We fail to detect visual changes that occur slowly or during a change of scene.

5. Do stimulant drugs aid academic performance for people without ADHD?
   (a) Yes, about as much as they do for those with ADHD.
   (b) Yes, but only for mathematics and related fields.
   (c) Yes, but with a substantial probability of causing drug addiction.
   (d) Slightly at most. The apparent benefits are a placebo effect.

6. Priming a concept is responsible for which of the following?
   (a) Change blindness
   (b) The Stroop effect
   (c) The stop-signal task
   (d) Spreading activation

Answers: 1c, 2d, 3c, 4c, 5d, 6d.

module 8.2
Solving Problems and Making Decisions

After studying this module, you should be able to:

1. Distinguish between Type 1 and Type 2 processing.

2. Explain the advantages and disadvantages of maximizing and satisficing.

3. List common errors of thinking.

4. Discuss factors that lead to belief in conspiracy theories.

5. Discuss the bases for developing expertise, and what experts do that makes them experts.

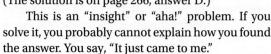

▼ **Figure 8.12** shows an object that was made by cutting and bending an ordinary piece of cardboard (Gardner, 1978). How was it made? Take a piece of paper and try to make it yourself. (The solution is on page 266, answer D.)

This is an "insight" or "aha!" problem. If you solve it, you probably cannot explain how you found the answer. You say, "It just came to me."

Here is another example of creative problem solving: A college physics exam asked how to use a barometer to determine the height of a building. One student answered that he would tie a long string to the barometer, go to the top of the building, and lower the barometer to the ground. Then he would cut the string and measure its length.

When the professor marked this answer incorrect, the student asked why. "Well," said the professor, "your method would work, but it's not the method I wanted you to use." When the student objected, the professor offered to let him try again.

"All right," the student said. "Take the barometer to the top of the building, drop it, and measure the time it takes to hit the ground. Then, from the formula for the speed of a falling object, using the gravitational constant, calculate the height of the building."

"Hmmm," replied the professor. "That too would work. And it does make use of physical principles. But it still isn't what I had in mind. Can you think of another way?"

"Another way? Sure," he replied. "Place the barometer next to the building on a sunny day. Measure the height of the barometer and the length of its shadow. Also measure the length of the building's shadow. Then use this formula:"

$$\frac{\text{height of barometer}}{\text{height of building}} = \frac{\text{length of barometer's shadow}}{\text{length of building's shadow}}$$

The professor was impressed but still reluctant to give credit, so the student persisted with another method: "Measure the barometer's height. Then walk up the stairs of the building, marking it off in units of the barometer's height. At the top, take the number of barometer units and multiply by the height of the barometer to get the height of the building."

The professor sighed: "Give me one more way—any other way—and I'll give you credit, even if it's not the answer I wanted."

"Really?" asked the student with a smile. "*Any* other way?"

"Yes, any other way."

"All right," said the student. "Go to the man who owns the building and say, 'Hey, buddy, if you tell me how tall the building is, I'll give you this great barometer!'"

Sometimes, people develop creative, imaginative solutions like the ones that the physics student proposed. At other times, they suggest creative ideas that couldn't possibly work. ▼ Figure 8.13 shows an example. Psychologists study problem-solving behavior and decision making partly to understand the thought processes and partly to look for ways to help people reason more effectively.

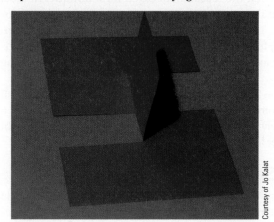

▲ **Figure 8.12** This object was made by cutting and folding an ordinary piece of cardboard with nothing left over. How was it done?

Courtesy of Jo Kalat

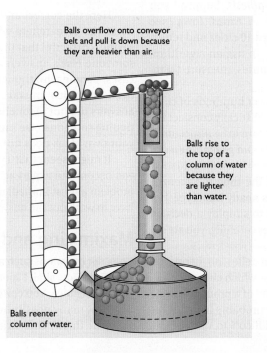

Balls overflow onto conveyor belt and pull it down because they are heavier than air.

Balls rise to the top of a column of water because they are lighter than water.

Balls reenter column of water.

◀ **Figure 8.13** An inventor applied for a patent on this "perpetual motion machine." Rubber balls, lighter than water, rise in a column of water and flow over the top. They are heavier than air, so they fall, moving a belt and generating energy. At the bottom, they reenter the water column. Why couldn't this system work? (Check answer E on page 266.)

Two Types of Thinking and Problem Solving

Daniel Kahneman (2011) described thinking in terms of two systems, System 1 and System 2. Many psychologists now prefer the terms Type 1 and Type 2. We use **Type 1 processing** *for tasks that are easy or that we think are easy.* We use **Type 2 processing** *for mathematical calculations and anything else that requires attention and effort.* As yet, psychologists have no consensus about the exact nature of the Type 1-Type 2 distinction (Bellini-Leite, 2018). Are we talking about different brain processes, or what? Nevertheless, the distinction is useful for descriptive purposes. Answer the following:

A bat and a ball together cost $1.10. The bat costs $1 more than the ball. What does the ball cost?

Type 1 processing suggests the intuitive answer that the ball costs $0.10, but that is wrong. If the ball costs $0.10 and the bat costs $1 more than the ball, the bat costs $1.10, and the total is $1.20. With a little effort, you can calculate that the ball must cost $0.05. But you might jump to a conclusion before realizing that you need Type 2 processing. If the question had been printed in small, blurry print, so that you had to exert some effort just to read it, you would be more likely to think about it and answer correctly (Alter, Oppenheimer, Epley, & Eyre, 2007). Yes, you actually do better if you have trouble reading the question! Anything that gets you to slow down and think about it improves performance on a tricky task like this one.

In many cases, Type 2 solves problems by an **algorithm**, *an explicit procedure for calculating an answer or testing every hypothesis.* Suppose you are a traveling salesperson in Ames, Iowa (see ▶ Figure 8.14). You want to visit 10 cities and return home by the shortest route. To use an algorithm, you would list all possible routes, measure them, and find the shortest.

However, if you had to visit hundreds of cities instead of 10, you could not realistically consider every possible route. You would turn to **heuristics**, *strategies for simplifying a problem and generating a satisfactory guess.* Heuristics provide quick guidance, and they work well most of the time (Gigerenzer, 2008). Not every decision fits neatly into Type 1 or Type 2. If you use heuristics to simplify a decision and then ponder a few choices carefully, you are using both types of thinking.

Type 1 processing often relies on heuristics. Examples: If you want to guess which child is oldest, choose the tallest. If one brand of a product is more expensive than another, it is probably better. If the instructions for a task are difficult to understand,

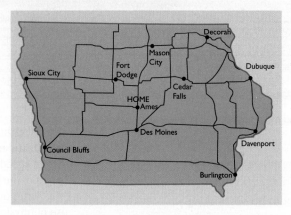

▲ **Figure 8.14** In the traveling salesperson task, you want to find the shortest route connecting all the points you need to visit.

the task is probably difficult but important (Labroo, Lambotte, & Zhang, 2009). However, we sometimes follow incorrect heuristics. For example, *if the instructions are written in an unfamiliar or unclear font,* people overestimate the difficulty of the task (Song & Schwarz, 2008). If you listen to a radio broadcast describing a scientific study, but the sound quality is poor, you might give the research a low rating (Newman & Schwarz, 2018).

Because Type 1 processing is easier, we tend to rely on it unless we see a need to override it. Here is an interesting study to illustrate that point: Participants answered a series of logic problems on which people sometimes give the wrong answer. For example,

A certain grocery sells apples that are not organic. What conclusion can we draw, if any?

A. The grocery has only organic products.

B. The grocery has only non-organic products.

C. The grocery has some organic products.

D. The grocery has some non-organic products.

E. We can draw no conclusion.

Here the correct answer is (D). After each person answered all the questions, the researchers waited and then handed back those answers, either saying (correctly) that these were the person's own answers, or that they were someone else's answers. Then the researchers asked for a critique. In most cases, people who thought they were critiquing someone else's answers noticed the logical mistakes. Those who knew they were looking at their own answers did not (Trouche, Johansson, Hall, & Mercier, 2016). The idea of critiquing someone else's ideas activates Type 2 processing, whereas reviewing your own ideas does not.

It might seem that Type 2 is better, but it is not always (Stanovich, 2018). If you become an expert at something, you can recognize the correct answer to a problem almost immediately (Type 1 processing), whereas someone else might have to work out the answer laboriously.

Maximizing and Satisficing

Consider questions such as, "Which college shall I attend?" or "Which job shall I take?" or "How shall I spend my money?" You cannot use an algorithm to evaluate every choice. You consider a few possibilities and try to evaluate them.

How many possibilities do you consider, and how thoroughly do you investigate them? One strategy, **maximizing**, is *thoroughly considering as many* choices as possible to find the best one. **Satisficing** is *searching only until you find something satisfactory.* If you have a choice with much at stake—for example, what is the safest design to build a nuclear power plant—you should consider each possibility as carefully as possible (maximizing). If your decision is less important, such as what to eat for lunch, you deliberate just briefly (satisficing). For intermediate cases, some people lean toward the maximizing strategy more often than others do. Researchers classify people as mainly maximizers or satisficers based on questions like the following (Schwartz et al., 2002). Rate yourself from 1 (not at all true) to 7 (definitely true):

- When I listen to the car radio, I frequently check other stations.
- I frequently channel-surf to find the best show.
- I shop at many stores before deciding which clothes to buy.
- I expect to interview for many jobs before I accept one.

The higher your score, the more you are a maximizer. Researchers find that high maximizers usually make better choices, according to objective criteria. They get jobs with higher starting pay than do satisficers, in spite of being about equal in their college grade point average. However, they have more difficulty making a choice (Paivandy, Bullock, Reardon, & Kelly, 2008), and they are usually *less* satisfied with their choices. Maximizers tend to believe that there is a "best" choice, and they are frustrated if they are not sure they found it (Shenhav & Buckner, 2014). Satisficers ordinarily doubt that any one choice is perfect, and they look for something "good enough." However, if you convince satisficers that there really is a best choice, they too spend more effort trying to find it (Luan & Li, 2017).

College students who are maximizers often brood about whether they chose the right major (Leach & Patall, 2013). Maximizers in romantic relationships tend to feel less satisfied with their partner and less committed to the relationship (Mikkelson & Pauley, 2013). However, being a maximizer has good features, too. Maximizers are more likely to consider the long-range consequences of their decisions. On average, they save more money and show more concern for future generations (Zhu, Dalal, & Hwang, 2017).

When you want to make a choice, how many options do you want to consider? Your local supermarket may offer 50 or more types of breakfast cereals and almost as many types of potato chips. As a rule, people make better choices if they consider no more than 20 possibilities, and people who face too many choices sometimes give up and choose nothing at all (Hadar & Sood, 2014; Schwartz, 2004; Shah & Wolford, 2007). In one study, researchers at a supermarket offered free samples of jams. If they offered 6 types of jam, 12 percent of people bought one. If they offered 24 types, more people stopped to sample them, but almost no one bought anything (Iyengar & Lepper, 2000). In another study, a bar varied the number of beers it listed on the menu. Customers were more likely to order a beer with six choices on the menu than with twelve choices, unless the menu included ratings to identify the best one (Malone & Lusk, 2017).

6. Why might dating be especially difficult for a maximizer in college?

Answer

6. It would be difficult to find the "best" person to date among the thousands of potential partners at a college.

The Representativeness Heuristic and Base-Rate Information

Although heuristic thinking is often helpful, it can lead us astray if we rely on it inappropriately. In 2002, Daniel Kahneman won the Nobel Prize in economics for his research showing examples of inappropriate use of heuristics. For example, consider the saying: "If something looks like a duck, waddles like a duck, and quacks like a duck, chances are it's a duck." This saying is an example of the **representativeness heuristic**, *the assumption that an item that resembles members of a category is probably also in that category.* This heuristic is usually correct, but not when we deal with uncommon categories. If you see something that looks, moves, and sounds like a rare bird, you should check carefully to make sure it isn't a similar, more common species. In general, to decide whether something belongs in one category or another, you should consider the **base-rate information**—that is, *how common the two categories are.*

When people apply the representativeness heuristic, they frequently overlook base-rate information. For example, consider the following question (modified from Kahneman & Tversky, 1973):

> Psychologists interviewed 30 engineers and 70 lawyers. One of them, Jack, is a 45-year-old married man with four children. He is generally conservative, cautious, and ambitious. He shows no interest in political and social issues and spends most of his free time on home carpentry, sailing, and solving mathematical puzzles. What is the probability that Jack is one of the 30 engineers in the sample of 100?

Most people estimate a rather high probability—perhaps 80 or 90 percent— because the description sounds more like engineers than lawyers. That estimate isn't wrong, as we cannot know the true probability. However, the key point is that if some people hear that the sample included 30 engineers and 70 lawyers, and others hear it included 70 engineers and 30 lawyers, both groups make about the same estimate for Jack (Kahneman & Tversky, 1973). Certainly, the base-rate information (the number of engineers in the sample) should have some influence.

Here is another example of misusing the representativeness heuristic:

> Linda was a philosophy major. She is 31, bright, outspoken, and concerned about issues of discrimination and social justice.

What would you estimate is the probability that Linda is a bank teller? What is the probability that she is a feminist bank teller? (Answer before you read on.)

The Availability Heuristic

When you estimate how common something is, you usually start by thinking of examples. If you remember more rainy days in your college town than in your home town, you assume your college town gets more rain. If you remember many summer days when mosquitoes bit you and no winter days when they bit you, you conclude that mosquitoes are more common in summer. The **availability heuristic** is *the tendency to assume that if we easily think of examples of a category, then that category must be common.* This heuristic leads us astray when uncommon events are highly memorable. You might remember the times when a hunch or dream seemed to predict a future event, and forget the times it did not, thereby incorrectly attributing value to your hunches or dreams.

Another example: How would you feel if your favorite team wins its next game? How would you feel if you missed your bus? Most people overestimate how good they would feel after good events and how bad they would feel after bad events. One reason is that you try to remember how you felt after similar experiences in the past, and memories of your most extreme experiences are easily available (Gilbert & Wilson, 2009). Because they are easily available, you assume they are typical.

Also, consider the widespread belief that "you should stick with your first impulse on a multiple-choice test." Researchers have consistently found this claim to be wrong (Johnston, 1975; Kruger, Wirtz, & Miller, 2005; Pagni et al., 2017). Changing an answer can help for several reasons. When you reread a question, you might discover that you misread it the first time. Sometimes, a question later in the test reminds you of the correct answer to an earlier item. Here is a reason why students believe that their first impulse is correct: When you get your test back, which questions do you check? You check the ones you got wrong. Therefore, you notice anything you changed from right to wrong. However, you overlook the ones you changed from wrong to right. Your availability heuristic leads you to believe that changing an answer hurts you. ■ **Table 8.1** summarizes the representativeness and availability heuristics.

In 2002, Princeton psychologist Daniel Kahneman won the Nobel Prize in economics. Although others have won Nobel Prizes for research related to psychology, Kahneman was the first winner who had a PhD in psychology.

Jonas Ekstromer/AFP/Getty Images

The true probabilities are not the point. The interesting result is that many people estimate a higher probability that Linda is a *feminist* bank teller than that she is a bank teller (Tversky & Kahneman, 1983). She couldn't be a feminist bank teller without being a bank teller. Apparently, the word "feminist" triggers people's representativeness heuristic to say, "Yes, that would fit" (Shafir, Smith, & Osherson, 1990).

concept check

7. **You assume that the driver who just honked and passed you is a hostile person. Is this an example of the representativeness heuristic or the availability heuristic?**

8. **Because certain types of crime receive much publicity, you overestimate how common they are. Is this an example of the representativeness heuristic or the availability heuristic?**

Answers

7. It is an example of the representativeness heuristic.
8. It is an example of the availability heuristic.

Table 8.1 The Representativeness Heuristic and the Availability Heuristic			
	A Tendency to Assume That	Leads Us Astray When	Example of Error
Representativeness Heuristic	An item that resembles members of a category probably belongs to that category.	Something resembles members of a rare category.	Something looks like it might be a UFO, so you decide it is.
Availability Heuristic	The more easily we can think of members of a category, the more common the category is.	One category gets more publicity than another or is more memorable.	You remember more reports of airplane crashes than car crashes, so you think air travel is more dangerous.

Additional Cognitive Errors

For decades, college professors have emphasized critical thinking, *the careful evaluation of evidence for and against any conclusion*. However, even professors (and textbook authors) who teach critical thinking sometimes find themselves making silly errors. Here are a few examples.

Overconfidence

How long is the Nile River? You probably don't know, but guess an approximate range, such as "between X and Y" in miles or kilometers. Then state your confidence in your answer. Do not say "0 percent," because that would mean that you *know* your answer is wrong. Widen the range until you are fairly sure of being right. Second question: In which country did people first cultivate potatoes? Answer, and state your percent confidence.

On difficult questions like this, most people are overconfident of their answers. When they say they are 90 percent confident, they are far less than 90 percent correct (Plous, 1993). On easy questions, the trend reverses, and people tend to be underconfident (Erev, Wallsten, & Budescu, 1994; Juslin, Winman, & Olsson, 2000). (Incidentally, the Nile River is 4,187 miles long, or 6,738 kilometers. And potatoes were first cultivated in Peru.) People also tend to be overconfident of their own opinions. Not only do they believe that most people agree with them now, but they also believe that an even higher percent will agree with them in the future (Rogers, Moore, & Norton, 2017). (After all, why not, if the opinion is right?)

Given almost any topic, most people overestimate how well they understand it, and given almost any task, most people overestimate how well they can do it, especially if they have watched someone else do it (Kardas & O'Brien, 2018). A survey of people who said they were "highly knowledgeable" in the field of personal finance found that more than 90 percent of them claimed to understand pre-rated stocks, fixed rate deduction, and annualized credit. Interesting, because none of those terms mean anything (Atir, Rosenzweig, & Dunning, 2015).

Overconfidence is sometimes helpful (Johnson & Fowler, 2011). Highly confident people tend to get good job offers and promotions. Highly confident politicians win elections. If you act certain of winning a fight, a stronger opponent may back down. However, overconfidence can be harmful, too. If the stronger opponent doesn't back down, you could get hurt. Overconfident leaders often blunder into costly mistakes, and overconfident investors lose money (Critcher & Rosenzweig, 2014). Most students believe that they study more than average, and become overconfident of success (Buzinski, Clark, Cohen, Buck, & Roberts, 2018).

Philip Tetlock (1992) studied government officials and consultants, foreign policy professors, newspaper columnists, and others who make their living by analyzing and predicting world events. He asked them to predict world events over the next 1 to 10 years. Later, he compared predictions to actual results and found very low accuracy, especially among those who were the most confident. Later research did, however, identify a small number of "superforecasters" who made reasonably accurate predictions. These people were characterized as open-minded, well-informed, well-read, apt to discuss issues with others, and always ready to revise their opinions based on new evidence (Mellers et al., 2015).

Confirmation Bias

We often err by *accepting a hypothesis and then looking for evidence to support it instead of considering other possibilities*. This tendency, the confirmation bias, occurs in all walks of life. People converse mostly with others who agree with them about politics, religion, and other controversial topics.

Once we have made a decision, we look for reasons to stick with it. Peter Wason (1960) asked students to discover a certain rule he had in mind for generating sequences of numbers. One example of the numbers the rule might generate, he explained, was "2, 4, 6." He told the students that they could ask about other sequences, and he would tell them whether or not those sequences fit his rule. They should tell him as soon as they thought they knew the rule.

Most students started by asking, "8, 10, 12?" When told "yes," they proceeded with "14, 16, 18?" Each time, they were told, "Yes, that sequence fits the rule." Soon they guessed, "The rule is three consecutive even numbers." "No," came the reply. "That is not the rule." Many students persisted, trying "20, 22, 24?" "26, 28, 30?" "250, 252, 254?" They continued testing sequences that fit their rule, ignoring other possibilities. The rule Wason had in mind was, "Any three positive numbers of increasing magnitude." For instance, 1, 2, 3 would be acceptable, and so would 21, 25, 601.

Confirmation bias is a threat to good science. Most scientists conduct one study after another to try to confirm the hypothesis they favor. Good science requires experiments that have a chance of supporting a rival hypothesis.

A special case of confirmation bias is functional fixedness, *the tendency to adhere to a single approach or a single way of using an item*. Here are three examples:

1. You are provided with a candle, a box of matches, some thumbtacks, and a tiny piece of string, as shown in ◀ Figure 8.15. Using no other equipment, find a way to mount the candle to the wall so that it can be lit.

2. Consider an array of nine dots:

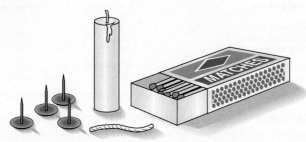

▲ **Figure 8.15** Given only these materials, what is the best way to attach the candle to a wall so that it can be lit?

Connect all nine dots with a series of connected straight lines, such that the end of one line is the start of the next. For example, one way would be: But use the fewest lines possible.

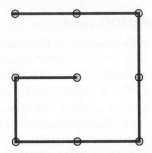

3. There are some students in a room. All but two of them are psychology majors, all but two are chemistry majors, and all but two are history majors. How many students are present? (If your System 1 blurts out, "two of each," try out your answer: It doesn't work.) Now here's the interesting part: There are two possible solutions. After you have found one solution, discard it and find another.

After you have either found solutions or given up, check answer F on page 266. (Solve these problems before reading further.)

Question 1 was difficult because most people think of the matchbox as a container for matches, not as a tool on its own. The box is "functionally fixed" for one way of using it. Question 2 was difficult because most people assume that the lines must remain within the area defined by the nine dots. On question 3, it is difficult to think of even one solution, and after thinking of it, it is hard to abandon it to think of another one.

Framing Questions

A logical person should give the same answer no matter how a question is worded, right? People often change their answers after a question is reworded. *The tendency to answer a question differently when it is worded differently* is called the **framing effect**.

An example: A company that provides health insurance will charge higher rates to overweight people. If they describe the difference as "a discount for lower weight," people like it better than if they call it "a penalty for higher weight" (Tannenbaum, Valasek, Knowles, & Ditto, 2013).

Another example: You are debating between two cars—let's call them B and C. Car B is better but more expensive. While you are pondering, the salesperson also suggests car A, which is even more luxurious and more expensive than B. You won't pick A, but now you are more likely to choose B, which seems like a compromise. If, instead of car A,

someone had suggested car D, which is cheap but of low quality, you would probably choose car C, because it seems like a compromise (Trueblood, Brown, Heathcote, & Busemeyer, 2013).

Another example of the framing effect: You have been appointed head of the Public Health Service, and you need to choose a plan to deal with a disease that endangers the lives of 600 people. Plan A will save the lives of 200 people. Plan B has a 33 percent chance to save all 600 and a 67 percent chance to save no one. *Choose plan A or B before reading further.*

Now another disease breaks out, and you must choose between plans C and D. If you adopt plan C, 400 people will die. If you adopt plan D, there is a 33 percent chance that no one will die and a 67 percent chance that 600 will die. *Choose plan C or D now.*

▼ Figure 8.16 shows the results for people who were given these choices. Most chose A over B and D over C. However, plan A is exactly the same as C (200 live, 400 die), and plan B is exactly the same as D. Why then did so many people choose both A and D? Most people are willing to take a risk to avoid loss (e.g., not letting people die), because any loss will feel bad (Tversky and Kahneman, 1981). Even a small loss will feel almost as bad as a big loss. But we risk less to gain something (e.g., saving more lives), because we know that even a small gain will feel good. The framing effect is larger when people have to decide quickly (Guo, Trueblood, & Diederich, 2017). Quick decisions, of course, relate to Type 1 processing.

For many decisions, people try to minimize the possibility of regret (Erev, Ert, Plonsky, Cohen, & Cohen, 2017). Suppose you can choose between $50 for sure and flipping a coin to determine whether you get $100 or nothing. If you flip the coin and lose, you will feel regret. If you take the $50, you do not flip the coin, and so you do not feel regret about the $100 you might have won (Gigerenzer & Garcia-Retamero, 2017). For a similar reason, you might not quit a safe job to take

Plan	How question was framed	Plan preferred by	Outcome
A	Save 200 people	72%	
C	400 people will die	22%	200 live, 400 die
B	33% chance of saving all 600; 67% chance of saving no one	28%	
D	33% chance no one will die; 67% chance all 600 will die	78%	33% chance 600 live or 67% chance 600 die

▲ **Figure 8.16** Most people chose plan A over B and D over C, although A produces the same result as C and B produces the same result as D. Amos Tversky and Daniel Kahneman (1981) proposed that most people play it safe to gain something but accept a risk to avoid a loss.

a less secure job that has a better chance for promotion. The situation is different when you are considering experiences instead of money. If you could choose either a safe, unexciting vacation or an exciting vacation that has some chance of being lost to bad weather, you might opt for the latter, because you know you would regret missing the better experience (Martin, Reimann, & Norton, 2016).

The Sunk Cost Effect

The sunk cost effect is a special case of the framing effect. Suppose that some time ago you bought an expensive ticket for today's football game, but the weather is cold and rainy. You wish you hadn't bought the ticket. Do you go to the game?

If you attend the game anyway because you don't want to waste the money, your action illustrates the sunk cost effect, *the willingness to do something undesirable because of money or effort already spent.* Even if someone else bought the tickets and gave them to you, you might go to the game so that the other person did not waste the money (Olivola, 2018). The sunk cost effect arises in many situations. A company or government continues investing money in an unsuccessful project because it doesn't want to admit that the money already spent was wasted. A professional sports team is disappointed with a high-salaried player's performance but keeps using that player to avoid wasting the money.

9. Someone says, "More than 90 percent of all college students like to watch late-night television, but only 20 percent of adults over 50 do. Therefore, most watchers of late-night television are college students." What error in thinking has this person made?

10. An advertiser says, "Just send $10 now, and you guarantee that you can buy our product at its current price, instead of the higher price that we might charge later." Why is this offer likely to be persuasive?

Answers

10. First, people will take a risk to avoid a loss—in this case, the loss associated with a possibly higher price later. Second, after you have committed yourself by sending $10, you are likely to buy the product, because otherwise you would have wasted $10. Remember the sunk-cost effect.

9. Failure to consider the base rate: 20 percent of all older adults is a larger number than 90 percent of all college students. This is an example of inappropriately using the representativeness heuristic.

Conspiracy Thinking

Some people believe, or at least say they believe, some very strange things: Pharmaceutical companies are hiding a cure for cancer so they can increase their profits. They also invented AIDS to increase their profits. NASA has a slave colony on Mars. Climate scientists are advancing a hoax for their own benefit. Reports of mass school shootings are a lie invented to outlaw gun ownership. The United States never really sent people to the moon, but instead faked the landing in a movie studio. The terrorist attacks of September 11, 2001, were planned by the U.S. government as a pretext to attack Iraq. And more.

Many people who believe in one conspiracy theory also believe in others, perhaps all of them, and sometimes even contradictory theories. For example, news sources reported that British Princess Diana died in an automobile accident in 1997. Of people who reject that report, some believe that she was murdered by an order from the British government, some believe she faked her own death and is still alive, and some report believing both! In 2011 news agencies reported that a U.S. raid had killed terrorist leader Osama bin Laden. Some who doubt that report insist that bin Laden had already been dead for years, some believe he is still alive, and (again) some endorse both of those ideas (Wood, Douglas, & Sutton, 2012). The unifying thread is that people who want to reject the "official" story will apparently accept almost anything that contradicts it.

Researchers have tried to characterize the type of people prone to conspiracy beliefs. They tend to be less educated, high in anxiety, and low in self-esteem. They also tend to be gullible. Psychologists asked people to evaluate a series of "B.S." statements that sound impressive but really mean nothing, such as "Wholeness quiets infinite phenomena," and "Hidden meaning transforms unparalleled abstract beauty." People prone to conspiracy beliefs were more likely than average to rate these sentences as "profound" (Pennycook, Cheyne, Barr, Koehler, & Fugelsang, 2005).

Conspiracy beliefs are especially likely to arise when people feel a loss of control, or a sense that everything they value is threatened. After all, if everything that is good is under attack, then evil forces must be at work. Under those conditions, people distrust the government and the established news sources, turn to any source that contradicts them, and increase their loyalty to their in-group (Federico, Williams, & Vitriol, 2018; van Prooijen, Staman, & Krouwel, 2018). In support of this interpretation, researchers asked one group of people (randomly assigned) to recall times when they felt in control, and asked another group to recall times when they felt they had no control. Then they posed questions about a possible conspiracy. People who

Contradicting a conspiracy belief is usually ineffective. Someone who believes in the conspiracy can simply decide that you are part of the conspiracy.

GARFIELD ©2019 Paws, Inc. Reprinted with permission of Andrews McMeel Syndication. All rights reserved.

were primed to feel lack of control were more likely to think that government officials had made decisions based on bribes (van Prooijen & Acker, 2015).

Conspiracy beliefs spread faster now than in the past because of the Internet and talk-show hosts. People are more likely to believe something if they hear it repeatedly (Unkelbach, Koch, Silva, & Garcia-Marques, 2019), and many people attend to sources that all express a similar viewpoint.

concept check

11. On average, would conspiracy beliefs be more likely for supporters of the political party in power, or for its opponents? Why?

Answer

11. Ordinarily, conspiracy beliefs should be more likely for supporters of the party out of power, because they feel a lack of control. An exception can arise if someone who supports conspiracy beliefs is elected.

Expertise

Many people develop expertise that enables them to solve problems quickly with a minimum of error. Reaching that point requires much effort.

Practice, Practice, Practice, but Have Some Talent, Too

Expert performance is impressive. Some people complete the most difficult crossword puzzles rapidly. Some physicians look at an X-ray and immediately notice a dot that indicates an illness. Someone might see a bird for a split second and identify its species, sex, and age. Are experts born, made, or some of each?

In fields ranging as diverse as chess, sports, and violin playing, expertise requires years of intense practice with feedback (Ericsson & Charness, 1994; Ericsson, Krampe, & Tesch-Römer, 1993). The top violin players practice three to four hours every day beginning in early childhood. World-class athletes spend hours at a time perfecting their skills. Whereas most average players like to practice the skills they do best, the best players practice to overcome their weaknesses. They also tend to alternate between practicing one skill and another (Coughlan, Williams, McRobert, & Ford, 2014). Varying your study within a session makes it more effective.

Hungarian author Laszlo Polgar set out to demonstrate that almost anyone can achieve expertise with sufficient effort. He devoted enormous efforts to nurturing his three daughters' chess skills. All three became outstanding, and one, Judit, became the first woman and at that time the youngest person ever to reach grand master status.

Based on these results, it became popular to say that expertise depends on 10,000 hours of practice. However, a few thousand hours starting in childhood count for more than the same number of hours in adulthood (Gobet & Campitelli, 2007). Also, the 10,000-hour rule overlooks individual differences (Campitelli & Gobet, 2011; Macnamara, Hambrick, & Oswald, 2014). Two people who practice a skill for the same number of hours are not necessarily equal at the end (Macnamara, Moreau, & Hambrick, 2016). Some chess players reach master level after barely 3,000 hours of practice, whereas others accumulate more than 25,000 hours without reaching master level (Gobet & Campitelli, 2007).

People who start off doing well at something are more likely than others to develop an interest and therefore devote the needed hours to improving their skill. Consider music: Many studies have found that highly practiced musicians are better than average at discriminating pitches, melodies, and rhythms (that is, detecting the difference between one and another). It seems natural to assume that their practice improved their recognition of sounds. However, the alternative is that people with better hearing were more likely than average to develop an interest in music. Miriam Mosing and colleagues compared thousands of pairs of adult twins. They found that even in cases where one twin had practiced a musical instrument extensively and the other one hardly at all, the twins were about equally good at discriminating pitches, melodies, and rhythms (Mosing, Madison, Pederson, Kuja-Halkola, & Ullén, 2014). That is, practice does not measurably improve hearing. Most good musicians hear well because people who hear well are more likely than average to become musicians.

For practice to be effective, people need feedback based on the practice (Kahneman & Klein, 2009). Athletes see at once how successful their performance was. Computer programmers get excellent feedback: If they program something correctly, it works. If they make a mistake, the computer crashes or does something it wasn't supposed to do. Weather forecasters also get good, quick feedback. People who get good feedback have a chance to improve with practice.

In contrast, consider psychotherapists. Some patients respond well to almost any treatment, and some respond poorly to almost any treatment. Consequently, a therapist gets uncertain feedback about whether some treatment is working well or not. On average, therapists show little improvement after years of experience (Tracey, Wampold, Lichtenberg, & Goodyear, 2014).

Rick Maiman/Sygma/Getty Images

Judit Polgar confirmed her father's confidence that prolonged effort could make her a grand master chess player.

12. Would you expect politicians to improve with practice? Why or why not?

Answer

12. Politicians do improve at their ability to win elections, because they get good feedback. However, experience in office doesn't greatly improve their ability to make good decisions on public policy, because they get poor feedback. When the government enacts a policy, we seldom know how much better or worse things might have been under some other policy.

Expert Pattern Recognition

What do experts do that sets them apart from others? Primarily, they can look at a pattern and recognize its important features quickly. In a typical experiment (de Groot, 1966), chess experts and novices briefly examined pieces on a chessboard, as in ▼ Figure 8.17, and tried to recall the positions. When the pieces were arranged as might occur in a normal game, expert players recalled 91 percent of the positions correctly, whereas novices recalled only 41 percent. When the pieces were arranged randomly, experts and novices were about equal at recalling the positions. That is, experts do not have a superior memory, but they have learned to recognize common chessboard patterns.

Another example comes from basketball. Imagine you watch a video clip of someone shooting a free throw, but the clip is interrupted before the ball reaches the net. How much would you have to see before you could guess whether the ball will go through the hoop? Most people aren't sure until the ball is well on the way to the basket. Professional basketball players usually know the answer before the ball leaves the shooter's hands (Aglioti, Cesari, Romani, & Urgesi, 2008; ▼ Figure 8.18). In areas from bird identification to reading X-rays to judging gymnastic competitions, experts recognize important patterns almost immediately (Murphy & Medin, 1985; Ste-Marie, 1999; Tanaka, Curran, & Sheinberg, 2005).

13. How does expertise relate to the concept of "chunking" in memory?

Answer

13. People can store more memory quickly if they group items into large chunks. Someone who has developed expertise recognizes more chunks and larger chunks than other people do.

Near Transfer and Far Transfer

Does practicing one skill help you with anything else? Educators have long assumed that it does. Long ago, college education in Europe and the United States focused on studying Latin and Greek, based on the assumption that learning them would add mental discipline that helps in other aspects of life. The premedical curriculum used to require calculus, and it still recommends it. How often do you suppose medical doctors use calculus? About as often as they use astronomy. The intention is to provide "mental exercise" that might help with other tasks. Many people recommend that old people do crossword puzzles to exercise their brains. The research finds that when older adults work crossword puzzles, they get better at crossword puzzles, but they don't get better at remembering where they left their keys (Salthouse, 2006).

Psychologists distinguish between near transfer and far transfer (Barnett & Ceci, 2002). **Near transfer**, *benefit to a skill from practicing a similar skill*, is a robust phenomenon, easy to demonstrate. For example, suppose you learn to solve problems like this in a physics course: A train going 25 meters per second (m/s) increases its velocity by 2 m/s each second. How fast will it be going 10 seconds from now? To solve, you multiply 2 m/s times 10 seconds (yielding an increase of 20 m/s) and add it to the original 25 m/s, for an answer of 45 m/s. If you now face new problems about cars that increase their velocity by a certain amount per second, you should solve them easily. That is near transfer.

In contrast, **far transfer**, *benefit from practicing something unrelated*, is at best a weak effect. Some studies have reported increases in overall memory or intelligence from practicing music, practicing chess, or playing action video games. However, the most positive results came from the weakest studies, using few participants or unsatisfactory control groups (Sala & Gobet, 2017; Sala, Tatlidil, & Gobet, 2018). Another problem is that studies that find a

(a)

(b)

◀ **Figure 8.17**
Master chess players quickly recognize and memorize chess pieces arranged as they might occur in a normal game **(a)**. However, they are no better than average at memorizing a random pattern **(b)**.

Most viewers can tell whether the ball will go in (above) or not (below) at about this point.

Professional players can tell whether the ball will go in or not at about this point.

▲ **Figure 8.18** Professional basketball players recognize whether or not the ball will go into the basket before the ball leaves the shooter's hands. The rest of us need longer.

benefit are more likely to be published than are the studies that do not find a benefit (Bediou et al., 2018). Several companies have marketed computer programs designed to train decision making or working memory. When people were randomly assigned to use these programs or to a control procedure, the people in the experimental groups showed gains in the trained tasks, but no consistent benefit for anything else (Kable et al., 2017; Melby-Lervåg, Redick, & Hulme, 2016).

Results have been mixed about whether bilingualism correlates with better overall cognitive performance. The hypothesis was that practice in shifting languages might improve attention and therefore produce far transfer to many other cognitive skills. Some studies showed significant benefits, but others did not, and again we have to worry that studies showing no effect are less likely

to be published (Bialystok, Craik, & Luk, 2008; de Bruin, Treccani, & Della Salla, 2015; Lehtonen et al., 2018). A possible explanation for the discrepant results is that many of the studies showing a benefit from bilingualism included families immigrating from Japan, Korea, or China—cultures that tend to do well academically for reasons other than bilingualism (Samuel, Roehr-Brackin, Pak, & Kim, 2018). Overall, the conclusion remains that far transfer is at best a weak effect.

concept check

14. Is exercising your brain similar to exercising a muscle?

Answer

14. No. Exercising a muscle builds strength that helps with anything that muscle can do. Practicing a brain task, even a difficult task, provides little if any benefit on unrelated tasks.

Successful and Unsuccessful Problem Solving

In this module, we have considered thinking at its best and worst—expertise and error. We all have to make decisions about topics in which we are not experts. We should at least hold ourselves to the standard of not doing anything foolish. Perhaps if we become more aware of common errors, we can be more alert to avoid them.

Summary

- *Two types of thinking.* We often make decisions quickly and automatically, using Type 1 processing. When we recognize a problem as being more difficult, we use more effortful Type 2 processing. (page 256)
- *Algorithms and heuristics.* Algorithms are ways of checking every possibility. Heuristics are ways of simplifying a problem. (page 256)
- *Maximizing and satisficing.* The maximizing strategy is to consider thoroughly every option to find the best one. The satisficing strategy is to accept a choice that seems good enough. People using the maximizing strategy usually make good choices but often second-guess themselves. (page 256)
- *Representativeness heuristic.* If something resembles members of some category, we usually assume it too belongs to that category. That assumption is risky if the category is a rare one. (page 257)
- *Availability heuristic.* Ordinarily we assume that the more easily we can think of examples of a category, the more common that category is. This heuristic misleads us if a rare event gets much publicity. (page 258)
- *Other errors.* People tend to be overconfident about their judgments on difficult questions. They tend to look for evidence that confirms their hypothesis instead of evidence that might reject it. They overlook new ways to use a familiar object. They answer the same question differently when it is framed differently. They sometimes take unpleasant actions to avoid admitting that previous actions were a waste of time or money. (page 259)
- *Conspiracy thinking.* Some people are prone to believe conspiracy theories, even contradictory ones. They tend to be less educated, more anxious, and more gullible than average. A major contributor to conspiracy thinking is a feeling of having one's values threatened and lacking control. (page 261)
- *Expertise.* Becoming an expert requires years of practice and effort, but a given amount of practice benefits some people more than others. Experts recognize and memorize familiar and meaningful patterns more rapidly than less experienced people do. (page 262)
- *Near and far transfer.* Developing skill at a task aids performance of a similar task. It seldom aids performance of a dissimilar task. (page 263)

Key Terms

algorithm (page 256)

availability heuristic (page 258)

base-rate information (page 257)

confirmation bias (page 259)

critical thinking (page 259)

far transfer (page 263)

framing effect (page 260)

functional fixedness (page 259)

heuristics (page 256)

maximizing (page 256)

near transfer (page 263)

representativeness heuristic (page 257)

satisficing (page 257)

sunk cost effect (page 261)

Type 1 processing (page 256)

Type 2 processing (page 256)

Answers to Other Questions in the Module

D. This illustration shows how to cut and fold an ordinary piece of paper or cardboard to match the figure with nothing left over. (page 255)

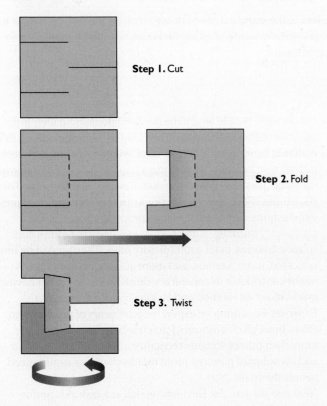

Step 1. Cut

Step 2. Fold

Step 3. Twist

E. A membrane heavy enough to keep the water in would also keep the rubber balls out. (page 255)

F. (1) The best way to attach the candle to the wall is to dump the matches from the box and thumbtack the side of the box to the wall, as shown in this picture. The tiny piece of string is irrelevant.

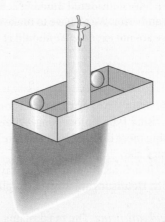

(2) The dots can be connected with four lines:

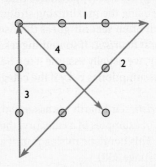

(3) One answer is three students: one psychology major, one chemistry major, and one history major. The other possibility is two students who are majoring in something else—music, for example. (If there are two music majors, all but two of them are indeed majoring in psychology, etc.) (page 260)

Review Questions

1. Which of the following is a likely result from developing expertise in a field?
   (a) Heavy reliance on the confirmation bias
   (b) Using both algorithms and heuristics for every type of problem
   (c) Frequently recognizing the correct answer by Type 1 processing
   (d) Carefully considering each answer by Type 2 processing

2. When is it best to use a heuristic instead of an algorithm?
   (a) When considering every possible choice would take too long
   (b) When it is important to find the best possible answer
   (c) When dealing with an unusual problem
   (d) When you feel discouraged and powerless

3. "Buyer's regret"—doubting that you made the right decision—is most likely under what circumstance?
   (a) Decisions based on heuristics
   (b) Decisions based on algorithms
   (c) Decisions made by maximizers
   (d) Decisions made by satisficers

4. What is meant by "base rate" information?
   (a) The frequency of some event under normal circumstances
   (b) The ease of thinking of examples of some event
   (c) The difference between results of heuristics and algorithms
   (d) The number of choices available in a certain situation

5. If you expect that violent behavior is more likely on nights of a full moon, and therefore you look for cases that fit, and remember those cases more than cases that don't fit, your behavior illustrates which two of the tendencies discussed in this chapter?
   (a) Confirmation bias and the availability heuristic
   (b) Confirmation bias and the representativeness heuristic
   (c) The framing effect and functional fixedness
   (d) The framing effect and the sunk cost effect

6. When are people most likely to show overconfidence?
   (a) When answering the most difficult questions
   (b) When answering the easiest questions
   (c) When they are aware of the base-rate information
   (d) When they use an algorithm to choose their answer

7. People will buy meat that claims "90 percent fat free," but not one that says "contains 10 percent fat." This observation is an example of which of the following?
   (a) Overconfidence
   (b) Framing effect
   (c) Sunk cost effect
   (d) Inappropriate use of the availability heuristic

8. When are people most likely to believe in conspiracy theories?
   (a) When they experience a change in status, such as a promotion
   (b) When they feel isolated from like-minded people
   (c) When their cherished values seem to be threatened
   (d) When they feel more confident than usual

9. Which of the following is essential for developing expertise?
   (a) Prolonged practice with feedback
   (b) Practicing working memory on tasks unrelated to the field of expertise
   (c) Intensive practice beginning in adulthood
   (d) Imagining yourself as a success

10. As people develop expertise in a skill such as chess, what improves?
    (a) Ability to recognize common patterns
    (b) The ratio of excitatory to inhibitory transmission
    (c) The accuracy of vision, hearing, and other senses
    (d) Overall memory and intelligence

11. What are the effects of working daily crossword puzzles?
    (a) Increases in overall intelligence
    (b) Improvement in working memory
    (c) Faster neural transmission in the cerebral cortex
    (d) Improvement on crossword puzzles, but not much else

Answers: 1c, 2a, 3c, 4a, 5a, 6a, 7b, 8c, 9a, 10a, 11d.

After studying this module, you should be able to:

1. Discuss attempts to teach language to chimpanzees.

2. Evaluate explanations for how humans are specialized to learn language.

3. Distinguish between types of language impairment after brain damage.

4. Describe how children develop language.

5. Explain the role of eye movements in reading.

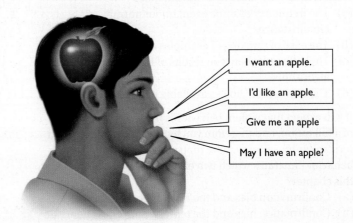

▲ **Figure 8.19** According to transformational grammar, we transform a given deep structure into any of several sentences with different surface structures.

Every species of animal has ways of communicating, but only human language has the property of **productivity**, *the ability to combine words into new sentences that express an unlimited variety of ideas* (Deacon, 1997). People constantly invent new sentences that no one has ever said before.

You might ask, "How do you know that no one has ever said that sentence before?" Well, of course, no one can be certain that a particular sentence is new, but we can be confident that many sentences are new, because of the vast number of ways to rearrange words. Imagine this exercise (but don't really try it unless you have nothing else to do with your life): Pick a sentence of more than 10 words from any book. How long would you need to keep reading, in that book or any other, until you found the exact same sentence again?

In short, we do not memorize all the sentences we use. We learn rules for making and understanding sentences. The famous linguist Noam Chomsky (1980) described those rules as a **transformational grammar**, *a system for converting a deep structure into a surface structure*. The deep structure is the underlying logic or meaning of a sentence. The surface structure is the sequence of words as they are actually spoken or written (see ▲ **Figure 8.19**). According to this theory, whenever we speak, we transform the deep structure of the language into a surface structure.

Two surface structures can resemble each other without representing the same deep structure, or they can represent the same deep structure without resembling each other. For example, "John is easy to please" has the same deep structure as "Pleasing John is easy" and "It is easy to please John." These sentences represent the same idea. In contrast, consider the sentence "Never threaten someone with a chain saw." The surface structure of that sentence maps into two deep structures, as shown in ▶ **Figure 8.20**.

Nonhuman Precursors to Language

Researcher Terrence Deacon once presented a talk about language to his 8-year-old's elementary school class. A child asked whether other animals have their own languages. Deacon explained that other species communicate but without anything like human language. The child persisted, asking whether other animals had at least a simple language with a few words and short sentences. No, he replied, they don't.

Then another child asked, "Why not?" (Deacon, 1997, p. 12). Deacon paused. Why not, indeed? If language is so useful to humans, why haven't other species evolved at least a little of it? And what makes humans so good at learning language?

Deep Structure No. 1:
You are holding a chain saw. Don't threaten to use it to attack someone!

Deep Structure No. 2:
Some deranged person is holding a chain saw. Don't threaten him!

▲ **Figure 8.20** The sentence "Never threaten someone with a chain saw" has one surface structure but two deep structures, corresponding to different meanings.

One way to examine humans' language specialization is to ask how far other species could progress toward language. Beginning in the 1920s, several psychologists reared chimpanzees in their homes and unsuccessfully tried to teach them to talk. In nature, chimpanzees communicate more by hand gestures than by sounds. R. Allen Gardner and Beatrice Gardner (1969) taught a chimpanzee named Washoe to use the sign language of the American deaf (Ameslan). Washoe eventually learned the symbols for about 100 words, and other chimps learned to communicate with other visual symbols (see ▼ Figure 8.21).

How much do these gestures resemble language? Washoe showed moderate understanding. She usually answered "Who" questions with names, "What" questions with objects, and "Where" questions with places, even when she specified the wrong name, object, or place (Van Cantfort, Gardner, & Gardner, 1989). However, she and other chimpanzees used gestures almost exclusively to make requests, not to describe, and rarely in original combinations (Pate & Rumbaugh, 1983; Terrace, Petitto, Sanders, & Bever, 1979; Thompson & Church, 1980). By contrast, a human child with a vocabulary of 100 words or so links them into short sentences and frequently uses words to describe. Furthermore, chimps seem not to understand gestures the same way children do. If you point at something, a child generally looks at it, understanding that you were trying to direct attention to something of interest. Chimps seldom look at where you are pointing. It is as if they assumed you were reaching out to get something for yourself (Tomasello & Call, 2019).

More impressive results have been reported for a related species, the bonobo chimpanzee, *Pan paniscus*. Bonobos' social behavior resembles that of humans in several regards: Males and females form strong attachments, females are sexually responsive outside their fertile period, males contribute to infant care, and adults often share food. Like humans, they stand comfortably on their hind legs, and they often copulate face-to-face. Several bonobos have learned to press keys on a board to make short sentences, as in Figure 8.21c and ▼ Figure 8.22. Unlike Washoe and other common chimpanzees, bonobos occasionally use symbols to describe events,

▲ **Figure 8.21** Psychologists have tried to teach chimpanzees to communicate with gestures or symbols. **(a)** A chimp arranges plastic chips to request food. **(b)** Another chimp in her human home. **(c)** Kanzi, a bonobo, presses symbols to indicate words. **(d)** A chimp signing *toothbrush*.

▲ **Figure 8.22** A bonobo points to symbols on a screen to communicate or to answer questions.

Language and General Intelligence

Did we evolve language as an accidental by-product of evolving bigger brains? Several observations argue against this idea. According to some estimates, as many as 7 percent of all children have normal intelligence in other ways but noticeable limitations in language. For example, they might not understand the difference between "Who was the girl pushing?" and "Who was pushing the girl?" (Leonard, 2007). People with a particular gene have even greater language impairments despite otherwise normal intelligence (Fisher, Vargha-Khadem, Watkins, Monaco, & Pembrey, 1998; Lai, Fisher, Hurst, Vargha-Khadem, & Monaco, 2001). They do not fully master even simple rules, such as how to form plurals of nouns.

At the opposite extreme, consider **Williams syndrome**, *a genetic condition characterized by mental retardation in most regards but good use of language relative to their other abilities* (Meyer-Lindenberg, Mervis, & Berman, 2006). One child, when asked to name as many animals as he could, started with "ibex, whale, bull, yak, zebra, puppy, kitten, tiger, koala, dragon . . ." Another child could sing more than 1,000 songs in 22 languages (Bellugi & St. George, 2000). However, these children prefer 50 pennies to 5 dollars and, when asked to estimate the length of a bus, give answers such as "3 inches or 100 inches, maybe" (Bellugi, Lichtenberger, Jones, Lai, & St. George, 2000). They often show problems in attention and planning (Greer, Riby, Hamiliton, & Riby, 2013). In short, language ability is not synonymous with intelligence.

without requesting anything (Lyn, Greenfield, Savage-Rumbaugh, Gillespie-Lynch, & Hopkins, 2011).

The most proficient bonobos seem to comprehend symbols about as well as a 2- to $2\frac{1}{2}$-year-old child understands language (Savage-Rumbaugh et al., 1993). They also understand simple spoken English, following such odd commands as "bite your ball" and "take the vacuum cleaner outside" (Savage-Rumbaugh, 1990; Savage-Rumbaugh, Sevcik, Brakke, & Rumbaugh, 1992). Why have bonobos been more successful than common chimpanzees? Apparently, bonobos have a greater predisposition for this type of learning. Also, they learned by observation and imitation, which promote better understanding than the formal training methods that previous studies used (Savage-Rumbaugh et al., 1992). Finally, the bonobos began their language experience early in life.

Language Learning as a Specialized Capacity

Susan Carey (1978) calculated that children between the ages of 1½ and 6 learn an average of nine new words per day. How do they infer the meanings of all those words? A parent points at a frog and says "frog." How does the child guess that the word means "frog" rather than "small thing," "green thing," or "this particular frog"? Indeed, why does the child assume the sound means anything at all?

Noam Chomsky and his followers have argued that people are born with a **language acquisition device**, *a built-in mechanism for acquiring language* (Pinker, 1994). One line of evidence for this theory is that deaf children who are not taught a sign language invent one of their own and try to teach it to their parents or to other deaf children (Goldin-Meadow, McNeill, & Singleton, 1996; Goldin-Meadow & Mylander, 1998). Further evidence is that children learn to use complex grammatical structures, such as "Is the boy who is unhappy watching Mickey Mouse?" even though they seldom hear that kind of expression. To understand grammar so quickly, children must have a predisposition of some sort. Still, the nature of that predisposition is uncertain.

concept check

15. **Theorists have proposed that human language evolved from gestures. What evidence supports this idea, and what would suggest skepticism?**

Answer

15. Chimpanzees, our nearest relatives, communicate by gestures instead of sounds. (Preverbal children do, also.) However, chimpanzee gestures differ from human gestures. For example, chimpanzees do not understand pointing as we do.

Human Specializations for Learning Language

Humans learn language easily and rapidly. We talk all the time, even when we have nothing worth saying. Why do we learn language so easily?

Language and the Human Brain

What aspect of the human brain enables us to learn language so easily? Fitch (2017a, 2017b) has argued persuasively that multiple evolutionary adaptations were necessary. Among them were increased breath control (to enable slow exhaling during a long utterance), a propensity to imitate, the ability to learn and

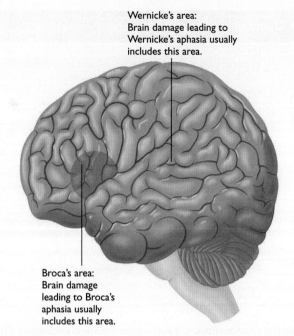

Wernicke's area: Brain damage leading to Wernicke's aphasia usually includes this area.

Broca's area: Brain damage leading to Broca's aphasia usually includes this area.

▲ **Figure 8.23** Brain damage that produces major deficits in language usually includes the left-hemisphere areas shown here. However, the deficits are severe only if the damage includes these areas but extends beyond them.

remember vocal patterns, and enhanced connections from certain cortical areas to the brain areas controlling the larynx.

Two cortical areas have long been recognized as important for language. People with damage in the frontal cortex, usually the left frontal cortex, including *Broca's area* (see ▲ Figure 8.23), develop Broca's aphasia, *a condition characterized by difficulties in language production.* Serious language impairment occurs only if the damage extends outside Broca's area and into the interior of the brain, but what matters here is the nature of the impairment, not the exact location of the damage. The person speaks slowly and inarticulately and is no better with writing or typing. Someone with Broca's aphasia is especially impaired with using and understanding grammatical devices such as prepositions and word endings. For example, one person who was asked about a dental appointment slowly mumbled, "Yes . . . Monday . . . Dad and Dick . . . Wednesday nine o'clock . . . 10 o'clock . . . doctors . . . and . . . teeth" (Geschwind, 1979, p. 186).

People with damage in the temporal cortex in and around *Wernicke's area* (see Figure 8.23) develop Wernicke's aphasia, *a condition marked by impaired recall of nouns and impaired language comprehension, despite fluent and grammatical speech.* Wernicke's aphasia is sometimes called *fluent aphasia.* Difficulty with nouns and impaired comprehension fit together: If you cannot remember what something is called, you cannot understand a sentence using that word. Because people with Wernicke's aphasia omit or misuse most nouns, their speech is hard to understand. For example, one patient responded to a question about his health, "I felt worse because I can no longer keep in mind from the mind of the minds to keep me from mind and up to the ear which can be to find among ourselves" (Brown, 1977, p. 29).

Language depends on more than just Broca's area and Wernicke's area. If you hear a story about sights and sounds, activity increases in the brain areas responsible for vision and hearing. If you hear a story with movement, activity increases in the areas responsible for body sensations and muscle control. If you hear a highly emotional story, activity increases in brain areas important for emotion (Chow et al., 2013). No brain area can do anything without connections to the rest of the brain.

16. **Brain-damaged patient A has trouble understanding other people's speech, and her own speech is often meaningless, although fluent. Patient B understands most speech, but he speaks slowly and inarticulately, omitting prepositions and word endings. Which kind of aphasia does each patient have?**

Answer
16. Patient A has Wernicke's aphasia. Patient B has Broca's aphasia.

Language Development

Children's language learning is amazing. Nearly every child learns language, even though the parents know nothing about how to teach it.

Language in Early Childhood

■ Table 8.2 lists the average ages at which children reach various language stages (Lenneberg, 1969; Moskowitz, 1978). Remember, these are averages, and children vary considerably. Progression through these stages depends largely on maturation (Lenneberg, 1967, 1969). Parents who expose their children to as much language as possible may increase the children's vocabulary, but they hardly affect the rate of progression through language stages. Hearing children of deaf parents are exposed to much less spoken language, but they too progress almost on schedule.

At first, infants babble only haphazard sounds, but soon they start repeating the sounds they have been hearing. A 1-year-old infant babbles mostly sounds that resemble the language the family speaks (Locke, 1994). One of an infant's first sounds is *muh,* and that sound or something similar has been adopted by many of the world's languages to mean "mother." Infants also make the sounds *duh, puh,* and *buh.* In many languages, the word for father is similar to *dada* or *papa. Baba* is the word for father in Chinese and for grandmother in several languages. In effect, infants tell their parents what words to use for these concepts.

By age 1½, most toddlers have a vocabulary of about 50 words, but they seldom link words together. A toddler says "Daddy" and "bye-bye" but not "Bye-bye, Daddy." In context, parents usually understand the single-word utterances. *Mama* might mean, "That's a picture of Mama," "Take me to Mama," "Mama went away and left me here," or "Mama, I'm hungry." Toddlers often combine a word with a gesture, such as pointing at a hat while saying "mama" to indicate mama's hat (Iverson & Goldin-Meadow, 2005). A word plus gesture constitute a primitive kind of sentence. Children who convey much information by gesture alone or word plus gesture at age 1½ are likely to develop better-than-average vocabulary and complex sentence structure by age 3½ (Rowe & Goldin-Meadow, 2009).

By age 2, children start producing phrases of two or more words, such as "more page" (read some more), "allgone sticky" (my hands are now clean), and "allgone outside" (someone has closed the door). Note the originality of such phrases. It is unlikely that the parents ever said "allgone sticky"!

By age 2½ to 3 years, most children generate sentences with idiosyncrasies. Many young children use their own rules for negative sentences. A common one is to add *no* or *not* to the beginning or end of a sentence, such as, "No I want to go to bed!" One little girl formed her negatives just by saying something louder and at a higher pitch. If she shrieked, "I want to share my toys!" she meant, "I do *not* want to share my toys." She had learned this rule by noting that people screamed when they told her not to do something. My son Sam made negatives for a while by adding the word *either* to the end of a sentence: "I want to eat lima beans either." He had heard people say, "I don't want to do that either."

When young children speak, they apply grammatical rules, although of course they cannot state the rules. For example, they apply the rules of English to say, "the womans goed and doed something," or "the mans getted their foots wet." Children *overregularize* or *overgeneralize* the rules. My son David invented the word *shis* to mean "belonging to a female." He apparently generalized the rule "He–his, she–shis." Clearly, children are not just repeating what they have heard.

People have an optimal period for learning language in early childhood (Werker & Tees, 2005). Adults can memorize the vocabulary of a second language, but children are better at mastering the pronunciation and acquiring the grammar (Huang, 2014). People who start a second language after early childhood only rarely approach the level of a native speaker. However, researchers find no sharp age cutoff when language suddenly becomes more difficult. The ease of learning a second language declines steadily from early childhood through old age (Vanhove, 2013).

17. What evidence shows that even very young children learn rules of grammar?

Answer

17. Children overgeneralize grammatical rules, creating such words as *womans* and *goed*.

Children Exposed to No Language or Two Languages

Would children who were exposed to no language make up a new one? In rare cases, an infant who was accidentally separated from other people grew up in a forest without human contact until discovered years later. Such children not only fail to show a language of their own but also fail to learn much language after

Table 8.2 Stages of Language Development

Age	Typical Language Abilities (Much Individual Variation)
3 months	Random vocalizations.
6 months	More distinct babbling.
1 year	Babbling that resembles the typical sounds of the family's language; probably one or more words including "mama"; language comprehension much better than production.
1½ years	Can say some words (mean about 50), mostly nouns; few or no phrases.
2 years	Speaks in two-word phrases.
2½ years	Longer phrases and short sentences with some errors and unusual constructions. Can understand much more.
3 years	Vocabulary near 1,000 words; longer sentences with fewer errors.
4 years	Close to adult speech competence.

they are given the chance (Pinker, 1994). However, their experiences have been so abnormal that we should hesitate to draw broad conclusions.

Better evidence comes from studies of children who are deaf. Children who cannot hear well enough to learn speech and who are not taught sign language invent their own sign language (Senghas, Kita, & Özyürek, 2004). Observations in Nicaragua found that sign language evolved over the decades. Deaf people learned sign language and taught it to the next generation, who, having learned it from early childhood, elaborated on it, made it more expressive, taught the enhanced sign language to the next generation, and so on (Senghas & Coppola, 2001).

If a deaf child learns sign language, it can be a bridge to later learning a spoken language. On average, the children who are best at sign language are also best at reading English or other written languages (Andrew, Hoshooley, & Joanisse, 2014). A deaf child who is given no opportunity to learn sign language until age 12 or so struggles to develop signing skills and never catches up with those who started earlier (Harley & Wang, 1997; Mayberry, Lock, & Kazmi, 2002). This observation is our best evidence for the importance of early development in language learning: A child who doesn't learn any language while young is permanently impaired at learning one.

Many children grow up in a **bilingual** environment, *learning two languages* (see ▼ Figure 8.24). You might guess that a bilingual person represents the languages in different brain areas. However, the research shows that both languages activate the same areas (Perani & Abutalebi, 2005). People who learn a second language after about age 6 use just one hemisphere, usually the left one, for both (Hull & Vaid, 2007). People who learn two languages beginning in infancy show activity in both hemispheres for both languages (Berken, Chai, Chen, Gracco, & Klein, 2016; Peng & Wang, 2011; Perani & Abutalebi, 2005; Polczynska, Japardi, & Bookheimer, 2017). If the brain represents two languages in the same places, how do bilingual people keep their languages separate? They don't, at least not completely (Thierry & Wu, 2007). They sometimes get confused when they switch between languages (Levy, McVeigh, Marful, & Anderson, 2007; Linck, Kroll, & Sunderman, 2009).

18. How does becoming bilingual from birth differ from becoming bilingual later?

Answer

18. A child who is bilingual from birth will be more fully fluent in both languages. Someone who becomes bilingual during early childhood activates both hemispheres for language, whereas someone who learned a second language later activates mainly one hemisphere, usually the left hemisphere.

▲ **Figure 8.24** Children who grow up in a bilingual or multilingual environment gain in their ability to communicate with more people.

Understanding Language

To understand a word, you have to imagine the experience to which it refers. Here are two examples: First, people examined pronounceable letter strings on a screen and identified each one as either a word (e.g., "glove") or a non-word (e.g., "gluve"). People with damage to the auditory portion of the cerebral cortex performed about as well as normal, except on words referring to sounds, such as "thunder." Often they regarded those as nonwords (Bonner & Grossman, 2012). Apparently, if you can't imagine thunder, then the word looks meaningless. Second example: Patients with Parkinson's disease have impaired movement. A group of cognitively intact Parkinson's patients were asked to name what they saw in a series of drawings. They performed as well as average for most drawings, but they were significantly below average in naming drawings of motion, such as dance, walk, run, or swim. Evidently if you can't imagine doing something, it is harder to think of the word (Bocanegra et al., 2017).

When we are in noisy places, we cannot hear every sound clearly. Watching lip movements helps us understand ambiguous sounds. If lip movements do not match the sound, we strike a compromise between what we see and what we hear (McGurk & MacDonald, 1976). If you search YouTube for "McGurk effect," you can find a marvelous demonstration.

Often we rely on context. Imagine a word that sounds halfway between *paper* and *pepper*. Let's call it "*pahper*." If someone says, "Please pass the salt and *pahper*," you perceive it as pepper. If someone says, "I need a pencil and *pahper*," then you hear it as paper. In one study, a computer generated a sound halfway between a normal *s* sound and a normal *sh* sound. When this intermediate sound replaced the *s* sound at the end of the word *embarrass*, people heard it as an *s* sound. When the same sound replaced *sh* at the end of *abolish*, people heard the same sound as *sh* (Samuel, 2001).

In another study, students listened to a tape recording of a sentence with a sound missing (Warren, 1970). The sentence was, "The state governors met with their respective legislatures convening in the capital city." However, the sound of the first *s* in the word *legislatures*, along with part of the adjacent *i* and *l*, had been replaced by a cough or a tone. The students were asked to listen to the recording and try to identify the location of the cough or tone. None of the 20 students identified the location correctly, and half thought the cough or tone interrupted one of the other words on the tape. Even those who were told that the *s* sound was missing insisted that they clearly heard the sound *s*. The brain uses context to fill in the missing sound.

Suppose you hear a tape-recorded word that is carefully engineered to sound halfway between *dent* and *tent*. The way you perceive it depends on the context:

1. When the *ent in the fender was well camouflaged, we sold the car.
2. When the *ent in the forest was well camouflaged, we began our hike.

Most people who hear sentence 1 report the word *dent*. Most who hear sentence 2 report *tent*. Now consider two more sentences:

3. When the *ent was noticed in the fender, we sold the car.
4. When the *ent was noticed in the forest, we stopped to rest.

For sentences 3 and 4, the context comes too late to help. People are as likely to report hearing *dent* in one sentence as in the other (Connine, Blasko, & Hall, 1991). Consider what this means: In the first two sentences, after *ent, the person heard only two intervening syllables before hearing fender or forest. In the second pair, five syllables intervened. Evidently, when you hear an ambiguous sound, you hold it briefly in an "undecided" state for the context to clarify it. After a couple more syllables, it is too late.

Although a delayed context cannot help you hear an ambiguous word correctly, it does help you understand its meaning. Consider the following sentence (Lashley, 1951):

> Rapid righting with his uninjured hand saved from loss the contents of the capsized canoe.

If you hear this sentence spoken aloud so that spelling provides no clues, you are likely at first to interpret the second word as *writing*, until you reach the final two words of the sentence. Suddenly, *capsized canoe* tells you that *righting* meant "pushing with a paddle." Only the immediate context can influence what you hear, but a delayed context can change the word's meaning.

19. What principle of Gestalt psychology pertains to filling in the missing sound in "legislatures"?

Answer

19. The Gestalt principle of closure is that we fill in a gap with what we assume must have been there.

Understanding a Sentence

Making sense of language requires knowledge about the world. For example, consider the following sentences (from Just & Carpenter, 1987):

That store sells horseshoes.
That store sells alligator shoes.

You interpret *horseshoes* to mean "shoes for horses to wear," but you interpret *alligator shoes* as "shoes made from alligator hide." Your understanding of the sentences depends on your knowledge of the world, not just the syntax of the sentences.

Here is another example:

I'm going to buy a pet hamster at the store, if it's open.
I'm going to buy a pet hamster at the store, if it's healthy.

Nothing about the sentence structure told you that *it* refers to the store in the first sentence and a hamster in the second sentence. You understood because you know that stores but not hamsters can be open, and hamsters but not stores can be healthy.

In short, understanding a sentence depends on your knowledge of the world and all the assumptions that you share with the speaker or writer of the sentence. Sometimes, you even have to remember where you are, because the meaning of a word differs from one place to another (see ▶ Figure 8.25).

Embedded Clauses and Negatives

Some grammatical sentences are almost incomprehensible. A singly embedded sentence is understandable, though difficult:

The dog the cat saw chased a squirrel.
The squirrel the dog chased climbed the tree.

In the first sentence, "the cat saw the dog" is embedded within "the dog chased a squirrel." In the second, "the dog chased the squirrel" is embedded within "the squirrel climbed the tree." So far, so good, but now consider a doubly embedded sentence, which is practically impossible to understand:

The squirrel the dog the cat saw chased climbed the tree.

Doubly embedded sentences overburden our memory. In fact, if your memory is already burdened with other matters, you may have trouble understanding a singly embedded sentence (Gordon, Hendrick, & Levine, 2002).

Double negatives are also difficult to understand. "I would not deny that . . ." means that I agree. "It is not false that . . ." means that something is true. People often misunderstand such sentences. Have you ever seen a multiple-choice test item that asks, "Which of the following is not true . . ." and then one of the choices includes the word *not*? With such items, confusion is almost certain.

▲ **Figure 8.25** In England, a *football coach* is a bus full of soccer fans. In the United States, it's the person who directs a team of American football players.

Consider the following sentence, which includes *four* negatives (emphasis added): "If you do *not* unanimously find from your consideration of all the evidence that there are *no* mitigating factors sufficient to *preclude* the imposition of a death sentence, then you should sign the verdict requiring the court to impose a sentence *other than* death." In Illinois some years ago, judges used to read those instructions to a jury to explain how to decide between a death penalty and life in prison. It means that if even one juror sees a reason to reject the death penalty, the jury should recommend prison instead. Do you think many jurors understood?

Even with a single negative, people often don't fully accept the meaning of the word *not*. Suppose a packaged food says, "Contains no rat pieces!" Would that notice encourage you to buy the product? Hardly! I was once on an airplane that turned around shortly after departure because one of its two engines failed. The attendant told the passengers what was happening, but until she said, "Please don't panic," we didn't realize there might be a reason to panic. If you ask someone for a favor and the person responds, "No problem," how do you react? The expression "no problem" implies there was almost a problem, or maybe there is a bit of a problem.

In one clever experiment, students watched an experimenter pour sugar into two jars. The students were then told to label one jar "sucrose, table sugar" and the other "not sodium cyanide, not poison." Then the experimenter made two cups of Kool-Aid, one from each jar of sugar, and asked the students to choose one to drink (see ▼ Figure 8.26). Of the 44 who expressed a preference, 35 wanted Kool-Aid made from the jar marked "sucrose," not from the one that denied having poison (Rozin, Markwith, & Ross, 1990).

Reading

Students of language distinguish between phonemes and morphemes. A **phoneme** is *a unit of sound*, such as *s* or *sh*. Machines that talk to you, such as a GPS, take a written word, break it into phonemes, and pronounce the phonemes. For words with irregular spellings, the machine's pronunciation may be wrong. A **morpheme**

▲ **Figure 8.26** Most students preferred Kool-Aid made with sugar labeled "sugar" instead of sugar labeled "not cyanide," even though they had placed the labels themselves. People don't always trust the word *not*. (Based on results of Rozin, Markwith, & Ross, 1990)

is *a unit of meaning*. For example, the noun *thrills* has two morphemes (*thrill* and *s*). The final *s* is a unit of meaning because it indicates that the noun is plural (see ▶ Figure 8.27). *Harp* has one morpheme, and *harping* has two, but *harpoon* has just one, as it is not derived from *harp*. Morphemes help us break an unfamiliar word into meaningful parts. For example, we can see *reinvigoration* as *re-in-vigor-ation*, meaning the process of increasing vigor again.

Readers of English and other European languages are accustomed to the idea that a letter or combination of letters represents a phoneme. However, in the Japanese *hiragana* style of writing, each character represents a syllable. In Chinese, a character represents a morpheme and ordinarily a whole word.

Phonemes
(units of sound):

Morphemes
(units of meaning):

▲ **Figure 8.27** The word *shamelessness* has nine phonemes (units of sound) and three morphemes (units of meaning).

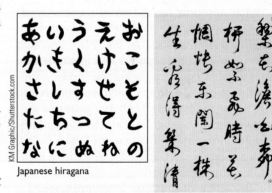

KM Graphic/Shutterstock.com

Japanese hiragana

Chinese characters

Illustration of Japanese hiragana writing and Chinese writing.

concept check

20. How many phonemes are in the word truthfully? How many morphemes?

Answer

20. It has eight phonemes: t-r-u-th-f-u-ll-y. It has three morphemes: truth-ful-ly.

Word Recognition

Expertise develops from years of practice, enabling someone to recognize complex patterns at a glance. Because you have been reading almost every day since childhood, you have developed expertise at reading. You may not think of yourself as an expert, because we usually reserve that term for someone who is far more skilled than others. Nevertheless, you recognize common words instantaneously, like an expert who recognizes chess patterns at a glance.

Consider the following experiment: The investigator flashes a letter on a screen for less than a quarter-second, shows an interfering pattern, and asks, "Was it *C* or *J*?" Then the experimenter flashes an entire word on the screen under the same conditions and asks, "Was the first letter of the word *C* or *J*?" (see ▼ Figure 8.28). Which question is easier? Most people *identify the letter more accurately when it is part of a word than when it is presented by itself* (Reicher, 1969; Wheeler, 1970). This is known as the **word-superiority effect**.

▲ **Figure 8.28** Either a word or a single letter flashed on a screen and then an interfering pattern. The observers were asked, "Which was presented: *C* or *J*?" More of them identified the letter correctly when it was part of a word.

James Johnston and James McClelland (1974) briefly flashed words on the screen and asked students to identify one letter at a marked position in each word (see ▼ Figure 8.29). On some trials, the experimenters told the students to try to see the whole word. On other trials, they showed the students exactly where the critical letter would appear on the screen and told them to focus on that spot and ignore the rest of the screen. Most students identified the critical letter more successfully when they looked at the whole word than when they focused on just the letter itself. This benefit occurs only with a real word, like COIN, not with a nonsense combination, like CXQF (Rumelhart & McClelland, 1982).

You may have experienced the word-superiority effect yourself. To pass time on long car trips, people sometimes try to find every letter of the alphabet on the billboards. It is easier to spot a letter by reading words than by checking letter by letter.

What accounts for the word-superiority effect? According to one model (McClelland, 1988; Rumelhart, McClelland, & the PDP Research Group, 1986), our perceptions and memories are represented by connections among "units" corresponding to sets of neurons. Each unit connects to other units (see ▶ Figure 8.30). Any activated unit excites some of its neighbors and inhibits others. Suppose units corresponding to the letters *C, O, I,* and *N* are moderately active. They excite a higher-order unit corresponding to the word *COIN*. Although none of the four letter units sends a strong message by itself, the collective impact is strong (McClelland & Rumelhart, 1981). The perception *COIN* then feeds excitation back to the individual letter-identifying units and confirms their tentative identifications.

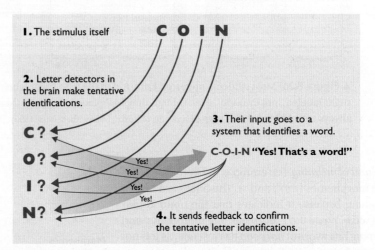

▲ **Figure 8.30** According to one model, a visual stimulus activates certain letter units, some more strongly than others. Those letter units then activate a word unit, which in turn strengthens the letter units that compose it. For this reason, we recognize a whole word more easily than a single letter.

This model helps explain our perception of ▼ Figure 8.31. You see the first and third words as *BIRD* and *PROOF*, not *BIPD* and *RROOF*. You see the second and fourth words as *DRIVE* and *FRIDAY*, not *DRIVF* and *EIRDAY*. Why? After all, the R in BIRD looks the same as the P in PROOF, and the E in DRIVE looks the same as the F in FRIDAY. When you tentatively perceive a word, the feedback strengthens the perception of the units that would make the word, and not those that would make a meaningless string of letters. Now consider the following sentence:

The boy cuold not slove the porblem so he aksed for help.

Most readers "recognize" the words *could, solve, problem, and asked*, although of course they read faster if all words are spelled correctly (Rayner, White, Johnson, & Liversedge, 2006; White, Johnson, Liversedge, & Rayner, 2008). When we read, we process the context so that even out-of-place letters activate identification of the correct words. (This tendency can pose a probelm for prooofreaders, who sometimes fail to notice a misspellling!)

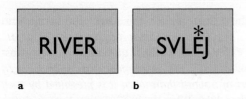

a   b

▲ **Figure 8.29** Students identified an indicated letter better when they focused on an entire word (**a**) than on a single letter in a designated spot (**b**).

21. What evidence indicates that we do *not* read a word one letter at a time?

Answer

21. Ambiguous letters, such as those in Figure 8.31, appear to be one letter in one context and another letter in a different context. Also, a reader sometimes "recognizes" a misspelled word even when certain letters are out of order.

BIRD DRIVE PROOF FRIDAY

▲ **Figure 8.31** The combination of possible letters enables us to identify a word. Word recognition in turn helps to confirm the letter identifications.

Reading and Eye Movements

When you are watching a moving object, you move your eyes steadily, but when you scan a stationary object, such as a page of print, you alternate between **fixations**, *when your eyes are stationary,* and **saccades** (sa-KAHDS), *quick eye movements from one fixation point to another.* You read during fixations, not during saccades. For an average adult reader, most fixations last about 200 to 250 milliseconds. Fixations are briefer on familiar words like *law* than on uncommon words like *luau* or words with more than one meaning like *lead* (Rodd, Gaskell, & Marslen-Wilson, 2002). Because all saccades last 25 to 50 ms, a normal reading pace is about four fixations per second (Rayner, 1998).

How much can someone read during a fixation? On average, the limit is about 11 characters at a time. To demonstrate, focus on the letter *i* marked by an arrow (↓) in these sentences:

↓

1. This is a sentence with no misspelled words.

↓

2. Xboc tx zjg rxunce with no mijvgab zucn.

If you permit your eyes to wander back and forth, you notice the gibberish in sentence 2. But as long as you dutifully keep your eyes on the fixation point, the sentence looks all right. You read the letter on which you fixated plus about three or four characters (including spaces) to the left and about seven to the right. The rest is uncertain. Therefore, you probably see *—ce with no m—* or *—nce with no mi—*. People vary, and you might be able to make out some additional letters.

This limit of about 11 letters depends partly on the lighting. In faint light, your span decreases to as little as 1 or 2 letters, and your reading ability suffers accordingly (Legge, Ahn, Klitz, & Luebker, 1997). However, your limit has little relationship to the size of the print (Miellet, O'Donnell, & Sereno, 2009). In the following display, again focus on the letter *i* in each sentence and check how many letters you can read to its left and right:

↓

This is a sentence with no misspelled words.

↓

This is a sentence with no misspelled words.

↓

is a sentence with no misspelled

If your reading span were limited by how many letters can fit into the fovea of your retina, you would read fewer letters as the print gets larger. In fact, you do at least as well, maybe even better, with larger print (up to a point).

The results vary from one language to another. In Japanese and Chinese, where each character conveys more information than English letters do, readers see fewer letters per fixation (Rayner, 1998). That is, the limit depends on how much meaning a reader sees at once. In Arabic, Hebrew, and Farsi, which are written right to left, readers see more letters to the left of fixation and fewer to the right (Brysbaert, Vitu, & Schroyens, 1996; Faust, Kravetz, & Babkoff, 1993; Melamed & Zaidel, 1993).

Reading is a strategic process of pausing longer on difficult or ambiguous words and sometimes looking back to previous words. In fact, of all eye movements while reading, about 10 to 15 percent are backward movements. An app you can get for your computer claims to increase reading speed by eliminating those backward movements. A device monitors your eye movements, so that whenever you move your eyes forward, every word you have already read goes blank. You therefore cannot go back. That procedure may indeed increase your reading speed, but sometimes you *need* to look back. Consider this sentence:

> While the woman ate the spaghetti on the table grew cold.

When you first read that sentence, you thought the woman ate the spaghetti. The rest of the sentence told you that you misunderstood, so you had to look back and reread (Schotter, Tran, & Rayner, 2014). Speed-reading courses train people to move their eyes rapidly, avoid backward movements, and infer meanings instead of reading every word. Speed-reading is a reasonable strategy for pleasure reading, when you do not need every detail. However, in many cases you can expect a decrease in comprehension (Rayner, Schotter, Masson, Potter, & Treiman, 2016).

22. What determines variations in people's reading speed, fixations or saccades?

Answer

22. People with longer fixations have slower reading speed. The duration of a saccade varies less.

Language and Humanity

At the start of this module, we considered the question, "If language is so useful to humans, why haven't other species evolved at least a little of it?" None of the research answers this question, but let's speculate.

Many adaptations are much more useful on a large scale than on a small scale. For example, stinkiness is useful to skunks, but being slightly stinky wouldn't help much.

Porcupines survive because of their long quills. Having a few short quills would be only slightly helpful. Similarly, a little bit of language development is probably an unstable condition, evolutionarily speaking. Once a species such as humans started to evolve language, those individuals with still better language abilities would have a huge selective advantage, leading to a cumulative growth of the ability.

Summary

- *Language training in nonhumans.* Chimpanzees, especially bonobo chimpanzees, have learned certain aspects of language. They communicate mostly by gestures, but they do not readily understand pointing at something in the same way humans do. (page 268)
- *Language and intelligence.* It is possible to have intelligence without language or impaired intelligence that largely spares language. (page 270)
- *Predisposition to learn language.* Noam Chomsky and others have argued that children's ease of learning language indicates that they are born with a predisposition for language learning. (page 270)
- *Brain organization and aphasia.* Brain damage, especially in the left hemisphere, impairs people's ability to understand or use language. (page 271)
- *Stages of language development.* Children advance through several stages of language development. From the start, their language is creative, using the rules of language to make new word combinations and sentences. (page 271)
- *Deaf children.* If deaf children are not exposed to language, they invent a sign language of their own. A deaf child who learns neither spoken language nor sign language in childhood is impaired on learning any language later. (page 272)
- *Bilingualism.* Children who are bilingual from the start increase the use of both brain hemispheres in language. Learning a second language becomes gradually more difficult as people age. (page 272)
- *Understanding language.* We use context to understand ambiguous words and sentences. (page 273)
- *Embedded clauses and negatives.* Many sentences are difficult to understand, especially those with embedded clauses or with one or more negatives. (page 274)
- *The word-superiority effect.* We recognize a letter more easily when it is part of a familiar word than when we see it by itself. (page 275)
- *Reading.* When we read, we alternate between fixation periods and saccadic eye movements. An average adult reads about 11 letters per fixation. (page 277)

Key Terms

bilingual (page 272)

Broca's aphasia (page 271)

fixation (page 277)

language acquisition device (page 270)

morpheme (page 274)

phoneme (page 274)

productivity (page 268)

saccade (page 277)

transformational grammar (page 268)

Wernicke's aphasia (page 271)

Williams syndrome (page 270)

word-superiority effect (page 275)

Review Questions

1. What do the observations on Williams syndrome tell us about language??
   (a) The two brain hemispheres contribute to language in different ways.
   (b) Language learning is easiest in early childhood and gradually declines.
   (c) Language is not a byproduct of overall intelligence.
   (d) Positive reinforcement is essential for language learning.

2. Someone with Wernicke's aphasia shows impairments most strongly with regard to which aspect of language?
   (a) Speech fluency
   (b) Use of prepositions, word endings, and other grammatical devices
   (c) Speech comprehension
   (d) Emotional intonation of speech

3. At what age do people begin to use rules of grammar?
   (a) Very early, even at ages 2 or 3
   (b) When start school
   (c) After a few years of school
   (d) As teenagers

4. What happens if a deaf child is prevented from learning sign language in childhood?
   (a) The child becomes more likely to learn lip reading.
   (b) The child begins babbling more and more.
   (c) The child will probably never develop good language of any type.
   (d) The child will have no trouble learning sign language later in life.

5. How does the brain of a bilingual person represent language?
   (a) One language in the left hemisphere and the other in the right hemisphere.
   (b) Both languages in the left hemisphere.
   (c) Both languages in both hemispheres.
   (d) Either both in the left hemisphere or both in both, depending on the age of becoming bilingual.

6. Suppose one sound in a word is engineered to sound halfway between *d* and *t*, or halfway between *s* and *sh*. What do you hear?
   (a) You hear both sounds.
   (b) You hear whichever sound is more common in your language.
   (c) You hear the sound that makes more sense in context, unless the context is delayed.
   (d) You hear the sound that makes more sense in context, even if the context is delayed.

7. What is meant by the "word-superiority effect"?
   (a) Children learn to read better by the whole word method than by phonics.
   (b) Familiar words activate more of the brain than less familiar words.
   (c) It is easier to recognize a letter when it is part of a familiar word.
   (d) People make faster saccades to words than to nonsensical strings of letters.

8. Which of the following would be a likely way to increase reading speed?
   (a) Decrease the time spent on each saccade.
   (b) Decrease the time spent on each fixation.
   (c) Double the number of characters seen in each fixation.
   (d) Read text that is written in a smaller font.

Answers: 1c, 2c, 3a, 4c, 5d, 6c, 7c, 8b.

9 Intelligence

$$\int_{-\infty}^{\infty} e^{-x^2} dx = \sqrt{\pi}$$

$$f(x) = a_0 + \sum_{n=1}^{\infty} (a_n \cos \frac{n\pi x}{L} + b_n \sin \frac{n\pi x}{L}$$

$$x = \frac{-b \pm \sqrt{b^2 - 4ac}}{2a}$$

sturti/E+/Getty Images

To repair a bicycle, you could use general problem-solving skills or specific expertise about bicycles. Either approach shows a kind of intelligence.

Bernd Opitz/The Image Bank/Getty Images

Alan Turing, a famous mathematician and pioneer in computer science, bicycled to and from work each day. Occasionally, the chain fell off his bicycle and he had to replace it. Turing kept records and noticed that the chain fell off at regular intervals, after a certain number of turns of the front wheel. He calculated that this number was the product of the number of spokes in the front wheel times the number of links in the chain times the number of cogs in the pedal. He deduced that the chain came loose whenever a particular link in the chain came in contact with a particular bent spoke on the wheel. He identified that spoke, repaired it, and had no more trouble with his bicycle (Stewart, 1987).

Turing's solution to his problem is impressive, but hold your applause. A good bicycle mechanic could have solved the problem without using mathematics at all. So, you might ask, what's the point? The point is that intelligence includes both the ability to solve unfamiliar problems, as Turing showed, and practiced skills, such as those of a bicycle mechanic.

Other chapters have dealt with learning, memory, and cognition, with an emphasis on theoretical understanding. Here, the emphasis shifts. Although the study of intelligence raises theoretical issues, the study of intelligence traditionally has been guided by the practical concern of measuring individual differences and predicting outcomes.

sturti/E+/Getty Images

After studying this module, you should be able to:

1. Describe *g*, the evidence for it, and explanations for it.

2. Distinguish between fluid and crystallized intelligence.

3. Describe three common IQ tests.

4. Evaluate the evidence for hereditary and environmental influences on intellectual development.

5. Discuss the relationship between intelligence and brain size.

Is there intelligent life in outer space? For decades, people have pointed arrays of dishes toward the stars, hoping to detect signals from alien civilizations. If we did intercept signals, could we make sense of them? If we replied, could alien civilizations understand our replies? The effort assumes that intelligent life in outer space resembles us enough to make communication possible. It is a remarkable assumption, considering that our communication with dolphins here on Earth is limited to such superficialities as "take the ball to the hoop."

Defining Intelligence

What is intelligence? Let's analyze that question before we try to answer it. If we ask what is gravity or what is magnetism, there can be only one correct answer, even if we are not sure what it is. But if we ask what is beauty, that's different. Beauty is in the eye of the beholder, and if you think something is beautiful, no one can say you are wrong. Is intelligence like gravity, with only one correct definition, or is it a subjective evaluation, like beauty?

Defining intelligence is not easy. Here are some attempts (Kanazawa, 2004; Sternberg, 1997; Wolman, 1989):

- The mental abilities that enable one to adapt to, shape, or select one's environment
- The ability to deal with novel situations
- The ability to judge, comprehend, and reason
- The ability to understand and deal with people, objects, and symbols
- The ability to act purposefully, think rationally, and deal effectively with the environment

None of these definitions is fully satisfactory. Note the use of terms such as *judge, comprehend, understand,* and *think rationally.* Those terms need definitions themselves.

It would be nice if we could say that psychologists first analyzed learning, memory, and cognition and then built upon that knowledge to understand intelligence. In fact, psychological researchers began by testing the ability to do well in school, and then conducted research to discover what the tests measure. It may seem odd to measure something before defining what it is. However, the same is true in other fields. Physicists measured gravity, electricity, magnetism, and other forces before studying what they were.

Spearman's Psychometric Approach and the *g* Factor

One of the first research programs in psychology was Charles Spearman's (1904) psychometric approach to intelligence, based on *the measurement of individual differences in performance.* Spearman measured how well people performed tasks such as following directions, judging musical pitch, matching colors, and doing arithmetic. He found that performance on any of his tasks correlated positively with performance on any of the others. He, therefore, inferred that all the tasks have something in common. To perform well on any test of mental ability, Spearman argued, people need a *"general"* ability, which he called *g.* The symbol *g* is always italicized and lowercase, like the mathematical terms *e* (the base of natural logarithms) and *i* (the square root of –1).

To account for the fact that performances on various tasks do not correlate perfectly, Spearman suggested that each task also requires a *"specific"* ability, *s* (see ▼ Figure 9.1). Thus, intelligence consists of a general ability plus an unknown number of specific abilities, such as mechanical, musical, arithmetical, logical, and spatial abilities. Spearman called his theory a "monarchic" theory of

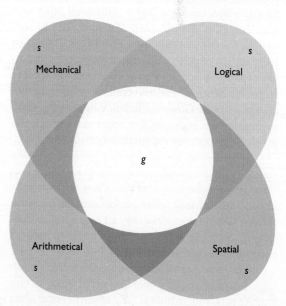

▲ **Figure 9.1** According to Spearman (1904), all intelligent abilities have an area of overlap, which he called *g* (for "general"). Each ability also depends on an *s* (for "specific") factor.

intelligence because it included a dominant ability, or monarch (*g*), that ruled over the lesser abilities.

Later researchers confirmed that scores on virtually all kinds of cognitive tests correlate positively with one another within almost any population (Johnson, Bouchard, Krueger, McGue, & Gottesman, 2004; Johnson, te Nijenhuis, & Bouchard, 2008), including non-Western nations (Warne & Burningham, 2019). You have probably noticed this trend yourself: A student who does well in one course generally does well in others also. Only under special conditions do most of the individuals with high scores on one test get low scores on another. For example, in one study, rural Kenyan children who did well on an academic test did poorly on a test of knowledge about traditional herbal medicines, and those who did well on the test of herbal medicines did poorly on the academic test (Sternberg et al., 2001). Evidently, the two groups of children had been exposed to different experiences.

Explanations for *g*

Why do people who perform well on one type of test generally perform well on others also? The simplest interpretation is that all the tasks measure a single underlying ability. Consider an analogy with the tasks shown in ▶ **Figure 9.2**. Most people who excel at running a 100-meter race also do well at the high jump and the long jump. They have to, because all three events depend on the same leg muscles.

Similarly, perhaps people perform well on a variety of intellectual tests because all the tests depend on one underlying skill. That underlying skill could be working memory capacity or processing speed, which correlate highly with each other and with cognitive performance (Kyllonen & Christal, 1990; Schubert, Hagemann, & Frischkorn, 2017). But what causes people to differ in their working memory capacity or speed of processing? One possibility is the efficiency of the mitochondria that generate energy in cells. Greater efficiency of mitochondria means greater potential for brain activity (Geary, 2018). Other possible explanations exist, of course.

Nevertheless, we need to take specialized skills seriously. Some people, especially those with brain damage or genetic mutations, show impairments on one type of task while performing normally on others. Could we explain why all cognitive abilities *usually* correlate highly with one another, without assuming a single underlying ability?

For one possibility, consider this analogy: Imagine you are making soups from twelve ingredients. You include at least seven in every soup, but a different set each time. Therefore, every soup will have some taste overlap with every other one, but not because all soups have one ingredient in common. A similar idea could be true for intelligence:

▲ **Figure 9.2** Measurements of sprinting, high jumping, and long jumping correlate with one another because they all depend on the same leg muscles. Similarly, the *g* factor that emerges in IQ testing could reflect a single ability.

Perhaps we have many abilities, and every cognitive task uses a combination of them, so that any pair of tasks uses at least a few overlapping abilities. The result would be a positive correlation between any pair of tasks, even without a single general factor (Kovacs & Conway, 2016).

Another possible explanation for *g* is that several types of intelligence correlate because they grow in the same ways (Petrill, Luo, Thompson, & Detterman, 1996). By analogy, consider the lengths of three body parts—the left leg, the right arm, and the left index finger: As a rule, most people with a long left leg also have a long right arm and a long left index finger, because the factors that increase the growth of one also help the others grow—factors such as genes, health, and nutrition. Similarly, all forms of intelligence depend on genes, health, nutrition, and education. Most people who have good support for developing one intellectual skill also have good support for developing others. However, just as it would be possible to damage your left index finger without harming your legs, it would be possible to impair one intellectual ability while sparing the others.

Which explanation applies to intelligence? Do the various intellectual skills correlate with one another because they all measure a single underlying ability (as do running and jumping, which require good leg muscles), or because any two tasks use a few overlapping abilities, or because all abilities grow together (as do your arms, legs, and fingers)? Each explanation is plausible, and indeed it is possible that all three are correct to some degree.

1. You read about three explanations for *g*. What would each of them say about Spearman's *s* factor?

Answer

1. If all intelligent abilities depend on a single underlying factor, then the *s* factor is something added to it for a specific task. The other two explanations propose that intelligence consists of *s* factors that correlate with one another.

Hierarchical Models of Intelligence

Regardless of whether a single *g* factor explains intelligence, it does not account for everything. Spearman suggested the existence of *s* factors, but the task fell on other psychologists to try to describe them. One option is to describe intelligence as a hierarchy of components. One analysis described them as language, perceptual processing, and spatial relationships (Johnson & Bouchard, 2005). Another analysis described them as language, short-term memory, and reasoning (Hampshire, Highfield, Parkin, & Owen, 2012). Each of those components might include subfactors (Cucina & Byle, 2017).

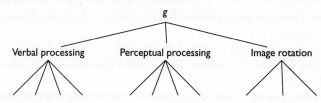

Raymond Cattell (1987) drew a distinction between fluid intelligence and crystallized intelligence. The analogy is to water: Fluid water fits into any shape of container, but an ice crystal has a fixed shape. **Fluid intelligence** is *the power of reasoning and using information.* It includes the ability to perceive relationships, solve unfamiliar problems, and gain new knowledge. **Crystallized intelligence** consists of *acquired skills and knowledge and the ability to apply that knowledge in familiar situations.* Fluid intelligence enables you to learn skills in a new job, whereas crystallized intelligence includes the job skills you have already acquired. Expertise is crystallized intelligence. The distinction between fluid and crystallized intelligence is sharper in theory than in practice, as almost any task taps some combination of fluid and crystallized intelligence.

Most aspects of fluid intelligence reach their peak before or soon after age 20, whereas many aspects of crystallized intelligence reach their peak in middle age and remain nearly constant, even in many older people (Hartshorne & Germine, 2015; Scheiber, Chen, Kaufman, & Weiss, 2017). Fluid intelligence declines on average in old age, as does speed of processing,

although individual differences are substantial. Results are sometimes misleading when older people are not sufficiently motivated to perform on seemingly unimportant tests (Metcalfe, Casal-Roscum, Radin, & Friedman, 2015).

2. Was Alan Turing's solution to the slipping bicycle chain, from the introduction to this chapter (page 282), an example of fluid or crystallized intelligence? Was the solution provided by a bicycle mechanic fluid or crystallized intelligence?

Answer

2. Turing's solution reflected fluid intelligence, a generalized ability that could apply to any topic. The solution provided by a bicycle mechanic reflected crystallized intelligence, an ability developed by practice.

Gardner's Theory of Multiple Intelligences

Certain critics propose to dispense with, or at least de-emphasize, the concept of *g*. According to Howard Gardner (1985, 1999), if we could test intellectual abilities in pure form, we might find **multiple intelligences**—*independent forms of intelligence,* such as language, musical abilities, logical and mathematical reasoning, spatial reasoning, ability to recognize and classify objects, body movement skills, self-control and self-understanding, and sensitivity to other people's social signals. Gardner argues that someone who seems intelligent in one way may be mediocre or worse in another because different skills require not only different kinds of practice but also different brain specializations.

Gardner makes the important point that people have different skills, and that we should value them all. However, he suggests that these types are different not just in the sense of Spearman's *s* factor—a specialization tacked onto a more general

According to Howard Gardner, we have many intelligences, including mathematical ability, artistic skill, muscle skills, and musical abilities.

ability. Gardner argues that the different abilities are independent and unrelated. To support Gardner's hypothesis, someone would need to demonstrate intellectual skills that are not strongly correlated with one another. In fact, each of Gardner's proposed types of intelligence correlates positively with the others, except for body movement skills and possibly music (Visser, Ashton, & Vernon, 2006). Gardner believes that the abilities would stop correlating so strongly if we could measure them in pure form, without the influence of language and other general skills. Perhaps so, but no one knows how to measure any intellectual ability in pure form. Gardner's theory is an appealing idea, but difficult to test.

Parallel to the claim of multiple intelligences, many educators have embraced the concept that people vary in their learning styles. According to this view, some people are visual learners, others are verbal learners, and others learn in other ways, and teaching should be adjusted to each student's style of learning. If so, some students would learn best in a classroom taught one way, and other students would learn best in a classroom taught a different way. The evidence fails to support that hypothesis (Pashler, McDaniel, Rohrer, & Bjork, 2008)—with the obvious exception that blind children don't learn from visual presentations and deaf children don't learn from spoken presentations. The idea of learning styles became popular without any research basis.

3. The text presented three possible explanations for *g*. Which of them is most consistent with Gardner's idea of multiple intelligences?

Answer

3. The third explanation holds that independent abilities correlate with one another because the same growth factors contribute to each of them. According to that idea, multiple intelligences could correlate with one another (as they do) and nevertheless be independent. The other two explanations for *g* assume that all intellectual tasks share at least some skills in common.

IQ Tests

We have been discussing intelligence and IQ tests in general, and the idea of IQ tests is no doubt familiar to you. The time has come to consider examples in more detail.

Let's start with this analogy: You have been put in charge of choosing the members of your country's next Olympic team, but the rules have been changed: Each country will send only 30 men and 30 women, and each athlete must compete in every event. The Olympic committee will not describe those events until after you choose the athletes. Clearly, you cannot hold the usual kind of tryouts, but neither will you choose people at random. How will you proceed?

Your best bet would be to devise a test of "general athletic ability." You might measure the abilities of applicants to run, jump, change direction, maintain balance, throw and catch, kick, lift weights, respond rapidly to signals, and perform other athletic feats. You would choose the applicants with the best scores.

No doubt, your test would be imperfect, but if you want your team to do well, you need some way to measure athletic ability. Later, other people begin to use your test also. Does its acceptance mean that athletic ability is a single quantity? Of course not. You found it useful to act as if it were a single quantity, but you know that most great basketball players are not great swimmers or gymnasts.

Intelligence tests resemble this imaginary test of athletic ability. If you were in charge of choosing which applicants a college should admit, you would want to select those who will be the best students. Because students will study subjects that they have not studied before, you will want to measure a range of academic skills, not knowledge of a single topic. That is, you want a test of **aptitude** (*ability to learn, or fluid intelligence*) in addition to **achievement** (*what people have already learned, or crystallized intelligence*). Aptitude and achievement are hard to separate because aptitude leads to achievement, and past achievement increases future ability to learn.

Two French psychologists, Alfred Binet and Theophile Simon (1904), devised the first IQ tests. The French Ministry of Public Instruction wanted a fair way to identify children who had such serious intellectual deficiencies that they needed to be placed in special classes, without leaving the decision to a teacher's opinion. Binet and Simon's test measured the skills that children need for success in school, such as counting, remembering, following instructions, and understanding language. When Stanford psychologists translated Binet's test into English, they changed the emphasis to identifying the best students, who would profit from accelerated classes. Objective tests help identify students with good abilities, including some whom their teachers had overlooked or underestimated.

Intelligence quotient (IQ) tests try to *predict people's performance in school and similar settings.* The term *quotient* originated when IQ was determined by dividing mental age by chronological age and then multiplying by 100. **Mental age** is *the average age of children who perform as well as this child.* Chronological age is time since birth. For example, an 8-year-old who performs like an average 10-year-old has a mental age of 10, a chronological age of 8, and an IQ of 10 / 8 × 100 = 125. Intelligence tests no longer use that formula, but the term IQ remains.

IQ tests make reasonably accurate predictions of academic success, as we shall consider in the second module of this chapter. But suppose a test correctly predicts that one student will perform better than another in school. Can we then say that the first student does better *because of* a higher IQ score? No, an IQ is a measurement, not an explanation. A child doesn't do poorly because of a low IQ score any more than a basketball player misses a shot because of a low shooting average.

The Stanford-Binet Test

The test that Binet and Simon designed was later modified for English speakers by Stanford psychologists and published as the **Stanford-Binet IQ test**. It has been revised several times, but much of today's test remains similar to the original test (Gibbons & Warne, 2019). Items on the version for children are designated by age (see ■ Table 9.1). An item designated as "age 8," for example, will be answered correctly by 60 to 90 percent of 8-year-olds. A higher percentage of older children answer it correctly and a lower percentage of younger children.

Table 9.1 Examples of the Types of Items on the Stanford-Binet Test

Age	Sample Test Items
2	Test administrator points at pictures of everyday objects and asks, "What is this?" "Here are some pegs of different sizes and shapes. See whether you can put each one into the correct hole."
4	"Why do people live in houses?" "Birds fly in the air; fish swim in the ___."
6	"Here is a picture of a horse. Do you see what part of the horse is missing?" "Here are some candies. Can you count how many there are?"
8	"What should you do if you find a lost puppy?" "Stephanie can't write today because she twisted her ankle. What is wrong with that?"
10	"Why should people be quiet in a library?" "Repeat after me: 4 8 3 7 1 4."
12	"What does regret mean?" "Here is a picture. Can you tell me what is wrong with it?"
14	"What is the similarity between high and low?" "Watch me fold this paper and cut it. Now, when I unfold it, how many holes will there be?"
Adult	"Make up a sentence using the words celebrate, reverse, and appointment." "What do people mean when they say, 'People who live in glass houses should not throw stones'?"

(Source: Modified from Nietzel and Bernstein, 1987.)

School psychologists are carefully trained on how to administer the test items and score the answers. A psychologist testing an 8-year-old might start with the items designated for 7-year-olds. Unless the child misses many of the 7-year-old items, the psychologist gives credit for all the 6-year-old items without testing them. If the child answers most of the 7-year-old items correctly, the psychologist proceeds to the items for 8-year-olds, 9-year-olds, and so forth, until the child begins missing most items. At that point, the test ends. This method is known as **adaptive testing,** because *the range of items used is adapted to the performance of the individual.* Individuals proceed at their own pace, usually finishing in 45 to 90 minutes.

Stanford-Binet IQ scores are computed from tables set up to ensure that a given IQ score means the same at different ages. The mean IQ at each age is 100. A 6-year-old with an IQ score of, say, 116 has performed better on the test than 84 percent of other 6-year-olds. Similarly, an adult with an IQ score of 116 has performed better than 84 percent of other adults. The Stanford-Binet provides an overall IQ score, a verbal IQ score, and a nonverbal IQ score based on items answered by handling objects. The test also provides subscores reflecting visual reasoning, short-term memory, and other skills.

The Wechsler Tests

The **Wechsler Intelligence Scale for Children–Fifth Edition (WISC–V)** and the **Wechsler Adult Intelligence Scale–Fourth Edition (WAIS–IV),** *originally devised by David Wechsler in 1939, and later modified by others,* produce the same average, 100, and almost the same distribution of scores as the Stanford-Binet. The WISC is for children up to age 16, and the WAIS is for everyone older. As with the Stanford-Binet, the Wechsler tests are administered to one person at a time (see ◄ Figure 9.3). The Stanford-Binet and Wechsler tests are the most widely used IQ tests.

A Wechsler test provides an overall IQ, a Verbal IQ, a Performance IQ (based on tasks that do not require a verbal response), and subtest scores representing working memory, verbal

© James Kalat

▲ **Figure 9.3** Most IQ tests are administered individually. Here, a psychologist (left) records the responses by a participant (right).

comprehension, processing speed, and others. Examples of working memory items are "Listen to these numbers and then repeat them: 3 6 2 5" and "Listen to these numbers and repeat them in reverse order: 4 7 6." An example of a processing speed item is "Put a slash (/) through all the circles on this page and an X through all the squares, as quickly as possible."

Subscores on either the Stanford-Binet or the Wechsler tests call attention to someone's strengths and weaknesses. For example, a child who learned English as a second language might do best on items that call for nonverbal answers. Educators can use either test to identify possible learning disabilities.

▲ **Figure 9.4** Items similar to those on Raven's Progressive Matrices test. Select the item that completes the pattern both going across and going down. (You can check your answers against answer A on page 292.)

Culture-Reduced Testing

If you learned English as a second language, or if you are hearing impaired, your score on the Stanford-Binet or Wechsler IQ test might seriously underestimate your abilities. "Why not translate the tests into other languages, including sign language?" you might ask. Psychologists do, but it is not practical to translate them into all the world's languages. Furthermore, a translated item may be easier or harder than the original. For example, some items refer to information that is more familiar in one culture than another. A direct translation would not produce an equivalent test.

Psychologists have therefore tried to devise a culture-fair or culture-reduced test. Although no task is free of cultural influences, some tests are fairer than others. *The most widely used culture-reduced test* is the Progressive Matrices test devised by John C. Raven. These matrices, which *progress*

gradually from easy to difficult items, attempt to measure abstract reasoning (fluid intelligence) without use of language or factual information. To answer questions on the Progressive Matrices, someone must generate hypotheses, test them, and infer rules. ▲ Figure 9.4 presents three matrices similar to those on this test. The first is relatively easy, the second is harder, and the third is harder still.

The Progressive Matrices test requires less information than the Wechsler or Stanford-Binet tests, and requires no use of language, but it does assume familiarity with pencil-and-paper, multiple-choice tests. No test can be totally free from cultural influences, but this comes closer than most. A limitation is that this test provides only a single score instead of identifying someone's strengths and weaknesses.

4. **What might a psychologist recommend if a student has a high score on the Wechsler performance scale but a low score on the verbal scale?**

Answer

4. One recommendation would be for language tutoring. Another recommendation would be to use the Progressive Matrices test to get a possibly more accurate IQ score. The Stanford-Binet and Wechsler tests underestimate the performance of people with language limitations.

Most first-generation immigrants do not score highly on English-language intelligence tests. As a rule, their children and grandchildren get higher scores.

Christian Science Monitor/Getty Images

Individual Differences in IQ Scores

Why do some people score higher than others on IQ tests? The British scholar Francis Galton (1869/1978)[1] was the first to argue for the importance of heredity. His evidence was that politicians, judges, and other eminent and distinguished people generally had distinguished relatives. You can quickly see why this evidence does not justify a conclusion about genetics. Let's consider the better evidence we have today.

[1]A slash like this indicates original publication date and the date of a revised printing, such as one in translation. It does not represent Galton's birth and death dates, which were 1822–1911.

Family Resemblances

■ Table 9.2, based on an extensive literature review (Plomin, DeFries, McClearn, & McGuffin, 2001), shows the correlations of IQ scores for people with various degrees of genetic relationship. These data are based on European and American families.

The scores of monozygotic ("identical") twins correlate with each other about 0.85, significantly higher than dizygotic twins or non-twin siblings (Bishop et al., 2003; McGue & Bouchard, 1998). Monozygotic twins also closely resemble each other in brain volume (Posthuma et al., 2002) and in working memory, attention, reading, and mathematics (Koten et al., 2009; Kovas, Haworth, Dale, & Plomin, 2007; Luciano et al., 2001). The greater similarity between monozygotic than dizygotic twins implies a genetic influence, although it may overstate the genetic impact, because monozygotic twins are more likely to be treated the same. In Table 9.2, note the high correlation between monozygotic twins reared apart. That is, they strongly resemble each other on IQ tests even though they were adopted by separate sets of parents (Bouchard & McGue, 1981; Farber, 1981). However, in most cases their environments were separate but similar.

Monozygotic twins continue to resemble each other throughout life, even beyond age 80 (Petrill et al., 1998). In fact, they become more similar to each other in IQ as they grow older (Davis, Haworth, & Plomin, 2009; Lyons et al., 2009). Why might that be? One explanation is that older individuals have more control of their environment. People who start with an intellectual advantage gravitate toward activities that sustain and increase that advantage. This is called the multiplier effect (Dickens & Flynn, 2001).

A limitation in this research is that most twin studies rely on data from middle-class families. Many, but not all, studies have found less evidence for a genetic influence in low-income families (Bates, Lewis, & Weiss, 2013; Gottschling et al., 2019; Nisbett et al., 2012; Selzam et al., 2017). When most children live in a good-enough environment, the differences among them relate largely to hereditary influences. When children live in less favorable environments, the differences in their quality of environment have a big impact.

concept check

5. How does the multiplier effect influence our estimates of the heritability of intelligence?

Answer

5. It increases measurements of heritability. The multiplier effect means that people with a genetic advantage, even a small one, will probably get an environmental advantage also.

Twins and Single Births

Notice in Table 9.2 that dizygotic twins resemble each other more closely than single-birth siblings do. This finding suggests an influence from being born at the same time and therefore sharing more of the environment. In support of this conclusion, researchers have found a higher correlation between the IQs of brothers born within a couple of years of each other than those born further apart (Sundet, Eriksen, & Tambs, 2008).

Adopted Children

In Table 9.2, note the correlation between unrelated children adopted into the same family, indicating an influence from shared environment (Plomin et al., 2001; Segal, 2000). However, this correlation is lower than the correlation between biological brothers or sisters. The IQs of young adopted children correlate moderately with those of their adoptive parents. As the children grow older, their IQ scores gradually correlate more with those of their biological parents and less with those of their adoptive parents (Loehlin, Horn, & Willerman, 1989; Plomin, Fulker, Corley, & DeFries, 1997; see ▼ Figure 9.5). Another interesting study examined "virtual twins"—unrelated children of the same age growing up in the same family. For example, parents might adopt two children of the same age, or have a child of their own and adopt another of the same age. In these cases, the virtual twins' IQs are moderately correlated in early childhood, and less as they grow older (Segal, McGuire, & Stohs, 2012).

The studies of adopted children imply a genetic influence from the biological parents, but another interpretation is possible. Some low-IQ parents who put their children up for adoption are impoverished and probably do not provide good prenatal care. Poor prenatal care correlates with decreased IQ for the offspring throughout life (Breslau, Dickens, Flynn, Peterson, & Lucia, 2006). In short, adopted children can resemble

Table 9.2 Mean Correlations for the IQs of Children with Various Degrees of Genetic and Environmental Similarity

Degree of Genetic or Environmental Similarity	Correlation of IQ Scores
Parent and child	0.41
Sibling	0.47
Parent & biological child who is adopted by another family	0.23
Biological siblings who are adopted in separate families	0.23
Adoptive parent & adopted child	0.19
Unrelated children adopted in the same family	0.31
Monozygotic twins adopted in separate families	0.78
Monozygotic twins reared together	0.85
Dizygotic twins reared together	0.6

(Adapted from Plomin, DeFries, McClearn, & McGuffin, 2001)

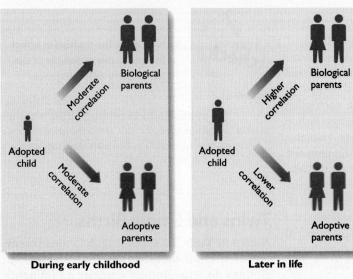

▲ Figure 9.5 As adopted children grow older, their IQs begin to correlate more strongly with those of their biological parents.

has the greatest effect on the youngest children (Beckett et al., 2006; Nelson et al., 2007; van IJzendoorn, Juffer, & Poelhuis, 2005).

Among environmental influences, much research emphasizes the role of physical health. Researchers have compared mean IQ scores across countries and across states within the United States. We need to be cautious here, as scores are not always comparable among countries speaking different languages. Still, the finding is that mean IQ is consistently lowest in the countries and states where children have the highest exposure to infectious diseases, such as tetanus, malaria, tuberculosis, hepatitis, cholera, and measles (Eppig, Fincher, & Thornhill, 2010, 2011). ▼ Figure 9.6 shows the results across countries. After public health programs reduced the prevalence of malaria in Tanzania, children showed substantial improvements in language performance (Klejnstrupl, Buhl-Wiggers, Jones, & Rand, 2018). Randomized controlled studies have demonstrated IQ benefits from dietary supplements (Protzko, 2017). In short, health is important for intellectual development.

Education also promotes intelligence. Evidence includes the fact that intellectual performance declines during summer vacation, for college students as well as for young children (Dills, Hernandez-Julian, & Rotthoff, 2016). Also, a comparison between children who were just barely old enough to start first grade and those just barely too young found that the children who went to school made more intellectual progress during that year (Brod, Bunge, & Shing, 2017). A variety of programs have provided special interventions for children from deprived homes to foster their intellectual development. Although no brief educational program helps much, intensive programs occupying many hours per week for several years do produce significant, lasting benefits (Barnett, 2011; Reynolds, Temple, Ou, Arteaga, & White, 2011).

their biological parents for nongenetic as well as genetic reasons.

Gene Identification

Modern research methods make it possible to identify particular genes that correlate with intelligence or anything else. The strategy is to locate genes that are more common among those with higher IQ scores than in people with lower scores. Studies on large populations have identified more than a thousand genetic variations that correlate with intelligence (Plomin & von Stumm, 2018; Savage et al., 2018). However, although certain rare genetic variants produce a big effect (because the rare form produces a severe deficit), all the common genetic variants produce such tiny effects that researchers have to compare results over thousands, tens of thousands, or even hundreds of thousands of people before they can demonstrate a statistically significant effect.

In that case, how can we explain the results showing such high heritability? One possibility is that the key factor is how genes are expressed (that is, epigenetic effects) rather than differences in the genes themselves.

Environmental Influences

Heredity is not the whole story. The importance of the environment for intelligence is especially apparent when children from a low-quality orphanage get adopted into a good home, or when a family with small children moves to a more prosperous country. In such cases, IQ scores can increase substantially (Sauce & Matzel, 2018). The improved environment

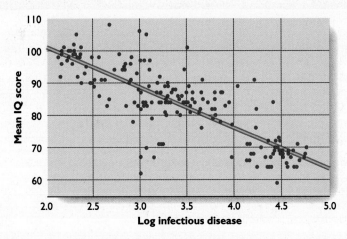

▲ Figure 9.6 Each dot represents the results for one country. Along the *x*-axis is the degree of exposure to infectious disease. Along the *y*-axis is the mean IQ score. The correlation was –0.82. (Figure 1 part (a) from "Parasite prevalence and the worldwide distribution of cognitive ability," by C. Eppig, C. L. Fincher, & R. Thornhill, 2010. *Proceedings of the Royal Society B, 277*, pp. 3801–3808. Copyright © 2010 by the Royal Society. Reprinted with permission.)

6. What types of evidence indicate an environmental contribution to individual differences in IQ scores?

Answer

6. Dizygotic twins resemble each other more than siblings born at separate times do. IQ appears to be less heritable for children in homes of low socioeconomic status. The mean IQ score is lowest in those countries and states where children have the highest exposure to infectious diseases. Orphans adopted into good homes show substantial increases in intelligence. Educational programs boost scores.

Brain Size and Intelligence

As a final point for this module, are you curious about the relation between brain size and intelligence? We would expect that, other things being equal, bigger brains are probably better than smaller ones. To some extent, they are, on average, although not strongly enough to make any prediction about an individual. Human brain volume correlates about 0.24 with IQ scores, according to one study (Pietschnig, Penke, Wicherts, Zeiler, & Voracek, 2015), and about 0.19 according to another, larger study (Nave, Jung, Linner, Kable, & Koellinger, 2019). A study within families found that, on average, the sibling with the larger brain also shows higher intelligence, with a correlation of 0.18 (Lee et al., 2019). This is a small tendency, but it becomes evident when researchers take an average over a large sample.

One puzzle is that, on average, men have larger brains than women, but women are equal to men in intelligence. Women have a more deeply folded cerebral cortex, and therefore the surface area of the cortex is nearly equal for men and women (Luders et al., 2004). Neuron cell bodies line the surface of the cortex, and therefore men and women have approximately the same number of neurons.

Elephants and whales have larger brains than humans, although we are more intelligent, at least in our own opinion. (We defined intelligence, so we get to make the rules.) Brain-to-body ratio does not put us in first place either, because some small monkey species have a greater ratio than humans do. However, humans have more total neurons than any other species. We have more than monkeys because we are larger than they are, and we have more neurons than elephants or whales because their neurons are larger and less numerous (Herculano-Houzel, 2011).

---

in closing | module 9.1

Measuring Intelligence

The standard IQ tests were first devised a century ago and revised by trial and error since then. Still today we cannot precisely define what we mean by intelligence. How useful are the tests? This is an empirical question, one to be decided by research. The next module explores ways of evaluating IQ tests.

Summary

- *Spearman's psychometric approach.* People's scores on almost any test of intelligent abilities correlate positively with scores on other tests. Charles Spearman inferred that all intellectual tasks use a general factor, referred to as *g*. (page 283)
- *Alternative explanations.* Many psychologists believe the *g* factor corresponds to a single ability, such as mental speed or working memory. Another possibility is that the many skills required for any task partly overlap the skills for any other. Still another explanation is that abilities correlate with one another because the same growth factors that promote one also support the others. (page 284)
- *Fluid and crystallized intelligence.* Psychologists distinguish between fluid intelligence (reasoning ability) and crystallized intelligence (acquired and practiced skills). (page 285)
- *One or many types of intelligence?* Howard Gardner argued that people have independent types of intelligence, such as social attentiveness, musical abilities, and motor skills. However, so far, no one has demonstrated this independence. (page 285)
- *IQ tests.* The Stanford-Binet and Wechsler IQ tests provide an overall score and subscores representing specialized skills. Culture-reduced tests such as Raven's Progressive Matrices are more appropriate for people not fluent in English. (page 286)
- *Hereditary influences.* Studies of twins and adopted children imply hereditary influences on individual differences in IQ performance. However, no common genetic difference has a major effect. Epigenetic influences are probably important. (page 289)
- *Environmental influences.* Intellectual development depends on many aspects of the environment, including health and nutrition. Moving a child from an impoverished environment such as an orphanage to a supportive environment increases intelligence significantly. (page 290)
- *Brain size.* Across animal species and among humans, intelligence appears to correlate with the number of neurons. Among humans, brain size does not correlate strongly enough with intelligence to provide a useful predictor for any individual. (page 291)

Key Terms

Answers to Other Question in the Module

A. 1. (8); 2. (2); 3. (4) For item 3, going either across or down, add any parts that are different and subtract any parts that are the same (page 288).

Review Questions

1. What evidence did Spearman have for the existence of *g*?
   (a) Scores of monozygotic twins correlate highly with each other.
   (b) Scores on any test of intelligent performance correlate positively with scores on other tests.
   (c) Children who are identified as intellectually gifted tend to become highly productive adults.
   (d) On average, intelligence scores are equal for males and females.

2. On average, how does intelligence change after age 20?
   (a) Both fluid and crystallized intelligence decline.
   (b) Fluid intelligence declines, but crystallized intelligence increases.
   (c) Fluid intelligence increases, but crystallized intelligence declines.
   (d) Both fluid and crystallized intelligence remain constant.

3. The research most strongly supports which of these conclusions?
   (a) It is important for educators to identify children's different learning styles.
   (b) The IQs of monozygotic twins become more similar as they grow older.
   (c) People have several independent, unrelated forms of intelligence.
   (d) IQ scores explain why some children do better than others in school.

4. What was the original purpose of Binet's first IQ test?
   (a) To select the brightest students for advanced training
   (b) To compare the performance of ethnic groups
   (c) To determine the relationship between intelligence and brain size
   (d) To identify slow learners who needed special education

5. What is the advantage of Raven's Progressive Matrices test?
   (a) It provides subscores that identify someone's strengths and weaknesses.
   (b) It can be used with people who do not understand English.
   (c) It can be used with people who are blind.
   (d) It directly measures the efficiency of each brain area.

6. What provides the main evidence for a genetic influence on intelligence?
   (a) Comparison of the chromosomes of people differing in intelligence
   (b) Measurements of changes in IQ scores as people grow older
   (c) Similarity of IQ scores between parents and children
   (d) Studies of twins and adopted children

7. In addition to schooling, which of the following is known to improve cognitive performance for many low-performing children?
   (a) Better nutrition
   (b) Sensitivity to a child's learning style
   (c) Longer vacations from school
   (d) Starting school at a later age

8. In what way do human brains exceed those of all other species?
   (a) Humans have the largest neurons.
   (b) Humans have the largest brain volume.
   (c) Humans have the largest number of neurons.
   (d) Humans have the largest ratio of axons to cell bodies.

Answers: 1b, 2b, 3b, 4d, 5b, 6d, 7a, 8c.

module 9.2

Evaluating Intelligence Tests

After studying this module, you should be able to:

1. Define standardization of a test.

2. Explain the Flynn effect and the evidence for it.

3. Describe the evidence that researchers use to measure reliability and validity.

4. Define test bias and describe how researchers look for it.

5. Discuss stereotype threat.

> Whatever exists at all exists in some amount.
> —E. L. Thorndike (1918, p. 16)

> Anything that exists in amount can be measured.
> —W. A. McCall (1939, p. 15)

> Anything which exists can be measured incorrectly.
> —D. Detterman (1979, p. 167)

The three quotes above apply to intelligence: If intelligence exists, it must exist in some amount. It must be measurable, but it can be measured either correctly or incorrectly. How accurate, useful, and fair are the IQ tests?

Standardizing IQ Tests

In the first module, we considered examples of IQ tests. To evaluate them or any other test, we need objective evidence. The evaluation begins with **standardization**, *the process of evaluating the questions, improving ambiguous items, and establishing rules for administering a test and interpreting the scores.* One step in this process is to find the **norms**, *descriptions of how frequently various scores occur.* Psychologists try to standardize a test on a large representative sample of the population.

You may sometimes hear someone use the term *standardized test* in a way that makes it sound threatening. The opposite of a standardized test is an unstandardized test, like nearly all the ones that professors give in class. Some of the questions might be confusing, and the test might be easier or harder than the professor intended. Standardizing a test improves it.

The Distribution of IQ Scores

Binet, Wechsler, and the others who devised IQ tests chose the items and arranged the scoring method to establish a mean score of 100. The standard deviation is 15 for the Wechsler test, and 16 for the Stanford-Binet. The standard deviation measures variance among individuals. It is small if most scores are close to the mean and large if scores vary widely. The scores for a large population approximate a *normal distribution*, or bell-shaped curve, as shown in ▶ Figure 9.7.

In a normal distribution, 68 percent of all people fall within one standard deviation above or below the mean, and about 95 percent are within

two standard deviations. Someone with a score of 115 on the Wechsler test exceeds the scores of people within one standard deviation from the mean plus all of those more than one standard deviation below the mean—a total of 84 percent, as shown in Figure 9.7. Such a person is "in the 84th percentile." Someone with an IQ score of 130 is in the 98th percentile, with a score higher than those of 98 percent of others.

In fact, however, the actual distribution of IQ scores isn't as symmetrical as the theoretical normal distribution. The mode (most common score) is about 105 instead of 100. More people score above 100 than below 100, but a slight bulge in the 60- to 85-range lowers the mean score to 100, as shown in ▼ Figure 9.8 (Johnson, Carothers, & Deary, 2008).

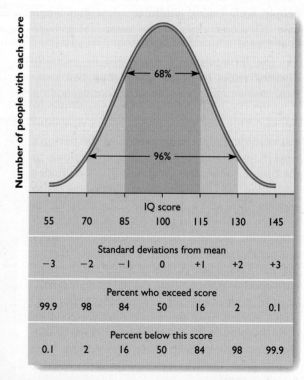

IQ score						
55	70	85	100	115	130	145

Standard deviations from mean						
−3	−2	−1	0	+1	+2	+3

Percent who exceed score						
99.9	98	84	50	16	2	0.1

Percent below this score						
0.1	2	16	50	84	98	99.9

▲ **Figure 9.7** The curve shown here represents the intended distribution of scores on the Wechsler IQ test, with a standard deviation of 15 (15 points above and below the mean, which is 100).

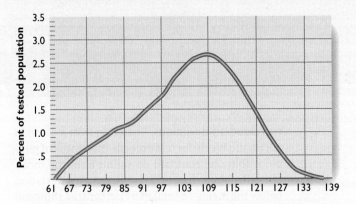

▲ **Figure 9.8** The actual distribution of scores is not quite symmetrical. The mode (most common score) is a bit higher than the mean, and more scores lie far below the mean than equally far above it. (Source: "Sex differences in variability in general intelligence," by W. Johnson, A. Carothers, & I. J. Deary, 2008. *Perspectives on Psychological Science, 3,* pp. 518–531.)

The bulge at the lower end represents people with disabilities, described as mentally challenged. For example, people with **Down syndrome** *have a variety of impairments as a result of having an extra copy of chromosome #21,* generally including impairments in speech development, motor skills, memory, and cognition. However, people with Down syndrome vary, and some have IQ scores close to the mean (Mégarbané et al., 2013).

The term *mentally challenged* or *mentally disabled* refers to people more than two standard deviations below average, corresponding to an IQ score less than 68 or 70, depending on the test. This cutoff is arbitrary, and a psychologist considers other observations of the person's level of functioning before making a diagnosis. In the United States, the Individuals with Disabilities Education Act (IDEA) requires public schools to provide "free and appropriate" education for all children regardless of their limitations. Children with mild physical or intellectual disabilities are mainstreamed as much as possible—that is, placed in the same classes as other children but with special consideration. On the plus side, children in mainstream classes develop better language abilities than those in classes for children with disabilities (Laws, Byrne, & Buckley, 2000). However, children with disabilities seldom form close friendships with their classmates (Webster & Carter, 2013).

An IQ score of 130 or more is the "gifted" range. As with a diagnosis of disabled, a label of gifted requires a judgment based on other behaviors, not just a test score. Gifted children learn rapidly without much help, seek to master knowledge, ask deep questions, and develop new ideas (Winner, 2000). Given adequate opportunities, most go on to earn advanced degrees and to make major accomplishments in science, the arts, business, or government (Kell, Lubinski, & Benbow, 2013).

Since the first IQ tests, psychologists have found that girls tend to do better than boys on certain language tasks, such as verbal fluency, whereas boys tend to do better than girls on visuospatial rotations. On the WAIS, men generally have higher scores on certain subtests, and women have higher scores on others (Irwing, 2012). On attention tasks, males more often focus on one item at a time whereas females spread their attention more broadly (Johnson & Bouchard, 2007). None of these differences are huge, and certainly none of them apply to all individuals. Still, by loading IQ tests with one type of item or another, test authors could have produced results favoring one gender or the other. Instead, they balanced various types of items to ensure that the mean scores of both females and males would be the same. On Raven's Progressive Matrices, even though it has only one type of item, researchers find no significant difference between males and females (Savage-McGlynn, 2012). In short, men and women are equal in intelligence.

concept check

7. **If you want to make a new standardized test, how should you start?**

Answer

7. Administer the test to a representative sample of people to determine the mean and the distribution of scores. Also examine any items that many of the people with high scores missed. Those items might be confusing ... or wrong!

People with Down syndrome vary in their degree of intellectual limitations.

The Flynn Effect

In 1920, the question "What is Mars?" was considered difficult, because most people knew little about the planets. Today, that question is easy. Researchers periodically restandardize tests to keep the overall difficulty about the same.

Eventually a pattern became clear: Every time the test authors restandardized an IQ test, they made it more difficult, to keep the mean score from rising above 100. That is, *decade by decade, generation by generation, people's raw scores on IQ tests gradually increased, and to keep up with this trend, test makers had to make the tests harder, either by changing the questions or revising the standards.* This tendency is known as the Flynn effect, after James Flynn, who called attention to it and made people take it seriously (Flynn, 1984, 1999), although other writers had noticed the trend since as early as 1936 (Lynn, 2013). The results vary, but a typical figure is a gain of about three IQ points per 10 years (Trahan, Stuebing, Fletcher, & Hiscock, 2014).

The size of the Flynn effect—that is, the rate of increase in IQ scores over time—varies from one test to another and one country to another. It also varies from one time to another. As ▼ Figure 9.9 illustrates, the effect was greatest during the 1920s (Pietschnig & Voracek, 2015). Since the 1970s, mean overall performance has stalled or reversed in several European countries. Crystallized IQ has been nearly flat worldwide since the 1970s (Dutton, van der Linden, & Lynn, 2016).

One consequence of the Flynn effect is that if you take an IQ test and later take a restandardized form, your score will probably drop! You did not deteriorate, but you are being compared to a higher standard. For most people, a few points' change makes little difference, but for people at the low end of the distribution, the loss of a few points might qualify them for special services (Kanaya, Scullin, & Ceci, 2003). In states that use the death penalty, courts have forbidden the death penalty for people who are mentally disabled. In borderline cases, eligibility for the death penalty depends on whether someone took an IQ test before or after it was revised.

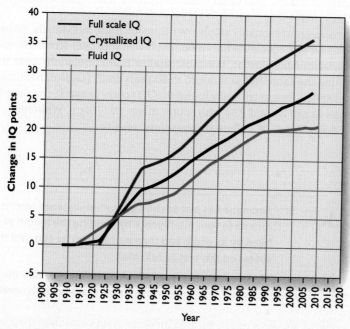

▲ **Figure 9.9** On average, IQ scores increased throughout the world over the decades. (Source: "One century of global IQ gains: A formal meta-analysis of the Flynn effect (1909-2013)," by J. Pietschnig & M. Voracek, 2015. *Perspectives on Psychological Science, 10,* pp. 282-306.)

The Flynn effect—increase in IQ scores over generations—has occurred in nearly every group for whom we have data, including people in rural Kenya (Daley, Whaley, Sigman, Espinosa, & Neumann, 2003) and deaf children in Saudi Arabia (Bakhiet, Barakat, & Lynn, 2014). Within the United States, the effect has occurred in all ethnic groups, with larger gains by black and Hispanic people than by non-Hispanic whites (Rindermann & Thompson, 2013).

What accounts for the Flynn effect? Here are some hypotheses, with their pros and cons (Pietschnig & Voracek, 2015; Trahan et al., 2014; Williams, 2013):

- **Improved education.** In the early 1900s, many children quit school after the eighth grade, if not before, and the quality of education was often poor. Improved education probably contributes to rising IQ performances, but it could not account for all of the Flynn effect, because the IQ improvement is evident for children who are just starting school, and for rural Kenyan children, who have little schooling (Daley et al., 2003). Furthermore, strong gains are apparent for scores on Raven's Progressive Matrices, which measures skills not taught in school.

- **Decreases in mental retardation.** Advances in medicine have decreased several types of mental retardation. However, over the decades we see an increase in the highest test scores as well as a decrease in low scores (Wai & Putallaz, 2011).

- **Improved health and nutrition** (Sigman & Whaley, 1998). People have been getting taller over the years, because of improved health and nutrition, decreased exposure to lead, and decreased smoking and drinking by pregnant women. Infants today on average hold their head up earlier than in past generations. They also sit up, stand, walk, say their first word, and so forth at a younger age (Lynn, 2009). Mean brain size is also somewhat larger now than in past decades (Menie, Penaherrera, Fernandes, Becker, & Flynn, 2016). Researchers studying intelligence agree that better health and nutrition is an important contributor to the Flynn effect (Rindermann, Becker, & Coyle, 2017).

- **Increased cognitive stimulation.** People have been exposed to more stimulation over the years, beginning with radio, and then movies, television, video games, and the Internet. Even in rural Kenya, some homes now have television (Daley et al., 2003).

- An increased tendency for people to marry outside their own neighborhood (Mingroni,

2004). Plant breeders have long noticed *hybrid vigor*, the improvement from crossing two genetic strains of a plant. For people, too, children have an advantage if their parents' genes are not too similar. A study in China found that a marriage between people from different provinces of the country yielded children who were taller and more academically successful than average (Zhu, Zhang, Zhao, & Chen, 2018).

Although performance on IQ tests has increased, have people really become that much more intelligent? Do we really believe that the average person of your grandparents' generation was, by today's standards, "intellectually challenged"? Flynn (1998) argued that the increase in IQ scores does not indicate equally increased intelligence over time. If so, we have to wonder exactly what IQ scores mean. At a minimum, it is clear that the IQ scores of people from different generations do not mean the same thing.

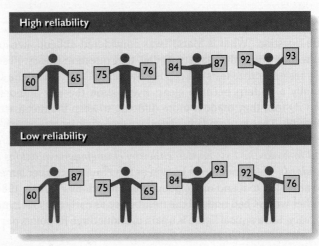
▲ **Figure 9.10** On a test with high reliability, people get similar scores each time they take the test. On a test with low reliability, scores fluctuate randomly.

on a scale from 0 to 1. Psychologists may test the same people twice and compare the two sets of scores, or they may compare the scores on the first and second halves of the test, or the scores on the test's odd-numbered and even-numbered items. If the test is reliable, one score correlates highly with the other. ▲ Figure 9.10 illustrates test–retest reliability, *the correlation between scores on a first test and a retest.*

If a test's reliability is perfect (+1), the person with the highest score on the first test also scores highest on the retest, the person who scores second highest on the first test scores second highest on the retest, and so forth. If the reliability is 0, scores vary randomly from the test to retest. For example, if the students in your class took a multiple-choice test in a language that none of you understand, so that everyone is just guessing on every item, we would expect a reliability of zero. The WISC, Stanford-Binet, Progressive Matrices, and other commonly used intelligence tests all have reliabilities above 0.9.

IQ scores are reasonably stable over time for most individuals. Scores for children under age 7 correlate only moderately well with later scores (Schneider, Niklas, & Schmiedeler, 2014), but most studies find correlations near 0.9 for adults taking the same test at times 10 to 20 years apart (Larsen, Hartmann, & Nyborg, 2008). A long-term study found that IQ scores at age 11 correlated 0.66 with scores at age 80 and 0.54 with scores at age 90 (Deary, Whiteman, Starr, Whalley, & Fox, 2004). ▼ Figure 9.11 shows those results.

8. If we want to evaluate explanations for the Flynn effect, why is it helpful to examine results from different countries and cultures?

Answer
8. If the Flynn effect is stronger in some places than others, we can relate it to what we know about those places. For example, some places have improved their health and nutrition more than others, some have had a bigger increase in marrying outside one's neighborhood, and some have increased cognitive stimulation more than others.

Evaluating Tests

Have you ever complained about a test in school that seemed unfair? *Seeming* unfair doesn't necessarily make it unfair—and seeming fair doesn't necessarily make it fair. When psychologists want to evaluate the accuracy or fairness of a test, they examine evidence related to its reliability and validity.

Reliability

The reliability of a test is defined as *the repeatability of its scores*. If a test is reliable, it produces similar results every time. To determine the reliability of a test, psychologists calculate a correlation coefficient. A correlation coefficient measures how accurately we can use one measurement to predict another,

9. Someone has just devised a new "intelligence test." It measures your intelligence by dividing the length of your head by its width and then multiplying by 100. Will the scores on this test be reliable?

10. Most students find that their scores on any standardized test increase the second time they take it. Does the improvement indicate that the test is unreliable?

Answers
10. Not necessarily. If most people's scores improve by about the same amount, then those who had the highest scores the first time still have the highest scores the second time.

9. Yes! To say that a test is "reliable" is simply to say that its scores are repeatable. This test will give useless scores, but they will be highly reliable (repeatable).

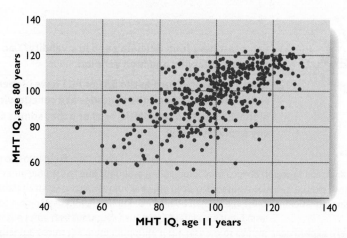

▲ **Figure 9.11** In this scatter plot, each point represents one person. The *x*-axis shows the IQ score at age 11, and the *y*-axis shows the IQ score at age 80. (MHT = the Moray House Test, a type of IQ test.) (Source: "The impact of childhood intelligence on later life: Following up the Scottish mental surveys of 1932 and 1947," by I. J. Deary, M. C. Whiteman, J. M. Starr, L. J. Whalley, & H. C. Fox, 2004. *Journal of Personality and Social Psychology, 86*, pp. 130–147.)

Validity

A test's validity is defined as *the degree to which evidence and theory support the interpretations of test scores for the intended purposes* (Joint Committee on Standards, 1999). In simpler terms, validity indicates how well the test measures what it claims to measure. To determine the validity of a test, researchers examine several types of evidence:

Content. The content of a test should match its purposes. A test given to job applicants should include only tasks that are important for the job. An end-of-grade test for fifth grade should correspond to the fifth-grade curriculum.

Response processes. If a test claims to measure a certain skill, then the test-takers should need to use that skill instead of using shortcuts. For example, tests of reading comprehension include something to read, followed by questions. If people can guess the correct answers without reading the passage, then the test isn't a valid measure of reading comprehension (Katz, Lautenschlager, Blackburn, & Harris, 1990).

Usefulness for prediction. Most importantly, if a test is valid, the scores predict some performance. For example, scores on an interest inventory should predict which jobs or activities someone would enjoy. Results of a personality test should predict aspects of social and emotional behavior. Scores on an IQ test should predict grades in school. Researchers determine the validity of an IQ test by measuring how well its scores correlate with students' grades. In fact, the correlations are positive for all academic subjects (Deary, Strand, Smith, & Fernandes, 2007).

Measuring the validity of adult IQ tests is more difficult, because adults do not go to school (Ackerman, 2017). However, people with higher IQ scores get better than average jobs and earn higher than average salaries (Strenze, 2007). They have fewer than average automobile accidents (O'Toole, 1990). They tend to be healthier than average, to live longer (Shalev et al., 2013), and to show more creativity and leadership (Kuncel & Hezlett, 2010). They are less likely to suffer post-traumatic stress disorder (Vasterling et al., 2002) and less likely to become depressed (Aichele et al., 2018). They do better than average at reading maps, understanding order forms, reading bus schedules, understanding nutrition labels on foods, and taking their medicines correctly (Gottfredson, 2002a; Murray, Johnson, Wolf, & Deary, 2011). They are more likely than average to hold attitudes that are antiracist and favorable to women's causes (Deary, Batty, & Gale, 2008). Although some of these correlations are small, they indicate that IQ scores do relate to real-world outcomes outside the classroom. Plomin and von Stumm (2018, p. 148) have said, "Life is an intelligence test."

As you might expect, high scores predict success in scientific fields. Even among people with a master's or PhD degree, those with higher scores usually have more patents and scientific publications (Park, Lubinski, & Benbow, 2008). IQ scores also predict success on jobs, especially if combined with other information (Schmidt & Hunter, 1998). According to Linda Gottfredson (2002b, pp. 25, 27), "The general mental ability factor—*g*—is the best single predictor of job performance . . . [It] enhances performance in all domains of work." According to Frank Schmidt and John Hunter (1981, p. 1128), "Professionally developed cognitive ability tests are valid predictors of performance on the job . . . for all jobs . . . in all settings." However, even if the validity is above zero, it is not always high enough to be useful. For example, no one would use IQ scores to predict success for singers or professional athletes, even if the validity is above zero.

Do IQ tests measure everything that we care about? Of course they don't, not even in academics. Success in school and elsewhere depends on self-control and persistence (Duckworth & Seligman, 2017). College grades correlate highly with measures of effort (Credé & Kuncel, 2008) and curiosity (von Stumm, Hell, & Chamorro-Premuzic, 2011). However, measuring self-control, persistence, and curiosity is difficult. Applicants can easily "fake" the right personality or misreport their motivation (Niessen & Meijer, 2017).

Consequences of testing. Tests produce benefits, but also certain unintended consequences. In the U.S. public school system, students' scores on end-of-grade tests determine whether they advance to the next grade. The scores also sometimes influence the teachers' salaries and the amount of government support that a school receives. As a result, the best qualified teachers don't want to work at schools with low-performing students. Many students and teachers concentrate heavily on preparing for the tests at the expense of other educational goals. Do the tests accomplish enough good to outweigh these costs? Although opinions are strong, good research on this issue is rare.

In some countries, test scores determine a student's future almost irrevocably. Students who perform well are almost assured future success, and those who perform poorly have limited opportunities.

11. Can a test have high reliability and low validity? Can a test have low reliability and high validity?

12. Would test scores such as the SAT or ACT have higher validity for predicting college grades at a college with the highest admission standards, or at one that admits almost any applicant? Why?

Answers

11. A test can have high reliability and low validity. Reliability means repeatability and nothing more. A test with low reliability cannot have high validity, however. Low reliability means that the scores fluctuate randomly. If the test scores cannot even predict a later score on the same test, then they can hardly predict anything else.

12. Scores would have higher validity at a college that admits almost anyone, because the scores would vary over a larger range. At the most competitive colleges, almost everyone has the same high score, and therefore the differences in college performance have to depend on something else.

Special Problems in Measuring Validity

Measuring the validity of a test can be difficult. At most colleges, students' grades correlate only modestly with their scores on the SAT or ACT. Why? Does that result imply a weakness of the tests? Not really. College students take different courses, and a B in a harder course is not comparable to a B in an easier course. If we examine data for only students taking the same courses, the test scores predict success reasonably well (Berry & Sackett, 2009).

Here is another issue: Consider data for the Graduate Record Examination (GRE), a test taken by graduate school applicants. According to one large study, grades for first-year graduate students in physics correlated 0.13 with their GRE quantitative scores and 0.19 with their verbal scores. That is, for students in physics, verbal scores predicted success better than quantitative scores did. For first-year students in English, the pattern was reversed. Their grades correlated 0.29 with their quantitative scores and 0.23 with their verbal scores (Educational Testing Service, 1994). These scores seem surprising, because physics is such a quantitative field and English is such a verbal field.

The explanation is simple: Almost all graduate students in physics have nearly the same (very high) score on the quantitative test, and almost all English graduate students have nearly the same (very high) score on the verbal test. If the students in a department have nearly the same score, their scores cannot predict who will do better than others. A test predicts performance only when scores vary over a substantial range.

Interpreting Fluctuations in Scores

Suppose on the first test in some course you get 94 percent correct. On the second test, which was equally difficult, your score is only 88 percent. Does that score indicate that you studied harder for the first test? Not necessarily. When tests are not perfectly reliable, your scores fluctuate. The lower the reliability, the greater the fluctuation.

When people lose sight of this fact, they sometimes draw unwarranted conclusions. In one study, Harold Skeels (1966) tested infants in an orphanage and identified those with the lowest IQ scores. He transferred those infants to an institution that provided more attention. Several years later, most of them showed major increases in their IQ scores. Should we conclude, as many psychologists did, that the extra attention improved the children's IQ performances? Other studies do support that conclusion, but this particular study had no control group (Longstreth, 1981). IQ tests for infants have low reliability—that is, low repeatability. If you had selected infants with the lowest scores and then said "hocus pocus" and tested them again a few days later, most of their scores would have improved, simply because they had nowhere to go but up.

Suppose we examine all the students who had close to a perfect score on the first test in some class. What scores should we expect on the second test? On average, their scores will go down. It is not because they got overconfident and failed to study. It is because the tests are not perfectly reliable, and a certain amount of fluctuation is inevitable. Similarly, for those with the lowest scores on the first test, we can predict that, on average, their scores will improve. This tendency is called *regression to the mean*. Some people misinterpret this pattern to mean that "everyone gets more mediocre over time." No, because many of the students with scores near the middle will go up or down on the second test. The second test has as many high scorers and low scorers as the first test, but they are not exactly the same students as the first test. ▼ Figure 9.12 illustrates this idea for a small sample of students.

A similar trend occurs wherever performance fluctuates. An athlete who performs extremely well or extremely poorly at one time will probably be closer to average the next time. If the value of a stock investment shoots way up today, the best guess is that it won't repeat its performance tomorrow. If a therapist starts treating patients who feel extremely depressed, some degree of improvement is likely, on average, regardless of the treatment. All of these changes reflect the low reliability of the measurements.

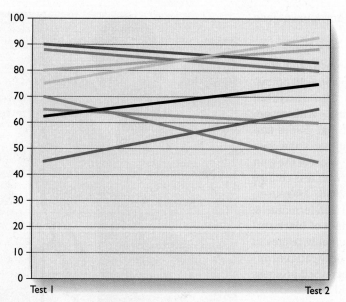

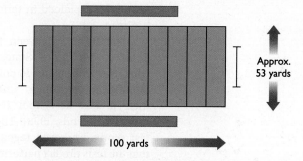

The diagram above represents a football field. What is the ratio of the distance between the goal lines to the distance between the sidelines?

a. 1.89
b. 1.53
c. 0.53
d. 5.3
e. 53

▲ **Figure 9.12** On a test with less than perfect reliability, scores fluctuate. On average, people with the highest scores will see decreased scores on a retest, and those with the lowest scores will see increased scores. This tendency is called *regression to the mean*. However, the overall distribution remains about the same, because of increases and decreases by those who had intermediate scores on the first test.

▲ **Figure 9.13** This item was eliminated from the SAT when researchers determined that it was biased against women. Some women who did very well on the rest of the test did not know which were the goal lines and which were the sidelines.

Measuring Test Bias

In addition to being reliable and valid, a test should also be unbiased—that is, equally fair and accurate for all groups. A **biased** test *overstates or understates the true performance of one or more groups.* If one group scores better than another, the difference by itself does not necessarily indicate bias. To take an extreme example, students who study hard in a course get better grades than those who don't study. Does that result mean the test is biased against students who don't study? No. (If you do think it is biased, then your idea of an unbiased test is one on which everyone gets the same score.) If groups really do differ in their performance, a test should report that fact. Driver's license examinations include vision tests. Are they biased against people who are blind? Again, no. The results accurately predict that blind people would be poor drivers. However, if someone were selecting applicants to be a high school guidance counselor, then a vision test *would* be biased against the blind, because it would understate their ability to do the job. The point is that bias means unfairness for a particular purpose. Researchers need to determine the bias, or lack of it, for any potential use of any test.

The question of bias is an empirical question—that is, one to be decided by the evidence. To measure possible test bias, psychologists conduct several kinds of research. They try to identify bias both in individual test items and in the test as a whole.

Evaluating Possible Bias in Single Test Items

Suppose on a test with 100 items, one item is the 10th easiest for group A but only the 42nd easiest for group B. This pattern suggests that the item taps information or skills that are more available to group A than group B. If so, the item is biased (Schmitt & Dorans, 1990). ▶ **Figure 9.13**, an item that once appeared on the SAT, diagrams an American football field and asks for the ratio of the distance between the goal lines to the distance between the sidelines. For men, this was one of the easiest items on the test. Many women missed it, including some

of the brightest women who missed almost no other questions.

The reason was that some women had so little interest in football that they did not know which were the goal lines and which were the sidelines. The publishers of the SAT saw that this item was biased and removed it from the test.

Evaluating Possible Bias in a Test as a Whole

By definition, a biased test misestimates the performance by members of some group. For example, if an IQ test is biased against black students, then black students who score, say, 100 will do better in school than white students with the same score.

Researchers have repeatedly looked for evidence of test bias but have never found that blacks' or Hispanics' mean performance in school is better than the scores would predict (Aguinis, Culpepper, & Pierce, 2016; Berry, 2015; Davis et al., 2013; McCornack, 1983; Pesta & Poznanski, 2008; Sackett, Borneman, & Connelly, 2008). However, most of the data in these studies were collected decades ago.

The unpleasant fact is that white students usually receive better grades in school than black students, as well as higher test scores. The difference in IQ scores approximately matches the difference in school performance. Presumably whatever is impairing performance in school is also impairing performance on the tests. The test scores make no implication about what that is. The difference cannot be explained in terms of any known gene (Colman, 2016).

The IQ gap between black and white students in the United States has decreased from what used to be about 16 points to about 10 points. Simultaneously, black students also increased their grades in school (Grissmer, Williamson, Kirby, & Berends, 1998). The fact that grades and test scores improved together supports the idea that the tests predict performance. Most of the gain occurred between 1970 and 1990, with less change since then (Dickens & Flynn, 2006; Magnuson & Duncan, 2006; Murray, 2007; Rindermann & Thompson, 2013). The improvement of black students' IQ scores and grades presumably relates to improved health, education, and occupational opportunities. The reason for the decreased progress since 1990 is not clear.

If IQ and SAT scores predict school performance about as well for blacks as for whites, then the tests are not biased, according to the definition of test bias. However, another possibility remains: Many black students may be performing at a lower level than they could, in *both* school and the tests.

If so, why? Poverty—which leads to poor prenatal health and nutrition, as well as distraction and worry—impairs intellectual performance (Mani, Mullainathan, Shafir, & Zhao, 2013), but it does not appear to be the whole explanation. If we compare blacks and whites of the same socioeconomic status, a difference in scores remains, although it is smaller than usual (Magnuson & Duncan, 2006). Another possibility is impairment by low expectations and aspirations. If you think you don't have a chance anyway, maybe you don't try. On average, black men score lower than black women, and are less likely than black women to attend college. That fact suggests that many black men are not giving a full effort academically (McKinnon & Bennett, 2005). We explore this possibility in the next section.

Are college entrance tests biased against women? On average, women get better college grades than do men who had the same SAT or ACT scores. That pattern is especially true for women who enter college or graduate school after age 25 (Swinton, 1987). Research results suggest that women tend to get better college grades for at least two reasons. First, women tend to be more conscientious. On average, they attend class more regularly, they turn in more of their assignments on time, and they do more extra credit activities. Second, women tend to take fewer math and science courses, which generally give lower grades (Fischer, Schult, & Hell, 2015; Keiser, Sackett, Kuncel, & Brothen, 2016).

Women who return to school after age 25 usually get better grades than their SAT scores predict. The tests are "biased" against them in the sense of underpredicting their performance.

13. **A company hiring salespeople proposes to test applicants on their ability to speak Spanish. Is this policy biased against people who don't speak Spanish?**

Answer

13. It depends. A test is biased if it underpredicts or overpredicts performance for a group of people. If the salespeople will be working in a neighborhood with many Spanish-speaking customers, this test will accurately predict success on the job, and it is unbiased. However, if the sales staff works in a neighborhood with no need to use Spanish, the test is biased.

Stereotype Threat

Test performance depends not only on the test itself but also on how the test is administered. Imagine you are about to take some test when someone says that "people like you"—left-handers, redheads, people who live in small towns, whatever it might be—usually don't do well on this kind of test. How will that statement affect you? Even if you don't believe the statement, it's a distraction. You worry that if you perform poorly, you confirm this hurtful expectation.

Claude Steele termed this idea **stereotype threat**—*people's perceived risk of performing poorly and thereby supporting an unfavorable stereotype about their group.* In particular, black students who take an IQ test may fear that a poor score would support prejudices about blacks. They become distracted and discouraged. Let's examine Steele's study.

Hypothesis If black students believe they are taking the kind of test on which black students on average do not perform well, then they worry that their own performance may reflect poorly on their group. They may also lose confidence. As a result, they fail to perform up to their abilities. If they are freed from this kind of concern, their performance may improve.

Method Participants were 20 black and 20 white undergraduate students at Stanford University, a prestigious, highly selective institution. They were given a set of 27 difficult verbal questions from the Graduate Record Exam, a test intended for college seniors applying to graduate schools. Before the test, two groups (randomly assigned) received different instructions. Those in the "nondiagnostic" group were told that the researchers were studying how people solve difficult verbal problems. Participants in the "diagnostic" group were told that the research was an attempt to find each participant's strengths and weaknesses in solving verbal problems. This latter instruction was an attempt to increase students' nervousness about being evaluated.

Results Instead of simply presenting the number of correct answers for each group, the researchers adjusted the scores based on participants' SAT scores. The results in ◀ Figure 9.14 show the number of correct answers for each group *relative to the scores predicted by their verbal SAT scores.* The mean for these black students on the verbal part of the SAT was 603, and the mean for these white students was 655. So, if the black and white students both did as well as their SAT scores predicted, the graph would show equal performances on the test, even if the white students answered a slightly higher percentage correctly.

The results for the "nondiagnostic" group do in fact show this pattern. However, black students who were given the "diagnostic" instructions performed below what their SAT scores predicted. They answered fewer questions overall, and answered fewer correctly, than black students who were given the "nondiagnostic" instructions. The instructions did not significantly affect the white students.

When interviewed afterward, the black students who received the "diagnostic" instructions said that they felt strongly aware of the stereotype about black students taking ability tests. They also said they felt self-doubts about possibly conforming to this stereotype (Steele & Aronson, 1995). Another study by the same researchers found that simply asking participants to indicate their race prior to the test impaired black students' scores (Steele & Aronson, 1995).

Interpretation The results confirmed that many black students are sensitive to a suggestion that they are taking a test on which black students do not excel. The worry distracts from their ability to concentrate on the questions. The limitation of this study is that it used only a small number of participants. However, further studies have replicated these results (Nguyen & Ryan, 2008; Steele, 2010). Stereotype threat also applies to other groups, such as the Turkish minority in Germany (Walton & Spencer, 2009).

More Research on Stereotype Threat

Many studies have tested whether stereotype threat impairs girls' performance on math tests, because of the (unfounded) belief that girls do not do well in math. Although many studies seemed to demonstrate this type of stereotype threat, most of the studies with larger numbers of participants did not. It is likely that the apparent support for stereotype threat for girls is a result of publication bias—the tendency to publish results that support the prediction and to disregard results that fail to support it (Flore & Wicherts, 2015).

Stereotype threat acts on older people, but in a different way. Most old people fully accept the stereotype that, in general, older

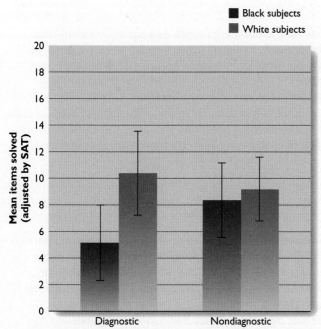

▲ **Figure 9.14** Black students who believed the test would identify their strengths and weaknesses failed to live up to their abilities. (From "Stereotype threat and the intellectual test performance of African Americans," by Claude M. Steele & Joshua Aronson, 1995. *Journal of Personality and Social Psychology, 69,* pp. 797–811.) Copyright © 1995 American Psychological Association. Reprinted with permission.

people have memory problems. They just want to deny that the stereotype is true for themselves! Therefore, a test of memory or problem solving threatens their image of being "different from those other old people," and that worry impairs their performance (Barber, 2017).

Given the goal of helping all people live up to their abilities, how can we combat stereotype threat? Researchers asked students who lacked confidence about their test performance to write about their most important values, their most valuable characteristics, or how it would feel to be highly successful. The result was enhanced test performance (Lang & Lang, 2010; Martens, Johns, Greenberg, & Schimel, 2006; Miyake et al., 2010). Writing about worries helped also, perhaps by getting them out in the open and then dismissing them (Ramirez & Beilock, 2011). The idea is that worrying about your performance leads to "choking under pressure," just as it does for athletes (Beilock, Jellison, Rydell, McConnell, & Carr, 2006).

Benefits of writing interventions can last surprisingly long. One group of black seventh-grade students completed a series of self-affirming writing assignments about their family, friendships, interests, and values. The result was improved grades in school for at least the next 2 years (Cohen, Garcia, Purdie-Vaughns, Apfel,

& Brzustoski, 2009). Another study found long-lasting benefits from self-affirmation writing by middle-school black and Hispanic students, mainly in what the researchers called "high threat" schools—schools with not many minority students and a history of minority students not performing well (Borman, Grigg, Rozek, Hanselman, & Dewey, 2018). Their interpretation was that affirming your values—such as family and friendships—decreases tension. Students who act with more self-confidence perform better and their teachers react to them more positively, thus magnifying the effect.

The effect of stereotype threat in a onetime experiment is the equivalent of about three IQ points. However, it is harder to estimate the cumulative effect over years. If students have been told year after year that they are not expected to do well, the discouragement may compound. Conversely, increasing early self-confidence could have a cumulative benefit. It could be interesting to see the results of longitudinal studies.

14. How does stereotype threat affect the validity of a test?

15. How would a belief that the tests are biased affect stereotype threat?

Answers

15. Believing that the tests are biased would increase stereotype threat by implying that a group has only a weak chance of success.

14. Because stereotype threat leads some people to perform at a lower level than they would otherwise, it decreases the validity of the test.

---

in closing | module 9.2

Consequences of Testing

Testing of some type is sure to continue for practical reasons. Just as a coach tries to choose the best players for an athletic team, colleges and employers try to choose the applicants who will perform best. When people make those judgments, we want them to use the best available methods and evaluate the results accurately.

Testing has consequences for the individuals who take the tests and the institutions that evaluate the scores, but it can also have another kind of consequence: If we begin to better understand the factors that influence intelligence, we may be able to

do something about these factors. As a society, we would like to intervene early to help children develop as well as possible, but to make those interventions work, we need research. How important are prenatal health and early childhood nutrition? Which kinds of environmental stimulation are most effective? Are different kinds of stimulation better for different kinds of children? To answer these questions, we need good measurements—measurements that can come only from testing of some kind.

Summary

- *Standardization.* To standardize a test is to evaluate its items for clarity and to determine what the scores mean. (page 293)
- *Distribution of IQ scores.* IQ tests have a mean of 100 and a standard deviation of about 15 or 16, depending on the test. However, the mode (most frequent score) is higher than 100 because of a bulge of lower scores. (page 293)
- *The Flynn effect.* To keep the mean score at 100, authors of IQ tests repeatedly increased the difficulty of the tests. If they had not done so, the mean score would have risen substantially. Several factors contribute to this trend. (page 295)
- *Reliability and validity.* Reliability is a measure of the repeatability of a test's scores. Validity is a determination of how well a test measures what it claims to measure. (page 296)

- *Consequences of low reliability.* The lower a measurement's reliability, the more fluctuation of performance will occur. Because of this tendency, individuals with the highest or lowest scores are likely to move toward the mean on a retest. (page 298)
- *Test bias.* Bias means inaccuracy of measurement. Psychologists try to remove from a test any item that tends to be easier for one group of people than for another. They also evaluate whether the test as a whole overestimates or underestimates the performance of any group. (page 299)
- *Test anxiety and stereotype threat.* Many black students perform worse on tests after a reminder of the stereotype of black students scoring poorly on such tests. (page 300)

Key Terms

bias (page 299)

Down syndrome (page 294)

Flynn effect (page 295)

norms (page 293)

reliability (page 296)

standardization (page 293)

stereotype threat (page 301)

test–retest reliability (page 296)

validity (page 297)

Review Questions

1. On average, how do males and females compare in IQ?
   (a) On average, males have a higher IQ.
   (b) On average, females have a higher IQ.
   (c) On average, males and females are equal on all subtests and on overall IQ.
   (d) On average, males and females differ on certain subscores, but are equal on overall IQ.

2. Which of the following is an accepted explanation for the Flynn effect?
   (a) More recent generations have better health and nutrition.
   (b) Revisions of the IQ tests have made them easier.
   (c) Richer people have more children than poorer people do.
   (d) Today's schools teach the material on the tests.

3. If people get approximately the same scores on a test and a retest, what if anything can we conclude about the test's reliability and validity?
   (a) Its reliability is high. We do not know about its validity.
   (b) Its reliability and validity are both high.
   (c) Its validity is high. We do not know about its reliability.
   (d) We do not know about either reliability or validity.

4. A measurement of a test's validity for predicting college grades will be low under which of these conditions?
   (a) If the reliability of the test is high
   (b) If the college admits students with a wide range of scores on the test
   (c) If the college admits only students with high scores on the test
   (d) If the test takes more than an hour to administer

5. Because measurements of athletic performance have less than perfect reliability, what if anything can we predict about changes in performance over time?
   (a) Most athletes who are near average at first will improve over time.
   (b) Most athletes who are near average at first will decline over time.
   (c) Most athletes who are at the top at first will decline over time.
   (d) We can make none of these predictions.

6. What evidence would demonstrate that a test is biased against some group?
   (a) Members of that group get lower than average scores on the test.
   (b) The authors of the test were all from some other group.
   (c) Members of that group perform worse than the scores predict.
   (d) Members of that group perform better than the scores predict.

7. The idea of stereotype threat implies that which of the following impairs performance?
   (a) Lack of familiarity with the content of the test
   (b) Poor health and nutrition
   (c) Other people's low expectations for your success
   (d) Your parents' lack of education

Answers: 1d, 2a, 3a, 4c, 5c, 6d, 7c.

10 Consciousness

iStock.com/Victor_Tongdee

What is consciousness? As William James (1892/1961) said, "Its meaning we know so long as no one asks us to define it" (p. 19).

Of all the questions that humans ask, two are the most profound. One is the existence of the universe. The thirteenth-century theologian Thomas Aquinas first pondered why anything exists, and the philosopher Gottfried Leibniz (1714) explicitly stated the question, "Why is there something rather than nothing?" A second profound question is why, in a universe of matter and energy, does consciousness exist? Does inanimate matter and energy become conscious? If so, how? Or does the existence of consciousness tell us something fundamental about the nature of matter and energy? Donald Hoffman (2019) has revived the idea by the eighteenth-century philosopher George Berkeley that consciousness is what really exists in the universe.

Fundamental questions about both the universe itself and consciousness remain elusive. Nevertheless, some important questions related to consciousness are amenable to research. What aspects of brain activity are associated with consciousness? How does your conscious experience change when you are sleeping, dreaming, or under hypnosis?

iStock.com/yanjf

We examine ourselves to try to understand consciousness.

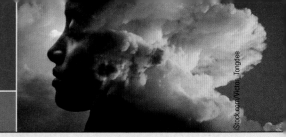

Conscious and Unconscious Processes

After studying this module, you should be able to:

1. Explain why early psychologists abandoned the study of consciousness and why new developments now make such a study possible.

2. List methods of presenting a stimulus while preventing conscious perception of it.

3. Describe how brain activity varies depending on whether a stimulus is consciously perceived.

4. Cite evidence that the brain processes some information unconsciously.

5. Discuss cases in which people in a vegetative state showed evidence of consciousness.

6. Evaluate evidence that brain activity responsible for a movement begins before the conscious decision to make that movement.

In the fall of 2013, the editors of *Science* invited young scientists to answer the question, "What recent discovery in your field will still be remembered 200 years from now?" They published some of the best replies in a later issue ("NextGen Speaks," 2014) and posted others online. Responses included suggestions for physics, astronomy, chemistry, biochemistry, and other fields, but no one offered a suggestion for psychology. So, what recent discovery in psychology, if any, will anyone remember 200 years from now?

Here is my guess: I predict that 200 years from now, people will remember that in the late twentieth and early twenty-first centuries, psychologists began to study consciousness as an empirical topic.

Psychology began in the late 1800s as the scientific study of the conscious mind. However, researchers soon abandoned that effort. (Someone quipped that psychology had "lost its mind.") The behaviorists argued that consciousness is an internal, private experience that researchers cannot observe or measure. At that time they were certainly right, as they had no method to measure brain activity or anything else that might correlate with a private experience. Therefore, psychologists redefined the field as the study of behavior. Many behaviorists went further, saying that consciousness was not important. Consider these quotes:

> The essence of behaviorism is the belief that the study of man will reveal nothing except what is adequately describable in the concepts of mechanics and chemistry. (Lashley, 1923a, p. 244)

> The behaviorist may go his way . . . with the conviction that the inclusion of "mind" will add nothing to scientific psychology. (Lashley, 1923b, p. 352)

> The epoch of the I is drawing to a close. . . . Consciousness contains almost no information. (Norretranders, 1991/1998, pp. ix–xi)

Several scientists and philosophers have gone still further, suggesting that consciousness doesn't even exist, defending the paradoxical claim that your mind is a figment of your imagination!

> Just as it turned out that there was no such thing as impetus, there may be no such thing as awareness. (P. S. Churchland, 1986, p. 309)

> [T]here is no subjective feeling inside. . . . Instead, there is a description of having a feeling and a computed certainty that the description is accurate. (Graziano, 2013, pp. 20–21)

Other psychologists and philosophers have made the point that consciousness does not help us explain behavior (Wegner, 2002). They are right, at least as of today, with one exception: the behavior of talking about consciousness. Presumably we wouldn't talk about it if it didn't exist. Except for that perhaps trivial exception, we don't need the concept of consciousness to explain behavior. But that statement misses the point: Consciousness is not something that psychologists invented to try to explain behavior. It is the thing we are trying to explain. What is consciousness and why does it exist?

Measuring Consciousness

Research on consciousness used to be impossible, but times have changed. Four advances have facilitated meaningful research.

An Operational Definition of Consciousness

A dictionary might define consciousness as *the subjective experience of perceiving oneself and one's surroundings.* However, that definition relies on the phrase "subjective experience," which is no better defined than consciousness itself. Researchers use this operational definition: *If a cooperative person reports being aware of one stimulus and not of another, then he or she was conscious of the first and not the second.* That definition may seem obvious, even silly, but it is useful for research purposes. An important limitation is that it applies only for people who speak. The definition does not apply to preverbal infants, animals, or people with certain types of brain damage. In those cases, we would need other types of evidence to infer the presence or absence of consciousness.

Limited, Answerable Questions

Important questions abound: Why does consciousness exist at all? Does it have elements, analogous to the elements of chemistry? What does it accomplish? For the time being, we postpone the most difficult questions and focus instead on answerable questions like, "How does brain activity differ depending on whether someone is or is not conscious of a stimulus?"

Among the stimuli striking your receptors at any moment, you are conscious of only a few. Right now, do you smell or taste anything? What do you feel in your left leg? The back of your neck? As you turn your attention to one sensation after another, you become aware of much that had been unconscious until then (Lambie & Marcel, 2002).

Modern Methods to Measure Brain Activity

Researchers today have several methods to record brain activity without invading the brain. The simplest are electroencephalography (EEG) and magnetoencephalography (MEG), which use detectors on the scalp to measure rapid changes in the brain's electrical or magnetic activity. They identify only the approximate location of the activity, but for many purposes approximate location is good enough, and these methods detect the timing of the activity within a millisecond. The functional magnetic resonance imaging (fMRI) method identifies the location of activity more precisely, but with less precision about timing. A researcher could use EEG, MEG, fMRI, or other methods, depending on the research question.

Ways of Controlling Consciousness of a Stimulus

The final advance comes from new methods of presenting a stimulus so that people are conscious of it at certain times and not others. One method is masking: *a word or other stimulus appears on the screen for a fraction of a second, preceded and/or followed by an interfering stimulus.* If *the interfering stimulus follows it*, we call the procedure backward masking. Participants in one study watched words flash on a screen for just 29 milliseconds (ms) each. On some trials, a blank screen preceded and followed the word:

Under those conditions, people usually identified the word, even though it flashed so briefly. On other trials, a masking pattern preceded and followed the word. Under these conditions, people almost never identified the word, and almost always insisted that they saw no word at all:

Here is a second method. Suppose you see a yellow dot surrounded by blue dots on a computer screen. Then the blue dots start moving rapidly in haphazard directions. They will grab your attention so strongly that the yellow dot disappears from your sight for seconds at a time (Bonneh, Cooperman, & Sagi, 2001). A similar possibility is for the *other dots*

▲ **Figure 10.1** To produce binocular rivalry, look through tubes and alter the focus of your eyes until the two circles seem to merge. You will alternate between seeing red lines and seeing green lines.

to flash on and off, rapidly. While they are flashing, you lose sight of the yellow dot (Kreiman, Fried, & Koch, 2002; Yuval-Greenberg & Heeger, 2013). This procedure is called flash suppression.

A third method is the attentional blink. Suppose you are viewing a series of items flashing rapidly on the screen, and you are to report whenever you see a particular type of item, such as a letter printed in purple ink. After you report one such item, you will probably miss a second such item if it appears a quarter to a half second later (Goodbourn et al., 2016). Your attention to the first stimulus blocks you from noticing the second one.

Here is a fourth method. Ordinarily, your two retinas see almost the same thing. Examine ▲ **Figure 10.1** to see what happens when the images conflict.

Find or make tubes like those in a roll of paper towels, so your left eye can look at Figure 10.1 through one roll and your right eye can look through the other. For a quick shortcut, you could cup your two hands to form viewing tubes, or touch your nose to the page so that your two eyes are right in front of the two images. Adjust your focus until the two circles appear to overlap. First, you will be conscious of what one eye sees—such as red and black lines. Within seconds, that perception fades and you start seeing green and black lines. Because you cannot see both images at the same time in the same place, your brain alternates between the two perceptions (Blake & Logothetis, 2002). The *alternation between seeing the pattern in the left retina and the pattern in the right retina* is known as binocular rivalry.

Brain Activity, Conscious and Unconscious

In each of the procedures just described, an observer is conscious of a stimulus under one condition and not the other, although the initial sensory processing is the same. The retina responds to the visual stimulus equally in both cases, and it sends equivalent messages to the visual cortex. For about the first 200 ms, the response in the visual cortex is about the same for stimuli destined for consciousness or unconsciousness. After that, the responses diverge. On trials when the observer does not become conscious of the stimulus, the response to it remains weak and localized mostly to the primary visual cortex. On trials when conscious processing results, the activation spreads quickly from the visual cortex to other brain areas, as shown in ▼ **Figure 10.2**, and then rebounds from the prefrontal cortex to the primary visual cortex, magnifying and prolonging the response there (Dehaene et al., 2001; Li, Hill, & He, 2014). That echo amplifies the conscious perception. People with an impaired prefrontal cortex are less likely than average to notice weak stimuli (Del Cul, Dehaene, Reyes, Bravo, & Slachevsky, 2009; Rounis, Maniscalco, Rothwell, Passingham, & Lau, 2010).

Researchers found a convenient way to label the brain response to a particular stimulus during binocular rivalry. Instead of using red and green stripes as in

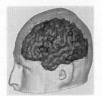

Visible words   Masked words

▲ **Figure 10.2** When people were conscious of a briefly flashed word, it activated the areas colored in the brain on the left. When masking prevented consciousness, the word activated only the areas colored on the right. (From "Cerebral mechanisms of word masking and unconscious repetition priming," by S. Dehaene, et al. *Nature Neuroscience, 4,* pp. 752–758. Copyright © 2001 Nature Publishing Group. Reprinted with permission.)

the example above, they exposed one eye to an unchanging face and the other eye to a circle that pulsated between large and small, seven times per second. Then they looked for patterns of brain activity that pulsated seven times per second. When a viewer reported seeing the flashing stimulus, researchers found a seven per second rhythm of activity throughout a large portion of the brain (Cosmelli et al., 2004; Lee, Blake, & Heeger, 2005). When the viewer reported seeing the face, the rhythmic activity faded, and a steadier pattern spread over the brain. In short, when you become conscious of a stimulus, it produces activity that spreads across brain areas. It also produces more inhibition of competing brain activity (Li et al., 2014; Moher, Lakshmanan, Egeth, & Ewen, 2014). A study using the attentional blink found that when you are conscious of a visual stimulus, it evokes simultaneous activity in many neurons, whereas the same stimulus without consciousness produces responses that are not only weaker, but also out of synchrony (Reber et al., 2017). Evidently precise timing contributes to consciousness.

The results suggest why it is hard to be conscious of several things at the same time: When you are conscious of something, it occupies much of your brain.

Unconscious Processing of a Suppressed Stimulus

During binocular rivalry, while you are conscious of one stimulus, is the brain representation of the other one lost altogether? No, even though the information doesn't spread widely, the brain does process it to a certain degree. If flash suppression or similar techniques block your awareness of a stimulus, you might still react to it emotionally—for example, if it is a picture of a spider, or a face with an emotional expression (Anderson, Siegel, White, & Barrett, 2012; Lapate, Rokers, Li, & Davidson, 2014). Suppose your eyes view two scenes on a computer screen, producing binocular rivalry. Then, while you are conscious of one eye, the experimenter gradually changes the scene in the other eye to show a face. A face with an emotional expression captures your attention faster than a neutral face does (Alpers & Gerdes, 2007). If a word emerges on one side, it captures your attention faster if it is in a language that you understand (Jiang, Costello, & He, 2007). That is, your brain notices that something is meaningful or important even before you become conscious of it, and then it routes that stimulus to consciousness. Unconscious processes do more than we once imagined (Hassin, 2013).

Consciousness as an All-or-None Phenomenon

Does consciousness come in degrees? That is, are you ever "partly" conscious of a stimulus? Suppose we flash blurry stimuli on the screen for a split second each. On some trials people say they were conscious of the stimulus and they accurately name or describe it. On other trials they say they did not see it, although they might be able to guess with accuracy slightly better than chance (Li et al., 2014). People almost never say they were "partly conscious" of the stimulus (Sergent & Dehaene, 2004).

Studies using brain scans point to the same conclusion. On trials where someone reports consciousness of a stimulus, its excitation spreads widely in the brain.

On other trials, the excitation spreads weakly and briefly. Intermediate cases do not occur. Evidently a stimulus either reaches a threshold necessary for spread, or it does not. Even with infants, the response to a stimulus is either strong and widespread, or weak and brief (Kouider et al., 2013). Consciousness of a stimulus appears to be an all-or-none phenomenon.

concept check

1. **Why is the study of consciousness more acceptable to researchers today than in the past?**

2. **What do people perceive during binocular rivalry?**

Answers

1. The main reasons are that researchers developed ways to measure brain activity and ways to present a stimulus without someone becoming conscious of it. 2. They perceive one stimulus and then the other, alternating every few seconds.

Consciousness as a Construction

When we see or hear something, we assume that we experience it *as it happens.* However, research casts doubt on that assumption. Suppose a word flashes on a screen for 29 ms followed by a masking stimulus, so that you are not conscious of the word. Then the experimenter repeats the procedure but extends the duration to 50 ms. With this longer presentation, you do see the word. More important, you don't have 29 ms of unconscious perception and 21 ms of conscious perception. Rather, the final part of that 50-ms presentation enabled you to become conscious of the first part retroactively. In some way, your brain constructed an experience of a 50-ms stimulus, even though it had to wait until the later part of the stimulus to perceive the first part.

Here is a related phenomenon. Suppose you see a display of two vertical lines:

|

|

After a delay of one- or two-tenths of a second, you see a display of circles like this:

o

o

When you report the appearance of the lines, you describe something like this:

|

|

That is, the lines appear to be displaced partly in the same direction that the circles were displaced (Ono & Watanabe, 2011). The later stimulus changed your perception of the earlier stimulus. Evidently, consciousness does not occur at exactly the same time as the events. You construct a conscious perception of events shortly after they happened.

Can We Use Brain Measurements to Infer Consciousness?

Physicians distinguish various gradations of brain activity that relate to arousal, responsiveness, and presumed consciousness. In **brain death**, *the brain shows no activity*. Recovery does not occur in such cases, and hospitals ordinarily remove life support. In a **coma** (KOH-muh), *caused by traumatic brain damage, the brain shows a steady but low level of activity and no response to any stimulus*, including potentially painful stimuli. In nearly all cases, someone in a coma either dies or begins to recover within a few weeks.

Someone starting to emerge from a coma enters a **vegetative state**, *marked by limited responsiveness, such as increased heart rate in response to pain*. The person alternates between sleeping and waking, but even in the waking state, brain activity is well below normal, and the person shows no purposeful behaviors. The next step up is a **minimally conscious state**, in which people have brief periods of purposeful actions and speech comprehension. A vegetative or minimally conscious state can last for months or years.

Because people in a vegetative state do nothing, they appear to be unconscious, but modern research methods challenge that assumption in certain cases. Researchers used fMRI to record the brain activity of a young woman who was in a persistent vegetative state following a traffic accident. When they instructed her to imagine playing tennis, activity increased in the same motor areas of the cortex as if she were getting ready to hit a tennis ball. An instruction to imagine walking through her house activated the brain areas responsible for spatial navigation. She showed a pattern of activation similar to what happens when uninjured people receive the same instructions (Owen et al., 2006). ▼ Figure 10.3 shows the results.

A follow-up study of 53 other patients in a vegetative state found results similar to this in 4 of them. One of them was asked questions about himself, and the investigator instructed him to imagine playing tennis if the answer was yes, and imagine walking through his house if the answer was no. His brain responses indicated the correct answers to the first five questions. His brain showed no response at all to the sixth question, suggesting that he had fallen asleep (Monti et al., 2010).

Several other patients demonstrated apparent consciousness in other ways. For example, one patient viewed a face superimposed on a picture of a house. When told to pay attention to the face, activity increased in a brain area important for perceiving faces. When told to attend to the house, activity increased in a different brain area. The researchers found that about 18 percent of patients who were in a vegetative state showed apparent indications of understanding spoken instructions (Fernández-Espejo & Owen, 2013). A study using EEG found brain activity in response to speech in some brain-injured patients and not others soon after the damage. Those showing brain responses were more likely than the others to show substantial recovery over the next year (Claassen et al., 2019).

These results suggest that at least a few patients in a vegetative state are conscious. It is an encouraging result, but also a scary one. How many times

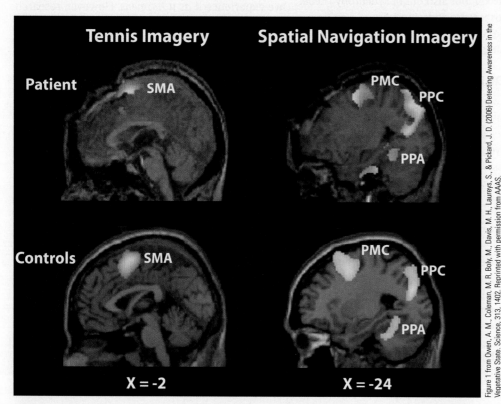

Figure 1 from Owen, A. M., Coleman, M. R., Boly, M., Davis, M. H., Laureys, S., & Pickard, J. D. (2006) Detecting Awareness in the Vegetative State. Science, 313, 1402. Reprinted with permission from AAAS.

▲ **Figure 10.3** The brain areas marked in red, orange, and yellow showed increased activity after instructions to imagine playing tennis or imagine walking through the house. Note the similarities between a patient in a persistent vegetative state and uninjured people. SMA = supplementary motor cortex, an area important for planning complex movements. PMC, PPC, and PPA = three areas responsible for spatial imagery and memory. (From Owen et al., 2006)

have people said something in the patient's presence, assuming that the patient didn't hear?

Consciousness and Action

You decide that three seconds from now you will pick up a pencil. Sure enough, three seconds later you pick up that pencil. You believe that your conscious decision controlled the action. But are you right? Do your conscious decisions control your behavior, or do they just predict something that unconscious processes caused? And how would you know?

We can fool ourselves about how much control we have. Psychologist Daniel Wegner (2002) described a time when he was manipulating a joystick at a video game display, making a monkey jump over barrels . . . or at least so it seemed. Then the notice "Start game" appeared, and he realized that he hadn't been controlling anything after all. Let's consider a famous experiment that poses a serious challenge to the idea of conscious control. Interest in this experiment followed an unusual trajectory. In the first 20 years after it was published, other researchers only rarely cited it. And then interest started increasing, among philosophers as well as psychologists.

what's the evidence?

Consciousness and Action

Benjamin Libet and his associates measured the time when people made a conscious decision to act, the time when brain activity preparing for the movement started, and the time of the act itself. What would you guess was the order of the three events in time?

Hypothesis The researchers considered three hypotheses, any one of which would be interesting: (1) Someone becomes aware of a decision to act before relevant brain activity begins, (2) awareness starts at the same time as the brain activity, and (3) the brain activity responsible for a movement starts before a conscious decision.

Method People were instructed to make a simple movement, flexing the wrist. Although they had no choice of movement, they had complete freedom for the timing. The instruction was to flex the wrist whenever they decided to, but spontaneously, with no planning. While waiting for that spontaneous urge to occur, they were to watch a special clock like the one in ▶ Figure 10.4, on which a spot of light moved around the edge every 2.56 seconds. When they suddenly decided to flex the wrist, they were to note the position of the light at that moment, so they could report it later. In this way, the study measured, as well as anyone knows how, the time of the conscious decision. Meanwhile, researchers used electrodes on the scalp to detect increased activity in the

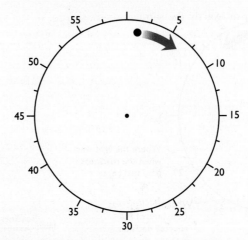

▲ **Figure 10.4** A spot of light rotated around the clock once every 2.56 seconds. Participants made a spontaneous decision to flex the wrist and noted the location of the light at the time of the decision. They remembered that time and reported it later. (From Libet, Gleason, Wright, & Pearl, 1983)

motor cortex, the brain area responsible for initiating muscle movements. *The increased motor cortex activity prior to the start of the movement* is known as the **readiness potential**. Researchers also measured when the wrist muscles began to flex. On certain trials, the participants were told to report when they felt the wrist flex instead of the time when they felt the intention to move it.

Results ▼ Figure 10.5 shows the mean result for a large sample. On average, people reported forming an intention of movement 200 to 300 ms before the movement (Libet, Gleason, Wright, & Pearl, 1983). (They noted the time on the clock then and reported it later.) For example, someone might report forming an intention when the light was at location 25 on the clock, 200 ms before the movement began at location 30. (Remember, the light zooms around the circle in 2.56 seconds.) In contrast, the readiness potential in the brain began 300 to 800 ms before the reported intention. Several other laboratories replicated this finding with varying procedures, confirming that the readiness potential comes before the reported time of the conscious intention (Haggard & Eimer, 1999; Lau, Rogers, Haggard, & Passingham, 2004; Pockett & Miller, 2007; Trevena & Miller, 2002).

Can people report these times accurately? Recall that on certain trials the participants reported the time of the wrist motion. On these trials, people usually reported the movement within 100 ms of the actual time (Lau et al., 2004; Libet et al., 1983). From this finding, the researchers concluded that people report the time of an experience with moderate accuracy.

Interpretation These results imply that your brain starts producing a voluntary movement before you are conscious of a decision to move. If so, your consciousness does not cause your action.

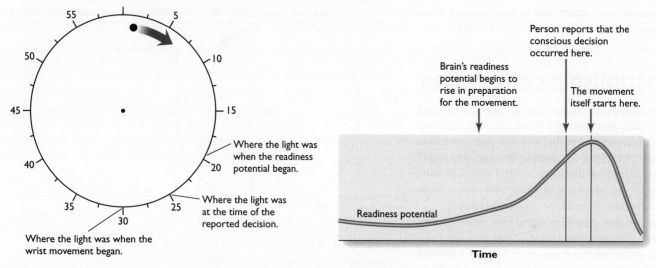

▲ **Figure 10.5** On average, the brain's readiness potential began 300 ms or more prior to the reported decision, which occurred 200 to 300 ms before the movement.

4. **In Libet's experiment described in the "What's the Evidence?" section, what did participants report, and when did they report it?**

5. **What was the order of these events: conscious decision to move, brain activity relevant to movement, and the movement itself?**

Answers

4. Participants watched a special fast clock and noted the time when they made a spontaneous decision to flex the wrist. They reported it a few seconds later.
5. Measurable brain activity came first, then the perception of the conscious decision, and then the movement.

An Additional Study

Imagine yourself in this follow-up study: You watch a screen that displays a different letter of the alphabet every half-second. You choose not only when to act but which of two acts to do. At some point you spontaneously decide whether to press a button on the left or one on the right. As soon as you decide, you press the button, and you remember what letter is on the screen when you decided which button to press. Researchers record your brain activity. The result: You usually report a letter you saw within a second of making the response. The letters changed only twice per second, so the researchers could not determine the time of decision with greater accuracy. However, it wasn't necessary, because areas in the frontal and parietal cortex showed activity related to the left or right hand 7 to

10 seconds before your response (Soon, Brass, Heinze, & Haynes, 2008). That is, someone monitoring your cortex could predict your choice a few seconds before you were aware of having decided.

How Well Can We Measure the Time of a Conscious Decision?

Although the results are clear, questions remain about the interpretation. People can fairly accurately report the time of a light, sound, or muscle movement, but reporting the time of a voluntary decision may be different. Perhaps people notice when they make a movement and merely guess that the decision came shortly before it. Researchers found that if they sounded a beep shortly after someone's movement, the person guessed the time of the movement later than it really was, and also guessed the time of the decision later than people usually do (Banks & Isham, 2009). That result supports the idea that reported decision times are little more than guesses.

A related objection is this: A spontaneous, voluntary decision is not a sudden event at a discrete time. Let's digress for a moment to discuss two types of movement. It will seem that we are way off topic, but the relevance will be clear later.

The movements we make in response to a stimulus differ from the movements we make spontaneously. The ones we make in response to a stimulus can be quick, but spontaneous movements are almost always slower and gradual. Imagine yourself driving along when suddenly a deer darts into the road. You swerve immediately to avoid it. In contrast, if you decide you need to get into the left lane to make a turn, you think about it and eventually move slowly into the left lane. Suppose your professor says, "When I count to three, please raise your hand." You will raise it swiftly at the count of three, in contrast to the way you slowly raise your hand when you want to ask a question. Gradual, spontaneous movements depend on a set of brain areas called the basal ganglia, which contribute much less when you act in response to a stimulus (Jueptner & Weiller, 1998; Turner & Anderson, 2005). People with Parkinson's disease suffer from decreased excitation into the basal ganglia. Their spontaneous, self-initiated movements are weak and slow, but they move faster when responding to signals (Teitelbaum, Pellis, & Pellis, 1991).

Distinguishing between stimulus-elicited and self-initiated movements has an interesting consequence. Many of the old western movies featured a gunfight between a good guy and a bad guy. Always the bad guy drew his gun first, but the good guy drew faster and won the fight. Plausible? Yes. The first one to draw his gun makes a spontaneous, self-initiated movement and the second one reacts to a stimulus (the sight of the other guy going for his gun). The second one therefore draws his gun faster. It might even be an advantage to draw second (Welchman, Stanley, Schomers, Miall, & Bülthoff, 2010). Remember that the next time you get into a gunfight.

Now, let's go back to Libet's experiment. When someone made a voluntary decision to flex the wrist, what type of movement was it? It was a spontaneous, self-initiated movement, the type that develops slowly and gradually. Asking for the time of the decision assumes, falsely, that the decision occurred suddenly. Similarly, if you asked a romantic couple when they fell in love, they might tell you the time when they were sure of it, but a good observer would have seen it developing long before. Perhaps what happens in Libet's study is that a conscious decision develops gradually, and the brain activity also develops gradually.

concept check

6. **How do self-initiated movements differ from movements in response to a signal?**

Answer

6. Self-initiated movements are slower and more gradual. They depend on the brain areas called the basal ganglia, which are less central to the movements we make in response to a stimulus.

What Is the Purpose of Consciousness?

Given that the role of consciousness in decisions remains unclear, why do we have it at all? Some theorists have argued that consciousness is an *epiphenomenon*—an accidental by-product with no purpose, like the noise a machine makes. But if consciousness does serve a purpose, what might that purpose be?

One hypothesis is that conscious thought is a way of rehearsing possibilities for future actions (Baumeister & Masicampo, 2010; Baumeister, Masicampo, & Vohs, 2011). After you do something, you might ponder, "That didn't go well. What could I have done differently? Then what would have happened? Ah, I see. The next time I'm in a situation like this, here is what I'll do. . . ." In that way your conscious thinking modifies your behavior on some future occasion.

That sort of process occurs only when we think about something consciously. Still, the question remains, must it depend on consciousness? Could someone build a robot (presumably unconscious) that calculated possible outcomes of its future actions? If so, why do humans need to be conscious? And what, if anything, is the function of simple awareness, such as the experience you have when you see a flower or hear a melody—the kind of consciousness we probably share with many other animal species?

Many theorists seem to see the role of consciousness as an either–or question: Either consciousness is useless, or it evolved to serve a special purpose. The identity position on the mind–brain relationship suggests another possibility: If a certain type of brain activity *is* mental activity, then they are inseparable. You cannot have consciousness without brain activity, but you also cannot have certain kinds of brain activity without consciousness. Brains didn't evolve consciousness to solve a special task any more than brains evolved mass to solve a special task.

Still, that idea doesn't answer the fundamental question of *why* brain activity is mental activity. In a universe of matter and energy, why is there such a thing as consciousness?

The questions will keep both scientists and philosophers busy for much time to come. But at least we now see consciousness as a legitimate topic for research.

in closing | module 10.1

Research on Consciousness

What outcomes can result from research on consciousness? If we better understand the types of brain activity associated with consciousness, we will be in a better position to infer consciousness, or lack of it, in people with brain damage and in infants, fetuses, and nonhuman animals. We may also be in a position to improve our speculations on the age-old philosophical question of the relationship between mind and brain.

Summary

- *Consciousness.* Consciousness, long ignored by researchers, became a respectable research topic because of modern methods to measure brain activity and newly developed ways to manipulate whether someone becomes aware of a stimulus. (page 307)

- *Ways to block consciousness.* Masking, flash suppression, and binocular rivalry are among the methods to present a stimulus while preventing conscious perception of it. (page 308)
- *The spread of consciousness.* When someone is conscious of a stimulus, the response to it spreads through much of the brain and echoes back to the original location to strengthen it. (page 308)
- *Unconscious activity.* The brain processes much information unconsciously and directs consciousness to the important information. (page 309)
- *No intermediates detected.* Consciousness of a stimulus appears to be an all-or-none process. Either the brain activity spreads strongly through the brain, or it does not. (page 309)
- *The timing of consciousness.* Conscious experience of a stimulus is a construction that can occur slightly after the stimulus itself, rather than simultaneously with it. (page 309)
- *Detecting consciousness in unresponsive people.* Some patients who show no voluntary behavior do show brain activity responsive to what they hear, suggesting they are conscious. (page 310)
- *Consciousness and movement.* Benjamin Libet's study reported that brain activity preparing for a movement begins before the time that people report making a decision to move. (page 311)
- *Limitations of Libet's study.* People are probably unable to report accurately the time of a decision because a decision to move is a gradual process. (page 312)

Key Terms

attentional blink (page 308)

backward masking (page 308)

binocular rivalry (page 308)

brain death (page 310)

coma (page 310)

consciousness (page 307)

flash suppression (page 308)

masking (page 308)

minimally conscious state (page 310)

readiness potential (page 311)

vegetative state (page 310)

Review Questions

1. At what point does the response to a visual stimulus begin to differ between times when it becomes conscious and times when it does not?
   (a) In the receptors of the eye
   (b) During transmission from the eye to the brain
   (c) As soon as the information reaches the visual cortex
   (d) After the initial processing in the visual cortex

2. What is meant by the "attentional blink"?
   (a) Attention span has a maximum duration that varies among people.
   (b) You tend to shift attention between one eye and the other.
   (c) Paying attention to one event causes you to ignore a slightly later event.
   (d) You do not notice changes that occur while you are blinking your eyes.

3. At any given moment, what do you see during binocular rivalry?
   (a) You see the stimuli in both eyes.
   (b) You see the stimulus in one eye or the other.
   (c) You see something that is a compromise between the two stimuli.
   (d) You see flashing lights.

4. What evidence suggests that consciousness is an all-or-none process?
   (a) You are as likely to attend to something unimportant as something important.
   (b) Many messages from the eyes stop before they reach the brain.

   (c) Brain responses either spread widely in the brain or they don't.
   (d) Perception of an ambiguous stimulus can vary depending on the context.

5. The inference that one woman in a vegetative state might be conscious depended on what type of evidence?
   (a) Her hand movements
   (b) The sounds that she made
   (c) Measurements of brain activity
   (d) Slow movements of her eyes

6. In Libet's experiment, in which people reported the time of a decision to flex the wrist, why were the results relevant to philosophical questions?
   (a) The results implied that heredity and environment are equally important for controlling behavior.
   (b) The results implied that the mind is separate from the body.
   (c) The results implied that conscious decisions do not control behavior.
   (d) The results implied that human behavior depends on the same influences as the rest of the animal kingdom.

7. Why is it difficult to report the time of a decision for a self-initiated movement?
   (a) A decision to move is a gradual process.
   (b) Making the movement interferes with vision.
   (c) People prefer not to talk about their private experiences.
   (d) Moving one hand interferes with movement of the other hand.

Answers: 1d, 2c, 3b, 4c, 5c, 6c, 7a.

module 10.2

Sleep and Dreams

After studying this module, you should be able to:

1. Describe how circadian rhythms affect alertness and other functions.

2. Distinguish between morning and evening people.

3. Discuss the consequences of jet lag and shift work.

4. Explain the brain mechanisms that control the circadian rhythm.

5. List functions of sleep.

6. Describe the stages of sleep, including REM sleep.

7. Discuss insomnia and other sleep problems.

8. Evaluate theories of dreaming.

During sleep, we become less aware of our surroundings. Dreams take us to a fantasy world of impossible events. Why do we have these periods of altered consciousness?

Circadian Rhythms

Animal life follows cycles. Consider hibernation. Ground squirrels hibernate in winter, when they would have trouble finding food. The females awaken in spring as soon as food is available. The males also need to eat, but they have a reason to awaken earlier: The females are ready to mate as soon as they come out of their winter burrows, and each female mates only once a year.

The rising and setting of the sun do not produce our daily rhythm of wakefulness and sleepiness, but they synchronize the rhythm. We adjust our internally generated cycles so that we feel alert during the day and sleepy at night.

A male who awakens after the females pays for his extra rest by missing his only mating opportunity of the *entire year*. To avoid that risk, males awaken a week before the females do. They spend that week waiting—with no females, nothing to eat, and little to do except fight with one another (French, 1988).

The point is that animals have evolved internal timing mechanisms to prepare them for predictable needs. Male ground squirrels awaken not in response to their current situation but in preparation for what will happen a few days later. Similarly, birds start migrating south in the fall long before their northern homes become inhospitable.

Humans have mechanisms that prepare us for activity during the day and sleep at night. Like other animals, we generate a **circadian rhythm**, a *rhythm of activity and inactivity lasting about a day.* (The term *circadian* comes from the Latin roots *circa* and *dies*, meaning "about a day.") The rising and setting of the sun provide cues to reset our rhythm, but we generate the rhythm ourselves. In an environment where the sun does not provide a cue for time, such as near-polar regions in summer or winter, most people generate a waking–sleeping rhythm a little longer than 24 hours, which gradually drifts out of phase with the clock (Palinkas, 2003).

Your circadian rhythm controls more than sleeping and waking. Over the course of a day, you vary in your hunger, thirst, urine production, blood pressure, and alertness. Your body temperature varies from 37.2°C (98.9°F) in late afternoon to 36.7°C (98.1°F) in the middle of the night (Morris, Lack, and Dawson, 1990). Most young people's mood varies over the day, reaching a peak of happiness in late afternoon (Murray et al., 2009).

Variations in certain genes can alter circadian rhythms (Jones, Huang, Ptácek, & Fu, 2013). People with genes causing a 23-hour cycle instead of the usual 24-hour cycle get sleepy early in the evening and wake up early. They act as if they were moving about one time zone west every day. They look forward to weekends so that they can go to bed *early!* Other people have genes causing a longer-than-24-hour cycle, or genes decreasing the total need for sleep.

Your sleepiness and alertness depend on your circadian rhythm, and not just on how long you have gone without sleep. If you have ever gone all night without sleep—as most college students do on occasion—you probably felt very sleepy between 2 and 6 A.M. But later that morning, you began feeling less sleepy, not more. You became more alert because of your circadian rhythm, despite your sleep deprivation.

In one study, volunteers went without sleep for three nights. Their body temperature and performance on reasoning tasks declined during the first night and then increased the next morning. During the second and third nights, their temperature and reasoning decreased even more than on the first night, but they rebounded somewhat in the day (see ▼ Figure 10.6). Thus, sleep deprivation produces a pattern of progressive deterioration superimposed on the normal circadian cycle of rising and falling body temperature and alertness (Babkoff, Caspy, Mikulincer, & Sing, 1991).

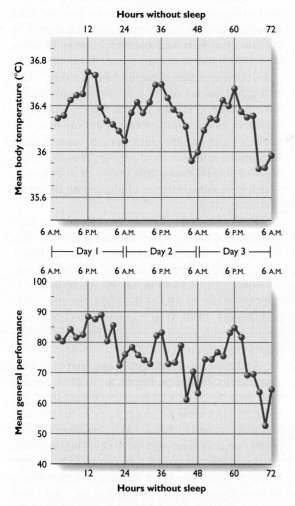

▲ Figure 10.6 Cumulative effects of three nights without sleep: Body temperature and reasoning decrease each night and increase the next morning. They also deteriorate from one day to the next. (From Babkoff, Caspy, Mikulincer, & Sing, 1991)

concept check

7. If you were on a submarine deep in the ocean with only artificial light that was the same at all times, what would happen to your rhythm of wakefulness and sleepiness?

Answer

7. You would continue to produce a wake–sleep rhythm of approximately 24 hours, although it would drift out of phase with the submarine's clock.

Morning People and Evening People

People vary in their circadian rhythms. "Morning people" awaken easily, become alert quickly, and do their best work early. "Evening people" take longer to warm up in the morning, literally as well as figuratively, and do their best work in the afternoon or evening (Horne, Brass, & Pettitt, 1980). You can probably classify yourself as a morning person, evening person, or intermediate.

Morning people have advantages in several ways, especially if school or work starts early in the morning. On average, morning-type students maintain attention better in the morning, do better on tests in the morning, and get better grades, even when compared to evening-type students with the same cognitive ability and motivation (Haraszti, Ella, Gyöngyösi, Roenneberg, & Káldi, 2014; Lara, Madrid, & Correa, 2014; Preckel et al., 2013). In the United States, high schools start classes early in the morning, despite the fact that most teenagers, especially boys, tend to stay up late and awaken late. As a result, many are inefficient during class and chronically sleep deprived. Sleep deprivation magnifies the effects of stressful experiences, leading to emotional difficulties as well as academic problems (Chue, Gunthert, Kim, Alfano, & Ruggiero, 2018).

Evening types have this advantage: They tend to be more extraverted, with more social life and sexual activity (Matchock, 2018; Randler et al., 2012). Benjamin Franklin said, "Early to bed and early to rise makes a man healthy, wealthy, and wise." Maybe so, but someone else quipped, "Early to bed and early to rise and the girls will go out with other guys!"

Most young adults are either evening people or intermediate, whereas most people over age 65 are morning people. If you ask people at what time they like to go to bed when they have no obligations, their mean answer shifts later and later during the teenage years, reaches 1 to 2 A.M. at age 20, and then starts reversing, slowly and steadily over decades (Roenneberg et al., 2004). If the shift toward earlier bedtimes after age 20 were a reaction to job requirements, we might expect a sudden change, and we might predict the trend to reverse at retirement. The fact that the trend continues gradually over a lifetime suggests a biological basis. Furthermore, the same pattern occurs in other species. Older rats wake up promptly, whereas younger rats awaken more slowly and improve their performance later (Winocur & Hasher, 1999, 2004). A reason for this trend is not obvious.

Age differences in circadian rhythms affect behavior in many ways. Researchers in one study compared the memories of young adults (18 to 22 years old) and older adults (66 to 78 years old). Early in the morning, the older adults did about as well as the younger ones. Later in the day, the younger adults remained steady or improved, whereas the older adults deteriorated (May, Hasher, & Stoltzfus, 1993). ▼ Figure 10.7 shows the results.

concept check

8. If you are an evening person, what might you do to maximize your chances for success?

Answer

8. If you are in school, try to schedule your important classes in the afternoon instead of the morning. If you are looking for a job, prefer one that does not start too early in the morning.

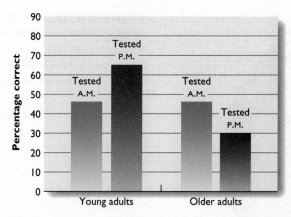

▲ **Figure 10.7** Early in the morning, older people perform as well as younger people on memory tasks. On average, young people improve later in the day, and older people deteriorate.

Shifting Sleep Schedules

Ordinarily, the light of early morning resets the body's clock each day to keep it in synchrony with the outside world. If you travel across time zones, your internal rhythm is temporarily out of phase with your new environment. For example, if you travel from California to France, it is 7 A.M. (time to wake up) when your body says it is 10 P.M. (getting close to bedtime). You experience **jet lag**, *a period of discomfort and inefficiency while your internal clock is out of phase with your new surroundings*. Most people find it easier to adjust when flying west, where they go to bed later, than when flying east, where they go to bed earlier (see ▼ **Figure 10.8**). If you fly west, your circadian rhythm shifts a bit later each day until it catches up; if you fly east, your rhythm shifts a bit earlier each day. If you fly beyond a certain number of time zones one way or the other, it is as if your rhythm isn't sure whether to move forward or backward, and you may need a long time to readjust (Leloup & Goldbeter, 2013). It is also possible to experience jet lag from long distance travel between north and south. For example, if you fly between New York and Santiago, Chile, in June or December, the sun rises and sets at times different from what your biological clock expects (Diekman & Bose, 2018).

People voluntarily control their sleeping and waking times when they have to go to school or work, but the sun continues to rule the internal clock. Researchers asked people in Germany the times they prefer to go to bed and wake up. On business days, people throughout Germany awaken at the same time because they are all in the same time zone. However, on weekends and holidays, people in eastern Germany prefer to go to bed and wake up about half an hour earlier than those in western Germany, corresponding to the fact that the sun rises half an hour earlier in eastern Germany (Roenneberg, Kumar, & Merrow, 2007).

People in most of the United States have to shift their clock ahead an hour on a Sunday in March because of daylight saving time. On Monday morning, they awaken when the clock tells them to, even though their internal clock thinks it is an hour earlier. For the next few days, many people have sleep problems, fatigue, and a decrease in overall well-being. Several reports also suggest possible increases in health problems, traffic accidents, and heart attacks during the week after the switch (Harrison, 2013; Kountouris & Remoundou, 2014; Manfredini, Fabbian, Cappadona, & Modesti, 2018).

Some businesses run three work shifts, such as midnight to 8 A.M., 8 A.M. to 4 P.M., and 4 P.M. to midnight. Because few people want to work regularly on the midnight to 8 A.M. shift, many companies rotate their workers among the three shifts. Employers can ease the burden on their workers in two ways: First, when they transfer workers from one shift to another, they should transfer them to a *later* shift (Czeisler, Moore-Ede, & Coleman, 1982; see also ▼ **Figure 10.9**). That is, someone working from 8 A.M. to 4 P.M. shifts to the 4 P.M. to midnight time (like traveling west) instead of midnight to 8 A.M. (like traveling east). Second, employers can help workers on the night shift by providing bright lights that resemble sunlight. In one study, young people exposed to very bright lights at night adjusted their circadian rhythms to the new schedule within 6 days. A group who worked under dimmer lights failed to alter their circadian rhythms (Czeisler et al., 1990).

9. What does jet lag tell us about the sleep problems of a newborn baby?

Answer

9. A newborn is adjusting to a new time zone!

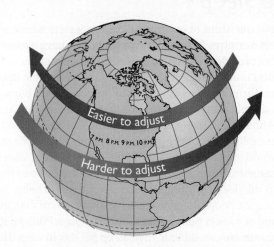

▲ **Figure 10.8** Most people suffer more serious jet lag when traveling east than when traveling west.

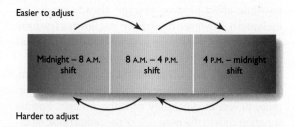

Easier to adjust

| Midnight – 8 A.M. shift | 8 A.M. – 4 P.M. shift | 4 P.M. – midnight shift |

Harder to adjust

▲ **Figure 10.9** The graveyard shift is aptly named: Serious industrial accidents usually occur at night, when workers are least alert. As in jet lag, the direction of change is critical. Moving forward—clockwise—is easier than going backward.

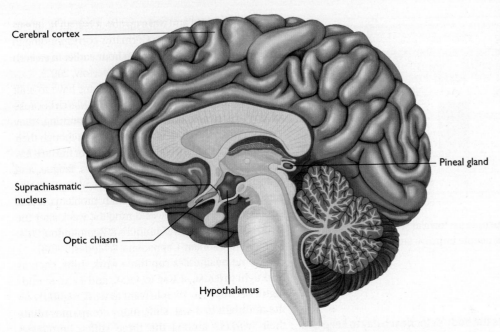

Cerebral cortex

Pineal gland

Suprachiasmatic nucleus

Optic chiasm

Hypothalamus

▲ **Figure 10.10** The suprachiasmatic nucleus, a small area at the base of the brain, produces the circadian rhythm. Information from the optic nerves resets the timing but doesn't produce it.

Brain Mechanisms of Circadian Rhythms

An animal continues following a circadian rhythm of wakefulness and sleep even in an unchanging environment with a constant temperature and constant light or darkness, even if it is blind or deaf, and after almost any intervention that changes its activity level (Richter, 1967, 1975). The circadian rhythm of sleep and wakefulness is generated within the brain by a tiny structure known as the *suprachiasmatic nucleus (SCN)*. If it is damaged, the body's activity cycles become erratic (Rusak, 1977). If cells from the SCN are kept alive outside the body, they generate a 24-hour rhythm on their own (Earnest, Liang, Ratcliff, & Cassone, 1999; Inouye & Kawamura, 1979). Cells in other areas also produce daily rhythms, but the suprachiasmatic nucleus is the body's main clock that synchronizes the others (see ▲ Figure 10.10).

The suprachiasmatic nucleus exerts its control partly by regulating the pineal gland's secretions of the hormone *melatonin*. Ordinarily, the human pineal gland starts releasing melatonin 2 or 3 hours before bedtime. Taking a melatonin pill in the evening has little effect because you are already producing melatonin. However, if you have just flown a few time zones east and want to get to sleep early, then a melatonin pill can help (Deacon & Arendt, 1996).

Although the SCN generates a circadian rhythm, light resets the internal clock, causing you to wake up more or less in synchrony with the sunlight. Special ganglion cells in the nose side of the retina (looking toward the periphery) respond to the average amount of bright light over a period of time, and send their output to the SCN, unlike the retinal cells that respond to instantaneous changes in light and send their output to the visual cortex (Berson et el., 2002). These special

ganglion cells respond mainly to short-wavelength light, which computers and televisions emit in abundance. A consequence is that people who watch television or use computers late in the evening often have trouble falling asleep (Czeisler, 2013; Fossum, Nordnes, Storemark, Bjorvatn, & Pallesen, 2014). For most people, moderate light in the evening delays melatonin release for an hour or more, but some people are much more sensitive or much less sensitive than average (Phillips et al., 2019).

concept check

10. **Suppose two people become blind, one because of damage to the eyes and the other because of damage to the visual cortex. Which one, if either, will synchronize the waking/sleeping schedule to sunlight? Explain.**

Answer

10. Someone with damage to the eyes will not synchronize to sunlight, but someone with blindness because of cortical damage does. If the eyes are intact, light activates certain ganglion cells that send their output not to the visual cortex, but to the suprachiasmatic nucleus, which controls the circadian rhythm.

Why We Sleep

We spend about one-third of our lives asleep, in a state where we cannot eat, mate, or protect ourselves from attack. We would not have evolved this mechanism if it did not provide important benefits. What are they?

The simplest is that sleep saves energy at a time when the individual would be relatively inefficient (Siegel, 2009). Even insects, nematodes, jellyfish, and bacteria have a daily sleep-like period of decreased activity (Anafi, Kayser, & Raizen, 2019; Mihalcescu, Hsing, & Leibler, 2004; Nath et al., 2017). When NASA sent a robot to explore Mars, they programmed it to shut down at nights, when exploration would waste energy. Presumably, our ancient ancestors evolved sleep for the same reason. Sleeping mammals and birds lower their body temperatures, and all sleeping animals decrease muscle activity, saving energy. When food is scarce, people need to conserve energy more than usual, and they sleep longer and at a lower body temperature (Berger & Phillips, 1995).

Various animal species differ in their sleep per day in ways that make sense based on their way of life (Campbell & Tobler, 1984; Siegel, 2005). Predatory animals, including cats and bats, sleep most of the day. They get the nutrition they

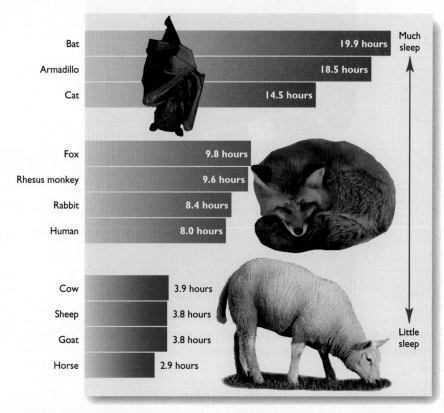

Bat	19.9 hours	Much sleep
Armadillo	18.5 hours	
Cat	14.5 hours	
Fox	9.8 hours	
Rhesus monkey	9.6 hours	
Rabbit	8.4 hours	
Human	8.0 hours	
Cow	3.9 hours	
Sheep	3.8 hours	
Goat	3.8 hours	
Horse	2.9 hours	Little sleep

▲ **Figure 10.11** Predatory mammals sleep more than prey animals. Predators are seldom attacked during their sleep, but prey species need to arouse quickly from sleep to avoid being attacked. (Based on data from Zepelin & Rechtschaffen, 1974; Image credits: EcoPrint/Shutterstock.com, Ilya D. Gridnev/Shutterstock.com, Photodisc/Getty Images)

need from brief, energy-rich meals, and they face little danger of attack during their sleep. In contrast, horses need to spend many hours grazing, and their survival depends on running away from attackers (see ▲ **Figure 10.11**). They sleep little and rouse easily. Woody Allen once wrote, "The lion and the calf shall lie down together, but the calf won't get much sleep."

Animals show other sleep specializations. Great frigatebirds spend weeks or months at a time flying over the ocean, eating flying fish. They never land on the water, but continue flying all night, sleeping very little. When they do sleep, they sleep on one side of the brain at a time (Rattenborg et al., 2016). Most migratory birds forage for food during the day and do their migratory flying at night, when it is cooler. That schedule leaves no time for sleep. Somehow the birds temporarily turn off their need for sleep (Rattenborg et al., 2004). They hardly sleep at all during the migratory season, even if they are kept in cages, and they show no sign of sleep deprivation (Fuchs, Haney, Jechura, Moore, & Bingman, 2006).

Whales and dolphins face a different problem: Throughout the night, they have to swim to the surface to breathe. Their solution is to sleep in half of the brain at a time so that one half or the other is always alert (Lyamin et al., 2002; Rattenborg, Amlaner, & Lima, 2000). Seals sleep this way too when they are at sea, but they shift to sleeping on both sides when they are on land (Lyamin, Kosenko, Lapierre, Mukhametov, & Siegel, 2008). During the first month after a baby whale or dolphin is born, it doesn't sleep at all, and neither does its mother (Lyamin, Pryaslova, Lance, & Siegel, 2005). Evidently, they have the secret for temporarily suppressing the need for sleep.

Among humans, some need less sleep than others (Meddis, Pearson, & Langford, 1973), but anyone suffers if they don't get enough sleep, regardless of what "enough" is for a given person. Sleep-deprived people become more vulnerable to physical and mental illnesses, including depression (Roberts & Duong, 2014; Wulff,

Gatti, Wettstein, & Foster, 2010). They suffer lapses of attention (Åkerstedt, 2007; Gvilia, Xu, McGinty, & Szymusiak, 2006) and lapses of ethical behavior (Barnes, Schaubroeck, Huth, & Ghumman, 2011). After sleep deprivation, an "awake" person has some neurons that are active but many others that are inactive or only weakly responsive (Nir et al., 2017; Vyazovskiy et al., 2011). A sleep-deprived driver is as dangerous as a drunk driver (Falleti, Maruff, Collie, Darby, & McStephen, 2003).

Sleep enhances learning and memory to varying degrees, depending on the type of learning (Doyon et al., 2009). When you learn something, your memory improves if you sleep within the next 3 hours (even a nap), and it deteriorates after a sleepless night (Hu, Stylos-Allan, & Walker, 2006; Korman et al., 2007; Rasch & Born, 2008; Yoo, Hu, Gujar, Jolesz, & Walker, 2007). A good night's sleep also improves the next day's learning (Van der Werf et al., 2009). So beware of those all-night study sessions.

When people learn a difficult new motor task, such as a video game skill, the brain areas active during the learning become reactivated during sleep that night, replaying the same patterns they had during the day, only faster (and sometimes backward). The amount of activity in those areas during sleep predicts the amount of improvement the next day (Euston, Tatsuno, & McNaughton, 2007; Huber, Ghilardi, Massimini, & Tononi, 2004; Maquet et al., 2000; Peigneux et al., 2004). What happens during sleep is not strengthening the synapses that learned, but weakening other synapses, so that the ones strengthened during wakefulness stand out by contrast (de Vivo et al., 2017; Li, Ma, Yang, & Gan, 2017; Vyazovskiy, Cirelli, Pfister-Genskow, Faraguna, & Tononi, 2008).

concept check

11. Under what circumstances do certain animals apparently change their need for sleep?

Answer

11. Migratory birds decrease their need for sleep during migration season. Great frigatebirds sleep very little when at sea. Mother and infant whales and dolphins sleep very little.

Stages of Sleep

In the mid-1950s, French and American researchers independently discovered a stage of sleep called *paradoxical sleep*, or rapid eye movement (REM) sleep (Dement & Kleitman, 1957a, 1957b; Jouvet, Michel, & Courjon, 1959). *During this stage of sleep, the sleeper's eyes move rapidly back and forth under the closed lids.* The other stages of sleep are known as non-REM, or NREM, sleep. REM sleep is paradoxical (that is, apparently self-contradictory) because it is light in some ways and deep in others. It is light because the brain is active and the body's heart rate, breathing rate, and temperature fluctuate substantially (Parmeggiani, 1982). It is deep because the large muscles of the body that control posture and locomotion are fully relaxed and immobile. REM also has features that are hard to classify as deep or light, such as penis erections and vaginal lubrication.

William Dement's early research indicated that people who were awakened during REM sleep usually reported dreaming, and people who were awakened during other periods seldom reported dreaming. Later research weakened that link, however. Adults who are awakened during REM sleep report dreams about 85 to 90 percent of the time, whereas those awakened during NREM sleep report dreams on 50 to 60 percent of occasions (Foulkes, 1999). REM dreams are on average longer, more complicated, and more visual, with more action by the dreamer, but not always (McNamara, McLaren, Smith, Brown, & Stickgold, 2005). Furthermore, people with certain types of brain damage have REM sleep but no dreams, and other people have dreams but no REM sleep (Domhoff, 1999; Solms, 1997). Dreams occur during periods of high-frequency activity in the posterior cortex, which can occur during either REM or NREM sleep (Siclari et al., 2017).

Nevertheless, because vivid dreams are most common during REM sleep and because the postural muscles are paralyzed during REM sleep, people typically do not act out their dreams. A small number of people, with a condition called *REM behavior disorder*, fail to inhibit their muscular activity during REM, and as a result, they sometimes walk around flailing their arms.

▲ **Figure 10.12** Electrodes monitor the activity in a sleeper's brain, and an EEG then records and displays brain-wave patterns.

Sleep Cycles during the Night

The brain is more active during sleep than you might guess. Neurons' metabolic rate, spontaneous activity, and responsiveness to stimuli decrease less than 20 percent (Hobson, 2005). The main characteristic of sleep is an increase of inhibitory messages, preventing brain messages from reverberating widely (Massimini et al., 2005). Activity in any brain area becomes less likely to excite other areas (Esser, Hill, & Tononi, 2009). A spread of messages through the brain is central to conscious experience, so blocking that spread blocks consciousness.

Sleep researchers distinguish among sleep stages by recording brain waves with electrodes attached to the scalp (see ▲ **Figure 10.12**). An

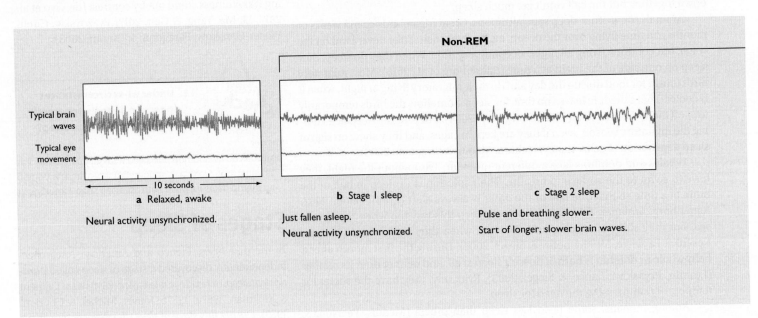

▲ **Figure 10.13** During sleep, people progress through stages of varying brain activity. The blue line indicates brain waves, as shown by an EEG. The red line shows eye movements. REM sleep resembles stage 1 sleep, except for the addition of rapid eye movements. (Courtesy of T. E. Le Vere)

electroencephalograph (EEG) *measures and amplifies tiny electrical changes on the scalp that reflect patterns of brain activity.* Sleep researchers *combine an EEG measure with a simultaneous measure of eye movements to produce a* **polysomnograph** (literally, "many-sleep measure"), as shown in Figure 10.13. A sleeper first enters stage 1, when the eyes are nearly motionless and the EEG shows short, choppy waves (see ▼ **Figure 10.13b**) that indicate a fair amount of brain activity. Because brain cells fire out of synchrony, their activities nearly cancel each other out, like the sound of many people talking at the same time.

As sleep continues, a person progresses into stage 2 and then slow-wave sleep, as shown in ▼ **Figure 10.13c** and **10.13d**. Stage 2 is marked by **sleep spindles**, *waves of activity at about 12 to 14 per second* that result from an exchange of information between the cerebral cortex and the underlying thalamus. Sleep spindles are important for storing memory, and the improvement of memory that often occurs after sleep depends on the sleep spindles (Barakat et al., 2013; Eschenko, Mölle, Born, & Sara, 2006). Preschool children's naps, which generally include much stage 2 sleep, are important for the children's memory storage (Kurdziel, Duclos, & Spencer, 2013).

Slow-wave sleep is marked by long, slow waves that indicate *decreased* brain activity. The waves grow larger because neurons synchronize their activity, with little outside input to disrupt them. Some authorities divide slow-wave sleep into stages 3 and 4, depending on the amount of slow waves.

After slow-wave sleep, a sleeper returns to stage 2, and then proceeds to REM sleep. In ▼ **Figure 10.13e**, the EEG in REM sleep resembles that of stage 1, but the eyes move steadily. At the end of REM sleep, the cycle repeats. In a healthy young adult, each cycle lasts 90 to 100 minutes on average. As shown in ▼ **Figure 10.14**, slow-wave sleep dominates the first half of the night, whereas REM and stage 2 increase in duration later. You may sometimes hear someone say that to benefit from sleep, you have to sleep through a full 90-minute cycle. They are either making that up, or quoting someone else who made it up. No evidence supports that statement.

concept check

12. **During which sleep stage is the brain most active? During which stage are the muscles least active? What is the advantage of this pattern?**

Answer

12. The brain is most active during REM sleep and the muscles are least active during this period. Inhibiting muscle activity prevents potentially risky movements while the brain is active but disengaged from the real world.

Sleep Problems

Comedian Steven Wright says that someone asked him, "Did you sleep well last night?" He replied, "No, I made a few mistakes."

We laugh because sleep isn't the kind of activity on which people make mistakes. Sometimes, however, we fail to sleep, feel poorly rested, or have bad dreams. These experiences are not "mistakes," but our sleep is not what we wanted it to be.

Insomnia

Insomnia means "lack of sleep." However, how much sleep you need may differ from someone else, or from how much you need at a different

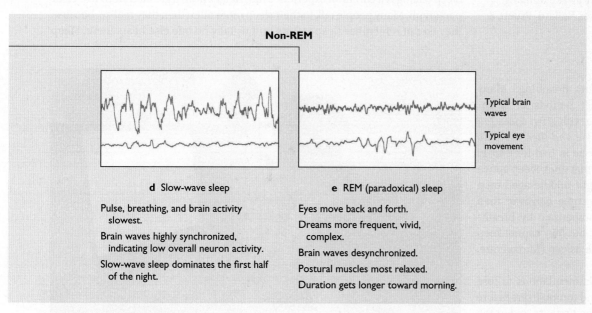

Non-REM

| Typical brain waves |
| Typical eye movement |

d Slow-wave sleep

Pulse, breathing, and brain activity slowest.

Brain waves highly synchronized, indicating low overall neuron activity.

Slow-wave sleep dominates the first half of the night.

e REM (paradoxical) sleep

Eyes move back and forth.

Dreams more frequent, vivid, complex.

Brain waves desynchronized.

Postural muscles most relaxed.

Duration gets longer toward morning.

▲ **Figure 10.13** *continued*

▲ Figure 10.14 This sleeper had five cycles of REM and non-REM sleep and awakened (A) briefly three times during the night. Slow-wave sleep (SWS) occupies more time earlier in the night than later. REM and stage 2 become more prevalent as the night progresses. (From Dement, 1972)

time. The best definition is that **insomnia** means *consistently not getting enough sleep to feel rested the next day*. The causes include noise, worries, indigestion, uncomfortable temperatures, use of caffeine or other substances, and medical or psychological disorders (Ohayon, 1997). If you have persistent insomnia, consult a physician, but for occasional insomnia, you can try a few things yourself:

- Keep a regular time schedule for going to bed and waking up each day.
- Spend some time in the sunlight to set your circadian rhythm.
- Minimize exposure to television, computers, and other bright lights in the hours before bedtime.
- Avoid caffeine, nicotine, and other stimulants, especially in the evening.
- Don't rely on alcohol or tranquilizers to fall asleep. After repeated use, you may be unable to sleep without them.
- Keep your bedroom cool and quiet.
- Exercise daily but not shortly before bedtime.
- Write a list of the tasks you need to do in the next few days. After you have recorded those tasks, you don't need to stay awake thinking about them (Scullin, Krueger, Ballard, Pruett, & Bliwise, 2018).

Sleep Apnea

Apnea (AP-nee-uh) means "no breathing." Many people have occasional brief periods of sleeping without breathing. People with **sleep apnea** *fail to breathe for a minute or more and then wake up gasping for breath*. They may lie in bed for 8 to 10 hours but sleep less than half that time. Sleep apnea is most common in overweight middle-aged men whose breathing passages become narrower than usual. While awake, they compensate by breathing frequently and vigorously, but they cannot keep up this pattern while they are asleep (Mezzanotte, Tangel, & White, 1992).

Treatment includes recommendations to lose weight and to avoid alcohol and tranquilizers before bedtime. Surgeons can remove tissue to widen the airways. Some people with sleep apnea use a device that pumps air into a mask covering the nose and

mouth during sleep, forcing the person to breathe. That procedure improves sleep, but it only slightly improves health if the person continues to be seriously overweight (Guo et al., 2016).

Narcolepsy

Infants alternate between brief waking periods and brief sleeping periods (Blumberg, Gall, & Todd, 2014). As they grow older, they consolidate into one long waking period during the day, possibly interrupted by a nap, and one long sleeping period at night. A neurotransmitter called *orexin* is important for maintaining long periods of wakefulness. People with **narcolepsy** lose the brain cells that produce orexin, and therefore return to a pattern resembling infants (Mahoney, Cogswell, Koralnik, & Scammell, 2019). They experience *sudden attacks of sleepiness during the day*. They also experience sudden attacks of muscle weakness or paralysis and occasional dreamlike experiences while awake. These symptoms represent intrusions of REM sleep into the waking period (Guilleminault, Heinzer, Mignot, & Black, 1998). Narcolepsy has a genetic predisposition that can be triggered by certain types of infection, causing the immune system to attack the brain cells that make orexin (Mahoney et al., 2019).

A combination of stimulant and antidepressant drugs maintains wakefulness during the day and blocks the attacks of muscle weakness. Clinical trials are attempting to develop new drugs that resemble the effects of orexin.

Other Sleep Experiences

Sleep talking is a common experience that ranges from a grunted word to a clear paragraph. Many people talk in their sleep more often than they realize, because they do not remember sleep talking and usually no one else hears them. Sleep

Insomnia is identified by how sleepy the person is the following day.

3 A.M.		4 A.M.		5 A.M.		6 A.M.		7 A.M.
2 SWS 2		REM	I 2 SWS 2 A I		REM	A	A 2		REM

talking occurs in all stages, but most commonly during stage 2 sleep (Moorcroft, 2003). Sleep talkers sometimes pause between utterances, as if they were carrying on a conversation. In fact, it is possible to engage some sleep talkers in a dialogue. Sleep talking is not related to mental or emotional disorders, and sleep talkers rarely say anything embarrassing. If you talk in your sleep, don't worry about it.

Have you ever had the experience of waking up and finding yourself unable to move? If so, don't be alarmed. When you awaken, all brain areas may not awaken at once (Krueger et al., 2008; Silva & Duffy, 2008). Occasionally, your cortex awakens but part of your medulla continues sending inhibitory messages to the spinal cord, just as it does during REM sleep. You then find yourself alert, with your eyes open, but temporarily unable to move your arms or legs.

Sleepwalking tends to run (walk?) in families, mostly in children and mainly during slow-wave sleep (Dement, 1972). Some adults sleepwalk also, mostly during the first half of the night's sleep, and not while dreaming. They have clumsy movements with only limited responsiveness to their surroundings. Contrary to what you may have heard, wakening a sleepwalker is not dangerous, although it is not helpful either (Moorcroft, 2003). A better idea is to guide the person gently back to bed. In addition to walking during sleep, some people have been known to eat, rearrange furniture, drive cars, or engage in sex (either by masturbation or with a partner) during sleep (Mangan, 2004). You might wonder, is the person really asleep? The answer is, "sort of." As mentioned earlier, the entire brain doesn't necessarily wake up or go to sleep all at once. Sleep can be localized to one brain area more than another. Sleepwalking occurs when the motor cortex and a few other areas are active while other brain areas remain asleep (Terzaghi et al., 2012; Zadra, Desautels, Petit, & Montplaisir, 2013).

Lucid dreaming is another instance in which part of the brain is awake and another part asleep. Someone having a lucid dream is aware that it is a dream. Lucid dreaming occurs during periods of increased activity in the frontal and temporal cortex, with less arousal in the rest of the brain (Voss et al., 2014).

Do you ever lie in bed, trying to fall asleep, when suddenly a leg kicks? An occasional leg jerk while trying to fall asleep is common and no cause for concern. However, some people have *prolonged "creepy-crawly" sensations in their legs, accompanied by repetitive leg movements strong enough to awaken the person, especially during the first half of the night* (Moorcroft, 1993). This condition, known as periodic limb movement disorder, interrupts sleep in many people, mostly over age 50. The causes are unknown, and the best advice is to avoid factors that make the condition worse, such as caffeine, stress, or fatigue.

Nightmares are intensely unpleasant dreams, most often about accidents, injuries to self or loved ones, or being chased (Schredl & Goeritz, 2018). A night terror, however, *causes someone to awaken screaming and sweating with a racing heart rate, sometimes flailing with the arms and pounding the walls.* Night terrors occur during slow-wave sleep, not REM, and their dream content, if any, is usually simple, such as a single image. Comforting or reassuring people during a night terror is futile, and the terror simply has to run its course. Many children have night terrors, as do nearly 3 percent of adults (Mahowald & Schenck, 2005). Treatments include psychotherapy, antidepressant and antianxiety drugs, and advice to minimize stress.

concept check

13. What experience reflects the fact that part of the brain can be awake while another is asleep?

Answer

13. Any of the following: waking up but finding oneself unable to move, sleepwalking, or lucid dreaming.

Dreams

Even a saint is not responsible for what happens in his dreams.
—St. Thomas Aquinas

In ancient times, people believed that dreams foretold the future. Occasionally, of course, they do, either by coincidence or because the dreamer had a reason to expect some outcome. Today, scientists do not believe dreams tell us about the future, although many other people do. If you dream about a plane crash tonight, will you hesitate to take a plane trip tomorrow? If you dream your friend treats you badly or your lover is unfaithful, will you become suspicious in real life? If so, you have plenty of company (Morewedge & Norton, 2009).

If dreams do not tell us the future, what do they tell us? Can we explain or interpret dreams? Let's consider dream content.

Descriptive Studies of Dreaming

One research method is to ask people to keep dream diaries. Another method is to awaken people in the laboratory and ask for immediate dream reports (Domhoff, 2003). ■ Table 10.1 lists common dream themes of college students in five countries. Note the similarities across samples.

Dreams differ among cultures in several regards (Domhoff & Schneider, 2008). People in the United States often dream of people they don't know, whereas people in India, Iran, and Japan more often dream only of the people they know (Mazandarani, Aguilar-Vafaie, & Domhoff, 2013). People in hunter-gatherer societies have many dreams about animals, and people in dangerous societies have dreams about being victims of violent aggression. In the United States, adolescents also have frequent dreams about being victims of aggression (Dale, Lafreniere, & De Koninck, 2017).

Table 10.1 Percentages of College Students Who Reported Certain Dream Topics

Dream Topic	U.S. 1958	Japan 1958	Canada 2003	Germany 2004	China 2008
Falling	83%	74%	74%	74%	87%
Being attacked or pursued	77%	91%	82%	89%	92%
Repeatedly trying to do something	71%	87%	54%	30%	74%
Schoolwork	71%	86%	67%	89%	94%
Sex	66%	68%	76%	87%	70%
Arriving too late	64%	49%	60%	68%	80%
Eating delicious food	62%	68%	31%	42%	69%
Frozen with fright	58%	87%	41%	56%	71%
Loved one dying	57%	42%	54%	68%	75%

(Based on Griffith, Miyagi, & Tago (1958); Nielsen et al. (2003); Schredl, Ciric, Götz, & Wittman, 2004; Yu, 2008.)

Common usage implies that dreams are happy. In the Disney movie, Cinderella sings, "A dream is a wish your heart makes." Martin Luther King Jr.'s famous "I Have a Dream" speech described a wonderful future. Calling your boyfriend or girlfriend "dreamy" is a compliment. Sigmund Freud claimed that dreams are based on wish fulfillment. However, Table 10.1 shows that most dream content is unpleasant, such as falling, being chased, or being unable to do something. An analysis of college students' dream reports found that misfortune and negative emotions outnumbered good fortune and positive emotions by more than three to one (Dale, Lortie-Lussier, Wong, & De Koninck, 2016). Happy dreams are most common among 11- to 13-year-olds (Foulkes, 1999), but from then on, dreams get worse. Sorry about that.

Most dreams are similar to what we think about in everyday life, and they often relate to a recent experience (Domhoff, 1996; Hall & Van de Castle, 1966). Unusual or emotional experiences are especially likely to be incorporated into a dream, whereas people seldom dream about reading, writing, using a computer, or watching television (Malinowski & Horton, 2014; Schredl, 2000). For the best research on dream content, visit this website: **dreams.ucsc.edu**.

Many questions about dreaming are difficult to answer. For example, "How accurately do we remember our dreams?" Well, how would we find out? We have no way to compare actual dreams to what people remember about their dreams. Or consider this apparently simple question: "Do we dream in color?" People ask because they do not remember. But how could an investigator answer the question except by asking people to remember? The best evidence we have is that, when people are awakened and asked immediately, they report color at least half of the time (Herman, Roffwarg, & Tauber, 1968; Padgham, 1975). This result does not mean that other dreams are in black and white. Perhaps the colors in those dreams were not memorable.

Do blind people have visual dreams? It depends. People who become blind because of damage to the visual cortex lose visual dreaming as well as visual imagery. People who experience eye damage after about age 5 to 7 continue to have visual dreams, although their frequency of visual dreams declines over time. People who were born blind or who became blind in early childhood have no visual imagery in their dreams. Instead, they dream of sounds, touch, smells, and tastes (Hurovitz et al., 1999).

14. How do dreams resemble waking experience, and how do they differ?

Answer

14. Dreams incorporate recent experiences, but mostly the novel and emotional ones. Adults' dreams are more often unpleasant than pleasant.

Freud's Theory of Dreams

The Austrian physician Sigmund Freud, founder of psychoanalysis, maintained that dreams reveal the dreamer's unconscious thoughts and motivations. To understand a dream, he said, one must probe for hidden meanings. Each dream has a manifest content—*the content that appears on the surface*—and a latent content—*the hidden ideas that the dream experience represents symbolically.*

For example, Freud (1900/1955) once dreamed that one of his friends was his uncle. He worked out these associations: Both this friend and another friend had been recommended for an appointment as professor at the university. Both had been turned down, probably because they were Jews. Freud himself had been recently recommended for the same appointment, and he feared that he too would be rejected because he was Jewish. Freud's only uncle had once been convicted of illegal business dealings. Freud's father had said, however, that the uncle was not bad but just a simpleton.

How did the two friends relate to the uncle? One of the friends was in Freud's judgment a bit simpleminded. The other had once been accused of sexual misconduct. By linking these two friends to his uncle, Freud interpreted the dream as meaning, "Maybe they didn't get the university appointment because one was a simpleton (like my uncle) and the other was regarded as a criminal (like my uncle). If so, my being Jewish might not stop me from getting the appointment."

In some cases, Freud relied on individual associations, as in the dream just described, but he also assumed that certain elements have predictable meanings for most dreams. For example, he claimed that the number three in a dream represents a man's penis and testes. Anything long, such as a stick, represents a penis. So does anything that could penetrate the body, anything from which water flows, anything that can be lengthened, almost any tool, and anything that can fly or float—because rising is like an erection (Freud, 1935). He admitted that if you dream about a knife or an airplane, you really might be dreaming about a knife or airplane instead of a penis, but he was confident that a skilled psychoanalyst could tell the difference, even if the dreamer could not. (How would the psychoanalyst know? Freud did not tell us.)

One of Freud's most famous dream analyses concerned a man who reported remembering a dream from when he was 4 years old (!) in which he saw six or seven white dogs with large tails sitting motionlessly in a tree outside his window. (The actual dream was of spitz dogs, although Freud wrote about them as wolves.) After a laborious line of reasoning, Freud concluded that the child had dreamed about his parents in their bedclothes—presumably white, like the dogs in the dream. The dogs' lack of motion represented its opposite—frantic sexual activity. The big tails also represented their opposite—the boy's fear of having his penis cut off. In short, said Freud, the boy had dreamed about watching his parents have sex, doggy style. Decades later, researchers located the man who had told Freud this dream. He reported that he regarded Freud's interpretation of his dream as far-fetched, and Freud's treatment did him no apparent good, as he spent many later years in continued treatment (Esterson, 1993).

Can anyone listen to dreams and determine hidden aspects of the dreamer's personality? Many therapists offer dream interpretations that their clients find meaningful. However, there is no way to check which interpretations are accurate and which ones are not. Freud's approach to dream analysis has been on the decline, although it continues to influence some therapists (Domhoff, 2003).

15. Does Freud's dream theory make any testable predictions?

Answer

15. No. Given any dream, he could state an interpretation, but we have no way to test the accuracy of the interpretation. Because the theory makes no clear predictions, it is not "falsifiable."

Modern Theories of Dreaming

According to the **activation-synthesis theory of dreams**, dreams occur because the cortex takes the haphazard activity that occurs during REM sleep plus whatever stimuli strike the sense organs and does its best to make sense of the activity (Hobson & McCarley, 1977). Some aspects of dreams do appear to relate to stimuli. For example, when people dream of using a toilet or trying to find a toilet, they often awaken and discover that they really do need to use a toilet. Do you ever dream that you are trying to walk or run, but you cannot move? One explanation is that the major postural muscles are really paralyzed during REM sleep. Your brain sends messages telling your muscles to move but receives sensory feedback indicating they have not moved.

However, dreams that relate to current sensations are the exception, not the rule (Foulkes & Domhoff, 2014; Nir & Tononi, 2010). Also, the muscles are always paralyzed during REM sleep. Why don't we always dream that we cannot move?

A modified view, known as the neurocognitive theory, is that dreaming is a kind of thinking, similar to daydreaming or mind wandering, that occurs under these conditions (Fox, Nijeboer, Solomonova, Domhoff, & Christoff, 2013; Solms, 2000):

- reduced sensory stimulation, especially in the brain's primary sensory areas
- reduced activity in the cortical areas important for planning and working memory
- loss of voluntary control of thinking
- enough activity in other brain areas, including those responsible for face recognition, motivation, and emotion

In contrast to the activation-synthesis theory, which regards dreaming as a bottom-up process beginning with sensations or random activation, the neurocognitive theory regards dreaming as a top-down process, controlled by the same mechanisms as any other thought. William Domhoff (2011) compares dreaming to activity of the brain's "default network," the system active during mind wandering and daydreaming. The default network drifts from thought to thought without plan or control, much as a dream does. A sleeper's brain receives only a limited amount of sensory information. Because the primary visual and auditory areas of the brain are inactive during sleep, the rest of the brain constructs images without interference, usually focusing on something the dreamer has seen, heard, or thought about in the last several days. Because of low activity in the prefrontal cortex, which is important for planning and working memory, the dream story jumps from one event to another without much continuity and without much sense of intention.

Dreams do reveal something about the dreamer's interests and personality. That is, you dream about issues that interest or worry you. However, that kind of interpretation is different from finding hidden symbolic meanings, as Freud attempted to do.

16. How does the neurocognitive theory differ from the activation-synthesis theory?

Answer

16. The activation-synthesis theory puts more emphasis on input coming into the brain from sense organs. The neurocognitive theory treats dreaming as similar to mind wandering.

The Mysteries of Sleep and Dreams

Sleep and dreams are not a state of unconsciousness but a state of reduced or altered consciousness. A healthy brain is never completely off duty, never completely relaxed.

Although our understanding of sleep and dreams continues to grow, major questions remain. Even such basic issues as the function of REM sleep remain in doubt. People have long found their dreams a source of wonder, and researchers continue to find much of interest and mystery.

Summary

- *Circadian rhythms.* A self-generated rhythm of approximately 24 hours governs wakefulness, sleepiness, and many body functions. (page 315)
- *Setting the rhythm.* Bright light resets the rhythm, like resetting a clock. (page 315)
- *Morning and evening people.* Some people arouse quickly and reach their peak alertness early. Others increase alertness more slowly and reach their peak in late afternoon or early evening. Young adults tend to be morning people, whereas older adults are more likely to be evening people. (page 316)
- *Brain mechanisms of circadian rhythms.* A brain area called the suprachiasmatic nucleus generates an approximately 24-hour rhythm. (page 318)
- *The need for sleep.* Sleep serves functions including conservation of energy and an opportunity to strengthen memories. (page 318)

- *Sleep stages.* During sleep, people cycle from sleep stages 1 and 2 to slow-wave sleep and back again. A cycle lasts about 90 to 100 minutes. (page 319)
- *REM sleep.* REM sleep replaces the stage 1 periods after the first one. REM sleep is characterized by rapid eye movements, a high level of brain activity, and relaxed muscles. Dreams are common in this stage but not limited to it. (page 319)
- *Insomnia.* Insomnia—subjectively unsatisfactory sleep—results from many influences. Sleep abnormalities include sleep apnea and narcolepsy. (page 321)
- *Dream content.* More dreams are threatening than pleasant. Freud proposed that dreams are the product of unconscious motivations. Modern theorists describe dreaming as a kind of thinking that occurs under conditions of low sensory input and no voluntary control of thinking. (page 323)

Key Terms

activation-synthesis theory of dreams (page 325)

circadian rhythm (page 315)

electroencephalograph (EEG) (page 321)

insomnia (page 322)

jet lag (page 317)

latent content (page 324)

manifest content (page 324)

narcolepsy (page 322)

night terror (page 323)

periodic limb movement disorder (page 323)

polysomnograph (page 321)

rapid eye movement (REM) sleep (page 319)

sleep apnea (page 322)

sleep spindles (page 321)

Review Questions

1. If someone remains awake nonstop for 3 days, what happens to alertness?
   (a) It decreases steadily throughout the three days.
   (b) It decreases for about one day and then remains constant.
   (c) It remains constant until the third day.
   (d) It rises and falls on a 24-hour schedule, superimposed on a downward slope.

2. Who are most likely to be morning people?
   (a) Young adults
   (b) Old adults
   (c) Athletes
   (d) Musicians

3. Why does the circadian rhythm continue even in an unchanging environment?
   (a) It is a habit learned in childhood.
   (b) A brain area generates it.
   (c) The earth's magnetic field generates it.
   (d) The heart generates it.

4. What happens during sleep to improve memory?
   (a) Synapses appropriate to a memory become stronger.
   (b) Synapses inappropriate to a memory become weaker.
   (c) Metabolic rate in the brain increases.
   (d) Long-distance axons in the brain increase their conduction velocity.

5. The sleep spindles of stage 2 sleep are important for what?
   (a) Emotional regulation
   (b) Increased metabolic rate
   (c) Memory storage
   (d) Formation of dreams

6. What do the long waves of brain activity during slow-wave sleep indicate?
   (a) Increased brain activity
   (b) Synchrony among neurons
   (c) Increased amplitude and velocity of action potentials
   (d) Muscle activity

7. Which of the following increases the risk of sleep apnea?
   (a) Prolonged exercise
   (b) Drinking beverages with caffeine
   (c) A loss of neurons containing orexin
   (d) Being overweight

8. If you awaken but cannot move your arms or legs, what is the probable reason?
   (a) You did not breathe enough while sleeping.
   (b) Not all parts of your brain awakened at once.
   (c) Your heart rate is not yet high enough for muscle movements.
   (d) You are in the early stages of mental illness.

9. Freud said that dreams are based on wish fulfillment. What is evidence either for or against this view?
   (a) Evidence for: Freud's interpretations consistently helped his patients.
   (b) Evidence for: Dreams originate in the prefrontal cortex.
   (c) Evidence against: Most dreams are unpleasant.
   (d) Evidence against: Most dreams repeat the most boring parts of the day.

10. The neurocognitive theory of dreams compares dreams to what?
    (a) Mind wandering and daydreaming
    (b) Hypnosis
    (c) Repressed thoughts and memories
    (d) Meditation

Answers: 1d, 2b, 3b, 4b, 5c, 6b, 7d, 8b, 9c, 10a.

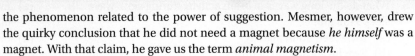

After studying this module, you should be able to:

1. Describe methods of inducing hypnosis.

2. List uses of hypnosis that the evidence supports, and those that it does not support.

3. Describe evidence that hypnosis does not improve memory.

4. Discuss whether we should regard hypnosis as an altered state of consciousness.

> Truth is nothing but a path traced between errors.[1]
> —Franz Anton Mesmer

If a hypnotist told you that you were 4 years old and you started acting like a 4-year-old, we would say that you are a good hypnotic subject. If the hypnotist said your cousin was sitting in the empty chair in front of you and you agreed that you see her, then again, we would remark on the depth of your hypnotism.

But what if you had *not* been hypnotized and you suddenly started acting like a 4-year-old or insisted that you saw someone in an empty chair? Then psychologists would suspect that you were suffering from a serious psychological disorder. Hypnosis induces behavior that is sometimes bizarre. No wonder we find it so fascinating.

Hypnosis is *a condition of focused attention and increased suggestibility that occurs in the context of a special hypnotist–subject relationship.* The term *hypnosis* comes from Hypnos, the Greek god of sleep, although the similarity between hypnosis and sleep is superficial. Hypnotized people, like dreamers, accept contradictory information without protest, but they walk around and respond to objects in the real world. Their brain activity, unlike that during sleep, is characterized by increased activity in the prefrontal cortex, important for attention (Oakley & Halligan, 2013).

Hypnosis originated with the work of Franz Anton Mesmer (1734–1815), an Austrian physician. Mesmer sometimes treated illnesses by passing a magnet back and forth across a patient's body to redirect the flow of blood, nerve activity, and undefined "fluids." Some patients reported dramatic benefits. Later, Mesmer discovered that he could dispense with the magnet and use only his hand. From this observation, most people would conclude that the phenomenon related to the power of suggestion. Mesmer, however, drew the quirky conclusion that he did not need a magnet because *he himself* was a magnet. With that claim, he gave us the term *animal magnetism.*

After his death, others studied "animal magnetism" or "Mesmerism," eventually calling it "hypnotism." By that time, hypnosis was associated with charlatans and hocus-pocus. Still today, some stage performers use hypnosis for entertainment. We should carefully distinguish the exaggerated claims from the legitimate use of hypnosis by licensed therapists.

Ways of Inducing Hypnosis

Mesmer thought hypnosis was a power emanating from his body. If so, only special people could hypnotize others. Today, we find that successful hypnotists need practice but no unusual powers.

The first step toward being hypnotized is agreeing to give it a try. Contrary to what you may have heard, no one can hypnotize an uncooperative person. A hypnotist tells you to sit down and relax, and you do so because you would like to experience hypnosis. The whole point of hypnosis is following the hypnotist's suggestions, and when you sit down and relax, you are already following a suggestion.

A hypnotist might then monotonously repeat something like, "You are putting everything else out of your mind except what you hear from me. You are starting to fall asleep. Your eyelids are getting heavy. Your eyelids are getting

Although Mesmer is often depicted as being able to control people irresistibly, hypnosis depends on the person's willingness.

[1]Does this seem profound? Or is it nonsense? Many statements sound profound until we try to figure out exactly what they mean.

A hypnotist induces hypnosis by repeating suggestions, relying on the hypnotized person's cooperation and willingness to accept suggestions.

very heavy. They are starting to close. You are falling into a deep, deep sleep." A bit later (Udolf, 1981), the hypnotist might suggest something specific, such as, "After you go under hypnosis, your arm will begin to rise automatically." (Some people, eager for the hypnosis to succeed, shoot their arm up immediately and have to be told, "No, not yet. Just relax. That will happen later.") The hypnotist encourages you to relax and suggests that your arm is starting to feel lighter, as if it were tied to a helium balloon.

The hypnotist might suggest that your arm is beginning to feel strange and is beginning to twitch. The timing of this suggestion is important, because if you stand or sit in one position long enough, your limbs really do tingle and twitch. If the hypnotist's suggestion comes at the right moment, you think, "Wow, that's right. My arm does feel strange. This is starting to work!" Believing that you are being hypnotized is a big step toward actually being hypnotized.

The Uses and Limitations of Hypnosis

Hypnosis resembles ordinary suggestibility. If someone asked you to imagine a bright, sunny day, you almost certainly would, without being hypnotized. If you were asked to please stand and put your hands on your head, you probably would, again without being hypnotized. Then someone asks you to flap your arms and cluck like a chicken. You might or might not. People vary considerably in how far they will follow suggestions, either with or without hypnosis (Barnier, Cox, & McConkey, 2014). Hypnosis enhances suggestibility, but not enormously (Kirsch & Braffman, 2001). If you are easily hypnotizable, you probably also respond strongly to books and movies, reacting almost as if the events were really happening.

What Hypnosis Can Do

One well-established effect of hypnosis is to inhibit pain. Some people undergo medical or dental surgery with only hypnosis and no anesthesia. The benefits of hypnosis are most easily demonstrated for acute (sudden) pains, but hypnosis helps with chronic pains, too (Patterson, 2004). Hypnosis is particularly helpful for people who react unfavorably to anesthetic drugs and those who have developed a tolerance to painkilling opiates. Unfortunately, although hypnosis can relieve pain cheaply and without side effects, few physicians and hospitals use it (Yeh, Schnur, & Montgomery, 2014).

Pain has both sensory and emotional components, which depend on different brain areas. Hypnosis alters mostly the emotional components, although it somewhat decreases the response of brain areas responsive to the

sensation (Jensen & Patterson, 2014; ▼ Figure 10.15). Exactly how hypnosis reduces pain is not understood, but it does not depend entirely on relaxation or distraction.

Another use of hypnosis is the posthypnotic suggestion, *a suggestion to do or experience something after coming out of hypnosis.* Suppose you receive a suggestion under hypnosis that whenever you see the number 1, it will look red, and when you see the number 2, it will look yellow. After you emerge from hypnosis, the researcher shows you black numbers on various backgrounds and asks you to press a key as soon as you see a number. You will have no trouble seeing 1 or 2, but you will usually fail to see 1 or 2 (Kadosh, Henik, Catena, Walsh, & Fuentes, 2009). Until the hypnotist cancels the suggestion or it wears off, you will be like the people with synesthesia.

In one study, adults known to be easily hypnotized were randomly assigned to two groups. One group was handed a stack of 120 addressed stamped postcards and asked (without being hypnotized) to mail one back each day until they exhausted the stack. Another group was given a posthypnotic suggestion to mail one card per day. The nonhypnotized group actually mailed back more cards, but they reported that they had to remind themselves each day to mail a card. Those given the posthypnotic

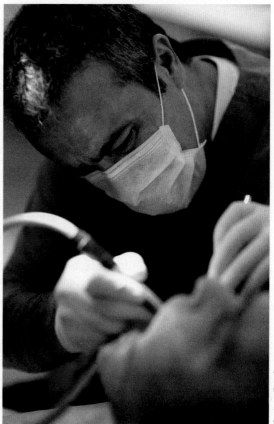

Some dentists use hypnosis to relieve pain, even for tooth extractions and root canal surgery.

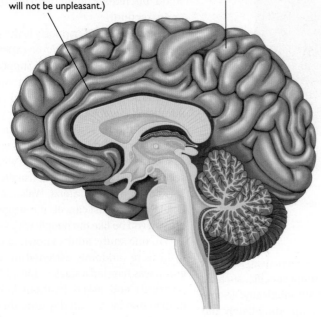

Area of frontal cortex responsive to emotional distress. (Activity decreased by hypnotic suggestion that stimulus will not be unpleasant.)

Area of parietal cortex responsive to painful stimulation.

▲ **Figure 10.15** A hypnotic suggestion to experience less pain decreases activity in the frontal cortex areas associated with emotional distress but has less effect on the sensory areas in the parietal cortex.

suggestion said they never made a deliberate effort. The idea of mailing a card just "popped into mind," providing a sudden compulsion to mail one (Barnier & McConkey, 1998).

Many therapists have given cigarette smokers a posthypnotic suggestion that they will not want to smoke. Only a few studies have compared the results to a placebo treatment. Overall, hypnosis appears to be a helpful treatment, but because of the small number of studies and their varying results, the amount of benefit is uncertain (Hasan, et al., 2014; Tahiri, Mottillo, Joseph, Pilote, & Eisenberg, 2012).

What Hypnosis Does Not Do

Some of the more spectacular claims about hypnosis become less impressive on closer scrutiny. For instance, as in ▶ Figure 10.16, people under hypnosis can balance their head and neck on one chair and their feet on another chair and even allow someone to stand on their body. Amazing? Not really. It's easier than it looks, with or without hypnosis. Give it a try. (But don't invite someone to stand on you. Someone who does not balance correctly could injure you.)

Many people have attempted to use hypnosis to enhance memory. For example, a distressed person tells a psychotherapist, "I don't know why I have such troubles. Maybe I had a bad experience when

I was younger. I just can't remember." Or a witness to a crime says, "I saw the culprit for a second or two, but now I can't give you a good description." Therapists and police officers have sometimes turned to hypnosis in the hope of uncovering lost memories.

Under hypnosis, people do report additional details, often with great confidence. However, most of the additional details are wrong. Hypnotized people have an "illusion of memory," but the evidence says that hypnosis is more harmful to memory than helpful (Mazzoni, Laurence, & Heap, 2014). Let's consider a typical study.

what's the evidence?

Hypnosis and Memory

The design of this study and several like it is simple: The experimenter presents material, tests people's memory of it, hypnotizes them, and tests their memory again (Dywan & Bowers, 1983).

Hypothesis People will remember additional details after hypnosis.

AP Images/Bookstaver

▲ **Figure 10.16** The U.S. Supreme Court ruled in 1987 that criminal defendants may testify about details they recalled under hypnosis. Its decision sparked this protest by the magician known as The Amazing Kreskin, who borrowed a stunt commonly used to demonstrate the power of hypnosis—standing on a person suspended between two chairs.

Method Fifty-four people looked at 60 drawings of simple objects (e.g., pencil, hammer, or bicycle), one every 3.5 seconds. Then they were given a sheet with 60 blank spaces and asked to recall as many items as possible. They viewed the drawings a second and third time, and after each session, they had another chance to recall items. Each day for the next week, they again wrote a list of all the items they could remember without seeing the slides again. Finally, a week after the original slide sessions, they returned to the laboratory. Half of them, chosen at random, were hypnotized and the others were just told to relax. All were asked to recall as many drawings as possible.

Results ▼ Figure 10.17 shows the means for the two groups. The hypnotized people reported some items that they had not recalled before and more than the nonhypnotized group did. However, the hypnotized group also reported more incorrect items than the nonhypnotized group did.

Interpretation These results show no evidence that hypnosis improves memory, contrary to the hypothesis. Rather, it decreases people's usual hesitance about reporting uncertain or doubtful memories. It may also cause people to confuse imagination with reality.

This study is an example of the signal-detection issue: A reported new memory is a "hit," but the number of hits, by itself, is useless information unless we also know the number of "false alarms"—reported memories that are incorrect.

In response to these results and similar ones, the American Medical Association (1986) recommended that courts of law should refuse to admit any testimony that was elicited under hypnosis, although hypnosis might be used as an investigative tool if all else fails. For example, if a hypnotized witness reports a license plate number and the police track down the car and find blood on it, the blood is certainly admissible evidence, even if the hypnotized report is not. Success stories of that type rarely if ever occur.

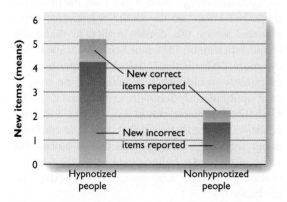

▲ **Figure 10.17** Hypnosis increased people's recall of items they had not recalled before. However, most of the new "memories" they confidently reported were incorrect. (From "The Use of Hypnosis to Aid Recall," J. Dwyan and K. Bowers, 1983. *Science, 222,* pp. 184–185. Copyright © 1983 American Association for the Advancement of Science. Reprinted with permission.)

You may encounter the astonishing claim that hypnosis enables people to recall memories from a previous life. Hypnotized young people who claim to be recollecting a previous life most often describe the life of someone similar to themselves, married to someone remarkably similar to the current boyfriend or girlfriend. They often tell good stories, but if they are asked about verifiable facts such as what kind of money the country of their previous life uses, their guesses are seldom correct (Spanos, 1987–1988).

17. What evidence says that hypnosis does not improve memory?

Answer

17. Under hypnosis, people report more items than before, but most of the new items are incorrect. They do not distinguish between correct memories and fantasies.

what's the evidence?

Hypnosis and Risky Acts

Most hypnotists will tell you, "You don't have to worry. People will not do anything under hypnosis that they would ordinarily refuse to do." That reassurance is important for persuading you to agree to hypnosis. But is it true? How would anyone know? Do you suppose hypnotists sometimes ask clients to perform dangerous or immoral acts, meet with refusals, and then report the results of these unethical experiments? Not likely. Furthermore, on the rare occasions when investigators did ask hypnotized people to perform dangerous acts, the results were hard to interpret. Here is an example.

Hypothesis Hypnotized people will sometimes perform acts that people would refuse to do otherwise.

Method Eighteen college students were randomly assigned to three groups. The investigator hypnotized those in one group, instructed the second group to pretend they were hypnotized, and simply asked the third group to participate in the study, without mentioning hypnosis. Each student was then asked to perform three acts: First, pick up a venomous snake from a box. Anyone who got too close was restrained at the last moment. Second, reach into a vat of fuming nitric acid to retrieve a coin (which was already starting to dissolve). Here, there was no last-second restraint. People who followed the instructions were told to wash their hands in warm soapy water immediately afterward. (Today's ethical procedures would prevent this study.) Third, throw the nitric acid into the face of the hypnotist's assistant. While the participant was washing hands, the researcher had replaced the nitric acid with water, but the participant had no way of knowing that.

Will hypnotized people do anything that they would otherwise refuse to do? The problem is that nonhypnotized people will sometimes perform some strange and dangerous acts either because an experimenter asked them to or on their own.

Results Five of the six hypnotized students followed all three directions (Orne & Evans, 1965). Moreover, so did all six of those who were pretending to be hypnotized! So did two of the six who were just told to take these actions as part of an experiment with no mention of hypnosis. Nonhypnotized subjects did, however, hesitate longer than the hypnotized subjects.

Why would people do such extraordinary things? They explained that they trusted the experimenter: "If he tells me to do something, it can't really be dangerous."

Interpretation We do not have evidence to decide whether people under hypnosis will do something that they would refuse to do otherwise because it is difficult to find something that people will refuse to do!

Notice the importance of control groups: We cannot simply assume what people would do without hypnosis. We need to test them.

Is Hypnosis an Altered State of Consciousness?

If a hypnotist tells you, "Your hand is rising; you can do nothing to stop it," your hand might indeed rise. If you were later asked why, you might reply that you lost control of your own behavior. Still, you were not a puppet. Was the act voluntary or not? To put the question differently, is hypnosis really different from normal wakefulness?

Over the years, psychologists have gone back and forth about whether to regard hypnosis as a special state of consciousness, and they have also wavered on exactly what a "state of consciousness" means (Lynn et al., 2015). It is possible to regard hypnosis as a special state in some ways but not others (Kirsch & Lynn, 1998). One way to determine whether hypnosis is a special state of consciousness is to find out whether nonhypnotized people can do everything that hypnotized people do. How convincingly could you act like a hypnotized person?

How Well Can Someone Pretend to Be Hypnotized?

In several experiments, one group of college students were hypnotized and others pretended to be hypnotized. An experienced hypnotist then examined them and tried to determine which ones were really hypnotized.

Fooling the hypnotist was easier than expected. The pretenders tolerated sharp pain without flinching. They pretended to recall old memories. When they were told to sit down, they did so immediately (as hypnotized people do) without first checking to make sure they had a chair behind them (Orne, 1959, 1979). When told to experience anger, they exhibited physiological changes such as increased heart rate and sweating, just as hypnotized people do (Damaser, Shor, & Orne, 1963). Even experienced hypnotists could not identify the pretenders.

A few differences between the hypnotized people and pretenders emerged, because the pretenders did not always know how a hypnotized subject would act (Orne, 1979). For instance, when the hypnotist suggested, "You see Professor Schmaltz sitting in that chair," some of the hypnotized subjects asked with puzzlement, "How is it that I see the professor there, but I also see the chair?" Pretenders never reported seeing this double reality. At that point in the experiment, Professor Schmaltz walked into the room. "Who is that?" asked the hypnotist. The pretenders would either say they saw no one, or they would identify Schmaltz as someone else. The hypnotized subjects would say, "That's Professor Schmaltz." Some then said that they were confused about seeing the same person in two places. For some of them, the hallucinated professor faded at that moment. Others continued to accept the double image.

One study reported a way to distinguish hypnotized people from pretenders more than 90 percent of the time. But it might not be the way you would expect. Simply ask people how deeply hypnotized they thought they were, how relaxed they were, and whether they were aware of their surroundings while hypnotized. People who rate themselves as "extremely" hypnotized, "extremely" relaxed, and "totally unaware" of their surroundings are almost always pretenders. Those who were really hypnotized rate themselves as only mildly influenced (Martin & Lynn, 1996).

So, what is our conclusion? Apparently, people pretending to be hypnotized can mimic almost any effect of hypnosis that they know about. However, hypnosis is ordinarily not just role-playing. The effects that role-players learn to imitate happen spontaneously for the hypnotized people.

18. Why is it hard to say whether hypnotized people will do anything they would refuse to do otherwise?

Answer

18. In certain experiments, hypnotized people did some strange things, but so did nonhypnotized people.

Other States of Consciousness

Meditation, *a systematic procedure for inducing a calm, relaxed state through the use of special techniques*, follows traditions that have been practiced in much of the world for thousands of years, especially in India. One variety of meditation seeks "mindfulness" or thoughtless awareness, in which the person is aware of the sensations of the moment but otherwise passive. While seeking this state, the person might concentrate on a single image, or repeat a sound or a short religious statement. Meditators may observe their own thoughts, attempt to modify them, or distance themselves from certain thoughts. Goals of meditation vary from the development of wisdom to general well-being (Walsh & Shapiro, 2006).

Many studies have reported that meditation increases relaxation and decreases pain, anxiety, and depression. It probably has benefits for attention, sleep, and other functions. However, most research studies have lacked an appropriate control group or have been weak in other ways (Leyland, Rowse, & Emerson, 2019; Van Dam et al., 2018). For anyone seeking help for physical or mental health problems, it is wisest to consider meditation in addition to well-established treatments, not instead of them.

The **déjà vu experience**, a *feeling that an event is uncannily familiar*, is fairly common in young adults and less so as people grow older (Brown, 2003). Because it takes several forms, a single explanation may not suffice. Occasionally, someone is somewhere for the first time and sees it as familiar, as if he or she had been there before. Perhaps the person really had seen something similar, possibly in a movie or a photo.

More commonly, people report déjà vu in a familiar setting. You might be sitting in your room, walking down a familiar road, or having an everyday conversation, when you suddenly feel, "This has happened before!" In a sense, of course it has happened before, but your sense is not that it's just similar to a past experience. Instead, it seems *this particular* event happened before. You feel that you know what will happen next, although in fact if you try to predict, your prediction is no more accurate than usual (Cleary & Claxton, 2018). Still, after something happens, you feel that you had been *about to* predict it. Apparently, something is triggering the brain to signal "familiar."

One man with epilepsy originating in his temporal cortex had a special feeling, an *aura*, before each of his seizures. Each aura included a strong sense of déjà vu that lasted long enough for him to move around and shift his attention from one item to another. During the aura, *whatever* he looked at seemed strangely familiar (O'Connor & Moulin, 2008). In a case like this, we can discard the hypothesis that what he saw was actually familiar. Another man with epilepsy experienced déjà vu constantly during his waking day. Everyone he met, anywhere he visited, and anything reported on a news program seemed familiar. Even when he was admitted to a hospital, he insisted that he had been treated there before. Anti-epileptic medication halted his déjà vu experiences. Brain scans suggested that his déjà vu experiences correlated with abnormal activity in parts of the temporal lobe that are important for memory (Takeda, et al., 2011).

fizkes/Shutterstock.com

Meditation excludes the worries and concerns of the day and thereby induces a calm, relaxed state.

19. What evidence shows that déjà vu does not always indicate that an experience was actually familiar?

Answer

19. A person with temporal lobe epilepsy reported an intense déjà vu experience immediately before his seizures, regardless of where he was or what he was seeing at the time.

What Hypnosis Is and Isn't

Researchers agree on a few general points: Hypnosis is not faking or pretending to be hypnotized, and it does not give people new mental or physical powers. Hypnosis enables people to relax, concentrate, and follow suggestions better than they usually do. Meditation also improves concentration, often in a more lasting way.

Summary

- *Nature of hypnosis.* Hypnosis is a condition of increased suggestibility. It is important to distinguish legitimate hypnotism from entertainment. (page 328)
- *Hypnosis induction.* To induce hypnosis, a hypnotist asks a person to concentrate and then makes repetitive suggestions. The first steps toward being hypnotized are the willingness to be hypnotized and the belief that one is becoming hypnotized. (page 328)
- *Uses.* Hypnosis can alleviate pain, and through posthypnotic suggestion, it sometimes helps people combat bad habits. (page 329)
- *Effects on memory.* When asked to report their memories under hypnosis, people report more information than usual, but most of the additional information is wrong. (page 330)

- *Uncertain limits.* Hypnotized people will sometimes do acts that seem dangerous, but other people will sometimes do the same things without being hypnotized. Therefore, it is uncertain whether hypnosis can get someone to do acts they would ordinarily refuse to do. (page 331)
- *Hypnosis as an altered state.* Hypnosis is not greatly different from normal wakefulness, but it is also not just something that people pretend. (page 332)
- *Meditation.* Meditation increases relaxation, decreases anxiety, and enhances attention. (page 333)
- *Déjà vu.* People sometimes feel that the current experience is uncannily familiar. In some cases, it relates to abnormal activity in brain areas responsible for memory. (page 333)

Key Terms

déjà vu experience (page 333)

meditation (page 333)

posthypnotic suggestion (page 329)

hypnosis (page 328)

Review Questions

1. Which of the following can hypnosis accomplish?
   (a) It can decrease pain.
   (b) It can improve memory.
   (c) It can give people superhuman strength.
   (d) It can help people recall a previous life.

2. Why does the medical profession recommend that courts of law refuse to admit testimony that was elicited under hypnosis?
   (a) Anything revealed under hypnosis is protected by physician-client privilege.
   (b) Most new information elicited by hypnosis is incorrect.
   (c) Relying on hypnosis would distract investigators from other approaches.
   (d) Most witnesses cannot be successfully hypnotized.

3. A researcher asked people, some hypnotized and some not, to do some dangerous acts. What happened?
   (a) Some of the hypnotized people performed the acts, but the others refused.
   (b) Only non-hypnotized people performed the acts.
   (c) Everyone in both groups refused.
   (d) Many people in both groups performed the acts.

4. An investigator asked a hypnotist to determine which people were hypnotized and which ones were just pretending. What happened?
   (a) Really hypnotized people could be identified, because they showed no response to pain.
   (b) Really hypnotized people could be identified, because they sat down without checking to see a chair behind them.
   (c) Really hypnotized people could be identified, because they showed physiological responses when told to feel anger.
   (d) The hypnotist could not reliably distinguish between the two groups.

5. During a state of meditation, what does a person practice?
   (a) Concentration on an image or sensation while remaining passive
   (b) Shifting attention among several activities
   (c) Maintaining a polite conversation
   (d) Self-criticism

Answers: 1a, 2b, 3d, 4d, 5a.

11 Motivated Behaviors

This flower is seldom cultivated, for good reasons. Would you stand in line to visit it?

During the summer of 1996, the proprietors of London's Kew Gardens announced that an unusual plant, native to Sumatra and rarely cultivated elsewhere, was about to bloom for the first time since 1963. If you had been in London then, would you have made a point of visiting Kew Gardens to witness this rare event? No? What if I told you that it was a truly beautiful flower? With a lovely, sweet smell? Still no?

Then what if I told you the truth—that the flower is called the *stinking lily* or *corpse plant* because it smells like a huge, week-old carcass of rotting meat or fish. One whiff of it can make a person retch. Now would you want to visit it? If so, you would have to wait in line. When Kew Gardens announced that the stinking lily was about to bloom, an enormous crowd gathered, forming a line that stretched to the length of a soccer field (MacQuitty, 1996). When another stinking lily bloomed in Davis, California, more than 3,000 visitors came during the 5 days it was in bloom (Cimino, 2007).

The visitors' behavior may seem puzzling, but it is not unusual. People seek new and interesting experiences out of curiosity. Even motivations with obvious biological value sometimes produce puzzling behaviors. We begin this chapter with an overview of motivation as it applies to ambition and work. Then we explore two representative and important motivations—hunger and sex.

module 11.1

Work Motivation

After studying this module, you should be able to:

1. Evaluate the drive, homeostasis, and incentive theories of motivation.

2. Evaluate theories of how we resolve conflicts among emotions.

3. Discuss the values of setting goals and deadlines.

4. Describe ways to overcome temptations, especially the temptation to procrastinate.

5. Distinguish between the scientific management and human relations approaches to job design.

6. List factors that correlate with job satisfaction.

7. Distinguish between transformational leaders and transactional leaders.

People compete at almost anything. One woman let her fingernails grow to 19 feet 9 inches (6 meters) to get her name in the *Guinness Book of World Records*. People compete in the mud pit belly flop contest, the wife-carrying contest, and cow-chip tossing. Did you know about the International Rock, Paper, Scissors Tournament? South Korea has a doing-nothing contest: People stare into space without doing anything, saying anything, or falling asleep for 90 minutes. The person with the most stable heart rate wins. For the Krispy Kreme Challenge, contestants run 2.5 miles, eat 12 Krispy Kreme donuts, and then run back. Anyone who vomits is disqualified.

Tapping into people's competitive nature can be useful. A father was trying to get his son to walk from a shopping mall to the car, while the son stubbornly refused. The father tried promises, pleadings, and threats, to no avail. Then the father's friend said, "Hey, kid, I'll race you to the car!" The son took off, won the race, and the problem was solved.

Striving for excellence in school or on the job is similar. People strive to beat someone else's performance or to top their own previous best.

Contestants at the South Korean Space Out competition.

Views of Motivation

Like many other important terms in psychology, motivation is difficult to define. Let's consider several possibilities: "Motivation is what activates and directs behavior." This description sounds good, but it also fits other phenomena. Light activates and directs plant growth, but we wouldn't say that light motivates plants.

"Motivation is what makes our behavior more vigorous and energetic." Alas, motivated behavior is not always vigorous. Sometimes you are motivated to go to sleep.

How about this: Based on the concept of reinforcement, we could define **motivation** as *the process that determines the reinforcement value of an outcome*. In everyday language, motivation is what makes you seek one thing more than another, or to seek something at one time more than another. Motivated behavior is goal-directed. If you are motivated by hunger, you try one approach after another until you find food. If you are cold, you put on heavier clothing, find a nice fireplace, ask someone to cuddle with you, or do whatever else you can to get warmer.

This definition works as a description, but it offers no theory. Let's briefly consider some influential theories with their strengths and weaknesses.

Drive Theories

One view regards motivation as a **drive**, *a state of unrest or irritation that energizes behaviors until they remove the irritation* (Hull, 1943). For example, if you get a splinter in your finger, the discomfort motivates you to try one action after another until you remove the splinter.

According to the *drive-reduction theory* that was popular among psychologists of the 1940s and 1950s, humans and other animals eat to reduce their hunger, drink to reduce their thirst, and have sexual activity to reduce their sex drive. According to this view, if you satisfy all your needs, you become inactive. That theory works well enough for reptiles. An alligator that has satisfied its needs may sit motionless for hours. Humans, however, dislike having nothing to do (unless they are in that Korean doing-nothing contest). In one study, young adults were asked to sit by themselves for up to 15 minutes doing nothing, unless they chose to flip a switch to give themselves

Table 11.1 Three Views of Motivation

View	Basic Position	Major Weaknesses
Drive Theories Motivation is an irritation that continues until we find a way to reduce it.	Motivations are based on needs or irritations that we try to reduce.	Implies that we always try to reduce stimulation, never to increase it. Also overlooks importance of external stimuli.
Homeostasis or Allostasis Motivation tries to maintain a variable such as body temperature within a set range.	Motivations may react to current needs and anticipate future needs.	Overlooks importance of external stimuli.
Incentive Theories Incentives are external stimuli that attract us even if we have no biological need for them.	Motivations respond to attractive stimuli.	Incomplete theory unless combined with drive or homeostasis.

a painful electrical shock. Even though all these people had previously said they would pay money to avoid such shocks, 12 of the 18 men and 6 of the 24 women gave themselves at least one shock, just to break the monotony (Wilson et al., 2014). Just try explaining that one in terms of drive-reduction theory.

Homeostasis

An advance on the idea of drive reduction is the concept of homeostasis, *the maintenance of an optimum level of biological conditions within an organism* (Cannon, 1929). The idea of homeostasis recognizes that we seek a state of equilibrium, which is not zero stimulation. For example, people make an effort to maintain a fairly constant body temperature, a steady body weight, a certain amount of water in the body, a moderate amount of sensory experience, and so on.

Our behavior also anticipates future needs. For example, you might eat a large breakfast even though you are not hungry, just because you know you will be too busy to stop for lunch. In fall, many animals put on extra fat and fur to protect against winter's cold weather. If you become frightened, you start to sweat in anticipation of the extra body heat you will generate while trying to escape a danger. A revised concept of homeostasis is allostasis, defined as *maintaining levels of biological conditions that vary according to an individual's needs and circumstances.* Allostasis acts to prevent difficulties instead of just correcting them after they occur (Sterling, 2012).

Incentive Theories

The drive-reduction and homeostasis concepts overlook the power of new stimuli to arouse behaviors. For example, if someone offers your favorite dessert, might you eat it even though you are not hungry? Motivation includes more than the internal forces that push us toward certain behaviors. It also includes incentives—*stimuli that pull us*

toward an action. Most motivated behaviors are controlled by a combination of drives and incentives. You eat because you are hungry (a drive) and because you see appealing food (an incentive). You jump into a swimming pool on a hot day to cool your body (a drive) and because you will enjoy splashing around in the water (an incentive). ■ Table 11.1 summarizes three views of motivation.

Psychologists draw an important distinction between extrinsic motivation and intrinsic motivation. An extrinsic motivation *is based on the rewards the act might bring or the punishments it might avoid.* A drive to eat, drink, or find a comfortable temperature is an extrinsic motivation. An intrinsic motivation *is based on enjoying the act itself.* For example, working a crossword puzzle, playing a video game, or taking a walk in the park is based on intrinsic motivation. Many acts combine both extrinsic and intrinsic motivations. As a rule, extrinsic motivation gets you to do just what is necessary. If you are taking a course just to pass a requirement or doing a job just for the paycheck, you do what you must and no more. Intrinsic motivation leads to persistence in the face of obstacles (van Egmond, Berges, Omarshah, & Benton, 2017) and efforts to achieve excellence.

People sometimes get misleading advice about motivation. Have you ever heard someone say that "you need to discover your passion"? That advice implies that your passion is out there, waiting for you to find it. In fact, new interests and passions develop gradually (O'Keefe, Dweck, & Walton, 2018). You have to nurture a new interest and practice its skills before it becomes a true passion, an intrinsic motivation.

1. **The introduction to this chapter described people who stood in line to visit a foul-smelling flower. Would that action make sense in terms of drive-reduction, incentive, or homeostasis views of motivation? Is it an extrinsic or intrinsic motivation?**

Answer

1. The action is a response to an incentive, the opportunity for an unusual experience. It is an intrinsic motivation, because they took the action for the sake of the experience itself, not for any reward.

Conflicting Motivations

When you have more than one motivation, sometimes they are in harmony. Imagine yourself outside on a hot day. You would like to cool off, you are thirsty and a bit hungry, and you would like to be with your friends. Someone

▲ **Figure 11.1** A person uses a mouse to send a cursor quickly toward one choice or the other. In this case the person started toward one choice and then shifted to the other. (From Stillman, P. E., Medvedev, D., & Ferguson, M. J., 2017. Resisting temptation: Tracking how self-control conflicts are successfully resolved in real time. *Psychological Science, 28*, 1240–1258.)

suggests going somewhere for a snack and a cool glass of lemonade. You agree, satisfying all four motives—temperature regulation, thirst, hunger, and socialization. At another time, your motivations might be in conflict. Perhaps you are sleepy when your friends want to watch a late-night movie. How do we resolve conflicts?

Researchers developed a clever way to track how people resolve a conflict on a moment-by-moment basis. Imagine you are the participant. You use a mouse to control a cursor on the computer screen, starting at a position in the lower center. Two objects appear, representing two types of food, such as ice cream bars and an apple. Your task is to move the cursor as quickly as possible to the choice that would help you meet your goal of health and fitness. ▲ **Figure 11.1** shows a typical result. As you can see, the participant started moving the cursor toward the ice cream bars (yummy!) but then shifted toward the apple (oh, yeah, I'm supposed to choose the healthful one). This procedure identifies how quickly someone resolves the conflict (Stillman, Medvedev, & Ferguson, 2017).

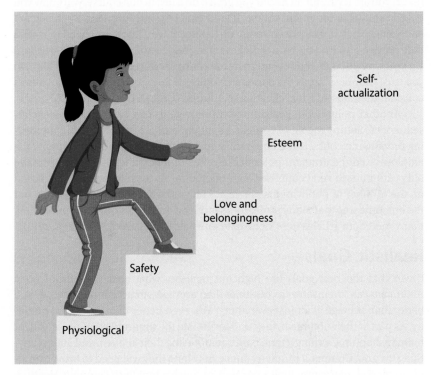

▲ **Figure 11.2** According to Maslow's hierarchy of needs, you satisfy your lower needs before moving on to your higher needs. (Based on Maslow, 1943)

Abraham Maslow (1943) proposed that we resolve conflicts by a **hierarchy of needs,** *a system in which the most insistent needs take priority over less urgent ones. For example,* if you are gasping for breath, your fight for oxygen takes priority over anything else. If you are extremely hungry or thirsty, or dangerously hot or cold, you pursue those needs until you satisfy them. As Maslow (1943, p. 375) said, "...man lives by bread alone—when there is no bread." After you satisfy your basic physiological needs, or at least bring them under control, you can move on to your safety needs, such as finding a safe place to spend the night. Next come your love and belongingness needs, followed by your need for esteem and recognition. At the apex of the hierarchy is the need for **self-actualization,** *becoming everything you are capable of being, to fulfill your potential.* Self-actualization consists of whatever is important to you, your intrinsic motivations. You cannot devote much attention to your intrinsic motivations when you are preoccupied with satisfying your basic needs (Deci & Ryan, 2008). Maslow further proposed that people who satisfy more of their higher needs tend to be mentally healthier than others. One reason, of course, could be that people who are mentally healthy are more likely to be able to concentrate on their higher needs.

Maslow himself never drew any diagram to represent these five levels of needs, but a later article (McDermid, 1960) presented them as a pyramid, and soon that diagram became popular. A critique has argued that a stair-step diagram, as in ◄ **Figure 11.2,** better captures Maslow's idea, because it shows that someone can be working on motivations on several levels at the same time (Bridgman, Cummings, & Ballard, 2019). Recall that on a hot, sunny day you and some friends stepped inside an ice-cream parlor for a treat. You satisfied your hunger and avoided overheating (physiological needs), got away from the sun that might lead to skin cancer (a safety need), and socialized with friends (a love and belongingness need).

Maslow's theory has been criticized for implying that lower-level needs always take priority over higher needs, and that the hierarchy is the same for everyone. He never said that, although later descriptions of his theory did. Maslow recognized, for example, that a martyr who accepts death to advance a political or religious cause is sacrificing physiological and safety needs to seek a higher-level need.

One criticism is that Maslow's theory omits motivations such as parenting and overemphasizes the vague idea of self-actualization (Kenrick, Griskevicius, Neuberg, & Schaller, 2010). Also, although

Maslow recognized the possibility of cultural differences, he did not elaborate on that idea. For many people in China, self-esteem and personal accomplishments are less important than the sense of belonging to one's group and one's family. ▶ Figure 11.3 presents an alternative hierarchy of needs (Yang, 2003). According to this model, anyone who satisfies the survival needs at the bottom can branch off in either of two directions or a combination of both. The arm at the right pertains to reproduction, an essential goal for all human cultures, although not for every person within a given culture. The arm at the left pertains to expressing one's own needs.

2. According to Maslow, would wealthier people or poorer people devote more effort to their intrinsic motivations? Why?

Answer

2. Wealthier people would devote more effort to their intrinsic motivations, because poorer people would have to spend more time trying to satisfy their basic needs for food, shelter, and safety.

Goals and Deadlines

We often try to improve ourselves by setting goals, especially at a birthday, the start of a new year, the start of a new semester, or some other landmark of time (Dai, Milkman, & Riis, 2015). We say, "I am disappointed with what I have done in the past, but from now on I am going to do better. Here is my new goal…" In the case of academics, which of these goals would be best?

- I will work for an A in every course.
- I will work for at least a C average.
- I will do my best.

The research says that "do your best" is the same as no goal at all. Although it sounds good, you are never behind schedule on achieving it, so it doesn't motivate extra work. The most effective goals are specific, difficult, and realistic (Locke & Latham, 2002). A goal should be specific because a vague goal does not tell you what to do. If a company sets a goal to "substantially increase sales," the goal does not say how much or how soon. In contrast, "increase sales by 10 percent within 2 years" is specific enough to be effective. A goal should also be difficult, or it inspires no work. For example, a student's goal of "at least a C average" would be worthless, except for a student whose previous performance was below that.

A goal must also be realistic. A student's goal of an A in every course might or might not be realistic,

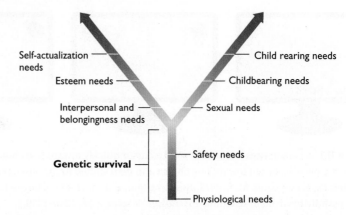

▲ **Figure 11.3** According to a revised model, people who satisfy their physiological and safety needs can branch off to emphasize one set of goals or another.

depending on previous performance and this semester's schedule. If you set an unrealistic goal, you soon see that you cannot achieve it, and you stop trying. Unrealistic goals for group work also backfire (Curseu, Janssen, & Meeus, 2014). Workers who are trying to achieve nearly impossible goals make risky, dangerous decisions and are tempted to dishonest dealing (Schiebener, Wegmann, Pawlikowski, & Brand, 2014).

Certain other conditions are necessary for a goal to be effective (Locke & Latham, 2002). One is to take the goal seriously, preferably by committing to it publicly. If you want better grades next semester, or if you want to quit smoking or cut back on alcohol, tell your friends about it. Then you will be less likely to ignore your goal. If you have a short-term goal, such as paying some bill before it is due, or cleaning your room before guests come, you might need a reminder. One trick that works well is to place an odd object somewhere that you are sure to notice (Rogers & Milkman, 2016). When you see that coffee mug in your underwear drawer, you will say, "What is that doing here? Oh, yeah, it's to remind me to …"

Another important condition is to receive periodic feedback about your progress. If you are trying for all A's but you get a B on a test in one course, you know you have to study harder in that course. If your goal is to increase sales by 10 percent and you learn that they are currently up 9 percent, you know you need to work a little harder. Finally, you have to believe that the reward will be worth the effort. Do you care enough about your grades to make sacrifices in your social life? Do you trust your boss to pay the bonus as promised? Some employees do, but others consider their bosses lying, cheating scoundrels (Craig & Gustafson, 1998).

Another point about goals: Inappropriate goals can have unfavorable consequences. Setting a goal of straight A's might lead a student to avoid interesting or valuable courses. If a company's goal is to get more new customers, the employees concentrate on potential new customers while largely ignoring the old customers. Several countries have offered raises to college professors based on the number of publications per year. The goal was to increase research, but the outcome was that many professors sacrificed quality for quantity, publishing many mediocre articles in seldom-read journals (Butler, 2002; Hedding, 2019).

Realistic Goals

Given that the best goals are high but realistic, what goal is realistic? Most Americans rate themselves as healthier than average, smarter, more creative, and better than average at almost everything. Yes, even better than average at humility. As part of their optimism, they underestimate the time and effort they need for holiday shopping, writing a term paper, remodeling their kitchen, and almost anything they do. Companies underestimate how long they will need to bring a product to market, reorganize their sales staff, or finish a building (Dunning, Heath, & Suls, 2004). Governments underestimate the time and cost of major projects. The Sydney Opera House in Australia was expected to be completed by 1963 at a cost

▲ **Figure 11.4** The Sydney Opera House is a classic example of underestimating the time and cost to complete a project.

of $7 million. It was finally completed in 1973 at a cost of $102 million (see ▲ Figure 11.4).

Senior students at one college were asked to estimate "realistically" how soon they would complete their senior honors thesis—a major research paper. They were also asked how late they might finish if everything went wrong. On average, they finished their papers 1 week *later* than what they said was the worst-case scenario (Buehler, Griffin, & Ross, 1994). The message is to allow yourself more time than you think you need and get started quickly. Major tasks almost always take more work than expected.

The Value of Deadlines

If you had no deadlines to meet, how hard would you work? When you have a deadline, do you sometimes wait until shortly before the deadline to start working in earnest? For example, are you reading this chapter now because you have to take a test on it tomorrow? Would anyone ever finish anything if they didn't have to meet a deadline?

Procrastination (putting off work until tomorrow) is a problem for many students and workers. Here is an experiment that beautifully illustrates the phenomenon.

what's the evidence?

The Value of Deadlines

A professor set firm deadlines for one class and let another class choose their own deadlines, to see whether those with evenly spaced deadlines would outperform those who gave themselves an opportunity to procrastinate (Ariely & Wertenbroch, 2002).

Hypothesis Students who are required, or who require themselves, to spread out their work will do better than those with an opportunity to wait until the end of the semester.

Method A professor taught two sections of the same course. Students were not randomly assigned to sections, but the students in the two sections had about equal academic records. The professor told one class that they had to write three papers, the first due after one-third of the semester, the second after two-thirds, and the third at the end of the semester. The other class was told that they could choose their own deadlines. They might make their three papers due after each third of the semester, all three at the end of the semester, or whatever else they chose. However, they had to decide by the second day of class, and whatever deadlines they chose would be enforced. That is, a paper that missed a deadline would be penalized, even though the student could have chosen a later deadline. At the end of the course, the professor graded all the papers blind to when they had been submitted.

Results If you were in the class that could choose the deadlines, what would you do? Twelve of the fifty-one students set all three deadlines on the final day of the semester. Presumably, they reasoned that they would try to finish their papers earlier, but they would have the opportunity for extra time if they needed it. Other students, however, saw that if they set their deadlines at the end, they would expose themselves to a temptation that would be hard to resist, so they imposed earlier deadlines. Some spaced the deadlines evenly at one-third, two-thirds, and the end of the semester, and others compromised, setting deadlines for the first two papers somewhat later but not at the end of the semester.

On average, the students in the section with assigned deadlines got better grades on their papers than those who were allowed to choose their own deadlines. Of those permitted to choose their own deadlines, those who set their deadlines at approximately one-third, two-thirds, and the end of the semester did about the same as those with assigned deadlines and much better than those who set all their deadlines at the end.

Interpretation If the professor had studied only one class and let them choose their own deadlines, we could draw no conclusion from the finding that those who spread out their deadlines did the best. It could mean that early deadlines help, but it could also mean that better students set earlier deadlines. However, the early-deadline students merely matched the assigned-deadline students, whereas the late-deadline students did worse. Therefore, the conclusion follows that deadlines do help. If you are required to do part of your work at a time, you manage your time to accomplish it. If your deadlines are all at the end, you face a powerful temptation to delay until the end.

3. What conclusion would have followed if the two classes on average did equally well, but within the class setting their own deadlines, those who set earlier deadlines did better than those setting later deadlines?

Answer

3. If students in the two sections had equal performance overall, we could not conclude that deadlines help. Instead, the conclusion would have been that brighter students tend to set earlier deadlines.

Overcoming Procrastination

You have a big assignment to do, but it isn't due immediately. When do you start on it? People who start work long before something is due achieve better than average outcomes in academics, work, or other endeavors (Duckworth, Taxer, Eskreis-Winkler, Galla, & Gross, 2019). We call this tendency self-control. A related trait is called grit, *the ability to persist despite setbacks* (Duckworth & Gross, 2014). However, the names do not explain anything.

Given the importance of working steadily toward a goal, how can you overcome the temptation to procrastinate? We tend to procrastinate big tasks that we know will take long to finish. If you have small tasks, you like to finish them quickly to get them out of the way (Rosenbaum et al., 2019). Therefore, one way to decrease procrastination is to break up a big task into little tasks. Start with the smallest part that you can finish, and get it out of the way.

You decrease procrastination if you make a detailed plan of what, when, where, and how you will do something (McCrea, Liberman, Trope, & Sherman, 2008). Suppose your goal is to exercise more. Decide what kind of exercise you will do, when you will do it, and where. If you want to eat a healthier diet, decide to eat a salad instead of a hamburger for lunch tomorrow. Place the order in advance, if you can, to avoid the temptation to eat a less healthful meal when the time comes. If you set specific plans, then the relevant situation will evoke the behavior (Milne, Orbell, & Sheeran, 2002; Verplanken & Faes, 1999).

Here is another strategy to combat procrastination: Identify an activity that you have been procrastinating, such as cleaning your room or calling your grandparents. *Yes, you. Please choose an activity, right now.* Next, estimate how likely you are to complete that activity within the next week. *Please make that estimate.* If you have followed instructions, you have just increased your probability of actually doing that activity! *Simply*

estimating your probability of doing some desirable activity increases your probability of completing the action (Levav & Fitzsimons, 2006). Psychologists call this phenomenon the mere measurement effect. (Of course, if you estimated your probability at zero, then this little trick isn't going to work.)

Another strategy for overcoming procrastination is to make a decision about something else first, even something unimportant. For example, please make these decisions: If you go to a zoo, which will you visit first, elephants or hippopotamuses? If someone offered you a free vacation, would you prefer the Caribbean or France? For a snack, would you rather have an Oreo cookie or a KitKat bar? Just after people have made quick decisions like these, they become more likely than usual to take action of other kinds, such as buying a new computer (Xu & Wyer, 2008). They get into the mind-set of deciding and acting instead of delaying and doing nothing. Of course, this procedure works only if you did make a quick decision. If you are still debating between that Oreo and the KitKat bar, then you probably won't make other decisions, either.

4. How could you increase your probability of getting a good start on writing a term paper?

5. Making a quick decision about anything increases your probability of action. If you were a salesperson, how could you use this principle to encourage someone to buy a product?

Answers

4. Start with the smallest part you can finish, such as choosing a topic or choosing materials to read. Make specific plans, such as, "I will spend Monday night at the library reading background material." You could also estimate your probability of completing the first part of the paper.

5. Get the person to make a decision related to the product. For example, ask, "If you did buy it, what color would you like? What size?"

Temptation

The conflict between doing work and procrastinating it until later, so you can do something fun right now, is an example of temptation, or what psychologists sometimes call a "*want* versus *should* conflict." They also refer to delay of gratification—*declining a pleasant activity now in order to get something better or more important later.* Temptation occurs in many settings. You might be tempted to cheat on a test, lie on your tax form, drive above the speed limit, or engage in risky sex. Every temptation is a battle between doing something enjoyable at the moment, or resisting it to gain a later benefit, or to avoid a later danger (Lopez, Hofmann, Wagner, Kelley, & Heatherton, 2014). Although many types of temptation don't pertain to work, it is convenient to discuss them here.

Walter Mischel and colleagues introduced a procedure for measuring children's resistance to temptation. It goes as follows: An experimenter seats a preschool child and explains, "Here is a marshmallow. You can eat it now, or you can wait until I come back. If you wait, I'll give you a second marshmallow." The choice is between one now and two later. Some children eagerly eat the first one, but others dutifully wait, often using strategies such as not looking at the marshmallow. If you do an Internet search for "marshmallow experiment," you can find entertaining videos. Long-term follow-up studies found significant advantages for the children who waited. As adolescents, they were less distractible, better able to handle frustration, and better able to resist temptations. Also, they had higher than average SAT scores (Shoda, Mischel, & Peake, 1990). As middle-aged people, they were less likely to be overweight (Schlam, Wilson, Shoda, Miscle, & Ayduk, 2013). On a task where middle-aged people were told to press a key quickly when they saw a face, but to avoid pressing if they saw a happy face, those who had waited for a second marshmallow as children were better able to inhibit pressing when they saw happy faces (Casey et al., 2011).

A limitation is that the original study drew their entire sample from the Stanford University community. A later, larger study with a more diverse sample did find a correlation between marshmallow-waiting time and later academic performance, but the correlation was weaker than in the first study (Watts, Duncan, & Quan, 2018). Still, the point is that the ability to delay gratification is a long-term personality characteristic.

Now let's consider adult examples. Would you prefer $5 now or $10 a year from now? Most people opt for the $5 now. But would you prefer $500 now or $1,000 a year from now? The ratios are the same, but a higher percentage of people choose to wait for the larger reward. One explanation is that people make less important choices impulsively, but they stop and think carefully when important outcomes are at stake (Ballard et al., 2017).

Suppose you would choose $500 now instead of $1,000 later. From an economic standpoint, this is a bad choice (unless you have a $500 gambling debt and someone is coming to break your legs if you don't pay right now). One way to discipline yourself is to make the decision in advance. If you know you will be offered this choice 3 months from now, commit yourself at once to the delayed reward, because you know that if you wait until the last minute to decide, you will probably take the smaller but quicker reward. Similarly, if you are going to ask someone to do you a big favor, ask in advance. It is easier to commit to doing something a few months from now than doing it tomorrow.

As people advance from childhood to adulthood, they gradually improve their ability to resist temptation and delay gratification (Steinberg et al., 2009), but most people overestimate their ability to resist temptation (Nordgren, van Harreveld, & van der Pligt, 2009). It is best to avoid tempting situations (Duckworth, Gendler, & Gross, 2016). If you want to lose weight, don't even look at the dessert menu, and don't keep snacks close at hand. If you want to avoid alcohol, don't walk past your favorite bar.

Imagine the following: You and another student show up for a research study. The researchers explain that two studies are available. One study will be short and enjoyable, and the other will be long and unpleasant. You are invited to flip a coin, examine it by yourself in private, and then announce who gets to be in the pleasant study. In this situation, nearly 90 percent of students claim they won the toss and get to be in the pleasant experiment. Obviously, many are lying. However, suppose you were asked whether you want to flip the coin and announce the results or let the experimenter do it. Now most people say, "Let the experimenter do it" (Batson & Thompson, 2001). They avoid putting themselves in a situation in which they know they will be tempted to cheat. They also make it clear that if they get to be in the pleasant study, it was *not* by cheating.

Does it help if you practice resisting temptations? Resisting a temptation sometimes helps you resist the same temptation later. For example, if you are trying to quit smoking, and you resist the temptation to smoke right now, you probably improve your ability to resist the next smoking temptation (O'Connell, Schwartz, & Shiffman, 2008). However, practice at avoiding dessert or other unhealthful foods is not consistently effective (Van Dessel, Hughes, & De Houwer, 2018).

Furthermore, resisting one temptation might make you more apt to yield to a different temptation (Hofmann, Vohs, & Baumeister, 2012; Inzlicht & Schmeichel, 2012). The explanation for this tendency is still uncertain. A simple, intuitive idea is that you have "used up your willpower." However, several studies indicate that simply facing many temptations weakens later resistance to a later temptation, regardless of whether you resisted the first temptations or not (Milyavskaya & Inzlicht, 2017; Wilkowski, Ferguson, Williamson, & Lappi, 2018). Self-control requires attention, and people find it difficult to continue

maintaining strong attention (Sripada, Kessler, & Jonides, 2014). The message is that it is better to avoid temptation than to practice resisting it.

Your ability to resist temptation depends on what you see other people doing. Imagine yourself in this study: An experimenter gives you a set of 20 math problems to try in the next 5 minutes. You are told to solve as many as you can, and then shred your answer sheet and report how many you solved, receiving a payment of 50 cents per answer. You see that you could easily exaggerate your number correct and increase your payment. Although an average person solves only about seven items in the 5 minutes, most people cheat a little and report a few more than that. But now suppose that after just 1 minute, someone stands up, shreds his paper, announces that he got them all correct, and takes the full payment of $10. Obviously, he must be cheating, and he got away with it. How do you react? His act would increase your own cheating... unless he is wearing a sweatshirt from another college that you consider a major rival. In that case, his cheating *decreases* your probability of cheating (Gino, Ayal, & Ariely, 2009). You say to yourself, "Hah. *Those* people act like that. We're better!" No doubt the same would happen if the person you saw cheating differed from you in religion, politics, or any other important way.

Here's another intervention that decreases cheating: You're in an experiment similar to the one just described, but right before it, you do a preliminary task of listing as many of the Ten Commandments as you can remember. Under those conditions, cheating is reduced to almost zero, even for nonreligious students. The simple reminder of ethical norms reduces the temptation to cheat (Mazar, Amir, & Ariely, 2008). One caution: These studies used U.S. and Canadian students. The results may be different in other cultures.

concept check

6. **What advice would you give someone who wants to resist a temptation?**

Answer

6. The best advice is to avoid situations in which you might feel temptation. Second, don't expose yourself to a temptation just after successfully resisting a different temptation. If it is possible to make a commitment far in advance, do so. Think of people who yield to the temptation as different from yourself. Also, remind yourself of ethical norms.

Job Design and Job Satisfaction

Let's turn to some research specifically dealing with work. People work harder, more effectively, and with more satisfaction at some jobs than at others. Why?

Two Approaches to Job Design

Imagine that you are starting or reorganizing a company, and you must decide how to divide the workload. Should you make the jobs challenging and interesting? Or should you make them simple and foolproof?

According to the scientific-management approach to job design, also known as *Theory X, you should experiment to find the best way to do the job, select appropriate workers, and train them to do it the right way* (Derksen, 2014). The employer should do research to find the most efficient way to do each task, to increase speed, decrease effort, and avoid injuries (see ▶ Figure 11.5). Employers following this approach don't expect workers to take initiative or to show creativity.

According to an alternative view, the human-relations approach to job design, also known as *Theory Y, employees like variety in their job, a sense of accomplishment, and a sense of responsibility.* Therefore, employers should enrich the jobs, giving each employee responsibility for meaningful tasks. For example, a financial services corporation that followed the scientific-management approach would let each employee keep just one kind of records for many clients, developing expertise at a narrow task. The same company, reorganized according to the human-relations approach, might put each employee in charge of fewer clients, keeping track of all the information about those clients. Employees with enriched jobs generally report greater satisfaction (Campion & McClelland, 1991). Designing jobs one way or the other becomes a self-fulfilling prophecy. Managers following the scientific-management approach exert control and punishment because they regard their workers as lazy and unmotivated, and the workers feel unappreciated and unmotivated. When managers follow the human-relations approach, many workers rise to the challenge.

Is the human-relations approach better? Often it is, but not always. Consider an analogy to education: Professor X tells students exactly what to read and precisely what to do to get a good grade. This course is analogous to the scientific-management approach. Professor Y outlines the issues, lists suggested readings, encourages class discussion, and invites students to create their own ideas for projects. This course is analogous to the human-relations approach, though perhaps more extreme. Which class would you like better?

It depends. If you are highly interested in the topic and have ideas of your own, you love Professor Y's course and consider Professor X's course tedious. But if you are taking the course just to satisfy a requirement, you appreciate the precise structure of Professor X's class. The same is true of jobs. The younger, brighter, more motivated workers thrive on

▲ **Figure 11.5** Adherents of the scientific-management approach tried to determine the best, safest, most efficient ways to perform even simple tasks. For example, the drawing on the left shows the right way to lift a brick, and the drawing on the right shows the wrong way, according to Gilbreth (1911).

the challenge of an enriched job, but some people prefer a simple, stable set of tasks (Arnold & House, 1980; Campion & Thayer, 1985; Hackman & Lawler, 1971).

7. **"I want my employees to enjoy their work and to feel pride in their achievements." Does that statement reflect a belief in the human-relations approach or the scientific-management approach?**

Answer

7. It reflects the human-relations approach.

Job Satisfaction

For most of your adult life, you will spend about half of your waking hours on the job. You want to spend that time on a job you like. How much you like your job correlates strongly with your interest in the job (Nye, Su, Rounds, & Drasgow, 2012). However, how much you like your job correlates only moderately with your skill at the job (Judge, Thoresen, Bono, & Patton, 2001). One reason why liking the job doesn't correlate highly with skill is that some of the people who are best at doing a job are eager to get an even better job.

Obviously, job satisfaction depends largely on the job itself, including the interest level, the pay, coworkers, and management. It also depends on the worker's personality. Some people are just easier to please than others. Comparisons of identical and fraternal twins indicate that job satisfaction is highly heritable (Arvey, McCall, Bouchard, Taubman, & Cavanaugh, 1994). If your close relatives say they are happy with their jobs, you probably are also, even though you have a different job. You don't inherit your job, but you inherit your disposition. Some people find much to like about their jobs, and others find much to complain about, even when it is the same job (Ilies & Judge, 2003; Judge & Larsen, 2001; Thoresen, Kaplan, Barsky, Warren, & de Chermont, 2003).

On average, older workers express higher job satisfaction than younger workers do (Pond & Geyer, 1991). Why? One explanation is that older workers have better, higher-paying jobs. Another is that many young workers start in the wrong job and find a more suitable one later. Yet another is that many young people are still considering the possibility of changing jobs. By middle age, most people reconcile themselves to whatever jobs they have.

Pay and Job Satisfaction

An employer who wants to keep workers satisfied gives careful attention to the pay scale. Obviously, workers want to be paid well, but they also need to perceive the pay scale as fair. In one classic experiment, some workers were led to believe that they had been hired in spite of less than average qualifications for the job. They worked harder than average, apparently to convince the employer that they deserved the job, but perhaps also to convince themselves that they earned their pay (J. S. Adams, 1963).

Employees who perceive their bosses as operating unfairly often start looking for another job. They also stop doing the "good citizen" behaviors that help the company, such as keeping the building tidy, helping other workers, and attending meetings after working hours (Simons & Roberson, 2003). At the opposite extreme, some workers develop an emotional commitment that leads them to work loyally and energetically, well beyond what they are paid to do (Meyer, Becker, & Vandenberghe, 2004; Seo, Barrett, & Bartunek, 2004).

Money is part of anyone's work motivation, but it is more effective at increasing the quantity than quality of work. Quality depends mainly on intrinsic motivation—enjoyment of the job itself and a feeling of accomplishment (Cerasoli, Nicklin, & Ford, 2014). For many people, work is an enjoyable, important part of who they are.

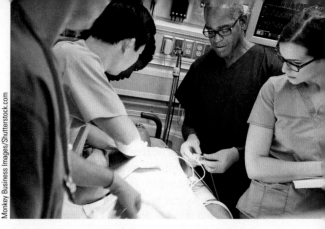

Job burnout is a serious problem for nurses and others who are expected to act positive while doing often unpleasant and challenging tasks.

8. Would the factors for class satisfaction in college be similar to the factors for job satisfaction?

Answer

8. Yes. Just as older workers generally have higher job satisfaction, older students (seniors) tend to enjoy their classes more, largely because they are taking the courses they like, in their major. Just as job satisfaction depends on high pay and a sense of fairness, course satisfaction relates to high grades and a sense of fairness. Also, just as job satisfaction depends on intrinsic motivation, so does course satisfaction.

Job Burnout

Almost any job produces some stress, but sometimes work stress gets so bad that it leaves people physically and emotionally exhausted. The term *burnout* should not be overused. If you have been working hard, but you recover after a nice vacation, you did not have burnout. **Job burnout** refers to a *long-lasting sense of mental and physical exhaustion and discouragement.* People with this condition feel detached from their job and their coworkers, and they lack any sense of accomplishment (Melamed et al., 2006). They become less effective on the job, and their health deteriorates. The long persistence of burnout has at least two possible explanations. One is that exhaustion and discouragement are a personality trait, related to depression. The other explanation is that burnout is like a severely shattered leg: After sustaining that kind of injury, you never completely recover, and it doesn't take much to reinjure that leg.

Burnout is common among people in the helping professions, such as nurses, teachers, and therapists, who are expected to be supportive and encouraging at all times. Consider the contrast: If you work an office job, you might come in one day and tell your coworkers, "I can still do my job, but I'm going to be in a bad mood today." You cannot do that in the helping professions. Imagine you are a nurse who just cleaned up vomit for the patient in room 1, blood for the patient in room 2, and bowel movements in room 3. The patient in room 4, whom you especially liked, just died. Next you have to go into room 5 and act cheerful

and supportive. Your training was in medicine, not acting, and this process of suppressing one emotion and substituting another requires enormous effort (Cheung & Tang, 2007).

Not everyone with a difficult job experiences burnout. People with a happy home life, enjoyable leisure activities, and high physical activity are unlikely to develop job burnout (Armon, 2014; Blom, Sverke, Vodin, Lindfors, & Svedberg, 2014; Sonnentag, Arbeus, Mahn, & Fritz, 2014).

9. What should someone do to prevent burnout?

Answer

9. Seek emotional support at home, be physically active, and spend time on pleasant leisure activities.

Leadership

Your motivation to work depends on how you perceive your organization's leadership. Some employers inspire deep loyalties and intense efforts, whereas others barely get their workers to do the minimum. The same is true of college professors, athletic coaches, and political leaders.

What does good leadership require? Psychological research has found no consistent personality difference between effective and ineffective leaders. Effective leaders are not consistently more gregarious, outspoken, or anything else. You know there has to be something wrong here. If good and poor leaders really do not differ, we could choose company executives, college presidents, or state governors at random. The reason that no single personality factor is decisive is that many qualities are important. A good leader has a combination of favorable personality, intelligence, expertise, motives, values, and people-handling skills (Zaccaro, 2007).

Furthermore, what constitutes good leadership depends on the situation. Just as no one is creative in all situations—a creative poet probably won't propose creative solutions to an automobile repair problem—the leadership style that succeeds in one situation may not be right for another (Vroom & Jago, 2007). A good leader of a committee meeting gives everyone a chance to express an opinion before putting an issue to a vote. Someone leading a field trip for a class of 6-year-olds makes the decisions and tells the children what to do.

Industrial-organizational psychologists distinguish between transformational and transactional leadership styles. A **transformational leader** *articulates a vision of the future, intellectually stimulates subordinates, and motivates them to use their imagination to advance the organization.* In most cases, organizations that talk about their "visionary leader" exaggerate that individual's importance. When all goes well and an organization is thriving, people tend to perceive their leader as visionary, inspiring, and transformational. Most organizations function best by sharing the leadership, with many people taking the lead as the situation changes (Eberly, Johnson, Hernandez, & Avolio, 2013; Wang, Waldman, & Zhang, 2014). Especially in a military setting, leaders are most effective if they share some of the same lifestyle and risks as their subordinates (Matthews, 2014).

A **transactional leader** *tries to make the organization more efficient at doing what it is already doing by providing rewards (mainly pay) for effective work.* Transactional leaders are often effective in organizations where activities stay the same from year to year (Lowe, Kroeck, & Sivasubramaniam, 1996). Someone can be either a transformational leader, a transactional leader, both, or neither.

Work and Ambition

Many workers do the same job every day, with little motivation to work harder. The most productive people see their work as a competition. They want to make a better product, sell more of their product, write a better novel, or do whatever else they are doing better than someone else, or better than their own previous performance. The best students have a similar ambition in their course work. This module has highlighted hints on how to facilitate the process.

Summary

- *Nature of motivation.* Motivation includes aspects of drive and incentive. It prepares the individual for anticipated needs. (page 337)
- *Extrinsic and intrinsic motivations.* Motivations include the possible rewards (extrinsic motivation) and the joy of the task itself (intrinsic motivation). Intrinsic motivation is more effective for producing persistent efforts and high-quality output. (page 338)
- *Motivation conflict.* In most cases, biological needs take priority over social needs, which take priority over self-expression. To some extent, need priorities vary over cultures. (page 339)
- *Goal setting.* A goal motivates strong effort if the goal is specific, difficult, and realistic. It is also important to make a serious commitment to the goal and to receive feedback on progress. (page 340)
- *Deadlines.* Deadlines motivate people to work harder. It is better to spread out the deadlines for parts of a task than to have only one deadline at the end. (page 341)
- *Overcoming procrastination.* We tend to procrastinate big tasks. To overcome this tendency, we should break the task into smaller bits, and make a detailed plan of what to do and when. (page 342)
- *Delayed gratification.* People vary in whether they choose a larger reward later or a smaller one now. Children who can delay gratification show long-term advantages when they reach adolescence. It is often easier to choose the delayed reward if you make the choice far in advance. (page 342)

- *Overcoming temptations.* It is better to avoid tempting situations than to try to combat temptation. Seeing another person yield to temptation increases the risk of also yielding, unless one sees the other person as an outsider, different from oneself. A reminder about ethical norms decreases cheating in some situations. (page 342)
- *Job design.* The scientific-management approach emphasizes finding the best, most efficient, safest way to do a job. According to the human-management approach, jobs should be made interesting enough to give workers a sense of achievement. (page 343)
- *Job satisfaction.* Job satisfaction is strongly correlated with an individual's interest in the job. People with a happy disposition are more likely than others to be satisfied with their jobs, as are older workers in general. Job satisfaction also requires a perception that the pay scale is fair. (page 344)
- *Job burnout.* Some people have a long-lasting discouragement that alienates them from their job and their coworkers. (page 345)
- *Leadership.* The demands of leadership depend on the situation. Organizations generally work best if many people can take a leadership role, depending on the situation. Leaders perceived as using rewards to get employees to do their work efficiently are effective in situations when the business is stable. (page 345)

Key Terms

allostasis (page 338)

delay of gratification (page 342)

drive (page 337)

extrinsic motivation (page 338)

grit (page 342)

hierarchy of needs (page 339)

homeostasis (page 338)

human-relations approach (page 344)

incentive (page 338)

intrinsic motivation (page 338)

job burnout (page 345)

mere measurement effect (page 342)

motivation (page 337)

scientific-management approach (page 344)

self-actualization (page 339)

transactional leader (page 346)

transformational leader (page 346)

Review Questions

1. How does the concept of allostasis differ from homeostasis?
   - (a) Allostasis maintains constancy within the body.
   - (b) Allostasis controls muscle movements.
   - (c) Allostasis anticipates future needs.
   - (d) Allostasis emphasizes the importance of incentives.

2. Which of the following is true, according to Maslow's hierarchy of needs?
   - (a) It is possible to strive toward more than one need at a time.
   - (b) Parenthood is the highest need.
   - (c) Children have one set of needs and adults have another.
   - (d) We need to satisfy one need completely before moving on to another.

3. Why is "do your best" not an effective goal?
   - (a) It is not specific.
   - (b) It is not realistic.
   - (c) It is too difficult.
   - (d) It is too common.

4. How could a professor get best results on a term paper assignment?
   - (a) Make the paper due at the middle of the semester.
   - (b) Require a partial paper or rough draft early in the semester.
   - (c) Allow students to set their own deadline for completion.
   - (d) Make the assignment sound intimidating.

5. What is a good strategy to minimize a temptation?
   - (a) Wait until the last moment to make your decisions.
   - (b) Prepare for the temptation by resisting other temptations.
   - (c) Avoid the situation in which temptations arise.
   - (d) Watch someone else yield to temptation.

6. What is the emphasis of the scientific-management approach to job design?
   - (a) Make the job interesting and fulfilling.
   - (b) Find the most efficient, foolproof way to do the job.
   - (c) Encourage workers to experiment with new methods.
   - (d) Rotate workers through different jobs every few months.

7. Job satisfaction correlates poorly with quality of job performance. Why?
   - (a) Workers who perform poorly are trying to do better.
   - (b) Young workers have the highest job performance.
   - (c) Many of the best workers want a better job.
   - (d) Job satisfaction depends on pay, and nothing else.

8. Why is it difficult to determine the qualities of a good leader?
   - (a) Most leaders change their policies too often.
   - (b) Almost everyone is an equally good leader.
   - (c) Leadership needs vary depending on the situation.
   - (d) Workers are afraid to complain about a poor leader.

Answers: 1c, 2a, 3a, 4b, 5c, 6b, 7c, 8c.

Hunger

After studying this module, you should be able to:

1. Describe short-term and long-term physiological influences on eating.

2. Cite an example of a social influence on the amount eaten.

3. Discuss possible causes of obesity.

4. Define anorexia nervosa and bulimia nervosa and discuss possible causes of each.

Small birds eat only what they need at the moment, mostly seeds or insects, storing almost no fat at all. Remaining as light as possible is important for flying away from predators. At the opposite extreme, predators such as lions, crocodiles, and sharks eat huge meals when they can, but have nothing to eat at other times. Their digestive systems are adapted to accept huge meals (Armstrong & Schindler, 2011).

Few humans eat as gluttonously as crocodiles, but we too apparently evolved a strategy of eating more than we need, in case food becomes scarce later, as was often the case during most of human existence. Today, however, prosperous countries have abundant food, and many people overeat (Pinel, Assanand, & Lehman, 2000).

Our eating depends on social motives as well as actual need. Imagine you visit your boyfriend's or girlfriend's family, and you want to make a good impression. "Dinner's ready!" You go to the dining room and find a huge meal, which your hosts clearly expect you to enjoy. Do you explain that you are not hungry because you made a pig of yourself at lunch? Probably not.

The Physiology of Hunger and Satiety

Hunger serves to keep fuel available for the body. How does your brain know how much fuel you need? The problem is more complex than keeping enough fuel in your car. You store fuel in your stomach, intestines, fat cells, liver cells, and bloodstream. Furthermore, each meal has different nutrients. It would be as if you were never sure how much fuel was already in your car's tank, exactly what you were filling it with, or how far you need to go before your next refueling. The complexity of hunger requires multiple mechanisms to control intake.

Short-Term Regulation of Hunger

The main factor for ending a meal is distension of the stomach and intestines. You feel full when your digestive system is full. The stomach signals its distension to the brain via the vagus nerve, and the intestines signal distension by releasing a hormone called *cholecystokinin* (Deutsch & Ahn, 1986; Gibbs, Young, & Smith, 1973). With familiar foods, you also calibrate approximately how much nutrition each bite contains (Deutsch & Gonzalez, 1980).

When the stomach is empty, it stimulates hunger by releasing the hormone *ghrelin* (GRELL-in). People who produce larger than average amounts of ghrelin, such as people with Praeder-Willi syndrome, are likely to overeat and become overweight (Karra et al., 2013). Another factor inducing hunger is a drop in how much glucose enters the cells (see ▼ **Figure 11.6**). Glucose, *the most abundant sugar in the blood, is the body's main energy source, especially for the brain.* The body makes glucose from almost any food. If you eat more than you need at the moment, your body converts the excess into fats and other stored fuels. If you eat too little, you convert the stored fuels into blood glucose. The flow of glucose from the blood into cells depends on insulin, a hormone released by the pancreas.

The hormone insulin *helps glucose and several other nutrients enter the cells.* At the beginning of a meal, before the nutrients in it begin to enter the blood, the brain sends messages to the pancreas to secrete insulin. Therefore, your cells start getting more nutrition at once.

As a meal continues, the digested food enters the blood, and almost as fast

Mealtime is more than an opportunity to satisfy hunger: It is an occasion to share a pleasant experience with family or friends, to discuss the events of the day, and even to pass on cultural traditions from one generation to the next.

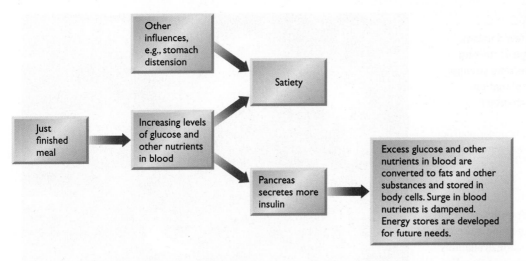

◄ **Figure 11.6** Varying secretions of insulin regulate the flow of nutrients from the blood into the cells or from storage back into the blood.

as it enters, insulin moves some of the nutrients out of the blood and into the liver or fat cells that store it for future use. Hours after a meal, when blood glucose levels start to drop, the pancreas secretes another hormone, *glucagon,* that stimulates the liver to release stored glucose back into the blood.

As insulin levels rise and fall, hunger decreases and increases, as shown in ► Figure 11.7. Insulin affects hunger partly by controlling the flow of glucose and also stimulating neurons of the hypothalamus that signal satiety (Brüning et al., 2000).

10. What is the effect of high insulin levels on hunger? Why?

Answer

10. High insulin levels decrease hunger, partly by increasing the flow of nutrients into cells and partly by stimulating parts of the hypothalamus. When the supply of nutrients in the blood decreases, hunger returns.

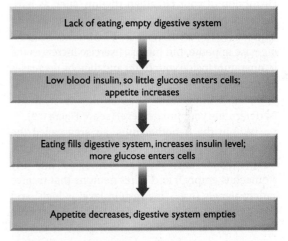

▲ **Figure 11.7** A feedback system between eating and insulin levels maintains homeostatic control of nutrition.

Long-Term Hunger Regulation

Stomach distension and other mechanisms for ending a meal are far from perfect. For your next meal, you may eat more than you need, or less. You have long-term mechanisms to correct short-term errors. After overeating, you feel less hungry until you get back to your normal weight. If you eat too little, you feel hungrier than usual until you get back to normal. Most people's weight fluctuates from day to day but remains fairly stable over long periods.

Your mean weight is called a **set point**—*a level that the body works to maintain* (see ► Figure 11.8). It's similar to the temperature at which you set the thermostat in your house. However, your body's set point for weight is like a thermostat that readjusts when you are not looking at it, especially after a splurge meal. The average young adult gains about 1 kg (2 pounds) per year (Kärkkäinen, Mustelin, Raevuori, Kaprio, & Keski-Rahkonen, 2018). That may not sound like much, but year after year it adds up.

Maintaining relatively constant body weight depends on *the hormone* **leptin**, *which the body's fat cells release in proportion to their mass.* When the body gains fat, the extra leptin alters activity in the hypothalamus, causing meals to satisfy hunger faster. Leptin is your fat cells' way to say, "You have enough fat already, so eat less." If you lose weight, your fat cells produce less leptin, and your hunger increases. Leptin also triggers the start of puberty: When the body reaches a certain weight, the increased leptin levels combine with other forces to induce the hormonal changes of puberty (Chehab, Mounzih, Lu, & Lim, 1997).

Those few people who lack the genes to produce leptin become obese (Farooqi et al., 2001). Their brains get no signals from their fat supplies, so they feel as if they are starving. They also fail to enter puberty (Clément et al., 1998). Leptin injections greatly reduce obesity for these few people (Williamson et al., 2005). However, for anyone else, extra leptin produces little effect. Low levels of leptin induce hunger, but beyond a certain point, extra leptin has little effect on satiety (Pan & Myers, 2018; Ravussin, Leibel, & Ferrante, 2014).

▲ **Figure 11.8** For most people, weight fluctuates around a set point, just as a diving board bounces up and down from a central position.

11. Over the past few decades, the average age of starting puberty has become younger. What is one explanation, based on this chapter?

Answer

11. People have been gaining weight and therefore producing more leptin. Leptin facilitates the onset of puberty.

Brain Mechanisms

Your appetite at any moment depends on your health, the taste and appearance of the food, the contents of your stomach and intestines, the availability of glucose to the cells, and your body's fat supplies. Disruption of your circadian rhythm, such as happens when you travel across time zones, alters your appetite (Karatsoreos et al., 2013). Mild exercise can increase appetite, but intense exercise increases the temperature inside your brain and thereby decreases appetite (Jeong et al., 2018). Several parts of the hypothalamus integrate all this information and thereby determine your hunger level (see ▼ Figure 11.9).

Within the hypothalamus, an area called the arcuate nucleus has one set of neurons that receive hunger signals (e.g., "the food looks good" and "my stomach is empty") and other neurons that receive satiety signals (e.g., "my insulin level is high" and "my leptin level is high enough"). The output from the arcuate nucleus directs other parts of the hypothalamus to enhance or weaken salivation, swallowing, digestion, and the pleasure of eating (Mendieta-Zéron, López, & Diéguez, 2008). Damage in the hypothalamus impairs regulation of eating. ▶ Figure 11.10 shows an example of a rat with damage to one part of the hypothalamus.

▲ **Figure 11.10** A rat with damage to part of the hypothalamus (left) has a constantly high insulin level that causes it to store most of its meal as fat. Because the nutrients do not circulate in the blood, the rat quickly becomes hungry again. This rat's excess fat prevents it from grooming its fur.

Social Influences on Eating

In addition to the need for nutrition, social factors also influence what, when, and how much we eat. If you eat while watching television, you tend to eat more than if you were paying full attention to your meal (van der Wal & van Dillen, 2013). When you dine with friends, on average you linger two or three times as long as you would if eating alone (Bell & Pliner, 2003), and you eat almost twice as much (de Castro, 2000). You eat a few more bites after you thought you were done, and then a few more, probably without realizing the other people's influence. Someone wants dessert, so you have one, too. Exceptions occur, of course, if you are dining with someone who might scold you for overeating (Herman, Roth, & Polivy, 2003).

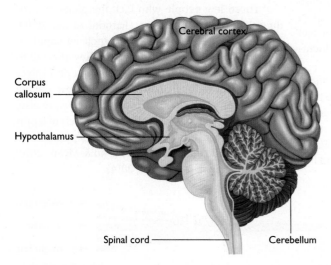

▲ **Figure 11.9** The hypothalamus, a small area on the underside of the brain, helps regulate eating, drinking, sexual behavior, and other motivated activities.

One reason for the increased obesity in the United States over recent decades is the increase in restaurant portion sizes. Instead of a simple cheeseburger, you can now get a colossal sandwich with several meat patties and many add-ons.

Even the name of the food can influence appetite. What we now call Chilean sea bass used to be called Patagonian toothfish. Changing the name greatly increased sales. Another fish, orange roughy, used to be called "slimehead." You can imagine the sales for a fish with that name.

concept check

12. **What evidence indicates important social influences on eating and weight gain?**

Answer

12. People eat more when in social groups than when eating alone. People's expectations about foods, based on such things as the name of the food, also influence intake.

Eating Too Much or Too Little

Obesity has become widespread but not universal. Why do some people become obese, whereas others do not? At the other extreme, why do some people eat too little? Abnormal eating reflects a combination of physiological and social influences.

Obesity

Obesity is *the excessive accumulation of body fat.* Physicians calculate a *body mass index,* defined as weight in kilograms divided by height in meters squared (kg/m^2). A ratio over 25 is considered overweight, over 30 is obese, and over 40 is extremely obese (National Institutes of Health, 2000). About 30 percent of U.S. adults are obese, and another 35 percent are overweight (Marx, 2003). Obesity is associated with deteriorating health, partly because of the weight itself, but also partly because of the stress of dealing with discrimination and hostility (Daly, Sutin, & Robinson, 2019).

People become overweight because they take in more calories than they use. But *why* do they do that? And why has overweight become more prevalent in recent decades? The increase in prevalence points to an environmental influence, because genetic changes do not happen that fast. The most obvious environmental influence is the ready availability of tasty, high calorie foods. Over the years, portion sizes have been steadily increasing, especially in the United States (Rozin, Kabnick, Pete, Fischler, & Shields, 2003). Overeating has spread in other cultures, too, as they became, as some people put it, "Coca-Colonized" by Western cultures (Friedman, 2000).

Consider the Native American Pima of Arizona (see ▼ Figure 11.11). The Pima have a high prevalence of obesity and type 2 diabetes, probably related to several genes (Norman et al., 1998). However, their ancestors—with the same genes—were not overweight. They ate the fruits and vegetables that grow in the Sonoran Desert, which are available only briefly during the year. To survive, they had to eat as much as they could whenever they could. Beginning in the 1940s, they switched to the same diet as other Americans, rich in calories and available year-round. The Pima still eat vigorously, and the result is weight gain. This is a superb example of the combined influence of genetics and environment. The Pima weight problem depends on both their genes and the change in diet.

The easy availability of high-calorie foods makes it easy to gain weight. Psychologists observed that restaurant customers tend to drink large amounts of sugary drinks if the wait staff keep refilling the glass. They drink less if they have to walk a few steps to refill the glass themselves (John, Donnelly, & Roberto, 2017). However, even in the same circumstances of food availability, some people gain weight and others do not. Again we see that weight gain depends on both hereditary and environmental influences (Albuquerque, Nóbrega, C., Manco, & Padez, 2017).

Studies of twins and adopted children support heritability estimates ranging from 47 percent to 80 percent. Only a small amount of that heritability can be linked to single, identified genes. More than a hundred genes make small contributions. Other hereditary influences include rare genetic variants (capable of producing big effects but too rare to be identified in typical research studies), copy-number

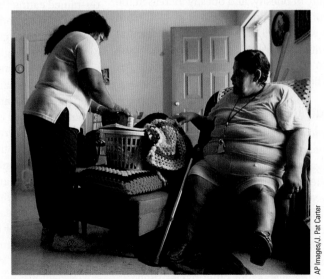

▲ **Figure 11.11** Until the 1940s, the Native American Pima remained thin eating their traditional diet of desert plants. Today, they eat the typical U.S. diet while remaining relatively inactive, and the result is high prevalence of obesity.

Many people with obesity feel distressed and suffer from low self-esteem because of how other people treat them.

variants (gene deletions or duplications), and epigenetics (Albuquerque et al., 2017).

The Limited Role of Emotional Disturbances

Many people react to emotional distress by overeating. Conversely, when people feel good, they tend to eat less (Sproesser, Schupp, & Renner, 2014). Data from people who kept an eating diary showed that shortly after an important football or soccer game, fans of the losing team ate more than usual whereas fans of the winning team ate less (Cornil & Chandon, 2013).

Eating binges in response to stress are particularly common among people who have been dieting to lose weight (Greeno & Wing, 1994). Evidently, dieters inhibit their desire to eat until a stressful experience breaks their inhibitions and releases a pent-up desire to eat. Is distress a major cause of obesity? A review of 15 studies found that depression increased the probability of obesity, and obesity increased the probability of depression (Luppino et al., 2010), but both effects were small. In one study, 19 percent of the people with a history of depression became obese compared to 15 percent of other people (McIntyre, Konarski, Wilkins, Soczynska, & Kennedy, 2006).

Energy Output

In addition to overeating, most overweight people have low energy output, including a low metabolic rate. Investigators compared the infants of 12 overweight mothers and 6 normal-weight mothers over their first year of life. The babies weighed about the same at birth, but six babies of the overweight mothers were less active than average and became overweight within their first year. During their first 3 months, they expended about 20 percent less energy per day than the average for other babies (Roberts, Savage, Coward, Chew, & Lucas, 1988).

Low energy expenditure is a good predictor of weight gain in adults as well. Researchers found that

obese people are less active than other people and spend more time sitting, even after they lose weight (J. A. Levine et al., 2005). Evidently, inactivity is a long-term habit, not just a reaction to being heavy.

13. What evidence indicates that overweight depends on both hereditary and environmental influences?

Answer

13. The Pima Indians tend to eat much, partly for a genetic predisposition, but they did not become overweight until they shifted to the typical American diet. Overweight has become more common over decades, indicating an environmental influence, but nevertheless some people become overweight and others do not, suggesting a hereditary influence.

Losing Weight

People trying to lose weight have a conflict between the motive to enjoy eating now and the motive to feel good about losing weight later. Certainly, it is possible to reduce meal size. One way to help is to include prominent statements about the calories of each item, as many restaurants now do (Lim, Penrod, Ha, Bruce, & Bruce, 2018). Another way is to include graphic warnings on sugary drinks, showing obesity, decayed teeth, and other dangers from excessive sugar (Donnelly, Zatz, Svirsky, & John, 2018).

However, reducing the size of a meal is not the same as losing weight in the long run. Advertisements for various diet programs report that many people lost a significant amount of weight. Let's assume they are telling the truth. If you hear that X number of people lost weight on some diet, how valuable is that information? It's almost worthless, unless you also know how long they kept it off and how many other people tried the diet without losing weight.

Many of the published statistics about dieting look discouraging. Those results are somewhat distorted, because the people who are most successful at losing weight don't keep seeking help. The people who fail to lose weight continue participating in one weight-loss program after another, biasing the statistics (Schachter, 1982). A survey of a large, representative sample of U.S. adults found that 17 percent of previously obese or overweight people did manage to lose at least 10 percent of their weight and maintain their weight loss for at least a year (Kraschnewski et al., 2010).

Dieting to combat obesity faces difficulties beyond the difficulty of restrained eating (Benton & Young, 2017). If you substantially reduce your calorie intake, your body decreases its metabolic rate, such that even normal eating can cause weight gain. Also, dieting leads to long-lasting changes in the release of leptin, insulin, ghrelin, and other hormones, resulting in increased appetite.

More successful treatments require a change of lifestyle. Increased exercise is an important part of any weight-loss program, although unfortunately most people overestimate how many calories they burn in an exercise session, and sometimes if they expect exercise to solve their weight problem, they continue to overeat (McFerran & Mukhopadhyay, 2013). An important lifestyle change is to eat more high-fiber fruits and vegetables, instead of trying to eat the same foods as before, only less of them. You are less likely to overindulge in a mostly vegetable meal than in a meal of meat, dairy, and dessert.

People are more likely to comply with recommendations for small changes: Consistently increase daily activity, but not so much that it becomes burdensome. Drink water instead of soda drinks, eat fewer and healthier snacks, store tempting treats out of sight, and always leave at least a few bites on the plate (Poelman, de Vet, Velema, Seidell, & Steenhuis, 2014).

Weight-loss pills are only mildly effective, they produce unwanted side effects, and there is one further disadvantage: People taking these pills no longer feel much obligation to control their appetite on their own. In one study, people trying to lose weight all took a placebo, but researchers told half of them, chosen randomly, that it was a weight-loss pill. A little later, all of them had a chance to sample some candies for a "taste preference" test. Those who thought they had taken a weight-loss pill ate, on average, 29 percent more candies (Chang & Chiou, 2014).

Anorexia Nervosa

The Duchess of Windsor once said, "You can't be too rich or too thin." She may have been right about too rich, but she was wrong about too thin. Some people are so strongly motivated to be thin that they threaten their health.

Anorexia nervosa is *a condition in which someone intensely fears gaining weight and refuses to eat a normal amount. Anorexia* means "loss of appetite," but the problem is not really lack of hunger. Most people with anorexia enjoy the taste of food and even enjoy preparing it, but they express fear of eating and gaining weight. The term *nervosa*, meaning "for reasons of the nerves," distinguishes this condition from digestive disorders.

In the United States, anorexia nervosa occurs in a little less than 1 percent of women at some point in life and in about 0.3 percent of men (Hudson, Hiripi, Pope, & Kessler, 2007). It usually begins in the teenage years, and almost never after the mid-20s. Unlike other starving people, most people with anorexia run long distances, compete at sports, or are extremely active in other ways. They usually deny or understate their problem. Even when they become dangerously thin, they often describe themselves as "looking fat" and "needing to lose weight."

Anorexia nervosa stands out from other psychiatric problems in several ways. Anyone with depression, schizophrenia, alcohol or drug abuse, or an anxiety disorder has at least a 50-50 chance to have one or more of the others also, and the genes that predispose to one disorder predispose to the others (Caspi et al., 2014; Cross-Disorder Group of the Psychiatric Genomics Consortium, 2013). Most people with anorexia have a perfectionistic, obsessive-compulsive personality, but otherwise have no more likelihood of anxiety disorders than the rest of the population. The rates of alcohol or drug abuse are very low at the onset of anorexia, although they increase to normal levels later in life. Many people with anorexia become depressed, and many therapists have therefore assumed that depression is the cause of anorexia, but few people had depression *before* becoming anorexic (Bühren et al., 2014; Zerwas et al., 2013), and the treatments appropriate for depression are seldom effective for anorexia (Berkman, Lohr, & Bulik, 2007). Furthermore, depression is associated with decreased activity, whereas people with anorexia tend to be highly active.

Another hypothesis is that weight loss is the primary problem, not a reaction to depression. Most cases of anorexia begin with strict dieting, often by ballet dancers, athletes, or others who are highly active and motivated to lose weight. It is remarkably easy to get rats to produce symptoms resembling anorexia, just by weight loss and an opportunity for exercise: Restrict a rat to just one hour a day of eating, and provide a running wheel. Ordinarily, laboratory rats are inactive for an hour or two after eating, and then run in a wheel until their next meal. That pattern works fine if the rats can eat again in a few hours, but if they have to wait 23 hours, they continue running most of that time and they lose weight. After losing much weight, they stop eating even when food becomes available. Unless rescued, they die of starvation. Why do they run so vigorously? Most laboratories are kept at about 21°C (70°F), comfortable for fully dressed human experimenters, but cool for a rat, especially a few hours after its last meal. Digesting food generates heat, but within a couple hours after eating, a rat starts feeling cold, and exercising helps it get warm. It has been known since the work of Curt Richter (1922) and confirmed later that rats in a warmer room run less, and they maintain normal weight even if they are limited to 1 hour of eating per day (Cerrato, Carrera, Vazquez, Echevarria, & Gutiérrez, 2012; Gutiérrez, 2013).

Extending this idea to humans, the hypothesis is that someone diets to lose weight, exercises extensively, partly to maintain body temperature,

loses further weight, and so forth, until the weight loss triggers other problems. People with anorexia are most active on the coldest days (Carrera et al., 2012), and anorexia is more common in cool climates than in warmer ones (Gutierrez, Carrera, Vazquez, & Birmingham, 2013). From this information, a treatment arose: Someone with anorexia stays in a warm room or wears a jacket to keep warm, and is required to limit physical activity. Medications, which are not very effective anyway, cease. At mealtimes, people with anorexia often fear that if they eat anything at all, they will overeat and become fat. To reduce this fear and maintain a sense of control, they eat with a scale under the plate, connected to a computer that reports the rate of eating compared to average (see ▼ Figure 11.12). Then eating is like a video game, as the person tries to eat at the recommended pace, neither too little nor too much. Six clinics using this approach with 571 patients, nearly all female, reported that 75 percent were fully recovered within 13 months of treatment and mostly remained in recovery 5 years later, a much better success rate than with typical forms of treatment (Bergh et al., 2013). This treatment is well established in Sweden, but so far it is not well known elsewhere (Södersten, Brodin, Zandian, & Bergh, 2019). Still, it sounds promising.

14. How does anorexia differ from depression?

Answer

14. People with anorexia tend to be highly active, whereas people with depression become inactive. Most people with anorexia had no psychiatric problems before developing anorexia. Standard treatments for depression are not very effective with anorexia.

Bulimia Nervosa

Another eating disorder is bulimia nervosa (literally, "ox hunger for nervous reasons"), in which people—again, mostly women—alternate *between self-deprivation and periods of excessive eating.* To compensate for overeating, they may force themselves to vomit or use laxatives or enemas, or they may go through long periods of dieting and exercising. That is, they "binge and purge." In extreme eating binges, people have been known to consume up to 20,000 calories at a time (Schlesier-Stropp, 1984). A meal of a cheeseburger, fries, and a milkshake constitutes about 1,000 calories, so imagine eating that meal 20 times at one

Place more food on the plate.

Place the plate on the scale and food on the plate.

Courtesy of Per Södersten

▲ **Figure 11.12** For treatment, someone with anorexia stays in a warm room, with restrictions on excessive activity. At mealtimes, a device connected to the plate monitors the rate of eating and compares it to the average rate. The patient tries to stay close to that rate.

sitting. Most binges feature sweets and fats (Latner, 2003), so a better illustration of 20,000 calories would be 5 kg (11 pounds) of chocolate fudge.

In the United States, about 1 percent of adult women and about 0.1 percent of adult men have bulimia nervosa (Hoek & van Hoeken, 2003). The incidence increased for several decades, although it has leveled out since about 1990 (Crowther, Armey, Luce, Dalton, & Leahey, 2008). Culture is a major contributor. Bulimia was rare until the mid-1900s, and it has not been recorded in any culture without a strong Western influence (Keel & Klump, 2003). Of course, eating binges are impossible without huge amounts of tasty food.

One hypothesis is that people with bulimia starve themselves for a while, fight their persistent feelings of hunger, and then go on an eating binge (Polivy & Herman, 1985). That idea may be on the right track, but it is incomplete. Of the people who starve themselves for days or weeks, some do develop eating binges, but others do not (Stice, 2002). The results may depend on what someone eats after a period of deprivation. Although most people end a fast by eating meat, fish, or eggs, people with bulimia start with desserts or snack foods (Latner, 2003).

In some ways, bulimia resembles drug addiction. The defining features of addiction are significant harm and repeated failures to quit. By that definition, people with bulimia nervosa can be described as addicted (Meule, van Rezori, & Blechert, 2014). Indulging in foods rich in fats and sugars can exert effects similar to those of addicting drugs (Hoebel, Rada, Mark, & Pothos, 1999). When someone consumes high quantities of rich foods, especially right after a period of abstention, the result is a "high" similar to what addictive drugs provide.

To test this idea, researchers put laboratory rats on a regimen of no food for 12 hours, including the first 4 hours of their waking day, followed by a meal of sweet syrup. With each repetition of this schedule, the rats consumed more and more of the syrup. Furthermore, if they were then deprived of this accustomed meal, they shook their heads and chattered their teeth much like rats going through morphine withdrawal (Colantuoni et al., 2001, 2002). The results suggest that a pattern of deprivation followed by overeating provides strong reinforcement that overwhelms other motivations.

concept check

Answer

15. **Under what circumstances would binge eating produce an experience similar to taking an addictive drug?**

15. Eating a meal high in sugars and fats right after a deprivation period produces an experience comparable to those produced by addictive drugs.

in closing | module 11.2

The Complexities of Hunger

The research in this module underscores the idea that our motivations reflect a complex mixture of physiological, social, and cognitive forces. People eat for many reasons and they abstain from food for many reasons also. To understand why

people become overweight or anorexic, we have to address many types of influence. The general point is that all our motivations interact and combine. We seldom do anything for just one reason.

Summary

- *Short-term regulation of hunger.* Distension of the stomach and intestines is the main mechanism for feeling satiated. Hunger resumes when the cells begin to receive less glucose and other nutrients. The hormone insulin regulates the flow of nutrients from the blood into cells. (page 348)
- *Long-term regulation of hunger.* When someone gains weight, the fat cells increase release of leptin, which decreases hunger. When someone loses weight, fat cells decrease leptin release and hunger increases. (page 349)
- *Brain mechanisms.* The hypothalamus integrates many types of information to regulate salivation, swallowing, digestion, and the pleasure of eating. (page 350)
- *Social influences on eating.* People eat more in groups than when eating alone. They eat more when they have high expectations for the meal, based on such things as the name of the food. (page 350)
- *Obesity.* Depression increases the probability of obesity, and obesity increases the probability of depression, but both effects are small. Obesity reflects environmental influences such as the ready availability of foods and hereditary influences including a tendency to be less active than average. (page 351)
- *Weight-loss techniques.* Losing weight requires a combination of diet and exercise, although the success rate is disappointing. (page 352)
- *Anorexia nervosa.* People suffering from anorexia nervosa deprive themselves of food, sometimes to a dangerous point. Most show extreme physical activity, which can be interpreted as a mechanism of temperature regulation. A therapy based on keeping the person warm, restricting exercise, and monitoring food intake has shown promise. (page 353)
- *Bulimia nervosa.* People suffering from bulimia nervosa alternate between periods of dieting and binge eating. Bulimia has been compared to drug addiction. (page 353)

Key Terms

anorexia nervosa (page 353)

bulimia nervosa (page 353)

glucose (page 348)

insulin (page 348)

leptin (page 349)

obesity (page 351)

set point (page 349)

Review Questions

1. How does the hormone insulin affect appetite?
   - (a) It helps glucose enter the cells.
   - (b) It increases sensitivity of the taste buds.
   - (c) It stimulates activity of the stomach and intestines.
   - (d) It increases salivation.

2. What body part produces leptin?
   - (a) The pancreas
   - (b) Fat cells
   - (c) The stomach
   - (d) The hypothalamus

3. Which of the following increases how much food people eat?
   - (a) People eat more after intense exercise.
   - (b) People eat more when the weather is hot.
   - (c) People eat more when eating in a group.
   - (d) People eat more after their favorite team wins a game.

4. What led to weight gain among the Pima?
   - (a) A genetic change
   - (b) Increased life stress
   - (c) Increased exercise
   - (d) A change in diet

5. How does anorexia relate to depression?
   - (a) Therapies for depression are equally effective for anorexia.
   - (b) People with depression or anorexia are about equal in activity level.
   - (c) Becoming depressed increases the probability of anorexia.
   - (d) Suffering from anorexia sometimes leads to depression.

6. Where is anorexia nervosa most common?
   - (a) Impoverished neighborhoods
   - (b) Neighborhoods with low physical activity
   - (c) Warm climates
   - (d) Cool climates

7. Research on rats suggests that bulimia nervosa resembles what other condition?
   - (a) Insomnia
   - (b) Addiction
   - (c) Bipolar disorder
   - (d) Phobia

Answers: 1a, 2b, 3c, 4d, 5d, 6d, 7b.

module 11.3

Sexual Motivation

After studying this module, you should be able to:

1. Describe the results of the Kinsey survey and other sex behavior surveys.

2. State how AIDS can and cannot be transmitted between people.

3. List the four stages of sexual arousal.

4. Explain the roles of testosterone and estradiol in prenatal sexual development.

5. Discuss the factors that cause an intersex appearance, and the policies for dealing with such people.

6. List differences between men and women with regard to sexual orientation.

7. Evaluate evidence about possible influences on sexual orientation.

Sexual motivation, like hunger, depends on both a physiological drive and incentives. Also like hunger, the sex drive increases during times of deprivation, at least up to a point, and people can inhibit the drive when they need to. However, the sex drive differs from hunger in important ways. We do not need to be around food to feel hungry, but many people need a partner to feel sexual arousal. We eat in public, but we have sexual activities in private.

Alfred C. Kinsey was an outstanding interviewer who put people at ease so they could speak freely, but he was also alert to probable lies.

Ultimately, hunger and sex serve important biological functions that we ordinarily don't even think about during the acts themselves. We evolved mechanisms that make us enjoy eating because eating keeps us alive. Similarly, we evolved mechanisms that make sex feel good because it leads to reproduction. It also leads to emotional satisfaction that strengthens a romantic bond (Meltzer et al., 2017).

What Do People Do and How Often?

Researchers have many reasons for studying the frequency of sexual behaviors. For example, if we want to predict the spread of AIDS, we need to know how many people are having unsafe sex and with how many partners. In addition to the scientific and medical reasons for studying sex, let's admit it: We're curious, aren't we?

The Kinsey Survey

The first important survey of human sexual behavior was conducted by Alfred C. Kinsey, an insect biologist who agreed to teach the biological portion of Indiana University's course on marriage. When he found that the library included little information about human sexuality, he conducted a survey. What started as a small-scale project for teaching purposes grew into a survey of 18,000 people.

Although Kinsey's sample was large, he obtained most of his interviews from members of cooperative organizations, ranging from fraternities to nunneries, mostly in the U.S. Midwest. Later researchers, trying harder to get representative samples of the population, obtained significantly different results.

Nevertheless, Kinsey did document the variability of human sexual behavior (Kinsey, Pomeroy, & Martin, 1948; Kinsey, Pomeroy, Martin, & Gebhard, 1953). He found some people who had rarely or never experienced orgasm. He also found several women who sometimes had 50 or more orgasms within 20 minutes, and one middle-aged man who reported an average of four or five orgasms per day, with a wide variety of male, female, and animal partners.

Sexual customs vary sharply from one society to another. At a Hmong festival, unmarried women toss tennis balls to potential suitors.

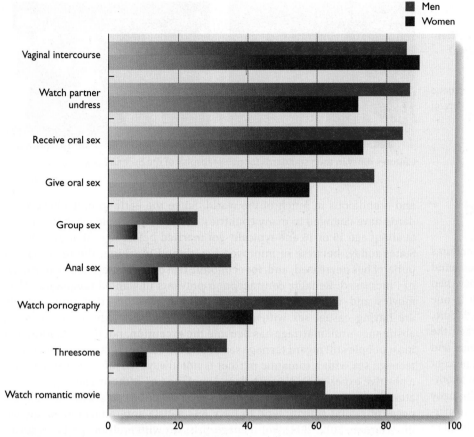

Figure 11.13 The percentage of U.S. adults who rate various sexual activities as appealing or very appealing. (Based on data of Herbenick et al., 2017)

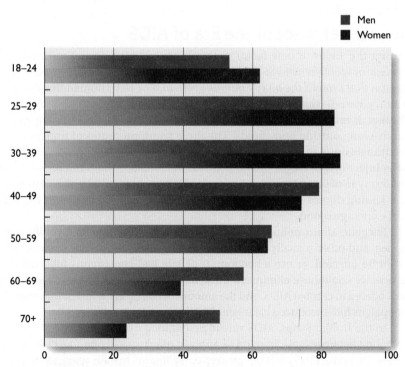

Figure 11.14 The percentage of people who have had vaginal intercourse within the last year. (Based on the data of Herbenick et al., 2017)

Kinsey found that most people were unaware of how much sexual behavior varies. When he asked people whether they believed that "excessive masturbation" causes physical and mental illness, most said "yes." (In fact, it does not.) He then asked what constitutes "excessive." For each person, excessive meant a little more than what he or she did. One young man who masturbated once a month said he thought three times a month would cause mental illness. A man who masturbated three times daily said he thought five times a day would be excessive. In reaction, Kinsey defined *nymphomaniac* as "someone who wants sex more than you do."

Later Surveys

Kinsey did not try to interview a random or representative sample of the population because he assumed that most people would refuse to cooperate. He may have been right in the 1940s, but in later years, researchers found that most people were willing to cooperate.

Some advice if anyone ever asks you to participate in a sex survey: Legitimate researchers present their credentials to show their affiliation with a research institute. They also take precautions to guarantee the confidentiality of your responses. Be wary of sex surveys by telephone. It is hard to distinguish a legitimate survey from an obscene phone call in disguise.

A survey of more than 2,000 U.S. adults with a wide range of ages (Herbenick et al., 2017) explored what people enjoy. ◄ Figure 11.13 shows the percentage of men and women who describe various sexual activities as appealing or very appealing. The percentages differ between men and women for certain activities, but in general, women report enjoying sex as much as men do, especially women who are in a committed, loving relationship (Barnett & Melugin, 2016; Conley, Moors, Matsick, Ziegler, & Valentine, 2011).

◄ Figure 11.14 presents the results from the same survey, showing differences by age. As the figure shows, frequency of sexual activity peaks in young adulthood and then declines (Herbenick et al., 2017). The sharply decreased sexual activity of older women reflects the fact that women usually outlive their partners. Another survey, including more than a thousand people, found that old people were, on average, as satisfied with their sex life as were young or middle-aged people. At all ages, the best predictor of sexual satisfaction was being in love with one's partner (Neto & Pinto, 2013).

16. Why did Kinsey's results differ from those of later surveys?

Answer

16. Kinsey interviewed a nonrepresentative sample of people.

Cultures differ in their standards for public display of the human body.

Comparisons by Culture and Cohort

Sexual customs vary considerably among cultures and subcultures. A survey of four U.S. colleges found that the percentage of undergraduates who have had sexual intercourse ranged from 54 percent at one college to 90 percent at another (Davidson, Moore, Earle, & Davis, 2008). At universities in Turkey, the percentage ranged from 32 percent of the men and 9 percent of the women at one college to 84 percent of the men and 33 percent of the women at another college (Askun & Ataca, 2007). Women in many countries in Asia and Africa have no sex before marriage, or no sex before becoming engaged. In all of these countries, more men than women have sex before marriage, some of them with prostitutes. In the United States and many countries in western Europe, men and women have sex, on average, 10 or more years before marriage (Parish, Laumann, & Mojola, 2007). Surveys in Finland, Brazil, and India have also found trends toward greater sexual freedom in more recent generations (Kontula & Haavio-Mannila, 2009; Paiva, Aranha, & Bastos, 2008; Sandhya, 2009).

Customs also vary by historical era. For most of human history, premarital sex was uncommon

To prevent AIDS, use condoms during sex and don't share injection needles. Advertisements such as this have prompted many people to change their behavior.

and scandalous in much of the world. Since the early to mid-1900s, standards have changed in many countries. Previously, people reached puberty at about age 15 or 16 and typically got married before age 20. In the United States today, because of improved health and nutrition, the mean age of puberty has decreased, and, for economic reasons, the mean age of marriage has increased. Reliable contraception prevents unwanted pregnancy. Also, movies and television bombard us with suggestions that other people are having casual sex with multiple partners. Under the circumstances, abstinence until marriage has become the exception, not the rule. Although most people still regard teenage sex as undesirable, others acknowledge that teenage sex with a romantic partner is not always harmful, and sometimes a positive experience. Nevertheless, "hooking up" without a strong personal attachment correlates with depression, and adolescents with the earliest onset of sexual activity tend to have less satisfactory attachments later in life (Harden, 2012, 2014). For teenage girls, sex with multiple partners correlates with symptoms of depression (Vasilenko, 2017). Because this result is a correlation, the result could mean either that having multiple partners leads to depression, or that girls feeling depressed are more likely to accept multiple partners.

Sexual Behavior in the Era of AIDS

During the 1980s, a new factor entered into people's sexual motivations: the fear of **acquired immune deficiency syndrome (AIDS)**, *a sexually transmitted disease that attacks the body's immune system.* For HIV (human immunodeficiency virus)—the virus that causes AIDS—to spread from one person to another, it must enter the other person's blood, because the virus does not survive long outside body fluids. The three common routes of transmission are transfusions of contaminated blood, sharing needles used for intravenous injections of illegal drugs, and sexual contact. Anal intercourse is the riskiest type of sexual contact, but vaginal intercourse is risky also. Touching and kissing do not spread the virus unless both people have open wounds that exchange blood.

For generations, people have known how to avoid contracting syphilis, gonorrhea, and other sexually transmitted diseases: Avoid sex with someone who might be infected, or use a condom. If people had consistently followed this advice, we could have eliminated those diseases long ago. The same advice is now offered to combat AIDS, and the amount of compliance varies. Information campaigns have produced clear benefits in many places.

In the United States, AIDS spread first among male homosexuals and later among heterosexuals. In parts of Africa, it affects up to one-fourth of young adults. One difficulty is that people remain symptom-free for years, so they can spread the virus long before they know they have it and before their partners have reason to suspect it.

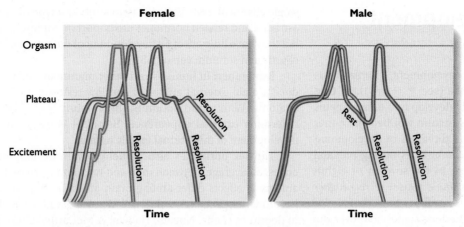

▲ **Figure 11.15** Sexual arousal usually proceeds through four stages—excitement, plateau, orgasm, and resolution. Each color represents the response of a different individual. Note the variation. (After Masters & Johnson, 1966)

Sexual Arousal

Sexual motivation depends on both physiological and cognitive influences—that is, not just hormones and such, but also the presence of a suitable partner, a willingness to be aroused, and a lack of anxiety. William Masters and Virginia Johnson (1966) pioneered the study of human sexual response by actually observing hundreds of men and women, many of them repeatedly, masturbating or having sexual intercourse in a laboratory. They monitored people's physiological responses to sex, including heart rate, breathing, muscle tension, blood engorgement of the genitals and breasts, and nipple erection. They estimated that they observed at least 10,000 sexual episodes. No one has attempted to replicate this study, and probably no one ever will.

Their research was considered shocking, but it revolutionized our understanding in many ways. Sigmund Freud had argued (based on no data) that vaginal orgasms were superior to clitoral orgasms, which he regarded as immature. Masters and Johnson found that clitoral stimulation was almost always essential to a woman's response. Although Kinsey had reported women with multiple orgasms, most psychiatrists and physicians writing about sex (men, as you might guess) ignored or doubted those reports. Masters and Johnson found that many women can have prolonged orgasms or repeated orgasms within a short time, unlike men. Furthermore, many psychiatrists had written that women had sex mainly to have babies or to please their partners. Masters and Johnson demonstrated that women can enjoy sex as much as men do, and possibly more. Clearly, this was research with important consequences.

Masters and Johnson identified four physiological stages in sexual arousal (see ▲ **Figure 11.15**). During the first stage, *excitement,* a man's penis becomes erect and a woman's vagina becomes lubricated. Breathing is rapid and deep. Heart rate and blood pressure increase. Many people experience a flush of the skin, resembling a rash. Women's nipples become erect, and the breasts swell slightly for women who have not nursed a baby. Nervousness interferes with sexual excitement, as do coffee and other stimulant drugs.

Excitement remains high during the second stage, the *plateau,* which lasts for varying lengths of time depending on age, health, and the intensity of stimulation. Excitement builds until the third stage, a sudden release of tension known as *climax* or *orgasm,* which the entire body feels. The fourth and final stage is *resolution*, or relaxation. At orgasm, the pituitary gland releases the hormone *oxytocin,* which induces relaxation, decreased anxiety, and increased sense of attachment to one's partner.

As Figure 11.15 shows, the pattern of excitation varies from one person to another. During a given episode, a woman may experience no orgasm, one, or

many. Most men have only one orgasm, although they can achieve orgasm again following a rest (or refractory) period that generally lasts at least an hour. Among both men and women, the intensity of an orgasm ranges from something like a sigh to an extremely intense experience.

Among men, levels of the hormone testosterone correlate only weakly with frequency of sexual activity, but one interesting pattern has been reported: On average, single men have higher testosterone levels than men in a committed relationship, such as marriage, but married men who are still seeking additional sex partners have a high testosterone level, similar to the average for single men (McIntyre, Gangestad, et al., 2006). How shall we interpret these results? One possibility is that when a man becomes completely faithful to a partner, his testosterone level drops. A longitudinal study supported a different interpretation: Men with lower testosterone levels are more likely to enter into a committed, monogamous relationship (van Anders & Watson, 2006). Women with relatively high testosterone levels also tend to seek multiple partners (van Anders, Hamilton, & Watson, 2007).

17. **Why was a longitudinal study more informative than a cross-sectional study?**

Answer

17. The cross-sectional study showed that married men who remain faithful to their partners tend to have lower testosterone levels than married men seeking additional partners, but those results don't tell us whether entering into a committed marriage changed their testosterone levels. The longitudinal study indicated that testosterone levels were already lower in those men who developed a committed, exclusive relationship.

Sexual Development and Identity

In the earliest stages of development, a human fetus has a unisex appearance (see ▼ **Figure 11.16**). One structure will eventually develop into either a penis or a clitoris. Another structure will become either a scrotum or labia. The direction of development depends on hormonal influences during prenatal development. Beginning in the seventh or eighth week after conception, *male fetuses secrete higher levels of the hormone* **testosterone** than do females (although both sexes produce some), and over the next couple of months, the testosterone causes the tiny fetal structures to expand into a penis and a scrotum. In female fetuses, with lower levels of testosterone, the structures develop into clitoris and labia instead. Levels of the *hormone* **estradiol** *increase more in females* than in males at this time. (*Estrogen* is a category of related chemicals, not a single chemical itself. Estradiol is an abundant type of estrogen.) Blood levels of estradiol and related hormones are important for internal female development, but they have little effect on development of the external anatomy—penis versus clitoris and scrotum versus labia.

Remember: In humans and other mammals, high testosterone levels produce a male external anatomy, and low testosterone levels produce a female anatomy. Within normal limits, the amount of circulating estradiol does not determine external appearance. Estradiol is essential, however, for normal development of the internal female organs.

The sex hormones also influence brain development, producing differences, on average, between men and women in several brain areas. The mechanisms of effects differ among brain areas. In one part of the hypothalamus, hormones regulate a chemical called prostaglandin, which influences the shape of dendrites (Lenz, Nugent, Haliyur, & McCarthy, 2013). In another part of the hypothalamus, hormones act by a chemical called PI3 kinase, and in still another area they act via histones (McCarthy & Arnold, 2011). Why is this important? Hormones are not the only influence on prostaglandins, PI3 kinase, or histones. Because the mechanism of sexual differentiation varies from one brain area to another and from one time period to another, it is common for someone's brain to be more strongly masculinized or feminized in one area than another. Most people's brains are not male-typical or female-typical in all regards. And that

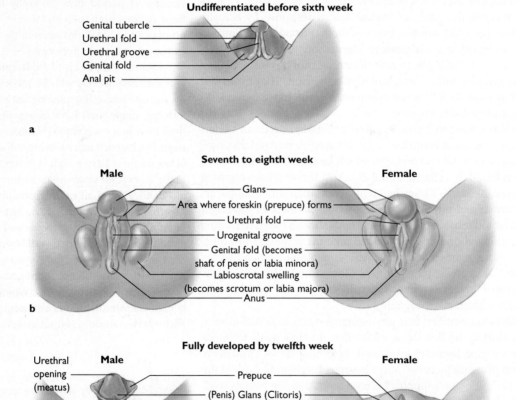

▲ **Figure 11.16** Male and female genitals look the same for the first 6 or 7 weeks after conception (**a**). Differences emerge over the next couple of months (**b**) and are clear at birth (**c**).

fact fits with what we know about behavior. You can be highly masculine or feminine in one aspect of your behavior, and not so much in another.

About 1 child in 2,000 is born with genitals that are hard to classify as male or female, and 1 or 2 in 100 have a slightly ambiguous external anatomy (Blackless et al., 2000). Ambiguity occurs most frequently if a genetic female's adrenal glands produce more than the usual amount of testosterone during a sensitive period before birth (Money & Ehrhardt, 1972). Less frequently, a genetic male develops an intermediate appearance because of an alteration in the gene that controls testosterone receptors (Misrahi et al., 1997). *People with an anatomy that appears intermediate between male and female* are known as intersexes. The Intersex Society of North America **(www.isna.org)** is devoted to increasing understanding and acceptance of people with ambiguous genitals.

How should parents and others treat intersexed children? For decades, the standard medical recommendation was, when in doubt, call the child female and perform surgery to make her anatomy look female. This surgery includes creating or lengthening a vagina and reducing the ambiguous penis/clitoris to the size of an average clitoris. Many cases required repeated surgery to obtain a satisfactory appearance.

This recommendation was based on the assumption that any child who looks like a girl and is treated like a girl will develop a female gender identity. Gender identity is *the sex that someone regards him- or herself as being*. No one ever had evidence for assuming that rearing was entirely responsible for gender identity, and later experience indicated otherwise. Follow-up studies on girls who were partly masculinized at birth but reared as females found that they are more likely than other girls to prefer boy-typical activities and interests during childhood and adolescence (Berenbaum, 1999; Berenbaum, Duck, & Bryk, 2000). The point is that rearing patterns do not entirely control psychological development.

Furthermore, the genital surgery—reducing or removing the penis/clitoris to make an intersex look more female—decreases sexual pleasure and the capacity for orgasm (Minto, Liao, Woodhouse, Ransley, & Creighton, 2003). An artificial vagina may be satisfactory to a male partner, but it provides no sensation or pleasure to the woman, and it requires frequent attention to prevent scar tissue. Many intersexes who underwent genital surgery report that they never had a love relationship of any type (Jürgensen et al., 2013), and most of those who did report very little sexual pleasure (van der Zwan et al., 2013). Finally, intersexed individuals object that, in many cases, physicians lied to them about the surgery and the reasons for it. Today, more and more physicians recommend that parents raise the child as the gender the appearance most resembles and perform no surgery until and unless the individual requests it. The result is that many are reared as males, instead of calling all such children female (Kolesinska et al., 2014). Many intersexed individuals prefer to remain as they are, without surgery (Dreger, 1998).

Related issues arise with regard to transgender youth (those who change sex assignment). Some children question their gender assignment, because of interests and behaviors that match the other gender. Someone originally assigned as a boy who transitions to being a girl generally acts similar to typical girls, and making the transition neither increases nor decreases that tendency (Rae et al., 2019). However, only about one-fourth of children who question their assignment will decide to make a transition final. Those who do transition will prefer not to have the physical changes that come with puberty, such as breast growth in chromosomal females and facial and chest hair for chromosomal males. Is it appropriate to provide hormones or surgery to prevent those changes? This is a difficult question for prepubertal children who are not yet ready to make a lifelong decision. Is it appropriate to give drugs that delay puberty, to give the young person more time to decide? Maybe, but those drugs have risky

Mark Dadswell/Getty Images Sport/Getty Images

Caster Semenya, a South African runner, has won several medals in the Olympics and in World Championships. She was subjected to a test to prove that she is a woman, and was judged eligible.

effects on health. Research on this topic has been sparse. Many people have strong opinions, but the opinions are not based on much factual information (Reardon, 2016).

concept check

18. If a human fetus is exposed to very low levels of both testosterone and estradiol throughout prenatal development, how does the sexual anatomy appear?

19. If a human fetus is exposed to high levels of both testosterone and estradiol throughout prenatal development, how does the sexual anatomy appear?

Answers

18. A fetus exposed to very low levels of both testosterone and estradiol throughout prenatal development develops a female appearance.
19. A fetus exposed to high levels of both testosterone and estradiol develops a male appearance. High levels of testosterone lead to male anatomy; low levels lead to female anatomy. Within normal limits, the level of estradiol has little effect on external anatomy.

Sexual Orientation

Sexual orientation is *the tendency to respond sexually to males, females, both, or neither.* People who prefer partners of their own sex have a homosexual (gay or lesbian) orientation.

Homosexual activity has also been observed at least occasionally in hundreds of animal species (Bagemihl, 1999). Exclusive, lifelong homosexuality has been documented in about 8 percent of male sheep. If "natural" means that something occurs in nature, then homosexual behavior is natural.

How many people have a homosexual orientation? You may have heard claims of 10 percent. That number is derived from Kinsey's report that about 13 percent of the men and 7 percent of the women he interviewed in the 1940s and 1950s stated a predominantly homosexual orientation. However, Kinsey did not have a random or representative sample, and later surveys have reported lower numbers.

In a random sample of 3,500 U.S. adults, 2.8 percent of men and 1.4 percent of women described themselves as having a gay or lesbian orientation (Laumann et al., 1994). As ▲ Figure 11.17 demonstrates, the results depend on the phrasing of the question. Many people who do not consider themselves gay or lesbian have had at least one homosexual experience in adulthood, and still more (especially males) had one in early adolescence (Laumann et al., 1994). Still more say they have felt

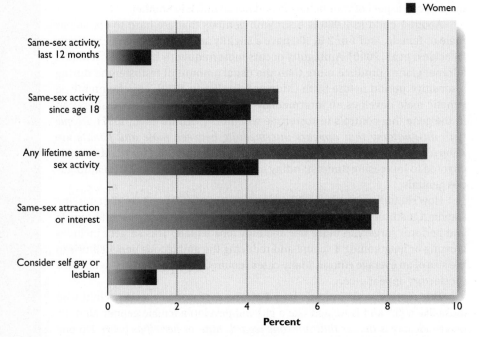

▲ **Figure 11.17** The percentages of U.S. adults who reported sexual activity or interest in sexual activity with people of their own sex. (Based on data of Laumann et al., 1994)

some sexual attraction to a member of their own sex (Dickson, Paul, & Herbison, 2003; Savin-Williams & Vrangalova, 2013). The percentages for women are somewhat misleading, because the data combine results across all ages. Surveys have found that the prevalence of same-sex contact increased gradually from less than 2 percent of women born before 1920 to about 7 percent of younger women born in the 1970s (Turner, Villaroel, Chromy, Eggleston, & Rogers, 2005).

Other large surveys reported that 1 to 6 percent of U.S. men have a gay or bisexual orientation (Billy, Tanfer, Grady, & Klepinger, 1993; Cameron, Proctor, Coburn, & Forde, 1985; Fay et al., 1989). That wide range of data indicates uncertainty about the actual prevalence. Surveys in other countries have reported the percentages shown in ▼ Figure 11.18 (Izazola-Licea, Gortmaker, Tolbert, De Gruttola, & Mann, 2000; Richters et al., 2014; Sandfort, de Graaf, Bijl, & Schnabel, 2001; Spira & Bajos, 1993; Wellings, Field, Johnson, & Wadsworth, 1994).

Differences between Men and Women

Sexual orientation differs on average between men and women in several regards. Most gay men have a history of childhood "gender-nonconforming" (i.e., feminine-type) behaviors (Rieger, Linsenmeier, Gygax, & Bailey, 2008), which observers confirmed by watching the families' home videos. Girls' early gender-nonconforming (i.e., "tomboyish") behaviors are relatively poor predictors of sexual orientation (Diamond, 2007; Udry & Chantala, 2006). Most men become aware of their sexual orientation by early adolescence, and they rarely change later. Masculine-looking and acting lesbians ("butches") also identify their sexual orientation in early adolescence, but more feminine lesbians ("femmes") typically discover their orientation in their early 20s (Luoto, Krams, & Rantala, 2019).

Also, women are more likely than men to experience some sexual attraction to both men and women, and they are more likely to show "fluidity" from one time to another (Bailey et al., 2016; Diamond, Dickenson, & Blair, 2017; Greaves et al., 2017). Psychologists used to think that bisexuality (*attraction to*

Attitudes toward homosexual relationships have varied among cultures and among historical eras.

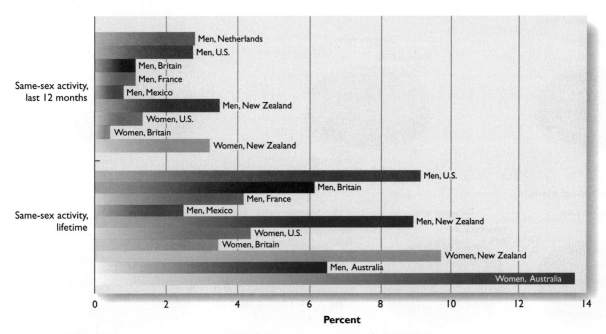

▲ **Figure 11.18** Results of surveys conducted in seven countries, in which people were asked about homosexual experiences. (Based on data of Dickson, Paul, & Herbison, 2003; Izazola-Licea, Gortmaker, Tolbert, De Gruttola, & Mann, 2000; Laumann, Gagnon, Michael, & Michaels, 1994; Richters et al., 2014; Sandfort, de Graaf, Bijl, & Schnabel, 2001; Spira & Bajos, 1993; Wellings, Field, Johnson, & Wadsworth, 1994)

both sexes) was just a temporary transition by someone switching between heterosexual and homosexual attraction. However, a longitudinal study found that female bisexuality is usually stable over many years, and more women switch *to* bisexuality than *from* it (Diamond, 2008). The prevalence of male bisexuality depends on how we define it. If bisexuality consists merely in having had sex with at least one man and at least one woman, then it is fairly common. Most gay men have had at least one heterosexual experience, and some "mostly" heterosexual men have had at least one homosexual experience. But if bisexuality consists of having sexual fantasies and sexual excitement almost equally toward men and women, then it is quite uncommon among men (Rieger, Chivers, & Bailey, 2005; Rieger et al., 2013).

Studying women's sexuality raised interesting problems for researchers. Studying men is easy, because penis erection is synonymous with sexual arousal. To find out whether a man is sexually excited by males or females, attach a device to his penis and measure erections while he views photos or films of naked men or women. If you want to know whether someone might be prone to sadistic sex, show pictures of sadistic sex and measure a possible erection (Seto, Lalumière, Harris, & Chivers, 2012). So, researchers tested women by measuring vaginal secretions or blood flow to the genital region in response to pornographic films. Most women showed about equal responses to depictions of naked men or women, regardless of whether they described themselves as heterosexual or lesbian, and despite protestations in many cases that they didn't enjoy any of the pictures (Chivers, Rieger, Latty, & Bailey, 2004; Peterson, Janssen, & Laan, 2010). At first, researchers were inclined to trust the physiological responses, but later research found that women also produced similar responses to descriptions of violent rape (Suschinsky & Lalumière, 2011). Evidently vaginal secretions and blood flow to the genitals are not synonymous with sexual arousal for women, the way penis erections are for men. The researchers speculated that the physiological responses may be a defensive reaction to prepare a woman for sexual contact, regardless of whether it is voluntary.

concept check

20. **What are some ways in which men's sexuality differs from women's?**

Answer

20. Nearly all men identify their sexual orientation early and cannot imagine switching. Some women discover their orientation later, and a fair number have a consistent bisexual response or fluid interest. Measuring penis erections can accurately indicate a man's sexual interest, but physiological responses are not a dependable way to measure a woman's sexual interest.

Possible Influences on Sexual Orientation

Why are some people heterosexual and others homosexual? The available research suggests that genetic factors contribute to sexual orientation for both men and women. ▼ Figure 11.19 shows the results of studies concerning homosexuality in twins and other relatives of adult gays and lesbians (Bailey & Pillard, 1991; Bailey, Pillard, Neale, & Agyei, 1993). Note that homosexuality is more prevalent in their monozygotic (identical) twins than in their dizygotic (fraternal) twins. Later studies have shown results in the same direction, but not always to the same degree. That is, all the research indicates that genes do influence sexual orientation, but the magnitude

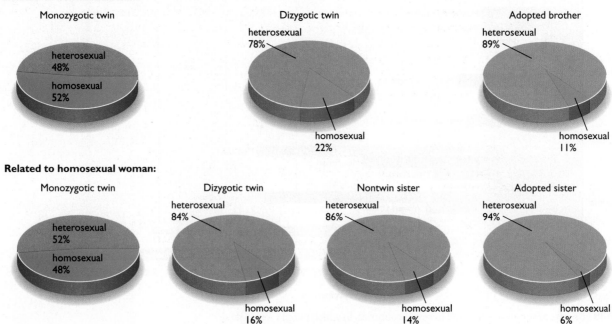

▲ Figure 11.19 The probability of a homosexual orientation is higher among monozygotic twins of adult homosexuals than among their dizygotic twins. The probability is higher among dizygotic twins than among adopted brothers or sisters who grew up together. These data suggest a genetic role in sexual orientation. (Based on results of Bailey & Pillard, 1991; Bailey, Pillard, Neale, & Agyei, 1993)

of that influence is uncertain (Bailey et al., 2016). Researchers who have compared the chromosomes of men varying in sexual orientation have located a few genes that differ on average between homosexual and heterosexual men, but their combined effect accounts for only a small portion of the variance (Ganna et al., 2019; Sanders et al., 2017). You could not look at someone's chromosomes and predict sexual orientation. Although the common genetic variants do not have a major effect, rare variants and epigenetic effects may be more important. The heritability appears to be higher for male than female sexual orientation.

The data on genetics raise an evolutionary question: How could a gene that increases homosexuality be widespread? Homosexual men have about one-fifth as many children as heterosexual men, and any gene that decreases the probability of reproducing will decline in prevalence. One hypothesis is that homosexual people who have no children of their own might help their brothers and sisters rear children, thus passing on some of their genes. Most gay men are not especially helpful to their relatives in the United States, although they are more helpful than average in Samoa (Bobrow & Bailey, 2001; Vasey & VanderLaan, 2010).

Another idea is that relatives of gay men may have larger than average families (Camperio-Ciani, Corna, & Capiluppi, 2004; Schwartz et al., 2010; Semenyna, Petterson, VanderLaan, & Vasey, 2017). A third possibility is that sexual orientation depends on epigenetics—activating or inactivating a gene rather than having a different gene (Rice, Friberg, & Gavrilets, 2012).

Another factor in sexual orientation is biological but not genetic: The probability of a homosexual orientation is slightly elevated among men who have an older brother. Having an older sister doesn't make a difference, nor does having an older adopted brother. It also doesn't make any difference whether the older brother lived in the same house with the younger brother or somewhere else. What matters is whether the mother had previously given birth to another son (Bogaert, 2006). A hypothesis to explain this tendency is that the first son sometimes causes the mother's immune system to build up antibodies that alter development of later sons (Bogaert, 2003).

Regardless of the role of genetics, prenatal environment, and everything else, the question arises of how the body differs. Adult hormone levels are *not* decisive. Most gays and lesbians have normal levels of testosterone and estradiol. Altering someone's hormone levels alters the strength of the sex drive but not sexual orientation (Tuiten et al., 2000). By analogy, changing your insulin or glucose levels affects your hunger but has little effect on what you consider good food.

However, it is possible that prenatal sex hormones influence later sexual orientation (McFadden, 2008). Presumably, if they do, they have some effect on the brain. One widely quoted and often misunderstood study reported a small but measurable difference between the brains of homosexual and heterosexual men. Let's examine the evidence.

what's the evidence?

Sexual Orientation and Brain Anatomy

Animal studies demonstrated that one section of the anterior hypothalamus is generally larger in males than in females. This brain area is necessary for male-typical sexual activity in many mammalian species, and its size depends on prenatal hormones. Might part of the anterior hypothalamus differ between homosexual and heterosexual men?

Hypothesis INAH3, a cluster of neurons in the anterior hypothalamus, will be larger on average in the brains of heterosexual than homosexual men or heterosexual women.

Method Simon LeVay (1991) examined the brains of 41 adults who died at ages 26 to 59. AIDS was the cause of death for all 19 of the homosexual men in the study, 6 of the 16 heterosexual men, and 1 of the 6 heterosexual women. No brains of homosexual women were available. LeVay measured the sizes of four clusters of neurons in the anterior hypothalamus, including two clusters for which sex differences are common and two that are the same between the sexes.

Results Three of the four neuron clusters did not consistently vary in size among the groups. However, area INAH3 was on the average about twice as large in heterosexual men as it was in homosexual men and about the same size in homosexual men as in heterosexual women. ▼ Figure 11.20 shows results for two representative individuals. The size of this area was about the same in heterosexual men who died of AIDS as in heterosexual men who died of other causes, so AIDS probably did not control the size of this area.

Interpretation These results suggest that the size of the INAH3 area may relate to heterosexual versus homosexual orientation, on average. Note, however, the variation within each group. The anatomy does not correlate perfectly with behavior.

Like most studies, this one has its limitations: We do not know whether the people that LeVay studied were typical of others. A later study found that the INAH3 of homosexual men was intermediate in size between that of heterosexual men and heterosexual women (Byne et al., 2001). That study extended our knowledge by finding that the INAH3 varied among people because of differences in the size of neurons, not the number of neurons.

A major limitation is that LeVay's study does not tell us whether brain anatomy influenced people's sexual orientation or whether their sexual activities altered brain anatomy. Extensive experience modifies brain anatomy, even in adults.

So where does the research leave us? The evidence points to both genetics and prenatal environment, which probably alter certain aspects of brain anatomy. However, we need to know far more about how these biological factors interact with experience. At this point, we don't even know what kinds of experience are most relevant.

Uncertainty and tentative conclusions are not unusual in psychology. If you decide to become a psychologist, you will need to get used to the words *maybe* and *probably*. Most researchers avoid the word *prove*. Results merely increase or decrease their confidence in a conclusion.

concept check

21. **Most studies find that gay men have approximately the same levels of testosterone in their blood as heterosexual men of the same age. Do such results conflict with the suggestion that prenatal hormonal conditions can predispose certain men to homosexuality?**

Answer

21. Not necessarily. The suggestion is that hormone levels can alter brain development at an early prenatal stage. The hormone could reach average levels later.

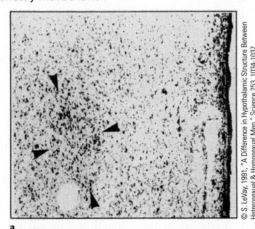

a

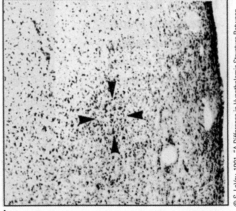

b

© S. LeVay, 1991. "A Difference in Hypothalamic Structure Between Heterosexual & Homosexual Men," Science 253, 1034–1037

▲ **Figure 11.20** One section of the anterior hypothalamus (marked by arrows) is larger on average in the brains of heterosexual men (**a**) than in the brains of homosexual men (**b**) or heterosexual women (LeVay, 1991). Review Figure 11.9 for the location of the hypothalamus.

The Biology and Sociology of Sex

Studies of sexual motivation remind us that important motives have multiple determinants, both biological and social. We engage in sexual activity because it feels good, and we evolved mechanisms that make it feel good because sex leads to reproduction. We also engage in sexual activity because it cements a relationship with another person. Sex is one of the most powerful ways of drawing people together or tearing a relationship apart.

Summary

- *Variability in human sexual behavior.* Although surveys differ in many regards, all of them agree that people vary greatly in their types and frequencies of sexual behavior. (page 356)
- *Age.* Although frequency declines with age, most people remain sexually active throughout life if they remain healthy and have a loving partner. (page 357)
- *Premarital sex.* In many countries the prevalence of premarital sex has increased over time, partly because of the growing gap between the onset of puberty and the average age of marriage. (page 358)
- *AIDS.* Acquired immune deficiency syndrome results from a virus that can result from sexual contact or from any other contact that lets the virus into someone's blood. (page 358)
- *Sexual arousal.* Masters and Johnson documented that sexual arousal proceeds through four stages: excitement, plateau, orgasm, and resolution. They also documented that female arousal depends on clitoral stimulation. (page 359)
- *Development of genitals.* In the early stages of development, the human fetus possesses anatomical structures that may develop into either male genitals (if testosterone levels are high enough) or female genitals (if testosterone levels are lower). (page 360)
- *Internal anatomy.* Both testosterone and estradiol modify anatomy of internal organs, including the brain. Few people have a male-typical or female-typical brain in all regards. (page 360)
- *Homosexuality.* The prevalence of homosexuality depends on how it is defined and measured. Sexual orientation varies in degree. (page 362)
- *Differences between men and women.* Bisexual orientation is more common in women than men. Measurements of penis erection accurately gauge a man's sexual interest, but physiological measurements do not accurately identify a woman's sexual interest. (page 362)
- *Origins of sexual orientation.* Genetic influences and prenatal environment affect sexual orientation. Homosexual and heterosexual people do not differ consistently in any one gene or in adult hormone levels. (page 363)

Key Terms

acquired immune deficiency syndrome (AIDS) (page 358)

bisexuality (page 362)

estradiol (page 360)

gender identity (page 361)

intersexes (page 361)

sexual orientation (page 362)

testosterone (page 360)

Review Questions

1. Under what condition can touching someone with AIDS spread the virus?
   - (a) Only if both people are male or both are female
   - (b) Only if both have open wounds that exchange blood
   - (c) Only if one of them is a drug user
   - (d) Only if they maintain contact for more than 5 seconds

2. If someone's brain is male-typical in one way and female-typical in another, which of the following is a likely explanation?
   - (a) The X and Y chromosomes control different brain areas.
   - (b) Brain areas differentiate based on the ratio of testosterone to estradiol.
   - (c) Brain areas differentiate at different times, controlled by different chemicals.
   - (d) The person is probably an intersex.

3. Which of the following results in a child with an "intersex" appearance of the genitals?
   - (a) Exposure of a female fetus to higher than average levels of testosterone
   - (b) Exposure of a male fetus to higher than average levels of estradiol
   - (c) Absence of the Y chromosome
   - (d) Stressful experiences to the mother during pregnancy

4. In which of these ways do women differ from men, on average?
   (a) Women identify their sexual orientation earlier in life.
   (b) Women show clearer physiological indications of sexual interest.
   (c) Women are more likely to remain sexually active in old age.
   (d) Women are more likely to be bisexual or fluid in their orientation.

5. What is known about the genetics of sexual orientation?
   (a) A gene on the X chromosome is primarily responsible for sexual orientation.
   (b) Sexual orientation depends on two genes, both of them recessive.

   (c) No common gene produces a large effect on sexual orientation.
   (d) Sexual orientation is unrelated to genetics.

6. In which of these ways do male homosexuals differ, on average, from male heterosexuals?
   (a) Concentration of testosterone in the blood and brain
   (b) Concentration of estradiol in the blood and brain
   (c) Anatomy of one part of the hypothalamus
   (d) Number of older sisters

Answers: 1b, 2c, 3a, 4d, 5c, 6c.

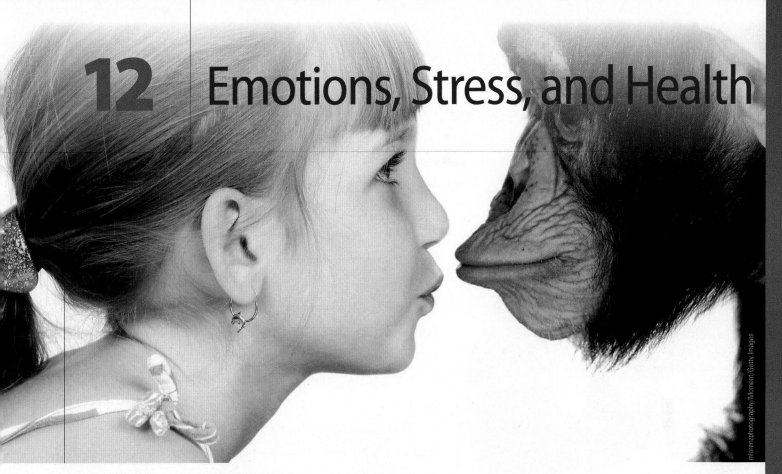

12 Emotions, Stress, and Health

Getty Images/Hulton Archive/Getty Images

Would you make more intelligent decisions if you could suppress your emotions, like the fictional character Spock? After brain damage that impairs emotion, people make worse than average decisions.

Suppose your romantic partner asks, "How much do you love me?" You reply, "Oh, compared to other loving couples, probably about average." "What?" your partner screams. "Average! Did you say *average*?" You are in deep trouble, even though your answer was probably true. It is for most people. That's what "average" means.

If that was the wrong answer, what would be better? "Forty-two cubic meters per second"? No, we don't measure love in physical units. So instead, you say, "I love you more than you can possibly imagine. More than any other person has ever loved." That was a good answer, and your partner is happy, even though the answer is almost certainly false. You get away with that answer because there is no way to check whether it is true.

When we are talking about emotions, measurement is a serious problem. Psychological researchers make satisfactory measurements of sensation, perception, learning, memory, and cognition. With regard to emotion, social behavior, and personality, the measurements become less reliable, and consequently, the progress has been slower. In this chapter, we consider what psychologists have learned about emotions despite the difficulties.

module 12.1

The Nature of Emotion

After studying this module, you should be able to:

1. Describe methods of measuring emotions, including the strengths and weaknesses of each method.

2. Evaluate the James-Lange theory of emotions, and the evidence relating to it.

3. Evaluate the Schachter and Singer theory, and the evidence relating to it.

4. Discuss whether it makes sense to distinguish a few "basic" emotions.

5. Describe an alternative to the idea of basic emotions.

6. Discuss the role of emotions in moral reasoning.

7. Define emotional intelligence and describe evidence relating to it.

Imagine trying to list all the emotions you feel during a day. You might include frightened, angry, sad, joyful, disgusted, worried, bored, ashamed, frustrated, awed, contemptuous, embarrassed, surprised, proud, and confused. But which of those states are really emotions? And how many are *different* emotions instead of overlapping or synonymous conditions?

Defining the term *emotion* is difficult. Psychologists usually define it in terms of a combination of cognitions, physiology, feelings, and actions (Keltner & Shiota, 2003; Plutchik, 1982). For example, you might have the *cognition* "he was unfair to me," *physiological* changes that include increased heart rate, a *feeling* you call anger, and *behaviors* such as a clenched fist. However, that definition implies that cognitions, physiology, feelings, and actions always occur together. Do they? Or might you sometimes feel frightened without knowing why, or experience anger without taking any action?

In fact, it is debatable whether emotion is a natural category at all. Lisa Feldman Barrett (2012) has argued that emotions are a category that we find useful, but only in the same way that we find "weeds" to be a useful category. Nature does not distinguish between emotions and motivations any more than between flowers and weeds.

Measuring Emotions

Research progress depends on good measurement. Psychologists measure emotions by self-reports, behavioral observations, and physiological measures. Each method has its strengths and weaknesses.

Self-Reports

Psychologists most often measure emotions by asking people how happy they are, how nervous, and so forth. Self-reports are quick and easy, but their accuracy is limited. If you rated your happiness 4 yesterday and 7 today, it seems clear that you have become happier. But if you rate your happiness 7 and your friend rates her happiness 6, are you happier than she is? Maybe, maybe not.

Behavioral Observations

We infer emotion from people's behavior and its context. If we see someone shriek and run away, we infer fear. When you were an infant, your parents must have inferred your emotions before you could report them verbally. They had to, in order to teach you the words for emotions! At some point, you screamed, and someone said you were "afraid." At another time, you smiled, and someone said you were "happy." Behavioral observations are often a better indicator than self-reports are. If you see someone making a fist, screaming, and frowning, while insisting, "I'm not angry," which do you believe, the observations or the words?

Observing the face is sometimes helpful. People control many expressions voluntarily, but *sudden, brief emotional expressions*, called microexpressions, are harder to control. For example, someone who is pretending to be calm or happy may show occasional brief signs of anger, fear, or sadness (Ekman, 2001). With practice, or a videotape that can be played slowly, psychologists infer emotions that people would like to hide. Still, it is an uncertain inference, as people's expressions do not always match what they feel.

Saeed Khan/AFP/Getty Images

Ordinarily, an emotional state elicits a tendency toward vigorous action, even if we suppress that tendency. Here, a soldier disarms a mine.

Physiological Measures

Originally, the term *emotion* referred to turbulent motion. Centuries ago, people described thunder as an "emotion of the atmosphere." Eventually, people limited the term to body motions and their associated feelings, but the idea still includes turbulent arousal.

Any stimulus that arouses emotion alters the activity of the autonomic nervous system, *the section of the nervous system that controls the organs* such as the heart and intestines. (See Figure 3.25.) The autonomic nervous system consists of the sympathetic and the parasympathetic nervous systems. *Chains of neuron clusters just to the left and right of the spinal cord* comprise the sympathetic nervous system, *which arouses the body for vigorous action*. It is often called the "fight-or-flight" system because it increases heart rate, breathing rate, sweating, and flow of epinephrine (EP-i-NEF-rin; also known as adrenaline), thereby preparing the body for vigorous activity.

The parasympathetic nervous system consists of *neurons whose axons extend from the medulla and the lower part of the spinal cord to neuron clusters near the organs. The parasympathetic nervous system decreases the heart rate and promotes digestion and other nonemergency functions.* Both the sympathetic and parasympathetic systems send axons to the heart, the digestive system, and most other organs. The adrenal gland, sweat glands, and muscles controlling blood vessels and "goosebumps" receive only sympathetic input.

Both systems are constantly active, although one system can temporarily dominate. If you spot danger at a distance (in either time or space), you pay attention to it with mainly parasympathetic activity. If the danger is close enough to require action, you shift to vigorous sympathetic activity (Löw, Lang, Smith, & Bradley, 2008). Many situations activate parts of both systems (Berntson, Cacioppo, & Quigley, 1993). For example, some emergency situations increase your heart rate and sweating (sympathetic responses) and also promote bowel and bladder evacuation (parasympathetic responses). Have you ever been so frightened that you thought you might lose your bladder control?

To measure emotion, researchers measure sympathetic nervous system arousal as indicated by heart rate, breathing rate, or momentary changes in the electrical conductivity across the skin. However, remember that the sympathetic nervous system is the fight-*or*-flight system, so its responses could indicate anger, fear, or any other intense emotion, as well as nonemotional influences such as exercise. Physiological measurements never tell us *which* emotion someone is feeling.

concept check

1. **Some theorists insist that we can discuss emotions only for humans because animals cannot tell us about their emotions. How might you argue against that position?**

Answer

1. We infer young children's emotions before they know the words to describe them. They could not learn the proper words if we did not infer the emotions directly from behavior. That is, we do not need self-reports to infer emotion.

Emotion, Arousal, and Action

How do emotional cognitions, feelings, behavior, and arousal relate to one another? William James, the founder of American psychology, proposed one of psychology's first theories.

The James-Lange Theory of Emotions

According to common sense, you feel sad and therefore you cry. You become afraid and therefore you tremble. You feel angry and therefore your face turns

The sympathetic nervous system prepares the body for a vigorous burst of activity.

red and you make a fist. In 1884 William James and Carl Lange independently proposed the opposite. According to the James-Lange theory, *your interpretation of a stimulus evokes autonomic changes and sometimes muscle actions. Your perception of those changes is the feeling aspect of your emotion.* In James's original article, he said simply that the situation (e.g., the sight of a bear) gives rise to an action (e.g., running away), and your perception of the action is the emotion. That is, you don't run away because you are afraid; you feel afraid because you perceive yourself running away. In response to his critics, he clarified his view (James, 1894): Obviously, the sight of a bear doesn't automatically cause you to run away. You first appraise the situation. If it is a caged bear, you do not run. If it appears dangerous, you do run. (Of course, it is stupid to try to outrun a bear, but you get the point.) Your appraisal of the situation is the cognitive aspect of the emotion. Your perception of your reaction is what you *feel* as the emotion. That perception includes your muscle reactions (running away), but also your autonomic reactions (heart rate, breathing, and so forth), and your facial expression. That is,

Situation →   **Appraisal →**   **Actions →**   **Perception of the actions**
           = cognitive   = physiological   = feeling aspect
           aspect of the   and behavioral   of the emotion
           emotion   aspects

Evaluation of this theory depends on two types of investigation: Do decreases in body reaction decrease emotional feelings? Do increases in body reaction increase emotional feelings?

Decreased Body Reaction

According to the James-Lange theory, people with weak physiological responses can still identify emotional situations cognitively, but they should have little emotional feeling. People with paralyzed muscles because of spinal cord injuries report normal or nearly normal emotions (Cobos, Sánchez, García, Vera, & Vila, 2002; Deady, North, Allan, Smith, & O'Carroll, 2010). However, they continue to feel changes in autonomic responses, such as heart rate, as well as movements in facial muscles. So, running away is not necessary for feeling fear, but other types of sensation may be.

What about people with weakened autonomic responses? In people with pure autonomic failure, *the autonomic nervous system stops regulating the organs.* That is, nothing in the nervous system influences heart rate, breathing rate, and so forth. One effect is that someone who stands up quickly faints because none of the usual reflexes kick in to prevent gravity from drawing blood from the head. With regard to emotions, affected people still recognize situations that call for anger, fear, or sadness, but they report that their emotions feel less intense than before (Critchley, Mathias, & Dolan, 2001). The cognitive aspect of emotion remains, but the feeling is weak, as the James-Lange theory predicts.

Further evidence comes from a study of people with BOTOX (botulinum toxin) injections that temporarily paralyzed all their facial muscles. Because they were unable to smile or frown, they reported weaker than usual emotional feelings while watching short videos (Davis, Senghas, Brandt, & Ochsner, 2010).

Increased Body Reaction

Suppose researchers mold your posture and breathing pattern into the pattern typical of an emotion. Will you then feel that emotion? Have someone read these instructions to you, or read them to someone else and check what happens:

Lower your eyebrows toward your cheeks. Sigh. Close your mouth and push your lower lip slightly upward. Sigh again. Sit back in your chair and draw your feet under the chair. Be sure you feel no tension in your legs or feet. Sigh again. Fold your hands in your lap, cupping one in the other. Drop your head, letting your rib cage fall, letting most of your body go limp, except for a little tension in the back of your neck and across your shoulder blades. Sigh again.

Most people who follow these directions report starting to feel sad (Flack, Laird, & Cavallaro, 1999; Philippot, Chapelle, & Blairy, 2002). Instructions to hold the posture and breathing pattern characteristic of happiness, anger, or fear tend to induce those emotions, too, although the instructions for fear sometimes induce anger and those for anger sometimes induce fear.

Does smiling make you happy, and does frowning make you unhappy? Researchers have used many ways to mold people's faces without actually saying "smile" or "frown." Then they took measures of the emotional experience. A review of 138 studies concluded that, yes, your facial movements can change your mood, a little. It is not a big effect, but the fact that it does occur (on average) is theoretically interesting, and supports the James-Lange approach (Coles, Larsen, & Lench, 2019). But don't overestimate the effect. Telling a depressed person to smile and cheer up will be irritating, not helpful.

More than a century after its proposal, the James-Lange theory remains controversial (Moors, 2009). Part of the resistance to the theory depends on misunderstandings, as Laird and Lacasse (2014) have argued. Disagreement also hinges on what we mean by "emotional feeling." William James meant emotional feeling as a sensation, and in fact it is hard to imagine where an emotional sensation could come from, other than from reactions of the body. Those who disagree with his theory seem to mean feeling in the sense of the whole experience of the emotion, including more cognitive aspects.

concept check

2. **According to the James-Lange theory, what should we predict about the emotions of people who have stronger than average reactions of their autonomic nervous system?**

Answer

2. People with stronger autonomic reactions should report more intense emotional experiences. For example, panic disorder relates to sudden strong reactions of heart rate and breathing rate.

Cognitive appraisal of the situation: This calls for fear.

Perception of autonomic responses: My heart is beating fast and I'm breathing hard. My fear must be intense.

▲ **Figure 12.1** According to Schachter and Singer's theory, physiological arousal determines the intensity of an emotion, but a cognitive appraisal determines which emotion one feels.

Schachter and Singer's Theory of Emotions

To assess your own emotion, you consider whether you feel angry, frightened, happy, or whatever, and how strongly you feel that way. Stanley Schachter and Jerome Singer (1962) proposed that different processes determine those two judgments. According to **Schachter and Singer's theory of emotions** (see ▲ Figure 12.1), *the intensity of the physiological state—that is, the response of the autonomic nervous system—determines the intensity of the emotion, but a cognitive appraisal of the situation identifies the type of emotion.* For example, when you feel your heart pounding, you might experience it as anger in one situation, fear in another, or overwhelming joy in still another. Schachter and Singer (1962) offered a demonstration in what became a famous study. Let's examine it in some detail.

what's the evidence?

The Cognitive Aspect of Emotion

Hypothesis A drug that increases arousal enhances whatever emotion a situation arouses, but the type of emotion depends on the situation.

Method The experimenters put college students in two situations and gave some of them injections of epinephrine to induce comparable, high levels of physiological arousal. (Epinephrine mimics the effects of the sympathetic nervous system.) They gave instructions to try to influence some participants to attribute their arousal to the situation and others to attribute it to the injection.

Specifically, the experimenters told certain participants that the injections would produce no important side effects. These participants would presumably notice their arousal and attribute it to the situation, feeling intense emotions. Others were told to expect side effects such as increased heart rate and butterflies in the stomach. When they felt the changes, they would presumably attribute them to the injections and not to emotional experiences. Additional participants were given either set of instructions but injected with a placebo instead of epinephrine.

Participants were then placed in situations to elicit euphoria or anger. Each student in the euphoria situation waited in a room with a playful young man who flipped paper wads into a trash can, sailed paper airplanes, built a tower with manila folders, shot paper wads at the tower with a rubber band, played with a hula hoop, and tried to get the other student to join his play. Each participant in the anger situation was asked to answer a questionnaire full of insulting items such as these:

Which member of your immediate family does not bathe or wash regularly?
With how many men (other than your father) has your mother had extramarital relationships?

4 or fewer   5–9   10 or more

Results Many students in the euphoria situation joined the playful partner (see ▼ Figure 12.2). One jumped up and down on the desk, and another opened a window and threw paper wads at passersby. The anger situation was less effective than expected, although a few students muttered angry comments or refused to complete the questionnaire.

Recall that some of the participants had been informed beforehand that the injections would produce certain autonomic effects. No matter which situation they were in, they showed only slight emotional responses. When they felt themselves sweating and their hands trembling, they said to themselves, "Aha! I'm getting the side effects, just as they said I would."

Interpretation Unfortunately, this experiment has problems that limit the conclusions. Recall that some participants were injected with a placebo instead of epinephrine. These participants showed about as much euphoria in the euphoria situation and as much anger in the anger situation as did the participants injected with epinephrine. Therefore, the epinephrine injections apparently had nothing to do with the results. If so, we are left with this summary of the results: People in a situation designed to induce euphoria act happy, and those in an anger situation act angry (Plutchik & Ax, 1967). Nevertheless, if they attribute their arousal to an injection, their response is more restrained.

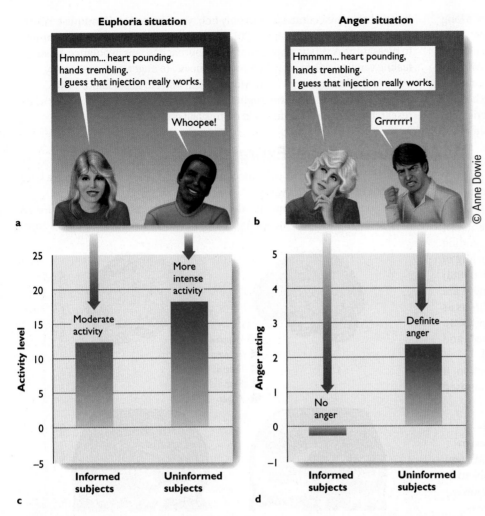

Euphoria situation

Hmmmm... heart pounding, hands trembling. I guess that injection really works.

Whoopee!

25
20
15
10
5
0
−5

Activity level

Moderate activity

More intense activity

a

c

Informed subjects

Uninformed subjects

Anger situation

Hmmmm... heart pounding, hands trembling. I guess that injection really works.

Grrrrrrr!

5
4
3
2
1
0
−1

Anger rating

No anger

Definite anger

b

d

Informed subjects

Uninformed subjects

© Anne Dowie

▲ **Figure 12.2** In Schachter and Singer's experiment, people who were uninformed about the effects of epinephrine reported strong emotions appropriate to the situation. People who were informed about the effects of epinephrine reported less intense emotions.

Despite the limitations of Schachter and Singer's experiment, the idea behind it is reasonable, and other research since then has supported it in many, though not all, cases (Reisenzein, 1983). That idea, to reiterate, is that feeling more highly aroused increases the intensity of your emotion, but you evaluate the situation to determine which emotion you feel. Still, some research results have been difficult to interpret. Consider this example: A young woman interviewed young men, either on a wide, sturdy bridge, or on the wobbly Capilano Canyon suspension bridge (see ◄ Figure 12.3). After the interview, she gave each man a card with her phone number in case he wanted to ask further questions about the study. Of those interviewed on the suspension bridge, 39 percent called her, as opposed to 9 percent from the sturdy, low bridge (Dutton & Aron, 1974). The interpretation was that men on the suspension bridge experienced high arousal from the situation and attributed it to the woman. ("Wow, what an exciting woman! My heart is racing!") There is, however, a problem. Might the woman herself have been more excited on the suspension bridge? Maybe the men were responding to her excitement, not just their own. You can begin to perceive the difficulty of research on emotion.

Chris Cheadle/All Canada Photos/Getty Images

▲ **Figure 12.3** How much excitement might you feel while crossing the Capilano Canyon suspension bridge? If you met an attractive person on this bridge, might you think that person was exciting?

3. You are going on a date and you hope this person will find you exciting. According to Schachter and Singer's theory, should you plan a date walking through an art gallery or riding on roller coasters?

Answer

3. You should plan a date riding on roller coasters, hoping that your date will attribute the arousal to you. (This strategy can backfire if your date gets nauseated on roller coasters!)

Do We Have a Few "Basic" Emotions?

How many emotions do humans experience? Do we have a few "basic" emotions that combine to form other experiences, analogous to the elements of chemistry? Or does one emotion blend into another, with no sharp boundaries? This controversy has a long history. Charles Darwin (1872/1965), noting that a few of the same facial expressions occur in other cultures, favored the idea of a few basic emotions. Wilhelm Wundt, who started the first psychology laboratory, and William James, founder of American psychology, both argued against the idea of distinct categories.

Some psychologists have proposed a short list of emotions, such as happiness, sadness, anger, fear, disgust, and surprise. Others add more candidates, such as contempt, shame, guilt, interest, hope, pride, relief, frustration, love, awe, boredom, jealousy, regret, or embarrassment (Keltner & Buswell, 1997). Japanese people include *amae*, translated as "the pleasant feeling of depending on someone else," also described as "the feeling of comfort in another person's acceptance" (Doi, 1981; Niiya, Ellsworth, & Yamaguchi, 2006). Japanese are also more likely than Americans to list loneliness as an emotion (Kobayashi, Schallert, & Ogren 2003). Hindus include heroism, amusement, peace, and wonder (Hejmadi, Davidson, & Rozin, 2000).

How can we decide what is a basic emotion, if there is such a thing? Psychologists have proposed the following criteria:

- Basic emotions should emerge early in life without requiring much experience. For example, nostalgia and pride emerge slowly and seem less basic than fear, anger, or joy. The problem with this criterion is that all emotional expressions emerge gradually. Infants' facial movements at first do not distinguish among distress, anger, and fear (Messinger, 2002).
- Basic emotions should be similar across cultures. Most psychologists agree that people throughout the world experience happiness, sadness, fear, anger, and so forth, but disagreement continues about whether the experiences fit distinct categories or blend into one another.
- Each basic emotion should have a distinct physiology. If we take this criterion seriously, we should abandon the idea of basic emotions. Physiological reactions such as heart rate and breathing rate do not distinguish between one emotion and another, and for a given emotion, such as fear or anger, autonomic responses vary from one instance to another (Siegel et al., 2018). Brain measurements also fail to identify which emotion someone feels. ▶ Figure 12.4 summarizes the results of many studies using PET and fMRI brain scans to measure brain activity when different emotions were aroused in various ways (Phan, Wager, Taylor, & Liberzon, 2002). As you can see, the areas aroused by any emotion largely overlap those aroused by other emotions. A thorough review of the literature concluded that no brain area is devoted exclusively to emotion, and

that no brain area contributes to only one type of emotion (Lindquist, Wager, Kober, Bliss-Moreau, & Barrett, 2012). A brain area might contribute mainly to pleasantness versus unpleasantness, approach versus avoidance, or strong feeling versus weak feeling, but not specifically to anger, sadness, or any other named category (Wilson-Mendenhall, Barrett, & Barsalou, 2013).

- Finally, each basic emotion might have its own facial expression. Most of the research and debate has focused on this last criterion.

Producing Facial Expressions

Does each emotion have its own special expression? And why do we have facial expressions of emotion anyway?

Emotional expressions are not altogether arbitrary, as shown in ▼ Figure 12.5. When you are frightened, you open your eyes wide, increasing your ability to see

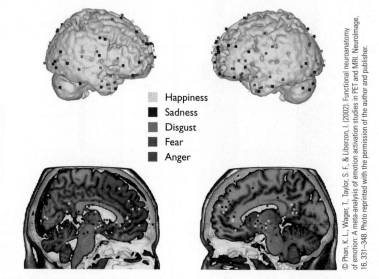

Happiness
Sadness
Disgust
Fear
Anger

© Phan, K. L., Wager, T., Taylor, S. F., & Liberzon, I. (2002). Functional neuroanatomy of emotion: A meta-analysis of emotion activation studies in PET and fMRI. NeuroImage, 16, 331–348. Photo reprinted with the permission of the author and publisher.

▲ **Figure 12.4** Researchers aroused emotions in various ways and then used positron emission tomography (PET) or functional magnetic resonance imaging (fMRI) scans to identify which brain areas became aroused. No brain area appears specific to one type of emotion. (Source: Phan, Wager, Taylor, & Liberzon, 2002)

Rainer Elstermann/The Image Bank/Getty Images

Digital Vision/Alamy Stock Photo

▲ **Figure 12.5** A disgust expression (left) decreases your exposure to something foul. A fear expression (right) increases your readiness to see dangers and take necessary actions.

▲ **Figure 12.6** Even children born deaf and blind show some of the typical facial expressions of emotion, including laughter.

and locate dangers, and you inhale deeply, preparing for possible action. If you see something disgusting, you partly close your eyes and turn your nose away from the offending object, decreasing your exposure to it (Susskind et al., 2008).

Emotional expressions are adapted for communication. Olympic medal winners generally smile when receiving the award publicly, or when they are waiting for the ceremony with others, but not if they are waiting alone (Fernández-Dols & Ruiz-Belda, 1997). Even 10-month-old infants smile more when their mothers are watching than when they are not (Jones, Collins, & Hong, 1991). Robert Provine (2000) spent many hours in shopping malls and elsewhere recording and observing laughter. He found that people laughed when they were with friends, but only rarely when they were alone.

Do we learn to make appropriate facial expressions, or are they part of our biological heritage? Irenäus Eibl-Eibesfeldt (1973, 1974) photographed people in various world cultures, documenting smiling, frowning, laughing, and crying, even in children who were born deaf and blind (see ▲ Figure 12.6). He also found that people in many societies make a friendly greeting by briefly raising their eyebrows (see ▶ Figure 12.7). The mean duration of that expression is one-third of a second in every society he examined. And so, at least a limited amount of similarity of expressions does occur across cultures. But questions remain: Does frowning or any other facial movement always mean the same thing? Do expressions fall into a limited number of discrete categories, corresponding to emotions that we can name?

Understanding Facial Expressions

To test the idea that humans have a few basic emotions, researchers asked people in several cultures to interpret six facial expressions like those in ▼ Figure 12.8. Look at each face and try to name the associated emotion. (Please try now.)

After researchers translated the labels into other languages, people in other cultures also identified them, though less accurately (Ekman, 1992; Ekman & Friesen, 1984; Russell, 1994). Cultural differences do occur. When Japanese and American people examined photos of Japanese faces for anger and disgust, 82 percent of the Japanese recognized the anger and 66 percent recognized the disgust, but only 34 percent of the Americans recognized the anger and 18 percent recognized disgust (Dailey et al., 2010).

▲ **Figure 12.7** In many cultures, people raise their eyebrows as a friendly greeting, indicating "I am glad to see you." The usual duration of the expression is one-third of a second, in all known cultures.

Because of the research method, the ability of people throughout the world to classify facial expressions into six categories is not strong evidence for the idea of basic emotions (Barrett, Mesquita, & Gendron, 2011; DiGirolamo & Russell, 2017). The usual procedure has been to list six emotion names and ask which face goes with which label. Obviously, if you can identify five of them, you get the sixth one also by process of elimination. In fact, even if you know just one or two for sure, you increase your chance of guessing other ones. If we change the procedure and simply ask people to say what each expression means, without any suggestions, people generally identify smiles as happy (or "laughing" or something similar). They show a little less agreement about angry, frightened, and sad expressions, and still less about disgust and surprise (Pochedly, Widen, & Russell, 2012; Widen & Naab, 2012). Agreement is even less for people from other cultures (Crivelli, Russell, Jarillo, & Fernández-Dols, 2017; Gendron, Crivelli, & Barrett, 2018; Gendron, Roberson, van der Vyver, & Barrett, 2014).

Facial expressions vary by context, and they do not invariably indicate someone's emotional state

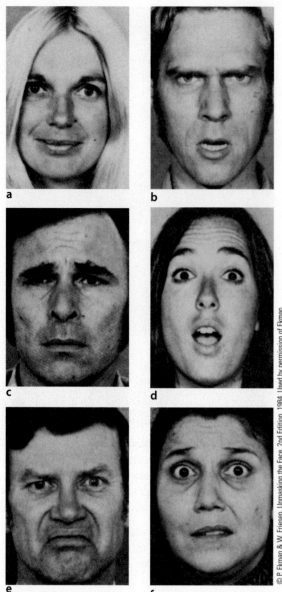

a

b

c

d

e

f

▲ **Figure 12.8** Paul Ekman has used these faces in experiments testing people's ability to recognize emotional expressions. Can you identify them? Check answer A on page 383. (From Ekman & Friesen, 1984)

© P. Ekman & W. Friesen, Unmasking the Face, 2nd Edition, 1984. Used by permission of Ekman.

From Angry, disgusted, or afraid? by Aviezer, H., Hassin, R. R., Ryan, J., Grady, C., Susskind, J., Anderson, A., et al (2008). Psychological Science, 19, 724–732.

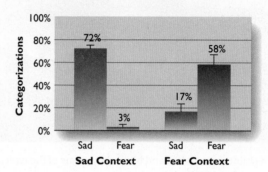

▲ **Figure 12.9** The same facial expression can look sad or frightened depending on someone's posture. (Source: Aviezer et al., 2008)

Halberstadt, & Shuster, 2018). Consider ▲ **Figure 12.9**. Out of context, most people would call the expression sadness. The posture on the left confirms that judgment. However, given the posture on the right, most people call the expression fear (Aviezer et al., 2008).

Another issue: The faces in Figure 12.8 are all posed looking at the viewer. From the standpoint of experimental design, putting all the faces in the same position seems right, but sad people almost always look down, not straight ahead. Frightened people stare at what frightens them. They make eye contact with you only if they are afraid of *you*. Examine the photos in ▼ **Figure 12.10**. Which expression is easier to identify? Most observers identify sad or frightened expressions faster when they see someone looking away (Adams & Kleck, 2003). In contrast, happy and angry expressions are easier to identify if the person is looking directly forward (Adams & Kleck, 2005).

Sad people not only look down, but also they cry. If you see someone with a sad face and tears, you immediately identify the

try it *your self*

(Barrett, Adolphs, Marsella, Martinez, & Pollak, 2019). People don't always smile when they are happy, and they sometimes smile without being happy. The same is true for other expressions. We infer someone's emotion from a combination of context, posture, touch, tone of voice, and gestures, and sometimes even smell, usually not by facial expression alone (de Groot, Semin, & Smeets, 2014; Edwards, 1998; Hertenstein, Keltner, App, Bulleit, & Jaskolka, 2006; Leppänen & Hietanen, 2003; Parkinson, Walker, Memmi, & Wheatley, 2017; Zhou & Chen, 2009). In fact, we often rely mainly on posture and body movements more than face (Abramson, Marom, Petranker, & Aviezer, 2017; Castro, Camras,

Fear

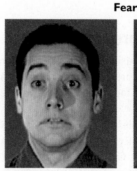

a Direct gaze   **b** Averted gaze

© Reginald B. Adams, Jr.

▲ **Figure 12.10** Most people identify fearful expressions more easily when the person is looking away.

expression as sadness, as in ▶ Figure 12.11. Take away the tears, and you might describe the same expression as awe, puzzlement, or concern (Provine, Krosnowski, & Brocato, 2009).

4. Why are people better at recognizing emotions in real life than when looking at a photograph of a facial expression?

Answer

4. In everyday life, we have other cues, including gestures, posture, tone of voice, and context.

Do Facial Expressions Indicate Basic Emotions?

Does emotion consist of a few basic and distinct categories, such as fear and anger? In everyday life, most expressions show a mixture of emotions. If we take photographs of spontaneous everyday expressions, observers often disagree with one another, they see more than one emotion in each face, and what they see doesn't always agree with what the person in the photograph was actually experiencing (Castro et al., 2018; Kayyal & Russell, 2013).

Furthermore, the ability of people to recognize expressions of six emotions could not tell us whether people have precisely six basic emotions. People can, with a little less accuracy, also identify expressions of contempt or pride (Tracy & Robins, 2004; Tracy, Robins, & Lagattuta, 2005). We also identify the facial expressions of sleepiness and confusion, although we probably would not classify sleep as an emotion and we would hesitate about confusion (Keltner & Shiota, 2003; Rozin & Cohen, 2003). Is surprise an emotion? Opinions differ. The fact that we can identify a facial expression for surprise does not mean it is an emotion, because we also identify a facial expression for sleepiness.

5. Why is the ability to recognize the facial expressions of six emotions not convincing evidence that these are basic emotions?

Answer

5. The apparent recognition of six expressions is inflated by use of a matching procedure. Most everyday expressions do not fit neatly into any of those six categories. We can also identify additional states, such as contempt and pride. Also, we can identify facial expressions of other conditions that may or may not be emotions.

An Alternative to Basic Emotions

Many psychologists doubt that it makes sense to talk about basic emotions (Barrett, 2006). Instead, we might regard emotion as a series of dimensions. According to the **circumplex model**, emotions range on a continuum from pleasure to misery and along another continuum from arousal to sleepiness (Russell, 1980). ▶ Figure 12.12 shows this idea. Note that this model deals with the feeling aspect of emotion, not the cognitive aspects. For example, both anger and fear would fit near "distress" on this graph, even though we associate anger and fear with different cognitions. Other psychologists have proposed different descriptions but maintain the idea that emotions range along continuous dimensions (Watson, Wiese, Vaidya, & Tellegen, 1999; Yik, Russell, & Steiger, 2011).

▲ **Figure 12.11** If you cover the tear with your finger, this face looks less sad. If you color the whites of the eyes slightly reddish, the face looks sadder.

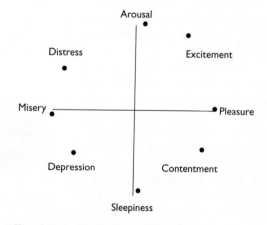

▲ **Figure 12.12** According to the circumplex model of emotion, emotional feelings occur along a continuum of arousal and another continuum of pleasure. (Figure 1 from "A circumplex model of affect," by J. A. Russell, 1980. *Journal of Personality and Social Psychology, 39,* pp. 1161–1178.)

6. What is the alternative to the concept of basic emotions?

Usefulness of Emotions

Presumably, emotions must be useful, or we would not have evolved the capacity to feel them. One function is that emotions focus our attention on important information. Images that evoke strong emotions grab your attention, even if you are trying to pay attention to something else (Kuhn, Pickering, & Cole, 2016; Schupp et al., 2007; Yoon, Hong, Joormann, & Kang, 2009). People who are prone to anxiety are especially likely to pay attention to something related to fear (Doty, Japee, Ingvar, & Ungerleider, 2013).

Emotions or moods adjust our priorities. If you are running away from an attacker, you don't stop to smell the roses. When you are in a happy mood, you expand your focus. According to Barbara Fredrickson's (2001) broaden-and-build hypothesis of positive emotions, *a happy mood increases your readiness to explore new ideas and opportunities.* You think creatively, notice the details in the background that you ordinarily overlook, and increase your pursuit of new experiences that will help maintain your happy mood (Fredrickson & Losada, 2005). That tendency relates to the fact that happiness is usually a low-intensity emotion. Intense emotions of any type tend to narrow your focus of attention (Gable & Harmon-Jones, 2010).

Although major depression impairs reasoning, a mildly sad mood aids reasoning under some conditions. Most people, especially happy people, overestimate their own abilities and underestimate how long a task will take. Sad people tend to be less optimistic, and therefore sometimes more realistic. They become more skeptical, and they usually examine the information in detail before making a decision (Forgas, 2019). In one study, students listened to a weaker and a stronger argument concerning possible increases in student fees at their university. Students

in a sad mood were more persuaded by the stronger argument, whereas students in a happy mood found both arguments about equally persuasive (Bless, Bohner, Schwarz, & Strack, 1990).

Emotions and Moral Reasoning

People sometimes advise us not to let our emotions get in the way of our decisions. Emotions do sometimes impair decisions, but often they provide a guide when we have to make a quick decision about right and wrong (Beer, Knight, & D'Esposito, 2006). Let's begin with two famous moral dilemmas:

The Trolley Dilemma. A trolley car with defective brakes is coasting downhill toward five people lying on the tracks. You could throw a switch to divert the trolley onto a different track, where one person is lying. If you flip the switch, the trolley will kill one instead of five. Should you do it?

The Footbridge Dilemma. Another trolley with defective brakes is coasting downhill and about to kill five people. This time you are standing on a footbridge over the track. You see a way to save those five people: A fat man is beside you, leaning over. If you push him off the bridge, he will land on the track and block the trolley. (You are, let's assume, too thin to block it yourself.) Again, your action would kill one to save five. Should you do it? (See ▼ Figure 12.13.)

Most people say "yes" to flipping the switch in the first dilemma, although they might find it difficult. We hesitate to do something that harms someone, even when failing to act harms a greater number (DeScioli, Christner, & Kurzban, 2011; Miller, Hannikainen, & Cushman, 2014). Fewer people say they would push someone off the bridge in the second dilemma (Greene, Sommerville, Nystrom, Darley, & Cohen, 2001). Logically, the answers might be the same because the act kills one person to save five, although the situations are not quite comparable.

▲ **Figure 12.13** (a) Should you flip a switch so the trolley goes down a track with one person instead of five? (b) Should you push a fat person off a bridge to save five people?

Can you be sure that pushing the man off the bridge would save five? What if you pushed him but the trolley killed the others anyway? Or what if they got out of the way, so that killing him was unnecessary? Still, even if you were fully confident that pushing someone off a bridge would save five others, it would be emotionally repulsive.

After people make moral decisions in cases like these, they often have trouble stating a reason for their decisions. They make a quick, emotional decision and then look for an explanation afterward (Haidt, 2001). Emotional guidance usually works for moral decisions. As a rule, pushing someone off a bridge is a horrendously bad idea. Your emotional reaction is a quick guide to making a decision that is almost always right, even if it might not be in this rare instance.

What would you do in these dilemmas? Are you sure? Students were asked whether they would flip a switch to deliver a painful shock to one mouse to prevent the same shock to five mice. Then they were put in the actual situation and had to choose. (They thought they controlled real shocks, but actually the mice were safe.) Many students flipped the switch who had said they would not (Bostyn, Sevenhant, & Roets, 2018). Be cautious about predicting what you would do in some situation you have never faced. You might be wrong.

Decisions by People with Impaired Emotions

Antonio Damasio (1994) described patients who suffered impoverished or inappropriate emotions following brain damage. One was the famous patient Phineas Gage, who in 1848 survived an accident in which an iron bar shot through his head (see ▶ Figure 12.14). More than a century and a half later, researchers examined his skull, which is still on display in a Boston museum, and reconstructed the route that the bar must have taken through his brain (Ratiu & Talos, 2004). The accident damaged part of his prefrontal cortex. During the first months after this accident, Gage often showed little emotion, and he made poor, impulsive decisions, although he apparently made some recovery later. Unfortunately, the reports at the time provided little detail. Over the years, people retold this story, elaborated on it, and exaggerated it (Kotowicz, 2007).

A patient known to us as "Elliot" provides a more recent, better documented example (Damasio, 1994). Elliot suffered damage to his prefrontal cortex during surgery to remove a brain tumor. After the operation, he showed almost no emotional expression, no impatience, no frustration, no joy from music or art, and almost no anger. He described his brain surgery and the resulting deterioration of his life with calm detachment, as if describing events that happened to a stranger. Besides his impaired emotions, he had trouble making or following reasonable plans. He could discuss the probable outcome of each possible choice but still had trouble deciding. As a result, he could not keep a job, invest his money intelligently, or maintain normal friendships.

As a rule, people with damage to one part of the prefrontal cortex (the ventromedial prefrontal cortex, to be precise) have trouble making decisions and seem particularly impaired in what we consider moral judgment. The moral deficit probably results from not being able to detect or imagine someone's emotional state (Roberts, Henry, & Molenberghs, 2019; Shenhav & Greene, 2014). If you can't imagine how someone else might feel, you have little inhibition about harming them. And if you can't imagine feeling guilty, then still less inhibition. Most people think it is okay to flip a switch to make a trolley car kill one person instead of five, but presumably you wouldn't think so if the one person who would die is your mother or your daughter. People with certain types of prefrontal brain damage generally say it would be okay, and they tend to make decisions like that with little hesitation (Ciaramelli, Muccioli, Làdavas, & diPellegrino, 2007; Thomas, Croft, & Tranel, 2011). If the brain damage occurs in childhood or early adolescence, the effects are even greater, such as saying it would be okay to kill a boss you disliked if you were sure you could get away with it (Taber-Thomas et al., 2014).

From the collection of Jack and Beverly Wilgus

▲ **Figure 12.14** Phineas Gage, holding the bar that shot through part of his prefrontal cortex. The damage impaired Gage's judgment and decision-making ability.

7. In what way might sadness be useful? In what way might guilt feelings be useful?

Answer

7. Sadness prompts people to be more cautious about future decisions. Guilt feelings, and the ability to imagine guilt feelings, are important for maintaining ethical behavior.

Emotional Intelligence

Is reasoning about emotional issues different from reasoning about anything else? The observations on patient Elliot imply a difference, as he answers questions normally when they have nothing to do with emotional consequences. Casual observations in everyday life also suggest that reasoning about emotional topics might be special. Some people know the right thing to say to make someone feel better. They notice subtle signals that indicate who needs reassurance or a pat on the back. They know when a smile is sincere or fake. They foresee whether their romantic attachments are going well or about to break up. Psychologists therefore speak of emotional intelligence, *the ability to perceive, imagine, and understand emotions and to use that information in making decisions* (Mayer & Salovey, 1995, 1997).

The idea of emotional intelligence quickly became popular, but the evidence has lagged behind. If the concept is going to be useful, emotional intelligence should have enough in common with other kinds of intelligence to deserve being called intelligence, but it should not overlap too heavily with academic intelligence, or we would have no reason to talk about it separately. Most importantly, it should predict outcomes that we cannot already predict with other measures.

First, we need a way to measure emotional intelligence. Several psychologists have devised pencil-and-paper tests. Here are two example questions, reworded slightly (Mayer, Caruso, & Salovey, 1999):

1. A man has been so busy at work that he spends little time with his wife and daughter. Recently, a relative who lost her job moved in with them. A few weeks later, they told her she had to leave because they needed their privacy.
On a scale from 1 to 5, rate how strongly this man feels each of the following:

Depressed   ___
Frustrated   ___
Guilty   ___
Energetic   ___
Happy   ___

2. A driver hit a dog that ran into the street. The driver and the dog's owner hurried to check on the dog.

On a scale from 1 to 5, where 5 means "extremely likely" and 1 means "extremely unlikely," how would the people probably feel?
The owner would feel angry at the driver. _____
The owner would feel embarrassed at not training the dog better. _____
The driver would feel guilty for not driving more carefully. _____
The driver would feel relieved that it was a dog and not a child. _____

To each of these questions, you might answer, "It depends!" You need more information about the people and the situation. Indeed, one of the key aspects of emotional intelligence is knowing what additional information to request. Still, you would do your best to answer the questions as stated. The problem then is, gulp, what are the correct answers? In fact, *are* there any correct answers, or do the answers depend on culture and circumstances?

Would you trust experts to decide the correct answers? Identifying the experts in a field like this is not so easy. Another method is "consensus": Researchers ask many people each question. Suppose on item 2, on the part about the driver

feeling guilty, 70 percent say "5" (it is extremely likely that the driver will feel guilty). That becomes the best answer. However, an answer of "4" isn't utterly wrong. Suppose 20 percent of people answer "4," 5 percent answer "3," 4 percent answer "2," and 1 percent answer "1." Instead of counting anything right or wrong, the test adds 0.70 point for everyone who answered 5, 0.20 for everyone who answered 4, and so on. In other words, you always get part credit on any question, and you get more credit depending on how many other people agreed with you. The problem is, what if only the wisest few people know the best answer to a difficult question? If the correct answer is uncommon, it will earn few points.

In short, an emotional intelligence question as currently constituted cannot identify an emotional genius. However, it does identify people who fail to answer easy questions. That by itself is worth something. People with certain kinds of brain damage or psychiatric disorders do poorly even on easy questions about emotional situations (Adolphs, Baron-Cohen, & Tranel, 2002; Blair et al., 2004; Edwards, Jackson, & Pattison, 2002; Townshend & Duka, 2003). The test does identify "emotional stupidity," even if it doesn't identify exceptional emotional intelligence.

The key criteria for any test are reliability and validity. The authors of the current tests of emotional intelligence claim that the tests have high reliability (Mayer, Salovey, Caruso, & Sitarenios, 2001), but other researchers find problems with many of the test items and report much lower reliability (Føllesdal & Hagtvet, 2009). With regard to validity, high emotional intelligence scores are associated with high quality of friendships (Lopes et al., 2004), ability to detect the emotional content of someone's voice (Trimmer & Cuddy, 2008), and good interpersonal communication (Libbrecht, Lievens, Carette, & Côté, 2014). However, emotional intelligence is a useful concept only if it predicts such outcomes better than we already could in other ways. Emotional intelligence scores correlate significantly with academic intelligence (Kong, 2014) and with conscientiousness and other personality factors. We can predict people's friendships, happiness, and life satisfaction moderately well from tests of academic intelligence and personality factors. What do emotional intelligence scores add to those predictions? Several studies have concluded "not much" (Amelang & Steinmayr, 2006; Gannon & Ranzijn, 2005; Karim & Weisz, 2010). Either emotional intelligence is not a useful concept, or we need to improve our measurements of it. Pencil-and-paper tests work well enough for academic intelligence, but they may not be ideal for measuring emotional intelligence.

8. What is the objection to "consensus" scoring?

Answer

8. A test based on consensus scoring cannot identify outstanding individuals because it rewards only the most common answer to each item.

Research on Emotions

Research on emotions is difficult. The best solution is to approach any question in multiple ways. Any study has limitations, but if several different kinds of research point to the same conclusion, we gain confidence in the overall idea. That principle

is, indeed, important throughout psychology: Seldom is any study fully decisive, so we strive for independent lines of research that converge on the same conclusion.

Summary

- *Measuring emotions.* Researchers infer emotions from self-reports, behavioral observations, and physiological measurements. (page 371)
- *James-Lange theory.* According to the James-Lange theory of emotions, the feeling aspect of an emotion is the perception of a change in the body's physiological state. (page 372)
- *Effects of arousal.* Weak arousal is associated with weak emotional feeling. Strong arousal is associated with strong emotional feeling. (page 373)
- *Schachter and Singer's theory.* According to Schachter and Singer, autonomic arousal determines the intensity of an emotion, but a cognitive appraisal of the situation determines whether we call the emotion happiness, anger, fear, or anything else. (page 374)
- *The controversy about basic emotions.* Certain psychologists propose that we have a few basic emotions. The main evidence is that people throughout the world can recognize certain emotional expressions. However, the usual research method overestimates accuracy. We ordinarily identify emotion from posture, context, and other cues and not by facial expressions alone, which vary too much to be fully reliable. (page 375)
- *The alternative.* Instead of basic emotions, an alternative is to consider emotional feelings as varying along continuous dimensions such as pleasantness and intensity. According to this view, one emotion blends into another. (page 379)
- *Usefulness of emotions.* Emotions call our attention to important information and they adjust our priorities. (page 380)
- *Emotions and moral decisions.* Emotions play a central role in moral decisions. Certain types of brain damage that impair emotional perception lead to moral decisions that most people consider deficient. (page 380)
- *Emotional intelligence.* People vary in their ability to perceive others' emotions and promote emotional health. However, it is not clear that current measurements of emotional intelligence predict much that we could not already predict in other ways. (page 381)

Key Terms

autonomic nervous system (page 372)

broaden-and-build hypothesis (page 380)

circumplex model (page 379)

emotional intelligence (page 381)

James-Lange theory (page 373)

microexpressions (page 371)

parasympathetic nervous system (page 372)

pure autonomic failure (page 373)

Schachter and Singer's theory of emotions (page 374)

sympathetic nervous system (page 372)

Answers to Other Questions in the Module

A. The faces correspond to (a) happiness, (b) anger, (c) sadness, (d) surprise, (e) disgust, and (f) fear (page 378).

Review Questions

1. What can physiological measurements tell us about someone's emotion?
   (a) They help us differentiate between fear and anger.
   (b) They help us differentiate between happiness and sadness.
   (c) They identify the cause of an emotional experience.
   (d) They gauge the intensity of an emotional experience.

2. According to the James-Lange theory, what causes the feeling aspect of an emotion?
   (a) Cognitive appraisal of the situation
   (b) Perception of body changes
   (c) Logical reasoning processes
   (d) Identification with other people

3. According to Schachter and Singer, how do you recognize which emotion you feel?
   (a) By monitoring the activity of your sympathetic nervous system
   (b) By monitoring the activity of your parasympathetic nervous system
   (c) By comparing your reactions to those of other people
   (d) By cognitive appraisal of the situation

4. Many studies overestimate people's ability to recognize emotions from facial expressions because they used which method?
   (a) Psychoanalysis
   (b) Imitation
   (c) Matching
   (d) Physiological responses

5. People experiencing which two emotions are unlikely to make eye contact with you?
   (a) Fear and sadness
   (b) Fear and happiness
   (c) Happiness and sadness
   (d) Happiness and anger

6. What do researchers propose as an alternative to the idea of six basic emotions?
   (a) Seven basic emotions
   (b) Two or more continuous dimensions

(c) A different set of emotions for each culture

(d) An unlimited number of basic emotions

7. What is one apparent advantage of feeling sad?

(a) Sad people become more active and more ambitious.

(b) In general, sad people are more optimistic about their future.

(c) Sadness improves the probability of maintaining good health.

(d) Sad people make more cautious decisions.

8. People with certain types of brain damage are impaired at perceiving or imagining other people's emotions. What is the effect on reasoning?

(a) They solve logical problems more rapidly and more accurately than average.

(b) They make the same decisions as other people, on average, but more slowly.

(c) They make decisions that others regard as morally unacceptable.

(d) They become more likely to conform to the majority opinion.

9. Tests of emotional intelligence ask questions about how someone would feel in various situations. Which of the following is a significant difficulty with such tests?

(a) The tests take too long to administer.

(b) They include too many difficult questions.

(c) It is hard to be sure what is the correct answer.

(d) Scores on these tests do not correlate with academic intelligence.

Answers: 1d, 2b, 3d, 4c, 5a, 6b, 7d, 8c, 9c.

Fear, Anger, Happiness, Sadness, and Other Experiences

mlorenzphotography/Moment/Getty Images

After studying this module, you should be able to:

1. Describe an objective way to measure anxiety.

2. Describe how amygdala damage alters fear and anxiety.

3. Evaluate the effectiveness of polygraphs ("lie detector tests").

4. Distinguish among anger, disgust, and contempt.

5. Discuss the role of wealth in happiness.

6. List factors that influence happiness and ways to enhance happiness.

7. Discuss how life satisfaction changes in old age.

The first module posed theoretical questions, but we do not have to wait until we answer them. Regardless of what we think about the concept of basic emotions, it remains convenient to talk about certain emotions separately, just as it is convenient to talk about Asia and Europe separately, even though they constitute a single landmass. Here we consider issues that are important to almost everyone, especially clinical psychologists, such as controlling fear and increasing happiness.

Fear and Anxiety

Fear is a response to an immediate danger, whereas *anxiety* is a vague sense that something bad might happen. The right level of anxiety depends on the situation. We readjust our anxiety based on our experiences.

Measuring Anxiety

Most studies of emotion rely largely on self-reports, because we have no reliable behavioral measure. However, for anxiety, researchers can use this operational definition based on behavior: **Anxiety** is *an increase in the startle reflex.* The startle reflex is the quick, automatic response that follows a sudden loud noise. Within a fifth of a second after the noise, you tense your muscles, especially your neck muscles, close your eyes, and mobilize your sympathetic nervous system to prepare for escape if necessary. The startle reflex itself is automatic, but experiences and context modify it.

Imagine yourself sitting with friends in a familiar place on a nice, sunny day when you hear a sudden loud noise. You startle, but just a bit. Now imagine yourself walking alone at night through a graveyard when

you notice someone following you . . . and then you hear the same loud noise. Your startle response will be greater. The increase in the startle reflex is an objective measurement of anxiety. As you would expect, the startle reflex is enhanced for people who are prone to frequent anxieties (McMillan, Asmundson, Zvolensky, & Carleton, 2012). Happiness and anger decrease the startle reflex (Amodio & Harmon-Jones, 2011).

Learned associations also alter the startle reflex in laboratory animals. Suppose a rat frequently sees one stimulus—a light or sound—before receiving a shock. Now that danger stimulus enhances the startle reflex to a loud noise. The increase in the startle reflex depends on activity of the amygdala (uh-MIG-duh-luh), shown in ▼ Figure 12.15 (Antoniadis, Winslow, Davis, & Amaral, 2007; Wilensky, Schafe, Kristensen, & LeDoux, 2006). The figure shows a human brain, but much of the research has been conducted with laboratory animals.

People vary in the responsiveness of the amygdala, and therefore in their tendency toward anxiety.

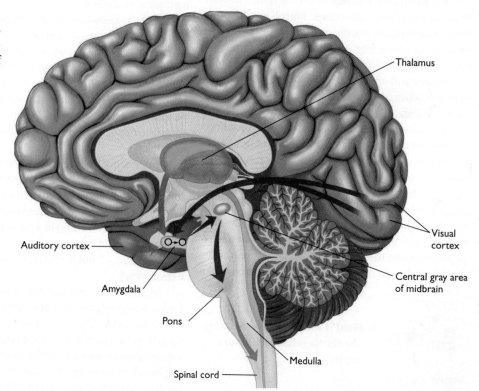

▲ **Figure 12.15** Structures in the pons and medulla control the startle response. The amygdala sends information that modifies activity in the pons and medulla. This drawing shows a human brain, although much of the research has used rats.

That tendency remains fairly consistent for an individual over time, based partly on genetics (Miu, Vulturar, Chis, Ungureanu, & Gross, 2013), and partly on epigenetics—that is, chemical changes that alter the expression of certain genes (Nikolova et al., 2014). It also depends on top-down connections from the frontal cortex that inhibit amygdala activity. People suffering from depression or severe anxiety have decreased activity in the frontal cortex, and therefore increased activity in the amygdala (Britton et al., 2013; Holmes et al., 2012).

People who have a highly responsive amygdala, for whatever reason, are more likely than others to report many emotionally unpleasant experiences (Barrett, Bliss-Moreau, Duncan, Rauch, & Wright, 2007). Soldiers with strong amygdala responses at the start of their service are more likely than others to report severe combat stress (Admon et al., 2009). Although soldiers experiencing a head wound leading to brain damage have a high probability of post-traumatic stress disorder (PTSD), those whose damage includes the amygdala apparently never experience PTSD (Koenigs et al., 2008). All these studies indicate that amygdala activity contributes to experiencing fear, and it also responds to other types of emotional information (Cunningham, Van Bavel, & Johnsen, 2008; Lumian & McRae, 2017).

A woman with damage to her amygdala in both brain hemispheres describes herself as fearless. When she watches horror movies, she experiences excitement but no fear. At an exotic pet store, people had to restrain her from trying to touch the venomous snakes and spiders. In everyday life, she enters dangerous situations without the caution other people would show. As a result, she has been robbed and assaulted several times. When she describes these events, she recalls feeling angry, but not frightened (Feinstein, Adolphs, Damasio, & Tranel, 2011). However, she did experience fear under one circumstance: When she breathed 35 percent carbon dioxide, which leaves a person gasping for breath, she reacted with panic and called it a terrible experience. Nevertheless, she agreed to do the same experiment again the next week. Furthermore, during that week she did not worry about going through the

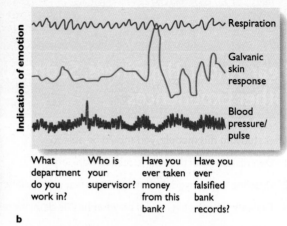

isifa/Getty Images

▲ **Figure 12.16** A polygraph operator (a) asks a series of nonthreatening questions to establish baseline readings of the subject's autonomic responses (b) and then asks questions relevant to an investigation.

ordeal again (Feinstein et al., 2013). Evidently her amygdala is not necessary for experiencing fear, but just for processing information that could lead to fear.

Anxiety, Arousal, and Lie Detection

Let's consider an attempt to use physiological measurement of anxiety for a practical purpose, lie detection. It is difficult to tell when someone is lying. Many people think they can detect lies by noticing fidgeting hands, or by watching whether someone looks them in the eye or looks away. Those techniques are, in fact, demonstrably worthless, and if anything, they interfere with our ability to identify lies (ten Brinke, Stimson, & Carney, 2014). The search is on for a reliable method of lie detection.

The best-known attempt is the **polygraph**, or "lie detector test," which records sympathetic nervous system arousal as measured by blood pressure, heart rate, breathing rate, and electrical conduction of the skin (see ▲ **Figure 12.16**). (Slight sweating increases electrical conduction of the skin.) The assumption is that when people lie, they feel nervous and therefore increase their sympathetic nervous system arousal. That assumption is often correct, but not always. Many people also get nervous while telling the truth, especially if they are worried that someone might not believe them, and many other people can lie without feeling nervous.

(Interesting trivia: William Marston, the inventor of the polygraph, was also the originator of the *Wonder Woman* cartoons. Wonder Woman used a "lasso of truth" to force people to stop lying.)

The polygraph sometimes accomplishes its goal simply because an accused person who is hooked up to a polygraph believes it will work, and therefore confesses, "Oh, what's the use. You're going to figure it out now anyway, so I may as well tell you. . . ." But if people do not confess, how effectively does a polygraph detect lying?

In one study, investigators selected 50 criminal cases where two suspects took a polygraph test and one suspect later confessed to the crime (Kleinmuntz & Szucko, 1984). Thus, they had data from 100 suspects, of whom 50 were later shown to be guilty and 50 shown to be innocent. Six professional polygraph administrators examined the polygraph results and judged which suspects appeared to be lying. ▼ **Figure 12.17** shows the results. The polygraph administrators identified 76 percent of the guilty suspects as liars but also classified 37 percent of the innocent suspects as liars.

The few other well-designed studies that have been done produced equally unimpressive results. Although many police officers still believe

9. What is the advantage of using the startle reflex to measure anxiety?

Answer

9. Using the startle reflex makes it possible to measure anxiety in animals or in people who cannot verbally describe their emotions. Using laboratory animals makes it possible to explore the biological mechanisms of anxiety.

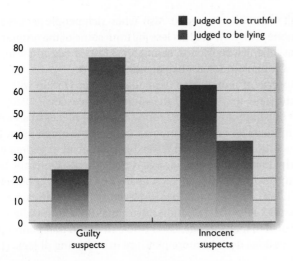

Legend:
■ Judged to be truthful
■ Judged to be lying

▲ **Figure 12.17** Polygraph examiners correctly identified 76 percent of guilty suspects as lying. However, they also identified 37 percent of innocent suspects as lying. (Based on data of Kleinmuntz & Szucko, 1984)

in polygraph testing, most researchers regard the accuracy as too uncertain for important decisions (Fiedler, Schmid, & Stahl, 2002). Polygraph results are only rarely admissible as evidence in U.S. courts. The U.S. Congress passed a law in 1988 prohibiting private employers from giving polygraph tests to employees or job applicants, except under special circumstances, and a commission of the U.S. National Academy of Sciences in 2002 concluded that polygraphs should not be used for national security clearances.

Alternative Methods of Detecting Lies

The **guilty-knowledge test**, *a modified version of the polygraph test,* produces more accurate results by *asking questions that should be threatening only to someone who knows the facts of a crime* (Lykken, 1979). Instead of asking, "Did you rob the gas station?" the interrogator asks, "Was the gas station robbed at 8 p.m.? At 10:30? At midnight? Did the robber carry a 22-caliber gun? A 45-caliber gun? A knife? Was the getaway car black? Red? Blue?" Someone who shows arousal only in response to the correct details is presumed to have "guilty knowledge" that only the guilty person or someone who had talked to the guilty person would possess. The guilty-knowledge test, when properly administered, rarely classifies an innocent person as guilty (Iacono & Patrick, 1999).

Another approach for detecting lies is to ask better questions. For example, if you ask, "What were you doing at the time of the crime?" someone can repeat a rehearsed lie. However, if you ask someone detailed, unexpected questions, or ask someone to draw a picture of where they were, innocent people generally do better than those who are lying (Vrij, Granhag, & Porter, 2010). Researchers also report that when people lie, they tend to provide few details, perhaps to avoid saying something that could be shown to be wrong (DePaolo et al., 2003). When people respond to questions on a computer so that investigators can measure their reaction times accurately, people usually respond faster when telling the truth than when lying (Suchotzki, Verschuere, Van Bockstaele, Ben-Shakhar, & Crombez, 2017; Verschuere, Kobis, Bereby-Meyer, Rand, & Shalvi, 2018). The interpretation is that people generally remember the truth quickly, but they need more cognitive effort to produce a lie. Still, none of these techniques is reliable enough to justify a confident decision about whether someone is lying or telling the truth.

10. How is a guilty-knowledge test better than the usual polygraph test?

Answer

10. A guilty-knowledge test asks questions that should cause nervousness only for someone with detailed knowledge about the crime. Therefore, it is less likely to classify an innocent person as guilty.

Anger and Related Emotions

Anger is associated with a desire to harm people or drive them away, usually in response to a belief that someone has caused harm or attempted to cause harm. Participants in one study kept an "anger diary" for a week (Averill, 1983). A typical entry was, "My roommate locked me out of the room when I went to the shower." They also described how they reacted, such as, "I talked to my roommate about it," or "I did nothing about it." Surveys across other cultures also find that people experience anger frequently but seldom consider resorting to violence (Ramirez, Santisteban, Fujihara, & Van Goozen, 2002).

Anger, contempt, and disgust are reactions to different types of offense. Anger occurs when someone interferes with your rights or expectations. Contempt is *a reaction to a violation of community standards,* such as when someone fails to do a fair share of the work or claims credit for something another person did (Rozin, Lowery, et al., 1999). Disgust is literally *dis* (bad) + *gust* (taste). In the English language, we often use the term loosely, but narrowly speaking, disgust refers to *a reaction to something that would make you feel contaminated if it got into your mouth* (Rozin, Lowery, et al., 1999*)*. Almost all people find the idea of eating feces highly disgusting, and most react with disgust to other things possible to eat—perhaps insects, animal brains, or their dead pets. On average, women experience disgust more readily than men do. One interpretation is that women need to be more careful to avoid risky behaviors in general (Sparks, Fessler, Chan, Ashokkumar, & Holbrook, 2018).

We also react with disgust to moral offenses, such as when one person cheats another (Chapman, Kim, Susskind, & Anderson, 2009; Danovitch & Bloom, 2009). Disgust related to contamination differs in some ways from disgust at moral offenses, such as producing different facial expressions (Yoder, Widen, & Russell, 2016). However, experiencing contamination disgust temporarily increases people's report of feeling disgusted by moral offenses, so evidently the two types of disgust are related (Erskine, Kacinik, & Prinz, 2014; Herz, 2014).

Happiness, Joy, and Positive Psychology

"What makes people happy?" is a more complicated question than it sounds. If we ask, "What *would* make you happy?" people often ask for more money, a better job, or other tangibles. If we ask, "What *does* make you happy?" people are more likely to cite family, friends, nature, a sense of accomplishment, music, or religious faith.

Positive psychology *studies the features that enrich life, such as happiness, hope, creativity, courage, spirituality, and responsibility* (Seligman & Csikszentmihalyi, 2000). It includes not only momentary happiness, but also subjective well-being, *a self-evaluation of one's life as pleasant, interesting, satisfying, and meaningful* (Diener, 2000). Happiness is not the only type of positive emotion. For some purposes it helps to distinguish among enthusiasm, amusement, pride, love, and awe (Griskevicius, Shiota, & Neufeld, 2010).

Research on happiness relies on self-reports, because we have no reliable physiological or behavioral measures. According to self-reports, most of the world's people report themselves to be happy more often than unhappy, and in fact most people say they are happier than average (Diener, Diener, Choi, & Oishi, 2018; Ong, Goodman, & Zaki, 2018). Isn't that nice? We are all above average. However, to a question about overall "life satisfaction," only about half report a positive score (Diener et al., 2018).

Influence of Wealth

Are rich people happier than poor people? On average, yes, but beyond a certain point, getting still richer does not add much. An increase in wealth makes more difference to poor people than to people who were already doing well (Jebb, Tay, Diener, & Oishi, 2018). Not all rich people are happy, but most poor people are unhappy, especially if their friends and relatives are doing better (Fliessbach et al., 2007; Frank, 2012; Lucas & Schimmack, 2009). Health also enters into the equation. It is possible to be poor and happy, or sick and happy, but it is hard to be happy if you are both poor and sick (Smith, Langa, Kabeto, & Ubel, 2005).

As you might guess, people who have just won a lottery call themselves very happy. As you might not guess, people who won a lottery a few months ago no longer rate themselves happier than average (Diener, Suh, Lucas, & Smith, 1999; Myers, 2000). Some have problems in handling their new wealth, including conflicts with relatives who expect a share of it. Another explanation is that lottery winners get used to their new level of happiness, so a given

rating doesn't mean what it used to. Also, when rich people get used to the fine things that money can buy, they get less joy from some of the ordinary pleasures of life, such as talking with friends, eating breakfast, or taking a walk in the park (Quoidbach, Dunn, Petrides, & Mikolajczak, 2010).

The influence of money also depends on what you do with the money. Someone said (and the origin of the quote is uncertain), "People who say money can't buy happiness haven't found the right places to shop!" How you spend your money can be more important than how much money you have. Psychologists initially reported that paying for special experiences—such as a vacation trip, tickets to a show, or a luxurious meal—generally brings more pleasure than buying an object, such as new clothing or a bigger television set (Dunn, Gilbert, & Wilson, 2011). However, as is often the case in psychology, "it depends." The original studies dealt mainly with middle-class people who already owned many things. Later research found that poorer people who had few possessions derived more pleasure from buying objects (Lee, Hall, & Wood, 2018).

Buying a present for someone else often brings more pleasure than buying something for yourself (Sheldon & Lyubomirsky, 2004). And that conclusion is something that most people wouldn't guess. In one study, experimenters asked people to rate their happiness in the morning, and then gave them money, instructing them to spend it by evening. Some (chosen randomly) were told to spend it on themselves. Others were told to buy a gift for someone else. When they were questioned that evening, those who gave presents were happier, on average, than those who spent the money on themselves (Dunn, Aknin, & Norton, 2008). Other studies confirmed that both adults and toddlers feel happy and act happy after acts of kindness to someone else (Aknin, Hamlin, & Dunn, 2012; Chancellor, Margolis, Bao, & Lyubomirsky, 2018; Mongrain, Chin, & Shapira, 2011; Nelson, Layous, Cole, & Lyubomirsky, 2016). Furthermore, whereas many other pleasures decline after repetition, the pleasure of doing kind deeds shows little or no decline over time (O'Brien & Kassierer, 2019). In the words of a Chinese proverb, if you want happiness for an hour, take a nap. If you want happiness for a day, go fishing. If you want happiness for a year, inherit a fortune. If you want happiness for a lifetime, help somebody.

Differences among Nations

Cross-cultural research on happiness is difficult, because it relies entirely on self-reports. Does "above-average happiness" mean the same thing to Venezuelans as it does to Bulgarians? Probably not, but for what it's worth, here are the results: In general, people in richer countries rate themselves happier than those in poorer countries, as shown in ▼ Figure 12.18 (Oishi & Schimmack, 2010). However, residents of poorer countries tend to report a higher sense of meaning and purpose in life, possibly because poorer countries tend to be more religious (Oishi & Diener, 2014).

As a rule, when the average wealth in a country increases, average satisfaction with life also increases. The United States has been an exception to that rule. From 1972 until 2012, the wealth of the average person approximately doubled, while reports of well-being slightly decreased. One explanation is the increasingly uneven distribution of wealth. It used to be that the chief executive officer of a large company earned about 20 times as much as the average worker. By 2012, the chief executive earned more than 350 times as much, a ratio higher than what almost anyone, liberal or conservative, considers fair (Kiatpongsan & Norton, 2014). When the statistics say that the mean wealth in the United States increased, most of the increase is due to increased wealth by the richest. Other people saw little change in their wealth, and if they compared themselves to the richest, it seemed they were doing worse than before (Sacks, Stevenson, & Wolfers, 2012). In other countries also, increased economic growth does not

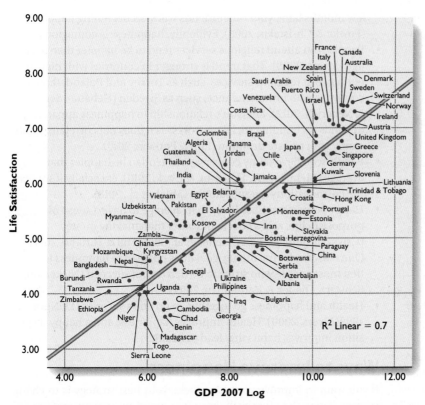

▲ **Figure 12.18** For each country, gross domestic product (GDP), a measure of wealth, is represented on the *x*-axis and an index of life satisfaction is on the *y*-axis. (From Oishi & Schimmack, 2010)

mean increased happiness, if the rich are gaining faster than everyone else (Oishi & Kesebir, 2015).

In addition to wealth, the mean level of happiness of a country correlates positively with individual freedoms, social equality, education, good opportunities for women, and a government with little corruption (Basabe et al., 2002; Oishi & Schimmack, 2010). Happiness also correlates with tolerance for minority groups (Inglehart, Foa, Peterson, & Welzel, 2008). It is likely that a tolerant attitude leads to happiness, but it is also true that feeling happy makes people more tolerant (Ashton-James, Maddux, Galinsky, & Chartrand, 2009).

11. Why did a doubling of the mean wealth of Americans over 30 years fail to increase mean happiness?

Answer

11. Most of the increased wealth went to rich people.

More Influences on Happiness

One of the strongest influences on happiness is people's temperament or personality. In one study, most pairs of monozygotic twins reported almost the same level of happiness, even if they differed in their wealth, education, and job prestige (Lykken & Tellegen, 1996). Another study found that most people's reports of life satisfaction fluctuate around a stable, moderately high level (Cummins, Li, Wooden, & Stokes, 2014). However, some people have wider fluctuations than others do. The degree of fluctuation shows a significant amount of heritability (Zheng, Plomin, & von Stumm, 2016).

How would you guess parenthood affects happiness? The answer depends on how we measure happiness. One way is to ask people to record what they are doing at various moments, in response to an unpredictable beeper, and how much they enjoy that activity. By that method, parenthood appears to be a negative influence. Being a parent means sometimes changing diapers, caring for pain or illness, and other unpleasant chores. Young or single parents are especially likely to find parenthood difficult. Nevertheless, if we ask people to describe their life satisfaction in general, most parents describe their children as a source of joy, because the occasional moments when a child gives a parent a hug and a smile outweigh all the tedious tasks. Parents are more likely than others to think frequently about the meaningfulness of life (Nelson, Kushlev, English, Dunn, & Lyubomirsky, 2013).

Several factors influence happiness less than we might expect. Wouldn't you guess that especially good-looking people would be happier than average? If you are good looking, many people smile at you and want to be your friend. However, researchers have found only a small correlation between attractiveness and happiness among college students—except that, on average, more attractive people are happier with their romantic life (Diener, Wolsic, & Fujita, 1995).

Weather also makes less difference than we might guess. People generally rate themselves happier on sunny days than cloudy days (Denissen, Butalid, Penke, & van Aken, 2008), but on a given day, happy people rate today's weather more pleasant than unhappy people do (Messner & Wänke, 2011). That is, most of happiness comes from inside, not from outside. On average, people in a cold state like Michigan rate themselves about as happy as those in sunny southern California (Schkade & Kahneman, 1998).

Certain life events produce long-term decreases in life satisfaction. People who get divorced show a gradual decrease in happiness in the years leading up to the divorce. They recover slowly and incompletely over the next few years (Diener & Seligman, 2004; Lucas, 2005). People who lose a spouse through death also have decreased happiness leading up to the event, because of the spouse's failing health, and on average they recover slowly and incompletely. ▼ Figure 12.19 shows the mean results. Naturally, the results vary from one person to another. Losing a job is a similar blow to life satisfaction, and many people do not fully recover (Lucas, Clark, Georgellis, & Diener, 2004).

Many aspects of life correlate with happiness or subjective well-being. In the following list, remember that correlations do not demonstrate causation, so alternative explanations are possible.

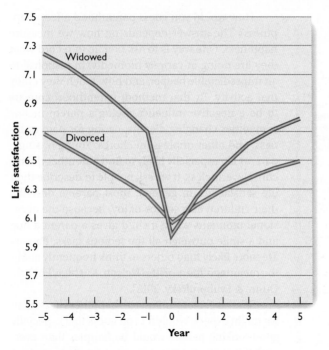

▲ **Figure 12.19** For each person, 0 marks the year of loss of a spouse through divorce or death. On average, life satisfaction declines until the loss and gradually but incompletely recovers afterward. (From "Beyond money: Toward an economy of well-being" by E. Diener and M. E. P. Seligman, 2004. *Psychological Science in the Public Interest, 5,* 1–31. Copyright © 2004 Blackwell Publishing. Reprinted by permission.)

- Married people tend to be happier than unmarried people (DeNeve, 1999; Myers, 2000), especially if it is a happy marriage (Carr, Freedman, Cornman, & Schwarz, 2014). (Well, duh!) A good marriage promotes happiness, but also happy people are more likely than sad people to get married. (Would you want to marry someone who was usually sad?) College students with close friendships and romantic attachments are usually happier than those without such attachments (Diener & Seligman, 2002). Friendships and romances are helpful in many ways, such as encouraging a variety of activities (Cacioppo, Hawkley, & Berntson, 2003; Stavrova, 2019). One study asked people how they might increase their happiness. Those who said they hoped to increase the time they spend with friends and family did in fact increase their life satisfaction over the following year (Rohrer, Richter, Brümmer, Wagner, & Schmulke, 2018).
- People who have happy friends tend also to be happy. A massive longitudinal study suggests a cause-and-effect relationship: If your friends or other people with whom you have frequent contact become happier, then within a few months, you will probably become happier also, and a

few months later, your other friends will start becoming happier (Fowler & Christakis, 2008). Evidently, happiness is contagious.

- People who attend religious services tend to be happier than average (Myers, 2000). That trend is stronger in countries with high attendance at religious services, such as Turkey and Poland, than in countries with low attendance, such as Sweden (Gebauer, Sedikides, & Neberich, 2012). Religion's relationship to happiness apparently depends on building social networks, as it does not correlate significantly with private devotion (Lim & Putnam, 2010).
- People who have many conversations tend to be happier than average (Mehl, Vazire, Holleran, & Clark, 2010), especially if some of the conversations are substantive (Milek et al., 2018).
- Happy people are more likely than average to have a sense of purpose in life, and a goal in life other than making money (Csikszentmihalyi, 1999; Diener et al., 1999; Hill & Turiano, 2014). One reason why the money goal does not lead to happiness is that most people who strive to be rich do not succeed (Nickerson, Schwarz, Diener, & Kahneman, 2003).
- Health and happiness go together, to no one's surprise (DeNeve, 1999; Myers, 2000). Health improves happiness, and a happy disposition improves habits that lead to health.

Ways to Improve Happiness

If you want to improve your happiness, your best strategy is to change your activities. A nature walk improves mood more than most people guess (Nisbet & Zelenski, 2011). People who live near a park or other natural area tend to be happier than those who don't (White, Alcock, Wheeler, & Depledge, 2013). For students, joining a club or starting better study habits yields long-term improvements in mood and satisfaction (Sheldon & Lyubomirsky, 2006).

Some advice that will help in the long run, though not necessarily today: Keep a diary where you record the events of the day, especially the pleasant ones. Later you will get pleasure—more than you expect—from looking back and reliving these events (Zhang, Kim, Brooks, Gino, & Norton, 2014). You can also enjoy anticipating future experiences, such as a vacation trip (Kumar, Killingsworth, & Gilovich, 2014).

Still more advice: Take out time once a week to list a few things about which you feel grateful. People who write about feeling grateful improve their life satisfaction (Emmons & McCullough, 2003; Lyubomirsky, Dickerhoof, Boehm, & Sheldon, 2011).

Age

Other things being equal, would you expect old people to be happier than young people, less happy, or about the same? ▼ Figure 12.20 shows the trend over age, according to a survey of more than 340,000 people in the United States (Stone, Schwartz, Broderick, & Deaton, 2010). Overall well-being declines from early adulthood until about age 50, on average, and then begins a steady increase as long as people remain healthy. The increase in old age relates more to a decrease in unhappy feelings than to an increase in happy ones (Mikels & Schuster, 2016). However, a later survey in other countries throughout the world found that life satisfaction was about steady from age 20 to 80, rather than showing the V-shaped function previously reported in the United States (Jebb, Morrison, Tay, & Diener, 2020).

To the extent that older people remain at least equal to younger people in life satisfaction, what is the explanation? One reason is decreased stress (Stone et al., 2010). Beyond a certain age, people can stop worrying about becoming a success, paying the bills, rearing a family, and so forth. They already know how successful they are or aren't, and they have little need to worry about it. Also, older people deliberately regulate their mood. They attend to happy events and turn away from

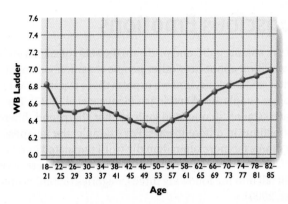

▲ **Figure 12.20** People's reported well-being reaches a low point at about age 50 and then increases, on average, as long as people remain healthy. These results represent a survey of more than 340,000 people in 2008. (Source: From "A snapshot of the age distribution of psychological well-being in the United States," by A. A. Stone, Schwartz, J. E., Broderick, J. E., & Deaton, A., 2010. *Proceedings of the National Academy of Sciences, U.S.A., 107,* pp. 9985–9990.)

unpleasant ones, especially if they are already in an unhappy mood (Isaacowitz, Toner, Goren, & Wilson, 2008). That trend varies somewhat across cultures, as older Americans are more likely to distance themselves from unpleasant information than Japanese people are (Grossmann, Karasawa, Kan, & Kitayama, 2014).

The age trend also depends on when someone was born. Over 20 to 30 years, researchers repeatedly asked several groups of people to rate their overall enjoyment of life. As ▼ Figure 12.21 shows, people reported greater enjoyment of life, on average, as they grew older, but people born in more recent decades started from a higher point than people born earlier (Sutin, et al., 2013). Those born in earlier decades had lived through the Great Depression, one or two World Wars, and other hard times that evidently left a lasting effect. These results are for the United States, and the data would of course differ for other countries.

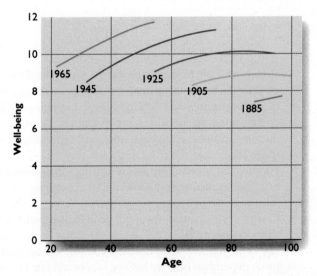

▲ **Figure 12.21** On average, people born in a given year (such as 1965 or 1945) reported greater well-being as they grew older. In addition, those born in more recent decades reported greater well-being than those born earlier. (From "The effect of birth cohort on well-being: The legacy of economic hard times," by A. R. Sutin, A. Terracciano, Y. Milaneschi, Y. An, L. Ferrucci, & A. B. Zonderman, 2013. *Psychological Science, 24,* pp. 379–385.)

concept check

12. Is asking about "happiness" the same as asking about "satisfaction with life"?

13. List some factors that correlate with happiness.

Answers

12. No. Most people rate themselves as happier than average, but only about average in satisfaction with life. Also, when parents report how happy they are right now, they often report low happiness, yet when asked about life satisfaction, they describe their children as a source of great joy.

13. Happiness correlates positively (though not in all cases strongly) with wealth, health, living in a country that tolerates minority groups and gives high status to women, having close personal relationships, having goals in life, having substantive conversations, having happy friends, expressing gratitude, and helping others. It also increases in old age, and it is greater for people born in recent decades (at least in the United States).

Sadness

If you ask people what makes them happy, you get many answers, but if you ask what makes them sad, most answers fit a pattern: People feel sad from a sense of loss. It could be death of a loved one, breakup of a romantic relationship, injury or illness, or a financial setback, but whatever it is, it is a serious loss. Sadness motivates people to restore their mood in whatever way possible, including a search for social support (Quoidbach, Taquet, Desseilles, de Montjoye, & Gross, 2019).

Crying

Sad people often react by crying. Just as cultures differ in their attitudes toward loud public laughter, they also differ in attitudes about adult crying. Adults in the United States cry far more often than those in China. Women reported crying more than men in each of 30 cultures (Becht & Vingerhoets, 2002).

Why do we cry? (Other animals don't.) Many people say that crying relieves tension and makes them feel better, but the actual effectiveness is uncertain. Certainly, people relax when they *stop* crying, but the relief from stopping doesn't necessarily mean that crying was beneficial (Gross, Fredrickson, & Levenson, 1994). In one experiment, one group was encouraged to cry, and another was instructed to hold back their tears while watching a sad film. Contrary to the idea that crying relieves tension, the two groups had equal tension at the end, and those who cried reported feeling more depressed (Kraemer & Hastrup, 1988).

An alternative view is that the main purpose of crying is to communicate a need for sympathy and social support (Gracanin, Bylsma, & Vingerhoets, 2014; Provine, Krosnowski, & Brocato, 2009). Seeing someone's eyes turn red adds to the appearance of sadness (Provine, Cabrera, Brocato, & Krosnowski, 2011). Robert Provine and colleagues have suggested that humans evolved white scleras (the whites of our eyes), in contrast to the dark scleras of other primates, to enhance emotional communication. When you see the sclera of someone's eyes turn red, you know the person is having some sort of problem and you might offer to help (Provine, Nave-Blodgett, & Cabrera, 2013).

14. What evidence conflicts with the idea that crying relieves tension?

Answer

14. People who cried during a sad movie had no less tension than people who restrained their crying, and they reported feeling more depressed.

Self-Conscious Emotions

Embarrassment, shame, guilt, and pride are the self-conscious emotions. They occur when we think about how other people regard us or might regard us if they knew what we had done, and we express these experiences most strongly when many other people are observing us (Sznycer et al., 2017). The distinctions among embarrassment, shame, and guilt are not sharp, and different cultures draw the distinctions in different ways. For example, the Japanese use a word translated as *shame* far more often than the word translated into English as *embarrassment* (Imahori & Cupach, 1994). For English speakers, most causes of **embarrassment** fall into the following three categories (Sabini, Siepmann, Stein, & Meyerowitz, 2000):

- *mistakes,* such as thinking someone was flirting with you when in fact they were flirting with the person behind you
- *being the center of attention,* such as having people sing "Happy Birthday" to you
- *sticky situations,* such as having to ask someone for a major favor

Sometimes, people also feel embarrassed out of sympathy for someone else who is in an embarrassing situation (Shearn, Spellman, Straley, Meirick, & Stryker, 1999). Imagining how the other person feels causes you embarrassment, too.

---

in closing | **module 12.2**

Emotions and the Richness of Life

We try to feel happy as much as possible and try to avoid feeling sad, angry, or frightened, right? Well, usually but not always. People go to movies that they know will make them feel sad or frightened. They ride roller coasters that advertise how scary they are. Sometimes people seem to enjoy being angry. Alcoholics and drug abusers experience wild swings of emotion, and many who quit say that although life is better since they quit, they sometimes miss the emotional swings. All of our emotions, within limits, provide richness to our experiences.

Summary

- *Measuring anxiety.* Anxiety can be operationally defined as variations in the startle reflex. That definition enables researchers to explore the biological basis of anxiety in laboratory animals. (page 385)
- *Role of the amygdala.* The amygdala processes information important for emotion. A woman with damage to her amygdala on both sides feels fear only when she is gasping for breath, and not in response to signals of danger. (page 385)
- *Polygraph.* The polygraph, sometimes intended to detect lies, measures the activity of the sympathetic nervous system. However, it too often classifies innocent people as guilty. (page 386)
- *Anger and similar states.* Anger, disgust, and contempt are similar feelings that arise in response to different types of offense. (page 387)
- *Wealth and happiness.* Increased wealth improves happiness for poorer people, but it has less effect for those who are already well-off. Mean happiness for a nation suffers when a great disparity exists between rich and poor. (page 388)
- *Increasing happiness.* Ways to increase happiness include doing something for others, social support, having meaningful conversations, enjoying nature, and expressing gratitude. (page 389)
- *Impaired happiness.* Happiness and life satisfaction suffer, usually for years, after divorce, death of a spouse, or loss of a job. (page 389)
- *Crying.* Crying communicates a need for sympathy and support. (page 391)
- *Self-conscious emotions.* Embarrassment, shame, guilt, and pride depend on how we believe others will react to our actions. (page 392)

Key Terms

anxiety (page 385)

contempt (page 387)

disgust (page 387)

embarrassment (page 392)

guilty-knowledge test (page 387)

polygraph (page 386)

positive psychology (page 388)

subjective well-being (page 388)

Review Questions

1. What typically causes the startle reflex?
   - (a) A sudden loud noise
   - (b) A scary movie or story
   - (c) Fear of abandonment
   - (d) Fear of falling

2. Why is the guilty-knowledge test preferable to the standard polygraph?
   - (a) It can be administered more quickly and inexpensively.
   - (b) It identifies a larger percentage of dishonest people.
   - (c) It can be used without requesting informed consent.
   - (d) It is less likely to mislabel innocent people.

3. What is the literal meaning of "disgust"?
   - (a) Distant emotion
   - (b) Lost face
   - (c) Bad taste
   - (d) Angry mouth

4. Which of the following makes a major, long-term contribution to happiness?
   - (a) Weather
   - (b) Being good-looking
   - (c) Temperament
   - (d) Birth order

5. What is the advantage of humans' white sclera of the eyes?
   - (a) To increase communication of sadness
   - (b) To improve perception of other people's emotions
   - (c) To improve blood circulation in the brain
   - (d) To shield the eyes from harmful radiation

Answers: 1a, 2d, 3c, 4c, 5a.

mlorenzphotography/Moment/Getty Images

module 12.3

Stress, Health, and Coping

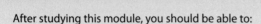

After studying this module, you should be able to:

1. Describe and evaluate Selye's concept of stress.

2. Discuss the difficulties of measuring stress.

3. Give examples of how stress can affect health by altering behavior.

4. Describe the role of cortisol and the immune system in stress effects on health.

5. Explain the evidence suggesting that some people are more predisposed than others to post-traumatic stress disorder.

6. List ways to cope with stress.

7. Describe procedures that might facilitate forgetting of a traumatic experience.

Imagine you meet a man suffering from multiple sclerosis. Would you say, "It's his own fault. He's being punished for his sins"? Many people in previous times believed just that. We congratulate ourselves today on having learned not to blame the victim.

Or have we? We think that cigarette smokers are at fault if they develop lung cancer. We note that AIDS is most common among people with a history of intravenous drug use or unsafe sex. As we learn more and more about the causes of various illnesses, we expect people to accept more responsibility for their own health. It is easy to overstate the effect of behavior on health. Even if you are careful about your diet, exercise regularly, and avoid all known risks, sooner or later you will become ill anyway.

Health psychology *addresses how people's behavior influences health.* In this module, we focus on stress, the effects of stress on health, and means of coping with stress. Stress is not itself an example of emotion, but it provokes strong emotions.

Stress

Have you ever gone without sleep several nights in a row trying to meet a deadline? Or waited in a dangerous area for someone who was supposed to pick you up? Or had a close friend suddenly not want to see you anymore? Or tried to explain why you no longer want to date someone? These experiences and countless others cause stress.

Selye's Concept of Stress

Hans Selye, an Austrian-born physician who worked at McGill University in Montreal, noticed that a wide variety of illnesses produce the same symptoms— fever, inactivity, sleepiness, loss of appetite, and release of the hormone cortisol, *which enhances metabolism and increases the supply of sugar to the cells.* While doing laboratory research with rats, he noted that the same symptoms followed many stressful experiences, including heat, cold, confinement, the sight of a cat, or an injection of anything. He inferred that the body reacts with fever, inactivity, and so forth to any threat, and that these symptoms were the body's way of defending itself. According to Selye (1979), stress is *the nonspecific response of the body to any demand made upon it.* Any demand evokes responses that prepare the body for fighting a threat.

Selye's concept of stress included any experience that changes someone's life. Getting married and getting a good job are presumably pleasant experiences, but they also require changes in your life, so in Selye's sense, they produce stress. However, Selye's definition does not include the effects of anything unchanging—such as poverty, racism, or a lifelong disability. It also ignores stress that we experience vicariously. Many people experience serious stress from watching television coverage of tragic events (Garfin, Holman, & Silver, 2015). An alternative definition of stress is *"an event or events that are interpreted as threatening to an individual and which elicit physiological and behavioral responses"* (McEwen, 2000, p. 173). Because this definition highlights what an individual interprets as threatening, it recognizes that an event might be stressful to you and not someone else, or to you at one time and not at another. For example, seeing a snake in the backyard could terrify one person but not another. A critical word from your boss might disturb you, but not as much if you know why your boss is in a bad mood.

Selye described the general adaptation syndrome, *the body's response to stressful events of any type.* It begins with the *alarm* stage, marked by activity of the

John Olson/The LIFE Picture Collection/Getty Images

Our emotions affect physiological processes and thereby influence health.

The stressfulness of an event depends on how we interpret it. Most people would be delighted to finish second in an Olympic event, but someone who hoped to finish first may consider it a defeat.

sympathetic nervous system to prepare the body for vigorous activity. Because the sympathetic nervous system cannot sustain long-term arousal, extended stress sends the body into the *resistance* stage, when the adrenal glands release cortisol and other hormones that maintain alertness. The body also saves energy by decreasing unnecessary activity. After even longer intense stress, the body enters *exhaustion*, marked by fatigue, inactivity, and decreased ability to resist illness. After an earthquake produced the Fukushima nuclear plant disaster in Japan, many families had to seek temporary shelter far from home. In the short run, they felt energized, but when they couldn't resume their normal lives, they became depressed (Brumfiel, 2013).

Table 12.1 Ten Common Hassles and Uplifts

Hassles	Uplifts
1. Concerns about weight	1. Relating well with your spouse or lover
2. Health of a family member	2. Relating well with friends
3. Rising prices of common goods	3. Completing a task
4. Home maintenance	4. Feeling healthy
5. Too many things to do	5. Getting enough sleep
6. Misplacing or losing things	6. Eating out
7. Yard work or outside home maintenance	7. Meeting your responsibilities
8. Property, investment, or taxes	8. Visiting, phoning, or writing someone
9. Crime	9. Spending time with family
10. Physical appearance	10. Home (inside) pleasing to you

Source: Kanner, Coyne, Schaefer, & Lazarus, 1981

Measuring Stress

To do research on stress, we need to measure it. One approach is to give people a checklist of stressful experiences. For example, the Social Readjustment Rating Scale lists 43 life-change events (Holmes & Rahe, 1967). The authors of this test asked people to rate how stressful each event would be, and on that basis, they assigned each event a certain number of points, such as 100 for death of a spouse and 11 for a traffic ticket. On this questionnaire, you check the events you experienced recently, and a psychologist totals your points to measure your stress.

Checklists of this sort have serious problems. One is the assumption that many small stressors add up to the same as one large stressor. For example, graduating from college, receiving unexpected money, moving to a new address, and starting a new job are all considered stressors. According to the checklist, this combination rates almost twice as many points as you would get from a divorce. Another problem is the ambiguity of many items. You get 44 points for "change in health of a family member." You would certainly check that item if you discover that your 5-year-old son or daughter has diabetes. Should you also check it if your aunt, whom you seldom see, recovers nicely from a bout of influenza? Apparently, you get to decide what counts and what doesn't.

Moreover, a given event has different meanings depending on how people interpret the event and what they can do about it (Lazarus, 1977). Becoming pregnant is not the same for a 27-year-old married woman as for an unmarried 16-year-old. Losing a job is shattering for a 50-year-old, mildly disappointing to a 17-year-old, and trivial for an actor who works in many plays each year and never expects any of them to last long. How would you feel about winning a silver medal in the Olympics? Most of us would feel great, but many silver medal winners are disappointed that they didn't win the gold (Medvec, Madey, & Gilovich, 1995). What matters is not the event itself but what it means to you.

Yet another problem with Selye's approach is that it considers all types of stressors to be equivalent, except in amount. Later research has found that personal rejection is especially troubling, such as comes from a romantic breakup, being fired from a job, or any other occasion when a person feels excluded and rejected. That type of stress is particularly likely to lead to health problems (Murphy, Slavich, Chen, & Miller, 2015).

The effects of stress depend not only on the unpleasant events ("hassles") that we have to deal with but also the pleasant events ("uplifts") that brighten our day (Kanner, Coyne, Schaefer, & Lazarus, 1981). ■ Table 12.1 presents one example of this approach.

15. Why is it difficult to measure stress?

Answer

15. The main reason is that an event can be highly stressful to one person and not to another. Also, people can have uplifts that soften the effect of stress.

How Stress Affects Health

People who have recently endured severe stress, such as divorce or the death of a husband or wife, have an increased risk of medical problems, ranging from life-threatening illnesses to tooth decay (Hugoson, Ljungquist, & Breivik, 2002; Lillberg et al., 2003; Manor & Eisenbach, 2003; Sbarra, Law, & Portley, 2011). The risk is greatest for the first 3 months, but still apparent a year after the event (Moon, Glymour, Vable, Liu, & Subramanian, 2014). How does stress lead to health problems?

Indirect Effects

Stress can influence health by altering people's behavior. For example, people who have just lost a husband or wife lose their appetite (Shahar, Schultz, Shahar, & Wing, 2001). They don't sleep well, they forget to take their medications, and they might engage in excessive drinking.

Stress also impairs health in roundabout ways. Back in the 1940s, a midwife who delivered three female babies on a Friday the 13th announced that all three were hexed and would die before their 23rd birthday. The first two did die young. As the third woman approached her 23rd birthday, she checked into a hospital and informed the staff of her fears. The staff noted that she dealt with her anxiety by extreme hyperventilation (deep breathing). Shortly before her birthday, she hyperventilated to death.

How did this happen? Ordinarily, when people do not breathe voluntarily, the carbon dioxide in their blood triggers reflexive breathing. By extreme hyperventilation, this woman exhaled so much carbon dioxide that she did not have enough left to trigger reflexive breathing. When she stopped breathing voluntarily, she stopped breathing altogether (Clinicopathologic Conference, 1967). This is a clear (but very unusual!) example of an indirect effect of emotions on health: The fact that she believed the hex caused its fulfillment.

Direct Effects

Stress also affects health more directly. Suppose you have a miserable job, you live in a war zone, or you live with someone who is often abusive. If you face a constant threat, you activate your adrenal glands

to release more cortisol, which enhances metabolism and enables cells to combat stress. A moderate, brief increase in cortisol improves attention and memory (Krugers, Hoogenraad, & Groc, 2010). Stress also activates parts of your immune system, preparing it to fight anything from infections to tumors (Benschop et al., 1995; Connor & Leonard, 1998). Presumably, the reason is that throughout our evolutionary history, stressful situations often led to injury, so the immune system must be ready to fight infections. That effect made more sense when injuries were people's main source of stress. Today, the immune system reacts to the stress of things that have nothing to do with infection or bacteria, such as giving a public lecture (Dickerson, Gable, Irwin, Aziz, & Kemeny, 2009). Still, when intense stress activates the immune system, the immune system activity can produce fever and sleepiness (Maier & Watkins, 1998). You feel ill and look ill, even if you are not.

Still more prolonged stress leads to exhaustion. You feel withdrawn, your performance declines, and you complain about low quality of life (Evans, Bullinger, & Hygge, 1998). Prolonged high release of cortisol damages the hippocampus, a key brain area for memory (de Quervain, Roozendaal, Nitsch, McGaugh, & Hock, 2000; Kleen, Sitomer, Killeen, & Conrad, 2006; Kuhlmann, Piel, & Wolf, 2005). Eventually, overuse of the immune system weakens it, and you become more vulnerable to illness (Cohen et al., 1998).

16. For many college students, the stress of taking final exams activates the immune system, resulting in increases in cortisol. Would that effect improve or impair performance on the exams?

Answer

16. It depends. A moderate increase in cortisol enhances memory and alertness. However, more extreme or prolonged cortisol damages the hippocampus, impairs memory, and exhausts the immune system. Different individuals react differently, of course. Be glad that final exams last only a week or two.

Heart Disease

An upholsterer repairing the chairs in a physician's waiting room once noticed that the fronts of the seats wore out before the backs. To figure out why, the physician began watching patients in the waiting room. He noticed that his heart patients habitually sat on the front edges of their seats, waiting impatiently to be called in for their appointments. This observation led to a hypothesis linking heart disease to an impatient, success-driven personality, now known as Type A personality (Friedman & Rosenman, 1974).

People with Type A personality are *highly competitive, insisting on always winning. They are impatient and often hostile.* By contrast, people with a Type B personality are *more easygoing, less hurried, and less hostile.* Heart disease correlates with Type A behavior, especially with the hostility aspect, but only weakly (Eaker, Sullivan, Kelly-Hayes, D'Agostino, & Benjamin, 2004). The best way to conduct the research is to measure personality now and heart problems later. (We want to know how personality affects heart problems, not how heart problems affect personality.) A study of that kind found a correlation of only 0.08 between hostility and heart disease (Rutledge & Hogan, 2002). However, another study found that heart disease is most common in the U.S. counties where people's tweets include more messages of hate and hostility (Eichstaedt et al., 2015).

The strongest known psychological influence on heart disease is social support. People with strong friendships and family ties usually take better care of themselves and keep their heart rate and blood pressure under control (Uchino, Cacioppo, & Kiecolt-Glaser, 1996). People who learn techniques for managing stress lower their blood pressure and decrease their risk of heart disease (Linden, Lenz, & Con, 2001).

a **b**

People in some cultures (a) live at a frantic pace. In other cultures (b), no one cares what time it is. Heart disease is more common in cultures with a hectic pace.

Variations in the prevalence of heart disease across cultures may depend on behavior (Levine, 1990). In some cultures, people walk fast, talk fast, wear watches, and tend to everything in a hurry. In other, more relaxed cultures, people are seldom in a rush. Almost nothing happens on schedule, but no one seems to care. As you might guess, heart disease is more common in countries with a hurried pace.

Post-Traumatic Stress Disorder

A profound result of severe stress is post-traumatic stress disorder (PTSD), *marked by prolonged anxiety and depression.* This condition has been recognized in post-war periods throughout history under such terms as "battle fatigue" and "shell shock." It also occurs in rape or assault victims, torture victims, survivors of life-threatening accidents, and witnesses to a murder. People with PTSD suffer from frequent nightmares, outbursts of anger, unhappiness, guilt, and impairments in both work and family life. A brief reminder of the tragic experience might trigger a flashback that borders on panic.

However, most people who endure a traumatic event do not develop PTSD. In fact, the probability of developing PTSD correlates poorly with the stressfulness of the event, and more strongly with previous anxiety and depression (Berntsen et al., 2012; Disner et al., 2017; Rubin & Feeling, 2013). It also correlates with "catastrophic thinking," characterized by often expecting the worst possible outcome (Seligman et al., 2019). Many soldiers who suffer post-traumatic stress disorder had already experienced "pre-traumatic stress disorder." Prior to military deployment, they reported disturbing images of what might happen in combat, disturbing dreams, and attempts to avoid any reminders of possible combat (Berntsen & Rubin, 2015).

Some people are more vulnerable than others. Most PTSD victims have a smaller than average hippocampus, and their brains differ from average in several other ways (Stein, Hanna, Koverola, Torchia, & McClarty, 1997; Yehuda, 1997). Given that stress releases cortisol and that high levels of cortisol damage the hippocampus, it would seem likely that high stress caused the smaller hippocampus. However, one study compared monozygotic twins in which one twin developed PTSD after wartime experiences and the other was not in battle and did not develop PTSD. The results: *Both* twins had a smaller than average hippocampus (Gilbertson et al., 2002). These results imply that the hippocampus was already small before the trauma, perhaps for genetic reasons, and having a small hippocampus increases the risk of PTSD.

Many psychologists have assumed that talking to a therapist soon after a traumatic experience might be helpful. However, most studies find that such interventions have little benefit (McNally, Bryant, & Ehlers, 2003), and often make people feel even worse (Bootzin & Bailey, 2005; Lilienfeld, 2007). If you have a traumatic experience, you might or might not want to talk about it, and you might want to talk just at certain times or to certain people. Talking about your trauma more than you wanted to just makes things worse.

17. What conclusion would follow if researchers had found that the twin without PTSD had a normal size hippocampus?

Answer

17. If the twin without PTSD had a normal hippocampus, the conclusion would be that severe stress had damaged the hippocampus of the twin with PTSD.

Coping with Stress

How you react to an event depends not only on the event itself but also on how you interpret it. Was it better or worse than you had expected? Do you think it was a onetime event or the start of a trend? Your reaction also depends on your personality. Some people keep their spirits high in the face of tragedy, whereas others are devastated by minor setbacks. Coping with stress is the process of getting through difficult times.

People cope with stress in many ways, grouped into three categories. One is problem-focused coping, *doing something to improve the situation.* Reappraisal is *reinterpreting a situation to make it seem less threatening.* Emotion-focused coping is *regulating one's emotional reaction.* Suppose you are nervous about an upcoming test. Studying harder is a problem-focused method of coping. Deciding that your grade is not very important is a reappraisal. Deep breathing exercises are an emotion-focused method. Each of these coping strategies works well under certain circumstances, and the best strategy is to be flexible in picking the strategy suited to the current situation (Bonanno & Burton, 2013). If you see a way to improve the situation, you should use problem-focused coping. If you have little or no control, you should shift to reappraisal or emotion-focused coping (Haines et al., 2016).

The distinction among coping styles is not a firm one (Skinner, Edge, Altman, & Sherwood, 2003). For example, if you seek help and support from friends, their support helps calm emotions (emotion-focused) but also may help deal with the problem itself (problem-focused).

Problem-Focused Coping

In many cases, the best way to handle stress is to do something about the problem. Often it helps to get *a small-scale preview of an upcoming experience*, a process called inoculation. Armies have soldiers practice combat skills under realistic conditions. A police trainee might pretend to intervene while two people enact a violent quarrel. If you are nervous about going to your landlord with a complaint, you might practice what you plan to say while your friend plays the part of the landlord. Some people are so nervous about saying or doing the wrong thing that they avoid dating opportunities. By role-playing, they practice dating behaviors with assigned partners and reduce their apprehension (Jaremko, 1983).

A feeling of control reduces stress. Suppose a snowstorm has trapped you in a small cabin. You have food and fuel, but you have no idea how long you will be stuck. The snow melts 5 days later, enabling you to leave. Contrast that with a case where you decide to isolate yourself in a cabin for 5 days so you can finish a painting. In both cases, you spend 5 days in a cabin, but when you do it voluntarily, you know what to expect, you feel in control, and you have less stress. Hospital patients who are told exactly what to expect show less anxiety and recover more quickly than average (Van Der Zee, Huet, Cazemier, & Evers, 2002).

Thinking that you have control is calming, even if you really don't. In one study, people received painfully hot stimuli to their arms while playing a video game. Participants in one group knew they had no control over the pain. Those in the other group were told (incorrectly) that they could decrease the painful stimuli if they made the correct joystick response quickly enough. In fact, the painful stimuli varied randomly, but whenever it decreased, these people

assumed they were responding "quickly enough." Those who *thought* they were in control reported less pain, and brain scans confirmed that the pain-sensitive areas of the brain responded less strongly (Salomons, Johnstone, Backonja, & Davidson, 2004).

18. Why does the mess that your roommate made bother you more than the mess you made yourself?

Answer

18. You have a feeling of control over your own mess, but not over your roommate's mess.

Coping by Reappraisal

Suppose you are in a situation that offers no control. You underwent medical tests, and you are nervously waiting for the results. While waiting, what can you do? You might reappraise the situation: "Even if the news is bad, I can handle it. It's an opportunity for me to rise to the occasion, to show how strong I can be." People who recover well from tragedies and defeats say that they try to see the positive side of any event (Tugade & Fredrickson, 2004). Most people like to maintain a moderately optimistic outlook even when it is not completely accurate (Armor, Massey, & Sackett, 2008).

Here is an example of reappraisal: Students were asked to restrain their emotions while examining pictures with disturbing images, such as injured people and crying children. Those who restrained their emotions most successfully relied on reinterpreting the pictures. For example, they might regard a picture of an injured person as "someone about to receive good medical care" (Jackson, Malmstadt, Larson, & Davidson, 2000). In another study, young adults in Israel who practiced reappraisal to control their anger became more inclined to approach the Israel-Palestinian conflict with conciliation, and less likely to advocate violence (Halperin, Porat, Tamir, & Gross, 2013).

Practicing self-defense serves as an inoculation against fear. The thought of being attacked is less frightening if you know how to handle a situation.

People who devote a short time each day to relaxation report diminished stress. Exercise works off excess energy, allowing greater relaxation.

husband's hand than did women reporting a less satisfactory marriage (Coan, Schaefer, & Davidson, 2006).

Relaxation

Relaxation is an excellent way to reduce unnecessary anxiety. Here are some suggestions (Benson, 1985):

- Find a quiet place, or at least one where the noise is not disturbing.
- Adopt a comfortable position, relaxing your muscles. If you are not sure how to do so, start with the opposite: Tense all your muscles so you notice how they feel. Then relax them one by one, starting from your toes and working toward your head.
- Reduce sources of stimulation, including your own thoughts. Focus your eyes on a simple, unexciting object. Or repeat something—a word, a phrase, a prayer, perhaps the Hindu syllable *om*—whatever feels comfortable to you.
- Don't worry about anything, not even about relaxing. If worrisome thoughts pop into your head, dismiss them with "oh, well."

Suppose you have to give a public speech tomorrow, or meet with your boss, and you feel such high arousal that your hands are shaking and your voice is trembling. An effective strategy is to reappraise your arousal: "I am not nervous. I am excited!" Embracing the arousal as a good thing leads to a more successful performance (Brooks, 2014).

Emotion-Focused Coping

Emotion-focused strategies do not solve a problem, but they help you manage your reaction to it. If you feel fear, anger, sadness, or disgust, would it help to simply suppress your emotion and act as if you are doing okay? It might, although suppressing your emotional expressions takes considerable effort (Segerstrom & Nes, 2007). Most Europeans and North Americans find it difficult and unpleasant to suppress their emotions. However, people in Asian cultures such as Japan and China routinely practice emotional suppression, especially in the presence of others, and they find it much less burdensome (Butler, Lee, & Gross, 2007; Mastracci & Adams, 2019). In addition to actively suppressing emotions, other ways of handling them include social support, relaxation, exercise, and distraction.

Social Support

When you feel bad, do you turn to others for support? This tendency varies across cultures. An American might discuss personal problems with a friend without necessarily expecting the friend to help. In Asian cultures, anyone who knows about your problem feels obligated to help. Therefore, many Asians avoid telling people about their difficulties for fear of burdening them with an obligation (Kim, Sherman, & Taylor, 2008).

Social support is helpful in many situations. A study found that people who had recently fallen in love reacted less strongly than usual to the stress of watching an unpleasant film, even if the loved one wasn't present (Schneiderman, Zilberstein-Kra, Leckman, & Feldman, 2011). Close contact with a loved one helps even more. Researchers recorded women's reactions while they waited to receive an electric shock. At various times, each woman held her husband's hand, an unfamiliar man's hand, or no hand. As shown in ▶ Figure 12.22, on average, a woman reported less unpleasantness and lower arousal while holding her husband's hand. Holding the hand of an unfamiliar man helped less. Women who reported a highly satisfactory marriage received more benefit from holding their

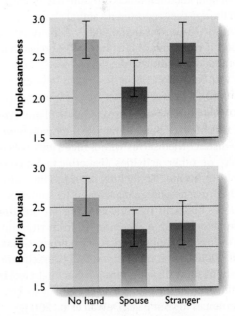

▲ **Figure 12.22** On average, a woman exposed to the threat of an upcoming shock reported less distress while holding her husband's hand. (From Coan, Schaefer, & Davidson, 2006)

People who practice this or other forms of meditation report that they feel less stress. Many improve their overall health (Benson, 1977, 1985). Teachers who went through an 8-week meditation program showed benefits in handling threatening situations and in showing compassion to other people (Kemeny et al., 2012).

Exercise

Exercise also reduces stress. It may seem contradictory to say that both relaxation and exercise reduce stress, but exercise helps people relax. Researchers found that students reported less stress on days when they exercised, and on days when they had a good sleep the night before (Flueckiger, Lieb, Meyer, Gitthauer, & Mata, 2016).

People in good physical condition react less strongly than average to stressful events. An event that would elevate heart rate enormously in other people elevates it only moderately in someone who has been exercising regularly. The exercise should be consistent, almost daily, but it does not need to be vigorous. In fact, strenuous activity often worsens someone's mood (Salmon, 2001).

The benefit of exercise depends partly on expectations. Researchers studied the female room attendants at seven hotels. They randomly chose certain hotels to inform these women (correctly) that their daily activities constitute good exercise that meets recommendations for a healthy, active lifestyle. When the researchers followed up 4 weeks later, they found that the women who were told that they were getting good exercise had in fact lost weight, and their blood pressure had decreased, even though they reported no actual change in their activities (Crum & Langer, 2007). Activity is more helpful if you think of it as healthy exercise than if you think of it as dull work.

Distraction

Another emotion-focused strategy is to distract yourself. Hospitalized patients handle their pain better if they distract themselves with a nice view, pleasant music, or other activities (Fauerbach, Lawrence, Haythornthwaite, & Richter, 2002). The Lamaze method teaches pregnant women to suppress the pain of childbirth by concentrating on breathing. Many people distract themselves from stressful or sad events by shopping (Cryder, Lerner, Gross, & Dahl, 2008; Hama, 2001). If you find yourself brooding about some disappointment, you might feel better after reminding yourself of pleasant or successful experiences in your past (DeWall et al., 2011).

Like exercise, the effectiveness of distraction depends partly on expectations. In one study, college students were asked to hold their fingers in ice water until the sensation became too painful to endure (Melzack, Weisz, & Sprague, 1963). Some of them listened to music of their own choice and were told that listening to music would reduce the pain. Others also listened to music but without the suggestion that it would ease the pain. Still others heard nothing but were told that a special "ultrasonic sound" was being transmitted that would lessen the pain. The group that heard music and expected it to reduce the pain tolerated the pain better than either of the other two groups did. Evidently, neither the music nor the suggestion of reduced pain is as effective as both are together.

All of us can learn to handle stress better by using the techniques just described, but some people handle it better naturally. We say they have resilience, *the ability to handle difficult situations with a minimum of distress.* A longitudinal study of police officers found that those who showed mostly positive emotions at the start were more likely than the others to handle their later stressful experiences well (Galatzer-Levy et al., 2013). A study of resilience among people of low socioeconomic status attributed part of their success to having good role models who taught them to persist through difficult situations by finding meaning in life and maintaining an optimistic viewpoint (Chen & Miller, 2012).

19. Under what conditions would emotion-focused coping be advisable?

Answer

19. It is best when problem-focused coping is not feasible.

Forgetting a Stressful Experience

Most problems related to anxiety or depression are precipitated by a stressful experience. If you have had a painfully stressful experience, would you want to forget it? You probably would not want to forget that it happened, but you might want to forget the emotional pain, and you might want to weaken the memory enough that fewer events will remind you of it.

A fair amount of animal research deals with ways to facilitate extinction of a fear memory. Suppose a rodent has had repeated experiences in which a visual or auditory stimulus predicts shock. That stimulus will now provoke fear, which the animal shows by freezing in place whenever it sees or hears that stimulus. If we now present the stimulus by itself repeatedly, we produce extinction of the learned fear, but the extinction is temporary. After a delay, the fear returns (spontaneous recovery). Similarly, when people undergo extinction training to combat PTSD, phobia, or other anxieties, the usual result is a temporary suppression followed by a later return of the anxiety.

Research on memory has discovered the following: Suppose stimulus A has been paired with shock (or anything else). Days later, present stimulus A again, by itself. At that time, the memory is in a malleable state. Ordinarily, the brain remembers the previous training and reconsolidates the memory at that point. However, a new experience can modify the original memory, and certain procedures can disrupt the reconsolidation. One way to disrupt reconsolidation is to administer drugs that block protein synthesis (Elsey, Van Ast, & Kindt, 2018). Another way is distraction, as research has demonstrated with both laboratory animals and humans. For example, show a film that reevokes a painful memory, and then 10 minutes later have the person play the video game *Tetris* for 12 minutes (James et al., 2015). Apparently, keeping working memory active at that point decreases reconsolidation and weakens the memory. Happily, it weakens the physiological response to the memory without destroying the declarative memory. That is, the person remembers the facts, but has less response to them (Kredlow, Eichenbaum, & Otto, 2018).

So far, most of the research has been with laboratory animals, and only a few studies have dealt with humans. The procedure seems promising, but the effectiveness depends on details of procedure. The previous paragraph mentioned a study in which people played *Tetris* 10 minutes after the reminder of a stressful experience. That 10-minute delay was crucial. With longer or shorter delays, the procedure failed. Similarly, in all other studies, the delay had to be right, and the right delay is not the same from one study to another (Drexler & Wolf, 2018; Treanor, Brown, Rissman, & Craske, 2017). Applying a procedure like this for treating human anxieties may be possible, but finding the correct parameters for each unique situation will be difficult.

in closing | module 12.3

Health Is Mental as Well as Medical

We have considered the ways people try to deal with stressful situations. How well do these strategies work? They work well for many people, but at a cost. The cost is that coping with serious stressors requires energy. Many people who have had to cope with long-lasting stressors break their diets, resume smoking and drinking habits that they had abandoned long ago, and they find it difficult to concentrate on challenging cognitive tasks (Muraven & Baumeister, 2000).

Still, in spite of the costs, an amazing number of people say that the experience of battling a chronic illness, tending to a loved one with a severe illness, or dealing with other painful experiences brought them personal strength and an enhanced feeling of meaning in life (Folkman & Moskowitz, 2000). They found positive moments even in the midst of fear and loss. Not everyone rises to the occasion, but many do.

Summary

- *Definitions of stress.* Hans Selye defined stress as the response to any change in life. An alternative definition is that stress comes from an event that someone considers threatening. (page 394)
- *General adaptation syndrome.* As Selye noticed, the body reacts to almost any illness or to severe stress with sleepiness, fatigue, and fever. (page 394)
- *Difficulties of measuring stress.* Stress is difficult to measure because a given event can be highly stressful to one person and much less to another. (page 395)
- *Indirect effects on health.* Stress affects health indirectly because people exposed to stressful events often change their eating, sleeping, and drinking habits. (page 396)
- *Direct effects on health.* Stress alters health by activating the immune system, including cortisol release. Mild or brief activation enhances health and alertness, but prolonged cortisol impairs the hippocampus and the immune system itself. (page 396)

- *Heart disease.* Research has found a small link between heart disease and emotional response, especially hostility. (page 396)
- *Post-traumatic stress disorder (PTSD).* Traumatic experiences can produce PTSD, but individuals differ in vulnerability. Increased vulnerability is linked to previous depression, a catastrophizing attitude, and a smaller than average hippocampus. (page 397)
- *Coping styles.* People cope with stress by fixing the problem, reappraising it, or trying to control emotions. (page 397)
- *Prediction and control.* Events are generally less stressful when people think they can predict or control them. (page 398)
- *Facilitated forgetting.* Research, mostly with laboratory animals, has found procedures that can weaken the physiological aspect of a fear memory. However, the effectiveness depends on details of the procedure, which will be difficult to apply to human anxieties. (page 400)

Key Terms

cortisol (page 394)

emotion-focused coping (page 397)

general adaptation syndrome (page 394)

health psychology (page 394)

inoculation (page 398)

post-traumatic stress disorder (PTSD) (page 397)

problem-focused coping (page 397)

reappraisal (page 397)

resilience (page 400)

stress (page 394)

Type A personality (page 396)

Type B personality (page 396)

Review Questions

1. According to Selye's definition of stress, which one of the following would be considered stressful?
   (a) Being born with a physical handicap
   (b) Getting married
   (c) Lifelong poverty
   (d) Being a member of a minority group

2. Intense, prolonged stress leads to fever, fatigue, and sleepiness by releasing which hormone?
   (a) Testosterone
   (b) Cortisol
   (c) Insulin
   (d) Cholecystokinin

3. Which of the following most strongly increases the probability of PTSD?
   (a) Previous history of depression
   (b) The severity of the stressful event itself
   (c) Inability to talk with a therapist soon after the event
   (d) Being older than 45 years old

4. What aspect of brain anatomy or function is associated with increased risk of PTSD?
   (a) Faster than average action potentials
   (b) Slower than average action potentials
   (c) Smaller than average hippocampus
   (d) Larger than average hippocampus

5. If people think they have control of a situation, but really they don't, what is the effect on stress, if any?
   (a) The stress becomes more severe.
   (b) The stress becomes less severe.
   (c) The stress is unchanged.

6. While a painful memory is undergoing reconsolidation, a distracting experience can weaken the emotional aspect of the memory, but the results depend critically on what?
   (a) Genetics
   (b) Age
   (c) Temperature
   (d) Timing

Answers: 1b, 2b, 3a, 4c, 5b, 6d.

13 Social Behavior

Hollie Adams/Getty Images

In the *Communist Manifesto*, Karl Marx and Friedrich Engels wrote, "Mankind are more disposed to suffer, while evils are sufferable, than to right themselves by abolishing the forms to which they are accustomed. But when a long train of abuses and usurpations, pursuing invariably the same object, evinces a design to reduce them under absolute despotism, it is their right, it is their duty, to throw off such government." Fidel Castro wrote, "A little rebellion, now and then, is a good thing." Do you agree with those statements? Why or why not? Can you think of anything that would change your mind?

What if I told you that the first statement is not from the *Communist Manifesto*, but from the United States' Declaration of Independence? And what if I told you that the second quotation is from Thomas Jefferson, not Castro? Would you agree more with these statements if they came from democratic revolutionaries instead of communist revolutionaries?

Well, those quotes did in fact come from the Declaration of Independence and Thomas Jefferson, so you can now consider one of the fundamental questions in social psychology: What influences your opinions?

Social psychology includes the study of attitudes, persuasion, self-understanding, and the everyday behaviors of people in their relationships with others. **Social psychologists** *study social behavior and how people influence one another.*

Bettmann/Getty Images

Influence depends not only on what someone says but also on what the listeners think of the speaker.

Prosocial and Antisocial Behavior

Hollie Adams/Getty Images

After studying this module, you should be able to:

1. Evaluate Kohlberg's approach to moral reasoning.

2. Describe the prisoner's dilemma task.

3. Explain logical reasons for cooperative behavior.

4. Discuss why people sometimes help each other and sometimes don't.

5. List factors related to aggressive behavior.

Young people, especially in the United States, look forward to becoming adults and being independent. But how independent are any of us, really? Do you make your own clothing? Will you build your own home? How much of your food do you hunt or gather? Do you perform your own medical care? Will you build your own car and pave your own roads? Of all the acts you need for survival, do you do *any* of them entirely by yourself, other than breathe? Even for that, you count on the government to prevent excessive air pollution. Humans are *inter*dependent. Our survival depends on cooperation.

Furthermore, most of us at least occasionally give to charity, volunteer time for worthy projects, offer directions to a stranger who appears lost, and in other ways help people who will never pay us back. Why?

Morality: Logical or Emotional?

Psychologists once regarded morality as a set of arbitrary rules, like learning to stop at a red light and go at a green light. Lawrence Kohlberg (1969; Kohlberg & Hersh, 1977) proposed instead that moral reasoning matures through a series of stages, similar to Piaget's stages of cognitive development. For example, children younger than about 6 years old say that accidentally breaking a valuable object is worse than intentionally breaking a less valuable object. Older children and adults make judgments based on intentions more than results. The change is a natural unfolding, according to Kohlberg, not a matter of memorizing rules.

According to Kohlberg, to evaluate people's moral reasoning, we should ask about the reasons for their decisions, not just the decisions themselves. In George Bernard Shaw's (1911) play *The Doctor's Dilemma*, two men are dying. The only doctor in town has enough medicine to save one of them but not both. One man is an artistic genius but dishonest, rude, and disagreeable. The other will make no great accomplishments, but he is honest and decent. The doctor, forced to choose between them, saves the honest but untalented man. Did he make the right choice? According to Kohlberg, this is the wrong question. The right question is *why* he made that choice. In the play, the doctor made this choice because he hoped to marry the wife of the artistic genius after letting him die. What do you think about the quality of the doctor's moral reasoning?

Kohlberg focused psychologists' attention on the reasoning processes behind moral decisions, but people don't often deliberate about right and wrong before they act. More often, they make a quick decision and then look for reasons afterward. In the terminology of cognitive psychology, we use Type 1

reasoning for the initial decision, and we call upon Type 2 reasoning to generate logical-sounding explanations. Consider the following: Mark and his sister Julie are college students. One summer, they traveled together, and one night they stayed at a cabin in the woods. They decided it would be fun to have sex together, so they did. Julie was taking birth control pills, but Mark used a condom anyway just to be sure. Both enjoyed the experience, and neither felt hurt in any way. They decided not to do it again but to keep it as their little secret. They feel closer than ever as brother and sister. Was their action okay?

Almost everyone reacts immediately, "No! No! No!" But why? Mark and Julie used reliable methods of birth control, and both said they enjoyed the experience and did not feel hurt. If their act was wrong, why was it wrong? When you (presumably) said that they were wrong, did you reason it out logically? You probably decided at once, emotionally, and then looked for a justification (Haidt, 2001, 2007).

In addition to the fact that most moral decisions are more emotional than logical, Kohlberg's analysis falls short in another way. According to Kohlberg, morality means seeking justice and avoiding harm to others. That description seems right to most Americans and Europeans, especially political liberals, but most people in the rest of the world also consider loyalty to their group, respect for authority, and spiritual purity. They would insist that incest between Mark and Julie was an impure act that defiles them spiritually, regardless of whether they enjoyed it (Haidt, 2012). Particularly in India, people regard moral behavior as a duty to be performed without question, not as a voluntary choice (Miller, Goyal, & Wice, 2017). If we care about moral thinking by all people, and not just certain types of people, we need to consider more than Kohlberg did.

concept check

1. **In what way was Kohlberg's approach an advance, and in what way is it limited?**

Answer

1. Kohlberg called attention to moral reasoning as a special process, not just memorizing rules. However, he ignored the emotional component of moral reasoning and the cultural differences in moral reasoning.

Altruistic Behavior

Altruistic behavior is *helping someone without any direct benefit to yourself.* Theoretically, it is a puzzle. The principles of operant conditioning say that you repeat behaviors that bring reinforcements to yourself. The principles of evolution say that natural selection favors behaviors that increase the probability of spreading your own genes, not those of someone else. So why would anyone help another person? One reason is a belief in a god who rewards good acts and punishes bad ones (Purzycki et al., 2016), but altruistic behavior also occurs in nonbelievers, children too young to know about religion, and at least some nonhuman animals, so we need to look for additional explanations.

In a great variety of species, animals devote great energies and even risk their lives to help their babies and sometimes other relatives. Helping unrelated others is much less common but it does occur at least occasionally, in species including chimpanzees, monkeys, dolphins, elephants, and of course your pet dog that acts as if it is related to you (de Waal & Preston, 2017; Schmelz, Grueneisen, Kabalak, Jost, & Tomasello, 2017). Chimpanzees learn to cooperate toward a common goal, at least sometimes (Suchak et al., 2016; Tomasello, 2018). But humans are the champions at cooperation and helping behavior, beginning in early childhood (Grossman, Missana, & Krol, 2018; Sebastián-Enesco, Hernández-Lloreda, & Colmenares, 2013), and increasing as children grow older (House et al., 2013). Given a choice between two treats to themselves or one to self and one to another, 6- to 8-year-old children generally choose two for themselves, but older children in most societies shift toward the sharing option, and they object if they are given more or better treats than someone else (Blake et al., 2015; House et al., 2013).

Nearly all people—even toddlers and young children—are more helpful toward familiar people than toward strangers (Wynn, Bloom, Jordan, Marshall, & Sheskin, 2018), but a few rare individuals will go to great lengths to help a stranger, even donate a kidney. What do we know about those extreme altruists? Suppose a researcher measures your brain responses while you experience pain, and while you watch someone else endure the same pain. Most people's brains respond much more strongly to their own pain, but people who have donated a kidney to a stranger respond nearly as much to watching a stranger's pain as they do to their own pain (Brethel-Haurwitz et al., 2018). Presumably this type of extreme empathy motivates their self-sacrificing behavior.

The Prisoner's Dilemma

To investigate cooperation and competition, social psychologists have used the **prisoner's dilemma**, *a*

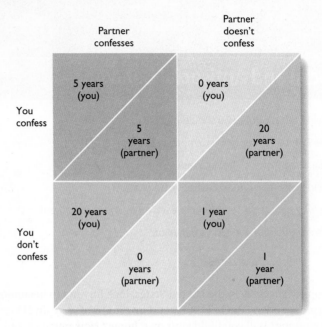

▲ **Figure 13.1** In the prisoner's dilemma, each person has an incentive to confess. But if both people confess, they suffer worse than if both had refused to confess.

situation where people choose between a cooperative act and a competitive act that benefits themselves but hurts others. Imagine that you and a partner are arrested and charged with armed robbery. The police take you into separate rooms and urge each of you to confess. If neither of you confesses, the police do not have enough evidence to convict you of robbery, but they can convict you of a lesser offense with a sentence of a year in prison. If either of you confesses and testifies against the other, the confessor goes free and the other gets 20 years in prison. If you both confess, you each get 5 years in prison. Each of you knows that the other person has the same options. ▲ **Figure 13.1** illustrates the choices.

If your partner does not confess, your better choice is to confess so that you can go free. (Let's assume you care only about yourself and not about your partner.) If your partner confesses, you still gain by confessing because you will get only 5 years in prison instead of 20. Therefore, you confess. Your partner, reasoning the same way, also confesses, and the result is that you both get 5 years in prison. If you had both kept quiet, you would have served only 1 year in prison. The situation trapped both of you into uncooperative behavior.

If you and your partner could discuss your strategy, you would agree not to confess. Then, when the police took you to separate rooms, you each hope that the other keeps the bargain. But can you be sure? Maybe your partner will double-cross you and confess. If so, you should confess, too. And if your partner does keep the bargain, what should you do? Again, it's to your advantage to confess! You are back where you started.

The two of you are most likely to cooperate if you stay in constant communication (Nemeth, 1972). If you overhear each other, you know that, if one confesses, the other will retaliate immediately. This kind of situation occurs in real life among nations as well as individuals. During the arms race between the United States and the Soviet Union, both sides wanted a treaty to stop building nuclear weapons. However, if one country kept the agreement while the other made additional weapons, the cheater could build a military advantage. The only way to keep an agreement was to allow each side to inspect the other. Eventually, spy satellites made it possible to monitor the agreement.

The prisoner's dilemma can also be stated in terms of gains. Suppose you and another person have a choice between two moves, which we call *cooperate* and *compete.* Depending on your choices, here are the payoffs:

Here are the payoffs:

	Other person cooperates	Other person competes
You cooperate	Both win $1	Other person gains $2; you lose $2
You compete	You gain $2; other person loses $2	Both lose $1

Suppose you play this game only once with someone you will never meet. Both of you will reveal your answers by telephone to a third person. Which move do you choose? If the other person cooperates, your winning choice is *compete* because you will get $2 instead of $1. If the other person competes, again you gain by competing because you will lose just $1 instead of $2. Logically, you should choose to compete, as should the other person, and you both lose $1. (Try to avoid getting into situations like this!)

In real life, people do cooperate most of the time. What is the difference between real-life situations and the prisoner's dilemma? The main difference is that we deal with people repeatedly, not just once. If you play the prisoner's dilemma many times with the same partner, the two of you will probably learn to cooperate, especially if real rewards are at stake. Furthermore, in real life you want a reputation for cooperating, or people will stop doing business with you (Feinberg, Willer, & Schultz, 2014). Thus, here is one explanation for altruistic behavior: *People want a reputation for being fair and helpful* (McNamara, Barta, Fromhage, & Houston, 2008). Both children and adults are more cooperative and generous with others who have a reputation for cooperation, and people who do cooperate want other people to know they cooperated (Martin & Olson, 2015; Romano & Balliet, 2017).

A second reason for cooperation is that *people who cooperate punish those who don't*. In some cases, people will pay for an opportunity to punish an uncooperative person (Gächter, Renner, & Sefton, 2008), and people who pay to punish an uncooperative person improve their own reputation for trustworthiness (Jordan, Hoffman, Bloom, & Rand, 2016). However, if too many people become uncooperative, it becomes difficult or ineffective to punish them all (Dreber, Rand, Fudenberg, & Nowak, 2008; Herrmann, Thöni, & Gächter, 2008). Punishing uncooperative people works well in countries where most people trust one another, but not in countries with low trust and limited cooperation (Balliet & Van Lange, 2013).

2. You have read two explanations for humans' altruistic behavior. Why do both of them require the ability to recognize one person from another?

Answer

2. One explanation for altruistic behavior is that cooperating builds a reputation, and a reputation requires individuals to recognize one another. The other explanation is that people who cooperate will punish those who do not. Again, to retaliate, they need to recognize who has failed to cooperate. It is noteworthy that humans, which are so good at cooperating, are also excellent at facial recognition.

Accepting or Denying Responsibility toward Others

What determines whether someone helps or ignores a person in need? The outcome relates to personality, but it also depends on the situation.

Bystander Helpfulness and Apathy

Suppose while you are waiting at a bus stop, you see me trip and fall down, not far away. I am not screaming in agony, but I don't get up either, so you are not sure whether I need help. Would you come over and offer to help? Before you answer, imagine the situation in two ways: First, you and I are the only people in sight. Second, many other people are nearby, and none of them are rushing to my aid. Does the presence of those other people make any difference to you? (It doesn't to me. I am in the same pain regardless of how many people ignore me.)

A real-life event illustrates the issue. Late one night in March 1964, Kitty Genovese was stabbed to death near her apartment in Queens, New York. A newspaper article at the time reported that 38 of her neighbors heard her screaming for more than half an hour, but none of them called the police, each of them either declining to get involved or assuming that someone else had already called the police. This episode popularized the concept of **bystander apathy**, the tendency to ignore someone's need when other people had an equal opportunity to help. However, later investigations indicated that the report about Kitty Genovese was distorted and exaggerated (Manning, Levine, & Collins, 2007). About six people saw someone attack her, and at least one or two did call the police, who failed to respond. Genovese went into the building on her own, and her attacker returned to attack again half an hour later, out of sight of witnesses, while she was too weak to scream.

And there is still more to the story. Five days after the attack, the police arrested a man, Winston Moseley, who not only confessed to the crime, but also led the police to her wallet and keys. He then confessed to two other murders and provided accurate details, including one murder for which the police had arrested another man and coerced a confession after exhausting him by several days of grilling. (This happened before the ruling that the police must advise suspects of their rights.) Despite Moseley's voluntary and detailed confession, and the other man's insistence that his confession was false, the police persisted with the prosecution of the other man. Possibly to distract attention from this dubious tactic, the police told a newspaper reporter that 38 neighbors had seen the attack on Genovese but failed to respond. Suddenly, that became the focus of attention (Kassin, 2017).

Although the newspaper article about 38 witnesses was full of errors, it prompted interest in why people often fail to help someone in distress. Are we less likely to act when we know that someone else could act? Bibb Latané and John Darley (1969) proposed that being in a crowd decreases our probability of action because of **diffusion of responsibility**: *We feel less responsibility to act when other people are equally able to act.*

In an experiment designed to test this hypothesis, a young woman ushered one or two students into a room and asked them to wait for the start of a market research study (Latané & Darley, 1968, 1969). She went into the next room, closing the door behind her. Then she played a tape recording that sounded as though she climbed onto a chair, fell off, and moaned, "Oh . . . my foot . . . I can't move it. Oh . . . my ankle . . ." Of the participants who were waiting alone, 70 percent went next door and offered to help. Of the participants who were waiting with someone else, only 13 percent offered to help. Similar results have been reported many times, including with young children (Plötner, Over, Carpenter, & Tomasello, 2015).

Diffusion of responsibility is one explanation. Each person thinks, "It's not my responsibility to help any more than someone else's." In fact, someone else might be better qualified to help. Bystander apathy is less likely if the bystanders know one another, because everyone knows that no one else is an expert (Hortensius & de Gelder, 2018). A second explanation is that the presence of other people who are doing nothing provides information (or misinformation). The situation is ambiguous: "Do I need to act or not? Does this person really need help?" Other people's inaction implies that the situation requires no action. In fact, the others, who are just as uncertain as you are, draw the same conclusion from *your* inaction. Social psychologists use the term **pluralistic ignorance** to describe *a situation in which each person falsely assumes that others have a better-informed opinion.* Other people's inactivity implies that that the situation is not an emergency.

Social Loafing

When you take a test, you work alone, and your success depends on your own effort. However, if you work for a company that gives workers a share of the profits, your rewards depend on other workers' productivity as well as your own. Do you work as hard as possible when the rewards depend on the group's productivity?

In many cases, you do not. In one experiment, students were told to scream, clap, and make as much noise as possible, like cheerleaders at a sports event. Students either screamed and clapped alone, or acted in groups, or acted alone but *thought* other people were screaming and clapping, too. (They wore headphones so they could not hear anyone else.) Most of the students who screamed and clapped alone made more noise than those who were, or thought they were, part of a group (Latané, Williams,

People watch other people's responses to decide how they should respond. When a group of sidewalk Santas—who had gathered in Manhattan to promote a back-rub business—came to the aid of an injured cyclist, a few Santas made the first move and the others followed.

& Harkins, 1979). Social psychologists call this phenomenon **social loafing**—*the tendency to "loaf" (or work less hard) when sharing work with other people.*

Social loafing has been demonstrated in many situations. Suppose you are asked to "name all the uses you can think of for a brick" (crack nuts, anchor a boat, use as a doorstop, etc.) and write each one on a card. You probably fill out many cards by yourself but fewer if you are tossing cards into a pile along with other people's suggestions (Harkins & Jackson, 1985). You don't bother submitting ideas that you assume other people have already suggested.

At this point, you may be thinking, "Wait a minute. When I'm playing basketball or soccer, I try as hard as I can. I don't think I loaf." You are right. Social loafing is rare in team sports because observers, including teammates, watch your performance. People work hard in groups if they expect other people to notice their effort or if they think they can contribute something that other group members cannot (Shepperd, 1993; Williams & Karau, 1991).

3. **In a typical family, one or two members have jobs, but their wages benefit all. Why do the wage earners *not* engage in social loafing?**

Answer

3. The main reason is that the wage earners see they can make a special contribution that the others (children, injured, or retired) cannot. Also, others can easily observe their contributions.

Violent and Aggressive Behavior

During World War II, nearly all the industrialized nations were at war, the Nazis were exterminating the Jews, and the United States was preparing a nuclear bomb that it later dropped on Japan. Meanwhile, Mohandas K. Gandhi was in jail for leading a nonviolent protest march against British rule in India. The charge against Gandhi was, ironically, "disturbing the peace." Someone asked Gandhi what he thought of Western civilization. He replied that "it might be a good idea."

Cruelty and violence have always been part of human experience, just as kindness and altruism have been. But the balance between kindness and cruelty has not always remained the same. As Steven Pinker (2011) has argued, since World War II, the worldwide rate of death by war and murder has declined to its lowest level ever. Education is a major contributor to the decline, as are travel and communication. It's hard to hate people after you have visited their country or played Internet games with them. Violence is still a problem, but we can do much about it.

Causes of Anger and Aggression

According to the **frustration-aggression hypothesis**, *the main cause of anger and aggression is frustration—an obstacle that stands in the way of doing something or obtaining something* (Dollard, Miller, Doob, Mowrer, & Sears, 1939). However, frustration makes you angry only when you believe the other person acted intentionally. You might feel angry if someone ran down the hall and bumped into you, but probably not if someone slipped on a wet spot and bumped into you.

Leonard Berkowitz (1983, 1989) proposed a more comprehensive theory: Any unpleasant event—frustration, pain, heat, foul odors, bad news, whatever—excites both the impulse to fight and the impulse to flee. It excites the sympathetic nervous system and its fight-or-flight response. Your choice to fight or flee depends on the circumstances. If the person who just bumped into you looks weak, you express anger. If that person looks intimidating, you suppress your anger. And if it is the loan and scholarship officer at your college, you smile and apologize for getting in the way.

Individual Differences in Aggression

Why are some people more aggressive than others? One hypothesis has been that low self-esteem leads to violence. According to this idea, people who think little of themselves try to build themselves up by tearing someone else down. Some studies find a small relationship between aggressive behaviors and low self-esteem, but others find virtually no relationship between the two (Baumeister, Campbell, Krueger, & Vohs, 2003; Donnellan, Trzesniewski, Robins, Moffitt, & Caspi, 2005). A stronger possibility is that people who are accustomed to feeling powerful become aggressive when they find their self-confidence threatened, or when their self-esteem wavers (Fast & Chen, 2009; Zeigler-Hill, Enjaian, Holden, & Southard, 2014).

Are mentally ill patients prone to violence? Swedish researchers examined the whole country's medical and criminal records and found that people with severe mental illnesses, who constituted 1.4 percent of the population, committed 5 percent of the violent crimes (Fazel & Grann, 2006). However, as illustrated in ◀ **Figure 13.2**, the increased danger is associated mainly with those mental patients who are also alcohol or substance abusers (Elbogen & Johnson, 2009; Elbogen, Dennis, & Johnson, 2016).

If low self-esteem and mental illness do not predict violence, what does? Many genes associated with the neurotransmitter serotonin have been linked to aggressive behavior, but each has only small effects (Xiang et al., 2019). A few rare genetic variants have been found in men with extreme impulsive violent behavior (Vevera et al., 2019).

Several other factors are correlated with a tendency toward violent behavior (Bushman & Anderson, 2009; Davidson, Putnam, & Larson, 2000; Glenn & Raine, 2014; Grotzinger et al., 2018; Hay et al., 2011; D. O. Lewis et al., 1985; Lynam, 1996; Muris, Merckelbach, Otgaar, & Meijer, 2017; Osofsky, 1995):

- Growing up in a violent neighborhood
- Having parents with a history of antisocial behavior
- Having a mother who smoked cigarettes or drank alcohol during pregnancy
- Poor nutrition or exposure to lead or other toxic chemicals early in life
- A history of head injury
- Not feeling guilty after hurting someone
- Weaker than normal sympathetic nervous system responses (which correlates with not feeling bad after hurting someone)
- A history of suicide attempts
- A psychopathic personality (hardly surprising, as antisocial behavior is part of the definition of psychopathic personality)

Culture is also a powerful influence, and not only for humans. A fascinating study documented the influence of culture on aggressive behavior even in nonhuman primates. Researchers observed a troop of baboons for 25 years. At one point, the most aggressive males in the troop took food away from a neighboring troop. The food happened to be contaminated, and those males died. The surviving

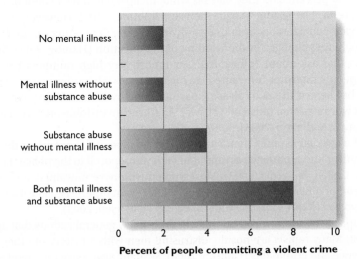

▲ **Figure 13.2** People with mental illness who are also substance abusers have an 8 percent chance of committing a violent crime within 2 to 3 years. Those who are not substance abusers are similar to the rest of the population. (Based on data from "The intricate link between violence and mental disorder," by E. B. Elbogen & S. C. Johnson, 2009. *Archives of General Psychiatry, 66,* pp. 152–161.)

troop then consisted of females, juveniles, and the less aggressive males. All got along well, stress levels decreased, and health improved. Over the years, new males occasionally entered the troop and adopted this troop's customs. Years later, none of the original males remained there, but the troop continued its nonaggressive tradition (Sapolsky & Share, 2004).

4. One proposal to reduce violence in the United States is to prevent mentally ill people from buying guns. How effective would that act be, probably?

Answer

4. It probably would not accomplish a great deal, because mentally ill people are responsible for only a small percentage of overall crime. Among the mentally ill, only those who are also drug or alcohol abusers are substantially more dangerous than average.

Even a baboon troop can develop a culture of peaceful behavior.

Cognitive Influences on Violence and Aggressive Behavior

Most people think of themselves as good. Most of the time you treat other people fairly, right? You know it is wrong to hurt or cheat anyone. But at times, you might make an exception. If you serve in the police or military, certain situations might require you to shoot someone. In business, you might yield to a temptation to raise profits by doing something unfair to your competitors or risky to your customers. If so, you want to justify your actions to make them seem acceptable.

People often justify their acts by thinking of themselves as better than the people they are hurting. In war, soldiers give their enemies a derogatory name and discuss them with contempt (Lewandowsky, Stritzke, Freund, Oberauer, & Krueger, 2013). The same occurs for violence against racial minorities or other groups. Psychologists describe this process as *deindividuation* (perceiving others as anonymous, without any real personality) and *dehumanization* (perceiving others as less than human). The result is greater acceptance of violence and injustice against those groups. Certain brain areas are known to respond strongly when you interact socially with someone, or even when you see someone with whom you would like to interact socially. These brain areas hardly respond at all when you see homeless people, drug addicts, or others for whom you have a low regard (Harris & Fiske, 2006). In effect, you don't see them as human. That study is one example of *social neuroscience*—the use of brain measurements to shed light on social behavior.

People also justify their violent behavior by decreasing their own sense of identity. A soldier on duty is no longer acting as an individual making his or her own decisions. A Ku Klux Klansman wearing a hood suppresses a sense of personal identity. A criminal wearing a mask not only decreases the probability of witness identification, but also creates a distance between the "real self" and the perpetrator of the act. Also, just as dehumanizing other people seems to justify treating them badly, dehumanizing yourself increases aggression. When prisoners or others are treated like "brute animals," they start thinking of themselves that way, and they behave in less moral ways (Kouchaki, Dobson, Waytz, & Kteily, 2018).

Sexual Aggression

Rape is *sexual activity without the consent of the partner*. In one survey, about 10 percent of adult women reported that they had been forcibly raped, and another 10 percent said they had sex while incapacitated by alcohol or other drugs (Testa, Livingston, Vanzile-Tamsen, & Frone, 2003). However, the statistics vary considerably from one study to another, depending on many factors, including changes in the wording of the question (Hamby, 2014). Some surveys that ask about "unwanted" sex report very high numbers because many people interpret "unwanted" to include times when they weren't in the mood but agreed to sex to please a partner (Hamby & Koss, 2003). With that type of wording, even most men answer yes (Struckman-Johnson, Struckman-Johnson, & Anderson, 2003).

Of all sexual assaults that legally qualify as rape, only about half the victims think of the experience as rape, and far fewer report it to the police (Fisher, Daigle, Cullen, & Turner, 2003). Most women who have unwanted sex with a boyfriend or other acquaintance do not call the event rape, especially if alcohol was involved (Kahn, Jackson, Kully, Badger, & Halvorsen, 2003).

Rapists are not all alike, but we can draw a few generalizations that apply to most. Many rapists are hostile, distrustful men with a history of other acts of violence and criminality (Hanson, 2000). Sexually aggressive men tend to be high users of pornography (Vega & Malamuth, 2007), and rapists are much more likely than other men to enjoy violent pornography (Donnerstein & Malamuth, 1997). Another element in rape is extreme self-centeredness, or lack of concern for others (Dean & Malamuth, 1997).

Is Cooperative Behavior Logical?

The research on the prisoner's dilemma and similar games attempts to demonstrate that cooperation and mutual aid are logical under certain conditions. You cooperate to develop a good reputation so that others will cooperate with you and not penalize you.

Do you find this explanation completely satisfactory? Sometimes, you make an anonymous contribution to a worthy cause with no expectation of personal gain, not even an improvement of your reputation. You simply wanted to help that cause. You occasionally help someone you'll never see again while no one else is watching. Perhaps these acts require no special explanation. You have developed habits of helping for all the reasons that investigators have identified, and having developed those habits, you generalize them to other circumstances. Yes, perhaps. Or maybe researchers are still overlooking something. Conclusions in psychology are seldom final. You are invited to think about these issues yourself and develop your own hypotheses.

Summary

- *Kohlberg's view of moral reasoning.* Lawrence Kohlberg identified morality as a type of reasoning, to be evaluated by the reasons people give for a decision. (page 405)
- *Other aspects of morality.* Kohlberg overlooked the importance of emotions in moral judgments and the differences among cultures. (page 405)
- *Altruism.* From the standpoint of either operant conditioning or evolution, the reasons for helping unrelated people are not obvious. (page 406)
- *Reasons for cooperation.* Studies of the prisoner's dilemma and similar games show that people cooperate to establish a reputation for cooperation, and to avoid possible retaliation. (page 407)
- *Bystander apathy.* People are less likely to help someone if other people are in an equally good position to help. (page 407)
- *Social loafing.* People often work less hard when other people with equal or greater abilities are working on the same task. (page 408)
- *Aggressive behavior.* Frustration or discomfort of any kind increases the probability of anger and aggression, especially if one perceives that others have caused their frustration intentionally. (page 408)
- *Factors related to aggressive behavior.* Self-esteem has less effect than we might expect on aggressiveness. Mental illness has only a weak relationship to violence, unless it is combined with alcohol or drug abuse. (page 409)
- *Cognitive factors in aggression.* People sometimes justify cruel or uncooperative behavior by lowering their opinion of the victims. People also decrease their own sense of personal responsibility. (page 410)
- *Sexual aggression.* Most men who commit sexual aggression have a history of previous antisocial behavior. (page 410)

Key Terms

altruistic behavior (page406)

bystander apathy (page 407)

diffusion of responsibility (page 408)

frustration-aggression hypothesis (page 409)

pluralistic ignorance (page 408)

prisoner's dilemma (page 406)

rape (page 410)

social loafing (page 408)

social psychologists (page 404)

Review Questions

1. What aspect of moral reasoning did Lawrence Kohlberg overlook or understate?
   (a) Stages
   (b) Development
   (c) Logical thinking
   (d) Emotional reactions

2. The principles of operant conditioning have trouble explaining which of the following?
   (a) Aggressive behavior
   (b) Altruistic behavior
   (c) Social loafing
   (d) Bystander apathy

3. What happens in real life that leads to more cooperation than in a single trial of the prisoner's dilemma?
   (a) People compete for benefits.
   (b) People seek to enhance their reputation.
   (c) People avoid expending extra effort.
   (d) People understand the payoff matrix.

4. Diffusion of responsibility is a plausible explanation for which of the following?
   (a) Altruism
   (b) Intergroup aggressive behavior
   (c) Low self-esteem
   (d) Bystander apathy

5. Under what circumstance, if any, does mental illness greatly increase the probability of violent behavior?
   (a) Under all circumstances
   (b) If the person abuses alcohol or other drugs
   (c) If the person is not receiving psychotherapy
   (d) Under no circumstances

6. How do deindividuation and dehumanization increase aggressive behavior?
   (a) They increase the perpetrator's sense of righteousness.
   (b) They make the victim seem less worthy.
   (c) They decrease the perpetrator's self-esteem.
   (d) They impair memory.

Answers: 1d, 2b, 3b, 4d, 5b, 6b.

module 13.2

Social Perception and Cognition

After studying this module, you should be able to:

1. Define the primacy effect in social psychology and give an example.

2. Describe how the implicit association test measures prejudices.

3. Discuss methods of overcoming prejudice.

4. Distinguish among three types of influence on attributions.

5. Describe the actor-observer effect and the fundamental attribution error.

6. Discuss cultural differences in attribution.

To live in our complex society, we need to predict how others will act and whom we can trust. Social perception and cognition are *the processes for learning about others and making inferences from that information.*

First Impressions

Other things being equal, *the first information we learn about someone influences us more than later information does* (Jones & Goethals, 1972). This tendency is known as the primacy effect. For example, if you hear both favorable and unfavorable reports about a restaurant, the reports you hear first influence you the most (Russo, Carlson, & Meloy, 2006). The term *primacy effect* also applies to memory, where it refers to the tendency to remember the first items on a list better than those in the middle.

We form first impressions quickly, and often more accurately than we might guess. People watching 6-second videos of music ensembles or orchestras, without sound, performed at better than chance levels at identifying the more successful group (Tsay, 2014). People viewing faces for just 39 milliseconds fairly accurately guessed how aggressive those people were (Carré, McCormick, & Mondloch, 2009). People who looked at photos of government officials guessed with greater than chance accuracy which ones had been convicted of corruption (Lin, Adolphs, & Alvarez, 2018). From just hearing a recording of "How are you doing?" listeners were 60 percent accurate at guessing whether someone was making a call to a friend or a romantic partner (Farley, Hughes, & LaFayette, 2013). From hearing a recording of people laughing together, listeners had better than chance accuracy of guessing whether the laughers were friends or strangers (Bryant et al., 2016).

However, don't overestimate the accuracy of first impressions. Researchers asked observers to estimate the trustworthiness of people in photos. Generally, they gave high ratings to someone who was smiling, but if they later saw the same person not smiling, they gave a lower rating (Todorov & Porter, 2014). Clearly, a temporary smile does not change someone's trustworthiness.

First impressions can become self-fulfilling prophecies, *expectations that increase the probability of the predicted event.* Suppose a psychologist hands you a cell phone and asks you to talk with someone, while showing you a photo supposedly of that person. Unknown to the person you are talking to, the psychologist might hand you a photo of a very attractive person or someone less attractive. Not surprisingly, you act friendlier to someone you regard as attractive. Furthermore, if you think you are talking to someone attractive, that person reacts by becoming more cheerful

and talkative. In short, your first impression changes how you act and influences the other person to live up to, or down to, your expectations (Snyder, Tanke, & Berscheid, 1977).

The Enduring Effect of a Bad Reputation

Suppose you are a personnel officer evaluating a potential employee. You learn about many neutral things, one good deed (volunteering one evening a week for a charity) and one bad deed (dumping hazardous chemicals into a lake). Does it matter to you whether the good deed was recent or long ago? Probably yes. Recent good deeds are better. Does it matter to you whether the bad deed was recent or long ago? Not so much. An immoral act is considered

What's your first impression of this man—rich or poor? Businessman, professional athlete, or manual laborer? (Yeah, you got it right.)

a sign of permanently bad character, even if it was done long ago (Brandimarte, Vosgerau, & Acquisti, 2018). Consider the celebrities whose reputations and careers have been tarnished by charges of something they did decades ago. So be careful about what you do in your youth.

5. How might self-fulfilling prophecies increase prejudice?

Answer

5. If you expect little of certain people, you might influence them to perform less well (a self-fulfilling prophecy), thereby confirming your prejudice.

Stereotypes and Prejudices

A **stereotype** is *a belief or expectation about a group of people.* A **prejudice** is *an unfavorable attitude toward a group of people.* It is usually associated with **discrimination**, which is *unequal treatment of different groups.*

You may sometimes hear someone say that we should avoid all stereotypes. Well, good luck with that one. Human brains, and indeed all animal brains, are set up to form generalizations. And,

The stereotype of old people as inactive has many exceptions.

indeed, stereotypes are not always wrong. Would you plan a different kind of party for a group of 80-year-olds than for a group of 20-year-olds? If so, you are guided by a stereotype about age—a mostly correct one. Do you have an opinion about the people who join the Ku Klux Klan or other racist organizations? If so, that is a stereotype—again, one that is probably more or less correct. Do you believe that culture influences behavior? If so, then you say that members of a given culture tend to behave in a particular way, on average.

Nevertheless, many stereotypes are exaggerated or wrong (Eyal & Epley, 2017; Fiske, 2017; Ranganath & Nosek, 2008). Even when a stereotype is correct on average, remember that phrase "on average." It is important to guide our responses to someone based on that individual, not the average for a group. Even when a stereotype is positive (e.g., "Asians are hard-working"), people like to be evaluated for their own accomplishments, not taken for granted because of their group affiliation (Czopp, Kay, & Cheryan, 2015).

Implicit Measures of Prejudice

Decades ago, Americans admitted their prejudices openly. Today, almost all people believe in fair treatment for everyone, or so they say. But are people as unprejudiced as they claim to be? Researchers have sought ways to measure subtle prejudices that people do not want to admit.

A popular method is the **implicit association test (IAT)**, which *measures reactions to combinations of categories.* Let's start with this example: You rest your left and right forefingers on a keyboard while you view words on a computer screen. You should press with your left finger if you see an unpleasant word, such as *death,* and press with your right finger if you see a pleasant word, such as *joy.* After a while, the instructions change. Now you should press the left key if you see the name of an insect and the right key if you see the name of a flower. Next you combine two categories: Press the left key for unpleasant words or insects, and the right key for pleasant words or flowers. Then the pairings switch: Press the left key for unpleasant words or flowers and the right key for pleasant words or insects. The procedure might continue, alternating between the two instructions.

Most people respond faster to the combination "pleasant or flowers" than to "pleasant or insects." The conclusion is that most people like flowers more than insects. This procedure may seem more trouble than it is worth, as people readily agree that they like flowers more than insects. However, the research establishes the validity of the method, which researchers can use to measure other preferences or prejudices that people might not want to admit (Greenwald, Nosek, & Banaji, 2003).

Imagine yourself in this experiment: You view a computer screen that sometimes shows a photo and sometimes a word. If it is a photo of a black person or a pleasant word, press the left key. If it is a photo of a white person or an unpleasant word, press the right key. After you respond that way for a while, the rule switches to the opposite pairing. ▼ **Figure 13.3** illustrates the procedures and ▼ **Figure 13.4** summarizes the results for a group of white people. Most of them responded faster to the combinations *black/unpleasant* and *white/pleasant,* even though they claimed to have no racial prejudice (Phelps et al., 2000). With enough practice, people learn to respond the same to each combination, so the test is most useful for the first few trials (Hu, Rosenfeld, & Bodenhausen, 2012). In similar studies, black participants show smaller differences in their responses to blacks and whites—that is, less prejudice one way or the other (Stewart, von Hippel, & Radvansky, 2009).

The results of the implicit association test correlate only weakly with people's expressed attitudes (Greenwald, Poehlman, Uhlmann, & Banaji, 2009), but the prejudices are not unconscious. When people are asked to state their prejudices but urged to answer *honestly,* their answers correlate more strongly with their IAT results (Phillips & Olson, 2014). Also, if people are asked to predict their IAT results, they do so fairly accurately, and then they more readily

Lisa-S/Shutterstock.com

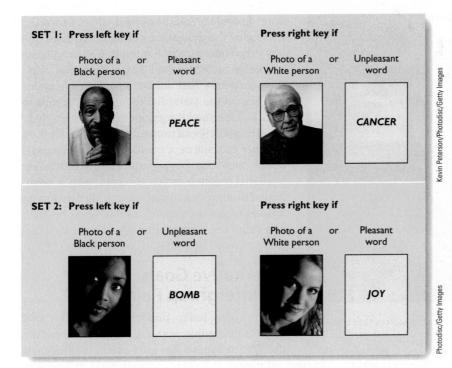

SET 1: Press left key if ... Press right key if

Photo of a Black person or Pleasant word ... Photo of a White person or Unpleasant word

PEACE ... CANCER

SET 2: Press left key if ... Press right key if

Photo of a Black person or Unpleasant word ... Photo of a White person or Pleasant word

BOMB ... JOY

▲ **Figure 13.3** Procedures for an implicit association test to measure prejudices.

admit their prejudices (Hahn & Gawronski, 2019; Hahn, Judd, Hirsh, & Blair, 2014). In short, most people do know their prejudices, even if they hesitate to admit them.

Is it possible to change implicit attitudes? Several brief procedures do work, temporarily. For example, after white people view a series of photos of highly respected black people and contemptible white people, their results on the IAT shift favorably toward blacks. Similar results occur after listening to a story in which a black person intervenes to stop a criminal action by a white person. However, the changes in implicit attitude last only briefly, a few days at most, and they fail to produce a noticeable change in actual behavior (Forscher et al., 2019; Lai et al., 2016). A lasting change in attitudes is possible, but it requires more extensive experiences.

How useful is the IAT? The results have modest test-retest reliability and positive, but not outstanding, correlations with actual behavior. Many changes in context can influence both the IAT results and actual behavior (Gawronski, 2019; Jost, 2019; Kurdi et al., 2019). If we want to identify prejudices, the IAT provides information we cannot get by just asking people, but it is not sufficiently accurate that anyone should use it for such purposes as, say, selecting among job applicants.

Researchers have also used the IAT to gauge attitudes toward men and women (Nosek & Banaji, 2001; Rudman & Goodwin, 2004), and toward obese people (Agerström & Rooth, 2011), politicians, old people, and other groups. Project Implicit on Harvard University's website provides implicit association tests that you can try yourself.

6. **Does the IAT measure prejudices that people don't want to admit to others, or that they don't want to admit to themselves?**

Answer

6. It measures prejudices that people don't want to admit to others. When they are urged to be honest, they reveal their awareness of prejudice.

Overcoming Prejudice

When someone forms a prejudice, what can overcome it? Increasing contact between groups does not always help. In fact, brief or superficial contact often increases tensions by calling attention to the differences between groups (Condra & Linardi, 2019). Prolonged, close contacts are more beneficial. A study of white and black college students who were assigned to be roommates found that they spent little time together at first, but gradually formed favorable attitudes over the course of a semester (Shook & Fazio, 2008). Voluntarily taking part in a Mexican cultural activity reduces prejudice against Mexicans (Brannon & Walton, 2013).

Another strategy is to get groups to work toward a common goal (Dovidio & Gaertner, 1999). A famous study by Muzafer Sherif (1966) set out to demonstrate the power of this technique using arbitrarily chosen groups. At a summer camp at Robbers Cave, Oklahoma, 11- and 12-year-old boys from similar backgrounds were divided into two groups in separate cabins. The groups competed for prizes in sports, treasure hunts, and other activities. With each competition, the antagonism between the two groups grew more intense. The boys made threatening posters, shouted insults, and engaged in food fights. Then the counselors set out to reverse the hostility. First, they asked the two groups to work together to find and repair a leak in the water pipe that supplied the camp. Then they

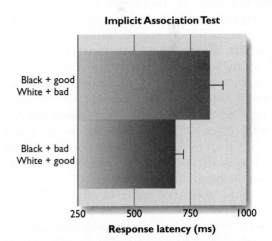

Implicit Association Test

Black + good White + bad

Black + bad White + good

250   500   750   1000

Response latency (ms)

▲ **Figure 13.4** On average, white people who claimed to have no racial prejudice responded slower if they had to make one response for "black face or pleasant word" and a different response for "white face or unpleasant word" than if the pairings were reversed—black and unpleasant, white and pleasant. (From "Performance on indirect measures of race evaluation predicts amygdala activation," by E. A. Phelps, K. J. O'Connor, W. A. Cunningham, E. S. Funayama, J. C. Gatenby, J. C. Gore & M. R. Banaji, 2000. Journal of Cognitive Neuroscience, 12, pp. 729–738.)

People who work together for a common goal can overcome prejudices that initially divide them.

had the two groups pool their treasuries to rent a movie that both groups wanted to see. Later, they had the boys pull together to get a truck out of a rut. Gradually, hostility declined and turned into friendship. The point was that competition breeds hostility, and cooperation leads to friendship.

So Sherif said, at least. Alas, this famous study has serious flaws. One is that Sherif did not mention his earlier study at a summer camp that failed to support his hypothesis. Decades later, Gina Perry (2018) pored through all the old notes to find the story. In the first study, the "counselors," who did no counseling and gave the boys almost no direction about what to do, set up competitions that produced no hostility. Then the counselors vandalized one of the tents and tried to get the boys in that tent to blame the other boys. But when the others vigorously denied it, their denial was accepted. The counselors rigged several of the competitions to favor one side or the other, but the only hostility they generated was by the boys against the counselors! The groups of boys that were expected to become hostile toward each other had bonded in friendship.

Sherif then tried again, in what became the famous Robbers Cave study, the one that he published. Two groups of boys arrived separately, unaware of the others, and settled in cabins a mile apart. After a few days, the two groups met. Then the counselors did what they could to stir animosity. They had a birthday party with cake for one cabin, and made sure the other cabin knew they were not invited. They arranged a tournament of 16 events over 4 days, in blazing summer heat, with big prizes for the winning team and nothing for the losers. The groups began to show hostility, which the counselors encouraged rather than simply observing

it, or discouraging it, as normal adults would do. Eventually the groups took to fighting. When one boy suggested a peaceful resolution to a conflict, a counselor recommended attacking instead. After the counselors had stirred up enough hostility, they set up the tasks that required the groups to work together, and the groups became reconciled.

The point Sherif wanted to make, that working together can reduce a conflict between groups, is a reasonable one. But perhaps a bigger conclusion from this research is that someone who is determined to support a hypothesis can rig the circumstances to get the desired results. Good research sets out to test a hypothesis, not to make sure that the results will support it.

Alternative Goals for Intergroup Relations

Most people today publicly endorse the goal of treating people without prejudice. However, the way of stating this goal makes a difference. Although saying, "We treat all people the same" sounds good, it seems to imply, "We expect all people to act the same." What if you are *not* the same as everyone else? You might differ from others in racial or ethnic background, sexual orientation, or other regards. You might be older or younger than everyone else, or the only man or only woman in the organization. Under a policy of treating everyone the same, people are supposed to ignore the fact that you are different. When people try not to notice skin color, sexual orientation, or anything else, they find the effort unpleasant and tiring, and the result is often an *increase* in prejudice (Legault, Gutsell, & Inzlicht, 2011; Trawalter & Richeson, 2006; Wegner, 2009). "Treating all people the same" can also be an excuse for those in power to justify the status quo (Plaut, Thomas, Hurd, & Romano, 2018).

An alternative is multiculturalism—*accepting, recognizing, and enjoying the differences among groups and the unique contributions that each person can offer.* For example, a multiculturalist approach to education encourages teachers to include class displays that represent many groups (Aragón, Dovidio, & Graham, 2017). When a company or other organization endorses a multiculturalist position, members of both majority and minority groups feel more comfortable (Meeussen, Otten, & Phalet, 2014; Plaut, Thomas, & Goren, 2009).

7. Why are training sessions to decrease racism or sexism often ineffective?

Answer

7. Trying to avoid seeming prejudiced is unpleasant and tiring. Such training sessions often backfire, especially when people feel they are being accused of misbehavior.

Attribution

Yesterday, you won the state lottery, and today, classmates who previously ignored you want to be your friends. You draw inferences about their reasons. Attribution is *the set of thought processes we use to explain our own behavior and that of others.*

Internal versus External Causes

Fritz Heider, the founder of attribution theory, emphasized the distinction between internal and external causes of behavior (Heider, 1958). **Internal attributions** are *explanations based on someone's abilities, personality, or other characteristics.* **External attributions** are *explanations based on the situation, including events that would influence almost anyone.* An example of an internal attribution is saying that your brother walked to work this morning "because he likes the exercise." An external attribution would be that he walked "because his car wouldn't start." Internal attributions are also known as *dispositional* (i.e., relating to the person's disposition). External attributions are also known as *situational* (i.e., relating to the situation).

You tend to make internal attributions when someone's act surprises you. For example, you draw no conclusions about someone who would like to visit Hawaii. After all, who wouldn't? However, if someone wants to visit northern Norway in winter, you look for something special about that person. When a man gets angry in public, most people assume he had a reason. When a woman gets equally angry in public, her behavior is more surprising, and people are more likely to attribute it to her personality (Brescoll & Uhlmann, 2008).

This tendency sometimes leads to misunderstandings between members of different cultures. Each person views the other's behavior as "something I would not have done" and therefore a reason to make an attribution about personality. For example, some cultures expect people to cry loudly at funerals, whereas others expect more restraint. People who are unfamiliar with other cultures may attribute a behavior to personality, when in fact it is a dictate of culture.

Harold Kelley (1967) proposed that three types of information influence us to make an internal or external attribution:

- **Consensus information** *(how someone's behavior compares with other people's behavior).* If someone behaves the same way you believe other people would in the same situation, you make an external attribution, recognizing that the situation led to the behavior. When a behavior seems unusual, you look for an internal attribution. Of course, you can be wrong if you misunderstand the situation.

- **Consistency information** *(how someone's behavior varies from one time to the next).* If someone almost always seems friendly, you make an internal attribution ("friendly person"). If someone's friendliness varies, you make external attributions, looking for events that elicited a good or bad mood.

- **Distinctiveness** *(how someone's behavior varies from one situation to another).* If your friend is pleasant to all but one individual, you assume that person has done something to irritate your friend (an external attribution).

8. **Why are you more likely to make internal attributions for someone from another culture than for members of your own culture?**

9. **Juanita returns from watching *The Return of the Son of Sequel Strikes Back Again Part 2* and says it was excellent. Most other people disliked the movie. Will you make an internal or external attribution for Juanita's opinion? Why (distinctiveness, consensus, or consistency)?**

Answers

8. You are more likely to be surprised by the behavior of someone from another culture. Whenever you find someone's behavior surprising, you tend to favor a internal attribution.

9. You probably will make an internal attribution because of consensus. When someone's behavior differs from others, we make an internal attribution.

The Actor-Observer Effect

If you see someone complaining loudly to a sales clerk, how do you react? You probably think, "Such an aggressive loudmouth!" When you complain equally loudly, how do you explain it? You say, "I was treated unfairly!" *People are more likely to make internal attributions for other people's behavior and more likely to make external attributions for their own* (Jones & Nisbett, 1972). This tendency is called the **actor-observer effect.** You are an "actor" when you try to explain the causes of your own behavior and an "observer" when you try to explain someone else's behavior.

We can account for this tendency in terms of the three influences just mentioned. First, *consensus:* When you see someone angry with a sales clerk, would you be equally angry in that situation? You don't know, because you don't know the situation. But usually you are polite to salespeople, so maybe there is something unusual about that other person.

In the United States, a funeral usually calls for reserved behavior. Many other places expect loud wailing.

Second, *consistency:* Is that other person angry all the time? Could be, so far as you know. But you know you get angry only on rare occasions. Third, *distinctiveness:* Is that other person aggressive in many situations? Could be, so far as you know. Are you aggressive in many situations? You know that you aren't.

Another explanation for the actor-observer effect is perceptual. We see other people as objects in our visual field, and we tend to think that whatever we are watching is the cause of the action. If you watch a videotape of your own behavior, you make more references to your personality than you ordinarily do (Storms, 1973), although still not as much as other people do (Hofmann, Gschwendner, & Schmitt, 2009).

An application of this idea: Suppose you watch a videotape of two people who participate equally in a conversation. You are randomly given a version of the videotape with the camera focused on one person or the other. You tend to perceive that the person you are watching dominates the conversation. Similarly, if you watch a videotape of an interrogation between a detective and a suspect, you judge the suspect's confession to be more voluntary if the camera focuses on the suspect and more coerced if the camera focuses on the detective (Lassiter, Geers, Munhall, Ploutz-Snyder, & Breitenbecher, 2002).

Another application: Police sometimes wear a body camera to record their actions in case a dispute arises. In other cases, a camera is mounted on the dashboard of the police car. When it is a body camera, viewers focus on the situation, and they tend to make an external attribution. When it is a dashboard camera, viewers watch the police officer and tend more toward an internal attribution (Turner, Caruso, Dilich, & Roese, 2019).

The Fundamental Attribution Error

A common error is *to make internal attributions for people's behavior even when we see evidence for an external influence on behavior.* This tendency is known as the fundamental attribution error (Ross, 1977). It is also known as the *correspondence bias,* meaning a tendency to assume a strong similarity between someone's current actions and his or her dispositions.

Imagine yourself in a classic study demonstrating this phenomenon. You are told that U.S. college students were randomly assigned to write essays praising or condemning Fidel Castro, then the communist leader of Cuba. You read an essay that praises Castro. What's your guess about the actual attitude of the student who wrote this essay?

|—|—|—|—|—|—|—|—|—|—|

very anti-Castro   neutral   very pro-Castro

Most U.S. students in one study guessed that the student was at least mildly pro-Castro, even though they were informed, as you were, that the author had been required to praise Castro (Jones & Harris, 1967). In a later study, experimenters explained that one student in a creative writing class had been assigned to write a pro-Castro essay and an anti-Castro essay at different times. When the participants read the two essays, most thought that the writer had changed attitudes between the two essays (Allison, Mackie, Muller, & Worth, 1993). That is, even when people are told of a powerful external reason for someone's behavior, they seem to believe the person probably had internal reasons as well.

Here is another example: Suppose you and another student are randomly assigned to be the "questioner" and the "answerer." If you are the questioner, you are to write questions about a topic that you know well, and then pose them to the other person. For example, if astronomy is your hobby, you might ask detailed questions about astronomy. Chances are, the other person answers only a few of them correctly, so all the observers think you are the smarter, more knowledgeable person. However, if the other person had been assigned the role of questioner, he/she would ask questions about a different field of interest, maybe bird identification. You would answer only a few, and everyone, probably even you, would think the other person was the more impressive. Observers usually ignore the fact that the questioner got to choose the type of question (Ross, Amabile, & Steinmetz, 1977).

The fundamental attribution error emerges in many settings. When we see crime, we tend to think "bad person," even when the truth might be closer to "bad situation." When we see poverty and failure, we think "lack of effort," even if "lack of opportunity" might be more accurate. We think our political opponents adopted their wrongheaded opinions because they are biased, whereas we formed our own opinions based on the evidence. My opinions are right, so of course something must be wrong with anyone who disagrees (Ross, 2018).

concept check

10. If instead of watching someone, you close your eyes and imagine yourself in that person's position, will you be more likely to explain the behavior with internal or external attributions? Why?

11. How would the fundamental attribution error affect people's opinions of actors and actresses who portray doctors?

Answers

11. Because of the fundamental attribution error, many people tend to think that performers who portray doctors actually know something about medicine.

10. You will be more likely to give an external attribution because you will become more like an actor and less like an observer.

Cultural Differences in Attribution and Related Matters

The fundamental attribution error varies by culture. People in Western cultures tend to make more internal (personality) attributions, whereas people in China and other Asian countries tend to make more external (situational) attributions. How would you explain the behavior of the fish designated with an arrow in the drawing on the next page? Most Americans say it is leading the others, whereas many Chinese say the other fish are chasing it (Hong, Morris, Chiu, & Benet-Martinez, 2000). That is, the cultures differ in whether they think the fish controls its own behavior or obeys the influence of the others.

try it yourself

In many ways, most Asian people tend to focus more on the situation and less on personality than do most people in Western cultures (Nisbett, Peng, Choi, & Norenzayan, 2001). As a result, Asians expect less consistency in people's behavior from one situation to another. They are less guided by first impressions than Americans are (Noguchi, Kamada, & Shrira, 2014). They are also more likely to accept contradictions and look for compromises instead of viewing one position as correct and another as incorrect. Here are a few examples:

- When given a description of a conflict, such as one between mother and daughter, Chinese students are more likely than Americans to see merit in both arguments (Peng & Nisbett, 1999).
- Far more Chinese than English-language proverbs include apparent self-contradictions, such as "beware of your friends, not your enemies" and "too humble is half proud" (Peng & Nisbett, 1999).
- Chinese people are more likely than Americans to predict that current trends—whatever they might be—will reverse themselves. If life seems to have been getting better lately, most Americans predict that things will continue getting better, whereas Chinese expect them to get worse (Ji, Nisbett, & Su, 2001).

The reported differences are interesting. Still, an important question remains: To the extent that Asian people respond differently from Western-culture people, is that difference due to ancient traditions or current conditions? Perhaps Asians notice the influence of their environment more just because their environment looks different from that of Western countries. Most Asian cities are more cluttered than American and European cities (see ▼ Figure 13.5). Researchers found that Japanese students tended to notice the background of photographs more than Americans, who focused heavily on objects in the foreground. However, after Americans viewed a series of pictures of Japanese cities, they too began paying more attention to the backgrounds (Miyamoto, Nisbett, & Masuda, 2006).

Using Attributions to Manage Perceptions of Ourselves

Most people vary their attributions to try to present themselves in a favorable light. For example, you might credit your good grades to your intelligence and hard work (an internal attribution) but blame your worst grades on unfair tests (an external attribution). *Attributions that we adopt to maximize credit for success and minimize blame for failure* are called self-serving biases. If you call someone's attention to the fact that an attribution is a self-serving bias, the person might reconsider, but often not. People say, "Yes, my belief is self-serving, but it is true anyway" (Rosenzweig, 2016).

Self-serving biases are less prominent among Asians. One reason is that Asian culture defines self-worth in terms of fitting into the group rather than

▲ **Figure 13.5** On average, Asian cities are more crowded and cluttered than U.S. and European cities.

outcompeting one's peers (Balcetis, Dunning, & Miller, 2008; Heine & Hamamura, 2007). Also, bragging is taboo in most Asian cultures.

People sometimes protect their images with **self-handicapping strategies**, in which they *intentionally put themselves at a disadvantage to provide an excuse for failure.* Suppose you fear you will do poorly on a test. If you stay out late at a party the night before, you can blame your low score on your lack of sleep without admitting that you might have done poorly anyway.

In one study, one group of students worked on solvable problems while others worked on a mixture of solvable and unsolvable problems. The students did not know that some of the problems were impossible. The experimenters told all students that they had done well. The students who had been given solvable problems (and solved them) felt good. Those who had worked on unsolvable problems were unsure in what way they had "done well." They had no confidence that they could continue to do well.

Next the experimenters told the participants that the purpose of the experiment was to investigate the effects of drugs on problem solving. Before starting on the next set of problems, each student could choose between taking a drug that supposedly impaired problem-solving abilities and another drug that supposedly improved them. The participants who had worked on unsolvable problems were more likely than the others to choose the drug that supposedly impaired performance. Because they were not sure they could continue their supposedly "good" performance, they provided themselves with an excuse (Berglas & Jones, 1978).

---

in closing | module 13.2

How Social Perceptions Affect Behavior

We are seldom fully aware of the reasons for our own behavior, much less someone else's, but we make our best guesses. If someone you know passes by without saying "hello," you might attribute that person's behavior to absentmindedness, indifference, or hostility.

You might attribute someone's friendly response to your own personal charm, the other person's extraverted personality, or that person's devious and manipulative tendency. The attributions you make are sure to influence your own social behaviors.

Summary

- *First impressions.* Other things being equal, we pay more attention to the first information we learn about someone than to later information. After a bad reputation forms because of a misdeed, it is hard to overcome. (page 413)
- *Stereotypes and prejudices.* Stereotypes are generalized beliefs about groups of people. A prejudice is an unfavorable stereotype. (page 414)
- *The implicit association test.* The implicit association test (IAT) measures subtle prejudices that people hesitate to admit. Implicit prejudices correlate with observed behavior, although not strongly. They are difficult to change. (page 414)
- *Overcoming prejudice.* One way to weaken a prejudice is to get groups to cooperate toward a common goal. However, Sherif's famous experiment to demonstrate this point was flawed. (page 415)
- *Enjoying diversity.* The goal of treating everyone the same tends to imply that everyone should act the same. As a rule, multiculturalism—accepting and enjoying diversity among people—is a better policy. (page 416)

- *Attribution.* Attribution is the set of thought processes by which we try to explain behavior. According to Harold Kelley, we attribute behavior to an internal cause if it is consistent over time, different from most other people's behavior, and directed toward a variety of other people or objects. (page 416)
- *Actor-observer effect.* We are more likely to attribute internal causes to other people's behavior than to our own. (page 417)
- *Fundamental attribution error.* People frequently attribute someone's behavior to internal causes, even when they see evidence of external influences. (page 418)
- *Cultural differences.* People in Asian cultures tend to attribute more of behavior to the situations. (page 418)
- *Self-serving bias and self-handicapping.* People often try to protect their self-esteem by attributing their successes to skill and their failures to outside influences. They sometimes place themselves at a disadvantage to provide an excuse for failure. (page 419)

Key Terms

actor-observer effect (page 417)

attribution (page 416)

consensus information (page 417)

consistency information (page 417)

discrimination (page 414)

distinctiveness (page 417)

external attributions (page 417)

fundamental attribution error (page 418)

implicit association test (IAT) (page 414)

internal attributions (page 417)

multiculturalism (page 416)

prejudice (page 414)

primacy effect (page 413)

self-fulfilling prophecies (page 413)

self-handicapping strategies (page 420)

self-serving biases (page 419)

social perception and cognition (page 413)

stereotype (page 414)

Review Questions

1. What does an implicit association test (IAT) measure?
   (a) Reaction times.
   (b) Percent correct
   (c) Brain activity
   (d) Word usage

2. What is known about the implicit attitudes that the IAT measures?
   (a) They are easy to modify.
   (b) They correlate with behavior, but not strongly.
   (c) People are not conscious of them.
   (d) They almost perfectly match the attitudes that people state explicitly.

3. What is the primary objection to Sherif's "Robbers Cave" study?
   (a) The results apply to boys but not girls.
   (b) Sherif manipulated the situation to get the desired results.
   (c) Studies in other cultures failed to replicate the results.
   (d) Several participants suffered psychological damage from the study.

4. Many people dislike the goal of "treating everyone the same" for what reason?
   (a) It implies that everyone should act the same.
   (b) It contradicts the law in several states.
   (c) It allows too much freedom to express group differences.
   (d) It relies too heavily on attribution theory.

5. Which of the following is an example of an external attribution?
   (a) She contributed money to charity because she is generous.
   (b) She contributed money to charity to impress her boss, who was watching.
   (c) She contributed money to charity because she formed that habit.
   (d) She contributed money to charity because of a pattern of brain activity.

6. Of the following, which type of people are most likely to rely on external (situational) attributions?
   (a) Asians
   (b) Teenagers
   (c) Uneducated people
   (d) Librarians

7. If you watch a movie of your own behavior, you give an internal attribution more often than you would normally. Why?
   (a) Actor-observer effect
   (b) Primacy effect
   (c) Self-handicapping strategy
   (d) Self-fulfilling prophecy

8. According to the text, why do people sometimes do something that they know will harm their own performance?
   (a) To conform to what they observe in others
   (b) To make a successful performance even more impressive
   (c) To support an internal attribution for failure
   (d) To support an external attribution for failure

Answers: 1a, 2b, 3b, 4a, 5b, 6a, 7a, 8d.

Hollie Adams/Getty Images

After studying this module, you should be able to:

1. Explain how psychologists measure attitudes.

2. Define cognitive dissonance and describe an experiment that demonstrates it.

3. Distinguish between the peripheral and central routes to persuasion.

4. List techniques of persuasion.

5. Discuss the effectiveness or ineffectiveness of fear messages.

6. Describe why coercive persuasion leads to unreliable information.

You may have heard people say, "If you want to change people's behavior, you have to change their attitudes first." That sounds reasonable, but let's test it out with these questions: (1) What is your attitude about paying higher taxes? (2) If the government raises taxes, will you pay them?

Nearly all people say their attitude is opposed to higher taxes. However, if the government does raise the taxes, people would pay them. In this case, it was easier to change behavior than to change attitudes. Also, as we shall see, changing behavior often leads to a change in attitudes.

Attitudes and Behavior

An attitude is *a like or dislike that influences behavior* (Allport, 1935; Petty & Cacioppo, 1981). Your attitudes include an evaluative or emotional component (how you feel about something), a cognitive component (what you know or believe), and a behavioral component (what you will do). Psychologists in Western cultures have typically interpreted attitudes in terms of an individual's likes and dislikes. In Asian cultures people's attitudes vary according to the situation and align more closely with the goals of their family or their society (Riemer, Shavitt, Koo, & Markus, 2014).

Attitude Measurement

Psychologists commonly measure attitudes through scales such as a Likert scale (named after psychologist Rensis Likert), on which you would check a

point along a line from 1, meaning "strongly disagree," to 7, meaning "strongly agree," for each statement, as illustrated in ▼ Figure 13.6.

When psychologists use this method to measure someone's attitudes, and then measure them again a few months later, how stable would you guess people's attitudes are? It depends, but it depends in a way that you would probably predict. When people say they have a confident, firm attitude, it remains stable. When they are not sure, or that they feel some conflict, then their expressed attitude might change (Luttrell, Petty, & Briñol, 2016).

How stable would be the average attitudes of a whole society? The originators of the implicit association test, discussed earlier in this chapter, have for many years operated a website where millions of people have tested their implicit attitudes while also stating their explicit attitudes. Over the years, attitudes toward gays and lesbians, old people, and disabled people, and white peoples' attitudes toward black people, have all moved from negative toward neutral. In each case, the explicit attitudes changed more than did the implicit attitudes (Charlesworth & Banaji, 2019). That is, people have become more accepting of all types of diversity, but old attitudes tend to linger in implicit form. Part of the change in society's attitudes comes from individuals changing their attitudes, but also part comes from a change in cohorts. A new generation of young people has replaced some of the most prejudiced older people.

People's reported attitudes do not always match their behaviors. Many people say one thing and do another with regard to alcohol, safe sex, or conserving natural resources. Your attitudes are most likely to match your behavior if you have personal experience with the topic (Glasman & Albarracín, 2006). For example, if you have had experience dealing with mental patients, then you know how you react to them, and you state your attitude accordingly. Someone without experience states a hypothetical attitude, which is less certain. But even with regard to something you know well, such as your attitude about studying hard

Indicate your level of agreement with the items below, using the following scale:

	Strongly disagree		Neutral			Strongly agree
1. Labor unions are necessary to protect the rights of workers.	1	2	3	4	5	6	7
2. Labor union leaders have too much power.	1	2	3	4	5	6	7
3. If I worked for a company with a union, I would join the union.	1	2	3	4	5	6	7
4. I would never cross a picket line of striking workers.	1	2	3	4	5	6	7
5. Striking workers hurt their company and unfairly raise prices for the consumer.	1	2	3	4	5	6	7
6. Labor unions should not be permitted to engage in political activity.	1	2	3	4	5	6	7
7. America is a better place for today's workers because of the efforts by labor unions in the past.	1	2	3	4	5	6	7

Note: Items 2, 5, and 6 are scored the opposite of 1, 3, 4, and 7.

▲ **Figure 13.6** This Likert scale assesses attitudes toward labor unions.

for tests, you might report what you think your attitude should be, rather than what your usual behavior actually is.

12. Suppose someone expresses a positive attitude on a Likert scale but you suspect the person really has a negative attitude. Which method from an earlier module of this chapter might confirm your suspicion?

Answer

12. The implicit association test measures attitudes that don't match what people say.

Cognitive Dissonance and Attitude Change

Much research measures how well attitudes influence behavior. The theory of cognitive dissonance reverses the direction: It holds that changing someone's behavior changes an attitude (Festinger, 1957). **Cognitive dissonance** is *a state of unpleasant tension that people experience when they hold contradictory attitudes or when their behavior contradicts their attitudes.*

Imagine yourself as a participant in this classic experiment on cognitive dissonance (Festinger & Carlsmith, 1959). The experimenters say they are studying motor behavior. They show you a board full of pegs. Your task is to take each peg out of the board, rotate it one-fourth of a turn, and return it to the board. When you finish all the pegs, you start over, rotating all the pegs again as quickly and accurately as possible. As you proceed, an experimenter silently takes notes, or at least pretends to take notes. You find the task immensely tedious. In fact, the researchers chose this task because it was so boring.

At the end of the session, the experimenter thanks you for participating and "explains" (falsely) that the study's purpose is to determine whether people's performance depends on their attitudes toward the task. You were in the neutral-attitude group, but those in the positive-attitude group are told before they start that they will enjoy the experience.

In fact, the experimenter continues, right now the research assistant is supposed to give that instruction to the next participant, who is waiting in the next room. The experimenter excuses himself to find the research assistant and returns distraught. The assistant is nowhere to be found, he says. He turns to you and asks, "Would you be willing to tell the next participant that you thought this was an interesting, enjoyable experiment? If so, I will pay you." Assume that you consent. After you have told someone that you enjoyed the study, what would you really think of it, assuming the experimenter paid you $1? What if he paid you $20? (This study occurred in the 1950s, before a great deal of inflation. At the time $20 would buy all of your textbooks for a semester.)

After you finished describing how much fun the experiment was, you leave and walk down the hall. A representative from the psychology department greets you and explains that the department wants to learn about all the experiments and their educational value. The answers to these questions are the real point of the experiment. The questions are how much you enjoyed the experiment and whether you would be willing to participate in a similar experiment later.

The students who received $20 said the experiment was boring and they wanted nothing to do with another such experiment. Contrary to what you might guess, most of those who received $1 said they enjoyed the experiment and would be willing to participate again (see ◄ Figure 13.7).

Why did those who received less pay say that they enjoyed participating? According to the theory of cognitive dissonance, if you accept $20 to tell a lie, you experience little conflict. You are lying, but you know why. You are doing it for the $20. However, if you tell a lie for $1, do you want to think you can be bribed so cheaply? You feel cognitive dissonance—unpleasant tension from the conflict between your true attitude and what you said about the experiment. You can reduce your tension by changing your attitude, deciding that the experiment really was interesting after all. ("I learned so much about myself, like . . . uh . . . how good I am at rotating pegs.")

The idea of cognitive dissonance attracted much attention and inspired a great deal of research (Aronson, 1997). Here are two examples:

- An experimenter left a child in a room with toys but forbade the child to play with one particular toy. If the experimenter threatened the child with severe punishment for playing with the toy, the child avoided it but still regarded it as desirable. However, if the experimenter merely said, "I would be disappointed" if the child played with that toy, the child avoided the toy and said (even weeks later) that it was not a good toy (Aronson & Carlsmith, 1963).
- An experimenter asked college students to write an essay defending a position that the experimenter knew, from previous information, contradicted the students' beliefs. For example, college students who favored freer access to alcohol might be asked to write essays on why the college should increase restrictions on alcohol. Those who were told they must write the essays did not change their views significantly, but those who were asked to "please" voluntarily write the essay generally came to agree with what they wrote (Croyle & Cooper, 1983).

The general principle is that, if you entice people to do something by a minimum reward or a tiny threat so that they are acting almost voluntarily, they change their attitudes to support what they are doing. People want to seem consistent. You might be able to use this principle to your advantage: At the

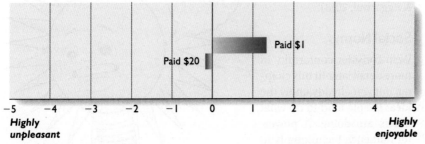

▲ **Figure 13.7** Participants were paid either $1 or $20 for telling another subject that they enjoyed an experiment that was actually boring. Later, they were asked for their real opinions. Participants who were paid the smaller amount said that they enjoyed the study. (Based on data from Festinger & Carlsmith, 1959)

start of a job interview, ask why the employer chose to interview you. That question prompts the interviewer to cite something positive about you. Once you get someone to compliment you, that person seeks evidence to support the compliment.

Back to this question: If you want to change people's behavior, do you have to change their attitudes first? The results of cognitive dissonance experiments say quite the opposite: If you change people's behavior first, their attitudes will change, too.

Attitude Change and Persuasion

How we form an attitude depends on many factors, especially the importance of the topic. Consider your less important attitudes. You probably didn't form your attitudes toward brands of drinks or potato chips by carefully evaluating the ingredients. You might like the colorful packaging, or you saw an entertaining commercial on television, or you saw other people enjoying a product. When a decision seems unimportant, or when you have so many more serious concerns that you cannot devote much effort to a decision, you form or change an attitude by the **peripheral route to persuasion** that is based mostly on emotions: *If for any reason you associate something with feeling happy, you form a favorable attitude toward it* (Petty & Briñol, 2015).

In contrast, consider your approach to an important decision. If you are buying a new home, you carefully examine the quality of the house, the price, the neighborhood, and more. The **central route to persuasion** *requires investing enough time and effort to evaluate the evidence and reason logically about a decision.* Your emotions can still enter into the decision, but only if they are relevant. You might be in a better mood when you see one house than another just because of nicer weather, but you don't let that kind of emotion influence your decision. However, if the appearance of one house makes you feel cheerful, that feeling is relevant and worth considering. Similarly, you might decide to marry someone because that person always makes you feel good, but not because you feel happy for some other reason at the moment.

Special Techniques of Persuasion

Many people will try to persuade you to buy something, contribute to a cause, or do something else that may or may not be in your best interests. Robert Cialdini (1993) has described many techniques of persuasion. Let's consider a few. The goal is to help you recognize and resist certain kinds of manipulation.

Liking and Similarity

People are more successful at persuading you if you like them or see them as similar to yourself. Suppose someone you don't know calls and asks, "How are you today?" You reply, "Okay." The reply: "Oh, I'm so glad to hear that!" Is this caller, who doesn't even know you, really delighted that you are "okay"? Or is this an attempt to seem friendly so that you will buy something? Salespeople, politicians, and others also try to emphasize the ways in which they are similar to you. For example, "I grew up in a small town, much like this one."

Here is a surprising use of this principle: If you see a lightbulb with a face on it and a message "I'm burning hot; turn me off when you leave," you are more likely to comply than if it has no face and the message "Our bulbs are burning hot; turn them off when you leave!" Simply putting a face on the bulb makes it seem more like *you* and therefore more worthy of your support. Similarly, a trash can with a face and the words "Please feed me food waste only" gets more compliance than a faceless can with the words "Please put in food waste only" (Ahn, Kim, & Aggarwal, 2013).

Social Norms

We'll consider conformity in more detail later in this chapter, but you already know the idea: People tend to do what others are doing. A powerful influence technique is to show that many other people are doing what you want them to do. A bartender or singer puts a few dollars in

If you perceive an inanimate object as similar to yourself, you are more likely to help it.

his or her tip jar at the start to imply that other people have left tips. A politician publishes photographs showing crowds of enthusiastic supporters.

Many hotels try to influence guests to agree to use towels more than once instead of expecting daily replacements. A typical message in the room points out that reusing towels saves energy, reduces the use of detergents that pollute the water supply, and helps protect the environment. More people agree to re-use their towels if the message adds that other guests have agreed to reuse their towels. It works even better to say that most other guests using *this room* have agreed (N. J. Goldstein, Cialdini, & Griskevicius, 2008). You conform to people similar to yourself.

Reciprocation

Civilization is based on the concept of reciprocation: If you do me a favor, then I owe you one. However, it is possible to abuse this principle. Someone gives you something that you might or might not want, and then tells you what favor you should do in return. Charities will send you colorful calendars or other inexpensive gifts, accompanied by a request for a donation.

Here's another version of reciprocation: An alumni organization once called me asking for a contribution. Their representative said that many other alumni were pledging $1,000, and he hoped he could count on me for the same. No, I explained, I wasn't prepared to make that kind of contribution. Oh, he responded, with a tone that implied, "too bad you don't have a *good* job like the other alumni." He then said that if I couldn't afford $1,000, how about $500? The suggestion was that we should compromise. He was giving in $500 from his original proposal, so I should give in $500 from my end.

Active Participation

Compare these procedures: One is, someone explains to you the advantages of including more vegetables and less meat in your diet. The other is, someone asks you to explain to another person the advantages of eating more vegetables and less meat. Which method has more influence on you? The second does. If you are actively advocating something, even if you can't generate many good reasons, you persuade yourself and you become more likely to do what you were recommending (Eskreis-Winkler, Fishbach, & Duckworth, 2018).

Contrast Effects

An offer can seem good or bad, depending on how it compares to something else. If a restaurant menu lists one entrée at an extraordinarily high price, almost no one orders it, but sales increase for the second most expensive item, because it seems more reasonable by contrast. A realtor might start by showing you several overpriced houses in bad condition, before showing a nicer house at a more reasonable price. If you had seen that house first, you might not have been impressed, but by contrast it seems like a good deal. Almost anything seems good by contrast to something worse.

Another example: At one food-processing plant in China, workers were supposed to wash their hands with a spray bottle hourly, but most were inconsistent. After the company offered a sink as an alternative way to wash hands, the simpler task of using the spray bottle seemed more attractive, and compliance increased (Li, Sung, & Chen, 2019).

Foot in the Door

Someone *starts with a modest request, which you accept, and follows with a larger request.* This procedure is called the foot-in-the-door technique. When Jonathan Freedman and Scott Fraser (1966) asked suburban residents in Palo Alto, California, to put a small "Drive Safely" sign in their windows, most agreed to do so. A couple of weeks later, other researchers asked the same residents to let them set up a large "Drive Safely" billboard in their front yards for 10 days. They also made the request to residents who had not been approached by the first researchers. Of those who had already agreed to display the small sign, 76 percent agreed to the billboard. Only 17 percent of the others agreed. Those who agreed to the first request felt they were already committed to the cause, and to be consistent, they agreed to further participation. Another study found that people who agreed to fill out a 20-minute survey became more willing a month later to take a 40-minute survey on the same topic. However, although this tendency was strong for Americans, it was weak for Chinese students. An interpretation was that Chinese culture puts less emphasis on individual consistency from one time to another (Petrova, Cialdini, & Sills, 2007).

Bait and Switch

Someone using the bait-and-switch technique *first offers an extremely favorable deal, gets the other person to commit to the deal, and then makes additional demands.* Alternatively, the person might offer a product at a low price to get customers to the store but then claim to be out of the product and try to sell something else. For example, a car dealer offers you an excellent price on a new car and a generous price for the trade-in of your old car. The deal seems too good to resist. After you have committed yourself to buying, the dealer checks with the boss and returns, saying, "I'm so sorry. I forgot that this car has some special features that raise the value. If we sold it for the price I quoted, we'd lose money." So you agree to a higher price. Then the company's used car specialist looks at your old car and "corrects" the trade-in value to a lower amount. Still, you have committed yourself. You leave with a deal that you would not have accepted at the start.

That's Not All!

In the that's-not-all technique, *someone makes an offer and then improves the offer before you have a chance to reply.* The television announcer says, "Here's your chance to buy this amazing combination paper shredder and coffeemaker for only $39.95. But wait, there's more! We'll throw in a can of dog deodorant! Also this handy windshield wiper cleaner and a so-lar-powered flashlight and a subscription to *Modern Lobotomist!* And if you call now, you get this amazing offer, which usually costs $39.95, for only $19.95! Call now!" People who hear the first offer and then the "improved" offer are more likely to comply than are people who hear the "improved" offer from the start (Burger, 1986).

You may notice a similarity among the foot-in-the-door, bait-and-switch, and that's-not-all techniques: The persuader starts with one proposal and then switches to another. The first proposal changes the listeners' state of mind, making them more open for the second proposal.

16. Identify each of the following as an example of reciprocation, the contrast effect, foot-in-the-door technique, the bait-and-switch technique, or the that's-not-all technique.

a. A credit card company offers you a card with a low introductory rate. After a few months, the interest rate on your balance doubles.

b. A store marks its prices "25 percent off," scratches that out and marks them "50 percent off!"

c. A friend asks you to help carry some supplies over to the elementary school for an afternoon tutoring program. When you get there, the principal says that one of the tutors is late and asks whether you could take her place until she arrives. You agree and spend the rest of the afternoon tutoring. The principal then talks you into coming back every week as a tutor.

Answer

16. a. bait-and-switch technique; b. either the contrast effect or the that's-not-all technique; c. foot-in-the-door technique.

Nudges

Nudges are *acts intended to encourage beneficial actions, without using significant rewards or penalties.* For example, if you agree to be an organ donor, physicians can remove any of your organs after you die and transplant them to someone else. Being an organ donor neither helps you nor harms you, but it helps someone else. No one wants to pay you for being an organ donor or penalize you if you refuse, but a shift in policy, a nudge, makes a big difference: In some countries, you are assumed to be an organ donor unless you refuse (opt out), whereas in other countries, you are assumed to refuse unless you say you want to be a donor (opt in). Donation rates are considerably higher in the opt-out countries (Shepherd, O'Carroll, & Ferguson, 2014). In both cases, you still have a choice.

Here are other examples of nudges: Instead of offering employees an opportunity to put part of their income into a retirement account, tell them that part will be put into a retirement account unless they opt out. Instead of inviting people to sign up for influenza vaccinations, give them an appointment, which they have the option to cancel. To encourage people to pay their taxes on time, simplify the paperwork. (Yeah, don't you wish.) To encourage energy conservation, mail homeowners an occasional report of their energy use and how it compares to their neighbors' use (see ▼ Figure 13.8). To encourage exercise, give people devices that report how many steps they have taken today. Nudges are a good policy whenever many people are failing to do something that they agree would be a good idea (Benartzi et al., 2017).

Fear Messages

Some attempts at persuasion use threats, such as, "If you don't send money to support our cause, our political opponents will gain power and do terrible things." One organization appealed for contributions with a message on the envelope, "Every day an estimated 800 dolphins, porpoises, and whales will die . . . unless you act now!" (What, my contribution would save 800 marine mammals per day? How much did they think I was going to contribute?)

As you would guess, the effectiveness of fear messages varies. Some countries require cigarette packages to include photos of damaged lungs or blackened teeth, and these frightening displays appear to be effective (Nan, Zhao, Yang, & Iles, 2015). Telling physicians about patients who died from an opiate overdose leads to fewer prescriptions for high doses of opioid drugs (Doctor et al., 2018). However, if a message is too frightening, many people simply don't want to listen to it, or if they do listen, they don't believe it (Petty & Briñol, 2015). An extreme fear message, about global climate change, for example, may suggest that the problem is so severe that one person's action could not make a difference (Cialdini, 2003).

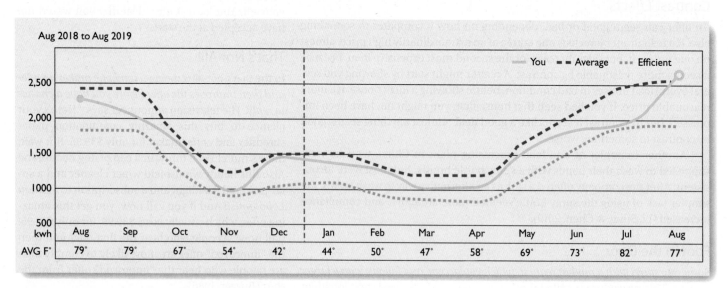

▲ **Figure 13.8** A mailing that compares your energy use to those of other people nudges you toward better efficiency.

Delayed Influence

Some messages have little influence at first but more later. Here are two examples.

The Sleeper Effect

Suppose you hear an idea from someone with poor qualifications. Because you don't respect the speaker, you reject the idea. Weeks later, you remember the idea but forget where you heard it (*source amnesia*). At that point, its persuasive impact may increase (Kumkale & Abarracín, 2004). If you completely forget the source, you might even claim it as your own idea. The **sleeper effect** is *delayed persuasion by an initially rejected message*. The sleeper effect is usually small for information heard in a speech, but larger for information heard on a television show (Jensen, Bernat, Wilson, & Goonewardene, 2011).

Minority Influence

Delayed influence also occurs when a minority group proposes a worthwhile idea. It could be a religious or political minority, or any other type. The majority rejects the idea at first but reconsiders it later. If the minority continually repeats a simple message and its members seem united, the influence often increases gradually, even if the majority hesitates to admit that the minority has swayed them (Wood, Lundgren, Ouellette, Busceme, & Blackstone, 1994). Also, by demonstrating the possibility of disagreeing with the majority, the minority may prompt others to offer additional proposals (Nemeth, 1986).

One powerful example of minority influence is that of the Socialist Party of the United States, which ran candidates for elective offices from 1900 through the 1950s, losing almost always (Shannon, 1955). Support gradually dwindled, until the party stopped nominating candidates. Had they failed? No! Most of their major proposals had been enacted into law (see ■ Table 13.1). Of course, those who voted for these changes claimed the ideas as their own rather than crediting the Socialists.

17. When does forgetting increase persuasion?

Answer

17. If you remember an idea but forget that it came from an unreliable source, it becomes more persuasive than if you remembered the source.

Resistance to Persuasion

You may be more easily influenced at certain times than at others. *Simply informing people that someone is going to try to persuade them activates resistance and weakens the persuasion* (Petty & Cacioppo, 1979). This tendency is called the **forewarning effect**. Actually, the results are somewhat complex. Suppose you have a strongly unfavorable attitude toward something—increased tuition at your college, for example. Now someone tells you that a well-informed person is going to try to persuade you in favor of higher tuition. At once, before the speech even begins, your attitudes shift slightly in the direction of favoring higher tuition. Exactly why is unclear, but perhaps you are telling yourself, "I guess there must be some good reason for that opinion." Then when you hear the speech itself, it does have some influence, and your attitudes shift still further, but not as much as if you had not been forewarned. The warning alerts you to resist the persuasion, to criticize weak arguments, and to reject weak evidence (Wood & Quinn, 2003).

Table 13.1 Political Proposals of the U.S. Socialist Party, Early 1900s	
Proposal	**Eventual Fate of Proposal**
Women's right to vote	Established by 19th Amendment to U.S. Constitution; ratified in 1920
Old-age pensions	Included in the Social Security Act of 1935
Unemployment insurance	Included in the Social Security Act of 1935; also guaranteed by other state and federal legislation
Health and accident insurance	Included in part in the Social Security Act of 1935 and in the Medicare Act of 1965
Increased wages, including minimum wage	First minimum-wage law passed in 1938; periodically updated since then
Reduction of working hours	Maximum 40-hour workweek (with exceptions) established by the Fair Labor Standards Act of 1938
Public ownership of electric, gas, and other utilities and of the means of transportation and communication	Utilities not owned by government but heavily regulated by federal and state government since the 1930s
Initiative, referendum, and recall (mechanisms for private citizens to push for changes in legislation and for removal of elected officials)	Adopted by most state governments

In the closely related inoculation effect, *people who hear and reject a weak argument are then disposed to resist a stronger argument suggesting the same conclusion.* In one experiment, people listened to speeches *against* brushing their teeth after every meal. Some of them heard just a strong argument (e.g., "Brushing your teeth too frequently wears away tooth enamel, leading to serious disease"). Others first heard a weak argument and then the strong argument 2 days later. Still others first heard an argument *for* brushing teeth and then the strong argument against it. Only those who heard the weak argument against brushing resisted the influence of the strong argument (McGuire & Papageorgis, 1961).

The inoculation effect can combat misinformation. For example, teenagers may face peer pressure to smoke cigarettes. They are more likely to resist if they have been told, "Someone will tell you that smoking isn't dangerous. But it is, and here is why..." A similar approach can help parents resist those who tell them not to vaccinate their children against diseases (Compton, Jackson, & Dimmock, 2016).

Coercive Persuasion

Finally, let's consider the most unfriendly kinds of persuasion. In some places, military or police interrogators have used torture (more generously known as "enhanced interrogation techniques") until suspects confessed or revealed information about subversive plots. If you were innocent, might you confess anyway, just to end the torture? Most people underestimate how painful torture can be (Nordgren, McDonnell, & Loewenstein, 2011). Any technique strong enough to get guilty people to confess gets innocent people to confess also.

Similar problems occur with what we might call "psychological torture." Suppose the police want you to confess to some crime. You agree to talk with them. After all, what do you have to lose? You're innocent, so you have nothing to hide. First the police claim your crime is horrendous and you face a stiff sentence. They offer sympathy and excuses, implying that if you confess, you can get a lighter sentence. They claim that you failed a polygraph test. You stay in isolation, without food or sleep for many hours, with no promise of when, if ever, this ordeal will end. Apparently,

confession is the only way you can get them to stop badgering you. Might you confess, even though you are innocent? Researchers agree that a procedure like this increases the chance of a false confession (Kassin, Redlich, Alceste, & Luke, 2018). You think, "Oh, well, eventually they will realize their mistake. They can't really convict me, because they won't have any other evidence." If the interrogators claim that they are awaiting analysis of fingerprints or DNA testing, you are even more likely to confess, just to end the interrogation, because you are sure the results of those tests will show your innocence. Ah, but then you learn that there were no fingerprints or DNA tests. Too late, you confessed.

Unfortunately, juries consider a confession to be strong evidence, even if they know it was coerced (Kassin & Gudjonsson, 2004). Furthermore, a forced confession biases the rest of the investigation. The police look only for further evidence of your guilt, not for evidence implicating someone else. Any witness who had been in doubt now testifies confidently that you were the perpetrator (Kassin, Bogart, & Kerner, 2012).

To test the effects of coercive persuasion, researchers set up this experiment: They asked pairs of students to work independently on logic problems. For half of the pairs, one of them (a confederate of the experimenter) asked for help, which the first person usually gave. Later, they were told that offering help was considered cheating. For the other pairs, the confederate did not ask for help and therefore no cheating occurred. After both completed the problems, the experimenter entered the room, accused the participant of cheating, and threatened to treat this event as harshly as any other case of academic cheating. However, the experimenter suggested they could settle the problem quickly if the student signed a confession. Under these circumstances, 87 percent of the guilty students and 43 percent of the innocent ones agreed to confess, as illustrated in ▼ Figure 13.9 (Russano, Meissner, Narchet, & Kassin, 2005). The message is that coercive techniques increase confessions by both guilty and innocent people, and therefore make the confessions unreliable evidence.

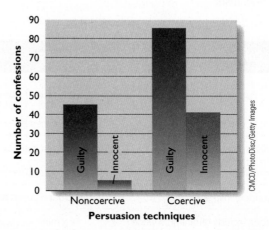

▲ **Figure 13.9** Coercive persuasion techniques increased the number of confessions by both guilty and innocent people. (Based on data of Russano, Meissner, Narchet, & Kassin, 2005)

Persuasion and Manipulation

Broadly defined, attitudes influence almost everything we do. It is important to be alert to some of the influences that might throw you off course. Advertisers, politicians, and others try to polish their techniques of persuasion, and not everyone has your best interest at heart.

Summary

- *Attitude measurement.* Psychologists usually measure attitudes by a Likert scale or something similar. (page 422)
- *Cognitive dissonance.* Cognitive dissonance is a state of tension when a behavior conflicts with an attitude. People try to reduce the inconsistency, often by changing their attitudes to match the behavior. (page 423)
- *Two routes to persuasion.* Persuasion based on superficial matters such as a television advertisement or a celebrity endorsement can be effective for unimportant decisions. For more important decisions, we take the effort to gather and evaluate information. (page 424)
- *Influence.* Many techniques increase influence, especially for less important decisions. Examples include reciprocation, contrast effects, foot in the door, bait and switch, and "that's not all." (page 424)
- *Nudges.* A nudge is a technique of making a desirable option easier, or making it seem like the normal thing to do. (page 426)
- *Influence of fear.* Messages that appeal to fear can be effective, but not if the message is too extreme or if it suggests that the problem is hopeless. (page 426)
- *Sleeper effect and minority influence.* In some cases, a suggestion that people initially reject becomes more influential later. (page 427)
- *Forewarning and inoculation effects.* Warning people about an attempt to influence them can increase their resistance. (page 427)
- *Coercive persuasion.* Techniques designed to pressure a suspect into confessing decrease the reliability of the confession because, under these circumstances, many innocent people confess also. (page 428)

Key Terms

attitude (p. 422)

bait-and-switch technique (p. 425)

central route to persuasion (p. 424)

cognitive dissonance (p. 423)

foot-in-the-door technique (p. 425)

forewarning effect (p. 427)

inoculation effect (p. 428)

nudges (p. 426)

peripheral route to persuasion (p. 424)

sleeper effect (p. 427)

that's-not-all technique (p. 425)

Review Questions

1. What does cognitive dissonance produce?
   (a) A change of an attitude
   (b) An undesirable behavior
   (c) Boredom
   (d) Disagreement between attitude and behavior

2. Which of these is an example of the central route to persuasion?
   (a) Buying something because of the bait-and-switch technique
   (b) Copying the preferences of someone who endorses a product

   (c) Reading *Consumer Reports* evaluations of a product
   (d) Preferring the product with the most colorful package

3. A company withholds a small part of each paycheck to apply to a retirement account, unless someone opts out. What is this procedure called?
   (a) A sleeper effect
   (b) A nudge
   (c) A contrast effect
   (d) Active participation

4. Suppose you want to persuade people to buy some product. Which of the following statements would probably be the most persuasive?
   (a) Most of the people who have bought this product like it.
   (b) More people have bought this product this year than last year.
   (c) Ten other people that I talked to today have bought this product.
   (d) Ten neighbors on your street have bought this product.

5. When are fear messages LEAST persuasive?
   (a) When they describe an extreme danger
   (b) When they imply that other people are already taking action
   (c) When they suggest what would be an effective action
   (d) When they are stated by a person similar to yourself

6. A friend asks you to drive him to the mall. When you get there, he asks whether you could wait while he shops and then drive him home. Which of these persuasion techniques did he use?
   (a) Foot-in-the-door technique
   (b) Contrast effect
   (c) That's-not-all technique
   (d) Reciprocation

7. What is the main objection to coercive methods of persuading a suspect to confess?
   (a) They require substantial effort and sometimes expensive equipment.
   (b) They produce confessions that are not admissible in court.
   (c) They might make an innocent person confess.
   (d) They create an adversarial relationship between suspect and police.

Answers: 1a, 2c, 3b, 4d, 5a, 6a, 7c.

Hollie Adams/Getty Images

After studying this module, you should be able to:

1. Explain a theory about why people and other animals care about physical attractiveness when choosing a mate.

2. List factors that increase the probability of forming a friendship or romantic relationship.

3. Distinguish between passionate and companionate love.

From 1975 to 1988, U.S. senator William Proxmire gave "Golden Fleece" awards to those who, in his opinion, most flagrantly wasted the taxpayers' money. He once bestowed an award on psychologists who had received a federal grant to study how people fall in love. According to Proxmire, the research was pointless because people do not want to understand love. They prefer, he said, to let such matters remain a mystery. This module describes the information that Senator Proxmire thought you didn't want to know.

Establishing Relationships

How do you choose your friends or romantic attachments? How do they choose you? Most people have many of the same preferences regardless of whether they are male or female, homosexual or heterosexual (Holmberg & Blair, 2009).

Proximity and Familiarity

Proximity means *closeness*. (It comes from the same root as *approximate*.) Not surprisingly, we are most likely to become friends with people who live or work in proximity to us. A professor assigned students to seats randomly and followed up on them a year later. Students most often became friends with those who sat in adjacent seats (Back, Schmulkle, & Egloff, 2008). Researchers analyzed the publications and patents by professors at Massachusetts Institute of Technology. Professors whose offices were closer to each other were more likely to work together on their research (Claudel, Massaro, Santi, Murray, & Ratti, 2017). (See ▼ Figure 13.10.)

One reason why proximity is important is that people who live nearby, or work nearby, have an opportunity to discover what they have in common. Another reason is the mere exposure effect, the principle that *coming into contact with someone or something increases how much we like that person or object* (Saegert, Swap, & Zajonc, 1973; Zajonc, 1968). Well, not always. Researchers contacted people who were about to go on a date arranged by an online dating service. Prior to the date, most people gave moderately high ratings on how much they expected to like the person they were about to date. After the date, more ratings went down than up (Norton, Frost, & Ariely, 2007). As you get to know someone better, you find how much you have in common, but you also find irritating quirks (Finkel et al., 2015). Proximity gives people the chance to become friends, but it doesn't guarantee anything.

Similarity

The saying "opposites attract" is true for magnets. It doesn't apply to people. Most romantic partners and close friends resemble each other in age, political and religious beliefs, intelligence, education, attitudes, and physical attractiveness (Eastwick, Finkel, Mochon, & Ariely, 2007; Laumann, 1969; Lee et al., 2008; Montoya, 2008; Rushton & Bons, 2005). They also have similar interests, and that similarity increases over time as a result of shared experiences (Anderson, Keltner, & John, 2003). With regard to physical attractiveness, note an interesting exception: For people who started dating shortly after they met, couples almost always resemble each other in physical attractiveness. However, for couples who had been good friends for a long time before dating, it sometimes happens that one is noticeably more attractive than the other (Hunt, Eastwick, & Finkel, 2015).

Although similarity is important in many regards, similarity of personality is less important (Montoya, Horton, & Kirchner, 2008). With careful measurement, researchers do find some personality similarities in most romantic couples (Wu, Stillwell, Schwartz, & Kosinski, 2017), but many happy couples have one who is more extraverted and one who is more introverted. In fact, couples with highly similar personalities sometimes find their relationship deteriorating over time (Shiota & Levenson, 2007). Another point on which similarity doesn't help is smell: Most women (unconsciously) prefer a romantic partner who does not smell too much like herself, her brothers, and other members of her family. That tendency is presumably a way to decrease the chance of mating with a close relative. Women taking birth control pills fail to show this tendency (Roberts, Gosling, Carter, & Petrie, 2008).

Members of minority groups face special difficulties. If your group is greatly outnumbered where you live, your choice of potential friends or romantic partners may be limited to members of your group who do not share your interests, or members of other groups who do (Hamm, 2000).

Even when friends differ in some ways, they generally have much in common, such as interests, attitudes, and level of education.

iStock.com/Olaser

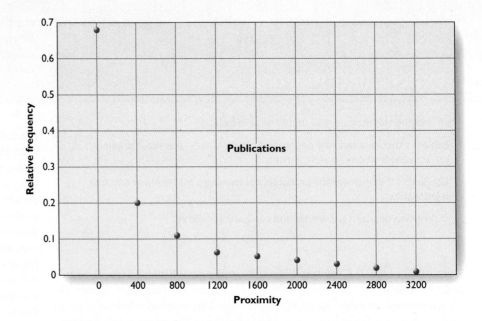

◀ **Figure 13.10** MIT professors were more likely to collaborate on research with a colleague whose office was nearby. (From "An exploration of collaborative scientific production at MIT through spatial organizational and institutional affiliation" by M. Claudel, E. Massaro, P. Santi, F. Murray, & C. Ratti, 2017. PLoS One, 12, 0179334.)

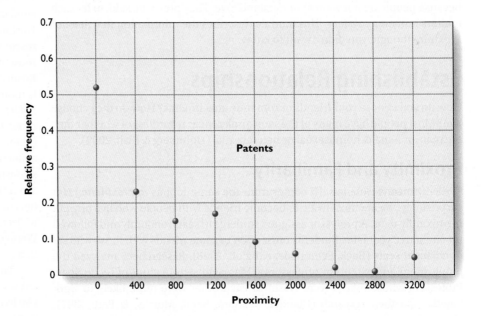

The Equity Principle

According to exchange or equity theories, *a friendship or romantic relationship is a transaction in which partners exchange goods and services.* As in business, a relationship is stable if both partners believe the deal is fair. It is easiest to establish a fair deal if the partners are about equally attractive and intelligent, contribute about equally to the finances and the chores, and so forth. In most couples, one partner contributes more in one way, and the other contributes more in another way.

The equity principle applies in the early stages of a friendship or romance but less so later. You might nurse your spouse or lifelong friend through a long illness without worrying about whether you are still getting a fair deal.

Physical Attractiveness

Finally, let's talk about the criterion that people notice first. If you ask people what they want in a partner, especially a romantic partner, they mention intelligence, honesty, a sense of humor, and other character traits. However, when people actually meet for the first time, as in speed dating, they mainly focus on appearance (Eastwick, Luchies, Finkel, & Hunt, 2014; Finkel & Eastwick, 2008).

In a study long ago, psychologists arranged blind dates for 332 freshman couples for a dance before the start of classes. They asked participants to fill out questionnaires, and then they ignored the questionnaires and paired students at random. Midway through the dance, the experimenters separated the men and women and asked them to rate how much they liked their dates. The only factor that influenced the ratings was physical attractiveness (Walster, Aronson, Abrahams, & Rottman, 1966). Surprising? Hardly. During the brief time they had spent together, the couples had little opportunity to learn about each other. Intelligence, personality, and character are critical for a lasting relationship but not for the first half of a first date (Keller, Thiessen, & Young, 1996).

The Value of Attractiveness: Birds

Why do we care about physical appearance? We take its importance so much for granted that we seldom consider the question, so for a moment let's consider other species.

In many bird species, early in the mating season, females shop around and choose a brilliantly colored male that sings vigorously from the treetops. In several species, females also prefer males with especially long tails (see ▼ Figure 13.11). From an evolutionary standpoint, aren't these foolish choices? The popular males are those that risk their lives by singing loudly from the treetops, where they call the attention of predators such as hawks and eagles. They waste energy by growing bright feathers. (It takes more energy to produce bright than dull colors.) A long tail may look pretty, but it interferes with flying. Why does the female prefer a mate who wastes energy and endangers his life?

Biologists eventually decided that wasting energy and risking life were precisely the point (Zahavi & Zahavi, 1997). Only a healthy, vigorous male has enough energy to make bright, colorful feathers (Blount, Metcalfe, Birkhead, & Surai, 2003). Only a strong male can fly despite a long tail, and only a vigorous male would risk predation by singing from an exposed perch. A colorful, singing male is more likely than average to have genes that produce a strong immune system (Pardal, Alves, Mota, & Ramos, 2018). The female presumably does not understand why she is attracted to colorful loudmouths. She just is, because throughout her evolutionary history, most females who chose such partners produced healthier offspring than those who chose dull-colored, quiet, inactive males.

The Value of Attractiveness: Humans

Are attractive humans more likely than others to be healthy and fertile? Theoretically, they should be. Illnesses decrease attractiveness. Also, *good-looking* means *normal*, and normal means good genes. Suppose a computer takes photographs of many people and averages their faces. The resulting composite face has about an average nose, average distance between the eyes, and so forth, and most people rate this face highly attractive (Langlois & Roggman, 1990; Langlois, Roggman, & Musselman, 1994; Rhodes, Sumich, & Byatt, 1999) (see ▼ Figure 13.12). An attractive person has nearly average features and few irregularities—no crooked teeth, skin blemishes, or other peculiarities that might indicate poor health or genetic abnormalities (Fink & Penton-Voak, 2002).

That is the theory, but do attractive people in fact tend to be healthier than average? An extensive study examined 15,000 young adults and found that those rated more attractive were healthier in almost all ways, except for having more sexually transmitted diseases (Nedelec & Beaver, 2014). (Tsk, tsk.) So, good appearance is evidently a cue to someone's health, and therefore a cue to favorable genes. It is far from a perfect cue, of course, but even a slightly valid cue is better than none at all.

18. **According to evolutionary theory, attractiveness is a sign of good health. Why would it be difficult for an unhealthy individual to produce "counterfeit" attractiveness?**

Answer

18. Attractive features such as bright feathers in a bird or large muscles in a man require much energy. It would be difficult for an unhealthy individual to devote enough energy to produce such features.

Dating and Modern Technology

The Internet has added a new dimension to dating. In the past, most couples met through friends or family. Today, more meet through Internet sites than by any other means (Rosenfeld, Thomas, & Hausen, 2019). Meeting online has advantages. Popular dating sites try to match people who might be compatible, and they introduce possible partners who would not have met otherwise. People can exchange information online before committing to meet in person. Disadvantages are present also. Many people are far from honest when describing themselves online. Also, having too many choices makes it hard to consider any of them carefully, tempts people to rely on superficial criteria, and sometimes leads to a habit of quickly rejecting

▲ **Figure 13.11** In some bird species, males with long tails attract more mates. Only a healthy male can afford this trait that impairs his flying ability.

▶ **Figure 13.12** Averaging or morphing many faces produces a generalized face that most people consider attractive. In this example, the first two faces were morphed to produce the one on the right.

possible matches (Finkel, Eastwick, Karney, Reis, & Sprecher, 2012). Despite all the information available on dating websites, both men and women react more strongly to the attractiveness of the photographs than to anything else (Sritharan, Heilpern, Wilbur, & Gawronski, 2010).

Young women tend to be highly selective. Women in their 40s, 50s, and beyond tend to be less selective (Whyte, Chan, & Torgler, 2018). They respond to the principle of supply and demand, as fewer men are available in the older age groups.

Some people also have Internet contacts with no intention of meeting face to face. They establish an online character (who may or may not look like the real person) who interacts with someone else's online character, sometimes even having on-screen sex. This type of activity apparently appeals mainly to people who do not have good real-life relationships (Scott, Mottarella & Lavooy, 2006).

Marriage and Long-Term Commitments

Most people hope to have a long-term loving relationship. Although the available research deals mainly with heterosexual marriages, the conclusions probably apply to other long-term commitments as well.

Is it possible to predict which marriages will succeed and which will not? To some extent, yes. Psychologists have studied newlywed couples and compared the results to how the marriages developed later. Couples whose arguments escalate to anger are likely to consider divorce later. Many people have been told that it is good to express their feelings fully, but venting anger at your partner makes both of you feel bad. If your partner retaliates by

screaming at you, nothing good will come of it (Fincham, 2003). Discussing a conflict calmly is important for maintaining a successful relationship (Bloch, Haase, & Levenson, 2014).

The best predictor of long-term satisfaction is much display of genuine affection (Graber, Laurenceau, Miga, Chango, & Coan, 2011). If your partner cheers you up when things are going badly, that's good, but often a better sign of affection is if your partner shows genuine pleasure at your successes.

Other subtle cues also distinguish successful from less successful relationships. In one study, 130 Dutch couples, mostly unmarried students, had a 7-minute discussion of some difference in their interests or preferred activities. Then other people watched videos of the discussion and rated the relationship. Their ratings were compared to implicit measures of the relationship, based on a variant of the IAT, and to self-reports of relationship satisfaction during the next week. The most accurate ratings of the relationship were by observers who do not speak Dutch, who therefore relied entirely on nonverbal behaviors (Faure, Righetti, Seibel, & Hofmann, 2018). That is, body language is often more revealing than words.

When you hear about how many marriages end in divorce, it is easy to despair, but many marriages remain strong for a lifetime. Psychologists have maintained that a romantic relationship begins with passionate love, *marked with sexual desire and excitement,* and gradually develops over many years

In a mature, lasting relationship, a couple can count on each other for care and affection through both good times and bad times.

into **companionate love**, *marked by sharing, care, and protection* (Bartels & Zeki, 2000; Hatfield & Rapson, 1993; Kim & Hatfield, 2004). However, research also found that one-third or more of people who have been married for more than 30 years report that they are still "very intensely" in love (O'Leary, Acevedo, Aron, Huddy, & Mashek, 2012). Brain scans show that when they see a photo of their spouse, they get excitation in the same brain areas that show excitation in the early stages of romance (Acevedo, Aron, Fisher, & Brown, 2012). Yes, love does fade for many couples, but for many others it remains strong for a lifetime.

19. What is the best predictor of long-term success for a marriage?

Answer

19. Consistent displays of affection and respect correlate with long-term success. Absence of angry displays is another strong correlate. Body language is often more reliable than what someone says.

---

in closing module 13.4

Choosing Your Partners Carefully

Life is like a roller-coaster ride in the dark: It has many ups and downs, and you never know what is going to happen next. You want to ride with someone you like and trust. In some regards, forming impressions of romantic partners is especially difficult.

A person you date is trying to make a good impression, and you *hope* to like the person. It is easy to form an attachment and regret it later. Choose carefully.

Summary

- *Forming relationships.* Important factors for starting a relationship include proximity, familiarity, and similarity. As in business, a relationship works best if both parties believe they are getting a fair deal. (page 431)
- *Similarity.* Friendships and romances are most likely to succeed if the partners are similar in education, interests, and beliefs. (page 431)
- *Physical attractiveness.* In humans as in birds, physical attractiveness is a partly valid cue to health and good genes. (page 432)

- *Internet dating.* Contrary to customs of the past, the most common way for romantic couples to meet today is by Internet dating sites. (page 433)
- *Marriage.* The best predictor of marriage success is consistent display of affection. (page 434)
- *Romantic love.* Psychologists distinguish passionate love and companionate love. For many people, love fades over a lifetime, but for a substantial number of people, it remains strong and passionate even after decades of marriage. (page 434)

Key Terms

companionate love (page 435)

exchange (or equity) theories (page 432)

mere exposure effect (page 431)

proximity (page 431)

passionate love (page 434)

Review Questions

1. According to equity theory, a social relationship is similar to what?
   (a) A high-stakes gamble
   (b) A business deal
   (c) An advice column
   (d) A visit to another country

2. According to evolutionary theory, why is a normal, average appearance considered attractive?
   (a) It avoids cognitive dissonance.
   (b) It puts less strain on the eyes.
   (c) It suggests similarity to yourself.
   (d) It implies good genetics.

3. Relationships work best if the partners are similar. Of the following, which type of similarity is LEAST important?
   (a) Similarity of education
   (b) Similarity of personality

   (c) Similarity of religious and political beliefs
   (d) Similarity of interests and activities

4. Of the following, which is the WORST advice?
   (a) When you are angry at your partner, express your anger fully.
   (b) Watch nonverbal body language when evaluating a relationship.
   (c) Consider using an Internet dating site.
   (d) Prefer a mate whose appearance is normal in most regards.

5. What is meant by "companionate" love?
   (a) Sexual desire and excitement
   (b) Weak, temporary attachment
   (c) Sharing, care, and protection
   (d) A relationship between people who never met in person

Answers: 1a, 2d, 3b, 4a, 5c.

Interpersonal Influence

After studying this module, you should be able to:

1. Describe Asch's classic experiment demonstrating conformity.

2. Discuss cultural differences in conformity.

3. Evaluate Zimbardo's prison experiment.

4. Describe Milgram's study on obedience.

5. Give examples of group polarization and groupthink.

People influence us constantly. First, people set *norms* that define the expectations of a situation. You watch how others dress and act in any situation, and you tend to do the same. Second, they provide us with *information*. For example, if you approach a building and find crowds quickly fleeing from it and screaming, they probably know something that you don't. However, people sometimes provide misinformation. In 2009, a man who had the wrong floor mat under the accelerator of his Toyota could not get his car to stop and therefore had a fatal accident. The publicity led people to believe there was something wrong with Toyotas, and suddenly a huge number of people reported problems with their Toyotas, and then with other models. Eventually people realized this was just mass hysteria, and none of the cars were defective (Fumento, 2014). Third, people influence us just by suggesting a possible action. Seeing people yawn makes you feel like yawning, too. Why? They haven't given you any new information, and you don't necessarily wish to resemble them. You copy just because seeing a yawn suggested the possibility.

Conformity

Conformity means *altering one's behavior to match other people's behavior or expectations.* In many situations, conformity is good. When you are driving, it is helpful if everyone going the same direction drives on the same side of the road at approximately the same speed. If you are having a discussion, it is helpful if everyone speaks the same language. If you go to a meeting, it is helpful if everyone arrives at about the same time.

Conformity is widespread in the animal kingdom. Consider fruit flies: Males genetically vary

between green and pink on part of the body. Ordinarily, a female shows no preference between the green and pink varieties, but one who has just watched another female mate with one or the other now prefers the same type (Danchin et al., 2018).

Don't underestimate the power of conformity. Koversada, Croatia, used to be an officially nudist town. If a first-time visitor walked around the city wearing clothes, other people stopped and stared, shaking their heads with disapproval. The visitor felt as awkward and self-conscious as a naked person would be in a city of clothed people. Most visitors quickly undressed (Newman, 1988). If you exclaim, "I wouldn't conform," compare your own clothing right now to what others around you are wearing. Professors have sometimes noted the irony of watching a class full of students in blue jeans insisting that they do not conform to other people's style of dress (Snyder, 2003).

On many websites, users post a comment and other users can then vote "thumbs up" or "thumbs down" to indicate their approval or disapproval. Researchers chose a few thousand new comments at random to give an initial "thumbs up." The result was a 25 percent increased percentage of "thumbs up" votes by later users, compared to average (Muchnik, Aral, & Taylor, 2013).

Do you think you conform about as much as most other people do, or more or less? *Most* U.S. students insist that they conform *less* than average. One group of students was asked, "Here is what most students at your college think about this issue . . . Now, what do you think?" Regardless of what the students were told the others thought, most students said they agreed with that position . . . while insisting that it was really their own opinion, and they were not just going along with the crowd (Pronin, Berger, & Molouki, 2007).

Conformity to an Obviously Wrong Majority

Someone in Iceland hung a bra on this fence, for unknown reasons. Since then, others have added bras to the fence. People conform, and not always for any clear reason.

Early research suggested that we conform our opinions when we are unsure of our own judgment (Sherif, 1935). Would we conform even we knew that everyone else was wrong? To answer that question, Solomon Asch (1951, 1956) conducted a now-famous series of experiments. He asked groups of students to look at a vertical bar, as shown in ▼ **Figure 13.13**, which he defined as the model. He showed them three other vertical bars (right half of Figure 13.13) and asked which bar was the same length as the model. As you can see, the task is simple. Asch asked the students to give their answers aloud. He repeated the procedure with 18 sets of bars.

In each group, only one student was a real participant. The others were confederates who had been instructed to give incorrect answers on 12 of the 18 trials. Asch arranged for the real participant to be the next to last person in the group to

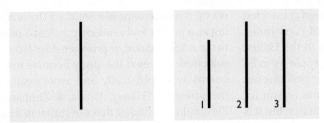

▲ **Figure 13.13** In Asch's conformity studies, a participant was asked which of three lines matched another line. Before answering, the participant heard other people answer incorrectly.

announce his answer so that he would hear most of the confederates' incorrect responses before giving his own (see ▼ Figure 13.14). Would he go along with the crowd?

To Asch's surprise, 37 of the 50 participants conformed to the majority at least once, and 14 conformed on most of the trials. Asch (1955) was disturbed by these results: "That we have found the tendency to conformity in our society so strong . . . is a matter of concern. It raises questions about our ways of education and about the values that guide our conduct" (p. 34).

Why did people conform so readily? When they were interviewed after the experiment, some said they thought the rest of the group was correct or they guessed that an optical illusion was influencing the appearance of the bars. Others said they knew their conforming answers were wrong but went along with the group for fear of ridicule. A few wanted to avoid embarrassing the others. The nonconformists were interesting, too. Some were nervous but felt duty bound to say how the bars looked to them. A few seemed socially withdrawn. Still others were supremely self-confident, as if to say, "I'm right and everyone else is wrong. It happens all the time." Experiments similar to Asch's have been repeated many times since then. A fair amount of conformity is generally present, although usually less than Asch found.

When Asch (1951, 1955) varied the number of confederates who gave incorrect answers, he found that people conformed to a group of three or four just as readily as to a larger group (see ▶ Figure 13.15). However, a participant with an ally giving correct answers conformed much less. Being a minority of one is painful, but being in a minority of two is not as bad (see ▶ Figure 13.16). Even among those who were

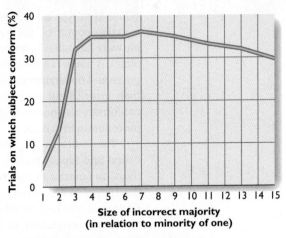

▲ **Figure 13.15** Asch found that conformity became more frequent as group size increased to about three, and then it leveled off. (Adapted from "Opinion and social pressure" by Solomon Asch, 1955 (November). *Scientific American*. Copyright © 1955 by Scientific American, Inc. All rights reserved.)

outnumbered many to one, not all people conformed. Situations have a powerful influence, but individual differences are important, too.

Cultural Differences

20. If your opinion is outnumbered, how does the size of the group make a difference?

Answer

20. Being outnumbered about 3 to 1 produces about as much influence as a larger group. However, having even one ally reduces the group influence.

▲ **Figure 13.14** Three of the participants in one of Asch's experiments on conformity. The one in the middle looking uncomfortable is the real participant. The others are the experimenter's confederates. (From Asch, 1951)

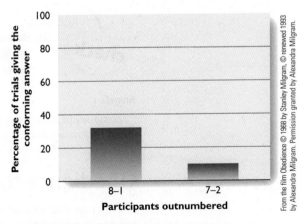

▲ **Figure 13.16** In Asch's experiments, participants who were faced with a unanimous incorrect majority conformed on 32 percent of trials. Participants who had an ally giving the correct answer were less likely to conform.

When Asch-type experiments have been conducted in Asian countries, the percentage of conforming answers has often been higher than in the United States. A major reason is that Asian people try to be polite and not embarrass the others by pointing out their error (Bond & Smith, 1996). That reason for conformity also occurs in the United States, but it is more common in Asia.

The cultures of southern Asia, including China and Japan, are often described as "collectivist" in contrast to the "individualist" cultures of the United States, Canada, Australia, and most of Europe. According to this view, Western culture encourages originality, individualism, and uniqueness, whereas Eastern culture favors subordination of the individual to the welfare of the family or society (Takemura, 2014). Children with a high tendency to conform are regarded as intelligent and well-behaved in Melanesia, but they are less highly evaluated in the United States (Clegg, Wen, & Legare, 2017).

However, making a sweeping generalization about Eastern versus Western cultures is an oversimplification. When investigators have directly observed conformist, cooperative, and competitive behaviors in various countries, the results have varied, depending on the type of question or the type of behavior observed. Japanese culture is more collectivist than American culture in some ways, but similar to American culture in other ways (Hamamura, 2012; Oyserman, Coon, & Kemmelmeier, 2002). Furthermore, each country has subcultures (Fiske, 2002). In many ways Tokyo resembles New York more than either city resembles the rural areas in their own countries.

21. How do the reasons for conformity in the United States differ from those in Asia?

Answer

21. Americans often conform to avoid embarrassing themselves. Asians more often conform to avoid embarrassing others.

Obedience to Authority

If someone told you to hurt an innocent person, would you refuse? Always? Are you sure?

In the early 1970s, psychologist Philip Zimbardo and his colleagues performed one of the best known studies in social psychology. They paid college students to play the roles of guards and prisoners for 2 weeks during a vacation period. The researchers set up the basement of a Stanford University building as a prison and randomly assigned participants to the roles of guard or prisoner. After 6 days, the researchers canceled the study because many of the guards were physically and emotionally bullying the prisoners (Haney, Banks, & Zimbardo, 1973). Zimbardo concluded that the situation had elicited cruel behavior. Normal, well-educated, middle-class young men, when given power over others, had quickly abused that power. The implication is that we shouldn't blame people who abuse their power, because most of us would do the same thing in that situation.

Although that conclusion may be true, the Stanford prison experiment is not solid evidence for it. Researchers should worry about demand characteristics, the cues that tell participants what the experimenter hopes to see. In this case, the demand characteristics were huge. After all, if the students were "playing prison" for 2 weeks, they must have inferred that they were expected to be rude and abusive (Banuazizi & Movahedi, 1975). One of the guards recalled, decades later, "I set out with a definite plan in mind, to try to force the action, force something to happen, so that the researchers would have something to work with. After all, what could they possibly learn from guys sitting around like it was a country club?" ("The Menace Within," 2011).

Furthermore, later and fuller descriptions of the study revealed that the guards didn't have to do much work to infer the experimenters' intentions. During the guards' orientation session, Zimbardo had instructed them to create fear, deprive the prisoners of privacy, and give them a sense of powerlessness. A few days later, some of the guards were told that they were supposed to act tougher (Zimbardo, 2007). Under the circumstances, the guards were doing what they thought they were supposed to do.

Regardless of the problems with the prison study, the question remains: How far would normal people go in following orders to hurt someone? Let's consider in detail another of psychology's most famous experiments.

what's the evidence?

Milgram's Obedience Experiment

If an experimenter asked you to deliver shocks to another person, starting with weak shocks and progressing to stronger ones, at what point, if any, would you refuse? Research by Stanley Milgram (1974) was inspired by reports of atrocities in the Nazi concentration camps during World War II. People who had committed the atrocities defended themselves by saying they were only obeying orders. International courts rejected that defense, and outraged people throughout the world

Irena Sendler, a Polish social worker, saved the lives of more than 2,500 Jewish children from the Nazis, not giving up their whereabouts even under torture. She was later able to reunite many of the children with their families by digging up thousands of jars in which she had buried their identities and information.

insisted, "If I had been there, I would have refused to follow such orders" or "I would have been like the woman in the movie *Schindler's List* who risked her life to save Jewish people from the Nazi Holocaust."

Well, maybe you would have, and maybe not. Milgram suspected that people might yield to pressure.

Hypothesis When an authority figure instructs people to do something that might hurt another person, some of them will obey.

Method Two adult men at a time arrived at the experiment—a real participant and a confederate of the experimenter pretending to be a participant. The experimenter told them that in this study on learning, one participant would be the "teacher" and the other would be the "learner." The teacher would read pairs of words through a microphone to the learner, sitting in another room. The teacher would then test the learner's memory for the associated words. Whenever the learner made a mistake, the teacher was to deliver an electric shock as punishment.

The experiment was rigged so that the real participant was always the teacher and the confederate was always the learner. The teacher watched as the learner was strapped into an escape-proof shock device (see ◄ Figure 13.17). The learner never received shocks, but the teacher was led to believe that he did. In fact, before the start of the study, the experimenter had the teacher feel a sample shock from the machine.

Throughout the experiment, the learner made many mistakes. The experimenter instructed the teacher to begin by punishing the learner with the 15-volt switch for his first mistake and increase by 15 volts for each successive mistake, up to the maximum of 450 volts (see ▼ Figure 13.18).

As the voltage went up, the learner in the next room cried out in pain. If the teacher asked who would take responsibility for any harm to the learner, the experimenter replied that he, the experimenter, would take responsibility but insisted, "while the shocks may be painful, they are not dangerous." When the shocks reached 150 volts, the learner begged to be let out of the experiment, complaining that his heart was bothering him. Beginning at 270 volts, he screamed in agony. At 300 volts, he shouted that he would no longer

▲ **Figure 13.17** In Milgram's experiment, a rigged selection chose a confederate of the experimenter to be the "learner." Here the learner is strapped to a device that supposedly delivers shocks. (Source: https://www.youtube.com/watch?v=Jqr5 -dWk6Gw)

▲ **Figure 13.18** The "teacher" in Milgram's experiment flipped switches on this box, apparently delivering stronger and stronger shocks for each successive error that the "learner" made. Although the device looked realistic, it did not actually shock the learner. (Source: https://www.youtube.com/watch?v=Jqr5-dWk6Gw)

answer any questions. After 330 volts, he made no response at all. Still, the experimenter ordered the teacher to continue asking questions and delivering shocks. (Failure to answer was considered a wrong answer, which called for another shock.) Remember, the learner was not really being shocked. The screams came from a recording.

Results Of 40 participants, 25 delivered shocks all the way to 450 volts. Most of those who quit did so early. Most of those who went beyond 150 volts and everyone who continued beyond 330 persisted all the way to 450. Those who delivered the maximum shock were not sadists, but normal adults recruited from the community through newspaper ads. They were paid a few dollars for their services, and if they asked, they were told that they could keep the money even if they quit. (Not many asked.) People from all walks of life obeyed the experimenter's orders, including blue-collar workers, white-collar workers, and professionals. Most became nervous and upset while they were supposedly delivering shocks to the screaming learner.

Interpretation Why did so many people obey orders? One reason was that the experimenter agreed to take responsibility. Remember the diffusion of responsibility principle. Another reason is that the teachers identified with the experimenter and saw themselves as his assistant (Reicher, Haslam, & Smith, 2012). Also, the experimenter started with a small request, a 15-volt shock, and gradually progressed to stronger shocks. It is easy to agree to the small request, and agreeing to that one facilitates agreeing to the next one. If you have already delivered many shocks it is difficult to quit, because if you quit, you take responsibility for your actions. If you quit after 300 volts, why didn't you quit earlier? You could no longer say, "I was just following orders."

▲ Figures 13.19 and ▼ 13.20 illustrate the results of variations in procedure. Participants were more obedient to an experimenter who remained in the same room than to one who left. They were less obedient if they needed to force the learner's hand back onto the shock plate. If additional "teachers" divided the task—the other "teachers" being confederates of the experimenter—a participant was likely to obey if the others obeyed but unlikely if the others refused.

The remarkable conclusion is that many normal people followed orders that they thought might hurt or even kill someone. If people in this study felt compelled to obey, just imagine the pressure to obey orders from a government or military leader.

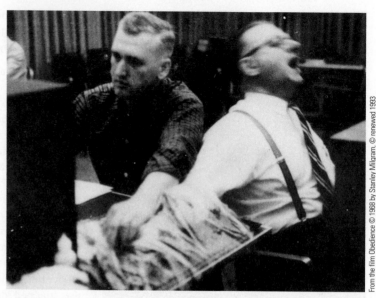

▲ **Figure 13.19** In one variation of the procedure, the experimenter asked the teacher to hold the learner's hand on the shock plate. This close contact with the learner decreased obedience to less than half its usual level. (From Milgram's 1965 film, *Obedience*)
(Source: https://www.youtube.com/watch?v=Jqr5-dWk6Gw)

Ethical Issues Milgram's experiment told us something about ourselves that we did not want to hear. No longer could we say, "What happened in Nazi Germany could never happen here." We found that most of us do follow orders, even offensive ones. We are indebted to Milgram's study for this unpleasant but important information. However, although it is good to know about Milgram's results, you would not have enjoyed participating in his experiment. Most people found the experience upsetting and some became very distressed (Perry, 2013).

A few years after Milgram's studies, the U.S. government established regulations to protect people participating in research. These regulations were a response to abusive experiments in medicine, not to Milgram's study (Benjamin & Simpson, 2009). Nevertheless, the rules apply to psychological research. In addition, psychologists have become more sensitive to the ethics of research. Today, before the start of any study—even the simplest and most innocuous—the researcher must submit a plan to an institutional committee that considers the ethics and approves or rejects the study. One of the main rules is *informed consent*. Before you participate, you must understand what is about to happen, and you must agree to it.

Could anyone replicate Milgram's research today? Psychologists long assumed that the ethical restraints would prohibit a replication (although reality television shows have submitted people to equal or worse experiences). However, one researcher found a way to replicate the essential aspect of the research. Milgram reported that most of the people who went beyond 150 volts continued all the way to 450. The teacher's

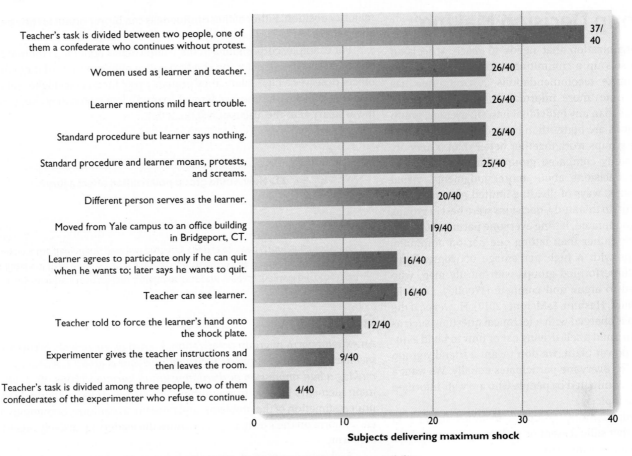

▲ **Figure 13.20** Milgram varied his procedure in many ways. Division of responsibility increased obedience. An implication of personal responsibility decreased obedience.

tension and stress increased as the learner screamed and protested at the higher voltages. Burger (2009) repeated the procedure but just until 150 volts. The result was that most people, both men and women, continued as far as 150 volts, as in Milgram's research more than 40 years earlier (Burger, 2009). The level of obedience was a bit lower than in Milgram's era, but the finding remains that most people followed orders that might hurt someone. Another study repeated Burger's procedure, but although the learner screamed, the learner did not mention heart problems or demand to quit the study. In this procedure, 90 percent continued through the 150-volt switch (Dolinski et al., 2017).

It is interesting to speculate about what would have happened under other conditions that Milgram didn't try. Would people quit earlier if they thought they were shocking a woman? (The learner in Milgram's studies was always a man.) How soon would they quit if they thought they were shocking a child? What if they were told that they would later trade places, so that the previous learner would start delivering shocks to the teacher? How do you think the teachers would behave then? What other changes in procedure can you imagine that might influence the degree of obedience?

At what point would you have quit in this experiment, if at all? It is difficult to estimate the influence of a situation you have never faced. To demonstrate, a professor came a few minutes late to class while an unfamiliar person entered, put down belongings, told the class, "I need you to put your cell phones in this box," and then walked around the room collecting phones, without any identification or explanation. In three of five classes, all the students obeyed, and in the other two, more than half obeyed. However, when other students were told about this procedure and asked how likely they would be to obey, their mean estimate was 22 percent (Farley, Carson, & Pope, 2019).

22. In what way did the obedience in Milgram's experiment resemble the foot-in-the-door procedure? How did it resemble Skinner's shaping procedure?

Answer

22. As with the foot-in-the-door procedure, Milgram started with a small request (give a small shock) and then built up. Skinner's shaping procedure also starts with an easy task and then builds to something more difficult.

Group Decision Making

An organization that needs to reach a decision often sets up a committee to consider the issues and make recommendations. A committee has more time, more information, and fewer peculiarities than any individual has. On average, group decisions are better than individual decisions, but some groups work together better than others do. One study compared groups that were asked to make decisions about moral judgments, visual problems, ways of dividing limited resources, and so forth. In this study, decisions were best in groups that cooperated, letting everyone participate about equally rather than letting one person dominate. Groups with a high percentage of women usually outperformed groups with mostly men, who tended to argue and compete (Woolley, Chabris, Pentland, Hashmi, & Malone, 2010). However, if the group is charged with a technical question, such as how to build a self-driving car or how to build a nuclear power plant, we don't want a friendly group in which everyone participates equally. We want a group dominated by people who are well-informed on the topic.

Furthermore, groups sometimes interact in ways that stifle dissent or rush to a judgment. Let's consider how this happens.

Group Polarization

If nearly all the people who compose a group lean in the same direction on a particular issue, then a group discussion moves the group as a whole even further in that direction. This phenomenon is known as group polarization. It occurs in homogeneous groups, not in groups that start with sharply divided opinions (Rodrigo & Ato, 2002).

The term *polarization* does not mean that the group breaks up into fragments favoring different positions. Rather, it means that the members of a group move *together* toward one pole (extreme position) or the other. For example, a group of people who are opposed to abortion or in favor of animal rights or opposed to gun regulations will, after discussing the issue among themselves, generally become more extreme in their views than they had been at the start (Lamm & Myers, 1978). During the discussion, if most of the members were already leaning in the same direction, people face peer pressure to conform, and they hear new information and arguments to support the

majority position. Either of those influences can be important for one person or another (Sieber & Ziegler, 2019).

For example, corporations in the United States appoint a committee of directors to set the salary for the chief executive officer. If most of them think the officer deserves a high salary, they probably vote for an even higher salary after discussing it with one another. If most favored a low salary, they choose an even lower salary after the discussion (Zhu, 2014).

23. How would group polarization affect a jury?

Answer

23. If most jury members lean toward a guilty or innocent verdict, they will become even more confident of their decision after a discussion. In a civil suit, if most jurors favor a strong penalty against the defendant, they will probably choose an even stronger penalty after a discussion.

Groupthink

An extreme form of group polarization, known as groupthink, occurs when *the members of a group suppress their doubts about a group's decision for fear of making a bad impression or disrupting group harmony* (Janis, 1972, 1985). The main elements leading to groupthink are overconfidence by the leadership, underestimation of the problems, and pressure to conform. Sometimes dissenters conform on their own, and sometimes the leadership actively urges them to conform.

A classic example of groupthink led to the Bay of Pigs fiasco of 1962. President John F. Kennedy and his advisers were considering a plan to support a small-scale invasion of Cuba at the Bay of Pigs. They assumed that a small group of Cuban exiles could overwhelm the Cuban army and trigger a spontaneous rebellion of the Cuban people against their government. Most of the advisers who doubted this assumption kept quiet. The only one who expressed doubts was told that he should loyally support the president. Within a few hours after the invasion began, all the invaders were killed or captured. The Bay of Pigs invasion led to the Cuban missile crisis that came close to starting a nuclear war. The decision makers wondered how they could have made such a stupid decision.

Another example was Japan's decision to attack the United States at Pearl Harbor in 1941. Most of the civilian leadership and the leaders of the navy doubted the wisdom of attacking, but a few army leaders strongly advocated the attack, and the opponents hesitated to speak out against the decision (Hotta, 2013).

Groupthink is not easy to avoid. We generally admire government or business leaders who are decisive and confident. Groupthink occurs when they become *too* decisive and confident, and when other group members hesitate to risk their status by objecting. Occasionally, some people do speak out, especially people who care deeply about an issue under discussion (Packer, 2009). To decrease groupthink, one strategy is for a leader to consult with advisers individually, to avoid influence from what other advisers say.

Fix the Situation, Not Human Nature

Certain situations bring out the worst in people, even well-educated people with good intentions. If we want to prevent people from panicking when a fire breaks out in a crowded theater, the best solution is not to remind people what to do. The solution is to build more exits. Similarly, it is difficult to teach people to behave ethically or intelligently when they are under strong pressure to conform or to obey orders. To avoid the temptation to make bad decisions, we need to choose our situations carefully.

Still, social psychologists have often concentrated so much on the power of the situation that they almost ignore individual differences. Not everyone in Asch's studies conformed, most of the guards in Zimbardo's prison study were not tyrannical, and not everyone in Milgram's study continued flipping shock switches. Situations are powerful, but personalities matter, too (Swann & Jetten, 2017).

Summary

- *Social influence.* People influence our behavior by setting norms and by offering information. We also follow others' examples just because they suggested a possible action. (page 436)
- *Conformity.* People sometimes conform to the majority opinion even when they are sure it is wrong. (page 436)
- *Cultural differences.* Although some cultures tend to be more collectivist or conforming than others, it is an over-generalization to regard all Asian cultures as collectivist or to assume that all members of a society are the same. (page 438)

- *Zimbardo's prison study.* The famous prison study should be interpreted with much caution, as the participants were encouraged to act as they did. (page 438)
- *Obedience.* In Milgram's obedience study, many people followed directions in which they thought they were delivering painful shocks to another person. (page 438)
- *Group polarization.* Groups of people who lean mostly in the same direction on a given issue tend to become more extreme after a group discussion. (page 442)
- *Groupthink.* Groupthink occurs when members of a cohesive group fail to express their opposition to a decision. (page 442)

Key Terms

conformity (p. 436)

group polarization (p. 442)

groupthink (p. 442)

Review Questions

1. When were people LEAST likely to conform in Solomon Asch's study?
   (a) If they had to speak their opinion publicly
   (b) If they were sure their own opinion was correct
   (c) If they had even one ally
   (d) If the majority group had only three members

2. Conformity tends to be greatest in which cultures, and why?
   (a) In collectivist cultures, because people do not want to embarrass others
   (b) In collectivist cultures, because people do not want to embarrass themselves
   (c) In individualist cultures, because people do not want to embarrass others
   (d) In individualist cultures, because people do not want to embarrass themselves

3. Which of these criticisms applies to Zimbardo's prison study?
   (a) The effect was too small to be statistically significant.
   (b) Participants were not randomly assigned to the two groups.
   (c) Later studies failed to replicate these results.
   (d) The participants were influenced by demand characteristics.

4. Which type of participants did Milgram use in his obedience study?
   (a) College students
   (b) A miscellaneous assortment of adults
   (c) A representative sample of several cultures
   (d) People with a previous history of antisocial behavior

5. How did recent replications differ from Milgram's original study?
   (a) The teacher watched the learner.
   (b) The learner complained about his heart and demanded to quit.
   (c) The research occurred in countries that do not demand ethical research.
   (d) The procedure stopped after 150 volts.

6. Under what circumstance does group polarization occur?
   (a) If people express their opinions anonymously
   (b) If no one in the group has a strong opinion at the start
   (c) If members of the group have sharp disagreements at the start
   (d) If members of the group lean the same direction at the start

Answers: 1c, 2a, 3d, 4b, 5d, 6d.

14 | Personality

WAYHOME studio/Shutterstock.com

A huge number of people are trying to assemble the world's largest jigsaw puzzle. Cody Conclusionjumper scrutinizes 20 pieces, stares off into space, and announces, "When the puzzle is fully assembled, it will be a picture of the Sydney Opera House!" Prudence Plodder says, "Well, I don't know what the whole puzzle will look like, but I think I've found two pieces that fit together."

Which of the two has made the greater contribution to completing the puzzle? We could argue either way. Clearly, the task requires an enormous number of small accomplishments like Prudence's. But if Cody is right, her flash of insight will be extremely valuable for assembling all the pieces. Of course, if the puzzle turns out to be a picture of a sailboat at sunset, then Cody will have misled us and wasted our time.

Some psychologists have offered grand theories about the nature of personality, while others have dealt with smaller, more detailed questions. In this chapter, we explore several approaches to personality. In the first module, we consider some famous theorists, including Sigmund Freud. The second module concerns descriptions of personality. Any description is a type of theory, but it differs from the kinds of theories in the first module. The final module concerns personality measurements.

Understanding personality is like assembling an extraordinarily complex jigsaw puzzle.

ASDF_MEDIA/Shutterstock.com

WAYHOME studio/Shutterstock.com

After studying this module, you should be able to:

1. Discuss and evaluate Sigmund Freud's theories.

2. List Freud's stages of psychosexual pleasure.

3. Define and give examples of Freud's defense mechanisms against anxiety.

4. Explain what Carl Jung meant by the collective unconscious.

5. Discuss how Alfred Adler advanced the idea that mental health is more than the absence of mental illness.

6. Explain how the learning approach deals with apparent inconsistencies in anyone's personality.

7. State the distinctive features of humanistic psychology.

people seek good and noble goals after they have been freed from unnecessary restraints.

Way down deep, are we good, bad, or both? Does the question even make sense? What is the basic nature of human personality?

The term *personality* comes from the Latin word *persona*, meaning "mask." In the plays of ancient Greece and Rome, actors wore masks to indicate their characters. **Personality** consists of *the consistent ways in which people differ from each other in their interests, attitudes, and social behaviors.* (Differences in learning, memory, sensation, or athletic skills are generally not considered personality.)

Sigmund Freud and the Psychodynamic Approach

Sigmund Freud (1856–1939), an Austrian physician, developed the first psychodynamic theory. A **psychodynamic theory** *relates personality to the interplay of conflicting forces, including unconscious ones, within the individual.* That is, internal forces that we don't always understand push us and pull us.

Freud's influence extends into sociology, literature, art, religion, and politics. And yet, here we are, approaching the end of this psychology textbook, and it has barely mentioned Freud so far. Why?

The reason is that most psychologists are highly skeptical of Freud's theories. According to Frederick Crews (1996, p. 63), "independent studies have begun to converge toward a verdict ... that there is literally nothing to be said, scientifically or therapeutically, to the advantage of the entire Freudian system or any of its constituent dogmas." Others have written, "the legend is losing its hold, fraying from all sides" (Borch-Jacobsen & Shamdasani, 2012). Freud's influence within psychology today is more limited than most people outside psychology imagine it to be.

> Every individual is virtually an enemy of civilization. . . . Thus civilization has to be defended against the individual. . . . For the masses are lazy and unintelligent . . . and the individuals composing them support one another in giving free rein to their indiscipline.
>
> —Sigmund Freud (1927/1961, pp. 6–8)

> It has been my experience that persons have a basically positive direction. In my deepest contacts with individuals in therapy, even those whose troubles are most disturbing, whose behavior has been most anti-social, whose feelings seem most abnormal, I find this to be true.
>
> —Carl Rogers (1961, p. 26)

What is human nature? The seventeenth-century philosopher Thomas Hobbes argued that humans are by nature selfish. Life in a state of nature, he said, is "nasty, brutish, and short." We need the government to protect us from one another. The eighteenth-century political philosopher Jean-Jacques Rousseau disagreed, maintaining that people are naturally good and that governments are the problem, not the solution. Rational people acting freely, he maintained, would advance the welfare of all.

The debate between those two viewpoints survives in theories of personality (see ▼ Figure 14.1). Sigmund Freud held that people are born with impulses that must be held in check if civilization is to survive. Carl Rogers believed that

Freud's Search for the Unconscious

Although Freud was a physician, he admitted in letters to his friends that he was never much interested in medicine. His goal was a theoretical understanding of the human mind. Early in his career, Freud worked with the psychiatrist Josef Breuer, who was treating a young woman with a fluctuating

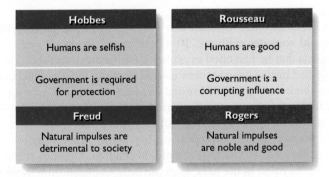

Hobbes		Rousseau	
Humans are selfish		Humans are good	
Government is required for protection		Government is a corrupting influence	
Freud		**Rogers**	
Natural impulses are detrimental to society		Natural impulses are noble and good	

▲ **Figure 14.1** Sigmund Freud, like the philosopher Thomas Hobbes, stressed the more destructive aspects of human nature. Carl Rogers, like Jean-Jacques Rousseau, emphasized the more favorable aspects.

Sigmund Freud interpreted dreams, slips of the tongue, and so forth to infer unconscious thoughts and motivations.

variety of physical complaints. As she talked with Breuer about her past, she described emotionally difficult experiences. Breuer, and later Freud, said that remembering these experiences produced catharsis, *a release of pent-up emotional tension,* thereby relieving her illness. However, later scholars who reexamined the medical records found that this woman who was so central to the history of psychoanalysis experienced little or no benefit from the treatment (Ellenberger, 1972). We should not take it for granted that catharsis is a good thing. Reliving painful experiences is painful, and ruminating about them leads to depression (Whisman, du Pont, & Butterworth, 2020).

Regardless of whether catharsis was helpful in this case, or any other, Freud began seeking a "talking cure" with other patients. He referred to *his method of explaining and dealing with personality, based on the interplay of conscious and unconscious forces,* as psychoanalysis. To this day, psychoanalysts remain loyal to some version of Freud's methods and theories, although their views have of course developed and diversified over the decades.

Central to Freud's theory was his concept of the unconscious, *a repository of memories, emotions, and thoughts, many of them illogical, that affect our behavior even though we do not acknowledge them.* According to this theory, people deal with traumatic experiences and unresolved childhood conflicts by forcing many thoughts and emotions into an unconscious mind. The goal of psychoanalysts is to bring those memories back to consciousness, producing catharsis and enabling the person to overcome irrational impulses. The psychoanalyst should listen intently to everything that patients say and help them explore possible meanings of each thought, memory, and action. The assumption is that simply understanding and bringing the unconscious material into consciousness will bring psychological improvement.

Freud said so, at any rate. Later interviews with his surviving ex-patients revealed that Freud often deviated from the procedure he recommended. Sometimes he administered morphine or other drugs. In many cases he gave explicit, and often harmful, advice. In one case he urged a client who was having an affair with a married woman to divorce his wife and marry the other woman. He also told the other woman it was essential that she divorce her husband and marry this other man to save him from what Freud claimed was his "latent homosexuality." When they followed his advice, the result was the breakup of two marriages and the substitute of a new one that ended in divorce two years later. Although Freud publicly claimed that his treatment always cured his patients, his private correspondence to friends admitted that many of his cases ended badly, and that few if any patients reached a full cure (Kramer, 2006).

Changes in Freud's Theory

Initially, Freud attributed neurotic behavior to recent traumatic experiences in his patients' lives. However, the recent events often seemed insufficient explanations. For a while in the early 1890s, Freud attributed patients' problems to sexual difficulties and recommended increased sexual activity as a cure (Macmillan, 1997). Then he abandoned that idea and suggested instead that the ultimate problem was sexual abuse during childhood. Freud's patients denied any such memories, but Freud drew inferences from his patients' symptoms, dream reports, slips of the tongue, and so forth and claimed that they pointed to early sexual abuse. He then tried to persuade his patients of these interpretations. Note the similarity to implanted memories or false memories.

A few years later, he abandoned the emphasis on childhood sexual abuse. According to Freud, he decided that his patients had "misled" him into believing they were sexually abused in early childhood (Freud, 1925). Why did Freud abandon his early theory? According to one view (Masson, 1984), Freud simply lost the courage to defend his theory. As other scholars insist, however, Freud never had any evidence for it (Esterson, 2001; Powell & Boer, 1994; Schatzman, 1992). Freud had inferred his patients' early sexual abuse despite their denials of such experiences. It was hardly fair, then, to complain that the patients had misled him into believing they had been abused.

Freud replaced the idea about early sexual abuse with theories focusing on children's sexual fantasies. Although he did not fully develop his views of girls' early sexual development, he was explicit about boys: According to Freud, every boy goes through an Oedipus complex, *when he develops a sexual interest in his mother and competitive aggression toward his father.* (Oedipus—EHD-ah-puhs— in the ancient Greek play by Sophocles unknowingly murdered his father and married his mother.) According to Freud, boys who fail to resolve these sexual fantasies develop long-term personality problems.

What evidence did he have for this view? Again, he had nothing that most people would consider evidence. He reinterpreted the same symptoms and dream reports that he had cited as evidence for his previous theory. Just as his patients denied having been sexually abused in childhood, they also denied his inferences about their childhood sexual fantasies. Freud's basis for his theories was only that he could construct coherent stories linking patients' symptoms, dreams, and so forth to the sexual fantasies that Freud imagined they must have had (Esterson, 1993). Developmental psychologists report that they almost never see evidence of an Oedipus complex in children. Although some psychoanalysts still see merit in the idea, most put little emphasis on it. Note also the difficulty of testing this theory. Determining whether a child had been sexually abused in childhood would be difficult, but determining a child's sexual fantasies (if any) is virtually impossible.

1. What was Freud's original view of the cause of personality problems, and what view did he substitute? What evidence did he have for either view?

Answer

1. After very early references to recent traumatic experiences or inadequate sex, Freud pointed to childhood sexual abuse. Later, he said the problem was childhood sexual fantasies, such as the Oedipus complex. His only evidence for either view was his inferences from his patients' symptoms, dream reports, and other statements.

According to Freud, if normal sexual development is blocked at the oral stage, the child seeks pleasure from drinking and eating and later from kissing and smoking. Like many of Freud's ideas, this one is difficult to test.

Stages of Psychosexual Development in Freud's Theory of Personality

Right or wrong, Freud's theory is so widely known that you should understand it. One of his central points was that psychosexual interest and pleasure begin in infancy. He used the term psychosexual pleasure broadly to include *all enjoyment arising from body stimulation.* He maintained that our psychosexual development influences nearly all aspects of personality.

According to Freud (1905/1925), people have a *psychosexual energy,* which he called libido (lih-BEE-doh), from a Latin word meaning "desire." During infancy, libido is focused in the mouth. As the child grows older, libido flows to other body parts. Children go through five stages of psychosexual development, and each leaves its mark on the adult personality. If normal sexual development is blocked or frustrated at any stage, Freud said, part of the libido is held in fixation at that stage, and the person *continues to be preoccupied with the pleasure area associated with that stage.* ■ Table 14.1 summarizes these stages.

The Oral Stage

In the oral stage, from birth to about age 1½, *infants derive intense pleasure from stimulation of the mouth, particularly while sucking at the mother's breast.* According to Freud, someone fixated at this stage continues to receive great

pleasure from eating, drinking, and smoking and may also have lasting concerns with dependence and independence.

The Anal Stage

At about age 1½, children enter the anal stage, when *they get psychosexual pleasure from the sensations of bowel movements.* If toilet training is either too strict or too lenient, the child becomes fixated at this stage. Someone fixated at the anal stage goes through life "holding things back"—being orderly, stingy, and stubborn—or less commonly, goes to the opposite extreme, becoming messy and wasteful. (A good theory should be falsifiable. Can you imagine any evidence that would contradict this aspect of Freud's theory?)

The Phallic Stage

Beginning at about age 3, in the phallic stage, children begin to *play with their genitals* and according to Freud they become sexually attracted to the opposite-sex parent. Freud claimed that every boy is afraid of having his penis cut off, whereas girls

Table 14.1 Freud's Stages of Psychosexual Development

Stage (approximate ages)	Sexual Interests	Effects of Fixation at This Stage
Oral stage (birth to 1½ years)	Sucking, swallowing, biting	Lasting concerns with dependence and independence; pleasure from eating, drinking, and other oral activities
Anal stage (1½ to 3 years)	Expelling feces, retaining feces	Orderliness or sloppiness, stinginess or wastefulness, stubbornness
Phallic stage (3 to 5 or 6 years)	Touching penis or clitoris; Oedipus complex	Difficulty feeling closeness. Males: fear of castration Females: penis envy
Latent period (5 or 6 to puberty)	Sexual interests suppressed	—
Genital stage (puberty onward)	Sexual contact with other people	—

develop "penis envy." These ideas have always been doubtful, and they have few defenders today.

The Latent Period

From about age 5 or 6 until adolescence, Freud said, most children enter a **latent period** in which they *suppress their psychosexual interest.* At this time, they play mostly with peers of their own sex. This period of suppressed sexual interest does not appear in all societies.

The Genital Stage

Beginning at puberty, people *develop a sexual interest in other people.* This is known as the **genital stage.** According to Freud, anyone who has fixated a great deal of libido in an earlier stage has little libido left for the genital stage. But people who have successfully negotiated the earlier stages now derive primary satisfaction from sexual intercourse.

Evaluation of Freud's Stages

It is undeniable that infants get pleasure from sucking, that toddlers go through toilet training, that older children begin to notice their genitals, and that adolescents become interested in sexual contact with other people. However, the idea of fixation at various stages, central to much of Freud's thinking, is difficult to test (Grünbaum, 1986; Popper, 1986). In fact, Freud resisted any attempt to test his ideas experimentally, insisting that the only relevant data were the observations he made during psychoanalytic sessions. To the extent that many of his followers have held the same position, the result has been alienation from scientific psychology (Chiesa, 2010).

2. According to Freud, what does it mean if someone is orderly and stingy? What does it mean if someone is messy and wasteful?

Answer

2. Freud would interpret both behaviors as fixations at the anal stage.

Structure of Personality

Personality, Freud claimed, consists of three aspects: id, ego, and superego. Actually, he used German words that mean *it, I,* and *over-I.* A translator used Latin equivalents instead of English words. The **id** consists of *sexual and other biological drives* that demand immediate gratification. The **ego** is *the rational, decision-making aspect of the personality.* It resembles the concept of central

executive or executive functioning. The **superego** contains *the memory of rules and prohibitions we learned from our parents and others,* such as, "Nice little boys and girls don't do that." If the id produces sexual desires that the superego considers repugnant, the result is guilty feelings. Most psychologists today find it difficult to imagine the mind in terms of three warring factions, although all agree that people do have conflicting impulses.

3. How would Freud interpret the behavior of someone who follows every impulse?

Answer

3. The lack of inhibition would indicate a weak superego.

Defense Mechanisms against Anxiety

According to Freud, *the ego defends itself against anxieties by relegating unpleasant thoughts and impulses to the unconscious mind.* Among the **defense mechanisms** that the ego employs are repression, denial, rationalization, displacement, regression, projection, reaction formation, and sublimation. He saw these as normal processes that sometimes went to extremes. His daughter, Anna, developed and elaborated the descriptions of these mechanisms.

Repression

The defense mechanism of **repression** is *motivated removal of something to the unconscious*—rejecting unacceptable thoughts, desires, and memories. For example, someone who has an unacceptable sexual impulse or a painful memory might repress it into the unconscious mind. Freud once compared a repressed thought to a rowdy person expelled from a polite room who continues banging on the door, trying to get back in.

Is repression real? The evidence for it is shaky. Most people remember all too well their miserable experiences, unless they were very young at the time. Laboratory attempts to demonstrate repression have produced, at best, weak and ambiguous evidence (Holmes, 1990). People can and often do intentionally suppress unwanted thoughts and memories (Erdelyi, 2006)—that is, they try not to think about them. However, suppression is not repression. According to most research, intentionally suppressing unpleasant memories *improves* psychological adjustment. It does not produce the distortions and pathologies that Freud linked to repression (Rofé, 2008). The evidence suggests much reason to be skeptical of the concept of repression.

Denial

The refusal to believe unpleasant information ("This can't be happening") is **denial.** Whereas repression is the motivated removal of information from consciousness, denial is an assertion that the information is incorrect. For example, someone with an alcohol problem may insist, "I'm not an alcoholic. I can take it or leave it." Someone whose marriage is headed for divorce may insist that all is going well. People who are about to get fired may insist that they are successful on the job.

Rationalization

When people *attempt to show that their actions are justifiable,* they are using **rationalization.** For example, a student who wants to go to the movies says, "More studying won't do any good anyway." People often try to rationalize

discrimination against women or minorities, or the ability of wealthy people to dominate the poor, or other injustices. Thereby, they maintain a belief that the world is a fair and just place (Laurin, 2018).

Displacement

By diverting a behavior or thought away from its natural target toward a less threatening target, displacement lets people engage in the behavior with less anxiety. For example, if you are angry with your employer or your professor, you might yell at someone else.

Regression

A *return to a more immature level of functioning,* regression is an effort to avoid the anxiety of the current situation. By adopting a childish role, a person returns to an earlier, more secure, way of life. For example, after a new sibling is born, an older child may cry or pout. An adult who has just gone through a divorce or lost a job may move in with his or her parents.

Projection

Attributing one's own undesirable characteristics to other people is known as projection. If someone tells you to stop being angry, you might reply, "I'm not angry! You're the one who's angry!" Suggesting that other people have your faults might make the faults seem less threatening. For example, someone who secretly enjoys pornography might accuse other people of enjoying it. However, the research finds that people using projection do not ordinarily decrease their anxiety or their awareness of their own faults (Holmes, 1978; Sherwood, 1981).

Reaction Formation

To avoid awareness of some undesirable characteristic, people sometimes use reaction formation to *present themselves as the opposite of what they really are.* A man troubled by doubts about his religious faith might try to convert others to the faith. Someone with unacceptable aggressive tendencies might join a group dedicated to preventing violence.

Sublimation

The transformation of sexual or aggressive energies into culturally acceptable, even admirable, behaviors is sublimation. According to Freud, sublimation lets someone express an impulse without admitting its existence. For example, painting and sculpture may represent a sublimation of sexual impulses. Someone may sublimate aggressive impulses by becoming a surgeon. Sublimation is the one proposed defense mechanism that is associated with socially constructive behavior. However, if the true motives of a painter are sexual and the true motives of a surgeon are violent, they are well hidden indeed.

concept check

4. Match each of the following situations to one of these Freudian defense mechanisms: regression, denial, projection, rationalization, reaction formation, and displacement.

a. An adult pouts and cries after losing an argument.
b. Someone who cheats on taxes says that everyone does it.
c. Someone justifies wasteful spending by saying that it boosts the economy.
d. A man hears something bad about someone he admires and insists it isn't true.
e. Someone embarrassed about enjoying pornography campaigns to have it banned.
f. A girl angry with her parents yells at her stuffed animals.

Answer

4. a. regression; b. projection; c. rationalization; d. denial; e. reaction formation; f. displacement.

Evaluating Freud

How much credit should we give Freud? He was right that people have conflicting impulses, but that idea was hardly original with him. He was also right that people have unconscious thoughts and feelings. However, that idea too had been around before Freud. Freud's elaboration on that idea was to say that the unconscious developed mostly from repressed sexual thoughts, such as boys' fear of losing the penis and girls' wish to have a penis (Borch-Jacobsen & Shamdasani, 2012; Kramer, 2006). The part that is original to Freud is the part that is the most doubtful. Later psychologists discovered implicit memories, which we could describe as unconscious, but implicit memories are far different from the unconscious forces that Freud proposed.

Freud did introduce a few new ideas that have stood the test of time, such as his recognition of transference: *You might react to your therapist, or your husband or wife, or other people in a particular way because they remind you of someone else, especially your parents.* Transference is an important insight that many therapists today find helpful. Still, Freud's main lasting contribution is that he popularized psychotherapy. Others had done psychotherapy before him, but he made it seem *interesting*. Many psychotherapists today, including some who acknowledge no allegiance to Freud, try to help their clients understand where their conflicts and emotional reactions come from. They help their clients think about their developmental history and what it means. In that way, Freud deserves credit, even if we doubt much of his theories.

© Freud Museum London

The idea behind the psychoanalytic couch is for the client to relax and say everything that comes to mind. This was Freud's couch.

Karen Horney, a neo-Freudian, revised some of Freud's theories and paid greater attention to cultural influences. She pioneered the study of feminine psychology.

Karen Horney, a Neo-Freudian

Psychologists known as neo-Freudians *kept much of Freud's theory while modifying other aspects.* One of the most influential was the German-born physician Karen Horney (HOR-nigh; 1885–1952), who kept Freud's concept of repression but argued that penis envy in women was no more likely than womb envy in men. She also argued that women have the same drive to achievement that men do, and that women feel frustrated when forced into subordinate roles. In that way she was a forerunner to later feminist thinkers. Contrary to Freud's idea of an Oedipus complex, Horney emphasized the detrimental effects a child might feel from parental neglect or indifference.

Horney focused on what happens when someone's unrealistic view of the *ideal self* contrasts with a low evaluation of the *real self.* The constant feeling that "I should be better in so many ways" tyrannizes the person, leading to psychological distress. In pronounced cases, the result is the emotional turbulence we call neurosis. Many later psychotherapists have emphasized the same idea.

Other theorists, including Carl Jung and Alfred Adler, disagreed more sharply with Freud. Jung and Adler were at one time associates of Freud, and they shared his interest in dreams and unconscious processes. However, their interpretations of dreams and their concepts of unconscious processes differed sharply from Freud's. Each broke with Freud's theory in such substantial ways that they should not be classified as neo-Freudians.

Carl Jung and the Collective Unconscious

Carl G. Jung (YOONG; 1875–1961) was a Swiss physician whom Freud regarded as the "heir apparent" or "crown prince" of the psychoanalytic movement, until their father–son relationship

deteriorated (Alexander, 1982). Jung's theory of personality emphasized people's search for a spiritual meaning in life. In contrast to Freud, who traced much of adult personality to childhood events, Jung stressed the possibility of personality changes in adulthood. He also discussed the way people adopt a *persona*, like a role in a play. That is, people try to make a certain impression while concealing parts of their true nature.

Jung was impressed that many of his patients described dreams with no clear relation to anything in their own lives. Instead, the dreams resembled images that are common in the myths, religions, and artworks of cultures throughout the world. He suggested that these images arise from inborn aspects of human nature. If you dream about a beetle, Jung might relate your dream to the important role beetles have played in human mythology dating back to the ancient Egyptians. If you dream about a baby, he might relate the symbolism to the possibility of psychological rebirth (Lawson, 2008).

According to Jung, people have not only a conscious mind and a "personal unconscious" (similar to the unconscious that Freud described) but also a collective unconscious mind. The **collective unconscious**, present at birth, relates to *the cumulative experience of preceding generations.* Whereas the conscious mind and the personal unconscious vary from one person to another, the collective unconscious is a constant. It contains **archetypes**, which are *vague images*—or at least the predisposition to form images—*that have always been part of the human experience.* As evidence for this view, Jung pointed out how cultures throughout the world have many similarities in their art, myths, and folklore (see ▼ **Figure 14.2**).

But how did the collective experiences of our ancestors become part of our unconscious minds? Jung offered little by way of explanation, and our current understanding of biology offers no route by which an experience could get into the genes. A more realistic hypothesis is that ancient people who thought in certain ways had advantages and therefore survived long enough to become our ancestors. As a result, we evolved a tendency to think in those same ways. An alternative is that cultures throughout the world have similar art and myths because they communicated, or because they faced similar experiences.

Another of Jung's contributions was the idea of psychological types. He believed that people's personalities fell into a few distinct categories, such as extraverted or introverted. The authors of the Myers-Briggs personality test revived this idea, as we shall see in the third module of this chapter.

Carl G. Jung rejected Freud's concept that dreams hide their meaning from the conscious mind: "To me dreams are a part of nature, which harbors no intention to deceive, but expresses something as best it can" (Jung, 1965, p. 161).

concept check

5. **How did Jung and Freud differ in their views of the unconscious?**

Answer

5. Freud believed the unconscious developed from repressed experiences. Jung thought some unconscious thoughts or motives came from personal experience, but he also thought we are born with a collective unconscious that reflects our ancestors' experiences.

▲ **Figure 14.2** Carl Jung was fascinated that similar images appear in the artworks of different cultures. One recurring image is the circular mandala, a symbol of unity and wholeness. These mandalas are: **(a)** a Hindu painting from Bhutan; and **(b)** a tie-dye tapestry created in California.

Alfred Adler and Individual Psychology

Alfred Adler (1870–1937) was an Austrian physician who broke away from Freud because he believed Freud neglected influences other than sex. They parted company in 1911, with Freud insisting that women experience "penis envy" and Adler replying that women were more likely to envy men's status and power.

Adler founded a rival school of thought, which he called individual psychology. Adler did not mean "psychology of the individual." Rather, he meant *"indivisible psychology," a psychology of the person as a whole rather than parts* such as id, ego, and superego. Adler emphasized the importance of conscious, goal-directed behavior.

Adler's Description of Personality

Several of Adler's early patients were acrobats who had suffered childhood injuries to an arm or leg. As they worked to overcome their disabilities, they continued until they developed unusual strength and coordination. Perhaps, Adler surmised, people in general try to overcome their weaknesses and transform them into strengths (Adler, 1932/1964). As infants, Adler noted, we are small, dependent, and surrounded by others who seem so powerful. We try to overcome that feeling of inferiority. Any experiences with failure goad us to try harder. However, persistent failures or excessive criticism can produce an inferiority complex, *an exaggerated feeling of weakness, inadequacy, and helplessness.*

Alfred Adler emphasized the ways in which personality depended on people's goals, especially their way of striving for a sense of superiority.

According to Adler, everyone has a natural striving for superiority, *a desire to seek personal excellence and fulfillment.* Each person creates a master plan for achieving a sense of superiority. A common strategy is to seek success in business, sports, or other competitive activities, but people also strive for success in other ways. Someone who withdraws from life gains a sense of superiority from being uncommonly self-sacrificing. Someone who constantly complains about illnesses or disabilities wins a measure of control over friends and family. Some people commit crimes to savor the attention the crimes bring. Many mass shootings are motivated at least in part by the publicity that the media seem eager to provide (Perrin, 2016). People also can get a feeling of superiority by making excuses. If you marry someone who is likely to thwart your ambitions, perhaps your underlying motivation is to maintain an illusion: "I would have been a great success if my spouse hadn't prevented me." Failure to study can have a similar motivation: "I could have done well on this test, but my friends talked me into partying the night before." According to Adler, people often engage in self-defeating behavior because they are not fully aware of their goals and strategies.

Adler tried to determine people's real motives. For example, he would ask someone who complained of a backache, "How would your life be different if you could get rid of your backache?" Those who eagerly said they would become more active were presumably trying to overcome their ailment. Those who said they could not imagine the change, or said only that they would get less sympathy, were probably exaggerating their discomfort if not imagining it.

Adler's View of Psychological Disorders

According to Adler, seeking success for yourself alone is unhealthy (Adler, 1928/1964). The healthiest goal is to seek success for a larger group, such as your family, your community, your nation, or all of humanity. Adler was ahead of his time, and many psychologists since then have rediscovered this idea (Crocker & Park, 2004).

According to Adler, people's needs for one another require a social interest, *a sense of solidarity and identification with other people that leads to constructive action.* Note that social interest does not mean a desire to socialize. It means an interest in the welfare of society. People with social interest want to cooperate. In equating mental health with social interest, Adler saw mental health as a positive state, not just a lack of impairments. In Adler's view, people with excessive anxieties are not suffering from an illness. Rather, they set immature goals, follow a faulty style of life, and show little social interest (Adler, 1932/1964).

6. According to Adler, what is people's main motivation? And what did he mean by "social interest"?

Answer

6. Adler said people's main motivation was striving for superiority. By "social interest," he meant an interest in the welfare of other people.

Adler's Legacy

Adler's influence exceeds his fame. His concept of the inferiority complex has become part of the common culture. He was the first to talk about mental health as a positive state rather than merely the absence of impairments. Several later forms of therapy drew upon Adler's emphasis on understanding the assumptions that people make and how those assumptions influence behavior. Many psychologists also followed Adler by urging people to take responsibility for their own behavior. According to Adler, the key to a healthy personality was not just freedom from disorders but a desire for the welfare of other people.

The Learning Approach

How did you develop your personality? According to the learning approach to personality, you developed much of what we call your personality by learning what to do in one situation after another, and as a result you might seem to have an inconsistent personality (Mischel, 1973, 1981). You might be honest about returning a lost wallet to its owner but lie to your professor about why your paper is late. You might always be on time for a date, but not always for your dental appointments.

We learn many social behaviors by vicarious reinforcement and punishment. We copy behaviors that were successful for other people and avoid behaviors that failed for others. We especially imitate people whom we want to resemble. For example, children watched adults choose between an apple and a banana. If all the men chose one fruit and all the women chose the other, the boys wanted what the men had, and the girls wanted what the women had (Perry & Bussey, 1979).

Much of what we think of as personality develops at least partly by imitation. Your attitudes toward alcohol, drugs, guns, and almost anything else depend on how you saw your parents and others in your neighborhood act. If you had lived in a different country, or if you had lived 100 years ago, you probably would have developed very different attitudes about women's roles, minority groups, sexual orientation, and much else.

7. According to the learning approach, do people have consistent personality traits, such as honesty or promptness?

Answer

7. Possibly, if someone happened to learn honesty or promptness in a wide variety of situations. However, the learning approach implies that a certain amount of inconsistency is more likely, because we learn how to act in one situation after another.

Humanistic Psychology

Another perspective on personality, humanistic psychology, *deals with consciousness, values, and abstract beliefs, including spiritual experiences and the beliefs that people live and die for.* According to humanistic psychologists, a psychologist can understand your personality only by asking you about your beliefs and how you interpret and evaluate the events of your life. If you *believe* that a particular experience was highly meaningful, then it *was* highly meaningful. (In theology, a *humanist* glorifies human potentials, generally denying or de-emphasizing a supreme being. The term *humanistic psychologist* implies nothing about someone's religious beliefs.)

Humanistic psychology emerged in the 1950s and 1960s as a protest against both behaviorism and psychoanalysis, the dominant psychological viewpoints at the time. Behaviorists and psychoanalysts often emphasize the less noble aspects of people's thoughts and actions, whereas humanistic psychologists see people as essentially good and striving to achieve their potential. Also, behaviorism and psychoanalysis, despite their differences, both assume *determinism* (the belief that every behavior has a cause) and *reductionism* (the attempt to explain behavior in terms of its component elements). Humanistic psychologists do not try to explain behavior in terms of its parts or hidden causes. They claim that people make deliberate, conscious decisions. For example, people might devote themselves to a great cause, sacrifice their own well-being, or risk their lives. To a humanistic psychologist, ascribing such behavior to past reinforcements or unconscious processes misses the point.

Humanistic psychology has much in common with positive psychology, in that both emphasize the factors that make life meaningful and joyful. However, the two fields follow different methods (Waterman, 2013). While researchers in positive psychology rely on surveys, experiments, and so forth to seek general principles, humanistic psychologists generally record narratives about individuals, using methods more like a biographer than like a scientist.

Carl Rogers and Unconditional Positive Regard

Carl Rogers, the most influential humanistic psychologist, studied theology before turning to psychology, and the influence of those early studies is apparent in his view of human nature. Rogers (1980) regarded human nature as basically good. According to Rogers, it is as natural for people to strive for excellence as it is for a plant to grow.

People evaluate themselves and their actions beginning in childhood. They develop a self-concept, *an image of what they really are,* and an ideal self, *an image of what they would like to be.* Rogers measured self-concept and ideal self by handing someone a stack of cards containing statements such as "I am honest" and "I am suspicious of others." The person would then sort the statements into piles representing *true of me* and *not true of me* or arrange them in a continuum from *most true of me* to *least true of me.* (This method is known as a *Q-sort.*) Then Rogers would provide an identical stack of cards and ask the person to sort them into two piles: *true of my ideal self* and *not true of my ideal self.* In this manner, he could compare someone's self-concept to his or her ideal self. People who perceive much discrepancy between the two generally feel distress. Humanistic psychologists try to help people overcome their distress by revising either their self-concept or their ideal self.

To promote human welfare, Rogers maintained that people should relate to one another with unconditional positive regard, a relationship that

Carl Rogers maintained that people naturally strive toward positive goals without special urging. He recommended that people relate to one another with unconditional positive regard.

Thomas Harris (1967) described as "I'm OK—You're OK." Unconditional positive regard is *the complete, unqualified acceptance of another person as he or she is,* much like the love of a parent for a child. If you feel unconditional positive regard, you might disapprove of someone's actions or intentions, but you would still accept and love the person. (This view resembles the Christian advice to "hate the sin but love the sinner.") The alternative is *conditional positive regard,* the attitude that "I shall like you if . . . ." People who are treated with conditional positive regard feel restrained about opening themselves to new ideas or activities for fear of losing someone else's support.

Abraham Maslow and the Self-Actualized Personality

Abraham Maslow, another humanistic psychologist, complained that most psychologists concentrate on disordered personalities, assuming that personality is either normal or worse than normal. Maslow insisted, as Alfred Adler had, that personality can also be better than normal. He emphasized self-actualization, *the achievement of one's full potential.*

As a first step toward describing the self-actualized personality, Maslow (1962, 1971) made a list of people who in his opinion were approaching their full potential. His list included people he knew personally and others from history.

Abraham Maslow, one of the founders of humanistic psychology, introduced the concept of a "self-actualized personality," a personality associated with high productivity and enjoyment of life.

He sought to discover what, if anything, they had in common.

According to Maslow (1962, 1971), people with a self-actualized (or self-actualizing) personality show the following characteristics:

- An accurate perception of reality: They perceive the world as it is, not as they would like it to be. They accept uncertainty and ambiguity.
- Independence, creativity, and spontaneity: They make their own decisions, even if others disagree.
- Acceptance of themselves and others: They treat people with unconditional positive regard.

Harriet Tubman, identified by Maslow as having a self-actualized personality, was a leader of the Underground Railroad, a system for helping slaves escape from the southern states before the Civil War. Maslow defined the self-actualized personality by first identifying admirable people, such as Tubman, and then determining what they had in common.

8. How does humanistic psychology resemble the ideas of Alfred Adler?

Answer

8. Like the later humanistic psychologists, Adler emphasized the importance of people's assumptions or beliefs and the possibility of a better than normal personality. The concept of self-actualization is similar to Adler's concept of striving for superiority. Adler's term "social interest" was the forerunner of unconditional positive regard.

- A problem-centered outlook rather than a self-centered outlook: They think about how to solve problems, not how to make themselves look good. They concentrate on significant philosophical or political issues, not just on getting through the day.
- Enjoyment of life: They are open to positive experiences, including "peak experiences" when they feel truly fulfilled and content.
- A good sense of humor.

Critics have noted that, because Maslow's description is based on his own choice of examples, it may simply reflect the characteristics that he himself admired. That is, his reasoning was circular: He defined certain people as self-actualized and then inquired what they had in common to decide what "self-actualized" means (Neher, 1991). In any case, Maslow emphasized the idea of a healthy personality as something more than the absence of disorder.

in closing | module 14.1

In Search of Human Nature

The three most comprehensive personality theorists—Freud, Jung, and Adler—lived and worked in Austria in the early 1900s. Here we are, a century later, and most specialists in personality research neither accept those theories nor try to replace them with anything better. Fundamental questions about human nature are extraordinarily interesting but not easily answerable.

Most researchers today try to answer smaller questions about specific, measurable aspects of behavior, as the next two modules will describe. After researchers answer many of the smaller questions, perhaps they may return to the big questions of "what makes people tick?"

Summary

- *Personality.* Personality consists of the stable, consistent ways in which each person's behavior differs from that of others, especially in social situations. (page 447)
- *Psychodynamic theories.* Several historically influential theories have described personality as the outcome of unconscious internal forces. (page 447)
- *Freud.* Sigmund Freud, the founder of psychoanalysis, proposed that much of what we do and say has hidden meanings. However, most psychologists today doubt most of his detailed interpretations of those hidden meanings. (page 447)
- *Freud's psychosexual stages.* Freud believed that many unconscious thoughts and motives are sexual in nature. He proposed that people progress through stages or periods of psychosexual development—oral, anal, phallic, latent, and genital—and that frustration at any stage fixates the libido at that stage. (page 449)
- *Defense mechanisms.* Freud and his followers argued that people defend themselves against anxiety by such mechanisms

as denial, repression, projection, and reaction formation. (page 450)
- *Jung.* Carl Jung believed that all people share a collective unconscious that represents the experience of our ancestors. (page 452)
- *Adler.* Alfred Adler proposed that people's primary motivation is a striving for superiority. Each person adopts his or her own method of striving, and to understand people, we need to understand their goals and beliefs. (page 453)
- *Adler's view of a healthy personality.* According to Adler, the healthiest style of life is one that emphasizes social interest—that is, concern for the welfare of others. (page 454)
- *The learning approach.* Much of what we call personality is learned through individual experience, imitation, or vicarious reinforcement and punishment. (page 454)
- *Humanistic psychology.* Humanistic psychologists emphasize conscious, deliberate decision making. (page 454)

Key Terms

anal stage (page 449)

archetypes (page 452)

catharsis (page 448)

collective unconscious (page 452)

defense mechanism (page 450)

denial (page 450)

displacement (page 451)

ego (page 450)

fixation (page 449)

genital stage (page 450)

humanistic psychology (page 454)

id (page 450)

ideal self (page 455)

individual psychology (page 453)

inferiority complex (page 453)

latent period (page 450)

libido (page 449)

neo-Freudians (page 452)

Oedipus complex (page 448)

oral stage (page 449)

personality (page 447)

phallic stage (page 449)

projection (page 451)

psychoanalysis (page 448)

psychodynamic theory (page 447)

psychosexual pleasure (page 449)

rationalization (page 450)

reaction formation (page 451)

regression (page 451)

repression (page 450)

self-actualization (page 455)

self-concept (page 455)

social interest (page 454)

striving for superiority (page 453)

sublimation (page 451)

superego (page 450)

transference (page 451)

unconditional positive regard (page 455)

unconscious (page 448)

Review Questions

1. Why are many psychologists skeptical of using catharsis to overcome distress?
   (a) Catharsis is difficult to achieve except by intensive psychoanalysis.
   (b) Catharsis is useful only if it occurs immediately after the painful experience.
   (c) Ruminating about painful experiences often leads to depression.
   (d) In his later works, Freud himself abandoned the idea.

2. What was Freud's evidence that childhood sexual fantasies led to later problems?
   (a) He observed the behavior of a large sample of children.
   (b) His patients described their childhood sexual fantasies.
   (c) He did a meta-analysis of research by developmental psychologists.
   (d) He inferred sexual fantasies from his patients' dreams and symptoms.

3. Which was the second of Freud's psychosexual stages?
   (a) Phallic
   (b) Genital
   (c) Oral
   (d) Anal

4. How does Freud's concept of repression differ from suppression?
   (a) Repression occurs unconsciously.
   (b) Repression is applied to other people, and suppression is to yourself.
   (c) Repression applies to ego impulses, and suppression to id impulses.
   (d) Repression is temporary and suppression is permanent.

5. What is meant by "reaction formation"?
   (a) Going to the opposite extreme
   (b) Attributing your undesirable qualities to other people

   (c) Offering a noble sounding excuse for disreputable acts
   (d) Directing a behavior toward a less threatening target

6. What is meant by "projection"?
   (a) Going to the opposite extreme
   (b) Attributing your undesirable qualities to other people
   (c) Offering a noble sounding excuse for a disreputable act
   (d) Directing a behavior toward a less threatening target

7. What did Carl Jung mean by the collective unconscious?
   (a) Material that remains unconscious even after psychotherapy
   (b) The residue of painful experiences from our childhood
   (c) Images created by the experiences of our ancestors
   (d) Material that became unconscious without being painful

8. According to Alfred Adler, what is people's main motivation?
   (a) Sex
   (b) Hunger
   (c) Trying to understand the universe
   (d) Striving for superiority

9. According to Adler, what is the main cause of psychological distress?
   (a) Conflict between the ego and the superego
   (b) Failure to understand the collective unconscious
   (c) Reinforcement and extinction
   (d) Setting unhealthy goals

10. What did Carl Rogers recommend?
    (a) Unconditional acceptance of other people
    (b) Intensive analysis of unconscious motivations
    (c) Extinction of inappropriate learned behaviors
    (d) Finding the "inner child" within each of us

Answers: 1c, 2d, 3d, 4a, 5a, 6b, 7c, 8d, 9d, 10a.

module 14.2

Personality Traits

After studying this module, you should be able to:

1. Distinguish the nomothetic approach from the idiographic approach.

2. Distinguish states from traits.

3. Use self-esteem as an example to illustrate the difficulty of measuring personality.

4. Describe how psychologists identified the Big Five personality factors.

5. List and describe the Big Five personality factors.

6. Discuss the roles of heredity, age, culture, and cohort in personality development.

You will sometimes hear someone talk about the opinions or attitudes of "the average person." Are you an average person? In some ways, probably yes. You might have average height, an average amount of interest in Olympic sports, or an average attitude toward penguins. But I doubt that you or anyone you will ever meet is an average person in all regards. People's personalities differ in countless ways.

Fujifotos/The Image Works

Like this man playing the role of a woman in Japanese kabuki theater, actors can present personalities that are very different from their private ones. All of us occasionally display temporary personalities that are different from our usual selves.

For research purposes, psychologists want to identify the major dimensions along which personality varies, so that they can study the causes and effects of personality differences. They study personalities in two ways, the nomothetic and the idiographic approaches. The word *nomothetic* (NAHM-uh-THEHT-ick) comes from the Greek *nomothetes,* meaning "legislator." The nomothetic approach *seeks general principles of personality* based on studies of groups of people. For example, we might make the nomothetic statement that more extraverted people are more likely to introduce themselves to a stranger. Most personality research uses the nomothetic approach.

In contrast, the word *idiographic* is based on the root *idio-,* meaning "individual." The same root appears in the word *idiosyncratic,* meaning *peculiar to an individual.* The idiographic approach uses *intensive studies of individuals,* looking for what makes someone special (Allport, 1961). For example, a psychologist might study one person's goals, moods, and reactions. The conclusions would apply to only this person, but a series of idiographic studies might discover a pattern.

Personality Traits and States

Meteorologists distinguish between climate (the usual conditions) and weather (the current conditions). For example, the climate in Scotland is moister and cooler than the climate in Texas, although on a given day the weather might be warm in Scotland or cool in Texas. Similarly, psychologists distinguish between long-lasting personality conditions and temporary fluctuations.

A consistent tendency in behavior, such as shyness, hostility, or talkativeness, is a trait. In contrast, a state is *a temporary activation of a particular behavior.* Being nervous most of the time is a trait, and being afraid right now is a state. Being quiet habitually is a trait, and being quiet in the library is a state. A trait, like a climatic condition, is an average over time. However, just as climates can change, personality traits are not 100 percent permanent.

Both traits and states are descriptions of behavior, not explanations. To say that someone is nervous does not explain anything, regardless of whether the nervousness is a trait or a state.

concept check ✓

9. **If being with your family makes you cheerful, is this experience a trait or a state?**

Answer

9. It is a state because it is a response to the situation.

The Search for Broad Personality Traits

According to the trait approach to personality, *people have reasonably consistent behavioral characteristics.* Let's start with one example: belief in a just world. People with a strong belief in a just world *maintain that life is fair and people usually get what they deserve* (Lerner, 1980). However, it is important to distinguish two varieties of this belief. One is the *personal* belief in a just world, measured by items like these:

I usually deserve what happens to me.

Most events in my life have been fair.

The other is the *general* belief in a just world, measured by items like these:

People usually get the rewards and punishments they deserve.

Most people who meet with misfortune did something to bring it on themselves.

It is possible, indeed easy, to believe that life has been fair to you but not to everyone else. When the questionnaires have been administered to college students, most of them endorse the personal belief in a just world more than they endorse the general belief (Bartholomaeus & Strelan, 2019). The two varieties of belief correlate differently with behavior. On average, people who believe the world is fair to themselves have higher satisfaction with life, handle stress better, act more honestly, and do more to help others (Bartholomaeus & Strelan, 2019; Schindler, Wenzel, Dobiosch, & Reinhard, 2019). Because these are correlations, we cannot be sure about causation. For example, perhaps a belief in a just world makes people feel good, or perhaps people who have had many successes and satisfactions tend to believe that life has been fair to them.

In contrast, people who believe that it is a just world for everyone are no more likely than average to be honest (Schindler, Wenzel, Dobiosch, & Reinhard, 2019), and they tend to blame victims for illnesses, poverty, or other disadvantages (Ebneter, Latner, & O'Brien, 2011). After all, if it is a just world, then people get what they deserve. People with a strong general belief in a just world are less likely than average to support preferential hiring for blacks or women (Wilkins & Wenger, 2014). If life is already fair, we don't need to improve its fairness.

Here are two general points: First, what we might initially describe as a single personality trait, such as belief in a just world, might have aspects that we need to separate. Second, any personality trait correlates with many aspects of behavior. The way someone acts in one situation provides a clue to how that person will act in other situations.

10. Why do accident victims often respond, "It could have been worse"?

Answer

10. It seems unjust for an innocent person to sustain an injury. Saying "it could have been worse" makes the injustice seem less severe, and it therefore helps someone maintain a belief in a just world.

Issues in Personality Measurement

In personality as in other areas of psychology, research progress depends on good measurement. Personality researchers seldom rely on observing actual behavior. What they care about is your behavior on average. Because your behavior fluctuates, researchers would have to watch you probably longer than any of them wanted to, and longer than you wanted anyone to watch you. Instead, researchers use questionnaires to ask how you usually behave.

When people rate their own personality, some are more accurate than others. On questions of the form, "Is this true of you...," some people check yes on almost everything. On rating scales, some people always go for the highest or lowest values, whereas certain others habitually put themselves in the middle (Melchers Plieger, Montag, Reuter, & Spinath, 2018). These response styles interfere with accurate measurement. In some cases, your close friends might provide

a more accurate assessment of your personality than you would yourself, although the ratings are usually not far apart (Hofstee, 1994; Kim, Di Domenico, & Connelly, 2019; Vazire & Carlson, 2011).

An Example of Measurement Problems: Self-Esteem

Let's consider the difficulty of devising a good personality questionnaire, using the example of self-esteem. **Self-esteem** is *the evaluation of one's own abilities, performance, and worth.* Most people, and Americans in particular, try to maintain good self-esteem, either by improving their skills, or reminding themselves that they are successful in one way or another (Nussbaum & Dweck, 2008). People who are highly productive tend to have high self-esteem, and psychologists have tested whether the opposite is also true: Does increasing self-esteem increase productivity? The result, contrary to many people's expectations, has been that praising people in an attempt to raise their self-esteem sometimes *decreases* school and job performance (Baumeister et al., 2003). Evidently, after people are told they are already wonderful, they feel little need to prove it.

One of the puzzles in self-esteem research is that, on average, teenage and college-age women report slightly lower self-esteem than men of the same age (Zuckerman, Li, & Hall, 2016). To evaluate that finding, we need to consider how self-esteem is measured (Blascovich & Tomaka, 1991). Here are example items from one self-esteem questionnaire:

- I feel that I have a number of good qualities.
- I can do things as well as most other people.
- At times I think I'm no good at all.
- I'm a failure.

Answers of "true" to the first two items or "false" to the second two items count toward a high self-esteem score. Contrast those items to another self-esteem questionnaire:

- I feel that I am a beautiful person.
- I think that I make a good impression on others.
- I think that I have a good sense of humor.
- I feel that people really like me very much.

Do those items measure self-esteem? Or do they measure bragging? Here are items from a third test of self-esteem:

- There are lots of things about myself I'd change if I could.
- I'm often sorry for the things I do.
- I'm not doing as well in school as I'd like.
- I wish I could change my physical appearance.

Do "true" answers on these items indicate low self-esteem or do they indicate high goals? Someone who says "true" is striving for self-improvement.

People who say "false" think they are just about perfect already.

How concerned should we be about the young women who report somewhat low self-esteem? Maybe it means low self-esteem, maybe it means low bragging, or maybe it means high goals. According to an analysis of answers to individual items, women's self-esteem is equal to men's or higher with regard to academics, emotional control, moral behavior, and many other regards. Women tend to have lower self-esteem only with regard to athletic ability (where, in fact, more men concentrate their efforts) and physical appearance, where most women strive for a higher standard than men do (Gentile, Grabe, Dolan-Pascoe, Twenge, & Wells, 2009). Physical appearance is, of course, especially salient for teenage and college-age women, the ages where the difference in self-esteem occurs.

High self-esteem is not always accurate.

Lucia Heffernan

The general message is this: Personality is difficult to measure, and we should look carefully at how it was measured before we draw conclusions.

concept check

11. If someone scores higher on self-esteem with one questionnaire than with another, what is a likely explanation?

Answer

11. Some questionnaires include items that might be measuring bragging or high goals, as opposed to pure self-esteem.

The Big Five Model of Personality

Psychologists have devised questionnaires to measure hundreds of traits, but no one wants to answer hundreds of questionnaires. Are some traits more central than others? If we can adequately describe personality with a few traits, we do not need to measure more.

One way to begin is to examine our language. The English language probably has a word for every important personality trait. Although this assumption is not self-evident, it seems likely, considering how much attention people pay to other people's personalities. When 168 people were asked to describe the personalities of people they knew, they generated 758 terms (Leising, Scharloth, Lohse, & Wood, 2014).

Gordon Allport and H. S. Odbert (1936) plodded through an English dictionary and found almost 18,000 words that might be used to describe personality. They deleted from this list words that were merely evaluations, such as *nasty*, and terms referring to temporary states, such as *confused*. (At least, we hope that being confused is temporary.) In the remaining list, they looked for clusters of synonyms, such as *affectionate*, *warm*, and *loving*, and kept only one of the terms. When they found opposites, such as *honest* and *dishonest*, they also kept just one term. After eliminating synonyms and antonyms, Raymond Cattell (1965) narrowed the original list to 35 traits.

Derivation of the Big Five Personality Traits

Although none of the 35 personality traits that Cattell identified are synonyms or antonyms of one another, many of them overlap. Psychologists looked for clusters of traits that correlate strongly with one another. Using this approach, researchers found what they call the Big Five personality traits or five-factor model: *emotional stability, extraversion, agreeableness, conscientiousness, and openness to new experience* (McCrae & Costa, 1987). The case for these five traits is that (1) each correlates with many personality dimensions for which the English language has a word and (2) none of these traits correlates highly with any of the other four. However, although they do not correlate highly, they do correlate somewhat. Generally, all five aspects—stable, extraverted, agreeable, conscientious, and open to experience—correlate positively with each of the others (van der Linden, Dunkel, & Figuerdo, 2018). The Big Five dimensions are described as follows (Costa, McCrae, & Dye, 1991):

Emotional stability is *a tendency to minimize unpleasant emotions*. The opposite term is neuroticism. Neuroticism correlates positively with anxiety, depression, hostility, self-consciousness, frequent conflicts with other people, many physical and mental illnesses, and decreased life expectancy (Lahey, 2009; O'Suilleabhain & Hughes, 2018; Watson & Naragon-Gainey, 2014). Emotional stability correlates with self-control, good relations with others, and mental health.

Extraversion is *a tendency to seek stimulation and to enjoy the company of other people*. The opposite of extraversion is introversion. Extraversion is associated with warmth, gregariousness, assertiveness, impulsiveness, and a need for excitement. The disadvantage of extraversion is an increased probability of alcohol abuse and other risky behaviors (Martsh & Miller, 1997). The advantage is that extraverts tend to feel good, and they report high life satisfaction (Gale, Booth, Mottus, Kuh, & Deary, 2013). The relationship goes in both directions: Feeling happy makes people more outgoing, and outgoing behavior makes people feel happy (Lucas, Le, & Dyrenforth, 2008). Even pretending to be extraverted makes introverted people feel happier (Fleeson, Malanos, & Achille, 2002; Zelenski, Santoro, & Whelan, 2012). Many people have assumed that extraverts are the best salespeople, but the research says the best salespeople are only mildly extraverted—somewhat assertive and enthusiastic, but not overconfident or domineering (Grant, 2013). In fact, an extreme along almost any personality dimension can cause problems (Carter, Miller, & Widiger, 2018).

Active, outgoing behavior → Happy feelings

Agreeableness is *a tendency to be compassionate toward others.* It implies a concern for the welfare of other people and is closely related to Adler's concept of social interest. People high in agreeableness trust other people and expect other people to trust them. They are more likely than average to have stable marriages and stable employment (Roberts et al., 2007). They are less likely than average to have prejudices (Akrami, Ekehammar, & Bergh, 2011). They recover better than average from an injury, partly because of good social support (Boyce & Wood, 2011). Again, you see that an extreme of a personality dimension can be a problem. Trusting people is good, but trusting everyone all the time? That would be asking for trouble.

Conscientiousness is *a tendency to show self-discipline, to be dutiful, and to strive for achievement and competence.* People high in conscientiousness work hard and complete their tasks on time (Judge & Ilies, 2002). They exercise, eat a healthy diet, and in general act in ways that improve health and longevity (Bogg & Roberts, 2013). Agreeableness and conscientiousness both correlate with success in many jobs (Sackett & Walmsley, 2014).

Openness to experience is *a tendency to enjoy new intellectual experiences and new ideas.* People high in this trait enjoy many varieties of art, music, films, and books. They enjoy meeting unusual people and exploring new ideas (McCrae, 1996). ■ Table 14.2 summarizes the five-factor model.

The Big Five approach has been tested in many countries, and it generally fits reasonably well (Kajonius & Mac Giolla, 2017; McCrae & Costa, 1997; Yamagata et al., 2006). However, the fit is better in educated, industrial societies than it is elsewhere. A study in China identified traits corresponding to extraversion, neuroticism, conscientiousness, and loyalty to Chinese traditions (Cheung et al., 1996). A study of an illiterate forager-farmer society in the Bolivian Amazon identified just two reliable factors, prosociality and industriousness (Gurven, von Rueden, Massenkoff, Kaplan, & Lero Vie, 2013).

Strengths and Limitations

If we want to predict who pays their bills on time, a measure of conscientiousness works well. To predict who will try an exotic new restaurant, we

The Japanese artist Morimura Yasumasa recreates famous paintings, substituting his own face for the original. People high in "openness to experience" delight in new, unusual art forms such as this.

can rely on openness to experience. If we measure agreeableness, we can identify people who are most likely to be forgiving. Personality correlates with which people will do best at particular jobs. For example, extraversion and openness to experience are important for stage actors, but not for bookkeepers or government tax officers (Denissen et al., 2018). Psychologists have conducted many studies relating one trait or another to life outcomes, and most of those results have been replicable (Soto, 2019).

But do the Big Five capture everything of importance about human behavior? If you knew precisely where someone stands on each of these five factors, would you completely understand that person's personality? Several researchers have argued for a sixth "big" factor, *selfishness* (Diebels, Leary, & Chon, 2018). Another possibility is *integrity* (honesty and virtue), which goes beyond just conscientiousness (O'Neill & Hastings, 2011). Other researchers fault the Big Five approach for overlooking sense of humor, religiousness, sexiness, thriftiness, conservativeness, masculinity–femininity, and snobbishness (Paunonen & Jackson, 2000). We have already considered belief in a just world and self-esteem. In short, the Big Five description accounts for a great deal of the variability in personality, but for specific purposes we might need additional dimensions.

Table 14.2 The Five-Factors Model of Personality		
Trait	**Description**	**Typical true–false question to measure it**
Emotional Stability	Resistance to unpleasant emotions	I have few major worries.
Extraversion	Seeking excitement and social contact	I make friends easily.
Agreeableness	Compassionate and trusting	I believe others have good intentions.
Conscientiousness	Self-disciplined and dutiful	I complete most tasks on time or early.
Openness	Stimulated by new ideas	I believe art is important for its own sake.

© Morimura Yasumasa

12. What type of research is necessary to decide whether to consider selfishness or integrity as a sixth big factor of personality?

Answer

12. Researchers need to determine two things: First, does selfishness or integrity correlate with many important behaviors? Second, does selfishness or integrity correlate strongly with any of the currently accepted Big Five factors? We should accept an additional big factor if the answer to the first question is yes and the answer to the second question is no.

The Origins of Personality

A description of personality differences is not an explanation. What makes some people more extraverted, emotionally stable, agreeable, conscientious, or open to experience than other people are?

Heredity and Environment

If you want evidence that heredity can influence personality, you need look no further than the nearest pet dog. For centuries, people have selectively bred dogs for their personalities, ranging from shy lapdogs to watchdogs that attack intruders.

To evaluate the role of heredity in human personality, much research relies on studies of twins. As ▶ Figure 14.3 shows, studies in five locations indicated greater similarities in extraversion between monozygotic pairs than dizygotic pairs (Loehlin, 1992). Similar research found hereditary components to neuroticism (Lake, Eaves, Maes, Heath, & Martin, 2000), conscientiousness (Luciano, Wainwright, Wright, & Martin, 2006), and other personality traits. Certain genetic markers that correlate with openness and emotional stability also correlate with academic success (Mottus, Realo, Vainik, Allik, & Esko, 2017). Examination of chromosomes has located at least 20 genes linked with neuroticism or extraversion, although no common gene by itself has a major influence (Aluja, Balada, Blanco, Fibla, & Blanch, 2019; Balestri, Calati, Serretti, & De Ronchi, 2014; D. J. Smith et al., 2016). At one point it appeared that a gene linked to serotonin levels in the brain might control responses to frightening stimuli. However, apparently most of the researchers who did not find the effect failed to publish their results. If we take into account all the results, published and unpublished, that gene appears to have no more than a small effect (Bastiaansen et al., 2014). In short, a great many genes influence personality, each in small ways, combined with environmental influences (Barlow, Ellard, Sauer-Zavala, Bullis, & Carl, 2014).

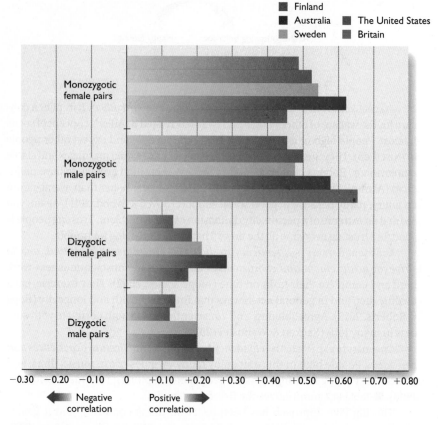

▲ **Figure 14.3** The length of each bar indicates the strength of a correlation between pairs of twins in their degree of extraversion. Correlations were greater between monozygotic twins (who share all their genes) than between dizygotic twins (who share half their genes). (Based on data summarized by Loehlin, 1992)

Researchers have compared personalities of parents, their biological children, and their adopted children. As ▼ Figure 14.4 shows, parents' extraversion levels correlate moderately with those of their biological children but hardly at all with their adopted children. Similarly, biologically related brothers or sisters growing up together resemble each other moderately in personality, but unrelated children adopted into the same family do not (Loehlin, 1992). The results shown in Figures 14.3 and 14.4 pertain to extraversion. Other studies provide a largely similar pattern for other personality traits (Heath, Neale, Kessler, Eaves, & Kendler, 1992; Loehlin, 1992; Viken, Rose, Kaprio, & Koskenvuo, 1994).

The low correlations between adopted children and adoptive parents imply that children learn rather little of their personalities from what researchers call the *shared environment*. More of the variation in personality relates to the **unshared environment**, *the aspects of environment that differ from one individual to another, even within a family*. Unshared environment could include the effects of a particular playmate, a particular teacher, an injury or illness, or any other special experience. Because of its idiosyncratic nature, unshared environment is difficult to investigate.

One aspect of environment that has a clear effect on personality is schooling. In Germany, students decide after grade 10 whether to enter a vocational track or a higher-education track. Comparisons of personality at grade 10 and 6 years later find that those choosing the vocational path increase in conscientiousness, whereas those choosing the higher-education track are more likely to increase in social and investigative tendencies (Golle et al., 2019).

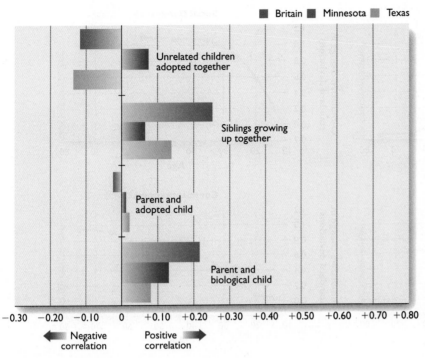

Britain ■ Minnesota ■ Texas

Unrelated children
adopted together

Siblings growing
up together

Parent and
adopted child

Parent and
biological child

−0.30 −0.20 −0.10 0 +0.10 +0.20 +0.30 +0.40 +0.50 +0.60 +0.70 +0.80

◀ Negative
correlation

Positive ▶
correlation

▲ **Figure 14.4** The length and direction of each bar indicate the correlations between pairs of people in their degree of extraversion. Biological relatives showed low positive correlations. People related by adoption had close to zero correlations. (Based on data summarized by Loehlin, 1992)

concept
check

13. What evidence would indicate an important role of the shared environment?

Answer

13. The best evidence for the role of shared environment would be any similarity between children adopted into the same family, or a similarity between adopted children and their adoptive parents.

Influences of Age and Culture

How much does your personality now resemble what it was in early childhood? In one study, investigators followed people's behavior from age 3 to 26. Children who were fearful and easily upset at age 3 were, on average, more nervous and inhibited than others at age 26. Those who were impulsive and restless at age 3 tended to have trouble with others from then on and felt alienated from society. Those who were confident, friendly, and eager to explore their environment at 3 tended to be confident adults, eager to take charge of events (Caspi et al., 2003). Another study followed young people from age 12 to 22. Each of the Big Five personality traits showed reasonable stability for most people (Borghuis et al., 2017). An even longer study compared the answers to personality questionnaires people gave during high school to their answers to the same questionnaires 50 years later. On every trait measured, most people were reasonably consistent over that period of time (Damian, Spengler, Sutu, & Roberts, 2019).

How will your personality change in the future? The older people get, the more slowly they change. In childhood, answers on a personality questionnaire correlate a modest 0.34 with a second test given 6 or 7 years later. By college age, the correlation is 0.54. It increases to 0.64 at age 30 and 0.74 at age 60 (Roberts & DelVecchio, 2000). One reason for personality to become more fixed is that older people usually stay in the same environment, doing the same things year after year.

Although the differences that occur over age are usually not large, a few trends are consistent. One trend, found in cultures throughout the world, is that middle-aged people tend to be more conscientious than teenagers (Donnellan & Lucas, 2008; McCrae et al., 2000). A simple hypothesis (not necessarily the whole explanation) is that adults are forced, whether they like it or not, to hold a job, pay the bills, repair the house, care for children, and take responsibility in other ways. Emotional stability also tends to increase with age. That is, neuroticism decreases (Cramer, 2003; Damian et al., 2019; McCrae et al., 2000). Most people reach their peak of social vitality and sensation seeking during adolescence or early adulthood and then decline gradually with further age (Roberts, Walton, & Viechtbauer, 2006). In other words, teenagers ride roller coasters more than their grandparents do. ▼ **Figure 14.5** shows mean changes in six aspects of personality over age (Roberts, Walton, & Viechtbauer, 2006). Note that this research distinguished between two aspects of extraversion—social vitality and social dominance.

Does personality vary among cultures or countries? Self-reports are not always easy to interpret. Outsiders think of Puerto Ricans as highly extraverted and Mexicans as highly sociable, but the Puerto Ricans and Mexicans don't rate themselves that way (Ramírez-Esparza, Mehl, Álvarez-Bermúdez, & Pennebaker, 2009; Terracciano et al., 2005). Countries' self-ratings on conscientiousness don't match the way outsiders would rank them, either. To some extent, the explanation may be that many of our stereotypes about national character are wrong (McCrae et al., 2013). However, problems also exist in the measurement techniques. When you rate your own personality, you of course rate yourself in comparison to people you know. If you are highly sociable, extraverted, or conscientious, but so is everyone else in your community, you rate yourself about average. Another problem relates to the way people handle rating scales. If you rated your own personality, or that of others you know, on a 1-to-7 scale, would you stay close to 4, or would you use many 1s and 7s? Most people in Japan, Hong Kong, and South Korea tend to rate themselves and other people close to average in most regards. People in Poland, Malaysia, and several African countries tend to use the top and bottom of each scale (Mottus et al., 2012). The result is that self-ratings from one country are not easily comparable to those from another. The best way to compare personalities across cultures is to observe actual behavior (Heine, Buchtel, & Norenzayan, 2008).

Within the United States, personality varies, on average, among geographical areas. "Creative productivity" tends to be highest in the Northeast, Midwest, and West Coast. People in the Southeast

MODULE 14.2 PERSONALITY TRAITS / **463**

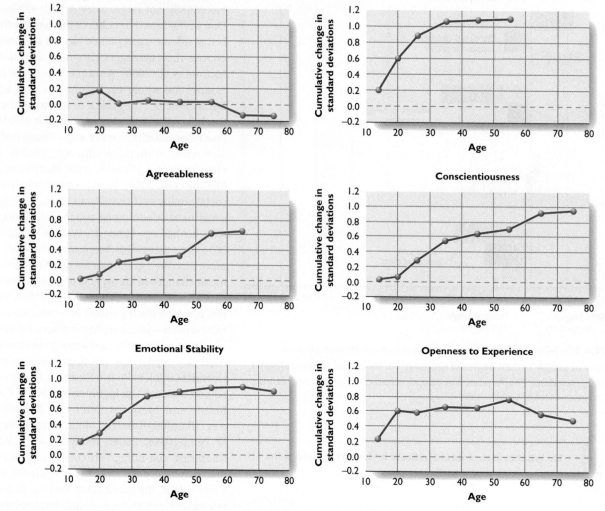

▲ **Figure 14.5** Six aspects of personality show different patterns of change over age based on the means of longitudinal research studies. The numbers along the vertical axis represent changes from the earliest age tested, measured in terms of standard deviations. (From Roberts, Walton, & Viechtbauer, 2006)

are more likely to defend their reputation vigorously. People in cities tend to be more extraverted than those in rural areas. These are just a few of the differences. One reason for the differences is that the reputation of a place tends to attract like-minded people. If what you read about people in Portland, Oregon, sounds much like yourself, you might want to move there, too.

Finally, does personality change from one generation to the next? Remember the Flynn effect: Over decades, mean performance on IQ tests gradually increased. Researchers have also found generational differences in personality. For example, beginning in the 1950s, self-reports of anxiety

steadily increased, at least in the United States (Schuermann & Margraf, 2018; Twenge, 2000). Perfectionism also increased. On average, people today perceive other people as being more demanding than before, both more demanding of themselves and more demanding of others (Curran & Hill, 2019). In many ways, life has become more competitive.

14. Why is it difficult to compare personality traits among countries or among generations?

Answer

14. The research relies on self-reports, and people from different countries or different generations may interpret the questions differently or may adopt different styles of answering questions.

The Challenges of Classifying Personality

Personality descriptions refer to trends over time. We don't expect anyone to be equally extraverted at all times, equally conscientious, or anything else. What you do at any moment depends largely on the situation as well as your personality.

In a sufficiently novel situation, you may be surprised by the actions of people you know well and even by your own behavior. The variation across situations makes personality research difficult.

Summary

- *Nomothetic and idiographic research.* Nomothetic studies look for general trends, whereas idiographic studies examine one or a few individuals intensively. (page 458)
- *Traits and states.* Traits are persistent personality characteristics. States are temporary responses to a situation. (page 458)
- *Measuring traits such as self-esteem.* Sometimes a questionnaire designed to measure a trait is measuring something else instead. (page 459)
- *Five major traits.* Based on an analysis of words to describe personality, psychologists identified five traits that cover the largest territory: emotional stability, extraversion, agreeableness, conscientiousness, and openness to new experience. (page 460)
- *Other traits.* Selfishness and integrity have been nominated as possible sixth or seventh major traits. For special purposes, psychologists need to consider smaller but more specific traits, such as sense of humor or religiousness. (page 461)

- *Determinants of personality.* Studies of twins and adopted children indicate an important role for heredity, although no identifiable gene produces a large effect. Family environment evidently contributes rather little. Some variation relates to unshared environment, the special experiences that vary from one person to another even within a family. (page 462)
- *Effects of age.* Personality traits are moderately stable over age, and they become even more consistent as people grow older. As people grow older, they tend to become more conscientious, more emotionally stable, and less open to new experiences. (page 463)
- *Culture and geography.* Personality tends to vary among cultures and among geographic areas within a country. However, we cannot be sure that everyone interprets the questions the same way. (page 463)
- *Effects of cohorts.* According to questionnaire research, more recent generations score higher on anxiety (at least in the United States) and higher in perfectionism. (page 464)

Key Terms

agreeableness (page 461)

belief in a just world (page 458)

Big Five personality traits or five-factor model (page 460)

conscientiousness (page 461)

emotional stability (page 460)

extraversion (page 460)

idiographic approach (page 458)

neuroticism (page 460)

nomothetic approach (page 458)

openness to experience (page 461)

self-esteem (page 459)

state (page 458)

trait (page 458)

trait approach to personality (page 458)

unshared environment (page 462)

Review Questions

1. People—college students, at least—are most likely to believe that the just world hypothesis applies to whom?
   (a) People in other countries
   (b) People who lived long ago
   (c) Poor people
   (d) Themselves

2. The difference between males and females in their self-esteem is greatest at what point in life?
   (a) Adolescence
   (b) Early career
   (c) Late career
   (d) Retirement

3. Some of the questions on certain self-esteem surveys seem to be measuring what, instead of self-esteem?
   (a) Belief in a just world
   (b) Sexual experience
   (c) High goals
   (d) Hostility

4. The research leading to the Big Five model of personality began with an analysis of what?
   (a) Children's playground activities
   (b) Words in the English language
   (c) Dating habits of college students
   (d) Symptoms of mental illness

5. Extraversion correlates most highly with which of the following?
   (a) Racial prejudice
   (b) Life expectancy
   (c) Job success
   (d) Happiness

6. What evidence indicates that "shared environment" has not much effect on personality?
   (a) Significant effects on personality from certain identified genes
   (b) Significant changes in personality between one generation and another
   (c) Equal similarity of personality for dizygotic twins or monozygotic twins
   (d) Low similarity between personality of adopted children and adoptive parents

7. Which of the following has been demonstrated to affect personality?
   (a) Swimming
   (b) Barometric pressure
   (c) Eye color
   (d) Schooling

Answers: 1d, 2a, 3c, 4b, 5d, 6d, 7d.

WAYHOME studio/Shutterstock.com

After studying this module, you should be able to:

1. Explain why we should not trust people's testimonials that a personality test described them accurately.

2. Describe several objective personality tests.

3. Explain how the MMPI detects lying.

4. Describe the pros and cons of projective personality tests.

5. Discuss the difficulty of using a personality test to diagnose an uncommon psychological disorder.

6. Evaluate the usefulness of criminal profiling.

A new P. T. Barnum Psychology Clinic that just opened at your local shopping mall is offering a grand opening special on personality tests. You would like to know more about yourself, so you sign up. Here is Barnum's test:

Questionnaire for Universal Assessment of Zealous Youth (QUAZY)

1.	I have never met a cannibal that I didn't like.	T F
2.	Robbery is the only felony I have ever committed.	T F
3.	I eat "funny mushrooms" less frequently than I used to.	T F
4.	I don't care what people say about my nose-picking habit.	T F
5.	Sex with vegetables no longer disgusts me.	T F
6.	This time I am quitting glue sniffing for good.	T F
7.	I generally lie on questions like this one.	T F
8.	I spent much of my childhood sucking on computer cables.	T F
9.	I find it impossible to sleep if I think my bed might be clean.	T F
10.	Naked bus drivers make me nervous.	T F
11.	I spend my spare time playing strip solitaire.	T F

You turn in your answers. A few minutes later, a computer prints out your personality profile:

> You have a need for other people to like and admire you, and yet you tend to be critical of yourself. While you have some personality weaknesses, you are generally able to compensate for them. You have considerable unused capacity that you have not turned to your advantage. Disciplined and self-controlled on the outside, you tend to be worrisome and insecure on the inside. At times, you have serious doubts as to whether you have made the right decision or done the right thing. You prefer a certain amount of change and variety and become dissatisfied when hemmed in by restrictions and limitations. You also pride yourself as an independent thinker and do not accept others' statements without satisfactory proof. But you have found it unwise to be too frank in revealing yourself to others. At times you are extraverted, affable, and sociable, while at other times you are introverted, wary, and reserved. Some of your aspirations tend to be rather unrealistic. (Forer, 1949, p. 120)

Do you agree with this assessment? Did it capture your personality? Several experiments have been conducted along these lines with psychology classes (Forer, 1949; Marks & Kammann, 1980; Ulrich, Stachnik, & Stainton, 1963). Students filled out a questionnaire that looked reasonable, not as ridiculous as the one you saw here (which was included just for your amusement). Several days later, each student received a sealed envelope containing a personality

Eva Hambach/AFP/Getty Images

People tend to accept almost any personality assessment, especially if it is stated in vague terms that people can interpret to fit themselves.

profile supposedly based on his or her answers to the questionnaire. The students were asked, "How accurately does this profile describe you?" About 90 percent rated it as good or excellent, and some expressed amazement at its accuracy. They didn't know that everyone had received exactly the same personality profile—the same one you just read.

The students accepted this personality profile partly because it applies approximately to most people, and partly because people accept almost *any* statement that a psychologist makes about them (Marks & Kammann, 1980). This *tendency to accept vague descriptions of our personality is known as the* Barnum effect, named after P. T. Barnum, the circus owner who specialized in fooling people out of their money.

The conclusion: Psychological testing must be done carefully. If we want to know whether a test measures personality, we cannot simply ask for people's opinions. Psychologists need to design a test carefully and then determine its reliability and validity.

Standardized Personality Tests

A **standardized test** is *one that is administered according to rules that specify how to interpret the results.* An important step for standardizing a test is to determine the distribution of scores. We need to know the mean score, the range of scores for a representative sample of the population, and how the scores differ for special populations, such as people with severe depression. Given such information, we can interpret what a particular score means.

Most of the tests published in popular magazines have not been standardized. A magazine may herald an article: "Test Yourself: How Good Is Your Marriage?" or "Test Yourself: How Well Do You Control Stress?" Unless the magazine states otherwise, you can assume that the author made up the scoring rules with no supporting research.

Over the years, psychologists have developed a great variety of tests to measure normal and abnormal personality. Let's examine a few prominent examples.

An Objective Personality Test: The Minnesota Multiphasic Personality Inventory

A widely used personality test, the **Minnesota Multiphasic Personality Inventory** (mercifully abbreviated **MMPI**), consists of *true-false questions intended to measure certain personality dimensions that relate to clinical conditions.* The original MMPI, developed in the 1940s and still in use, has 550 items. *The second edition,* MMPI–2, published in 1990, has 567. Example items are "my mother never loved me" and "I think I would like the work of a pharmacist." (The items stated in this text are rewordings of actual items.)

The MMPI was devised *empirically*—that is, based on trial-and-error rather than theory (Hathaway & McKinley, 1940). The authors wrote hundreds of questions that they thought might relate to personality. They put these questions to people with various psychological disorders and to a group of hospital visitors, who they assumed were psychologically normal. The researchers selected the items that most people with a disorder answered differently from most normal people. They assumed, for example, that if your answers resemble those of people with depression, you probably are depressed also. The MMPI includes scales for depression, paranoia, schizophrenia, and others.

Some of the items on the MMPI make sense theoretically, but others do not. For example, some items on the depression scale ask about feelings of helplessness or worthlessness, an important part of depression. But two other items on the original MMPI are "I attend religious services frequently" and "occasionally I tease animals." If you answer *false* to either of those items, you get a point on the depression scale! These items were included simply because many people with depression answered *false.* The reason is not clear, except that people feeling depressed seldom do anything they don't have to do.

Revision of the Test

The MMPI was standardized in the 1940s. As time passed, the meaning of certain items changed. For example, how would you respond to the following item?

I believe I am important.   T   F

In the 1940s, fewer than 10 percent of all people marked *true.* At the time, the word *important* implied *famous,* and people who called themselves important were thought to have an inflated view of themselves. Today, we stress that every person is important.

What about this item?

I like to play drop the handkerchief.   T   F

Drop the handkerchief, a game similar to tag, fell out of popularity in the 1950s. Most people today have never heard of the game, much less played it.

To bring the MMPI up to date, psychologists eliminated obsolete items and added new ones to deal with drug abuse, suicidal thoughts, and other issues (Butcher, Graham, Williams, & Ben-Porath, 1990). They also removed most of the items that made little sense theoretically, such as the one about teasing animals. Then they standardized the new MMPI–2 on a large representative sample of the U.S. population. The MMPI–2 has 10 clinical scales, as shown in ■ Table 14.3. The items of any type are scattered throughout the test so that people won't see that "oh, this seems to be a set of items about depression." Most people get at least a few points on each scale. Unusually high scores indicate greater probability of psychological distress.

Table 14.3 The 10 MMPI–2 Clinical Scales	
Scale	**Typical Item**
Hypochondria (Hs)	I have chest pains several times a week. (T)
Depression (D)	I am glad that I am alive. (F)
Hysteria (Hy)	My heart frequently pounds so hard I can hear it. (T)
Psychopathic Deviation (Pd)	I get a fair deal from most people. (F)
Masculinity–Femininity (Mf)	I like to arrange flowers. (T = female)
Paranoia (Pa)	There are evil people trying to influence my mind. (T)
Psychasthenia (Obsessive–Compulsive) (Pt)	I save nearly everything I buy, even after I have no use for it. (T)
Schizophrenia (Sc)	I see, hear, and smell things that no one else knows about. (T)
Hypomania (Ma)	When things are dull I try to get some excitement started. (T)
Social Introversion (Si)	I have the time of my life at parties. (F)

Detecting Deception

If you take the MMPI, could you lie to make yourself look mentally healthier than you really are? Yes. Could someone catch your lies? Probably.

The designers of the MMPI and MMPI–2 included items designed to identify lying (Woychyshyn, McElheran, & Romney, 1992). For example, consider the items "I like every person I have ever met" and "Occasionally I get angry at someone." If you answer *true* to the first question and *false* to the second, you are either a saint or a liar. On the theory that liars outnumber saints, the test counts such answers on a "lie" scale. If you get too many points on the lie scale, a psychologist distrusts your answers to the other items. Strangely enough, some people lie to try to look bad. For example, a criminal defendant might want to be classified as mentally ill. The MMPI includes items to detect that kind of faking also (Bagby, Nicholson, Bacchiochi, Ryder, & Bury, 2002).

Several other questionnaires also try to detect deception. Suppose an employer's questionnaire asks you to state how much experience you have at various skills. One of them is "determining myopic weights for periodic tables." You're not sure what that means, but you want the job. Do you claim to have extensive experience? If so, your claimed expertise will count *against* you because "determining myopic weights for periodic tables" is nonsense. The employer asked about it just to see whether you were exaggerating your qualifications on other items.

15. **Suppose you want to devise a test of curiosity. How would you choose items for your test, presuming you use the same method as the MMPI?**

Answer

15. Identify people who have unusually high curiosity. Then give questions to these people and a representative sample of the population and find questions that the highly curious people tend to answer differently from everyone else.

The NEO PI-R

A more recent personality test is based on the Big Five personality model. An early version of this test measured neuroticism, extraversion, and openness to experience, abbreviated NEO. A revised test added scales for conscientiousness and agreeableness, but kept the name NEO, which is now considered just the name of the test and not an abbreviation. (It's like the company AT&T, which no longer stands for American Telephone and Telegraph.) The NEO PI-R (NEO Personality Inventory-Revised) *includes 240 items to measure neuroticism, extraversion, openness, agreeableness, and conscientiousness.* A typical conscientiousness item resembles this:

Very inaccurate	Moderately inaccurate	Neither	Moderately accurate	Very accurate

I keep my promises.

Scores on this test have good reliability, about 0.9 (Gnambs, 2014). They correlate with observable behaviors, too. For example, students who score high on conscientiousness tend to spend much time studying (Chamorro-Premuzic, & Furnham, 2008). People who score high on openness are more likely than others to visit an art gallery (Church et al., 2008). The test has been translated into several other languages and seems to work reasonably well in other cultures (Ispas, Iliescu, Ilie, & Johnson, 2014; Wu, Lindsted, Tsai, & Lee, 2008). It is intended mainly to measure normal personality, as contrasted to the MMPI, which is used mainly to identify clinical problems.

16. **For what purposes might the NEO PI-R be more suitable, and for what purposes might the MMPI be more suitable?**

Answer

16. The NEO PI-R is designed to measure normal personality. The MMPI is intended to detect possible abnormalities.

The Myers-Briggs Type Indicator

The Myers-Briggs Type Indicator (MBTI) is *a test of normal personality, loosely based on Carl Jung's theories.* It was devised by a mother and daughter, Katherine Briggs and Isabel Briggs Myers. Neither of them had any formal training in psychology, nor any background in research or statistics. What they lacked in knowledge they made up for with enthusiasm (Emre, 2018).

Jung emphasized the distinction between extraversion, which he defined as attending to the outside world, and introversion, concentrating on one's inner world. Note the difference between his definitions and the ones more commonly used today. Jung also discussed thinking, feeling, sensation, and intuition. Myers and Briggs set these as paired opposites, thinking versus feeling, and sensing versus intuiting, in addition to the extraversion-introversion dimension. They also added a fourth distinction that was not part of Jung's thinking, a distinction between judging and perceiving. The Myers-Briggs Type Indicator uses a series of two-choice questions to classify each person to one side or the other of the four dimensions, yielding a total of 16 personality types. For example, you might be classified as introverted-intuitive-thinking-judging.

Jung had speculated that each person remained throughout life either extraverted or introverted. Myers and Briggs assumed that the other three dimensions have lifelong consistency also. They also assumed a bimodal distribution for each category—that is, they assumed that most people fall clearly into one category or the other. However, most people in fact score close to the middle on any dimension. If you take the questionnaire twice and change one or two of your answers, as people often do, the result could be to classify you as a different "type."

Because all aspects of personality vary as continuous dimensions, personalities do not cluster into discrete types (Loehlin & Martin, 2018). However, although most psychological researchers hold the MBTI in low regard, it is amazingly popular with businesses, organizations, and job counselors. One reason for its appeal is that it classifies all personalities as normal. Regardless of how it might classify you, it would give a description of your probable interests, strengths, and desires, and it would offer advice about what type of job to seek, what type of romantic partner would be best, and so forth. The descriptions are sufficiently vague, almost like horoscopes, that almost anyone can say, "yes, that fits me reasonably well."

Projective Techniques

The MMPI, NEO PI-R, and Myers-Briggs Type Indicator analyze personalities based on self-reports. However, people don't always describe themselves honestly, and even when they intend to be honest, they might have distorted or incomplete views of themselves. Therefore, many psychologists want to supplement objective tests with other ways of assessing personality.

Sometimes when people are embarrassed to admit something about themselves, they say something like, "Let me tell you about my friend's problem and ask what my friend should do." They then describe their own problem. They are "projecting" their problem onto someone else in Freud's sense of the word—that is, attributing it to someone else.

Rather than discouraging projection, psychologists make use of it with projective techniques, *procedures designed to encourage people to project their personality characteristics onto ambiguous stimuli.* Let's consider two popular projective techniques: the Rorschach inkblots and the Thematic Apperception Test.

The Rorschach Inkblots

The Rorschach inkblots, *a technique based on people's interpretations of 10 ambiguous inkblots,* is the most famous, most widely used, and most controversial projective personality technique. It was created by Hermann Rorschach (ROAR-shock), a Swiss psychiatrist, who showed people inkblots and asked them to say whatever came to mind (Pichot, 1984). Other psychiatrists and psychologists gradually developed the Rorschach into the technique we know today.

Administering the Rorschach

The Rorschach inkblot technique consists of 10 cards similar to those in ▼ Figure 14.6, 5 of them in

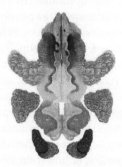

▲ **Figure 14.6** In the Rorschach inkblot technique, people examine an abstract pattern and say what it looks like.

color. A psychologist hands you a card and asks, "What might this be?" The instructions are intentionally vague on the assumption that you reveal more about your personality in an ill-defined situation. (If you would like to watch a psychologist squirm, ask for an example of how to answer. Someone administering the Rorschach is never supposed to give an example.)

Sometimes, people's answers are revealing, either immediately or in response to a psychologist's probes. Here is an example (Aronow, Reznikoff, & Moreland, 1995):

Client: Some kind of insect; it's not pretty enough to be a butterfly.

Psychologist: Any association to that?

Client: It's an ugly black butterfly, no colors.

Psychologist: What does that make you think of in your own life?

Client: You probably want me to say "myself." Well, that's probably how I thought of myself when I was younger—I never thought of myself as attractive—my sister was the attractive one. I was the ugly duckling—I did get more attractive as I got older.

Evaluation of the Rorschach

When you describe what you see on an inkblot, your answer undoubtedly has something to do with your experiences, concerns, or personality. But how accurately can psychologists perceive that relationship? And if they perceive a relationship, did they really get the information from the Rorschach or from something they already knew about you?

One man described a particular inkblot as "like a bat that has been squashed on the pavement under the heel of a giant's boot" (Dawes, 1994, p. 149). Psychologist Robyn Dawes initially was impressed with how the Rorschach had revealed this client's sense of being overwhelmed and crushed by powers beyond his control. But then he realized that he had already known the man was depressed. If a client with a history of violence had made the same response, he would have focused on the aggressive nature of the giant's foot stomp. Psychologists often believe the Rorschach gave them an insight, when in fact it just confirmed an opinion they already had (Wood, Nezworski, Lilienfeld, & Garb, 2003).

James Exner (1986) and others have developed methods to standardize the interpretations of Rorschach responses, such as counting the number of times a client mentions aggressive themes. Clinicians using such methods achieve reasonably high agreement in most regards (Kivisalu, Lewey, Shaffer, & Canfield, 2017; Viglione & Taylor, 2003). However, a high level of agreement does not necessarily indicate useful information. One problem that critics have noticed is that using the Rorschach identifies an unrealistically large percentage of people as disturbed or pathological (Garb, Wood, Lilienfeld, & Nezworski, 2005; Lilienfeld, Wood, & Garb, 2000; Wood et al., 2003).

Critics of the Rorschach stop short of calling it completely invalid. The Rorschach does detect thought disorders (as are common in schizophrenia). It has moderate validity for detecting risk of suicide, and it identifies certain other personality characteristics with low to moderate accuracy (Mihura, Meyer, Dumitrascu, & Bombel, 2013). Its defenders insist that when the Rorschach is used properly, its validity is comparable to that of many other psychological tests (Society for Personality Assessment, 2005). Unfortunately, the other tests also have only low to moderate validity. Furthermore, critics reply, the Rorschach seldom gives information that one could not obtain just as well or better from biographical reports or other sources. Critics insist that the Rorschach is not accurate enough for making important decisions, such as which parent should get custody of a child or which prisoners should get parole (Erickson, Lilienfeld, & Vitacco, 2007). Unfortunately, courts do sometimes allow testimony based on the Rorschach, in spite of the questionable validity (Neal et al., 2019).

17. The belief is that you reveal the most about your personality in an ill-defined, unstructured situation.

The Thematic Apperception Test

The **Thematic Apperception Test (TAT)**, or *Thematic Apperception Technique*, consists of pictures similar to the one shown in ▼ Figure 14.7. *The person is asked to make up a story for each picture, describing what events led up to this scene, what is happening now, and what will happen in the future.* Christiana Morgan and Henry Murray devised this test to measure people's needs (Murray, 1943). It includes 31 pictures, including some showing women, some showing men, some with both or neither, and one that is totally blank. A psychologist selects a few cards to use with a given client (Lilienfeld, Wood, & Garb, 2000).

The assumption is that when you tell a story about someone in the drawing, you probably identify with that person, and so the story is really about yourself. You might describe events and concerns that you might be reluctant to discuss openly. For example, one young man told the following story about a picture of a man clinging to a rope:

> This man is escaping. Several months ago, he was beat up and shanghaied and taken aboard ship. Since then, he has been mistreated and unhappy and has been looking for a way to escape. Now the ship is anchored near a tropical island and he is climbing down a rope to the water. He will get away successfully and swim to shore. When he gets there, he will be met by a group of beautiful native women with whom he will live the rest of his life in luxury and never tell anyone what happened. Sometimes he will feel that he should go back to his old life; but he will never do it. (Kimble & Garmezy, 1968, pp. 582–583)

This young man had entered divinity school to please his parents but was unhappy there. He was wrestling with a secret desire to escape to a new life with greater worldly pleasures. In his story, he described someone doing what he wanted to do.

The TAT is not easy to evaluate. Because a clinician might use one set of pictures at one time and a different set at another, we cannot easily determine reliability or validity. Furthermore, it is sensitive to what a client is thinking about right now, as opposed to more persistent personality traits, and many therapists interpret the results according to their clinical judgment, without any clear rules. If you took the TAT with two psychologists and said the same thing both times, they might reach different conclusions about you (Cramer, 1996). Nevertheless, regardless of whether the TAT is a valid "test," it can be a way to open a conversation with a client.

Researchers also use the TAT to measure people's need for achievement, need for power, or need for affiliation, by counting all the times someone mentions related terms. These results are useful for research purposes, although not necessarily for making decisions about an individual (Lilienfeld, Wood, & Garb, 2000).

Handwriting as a Projective Technique

Based on the theory that your personality affects everything you do, might your handwriting reveal something important about you? Hypothetically, perhaps people who dot their i's with a dash—*i*—might be especially energetic, or perhaps people who draw large loops above the line—as in *allow*—might be highly idealistic. Carefully collected data, however, show no dependable relationship between handwriting and personality (Tett & Palmer, 1997).

Implicit Personality Tests

Although projective tests have debatable usefulness, the motivation behind them remains: Psychologists would like to measure personality aspects that people avoid discussing openly, and researchers continue to search for other kinds of personality tests.

Cognitive psychologists distinguish between explicit and implicit memory. If you hear a list of words and try to repeat them, your recall is explicit memory. If you later use words from the list in your conversation, your use of those words constitutes implicit memory. Implicit memory can affect you without your awareness.

Analogous to that, an **implicit personality test** *measures some aspect of your personality based on subtle changes in your behavior, rather than a self-report.* An implicit personality test resembles the implicit association test (IAT) that social psychologists use to measure prejudices. They might ask people to press one key if they see either a "good"

▲ **Figure 14.7** In the Thematic Apperception Test, people tell a story about what is going on in a picture, including what led up to this event, what is happening now, and what will happen in the future.

word or a photo of a white person, and another key if they see either a "bad" word or a photo of a black person. Then they try the reverse pairing and determine which pairing produces faster responses.

An implicit personality test uses a similar method. For example, suppose the instruction is to press the left key if you see either a picture of people having sex or a word associated with guilt (such as *shameful* or *wrong*) and the right key if you see either a picture of people exercising or a word associated with innocence (such as *virtuous* or *moral*). Almost everyone responds faster to these pairings than to the reverse (sex-innocence and exercise-guilt), but people with the biggest difference tend to have the most intense guilt feelings about sex (Totonchi, Derlega, & Janda, 2019). Tests like this have moderate accuracy, especially if we take an average over a fair number of people, but they are not accurate enough to tell us much about a given individual (DeHouwer, Teige-Mocigemba, Spruyt, & Moors, 2009; Horcajo, Rubio, Aguado, Hernandez, & Marquez, 2014).

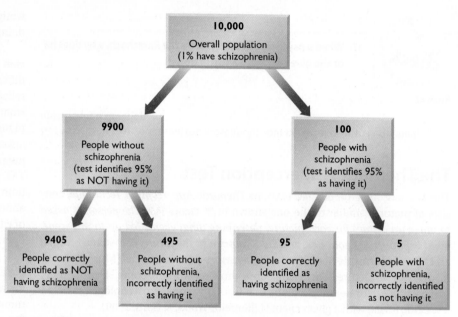

▲ **Figure 14.8** Assume that a certain profile occurs in 95 percent of people with schizophrenia and 5 percent of other people. If we relied entirely on this test, we would correctly identify 95 people with schizophrenia and misidentify 495 normal people.

18. Are implicit personality tests more useful to researchers or clinicians? Why?

Answer

18. They are more useful to researchers, because they demonstrate trends on average. They are not accurate enough to say anything for sure about an individual.

Uses and Misuses of Personality Tests

Personality tests serve several functions. Researchers use them to investigate how personality develops. Some businesses use them to help select among job applicants. Clinicians use them to help identify disorders and to measure improvement during therapy.

Personality tests are useful up to a point, but we need to be aware of their limits. Suppose someone's MMPI personality profile resembles the profile typical for schizophrenia. Identifying schizophrenia or any other unusual condition is a signal-detection problem: We want to report something when it is present but not when it is absent. People without schizophrenia outnumber people with schizophrenia by approximately 100 to 1. Suppose a particular score on some personality test is characteristic of 95 percent of people with schizophrenia, but also for 5 percent of other people. As ▶ Figure 14.8 shows,

5 percent of the non-schizophrenic population is a larger group than 95 percent of the people with schizophrenia. Thus, if we label as "schizophrenic" everyone with a high score, we are wrong more often than right. Recall the representativeness heuristic and the issue of base-rate information: Someone who seems representative of people in a rare category does not necessarily belong to that category. Therefore, although the personality test provides a helpful clue, a psychologist looks for evidence beyond the test score before drawing a conclusion.

Personality Tests in Action: Offender Profiling

When we observe certain behaviors, we infer a personality trait. For example, if we see someone mingling in a crowd and talking to many people, we infer extraversion. If we notice that someone always completes assignments on time, we infer conscientiousness. But how far can we go in this regard? In particular, if we see evidence of a crime, how much if anything can we infer about the personality of the person who committed the crime? *Offender profiling*, also known as *behavioral investigative advice*, attempts to infer something about the criminal from the crime itself. The field assumes that people who commit similar crimes have similar personalities or backgrounds.

In 1956, the New York City police asked psychiatrist James Brussel to help them find the "mad bomber" who had planted more than 30 bombs over 16 years. Brussel examined the evidence and told police the mad bomber hated the power company, Con Ed. The bomber was probably unmarried, foreign-born, probably Slavic, 50 to 60 years old, and living in Bridgeport, Connecticut. Brussel said to look for a man who dresses neatly and wears a buttoned double-breasted suit. That evidence led police directly to a suspect, George Metesky, who was wearing a buttoned double-breasted suit! Metesky confessed, and offender profiling established itself as an investigative tool.

Well, that's the way James Brussel told the story, anyway. Evidently, he had some memory distortions. According to police records, Brussel didn't say the bomber was Slavic; he said German. Metesky, in fact, was Lithuanian.

Brussel didn't say the bomber lived in Bridgeport, Connecticut; he said White Plains, New York, and the police spent much time fruitlessly searching for suspects in White Plains. Metesky, in fact, lived in Waterbury, Connecticut. Brussel said the bomber was 40 to 50 years old and revised his memory when Metesky turned out to be older. Brussel also said the bomber had a facial scar, had a night job, and was an expert on civil or military ordnance (none of which was true). And Metesky was not wearing a buttoned double-breasted suit when the police arrested him. He was wearing pajamas. Nothing that Brussel said helped the police find the mad bomber. They found Metesky because a clerk from Con Ed patiently went through years of letters the company had received until she found a threatening letter that resembled messages that Metesky had planted with his bombs (Foster, 2000).

Brussel's *reported* success in helping the police (which was really no success at all) inspired interest in offender profiling, and today, profilers consult with police on a thousand or so cases per year. The police often report satisfaction with the profilers' reports, but the satisfaction could be an example of the Barnum effect—the tendency to accept almost any personality description as being accurate. How accurate are offender profiles, really? Researchers examined 21 profiles that various police departments had obtained. Most statements in those profiles were useless to investigators, such as, "The offender felt no remorse" (Alison, Smith, Eastman, & Rainbow, 2003). It is possible to list many correct statements that profilers have made (Snook, Cullen, Bennell, Taylor, & Gendreau, 2008), but the number of correct statements is meaningless unless we also know the number of incorrect statements. We also need to compare professional profilers' surmises to the accuracy of other people's guesses. Only a few studies have investigated these questions. Let's examine two of the best such studies.

what's the evidence?

Offender Profiling

Richard Kocsis and his associates first did a study of profiling in a murder case. They provided extensive details about the murder to five professional profilers and larger numbers of police officers, psychologists, college students, and people who claimed to be psychics. Then each person tried to guess the murderer's sex, height, age, religion, and so forth in 30 multiple-choice questions, with varying numbers of choices per item. Researchers compared those answers to the facts learned about the actual murderer, who had in fact been caught. Random guessing would produce 8.1 correct answers for the 30 items, but no one would guess

at random. Even without knowing any details about the crime, aren't you more likely to guess the murderer was a young man than an 80-year-old woman? If the crime was in the United States, you probably won't guess that the criminal's religion was Buddhist. And so forth. All groups did better than the random score of 8.1, but none did well. The professional profilers did the best, at 13.8 correct out of 30, and psychics did the worst, at 11.3 (Kocsis, Irwin, Hayes, & Nunn, 2000).

However, it may be hard to profile a criminal from a single crime. Kocsis (2004) therefore did a similar study concerning someone who had committed a series of 13 cases of arson (setting fires).

Hypothesis Professional profilers will guess correctly more facts about the arsonist than other people will.

Method As in Kocsis's first study, most profilers refused to participate, but three were willing. Other groups were police officers with much experience investigating arson, professional fire investigators, and sophomore chemistry majors. Each person examined all the evidence that police had assembled, including photos and descriptions of the crime scenes, statements by witnesses, shoe prints, information about how the fires were set, and so forth. The study also included a group of community college students who received no information about the crimes, except that they were arson. Then each participant answered 33 questions about the probable arsonist. All were questions to which the researcher knew the correct answer. Examples (reworded slightly for brevity):

- The offender is: (1) male, (2) female.
- The offender is: (1) thin, (2) average, (3) solid/muscular, (4) fat.
- The offender was: (1) highly familiar with the crime locations, (2) somewhat familiar, (3) unfamiliar.
- The offender is: (1) single, (2) married, (3) living with someone, (4) divorced.
- The offender is: (1) a student, (2) unemployed, (3) employed part time, (4) a blue-collar worker, (5) a semiskilled worker, (6) a skilled or white-collar worker.
- The offender's alcohol use is: (1) none, (2) low, (3) medium, (4) in binges, (5) high.
- The offender: (1) has a previous criminal record, (2) has no previous criminal record.

Results Questions had between 2 and 9 choices each, and random guessing would produce a bit more than 10 correct answers out of 33. ▼ Figure 14.9 shows the results. The three professional profilers did the best, 3 to 4 items better than the chemistry majors. (Chemistry majors were used to represent people with no relevant experience but high intelligence. Take a bow, chemistry majors.) Police and firefighters, despite their experience, did only slightly better than the community college students who had no information about the crimes.

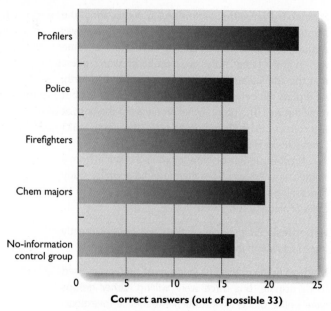

▲ **Figure 14.9** Of 33 multiple-choice questions, many of them with only 2 or 3 choices, profilers answered a mean of 23 items correctly. Random guessing would produce 10 correct. People with no information about the crime guessed more than 16 correct. (Source: Based on data from Kocsis, 2004)

Interpretation This study has clear limitations, especially that it included only three professional profilers, just one criminal, and a set of questions that may not have been ideal. Still, the profilers did better than the other groups, so it appears that the field is not entirely bogus. A few

other studies yielded similar results: Professional profilers do better than other people, and police investigators do no better than inexperienced people. However, in no case did anyone answer a very high percentage of questions correctly (Snook, Eastwood, Gendreau, Goggin, & Cullen, 2007).

A critical question remains: Did the profilers do well *enough*? On average, in the study just described, they answered 23 questions correctly, which is closer to the scores of people who knew nothing (16+) than to a perfect score (33). If profilers provide the police with a mixture of correct and incorrect information, does the net result advance the investigation or lead the police astray?

Research to improve profiling has progressed, but it remains weak by scientific standards. Improved offender profiling is certainly possible because people who commit certain crimes do tend to resemble each other in certain ways (Cole & Brown, 2014; Fujita et al., 2013), but we need much more research, both to improve the profiles themselves, and to determine how much confidence they merit (Fox & Farrington, 2018).

19. **In what way is offender profiling similar to a projective personality test?**

Answer

19. In each case, a psychologist tries to infer someone's personality from behavior, instead of from self-reports.

---

in closing | module 14.3

Possibilities and Limits of Personality Tests

One of the most common topics of conversation could be described uncharitably as "gossip" or more generously as "understanding other people." Understanding people's personality is important. You need to know whom to trust and whom to distrust.

Given our focus on personality, most of us tend to believe that personality is highly stable and governs a great deal of behavior. If so, someone might be able to look at a crime scene and infer

the personality of the perpetrator. Psychologists might be able to listen to people's answers to the Rorschach inkblots and discern their innermost secrets. So it might seem, at least, but the research suggests we should be cautious. Personality is not always consistent, and inferring someone's personality is not always accurate. People's actions depend on the situations at least as much as they depend on personality.

Summary

- *The Barnum effect.* Because most people accept almost anything they are told about their personality, tests must be carefully evaluated to ensure that they measure what they claim to measure. (page 467)
- *The MMPI.* The MMPI, a widely used personality test, consists of true–false questions selected to identify signs of possible psychological problems. The MMPI–2 is a modern version. (page 468)

- *Derivation of the MMPI.* The MMPI was developed by selecting items that people with a disorder tended to answer differently from other people. (page 468)
- *Detection of lying.* The MMPI includes items about common faults and rare virtues. People who deny common faults or claim rare virtues are probably lying on that item, and therefore probably on others also. (page 469)

- *Other objective tests.* The NEO-PI-R measures the Big Five personality traits. The Myers-Briggs Type Indicator divides people into 16 types. Because personality traits follow continuous dimensions instead of tending toward one extreme or the other, most psychologists hold the Myers-Briggs in low regard. (page 469)
- *Projective techniques.* A projective technique, such as the Rorschach inkblots or the Thematic Apperception Test, lets people describe their concerns indirectly while talking about ambiguous stimuli. The usefulness of these procedures is controversial. (page 470)

- *Uses and misuses of personality tests.* Because the tests are not entirely accurate, a score that seems characteristic of a psychological disorder may occur also in many people without that disorder. A test score by itself should not be the basis for a diagnosis of mental disorder. (page 472)
- *Offender profiling.* From inspection of a crime, it is possible to draw inferences about the probable offender, but at this point, offender profiling has only limited validity. (page 472)

Key Terms

Barnum effect (page 467)

implicit personality test (page 471)

Minnesota Multiphasic Personality Inventory (MMPI) (page 468)

MMPI-2 (page 468)

Myers-Briggs Type Indicator (MBTI) (page 469)

NEO PI-R (NEO Personality Inventory-Revised) (page 469)

projective techniques (page 470)

Rorschach inkblots (page 470)

standardized test (page 468)

Thematic Apperception Test (TAT) (page 471)

Review Questions

1. Suppose a job interviewer asks how much experience you have had at operating a matriculation machine and planning basic entropy programs. What is the probable point of these questions?
   - (a) To test your vocabulary
   - (b) To find out about your computer skills
   - (c) To see whether you exaggerate your qualifications
   - (d) To assess your interest in getting the job

2. Which test is based on the Big Five model of personality?
   - (a) The MMPI
   - (b) Rorschach Inkblots
   - (c) The Thematic Apperception Test
   - (d) The NEO-PI-R

3. Who devised the Myers-Briggs Type Indicator?
   - (a) The followers of Sigmund Freud
   - (b) A mother and daughter with no training in psychology or statistics
   - (c) An assembly of psychological researchers
   - (d) Two psychiatrists

4. The instructions for the Rorschach inkblots are vague, because of what assumption?
   - (a) Your personality emerges best in an ill-defined situation.
   - (b) Most people have trouble remembering and following specific instructions.
   - (c) People will become more interested after they ask for clarification.
   - (d) Most people are already familiar with the procedure.

5. Why are many psychological researchers skeptical of using the Rorschach?
   - (a) It often just confirms an opinion based on other evidence.
   - (b) It penalizes people who cannot think of many answers.
   - (c) It is based entirely on the Big Five personality model.
   - (d) People with schizophrenia give the same answers as anyone else.

6. Why is it difficult to evaluate the reliability of the TAT?
   - (a) Researchers have not been able to try it on a representative sample.
   - (b) The procedure varies from one instance to another.
   - (c) People are encouraged to vary their responses.
   - (d) The statistics are difficult to calculate.

7. Suppose your answers on some test resemble the typical responses of people with a rare syndrome. Before rushing to a diagnosis, what else would a psychologist need to know?
   - (a) How many people without the syndrome also give these answers?
   - (b) How many people with that syndrome do not answer this way?
   - (c) Have you recently met someone who has the syndrome?
   - (d) What answers did you give on the Rorschach?

Answers: 1c, 2d, 3b, 4a, 5a, 6b, 7a.

15 Abnormal Psychology: Disorders and Treatment

Over the past 4 months, George has injured dozens of people whom he hardly knew. Two of them needed hospital treatment. George expresses no guilt, no regrets. He says he would hit every one of them again if he got the chance. What should society do with George?

1. Send him to prison.

2. Commit him to a mental hospital.

3. Give him an award for being the best defensive player in the National Football League.

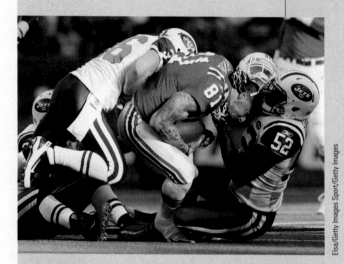

American football players such as Aaron Hernandez risk head trauma or other injury to themselves and others. How does the context of this behavior influence our opinion of it? Would we accept similar behavior outside of the sport?

Elsa/Getty Images Sport/Getty Images

You cannot answer the question unless you know the context of George's behavior. Behavior that seems normal at a party is bizarre at a business meeting. Behavior expected of a rock star might earn a trip to the mental hospital for a college professor. Refusing to leave your home for days at a time would seem strange ordinarily, but not during a coronavirus pandemic.

Even knowing the context of someone's behavior may not tell us whether the behavior is normal. Suppose your rich aunt Tillie starts passing out money to strangers on a street corner and plans to continue until she has exhausted her fortune. Does that sound crazy? Should you urge her to seek therapy? If so, for her sake or for yours? How is she different than Warren Buffet, one of the richest men in the world, saying he will donate half of his multibillion-dollar estate to charity?

Assessing abnormal behavior is difficult. What seems abnormal for one person or in one context may be normal for someone else. Deciding what to do about abnormal behavior is often difficult.

An Overview of Abnormal Behavior

iStock.com/SDI Productions

After studying this module, you should be able to:

1. Discuss the difficulty of defining mental illness.

2. Describe the biopsychosocial model of mental illness.

3. Give examples of cultural influences on abnormal behavior.

4. Describe *DSM-5* and give examples of the categories it lists.

5. Evaluate the assumptions behind *DSM* and the categorical approach to mental illness.

Many students in medical school develop what is called "medical students' disease." Imagine reading a medical textbook that describes, say, Cryptic Ruminating Umbilicus Disorder (CRUD): "The symptoms are hardly noticeable until the condition becomes hopeless. The first symptom is a pale tongue." (You go to the mirror. You cannot remember what your tongue is supposed to look like, but it *does* look a little pale.) "Later, a hard spot forms in the neck." (You feel your neck. "Wait! I never felt *this* before! I think it's something hard!") "Just before the arms and legs fall off, the person has shortness of breath, increased heart rate, and sweating." (Already distressed, you *do* have shortness of breath, your heart *is* racing, and you *are* sweating profusely.)

Sooner or later, most medical students misunderstand the description of some disease and confuse it with their own normal condition. When my brother was in medical school, he diagnosed himself as having a rare, fatal illness, checked himself into a hospital, and wrote out his will. (He finished medical school and is still doing fine today, decades later.)

Students of psychological disorders are particularly vulnerable to medical students' disease. As you read this chapter, you may decide that you are suffering from one of the disorders you read about. Perhaps you are, but recognizing a little of yourself in the description of a disorder does not necessarily mean that you have it. Most people feel nervous occasionally, and most have mood swings and a peculiar behavior or two. A diagnosis of a psychological disorder should be reserved for people whose problems seriously interfere with their lives.

Defining Abnormal Behavior

The American Psychiatric Association (2013, p. 20) defined mental disorder as a "clinically significant disturbance in an individual's cognition, emotion regulation, or behavior that reflects a dysfunction in the psychological, biological, or developmental processes underlying mental functioning." That seems a reasonable definition, but it is not always easy in practice. Who decides whether a disturbance is clinically significant? Do people themselves decide? Does a psychiatrist or psychologist decide? Furthermore, does the second part of that definition ("reflects a dysfunction in the psychological, biological, or developmental processes . . .") add anything?

In previous eras, people have held many views of abnormal behavior and its causes. The idea of demon possession was popular in medieval Europe and is still common in much of the world today

(van Duijl, Nijenhuis, Komproe, Gernaat, & de Jong, 2010). Although it conflicts with a scientific worldview, we understand its appeal: If someone's behavior changes drastically, we feel like saying, "That's not the person I knew."

The ancient Greeks explained behavior in terms of four fluids: An excess of blood caused a sanguine (courageous and loving) personality. An excess of phlegm caused a phlegmatic (calm) personality. Too much yellow bile made one choleric (easily angered). Too much black bile made one melancholic (sad). Although the four-fluids theory is obsolete, the terms *sanguine*, *phlegmatic*, *choleric*, and *melancholic* persist.

Traditional Chinese philosophy held that personality progresses through five states of change, analogous to the seasons: Winter rain helps the trees (wood) grow in spring. The trees burn (fire) in summer, and the ashes return to earth in late summer. The earth can be mined for metal in autumn, and melted metal becomes a liquid, like water, completing the cycle. According to this view, personality also cycles with the seasons, and an excessive response could cause too much fear, anger, and so forth. ▼ **Figure 15.1** illustrates the idea.

FineArt/Alamy Stock Photo

Edvard Munch (1863–1944), *Evening Melancholy* (1896). Like many of Munch's paintings, this one depicts depression and despair.

The Biopsychosocial Model

Psychologists in Western cultures today endorse the biopsychosocial model that emphasizes *biological, psychological, and sociological aspects of abnormal behavior.* The *biological* roots of abnormal behavior include genetic factors, infectious diseases, poor nutrition, inadequate sleep, drugs, and other influences on brain functioning.

The *psychological* component includes reactions to stressful experiences. For example, people who were physically or sexually abused in childhood, bullied, or neglected are more likely than others to develop psychological problems in adulthood (J. G. Johnson, Cohen, Brown, Smailes, & Bernstein, 1999; Schaefer et al., 2018). A current stress, such as dealing with the coronavirus pandemic, aggravates any tendency toward anxiety or depression. Finally, behavior must be understood in a *social* and cultural context. Behavior that is considered acceptable in one society might be labeled abnormal in another. For example, loud wailing at a funeral is expected in some societies, but not in others. Public drunkenness is acceptable in some cultures, but strictly forbidden in others.

Cultural Influences on Abnormality

We learn from our culture how to behave normally, but we also learn some of the options for behaving abnormally. In part of Sudan some years ago, women had low status and very limited rights. If a woman's husband mistreated her, she had no defense.

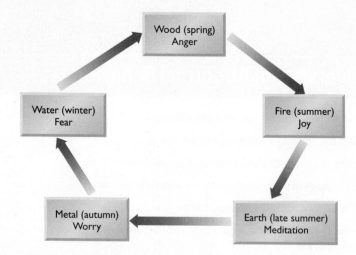

▲ **Figure 15.1** In traditional Chinese philosophy, personality cycles through five stages or elements, just as the seasons do. An excessive response could lead to abnormalities.

However, people believed that a woman could be possessed by a demon that caused her to lose control and scream "crazy" things that she "could not possibly believe," including insults against her own husband (!). Her husband could not scold or punish her because, after all, it was not she who was speaking, but a demon. The standard way to remove the demon was to provide the woman with the best available food, new clothing, an opportunity to spend much time with other women, freedom from work responsibilities, and almost anything else she demanded until the demon departed. You can imagine how common demon possession became (Constantinides, 1977).

More examples: *Koro*, said to be common in China, is a fear that a man's penis will retract into the body, causing death. Some men have been known to hold onto their penis constantly to prevent it from disappearing into the body (Bracha, 2006). You have probably heard the expression "to run amok." *Running*

What we consider abnormal depends on the context. **(a)** People dressed as witches ski down a mountain as part of an annual festival in Belalp, Switzerland, in which dressing as witches is supposed to chase away evil spirits. **(b)** People parade through Stockholm, Sweden, on "Zombie Day." Unusual behavior is not necessarily a sign of psychological disorder.

Fans sometimes celebrate a major sports victory with a destructive rampage. In some ways, it is like running amok. People copy abnormal behavior from other people's example.

amok occurs in parts of Southeast Asia, where someone (usually a young man) runs around engaging in indiscriminate violent behavior (Berry, Poortinga, Segal, & Dasen, 1992). Such behavior is considered an understandable reaction to psychological stress.

An Australian psychiatrist found that three mental patients in a hospital had cut off one of their ears. Assuming that this behavior must be a common symptom of mental illness, he asked other psychiatrists how often they had

seen the same thing. He found that ear removal occurred only at his own hospital. Apparently, after one patient cut off his ear, the others copied (Alroe & Gunda, 1995).

DSM and the Categorical Approach to Psychological Disorders

If you go to a doctor's office complaining of headache, the doctor will ask questions and run tests to determine the cause. Most headaches are due to tension, sleeplessness, or other simple problems, but some are due to an infection or blood clot in the brain, a tumor, or migraine. In any case, the doctor pinpoints a cause before recommending a treatment. For many years, psychiatrists and clinical psychologists expected to reach the same point: They would precisely diagnose someone's psychological problem, determine the cause, and recommend the most effective therapy. Over time, that goal has become more and more elusive.

To standardize their definitions and diagnoses, psychiatrists and psychologists developed *reference books that set criteria for each psychiatric diagnosis.* The World Health Organization (WHO) published

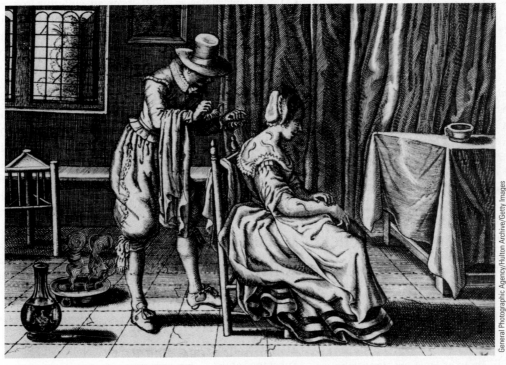

In the early days of medicine, physicians provided the same treatments for all diseases (e.g., applying leeches to draw blood, as shown). Progress depended on differentiating particular disorders and developing individual treatments for each. Can we also find specific treatments for psychological disorders?

Table 15.1 Categories of Psychological Disorders According to *DSM–5*

Neurodevelopmental Disorders

Schizophrenia Spectrum

Bipolar and Related Disorders

Depressive Disorders

Anxiety Disorders

Obsessive-Compulsive Disorders

Trauma-Related Disorders

Dissociative Disorders

Somatic Symptom Disorders

Eating Disorders

Elimination Disorders

Sleep-Wake Disorders

Sexual Dysfunctions

Gender Dysphoria

Impulse Control Disorders

Substance Abuse and Addictions

Neurocognitive Disorders

Personality Disorders

Paraphilias

Others

the *International Statistical Classification of Diseases and Related Health Problems* tenth edition (ICD-10), which includes diagnoses for all types of illness, not just those of psychiatry. Most of the world uses the ICD-10, but the United States and a few other countries use the *Diagnostic and Statistical Manual of Mental Disorders (DSM)*, for which the fifth edition, *DSM-5*, was published in 2013 (American Psychiatric Association, 2013). The ICD and DSM are similar, except that ICD describes typical examples of each disorder instead of specific criteria (Clark, Cuthbert, Lewis-Fernández, Narrow, & Reed, 2017). ■ Table 15.1 lists categories of disorder, in the order that *DSM-5* lists them.

For each disorder, *DSM-5* sets the criteria for a diagnosis. For example, to qualify for a diagnosis of attention deficit/hyperactivity disorder, someone must frequently show at least six symptoms (or four if over age 17) from either of the following columns:

Inattention	Hyperactivity/Impulsivity
Fails to attend to details	Often fidgets
Difficulty sustaining attention	Restless while others sit quietly
Seems not to listen	Runs about inappropriately
Fails to finish tasks	Excessively loud during play
Difficulty organizing an activity	Acts as if driven by a motor
Avoids tasks requiring sustained effort	Talks excessively
Frequently loses objects	Blurts out answer before question is complete
Easily distracted	Difficulty waiting his/her turn
Forgetful in daily tasks	Interrupts others

This "either–or" style of diagnosis means that people can qualify for the same diagnosis in many ways. *DSM-5* offers 227 possible combinations of symptoms for major depression, more than 23,000 for panic disorder, and more than 636,000 for post-traumatic stress disorder (PTSD) (Galatzer-Levy & Bryant, 2013). Note also that each criterion is imprecise. For example, how much fidgeting constitutes "often"? How much talk counts as "excessive"? How often would you have to fail to finish a task before it becomes a symptom? In all psychiatric diagnoses, many people are near the borderline between normal and abnormal. In other areas of medicine, a physician can run laboratory tests to confirm or rule out a possible diagnosis. Psychiatrists, however, have no valid laboratory tests, and they have to rely on their assessments of behavior.

DSM has helped standardize psychiatric diagnoses so that psychologists use terms like *depression, schizophrenia,* and so forth in more consistent ways than they would otherwise. However, this approach assumes that each case fits into one category or another, and that each troubled person can receive a clear diagnosis. In fact, many and perhaps most troubled people fit several diagnoses partly and none of them perfectly (Ahn, Flanagan, Marsh, & Sanislow, 2006; Kupfer, First, & Regier, 2002). If you are suffering from depression, bipolar disorder, anxiety, attention deficit disorder, substance abuse, conduct disorder, obsessive-compulsive disorder, schizophrenia, or migraine headaches, the chances are high that you suffer from one or more of the others also, at least to some degree (Brainstorm Consortium, 2018; Caspi et al., 2014), and you probably have physical ailments as well (Hagerty et al., 2019). You might fit mainly into one diagnosis now but a different one later. Furthermore, different disorders result from the same genetic predispositions and the same kinds of stressful experiences (Cross-Disorder Group, 2013; Duncan, Pollastri, & Smoller, 2014; Gandal et al., 2018; Keyes et al., 2014; Nolen-Hoeksema & Watkins, 2011; Schneider et al., 2014; Schork et al., 2019). Even when a single diagnosis seems reasonable, the diagnosis doesn't reliably point the way to a treatment. Antidepressant drugs sometimes help people with disorders other than depression, and antipsychotic drugs sometimes help with nonpsychotic disorders (Dean, 2011).

Many psychologists who are dissatisfied with the *DSM* approach would prefer to rate each client's problems along several dimensions, instead of trying to give each person a label (Watson & Clark, 2006). For example, instead of a single diagnosis, a therapist might use ratings like this:

	Mild	Moderate	Strong	Severe
Depressed mood				
Anxiety				
Violent temper				
Substance abuse				
Thought disorder				

Table 15.2 Six Personality Disorders

Personality Disorder	Description
Antisocial personality disorder	Lack of affection for others, lack of guilt feelings
Avoidant personality disorder	Avoidance of social contact, lack of friends
Borderline personality disorder	Unstable self-image, no lasting relationships or firm decisions, repeated self-endangering behaviors
Narcissistic personality disorder	Exaggerated self-regard, disregard for others
Obsessive-compulsive personality disorder	Excessive preoccupation with details
Schizotypal personality disorder	Cognitive impairments and interpersonal deficits

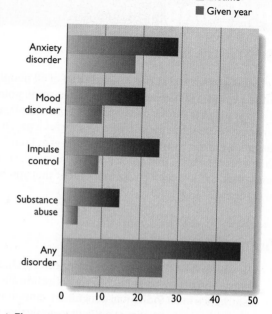

▲ **Figure 15.2** According to this survey, just over one-fourth of U.S. adults suffer a psychological disorder in any given year, and nearly half do at some time in life. (Based on data of Kessler, Berglund, et al., 2005; Kessler, Chiu, et al., 2005)

The authors of *DSM-5* considered switching to dimensions instead of categories, but they decided against that approach for several reasons. One is that although the categorical approach is not entirely correct, it is not entirely wrong either. Many people, after all, do fit into a single category reasonably well. A second reason is that if we switch to dimensions, psychologists and psychiatrists do not yet have a consensus on what those dimensions are. A third reason, probably the most important, is that currently the health insurance companies will pay for treatment only if someone has a specific diagnosis.

DSM-5 did accept a dimensional approach for personality disorders. A **personality disorder** is *a maladaptive, inflexible way of dealing with the environment and other people,* such as being unusually self-centered. A previous edition of *DSM* listed ten personality disorders, but clinicians found that few clients fit neatly into just one of them (Lenzenweger, Johnson, & Willett, 2004). *DSM-5* gives clinicians two options. First, they can classify someone in terms of six personality disorders, as briefly described in ■ Table 15.2. Second, if they prefer, they can dispense with labels and rate someone along several dimensions, including impulsivity, suspiciousness, withdrawal, and hostility. It is fair to say that our understanding of personality disorders is in a state of flux, and so is the whole concept of mental illness, but the trend is toward doubting the categorical approach to mental illness.

A further criticism is that *DSM* labels too many conditions as mental illnesses. If you seek help to increase your enjoyment of sex, you have *sexual interest/arousal disorder* or *hypoactive sexual desire disorder.* A woman with premenstrual distress can get a diagnosis of *premenstrual dysphoric disorder.* If you get at least 7 hours of sleep per night but still feel sleepy during the day, and you have trouble feeling fully awake after a sudden awakening, you have *hypersomnolence disorder.* The list goes on, with hundreds of possibilities. Surveys have found that almost half of all people in the United States qualify for at least one *DSM* diagnosis of mental illness at some time in life (Kessler, Berglund, Demler, Jin, & Walters, 2005; Kessler, Chiu, Demler, & Walters, 2005). Most people would prefer to avoid any label, because of the stigma attached to mental illness (Corrigan, Druss, & Perlick, 2014). Once you have been labeled as mentally ill, people interpret almost anything you do as a further manifestation of your illness. Therapist Jack Huber (personal communication) said that if

it were up to him, he would eliminate all the other diagnoses and just label *everyone* with "chronic human imperfection."

The most common disorders are anxiety disorders, mood disorders (e.g., depression), impulse control problems (including attention deficit disorder), and substance abuse, as shown in ▲ Figure 15.2. Throughout this chapter we shall discuss several of the common diagnoses listed in *DSM-5*, but remember that many troubled people don't exactly fit into any of them.

concept check

1. **Is it possible for people with different symptoms to get the same diagnosis?**

2. **What is the advantage of rating a person along several dimensions, instead of giving a categorical diagnosis?**

Answers

1. Yes. In *DSM-5*, many diagnoses are based on variable combinations of symptoms, such as six out of column A or six out of column B.

2. Rating someone along several dimensions recognizes that a person can have any symptom to various degrees, and can have symptoms that would fit the descriptions of more than one disorder.

Is Anyone Normal?

According to several surveys, nearly half of all people in the United States will have a *DSM* disorder at some point in life. If that statistic is even close to accurate, one implication is obvious: Most of the people who qualify for a psychological diagnosis are not a rare group who would stand out immediately from everyone else. If at some point in your life, you have a bout of psychological distress, remember that you have plenty of company.

This module has suggested skepticism about whether mental illnesses fall into discrete categories. Nevertheless, the rest of this chapter presents research on anxiety disorders, depression, schizophrenia, and so forth as if the categorical approach were valid. The reason is that most research so far has focused on specific categories. A further reason is that research on anxiety or depression is equally applicable regardless of whether we consider them to be categories or dimensions.

Summary

*   *The biopsychosocial model.* The American Psychiatric Association defines mental disorder as a clinically significant disturbance in an individual's cognition, emotion regulation, or behavior. It is sometimes difficult to apply that definition, because of disagreements over what constitutes a significant disturbance. (page 480)
*   *Cultural differences.* Patterns of abnormality vary among cultures, partly because people copy one another's behaviors, including abnormal ones. (page 480)
*   *The categorical approach.* The *Diagnostic and Statistical Manual of Mental Disorders (DSM-5)* and the *International Statistical Classification of Diseases and Related Health Problems* tenth edition (ICD-10) list categories of mental illness and the criteria for diagnosing them. (page 481)

*   *Difficulties of diagnosis.* Diagnosis of mental disorder is difficult because no laboratory test is sufficiently valid, and because the line separating normal from abnormal is a matter of judgment. (page 482)
*   *Problems with the categorical approach.* Most troubled people fit two or more diagnoses at least partly. Also, the causes of various disorders overlap, and the treatment designed for one disorder may help with another. (page 482)
*   *An alternative.* Many psychologists believe it would be better to rate each person along several continuous dimensions of symptoms instead of applying a categorical diagnosis. (page 482)
*   *Personality disorders.* A personality disorder is a maladaptive way of dealing with the environment or other people. (page 483)

Key Terms

biopsychosocial model (page 480)

Diagnostic and Statistical Manual of Mental Disorders (DSM) (page 482)

International Statistical Classification of Diseases and Related Health Problems tenth edition (ICD-10) (page 482)

personality disorder (page 483)

Review Questions

1. How is *DSM* useful to researchers?
    (a) It explains the statistical tests for evaluating experimental results.
    (b) It identifies the places where it will be easy to find people with any disorder.
    (c) It clarifies the procedures for obtaining informed consent.
    (d) It increases consistency in how disorders are diagnosed.

2. Why is it easy for people with different symptoms to get the same diagnosis?
    (a) When in doubt, a therapist calls anyone "psychotic."
    (b) Behavioral observations do not always match the laboratory results.
    (c) Many disorders are characterized in an either-or fashion.
    (d) Many therapists do not rely on DSM.

3. Why is it often difficult to give a clear diagnosis?
    (a) Some therapists rely on behavior, and others use laboratory tests.
    (b) Many people have rare disorders that are unfamiliar to a therapist.
    (c) *DSM* does not list enough categories.
    (d) Many people have symptoms that partly match more than one category.

4. What is an alternative to the categorical approach to diagnosis?
    (a) Wait until laboratory tests are validated before making a diagnosis.
    (b) Rate each person's symptoms along several dimensions.
    (c) Use the MMPI, Rorschach, and other personality tests.
    (d) Let each therapist use his or her own system.

Answers: 1d, 2c, 3d, 4b.

module 15.2

Anxiety Disorders and Obsessive-Compulsive Disorder

After studying this module, you should be able to:

1. Describe generalized anxiety disorder and panic disorder.
2. Explain why learned avoidance responses are so resistant to extinction.
3. Evaluate the classical conditioning explanation for a phobia.
4. Describe obsessive-compulsive disorder.
5. Explain how therapists treat phobias and obsessive-compulsive disorder.

You go to the beach, looking forward to an afternoon of swimming and surfing. Will you stay out of the water if someone tells you that a shark attacked a swimmer yesterday? What if the shark attack was a month ago? What if someone saw a small shark that did not attack anyone?

Staying out of the water because you see a shark is reasonable. Staying out because a small shark was present a few days ago is less sensible. If you refuse to look at ocean photographs because they might *remind* you of sharks, you have a serious problem. Anxiety varies in degree, and excessive anxiety interferes with life in many ways.

Disorders with Excessive Anxiety

Many people are troubled by anxiety and by their attempts to avoid anxiety. The distinction between fear and anxiety is that fear is tied to a specific situation, whereas anxiety is a persistent apprehensive feeling you cannot easily escape. ▼ Figure 15.3 shows how many people in six countries have an anxiety

disorders within a year (Bijl et al., 2003; Murali, 2001). Although the prevalence varies, all surveys agree that anxiety disorders occur throughout the world, that they are more common in women than in men, more common in young adults than old, more common in English-speaking countries than in others, and more common in white people than in blacks (Nay, Brown, & Roberson-Nay, Remes, Brayne, van der Linde, & Lafortune, 2016; Somers, Goldner, Waraich, & Hsu, 2006). People with either anxiety or depression are likely to have the other one also (Jacobson & Newman, 2017).

Several explanations have been offered for why women experience more anxiety than men. From an evolutionary standpoint, one explanation is that women have always been more vulnerable, and therefore evolution may have favored increased anxiety to avoid dangerous situations. Another explanation is that women learn to be anxious, because of more vulnerability here and now. The greater prevalence of anxiety in whites than in blacks is puzzling, because blacks are more likely to face stressful experiences (Erving, Thomas, & Frazier, 2019; Gibbs et al., 2013; ▼ Figure 15.4).

Anxiety disorders are also more common among people with physical ailments or abnormalities. People with *joint laxity* (the ability to bend fingers farther than usual, popularly called "double-jointedness") tend to experience more fears than average, and they are more likely than average to develop anxiety disorders (T. O. Smith et al., 2014).

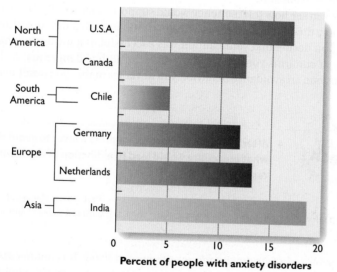

▲ **Figure 15.3** Percentage of people in six countries who have an anxiety disorder within a given year. (Based on data from "The prevalence of treated and untreated mental disorders in five countries," by R. V. Bijl, R. de Graaf, E. Hiripi, R. C. Kessler, R. Kohn, D. R. Offord, et al., 2003. *Health Affairs, 22,* pp. 122–133; and "Epidemiological study of prevalence of mental disorders in India," by M. S. Murali, 2001. *Indian Journal of Community Medicine, 26,* p. 198.)

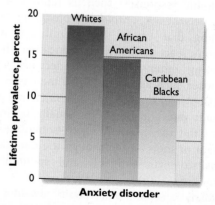

▲ **Figure 15.4** Lifetime prevalence of anxiety disorders for whites in the United States, African Americans, and Caribbean blacks who immigrated to the United States. (Based on data of Gibbs et al., 2013)

Generalized Anxiety Disorder (GAD)

People with **generalized anxiety disorder (GAD)** have *frequent, exaggerated worries*. They worry that "I might get sick," "My daughter might get sick," "I might lose my job," or "I might not be able to pay my bills." Although they face no more actual danger than anyone else, they grow so tense, irritable, and fatigued that they have trouble enjoying life (Henning, Turk, Mennin, Fresco, & Heimberg, 2007). Generalized anxiety disorder often overlaps with other anxiety disorders or with depression.

Panic Disorder (PD)

Suddenly, you feel warm all over. You breathe faster and faster, and your heart is pounding vigorously for no apparent reason. You feel dizzy and nauseated, you sweat profusely, and your hands are shaking. A few minutes later, you return to normal. No heart attack would end so quickly. What happened?

You have just read about a panic attack. People with **panic disorder (PD)** *have frequent anxiety and occasional attacks of panic—rapid breathing, increased heart rate, chest pains, sweating, faintness, and trembling.* As with all anxiety disorders, research shows clear signs of heritability, but no identified gene produces a large effect, and even the genes with small effects overlap the genes that predispose to depression and other disorders (Ohi et al., 2020; Shimada-Sugimoto, Otowa, & Hettema, 2015). You may as well get used to that statement. Every psychological disorder has at least moderate heritability, but except for one gene related to alcohol use, no identifiable gene controls much of the variance.

Panic disorder is linked to having strong autonomic responses, such as rapid heartbeat and **hyperventilation**, *rapid deep breathing*. Almost anything that causes hyperventilation makes the body react as if it were suffocating, thereby triggering other sympathetic nervous system responses such as sweating and increased heart rate (Coplan et al., 1998; Klein, 1993). Fluctuations in heart rate and breathing usually begin well before the panic attack itself—sometimes half an hour or more—even though the panic attack seems to occur suddenly and spontaneously (Meuret et al., 2011).

Many people with panic disorder also develop **agoraphobia** (from *agora*, the Greek word for "marketplace"), *an excessive fear of open or public places*, or **social phobia**, *a severe avoidance of other people and a fear of doing anything in public.* They

develop these fears because they are afraid of being incapacitated or embarrassed by a panic attack in a public place. In a sense, they are afraid of their fear itself (McNally, 1990).

A common treatment focuses on teaching the patient to control breathing and learn to relax (Marchand et al., 2008). Controlling stress helps also. A stressful experience doesn't trigger an immediate panic attack, but it increases the frequency of future attacks (Moitra et al., 2011). In addition, therapists help the person experience sweating and increased heart rate in a controlled setting, showing that these symptoms need not lead to a full-scale panic attack. Panic disorder often follows a pattern of remission and relapse—that is, disappearing for some time and then returning (Nay, Brown, & Roberson-Nay, 2013). Nevertheless, most people experience improvement over time.

3. Why would control of breathing be important in treating panic disorder?

Answer

3. A feeling of being unable to breathe triggers increased heart rate and fear. Getting control of breathing helps calm a person.

Phobia

Sometimes an extreme effort to avoid harm can be harmful itself. Let's begin with avoidance learning, which is relevant to phobias and compulsions. Suppose you learn to press a lever at least once every 15 seconds to avoid electric shocks. After you are responding consistently, the experimenter disconnects the shock generator without telling you. What will you do? You continue pressing, of course. As far as you can tell, nothing has changed, and the response still works. What if you continue dutifully pressing the lever but the experimenter gives you a shock anyway, just for the heck of it? In that case, you probably assume you weren't pressing often enough, and you press even harder. After you have developed an avoidance behavior, it becomes very resistant to extinction.

You can see how this tendency would support superstitions. If you believe that Friday the 13th is dangerous, you are cautious on that day. If nothing goes wrong, you decide that your caution was successful. If a misfortune happens anyway, it confirms your belief that Friday the 13th is dangerous. As long as you continue an avoidance behavior, you never learn that you don't need it.

4. After someone has learned to press a lever to avoid shock, what procedure would lead to extinction of the learned response?

Answer

4. Temporarily prevent pressing the lever. Only by ceasing to press it does anyone discover that pressing is not necessary.

A **phobia** is *a fear that interferes with normal living.* It is not necessarily irrational. A fear of snakes or spiders, for example, is not irrational. Phobia is defined by the degree of the fear. Most people with phobias are not so much afraid of the object itself but of their own reactions (Beck & Emery, 1985). They fear that they will have a heart attack or that they will embarrass themselves by trembling or fainting. Consequently, they vigorously avoid the object and any reminder

Many people who watched the famous shower scene in the movie *Psycho* became afraid to take showers. Actress Janet Leigh, who portrayed the woman killed in that scene, subsequently avoided showers herself.

of it. And as long as they continue avoiding it, they don't learn that the avoidance is unnecessary or exaggerated.

Prevalence

Reportedly, about 7 percent of people suffer a phobia at some time in life, and 5 to 6 percent have a phobia at any given time (Wardenaar, et al., 2017). However, phobias vary from mild to extreme, so the apparent prevalence depends on how many marginal cases we include. Common objects of phobias include public places, public speaking, heights, air travel, water travel, snakes or other dangerous animals, blood, lightning storms, and being observed by strangers (Cox, McWilliams, Clara, & Stein, 2003). Social phobia—avoidance of contact with unfamiliar people—is also common.

Acquiring Phobias

John B. Watson, one of the founders of behaviorism, was the first to argue that phobias and intense fears are learned (Watson & Rayner, 1920). To demonstrate the point, Watson set out to teach a child an intense fear. (He worked before the day of institutional review boards that oversee research ethics.) Watson and Rosalie Rayner studied an 11-month-old child, "Albert B.," who

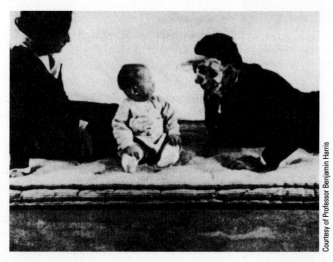

▲ **Figure 15.5** John B. Watson first demonstrated that Albert B. showed little fear of small animals. Then Watson paired a white rat with a loud, frightening noise. Albert became afraid of the white rat, as well as other small animals and odd-looking masks.

had previously shown no fear of animals (see ◄ **Figure 15.5**). They set a white rat in front of him and then struck a large steel bar behind him with a hammer. The sound made Albert whimper and cover his face. After a few repetitions, the presence of the rat made him cry and crawl away. Watson and Rayner declared that they had created a strong fear. Unfortunately, they made no attempt to extinguish it.

Almost a century later, scholars tried to discover Albert's true identity. An initial report pointed to Douglas Merritte, the young son of an unmarried woman who worked at Watson's university, Johns Hopkins. Merritte was almost exactly the same age as the child Watson and Rayner had described, so he seemed a likely candidate (Beck, Levinson, & Irons, 2009). However, a later study identified another child, also the son of an unmarried woman working at Johns Hopkins. This child, named Albert Barger, was almost exactly the same age as Douglas Meritte, matched the weight that Watson had recorded for "Albert B.," and now seems almost certainly to have been the child Watson studied. Albert lived a long, mentally healthy life. He did dislike being around dogs and other animals, but we will never know whether that mild avoidance had anything to do with Watson's research study (Powell, Digdon, Harris, & Smithson, 2014).

Regardless of the questionable ethics and scientific weaknesses of the study, Watson and Rayner's explanation of phobias ignored important questions: First, why do many people develop phobias toward objects that have never injured them? Some people with phobias can indeed trace them to a specific frightening event, but many other people cannot, and many people who do have traumatic experiences fail to develop phobias (Field, 2006). Genetic predisposition to fearfulness is part of the answer, but certainly not the whole story (Van Houtem et al., 2013).

Furthermore, why are some phobias more common than others? And why are phobias so persistent?

concept check

5. In classical conditioning terms, what was the conditioned stimulus (CS) in Watson and Rayner's experiment? The unconditioned stimulus (UCS)? If they had tried to extinguish the fear, what would have been the procedure?

Answer

5. The CS was the white rat. The UCS was the loud noise. To extinguish the fear, they could have presented the rat repeatedly without the loud noise.

what's the evidence?

Learning Fear by Observation

Given that many people develop phobias without any traumatic experience, maybe they learn their phobias by watching others. Susan Mineka and her colleagues demonstrated that monkeys learn fears by observing other monkeys (Mineka, 1987; Mineka, Davidson, Cook, & Keir, 1984). This animal study sheds light on important human issues.

First Study

Hypothesis Monkeys that see other monkeys avoid a snake will develop the same fear.

Method Nearly all wild-born monkeys show a fear of snakes, but laboratory monkeys do not. Mineka put a laboratory-reared monkey with a wild-born monkey and let them both see a snake (see ▼ Figure 15.6). The lab monkey

Wild-reared monkey   **Lab-reared monkey**

a   Wild-reared monkey shows fear of snake.   Lab-reared monkey shows no fear of snake.

b   Lab-reared monkey learns fear of snake by observing wild-reared monkey and snake.

c   Barrier masks snake from view of lab-reared monkey.   Lab-reared monkey does not learn fear when snake is not visible.

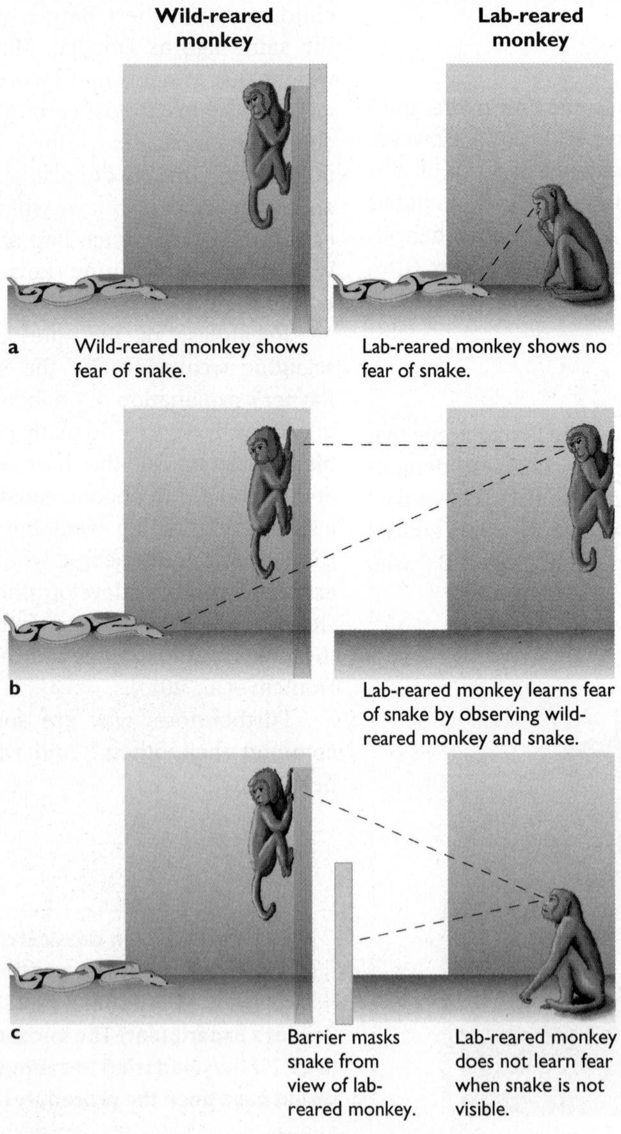

▲ **Figure 15.6** A lab-reared monkey learns to fear snakes from the reactions of a wild-reared monkey. But if the snake is not visible, the lab-reared monkey learns no fear.

watched the wild monkey shriek and run away. Later, Mineka tested the lab monkey's response to a snake.

Results When the lab monkey saw its partner shriek and run away from the snake, it too shrieked, ran away, and turned to see what was frightening (see **Figure 15.6b**). ("Aha! Learned something today. Snakes are bad for monkeys.") It continued to fear the snake when tested by itself, even months later.

Interpretation The lab monkey learned a fear because it saw its partner's fear. But Mineka asked a further question: What was the critical experience—seeing the other monkey show fear *of snakes* or seeing the other monkey show fear *of anything*? To find out, Mineka conducted a second experiment.

Second Study

Hypothesis A monkey learns a fear from another monkey only if it sees *what* the other monkey fears.

Method A lab-reared monkey watched a wild-reared monkey through a window. The wild monkey saw a snake, and it reacted with fear. The lab monkey saw the wild monkey's fear without seeing the snake. Later, the lab monkey was placed with a snake.

Results The lab monkey showed no fear of the snake.

Interpretation To develop a fear of snakes, the observer monkey needed to see that the other monkey was frightened of snakes, not just that it was frightened (see Figure 15.5c). Similarly, children learn fears by observing adults' fears (Dunne & Ashew, 2013).

Some Phobias Are More Common Than Others

Imagine that you survey your friends. You can actually survey them, if you wish, but it's easy enough to imagine the results. You ask them:

- Are you afraid of snakes?
- Are you afraid of cars?
- Have you ever been bitten by a snake or seen someone else bitten?
- Have you ever been injured in a car accident or seen someone else injured?

You know what to expect. Far more people have been injured or seen someone injured by cars than by snakes, but far more are afraid of snakes than cars. Few people have phobias of cars, guns, tools, or electricity, even though they produce many injuries. When my son Sam was a toddler, three times that we know about he stuck his finger into an electric outlet. He even had a name for it: "Smoky got me again." But he never developed a fear of electricity or electric devices.

Why do people develop fears of some objects more readily than other objects? One explanation

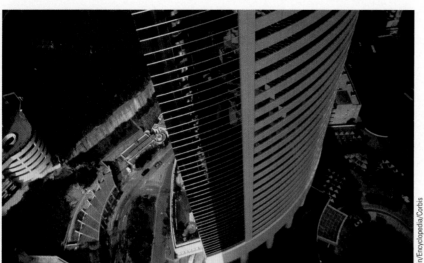

Many people are afraid of extreme heights, partly because the danger is hard to control.

is that we may be evolutionarily prepared to learn certain fears easily (Öhman & Mineka, 2003; Seligman, 1971). Nearly every infant develops a fear of heights and unfamiliar people, especially men. Heights and unfamiliar adult males have been dangerous throughout mammalian evolution. Less universal but still widespread are the fears of snakes, darkness, and confined spaces, which have been dangerous throughout primate (monkey and ape) evolution. Cars, guns, and electricity became dangerous only within the last few generations. Our predisposition to develop fears and phobias corresponds to how long various items have been dangerous in our evolutionary history (Bracha, 2006). In support of this idea, people who receive electric shocks paired with snake pictures quickly develop a strong conditioned response. People who receive shocks paired with pictures of houses learn a much weaker response (Öhman, Eriksson, & Olofsson, 1975). People are also slow to associate shock with a photo of a close friend or family member (Hornstein, Fanselow, & Eisenberger, 2016).

However, evolution is not the only explanation for why you learn a snake or spider fear more easily than a fear of houses. Yes, you have hurt yourself with tools and you have been in a car accident or seen others injured in a car accident. But how many safe experiences have you had with tools and cars? In contrast, how many safe experiences have you had with snakes or spiders? What matters is not just the number of bad experiences but also the number of safe experiences.

Also, people most often develop phobias of objects that they cannot predict or control. If you are afraid of spiders, you must be constantly on the alert, because they could be anywhere. Lightning is also unpredictable and uncontrollable. In contrast, you don't have to worry that hammers, saws, or electric outlets will take you by surprise.

6. Why are we more likely to develop phobias of snakes and spiders than of cars or electric outlets? Offer three explanations.

Treatment for Phobias

Phobias sometimes last for years. Remembering the discussion about avoidance learning, you see why phobias are difficult to extinguish: If you have learned to press a lever to avoid shock, you may not stop pressing long enough to find out that you no longer need to respond. Similarly, if you always avoid snakes or heights or open places, you don't learn that your avoidance is unnecessary or excessive.

A common, successful type of therapy for phobia is exposure therapy, also known as systematic desensitization, *a method of gradually exposing people to the object of their fear* (Wolpe, 1961). Someone with a phobia of snakes, for example, is exposed to pictures of a snake in the reassuring environment of a therapist's office. The therapist might start with a cartoon drawing and gradually work up to a black-and-white photograph, a color photograph, and then a real snake (see ▼ Figure 15.7). Or the therapist might start with the snake itself (with the client's consent). The client is terrified at first, but the autonomic nervous system is not capable of sustaining a permanent panic. Gradually, the person becomes calmer and learns, "It's not that bad after all. Here I am, not far from that horrid snake, and I'm not having a heart attack." Getting the client to actively approach the

▲ Figure 15.7 Here a therapist treats fear of water by exposing someone to the fear under calming conditions.

feared object makes the procedure even more effective (Jones, Vilensky, Vasey, & Fazio, 2013).

Exposure therapy resembles Skinner's shaping procedure. The person masters one step before going on to the next. If the distress becomes too great, the therapist goes back several steps. Exposure is combined with social learning: The person with a phobia watches the therapist or other people display a fearless response to the object.

However, most therapists do not keep handy a supply of snakes, spiders, and so forth. Increasingly, they use virtual reality (Coelho, Waters, Hine, & Wallis, 2009): The client wears a helmet that displays a virtual-reality scene, as shown in ▶ **Figure 15.8**. For example, a client with a phobia of heights can view going up a glass elevator or crossing a narrow bridge over a chasm. This technology provides control of the situation, including the option of quickly turning off the display. Research has found this method to be highly effective, and most clients prefer confronting their fears with virtual reality than with the real thing (Carl et al., 2019).

Exposure therapy is effective in most cases, especially if someone's anxiety is not too severe (Böhlein et al., 2020). However, phobias sometimes return. For an explanation, recall the discussion of classical and operant conditioning. Exposure therapy is extinction of the original learning, but extinction just competes with original learning, without erasing it. When time passes after an extinction procedure, spontaneous recovery is likely—that is, a return of the original learned response. In animal learning, a good way to minimize spontaneous recovery is to repeat the extinction procedure in several environments (Laborda & Miller, 2013). Similarly, exposure therapy is likely to be more effective if it is repeated in as many ways, places, and times as possible, even after the phobia appears to be gone.

Boris Horvat/AFP/Getty Images

▲ **Figure 15.8** Virtual reality lets a patient with a phobia of heights experience heights without leaving the therapist's office.

7. How does exposure therapy resemble extinction of a learned shock-avoidance response?

Answer

7. To extinguish a learned shock-avoidance response, prevent the response so that the individual learns that a failure to respond is not dangerous. Similarly, in exposure therapy, the patient is prevented from fleeing the feared stimulus. He or she learns that the danger is not as great as imagined.

Obsessive-Compulsive Disorder

People with **obsessive-compulsive disorder (OCD)** have two problems. An **obsession** is a *repetitive, unwelcome stream of thought*, such as worrying about doing something shameful. A **compulsion** is a *repetitive, almost irresistible urge to an action*. Obsessions generally lead to compulsions, just as an itching sensation leads to scratching. For example, someone obsessed about dirt and disease develops compulsions of continual cleaning and washing. Someone obsessively worried about doing something shameful develops compulsive rituals that maintain rigorous self-control.

An estimated 2 to 3 percent of all people in the United States suffer from obsessive-compulsive disorder at some time in life, most of them to a mild degree, although the severe cases can be disabling (Karno, Golding, Sorenson, & Burnam, 1988). The usual age of onset is between the ages of 10 and 25. Twin studies indicate a moderate degree of genetic influence, but no common genetic variant has a large effect (Lopez-Sola et al., 2014).

Earlier editions of *DSM* listed OCD among the anxiety disorders, but *DSM-5* lists it separately. Although people with OCD do show anxiety, they tend to experience disgust more often (Pauls, Abramovitch, Rauch, & Geller, 2014). They also feel guilty about certain impulses—perhaps an impulse to engage in a sexual act that they consider shameful, an impulse to hurt someone, or an impulse to commit suicide. Often they believe that thinking something makes it more likely to happen, or that thinking about a contemptible act is as bad as actually doing it (Coughtrey, Shafran, Lee, & Rachman, 2013). They decide, "I don't want to ever think that terrible thought again."

However, vigorously trying to avoid a thought can make it even more intrusive. As a child, the Russian novelist Leo Tolstoy once organized a club with an unusual qualification: A prospective member had to stand alone in a corner *without thinking about a white bear* (Simmons, 1949). If you think that sounds easy, try it. Ordinarily, you might go months between thoughts about polar bears, but when you try *not* to think about them, you can think of little else.

Dan Guravich/Documentary Value/Corbis

try it yourself

It's probably a long time since you last thought about polar bears. But see what happens if you are trying as hard as possible to *avoid* thinking about them.

The most common compulsions are cleaning and checking. Another common one is counting one's steps, counting objects, or counting almost anything. One man with obsessive-compulsive disorder could not go to sleep at night until he had counted the corners of every object in the room to make sure that the total was evenly divisible by 16. Others have odd habits such as touching everything they see, trying to arrange objects in a completely symmetrical manner, or walking back and forth through a doorway nine times before leaving a building. Hoarding is yet another common compulsion.

Distrusting Memory

Many obsessive-compulsive people repeatedly check whether the doors and windows are locked and the water faucets are turned off. But then they worry, "Did I *really* check them all, or did I only imagine it?" Because they distrust their memory, they check again and again.

Why do obsessive-compulsive checkers distrust their memory? Several studies found that repeated checking makes the memories less distinct. Suppose you check the kitchen stove to make sure it is turned off. Then you do it again and again several times. The more times you do it, the less distinctly you remember the most recent time you did so, and you might distrust your memory (Radomsky, Dugas, Alcolado, & Lavoie, 2014; van den Hout & Kindt, 2003). A vicious cycle results: Because of repeated checking, you doubt your memory, and because you doubt your memory, you want to check again.

Therapies

Most people with obsessive-compulsive disorder eventually improve to some extent even without treatment (Skoog & Skoog, 1999). Still, no one wants to wait years for recovery. The therapy best supported by the evidence is *exposure therapy with response prevention:* The person is simply prevented from performing the obsessive ritual (Rosa-Alcázar, Sánchea-Meca, Gómez-Conesa, & Marín-Martínez, 2008). Someone might be prevented from cleaning the house or checking the doors more than once before going to sleep. The point is to demonstrate that nothing catastrophic occurs if one leaves a little mess in the house or runs a slight risk of leaving a door unlocked.

Also, many people with obsessive-compulsive disorder respond well to a cognitive intervention to help them reinterpret their thoughts and images (Coughtrey et al., 2013). In some cases, antidepressant drugs also help (Kotapati, 2019).

8. Suppose someone reports that a new therapy relieves many cases of obsessive-compulsive disorder. Why would it be important to have a no-treatment or waiting-list control group?

Answer

8. A certain degree of recovery over time is common even without treatment. We need to see whether the new therapy produces the outcome better than just waiting.

---

in closing | module 15.2

Emotions and Avoidance

Phobias and obsessive-compulsive disorder illustrate some of the complex links between emotions and cognitions. People with phobias experience emotional attacks associated with a particular thought, image, or situation. People with obsessive-compulsive disorder experience repetitive thoughts that produce emotional distress. In both conditions, most people know that their reactions are exaggerated, but mere awareness of the problem does not correct it. Dealing with such conditions requires attention to emotions, cognitions, and the links between them.

Summary

- *Anxiety disorders.* Anxiety disorders tend to overlap with depression. Anxiety disorders are more common for women than men, and more for white people than black people. Many physical illnesses are associated with increased anxiety. (page 485)
- *Panic disorder.* Panic disorder is characterized by bouts of hyperventilation and increased heart rate. It often accompanies agoraphobia, fear of public places. (page 486)
- *Avoidance learning.* A learned avoidance response is slow to extinguish, unless the response is prevented. Similarly, phobias persist because people do not discover that the avoidance is unnecessary. (page 486)
- *Phobia.* A phobia is a fear so extreme that it interferes with normal living. Phobias are learned through observation as well as through experience. (page 486)
- *Common phobias.* People often develop phobias for items that have been dangerous throughout human existence, suggesting an evolutionary predisposition. Alternative explanations are that we develop phobias for items that are difficult to predict or control, and items with which we have had few safe experiences. (page 488)
- *Exposure therapy.* A common therapy for phobia is exposure therapy. The patient relaxes while being exposed to the object

of the phobia. The procedure is generally successful, although the phobia may return later. (page 489)

- *Obsessive-compulsive disorder (OCD).* People with obsessive-compulsive disorder have distressing thoughts or impulses. Many also perform repetitive behaviors. (page 490)

- *Compulsive checking.* Compulsive checkers constantly double-check their actions and invent elaborate rituals. Repeatedly checking something leads to decreased confidence in the memory of having checked it. (page 491)

Key Terms

agoraphobia (page 486)

compulsion (page 490)

exposure therapy (page 489)

generalized anxiety disorder (GAD)
  (page 486)

hyperventilation (page 486)

obsession (page 490)

obsessive-compulsive disorder (OCD)
  (page 490)

panic disorder (PD) (page 486)

phobia (page 486)

social phobia (page 486)

systematic desensitization (page 489)

Review Questions

1. Which of the following is most common for people with panic disorder?
   (a) Bipolar disorder
   (b) Obsessive-compulsive disorder
   (c) Agoraphobia
   (d) Anorexia nervosa

2. Panic disorder is associated with bursts of overactivity by which of these?
   (a) Corpus callosum
   (b) Primary visual cortex
   (c) Sympathetic nervous system
   (d) Parasympathetic nervous system

3. What is unusual about avoidance learning, compared to other learning?
   (a) It continues even when there is no need for it.
   (b) It develops more rapidly in older than in younger individuals.
   (c) It requires simultaneous activation of the sympathetic and parasympathetic nervous systems.
   (d) It does not generalize to other stimuli.

4. In Watson and Rayner's experiment, what was the conditioned response?
   (a) A white rat
   (b) A loud noise

   (c) Fear responses
   (d) Relaxation

5. What happens if a monkey watches another monkey show fear?
   (a) It increases its own fear of almost everything.
   (b) It develops a fear of the same thing the other monkey fears.
   (c) It tries to comfort the other monkey.
   (d) It decreases its own fear of almost everything.

6. The return of a phobia long after exposure therapy is comparable to which aspect of classical conditioning?
   (a) Acquisition
   (b) Extinction
   (c) Spontaneous recovery
   (d) Generalization

7. What is one reason why obsessive-compulsive checkers continue checking?
   (a) They distrust their memory.
   (b) They experience pleasure and relief from checking.
   (c) They impress other people with their conscientiousness.
   (d) They experience spontaneous recovery.

Answers: 1c, 2c, 3a, 4c, 5b, 6c, 7a.

iStock.com/SDI Productions

module 15.3

Substance-Use Disorders

After studying this module, you should be able to:

1. Define substance dependence and addiction.

2. Discuss possible explanations for addiction.

3. Describe a way to identify young people who may be at increased risk of alcohol abuse.

4. Describe treatments for alcoholism and opiate abuse.

How would you like to volunteer for an experiment? I want to implant into your brain a little device that will automatically lift your mood. There are still a few kinks in it, but most people who have tried it say that it makes them feel good at least some of the time, and some people like it a great deal.

I should tell you about the possible risks. My device will endanger your health and reduce your life expectancy. Some people believe it causes brain damage, but they haven't proved that charge, so I don't think you should worry about it. Your behavior will change a good bit, though. You may have difficulty concentrating, for example. The device affects some people more than others. If you happen to be strongly affected, you will have difficulty completing your education, getting or keeping a job, and carrying on a satisfactory personal life. But if you are lucky, you might avoid all that. Anyway, you can quit the experiment anytime you decide. You should know, though, that the longer the device remains in your brain, the harder it is to remove.

I cannot pay you for taking part in this experiment. In fact, you will have to pay me. But I'll give you a bargain rate: only $10 for the first week and then a little more each week as time passes. One other thing: Technically speaking, this experiment is illegal. We probably won't get caught, but if we do, we could both go to prison.

What do you say? Is it a deal? I presume you will say "no." I get very few volunteers. And yet, if I change the term *brain device* to *drug* and change *experiment* to *drug deal*, it is amazing how many volunteers come forward. In this module, we focus on addiction.

Dependence and Substance Use Disorder

People who *suffer withdrawal symptoms when they abstain from a drug* have a **physical dependence** on it. People who *are unable to quit a self-destructive habit* are said to have an **addiction** or **substance use disorder**. Dependence usually leads to substance use disorder, but the terms are not synonymous.

Heroin withdrawal resembles a week-long bout of severe flu, with aching limbs, intense chills, vomiting, and diarrhea. Unfortunately, even after people have endured withdrawal, they still sometimes crave the drug.

Ed Kashi/Terra /Corbis

Opiate dependence generally has the most rapid onset. At one time it was widely believed that addiction was not likely when opiates were used for pain relief. As a result, opiates were over-prescribed and opiate addiction became more widespread, especially in certain parts of the United States. Many people who began using prescription opiates for pain relief continued using the opiates after the pain was gone, and some of them later switched to heroin, fentanyl, or other drugs. Publicity about this problem led to more restraint in opiate prescriptions, beginning around 2016, but the problem of massive opiate use lingers.

The difference between drug use and drug addiction relates mainly to how much the drug disrupts one's life. People who attend Alcoholics Anonymous for the first time often ask, "How can I tell whether I am an alcoholic?" You should consider yourself an alcoholic if you answer yes to these two questions: Does alcohol use cause serious trouble in your life? And do you sometimes decide you will quit after a certain amount, and then find yourself unable to stop at that point? The same questions apply to any other addiction.

Most people who use a drug do not develop an addiction, and a major scientific question is, what causes drug use to develop into an addiction? Addictive drugs increase the release of dopamine in a small brain area called the *nucleus accumbens,* which is essential for attention and reinforcement (Berridge & Robinson, 1998; Koob & LeMoal, 1997; Robinson & Berridge, 2000). ▼ Figure 15.9 shows the location of the nucleus accumbens. Dopamine release increases after an unexpected reward or a greater-than-expected reward, and it is important for motivation to seek food, sex, or other rewards (Solinas, Belujon, Fernagut, Jaber, & Thiriet, 2019).

However, beware of assuming that a drug becomes addictive simply because it increases the release of dopamine. Compulsive gambling and video game playing, which have much in common with drug addictions (Gentile, 2009), release dopamine in the nucleus accumbens after they become addictive (Ko et al., 2009; Koepp et al., 1998). It would be

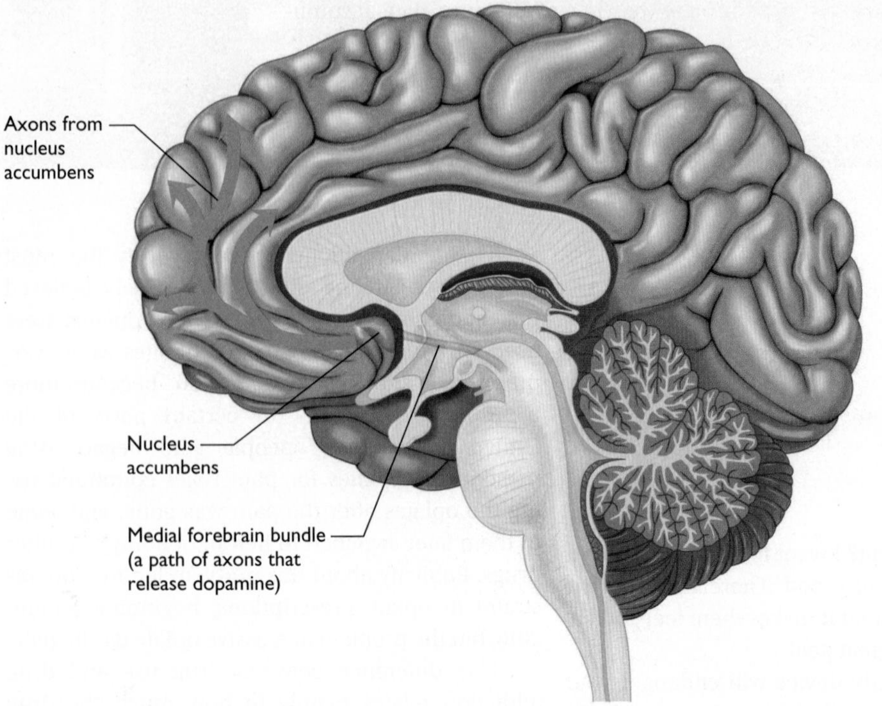

Axons from nucleus accumbens

Nucleus accumbens

Medial forebrain bundle (a path of axons that release dopamine)

▲ **Figure 15.9** The nucleus accumbens is a small brain area that is critical for the motivating effects of many experiences, including drugs, food, and sex. Abused drugs increase the activity of the neurotransmitter dopamine in this area.

What Motivates Addictive Behavior?

People use alcohol or other drugs initially for pleasure, but an addiction is more insistent. Terry Robinson and Kent Berridge (2000, 2001) distinguished between "liking" and "wanting." Ordinarily, you like the things you want, but not always. You might *want* to eat a healthy diet instead of a plate of chocolate fudge, no matter how much you would *like* the fudge. Addicted drug users want the drug more and more, but they usually do not like it as much as before, and certainly they do not like the consequences for their lives (Berridge & Robinson, 2016). Why do addictive behaviors continue with such intensity? Many explanations have been offered, and all contribute to some extent (Bechara et al., 2019).

One reason is to escape unpleasant feelings. Abstaining from a drug leads to withdrawal symptoms. Withdrawal symptoms from prolonged alcoholism include sweating, nausea, sleeplessness, and sometimes hallucinations or seizures. With opiate drugs, the withdrawal symptoms include anxiety, insomnia, vomiting, diarrhea, and sweating. Consistent cigarette smokers experience unpleasant mood when they abstain (Baker et al., 2012). Abstaining from gambling or similar habits can lead to *an insistent craving without physical withdrawal symptoms*, a pattern called psychological dependence.

Another explanation for addiction is that someone who takes a drug to relieve withdrawal symptoms learns its power to relieve distress, and then begins using it to relieve other kinds of displeasure. After people have quit drugs, they often relapse during periods of financial or social difficulties (Baker, Piper, McCarthy, Majeskie, & Fiore, 2004). The relief-from-distress explanation works, but it seems incomplete. People often use a substance so obsessively that its effect on their lives produces more distress than it relieves.

Neuroscientists have demonstrated that when an addictive behavior strongly activates the nucleus accumbens, it stimulates synaptic changes of the same type that occur in learning. For example, after repeated cocaine use, the synapses learn to respond strongly to cocaine and reminders of cocaine, but they decrease their response to other reinforcers. The result is a craving for cocaine, increased sensitivity to cues for cocaine, and decreased interest in most other activities (Lubman et al., 2009; Mameli & Lüscher, 2011). Cocaine use then becomes the most efficient way to produce the synaptic activities normally associated with pleasure (Willuhn, Burgeno, Groblewski, & Phillips, 2014). Similarly, nicotine addiction, alcohol abuse, and other addictions sometimes reduce the pleasure from other activities (Augier et al., 2018; Leventhal et al., 2014). Persistent use of cocaine or other drugs can also impair the activity of the prefrontal cortex, an area that is important for inhibiting impulses (Luescher, Robbins, & Everitt, 2020; Volkow et al., 1993).

Unfortunately, this description of brain changes makes the situation sound hopeless, as if exposure to a drug leads automatically to addiction. Addiction depends on other circumstances besides the drug itself. Long ago, research found that rats exposed to cocaine always developed a strong addiction. But then other researchers noted that the rats in those studies lived in small,

misleading to say they became addictive *because* they release dopamine. They began releasing dopamine as they became addictive. Furthermore, although addictive drugs increase dopamine release, some of them do not increase it by much, and the probability of addiction does not correlate strongly with the amount of dopamine release. Furthermore, drugs that block dopamine release do not eliminate the reward value of opiate drugs. In short, although dopamine release is certainly part of addiction, it cannot be the whole story (Nutt, Lingford-Hughes, Erritzoe, & Stokes, 2015).

It is hard to put limits on what can or cannot be addictive. In a hospital ward for treating alcoholism, one patient moved his bed into the men's room (Cummings, 1979). At first, the hospital staff ignored his curious behavior. Then, more and more patients moved their beds into the men's room. Eventually, the staff discovered what was happening. These men, deprived of alcohol, had found that by drinking about 30 liters of water per day and urinating the same amount (which was why they moved into the men's room), they could alter the acid-to-base balance of their blood enough to produce a sensation like drunkenness. (Do *not* try this yourself. Some people have died from an overdose of water.)

concept check

9. **Does it make sense to distinguish between substances that are and are not addictive?**

solitary-confinement cages with nothing else to do. When researchers studied rats living in larger cages with other rats and objects to explore, the rats used less of the drugs (Alexander, Coambs, & Hadaway, 1978; Solinas, Thiriet, El Rawas, Lardeux, & Jaber, 2009). Later research also found that intermittent use of cocaine produced more addiction than extensive use all at one time (Kawa, Valenta, Kennedy, & Robinson, 2019). In short, addiction depends on more than just total amount of exposure to the drug.

concept check

10. How do stressful experiences relate to addiction?

Answer

10. People who at first use a drug for pleasure discover that it can help reduce stress. Then, even after they have quit using the drug for some time, stressful experiences reawaken a craving.

Genetics and Family Background

Twin studies indicate a substantial genetic influence on abuse of alcohol or other drugs, in combination with important environmental influences, especially the influence of neighborhood quality (Kendler, Maes, Sundquist, Ohlsson, & Sundquist, 2014; Liu, Blacker, Xu, Fitzmaurice, Lyons, & Tsuang, 2004; Volkow & Boyle, 2018).

Although many genetic variations have small influences on the vulnerability to alcoholism, only one is known to produce substantial effects. That gene affects the liver's ability to metabolize alcohol. The liver converts alcohol into a toxic substance, *acetaldehyde* (ASS-eh-TAL-de-hide), and then uses another enzyme to convert acetaldehyde into harmless *acetic acid*. People vary in the gene for that second enzyme. Those with one form of that gene are slow to convert acetaldehyde into acetic acid.

iStock.com/shironosov

Alcohol abuse is more common in cultures that tolerate it than in cultures that emphasize moderation.

If they drink much alcohol at a time, they accumulate acetaldehyde, feel ill, and experience an extreme hangover. Consequently, they learn to avoid excessive alcohol (Biernacka et al., 2013). Nearly half of Southeast Asians have that genetic variant, and relatively few Asians become alcoholics or binge drinkers (Harada, Agarwal, Goedde, Tagaki, & Ishikawa, 1982; Luczak et al., 2014). A nationwide sample in China found that only 3 percent of people develop alcohol abuse (Huang et al., 2019).

Environmental influences are important also, of course. For example, alcohol abuse is more prevalent in Irish culture, which tolerates heavy drinking, than among Jews or Italians, who emphasize drinking in moderation (Cahalan, 1978; Vaillant & Milofsky, 1982). Childhood physical or sexual abuse increases the risk of later alcoholism or substance abuse (Halpern et al., 2018; Schulsinger, Knop, Goodwin, Teasdale, & Mikkelsen, 1986).

what's the evidence?

Predicting Alcoholism

After someone has developed a strong habit of alcohol abuse, quitting is difficult. If we could identify the young people who are at the highest risk for alcoholism, perhaps we could encourage early prevention. At least, psychologists would like to try.

It is useful to distinguish between early-onset and late-onset alcoholism. Early-onset alcoholism develops rapidly, usually by age 25, and usually in men. It is often severe, and it shows a clear genetic basis (Devor, Abell, Hoffman, Tabakoff, & Cloninger, 1994; McGue, 1999). Late-onset alcoholism develops gradually over the years, affects about as many women as men, is generally less severe, and often occurs in people with no family history of alcoholism. Late-onset alcoholism is more a product of painful experiences than of a predisposition that we might measure in young adults. Naturally, not everyone with alcoholism fits neatly into one category or the other, but the research we discuss here focuses on men who might have a predisposition to early-onset alcoholism. Perhaps their behavior might indicate who is more likely to develop alcoholism (Schuckit & Smith, 1997).

Hypothesis Men who underestimate their intoxication after moderate drinking are more likely than others to develop alcoholism later.

Method This study was limited to 18- to 25-year-old men who had a close relative with alcoholism. Presumably, many of these young men, but not all, had inherited a predisposition toward alcoholism. After each of them drank a fixed amount of alcohol, they were asked to walk and to describe how intoxicated they felt. Experimenters measured the stagger or sway when the men walked. Ten years later, the experimenters located as many of these men as possible and asked them about their alcohol use.

Results Of the 81 who either did not sway much when walking or stated that they did not feel intoxicated, 51 (63 percent) became alcoholics within 10 years. Of those who clearly swayed and reported feeling intoxicated, 9 of 52 (17 percent) became alcoholics (Schuckit & Smith, 1997).

Interpretation Someone who starts to stagger and feel intoxicated after drinking a moderate amount may stop drinking at that point. Someone who shows less effect thinks, "I hold my liquor well," and continues drinking. By the time he begins to stagger, he may have drunk enough to impair his judgment. People who don't show much effect of alcohol on their movement nevertheless show a normal amount of impairment in their cognition and self-control (Fillmore & Weafer, 2012; Miller, Hays, & Fillmore, 2012).

Although the original study examined only men, a later study found similar results for women: Women with a family history of alcoholism are more likely than average to report low intoxication, and to experience little body sway after drinking a moderate amount (Eng, Schuckit, & Smith, 2005).

Measuring body sway after people drink alcohol is a time-consuming process. Later research found it possible to achieve similar result just by asking people a few questions, such as how many drinks before you feel dizzy, how many before you stumble, and how many before you slur your speech. Those who report needing more drinks to produce these effects are more likely than average to become heavy drinkers (Schuckit et al., 2007; Schuckit & Smith, 2013).

11. **If you "hold your liquor well" and do not quickly feel intoxicated, is that something to feel good about or something to worry about?**

Answer

11. It is cause for worry. Young people who do not quickly feel intoxicated are more likely than average to develop a habit of alcohol abuse.

Treatments

My mind is a dark place, and I should not be left alone there at night.
—Participant at Alcoholics Anonymous meeting

Many young people who abuse alcohol or other drugs manage to quit or greatly reduce their use later, even without treatment (Genberg et al., 2011; Heyman, 2011). They might have some ups and downs along the way. Quitting is easier for marijuana or amphetamine users than for heroin or cocaine users, but even for the stronger drugs, lifetime addiction is not inevitable (Calabria et al., 2010).

However, many other people find that they cannot quit substance abuse on their own. Eventually, they "hit bottom," discovering that they have damaged their health, their ability to hold a job, and their relationships with friends and family. At that point, they might seek help.

Sometimes you will hear people say that alcoholism or drug addiction is a disease. That is an ambiguous statement, because medicine has no firm definition of "disease." Classifying addiction as a disease helps people feel it is not something to be ashamed of, but it has the unfortunate consequence of implying that it requires a medical intervention. In many cases, behavioral methods of treatment are preferable (Grifell & Hart, 2018).

Alcoholics Anonymous

The most popular treatment for alcoholism in North America is **Alcoholics Anonymous (AA)**, *a self-help group of people who are trying to abstain from alcohol use and help others to do the same.* AA meetings take place in community halls, church basements, and other available spaces. The meeting format varies but often includes study of the book *Alcoholics Anonymous* (Anonymous, 1955) and discussions of participants' individual problems. Some meetings feature an invited speaker. The group has a spiritual focus, including a reliance on "a power greater than ourselves," but it has no affiliation with any particular religion. Although AA imposes no requirements on its members other than an effort to quit alcohol, new members are strongly encouraged to attend 90 meetings during the first 90 days. The idea is to make a strong commitment. If you can discipline yourself to get to that many meetings, you can discipline yourself to make a change in your life. From then on, members attend as often as they like.

Millions of people have participated in the AA program. One reason for its appeal is that all its members have had similar experiences. If someone makes an excuse for drinking and says, "You just don't understand how I feel," others can retort, "Oh, yes we do!" A member who feels the urge to take a drink can phone a fellow member day or night for support. However, the other member offers support, not pampering. Fellow members help someone resist the urge to drink, but they generally won't do much for someone who is already drunk. Membership is free, but members make voluntary contributions toward the cost of renting the meeting place. AA has inspired Narcotics Anonymous (NA), Gamblers Anonymous (GA), and similar self-help groups.

Researchers find that people who regularly attend AA or similar meetings, and who have a strong commitment to the program, are more likely than others to abstain from alcohol and drugs (Gossop, Stewart, & Marsden, 2008; Laffaye, McKellar, Ilgen, & Moos, 2008). However, it is impossible to conduct controlled experiments. AA and NA are voluntary organizations, and people cannot be randomly assigned to participate or not. People who participate probably differ in many ways from those who do not.

Contingency Management

Another approach to treating addictions is *contingency management*. Therapists emphasize the importance of minimizing exposure to the situations that evoke the greatest temptation (Witkiewitz & Marlatt, 2004), and the therapists provide reinforcements, such as a movie pass or a voucher for a pizza, when a breathalyzer or urine sample indicates the absence of alcohol or other drug.

The effectiveness of contingency management is surprising, as the rewards are small. People could have abstained from alcohol and drugs and then used the money they saved to give themselves the same or greater rewards. Evidently, there is something powerful about testing negative for drugs and then receiving an immediate reinforcement.

Medications

Given that addictive drugs release dopamine, many attempts have been made to combat drug abuse by giving drugs that impair transmission at dopamine synapses. These attempts have produced little benefit. Generally, someone with an addiction reacts to the dopamine blocker by increasing the dose of the addictive drug (Solinas et al., 2019).

A more successful treatment for opiate abuse is the drug methadone (METH-uh-don) *which can be offered as a substitute for other opiates.* Chemically similar to morphine and heroin, methadone would produce the same effects if it were taken as an injection. However, when methadone is taken as a pill, it enters the bloodstream gradually and departs gradually. (If morphine or heroin is taken as a pill, much of it is digested without reaching the brain.) Thus, methadone satisfies the craving without producing the "rush" associated with injected opiates. Therefore, methadone does not strongly interfere with important behaviors, such as keeping a job. ■ Table 15.3 compares methadone and morphine.

Methadone does not eliminate the addiction. Most people who try to reduce their use of methadone report that their drug craving returns. Therefore, methadone is a long-term treatment. The drug *buprenorphine* has effects similar to those of methadone. Although methadone or buprenorphine is the most effective known treatment for opiate abuse, it is not always offered.

Another possible treatment for opiate abuse is *cannabidiol*, a non-intoxicating component of marijuana. Small-scale studies have reported that it can decrease the craving caused by drug-related cues (Hurd et al., 2019).

Disulfiram, available under the trade name Antabuse, is often *effective in treating alcoholism*, although it is not widely used (Brewer, Streel, & Skinner, 2017). It was discovered long ago when someone noticed that the workers in a certain rubber manufacturing plant drank very little alcohol. Investigators linked this behavior to *disulfiram*, a chemical that was used in the manufacturing process. The liver converts alcohol into toxic acetaldehyde and then converts acetaldehyde into acetic acid. Disulfiram blocks the conversion of acetaldehyde to acetic acid. When the workers who were exposed to disulfiram drank alcohol, they accumulated acetaldehyde, became ill, suffered severe hangovers, and learned to avoid alcohol.

Alcoholics who agree to take a daily Antabuse pill (disulfiram) know that they will become severely sick if they have a drink. The threat of sickness deters drinking (Fuller & Roth, 1979). By taking a daily Antabuse pill, a recovering alcoholic renews the decision not to drink, and in most cases the person never experiences the sickness. The key to success is compliance with taking the daily pill. Many alcoholics will quit taking Antabuse unless a family member or someone else is supervising.

concept checks

12. Why is it important to supervise both the people taking methadone and the people taking Antabuse?

13. In what way are many southeast Asians similar to someone taking Antabuse?

Answers

12. Someone who didn't swallow the methadone pill could dissolve it in water and inject it to get a high similar to that of heroin or morphine. Or the person could spit it out and later use heroin or morphine. Similarly, someone who omitted the daily Antabuse pill could resume drinking alcohol.

13. Many southeast Asians have a gene that slows the breakdown of acetaldehyde into acetic acid. Therefore, they get sick if they drink much alcohol and they learn to abstain or greatly limit their intake. Antabuse produces effects similar to the gene.

Table 15.3 Comparison of Methadone and Morphine

	Morphine	Methadone by Injection	Methadone Taken Orally
Addictive?	Yes	Yes	Maintains an addiction
Onset	Rapid	Rapid	Slow
"Rush"?	Yes	Yes	No
Relieves craving?	Yes	Yes	Yes

in closing | module 15.3

Substances, the Individual, and Society

Substance abuse is a problem for everyone because of its link to crime, unemployment, drunk driving, and other threats. In the 1970s, the U.S. government declared a "war on drugs." It seems unlikely that we shall ever declare victory in that war. Fighting addiction is more like fighting weeds in your garden. You cannot expect to eliminate all weeds forever. Your best hope is to suppress the weeds enough that they don't seriously interfere with the plants you are trying to cultivate.

Summary

- *Addiction or substance use disorder.* The marks of addiction or substance use disorder are that the activity causes serious trouble in someone's life, and that the person finds it difficult to stop. (page 493)
- *Dopamine.* Addictive substances stimulate dopamine synapses in the nucleus accumbens, a brain area that is associated with attention. However, dopamine alone does not explain addiction. (page 493)
- *Liking and wanting.* People with an addiction intensely want the substance, even if they do not like it as much as before. (page 494)
- *Motivations.* Drug users discover that the drug relieves withdrawal symptoms, and later use it to relieve other distress. Also, addiction sensitizes the brain to that substance and reminders of it. Addiction depends on factors other than the drug itself, such as the social environment. (page 494)
- *Genetics.* Vulnerability to substance abuse is partly heritable. However, the only gene known to produce a large influence on vulnerability is one that influences the breakdown of alcohol. (page 495)
- *Predisposition to alcoholism.* People who are slower than average to feel intoxication from alcohol are more likely than average to become heavy drinkers. (page 495)
- *Alcoholics Anonymous.* The self-help group Alcoholics Anonymous provides the most common treatment for alcoholism in North America. (page 496)
- *Contingency management.* Rewarding people for abstaining from drugs can be an effective treatment. (page 497)
- *Methadone.* Methadone and similar drugs can help opiate abusers by substituting a less disruptive way of stimulating opiate synapses. (page 497)
- *Antabuse.* Antabuse (disulfiram) is effective, though not often used, as a treatment for alcoholism. (page 497)

Key Terms

addiction (page 493)

Alcoholics Anonymous (AA) (page 496)

Antabuse (page 497)

methadone (page 497)

physical dependence (page 493)

psychological dependence (page 494)

substance use disorder (page 493)

Review Questions

1. What characterizes physical dependence on a drug?
   (a) The drug produces increasing amounts of pleasure.
   (b) The drug blocks dopamine synapses in the nucleus accumbens.
   (c) Abstaining from the drug produces withdrawal symptoms.
   (d) The person uses the drug almost every day.

2. Why do many south Asians avoid drinking much alcohol?
   (a) They have a gene that slows the breakdown of alcohol.
   (b) Alcohol does not stimulate the dopamine synapses in their brains.
   (c) They do not experience the withdrawal symptoms that other people do.
   (d) Their taste buds respond more slowly to alcohol, relative to other people.

3. How does early-onset alcoholism differ from later-onset alcoholism?
   (a) Early-onset alcoholism is mostly male, and it has a stronger genetic influence.
   (b) Early-onset alcoholism is mostly male, and it has a weaker genetic influence.
   (c) Early-onset alcoholism is mostly female, and it has a stronger genetic influence.
   (d) Early-onset alcoholism is mostly female, and it has a weaker genetic influence.

4. What kind of people are more likely than average to develop alcohol abuse?
   (a) People for whom alcohol has little influence on dopamine synapses
   (b) People who have a greater than average density of taste buds on the tongue
   (c) People who get intoxicated easily
   (d) People who can drink a fair amount before feeling intoxicated

5. If someone injected methadone instead of swallowing it, what would happen?
   (a) It would have no effect.
   (b) It would produce effects similar to heroin or morphine.
   (c) It would interfere with opiate synapses.
   (d) It would decrease the metabolic breakdown of heroin or morphine.

6. If someone takes a placebo, but believes it is Antabuse, it can be effective anyway. Why?
   (a) Antabuse acts by strengthening inhibitory pathways.
   (b) Antabuse acts to reinforce a decision to avoid alcohol.
   (c) Placebos alter the breakdown of alcohol.
   (d) Antabuse and placebos both stimulate increased cortical activity.

Answers: 1c, 2a, 3a, 4d, 5b, 6b.

iStock.com/SDI Productions

After studying this module, you should be able to:

1. Describe the symptoms and possible causes of major depression.

2. Evaluate the advantages and disadvantages of several treatments for depression.

3. Distinguish bipolar disorder from major depression.

4. List the primary symptoms of schizophrenia.

5. Cite evidence that supports the neurodevelopmental hypothesis of schizophrenia.

6. Describe therapies for schizophrenia.

7. Describe and discuss autism spectrum disorder.

8. Discuss the genetic basis of depression, schizophrenia, and autism spectrum disorder.

All psychological disorders range in severity, but depression, bipolar disorder, and schizophrenia are the most likely to become severe. We shall consider these conditions, along with autism, which also produces long-term limitations.

Depression

People sometimes call themselves depressed when they mean that they are discouraged or disappointed. A **major depression** is a *more extreme condition lasting weeks at a time, during which the person experiences sadness and a lack of interest, pleasure, or motivation.* Many people with depression say they cannot even imagine anything that would make them happy. Depression is usually linked to other problems, especially anxiety (Jacobson & Newman, 2017). About 20 percent of U.S. adults are depressed at some time in life (Kessler, Berglund, Demler, Jin, & Walters, 2005). The reported prevalence is lower in most other countries (Steel et al., 2014). Women experience depression more than men in all cultures for which we have data (Steel et al., 2014).

If you feel miserable after the death of a friend or relative, should your great sadness count as depression? The answer to that question has become controversial (Zachar, First, & Kendler, 2017). The third and fourth editions of *DSM* specified that bereavement following the death of a loved one should not be considered depression, unless the symptoms were severe or if they lasted for more than 2 months. In *DSM-5*, bereavement lasting even 2 weeks can lead to a diagnosis of major depression, although the book does recommend "clinical judgment" to distinguish between a normal response and a psychiatric condition. The argument in favor of this decision was that almost all depression follows a loss of some sort, and therefore, if the symptoms look like depression, then the person is depressed. The contrary view is that bereavement varies from one person to another, and we should not label someone with a "mental illness" because of a more serious than average bereavement.

Nearly all people experiencing depression have sleep abnormalities (Carroll, 1980; Healy & Williams, 1988) (see ◄ **Figure 15.10**). They enter REM sleep faster than average. They wake up early and cannot get back to sleep. Two longitudinal studies found that adolescents who had trouble sleeping were more likely than average to become depressed later (Roane & Taylor, 2008; Roberts & Duong, 2014).

The second module of this chapter noted that anxiety disorders are more common for whites than blacks in the United States. The same is true of depression, as shown in ▼ **Figure 15.11** (Erving et al., 2019; Gibbs et al., 2013). The statistics come from surveys of representative populations, not from therapists' records. This tendency is surprising, because much evidence shows that highly stressful experiences increase the probability of depression (Sasson & Umberson, 2014; Slavich & Irwin, 2014), and blacks in the United States face stressful experiences more often than whites do (Barnes & Bates, 2017). Therefore, psychologists try to explain the "black-white paradox." Many hypotheses have been offered. Perhaps blacks react to stress physically instead of emotionally. Perhaps they get greater social support, or greater benefits from religion. Perhaps they are more likely than whites to react to stress by smoking cigarettes or overeating, sacrificing physical health to improve mood (Mezuk et al., 2010). Perhaps the surveys have overlooked homeless or imprisoned black people with depression. All these hypotheses are difficult to test, but to the

Normal sleep

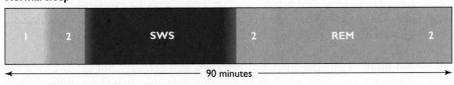

| 1 | 2 | SWS | 2 | REM | 2 |

90 minutes

Depressed sleep

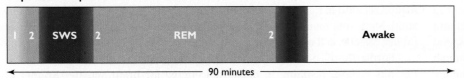

| 1 | 2 | SWS | 2 | REM | 2 | Awake |

90 minutes

▲ **Figure 15.10** During a bout of depression, people enter REM sooner than average and awaken frequently during the night.

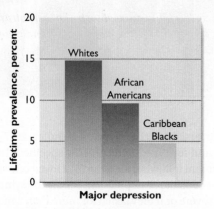

▲ **Figure 15.11** Lifetime prevalence of major depression for whites in the United States, African Americans, and Caribbean blacks who immigrated to the United States. (Based on data of Gibbs et al., 2013)

extent that they have been tested, the evidence so far is not decisive (Barnes & Bates, 2017; Erving et al., 2019; Mouson, 2013, 2014). The explanation remains uncertain.

Although depression is a widespread problem, the good news is that few people remain permanently depressed. Typically, people have an episode of depression that lasts months or maybe years, and then they start feeling better. In perhaps as many as half of cases, people have just one episode and then maintain a satisfactory level of functioning (Rottenberg, Devendorf, Kashdan, & Disabato, 2018).

In other cases, depression may return, perhaps repeatedly. It was at one time reported that later episodes of depression tend to be briefer but more frequent (Post, 1992; Solomon et al., 1997). We now understand that the apparent tendency toward briefer episodes was a statistical artifact: A single episode could be either brief or long, but if someone has a great many episodes, they had to be brief. (It would be hard to get to a tenth episode if each episode lasted many years.) Therefore, the average for first episodes is not comparable to the average for fifth or tenth episodes, unless we look only at the data for people who had at least five or ten episodes. In fact, for people who do have several episodes, the length of the early ones is generally about the same as that of the later ones (Anderson, Monroe, Rohde, & Lewinsohn, 2016).

In a related condition, **seasonal affective disorder (SAD)**, *people repeatedly become depressed during a particular season of the year.* It is common in Scandinavia, which has many hours of sunlight in summer and few in winter (Haggarty et al., 2002), and it is almost universal among explorers who spend long times in Antarctica (Palinkas, 2003). Although annual winter depressions receive the most publicity, annual summer depressions also occur (Faedda et al., 1993). People with seasonal affective disorder

tend to have increased appetite and weight gain, unlike most people with non-seasonal depression (Wirz-Justice, Ajdacic, Rossler, Steinhausen, & Angst, 2019). The most common treatment is a couple extra hours per day of bright light (by special lamps that you could order by the Internet). Bright light therapy appears to be effective, although the research has been limited (Mårtensson, Pettersson, Berglund, & Ekselius, 2015).

14. **If an advocate of some new therapy for depression reports that most people undergoing this therapy feel better a few months later, what if anything can we conclude?**

Answer

14. Unless the report included a control group not receiving the therapy, we cannot conclude anything. Most people show some recovery over time, with or without treatment.

Biological Aspects of Depression

Why do some people become depressed more easily than others? Studies of twins and relatives of patients with depression indicate a moderate degree of heritability (Wilde et al., 2014). Researchers identified dozens of genetic variants that differed between depressed and nondepressed people in at least one sample of the population (Howard et al., 2019). However, the results vary from one sample to another. A study of more than 400,000 people examining the effects of 18 genes that were reportedly linked to depression found slight support for one of the genes and no support for any of the others (Border et al., 2019).

Given the failure to find a single gene with a major effect, another attractive hypothesis was that certain genes might increase the risk of depression only in people who endured major stressful experiences. After one study reported this finding (Caspi et al., 2003), many other researchers attempted to replicate it, some successfully and some not (Karg, Burmeister, Shedden, & Sen, 2011). Many of these studies used small samples. The study with the largest sample found no support for the hypothesis (Border et al., 2019). The emerging conclusion is that no common genetic variant contributes substantially to the risk of depression. Rare genes, however, may be a significant factor. The usual methods of trying to link genetic variants to depression (or to anything else) overlook rare variants.

Most people with depression have relatives with depression (Kendler, Gardner, & Prescott, 1999; Lyons et al., 1998), and also relatives with other problems, including substance abuse, antisocial personality disorder, attention deficit disorder, bulimia nervosa, migraine headaches, asthma, arthritis, and others (Fu et al., 2002; Hudson et al., 2003; Kendler et al., 1995). In other words, whatever it is that predisposes to depression also increases the vulnerability to other disorders.

One thing depression has in common with many other disorders is a cascade of events that lead to inflammation. Highly stressful experiences activate the immune system, preparing the body to attack an infection. In a stressful situation, your body reacts as if it expects to be injured, and it prepares to fight the infection. The immune system increases the release of cytokines that fight infection and produce inflammation, but cytokines also conserve energy by producing sleepiness, inactivity, and loss of appetite—common symptoms of depression. Inflammation can also lead to asthma, arthritis, and other disorders. Brain inflammation is found in many cases of depression (Woelfer, Kasties, Kahlfuss, & Walter, 2019). Many treatments that decrease inflammation also help relieve depression (Miller, Maletic, & Raison, 2009).

Furthermore, prolonged inflammation impairs the mitochondria in the nervous system, resulting in decreased energy for brain activity (Kramer & Bressan, 2018). Mitochondrial damage is a plausible explanation for many cases of depression (Allen, Romay-Tallon, Brymer, Caruncho, & Kalynchuk, 2018).

Depression is common among people who have little social support.

15. Some of the same factors that predispose to depression also increase vulnerability to other disorders. How might that fact complicate the search for genes linked to depression?

Answer

15. Researchers compare the genes of people with depression to those without depression. If certain genes sometimes lead to depression and sometimes lead to different problems, then some of the genes linked to depression will also show up frequently in the population of people without depression.

Treatments for Major Depression

The common treatments for depression are antidepressant medications and psychotherapy. Much research has addressed the effectiveness of each.

Antidepressant Medications

Three common classes of antidepressants are tricyclics, serotonin reuptake inhibitors, and monoamine oxidase inhibitors. **Tricyclic drugs** *interfere with*

the axon's ability to reabsorb the neurotransmitters dopamine, norepinephrine, and serotonin after releasing them (see ▼ Figure 15.12b). Thus, tricyclics prolong the effect of these neurotransmitters at the synapses. **Selective serotonin reuptake inhibitors (SSRIs)** (e.g., fluoxetine, trade name Prozac) have a similar effect, but *block reuptake of only serotonin*. **Monoamine (MAHN-oh-ah-MEEN) oxidase inhibitors (MAOIs)** *block the metabolic breakdown of dopamine, norepinephrine, and serotonin* by the enzyme monoamine oxidase (MAO) (see ▼ Figure 15.12c). Thus, MAOIs also increase the effects of these neurotransmitters. People taking MAOIs must be careful with their diet, avoiding red wine, raisins, and many kinds of cheese. Psychiatrists seldom prescribe MAOIs except for patients who did not respond to the other drugs. Additional drugs called *atypical antidepressants* do not fall into any of these three categories.

Based on these descriptions of antidepressants, researchers at one time assumed that the cause of depression was inadequate release of serotonin or other transmitters. However, antidepressant drugs alter synaptic activity within an hour or so, whereas mood improvement begins 2 to 3 weeks later. Evidently the effect on serotonin and other transmitters is not the whole explanation of how the drugs work. It may not even be relevant. In addition to altering the neurotransmitters, prolonged use of antidepressants increases production of a chemical called BDNF (brain-derived neurotrophic factor) that over a period of weeks leads to expansion of dendrites, improved learning, and increased cognitive flexibility (Anacker & Hen, 2017). The increased learning and flexibility may be the main reason for how antidepressants help, although researchers are not yet certain.

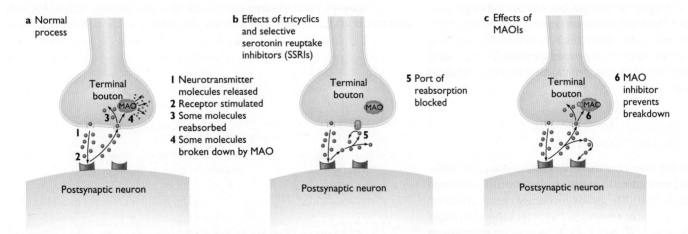

▲ **Figure 15.12** **(a)** Ordinarily, after the release of a neurotransmitter, some of the molecules are reabsorbed, and some are broken down by the enzyme monoamine oxidase (MAO). **(b)** Selective serotonin reuptake inhibitors (SSRIs) prevent reabsorption of serotonin. Tricyclic drugs prevent reabsorption of dopamine, norepinephrine, and serotonin. **(c)** MAO inhibitors (MAOIs) block the enzyme monoamine oxidase and thereby increase the availability of the neurotransmitter.

16. How do the effects of tricyclics and SSRIs resemble those of cocaine?

Answer

16. As discussed in another chapter, cocaine also blocks reuptake of certain neurotransmitters, especially dopamine. However, the antidepressant drugs produce much slower and milder effects.

Depressed Cognition and Cognitive Therapy

Suppose you fail a test. Choose your probable explanation:

- The test was difficult. Probably other students did poorly, too.
- Other students had a better previous background in this topic than I did.
- I didn't study hard enough.
- I'm just stupid. I always do badly no matter how hard I try.

The first three explanations attribute your failure to something temporary, specific, or correctable, but the fourth leaves you feeling hopeless. If you consistently make that type of attribution for your disappointments, you have a *pessimistic explanatory style*. People with a pessimistic style are likely to be depressed now or to become depressed later (Alloy et al., 1999; Haeffel et al., 2005). Depressed people tend to persist with their pessimistic attributions even when they see evidence to the contrary (Everaert, Bronstein, Cannon, & Joormann, 2018). Ruminating about pessimistic attributions prolongs sadness and increases depression and anxiety (Grafton, Southworth, Watkins, & MacLeod, 2016; Hong & Cheung, 2015).

Cognitive therapy focuses on changing people's thoughts and encouraging a more active life. According to Aaron Beck, a pioneer in cognitive therapy, depressed people are guided by thoughts that he calls the "negative cognitive triad of depression":

- I am deprived or defeated.
- The world is full of obstacles.
- The future is devoid of hope.

People who have these "automatic thoughts" interpret ambiguous situations to their own disadvantage (Beck, 1991). Therapists encourage clients to reinterpret events in a more positive way. A therapist might invite the client to regard the negative thoughts as charges by a prosecuting attorney, and then act as the defense attorney to produce counterarguments.

Research finds that most people undergoing cognitive therapy show improvements in both cognition and mood, but the improvements occur

simultaneously. That is, the changes in cognition do not precede the changes in mood, as we might expect if changes in cognition cause the changes in mood (Vittengl, Clark, Thase, & Jarrett, 2014). An important aspect of cognitive therapy is encouraging people to become more active—to take part in more activities that might bring pleasure or a sense of accomplishment (Jacobson et al., 1996). An experiment randomly assigned patients with major depression to full cognitive therapy with a trained therapist, or just encouragement for more behavioral activity, led by a less-trained mental health worker. The two procedures were equally effective, implying that increased activity is the main key to success (Richards et al., 2016).

Most people who become depressed after a highly stressful event find it helpful to talk with a therapist, and all of the common types of psychotherapy appear to be nearly equal in effectiveness (Barth et al., 2013). However, continuing to talk about a stressful experience month after month can sometimes do more harm than good (Curci & Rimé, 2012). Discussing a bad experience too long is rumination, which interferes with recovery. Often it is best to put a bad experience behind you and move on with life.

Effectiveness or Ineffectiveness of Treatments

Psychotherapy and antidepressant drugs are about equally effective for depression of any level of severity, but neither is highly reliable (Bortolotti, Menchetti, Bellini, Montaguti, & Berardi, 2008; Furukawa et al., 2017). Depression is characterized by feeling bad and failing to feel good, and therapies tend to reduce the bad feelings more than increase the good feelings (Dunn et al., 2020).

If we ask what percentage of people with depression show significant improvement, the result depends on how long the treatment lasts and how someone measures improvement, but in most studies, about half improve noticeably. Even saying that half of the people show improvement overstates the effectiveness of the treatments. Because depression occurs in episodes, most people with no treatment at all improve, given enough time, and some improve within a short time. Giving a placebo increases the chance of recovery, just by the expectation of improvement. If we look at results a few months after the onset of depression, about a third of patients improve with a placebo, and about half improve with either antidepressant drugs or psychotherapy (Hollon, Thase, & Markowitz, 2002). And even that statement might overstate effectiveness. Some research studies use only the type of patients who are expected to respond well, and the studies showing the weakest results are seldom published (Bschor & Kilarski, 2016).

▼ Figure 15.13 summarizes the results of many studies with many antidepressant drugs. The drugs are better than placebos for people with severe

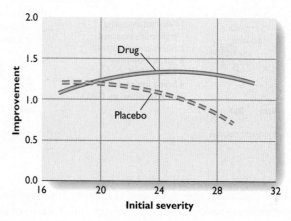

▲ **Figure 15.13** For people with mild to moderate depression, antidepressant drugs produce little measurable benefit, as compared to placebos. The benefit is clearer for people with severe depression. (From Kirsch et al., 2008)

depression, mainly because those people don't respond well to placebos (Kirsch et al., 2008). The effectiveness for people with mild to moderate depression is controversial (Fournier et al., 2010; Furukawa et al., 2018; Zimmerman, 2019). It may be more difficult to measure the improvement by the least depressed people, simply because they have less room for improvement. In any case, it is clear that antidepressant drugs are only moderately effective.

When patients fail to respond to a drug, psychiatrists sometimes increase the dosage or switch to a different drug, but no solid research supports this strategy. One study took people who failed to respond to a drug, switched them to another drug, and found that 21 percent of them improved within the next few weeks (Rush et al., 2006). Do you see a problem with this design? The problem is the lack of a control group that stayed on the first drug. We don't know whether switching drugs was the key, or whether people recovered because of more total time of treatment.

Choosing between Psychotherapy and Antidepressant Drugs

Might it be that some people respond better to psychotherapy and others respond better to antidepressant drugs? If so, no one has found a way to identify which are which. Many if not most of the people who would respond well to one would respond well to the other, also. Furthermore, although combining both types of treatment is, on average, a bit more effective than either one alone, it is not much better (Hollon et al., 2014; Thase, 2014; van Bronswijk, Moopen, Beijers, Ruhe, & Peeters, 2019).

Antidepressant drugs usually show benefits a little faster. They are less expensive, and it's more convenient to take a pill than to spend time with a therapist. However, the drugs produce unpleasant side effects, such as dry mouth, difficulty urinating, or increased blood pressure. An advantage of psychotherapy is that its benefits usually last longer after the end of treatment (Imel, Malterer, McKay, & Wampold, 2008).

In 2019, the U.S. Food and Drug Administration (FDA) approved a new type of antidepressant medication, esketamine, a nasal spray, for patients who failed to respond to other treatments. Esketamine acts by increasing activity in parts of the prefrontal cortex and increasing dendritic growth there (Moda-Sava et al., 2019). Unlike other antidepressants, esketamine improves mood and behavior within hours, not weeks. However, its side effects include sedation, thought disorder, and the risk of addiction.

Other Treatments

For those who don't respond to either psychotherapy or antidepressant drugs, another option is electroconvulsive therapy (ECT) (see ◀ Figure 15.14), in which *a brief electrical shock is administered across the patient's head to induce a convulsion similar to epilepsy.* ECT, widely used in the 1940s and 1950s, fell out of favor because of a history of abuse. Some patients were subjected to ECT hundreds of times without informed consent, and ECT was sometimes used more as a punishment than a therapy.

Beginning in the 1970s, ECT made a comeback in modified form, mostly for people with severe depression who failed to respond to antidepressant drugs or for patients with strong suicidal tendencies (Scovern & Kilmann, 1980). For suicidal patients, ECT has the advantage of acting faster, often within a week. When a life is at stake, rapid relief is important. However, up to half of those who respond to ECT will relapse into depression within 6 months or less, unless they receive some other therapy to prevent it (Riddle & Scott, 1995).

ECT is used only after patients have given their informed consent. The shock is less intense than previously, and the patient is given muscle relaxants to prevent injury and anesthetics to reduce discomfort. The main side effect is temporary memory impairment. How ECT works is uncertain, but it is not by causing people to forget depressing memories. ECT that is administered to just the frontal part of the brain or just the right hemisphere is as effective as whole-brain ECT but without significant memory loss (Lisanby, Maddox, Prudic, Devanand, & Sackeim, 2000; Sackeim et al., 2000).

ECT produces faster benefits than psychotherapy or antidepressant drugs, but its benefits are the least enduring. Although it has a high success rate for patients who did not respond to other treatments, only about 10 percent of hospitals in the United States offer it (Case et al., 2013).

Another option for treatment is the simplest. We have good reasons to expect exercise to help. Animal research has shown that steady, nonstrenuous exercise increases plasticity in the hippocampus, known to be an important part of recovery from depression. Research with humans has shown that increased physical activity predicts a lower probability of later depression, whereas depression predicts a decrease in physical activity (Pereira, Geoffroy, & Power, 2014; Yeatts, Martin, & Petrie, 2017). That is, people who exercise feel good, and people who feel bad stop exercising.

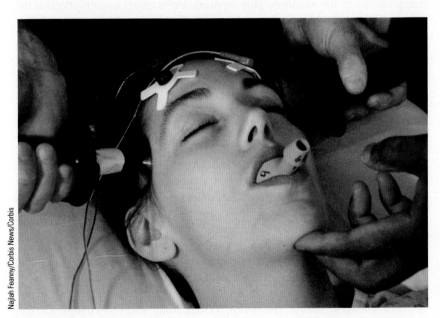

Najah Feanny/Corbis News/Corbis

▲ **Figure 15.14** Electroconvulsive therapy is administered today only with the patient's informed consent. ECT is given in conjunction with muscle relaxants and anesthetics to minimize discomfort.

17. Of the various treatments recommended for depression, which one might be helpful for prevention, as opposed to treating a disorder that has already occurred?

Answer

17. Exercise is suitable for prevention.

Bipolar Disorder

Bipolar disorder, previously known as manic-depressive disorder, is a condition in which someone alternates between mood extremes. Lifetime prevalence rates vary from less than 0.5 percent in Asia to about 1 percent in the United States and almost 1.5 percent in Europe (Johnson & Johnson, 2014). In certain respects, mania is the *opposite of depression.* In mania, people are *constantly active, uninhibited, often irritable, and sometimes cheerful but not necessarily.* They are sometimes dangerous to themselves or others. Some mental hospitals have had to disable the fire alarms, because manic patients would impulsively pull the alarm whenever they passed it. People with a mild degree of mania, *hypomania,* are also energetic and uninhibited, but to a lesser degree. Bipolar disorder 1 is associated with depression and mania, whereas bipolar disorder 2 is associated with depression and hypomania. Research has found a small positive correlation between bipolar disorder and creativity (Taylor, 2017).

As mentioned earlier in the chapter, many people do not fit neatly into one category. Some patients straddle the border between depression and bipolar

Treatment for bipolar disorder enables people to lead successful lives. Dr. Alice W. Flaherty is a neurologist who says having the disorder has made her more empathetic to her patients.

disorder, many have bipolar disorder plus anxiety problems, and some have both the mood swings of bipolar disorder and the thought problems associated with schizophrenia.

Effective treatments for bipolar disorder include lithium salts and anticonvulsant drugs, such as valproate (trade names Depakene, Depacote), all of which can be tolerated for long-term treatment if the dose is carefully monitored. Psychotherapy is helpful for handling the anxiety that many patients experience (Deckersbach et al., 2014). Bright lights, a typical treatment for seasonal affective disorder, can also help in some cases (Sit et al., 2018).

18. What are the similarities and differences between seasonal affective disorder and bipolar disorder?

Answer

18. Both conditions have repetitive cycles. However, people with bipolar disorder swing back and forth between depression and mania, whereas people with seasonal affective disorder alternate between depression and normal mood. Also, people with seasonal affective disorder show symptoms that depend on time of year.

Schizophrenia

Many people mistakenly use the term *schizophrenia* when they mean *dissociative identity disorder,* or *multiple personality,* a rare condition in which people alternate personalities. In fact, calling it "rare" may give it more credence than it deserves. Many researchers doubt that it occurs at all, or believe that when it apparently occurs, it was the result of hypnosis or other suggestions by a therapist, rather than a spontaneous occurrence (Boysen & Van Bergen, 2013; Paris, 2012).

People with schizophrenia do not alternate between one personality and another. The term *schizophrenia* does come from Greek roots meaning "split mind" or "shattered mind," but the original idea was a split between the intellectual and emotional aspects of a personality, as if the intellect had lost contact with the emotions. That is, someone suffering from schizophrenia might express an emotion that is inappropriate to the situation, or fail to show an emotion that is appropriate to the situation. This separation of intellect and emotions is no longer considered a defining feature of schizophrenia, but the term remains.

To be diagnosed with **schizophrenia,** someone must exhibit a prolonged deterioration of daily activities such as work, social relations, and self-care, and some combination of the following: hallucinations, delusions, disorganized speech and thought, movement disorder, and loss of normal emotional responses and social behaviors. The symptoms must include at least two symptoms, including at least one of the first three (delusions, hallucinations, and disorganized speech). As you can see, two people diagnosed with schizophrenia might have no symptoms in common.

Hallucinations, delusions, thought disorder, and movement disorder are considered **positive symptoms,** meaning that they are *defined by the presence of some behavior.* In contrast, negative symptoms are *defined by the absence of a behavior.* Common **negative symptoms** include lack of emotional expression, lack of motivation, and lack of social interactions.

Studies of emotional experience find that people with schizophrenia experience a normal amount of pleasure in response to highly pleasant events. The difference is that most other people feel moderately happy even when nothing much is happening, whereas people with schizophrenia feel happy only in response to an event (Strauss, Visser, Lee, & Gold, 2017). Also, most people feel excited when they expect that something good is about to happen, whereas people with schizophrenia show little emotional anticipation—actually, not much response to expecting either good or bad (Moran & Kring, 2018).

Hallucinations

Hallucinations are *perceptions that do not correspond to anything in the real world*, such as hearing voices that no one else hears. People with schizophrenia sometimes think the voices are real, sometimes they know the voices are unreal, and sometimes they are not sure (Junginger & Frame, 1985). Spontaneous activity in the auditory cortex accompanies auditory hallucinations (Shergill, Brammer, Williams, Murray, & McGuire, 2000).

Have you ever heard a voice when you knew you were alone? I asked my class this question. At first, just a few people hesitantly raised their hands, and then more and more, until about one-fourth of the class—including myself—admitted to hearing a voice at least once. Often, the experience occurred while someone lay in bed, just waking up. Having an auditory hallucination is not necessarily a sign of trouble. For people with schizophrenia, the hallucinations are frequent and disturbing.

Delusions

A delusion is a *belief that someone holds strongly despite evidence against it.* For example, a delusion of persecution is *a belief that enemies are persecuting you.* A delusion of grandeur is *a belief that you are unusually important,* perhaps a special messenger from God. A delusion of reference is *a tendency to take all sorts of messages personally.* For example, someone might interpret a newspaper headline as a coded message of what he or she should do today.

One should hesitate to make a diagnosis of schizophrenia if the main symptom is a delusion. Suppose someone constantly sees evidence of government conspiracies in everyday events. Is that belief a psychotic delusion or just an unusual opinion? Most people who believe they have been abducted by outer space aliens do not seem mentally ill, despite their implausible beliefs (Clancy, 2005). Probably most people believe something that someone else might consider ridiculous. The difference between a questionable belief and a psychotic delusion is a matter of degree, and a matter of how much it interferes with living.

Disordered Speech and Cognition

Many people with schizophrenia show various problems with communication, including illogical, incoherent, distracted, or tangential speech, as if they started speaking but quickly forgot what they were trying to say. Here is a quote from a person with schizophrenia (Andreasen, 1986, p. 477):

> They're destroying too many cattle and oil just to make soap. If we need soap when you can jump into a pool of water, and then when you go to buy your gasoline, my folks always thought they should get pop but the best thing to get, is motor oil, and, money.

Most but not all people with schizophrenia show intellectual impairments of attention and working memory, especially on more difficult tasks (M. L. Thomas et al., 2017). For example, the Wisconsin Card Sorting Test asks people to sort a stack of cards by one rule (such as piles by color) and then shift to a different rule (piles by number or shape). Most people with schizophrenia have trouble shifting, as do people with frontal cortex damage.

Another characteristic of schizophrenic thought is difficulty using abstract concepts, such as interpreting proverbs literally instead of seeing the intended meaning. Here are examples (Krueger, 1978, pp. 196–197):

Proverb: People who live in glass houses shouldn't throw stones.
Interpretation: "It would break the glass."
Proverb: All that glitters is not gold.
Interpretation: "It might be brass."

19. What are the positive and negative symptoms of schizophrenia?

Answer

19. Positive symptoms of schizophrenia include hallucinations, delusions, thought disorder, and movement disorder. Negative symptoms include lack of speech, lack of emotional expression, and lack of social contact.

Prevalence

Estimates of the worldwide incidence of schizophrenia range from one in a hundred to one in a thousand at some point in life (Brown, 2011; He et al., 2020). As with all statistics about mental illness, the figures increase or decrease depending on how many mild cases we count. Schizophrenia is most often diagnosed when people are in their 20s or late teens, and less often as people grow older. It is 10 to 20 percent more common in men than women, and on average it is more severe in men (Brown, 2011; He et al., 2020). Schizophrenia occurs more often among people who grew up in large cities than among people who grew up in rural areas or small towns (Brown, 2011). Several explanations are possible, including decreased social support in large cities, differences in diet, exposure to toxic substances, and decreased exposure to sunlight, resulting in less absorption of vitamin D. (Right, that means we don't know the explanation.)

Decades ago, psychiatrists believed that people with schizophrenia almost invariably continued deteriorating throughout life. At the time, most such patients lived in poorly staffed, poorly funded, overcrowded mental hospitals, and it is not surprising that they deteriorated. Anybody would have. Today, the prospects are less dismal. Although most people with schizophrenia remain permanently impaired to some degree, few get steadily worse over time and many show some degree of improvement. Some show long-term recovery after a first episode, especially people who do not have severe negative symptoms (Hui et al., 2019). Others alternate between periods of remission and periods of relapse (Lally et al., 2017). The percentages of people who recover or relapse vary from one study to another.

Causes

Schizophrenia develops from a variety of influences. The main contributors are genetics and prenatal environment, aggravated by stress later in life.

Genetics

The original evidence for a genetic basis came from studies of twins and adopted children. Monozygotic twins have much higher overlap than dizygotic twins

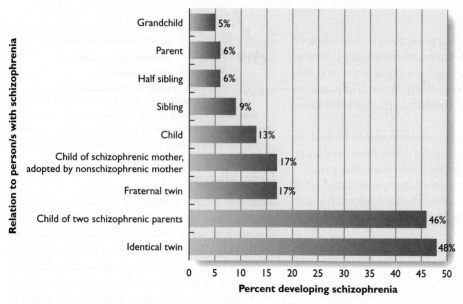

▲ **Figure 15.15** The relatives of someone with schizophrenia have an increased probability of developing schizophrenia. (Based on data from Gottesman, 1991)

effect. Another approach is to examine the chromosomes of one person at a time. Studies using that method have found that many people with schizophrenia have a rare mutation of one gene or another that affects synaptic transmission, or they have a copy number variant—that is, *a deletion or duplication of a small part of a chromosome* (Buizer-Voskamp et al., 2011; Gulsuner, et al., 2020; International Schizophrenia Consortium, 2008; Singh, Neale, Daly, & Schizophrenia Exome Meta-Analysis Consortium, 2019; Stefansson et al., 2008, 2014). Because all of these individual mutations or copy number variants are rare, indeed "ultra-rare," they do not show up in studies comparing whole populations. Note another implication: Because various cases of schizophrenia depend on different rare genetic variations, it is not surprising that the symptoms vary so much.

(Cardno et al., 1999; Gottesman, 1991; Sullivan, Kendler, & Neale, 2003), and close relatives in general have an increased similarity (see ▲ Figure 15.15). Brothers and sisters of someone with schizophrenia have an increased probability of impaired memory and attention, even if they do not have other symptoms (Barch, Cohen, & Csernansky, 2014). Adopted children with schizophrenia have more biological relatives than adoptive relatives with schizophrenia (Kety et al., 1994). However, the data on adopted children are subject to another interpretation. Many women with schizophrenia use drugs during pregnancy, take poor care of their health, and fail to eat a good diet. That prenatal environment can unfavorably affect a fetus's brain development.

Modern methods enable researchers to look for particular genes associated with schizophrenia. A massive study comparing nearly 37,000 people with schizophrenia to more than 100,000 others identified more than a hundred genes that differed in frequency between the two groups. Most of these genes influence some aspect of brain activity, but many others related to the immune system (Schizophrenia Working Group, 2014). However, most of these genes raise the risk of schizophrenia only slightly. A typical result is that one of these genes is just 1 or 2 percent more common among people with schizophrenia than in the rest of the population (Birnbaum & Weinberger, 2017).

That type of research—trying to find a gene that is more common in the schizophrenia population than in the rest of the population—is limited to finding a fairly common gene with a noticeable

20. How can schizophrenia have a strong genetic basis, even though no single gene is strongly linked with schizophrenia?

Answer

20. Brain development depends on many genes, and a disruption of any of them (including a spontaneous deletion or duplication of part of a gene) can increase the risk of schizophrenia. That is, a huge number of possible genetic variations can predispose to schizophrenia.

The Neurodevelopmental Hypothesis

Many cases of schizophrenia may not result from genetic factors at all. According to the neurodevelopmental hypothesis, *schizophrenia originates with nervous system impairments that develop before birth or in early childhood, influenced by either genetics or early environment, especially prenatal environment* (McGrath, Féron, Burne, Mackay-Sim, & Eyles, 2003; Weinberger, 1996). Schizophrenia is known to be more common in any of these cases (Brown, 2011):

- The mother had a difficult pregnancy, labor, or delivery.
- The mother was poorly nourished during pregnancy.
- The mother had influenza, rubella, or other infection during early to mid-pregnancy.
- The mother had an extremely stressful experience early in her pregnancy.
- A mother with Rh-negative blood type has given birth to more than one baby with Rh-positive blood.
- The patient was exposed to lead or other toxins in early childhood.
- The patient was infected during childhood with the parasite *Toxoplasma gondii*, which attacks parts of the brain (Yolken, Dickerson, & Torrey, 2009). People acquire this parasite by handling cat feces (Leweke et al., 2004; Torrey & Yolken, 2005).

Furthermore, consider the season-of-birth effect: *a person born in the winter or early spring is slightly more likely to develop schizophrenia than a person born at other times* (Bradbury & Miller, 1985; Davies, Welham, Chant, Torrey, & McGrath, 2003). No other psychological disorder has this characteristic.

(c) They alter synaptic activity within hours, but they take weeks to alter mood.

(d) They alter mood within hours, but they take weeks to alter synaptic activity.

6. Which of the following is a major disadvantage of ECT for depression?

(a) Its benefits are usually temporary.

(b) Its benefits emerge slowly after many repetitions.

(c) It is so painful that most patients refuse a second treatment.

(d) It is illegal in most states.

7. Which of the following helps to relieve depression?

(a) Exercise

(b) A vegan diet

(c) Homeopathic medicines

(d) Rumination

8. Which of the following is NOT a symptom of schizophrenia?

(a) Alternating between one personality and another

(b) Hallucinations and delusions

(c) Lack of motivation

(d) Deterioration of daily activities

9. What is meant by a "positive" symptom of schizophrenia?

(a) Something noted by its presence instead of its absence

(b) Something that is present in every individual

(c) Something that causes more good than harm

(d) Something that the patient is willing to discuss

10. Schizophrenia is more common in what kind of people?

(a) More in women than men, more in rural people than city people.

(b) More in men than women, more in rural people than city people.

(c) More in men than women, more in city people than rural people.

(d) More in women than men, more in city people than rural people.

11. How do first-generation antipsychotic drugs affect the brain?

(a) They block reuptake of serotonin.

(b) They block dopamine synapses.

(c) They improve synaptic plasticity.

(d) They suppress activity in sensory areas of the cortex.

12. Research indicates that some cases of autism probably result from which of the following?

(a) Cold, distant parents

(b) A smaller than average brain

(c) Exposure to bullying in elementary school

(d) Excessive exposure to pesticides and air pollutants in prenatal development

13. Why do many people with autism act more normally when they have a fever?

(a) Suppressed activity in the sensory cortex

(b) Lack of energy to do anything

(c) Increased activity at dopamine synapses

(d) Increased blood flow to the brain

Answers: 1c, 2d, 3a, 4b, 5c, 6a, 7a, 8a, 9a, 10c, 11b, 12d, 13a.

iStock.com/SDI Productions

After studying this module, you should be able to:

1. Distinguish among forms of psychotherapy.

2. Describe how researchers evaluate the effectiveness of psychotherapy.

3. Describe possible ways of providing psychotherapeutic help less expensively to more people.

4. List and evaluate possible methods to prevent psychological disorders.

5. Discuss the insanity defense and other societal issues related to mental illness.

Nearsighted people lost in the woods were trying to find their way home. One of the few who wore glasses said, "I think I know the way. Follow me." The others burst into laughter. "That's ridiculous," said one. "How could anybody who needs glasses be our leader?"

In 1972 the Democratic Party nominated Senator Thomas Eagleton for vice president of the United States. Shortly after his nomination, he re-vealed that he had once received psychiatric treat-ment for depression. He was ridiculed mercilessly: "How could anybody who needed a psychiatrist be our leader?"

Many troubled people decline to seek help, partly because of the stigma (Corrigan, Druss, & Perlick, 2014). All of us need to consider our reac-tions toward the idea of therapeutic help. We also need to deal with other issues. Can society as a whole take steps to prevent psychological disorders? Under what circumstances, if any, should a criminal defendant be acquitted because of "insanity"?

Overview of Psychotherapy

Treatments for psychological disorders are of two types, medications and psy-chotherapy. We have already considered psychotherapy in the previous module, but now it is time to examine it in more detail. **Psychotherapy** is *a treatment of psychological disorders by methods that include a personal relationship between a trained therapist and a client.*

Treatment of mental illness has changed greatly since the mid-1900s, for both scientific and economic reasons (Sanchez & Turner, 2003). If you had sought treat-ment in the mid-1900s, you probably would have gone to a psychiatrist, because clinical psychology was just getting started. Freud's theories were dominant, and if you went to a Freudian therapist (a psychoanalyst), you would schedule 1-hour sessions, 4 or 5 days a week, for months or years. You had to pay for it yourself, because few people had health insurance, and even if you did have health insur-ance, it didn't cover psychiatric care. In other words, hardly anyone but the wealthy could get psychotherapy. No research had tested the effectiveness of treatments, and so you had to hope and trust that your treatment was appropriate. Your thera-pist might give you no diagnosis at all, or a vague diagnosis like "neurotic."

Today, all of that has changed. If you want treatment, you can choose among psychiatrists, clinical psychologists, clinical social workers, and others. Therapists use many methods, not just psychoanalysis. Instead of paying for your treatment, you will probably charge it to an insurance program. Insurers will pay for only as much treatment as necessary, and only for dependable tech-niques. If you want to crawl naked into a hot tub with your psychotherapist to reenact the moment of birth, you are welcome to do it as often as you like, if you pay for it yourself. But if you expect insurance to pay for it, someone needs to demonstrate that the treatment is effective. Consequently, therapists have felt pressure to test their methods and adopt **empirically supported treatments**, *thera-pies demonstrated to be helpful* (APA Presidential Task Force on Evidence-Based Practice, 2006). Many therapists follow published manuals that specify exactly how to treat various disorders. Because insurers limit the number of sessions that they will reimburse, therapists developed briefer therapies, in which they accomplish as much as they can in a moderate number of sessions. Having a deadline urges both client and therapist to address all issues promptly and efficiently. As ▼ Figure 15.18 shows, about half of all people who enter psycho-therapy show significant improvement within eight sessions (Howard, Kopta, Krause, & Orlinsky, 1986), although the results depend on the disorder. For most people, the rate of improvement declines over time (Stulz, Lutz, Kopta, Minami, & Saunders, 2013). Two brief sessions per week for a few weeks might be bet-ter than one session a week for many weeks (Cuijpers, Huibers, Ebert, Koole, & Andersson, 2013).

Insurance companies might pay for a session or two if you just feel bad and want to talk to someone, but they pay for more if you have a diagnosed mental disorder. As you might guess, the consequence is that a therapist is almost certain to give you a diagnosis of some sort, no matter what your prob-lem is. ■ Table 15.4 summarizes these changes.

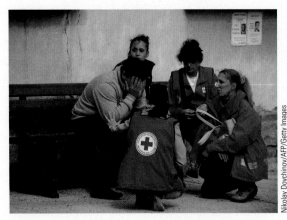

Psychologists offer help for many problems. Here, psychologists comfort the relatives of people killed in an explosion.

Nikolay Doychinov/AFP/Getty Images

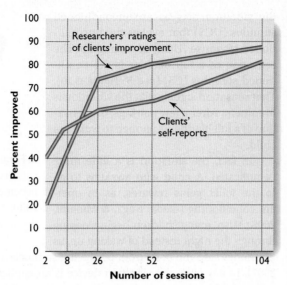

► **Figure 15.18** The relationship of the number of psychotherapy sessions to the percentage of clients who improved. (From "The dose-effect relationship in psychotherapy," by K. I. Howard et al., 1986. *American Psychologist*, 41, pp. 159–164. By the American Psychological Association.)

Researchers' ratings of clients' improvement

Clients' self-reports

Percent improved

Number of sessions

concept check

25. How has treatment of psychological disorders changed since the 1950s?

Answer

25. In the 1950s, psychiatrists conducted almost all psychotherapy. Today, clinical psychologists and other specialists also provide treatment. Today's therapists use a variety of empirically supported treatments, with less reliance on Freudian methods. Therapists try to achieve good results in fewer sessions, when possible. Today's therapists assign diagnoses for almost all clients.

Types of Psychotherapy

Many types of psychotherapy are available, differing in their procedures and assumptions. The discussion here focuses on psychotherapy as it is practiced in the United States and Europe. Customs vary in other countries. For example, most Chinese consider it shameful to discuss personal or family matters with a stranger (Bond, 1991). Psychologists in India have to respect beliefs in astrology and other concepts that most Western psychologists dismiss (Clay, 2002).

Psychodynamic Therapies

Psychodynamic therapies *attempt to understand conflicting impulses, including unconscious ones.* Both Sigmund Freud's procedure (looking for sexual motives) and Alfred Adler's procedure (looking for power and superiority motives) are psychodynamic, despite the differences between them.

Psychoanalysis *tries to bring unconscious thoughts, motivations, and emotions to consciousness.* It is therefore an insight-oriented therapy. Psychoanalysts offer interpretations of what the client says—that is, they try to explain the underlying meaning—and sometimes argue with a client about interpretations. They may regard a client's disagreement with an interpretation as resistance. A client could also show resistance by turning the conversation to something trivial or simply "forgetting" to come to the next session.

One technique used in psychoanalysis is **free association**, in which *the client says everything that comes to mind*—a word, phrase, or image—without censoring anything or even speaking in complete sentences. The psychoanalyst listens for links that might tie the remarks together, on the assumption that every jump from one thought to another reveals a relationship between them. Another technique is **dream analysis**, *seeking to understand symbolism in reported dreams.* Even a therapist who doesn't look for deep symbolism can use dreams to understand how the client understands the world. Psychoanalysts also attend to **transference**, in which clients *transfer onto the therapist the behaviors and feelings they originally established toward their father, mother, or other important person.*

Psychoanalysts today modify Freud's approach in many ways. The goal is still to bring about a reorganization of the personality, changing a person from the inside out, by helping people understand

Table 15.4 Changes in Psychotherapy Between the 1950s and the 21st Century		
Aspect of Therapy	**1950s**	**Early 21st Century**
Payment	By the patient or family	Usually by health insurance
Types of therapist	Psychiatrists	Psychiatrists, clinical psychologists, others
Types of treatment	Mostly Freudian	Many types; emphasis on evidence-based treatments
Duration of treatment	Usually long, often years	A few sessions if effective; more if necessary
Diagnoses	Usually vague, such as "neurosis" or "psychosis." Often, no diagnosis.	Many diagnoses, carefully defined
Treatment decisions	By the therapist and patient	By the insurer, unless the patient pays for more

the hidden reasons behind their actions. The duration of treatment varies, sometimes lasting just weeks, but possibly continuing for years.

26. What methods do psychoanalysts use to try to gain access to the unconscious?

Answer

26. Psychoanalysts try to infer the contents of the unconscious by using free association, dream analysis, and transference.

Behavior Therapy

Behavior therapists emphasize that abnormal behavior is learned and can be unlearned. They identify the behavior that needs to be changed, such as a fear or a bad habit, and then set about changing it through positive reinforcement and other principles of learning. They may try to understand the causes of a behavior as a first step toward changing it, but unlike psychoanalysts, they are more interested in changing a behavior than in understanding its hidden meanings.

Behavior therapy *begins with a clear, well-defined goal, such as eliminating test anxiety, and then attempts to achieve it through learning.* A behavior therapist is more likely than any other type of therapist to set a specific goal. Setting a clear goal enables the therapist to evaluate progress. If the client shows no improvement, the therapist changes the procedure.

One example of behavior therapy is for children who continue wetting the bed after the usual age of toilet training. The most effective procedure uses classical conditioning to train the child to wake up when the bladder is full. A small battery-powered device is attached to the child's underwear at night (see ▶ Figure 15.19). If the child urinates, the device detects the moisture and produces a vibration that awakens the child. According to one interpretation,

the vibration acts as an unconditioned stimulus (UCS) that evokes the unconditioned response (UCR) of waking up. The sensation of a full bladder is the conditioned stimulus (CS) (see ▼ Figure 15.20). That sensation signals that the vibration is imminent. After a few pairings, the sensation of a full bladder is enough to wake the child.

In fact, the situation is a little more complicated. A child who awakens to go to the toilet gains rewards, as in operant conditioning (Ikeda, Koga, & Minami, 2006). Also, many children begin sleeping through the night instead of waking up, as hormones stop the body from producing so much urine at night (Butler et al., 2007). In any case, the vibration device is an application of behavior therapy, successful for at least two-thirds of bed-wetting children, sometimes after as few as one or two nights.

▲ **Figure 15.19** A Potty Pager in a child's underwear vibrates when it becomes moist. This awakens the child, who learns to awaken when the bladder is full.

© Ideas for Living, Inc.

27. In the behavior therapy for bed-wetting, what is the conditioned stimulus? What is the unconditioned stimulus? What is the conditioned response?

Answer

27. The conditioned stimulus is the sensation of a full bladder. The unconditioned stimulus is the alarm. The conditioned response (and the unconditioned response) is waking up.

Cognitive Therapies

Suppose someone asks for your opinion and then asks another person also. You might react, "It's good to get several opinions." Or you might feel hurt that your opinion wasn't good enough. Your emotions depend not only on the events but also on how you interpret them. **Cognitive therapy** *seeks to improve psychological well-being by changing people's interpretation of events* (Hofmann, Asmundson, & Beck, 2013). A cognitive therapist identifies distressing thoughts (such as "people don't like me" or "my enemies are out to get me") and encourages the client to explore the evidence behind them, much as a scientist would evaluate evidence. The therapist isn't necessarily promoting an optimistic outlook, but a realistic outlook. After all, if people really don't like you, or if you really do have enemies, you should know about it! Usually, however, the client discovers that

▶ **Figure 15.20** At first, the sensation of a full bladder (the CS) produces no response, and the child wets the bed. The moisture causes a vibration (the UCS), and the child wakes up (the UCR). Soon the sensation of a full bladder wakens the child (CR).

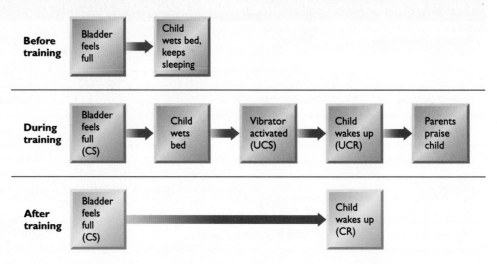

An event can be upsetting or not, depending on how we interpret it.

e. Which one might continue for years?
Answer

28. a. behavior therapy; b. cognitive therapy and psychoanalysis; c. humanistic therapy; d. cognitive therapy;
e. psychoanalysis.

the beliefs are unjustified. The therapist helps people identify unrealistic beliefs and abandon unrealistic goals, such as a need to excel all the time. Cognitive therapy also encourages people to find opportunities for activity, pleasure, or a sense of accomplishment.

Many therapists combine features of behavior therapy and cognitive therapy into cognitive-behavior therapy, in which therapists *set explicit behavioral goals, but also try to change people's interpretation of situations.* For example, they help clients distinguish between serious problems and imagined or exaggerated problems. Then they try to change clients' behavior in handling the more serious problems.

Humanistic Therapy

Humanistic psychologists believe that people can decide deliberately what kind of person to be. According to humanistic therapists, once people are freed from a feeling of rejection or failure, they can solve their own problems.

In Carl Rogers's version of humanistic therapy, person-centered therapy, also known as *nondirective* or *client-centered therapy, the therapist listens to the client with total acceptance and unconditional positive regard.* Most of the time, the therapist paraphrases and clarifies what the client has said, conveying the message, "I'm trying to understand the experience from your point of view." The therapist strives to be genuine, empathic, and caring, seldom if ever offering interpretation or advice. Few therapists today rely entirely on person-centered therapy, but most therapists, regardless of their other methods, follow the emphasis on listening carefully to the client and developing a caring, honest relationship between therapist and client.

concept check

28. **Answer the following questions with reference to psychoanalysis, cognitive therapy, humanistic therapy, and behavior therapy.**

a. Which one concentrates on actions more than thoughts?
b. Which two of them try to change what people think?
c. Which one focuses entirely on sympathetic listening?
d. Which one tries to change how people interpret events?

Family Systems Therapy

In family systems therapy, *the guiding assumption is that most people's problems develop in a family setting and that the best way to deal with them is to improve family relationships and communication.* A family therapist may use behavior therapy, cognitive therapy, or other techniques. What distinguishes family therapists is that they prefer to talk with two or more members of a family together. Solving most problems requires changing the family dynamics as well as any individual's behavior.

We have examined five types of psychotherapy. About half of U.S. psychotherapists profess no strong allegiance to any single method. Instead, they practice eclectic therapy, in which they *use a combination of methods and approaches.*

Group Therapies

The pioneers of psychotherapy saw their clients individually. Individual treatment has advantages, such as privacy. Group therapy *is administered to several people at once.* It first became popular for economic reasons. Spreading the costs among several people makes it more affordable. Soon therapists discovered other advantages to group therapy. Simply meeting other people with similar problems is reassuring. Also, group therapy lets people examine how they relate to others, practice social skills, and receive feedback (Ballinger & Yalom, 1995).

In group therapy, participants can explore how they relate to other people.

A self-help group, such as Alcoholics Anonymous, *operates much like group therapy, except without a therapist.* Each participant both gives and receives help. People who have experienced a problem can offer special insights to others with the same problem. In some places, people with mental health issues have organized self-help centers as an alternative to mental hospitals. These small, homelike environments may or may not include professional therapists. Instead of treating people as patients who need medical help, they expect people to take responsibility for their own actions. For most types of disorder, these facilities produce results equal to or better than those of mental hospitals, and the clients certainly like them better (Greenfield, Stoneking, Humphreys, Sundby, & Bond, 2008).

29. Why is brief therapy a less important goal for self-help groups such as Alcoholics Anonymous?

Answer

29. One advantage of brief therapy is that it limits the expense. Expense is not an issue for self-help groups because they charge nothing other than a voluntary contribution toward rental of the facilities. Also, a problem like alcoholism is generally a long-term issue requiring long-term help.

How Effective Is Psychotherapy?

Suppose you enter therapy, and 6 months later you and your therapist agree that you are much improved. Can we conclude that the therapy was effective? No, for several reasons (Lilienfeld, Ritschel, Lynn, Cautin, & Latzman, 2014). First, both you and your therapist want to believe the therapy worked, and so you may overestimate the degree of improvement. Second and more importantly, most psychological crises are temporary, and most people improve to some extent, with or without therapy. *Improvement without therapy* is called spontaneous remission. We cannot conclude that the therapy was effective unless its benefits were greater than those of spontaneous remission, which we might see in a control group.

To evaluate psychotherapy, we cannot simply compare people who did or did not receive therapy. Those who sought help might differ from the others in the severity of their problems or their motivation for improvement. In the best studies, people who contact a clinic are randomly assigned to receive therapy at once or to wait for therapy later. A few months later, the investigators compare the improvement for the two groups. For ethical reasons, such research is limited to less severe disorders. No one would ask people with a risk of suicide to wait a few months before treatment.

Most experiments have included only a moderate number of people. To draw a conclusion, researchers use a meta-analysis, *taking the results of many experiments, weighting each one in proportion to the number of participants, and determining the overall average effect.* According to a meta-analysis that pooled the results of 475 experiments, the average person in therapy showed greater improvement than 80 percent of similar people who did not receive therapy (Smith, Glass, & Miller, 1980).

One could easily complain that investigators invested much effort for little payoff. From 475 experiments, we conclude that therapy is usually better than no therapy for mild disorders. This outcome is like saying that medicine is usually better than no medicine. However, the research paved the way for more detailed studies about how therapy produces its benefits and which types of therapy are or are not effective.

Still, although psychotherapy is beneficial on average, the amount of effect is sometimes disappointing. Since the onset of empirically supported therapies, we would expect that therapy is more effective today than it was in the past. However, a comparison of psychotherapy results for children and adolescents from 1960 through 2017 found that effectiveness had actually decreased over the years for depression and conduct problems, while failing to change significantly for anxiety and attention-deficit disorder (Weisz et al., 2019). The unimproved

a   b

Because everyone's moods and behavior fluctuate over time, an apparent improvement between **(a)** the start of therapy and **(b)** the end is hard to interpret. How much improvement is due to therapy and how much would have occurred without it?

effectiveness could relate to differences in the people being treated rather than the treatment itself, but nevertheless we have to be disappointed that we are not seeing a clear improvement.

Comparing Therapies

Next, we would like to know which kinds of therapy are most effective, or under what conditions. At first the conclusion appeared stunningly simple: For a variety of disorders relating to anxiety or depression, all the mainstream types of therapy appeared nearly equal in effectiveness (Benish, Imel, & Wampold, 2008; Cuijpers, van Straten, Andersson, & van Oppen, 2008; Wampold et al., 1997). Later research qualified this statement somewhat: For certain types of disorder, one or another type of therapy produces better results for relieving target symptoms. Still, all the common types of treatment are roughly equal for less specific goals, such as overall quality of life (Marcus, O'Connell, Norris, & Sawaqeh, 2014).

How could we explain why different types of psychotherapy produce similar results, despite differences in their assumptions, methods, and goals? Possibly they produce the same result in different ways, just as several roads from different directions all arrive in your hometown. The other possibility is that the various therapies have more in common than we might have thought. One feature they share is a *therapeutic alliance*—a relationship between therapist and client characterized by acceptance, caring, respect, and attention. Second, nearly all forms of therapy encourage clients to talk openly about their beliefs, emotions, and other aspects of themselves that they usually take for granted. Third, the mere fact of entering therapy improves clients' morale. Just taking action—any action—suggests that things will get better.

Finally, every form of therapy requires clients to commit themselves to change their lifestyle. Simply by coming to a therapy session, they reaffirm their commitment to feel less depressed, overcome their fears, or conquer some bad habit. Between sessions, they work to make progress that they can report at the next session. ■ Table 15.5 highlights similarities and differences among four types of therapy.

concept check

30. What do nearly all standard types of psychotherapy have in common?

Answer

30. They all include a close relationship between client and therapist, an effort to discuss personal difficulties openly, an expectation of improvement, and a commitment to make changes.

Advice for Potential Clients

At some point, you or someone close to you may consider seeing a psychotherapist. If so, here are some points to remember:

- Consulting a therapist does not mean that something is wrong with you. Many people need to talk with someone during a crisis.
- If you live in the United States, you can look up the telephone number for the Mental Health Association. Call and ask for a recommendation. You can specify how much you can pay, what kind of problem you have, and even what type of therapy you prefer. On average, people who choose their form of treatment persist with it longer and show greater benefits (Lindhiem, Bennett, Trentacosta, & McLear, 2014).
- Effective therapy depends on a good relationship between client and therapist. If you feel more comfortable talking with someone from your own culture, ethnic group, or religious

Table 15.5 Similarities and Differences among Four Types of Psychotherapy				
Procedure	**Psychoanalysis**	**Behavior Therapy**	**Cognitive Therapy**	**Person-Centered Therapy**
Therapeutic alliance	√	√	√	√
Discuss problems openly	√	√	√	√
Expect improvement	√	√	√	√
Commit to make changes	√	√	√	√
Probe unconscious	√			
Specific goals		√	√	
Emphasize new learning		√		
Reinterpret situation			√	
Unconditional positive regard				√
Change thinking	√		√	

background, look for such a person (La Roche & Christopher, 2008; Worthington, Kurusu, McCullough, & Sandage, 1996).

• Be skeptical of any therapist who seems overconfident. Clinical experience does not give anyone quick access to your private thoughts.

The Future of Psychotherapy and Prospects for Prevention

Sigmund Freud's procedure featured a therapist and a client for an hour at a time, four or five times a week, month after month. Most therapists today provide briefer treatments, often with a group of people at a time, and the prices have come down. Still, Alan Kazdin and his associates have argued that we will never have enough psychologists and psychiatrists to have personal meetings with everyone who needs help (Kazdin & Rabbitt, 2013). So, what should we do instead? Kazdin suggests therapy by telephone or the Internet, good self-help books, and informative movie and television programs. Computer programs to provide cognitive-behavioral therapy have made great advances, especially for treating anxiety (Rooksby, Elouafkaoui, Humphris, Clarkson, & Freeman, 2015). A website to help people quit smoking had good success for those who completed the program, although a high percentage dropped out after starting (Muñoz et al., 2016).

A still better goal should be to prevent disorders as much as possible. Just as our society puts fluoride into drinking water to prevent tooth decay and immunizes people against contagious diseases, it can take action to prevent certain types of psychological disorders (Albee, 1986; Wandersman & Florin, 2003).

Let's distinguish prevention from intervention and maintenance. Prevention is *avoiding a disorder from the start.* Intervention is *identifying a disorder in its early stages and relieving it,* and maintenance is *taking steps to keep a disorder from becoming more serious.* Prevention takes several forms. A *universal* program targets everyone, such as an antismoking campaign, or abolition of lead-based paints and leaded gasoline. A *selective* program includes only people at risk, such as people with a family history of some disorder. An *indicated* program identifies people in the early stages of a disorder and tries to stop it. An indicated program is closer to intervention than to prevention.

Community psychologists *try to help people change their environment, both to prevent disorders and to promote a positive sense of mental well-being,* analogous to the goals set by Alfred Adler (Trickett, 2009). For example, many schools have instituted social and emotional learning programs (SEL) to teach self-management, social relationship skills, and responsible decision making. These programs reliably reduce the prevalence of conduct problems and emotional distress, but in addition they improve social skills, emotional control, and academic performance even for students who were already doing reasonably well (Durlak, Weissberg, Dymncki, Taylor, & Schellinger, 2011). Success of this type shows the potential of well-designed universal prevention programs.

However, many prevention programs that sound good don't work. For example, prolonged discussions of a dreadful experience shortly after the event are more likely to cause than prevent post-traumatic stress disorder. "Scared straight" interventions tend to increase, not decrease, criminal behavior. Group therapy for aggressive teenagers often backfires by introducing them to potential partners. Several programs intended to prevent anorexia nervosa or to decrease suicide rates have in fact increased the rates (Joiner, 1999; Mann et al., 1997; Moller, 1992; Stice & Shaw, 2004; Taylor et al., 2006). The point is that we need careful research to identify effective methods of prevention (Lilienfeld, 2007; Nicholson, Foote, & Gigerick, 2009). Good intentions are not enough.

The best programs give participants active practice at specific behaviors, such as resisting peer pressure to risky behaviors. They build up step by step from simpler skills to more complex ones, analogous to Skinner's method of shaping. And they work with people at appropriate times in their lives. For example, AIDS prevention or pregnancy prevention should start at an age when students might begin to be sexually active, not several years earlier or several years later.

Here are examples of effective prevention programs:

• **Ban toxins.** The sale of lead-based paint was banned because children who eat flakes of it sustain brain damage.
• **Educate pregnant women about prenatal care.** The developing brain is vulnerable. It develops best if the mother avoids or minimizes alcohol, other drugs, and bacterial and viral infections.
• **Outlaw smoking in public places and educate people about the risks of smoking.** Improvements in physical health improve psychological well-being, too.
• **Help people get jobs.** People who lose their jobs lose self-esteem and increase their risk of depression and substance abuse. Summer jobs for low-income teenagers decrease their probability of violent crime, not only during the summer but also long after (Heller, 2014).
• **Neighborhood improvement.** Low-income people who move from a crime-ridden neighborhood to a less distressed neighborhood experience long-term benefits in mental health (Ludwig et al., 2012).
• **Prevent bullying in school.** Children who are frequently bullied have an increased risk of anxiety, depression, and other distress throughout life (Takizawa, Maughan, & Aarseneault, 2014).

31. Why is it important to do careful research before initiating a new program to prevent a psychological disorder?

Answer

31. Some programs intended for prevention have been ineffective or counterproductive.

Social Issues Related to Mental Illness

Finally, let's consider some public policy issues you may face as a citizen. First, mental hospitals: Long ago, huge numbers of troubled people were confined in understaffed, overcrowded mental hospitals. Residents included not only mental patients but also people with Alzheimer's disease and other intellectual disabilities.

Beginning in the 1950s, the policy moved toward deinstitutionalization, *the removal of patients from mental hospitals,* to give them the least restrictive care possible—an idea that many people had been advocating for 100 years or more (Tuntiya, 2007). The hope was that patients would go home, free to live as normal a life as possible, while receiving outpatient care at community mental health centers, which are both cheaper and more effective than residential mental hospitals. England and Wales had 130 psychiatric hospitals in 1975 but only 12 in 2000 (Leff, 2002). The United States had almost 200,000 people in mental hospitals in 1967 and fewer than 40,000 in 2007 (Scott, Lakin, & Larson, 2008).

But what happened to people after release from the mental hospitals? Implementing good alternative care wasn't easy. Policies vary from one place to another, and the effectiveness has been undependable (Markström, 2014). Too often, patients were just released with little or no alternative care. Deinstitutionalization was and is a good idea in principle, but only if implemented well, and in many cases it has not been.

The Duty to Protect

Suppose you are a therapist, and someone tells you that he is thinking about killing a woman who refused his attentions. Later, he really does kill her. Should her family be able to sue you for not warning them?

In the 1976 Tarasoff case, a California court ruled that *a therapist who has reason to believe that a client is dangerous to someone must warn the endangered person or take other steps to prevent harm.* That rule has become widely accepted in most of the United States and Canada, although its application is sometimes unclear (Quattrocchi & Schopp, 2005). Imagine you are the therapist. If someone says he is thinking about killing someone, would you know how seriously to

Deinstitutionalization moved people out of mental hospitals, but many received little or no treatment after their release.

take that threat? Therapists don't always know who is dangerous and who is just expressing a moment of frustration. An unintended result of the *Tarasoff* rule is that many therapists are now hesitant to take potentially violent clients, for fear of legal responsibility, and many clients decline to discuss their violent impulses, for fear of involuntary commitment (Bersoff, 2014; Edwards, 2014).

The Insanity Defense

Suppose someone slips into your drink a drug that causes you to hallucinate wildly. Suddenly you see what looks like a hideous giant cockroach, and you kill it. Later when you feel normal, you discover it was not a cockroach but a person. Should you be convicted of murder? Of course not. Now suppose your own brain chemistry causes the same hallucination. You kill what you think is a giant cockroach, but it is actually a human being. Are you guilty of murder?

The tradition since Roman times has been that you are "not guilty, by reason of insanity." You had no intention to do harm, and you did not know what you were doing. You should go to a mental hospital, not a prison. Most people agree with that principle in extreme cases. The problem is where to draw the line. *Insanity* is a legal term, not a psychological or medical term. According to the most famous definition of insanity, the M'Naghten rule, written in Great Britain in 1843,

> [t]o establish a defense on the ground of insanity, it must be clearly proved that, at the time of the committing of the act, the party accused was laboring under such a defect of reason, from disease of the mind, as not to know the nature and quality of the act he was doing; or if he did know it, that he did not know he was doing what was wrong.

Would a diagnosis of schizophrenia or another mental illness demonstrate that someone was insane? Not by itself. What if someone committed a bizarre crime that most people couldn't imagine committing? Still no. Jeffrey Dahmer, arrested in 1991

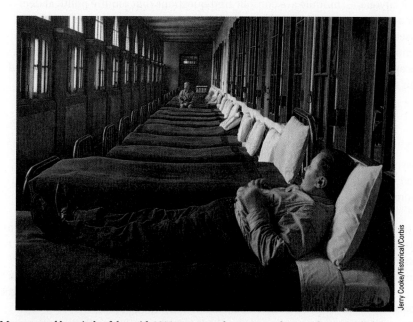

Most mental hospitals of the mid-1900s were unpleasant warehouses that provided minimal care.

for murdering and cannibalizing several men, was ruled sane and sentenced to prison. *To be regarded as insane under the M'Naghten rule, people must be so disordered that they do not understand what they are doing.* Someone who tries to prevent the police from detecting a criminal act presumably did understand what he or she was doing.

An insanity verdict requires a difficult judgment about the defendant's state of mind at the time of the act. To help make that judgment, psychologists and psychiatrists testify as expert witnesses. The insanity cases that come to a jury trial are the difficult ones in which the experts disagree. In the United States, fewer than 1 percent of accused felons plead insanity, and of those, fewer than one-fourth are found not guilty (Knoll & Resnick, 2008). However, those rare cases get enough publicity that many people overestimate how common they are.

Another misconception is that defendants found not guilty by reason of insanity simply go free. In fact, they are almost always committed to a mental hospital, where their average stay is at least as long as the average prison term (Silver, 1995). If and when they are eventually released, it is usually a "conditional release" that requires them to follow certain rules, such as continuing to take their medicine or to abstain from alcohol (Marshall, Vitaco, Read, & Harway, 2014).

Answer

32. How does the concept of mental illness differ from the concept of insanity?

32. Mental illness is a psychological or psychiatric concept indicating that someone has emotional or behavioral problems. Insanity is a legal concept indicating that someone is so disturbed as to not understand what he or she is doing. Mental illness is common, and legal insanity is rare.

Jeffery Dahmer, who murdered and cannibalized several men, was ruled sane. The bizarreness of the crime itself does not demonstrate legal insanity.

in closing module 15.5

The Science and Politics of Mental Illness

Suppose you are a storekeeper. Someone dressed as Batman stands outside your store every day shouting gibberish at anyone who comes by. Your once thriving business draws fewer and fewer customers. The disturbing man outside does not seem to be breaking any laws. He wants nothing to do with psychologists or psychiatrists. Should he nevertheless be forced to accept treatment for his odd behavior? If so, are we doing that for his sake or for yours as a storekeeper?

Similarly, the insanity defense and the other issues in this module are complicated questions that require political decisions by society as a whole, not just the opinions of psychologists or psychiatrists. Regardless of what career you enter, you will be a voter and potential juror, and you will have a voice in deciding these issues. The decisions deserve serious, informed consideration.

Summary

- *Historical trends.* Contrary to practices of the past, psychotherapy today uses a variety of empirically supported methods and tries to achieve results with brief treatments that insurance will support. (page 512)
- *Psychodynamic therapies.* Psychodynamic therapies, including psychoanalysis, tries to uncover the unconscious reasons behind self-defeating behaviors. Psychoanalysts rely on methods that include free association, dream analysis, and transference. (page 513)
- *Behavior therapy.* Behavior therapists set specific goals for changing a client's behavior and use learning techniques to help clients achieve those goals. (page 514)
- *Cognitive therapies.* Cognitive therapists try to get clients to replace defeatist thinking with more favorable views of themselves and the world. They also encourage greater activity. (page 514)
- *Humanistic therapy.* Humanistic therapists, including person-centered therapists, listen empathically without giving advice or interpretations. (page 515)
- *Family systems therapy.* Many individual problems relate to a disorder of family communications. Family systems therapists try to work with a whole family. (page 515)
- *Group therapies and self-help groups.* Psychotherapy is sometimes provided to people in groups, often composed of

individuals with similar problems. Self-help groups are similar to group therapy sessions, but without a therapist. (page 515)

- *Effectiveness of psychotherapy.* Mainstream forms of therapy are about equally effective for most problems, because they share several features: a caring relationship with a therapist, an effort at self-understanding, improved morale, and a commitment to make changes. (page 516)
- *Prevention.* Psychologists, especially community psychologists, seek to help people change their environment to promote mental health. Prevention requires research, because many well-meaning attempts at prevention can be ineffective or harmful. (page 518)
- *Deinstitutionalization.* Ideally, mental patients should get good care without being in a mental hospital, but the availability of such care is undependable. (page 519)
- *Duty to warn.* The courts have ruled that a therapist who is convinced that a client is dangerous should warn the endangered person. However, it is difficult to be certain about whether someone is dangerous. (page 519)
- *The insanity defense.* A criminal defendant can be acquitted because of insanity. In most cases the insanity defense is limited to people so disturbed that they do not understand what they are doing. (page 519)

Key Terms

behavior therapy (page 514)

cognitive therapy (page 514)

cognitive-behavior therapy (page 515)

community psychologist (page 518)

deinstitutionalization (page 519)

dream analysis (page 513)

eclectic therapy (page 515)

empirically supported treatments (page 512)

family systems therapy (page 515)

free association (page 513)

group therapy (page 515)

intervention (page 518)

maintenance (page 518)

M'Naghten rule (page 519)

person-centered therapy (page 515)

prevention (page 518)

psychoanalysis (page 513)

psychodynamic therapies (page 513)

psychotherapy (page 512)

self-help group (page 516)

spontaneous remission (page 516)

Tarasoff case (page 519)

transference (page 513)

Review Questions

1. What happens during free association?
   - (a) People join a self-help group without an obligation to pay.
   - (b) A therapist shows ambiguous pictures and asks what they mean.
   - (c) People in group therapy walk around and talk.
   - (d) A client says everything that comes to mind.

2. Which type of therapist uses positive reinforcement to achieve specific goals?
   - (a) Cognitive therapist
   - (b) Humanistic therapist
   - (c) Psychodynamic therapist
   - (d) Behavior therapist

3. In the behavior-therapy method used for bed-wetting children, what does the device do?
   - (a) It punishes the child for wetting the bed.
   - (b) It plays soothing music.
   - (c) It alerts the parents when the child wets the bed.
   - (d) It wakes a child when he/she wets the bed.

4. How does a self-help group differ from group therapy?
   - (a) A self-help group has people with more serious disorders.
   - (b) A self-help group has no therapist.
   - (c) A self-help group distributes readings instead of having meetings.
   - (d) A self-help group charges every participant the same amount.

5. To show that a new form of therapy is effective, researchers need to show that it produces better results than what?
   - (a) The researchers' predictions
   - (b) Other forms of therapy
   - (c) Spontaneous remission
   - (d) The clients' expectations

6. Which of the following is characteristic of community psychologists?
   - (a) They try to prevent mental disorders before they start.
   - (b) They live in the same neighborhood as their patients.
   - (c) They provide therapy to large groups of people at once.
   - (d) They rely on telephone and Internet services.

7. What does the *Tarasoff* ruling require?
   - (a) Communities should be free from lead paint and other pollutants.
   - (b) People who commit a crime but do not understand what they are doing should be considered not guilty by reason of insanity.
   - (c) Mentally ill people should be released from mental hospitals and given alternative care.
   - (d) A therapist should alert someone whom a client has threatened.

Answers: 1d, 2d, 3d, 4b, 5c, 6a, 7d.

Here we are at the end of the book. As I've been writing and revising, I've imagined you sitting there reading. I've imagined a student much like I was in college, reading about psychology for the first time and often growing excited about it. I remember periodically telling a friend or relative, "Guess what I just learned about psychology! Isn't this interesting?" (I still do the same today.) I also remember occasionally thinking, "Hmm. The book says such-and-so, but I'm not convinced. I wonder whether psychologists ever considered a different explanation. . . ." I started thinking about research I might do if I became a psychologist.

I hope that you've had similar experiences yourself. I hope you've occasionally become so excited about something you read that you thought about it and told other people about it. In fact, I hope you told your roommate so much about psychology that you started to become mildly annoying. I also hope you've sometimes doubted a conclusion, imagining a research project that might test it or improve on it. Psychology is still a work in progress.

Now, as I picture you reaching the end of the course, I'm not sure how you'll react. You might be thinking, "Wow, I sure have learned a lot!" Or you might be thinking, "Is that *all*?" Maybe you are reacting both ways: "Yes, I learned a lot. But it seems like there should be more. I still don't understand what conscious experience is all about, and I don't understand why I react the way I do sometimes. However, this book—*wonderful as it is!*—hardly mentioned certain topics. Why do we laugh? How do we sense the passage of time? Why do people like to watch sports? Why are some people religious and others not?"

I have two good reasons for not answering all of your questions. One is that this is an introductory text and it can't go on forever. If you want to learn more, you should take other psychology courses or do additional reading. The other reason is that psychologists do not know all the answers.

Perhaps someday you'll become a researcher yourself and add to our knowledge. If not, you can try to keep up to date on current developments in psychology by reading good books and magazine articles. The magazine *Scientific American Mind* is an excellent source. One of my main goals has been to prepare you to continue learning about psychology.

Try to read critically: Is a conclusion based on good evidence? If you read about a survey, were the questions worded clearly? How reliable and valid were the measurements? Did the investigators obtain a representative or random sample? If someone draws a cause-and-effect conclusion, was the evidence based on experiments or only correlations? Even if the evidence looks solid, is the author's explanation the best one?

Above all, remember that *any* conclusion is tentative. Psychological researchers seldom use the word *prove;* their conclusions are almost always tentative. I once suggested to my editor, half seriously, that we should include in the index to this book the entry "*maybe*—see pages 1–522." We did not include such an entry, partly because I doubt anyone would have noticed the humor, and partly because our understanding of psychology isn't really that bad. Still, be leery of anyone who seems a little too certain about a great new insight in psychology. It's a long route from *maybe to definitely.*

Numbers in parentheses indicate the chapter in which a source is cited.

Abramson, L., Marom, I., Petranker, R., & Aviezer, H. (2017). Is fear in your head? A comparison of instructed and real-life expressions of emotion in the face and body. *Emotion, 17,* 557–565. (12) doi: 10.1037/emo0000252

Acevedo, B. P., Aron, A., Fisher, H. E., & Brown, L. L. (2012). Neural correlates of long-term intense romantic love. *Social Cognitive and Affective Neuroscience, 7,* 145–159. (13) doi: 10.1093/scan/nsq092

Ackerman, P. L. (2017). Adult intelligence: The construct and the criterion problem. *Perspectives on Psychological Science, 12,* 987–998. (9) doi: 10.1177/1745691617703437

Ackil, J. K., Van Abbema, D. L., & Bauer, P. J. (2003). After the storm: Enduring differences in mother-child recollections of traumatic and nontraumatic events. *Journal of Experimental Child Psychology, 84,* 286–309. (7) doi: 10.1016/S0022-0965(03)00027-4

Adam, H., Shirako, A., & Maddux, W. W. (2010). Cultural variance in the interpersonal effects of anger in negotiations. *Psychological Science, 21,* 882–889. (5) doi: 10.1177/0956797610370755

Adams, J. S. (1963). Wage inequities, productivity, and work quality. *Industrial Relations, 3,* 9–16. (11) doi: 10.1111/j.1468-232X.1963.tb00805.x

Adams, R. B., & Kleck, R. E. (2003). Perceived gaze direction and the processing of facial displays of emotion. *Psychological Science, 14,* 644–647. (12) doi: 10.1046/j.0956-7976.2003.psci_1479.x

Adams, R. B., & Kleck, R. E. (2005). Effects of direct and averted gaze on the perception of facially communicated emotion. *Emotion, 5,* 3–11. (12) doi: 10.1037/1528-3542.5.1.3

Adler, A. (1964). Brief comments on reason, intelligence, and feeble-mindedness. In H. L. Ansbacher & R. R. Ansbacher (Eds.), *Superiority and social interest* (pp. 41–49). New York: Viking Press. (Original work published 1928) (14)

Adler, A. (1964). The structure of neurosis. In H. L. Ansbacher & R. R. Ansbacher (Eds.), *Superiority and social interest* (pp. 83–95). New York: Viking Press. (Original work published 1932) (14)

Adler, E., Hoon, M. A., Mueller, K. L., Chandrashekar, J., Ryba, N. J. P., & Zuker, C. S. (2000). A novel family of mammalian taste receptors. *Cell, 100,* 693–702. (4) doi: 10.1016/S0092-8674(00)80705-9

Admon, R., Lubin, G., Stern, O., Rosenberg, K., Sela, L., Ben-Ami, H., & Hendler, T. (2009). Human vulnerability to stress depends on amygdala's predisposition and hippocampal plasticity. *Proceedings of the National Academy of Sciences, U.S.A., 106,* 14120–14125. (12) doi: 10.1073/pnas.0903183106

Adolph, K. E. (2000). Specificity of learning: Why infants fall over a veritable cliff. *Psychological Science, 11,* 290–295. (5) doi: 10.1111/1467-9280.00258

Adolphs, R., Baron-Cohen, S., & Tranel, D. (2002). Impaired recognition of social emotions following amygdala damage. *Journal of Cognitive Neuroscience, 14,* 1264–1274. (12) doi: 10.1162/089892902760807258

Adolphs, R., Damasio, H., & Tranel, D. (2002). Neural systems for recognition of emotional prosody: A 3-D lesion study. *Emotion, 2,* 23–51. (3) doi: 10.1037/1528-3542.2.1.23

Agar, W. E., Drummond, F. H., Tiegs, O. W., & Gunson, M. M. (1954). Fourth (final) report on a test of McDougall's Lamarckian experiment on the training of rats. *Journal of Experimental Biology, 31,* 307–321. (2) https://jeb.biologists.org/content/31/3/307

Agerström, J., & Rooth, D. O. (2011). The role of automatic obesity stereotypes in real hiring decisions. *Journal of Applied Psychology, 96,* 790–805. (13) doi: 10.1037/a0021594

Aglioti, S. M., Cesari, P., Romani, M., & Urgesi, C. (2008). Action anticipation and motor resonance in elite basketball players. *Nature Neuroscience, 11,* 1109–1116. (8) doi: 10.1038/nn.2182

Aguinis, H., Culpepper, S. A., & Pierce, C. A. (2016). Differential prediction generalization in college admission testing. *Journal of Educational Psychology, 108,* 1045–1059. (9) doi: 10.1037/edu0000104

Ahn, W., Flanagan, E. H., Marsh, J. K., & Sanislow, C. A. (2006). Beliefs about essences and the reality of mental disorders. *Psychological Science, 17,* 759–766. (15) doi: 10.1111/j.1467-9280.2006.01779.x

Ahn, H.-K., Kim, H. J., & Aggarwal, P. (2013). Helping fellow beings: Anthropomorphized social causes and the role of anticipatory guilt. *Psychological Science, 25,* 224–229. (13) doi: 10.1177/0956797613496823

Aichele, S., Ghisletta, P., Corley, J., Pattie, A., Taylor, A. M., Starr, J. M., & Deary, I. J. (2018). Fluid intelligence predicts change in depressive symptoms in later life: The Lothian birth cohort 1936. *Psychological Science, 29,* 1984–1995. (9) doi: 10.1177/0956797618804501

Ainsworth, M. D. S. (1979). Attachment as related to mother-infant interaction. In J. S. Rosenblatt, R. A. Hinde, C. Beer, & M. Busnel (Eds.), *Advances in the study of behavior* (Vol. 9, pp. 1–51). New York: Academic Press. (5)

Ainsworth, M. D. S., Blehar, M., Waters, E., & Wall, S. (1978). *Patterns of attachment.* Hillsdale, NJ: Erlbaum. (5)

Ajina, S., Pestilli, F., Rokem, A., Kennard, C., & Bridge, H. (2015). Human blindsight is mediated by an intact geniculo-extrastriate pathway. *eLife, 4,* article 08935. (3) doi: 10.7554/eLife.08935

Akers, K. G., Martinez-Canabal, A., Restivo, L., Yiu, A. P., De Cristofaro, A., Hsiang, H.-L., Wheeler, A. L., Guskjolen, A., Niibori, Y., Shoji, H., Ohira, K., Richards, B. A., Miyakawa, T., Josselyn, S. A., & Frankland, P. W. (2014). Hippocampal neurogenesis regulates forgetting during adulthood and infancy. *Science, 344,* 598–602. (7) doi: 10.1126/science.1248903

Åkerstedt, T. (2007). Altered sleep/wake patterns and mental performance. *Physiology and Behavior, 90,* 209–218. (10) doi: 10.1016/j.physbeh.2006.09.007

Aknin, L. B., Hamlin, J. K., & Dunn, E. W. (2012). Giving leads to happiness in young children. *PLoS One, 7,* e39211. (12) doi: 10.1371/journal.pone.0039211

Akrami, N., Ekehammar, B., & Bergh, R. (2011). Generalized prejudice: Common and specific components. *Psychological Science, 22,* 57–59. (14) doi: 10.1177/0956797610390384

Albee, G. W. (1986). Toward a just society: Lessons from observations on the primary prevention of psychopathology. *American Psychologist, 41,* 891–898. (15) doi: 10.1037/0003-066X.41.8.891

Albuquerque, D., Nóbrega, C., Manco, L., & Padez, C. (2017). The contribution of genetics and environment to obesity. *British Medical Bulletin, 123,* 159–173. (11) doi: 10.1177/1745691617703437

Alcock, J. E. (2011, March/April). Back from the future: Parapsychology and the Bem affair. *Skeptical Inquirer, 35*(2), 31–39. (2) https://skepticalinquirer.org/exclusive/back-from-the-future/

Alexander, B. K., Coambs, R. B., & Hadaway, P. F. (1978). The effect of housing and gender on morphine self-administration in rats. *Psychopharmacology, 58,* 175–179. (15) doi: 10.1007/BF00426903

Alexander, G. M., & Hines, M. (2002). Sex differences in response to children's toys in nonhuman primates (*Cercopithecus aethiops sabaeus*). *Evolution and Human Behavior, 23,* 467–479. (5) doi: 10.1016/S1090-5138(02)00107-1

Alexander, G. M., Wilcox, T., & Woods, R. (2009). Sex differences in infants' visual interest in toys. *Archives of Sexual Behavior, 38,* 427–433. (5, 14) doi: 10.1007/s10508-008-9430-1

Alexander, I. E. (1982). The Freud-Jung relationship—the other side of Oedipus and countertransference. *American Psychologist, 37,* 1009–1018. (14) doi: 10.1037//0003-066x.37.9.1009

Alexander, K. W., Quas, J. A., Goodman, G. S., Ghetti, S., Edelstein, R. S., Redlich, A. D., Cordon, I. M., & Jones, D. P. H. (2005). Traumatic impact predicts long-term memory for documented child sexual abuse. *Psychological Science, 16,* 33–40. (7) doi: 10.1111/j.0956-7976.2005.00777.x

Alison, L. J., Smith, M. D., Eastman, O., & Rainbow, L. (2003). Toulmin's philosophy of argument and its relevance to offender profiling. *Psychology, Crime and Law, 9,* 173–183. (14) doi: 10.1080/1068316031000116265

Allen, J., Romay-Tallon, R., Brymer, K. J., Caruncho, H. J., & Kalynchuk, L. E. (2018). Mitochondria and mood: Mitochondrial dysfunction as a key player in the manifestation of depression. *Frontiers in Neuroscience, 12,* article 386. (15) doi: 10.3389/fnins.2018.00386

Allison, S. T., Mackie, D. M., Muller, M. M., & Worth, L. T. (1993). Sequential correspondence biases and perceptions of change: The Castro studies revisited. *Personality and Social Psychology Bulletin, 19,* 151–157. (13) doi: 10.1177/0146167293192003

Alloy, L. B., Abramson, L. Y., Whitehouse, W. G., Hogan, M. E., Tashman, N. A., Steinberg, D. L., Rose, D. T., & Donovan, P. (1999). Depressogenic cognitive styles: Predictive validity, information processing and personality characteristics, and developmental origins. *Behaviour Research and Therapy, 37*, 503–531. (15) doi: 10.1016/S0005-7967(98)00157-0

Allport, G. W. (1935). Attitudes. In C. Murchison (Ed.), *A handbook of social psychology* (pp. 798–844). Worcester, MA: Clark University Press. (13)

Allport, G. W. (1961). *Pattern and growth in personality.* New York: Holt, Rinehart & Winston. (14)

Allport, G. W., & Odbert, H. S. (1936). Traitnames: A psycholexical study. *Psychological Monographs, 47*(Whole No. 211). (14) doi: 10.1037/h0093360

Alpers, G. W., & Gerdes, A. B. M. (2007). Here is looking at you: Emotional faces predominate in binocular rivalry. *Emotion, 7*, 495–506. (10) doi: 10.1037/1528-3542.7.3.495

Alpert, J. L., Brown, L. S., & Courtois, C. A. (1998). Symptomatic clients and memories of childhood abuse. *Psychology, Public Policy, and Law, 4*, 941–995. (7) doi: 10.1037/1076-8971.4.4.941

Alroe, C. J., & Gunda, V. (1995). Self-amputation of the ear. *Australian and New Zealand Journal of Psychiatry, 29*, 508–512. (15) doi: 10.3109/00048679509064962

Alter, A. L., Oppenheimer, D. M., Epley, N., & Eyre, R. N. (2007). Overcoming intuition: Metacognitive difficulty activates analytic reasoning. *Journal of Experimental Psychology: General, 136*, 569–576. (8) doi: 10.1037/0096-3445.136.4.569

Altmann, E. M., & Gray, W. D. (2002). Forgetting to remember: The functional relationship of decay and interference. *Psychological Science, 13*, 27–33. (7) doi: 10.1111/1467-9280.00405

Aluja, A., Balada, F., Blanco, E., Fibla, J., & Blanch, A. (2019). Twenty candidate genes predicting neuroticism and sensation seeking personality traits: A multivariate analysis association approach. *Personality and Individual Differences, 140*, 90–102. (14) doi: 10.1016/j.paid.2018.03.041

Ambady, N., & Rosenthal, R. (1993). Half a minute: Predicting teacher evaluations from thin slices of nonverbal behavior and physical attractiveness. *Journal of Personality and Social Psychology, 64*, 431–441. (13) doi: 10.1037/0022-3514.64.3.431

Amelang, M., & Steinmayr, R. (2006). Is there a validity increment for tests of emotional intelligence in explaining the variance of performance criteria? *Intelligence, 34*, 459–468. (12) doi: 10.1016/j.intell.2006.03.003

American Medical Association. (1986). Council report: Scientific status of refreshing recollection by the use of hypnosis. *International Journal of Clinical and Experimental Hypnosis, 34*, 1–12. (10) doi: 10.1080/00207148608407388

American Psychiatric Association (2013). *Diagnostic and Statistical Manual of Mental Disorders* (fifth edition). Washington, DC: American Psychiatric Publishing. (15)

Amodio, D. M., & Harmon-Jones, E. (2011). Trait emotions and affective modulation of the startle eyeblink: On the unique relationship of trait anger. *Emotion, 11*, 47–51. (12) doi: 10.1037/a0021238

Anacker, C., & Hen, R. (2017). Adult hippocampal neurogenesis and cognitive flexibility—linking memory and mood. *Nature Reviews Neuroscience, 18*, 335–346. (15) doi: 10.1038/nrn.2017.45

Anafi, R. C., Kayser, M. S., & Raizen, D. M. (2019). Exploring phylogeny to find the function of sleep. *Nature Reviews Neuroscience, 20*, 109–116. (10) doi: 10.1038/s41583-018-0098-9

Anderson, A., & Phelps, E. A. (2000). Expression without recognition: Contributions of the human amygdala to emotional communication. *Psychological Science, 11*, 106–111. (12) doi: 10.1111/1467-9280.00224

Anderson, C., Keltner, D., & John, O. P. (2003). Emotional convergence between people over time. *Journal of Personality and Social Psychology, 84*, 1054–1068. (13) doi: 10.1037/0022-3514.84.5.1054

Anderson, D. I., Campos, J., Witherington, D. C., Dahl, A., Rivera, M., He, M., Uchiyama, I., & Barbu-Roth, M. (2013). The role of locomotion in psychological development. *Frontiers in Psychology, 4*, Article 440. (5) doi: 10.3389/fpsyg.2013.00440

Anderson, E., Siegel, E., White, D., & Barrett, L. F. (2012). Out of sight but not out of mind: Unseen affective faces influence evaluations and social impressions. *Emotion, 12*, 1210–1221. (10) doi: 10.1037/a0027514

Anderson, S., Parbery-Clark, A., White-Schwoch, T., & Kraus, N. (2012). Aging affects neural precision of speech encoding. *Journal of Neuroscience, 32*, 14156–14164. (4) doi: 10.1523/JNEUROSCI.2176-12.2012

Anderson, S. F., Monroe, S. M., Rohde, P., & Lewinsohn, P. M. (2016). Questioning kindling: An analysis of cycle acceleration in unipolar depression. *Clinical Psychological Science, 4*, 229–238. (15) doi: 10.1177/2167702615591951

Andreano, J. M., & Cahill, L. (2006). Glucocorticoid release and memory consolidation in men and women. *Psychological Science, 17*, 466–470. (7) doi: 10.1111/j.1467-9280.2006.01729.x

Andreasen, N. C. (1986). Scale for the assessment of thought, language, and communication. *Schizophrenia Bulletin, 12*, 473–482. (15) doi: 10.1093/schbul/12.3.473

Andrew, D., & Craig, A. D. (2001). Spinothalamic lamina I neurons selectively sensitive to histamine: A central neural pathway for itch. *Nature Neuroscience, 4*, 72–77. (4) doi: 10.1038/82924

Andrew, K. N., Hoshooley, J., & Joanisse, M. F. (2014). Sign language ability in young deaf signers predicts comprehension of written sentences in English. *PLoS One, 9*, e89994. (8) doi: 10.1371/journal.pone.0089994

Andrews, T. J., Halpern, S. D., & Purves, D. (1997). Correlated size variations in human visual cortex, lateral geniculate nucleus, and optic tract. *Journal of Neuroscience, 17*, 2859–2868. (4) doi: 10.1523/JNEUROSCI.17-08-02859.1997.

Andino, S. L. G., de Peralta Menendez, R. G., Khateb, A., Landis, T., & Pegna, A. J. (2009). Electrophysiological correlates of affective blindsight. *NeuroImage, 44*, 581–589. (3) doi: 10.1016/j.neuroimage.2008.09.002

Anglin, S. M. (2014). From avoidance to approach: The effects of mortality salience and attachment on the motivation to repair troubled relationships. *Personality and Individual Differences, 66*, 86–91. (5) doi: 10.1016/j.paid.2014.03.012

Anglin, D., Spears, K. L., & Hutson, H. R. (1997). Flunitrazepam and its involvement in date or acquaintance rape. *Academy of Emergency Medicine, 4*, 323–326. (3) doi: 10.1111/j.1553-2712.1997.tb03557.x

Anonymous. (1955). *Alcoholics anonymous* (2nd ed.). New York: Alcoholics Anonymous World Services. (15)

Antoniadis, E. A., Winslow, J. T., Davis, M., & Amaral, D. G. (2007). Role of the primate amygdala in fear-potentiated startle. *Journal of Neuroscience, 27*, 7386–7396. (12) doi: 10.1523/JNEUROSCI.5643-06.2007

APA Presidential Task Force on Evidence-Based Practice. (2006). Evidence-based practice in psychology. *American Psychologist, 61*, 271–285. (15) 10.1037/0003-066X.61.4.271

Arágon, O. R., Dovidio, J. F., & Graham, M. J. (2017). Colorblind and multicultural ideologies are associated with faculty adoption of inclusive teaching practices. *Journal of Diversity in Higher Education, 10*, 201–215. (13) doi: 10.1037/dhe0000026

Arden, R., Trzaskowski, M., Garfield, V., & Plomin, R. (2014). Genes influence young children's human figure drawings and their association with intelligence a decade later. *Psychological Science, 25*, 1843–1850. (3) doi: 10.1177/0956797614540686

Ariely, D., & Wertenbroch, K. (2002). Procrastination, deadlines, and performance: Self-control by precommitment. *Psychological Science, 13*, 219–224. (11) doi: 10.1111/1467-9280.00441

Arkes, H. R. (2013). The consequences of the hindsight bias in medical decision making. *Current Directions in Psychological Science, 22*, 356–360. (7) doi: 10.1177/0963721413489988

Arkes, H. R., & Ayton, P. (1999). The sunk cost and Concorde effects: Are humans less rational than lower animals? *Psychological Bulletin, 125*, 591–600. (8) doi: 10.1037/0033-2909.125.5.591

Armon, G. (2014). Type D personality and job burnout: The moderating role of physical activity. *Personality and Individual Differences, 58*, 112–115. (11) doi: 10.1016/j.paid.2013.10.020

Armor, D. A., Massey, C., & Sackett, A. M. (2008). Prescribed optimism: Is it right to be wrong about the future? *Psychological Science, 19*, 329–331. (12) doi: 10.1111/j.1467-9280.2008.02089.x

Armstrong, J. B., & Schindler, D. E. (2011). Excess digestive capacity in predators reflects a life of feast and famine. *Nature, 476*, 84–87. (11) doi: 10.1038/nature10240

Arnell, K. M., Killman, K. V., & Fijavz, D. (2007). Blinded by emotion: Target misses follow attention capture by arousing distractors in RSVP. *Emotion, 7*, 465–477. (7) doi: 10.1037/1528-3542.7.3.465

Arnold, H. J., & House, R. J. (1980). Methodological and substantive extensions to the job characteristics model of motivation. *Organizational Behavior and Human Performance, 25*, 161–183. (11) doi: 10.1016/0030-5073(80)90062-8

Aronow, E., Reznikoff, M., & Moreland, K. L. (1995). The Rorschach: Projective technique or psychometric test? *Journal of Personality Assessment, 64*, 213–228. (14) doi: 10.1207/s15327752jpa6402_1

Aronson, E. (1997). The theory of cognitive dissonance: The evolution and vicissitudes of an idea. In C. McGarty & S. A. Haslam (Eds.),

The message of social psychology (pp. 20–35). Cambridge, MA: Blackwell. (13)

Aronson, E., & Carlsmith, J. M. (1963). Effect of the severity of threat on the devaluation of forbidden behavior. *Journal of Abnormal and Social Psychology, 66,* 584–588. (13) doi: 10.1037/h0039901

Arvey, R. D., McCall, B. P., Bouchard, T. J., Jr., Taubman, P., & Cavanaugh, M. A. (1994). Genetic influences on job satisfaction and work values. *Personality and Individual Differences, 17,* 21–33. (11) doi: 10.1016/0191-8869(94)90258-5

Asch, S. E. (1951). Effects of group pressure upon the modification and distortion of judgments. In H. Guetzkow (Ed.), *Groups, leadership, and men* (pp. 177–190). Pittsburgh, PA: Carnegie Press. (13)

Asch, S. E. (1955, November). Opinions and social pressure. *Scientific American, 193*(5), 31–35. (13) doi: 10.1038/scientificamerican1155-31

Asch, S. E. (1956). Studies of independence and conformity: I. A minority of one against a unanimous majority. *Psychological Monographs, 70*(9, Whole No. 416). (13) doi: 10.1037/h0093718

Ash, R. (1986, August). An anecdote submitted by Ron Ash. *The Industrial-Organizational Psychologist, 23*(4), 8. (6)

Ashton-James, C. E., Maddux, W. W., Galinsky, A. D., & Chartrand, T. L. (2009). Who I am depends on how I feel. *Psychological Science, 20,* 340–346. (12) doi: 10.1111/j.1467-9280.2009.02299.x

Askun, D., & Ataca, B. (2007). Sexuality related attitudes and behaviors of Turkish university students. *Archives of Sexual Behavior, 36,* 741–752. (11) doi: 10.1007/s10508-007-9186-z

Athos, E. A., Levinson, B., Kistler, A., Zemansky, J., Bostrom, A., Freimer, N., & Gitschier, J. (2007). Dichotomy and perceptual distortions in absolute pitch ability. *Proceedings of the National Academy of Sciences, USA, 104,* 14795–14800. (4) doi: 10.1073/pnas.0703868104

Atir, S., Rosenzweig, E., & Dunning, D. (2015). When knowledge knows no bounds: Self-perceived expertise predicts claims of impossible knowledge. *Psychological Science, 26,* 1295–1303. (8) doi: 10.1177/0956797615588195

Atkinson, R. C., & Shiffrin, R. M. (1968). Human memory: A proposed system and its control. In K. W. Spence & J. T. Spence (Eds.), *The psychology of learning and motivation* (Vol. 2, pp. 89–105). New York: Academic Press. (7) http://www.rca.ucsd.edu/selected_papers/2_Human%20memory_A%20proposed%20system%20and%20its%20control%20processes.pdf

Augier, E., Barbier, E., Dulman, R. S., Licheri, V., Augier, G., Domi, E., Barchiesi, R., Farris, S., Natt, D., Mayfield, R. D., Adermark, L., & Heilig, M. (2018). A molecular mechanism for choosing alcohol over an alternative reward. *Science, 360,* 1321–1326. (15) doi: 10.1126/science.aao1157

Averill, J. R. (1983). Studies on anger and aggression: Implications for theories of emotion. *American Psychologist, 38,* 1145–1160. (12) doi: 10.1037/0003-066X.38.11.1145

Aviezer, H., Hassin, R. R., Ryan, J., Grady, C., Susskind, J., Anderson, A., Moscovitch, M., & Bentin, S. (2008). Angry, disgusted, or afraid? *Psychological Science, 19,* 724–732. (12) doi: 10.1111/j.1467-9280.2008.02148.x

Babkoff, H., Caspy, T., Mikulincer, M., & Sing, H. C. (1991). Monotonic and rhythmic influences: A challenge for sleep deprivation research. *Psychological Bulletin, 109,* 411–428. (10) doi: 10.1037/0033-2909.109.3.411

Back, M. D., Schmulkle, S. C., & Egloff, B. (2008). Becoming friends by chance. *Psychological Science, 19,* 439–440. (13) doi: 10.1111/j.1467-9280.2008.02106.x

Baddeley, A. D. (2001). Is working memory still working? *American Psychologist, 56,* 851–864. (7) doi: 10.1037/0003-066X.56.11.851

Baddeley, A., & Hitch, G. J. (1994). Developments in the concept of working memory. *Neuropsychology, 8,* 485–493. (7) doi: 10.1037/0894-4105.8.4.485

Bagby, R. M., Nicholson, R. A., Bacchiochi, J. R., Ryder, A. G., & Bury, A. S. (2002). The predictive capacity of the MMPI-2 and PAI validity scales and indexes to detect coached and uncoached feigning. *Journal of Personality Assessment, 78,* 69–86. (14) doi: 10.1207/S15327752JPA7801_05

Bagemihl, B. (1999). *Biological exuberance.* New York: St. Martin's Press. (11)

Bahrick, H. (1984). Semantic memory content in permastore: 50 years of memory for Spanish learned in school. *Journal of Experimental Psychology: General, 113,* 1–29. (7) doi: 10.1037/0096-3445.113.1.1

Bailey, A., Le Couteur, A., Gottesman, I., Bolton, P., Simonoff, E., Yuzda, E., & Rutter, M. (1995). Autism as a strongly genetic disorder: Evidence from a British twin study. *Psychological Medicine, 25,* 63–78. (15) doi: 10.1017/S0033291700028099

Bailey, J. M., & Pillard, R. C. (1991). A genetic study of male sexual orientation. *Archives of General Psychiatry, 48,* 1089–1096. (11) doi: 10.1001/archpsyc.1991.01810360053008

Bailey, J. M., Pillard, R. C., Neale, M. C., & Agyei, Y. (1993) Heritable factors influence sexual orientation in women. *Archives of General Psychiatry, 50,* 217–223. (11) doi: 10.1001/archpsyc.1993.01820150067007

Bailey, J. M., Vasey, P. L., Diamond, L. M., Breedlove, S. M., Vilain, E., & Epprecht, M. (2016). Sexual orientation, controversy, and science. *Psychological Science in the Public Interest, 17,* 45–101. (11) doi: 10.1177/1529100616637616

Baillargeon, R. (1986). Representing the existence and the location of hidden objects: Object permanence in 6- and 8-month-old infants. *Cognition, 23,* 21–41. (5) doi: 10.1016/0010-0277(86)90052-1

Baillargeon, R., Li, J., Ng, W., & Yuan, S. (2009). An account of infants' physical reasoning. In A. Woodward & A. Needham (Eds.), *Learning and the infant* (pp. 66–116). New York: Oxford University Press. (5) doi: 10.1093/acprof:oso/9780195301151.003.0004

Baird, J. C. (1982). The moon illusion: A reference theory. *Journal of Experimental Psychology: General, 111,* 304–315. (4) doi: 10.1037/0096-3445.111.3.304

Baker-Ward, L., Gordon, B. N., Ornstein, P. A., Larus, D. M., & Clubb, P. A. (1993). Young children's long-term retention of a pediatric examination. *Child Development, 64,* 1519–1533. (7) doi: 10.2307/1131550

Baker, T. B., Piper, M. E., McCarthy, D. E., Majeskie, M. R., & Fiore, M. C. (2004). Addiction motivation reformulated: An affective processing model of negative reinforcement.

Psychological Review, 111, 33–51. (15) doi: 10.1037/0033-295X.111.1.33

Baker, T. B., Piper, M. E., Shlam, T. R., Cook, J. W., Smith, S. S., Loh, W.-Y., & Bolt, D. (2012). Are tobacco dependence and withdrawal related amongst heavy smokers? Relevance to conceptualizations of dependence. *Journal of Abnormal Psychology, 121,* 909–921. (15) doi: 10.1037/a0027889

Bakhiet, S. E. F. A., Barakat, S. M. R., & Lynn, R. (2014). A Flynn effect among deaf boys in Saudi Arabia. *Intelligence, 44,* 75–77. (9) doi: 10.1016/j.intell.2014.03.003

Balcetis, E., Dunning, D., & Miller, R. L. (2008). Do collectivists know themselves better than individualists? Cross-cultural studies of the holier than thou phenomenon. *Journal of Personality and Social Psychology, 95,* 1252–1267. (13) doi: 10.1037/a0013195

Baldauf, D., & Desimone, R. (2014). Neural mechanisms of object-based attention. *Science, 344,* 424–427. (3) doi: 10.1126/science.1247003

Baldessarini, R. J. (1984). Antipsychotic drugs. In T. B. Karasu (Ed.), *The psychiatric therapies: I. The somatic therapies* (pp. 119–170). Washington, DC: American Psychiatric Press. (15)

Balestri, M., Calati, R., Serretti, A., & De Ronchi, D. (2014). Genetic modulation of personality traits: A systematic review of the literature. *International Clinical Psychopharmacology, 29,* 1–15. (14) doi: 10.1097/YIC.0b013e328364590b

Ballard, I. C., Kim, B., Liatsis, A., Aydogan, G., Cohen, J. D., & McClure, S. M. (2017). More is meaningful: The magnitude effect in intertemporal choice depends on self-control. *Psychological Science, 28,* 1443–1454. (11) doi: 10.1177/0956797617711455

Balliet, D., & Van Lange, P. A. M. (2013). Trust, punishment, and cooperation across 18 societies: A meta-analysis. *Perspectives on Psychological Science, 8,* 363–379. (13) doi: 10.1177/1745691613488533

Ballinger, B., & Yalom, I. (1995). Group therapy in practice. In B. Bongar & L. E. Beutler (Eds.), *Comprehensive textbook of psychotherapy: Theory and practice* (pp. 189–204). Oxford, England: Oxford University Press. (15)

Bandura, A. (1977). *Social learning theory.* Upper Saddle River, NJ: Prentice Hall. (6)

Bandura, A. (1986). *Social foundations of thought and action.* Upper Saddle River, NJ: Prentice Hall. (6)

Bandura, A., Barbaranelli, C., Caprara, G. V., & Pastorelli, C. (2001). Self-efficacy beliefs as shapers of children's aspirations and career trajectories. *Child Development, 72,* 187–206. (6) doi: 10.1111/1467-8624.00273

Bandura, A., & Ross, S. A. (1963). Imitation of film-mediated aggressive models. *Journal of Abnormal and Social Psychology, 66,* 3–11. (6) doi: 10.1037/h0048687

Banks, W. P., & Isham, E. A. (2009). We infer rather than perceive the moment we decided to act. *Psychological Science, 20,* 17–21. (10) doi: 10.1111/j.1467-9280.2008.02254.x

Banuazizi, A., & Movahedi, S. (1975). Interpersonal dynamics in a simulated prison. *American Psychologist, 30,* 152–160. (13) doi: 10.1037/h0076835

Barakat, M., Carrier, J., Debas, K., Lungu, O., Fogel, S., Vanderwalle, G., Hoge, R. D., Bellec, P., Karni, A., Ungerleider, L. G., Benali, H., & Doyon, J. (2013). Sleep spindles predict neural and behavioral changes in motor sequence consolidation. *Human Brain Mapping, 34,* 2918–2928. (10) doi: 10.1002/hbm.22116

Barber, S. J. (2017). An examination of age-based stereotype threat about cognitive decline: Implications for stereotype-threat research and theory development. *Perspectives on Psychological Science, 12,* 62–90. (9) doi: 10.1177/1745691616656345

Barch, D. M., Cohen, R., & Csernansky, J. G. (2014). Altered cognitive development in the siblings of individuals with schizophrenia. *Clinical Psychological Science, 2,* 138–151. (15) doi: 10.1177/2167702613496244

Barlow, D. H., Ellard, K. K., Sauer-Zavala, S., Bullis, J. R., & Carl, J. R. (2014). The origins of neuroticism. *Perspectives on Psychological Science, 9,* 481–496. (14) doi: 10.1177/1745691614544528

Barnes, C. M., Schaubroeck, J., Huth, M., & Ghumman, S. (2011). Lack of sleep and unethical conduct. *Organizational Behavior and Human Decision Processes, 115,* 169–180. (10) doi: 10.1016/j.obhdp.2011.01.009

Barnes, D. M., & Bates, L. M. (2017). Do racial patterns in psychological distress shed light on the Black-White depression paradox? A systematic review. *Social Psychiatry and Psychiatric Epidemiology, 52,* 913–928. (15) doi: 10.1007/s00127-017-1394-9

Barnett, K. J., Finucane, C., Asher, J. E., Bargary, G., Corvin, A. P., Newell, F. N., & Mitchell, K. J. (2008). Familial patterns and the origins of individual differences in synaesthesia. *Cognition, 106,* 871–893. (4) doi: 10.1016/j.cognition.2007.05.003

Barnett, M. D., & Melugin, P. R. (2016). Reported sexual pleasure among heterosexual men and women: An empirical investigation. *Personality and Individual Differences, 98,* 62–68. (11) doi: 10.1016/j.paid.2016.03.061

Barnett, S. M., & Ceci, S. J. (2002). When and where do we apply what we learn? A taxonomy for far transfer. *Psychological Bulletin, 128,* 612–637. (8) doi: 10.1037//0033-2909.128.4.612

Barnett, W. S. (2011). Effectiveness of early educational intervention. *Science, 333,* 975–978. (9) doi: 10.1126/science.1204534

Barnier, A. J., Cox, R. E., & McConkey, K. M. (2014). The province of "highs": The high hypnotizable person in the science of hypnosis and in psychological science. *Psychology of Consciousness, 1,* 168–183. (10) doi: 10.1037/cns0000018

Barnier, A. J., & McConkey, K. M. (1998). Posthypnotic responding away from the hypnotic setting. *Psychological Science, 9,* 256–262. (10) doi: 10.1111/1467-9280.00052

Baron, A., & Galizio, M. (2005). Positive and negative reinforcement: Should the distinction be preserved? *Behavior Analyst, 28,* 85–98. (6) doi: 10.1007/BF03392107

Barrett, L. F. (2006). Are emotions natural kinds? *Perspectives on Psychological Science, 1,* 28–58. (12) doi: 10.1111/j.1745-6916.2006.00003.x

Barrett, L. F. (2012). Emotions are real. *Emotion, 12,* 413–429. (12) doi: 10.1037/a0027555

Barrett, L. F., Adolphs, R., Marsella, S., Martinez, A. M., & Pollak, S. D. (2019). Emotional expressions reconsidered: Challenges to inferring emotion from human facial movements. *Psychological Science in the Public Interest, 20,* 1–68. (12) doi: 10.1177/1529100619832930

Barrett, L. F., Bliss-Moreau, E., Duncan, S. L., Rauch, S. L., & Wright, C. I. (2007). The amygdala and the experience of affect. *Social Cognitive and Affective Neuroscience, 2,* 73–83. (12) doi: 10.1093/scan/nsl042

Barrett, L. F., Mesquita, B., & Gendron, M. (2011). Context in emotion perception. *Current Directions in Psychological Science, 20,* 286–290. (12) doi: 10.1177/0963721411422522

Barrett, L. F., Tugade, M. M., & Engle, R. W. (2004). Individual differences in working memory capacity and dual-process theories of the mind. *Psychological Bulletin, 130,* 553–573. (7) doi: 10.1037/0033-2909.130.4.553

Barron, E., Riley, L. M., Greer, J., & Smallwood, J. (2011). Absorbed in thought: The effect of mind wandering on the processing of relevant and irrelevant events. *Psychological Science, 22,* 596–601. (8) doi: 10.1177/0956797611404083

Bartels, A., & Zeki, S. (2000). The neural basis of romantic love. *NeuroReport, 11,* 3829–3834. (13) doi: 10.1097/00001756-200011270-00046

Barth, J., Munder, T., Gerger, H., Nüesch, E., Trelle, S., Znoj, H., Juni, P., & Cuijpers, P. (2013). Comparative efficacy of seven psychotherapeutic interventions for patients with depression: A network meta-analysis. *PLoS Medicine, 10,* e1001454. (15) doi: 10.1371/journal.pmed.1001454

Bartholomaeus, J., & Strelan, P. (2019). The adaptive, approach-oriented correlates of belief in a just world for the self: A review of the research. *Personality and Individual Differences, 151,* article 109485. (14) doi: 10.1016/j.paid.2019.06.028

Bartlett, F. C. (1932). *Remembering.* Cambridge, England: Cambridge University Press. (7) doi: 10.1017/S0031819100033143

Bartoshuk, L. M. (1991). Taste, smell, and pleasure. In R. C. Bolles (Ed.), *The hedonics of taste* (pp. 5–28). Hillsdale, NJ: Erlbaum. (4)

Bartoshuk, L. M., Duffy, V. B., Lucchina, L. B., Prutkin, J., & Fast, K. (1998). PROP (6-n-propyl-thiouracil) supertasters and the saltiness of NaCl. *Annals of the New York Academy of Sciences, 855,* 793–796. (1) doi: 10.1111/j.1749-6632.1998.tb10660.x

Bartz, J. A., Simeon, D., Hamilton, H., Kim, S., Crystal, S., Braun, A., Vicens, V., & Hollander, E. (2011). Oxytocin can hinder trust and cooperation in borderline personality disorder. *Social, Cognitive, and Affective Neuroscience, 6,* 556–563. (3) doi: 10.1093/scan/nsq085

Basabe, N., Paez, D., Valencia, J., Gonzalez, J. L., Rimé, B., & Diener, E. (2002). Cultural dimensions, socioeconomic development, climate, and emotional hedonic level. *Cognition & Emotion, 16,* 103–125. (12) doi: 10.1080/02699930143000158

Bastiaansen, J. A., Servaas, M. N., Bernard, J., Marsman, C., Ormel, J., Nolte, I. M., Riese, H., & Aleman, A. (2014). Filling the gap: Relationship between the serotonin-transporter-linked polymorphic region and amygdala activation. *Psychological Science, 25,* 2058–2066. (14) doi: 10.1177/0956797614548877

Bates, T. C., Lewis, G. J., & Weiss, A. (2013). Childhood socioeconomic status amplifies genetic effects on adult intelligence. *Psychological Science, 24,* 2111–2116. (9) doi: 10.1177/0956797613488394

Batson, C. D., & Thompson, E. R. (2001). Why don't people act morally? Motivational considerations. *Current Directions in Psychological Science, 10,* 54–57. (11) doi: 10.1111/1467-8721.00114

Baugerud, G. A., Magnussen, S., & Melinder, A. (2014). High accuracy but low consistency in children's long-term recall of a real life stressful event. *Journal of Experimental Child Psychology, 126,* 357–368. (7) doi: 10.1016/j.jecp.2014.05.009

Baumeister, R. F. (2008). Free will in scientific psychology. *Perspectives on Psychological Science, 3,* 14–19. (1) doi: 10.1111/j.1745-6916.2008.00057.x

Baumeister, R. F., Campbell, J. D., Krueger, J. I., & Vohs, K. D. (2003). Does high esteem cause better performance, interpersonal success, happiness, or healthier lifestyles? *Psychological Science, 4,* 1–44. (13) doi: 10.1111/1529-1006.01431

Baumeister, R. F., & Masicampo, E. J. (2010). Conscious thought is for facilitating social and cultural interactions: How mental simulations serve the animal-culture interface. *Psychological Review, 117,* 945–971. (10) doi: 10.1037/a0019393

Baumeister, R. F., Masicampo, E. J., & Vohs, K. D. (2011). Do conscious thoughts cause behavior? *Annual Review of Psychology, 62,* 331–361. (10) doi: 10.1146/annurev.psych.093008.131126

Bäuml, K.-H. T., & Samenieh, A. (2010). The two faces of memory retrieval. *Psychological Science, 21,* 793–795. (7) doi: 10.1177/0956797610370162

Baumrind, D. (1971). Current patterns of parental authority. *Developmental Psychology Monographs, 4*(1, Pt. 2). (5) doi: 10.1037/h0030372

Baxter, M. G., & Murray, E. A. (2002). The amygdala and reward. *Nature Reviews Neuroscience, 3,* 563–573. (3, 12) doi: 10.1038/nrn875

Bayley, T. M., Dye, L., & Hill, A. J. (2009). Taste aversions in pregnancy. In S. Reilly & T. R. Schachtman (Eds.), *Conditioned taste aversion* (pp. 497–512). New York: Oxford University Press.

Beaman, L., Duflo, E., Pande, R., & Topalova, P. (2012). Female leadership raises aspirations and educational attainment for girls: A policy experiment in India. *Science, 335,* 582–586. (6) doi: 10.1126/science.1212382

Beauchamp, G. K., Cowart, B. J., Mennella, J. A., & Marsh, R. R. (1994). Infant salt taste: Developmental, methodological, and contextual factors. *Developmental Psychobiology, 27,* 353–365. (1) doi: 10.1002/dev.420270604

Bechara, A., Berridge, K. C., Bickel, W. K., Morón, J. A., Williams, S. B., & Stein, J. S. (2019). A neurobehavioral approach to addiction: Implications for the opioid epidemic and the psychology of addiction. *Psychological Science in the Public Interest, 20,* 96–127. (15) doi: 10.1177/1529100619860513

Becht, M. C., & Vingerhoets, A. J. J. M. (2002). Crying and mood change: A cross-cultural study. *Cognition & Emotion, 16,* 87–101. (12) doi: 10.1080/02699930143000149

Beck, A. T. (1991). Cognitive therapy: A 30-year retrospective. *American Psychologist, 46,* 368–375. (15) doi: 10.1037/0003-066X.46.4.368

Beck, A. T., & Emery, G. (1985). *Anxiety disorders and phobias.* New York: Basic Books. (15)

Beck, H. P., Levinson, S., & Irons, G. (2009). Finding Little Albert: A journey to John B. Watson's infant laboratory. *American Psychologist, 64,* 605–614. (15) doi: 10.1037/a0017234

Beckett, C., Maughan, B., Rutter, M., Castle, J., Colvert, E., Groothues, C., Kreppner, J., Stevens, S., O'Connor, T. G., & Sonuga-Barke,

E. J. S. (2006). Do the effects of early severe deprivation on cognition persist into early adolescence? Findings from the English and Romanian adoptees study. *Child Development, 77,* 696–711. (9) doi: 10.1111/j.1467-8624.2006.00898.x

Bediou, B., Adams, D. M., Mayer, R. E., Tipton, E., Green, C. S., & Bavelier, D. (2018). Meta-analysis of action video game impact on perceptual, attentional, and cognitive skills. *Psychological Bulletin, 144,* 77–110. (8) doi: 10.1037/bul0000130

Beer, J. S., Knight, R. T., & D'Esposito, M. (2006). Controlling the integration of emotion and cognition. *Psychological Science, 17,* 448–453. (12) doi: 10.1111/j.1467-9280.2006.01726.x

Behrens, M., Foerster, S., Staehler, F., Raguse, J.-D., & Meyerhof, W. (2007). Gustatory expression pattern of the human TAS2R bitter receptor gene family reveals a heterogenous population of bitter responsive taste receptor cells. *Journal of Neuroscience, 27,* 12630–12640. (4) doi: 10.1523/JNEUROSCI.1168-07.2007

Beilock, S. L., Jelllison, W. A., Rydell, R. J., McConnell, A. R., & Carr, T. H. (2006). On the causal mechanisms of stereotype threat: Can skills that don't rely heavily on working memory still be threatened? *Personality and Social Psychology Bulletin, 32,* 1059–1071. (9) doi: 10.1177/0146167206288489

Bell, R., & Pliner, P. L. (2003). Time to eat: The relationship between the number of people eating and meal duration in three lunch settings. *Appetite, 41,* 215–218. (11) doi: 10.1016/S0195-6663(03)00109-0

Bellini-Leite, S. C. (2018). Dual process theory: Types, minds, modes, kinds or metaphors? A critical review. *Review of Philosophy and Psychology, 9,* 213–225. (8) doi: 10.1007/s13164-017-0376-x

Bellugi, U., & St. George, M. (2000). Preface. *Journal of Cognitive Neuroscience, 12*(Suppl.), 1–6. (8) doi: 10.1162/089892900561940

Bellugi, U., Lichtenberger, L., Jones, W., Lai, Z., & St. George, M. (2000). The neurocognitive profile of Williams syndrome: A complex pattern of strengths and weaknesses. *Journal of Cognitive Neuroscience, 12*(Suppl.), 7–29. (8) doi: 10.1162/089892900561959

Belsky, J. (1996). Parent, infant, and social-contextual antecedents of father-son attachment security. *Developmental Psychology, 32,* 905–913. (5) doi: 10.1037/0012-1649.32.5.905

Bem, D. J. (2011). Feeling the future: Experimental evidence for anomalous retroactive influences on cognition and affect. *Journal of Personality and Social Psychology, 100,* 407–425. (2) doi: 10.1037/a0021524

Bem, D. J., & Honorton, C. (1994). Does psi exist? Replicable evidence for an anomalous process of information transfer. *Psychological Bulletin, 115,* 4–18. (2) https://psycnet.apa.org/record/1994-20287-001

Benartzi, S., Beshears, J., Milkman, K. L., Sunstein, C. R., Thaler, R. H., Shankar, M., Tucker-Ray, W., Congdon, W. J., & Galing, S. (2017). Should governments invest more in nudging? *Psychological Science, 28,* 1041–1055. (13) doi: 10.1177/0956797617702501

Benish, S. G., Imel, Z. E., & Wampold, B. E. (2008). The relative efficacy of bona fide psychotherapies for treating post-traumatic stress disorder: A meta-analysis of direct comparisons. *Clinical Psychology Review, 28,* 746–758. (15) doi: 10.1016/j.cpr.2007.10.005

Benjamin, L. T., Jr., & Simpson, J. A. (2009). The power of the situation. *American Psychologist, 64,* 12–19. (13) doi: 10.1037/a0014077

Benschop, R. J., Godaert, G. L. R., Geenen, R., Brosschot, J. F., DeSmet, M. B. M., Olff, M., Heijnen, C. J., & Ballieux, R. E. (1995). Relationships between cardiovascular and immunologic changes in an experimental stress model. *Psychological Medicine, 25,* 323–327. (12) doi: 10.1017/S0033291700036229

Benson, H. (1977). Systemic hypertension and the relaxation response. *New England Journal of Medicine, 296,* 1152–1156. (12) doi: 10.1056/NEJM197705192962008

Benson, H. (1985). Stress, health, and the relaxation response. In W. D. Gentry, H. Benson, & C. J. de Wolff (Eds.), *Behavioral medicine: Work, stress and health* (pp. 15–32). Dordrecht, The Netherlands: Martinus Nijhoff. (12)

Benton, D., & Young, H. A. (2017). Reducing calorie intake may not help you lose weight. *Perspectives on Psychological Science, 12,* 703–714. (11) doi: 10.1177/1745691617690878

Benton, T. R., Ross, D. F., Bradshaw, E., Thomas, W. N., & Bradshaw, G. S. (2006). Eyewitness memory is still not common sense: Comparing jurors, judges and law enforcement to eyewitness experts. *Applied Cognitive Psychology, 20,* 115–129. (7) doi: 10.1002/acp.1171

Berenbaum, S. A. (1999). Effects of early androgens on sex-typed activities and interests in adolescents with congenital adrenal hyperplasia. *Hormones and Behavior, 35,* 102–110. (11) doi: 10.1006/hbeh.1998.1503

Berenbaum, S. A., Duck, S. C., & Bryk, K. (2000). Behavioral effects of prenatal versus postnatal androgen excess in children with 21-hydroxylase-deficient congenital adrenal hyperplasia. *Journal of Clinical Endocrinology and Metabolism, 85,* 727–733. (5, 11) doi: 10.1210/jc.85.2.727

Berger, R. J., & Phillips, N. H. (1995). Energy conservation and sleep. *Behavioural Brain Research, 69,* 65–73. (10) doi: 10.1016/0166-4328(95)00002-B

Bergh, C., Callmar, M., Danemar, S., Hölcke, M., Isberg, S., Leon, M., Lindgren, J., Lundqvist, A., Niinimaa, M., Olofsson, B., Palmberg, K., Pettersson, A., Zandian, M., Asberg, K., Brodin, U., Maletz, L., Court, J., Iafeta, I., Bjornstrom, M., ... Södersten, P. (2013). Effective treatment of eating disorders: Results at multiple sites. *Behavioral Neuroscience, 127,* 878–889. (11) doi: 10.1037/a0034921

Berglas, S., & Jones, E. E. (1978). Drug choice as a self-handicapping strategy in response to noncontingent success. *Journal of Personality and Social Psychology, 36,* 405–417. (13) doi: 10.1037/0022-3514.36.4.405

Berken, J. A., Chai, X., Chen, J.-K., Gracco, V. L., & Klein, D. (2016). Effects of early and late bilingualism on resting-state functional connectivity. *Journal of Neuroscience, 36,* 1165–1172. (8) doi: 10.1523/JNEUROSCI.1960-15.2016

Berkowitz, L. (1983). Aversively stimulated aggression: Some parallels and differences in research with animals and humans. *American Psychologist, 38,* 1135–1144. (13) doi: 10.1037/0003-066X.38.11.1135

Berkowitz, L. (1989). Frustration-aggression hypothesis: Examination and reformulation. *Psychological Bulletin, 106,* 59–73. (13) doi: 10.1037/0033-2909.106.1.59

Bernardi, F., & Radl, J. (2014). The long-term consequences of parental divorce for children's educational attainment. *Demographic Research, 30,* Article 61. (5) doi: 10.4054/DemRes.2014.30.61

Bernstein, D. M., & Loftus, E. F. (2009). The consequences of false memories for food preferences and choices. *Perspectives on Psychological Science, 4,* 135–139. (7) doi: 10.1111/j.1745-6924.2009.01113.x

Bernstein, D. M., Atance, C., Loftus, G. R., & Meltzoff, A. (2004). We saw it all along. *Psychological Science, 15,* 264–267. (7) doi: 10.1111/j.0963-7214.2004.00663.x

Bernstein, I. L. (1991). Aversion conditioning in response to cancer and cancer treatment. *Clinical Psychology Review, 11,* 185–191. (6) doi: 10.1016/0272-7358(91)90095-C

Berntsen, D., Johannessen, K. B., Thomsen, Y. D., Bertelsen, M., Hoyle, R. H., & Rubin, D. C. (2012). Peace and war: Trajectories of posttraumatic stress disorder symptoms before, during, and after military deployment in Afghanistan. *Psychological Science, 23,* 1557–1565. (12) doi: 10.1177/0956797612457389

Berntsen, D., & Rubin, D. C. (2015). Pretraumatic stress reactions in soldiers deployed to Afghanistan. *Clinical Psychological Science, 3,* 663–674. (12) doi: 10.1177/2167702614551766

Berntson, G. G., Cacioppo, J. T., & Quigley, K. S. (1993). Cardiac psychophysiology and autonomic space in humans: Empirical perspectives and conceptual implications. *Psychological Bulletin, 114,* 296–322. (12) doi: 10.1037/0033-2909.114.2.296

Berridge, K. C., & Robinson, T. E. (1998). What is the role of dopamine in reward: Hedonic impact, reward learning, or incentive salience? *Brain Research Reviews, 28,* 309–369. (15) doi: 10.1016/S0165-0173(98)00019-8

Berridge, K. C., & Robinson, T. E. (2016). Liking, wanting, and the incentive-sensitization theory of addiction. *American Psychologist, 71,* 670–679. (15) doi: 10.1037/amp0000059

Berry, C. M., & Sackett, P. R. (2009). Individual differences in course choice result in underestimation of the validity of college admission systems. *Psychological Science, 20,* 822–830. (9) doi: 10.1111/j.1467-9280.2009.02368.x

Berry, C. M. (2015). Differential validity and differential prediction of cognitive ability tests: Understanding test bias in the employment context. *Annual Review of Organizational Psychology and Organizational Behavior, 2,* 435–463. (9) doi: 10.1146/annurev-orgpsych-032414-111256

Berry, J. W., Poortinga, Y. H., Segal, H., & Dasen, P. R. (1992). *Cross-cultural psychology.* Cambridge, England: Cambridge University Press. (15)

Bersoff, D. N. (2014). Protecting victims of violent patients while protecting confidentiality. *American Psychologist, 69,* 461–467. (15) doi: 10.1037/a0037198

Berson, D. M., Dunn, F. A., & Takao, M. (2002). Phototransduction by retinal ganglion cells that set the circadian clock. *Science, 295,* 1070–1073. (10) doi: 10.1126/science.1067262

Beuming, T., Kniazeff, J., Bergmann, M. L., Shi, L., Gracia, L., Raniszewska, K., Newman, A. H., Javitch, J. A., Weinstein, H., Gether, U., & Loland, C. J. (2008). The binding sites for cocaine and dopamine in the dopamine transporter overlap. *Nature Neuroscience, 11,* 780–789. (3) doi: 10.1038/nn.2146

Bialystok, E., Craik, F., & Luk, G. (2008). Cognitive control and lexical access in younger and older bilinguals. *Journal of Experimental Psychology: Learning, Memory, and Cognition, 34,* 859–873. (8) doi: 10.1037/0278-7393.34.4.859

Bidwell, L. C., Gray, J. C., Weafer, J., Palmer, A. A., de Wit, H., & MacKillop, J. (2017). Genetic influences on ADHD symptom dimensions: Examination of a priori candidates, gene-based tests, genome-wide variation, and SNP heritability. *American Journal of Medical Genetics, B, 174,* 458–466. (8) doi: 10.1002/ajmg.b.32535

Biederman, I., Yue, X., & Davidoff, J. (2009). Representation of shape in individuals from a culture with minimal exposure to regular, simple artifacts. *Psychological Science, 20,* 1437–1442. (4) doi: 10.1111/j.1467-9280.2009.02465.x

Biernacka, J. M., Geske, J. R., Schneekloth, T. D., Frye, M. A., Cunningham, J. M., Choi, D.-S., Tapp, C. L., Lewis, B. R., Drews, M. S., Pietrzak, T. L., Colby, C. L., Hall-Flavin, D. K., Loukianova, L. L., Heit, J. A., Mrazek, D. A., & Karpyak, V. M. (2013). Replication of genome wide association studies of alcohol dependence: Support for association with variation in *ADH1C. PLoS One,* e58798. (15) doi: 10.1371/journal.pone.0058798

Bijl, R. V., de Graaf, R., Hiripi, E., Kessler, R. C., Kohn, R., Offord, D. R., Ustun, T. B., Vicente, B., Vollebergh, W. A. M., Walters, E. E., & Wittchen, H. U. (2003). The prevalence of treated and untreated mental disorders in five countries. *Health Affairs, 22,* 122–133. (15) doi: 10.1377/hlthaff.22.3.122

Billy, J. O. G., Tanfer, K., Grady, W. R., & Klepinger, D. H. (1993, March/April). The sexual behavior of men in the United States. *Family Planning Perspectives, 25,* 52–60. (11) doi: 10.2307/2136206

Binet, A., & Simon, T. (1904). Méthodes nouvelles pour le diagnostic du niveau intellectual des anormaux [New methods for the measurement of an abnormal intellectual level]. *L'Année Psychologique, 11,* 191–244. (9) https://psychclassics.yorku.ca/Binet/binet1.htm

Birak, K. S., Higgs, S., & Terry, P. (2011). Conditioned tolerance to the effects of alcohol on inhibitory control in humans. *Alcohol and Alcoholism, 46,* 686–693. (6) doi: 10.1093/alcalc/agr084

Birnbaum, R., & Weinberger, D. R. (2017). Genetic insights into the neurodevelopmental origins of schizophrenia. *Nature Reviews Neuroscience, 18,* 727–740. (15) doi: 10.1038/nrn.2017.125

Bishop, E. G., Cherny, S. S., Corley, R., Plomin, R., DeFries, J. C., & Hewitt, J. K. (2003). Development genetic analysis of general cognitive ability from 1 to 12 years in a sample of adoptees, biological siblings, and twins. *Intelligence, 31,* 31–49. (9) doi: 10.1016/S0160-2896(02)00112-5

Bjerkedal, T., Kristensen, P., Skjeret, G. A., & Brevik, J. I. (2007). Intelligence test scores and birth order among young Norwegian men (conscripts) analyzed within and between families. *Intelligence, 35,* 503–514. (5) doi: 10.1016/j.intell.2007.01.004

Bjorklund, D. F., & Shackelford, T. K. (1999). Differences in parental investment contribute to important differences between men and women. *Current Directions in Psychological Science, 8,* 86–89. (3) doi: 10.1111/1467-8721.00020

Blackless, M., Charuvastra, A., Derryck, A., Fausto-Sterling, A., Lauzanne, K., & Lee, E. (2000). How sexually dimorphic are we? Review and synthesis. *American Journal of Human Biology, 12,* 151–166. (11) doi: 10.1002/(SICI)1520-6300(200003/04)12:2<151::AID-AJHB1>3.3.CO;2-6

Blair, R. J. R., Mitchell, D. G. V., Peschardt, K. S., Colledge, E., Leonard, R. A., Shine, J. H., Murray, L. K., & Perrett, D. I. (2004). Reduced sensitivity to others' fearful expressions in psychopathic individuals. *Personality and Individual Differences, 37,* 1111–1122. (12) doi: 10.1016/j.paid.2003.10.008

Blake, P. R., McAuliffe, K., Corbit, J., Callaghan, T. C., Barry, O., Bowie, A., Kleutsch, L., Kramer, K. L., Ross, E., Vongsachang, H., Wrangham, R., & Warneken, F. (2015). The ontogeny of fairness in seven societies. *Nature, 528,* 258–261. (13) doi: 10.1038/nature15703

Blake, R., & Logothetis, N. K. (2002). Visual competition. *Nature Reviews Neuroscience, 3,* 13–23. (10) doi: 10.1038/nrn701

Blakemore, C., & Sutton, P. (1969). Size adaptation: A new aftereffect. *Science, 166,* 245–247. (4) doi: 10.1126/science.166.3902.245

Blascovich, J., & Tomaka, J. (1991). Measures of self-esteem. In J. P. Robinson, R. R. Shaver, & L. S. Wrightsman (Eds.), *Measures of personality and social psychological attitudes* (Vol. 1, pp. 115–160). San Diego, CA: Academic Press. (14)

Bless, H., Bohner, G., Schwarz, N., & Strack, F. (1990). Mood and persuasion: A cognitive response analysis. *Personality and Social Psychology Bulletin, 16,* 331–345. (12) doi: 10.1177/0146167290162013

Bloch, L., Haase, C. M., & Levenson, R. W. (2014). Emotion regulation predicts marital satisfaction: More than a wives' tale. *Emotion, 14,* 130–144. (13) doi: 10.1037/a0034272

Blom, V., Sverke, M., Bodin, L., Lindfors, P., & Svedberg, P. (2014). Work-home interference and burnout: A study based on Swedish twins. *Journal of Occupational and Environmental Medicine, 56,* 361–366. (11) doi: 10.1097/JOM.0000000000000128

Bloomfield, M. A. P., Hindocha, C., Green, S. F., Wall, M. B., Lees, R., Petrilli, K., Costello, H., Ogunbiyi, M. O., Bossong, M. G., & Freeman, T. P. (2019). The neuropsychopharmacology of cannabis: A review of human imaging studies. *Pharmacology & Therapeutics, 195,* 132–161. (3) doi: 10.1016/j.pharmthera.2018.10.006

Blount, J. D., Metcalfe, N. B., Birkhead, T. R., & Surai, P. F. (2003). Carotenoid modulation of immune function and sexual attractiveness in zebra finches. *Science, 300,* 125–127. (13) doi: 10.1126/science.1082142

Blum, D. (1994). *The monkey wars.* New York: Oxford University Press. (2)

Blum, G. S., & Barbour, J. S. (1979). Selective inattention to anxiety-linked stimuli. *Journal of Experimental Psychology: General, 108,* 182–224. (4) doi: 10.1037/0096-3445.108.2.182

Blumberg, M. S., Gall, A. J., & Todd, W. D. (2014). The development of sleep-wake rhythms and the search for elemental circuits in the infant brain. *Behavioral Neuroscience, 128,* 250–263. (10) doi: 10.1037/a0035891

Bobrow, D., & Bailey, J. M. (2001). Is male homosexuality maintained via kin selection? *Evolution and Human Behavior, 22,* 361–368. (11) doi: 10.1016/S1090-5138(01)00074-5

Bocanegra, Y., García, A. M., Lopera, F., Pineda, D., Baena, A., Ospina, P., ... Cuetos, F. (2017). Unspeakable motion: Selective action-verb impairments in Parkinson's disease patients without mild cognitive impairment. *Brain & Language, 168,* 37–46. (8) doi: 10.1016/j.bandl.2017.01.005

Boccio, C. M., & Beaver, K. M. (2019). Further examining the potential association between birth order and personality: Null results from a national sample of American siblings. *Personality and Individual Differences, 139,* 125–131. (5) doi: 10.1016/j.paid.2018.11.017

Bogaert, A. F. (2003). The interaction of fraternal birth order and body size in male sexual orientation. *Behavioral Neuroscience, 117,* 381–384. (11) doi: 10.1037/0735-7044.117.2.381

Bogaert, A. F. (2006). Biological versus nonbiological older brothers and men's sexual orientation. *Proceedings of the National Academy of Sciences, USA, 103,* 10771–10774. (11) doi: 10.1073/pnas.0511152103

Bogg, T., & Roberts, B. W. (2013). The case for conscientiousness: Evidence and implications for a personality trait marker of health and longevity. *Annals of Behavioral Medicine, 45,* 278–288. (14) doi: 10.1007/s12160-012-9454-6

Böhlein, J., Altegoer, L., Muck, N. K., Poesmann, K., Redlich, R., Dannlowski, U., & Leehr, E. J. (2020). Factors influencing the success of exposure therapy for specific phobia: A systematic review. *Neuroscience and Biobehavioral Reviews, 108,* 796–820. (15) doi: 10.1016/j.neubiorev.2019.12.009

Boldrini, M., Fulmore, C. A., Tartt, A. N., Simeon, L. R., Pavlova, I., Poposka, V., Rosoklija, B. B., Stankov, A., Arango, V., Dwork, A. J., Hen, R., & Mann, J. J. (2018). Human hippocampal neurogenesis persists throughout aging. *Cell Stem Cell, 22,* 589–599. (3) doi: 10.1016/j.stem.2018.03.015

Bonanno, G. A., & Burton, C. L. (2013). Regulatory flexibility: An individual differences perspective on coping and emotion regulation. *Perspectives on Psychological Science, 8,* 591–612. (12) doi: 10.1177/1745691613504116

Bonanno, G. A., & Mancini, A. D. (2008). The human capacity to thrive in the face of potential trauma. *Pediatrics, 121,* 369–375. (5) doi: 10.1542/peds.2007-1648

Bond, M. H. (1991). *Beyond the Chinese face.* New York: Oxford University Press. (15)

Bond, R., & Smith, P. B. (1996). Culture and conformity: A meta-analysis of studies using Asch's (1952, 1956) line judgment task. *Psychological Bulletin, 119,* 111–137. (13) doi: 10.1037/0033-2909.119.1.111

Bonneh, Y. S., Cooperman, A., & Sagi, D. (2001). Motion-induced blindness in normal observers. *Nature, 411,* 798–801. (10) doi: 10.1038/35081073

Bonnie, R. J. (1997). Research with cognitively impaired subjects: Unfinished business in the regulation of human research. *Archives of General Psychiatry, 54,* 105–111. (2) doi: 10.1001/archpsyc.1997.01830140013002

Boot, W. R., Simons, D. J., Stothart, C., & Stutts, C. (2013). The pervasive problem with placebos in psychology: Why active control groups are not sufficient to rule out placebo effects. *Perspectives on Psychological Science, 8,* 445–454. (2) doi: 10.1177/1745691613491271

Bootzin, R. R., & Bailey, E. T. (2005). Understanding placebo, nocebo, and iatrogenic treatment effects. *Journal of Clinical Psychology, 61,* 871–880. (12) doi: 10.1002/jclp.20131

Borch-Jacobsen, M., & Shamdasani, S. (2012). *The Freud files: An inquiry into the history of psychoanalysis.* New York: Cambridge University Press. (1, 14)

Border, R., Johnson, E. C., Evans, L. M., Smolen, A., Berley, N., Sullivan, P. F., & Keller, M. C. (2019). No support for historical candidate gene or candidate gene-by-interaction hypotheses for major depression across multiple large samples. *American Journal of Psychiatry, 176,* 376–387 (15) doi: 10.1176/appi.ajp.2018.18070881

Borghi, A. M., Binkofski, F., Castelfranchi, C., Cimatti, F., Scorolli, C., & Tummolini, L. (2017). The challenge of abstract concepts. *Psychological Bulletin, 143,* 263–292. (8) doi: 10.1037/bul0000089

Borghuis, J., Denissen, J. J. A., Oberski, D., Sijtsma, K., Meeus, W. H. J., Branje, S., Koot, H. M., & Bleidorn, W. (2017). Big five personality stability, change, and codevelopment across adolescence and early adulthood. *Journal of Personality and Social Psychology, 113,* 641–657. (14) doi: 10.1037/pspp0000138

Boring, E. G. (1930). A new ambiguous figure. *American Journal of Psychology, 42,* 444–445. (4) doi: 10.2307/1415447

Borman, G. D., Grigg, J., Rozek, C. S., Hanselman, P., & Dewey, N. A. (2018). Self-affirmation effects are produced by school context, student engagement with the intervention, and time: Lessons from a district-wide implementation. *Psychological Science, 29,* 1773–1784. (9) doi: 10.1177/0956797618784016

Boroditsky, L., & Gaby, A. (2010). Remembrances of times east: Absolute spatial representations of time in an Australian aboriginal community. *Psychological Science, 21,* 1635–1639. (2) doi: 10.1177/0956797610386621

Borota, D., Murray, E., Keceli, G., Chang, A., Watabe, J. M., Ly, M., Toscano, J. P., & Yassa, M. A. (2014). Post-study caffeine administration enhances memory consolidation in humans. *Nature Neuroscience, 17,* 201–203. (7) doi: 10.1038/nn.3623

Borsutzky, S., Fujiwara, E., Brand, M., & Markowitsch, H. J. (2008). Confabulations in alcoholic Korsakoff patients. *Neuropsychologia, 46,* 3133–3143. (7) doi: 10.1016/j.neuropsychologia.2008.07.005

Bortolotti, B., Menchetti, M., Bellini, F., Montaguti, M. B., & Berardi, D. (2008). Psychological interventions for major depression in primary care: A meta-analytic review of randomized controlled trials. *General Hospital Psychiatry, 30,* 293–302. (15) doi: 10.1016/j.genhosppsych.2008.04.001

Bos, H. M. W., van Balen, F., & van den Boom, D. C. (2007). Child adjustment and parenting in planned lesbian-parent families. *American Journal of Orthopsychiatry, 77,* 38–48. (5) doi: 10.1037/0002-9432.77.1.38

Bos, H., & Gartrell, N. (2010). Adolescents of the USA National Longitudinal Lesbian Family Study: Can family characteristics counteract the negative effects of stigmatization. *Family Process, 49,* 559–572. (5) doi: 10.1111/j.1545-5300.2010.01340.x

Bostyn, D. H., Sevenhant, S., & Roets, A. (2018). Of mice, men, and trolleys: Hypothetical judgment versus real-life behavior in trolley-style moral dilemmas. *Psychological Science, 29,* 1084–1093. (12) doi: 10.1177/0956797617752640

Bouchard, T. J., Lykken, D. T., McGue, M., Segal, N. L., & Tellegen, A. (1990). Sources of psychological differences: The Minnesota study of twins reared apart. *Science, 250,* 223–228. (5) doi: 10.1126/science.2218526

Bouchard, T. J., Jr., & McGue, M. (1981). Familial studies of intelligence: A review. *Science, 212,* 1055–1059. (9) doi: 10.1126/science.7195071

Bouchard, T. J., Jr., & McGue, M. (2003). Genetic and environmental influences on human psychological differences. *Journal of Neurobiology, 54,* 4–45. (5, 14) doi: 10.1002/neu.10160

Bowlby, J. (1973). *Attachment and loss: Vol. II. Separation.* New York: Basic Books. (5)

Bowers, J. S. (2016). The practical and principled problems with educational neuroscience. *Psychological Review, 123,* 600–612. (3) doi: 10.1037/rev0000025

Bowmaker, J. K. (1998). Visual pigments and molecular genetics of color blindness. *News in Physiological Sciences, 13,* 63–69. (4) doi: 10.1152/physiologyonline.1998.13.2.63

Bowmaker, J. K., & Dartnall, H. J. A. (1980). Visual pigments of rods and cones in a human retina. *Journal of Physiology* (London), *298,* 501–511. (4) doi: 10.1113/jphysiol.1980.sp013097

Boyce, C. J., & Wood, A. M. (2011). Personality prior to disability determines adaptation: Agreeable individuals recover lost life satisfaction faster and more completely. *Psychological Science, 22,* 1397–1402. (14) doi: 10.1177/0956797611421790

Boyer, P., Firat, R., & van Leeuwen, F. (2015). Safety, threat, and stress in intergroup relations: A coalitional index model. *Perspectives on Psychological Science, 10,* 434–450. (5) doi: 10.1177/1745691615583133

Boyke, J., Driemeyer, J., Gaser, C., Büchel, C., & May, A. (2008). Training-induced brain structure changes in the elderly. *Journal of Neuroscience, 28,* 7031–7035. (3) doi: 10.1523/JNEUROSCI.0742-08.2008

Boysen, G. A., & Van Bergen, A. (2013). A review of published research on adult dissociative identity disorder 2000–2010. *Journal of Nervous and Mental Disease, 201,* 5–11. (15) doi: 10.1097/NMD.0b013e31827aaf81

Bracha, H. S. (2006). Human brain evolution and the "neuroevolutionary time-depth principle": Implications for the reclassification of fear-circuitry-related traits in *DSM–V* and for studying resilience to warzone-related posttraumatic stress disorder. *Progress in Neuro-Psychopharmacology and Biological Psychiatry, 30,* 827–853. (15) doi: 10.1016/j.pnpbp.2006.01.008

Bradbury, T. N., & Miller, G. A. (1985). Season of birth in schizophrenia: A review of evidence, methodology, and etiology. *Psychological Bulletin, 98,* 569–594. (15) doi: 10.1037/0033-2909.98.3.569

Brainstorm Consortium (2018). Analysis of shared heritability in common disorders of the brain. *Science, 360,* 1313. (15) doi: 10.1126/science.aap8757

Brandimarte, L., Vosgerau, J., & Acquisti, A. (2018). Differential discounting and present impace of past information. *Journal of Experimental Psychology: General, 147,* 74–92. (13) doi: 10.1037/xge0000372

Brang, D., Edwards, L., Ramachandran, V. S., & Coulson, S. (2008). Is the sky 2? Contextual priming in grapheme-color synesthesia. *Psychological Science, 19,* 421–428. (4) doi: 10.1111/j.1467-9280.2008.02103.x

Brannon, T. N., & Walton, G. M. (2013). Enacting cultural interests: How intergroup contact reduces prejudice by sparking interest in an out-group's culture. *Psychological Science, 24,* 1947–1957. (13) doi: 10.1177/0956797613481607

Braungart-Rieker, J. M., Zentall, S., Lickenbrock, D. M., Ekas, N. V., Oshio, T., & Planalp, E. (2014). Attachment in the making: Mother and father sensitivity and infants' responses during the Still-Face Paradigm. *Journal of Experimental Child Psychology, 125,* 63–84. (5) doi: 10.1016/j.jecp.2014.02.007

Braunschweig, D., Krakowiak, P., Duncanson, P., Boyce, R., Hansen, R. L., Ashwood, P., Hertz-Picciotto, I., Pessah, I. N., & Van de Water, J. (2013). Autism-specific maternal autoantibodies recognize critical proteins in developing brain. *Translational Psychiatry, 3,* e277. (15) doi: 10.1038/tp.2013.50

Breda, T., Jouini, E., & Napp, C. (2018). Societal inequalities amplify gender gaps in math. *Science, 359,* 1219–1220. (5) doi: 10.1126/science.aar2307

Brédart, S., Delchambre, M., & Laureys, S. (2006). One's own face is hard to ignore. *Quarterly Journal of Experimental Psychology, 59,* 46–52. (8) doi: 10.1080/17470210500343678

Bregman, A. S. (1981). Asking the "what for" question in auditory perception. In M. Kubovy & J. R. Pomerantz (Eds.), *Perceptual organization* (pp. 99–118). Hillsdale, NJ: Erlbaum. (4)

Bremmer, F., Kubischik, M., Hoffmann, K.-P., & Krekelberg, B. (2009). Neural dynamics of saccadic suppression. *Journal of Neuroscience, 29,* 12374–12383. (3) doi: 10.1523/JNEUROSCI.2908-09.2009

Brescoll, V. L., & Uhlmann, E. L. (2008). Can an angry woman get ahead? *Psychological Science, 19,* 268–275. (13) doi: 10.1111/j.1467-9280.2008.02079.x

Breslau, N., Dickens, W. T., Flynn, J. R., Peterson, E. L., & Lucia, V. C. (2006). Low birthweight and social disadvantage: Tracking their relationship with children's IQ during the period of school attendance. *Intelligence, 34,* 351–362. (9) doi: 10.1016/j.intell.2005.10.003

Brethel-Haurwitz, K. M., Cardinale, E. M., Vekaria, K. M., Robertson, E., Walitt, B., VanMeter, J. W., & Marsh, A. A. (2018). Extraordinary altruists exhibit enhanced self-other overlap in neural responses to distress. *Psychological Science, 29,* 1631–1641. (13) doi: 10.1177/0956797618779590

Brewer, C., Streel, E., & Skinner, M. (2017). Supervised disulfiram's superior effectiveness in alcoholism treatment: Ethical, methodological, and psychological aspects. *Alcohol and Alcoholism, 52,* 213–219. (15) doi: 10.1093/alcalc/agw093

Brewer, M. B., & Chen, Y.-R. (2007). Where (who) are collectives in collectivism? Toward conceptual clarification of individualism and collectivism. *Psychological Review, 114,* 131–151. (5) doi: 10.1037/0033-295X.114.1.133

Brewer, N., Weber, N., Wootton, D., & Lindsay, D. S. (2012). Identifying the bad guy in a lineup using confidence judgments under deadline pressure. *Psychological Science, 23,* 1208–1214. (7) doi: 10.1177/0956797612441217

Bridgman, T., Cummings, S., & Ballard, J. (2019). Who built Maslow's pyramid? A history of the creation of management studies' most famous symbol and its implications for management education. *Academy of Management Learning & Education, 18,* 81–98. (11) doi: 10.5465/amle.2017.0351

Britton, J. C., Grillon, C., Lissek, S., Norcross, M. A., Szuhany, K.L., Chen, G., Ernst, M., Nelson, E. E., Leibenluft, E., Shechner, T., & Pine, D. S. (2013). Response to learned threat: An fMRI study in adolescent and adult anxiety. *American Journal of Psychiatry, 170*, 1195–1204. (12) doi: 10.1176/appi.ajp.2013.12050651

Brod, G., Bunge, S. A., & Shing, Y. L. (2017). Does one year of schooling improve children's cognitive control and alter associated brain activation? *Psychological Science, 28*, 967–978. (9) doi: 10.1177/0956797617699838

Brooks, A. W. (2014). Get excited: Reappraising pre-performance anxiety as excitement. *Journal of Experimental Psychology: General, 143*, 1144–1158. (12) doi: 10.1037/a0035325

Brower, K. J., & Anglin, M. D. (1987). Adolescent cocaine use: Epidemiology, risk factors, and prevention. *Journal of Drug Education, 17*, 163–180. (3) doi: 10.2190/BQY5-MBLW-PNQF-XFWB

Brown, A. S. (2003). A review of the déjà vu experience. *Psychological Bulletin, 129*, 394–413. (10) doi: 10.1037/0033-2909.129.3.394

Brown, A. S. (2011). The environment and susceptibility to schizophrenia. *Progress in Neurobiology, 93*, 23–58. (15) doi: 10.1016/j.pneurobio.2010.09.003

Brown, G. W. (1989). Life events and measurement. In G. W. Brown & T. O. Harris (Eds.), *Life events and illness* (pp. 3–45). New York: Guilford Press. (12)

Brown, J. (1977). *Mind, brain, and consciousness.* New York: Academic Press. (8)

Brown, R., & McNeill, D. (1966). The "tip of the tongue" phenomenon. *Journal of Verbal Learning and Verbal Behavior, 5*, 325–337. (7) doi: 10.1016/S0022-5371(66)80040-3

Bruck, M., Cavanagh, P., & Ceci, S. J. (1991). Fortysomething: Recognizing faces at one's 25th reunion. *Memory & Cognition, 19*, 221–228. (4) doi: 10.3758/BF03211146

Bruder, C. E. G., Piotrowski, A., Gijsbers, A. A. C. J., Andersson, R., Erickson, S., de Staal, T. D., Menzel, U., Sandgren, J., von Tell, D., Poplawski, A., Crowley, M., Crasto, C., Partridge, E. D., Tiwari, H., Allison, D. B., Komorowski, J., van Ommen, G. J. B., Boomsma, D. I., Pedersen, N. L., ... Dumanski, J. P. (2008). Phenotypically concordant and discordant monozygotic twins display different DNA copy-number-variant profiles. *American Journal of Human Genetics, 82*, 763–771. (15) doi: 10.1016/j.ajhg.2007.12.011

Brumfiel, G. (2013). Fallout of fear. *Nature, 493*, 290–293. (12) doi: 10.1038/493290a

Brüning, J. C., Gautham, D., Burks, D. J., Gillette, J., Schubert, M., Orban, P. C, Klein, R., Krone, W., Muller-Wieland, D., & Kahn, C. R. (2000). Role of brain insulin receptor in control of body weight and reproduction. *Science, 289*, 2122–2125. (11) doi: 10.1126/science.289.5487.2122

Bryant, F. B., & Guilbault, R. L. (2002). "I knew it all along" eventually: The development of hindsight bias in the Clinton impeachment verdict. *Basic and Applied Social Psychology, 24*, 27–41. (7) doi: 10.1207/S15324834BASP2401_3

Bryant, G. A., Fessler, D. M. T., Fusaroli, R., Clint, E., Aaroe, L., Apicella, C. L., Petersen, M. B., Bickham, S. T., Bolyanatz, A., Chavez, B., De Smet, D., Diaz, D., Fancovicova, J., Fux, M., Giraldo-Perez, P., Hu, A. N., Kamble, S. V., Kameda, T., Li, N. P., ... Zhou, Y. (2016). Detecting affiliation in colaughter across 24 societies. *Proceedings of the National Academy of Sciences, 113*, 4682–4687. (13) doi: 10.1073/pnas.1524993113

Bryant, R. A., Creamer, M., O'Donnell, M., Forbes, D., Felmingham, K. L., Silove, D., Malhi, G., van Hoof, M., McFarlane, A. C., & Nickerson, A. (2017). Separation from parents during childhood trauma predicts adult attachment security and post-traumatic stress disorder. *Psychological Medicine, 47*, 2028–2035. (5) doi: 10.1017/S0033291717000472

Brysbaert, M., Vitu, F., & Schroyens, W. (1996). The right visual field advantage and the optimal viewing position effect: On the relation between foveal and parafoveal word recognition. *Neuropsychology, 10*, 385–395. (8) doi: 10.1037/0894-4105.10.3.385

Bryson, S. E. (2005). The autistic mind. In M. L. Bauman & T. L. Kemper (Eds.), *The neurobiology of autism* (pp. 34–44). Baltimore: Johns Hopkins University Press. (15)

Bschor, T., & Kilarski, L. L. (2016). Are antidepressants effective? A debate on their efficacy for the treatment of major depression in adults. *Expert Review of Neurotherapeutics, 16*, 367–374. (15) doi: 10.1586/14737175.2016.1155985

Buck, L., & Axel, R. (1991). A novel multigene family may encode odorant receptors: A molecular basis for odor recognition. *Cell, 65*, 175–187. (4) doi: 10.1016/0092-8674(91)90418-X

Buehler, R., Griffin, D., & Ross, M. (1994). Exploring the "planning fallacy": Why people underestimate their task completion times. *Journal of Personality and Social Psychology, 67*, 366–381. (11) doi: 10.1037/0022-3514.67.3.366

Bühren, K., Schwarte, R., Fluck, F., Timmesfeld, N., Krei, M., Egberts, K., Pfeiffer, E., Fleischhaker, C., Wewetzer, C., & Herpertz-Dahlmann, B. (2014). Comorbid psychiatric disorders in female adolescents with first-onset anorexia nervosa. *European Eating Disorders Review, 22*, 39–44. (11) doi: 10.1002/erv.2254

Buizer-Voskamp, J. E., Muntjewerff, J. W., Strengman, E., Sabatti, C., Stefansson, H., Vorstman, J. A. S., & Ophoff, R. A. (2011). Genome-wide analysis shows increased frequency of copy number variations deletions in Dutch schizophrenia patients. *Biological Psychiatry, 70*, 655–662. (15) doi: 10.1016/j.biopsych.2011.02.015

Burger, J. M. (1986). Increasing compliance by improving the deal: The that's-not-all technique. *Journal of Personality and Social Psychology, 51*, 277–283. (13) doi: 10.1037/0022-3514.51.2.277

Burger, J. M. (2009). Replicating Milgram: Would people still obey today? *American Psychologist, 64*, 1–11. (13) doi: 10.1037/a0010932

Burke, K. A., Franz, T. M., Miller, D. N., & Schoenbaum, G. (2008). The role of the orbitofrontal cortex in the pursuit of happiness and more specific rewards. *Nature, 454*, 340–344. (6) doi: 10.1038/nature06993

Burr, D. C., Morrone, M. C., & Ross, J. (1994). Selective suppression of the magnocellular visual pathway during saccadic eye movements. *Nature, 371*, 511–513. (8) doi: 10.1038/371511a0

Bushdid, C., Magnasco, M. O., Vosshall, L. B., & Keller, A. (2014). Humans can discriminate more than 1 trillion olfactory stimuli. *Science, 343*, 1370–1372. (4) doi: 10.1126/science.1249168

Bushman, B. J., & Anderson, C. A. (2009). Comfortably numb: Desensitizing effects of violent media on helping others. *Psychological Science, 20*, 273–277. (13) doi: 10.1111/j.1467-9280.2009.02287.x

Buss, D. M. (2000). Desires in human mating. *Annals of the New York Academy of Sciences, 907*, 39–49. (3) doi: 10.1111/j.1749-6632.2000.tb06614.x

Butcher, J. N., Graham, J. R., Williams, C. L., & Ben-Porath, Y. S. (1990). *Development and use of the MMPI-2 content scales.* Minneapolis: University of Minnesota Press. (14)

Butler, A. C., Chapman, J. E., Forman, E. M., & Beck, A. T. (2006). The empirical status of cognitive-behavioral therapy: A review of meta-analyses. *Clinical Psychology Review, 26*, 17–31. (15) doi: 10.1016/j.cpr.2005.07.003

Butler, E. A., Lee, T. L., & Gross, J. J. (2007). Emotion regulation and culture: Are the social consequences of emotion suppression culture-specific? *Emotion, 7*, 30–48. (12) doi: 10.1037/1528-3542.7.1.30

Butler, L. (2002). A list of published papers is no measure of value. *Nature, 419*, 877. (11) doi: 10.1038/419877a

Butler, R. J., Holland, P., Gasson, S., Norfolk, S., Houghton, L., & Penney, M. (2007). Exploring potential mechanisms in alarm treatment for primary nocturnal enuresis. *Scandinavian Journal of Urology and Nephrology, 41*, 407–413. (15) doi: 10.1080/00365590701571506

Buzinski, S. G., Clark, J., Cohen, M., Buck, B., & Roberts, S. P. (2018). Insidious assumptions: How pluralistic ignorance of studying behavior relates to exam performance. *Teaching of Psychology, 45*, 333–339. (8) doi: 10.1177/0098628318796919

Byne, W., Tobet, S., Mattiace, L. A., Lasco, M. S., Kemether, E., Edgar, M. A., Morgello, S., Buchsbaum, M. S., & Jones, L. B. (2001). The interstitial nuclei of the human anterior hypothalamus: An investigation of variation with sex, sexual orientation, and HIV status. *Hormones and Behavior, 40*, 86–92. (11) doi: 10.1006/hbeh.2001.1680

Cacioppo, J. T., Hawkley, L. C., & Berntson, G. G. (2003). The anatomy of loneliness. *Current Directions in Psychological Science, 12*, 71–74. (12) doi: 10.1111/1467-8721.01232

Cahalan, D. (1978). Subcultural differences in drinking behavior in U.S. national surveys and selected European studies. In P. E. Nathan, G. A. Marlatt, & T. Løberg (Eds.), *Alcoholism: New directions in behavioral research and treatment* (pp. 235–253). New York: Plenum Press. (15)

Cahill, L. (2006). Why sex matters for neuroscience. *Nature Reviews Neuroscience, 7*, 477–484. (3, 5) doi: 10.1038/nrn1909

Calabria, B., Degenhardt, L., Briegleb, C., Vos, T., Hall, W., Lynskey, M., Callaghan, B., Rana, U., & McLaren, J. (2010). Systematic review of prospective studies investigating "remission" from amphetamine, cannabis, cocaine or opioid dependence. *Addictive Behaviors, 35*, 741–749. (15) doi: 10.1016/j.addbeh.2010.03.019

Calipari, E. S., & Ferris, M. J. (2013). Amphetamine mechanisms and actions at the dopamine terminal revisited. *Journal of Neuroscience, 33*, 8923–8925. (3) doi: 10.1523/JNEUROSCI.1033-13.2013

Callan, A., Callan, D., & Ando, H. (2015). An fMRI study of the ventriloquism effect. *Cerebral Cortex, 25*, 4248–4258. (4) doi: 10.1093/cercor/bhu306

Cameron, P., Proctor, K., Coburn, W., & Forde, N. (1985). Sexual orientation and sexually transmitted disease. *Nebraska Medical Journal, 70*, 292–299. (11)

Campbell, S. S., & Tobler, I. (1984). Animal sleep: A review of sleep duration across phylogeny. *Neuroscience and Biobehavioral Reviews, 8*, 269–300. (10) doi: 10.1016/0149-7634(84)90054-X

Camperio-Ciani, A., Corna, F., & Capiluppi, C. (2004). Evidence for maternally inherited factors favouring male homosexuality and promoting female fecundity. *Proceedings of the Royal Society of London*, B, *271*, 2217–2221. (11) doi: 10.1098/rspb.2004.2872

Campion, M. A., & McClelland, C. L. (1991). Interdisciplinary examination of the costs and benefits of enlarged jobs: A job design quasi-experiment. *Journal of Applied Psychology, 76*, 186–198. (11) doi: 10.1037/0021-9010.76.2.186

Campion, M. A., & Thayer, P. W. (1985). Development and field evaluation of an interdisciplinary measure of job design. *Journal of Applied Psychology, 70*, 29–43. (11) doi: 10.1037/0021-9010.70.1.29

Campion, M. A., & Thayer, P. W. (1989). How do you design a job? *Personnel Journal, 68*, 43–46. (1) https://search-proquest-com.prox.lib.ncsu.edu/docview/219766538/5217FC4E26174A52PQ/19?accountid=12725

Campitelli, G., & Gobet, F. (2011). Deliberate practice: Necessary but not sufficient. *Current Directions in Psychological Science, 20*, 280–285. (8) doi: 10.1177/0963721411421922

Campolattaro, M. M., Savage, S. W., & Lipatova, O. (2017). Auditory cue absence as a conditioned stimulus for delay eyeblink conditioning. *Behavioral Neuroscience, 131*, 149–154. (6) doi: 10.1037/bne0000188

Cannon, W. B. (1929). Organization for physiological homeostasis. *Physiological Reviews, 9*, 399–431. (11) doi: 10.1152/physrev.1929.9.3.399

Cardno, A. G., Marshall, E. J., Coid, B., Macdonald, A. M., Ribchester, T. R., Davies, N. J., Venturi, P., Jones, L. A., Lewis, S. W., Sham, P. C., Gottesman, I. I., Farmer, A. E., McGuffin, P., Reveley, A. M., & Murray, R. M. (1999). Heritability estimates for psychotic disorders. *Archives of General Psychiatry, 56*, 162–168. (15) doi: 10.1001/archpsyc.56.2.162

Carey, S. (1978). The child as word learner. In M. Halle, J. Bresnan, & G. A. Miller (Eds.), *Linguistic theory and psychological reality* (pp. 264–293). Cambridge, MA: MIT Press. (8)

Carl, E., Stein, A. T., Levihn-Coon, A., Pogue, J. R., Rothbaum, B., Emmelkamp, P., Asmundson, G. J. G., Carlbring, P., & Powers, M. B. (2019). Virtual reality exposure therapy for anxiety and related disorders: A meta-analysis of randomized controlled trials. *Journal of Anxiety Disorders, 61*, 27–36. (15) doi: 10.1016/j.janxdis.2018.08.003

Carlson, E. A., Hostinar, C. E., Mlinar, S. B., & Gunnar, M. R. (2014). The emergence of attachment following early social deprivation. *Development and Psychopathology, 26*, 479–489. (5) doi: 10.1017/S0954579414000078

Carlsson, K., Petrovic, P., Skare, S., Petersson, K. M., & Ingvar, M. (2000). Tickling expectations: Neural processing in anticipation of a sensory stimulus. *Journal of Cognitive Neuroscience, 12*, 691–703. (4) doi: 10.1162/089892900562318

Carney, R. N., & Levin, J. R. (1998). Coming to terms with the keyword method in introductory psychology: A "neuromnemonic"

example. *Teaching of Psychology, 25*, 132–134. (7) doi: 10.1207/s15328023top2502_15

Carr, D., Freedman, V. A., Cornman, J. C., & Schwarz, N. (2014). Happy marriage, happy life? Marital quality and subjective well-being in later life. *Journal of Marriage and Family, 76*, 930–948. (12) doi: 10.1111/jomf.12133

Carré, J. M., McCormick, C. M., & Mondloch, C. J. (2009). Facial structure is a reliable cue of aggressive behavior. *Psychological Science, 20*, 1194–1198. (13) doi: 10.1111/j.1467-9280.2009.02423.x

Carreiras, M., Seghier, M. L., Baquero, S., Estévez, A., Lozano, A., Devlin, J. T., & Price, C. J. (2009). An anatomical signature for literacy. *Nature, 461*, 983–986. (3) doi: 10.1038/nature08461

Carrera, O., Adan, R. A. H., Gutiérrez, E., Danner, U. N., Hoek, H. W., van Elburg, A. A., & Kas, M. J. H. (2012). Hyperactivity in anorexia nervosa: Warming up not just burning-off calories. *PLoS One, 7*, e41851. (11) doi: 10.1371/journal.pone.0041851

Carroll, B. J. (1980). Implications of biological research for the diagnosis of depression. In J. Mendlewicz (Ed.), *New advances in the diagnosis and treatment of depressive illness* (pp. 85–107). Amsterdam: Excerpta Medica. (15)

Carstensen, L. L., Mikels, J. A., & Mather, M. (2006). Aging and the intersection of cognition, motivation, and emotion. In J. E. Birren & K. W. Schaie (Eds.), *Handbook of the psychology of aging* (6th ed., pp. 343–362). Burlington, MA: Elsevier. (5) https://www.sciencedirect.com/science/article/pii/B9780121012649500185

Carter, N. T., Miller, J. D., & Widiger, T. A. (2018). Extreme personalities at work and in life. *Current Directions in Psychological Science, 27*, 429–436. (14) doi: 10.1177/0963721418793134

Case, B. G., Bertollo, D. N., Laska, E. M., Price, L. H., Siegel, C. E., Olfson, M., & Marcus, S. C. (2013). Declining use of electroconvulsive shock in United States general hospitals. *Biological Psychiatry, 73*, 119–126. (15) doi: 10.1016/j.biopsych.2012.09.005

Casey, B. J., Somerville, L. H., Gotlib, I. H., Ayduk, O., Franklin, N. T., Askren, M. K., Jonides, J., Berman, M. G., Wilson, N. L., Teslovich, T., Glover, G., Zayas, V., Mischel, W., & Shoda, Y. (2011). Behavioral and neural correlates of delay of gratification 40 years later. *Proceedings of the National Academy of Sciences (U.S.A.), 108*, 14998–15003. (11) doi: 10.1073/pnas.1108561108

Caspi, A., Houts, R. M., Belsky, D. W., Goldman-Mellor, S. J., Harrington, H. L., Israel, S., Meieer, M. H., Ramrakha, S., Shalev, I., Poulton, R., & Moffitt, T. E. (2014). The *p* factor: One general psychopathology factor in the structure of psychiatric disorders? *Clinical Psychological Science, 2*, 119–137. (11, 15) doi: 10.1177/2167702613497473

Caspi, A., Sugden, K., Moffit, T. E., Taylor, A., Craig, I. W., Harrington, H. L., McClay, J., Mill, J., Martin, J., Braithwaite, A., & Poulton, R. (2003). Influence of life stress on depression: Moderation by a polymorphism in the 5-HTT gene. *Science, 301*, 386–389. (14, 15) doi: 10.1126/science.1083968

Cassia, V. M., Turati, C., & Simion, F. (2004). Can a nonspecific bias toward top-heavy patterns explain newborns' face preference? *Psychological Science, 15*, 379–383. (5) doi: 10.1111/j.0956-7976.2004.00688.x

Castro, V. L., Camras, L. A., Halberstadt, A. G., & Shuster, M. (2018). Children's prototypic facial expressions during emotion-eliciting

conversations with their mothers. *Emotion, 18*, 260–276. (12) doi: 10.1037/emo0000354

Catalá-López, F., Hutton, B., Nuñez-Beltrán, A., Page, M. J., Ridao, M., Saint-Gerons, D. M., Catala, M. A., Tabares-Seisdedos, R., & Moher, D. (2017). The pharmacological and non-pharmacological treatment of attention deficit hyperactivity disorder in children and adolescents: A systematic review with network meta-analyses of randomised trials. *PLoS One, 12*, e0180355. (8) doi: 10.1371/journal.pone.0180355

Catmur, C., Walsh, V., & Heyes, C. (2007). Sensorimotor learning configures the human mirror system. *Current Biology, 17*, 1527–1531. (3) doi: 10.1016/j.cub.2007.08.006

Cattell, R. B. (1965). *The scientific analysis of personality*. Chicago, IL: Aldine. (14)

Center for Psychology Workforce Analysis and Research. (2007). Doctorate Employment Survey. Washington, DC: American Psychological Association. (1) https://www.apa.org/workforce/publications/07-doc-empl/

Cepeda, N. J., Pashler, H., Vul, E., Wixted, J. T., & Rohrer, D. (2006). Distributed practice in verbal recall tasks: A review and quantitative synthesis. *Psychological Bulletin, 132*, 354–380. (7) doi: 10.1037/0033-2909.132.3.354

Cepeda, N. J., Vul, E., Rohrer, D., Wixted, J. T., & Pashler, H. (2008). Spacing effects in learning. *Psychological Science, 19*, 1095–1102. (7) doi: 10.1111/j.1467-9280.2008.02209.x

Cerasoli, C. P., Nicklin, J. M., & Ford, M. T. (2014). Intrinsic motivation and extrinsic incentives jointly predict performance: A 40-year meta-analysis. *Psychological Bulletin, 140*, 980–1008. (11) doi: 10.1037/a0035661

Cerrato, M., Carrera, O., Vazquez, R., Echevarria, E., & Gutiérrez, E. (2012). Heat makes a difference in activity-based anorexia: A translational approach to treatment development in anorexia nervosa. *International Journal of Eating Disorders, 45*, 26–35. (11) doi: 10.1002/eat.20884

Cesarini, D., Dawes, C. T., Fowler, J. H., Johanesson, M., Lichtenstein, P., & Wallace, B. (2008). Heritability of cooperative behavior in the trust game. *Proceedings of the National Academy of Sciences, USA, 105*, 3721–3726. (5) doi: 10.1073/pnas.0710069105

Chabris, C. F., & Glickman, M. E. (2006). Sex differences in intellectual performance: Analysis of a large cohort of competitive chess players. *Psychological Science, 17*, 1040–1046. (5) doi: 10.1111/j.1467-9280.2006.01828.x

Chamorro-Premuzic, T., & Furnham, A. (2008). Personality, intelligence and approaches to learning as predictors of academic performance. *Personality and Individual Differences, 44*, 1596–1603. (14) doi: 10.1016/j.paid.2008.01.003

Chancellor, J., Margolis, S., Bao, K. J., & Lyubomirsky, S. (2018). Everyday prosociality in the workplace: The reinforcing benefits of giving, getting, and glimpsing. *Emotion, 18*, 507–517. (12) doi: 10.1037/emo0000321

Chang, Y. Y.-C., & Chiou, W.-B. (2014). Taking weight-loss supplements may elicit liberation from dietary control. A laboratory experiment. *Appetite, 72*, 8–12. (11) doi: 10.1016/j.appet.2013.09.021

Chapman, H. A., Kim, D. A., Susskind, J. M., & Anderson, A. K. (2009). In bad taste: Evidence for the oral origins of moral disgust. *Science, 323*, 1222–1226. (12) doi: 10.1126/science.1165565

Charlesworth, T. E. S., & Banaji, M. R. (2019). Patterns of implicit and explicit attitudes: I. Long-term change and stability from 2007 to 2016. *Psychological Science, 30,* 174–192. (13) doi: 10.1177/0956797618813087

Chaudhari, N., Landin, M. A., & Roper, S. D. (2000). A metabotropic glutamate receptor variant functions as a taste receptor. *Nature Neuroscience, 3,* 113–119. (4) doi: 10.1038/72053

Cheetham, E. (1973). *The prophecies of Nostradamus.* New York: Putnam's. (2)

Chehab, F. F., Mounzih, K., Lu, R., & Lim, M. E. (1997). Early onset of reproductive function in normal female mice treated with leptin. *Science, 275,* 88–90. (11) doi: 10.1126/science.275.5296.88

Chen, A. T., & Nasrallah, H. A. (2019). Neuroprotective effects of the second generation antipsychotics. *Schizophrenia Research, 208,* 1–7. (15) doi: 10.1016/j.schres.2019.04.009

Chen, D., & Haviland-Jones, J. (2000). Human olfactory communication of emotion. *Perceptual and Motor Skills, 91,* 771–781. (5) doi: 10.2466/pms.2000.91.3.771

Chen, E., & Miller, G. E. (2012). "Shift-and-persist" strategies: Why low socioeconomic status isn't always bad for health. *Perspectives on Psychological Science, 7,* 135–158. (12) doi: 10.1177/1745691612436694

Chen, W.-J., Du, J-K., Hu, X., Yu, Q., Li, D.-X., Wang, C. N., Zhu, X. Y., & Liu, Y.-J. (2017). Protective effects of resveratrol on mitochondrial function in the hippocampus improves inflammation-induced depressive-like behavior. *Physiology & Behavior, 182,* 54–61. (15) doi: 10.1016/j.physbeh.2017.09.024

Chen, Y-C., Sudre, G., Sharp, W., Donovan, F., Chandrasekharappa, S. C., Hansen, N., Elnitski, L., & Shaw, P. (2018). Neuroanatomic, epigenetic, and genetic differences in monozygotic twins discordant for attention deficit hyperactivity disorder. *Molecular Psychiatry, 23,* 683–690. (8) doi: 10.1038/mp.2017.45

Cheung, B. Y., Chudek, M., & Heine, S. J. (2011). Evidence for a sensitive period for acculturation: Younger immigrants report acculturating at a faster rate. *Psychological Science, 22,* 147–152. (5) doi: 10.1177/0956797610394661

Cheung, F. M., Leung, K., Fang, R. M., Song, W. Z., Zhang, J. X., & Zhang, J. P. (1996). Development of the Chinese Personality Assessment Inventory (CPAI). *Journal of Cross-Cultural Psychology, 27,* 181–199. (14) doi: 10.1177/0022022196272003

Cheung, F. Y.-L., & Tang, C. S.-K. (2007). The influence of emotional dissonance and resources at work on job burnout among Chinese human service employees. *International Journal of Stress Management, 14,* 72–87. (11) doi: 10.1037/1072-5245.14.1.72

Chiesa, M. (2010). Research and psychoanalysis: Still time to bridge the great divide? *Psychoanalytic Psychology, 27,* 99–114. (14) doi: 10.1037/a0019413

Chiu, C.-D. (2018). Phenomenological characteristics of recovered memory in nonclinical individuals. *Psychiatry Research, 259,* 135–141. (7) doi: 10.1016/j.psychres.2017.10.021

Chivers, M. L., Rieger, G., Latty, E., & Bailey, J. M. (2004). A sex difference in the specificity of sexual arousal. *Psychological Science, 15,* 736–744. (11) doi: 10.1111/j.0956-7976.2004.00750.x

Choi, D., Black, A. K., & Werker, J. F. (2018). Cascading and multisensory influences on speech perception and development. *Mind, Brain, and Education, 12,* 212–223. (5) doi: 10.1111/mbe.12162

Chomsky, N. (1980). *Rules and representations.* New York: Columbia University Press. (8)

Chow, H. M., Mar, R. A., Xu, Y., Liu, S., Wagage, S., & Braun, A. R. (2014). Embodied comprehension of stories: Interactions between language regions and modality-specific neural systems. *Journal of Cognitive Neuroscience, 26,* 279–295. (8) doi: 10.1162/jocn_a_00487

Chue, A. E., Gunthert, K. C., Kim, R. W., Alfano, C. A., & Ruggiero, A. R. (2018). The role of sleep in adolescents' daily stress recovery: Negative affect spillover and positive affect bounce-back effects. *Journal of Adolescence, 66,* 101–111. (10) doi: 10.1016/j.adolescence.2018.05.006

Church, A. T., Katigbak, M. S., Reyes, J. A. S., Salanga, M. G. C., Miramontes, L. A., & Adams, N. B. (2008). Prediction and cross-situational consistency of daily behavior across cultures: Testing trait and cultural psychology perspectives. *Journal of Research in Personality, 42,* 1199–1215. (14) doi: 10.1016/j.jrp.2008.03.007

Churchland, P. S. (1986). *Neurophilosophy.* Cambridge, MA: MIT Press. (10)

Cialdini, R. B. (1993). *Influence: The psychology of persuasion* (Rev. ed.). New York: Morrow. (6, 13)

Cialdini, R. B. (2003). Crafting normative messages to protect the environment. *Current Directions in Psychological Science, 12,* 105–109. (13) doi: 10.1111/1467-8721.01242

Ciaramelli, E., Muccioli, M., Làdavas, E., & DiPellegrino, G. (2007). Selective deficit in personal moral judgment following damage to ventromedial prefrontal cortex. *Social Cognitive and Affective Neuroscience, 2,* 84–92. (12) doi: 10.1093/scan/nsm001

Cimino, K. (2007, June 20). After it blooms, it will smell as bad as a blooming corpse. *News and Observer* (Raleigh, NC), p. 4B. (11)

Cislo, A. M. (2008). Ethnic identity and self-esteem: Contrasting Cuban and Nicaraguan young adults. *Hispanic Journal of Behavioral Sciences, 30,* 230–250. (5) doi: 10.1177/0739986308315297

Clancy, S. A. (2005). *Abducted: How people come to believe they were kidnapped by aliens.* Cambridge, MA: Harvard University Press. (15)

Clark, L. A., Cuthbert, B., Lewis-Fernández, R., Narrow, E., & Reed, G. M. (2017). Three approaches to understanding and classifying mental disorder: ICD-11, DSM-5, and the National Institute of Mental Health's Research Domain Criteria (RDoC). *Psychological Science in the Public Interest, 18,* 72–145. (15) doi: 10.1177/1529100617727266

Clark, S. E. (2012). Costs and benefits of eyewitness identification reform: Psychological science and public policy. *Perspectives on Psychological Science, 7,* 238–259. (7) doi: 10.1177/1745691612439584

Claassen, J., Doyle, K., Matory, A., Couch, C., Burger, K. M., Velazquez, A., … Rohaut, B. (2019). Detection of brain activation in unresponsive patients with acute brain injury. *New England Journal of Medicine, 380,* 2497–2505. (10) doi: 10.1056/NEJMoa1812757

Claudel, M., Massaro, E., Santi, P., Murray, F., & Ratti, C. (2017). An exploration of collaborative scientific production at MIT through spatial organizational and institutional affiliation. *PLoS One, 12,* e0179334. (13) doi: 10.1371/journal.pone.0179334

Clay, R. A. (2002, May). An indigenized psychology. *Monitor on Psychology, 33*(5), 58–59. (15) https://www.apa.org/monitor/may02/india.html

Clearfield, M. W., & Nelson, N. M. (2006). Sex differences in mothers' speech and play behavior with 6-, 9-, and 14-month-old infants. *Sex Roles, 54,* 127–137. (5) doi: 10.1007/s11199-005-8874-1

Cleary, A. M., & Claxton, A. B. (2018). Déjà vu: An illusion of prediction. *Psychological Science, 29,* 635–644. (10) doi: 10.1177/0956797617743018

Clegg, J. M., Wen, N. J., & Legare, C. H. (2017). Is non-conformity WEIRD? Cultural variation in adults' beliefs about children's competency and conformity. *Journal of Experimental Psychology: General, 146,* 428–441. (13) doi: 10.1037/xge0000275

Clément, K., Vaisse, C., Lahlou, N., Cabrol, S., Pelloux, V., Cassuto, D., Gourmelen, M., Dina, C., Chambaz, J., Lacorte, J. M., Basdevant, A., Bougneres, P., Lebouc, Y., Froguel, P., & Guy-Grand, B. (1998). A mutation in the human leptin receptor gene causes obesity and pituitary dysfunction. *Nature, 392,* 398–401. (11) https://www.nature.com/articles/32911

Clinicopathologic Conference. (1967). *Johns Hopkins Medical Journal, 120,* 186–199. (12)

Coan, J. A., Schaefer, H. S., & Davidson, R. J. (2006). Lending a hand: Social regulation of the neural response to threat. *Psychological Science, 17,* 1032–1039. (12) doi: 10.1111/j.1467-9280.2006.01832.x

Coatsworth, J. D., Maldonado-Molina, M., Pantin, H., & Szapocznik, J. (2005). A person-centered and ecological investigation of acculturation strategies in Hispanic immigrant youth. *Journal of Community Psychology, 33,* 157–174. (5) doi: 10.1002/jcop.20046

Cobos, P., Sánchez, M., García, C., Vera, M. N., & Vila, J. (2002). Revisiting the James versus Cannon debate on emotion: Startle and autonomic modulation in patients with spinal cord injuries. *Biological Psychology, 61,* 251–269. (12) doi: 10.1016/S0301-0511(02)00061-3

Coelho, C. M., Waters, A. M., Hine, T. J., & Wallis, G. (2009). The use of virtual reality in acrophobia research and treatment. *Journal of Anxiety Disorders, 23,* 563–574. (15) doi: 10.1016/j.janxdis.2009.01.014

Cohen, G. L., Garcia, J., Purdie-Vaughns, V., Apfel, N., & Brzustoski, P. (2009). Recursive processes in self-affirmation: Intervening to close the minority achievement gap. *Science, 324,* 400–403. (9) doi: 10.1126/science.1170769

Cohen, M. A., Alvarez, G. A., & Nakayama, K. (2011). Natural-scene perception requires attention. *Psychological Science, 22,* 1165–1172. (8) doi: 10.1177/0956797611419168

Cohen, M. A., Konkle, T., Rhee, J. Y., Nakayama, K., & Alvarez, G. A. (2014). Processing multiple visual objects is limited by overlap in neural channels. *Proceedings of the National Academy of Sciences (U.S.A.), 111,* 8955–8960. (8) doi: 10.1073/pnas.1317860111

Cohen, M. R., & Maunsell, J. H. R. (2011). When attention wanders: How uncontrolled fluctuations in attention affect performance. *Journal of Neuroscience, 31,* 15802–15806. (8) doi: 10.1523/JNEUROSCI.3063-11.2011

Cohen, N. J., & Squire, L. R. (1980). Preserved learning and retention of pattern-analyzing skill in amnesia: Dissociation of knowing how and knowing that. *Science, 210*, 207–211. (7) doi: 10.1126/science.7414331

Cohen, S., Frank, E., Doyle, W. J., Skoner, D. P., Rabin, B. S., & Swaltney, J. M., Jr. (1998). Types of stressors that increase susceptibility to the common cold in healthy adults. *Health Psychology, 17*, 214–223. (12) doi: 10.1037/0278-6133.17.3.214

Cohen, S., Lichtenstein, E., Prochaska, J. O., Rossi, J. S., Gritz, E. R., Carr, C. R., Orleans, C. T., Schoenbach, V. J., Biener, L., Abrams, D., DiClemente, C., Curry, S., Marlatt, G. A., Cummings, K. M., Emont, S. L., Giovino, G., & Ossip-Klein, D. (1989). Debunking myths about self-quitting: Evidence from 10 prospective studies of persons who attempt to quit smoking by themselves. *American Psychologist, 44*, 1355–1365. (15) doi: 10.1037/0003-066X.44.11.1355

Colantuoni, C., Rada, P., McCarthy, J., Patten, C., Avena, N. M., Chadcayne, A., & Hoebel, B. G. (2002). Evidence that intermittent, excessive sugar intake causes endogenous opioid dependence. *Obesity Research, 10*, 478–488. (11) doi: 10.1038/oby.2002.66

Colantuoni, C., Schwenker, J., McCarthy, J., Rada, P., Ladenheim, B., Cadet, J. L., Schwartz, G. J., Moran, T. H., & Hoebel, B. G. (2001). Excessive sugar intake alters binding to dopamine and mu-opioid receptors in the brain. *NeuroReport, 12*, 3549–3552. (11) doi: 10.1097/00001756-200111160-00035

Colcombe, S., & Kramer, A. F. (2003). Fitness effects on the cognitive function of older adults: A meta-analytic study. *Psychological Science, 14*, 125–130. (5) doi: 10.1111/1467-9280.t01-1-01430

Cole, T., & Brown, J. (2014). Behavioural investigative advice: Assistance to investigative decision-making in difficult-to-detect murder. *Journal of Investigative Psychology and Offender Profiling, 11*, 191–200. (14) doi: 10.1002/jip.1396

Coles, N. A., Larsen, J. T., & Lench, H. C. (2019). A meta-analysis of the facial feedback literature: Effects of facial feedback on emotional experience are small and variable. *Psychological Bulletin, 145*, 610–651. (12) doi: 10.1037/bul0000194

Colizoli, O., Muirre, J. M. J., & Rouw, R. (2013). A taste for words and sounds: A case of lexical-gustatory and sound-gustatory synesthesia. *Frontiers in Psychology, 4*, Article 775. (4) doi: 10.3389/fpsyg.2013.00775

Collins, A. M., & Loftus, E. F. (1975). A spreading-activation theory of semantic processing. *Psychological Review, 82*, 407–428. (8) doi: 10.1037/0033-295X.82.6.407

Collins, A. M., & Quillian, M. R. (1969). Retrieval time from semantic memory. *Journal of Verbal Learning and Verbal Behavior, 8*, 240–247. (8) doi: 10.1016/S0022-5371(69)80069-1

Collins, A. M., & Quillian, M. R. (1970). Does category size affect categorization time? *Journal of Verbal Learning and Verbal Behavior, 9*, 432–438. (8) doi: 10.1016/S0022-5371(70)80084-6

Colman, A. M. (2016). Race differences in IQ: Hans Eysenck's contribution to the debate in the light of subsequent research. *Personality and Individual Differences, 103*, 182–189. (9) doi: 10.1016/j.paid.2016.04.050

Coman, A., & Hirst, W. (2015). Social identity and socially shared retrieval-induced forgetting: The effects of group membership. *Journal of*

Experimental Psychology: General, 144, 717–722. (7) doi: 10.1037/xge0000077

Coman, A., Manier, D., & Hirst, W. (2009). Forgetting the unforgettable through conversation. *Psychological Science, 20*, 627–633. (7) doi: 10.1111/j.1467-9280.2009.02343.x

Compton, J., Jackson, B., & Dimmock, J. A. (2016). Persuading others to avoid persuasion: Inoculation theory and resistant health attitudes. *Frontiers in Psychology, 7*, article 122. (13) doi: 10.3389/fpsyg.2016.00122

Condra, L. N., & Linardi, S. (2019). Casual contact and ethnic bias: Experimental evidence from Afghanistan. *Journal of Politics, 81*, 1028–1042. (13) doi: 10.1086/703380

Conley, T. D., Moors, A. C., Matsick, J. L., Ziegler, A., & Valentine, B. A. (2011). Women, men, and the bedroom: Methodological and conceptual insights that narrow, reframe, and eliminate gender differences in sexuality. *Current Directions in Psychological Science, 20*, 296–300. (11) doi: 10.1177/0963721411418467

Connine, C. M., Blasko, D. G., & Hall, M. (1991). Effects of subsequent sentence context in auditory word recognition: Temporal and linguistic constraints. *Journal of Memory and Language, 30*, 234–250. (8) doi: 10.1016/0749-596X(91)90005-5

Connor, T. J., & Leonard, B. E. (1998). Depression, stress and immunological activation: The role of cytokines in depressive disorders. *Life Sciences, 62*, 583–606. (12) doi: 10.1016/S0024-3205(97)00990-9

Constantinides, P. (1977). Ill at ease and sick at heart: Symbolic behavior in a Sudanese healing cult. In I. Wilson (Ed.), *Symbols and sentiments* (pp. 61–84). New York: Academic Press. (15)

Constantinescu, M., Moore, D. S., Johnson, S. P., & Hines, M. (2018). Early contributions to infants' mental rotation abilities. *Developmental Science, 21*, e12613. (5) doi: 10.1111/desc.12613

Constantino, J. N., Kennon-McGill, S., Weichselbaum, C., Marrus, N., Haider, A., Glowinski, A. L., Gillespie, S., Klaiman, C., Klin, A., & Jones, W. (2017). Infant viewing of social scenes is under genetic control and is atypical in autism. *Nature, 547*, 340–344. (5) doi: 10.1038/nature22999

Cooper, J., & Cooper, G. (2002). Subliminal motivation: A story revisited. *Journal of Applied Social Psychology, 32*, 2213–2227. (4) doi: 10.1111/j.1559-1816.2002.tb01860.x

Coplan, J. D., Goetz, R., Klein, D. F., Papp, L. A., Fyer, A. J., Leibowitz, M. R., Davies, S. O., & Gorman, J. M. (1998). Plasma cortisol concentrations preceding lactate-induced panic. *Archives of General Psychiatry, 55*, 130–136. (15) doi: 10.1001/archpsyc.55.2.130

Corder, G., Ahanonu, B., Grewe, B. F., Wang, D., Schnitzer, M. J., & Scherrer, G. (2019). An amygdalar neural ensemble that encodes the unpleasantness of pain. *Science, 363*, 276–281. (4) doi: 10.1126/science.aap8586

Corkin, S. (1984). Lasting consequences of bilateral medial temporal lobectomy: Clinical course and experimental findings in H. M. *Seminars in Neurology, 4*, 249–259. (7) doi: 10.1055/s-2008-1041556

Corkin, S. (2002). What's new with the amnesic patient H. M.? *Nature Reviews Neuroscience, 3*, 153–159. (7) doi: 10.1038/nrn726

Cornil, Y., & Chandon, P. (2013). From fan to fat? Vicarious losing increases unhealthy eating, but self-affirmation is an effective remedy.

Psychological Science, 24, 1936–1946. (11) doi: 10.1177/0956797613481232

Corrigan, P. W., Druss, B. G., & Perlick, D. A. (2014). The impact of mental illness stigma on seeking and participating in mental health care. *Psychological Science in the Public Interest, 15*, 37–70. (15) doi: 10.1177/1529100614531398

Cosmelli, D., David, O., Lachaux, J.-P., Martinerie, J., Garnero, L., Renault, B., & Varela, F. (2004). Waves of consciousness: Ongoing cortical patterns during binocular rivalry. *NeuroImage, 23*, 128–140. (10) doi: 10.1016/j.neuroimage.2004.05.008

Costa, P. T., Jr., McCrae, R. R., & Dye, D. A. (1991). Facet scales for agreeableness and conscientiousness: A revision of the NEO personality inventory. *Personality and Individual Differences, 12*, 887–898. (14) doi: 10.1016/0191-8869(91)90177-D

Coughlan, E. K., Williams, A. M., McRobert, A. P., & Ford, P. R. (2014). How experts practice: A novel test of deliberate practice theory. *Journal of Experimental Psychology: Learning Memory and Cognition, 40*, 449–458. (8) doi: 10.1037/a0034302

Coughtrey, A. E., Shafran, R., Lee, M., & Rachman, S. (2013). The treatment of mental contamination: A case series. *Cognitive and Behavioral Practice, 20*, 221–231. (15) doi: 10.1016/j.cbpra.2012.07.002

Courage, M. L., & Howe, M. L. (2002). From infant to child: The dynamics of cognitive change in the second year of life. *Psychological Bulletin, 128*, 250–277. (5) doi: 10.1037//0033-2909.128.2.250

Cowan, N. (2010). The magical mystery four: How is working memory capacity limited, and why? *Current Directions in Psychological Science, 19*, 51–57. (7) doi: 10.1177/0963721409359277

Cox, B. J., McWilliams, L. A., Clara, I. P., & Stein, M. B. (2003). The structure of feared situations in a nationally representative sample. *Journal of Anxiety Disorders, 17*, 89–101. (15) doi: 10.1016/S0887-6185(02)00179-2

Cox, J. J., Reimann, F., Nicholas, A. K., Thornton, G., Roberts, E., Springell, K., Karbani, G., Jafri, H., Mannan, J., Raashid, Y., Al-Gazali, L., Hamamy, H., Valente, E. M., Gorman, S., Williams, R., McHale, D. P., Wood, J. N., Gribble, F. M.. & Woods, C. G. (2006). An *SCN9A* channelopathy causes congenital inability to experience pain. *Nature, 444*, 894–898. (4) doi: 10.1038/nature05413

Craig, A. D., Bushnell, M. C., Zhang, E. T., & Blomqvist, A. (1994). A thalamic nucleus specific for pain and temperature sensation. *Nature, 372*, 770–773. (4) doi: 10.1038/372770a0

Craig, M., & Dewar, M. (2018). Rest-related consolidation protects the fine detail of new memories. *Scientific Reports, 8*, article 6857. (7) doi: 10.1038/s41598-018-25313-y

Craig, S. B., & Gustafson, S. B. (1998). Perceived leader integrity scale: An instrument for assessing employee perceptions of leader integrity. *Leadership Quarterly, 9*, 127–145. (11) doi: 10.1016/S1048-9843(98)90001-7

Craik, F. I. M., & Lockhart, R. S. (1972). Levels of processing: A framework for memory research. *Journal of Verbal Learning and Verbal Behavior, 11*, 671–684. (7) doi: 10.1016/S0022-5371(72)80001-X

Cramer, P. (1996). *Storytelling, narrative, and the Thematic Apperception Test*. New York: Guilford Press. (14)

Cramer, P. (2003). Personality change in later adulthood is predicted by defense mechanism use in early adulthood. *Journal of Research in Personality, 37,* 76–104. (14) doi: 10.1016/S0092-6566(02)00528-7

Credé, M., & Kuncel, N. R. (2008). Study habits, skills, and attitudes. *Perspectives on Psychological Science, 3,* 425–453. (9) doi: 10.1111/j.1745-6924.2008.00089.x

Crews, F. (1996). The verdict on Freud. *Psychological Science, 7,* 63–68. (14) doi: 10.1111/j.1467-9280.1996.tb00331.x

Critcher, C. R., & Rosenzweig, E. L. (2014). The performance heuristic: A misguided reliance on past success when predicting prospects for improvement. *Journal of Experimental Psychology: General, 143,* 480–485. (8) doi: 10.1037/a0034129

Critchley, H. D., Mathias, C. J., & Dolan, R. J. (2001). Neuroanatomical basis for first- and second-order representations of bodily states. *Nature Neuroscience, 4,* 207–212. (12) doi: 10.1038/84048

Crivelli, C., Russell, J. A., Jarillo, S., & Fernández-Dols, J. M. (2017). Recognizing spontaneous facial expressions of emotion in a small-scale society of Papua New Guinea. *Emotion, 17,* 337–347. (12) doi: 10.1037/emo0000236

Crocker, J., & Park, L. E. (2004). The costly pursuit of self-esteem. *Psychological Bulletin, 130,* 392–414. (14) doi: 10.1037/0033-2909.130.3.392

Cropsey, K. L., Schiavon, S., Hendricks, P. S., Froelich, M., Lentowicz, I., & Ferguson, R. (2017). Mixed-amphetamine salts expectancies among college students: Is stimulant induced cognitive enhancement a placebo effect? *Drug and Alcohol Dependence, 178,* 302–309. (8) doi: 10.1016/j.drugalcdep.2017.05.024

Cross-Disorder Group of the Psychiatric Genomics Consortium. (2013). Genetic relationship between five psychiatric disorders estimated from genome-wide SNPs. *Nature Genetics, 45,* 984–994. (11, 15) doi: 10.1038/ng.2711

Crowley, K., Callanen, M. A., Tenenbaum, H. R., & Allen, E. (2001). Parents explain more often to boys than to girls during shared scientific thinking. *Psychological Science, 12,* 258–261. (5) doi: 10.1111/1467-9280.00347

Crowther, J. H., Armey, M., Luce, K. H., Dalton, G. R., & Leahey, T. (2008). The point prevalence of bulimic disorders from 1990 to 2004. *International Journal of Eating Disorders, 41,* 491–497. (11) doi: 10.1002/eat.20537

Croyle, R. T., & Cooper, J. (1983). Dissonance arousal: Physiological evidence. *Journal of Personality and Social Psychology, 45,* 782–791. (13) doi: 10.1037/0022-3514.45.4.782

Crum, A. J., & Langer, E. J. (2007). Mind-set matters. *Psychological Science, 18,* 165–171. (12) doi: 10.1111/j.1467-9280.2007.01867.x

Cryder, C. E., Lerner, J. S., Gross, J. J., & Dahl, R. E. (2008). Misery is not miserly: Sad and self-focused individuals spend more. *Psychological Science, 19,* 525–530. (12) doi: 10.1111/j.1467-9280.2008.02118.x

Cubillo, A., Halari, R., Smith, A., Taylor, E., & Rubia, K. (2012). A review of fronto-striatal and fronto-cortical brain abnormalities in children and adults with attention deficit hyperactivity disorder (ADHD) and new evidence for dysfunction in adults with ADHD during motivation and attention. *Cortex, 48,* 194–215. (8) doi: 10.1016/j.cortex.2011.04.007

Cucina, J., & Byle, K. (2017). The bifactor model fits better than the higher-order model in more than 90% of comparisons for mental abilities test batteries. *Journal of Intelligence, 5,* 27. (9) doi: 10.3390/jintelligence5030027

Cuijpers, P., Huibers, M., Ebert, D. D., Koole, S. L., & Andersson, G. (2013). How much psychotherapy is needed to treat depression? A metaregression analysis. *Journal of Affective Disorders, 149,* 1–13. (15) doi: 10.1016/j.jad.2013.02.030

Cuijpers, P., van Straten, A., Andersson, G., & van Oppen, P. (2008). Psychotherapy for depression in adults: A meta-analysis of comparative outcome studies. *Journal of Consulting and Clinical Psychology, 76,* 909–922. (15) doi: 10.1037/a0013075

Cumming, G. (2014). The new statistics: Why and how. *Psychological Science, 25,* 7–29. (2) doi: 10.1177/0956797613504966

Cumming, G. (2008). Replication and *p* intervals. *Perspectives on Psychological Science, 3,* 286–300. (2) doi: 10.1111/j.1745-6924.2008.00079.x

Cummings, N. A. (1979). Turning bread into stones: Our modern antimiracle. *American Psychologist, 34,* 1119–1129. (15) doi: 10.1037/0003-066X.34.12.1119

Cummins, R. A., Li, N., Wooden, M., & Stokes, M. (2014). A demonstration of set-points for subjective wellbeing. *Journal of Happiness Studies, 15,* 183–206. (12) doi: 10.1007/s10902-013-9444-9

Cunningham, W. A., Van Bavel, J. J., & Johnsen, I. R. (2008). Affective flexibility: Evaluative processing goals shape amygdala activity. *Psychological Science, 28,* 1193–1200. (12) doi: 10.1111/j.1467-9280.2008.02061.x

Curci, A., & Rimé, B. (2012). The temporal evolution of social sharing of emotions and its consequences on emotional recovery: A longitudinal study. *Emotion, 12,* 1404–1414. (15) doi: 10.1037/a0028651

Curran, T., & Hill, A. P. (2019). Perfectionism is increasing over time: A meta-analysis of birth cohort differences from 1989 to 2016. *Psychological Bulletin, 145,* 410–429. (14) doi: 10.1037/bul0000138

Curseu, P. L., Janssen, S. E. A., & Meeus, M. T. H. (2014). Shining lights and bad apples: The effect of goal setting on group performance. *Management Learning, 45,* 332–348. (11) doi: 10.1177/1350507613483425

Czeisler, C. (2013). Casting light on sleep deficiency. *Nature, 497,* S13. (10) doi: 10.1038/497S13a

Czeisler, C. A., Johnson, M. P., Duffy, J. F., Brown, E. N., Ronda, J. M., & Kronauer, R. E. (1990). Exposure to bright light and darkness to treat physiologic maladaptation to night work. *New England Journal of Medicine, 322,* 1253–1259. (10) doi: 10.1056/NEJM199005033221801

Czeisler, C. A., Moore-Ede, M. C., & Coleman, R. M. (1982). Rotating shift work schedules that disrupt sleep are improved by applying circadian principles. *Science, 217,* 460–463. (10) doi: 10.1126/science.7089576

Czopp, A. M., Kay, A. C., & Cheryan, S. (2015). Positive stereotypes are pervasive and powerful. *Perspectives on Psychological Science, 10,* 451–463. (13) doi: 10.1177/1745691615588091

Dahl, A., Campos, J. J., Anderson, D. I., Uchiyama, I., Witherington, D. C., Ueno, M., Poutrain-Lejeune, L., & Barbu-Roth, M. (2013). The epigenesis of wariness of heights. *Psychological Science, 24,* 1361–1367. (5) doi: 10.1177/0956797613476047

Dai, H., Milkman, K. L., & Riis, J. (2015). Put your imperfections behind you: Temporal landmarks spur goal initiation when they signal new beginnings. *Psychological Science, 26,* 1927–1936. (11) doi: 10.1177/0956797615605818

Dailey, M. N., Joyce, C., Lyons, M. J., Kamachi, M., Ishi, H., Gyoba, J., & Cottrell, G. W. (2010). Evidence and a computational explanation of cultural differences in facial expression recognition. *Emotion, 10,* 874–893. (12) doi: 10.1037/a0020019

Dale, A., Lafreniere, A., & De Koninck, J. (2017). Dream content of Canadian males from adolescence to old age: An exploration of ontogenetic patterns. *Consciousness and Cognition, 49,* 145–156. (10) doi: 10.1016/j.concog.2017.01.008

Dale, A., Lortie-Lussier, M., Wong, C., & De Koninck, J. (2016). Dreams of Canadian students: Norms, gender differences, and comparison with American norms. *Journal of Cross-Cultural Psychology, 47,* 941–955. (10) doi: 10.1177/0022022116655788

Daley, D., van der Oord, S., Ferrin, M., Danckaerts, M., Cortese, S., & Sonuga-Barke, E. J. S. (2014). Behavioral interventions in attention-deficit/hyperactivity disorder: A meta-analysis of randomized controlled trials across multiple outcome domains. *Journal of the American Academy of Child & Adolescent Psychiatry, 53,* 835–847. (8) doi: 10.1016/j.jaac.2014.05.013

Daley, T. C., Whaley, S. E., Sigman, M. D., Espinosa, M. P., & Neumann, C. (2003). IQ on the rise: The Flynn effect in rural Kenyan children. *Psychological Science, 14,* 215–219. (9) doi: 10.1111/1467-9280.02434

Dallenbach, K. M. (1951). A puzzle picture with a new principle of concealment. *American Journal of Psychology, 64,* 431–433. (4) doi: 10.2307/1419008

Daly, M., Sutin, A. R., & Robinson, E. (2019). Perceived weight discrimination mediates the prospective association between obesity and physiological dysregulation: Evidence from a population-based cohort. *Psychological Science, 30,* 1030–1039. (11) doi: 10.1177/0956797619849440

Damaser, E. C., Shor, R. E., & Orne, M. E. (1963). Physiological effects during hypnotically requested emotions. *Psychosomatic Medicine, 25,* 334–343. (10) doi: 10.1097/00006842-196307000-00002

Damasio, A. (1999). *The feeling of what happens.* New York: Harcourt Brace. (12)

Damasio, A. R. (1994). *Descartes' error: Emotion, reason, and the human brain.* New York: G. P. Putnam's Sons. (12)

Damian, R. I., Spengler, M., Sutu, A., & Roberts, B. W. (2019). Sixteen going on sixty-six: A longitudinal study of personality stability and change across 50 years. *Journal of Personality and Social Psychology, 117,* 674–695. (14) doi: 10.1037/pspp0000210

Danchin, E., Nöbel, S., Pocheville, A., Dagaeff, A.-C., Demay, L., Alphand, M., Ranty-Roby, S., van Renssen, L., Monier, M., Gazagne, E., Allain, M., & Isabel, G. (2018). Cultural flies: Conformist social learning in fruitflies predicts long-lasting mate-choice traditions. *Science, 362,* 1025–1030. (13) doi: 10.1126/science.aat1590

Danovitch, J., & Bloom, P. (2009). Children's extension of disgust to physical and moral events. *Emotion, 9,* 107–112. (12) doi: 10.1037/a0014113

Darst, C. R., & Cummings, M. E. (2006). Predator learning favours mimicry of a less-toxic model in poison frogs. *Nature, 440,* 208–211. (6) doi: 10.1038/nature04297

Darwin, C. (1859). *On the origin of species by means of natural selection.* New York: D. Appleton. (1)

Darwin, C. (1871). *The descent of man.* New York: D. Appleton. (1)

Darwin, C. (1965). *The expression of emotions in man and animals.* Chicago, IL: University of Chicago Press. (Original work published 1872) (12)

Davenport, J. L., & Potter, M. C. (2004). Scene consistency in object and background perception. *Psychological Science, 15,* 559–564. (8) doi: 10.1111/j.0956-7976.2004.00719.x

Davidson, J. K., Sr., Moore, N. B., Earle, J. R., & Davis, R. (2008). Sexual attitudes and behavior at four universities: Do region, race, and/or religion matter? *Adolescence, 43,* 189–220. (11)

Davidson, R. J., Putnam, K. M., & Larson, C. L. (2000). Dysfunction in the neural circuitry of emotion regulation—A possible prelude to violence. *Science, 289,* 591–594. (13) doi: 10.1126/science.289.5479.591

Davies, G., Welham, J., Chant, D., Torrey, E. F., & McGrath, J. (2003). A systematic review and meta-analysis of Northern Hemisphere season of birth studies in schizophrenia. *Schizophrenia Bulletin, 29,* 587–593. (15) doi: 10.1093/oxfordjournals.schbul.a007030

Davis, D., Dorsey, J. K., Franks, R. D., Sackett, P. R, Searcy, C. A., & Zhao, X. (2013). Do racial and ethnic group differences in performance on the MCAT exam reflect test bias? *Academic Medicine, 88,* 593–602. (9) doi: 10.1097/ACM.0b013e318286803a

Davis, J. I., Senghas, A., Brandt, F., & Ochsner, K. N. (2010). The effects of BOTOX injections on emotional experience. *Emotion, 10,* 433–440. (12) doi: 10.1037/a0018690

Davis, J. M., Chen, N., & Glick, I. D. (2003). A meta-analysis of the efficacy of second-generation antipsychotics. *Archives of General Psychiatry, 60,* 553–564. (15) doi: 10.1001/archpsyc.60.6.553

Davis, O. S. P., Haworth, C. M. A., & Plomin, R. (2009). Dramatic increase in heritability of cognitive development from early to middle childhood. *Psychological Science, 20,* 1301–1308. (9) doi: 10.1111/j.1467-9280.2009.02433.x

Dawes, R. M. (1994). *House of cards: Psychology and psychotherapy.* New York: Free Press. (14)

Dawson, M., Soulières, I., Gernsbacher, M. A., & Mottron, L. (2007). The level and nature of autistic intelligence. *Psychological Science, 18,* 657–662. (15) doi: 10.1111/j.1467-9280.2007.01954.x

Day, R. H. (1972). Visual spatial illusions: A general explanation. *Science, 175,* 1335–1340. (4) doi: 10.1126/science.175.4028.1335

de Abreu, P. M. J. E., Cruz-Santos, A., Tourinho, C. J., Martin, R., & Bialystok, E. (2012). Bilingualism enriches the poor: Enhanced cognitive control in low-income minority children. *Psychological Science, 23,* 1364–1371. (8) doi: 10.1177/0956797612443836

de Bruin, A., Treccani, B., & Della Salla, S. (2015). Cognitive advantage in bilingualism: An example of publication bias? *Psychological Science, 26,* 99–107. (8) doi: 10.1177/0956797614557866

de Castro, J. M. (2000). Eating behavior: Lessons from the real world of humans. *Nutrition,* 16, 800–813. (1, 11) doi: 10.1016/S0899-9007(00)00414-7

de Groot, A. D. (1966). Perception and memory versus thought: Some old ideas and recent findings. In B. Kleinmuntz (Ed.), *Problem solving* (pp. 19–50). New York: Wiley. (8).

de Groot, J. H. B., Semin, G. R., & Smeets, M. A. M. (2014). Chemical communication of fear: A case of male-female asymmetry. *Journal of Experimental Psychology: General, 143,* 1515–1525. (12) doi: 10.1037/a0035950

De Houwer, J., Teige-Mocigemba, S., Spruyt, A., & Moors, A. (2009). Implicit measures: A normative analysis and review. *Psychological Bulletin, 135,* 347–368. (14) doi: 10.1037/a0014211

de Quervain, D. J.-F., Roozendaal, B., Nitsch, R. M., McGaugh, J. L., & Hock, C. (2000). Acute cortisone administration impairs retrieval of long-term declarative memory in humans. *Nature Neuroscience, 3,* 313–314. (12) doi: 10.1038/73873

De Simoni, C., & von Bastian, C. C. (2018). Working memory updating and binding training: Bayesian evidence supporting the absence of transfer. *Journal of Experimental Psychology: General, 147,* 829–858. (7) doi: 10.1037/xge0000453

de Vivo, L., Bellesi, M., Marshall, W., Bushong, E. A., Ellisman, M. H., Tononi, G., & Cirelli, C. (2017). Ultrastructural evidence for synaptic scaling across the wake/sleep cycle. *Science, 355,* 507–510. (10) doi: 10.1126/science.aah5982

de Waal, F. B. M. (2002). Evolutionary psychology: The wheat and the chaff. *Current Directions in Psychological Science, 11,* 187–191. (1, 3) doi: 10.1111/1467-8721.00197

de Waal, F. B. M., & Preston, S. D. (2017). Mammalian empathy: Behavioural manifestatons and neural basis. *Nature Reviews Neuroscience, 18,* 498–509. (13) doi: 10.1038/nrn.2017.72

Deacon, S., & Arendt, J. (1996). Adapting to phase shifts: II. Effects of melatonin and conflicting light treatment. *Physiology and Behavior, 59,* 675–682. (10) doi: 10.1016/0031-9384(95)02148-5

Deacon, T. W. (1997). *The symbolic species.* New York: W. W. Norton. (8)

Deady, D.K., North, N. T., Allan, D., Smith, M. J. L., & O'Carroll, R. E. (2010). Examining the effect of spinal cord injury on emotional awareness, expressivity and memory for emotional material. *Psychology, Health & Medicine, 15,* 406–419. (12) doi: 10.1080/13548506.2010.482138

Dean, C. E. (2011). Psychopharmacology: A house divided. *Progress in Neuro-Psychopharmacology & Biological Psychiatry, 35,* 1–10. (15) doi: 10.1016/j.pnpbp.2010.08.028

Dean, K. E., & Malamuth, N. M. (1997). Characteristics of men who aggress sexually and of men who imagine aggressing: Risk and moderating variables. *Journal of Personality and Social Psychology, 72,* 449–455. (13) doi: 10.1037/0022-3514.72.2.449

Deary, I. J., Batty, G. D., & Gale, C. R. (2008). Bright children become enlightened adults. *Psychological Science, 19,* 1–6. (9) doi: 10.1111/j.1467-9280.2008.02036.x

Deary, I. J., Strand, S., Smith, P., & Fernandes, C. (2007). Intelligence and educational achievement. *Intelligence, 35,* 13–21. (9) doi: 10.1016/j.intell.2006.02.001

Deary, I. J., Whiteman, M. C., Starr, J. M., Whalley, L. J., & Fox, H. C. (2004). The impact of childhood intelligence on later life: Following up the Scottish mental surveys of 1932 and 1947. *Journal of Personality and Social Psychology, 86,* 130–147. (9) doi: 10.1037/0022-3514.86.1.130

DeCasper, A. J., & Fifer, W. P. (1980). Of human bonding: Newborns prefer their mothers' voices. *Science, 208,* 1174–1177. (5) doi: 10.1126/science.7375928

Deci, E. L., & Ryan, R. M. (2008). Self-determination theory: A macrotheory of human motivation, development, and health. *Canadian Psychology, 49,* 182–185. (11) doi: 10.1037/a0012801

Deckersbach, T., Peters, A. T., Sylvia, L., Urdahl, A., Magalhaes, P. V. S., Otto, M. W., Frank, E., Miklowitz, D. J., Berk, M., Kinrys, G., & Nierenberg, A. (2014). Do comorbid anxiety disorders moderate the effects of psychotherapy for bipolar disorder? Results from STEP-BD. *American Journal of Psychiatry, 171,* 178–186. (15) doi: 10.1176/appi.ajp.2013.13020225

Deese, J. (1959). On the prediction of occurrence of particular verbal intrusions in immediate recall. *Journal of Experimental Psychology, 58,* 17–22. (7) doi: 10.1037/h0046671

de Groot, J. H. B., Semin, G. R., & Smeets, M. A. M. (2017). On the communicative function of body odors: A theoretical integration and review. *Perspectives on Psychological Science, 12,* 306–324. (4) doi: 10.1177/1745691616676599

Dehaene, S., Naccache, L., Cohen, L., LeBihan, D., Mangin, J.-F., Poline, J. B., & Riviere, D. (2001). Cerebral mechanisms of word masking and unconscious repetition priming. *Nature Neuroscience, 4,* 752–758. (10) doi: 10.1038/89551

Dehaene, S., Pegado, F., Braga, L. W., Ventura, P., Nunez Filho, G., Jobert, A., Dehaene-Lambertz, G., Kolinsky, R., Morais, J., & Cohen, L. (2010). How learning to read changes the cortical networks for vision and language. *Science, 330,* 1359–1364. (3) doi: 10.1126/science.1194140

De Houwer, J., Teige-Mocigemba, S., Spruyt, A., & Moors, A. (2009). Implicit measures: A normative analysis and review. *Psychological Bulletin, 135,* 347–368. (14) doi: 10.1037/a0014211

Del Cul, A., Dehaene, S., Reyes, P., Bravo, E., & Slachevsky, A. (2009). Causal role of prefrontal cortex in the threshold for access to consciousness. *Brain, 132,* 2531–2540. (10) doi: 10.1093/brain/awp111

DeLoache, J. S. (1989). The development of representation in young children. *Advances in Child Development and Behavior, 22,* 1–39. (5) doi: 10.1016/S0065-2407(08)60411-5

DeLoache, J. S., Miller, K. F., & Rosengren, K. S. (1997). The credible shrinking room: Very young children's performance with symbolic and nonsymbolic relations. *Psychological Science, 8,* 308–313. (5) doi: 10.1111/j.1467-9280.1997.tb00443.x

Dement, W. C. (1972). *Some must watch while some must sleep.* Stanford, CA: Stanford Alumni Association. (10)

Dement, W., & Kleitman, N. (1957a). Cyclic variations in EEG during sleep and their relation to eye movements, body motility, and dreaming. *Electroencephalography and Clinical Neurophysiology, 9,* 673–690. (10) doi: 10.1016/0013-4694(57)90088-3

Dement, W., & Kleitman, N. (1957b). The relation of eye movements during sleep to dream activity: An objective method for the study of dreaming. *Journal of Experimental Psychology, 53,* 339–346. (10) doi: 10.1037/h0048189

DeNeve, K. M. (1999). Happy as an extraverted clam? The role of personality for subjective well-being. *Current Directions in Psychological Science, 8,* 141–144. (12) doi: 10.1111/1467-8721.00033

Denissen, J. J. A., Bleidorn, W., Hennecke, M., Luhmann, M., Orth, U., Specht, J., & Zimmermann, J. (2018). Uncovering the power of personality to shape income. *Psychological Science, 29,* 3–13. (14) doi: 10.1177/0956797617724435

Denissen, J. J. A., Butalid, L., Penke, L., & van Aken, M. A. G. (2008). The effects of weather on daily mood. A multilevel approach. *Emotion, 8,* 662–667. (12) doi: 10.1037/a0013497

Dennett, D. C. (2003). *Freedom evolves.* New York: Viking Press. (1)

Derksen, M. (2014). Turning men into machines? Scientific management, industrial psychology, and the "human factor." *Journal of the History of the Behavioral Sciences, 50,* 148–165. (11) doi: 10.1002/jhbs.21650

DeScioli, P., Christner, J., & Kurzban, R. (2011). The omission strategy. *Psychological Science, 22,* 442–446. (12) doi: 10.1177/0956797611400616

Detterman, D. K. (1979). Detterman's laws of individual differences research. In R. J. Sternberg & D. K. Detterman (Eds.), *Human intelligence* (pp. 165–175). Norwood, NJ: Ablex. (9)

Deutsch, D., Henthorn, T., Marvin, E., & Xu, H. S. (2006). Absolute pitch among American and Chinese conservatory students: Prevalence differences, and evidence for a speech-related critical period. *Journal of the Acoustical Society of America, 119,* 719–722. (4) doi: 10.1121/1.2151799

Deutsch, J. A., & Ahn, S. J. (1986). The splanchnic nerve and food intake regulation. *Behavioral and Neural Biology, 45,* 43–47. (11) doi: 10.1016/S0163-1047(86)80004-8

Deutsch, J. A., & Gonzalez, M. F. (1980). Gastric nutrient content signals satiety. *Behavioral and Neural Biology, 30,* 113–116. (11) doi: 10.1016/S0163-1047(80)90989-9

Devane, W. A., Hanus˘, L., Breuer, A., Pertwee, R. G., Stevenson, L. A., Griffin, G., Gibson, D., Mandelbaum, A., Ethinger, A., & Mechoulam, R. (1992). Isolation and structure of a brain constituent that binds to the cannabinoid receptor. *Science, 258,* 1946–1949. (3) doi: 10.1126/science.1470919

Devor, E. J., Abell, C. W., Hoffman, P. L., Tabakoff, B., & Cloninger, C. R. (1994). Platelet MAO activity in Type I and Type II alcoholism. *Annals of the New York Academy of Sciences, 708,* 119–128. (15) doi: 10.1111/j.1749-6632.1994.tb24704.x

de Waal, F. B. M., & Preston, S. D. (2017). Mammalian empathy: behavioural manifestations and neural basis. *Nature Reviews Neuroscience, 18,* 498–509. (13) doi: 10.1038/nrn.2017.72

DeWall, C. N., MacDonald, G., Webster, G. D., Masten, C. L., Baumeister, R. F., Powell, C., Combs, D., Schurtz, D. R., Stillman, T. F., Tice, D. M., & Eisenberger, N. I (2010). Acetaminophen reduces social pain: Behavioral and neural evidence.

Psychological Science, 21, 931–937. (4) doi: 10.1177/0956797610374741

DeWall, C. N., Twenge, J. M., Koole, S. L., Baumeister, R. F., Marquez, A., & Reid, R. W. (2011). Automatic emotion regulation after social exclusion: Turning to positivity. *Emotion, 11,* 623–636. (12) doi: 10.1037/a0023534

Dewar, M., Alber, J., Butler, C., Cowan, N., & Della Salla, S. (2012). Brief wakeful resting boosts new memories over the long term. *Psychological Science, 23,* 955–960. (7) doi: 10.1177/0956797612441220

Dewsbury, D. A. (1998). Celebrating E. L. Thorndike a century after *Animal Intelligence. American Psychologist, 53,* 1121–1124. (6) doi: 10.1037/0003-066X.53.10.1121

Dewsbury, D. A. (2000). Introduction: Snapshots of psychology circa 1900. *American Psychologist, 55,* 255–259. (1) https://psycnet.apa.org/buy/2000-13816-011

Di Pino, G., Guglielmelli, E., & Rossini, P. M. (2009). Neuroplasticity in amputees: Main implications on bidirectional interfacing of cybernetic hand prostheses. *Progress in Neurobiology, 88,* 114–126. (4) doi: 10.1016/j.pneurobio.2009.03.001

Diamond, L. M. (2007). A dynamical systems approach to the development and expression of female same-sex sexuality. *Perspectives on Psychological Science, 2,* 142–161. (11) doi: 10.1111/j.1745-6916.2007.00034.x

Diamond, L. M. (2008). Female bisexuality from adolescence to adulthood: Results from a 10-year longitudinal study. *Developmental Psychology, 44,* 5–14. (11) doi: 10.1037/0012-1649.44.1.5

Diamond, L.M., Dickenson, J. A., & Blair, K. L. (2017). Stability of sexual attractions across different timescales: The roles of bisexuality and gender. *Archives of Sexual Behavior, 46,* 193–204. (11) doi: 10.1007/s10508-016-0860-x

Diaz, M., Parra, A., & Gallardo, C. (2011). Serins respond to anthropogenic noise by increasing vocal activity. *Behavioral Ecology, 22,* 332–336. (6) doi: 10.1093/beheco/arq210

Dick, D. M., Agrawal, A., Keller, M. C., Adkins, A., Aliev, A., Monroe, S., Hewitt, J. K., Kendler, K. S., & Sher, K. J. (2015). Candidate gene-environment interaction research: Reflections and recommendations. *Perspectives on Psychological Science, 10,* 37–59. (3) doi: 10.1177/1745691614556682

Dickens, W. T., & Flynn, J. R. (2001). Heritability estimates versus large environmental effects: The IQ paradox resolved. *Psychological Review, 108,* 346–369. (3, 9) doi: 10.1037/0033-295X.108.2.346

Dickens, W. T., & Flynn, J. R. (2006). Black Americans reduce the racial IQ gap. *Psychological Science, 17,* 913–920. (9) doi: 10.1111/j.1467-9280.2006.01802.x

Dickerson, S. S., Gable, S. L., Irwin, M. R., Aziz, N., & Kemeny, M. E. (2009). Social-evaluative threat and proinflammatory cytokine regulation. *Psychological Science, 20,* 1237–1244. (12) doi: 10.1111/j.1467-9280.2009.02437.x

Dickson, N., Paul, C., & Herbison, P. (2003). Same-sex attraction in a birth cohort: Prevalence and persistence in early adulthood. *Social Science and Medicine, 56,* 1607–1615. (11) doi: 10.1016/S0277-9536(02)00161-2

Diebels, K. J., Leary, M. R., & Chon, D. (2018). Individual differences in selfishness as a major dimension of personality: A reinterpretation of

the sixth personality factor. *Review of General Psychology, 22,* 367–376. (14) doi: 10.1037/gpr0000155

Diekman, C. O., & Bose, A. (2018). Reentrainment of the circadian pacemaker during jet lag: East-west asymmetry and the effects of north-south travel. *Journal of Theoretical Biology, 437,* 261–285. (10) doi: 10.1016/j.jtbi.2017.10.002

Diener, E. (2000). Subjective well-being. *American Psychologist, 55,* 34–43. (12) doi: 10.1037/0003-066X.55.1.34

Diener, E., Diener, C., Choi, H., & Oishi, S. (2018). Revisiting "most people are happy"—and discovering when they are not. *Perspectives on Psychological Science, 13,* 166–170. (12) doi: 10.1177/1745691618765111

Diener, E., & Seligman, M. E. P. (2002). Very happy people. *Psychological Science, 13,* 81–84. (12) doi: 10.1111/1467-9280.00415

Diener, E., & Seligman, M. E. P. (2004). Beyond money: Toward an economy of well-being. *Psychological Science in the Public Interest, 5,* 1–31. (12) doi: 10.1111/j.0963-7214.2004.00501001.x

Diener, E., Suh, E. M., Lucas, R. E., & Smith, H. L. (1999). Subjective well-being: Three decades of progress. *Psychological Bulletin, 125,* 276–302. (12) doi: 10.1037//0033-2909.125.2.276

Diener, E., Wolsic, B., & Fujita, F. (1995). Physical attractiveness and subjective well-being. *Journal of Personality and Social Psychology, 69,* 120–129. (12) doi: 10.1037//0022-3514.69.1.120

DiGirolamo, M. A., & Russell, J. A. (2017). The emotion seen in a face can be a methodological artifact: The process of elimination hypothesis. *Emotion, 17,* 538–546. (12) doi: 10.1037/emo0000247

Dijksterhuis, A., & Bargh, J. A. (2001). The perception-behavior expressway: Automatic effects of social perception on social behavior. *Advances in Experimental Social Psychology, 33,* 1–40. (6) doi: 10.1016/S0065-2601(01)80003-4

DiLalla, D. L., Carey, G., Gottesman, I. I., & Bouchard, T. J., Jr. (1996). Heritability of MMPI personality indicators of psychopathology in twins reared apart. *Journal of Abnormal Psychology, 105,* 491–499. (5) doi: 10.1037/0021-843X.105.4.491

Dills, A., Hernandez-Julian, R., & Rotthoff, K. W. (2016). Knowledge decays between semesters. *Economics of Education Review, 50,* 63–74. (9) doi: 10.1016/j.econedurev.2015.12.002

Di Marzo, V., Goparaju, S. K., Wang, L., Liu, J., Bátkai, S., Járai, Z., Fezza, F., Miura, G. I., Palmiter, R. T., Sugiura, T., & Kunos, G. (2001). Leptin-regulated endocannabinoids are involved in maintaining food intake. *Nature, 410,* 822–825. (3) doi: 10.1038/35071088

Dinstein, I., Hasson, U., Rubin, N., & Heeger, D. J. (2007). Brain areas selective for both observed and executed movements. *Journal of Neurophysiology, 98,* 1415–1427. (3) doi: 10.1152/jn.00238.2007

Disner, S. G., Kramer, M. D., Nelson, N. W., Lipinski, A. J., Christensen, J. M., Polusny, M. A., & Sponheim, S. R. (2017). Predictors of postdeployment functioning in combat-exposed U.S. military veterans. *Clinical Psychological Science, 5,* 650–663. (12) doi: 10.1177/2167702617703436

Dobrzecka, C., Szwejkowska, G., & Konorski, J. (1966). Qualitative versus directional cues in two forms of differentiation. *Science, 153,* 87–89. (6) doi: 10.1126/science.153.3731.87

Doctor, J. N., Nguyen, A., Lev, R., Lucas, J., Knight, T., Zhao, H., & Menchine, M. (2018). Opioid prescribing decreases after learning of a patient's fatal overdose. *Science, 361,* 588–590. (13) doi: 10.1126/science.aat4595

Doi, T. (1981). *The anatomy of dependence.* Tokyo: Kodansha International. (12)

Dolinski, D., Grzyb, T., Folwarczny, M., Grzybala, P., Krzyszycha, K., Martynowska, K., & Trojanowski, J. (2017). Would you deliver an electric shock in 2015? Obedience in the experimental paradigm developed by Stanley Milgram in the 50 years following the original study. *Social Psychological and Personality Science, 8,* 927–933. (13) doi: 10.1177/1948550617693060

Dollard, J., Miller, N. E., Doob, L. W., Mowrer, O. H., & Sears, R. R. (1939). *Frustration and aggression.* New Haven, CT: Yale University Press. (13)

Domhoff, G. W. (1996). *Finding meaning in dreams: A quantitative approach.* New York: Plenum Press. (10)

Domhoff, G. W. (1999). Drawing theoretical implications from descriptive empirical findings on dream content. *Dreaming, 9,* 201–210. (10) doi: 10.1023/A:1021302118072

Domhoff, G. W. (2003). *The scientific study of dreams.* Washington, DC: American Psychological Association. (2, 10)

Domhoff, G. W. (2011). The neural substrate for dreaming: Is it a subsystem of the default network? *Consciousness and Cognition, 20,* 1163–1174. (10) doi: 10.1016/j.concog.2011.03.001

Domhoff, G. W., & Schneider, A. (2008). Similarities and differences in dream content at the cross-cultural, gender, and individual levels. *Consciousness and Cognition, 17,* 1257–1265. (10) doi: 10.1016/j.concog.2008.08.005

Dompnier, B., Darnon, C., & Butera, F. (2009). Faking the desire to learn. *Psychological Science, 20,* 939–943. (2) doi: 10.1111/j.1467-9280.2009.02384.x

Donnellan, M. B., & Lucas, R. E. (2008). Age differences in the big five across the life span: Evidence from two national samples. *Psychology and Aging, 23,* 558–566. (14) doi: 10.1037/a0012897

Donnellan, M. B., Trzesniewski, K. H., Robins, R. W., Moffitt, T. E., & Caspi, A. (2005). Low self-esteem is related to aggression, antisocial behavior, and delinquency. *Psychological Science, 16,* 328–335. (13) doi: 10.1111/j.0956-7976.2005.01535.x

Donnelly, G. E., Zatz, L. Y., Svirsky, D., & John, L. K. (2018). The effect of graphic warnings on sugary-drink purchasing. *Psychological Science, 29,* 1321–1333. (11) doi: 10.1177/0956797618766361

Donnerstein, E., & Malamuth, N. (1997). Pornography: Its consequences on the observer. In L. B. Schlesinger & E. Revitch (Eds.), *Sexual dynamics of antisocial behavior* (2nd ed., pp. 30–49). Springfield, IL: Charles C Thomas. (13)

Doty, R. L., & Kamath, V. (2014). The influences of age on olfaction: A review. *Frontiers in Psychology, 5,* Article 20. (4) doi: 10.3389/fpsyg.2014.00020

Doty, T. J., Japee, S., Ingvar, M., & Ungerleider, L. G. (2013). Fearful face detection sensitivity in healthy adults correlates with anxiety-related traits. *Emotion, 13,* 183–188. (12) doi: 10.1037/a0031373

Dovidio, J. E., & Gaertner, S. L. (1999). Reducing prejudice: Combating intergroup biases. *Current Directions in Psychological Science, 8,* 101–105. (13) doi: 10.1111/1467-8721.00024

Doyon, J., Korman, M., Morin, A., Dostie, V., Tahar, A. H., Benali, H., Karni, A., Ungerleider, L. G., & Carrier, J. (2009). Contribution of night and day sleep vs. simple passage of time to the consolidation of motor sequence and visuomotor adaptation learning. *Experimental Brain Research, 195,* 15–26. (10) doi: 10.1007/s00221-009-1748-y

Dreber, A., Rand, D. G., Fudenberg, D., & Nowak, M. A. (2008). Winners don't punish. *Nature, 452,* 348–351. (13) doi: 10.1038/nature06723

Dreger, A. D. (1998). *Hermaphrodites and the medical invention of sex.* Cambridge, MA: Harvard University Press. (11)

Drew, T., Võ, M. L.-H., & Wolfe, J. M. (2013). The invisible gorilla strikes again: Sustained inattentional blindness in expert observers. *Psychological Science, 24,* 1848–1853. (4) doi: 10.1177/0956797613479386

Drewnowski, A., Henderson, S. A., Shore, A. B., & Barratt-Fornell, A. (1998). Sensory responses to 6-n-propylthiouracil (PROP) or sucrose solutions and food preferences in young women. *Annals of the New York Academy of Sciences, 855,* 797–801. (1) doi: 10.1111/j.1749-6632.1998.tb10661.x

Drews, F. A., Pasupathi, M., & Strayer, D. L. (2008). Passenger and cell phone conversations in simulated driving. *Journal of Experimental Psychology: Applied, 14,* 392–400. (8) doi: 10.1037/a0013119

Drexler, S. M., & Wolf, O. T. (2018). Behavioral disruption of memory reconsolidation: From bench to bedside and back again. *Behavioral Neuroscience, 132,* 13–22. (12) doi: 10.1037/bne0000231

Dubois, F. (2007). Mate choice copying in monogamous species: Should females use public information to choose extrapair males? *Animal Behaviour, 74,* 1785–1793. (6) doi: 10.1016/j.anbehav.2007.03.023

Duckworth, A. L., Gendler, T. S., & Gross, J. J. (2016). Situational strategies for self-control. *Perspectives on Psychological Science, 11,* 35–55. (11) doi: 10.1177/1745691615623247

Duckworth, A., & Gross, J. J. (2014). Self-control and grit: Related but separable determinants of success. *Current Directions in Psychological Science, 23,* 319–325. (11) doi: 10.1177/0963721414541462

Duckworth, A. L., Taxer, J. L., Eskreis-Winkler, L., Galla, B. M., & Gross, J. J. (2019). Self-control and academic achievement. *Annual Review of Psychology, 70,* 373–399. (11) doi: 10.1146/annurev-psych-010418-103230

Duckworth, A. L., & Seligman, M. E. P. (2017). The science and practice of self-control. *Perspectives on Psychological Science, 12,* 715–718. (9) doi: 10.1177/1745691617690880

Duncan, L. E., Pollastri, A. R., & Smoller, J. W. (2014). Mind the gap. *American Psychologist, 69,* 249–268. (15) doi: 10.1037/a0036320

Dunlosky, J., Rawson, K. A., Marsh, E. J., Nathan, M. J., & Willingham, D. T. (2013). Improving students' learning with effective learning techniques: Promising directions from cognitive and educational psychology. *Psychological Science in the Public Interest, 14,* 1–58. (7) doi: 10.1177/1529100612453266

Dunn, B. D., German, R. E., Khazanov, G., Xu, C., Hollon, S. D., & DeRubeis, R. J. (2020). Changes in positive and negative affect during pharmacological treatment and cognitive therapy for major depressive disorder: A secondary analysis of two randomized trials. *Clinical Psychological Science, 8,* 36–51. (15) doi: 10.1177/2167702619863427

Dunn, E. W., Aknin, L. B., & Norton, M. I. (2008). Spending money on others promotes happiness. *Science, 319,* 1687–1688. (12) doi: 10.1126/science.1150952

Dunn, E. W., Gilbert, D. T., & Wilson, T. D. (2011). If money doesn't make you happy, then you probably aren't spending it right. *Journal of Consumer Psychology, 21,* 115–125. (12) doi: 10.1016/j.jcps.2011.02.002

Dunne, G., & Askew, C. (2013). Vicarious learning and unlearning of fear in childhood via mother and stranger models. *Emotion, 13,* 974–980. (15) doi: 10.1037/a0032994

Dunning, D., Heath, C., & Suls, J. M. (2004). Flawed self-assessment: Implications for health, education, and the workplace. *Psychological Science in the Public Interest, 5,* 69–106. (11) doi: 10.1111/j.1529-1006.2004.00018.x

Dunsmoor, J. E., Kroes, M. C.W., Braren, S. H., & Phelps, E. A. (2017). Threat intensity widens fear generalization gradients. *Behavioral Neuroscience, 131,* 168–175. (6) doi: 10.1037/bne0000186

Durgin, F. H. (2000). The reverse Stroop effect. *Psychonomic Bulletin and Review, 7,* 121–125. (8) doi: 10.3758/BF03210730

Durlak, J. A., Weissberg, R. P., Dymnicki, A. B., Taylor, R. D., & Schellinger, K. B. (2011). The impact of enhancing students' social and emotional learning: A meta-analysis of school-based universal interventions. *Child Development, 82,* 405–432. (15) doi: 10.1111/j.1467-8624.2010.01564.x

Durso, G. R. O., Luttrell, A., & Way, B. M. (2015). Over-the-counter relief from pains and pleasures alike: Acetaminophen blunts evaluation sensitivity to both negative and positive stimuli. *Psychological Science, 26,* 750–758. (4) doi: 10.1177/0956797615570366

Dutton, D. G., & Aron, A. P. (1974). Some evidence for heightened sexual attraction under conditions of high anxiety. *Journal of Personality and Social Psychology, 30,* 510–517. (12) doi: 10.1037/h0037031

Dutton, E., van der Linden, D., & Lynn, R. (2016). The negative Flynn effect: A systematic literature review. *Intelligence, 59,* 163–169. (9) doi: 10.1016/j.intell.2016.10.002

Dywan, J., & Bowers, K. (1983). The use of hypnosis to enhance recall. *Science, 22,* 184–185. (10) doi: 10.1126/science.6623071

Eagly, A. H., & Crowley, M. (1986). Gender and helping behavior: A meta-analytic review of the social psychological literature. *Psychological Bulletin, 100,* 283–308. (5) doi: 10.1037/0033-2909.100.3.283

Eagly, A. H., & Wood, W. (1999). The origins of sex differences in human behavior. *American Psychologist, 54,* 408–423. (3) doi: 10.1037/0003-066X.54.6.408

Eaker, E. D., Sullivan, L. M., Kelly-Hayes, M., D'Agostino, R. B., Sr., & Benjamin, E. J. (2004). Anger and hostility predict the development of atrial fibrillation in men in the Framingham Offspring Study. *Circulation, 109,* 1267–1271. (12) doi: 10.1161/01.CIR.0000118535.15205.8F

Earnest, D. J., Liang, F.-Q., Ratcliff, M., & Cassone, V. M. (1999). Immortal time: Circadian clock properties of rat suprachiasmatic cell lines.

Science, 283, 693–695. (10) doi: 10.1126/science.283.5402.693

Eastwick, P. W., Finkel, E. J., Mochon, D., & Ariely, D. (2007). Selective versus unselective romantic desire. *Psychological Science, 18,* 317–319. (13) doi: 10.1111/j.1467-9280.2007.01897.x

Eastwick, P. W., Luchies, L. B., Finkel, E. J., & Hunt, L. L. (2014). The predictive validity of ideal partner preferences: A review and meta-analysis. *Psychological Bulletin, 140,* 623–665. (13) doi: 10.1037/a0032432

Eaton, A. A., & Rose, S. (2011). Has dating become more egalitarian? A 35 year review using *Sex Roles. Sex Roles, 64,* 843–862. (5) doi: 10.1007/s11199-011-9957-9

Eaves, L. J., Martin, N. G., & Heath, A. C. (1990). Religious affiliation in twins and their parents: Testing a model of cultural inheritance. *Behavior Genetics, 20,* 1–22. (3) doi: 10.1007/BF01070736.

Ebbinghaus, H. (1913). *Memory.* New York: Teachers College Press. (Original work published 1885) (7)

Eberly, M. B., Johnson, M. D., Hernandez, M., & Arolio, B. J. (2013). An integrative process model of leadership. *American Psychologist, 68,* 427–433. (11) doi: 10.1037/a0032244

Ebneter, D. S., Latner, J. D., & O'Brien, K. S. (2011). Just world beliefs, causal beliefs, and acquaintance: Associations with stigma toward eating disorders and obesity. *Personality and Individual Differences, 51,* 618–622. (14) doi: 10.1016/j.paid.2011.05.029

Educational Testing Service. (1994). *GRE 1994–95 guide.* Princeton, NJ: Author. (9)

Edwards, G. (2014). Doing their duty: An empirical analysis of the unintended effect of *Tarasoff v. Regents* on homicidal activity. *Journal of Law and Economics, 57,* 321–348. (15) doi: 10.1086/675668

Edwards, J., Jackson, H. J., & Pattison, P. E. (2002). Emotion recognition via facial expression and affective prosody in schizophrenia: A methodological review. *Clinical Psychology Review, 22,* 789–832. (12) doi: 10.1016/S0272-7358(02)00130-7

Edwards, K. (1998). The face of time: Temporal cues in facial expressions of emotion. *Psychological Science, 9,* 270–276. (12) doi: 10.1111/1467-9280.00054

Eibl-Eibesfeldt, I. (1973). *Der vorprogrammierte Mensch* [The preprogrammed human]. Vienna: Verlag Fritz Molden. (12)

Eibl-Eibesfeldt, I. (1974). *Love and hate.* New York: Schocken Books. (12)

Eichenbaum, H. (2002). *The cognitive neuroscience of memory.* New York: Oxford University Press. (7)

Eichstaedt, J. C., Schwartz, H. A., Kern, M. L., Park, G., Labarthe, D. R., Merchant, R. M., Jha, S., Agrawal, M., Dziurzynski, L. A., Sap, M., Weeg, C., Larson, E. E., Ungar, L. H., & Seligman, M. E. P. (2015). Psychological language on Twitter predicts county-level heart disease mortality. *Psychological Science, 26,* 159–169. (12) doi: 10.1177/0956797614557867

Eimas, P. D., Siqueland, E. R., Jusczyk, P., & Vigorito, J. (1971). Speech perception in infants. *Science, 171,* 303–306. (5) doi: 10.1126/science.171.3968.303

Eisenberger, N. I., Lieberman, M. D., & Williams, K. D. (2003). Does rejection hurt? An fMRI study of social exclusion. *Science, 302,* 290–292. (4) doi: 10.1126/science.1089134

Ekman, P. (1992). Facial expressions of emotion: New findings, new questions. *Psychological*

Science, 3, 34–38. (12) doi: 10.1111/j.1467-9280.1992.tb00253.x

Ekman, P. (2001). *Telling lies* (3rd ed.). New York: W. W. Norton. (12)

Ekman, P., & Davidson, R. J. (1993). Voluntary smiling changes regional brain activity. *Psychological Science, 4,* 342–345. (12) doi: 10.1111/j.1467-9280.1993.tb00576.x

Ekman, P., & Friesen, W. V. (1984). *Unmasking the face* (2nd ed.). Palo Alto, CA: Consulting Psychologists Press. (12)

Ekroll, V., Sayim, B., & Wagemans, J. (2017). The other side of magic: The psychology of perceiving hidden things. *Perspectives on Psychological Science, 12,* 91–106. (4) doi: 10.1177/1745691616654676

El-Sheikh, M., Buckhalt, J. A., Mize, J., & Acebo, C. (2006). Marital conflict and disruption of children's sleep. *Child Development, 77,* 31–43. (5) doi: 10.1111/j.1467-8624.2006.00854.x

Elbert, T., Pantev, C., Wienbruch, C., Rockstroh, B., & Taub, E. (1995). Increased cortical representation of the fingers of the left hand in string players. *Science, 270,* 305–307. (3) doi: 10.1126/science.270.5234.305

Elbogen, E. B., Dennis, P. A., & Johnson, S. C. (2016). Beyond mental illness: Targeting stronger and more direct pathways to violence. *Clinical Psychological Science, 4,* 747–759. (13) doi: 10.1177/2167702615619363

Elbogen, E. B. & Johnson, S. C. (2009). The intricate link between violence and mental disorder. *Archives of General Psychiatry, 66,* 152–161. (13, 15) doi: 10.1001/archgenpsychiatry.2008.537

Elder, T. E. (2010). The importance of relative standards in ADHD diagnoses: Evidence based on exact birth dates. *Journal of Health Economics, 29,* 641–656. (8) doi: 10.1016/j.jhealeco.2010.06.003

Elicker, J., Englund, M., & Sroufe, L. A. (1992). Predicting peer competence and peer relationships in childhood from early parent-child relationships. In R. D. Parke & G. W. Ladd (Eds.), *Family-peer relationships* (pp. 77–106). Hillsdale, NJ: Erlbaum. (5)

Elkind, D. (1984). *All grown up and no place to go.* Reading, MA: Addison-Wesley. (5)

Ellenberger, H. F. (1972). The story of "Anna O": A critical review with new data. *Journal of the History of the Behavioral Sciences, 8,* 267–279. (14) doi: 10.1002/1520-6696(197202)8:3<267::aid-jhbs2300080302>3.0.co;2-c

Else-Quest, N. M., Hyde, J. S., Goldsmith, H. H., & Van Hulle, C. A. (2006). Gender differences in temperament: A meta-analysis. *Psychological Bulletin, 132,* 33–72. (5) doi: 10.1037/0033-2909.132.1.33

Elsey, J. W. B., Van Ast, V. A., & Kindt, M. (2018). Human memory reconsolidation: A guiding framework and critical review of the evidence. *Psychological Bulletin, 144,* 797–848. (12) doi: 10.1037/bul0000152

Emberson, L. L., Lupyan, G., Goldstein, M. H., & Spivey, M. I. (2010). Overheard cell-phone conversations: When less speech is more distracting. *Psychological Science, 21,* 1383–1388. (8) doi: 10.1177/0956797610382126

Emery, C. E., Jr. (1997, November/December). UFO survey yields conflicting conclusions. *Skeptical Inquirer, 21,* 9. (2)

Emmons, R. A., & McCullough, M. E. (2003). Counting blessings versus burdens: An experimental investigation of gratitude and subjective well-being in daily life. *Journal of*

Personality and Social Psychology, 84, 377–389. (12) doi: 10.1037/0022-3514.84.2.377

Emre, M. (2018). *The personality brokers: The strange history of Myers-Briggs and the birth of personality testing.* New York: Doubleday. (14)

Endress, A. D., & Potter, M. C. (2014). Large capacity temporary visual memory. *Journal of Experimental Psychology: General, 143,* 548–565. (7) doi: 10.1037/a0033934

Eng, M. Y., Schuckit, M. A., & Smith, T. L. (2005). The level of response to alcohol in daughters of alcoholics and controls. *Drug and Alcohol Dependence, 79,* 83–93. (15) doi: 10.1016/j.drugalcdep.2005.01.002

Engelhard, I. M., McNally, R. J., & van Schie, K. (2019). Retrieving and modifying traumatic memories: Recent research relevant to three controversies. *Current Directions in Psychological Science, 28,* 91–96. (7) doi: 10.1177/0963721418807728

Enns, J. T., & Rensink, R. A. (1990). Sensitivity to three-dimensional orientation in visual search. *Psychological Science, 1,* 323–326. (8) doi: 10.1111/j.1467-9280.1990.tb00227.x

Eppig, C., Fincher, C. L., & Thornhill, R. (2010). Parasite prevalence and the worldwide distribution of cognitive ability. *Proceedings of the Royal Society B, 277,* 3801–3808. (9) doi: 10.1098/rspb.2010.0973

Eppig, C., Fincher, C. L., & Thornhill, R. (2011). Parasite prevalence and the distribution of intelligence among the states of the USA. *Intelligence, 39,* 155–160. (9) doi: 10.1016/j.intell.2011.02.008

Erdelyi, M. H. (2006). The unified theory of repression. *Behavioral and Brain Sciences, 29,* 499–551. (14) doi: 10.1017/S0140525X06009113

Erdelyi, M. H. (2010). The ups and downs of memory. *American Psychologist, 65,* 623–633. (7) doi: 10.1037/a0020440

Erel, O., & Burman, B. (1995). Interrelatedness of marital relations and parent-child relations: A meta-analytic review. *Psychological Bulletin, 118,* 108–132. (5) doi: 10.1037/0033-2909.118.1.108

Erev, I., Ert, E., Plonsky, O., Cohen, D., & Cohen, O. (2017). From anomalies to forecasts: Toward a descriptive model of decisions under risk, under ambiguity, and from experience. *Psychological Review, 124,* 369–409. (8) doi: 10.1037/rev0000062

Erev, I., Wallsten, T. S., & Budescu, D. V. (1994). Simultaneous over- and underconfidence: The role of error in judgment processes. *Psychological Review, 101,* 519–527. (8) doi: 10.1037/0033-295X.101.3.519

Erickson, S. K., Lilienfeld, S. O., & Vitacco, M. J. (2007). A critical examination of the suitability and limitations of psychological tests in family court. *Family Court Review, 45,* 157–174. (14) doi: 10.1111/j.1744-1617.2007.00136.x

Ericsson, K. A., & Charness, N. (1994). Expert performance: Its structure and acquisition. *American Psychologist, 49,* 725–747. (8) doi: 10.1037/0003-066X.49.8.725

Ericsson, K. A., Chase, W. G., & Faloon, S. (1980). Acquisition of a memory skill. *Science, 208,* 1181–1182. (7) doi: 10.1126/science.7375930

Ericsson, K. A., Cheng, X. J., Pan, Y. F., Ku, Y. X., Ge, Y., & Hu, Y. (2017). Memory skills mediating superior memory in a world-class memorist. *Memory, 25,* 1294–1302. (7) doi: 10.1080/09658211.2017.1296164

Ericsson, K. A., Krampe, R. T., & Tesch-Römer, C. (1993). The role of deliberate practice in the acquisition of expert performance.

Psychological Review, 100, 363–406. (8) doi: 10.1037/0033-295X.100.3.363

Erikson, E. H. (1963). *Childhood and society* (2nd ed.). New York: W. W. Norton. (5)

Ernhart, C. B., Sokol, R. J., Martier, S., Moron, P., Nadler, D., Ager, J. W., & Wolf, A. (1987). Alcohol teratogenicity in the human: A detailed assessment of specificity, critical period, and threshold. *American Journal of Obstetrics and Gynecology, 156,* 33–39. (5) doi: 10.1016/0002-9378(87)90199-2

Ernst, A., Alkass, K., Bernard, S., Salehpour, M., Perl, S., Tisdale, J., & Frisén, J. (2014). Neurogenesis in the striatum of the adult human brain. *Cell, 156,* 1072–1083. (3) doi: 10.1016/j.cell.2014.01.044

Ernst, C., & Angst, J. (1983). *Birth order: Its influence on personality.* New York: Springer-Verlag. (5)

Erskine, K. J., Kacinik, N. A., & Prinz, J. J. (2011). A bad taste in the mouth: Gustatory disgust influences moral judgment. *Psychological Science, 22,* 295–299. (12) doi: 10.1177/0956797611398497

Erving, C. L., Thomas, C. S., & Frazier, C. (2019). Is the black-white mental health paradox consistent across gender and psychiatric disorders? *American Journal of Epidemiology, 188,* 314–322. (15) doi: 10.1093/aje/kwy224

Eschenko, O., Mölle, M., Born, J., & Sara, S. J. (2006). Elevated sleep spindle density after learning or after retrieval in rats. *Journal of Neurophysiology, 26,* 12914–12920. (10) doi: 10.1523/JNEUROSCI.3175-06.2006

Eskreis-Winkler, L., Fishbach, A., & Duckworth, A. L. (2018). Dear Abby: Should I give advice or receive it? *Psychological Science, 29,* 1797–1806. (13) doi: 10.1177/0956797618795472

Eskritt, M., & Ma, S. (2014). Intentional forgetting: Note-taking as a naturalistic example. *Memory & Cognition, 42,* 237–246. (7) doi: 10.3758/s13421-013-0362-1

Esser, S. K., Hill, S., & Tononi, G. (2009). Breakdown of effective connectivity during slow wave sleep; Investigating the mechanism underlying a cortical gate using large-scale modeling. *Journal of Neurophysiology, 102,* 2096–2111. (10) doi: 10.1152/jn.00059.2009

Esterson, A. (1993). *Seductive mirage.* Chicago, IL: Open Court. (10, 14)

Esterson, A. (2001). The mythologizing of psychoanalytic history: Deception and self-deception in Freud's accounts of the seduction theory episode. *History of Psychiatry, 12,* 329–352. (14) doi: 10.1177/0957154X0101204704

Etcoff, N. L., Ekman, P., Magee, J. J., & Frank, M. G. (2000). Lie detection and language comprehension. *Nature, 405,* 139. (3) doi: 10.1038/35012129

Euston, D. R., Tatsuno, M., & McNaughton, B. L. (2007). Fast-forward playback of recent memory sequences in prefrontal cortex during sleep. *Science, 318,* 1147–1150. (10) doi: 10.1126/science.1148979

Evans, G. W., Bullinger, M., & Hygge, S. (1998). Chronic noise exposure and physiological response: A prospective study of children living under environmental stress. *Psychological Science, 9,* 75–77. (12) doi: 10.1111/1467-9280.00014

Evans, J. S. T., & Stanovich, K. E. (2013). Dual-process theories of higher cognition: Advancing the debate. *Perspectives on Psychological Science, 8,* 223–241. (8) doi: 10.1177/1745691612460685

Evans, S. W., Owens, J. S., & Bunford, N. (2014). Evidence-based psychosocial treatments for children and adolescents with attention-deficit/hyperactivity disorder. *Journal of Clinical Child & Adolescent Psychology, 43,* 527–551. (8) doi: 10.1080/15374416.2013.850700

Everaert, J., Bronstein, M. V., Cannon, T. D., & Joormann, J. (2018). Looking through tinted glasses: Depression and social anxiety are related to both interpretation biases and inflexible negative interpretations. *Clinical Psychological Science, 6,* 517–528. (15) doi: 10.1177/2167702617747968

Exner, J. E., Jr. (1986). *The Rorschach: A comprehensive system* (2nd ed.). New York: Wiley. (14)

Eyal, T., & Epley, N. (2017). Exaggerating accessible differences: When gender stereotypes overestimate actual group differences. *Personality and Social Psychology Bulletin, 43,* 1323–1336. (13) doi: 10.1177/0146167217713190

Fabiano, G. A., Pelham, W. E., Jr., Gnagy, E. M., Burrows-MacLean, L., Coles, E. K., Chacko, A., Wymbs, B. T., Walker, K. S., Arnold, F., Garefino, A., Keenan, J. K., Onyango, A. N., Hoffman, M. T., Massetti, G. M., & Robb, J. A. (2007). The single and combined effects of multiple intensities of behavior modification and methylphenidate for children with attention deficit hyperactivity disorder in a classroom setting. *School Psychology Review, 36,* 195–216. (6)

Faedda, G. L., Tondo, L., Teicher, M. H., Baldessarini, R. J., Gelbard, H. A., & Floris, G. F. (1993). Seasonal mood disorders: Patterns of seasonal recurrence in mania and depression. *Archives of General Psychiatry, 50,* 17–23. (15) doi: 10.1001/archpsyc.1993.01820130019004

Falleti, M. G., Maruff, P., Collie, A., Darby, D. G., & McStephen, M. (2003). Qualitative similarities in cognitive impairment associated with 24 h of sustained wakefulness and a blood alcohol concentration of 0.05%. *Journal of Sleep Research, 12,* 265–274. (10) doi: 10.1111/j.1365-2869.2003.00363.x

Fan, P. (1995). Cannabinoid agonists inhibit the activation of 5-HT3 receptors in rat nodose ganglion neurons. *Journal of Neurophysiology, 73,* 907–910. (3) doi: 10.1152/jn.1995.73.2.907.

Fantz, R. L. (1963). Pattern vision in newborn infants. *Science, 140,* 296–297. (5) https://science.sciencemag.org/content/140/3564/296

Farber, S. L. (1981). *Identical twins reared apart: A reanalysis.* New York: Basic Books. (9)

Farley, S. D., Carson, D. H., & Pope, T. J. (2019). "I would never fall for that": The use of an illegitimate authority to teach social psychology principles. *Teaching of Psychology, 46,* 146–152. (13) doi: 10.1177/0098628319834200

Farley, S. D., Hughes, S. M., & LaFayette, J. N. (2013). People will know we are in love: Evidence of differences between vocal samples directed toward lovers and friends. *Journal of Nonverbal Behavior, 37,* 123–138. (13) doi: 10.1007/s10919-013-0151-3

Farmer-Dougan, V. (1998). A disequilibrium analysis of incidental teaching. *Behavior Modification, 22,* 78–95. (6) doi: 10.1177/01454455980221005

Farooqi, I. S., Keogh, J. M., Kamath, S., Jones, S., Gibson, W. T., Trussell, R., Jebb, S. A., Lip, G. Y. H., & O'Rahilly, S. (2001). Partial leptin deficiency and human adiposity. *Nature, 414,* 34–35. (11) doi: 10.1038/35102112

Farr, R. H. (2017). Does parental sexual orientation matter? A longitudinal follow-up of adoptive families with school-age children. *Developmental Psychology, 53,* 252–264. (5) doi: 10.1037/dev0000228

Farris, C., Treat, T. A., Viken, R. J., & McFall, R. M. (2008). Perceptual mechanisms that characterize gender differences in decoding women's sexual intent. *Psychological Science, 19,* 348–354. (5) doi: 10.1111/j.1467-9280.2008.02092.x

Fast, N. J., & Chen, S. (2009). When the boss feels inadequate. *Psychological Science, 20,* 1406–1413. (13) doi: 10.1111/j.1467-9280.2009.02452.x

Fatemi, S. H., Aldinger, K. A., Ashwood, P., Bauman, M. L., Blaha, C. D., Blatt, G. J., Chauhan, A., Chauhan, V., Dager, S. R., Dickson, P. E., Estes, A. M., Goldowitz, D., Heck, D. H., Kemper, T. L., King, B. H., Martin, L. A., Millen, K. J., Mittleman, G., Mosconi, M. W., ... Welsh, J. P. (2012). Consensus paper: Pathological role of the cerebellum in autism. *Cerebellum, 11,* 777–807. (15) doi: 10.1007/s12311-012-0355-9

Fauerbach, J. A., Lawrence, J. W., Haythornthwaite, J. A., & Richter, L. (2002). Coping with the stress of a painful medical procedure. *Behaviour Research and Therapy, 40,* 1003–1015. (12) doi: 10.1016/S0005-7967(01)00079-1

Faure, R., Righetti, F., Seibel, M., & Hofmann, W. (2018). Speech is silver, nonverbal behavior is gold: How implicit partner evaluations affect dyadic interactions in close relationships. *Psychological Science, 29,* 1731–1741. (13) doi: 10.1177/0956797618785899

Faust, M., Kravetz, S., & Babkoff, H. (1993). Hemispheric specialization or reading habits: Evidence from lexical decision research with Hebrew words and sentences. *Brain and Language, 44,* 254–263. (8) doi: 10.1006/brln.1993.1017

Fay, R. E., Turner, C. F., Klassen, A. D., & Gagnon, J. H. (1989). Prevalence and patterns of same-gender sexual contact among men. *Science, 243,* 338–348. (11) doi: 10.1126/science.2911744

Fazel, S., & Grann, M. (2006). The population impact of severe mental illness on violent crime. *American Journal of Psychiatry, 163,* 1397–1403. (13) doi: 10.1176/appi.ajp.163.8.1397

Fazio, L. K., Barber, S. J., Rajaram, S., Ornstein, P. A., & Marsh, E. J. (2013). Creating illusions of knowledge: Learning errors that contradict prior knowledge. *Journal of Experimental Psychology: General, 142,* 1–5. (7) doi: 10.1037/a0028649

Federico, C. M., Williams, A. L., & Vitriol, J. A. (2018). The role of system identity threat in conspiracy theory endorsement. *European Journal of Social Psychology, 48,* 927–938. (8) doi: 10.1002/ejsp.2495

Feeney, D. M. (1987). Human rights and animal welfare. *American Psychologist, 42,* 593–599. (2) doi: 10.1037/0003-066X.42.6.593

Feinberg, M., Willer, R., & Schultz, M. (2014). Gossip and ostracism promote cooperation in groups. *Psychological Science, 25,* 656–664. (13) doi: 10.1177/0956797613510184

Feinstein, J. S., Adolphs, R., Damasio, A., & Tranel, D. (2011). The human amygdala and the induction and experience of fear.

Current Biology, 21, 34–38. (12) doi: 10.1016/j.cub.2010.11.042

Feinstein, J. S., Buzza, C., Hurlemann, R., Follmer, R. L., Dahdaleh, N. S., Coryell, W. H., Welsh, M. J., Tranel, D., & Wemmie, J. A. (2013). Fear and panic in humans with bilateral amygdala damage. *Nature Neuroscience, 16,* 270–272. (12) doi: 10.1038/nn.3323

Felson, R. B., & Palmore, C. (2018). Biases in blaming victims of rape and other crime. *Psychology of Violence, 8,* 390–399. (7) doi: 10.1037/vio0000168

Feng, J., Spence, I., & Pratt, J. (2007). Playing an action video game reduces gender differences in spatial cognition. *Psychological Science, 18,* 850–855. (5) doi: 10.1111/j.1467-9280.2007.01990.x

Ferguson, C. J. (2015). Do angry birds make for angry children? A meta-analysis of video game influences on children's and adolescents' aggression, mental health, prosocial behavior, and academic performance. *Perspectives on Psychological Science, 10,* 646–666. (2) doi: 10.1177/1745691615592234

Fernald, D. (1984). *The Hans legacy: A story of science.* Hillsdale, NJ: Erlbaum. (2)

Fernandez, E., & Turk, D. C. (1992). Sensory and affective components of pain: Separation and synthesis. *Psychological Bulletin, 112,* 205–217. (4) doi: 10.1037/0033-2909.112.2.205

Fernández-Dols, J. M., & Ruiz-Belda, M. A. (1997). Spontaneous facial behavior during intense emotional episodes: Artistic truth and optical truth. In J. A. Russell & J. M. Fernández-Dols (Eds.), *The psychology of facial expression* (pp. 255–274). Cambridge, England: Cambridge University Press. (12)

Fernández-Espejo, D., & Owen, A. M. (2013). Detecting awareness after severe brain injury. *Nature Reviews Neuroscience, 14,* 801–809. (10) doi: 10.1038/nrn3608

Ferrari, C., Oldrati, V., Gallucci, M., Vecchi, T., & Cattaneo, Z. (2018). The role of the cerebellum in explicit and incidental processing of facial emotional expressions: A study with transcranial magnetic stimulation. *NeuroImage, 169,* 256–264. (3) doi: 10.1016/j.neuroimage.2017.12.026

Festinger, L. (1957). *A theory of cognitive dissonance.* Stanford, CA: Stanford University Press. (13)

Festinger, L., & Carlsmith, J. M. (1959). Cognitive consequences of forced compliance. *Journal of Abnormal and Social Psychology, 58,* 203–210. (13) doi: 10.1037/h0041593

Fiedler, K., Schmid, J., & Stahl, T. (2002). What is the current truth about polygraph lie detection? *Basic and Applied Social Psychology, 24,* 313–324. (12) doi: 10.1207/S15324834BASP2404_6

Field, A. P. (2006). Is conditioning a useful framework for understanding the development and treatment of phobias? *Clinical Psychology Review, 26,* 857–875. (15) doi: 10.1016/j.cpr.2005.05.010

Fillmore, M. T., & Weafer, J. (2012). Acute tolerance to alcohol in at-risk binge drinkers. *Psychology of Addictive Behaviors, 26,* 693–702. (15) doi: 10.1037/a0026110

Fincham, F. D. (2003). Marital conflict: Correlates, structure, and context. *Current Directions in Psychological Science, 12,* 23–27. (13) doi: 10.1111/1467-8721.01215

Fink, B., & Penton-Voak, I. (2002). Evolutionary psychology of facial attractiveness. *Current Directions in Psychological Science, 11,* 154–158. (13) doi: 10.1111/1467-8721.00190

Finkel, E. J., & Eastwick, P. W. (2008). Speed-dating. *Current Directions in Psychological Science, 17,* 193–197. (13) doi: 10.1111/j.1467-8721.2008.00573.x

Finkel, E. J., Eastwick, P. W., Karney, B. R., Reis, H. T., & Sprecher, S. (2012). Online dating: A critical analysis from the perspective of psychological science. *Psychological Science in the Public Interest, 13,* 3–66. (13) doi: 10.1177/1529100612436522

Finkel, E. J., Norton, M. I., Reis, H. T., Ariely, D., Caprariello, P. A., Eastwick, P. W., Frost, J. H., & Maniaci, M. R. (2015). When does familiarity promote verus undermine interpersonal attraction? A proposed integrative model from erstwhile adversaries. *Perspectives on Psychological Science, 10,* 3–19. (13) doi: 10.1177/1745691614561682

Fischer, F., Schult, J., & Hell, B. (2015). Unterschätzung der Studienleistungen von Frauen durch Studierfähigkeitstests. Erklärbar durch Persönlichkeitseigenschaften? [Underestimation of women's college grades by college admission tests: Explainable by personality traits?] *Diagnostica, 61,* 34–46. (9) doi: 10.1026/0012-1924/a000120

Fisher, A. V., Godwin, K. E., & Seltman, H. (2014). Visual environment, attention allocation, and learning in young children: When too much of a good thing may be bad. *Psychological Science, 25,* 1362–1370. (8) doi: 10.1177/0956797614533801

Fisher, B. S., Daigle, L. E., Cullen, F. T., & Turner, M. G. (2003). Acknowledging sexual victimization as rape: Results from a national-level survey. *Justice Quarterly, 20,* 535–574. (13) doi: 10.1080/07418820300095611

Fisher, R. P., Geiselman, R. E., & Amador, M. (1989). Field test of the cognitive interview: Enhancing the recollection of actual victims and witnesses of crime. *Journal of Applied Psychology, 74,* 722–727. (7) doi: 10.1037/0021-9010.74.5.722

Fisher, S. E., Vargha-Khadem, F., Watkins, K. E., Monaco, A. P., & Pembrey, M. E. (1998). Localisation of a gene implicated in a severe speech and language disorder. *Nature Genetics, 18,* 168–170. (8) doi: 10.1038/ng0298-168

Fiske, A. P. (2002). Using individualism and collectivism to compare cultures—A critique of the validity and measurement of the constructs: Comment on Oyserman et al. (2002). *Psychological Bulletin, 128,* 78–88. (13) doi: 10.1037/0033-2909.128.1.78

Fiske, S. T. (2017). Prejudices in cultural contexts: shared stereotypes (gender, age) versus variable stereotypes (race, ethnicity, religion). *Perspectives on Psychological Science, 12,* 791–799. (13) doi: 10.1177/1745691617708204

Fitch, W. T. (2017a). Empirical approaches to the study of language evolution. *Psychonomic Bulletin & Review, 24,* 3–33. (8) doi: 10.3758/s13423-017-1236-5

Fitch, W. T. (2017b). On externalization and cognitive continuity in language evolution. *Mind & Language, 32,* 597–606. (8) doi: 10.1111/mila.12162

Flack, W. F., Jr., Laird, J. D., & Cavallaro, L. A. (1999). Separate and combined effects of facial expressions and bodily postures on emotional feelings. *European Journal of Social Psychology, 29,* 203–217. (12) doi: 10.1002/(SICI)1099-0992(199903/05)29:2/3<203::AID-EJSP924>3.0.CO;2-8

Flanagin, V. L., Schörnich, S., Schranner, M., Hummel, N., Wallmeier, L., Stephan, T., & Wiegrebe, L. (2017). Human exploration of enclosed spaces through echolocation. *Journal of Neuroscience, 37,* 1614–1627. (4) doi: 10.1523/JNEUROSCI.1566-12.2016

Flatz, G. (1987). Genetics of lactose digestion in humans. *Advances in Human Genetics, 16,* 1–77. (3)

Flavell, J. (1986). The development of children's knowledge about the appearance–reality distinction. *American Psychologist, 41,* 418–425. (5) doi: 10.1037/0003-066X.41.4.418

Fleeson, W., Malanos, A. B., & Achille, N. M. (2002). An intraindividual process approach to the relationship between extraversion and positive affect: Is acting extraverted as "good" as being extraverted? *Journal of Personality and Social Psychology, 83,* 1409–1422. (14) doi: 10.1037//0022-3514.83.6.1409

Fletcher, R., & Voke, J. (1985). *Defective colour vision.* Bristol, England: Hilger. (4)

Fliessbach, K., Weber, B., Trautner, P., Dohmen, T., Sunde, U., Elger, C. E., & Falk, A. (2007). Social comparison affects reward-related brain activity in the human ventral striatum. *Science, 318,* 1305–1308. (12) doi: 10.1126/science.1145876

Flor, H., Elbert, T., Knecht, S., Wienbruch, C., Pantev, C., Birbaumer, N., Larbig, W., & Taub, E. (1995). Phantom-limb pain as a perceptual correlate of cortical reorganization following arm amputation. *Nature, 375,* 482–484. (4) doi: 10.1038/375482a0

Flore, P. C., & Wicherts, J. M. (2015). Does stereotype threat influence performance of girls in stereotyped domains? A meta-analysis. *Journal of School Psychology, 53,* 25–44. (9) doi: 10.1016/j.jsp.2014.10.002

Flournoy, T. (1903). F. W. H. Myers et son oeuvre posthume. *Archives de Psychologie, 2,* 269–296. (1) https://www.persee.fr/doc/psy_0003-5033_1903_num_10_1_3647

Flueckiger, L., Lieb, R., Meyer, A. H., Gitthauer, C., & Mata, J. (2016). The importance of physical activity and sleep for affect on stressful days: Two intensive longitudinal studies. *Emotion, 16,* 488–497. (12) doi: 10.1037/emo0000143

Flynn, J. R. (1984). The mean IQ of Americans: Massive gains 1932 to 1978. *Psychological Bulletin, 95,* 29–51. (9) doi: 10.1037/0033-2909.95.1.29

Flynn, J. R. (1998). IQ gains over time: Toward finding the causes. In U. Neisser (Ed.), *The rising curve* (pp. 25–66). Washington, DC: American Psychological Association. (9)

Flynn, J. R. (1999). Searching for justice: The discovery of IQ gains over time. *American Psychologist, 54,* 5–20. (9) doi: 10.1037/0003-066X.54.1.5

Folkman, S., & Moskowitz, J. T. (2000). Positive affect and the other side of coping. *American Psychologist, 55,* 647–654. (12) doi: 10.1037/0003-066X.55.6.647

Føllesdal, H., & Hagtvet, K. A. (2009). Emotional intelligence: The MSCEIT from the perspective of generalizability theory. *Intelligence, 37,* 94–105. (12) doi: 10.1016/j.intell.2008.08.005

Forer, B. R. (1949). The fallacy of personal validation: A classroom demonstration of gullibility. *Journal of Abnormal and Social Psychology, 44,* 118–123. (14) doi: 10.1037/h0059240

Forgas, J. P. (2019). Happy believers and sad skeptics? Affective influences on gullibility.

Current Directions in Psychological Science, 28, 306–313. (12) doi: 10.1177/0963721419834543

Forscher, P. S., Lai, C. K., Axt, J. R., Ebersole, C. R., Herman, M., Devine, P. G., & Nosek, B. A. (2019). A meta-analysis of procedures to change implicit measures. *Journal of Personality and Social Psychology, 117,* 522–559. (13) doi: 10.1037/pspa0000160

Forster, S., & Lavie, N. (2016). Establishing the attention-distractibility trait. *Psychological Science, 27,* 203–212. (8) doi: 10.1177/0956797615617761

Forster, S., & Spence, C. (2018). "What smell?" Temporarily loading visual attention indues a prolonged loss of olfactory awareness. *Psychological Science, 29,* 1642–1652. (8) doi: 10.1177/0956797618781325

Fossum, I. N., Nordnes, L. T., Storemark, S. S., Bjorvatn, B., & Pallesen, S. (2014). The association between use of electronic media in bed before going to sleep and insomnia symptoms, daytime sleepiness, morningness, and chronotype. *Behavioral Sleep Medicine, 12,* 343–357. (10) doi: 10.1080/15402002.2013.819468

Foster, D. (2000). *Author unknown.* New York: Henry Holt. (14)

Foster, W. Z. (1968). *History of the Communist Party of the United States.* New York: Greenwood Press. (13)

Foulkes, D. (1999). *Children's dreaming and the development of consciousness.* Cambridge, MA: Harvard University Press. (10)

Foulkes, D., & Domhoff, G. W. (2014). Bottom-up or top-down in dream neuroscience? A top-down critique of two bottom-up studies. *Consciousness and Cognition, 27,* 168–171. (10) doi: 10.1016/j.concog.2014.05.002

Fournier, J. C., DeRubeis, R. J., Hollon, S. D., Dimidjian, S., Amsterdam, J., Shelton, R. C., & Fawcett, J. (2010). Antidepressant drug effects and depression severity. *Journal of the American Medical Association, 303,* 47–53. (15) doi: 10.1001/jama.2009.1943

Fowler, J. H., Baker, L. A., & Dawes, C. T. (2008). Genetic variation in political participation. *American Political Science Review, 102,* 233–248. (5) doi: 10.1017/S0003055408080209

Fowler, J. H., & Christakis, N. A. (2008). Dynamic spread of happiness in a large social network: Longitudinal analysis over 20 years in the Framingham Heart Study. *British Medical Journal, 337,* a2338. (12) doi: 10.1136/bmj. a2338

Fox, B., & Farrington, D. P. (2018). What have we learned from offender profiling? A systematic review and meta-analysis of 40 years of research. *Psychological Bulletin, 144,* 1247–1274. (14) doi: 10.1037/bul0000170

Fox, K. C. R., Nijeboer, S., Solomonova, E., Domhoff, G. W., & Christoff, K. (2013). Dreaming as mind wandering: Evidence from functional neuroimaging and first-person content reports. *Frontiers in Human Neuroscience, 7,* Article 412. (10) doi: 10.3389/fnhum.2013.00412

Franconeri, S. L., Alvarez, G. A., & Enns, J. T. (2007). How many locations can be selected at once? *Journal of Experimental Psychology: Human Perception and Performance, 33,* 1003–1012. (8) doi: 10.1037/0096-1523.33.5.1003

Frank, R. H. (2012). The Easterlin paradox revisited. *Emotion, 12,* 1188–1191. (12) doi: 10.1037/a0029969

Franke, B., Faraone, S. V., Asherson, P., Buitelaaar, J., Bau, C. H. D., Ramos-Quiroga, J. A., Mick, E., Grevet, E. H., Johansson, S., Haavik, J., Lesch, K. P., Cormand, B., & Reif, A. (2012). The genetics of attention deficit/hyperactivity disorder in adults, a review. *Molecular Psychiatry, 17,* 960–987. (8) doi: 10.1038/mp.2011.138

Fredrickson, B. L. (2001). The role of positive emotion in psychology: The broaden-and-build theory of positive emotions. *American Psychologist, 56,* 218–226. (12) doi: 10.1037/0003-066X.56.3.218

Fredrickson, B. L., & Losada, M. F. (2005). Positive affect and the complex dynamics of human flourishing. *American Psychologist, 60,* 678–686. (12) doi: 10.1037/0003-066X.60.7.678

Freedman, J. L., & Fraser, S. C. (1966). Compliance without pressure: The foot in the door technique. *Journal of Personality and Social Psychology, 4,* 195–202. (13) doi: 10.1037/h0023552

Freedman, R., Hunter, S. K., & Hoffman, M. C. (2018). Prenatal primary prevention of mental illness by micronutrient supplements in pregnancy. *American Journal of Psychiatry, 175,* 607–619. (15) doi: 10.1176/appi.ajp.2018.17070836

French, A. R. (1988). The patterns of mammalian hibernation. *American Scientist, 76,* 568–575. (10)

Frensch, P. A., & Rünger, D. (2003). Implicit learning. *Current Directions in Psychological Science, 12,* 13–18. (7) doi: 10.1111/1467-8721.01213

Freud, S. (1935). *A general introduction to psycho-analysis.* New York: Liveright. (Original work published 1915) (1)

Freud, S. (1925). An autobiographical study. In J. Strachey, A. Freud, A. Strachey, & A. Tyson (Eds.), *The standard edition of the complete psychological works of Sigmund Freud* (Vol. 20, pp. 7–70). London: Hogarth Press and the Institute of Psycho-Analysis. (14)

Freud, S. (1925). *Three contributions to the theory of sex* (A. A. Brill, Trans.). New York: Nervous and Mental Disease Publishing. (Original work published 1905) (14)

Freud, S. (1955). *The interpretation of dreams* (J. Strachey, Trans.). New York: Basic Books. (Original work published 1900) (10)

Freud, S. (1961). *The future of an illusion* (J. Strachey, Trans.). New York: W. W. Norton. (Original work published 1927) (14)

Frey, S. H., Bogdanov, S. Smith, J. C., Watrous, S., & Breidenbach, W. C. (2008). Chronically deafferented sensory cortex recovers a grossly typical organization after allogenic hand transplantation. *Current Biology, 18,* 1530–1534. (3) doi: 10.1016/j.cub.2008.08.051

Fried, C. B. (2008). In-class laptop use and its effects on student learning. *Computers & Education, 50,* 906–914. (7) doi: 10.1016/j.compedu.2006.09.006

Friedman, J. M. (2000). Obesity in the new millennium. *Nature, 404,* 632–634. (11) https://www.nature.com/articles/35007504

Friedman, M., & Rosenman, R. H. (1974). *Type-A behavior and your heart.* New York: Knopf. (12)

Friedman, W. J., Reese, E., & Dai, X. (2011). Children's memory for the times of events from the past years. *Applied Cognitive Psychology, 25,* 156–165. (7) doi: 10.1002/acp.1656

Fritz, C. O., Morris, P. E., Bjork, R. A., Gelman, R., & Wickens, T. D. (2000). When further learning fails: Stability and change following repeated presentation of text. *British Journal of Psychology, 91,* 493–511. (7) doi: 10.1348/000712600161952

Fu, Q., Heath, A. C., Bucholz, K. K., Nelson, E., Goldberg, J., Lyons, M. J., True, W. R., Jacob, T., Tsuang, M. T., & Eisen, S. A. (2002). Shared genetic risk of major depression, alcohol dependence, and marijuana dependence. *Archives of General Psychiatry, 59,* 1125–1132. (15) doi: 10.1001/archpsyc.59.12.1125

Fuchs, T., Haney, A., Jechura, T. J., Moore, F. R., & Bingman, V. P. (2006). Daytime naps in night-migrating birds: Behavioural adaptation to seasonal sleep deprivation in the Swainson's thrush, *Catharus ustulatus. Animal Behaviour, 72,* 951–958. (10) doi: 10.1016/j.anbehav.2006.03.008

Fujita, G., Watanabe, K., Yokota, K., Kuraishi, H., Suzuki, M., Wachi, T., & Otsuka, Y. (2013). Multivariate models for behavioral offender profiling of Japanese homicide. *Criminal Justice and Behavior, 40,* 214–227. (14) doi: 10.1177/0093854812458425

Fuligni, A. J. (1998). The adjustment of children from immigrant families. *Current Directions in Psychological Science, 7,* 99–103. (5) doi: 10.1111/1467-8721.ep10774731

Fuller, R. A., Warren, P. H., & Gaston, K. J. (2007). Daytime noise predicts nocturnal singing in urban robins. *Biology Letters, 3,* 368–370. (6) doi: 10.1098/rsbl.2007.0134

Fuller, R. K., & Roth, H. P. (1979). Disulfiram for the treatment of alcoholism: An evaluation in 128 men. *Annals of Internal Medicine, 90,* 901–904. (15) doi: 10.7326/0003-4819-90-6-901

Fumento, M. (2014, September/October). Runaway hysteria. *Skeptical Inquirer, 42*(5), 42–49. (13) https://skepticalinquirer.org/2014/09/runaway-hysteria/

Furman, L. M. (2008). Attention-deficit hyperactivity disorder (ADHD): Does new research support old concepts? *Journal of Child Neurology, 23,* 775–784. (8) doi: 10.1177/0883073808318059

Furukawa, T. (1997). Cultural distance and its relationship to psychological adjustment of international exchange students. *Psychiatry and Clinical Neurosciences, 51,* 87–91. (1) doi: 10.1111/j.1440-1819.1997.tb02367.x

Furukawa, T. A., Maruo, K., Noma, H., Tanaka, S., Imai, H., Shinohara, K., Yamawaki, S., Levine, S. Z., Goldberg, Y., Leucht, S., & Cipriani, A. (2018). Initial severity of major depression and efficacy of new generation antidepressants: individual participation data meta-analysis. *Acta Psychiatrica Scandinavica, 137,* 450–458. (15) doi: 10.1111/acps.12886

Furukawa, T. A., Weitz, E. S., Tanaka, S., Hollon, S. D., Hofmann, S. G., Andersson, G., Twisk, J., DeRubeis, R. J., Dimidjian, S., Hegerl, U., Mergl, R., Jarrett, R. B., Vittengl, J. R., Watanabe, N., & Cuijpers, P. (2017). Initial severity of depression and efficacy of cognitive-behavioural therapy: Individual-participant data meta-analysis of pill-placebo-controlled tirals. *British Journal of Psychiatry, 210,* 190–196. (15) doi: 10.1192/bjp.bp.116.187773

Furuya-Kanamori, L., & Doi, S. A. R. (2016). Angry birds, angry children, and angry meta-analysis: A reanalysis. *Perspectives on Psychological Science, 11,* 408–414. (2) doi: 10.1177/1745691616635599

Gable, P., & Harmon-Jones, E. (2010). The blues broaden, but the nasty narrows: Attentional consequences of negative affects low and high in motivational intensity. *Psychological Science, 21,* 211–215. (12) doi: 10.1177/0956797609359622

Gabrieli, J. D. E., Cohen, N. J., & Corkin, S. (1988). The impaired learning of semantic knowledge following bilateral medial temporal-lobe resection. *Brain and Cognition, 7,* 157–177. (7) doi: 10.1016/0278-2626(88)90027-9

Gächter, S., Renner, E., & Sefton, M. (2008). The long-run benefits of punishment. *Science, 322,* 1510. (13) doi: 10.1126/science.1164744

Gage, F. H. (2000). Mammalian neural stem cells. *Science, 287,* 1433–1438. (3) doi: 10.1126/science.287.5457.1433

Galak, J., LeBoeuf, R. A., Nelson, L. D., & Simmons, J. P. (2012). Correcting the past: Failure to replicate psi. *Journal of Personality and Social Psychology, 103,* 933–948. (2) doi: 10.1037/a0029709

Galatzer-Levy, I. R., Brown, A. D., Henn-Haase, C., Metzler, T. J., Neylan, T. C., & Marmar, C. R. (2013). Positive and negative emotion prospectively predict trajectories of resilience and distress among high-exposure police officers. *Emotion, 13,* 545–553. (12) doi: 10.1037/a0031314

Galatzer-Levy, I. R., & Bryant, R. A. (2013). 636,120 ways to have posttraumatic stress disorder. *Perspectives on Psychological Science, 8,* 651–662. (15) doi: 10.1177/1745691613504115

Gale, C. R., Booth, T., Mottus, R., Kuh, D., & Deary, I. J. (2013). Neuroticism and extraversion in youth predict mental well-being and life satisfaction 40 years later. *Journal of Research in Personality, 47,* 687–697. (14) doi: 10.1016/j.jrp.2013.06.005

Galef, B. G., Jr. (1998). Edward Thorndike: Revolutionary psychologist, ambiguous biologist. *American Psychologist, 53,* 1128–1134. (6) doi: 10.1037/0003-066X.53.10.1128

Gallavotti, A., Zhao, Q., Kyozuka, J., Meeley, R. B., Ritter, M. K., Doebley, J. F., Pe, M. E., & Schmidt, R. J. (2004). The role of *barren stalk1* in the architecture of maize. *Nature, 432,* 630–635. (3) doi: 10.1038/nature03148

Gallistel, C. R., & Gibbon, J. (2000). Time, rate, and conditioning. *Psychological Review, 107,* 289–344. (6) doi: 10.1037/0033-295X.107.2.289

Galton, F. (1869/1978). *Hereditary genius.* New York: St. Martin's Press. (Original work published 1869) (1, 9)

Gandal, M. J., Haney, J. R., Parikshak, N. N., Leppa, V., Ramaswami, G., Hartl, C., Schork, A. J., Appadurai, V., Buil, A., Werge, T. M., Liu, C., White, K. P., Horvath, S., & Geschwind, D. H. (2018). Shared molecular neuropathology across major psychiatric disorders parallels polygenic overlap. *Science, 359,* 693–697. (15) doi: 10.1126/science.aad6469

Gangestad, S. W. (2000). Human sexual selection, good genes, and special design. *Annals of the New York Academy of Sciences, 907,* 50–61. (3) doi: 10.1111/j.1749-6632.2000.tb06615.x

Gangestad, S. W., & Simpson, J. A. (2000). The evolution of human mating: Trade-offs and strategic pluralism. *Behavioral and Brain Sciences, 23,* 573–644. (3) doi: 10.1017/S0140525X0000337X

Ganna, A., Verweij, K. J. H., Nivard, M. G., Maier, R., Wedow, R., Busch, A. S., Abdellaoui, A., Guo, S., Sathirapongsasuti, J. F., Lichtenstein, P., Lundstrom, S., Langstrom, N., Auton, A., Harris, K. M., Beecham, G. W., Martin, E. R., Sanders, A. R., Perry, J. R. B., Neale, B. M., ... Zietsch, B. P. (2019). Large-scale GWAS reveals insights into the genetic architecture of same-sex sexual behavior. *Science, 365,* 882. (11) doi: 10.1126/science.aat7693

Gannon, N., & Ranzijn, R. (2005). Does emotional intelligence predict unique variance in life satisfaction beyond IQ and personality? *Personality and Individual Differences, 38,* 1353–1364. (12) doi: 10.1016/j.paid.2004.09.001

Gantman, A. P., & Van Bavel, J. J. (2014). The moral pop-out effect: Enhanced perceptual awareness of morally relevant stimuli. *Cognition, 132,* 22–29. (8) doi: 10.1016/j.cognition.2014.02.007

Gapin, J. I., Labban, J. D., & Etnier, J. L. (2011). The effects of physical activity on attention deficit disorder symptoms: The evidence. *Preventive Medicine, 52,* S70–S74. (8) doi: 10.1016/j.ypmed.2011.01.022

Gapp, K., Jawaid, A., Sarkies, P., Bohacek, J., Pelczar, P., Prados, J., Farinelli, L., Miska, E., & Mansuy, I. M. (2014). Implication of sperm RNAs in transgenerational inheritance of the effects of early trauma in mice. *Nature Neuroscience, 17,* 667–669. (3) doi: 10.1038/nn.3695

Garb, H. N., Wood, J. N., Lilienfeld, S. O., & Nezworski, M. T. (2005). Roots of the Rorschach controversy. *Clinical Psychology Review, 25,* 97–118. (14) doi: 10.1016/j.cpr.2004.09.002

Garcia, J., Ervin, F. R., & Koelling, R. A. (1966). Learning with prolonged delay of reinforcement. *Psychonomic Science, 5,* 121–122. (6) https://link.springer.com/article/10.3758/BF03328311

Garcia, J., & Koelling, R. A. (1966). Relation of cue to consequence in avoidance learning. *Psychonomic Science, 4,* 123–124. (6) https://link.springer.com/article/10.3758/BF03342209

Gardner, H. (1985). *Frames of mind.* New York: Basic Books. (9)

Gardner, H. (1999). *Intelligence reframed.* New York: Basic Books. (9)

Gardner, M. (1978). Mathematical games. *Scientific American, 239*(5), 22–32. (8) doi: 10.1038/scientificamerican1178-22

Gardner, M. (1994). Notes of a fringe watcher: The tragedies of false memories. *Skeptical Inquirer, 18,* 464–470. (7) https://skepticalinquirer.org/1994/09/the-tragedies-of-false-memories-the-accused-are-striking-back/

Gardner, R. A., & Gardner, B. T. (1969). Teaching sign language to a chimpanzee. *Science, 165,* 664–672. (8) doi: 10.1126/science.165.3894.664

Garfin, D. R., Holman, E. A., & Silver, R. C. (2015). Cumulative exposure to prior collective trauma and acute stress responses to the Boston Marathon bombing. *Psychological Science, 26,* 675–683. (12) doi: 10.1177/0956797614561043

Gartrell, N. K., Bos, H. M. W., & Goldberg, N. G. (2011). Adolescents of the US national longitudinal Lesbian family study: Sexual orientation, sexual behavior, and sexual risk exposure. *Archives of Sexual Behavior, 40,* 1199–1209. (5) doi: 10.1007/s10508-010-9692-2

Gautam, L., Sharratt, S. D., & Cole, M. D. (2014). Drug facilitated sexual assault: Detection and stability of benzodiazepines in spiked drinks using gas chromatography-mass spectrometry. *PLoS One, 9,* e89031. (3) doi: 10.1371/journal.pone.0089031

Gawronski, B. (2019). Six lessons for a cogent science of implicit bias and its criticism. *Perspectives on Psychological Science, 14,* 574–595. (13) doi: 10.1177/1745691619826015

Gazzaniga, M. S. (2000). Cerebral specialization and interhemispheric communication: Does the corpus callosum enable the human condition? *Brain, 123,* 1293–1326. (3) doi: 10.1093/brain/123.7.1293

Geary, D. C. (2000). Evolution and proximate expression of human paternal investment. *Psychological Bulletin, 126,* 55–77. (3) doi: 10.1037/0033-2909.126.1.55

Geary, D. C. (2018). Efficiency of mitochondrial functioning as the fundamental biological mechanism of general intelligence (*g*). *Psychological Review, 125,* 1028–1050. (9) doi: 10.1037/rev0000124

Gebauer, J. E., Sedikides, C., & Neberich, W. (2012). Religiosity, social self-esteem, and psychological adjustment: On the cross-cultural specificity of the psychological benefits of religiosity. *Psychological Science, 23,* 158–160. (12) doi: 10.1177/0956797611427045

Gelman, R. (1982). Accessing one-to-one correspondence: Still another paper about conservation. *British Journal of Psychology, 73,* 209–220. (5) doi: 10.1111/j.2044-8295.1982.tb01803.x

Genberg, B. L., Gange, S. J., Go, V. F., Celentano, D. D., Kirk, G. D., & Mehta, S. H. (2011). Trajectories of injection drug use over 20 years (1988–2008) in Baltimore, Maryland. *American Journal of Epidemiology, 173,* 829–836. (15) doi: 10.1093/aje/kwq441

Gendron, M., Crivelli, C., & Barrett, L. F. (2018). Universality reconsidered: Diversity in making meaning of facial expressions. *Current Directions in Psychological Science, 27,* 211–219. (12) doi: 10.1177/0963721417746794

Gendron, M., Roberson, D., van der Vyver, J. M., & Barrett, L. F. (2014). Perceptions of emotion from facial expressions are not culturally universal: Evidence from a remote culture. *Emotion, 14,* 251–262. (12) doi: 10.1037/a0036052

Genoux, D., Haditsch, U., Knobloch, M., Michalon, A., Storm, D., & Mansuy, I. M. (2002). Protein phosphatase 1 is a molecular constraint on learning and memory. *Nature, 418,* 970–975. (7) doi: 10.1038/nature00928

Gentile, B., Grabe, S., Dolan-Pascoe, B., Twenge, J. M., & Wells, B. E. (2009). Gender differences in domain-specific self-esteem: A meta-analysis. *Review of General Psychology, 13,* 34–45. (14) doi: 10.1037/a0013689

Gentile, D. (2009). Pathological video-game use among youth ages 8 to 18: A national study. *Psychological Science, 20,* 594–602. (15) doi: 10.1111/j.1467-9280.2009.02340.x

Gentner, D. (2016). Language as cognitive tool kit: How language supports relational thought. *American Psychologist, 71,* 650–657. (8) doi: 10.1037/amp0000082

Geraerts, E., Schooler, J. W., Merckelbach, H., Jelicic, M., Hauer, B. J. A., & Ambadar, Z. (2007). The reality of recovered memories. *Psychological Science, 18,* 564–568. (7) doi: 10.1111/j.1467-9280.2007.01940.x

Gershoff, E. T., Goodman, G. S., Miller-Perrin, C. L., Holden, G. W., Jackson, Y., & Kazdin, A. E. (2018). The strength of the causal evidence against physical punishment of children and its implicagtions for parents, psychologists, and policymakers. *American Psychologist, 73,* 626–638. (6) doi: 10.1037/amp0000327

Geschwind, N. (1979). Specializations of the human brain. In *Scientific American* (Ed.), *The brain: A Scientific American book.* San Francisco: W. H. Freeman. (8)

Gheysen, F., Poppe, L., DeSmet, A., Swinnen, S., Cardon, G., De Bourdeaudhuij, I., Chastin, S., & Fias, W. (2018). Physical activity to improve cognition in older adults: can physical activity programs enriched with cognitive challenges enhance the effects? A systematic review and meta-analysis. *International Journal of Behavioral Nutrition and Physical Activity, 15,* 63. (5) doi: 10.1186/s12966-018-0697-x

Gibbons, A., & Warne, R. T. (2019). First publication of subtests in the Stanford-Binet 5, WAIS-IV, WISC-V, and WPPSI-IV. *Intelligence, 75,* 9–18. (9) doi: 10.1016/j.intell.2019.02.005

Gibbs, J., Young, R. C., & Smith, G. P. (1973). Cholecystokinin decreases food intake in rats. *Journal of Comparative and Physiological Psychology, 84,* 488–495. (11) doi: 10.1037/h0034870

Gibbs, T. A., Okuda, M., Oquendo, M. A., Lawson, W. B., Wang, S., Thomas, Y. F., & Blanco, C. (2013). Mental health of African Americans and Caribbean Blacks in the United States: Results from the national epidemiological survey on alcohol and related conditions. *American Journal of Public Health, 103,* 330–338. (15) doi: 10.2105/AJPH.2012.300891

Gibson, J. J. (1968). What gives rise to the perception of movement? *Psychological Review, 75,* 335–346. (4) doi: 10.1037/h0025893

Giebel, H. D. (1958). Visuelles Lernvermögen bei Einhufern [Visual learning capacity in hoofed animals]. *Zoologische Jahrbücher Abteilung für Allgemeine Zoologie, 67,* 487–520. (1)

Gigerenzer, G. (2008). Why heuristics work. *Perspectives on Psychological Science, 3,* 20–29. (8) doi: 10.1111/j.1745-6916.2008.00058.x

Gigerenzer, G., & Garcia-Retamero, R. (2017). Cassandra's regret: The psychology of not wanting to know. *Psychological Review, 124,* 179–196. (8) doi: 10.1037/rev0000055

Gilbert, D. T., & Wilson, T. D. (2009). Why the brain talks to itself: Sources of error in emotional prediction. *Philosophical Transactions of the Royal Society, B, 364,* 1335–1341. (8) doi: 10.1098/rstb.2008.0305

Gilbertson, M. W., Shenton, M. E., Ciszewski, A., Kasai, K., Lasko, N. B., Orr, S. P., & Pitman, R. K. (2002). Smaller hippocampal volume predicts pathological vulnerability to psychological trauma. *Nature Neuroscience, 5,* 1242–1247. (12) doi: 10.1038/nn958

Gilbreth, F. B. (1911). *Motion study.* London: Constable. (11)

Gillam, S., Holbrook, S., Mecham, J., & Weller, D. (2018). Pull the Andon rope on working memory capacity interventions until we know more. *Language Speech and Hearing Services in Schools, 49,* 434–448. (7) doi: 10.1044/2018_LSHSS-17-0121

Gino, F., Ayal, S., & Ariely, D. (2009). Contagion and differentiation in unethical behavior. *Psychological Science, 20,* 393–398. (11) doi: 10.1111/j.1467-9280.2009.02306.x

Glasman, L. R., & Albarracín, D. (2006). Forming attitudes that predict future behavior: A meta-analysis of the attitude–behavior relation. *Psychological Bulletin, 132,* 778–822. (13) doi: 10.1037/0033-2909.132.5.778

Glass, M. (2001). The role of cannabinoids in neurodegenerative diseases. *Progress in Neuro-Psychopharmacology and Biological Psychiatry, 25,* 743–765. (3) doi: 10.1016/S0278-5846(01)00162-2

Gleich, S., Nemergut, M., & Flick, R. (2013). Anesthetic-related neurotoxicity in young children: An update. *Current Opinion in Anesthesiology, 26,* 340–347. (5) doi: 10.1097/ACO.0b013e3283606a37

Glenn, A. L., & Raine, A. (2014). Neurocriminology: Implications for the punishment, prediction and prevention of criminal behaviour. *Nature Reviews Neuroscience, 15,* 54–63. (13) doi: 10.1038/nrn3640

Gnambs, T. (2014). A meta-analysis of dependability coefficients (test-retest reliabilities) for measures of the Big Five. *Journal of Research in Personality, 52,* 20–28. (14) doi: 10.1016/j.jrp.2014.06.003

Gobet, F., & Campitelli, G. (2007). The role of domain-specific practice, handedness, and starting age in chess. *Developmental Psychology, 43,* 159–172. (8) doi: 10.1037/0012-1649.43.1.159

Goetz, T. (2011, July). The feedback loop. *Wired, 19(7),* 125–133, 162–164. (6)

Gold, B. T., Kim, C., Johnson, N. F., Kryscio, R. J., & Smith, C. D. (2013). Lifelong bilingualism maintains neural efficiency for cognitive control in aging. *Journal of Neuroscience, 33,* 387–396. (8) doi: 10.1523/JNEUROSCI.3837-12.2013

Goldfarb, D., Goodman, G. S., Larson, R. P., Eisen, M. L., & Qin, J. (2019). Long-term memory in adults exposed to childhood violence: Remembering genital contact nearly 20 years later. *Clinical Psychological Science, 7,* 381–396. (7) doi: 10.1177/2167702618805742

Goldin, A. P., Hermida, M. J., Shalom, D. E., Costa, M. E., Lopez-Rosenfeld, M., Segretin, M. S., Fernandez-Slezak, D., Lipina, S. J., & Sigman, M. (2014). Far transfer to language and math of a short software-based gaming intervention. *Proceedings of the National Academy of Sciences (U.S.A.), 111,* 357–379. (8) doi: 10.1073/pnas.1320217111

Goldin-Meadow, S., McNeill, D., & Singleton, J. (1996). Silence is liberating: Removing the handcuffs on grammatical expression in the manual modality. *Psychological Review, 103,* 34–55. (8) doi: 10.1037/0033-295X.103.1.34

Goldin-Meadow, S., & Mylander, C. (1998). Spontaneous sign systems created by deaf children in two cultures. *Nature, 391,* 279–281. (8) doi: 10.1038/34646

Goldstein, E. B. (1989). *Sensation and perception* (3rd ed.). Belmont, CA: Wadsworth. (4)

Goldstein, E. B. (2007). *Sensation and perception* (7th ed.). Belmont, CA: Wadsworth. (4)

Goldstein, N. J., Cialdini, R. B., & Griskevicius, V. (2008). A room with a viewpoint: Using social norms to motivate environmental conservation in hotels. *Journal of Consumer Research, 35,* 472–482. (13) doi: 10.1086/586910

Golle, J., Rose, N., Gölner, R., Spenglerm M., Stoll, G., Hübner, N., Rieger, S., Trautwein, U., Ludtke, O., Roberts, B. W., & Nagengast, B. (2019). School or work? The choice may change your personality. *Psychological Science, 30,* 32–42. (14) doi: 10.1177/0956797618806298

Golombok, S., Perry, B., Burston, A., Murray, C., Mooney-Somers, J., Stevens, M., & Golding, J. (2003). Children with lesbian parents: A community study. *Developmental Psychology, 39,* 20–33. (5) doi: 10.1037//0012-1649.39.1.20

Golubock, J. L., & Janata, P. (2013). Keeping timbre in mind: Working memory for complex sounds that can't be verbalized. *Journal of Experimental Psychology: Human Perception and Performance, 39,* 399–412. (7) doi: 10.1037/a0029720

Golumbic, E. Z., Cogan, G. B., Schroeder, C. E., & Poepel, D. (2013). Visual input enhances selective speech envelope tracking in auditory cortex at a "cocktail party." *Journal of Neuroscience, 33,* 1417–1426. (4) doi: 10.1523/JNEUROSCI.3675-12.2013

Gómez-Pinilla, F. (2008). Brain foods: The effects of nutrients on brain function. *Nature Reviews Neuroscience, 9,* 568–578. (2) doi: 10.1038/nrn2421

Goodall, J. (1971). *In the shadow of man.* Boston: Houghton Mifflin. (2)

Goodbourn, P. T., Martini, P., Barnett-Cowan, M., Harris, I. M., Livesey, E. J., & Holcombe, A. O. (2016). Reconsidering temporal selection in the attentional blink. *Psychological Science, 27,* 1146–1156. (10) doi: 10.1177/0956797616654131

Goodman, G. S., Ghetti, S., Quas, J. A., Edelstein, R. S., Alexander, K. W., Redlich, A. D., Cordon, I. M., & Jones, D. P. H. (2003). A prospective study of memory for child sexual abuse: New findings relevant to the repressed-memory controversy. *Psychological Science, 14,* 113–118. (7) doi: 10.1111/1467-9280.01428

Gordon, P. C., Hendrick, R., & Levine, W. H. (2002). Memory-load interference in syntactic processing. *Psychological Science, 13,* 425–430. (8) doi: 10.1111/1467-9280.00475

Gossop, M., Stewart, D., & Marsden, J. (2008). Attendance at Narcotics Anonymous and Alcoholics Anonymous meetings, frequency of attendance and substance use outcomes after residential treatment for drug dependence: A 5-year follow-up study. *Addiction, 103,* 119–125. (15) doi: 10.1111/j.1360-0443.2007.02050.x

Gottesman, I. I. (1991). *Schizophrenia genesis.* New York: W. H. Freeman. (15)

Gottfredson, L. S. (2002a). *g:* Highly general and highly practical. In R. J. Sternberg & E. L. Grigorenko (Eds.), *The general intelligence factor: How general is it?* (pp. 331–380). Mahwah, NJ: Erlbaum. (9)

Gottfredson, L. S. (2002b). Where and why g matters: Not a mystery. *Human Performance, 15,* 25–46. (9) doi: 10.1207/S15327043HUP1501&02_03

Gottschling, J., Hahn, E., Beam, C. R., Spinath, F. M., Carroll, S., & Turkheimer, E. (2019). Socioeconomic status amplifies genetic effects in middle childhood in a large German twin sample. *Intelligence, 72,* 20–27. (9) doi: 10.1016/j.intell.2018.11.006

Graber, E. C., Laurenceau, J.-P., Miga, E., Chango, J., & Coan, J. (2011). Conflict and love: Predicting newlywed marital outcomes from two interaction contexts. *Journal of Family Psychology, 25,* 541–550. (13) doi: 10.1037/a0024507

Gracanin, A., Bylsma, L. M., & Vingerhoets, A. J. J. M. (2014). Is crying a self-soothing behavior? *Frontiers in Psychology, 5,* article 502. (12) doi: 10.3389/fpsyg.2014.00502

Graf, P., & Mandler, G. (1984). Activation makes words more accessible, but not necessarily more retrievable. *Journal of Verbal Learning and Verbal Behavior, 23,* 553–568. (7) doi: 10.1016/S0022-5371(84)90346-3

Graffi, J., Moss, E., Jolicoeur-Martineau, A., Moss, G., Lecompte, V., Pascuzzo, K., Babineau, V., Gordon-Green, C., Mileva-Seitz, V. R., Minde, K., Sassi, R., Steiner, M., Kennedy, J. L., Gaudreau, H., Levitan, R., Meaney, M. J., & Wazana, A. (2018). The dopamine D4 receptor gene, birth weight, maternal depression, and the prediction of disorganized attachment at 36 months of age: A prospective gene x environment analysis. *Infant Behavior and*

Development, 50, 64–77. (5) doi: 10.1016/j. infbeh.2017.11.004

Grafton, B., Southworth, F., Watkins, E., & MacLeod, C. (2016). Stuck in a sad place: Biased attentional disengagement in rumination. *Emotion, 16,* 63–72. (15) doi: 10.1037/emo0000103

Granier-Deferre, C., Bassereau, S., Ribeiro, A., Jacquet, A.-Y., & DeCasper, A. J. (2011). A melodic contour repeatedly experienced by human near-term fetuses elicits a profound cardiac reaction one month after birth. *PLoS One, 6,* e17304. (5) doi: 10.1371/journal. pone.0017304

Grant, A. M. (2013). Rethinking the extraverted sales ideal: The ambivert advantage. *Psychological Science, 24,* 1024–1030. (14) doi: 10.1177/0956797612463706

Graziadei, P. P., & deHan, R. S. (1973). Neuronal regeneration in the frog olfactory system. *Journal of Cell Biology, 59,* 525–530. (3) doi: 10.1083/jcb.59.2.525

Graziano, M. S. A. (2013). *Consciousness and the social brain.* New York: Oxford University Press. (10)

Greaves, L. M., Barlow, F. K., Lee, C. H. J., Matika, C. M., Wang, W. Y., Lindsay, C. J., Case, C. J. B., Sengupta, N. K., Huang, Y. S., Cowie, L. J., Stronge, S., Storey, M., De Souza, L., Manuela, S., Hammond, M. D., Milojev, P., Townrow, C. S., Muriwai, E., Satherley, N. ... Sibley, C. G. (2017). The diversity and prevalence of sexual orientation self-labels in a New Zealand national sample. *Archives of Sexual Behavior, 46,* 1325–1336. (11) doi: 10.1007/s10508-016-0857-5

Green, D. M., & Swets, J. A. (1966). *Signal detection theory and psychophysics.* New York: Wiley. (4)

Greenberg, J., Martens, A., Jonas, E., Eisenstadt, D., Pyszczynski, T., & Solomon, S. (2003). Psychological defense in anticipation of anxiety. *Psychological Science, 14,* 516–519. (5) doi: 10.1111/1467-9280.03454

Greene, J. D., Sommerville, R. B., Nystrom, L. E., Darley, J. M., & Cohen, J. D. (2001). An fMRI investigation of emotional engagement in moral judgment. *Science, 293,* 2105–2108. (12) doi: 10.1126/science.1062872

Greenfield, P. M. (2017). Cultural change over time: Why replicability should not be the gold standard in psychological science. *Perspectives on Psychological Science, 12,* 762–771. (2) doi: 10.1177/1745691617707314

Greenfield, T. K., Stoneking, B. C., Humphreys, K., Sundby, E., & Bond, J. (2008). A randomized trial of a mental health consumer-managed alternative to civil commitment for acute psychiatric crisis. *American Journal of Community Psychology, 42,* 135–144. (15) doi: 10.1007/s10464-008-9180-1

Greenhoot, A. F., Ornstein, P. A., Gordon, B. N., & Baker-Ward, L. (1999). Acting out the details of a pediatric check-up: The impact of interview condition and behavioral style on children's memory reports. *Child Development, 70,* 363–380. (7) doi: 10.1111/1467-8624.00027

Greeno, C. G., & Wing, R. R. (1994). Stress-induced eating. *Psychological Bulletin, 115,* 444–464. (11) doi: 10.1037/0033-2909.115.3.444

Greenwald, A. G., Nosek, B. A., & Banaji, M. R. (2003). Understanding and using the Implicit Association Test: I. An improved scoring algorithm. *Journal of Personality and Social Psychology, 85,* 197–216. (13) doi: 10.1037/0022-3514.85.2.197

Greenwald, A. G., Poehlman, A. T., Uhlmann, E. L., & Banaji, M. R. (2009). Understanding and using the Implicit Association Test: III. Meta-analysis of predictive validity. *Journal of Personality and Social Psychology, 97,* 17–41. (13) doi: 10.1037/a0015575

Greenwald, A. G., Spangenberg, E. R., Pratkanis, A. R., & Eskanazi, J. (1991). Double-blind tests of subliminal self-help audiotapes. *Psychological Science, 2,* 119–122. (4) doi: 10.1111/j.1467-9280.1991.tb00112.x

Greer, J., Riby, D. M., Hamilton, C., & Riby, L. M. (2013). Attentional lapse and inhibition control in adults with Williams syndrome. *Research in Developmental Disabilities, 34,* 4170–4177. (8) doi: 10.1016/j.ridd.2013.08.041

Gregersen, P. K., Kowalsky, E., Lee, A., Baron-Cohen, S., Fisher, S. E., Asher, J. E., Ballard, D., Freudenberg, J., & Li, W. T. (2013). Absolute pitch exhibits phenotypic and genetic overlap with synesthesia. *Human Molecular Genetics, 22,* 2097–2104. (4) doi: 10.1093/hmg/ddt059

Grifell, M., & Hart, C. L. (2018, May–June). Is drug addiction a brain disease? *American Scientist, 106(3),* 160–167. (15) https://www.americanscientist.org/article/is-drug-addiction-a-brain-disease

Griffith, R. M., Miyagi, O., & Tago, A. (1958). The universality of typical dreams: Japanese vs. Americans. *American Anthropologist, 60,* 1173–1179. (10) doi: 10.1525/aa.1958.60.6.02a00110

Grimm, O., Kittel-Schneider, S., & Reif, A. (2018). Recent developments in the genetics of attention-deficit hyperactivity disorder. *Psychiatry and Clinical Neurosciences, 72,* 654–672. (8) doi: 10.1111/pcn.12673

Griskevicius, V., Shiota, M. N., & Neufeld, S. L. (2010). Influence of different positive emotions on persuasion processing: A functional evolutionary approach. *Emotion, 10,* 190–206. (12) doi: 10.1037/a0018421

Grissmer, D. W., Williamson, S., Kirby, S. N., & Berends, M. (1998). Exploring the rapid rise in the Black achievement scores in the United States (1970–1990). In U. Neisser (Ed.), *The rising curve* (pp. 251–285). Washington, DC: American Psychological Association. (9)

Groenman, A. P., Janssen, T. W., & Oosterlaan, J. (2017). Childhood psychiatric disorders as risk factor for subsequent substance abuse: A meta-analysis. *Journal of the American Academy of Child and Adolescent Psychiatsry, 56,* 556–569. (3) doi: 10.1016/j.jaac.2017.05.004

Gross, J. J., Fredrickson, B. L., & Levenson, R. W. (1994). The psychophysiology of crying. *Psychophysiology, 31,* 460–468. (12) doi: 10.1111/j.1469-8986.1994.tb01049.x

Grossman, E. D., & Blake, R. (2001). Brain activity evoked by inverted and imagined biological motion. *Vision Research, 41,* 1475–1482. (4) doi: 10.1016/S0042-6989(00)00317-5

Grossman, I., Karasawa, M., Kan, C., & Kitayama, S. (2014). A cultural perspective on emotional experiences across the life span. *Emotion, 14,* 679–692. (12) doi: 10.1037/a0036041

Grossmann, T., Missana, M., & Krol, K. M. (2018). The neurodevelopmental precursors of altruistic behavior in infancy. *PLoS Biology, 16,* e2005281. (13) doi: 10.1371/journal. pbio.2005281

Grotzinger, A. D., Mann, F. D., Patterson, M. W., Tackett, J. L., Tucker-Drob, E. M., & Harden, K. P. (2018). Hair and salivary testosterone, hair cortisol, and externalizing behaviors in adolescents. *Psychological Science, 29,* 688–699. (13) doi: 10.1177/0956797617742981

Gruber, R., Wiebe, S., Montecalvo, L., Brunetti, B., Amsel, R., & Carrier, J. (2011). Impact of sleep restriction on neurobehavioral functioning of children with attention deficit hyperactivity disorder. *Sleep, 34,* 315–323. (8) doi: 10.1093/sleep/34.3.315

Grueter, M., Grueter, T., Bell, V., Horst, J., Laskowski, W., Sperling, K., Halligan, P. W., Ellis, H. D., & Kennerknecht, I. (2007). Hereditary prosopagnosia: The first case series. *Cortex, 43,* 734–749. (3) doi: 10.1016/S0010-9452(08)70502-1

Grünbaum, A. (1986). Précis of *The foundations of psychoanalysis:* A philosophical critique. *Behavioral and Brain Sciences, 9,* 217–228. (14) doi: 10.1017/S0140525X00022287

Guilleminault, C., Heinzer, R., Mignot, E., & Black, J. (1998). Investigations into the neurologic basis of narcolepsy. *Neurology, 50*(Suppl. 1), S8–S15. (10) doi: 10.1212/WNL.50.2_Suppl_1.S8

Guiso, L., Monte, F., Sapienza, P., & Zingales, L. (2008). Culture, gender, and math. *Science, 320,* 1164–1165. (5) doi: 10.1126/science.1154094

Gulsuner, S., Stein, D. J., Susser, E. S., Sibelko, G., Pretorius, A., Walsh, T., Majara, L., Mndini, M. M., Mqulwana, S. G., Ntola, O. A., Casadei, S, Ngqengelele, L. L., Korchina, V., van der Merwe, C., Malan, M., Fader, K. M., Feng, M., Willoughby, E., Muzny, D., ... McClellan, J. M. (2020). Genetics of schizophrenia in the South African Xhosa. *Science, 367,* 569–573. (15) https://science.sciencemag.org/content/367/6477/569

Guo, J., Sun, Y., Xue, L.-J., Huang, Z.-Y., Wang, Y.-S., Zhang, L., Zhou, G.-H., & Yuan, L.-X. (2016). Effect of CPAP therapy on cardiovascular events and mortality in patients with obstructive sleep apnea: A meta-analysis. *Sleep and Breathing, 20,* 965–974. (10) doi: 10.1007/s11325-016-1319-y

Guo, L. S., Trueblood, J. S., & Diederich, A. (2017). Thinking fast increases framing effects in risky decision making. *Psychological Science, 28,* 530–543. (8) doi: 10.1177/0956797616689092

Gur, R. E., Cowell, P. E., Latshaw, A., Turetsky, B. I., Grossman, R. I., Arnold, S. E., Bilkeer, W. B., & Gur, R. C. (2000). Reduced dorsal and orbital prefrontal gray matter volumes in schizophrenia. *Archives of General Psychiatry, 57,* 761–768. (15) doi: 10.1001/archpsyc.57.8.761

Gurven, M., von Rueden, C., Massenkoff, M., Kaplan, H., & Lero Vie, M. (2013). How universal is the big five? Testing the five-factor model of personality variation among forager-farmers in the Brazilian Amazon. *Journal of Personality and Social Psychology, 104,* 354–370. (14) doi: 10.1037/a0030841

Gustavson, C. R., Kelly, D. J., Sweeney, M., & Garcia, J. (1976). Prey-lithium aversions: I. Coyotes and wolves. *Behavioral Biology, 17,* 61–72. (6) doi: 10.1016/S0091-6773(76)90272-8

Gutiérrez, E. (2013). A rat in the labyrinth of anorexia nervosa: Contributions of the activity-based rodent model to the understanding of anorexia nervosa. *International Journal of Eating Disorders, 46,* 289–301. (11) doi: 10.1002/eat.22095

Gutiérrez, E., Carrera, O., Vazquez, R., & Birmingham, C. L. (2013). Climate might be considered as a risk factor for anorexia? A hypothesis worth another look. *Eating Behaviors, 14,* 278–280. (11) doi: 10.1016/j.eatbeh.2013.05.006

Gvilia, I., Xu, F., McGinty, D., & Szymusiak, R. (2006). Homeostatic regulation of sleep: A role for preoptic area neurons. *Journal of Neuroscience, 26,* 9426–9433. (10) doi: 10.1523/JNEUROSCI.2012-06.2006

Haarmeier, T., Thier, P., Repnow, M., & Petersen, D. (1997). False perception of motion in a patient who cannot compensate for eye movements. *Nature, 389,* 849–852. (4) doi: 10.1038/39872

Hackman, J. R., & Lawler, E. E., III (1971). Employee reactions to job characteristics. *Journal of Applied Psychology, 55,* 259–286. (11) doi: 10.1037/h0031152

Hadar, L., & Sood, S. (2014). When knowledge is demotivating: Subjective knowledge and choice overload. *Psychological Science, 25,* 1739–1747. (8) doi: 10.1177/0956797614539165

Haeffel, G. J., Abramson, L. Y., Metalsky, G. I., Dykman, B. M., Donovan, P., Hogan, M. E., Voelz, Z. R., Halberstadt, L., & Hankin, B. L. (2005). Negative cognitive styles, dysfunctional attitudes, and the remitted depression paradigm: A search for the elusive cognitive vulnerability to depression factor among remitted depressives. *Emotion, 5,* 343–348. (15) doi: 10.1037/1528-3542.5.3.343

Hagerty, S. L., Ellingson, J. M., Helmuth, T. B., Bidwell, L. C., Hutchinson, K. E., & Bryan, A. D. (2019). An overview and proposed research framework for studying co-occurring mental- and physical-health dysfunction. *Perspectives on Psychological Science, 14,* 633–645. (15) doi: 10.1177/1745691619827010

Haggard, P., & Eimer, M. (1999). On the relation between brain potentials and the awareness of voluntary movements. *Experimental Brain Research, 126,* 128–133. (10) doi: 10.1007/s002210050722

Haggarty, J. M., Cernovsky, Z., Husni, M., Minor, K., Kermean, P., & Merskey, H. (2002). Seasonal affective disorder in an arctic community. *Acta Psychiatrica Scandinavica, 105,* 378–384. (15) doi: 10.1034/j.1600-0447.2002.1o185.x

Hahn, A., & Gawronski, B. (2019). Facing one's implicit biases: From awareness to acknowledgment. *Journal of Personality and Social Psychology, 116,* 769–794. (13) doi: 10.1037/pspi0000155

Hahn, A., Judd, C. M., Hirsh, H. K., & Blair, I. V. (2014). Awareness of implicit attitudes. *Journal of Experimental Psychology-General, 143,* 1369–1392. (13) doi: 10.1037/a0035028

Hahn, B., Robinson, B. M., Kaiser, S. T., Matveeva, T. M., Harvey, A. N., Luck, S. J., & Gold, J. M. (2012). Kraepelin and Bleuler had it right: People with schizophrenia have deficits sustaining attention over time. *Journal of Abnormal Psychology, 121,* 641–648. (15) doi: 10.1037/a0028492

Haidt, J. (2001). The emotional dog and its rational tail: A social intuitionist approach to moral judgment. *Psychological Review, 108,* 814–834. (13) doi: 10.1037//0033-295X.108.4.814

Haidt, J. (2007). The new synthesis in moral psychology. *Science, 316,* 998–1002. (13) doi: 10.1126/science.1137651

Haidt, J. (2012). *The righteous mind.* New York: Pantheon. (13)

Haijma, S. V., Van Haren, H., Cahn, W., Koolschijn, C. M. P., Pol, H. E. H., & Kahn, R. S. (2013). Brain volumes in schizophrenia: A meta-analysis in over 18 000 subjects. *Schizophrenia Bulletin, 39,* 1129–1138. (15) doi: doi.org/10.1093/schbul/sbs118

Haines, S. J., Gleeson, J., Kuppens, P., Hollenstein, T., Ciarrochi, J., Labuschagne, I., Grace, C., & Koval, P. (2016). The wisdom to know the difference: Strategy-situation fit in emotion regulation in daily life is associated with well-being. *Psychological Science, 27,* 1651–1659. (12) doi: 10.1177/0956797616669086

Hall, C. S., & Van de Castle, R. L. (1966). *The content analysis of dreams.* New York: Appleton-Century-Crofts. (10)

Hall, J. A., & Matsumoto, D. (2004). Gender differences in judgments of multiple emotions from facial expressions. *Emotion, 4,* 201–206. (12) doi: 10.1037/1528-3542.4.2.201

Halperin, E., Porat, R., Tamir, M., & Gross, J. J. (2013). Can emotion regulation change political attitudes in intractable conflicts? From the laboratory to the field. *Psychological Science, 24,* 106–111. (12) doi: 10.1177/0956797612452572

Halpern, D. F., Benbow, C. P., Geary, D. C., Gur, R. C., Hyde, J. S., & Gernsbacher, M. A. (2007). The science of sex differences in science and mathematics. *Psychological Science in the Public Interest, 8,* 1–51. (5) https://journals.sagepub.com/doi/full/10.1111/j.1529-1006.2007.00032.x

Halpern, S. C., Schuch, F. B., Scherer, J. N., Sordi, A. O., Pachado, M., Dalbosco, C., Fara, L., Pechansky, F., Kessler, F., & Von Diemen, L. (2018). Child maltreatment and illicit substance abuse: A systematic review and meta-analysis of longitudinal studies. *Child Abuse Review, 27,* 344–360. (15) doi: 10.1002/car.2534

Halpern, S. D., Andrews, T. J., & Purves, D. (1999). Interindividual variation in human visual performance. *Journal of Cognitive Neuroscience, 11,* 521–534. (4) doi: 10.1162/089892999563580

Hama, Y. (2001). Shopping as a coping behavior for stress. *Japanese Psychological Research, 43,* 218–224. (12) doi: 10.1111/1468-5884.00179

Hamamura, T. (2012). Are cultures becoming individualistic? A cross-temporal comparison of individualism-collectivism in the United States and Japan. *Personality and Social Psychology Review, 16,* 3–24. (13) doi: 10.1177/1088868311411587

Hamann, S. B., & Squire, L. R. (1997). Intact perceptual memory in the absence of conscious memory. *Behavioral Neuroscience, 111,* 850–854. (7) doi: 10.1037/0735-7044.111.4.850

Hamby, S. (2014). Intimate partner and sexual violence research: Scientific progress, scientific challenges, and gender. *Trauma, Violence, and Abuse, 15,* 149–158. (13) doi: 10.1177/1524838014520723

Hamby, S. L., & Koss, M. P. (2003). Shades of gray: A qualitative study of terms used in the measurement of sexual victimization. *Psychology of Women Quarterly, 27,* 243–255. (13) doi: 10.1111/1471-6402.00104

Hamm, J. V. (2000). Do birds of a feather flock together? The variable bases for African American, Asian American, and European American adolescents' selection of similar friends. *Developmental Psychology, 36,* 209–219. (13) doi: 10.1037/0012-1649.36.2.209

Hampshire, A., Highfield, R. R., Parkin, B. L., & Owen, A. M. (2012). Fractionating human intelligence. *Neuron, 76,* 1225–1237. (9) doi: 10.1016/j.neuron.2012.06.022

Han, C. J., & Robinson, J. K. (2001). Cannabinoid modulation of time estimation in the rat.

Behavioral Neuroscience, 115, 243–246. (3) doi: 10.1037/0735-7044.115.1.243

Haney, C., Banks, C., & Zimbardo, P. (1973). Interpersonal dynamics in a simulated prison. *International Journal of Criminology and Penology, 1,* 69–97. (13)

Hannigan, L. J., Rijsdijk, F. V., Ganiban, J. M., Reiss, D., Spotts, E. L., Neiderhiser, J. M., Lichtenstein, P., McAdams, T. A., & Eley, T. C. (2018). Shared genetic influences do not explain the relationship between parent-offspring relationship quality and offspring internalizing problems: Results from a children-of-twins study. *Psychological Medicine, 48,* 592–603. (5) doi: 10.1017/S0033291717001908

Hanson, R. K. (2000). Will they do it again? Predicting sex-offense recidivism. *Current Directions in Psychological Science, 9,* 106–109. (13) doi: 10.1111/1467-8721.00071

Happé, F., Ronald, A., & Plomin, R. (2006). Time to give up on a single explanation for autism. *Nature Neuroscience, 9,* 1218–1220. (15) doi: 10.1038/nn1770

Harada, S., Agarwal, D. P. Goedde, H. W., Tagaki, S., & Ishikawa, B. (1982). Possible protective role against alcoholism for aldehyde dehydrogenase isozyme deficiency in Japan. *Lancet, ii,* 827. (15) doi: 10.1016/s0140-6736(82)92722-2

Haraszti, R. A., Ella, K., Gyöngyösi, N., Roenneberg, T., & Káldi, K. (2014). Social jetlag negatively correlates with academic performance in undergraduates. *Chronobiology International, 31,* 603–612. (10) doi: 10.3109/07420528.2013.879164

Harden, K. P. (2012). True love waits? A sibling-comparison study of age at first sexual intercourse and romantic relationships in young adulthood. *Psychological Science, 23,* 1324–1336. (11) doi: 10.1177/0956797612442550

Harden, K. P. (2014). A sex-positive framework for research on adolescent sexuality. *Perspectives on Psychological Science, 9,* 455–469. (11) doi: 10.1177/1745691614535934

Hariri, A. R., Mattay, V. S., Tessitore, A., Kolachana, B., Fera, F., Goldman, D., Egan, M. F., & Weinberger, D. R. (2002). Serotonin transporter genetic variation and the response of the human amygdala. *Science, 297,* 400–403. (3) doi: 10.1126/science.1071829

Harkins, S. G., & Jackson, J. M. (1985). The role of evaluation in eliminating social loafing. *Personality and Social Psychology Bulletin, 11,* 457–465. (13) doi: 10.1177/0146167285114011

Harley, B., & Wang, W. (1997). The critical period hypothesis: Where are we now? In A. M. B. deGroot & J. F. Knoll (Eds.), *Tutorials in bilingualism* (pp. 19–51). Mahwah, NJ: Erlbaum. (8)

Harris, J. C. (2016). The origin and natural history of autism spectrum disorders. *Nature Neuroscience, 11,* 1390–1391. (15) doi: 10.1038/nn.4427

Harris, J. R. (1995). Where is the child's environment? A group socialization theory of development. *Psychological Review, 102,* 458–489. (5) doi: 10.1037/0033-295X.102.3.458

Harris, J. R. (1998). *The nurture assumption.* New York: Free Press. (5)

Harris, J. R. (2000). Context-specific learning, personality, and birth order. *Current Directions in Psychological Science, 9,* 174–177. (5) doi: 10.1111/1467-8721.00087

Harris, L. T., & Fiske, S. T. (2006). Dehumanizing the lowest of the low: Neuroimaging responses to extreme out-groups. *Psychological Science, 17,* 847-853. (13) doi: 10.1111/j.1467-9280.2006.01793.x

Harris, R. J., Schoen, L. M., & Hensley, D. L. (1992). A cross-cultural study of story memory. *Journal of Cross-Cultural Psychology, 23,* 133-147. (7) doi: 10.1177/0022022192232001

Harris, T. (1967). *I'm OK—You're OK.* New York: Avon. (14)

Harrison, Y. (2013). The impact of daylight saving time on sleep and related behaviours. *Sleep Medicine Reviews, 17,* 285-292. (10) doi: 10.1016/j.smrv.2012.10.001

Hartshorne, J. K., & Germine, L. T. (2015). When does cognitive functioning peak? The asynchronous rise and fall of different cognitive abilities across the life span. *Psychological Science, 26,* 433-443. (9) doi: 10.1177/0956797614567339

Hasan, F. M., Zagarins, S. E., Pischke, K. M., Saiyed, S., Bettencourt, A. M., Beal, L., Macys, D., Aurora, S., & McCleary, N. (2014). Hypnotherapy is more effective than nicotine replacement therapy for smoking cessation: Results of a randomized controlled trial. *Complementary Therapies in Medicine, 22,* 1-8. (10) doi: 10.1016/j.ctim.2013.12.012

Hasel, L. E., & Kassin, S. M. (2009). On the presumption of evidentiary independence. *Psychological Science, 20,* 122-126. (7) doi: 10.1111/j.1467-9280.2008.02262.x

Hassabis, D., Kumaran, D., Vann, S. D., & Maguire, E. A. (2007). Patients with hippocampal amnesia cannot imagine new experiences. *Proceedings of the National Academy of Sciences, 104,* 1726-1731. (7) doi: 10.1073/pnas.0610561104

Hassett, J. M., Siebert, E. R., & Wallen, K. (2008). Sex differences in rhesus monkey toy preferences parallel those of children. *Hormones and Behavior, 54,* 359-364. (5) doi: 10.1016/j.yhbeh.2008.03.008

Hassin, R. R. (2013). Yes it can: On the functional abilities of the human unconscious. *Perspectives on Psychological Science, 8,* 195-207. (10) doi: 10.1177/1745691612460684

Hastie, R., Schkade, D. A., & Payne, J. W. (1999). Juror judgments in civil cases: Hindsight effects on judgments of liability for punitive damages. *Law and Human Behavior, 23,* 597-614. (7) doi: 10.1023/A:1022352330466

Hatfield, E., & Rapson, R. L. (1993). *Love, sex, and intimacy.* New York: HarperCollins. (13)

Hathaway, S. R., & McKinley, J. C. (1940). A multiphasic personality schedule (Minnesota): I. Construction of the schedule. *Journal of Psychology, 10,* 249-254. (14) doi: 10.1080/00223980.1940.9917000

Haueisen, J., & Knösche, T. R. (2001). Involuntary motor activity in pianists evoked by music perception. *Journal of Cognitive Neuroscience, 13,* 786-792. (6) doi: 10.1162/08989290152541449

Havlicek, J., & Roberts, S. C. (2009). MHC-correlated mate choice in humans: A review. *Psychoneuroendocrinology, 34,* 497-512. (4) doi: 10.1016/j.psyneuen.2008.10.007

Hay, D. F., Mundy, L., Roberts, S., Carta, R., Waters, C. S., Perra, O., Jones, R., Jones, I., Goodyer, I., Harold, G., Thapar, A., & van Goozen, S. (2011). Known risk factors for violence predict 12-month-old infants' aggressiveness with peers. *Psychological Science, 22,* 1205-1211. (13) doi: 10.1177/0956797611419303

Hayes, J. E., Bartoshuk, L. M., Kidd, J. R., & Duffy, V. B. (2008). Supertasting and PROP bitterness depends on more than the *TAS2R38* gene. *Chemical Senses, 33,* 255-265. (4) doi: 10.1093/chemse/bjm084

He, H., Liu, Q., Li, N., Guo, L., Gao, F., Bai, L., Gao, F., & Lyu, J. (2020). Trends in the incidence and DALYs of schizophrenia at the global, regional and national levels: Results from the Global Buren of Disease Study 2017. *Epidemiology and Psychiatric Sciences, 29,* e91, 1-11. (15) doi: 10.1017/S2045796019000891

Healy, D., & Williams, J. M. G. (1988). Dysrhythmia, dysphoria, and depression: The interaction of learned helplessness and circadian dysrhythmia in the pathogenesis of depression. *Psychological Bulletin, 103,* 163-178. (15) doi: 10.1037/0033-2909.103.2.163

Heath, A. C., Neale, M. C., Kessler, R. C., Eaves, L. J., & Kendler, K. S. (1992). Evidence for genetic influences on personality from self-reports and informant ratings. *Journal of Personality and Social Psychology, 63,* 85-96. (5, 14) doi: 10.1037/0022-3514.63.1.85

Hedding, D. W. (2019). Payouts push professors toward predatory journals. *Nature, 565,* 267. (11) doi: 10.1038/d41586-019-00120-1

Heider, F. (1958). *The psychology of interpersonal relations.* New York: Wiley. (13)

Heine, S. J., Buchtel, E. E., & Norenzayan, A. (2008). What do cross-national comparisons of personality traits tell us? *Psychological Science, 19,* 309-313. (14) doi: 10.1111/j.1467-9280.2008.02085.x

Heine, S. J., & Hamamura, T. (2007). In search of East Asian self-enhancement. *Personality and Social Psychology Review, 11,* 4-27. (13) doi: 10.1177/1088868306294587

Heinzel, S., Schulte, S., Onken, J., Duong, Q.-L., Riemer, T. G., Heinz, A., Kathmann, N., & Rapp, M. A. (2014). Working memory training improvements and gains in non-trained cognitive tasks in young and older adults. *Aging, Neuropsychology, and Cognition, 21,* 146-173. (8) doi: 10.1080/13825585.2013.790338

Heisz, J. J., Pottruff, M. M., & Shore, D. I. (2013). Females scan more than males: A potential mechanism for sex differences in recognition. *Psychological Science, 24,* 1157-1163. (5) doi: 10.1177/0956797612468281

Heit, E. (1993). Modeling the effects of expectations on recognition memory. *Psychological Science, 4,* 244-252. (7) doi: 10.1111/j.1467-9280.1993.tb00268.x

Heller, S. B. (2014). Summer jobs reduce violence among disadvantaged youth. *Science, 346,* 1219-1223. (15) doi: 10.1126/science.1257809

Hemond, C., Brown, R. M., & Robertson, E. M. (2010). A distraction can impair or enhance motor performance. *Journal of Neuroscience, 30,* 650-654. (8) doi: 10.1523/JNEUROSCI.4592-09.2010

Henderson, J. M. (2007). Regarding scenes. *Current Directions in Psychological Science, 16,* 219-222. (8) doi: 10.1111/j.1467-8721.2007.00507.x

Henderson, J. M., & Hollingworth, A. (2003). Global transsaccadic change blindness during scene perception. *Psychological Science, 14,* 493-497. (8) doi: 10.1111/1467-9280.02459

Henkel, L. A. (2011). Photograph-induced memory errors: When photographs make people claim they have done things they have not. *Applied Cognitive Psychology, 25,* 78-86. (7) doi: 10.1002/acp.1644

Henning, E. R., Turk, C. L., Mennin, D. S., Fresco, D. M., & Heimberg, R. G. (2007). Impairment and quality of life in individuals with generalized anxiety disorder. *Depression and Anxiety, 24,* 342-349. (15) doi: 10.1002/da.20249

Henrich, J., Heine, S. J., & Norenzayan, A. (2010). Most people are not WEIRD. *Nature, 466,* 29. (2) doi: 10.1038/466029a

Herbenick, D., Bowling, J., Fu, T. C., Dodge, B., Guerra-Reyes, L., & Sanders, S. (2017). Sexual diversity in the United States: Results from a nationally representative probability sample of adult women and men. *PLoS One, 12,* e0181198. (11) duo: 10.1371/journal.pone.0181198

Herculano-Houzel, S. (2011). Brains matter, bodies maybe not: The case for examining neuron numbers irrespective of body size. *Annals of the New York Academy of Sciences, 1225,* 191-199. (9) doi: 10.1111/j.1749-6632.2011.05976.x

Heres, S., Davis, J., Maino, K., Jetzinger, E., Kissling, W., & Leucht, S. (2006). Why olanzapine beats risperidone, risperidone beats quetiapine, and quetiapine beats olanzapine: An exploratory analysis of head-to-head comparison studies of second-generation antipsychotics. *American Journal of Psychiatry, 163,* 185-194. (2) doi: 10.1176/appi.ajp.163.2.185

Hergenhahn, B. R. (1992). *An introduction to the history of psychology* (2nd ed.). Belmont, CA: Wadsworth. (1)

Herkenham, M., Lynn, A. B., de Costa, B. R., & Richfield, E. K. (1991). Neuronal localization of cannabinoid receptors in the basal ganglia of the rat. *Brain Research, 547,* 267-274. (3) doi: 10.1016/0006-8993(91)90970-7

Herkenham, M., Lynn, A. B., Little, M. D., Johnson, M. R., Melvin, L. S., deCosta, B. R., & Rice, K. C. (1990). Cannabinoid receptor localization in brain. *Proceedings of the National Academy of Sciences, USA, 87,* 1932-1936. (3) doi: 10.1073/pnas.87.5.1932

Herman, C. P., Roth, D. A., & Polivy, J. (2003). Effects of the presence of others on food intake: A normative interpretation. *Psychological Bulletin, 129,* 873-886. (11) doi: 10.1037/0033-2909.129.6.873

Herman, J., Roffwarg, H., & Tauber, E. S. (1968). Color and other perceptual qualities of REM and NREM sleep. *Psychophysiology, 5,* 223. (10)

Herrmann, B., Thöni, C., & Gächter, S. (2008). Antisocial punishment across societies. *Science, 319,* 1362-1367. (13) doi: 10.1126/science.1153808

Hertenstein, M. J. (2002). Touch: Its communicative functions in infancy. *Human Development, 45,* 70-94. (5) doi: 10.1159/000048154

Hertenstein, M. J., Keltner, D., App, B., Bulleit, B. A., & Jaskolka, A. R. (2006). Touch communicates distinct emotions. *Emotion, 6,* 528-533. (12) doi: 10.1037/1528-3542.6.3.528

Hertzog, C., Kramer, A. F., Wilson, R. S., & Lindenberger, U. (2009). Enrichment effects on adult cognitive development. *Psychological Science in the Public Interest, 9,* 1-65. (8) https://journals.sagepub.com/doi/full/10.1111/j.1539-6053.2009.01034.x

Herz, R. (2007). *The scent of desire.* New York: HarperCollins. (4)

Herz, R. S. (2014). Verbal priming and taste sensitivity make moral transgressions gross. *Behavioral Neuroscience, 128,* 20-28. (12) doi: 10.1037/a0035468

Herz, R. S., & von Clef, J. (2001). The influence of verbal labeling on the perception of odors: Evidence for olfactory illusions? *Perception, 30,* 381–391. (4) doi: 10.1068/p3179

Hess, T. M. (2014). Selective engagement of cognitive resources: Motivational influences on older adults' cognitive functioning. *Perspectives on Psychological Science, 9,* 388–407. (5) doi: 10.1177/1745691614527465

Hetherington, E. M. (1989). Coping with family transitions. Winners, losers, and survivors. *Child Development, 60,* 1–14. (5) doi: 10.2307/1131066

Hetherington, E. M., Stanley-Hagan, M., & Anderson, E. R. (1989). Marital transitions: A child's perspective. *American Psychologist, 44,* 303–312. (5) doi: 10.1037/0003-066X.44.2.303

Heyman, G. M. (2011). Received wisdom regarding the roles of craving and dopamine in addiction: A response to Lewis's critique of *Addiction: A disorder of choice. Perspectives on Psychological Science, 6,* 156–160. (15) doi: 10.1177/1745691611400243

Hilchey, M. D., Taylor, E. T., & Pratt, J. (2016). Much ado about nothing: Capturing attention toward locations without new perceptual events. *Journal of Experimental Psychology: Human Perception and Performance, 42,* 1923–1927. (8) doi: 10.1037/xhp0000326

Hildreth, K., Sweeney, B., & Rovee-Collier, C. (2003). Differential memory-preserving effects of reminders at 6 months. *Journal of Experimental Child Psychology, 84,* 41–62. (5) doi: 10.1016/S0022-0965(02)00163-7

Hilgard, J., Engelhardt, C. R., & Rouder, J. N. (2017). Overstated evidence for short-term effects of violent games on affect and behavior: A reanalysis of Anderson (2010). *Psychological Bulletin, 143,* 757–774. (2) doi: 10.1037/bul0000074

Hill, P. L., & Turiano, N. A. (2014). Purpose in life as a predictor of mortality across adulthood. *Psychological Science, 25,* 1482–1486. (12) doi: 10.1177/0956797614531799

Hinze, S. R., Slaten, D. G., Horton, W. S., Jenkins, R., & Rapp, D. N. (2014). Pilgrims sailing the Titanic: Plausibility effects on memory for misinformation. *Memory & Cognition, 42,* 305–324. (7) doi: 10.3758/s13421-013-0359-9

Hirst, W., & Echterhoff, G. (2012). Remembering in conversations: The social sharing and reshaping of memories. *Annual Review of Psychology, 63,* 55–79. (7) doi: 10.1146/annurev-psych-120710-100340

Hirvonen, J., van Erp, T. G. M., Huttunen, J., Aalto, S., Någren, K., Huttunen, M., Lonqvist, J., Kaprio, J., Cannon, T. D., & Hietala, J. (2006). Brain dopamine D_1 receptors in twins discordant for schizophrenia. *American Journal of Psychiatry, 163,* 1747–1753. (15) doi: 10.1176/appi.ajp.163.10.1747

Hobson, J. A. (2005). Sleep is of the brain, by the brain and for the brain. *Nature, 437,* 1254–1256. (10) doi: 10.1038/nature04283

Hobson, J. A., & McCarley, R. W. (1977). The brain as a dream state generator: An activation-synthesis hypothesis of the dream process. *American Journal of Psychiatry, 134,* 1335–1348. (10) doi: 10.1176/ajp.134.12.1335.

Hoebel, B. G., Rada, P. V., Mark, G. P., & Pothos, E. (1999). Neural systems for reinforcement and inhibition of behavior: Relevance to eating, addiction, and depression. In D. Kahneman, E. Diener, & N. Schwartz (Eds.), *Well-being: Foundations of hedonic psychology* (pp. 560–574). New York: Russell Sage Foundation. (11, 15)

Hoek, H. W., & van Hoeken, D. (2003). Review of the prevalence and incidence of eating disorders. *International Journal of Eating Disorders, 34,* 383–396. (11) doi: 10.1002/eat.10222

Hoffman, D. (2019). *The case against reality.* New York: W. W. Norton. (10)

Hofmann, S. G., Asmundson, G. J. G., & Beck, A. T. (2013). The science of cognitive therapy. *Behavior Therapy, 44,* 199–212. (15) doi: 10.1016/j.beth.2009.01.007

Hofmann, W., Gschwendner, T., & Schmitt, M. (2009). The road to the unconscious self not taken: Discrepancies between self- and observer-inferences about implicit dispositions from nonverbal behavioural cues. *European Journal of Personality, 23,* 343–366. (13) doi: 10.1002/per.722

Hofmann, W., Vohs, K. D., & Baumeister, R. F. (2012). What people desire, feel conflicted about, and try to resist in everyday life. *Psychological Science, 23,* 582–588. (11) doi: 10.1177/0956797612437426

Hofstee, W. K. B. (1994). Who should own the definition of personality? *European Journal of Personality, 8,* 149–162. (14) doi: 10.1002/per.2410080302

Hollon, S. D., DeRubeis, R. J., Fawcett, J., Amsterdam, J. D., Shelton, R. C., Zajecka, J., Young, P. R., & Gallop, R. (2014). Effect of cognitive therapy with antidepressant medications vs antidepressants alone on the rate of recovery in major depressive disorder. *JAMA Psychiatry, 71,* 1157–1164. (15) doi: 10.1001/jamapsychiatry.2014.1054

Hollon, S. D., Thase, M. E., & Markowitz, J. C. (2002). Treatment and prevention of depression. *Psychological Science in the Public Interest, 3,* 39–77. (15) https://www.psychologicalscience.org/journals/pspi/pdf/pspi31101.pdf

Holmberg, D., & Blair, K. L. (2009). Sexual desire, communication, satisfaction, and preferences of men and women in same-sex versus mixed-sex relationships. *Journal of Sex Research, 46,* 57–66. (13) doi: 10.1080/00224490802645294

Holmes, A. J., Lee, P. H., Hollinshead, M. O., Bakst, L., Roffman, J. L., Smoller, J. W., & Buckner R. L. (2012). Individual differences in amygdala-medial prefrontal anatomy link negative affect, impaired social functioning, and polygenic depression risk. *Journal of Neuroscience, 32,* 18087–18100. (12) doi: 10.1523/JNEUROSCI.2531-12.2012

Holmes, D. S. (1978). Projection as a defense mechanism. *Psychological Bulletin, 85,* 677–688. (14) doi: 10.1037/0033-2909.85.4.677

Holmes, D. S. (1990). The evidence for repression: An examination of sixty years of research. In J. L. Singer (Ed.), *Repression and dissociation* (pp. 85–102). New York: Wiley. (7, 14)

Holmes, T., & Rahe, R. (1967). The social readjustment rating scale. *Journal of Psychosomatic Research, 11,* 213–218. (12) doi: 10.1016/0022-3999(67)90010-4

Hong, R. Y., & Cheung, M. W.-L. (2015). The structure of cognitive vulnerabilities to depression and anxiety: Evidence for a common core etiologic process based on a meta-analytic review. *Clinical Psychological Science, 3,* 892–912. (15) doi: 10.1177/2167702614553789

Hong, Y., Morris, M. W., Chiu, C., & Benet-Martinez, V. (2000). Multicultural minds: A dynamic constructivist approach to culture and cognition. *American Psychologist, 55,* 709–720. (13) doi: 10.1037//0003-066X.55.7.709

Hoover, D. W., & Milich, R. (1994). Effects of sugar ingestion expectancies on mother-child interactions. *Journal of Abnormal Child Psychology, 22,* 501–515. (2) doi: 10.1007/BF02168088

Hopman, E. W. M., & MacDonald, M. C. (2018). Production practice during language learning improves comprehension. *Psychological Science, 29,* 961–971. (7) doi: 10.1177/0956797618754486

Horcajo, J., Rubio, V. J., Aguado, D., Hernandez, J. M., & Marquez, M. O. (2014). Using the Implicit Association Test to assess risk propensity self-concept: Analysis of its predictive validity on a risk-taking behaviour in a natural setting. *European Journal of Personality, 28,* 459–471. (14) doi: 10.1002/per.1925

Horikawa, T., Tamaki, M., Miyawaki, Y., & Kamitani, Y. (2013). Neural decoding of visual imagery during sleep. *Science, 340,* 639–642. (3) doi: 10.1126/science.1234330

Horn, J. L. (1968). Organization of abilities and the development of intelligence. *Psychological Review, 75,* 242–259. (9) doi: 10.1037/h0025662

Horne, J. A., Brass, C. G., & Pettitt, A. N. (1980). Circadian performance differences between morning and evening "types." *Ergonomics, 23,* 29–36. (10) doi: 10.1080/00140138008924715

Hornstein, E. A., Fanselow, M. S., & Eisenberger, N. I. (2016). Investigating social-support figures as prepared safety stimuli. *Psychological Science, 27,* 1051–1060. (15) doi: 10.1177/0956797616646580

Hortensius, R., & de Gelder, B. (2018). From empathy to apathy: The bystander effect revisited. *Current Directions in Psychological Science, 27,* 249–256. (13) doi: 10.1177/0963721417749653

Hotta, E. (2013). *Japan 1941: Countdown to infamy.* New York: Knopf. (13)

Houben, K., Wiers, R. W., & Jansen, A. (2011). Getting a grip on drinking behavior: Training working memory to reduce alcohol abuse. *Psychological Science, 22,* 968–975. (7) doi: 10.1177/0956797611412392

House, B. R., Silk, J. B., Henrich, J., Barrett, H. C., Scelza, B. A., Boyette, A. H., Hewlett, B. S., McElreath, R., & Laurence, S. (2013). Ontogeny of prosocial behavior across diverse societies. *Proceedings of the National Academy of Sciences (U.S.A.), 110,* 14586–14591. (13) doi: 10.1073/pnas.1221217110

Howard, D. M., Adams, M. J., Clarke, T.-K., Hafferty, J. D., Gibson, J., Shirali, M., Coleman, J. R. I., Hagenaars, S. P., Ward, J., Wigmore, E. M., Alloza, C., Shen, X., Barbu, M. C., Xu, E. Y., Whalley, H. C., Marioni, R. E., Porteous, D. J., Davies, G., Deary, I. J., ... McIntosh, A. M. (2019). Genome-wide meta-analysis of depression identifies 102 independent variants and highlights the importance of the prefrontal brain regions. *Nature Neuroscience, 22,* 343–352. (15) doi: 10.1038/s41593-018-0326-7

Howard, K. I., Kopta, S. M., Krause, M. S., & Orlinsky, D. E. (1986). The dose-effect relationship in psychotherapy. *American Psychologist, 41,* 159–164. (15) doi: 10.1037/0003-066X.41.2.159

Howard, R. W. (1999). Preliminary real-world evidence that average human intelligence really is rising. *Intelligence, 27,* 235–250. (9) doi: 10.1016/S0160-2896(99)00018-5

Howe, M. L., & Courage, M. L. (1993). On resolving the enigma of infantile amnesia. *Psychological*

Bulletin, 113, 305–326. (7) doi: 10.1037/0033-2909.113.2.305

Howes, O. D., Montgomery, A. J., Asselin, M.-C., Murray, R. M., Valli, I., Tabraham, P., Bramon-Bosch, E., Valmaggia, L., Johns, L., Broome, M., McGuire, P. K., & Grasby, P. M. (2009). Elevated striatal dopamine function linked to prodromal signs of schizophrenia. *Archives of General Psychiatry, 66*, 13–20. (15) doi: 10.1001/archgenpsychiatry.2008.514

Hrdy, S. B. (2000). The optimal number of fathers. *Annals of the New York Academy of Sciences, 907*, 75–96. (3) doi: 10.1111/j.1749-6632.2000.tb06617.x

Hróbjartsson, A., & Gøtzsche, P. C. (2001). Is the placebo powerless? *New England Journal of Medicine, 344*, 1594–1602. (4) doi: 10.1056/NEJM200105243442106

Hu, P., Stylos-Allan, M., & Walker, M. P. (2006). Sleep facilitates consolidation of emotional declarative memory. *Psychological Science, 17*, 891–898. (10) doi: 10.1111/j.1467-9280.2006.01799.x

Hu, X. Q., Rosenfeld, J. P., & Bodenhausen, G. V. (2012). Combating automatic autobiographical associations: The effect of instruction and training in strategically concealing information in the autobiographical Implicit Association Test. *Psychological Science, 23*, 1079–1085. (13) doi: 10.1177/0956797612443834

Huang, B. H. (2014). The effects of age on second language grammar and speech production. *Journal of Psycholinguistic Research, 43*, 397–420. (8) doi: 10.1007/s10936-013-9261-7

Huang, Y., Wang, Y., Wang, H., Liu, Z. R., Yu, X., Yan, J., Yu, Y. Q., Kou, C. G., Xu, X. F., & Wu, Y. (2019). Prevalence of mental disorders in China: A cross-sectional epidemiological study. *Lancet Psychiatry, 6*, E11. (15) doi: 10.1016/S2215-0366(19)30074-4

Hubel, D. H., & Wiesel, T. N. (1968). Receptive fields and functional architecture of monkey striate cortex. *Journal of Physiology* (London), *195*, 215–243. (4) doi: 10.1113/jphysiol.1968.sp008455

Huber, R., Ghilardi, M. F., Massimini, M., & Tononi, G. (2004). Local sleep and learning. *Nature, 430*, 78–81. (10) doi: 10.1038/nature02663

Hudson, J. I., Hiripi, E., Pope, H. G., Jr., & Kessler, R. C. (2007). The prevalence and correlates of eating disorders in the National Comorbidity Survey Replication. *Biological Psychiatry, 61*, 348–358. (11) doi: 10.1016/j.biopsych.2006.03.040

Hudson, J. I., Mangweth, B., Pope, H. G., Jr., De Col, C., Hausmann, A., Gutweniger, S., Laird, N. M., Biebl, W., & Tsuang, M. T. (2003). Family study of affective spectrum disorder. *Archives of General Psychiatry, 60*, 170–177. (15) doi: 10.1001/archpsyc.60.2.170

Hudson, W. (1960). Pictorial depth perception in subcultural groups in Africa. *Journal of Social Psychology, 52*, 183–208. (4) doi: 10.1080/00224545.1960.9922077

Huff, D. (1954). *How to lie with statistics.* New York: W. W. Norton. (2)

Hughes, J., Smith, T. W., Kosterlitz, H. W., Fothergill, L. A., Morgan, B. A., & Morris, H. R. (1975). Identification of two related pentapeptides from the brain with potent opiate antagonist activity. *Nature, 258*, 577–579. (3) doi: 10.1038/258577a0

Hugoson, A., Ljungquist, B., & Breivik, T. (2002). The relationship of some negative events and psychological factors to periodontal disease

in an adult Swedish population 50 to 80 years of age. *Journal of Clinical Periodontology, 29*, 247–253. (12) doi: 10.1034/j.1600-051x.2002.290311.x

Hui, C. L. M., Honer, W. G., Lee, E. H. M., Chang, W. C., Chan, S. K. W, Chen, E. S.M., Pang, E. P. F., Lui, S. S. Y., Chung, D. W. S., Yeung, W. S., Ng, R. M. K., Lo, W. T. L., Jones, P. B., Shann, P., & Chen, E. Y. H. (2019). Predicting first-episode psychosis patients who will never relapse over 10 years. *Psychological Medicine, 49*, 2206–2214. (15) doi: 10.1017/S0033291718003070

Hull, C. L. (1932). The goal gradient hypothesis and maze learning. *Psychological Review, 39*, 25–43. (1) doi: 10.1037/h0072640

Hull, C. L. (1943). *Principles of behavior: An introduction to behavior theory.* New York: D. Appleton. (11)

Hull, R., & Vaid, J. (2007). Bilingual language lateralization: A meta-analytic tale of two hemispheres. *Neuropsychologia, 45*, 1987–2008. (8) doi: 10.1016/j.neuropsychologia.2007.03.002

Humphreys, K. L., Eng, T., & Lee, S. S. (2013). Stimulant medication and substance use outcome: A meta-analysis. *JAMA Psychiatry, 70*, 740–749. (3) doi: 10.1001/jamapsychiatry.2013.1273

Hunt, L. L., Eastwick, P. W., & Finkel, E. J. (2015). Leveling the playing field: Longer acquaintance predicts reduced assortative mating on attractiveness. *Psychological Science, 26*, 1046–1053. (13) doi: 10.1177/0956797615579273

Hunter, J. E. (1997). Needed: A ban on the significance test. *Psychological Science, 8*, 3–7. (2) doi: 10.1111/j.1467-9280.1997.tb00534.x

Hur, Y.-M., Bouchard, T. J., Jr., & Eckert, E. (1998). Genetic and environmental influences on self-reported diet: A reared-apart twin study. *Physiology and Behavior, 64*, 629–636. (5) doi: 10.1016/S0031-9384(98)00101-2

Hur, Y.-M., Bouchard, T. J., Jr., & Lykken, D. T. (1998). Genetic and environmental influence on morningness–eveningness. *Personality and Individual Differences, 25*, 917–925. (5) doi: 10.1016/S0191-8869(98)00089-0

Hurd, Y. L., Spriggs, S., Alishayev, J., Winkel, G., Gurgov, K., Kudrich, C., Oprescu, A. M., & Salsitz, E. (2019). Cannabidiol for the reduction of cue-induced craving and anxiety in drug-abstinent individuals with heroin use disorder: A double-blind randomized placebo-controlled trial. *American Journal of Psychiatry, 176*, 911–922. (15) doi: 10.1176/appi.ajp.2019.18101191

Hyde, J. S. (2005). The gender similarities hypothesis. *American Psychologist, 60*, 581–592. (5) doi: 10.1037/0003-066X.60.6.581

Hyde, K. L., Lerch, J., Norton, A., Forgeard, M., Winner, E., Evans, A. C., & Schlaug, G. (2009). Musical training shapes structural brain development. *Journal of Neuroscience, 29*, 3019–3025. (3) doi: 10.1523/JNEUROSCI.5118-08.2009

Hyland, M. E., Alkhalaf, A. M., & Whalley, B. (2013). Beating and insulting children as a risk for adult cancer, cardiac disease and asthma. *Journal of Behavioral Medicine, 36*, 632–640. (6) doi: 10.1007/s10865-012-9457-6

Iacono, W. G., & Patrick, C. J. (1999). Polygraph ("lie detector") testing: The state of the art. In A. K. Hess & I. B. Weiner (Eds.), *The handbook of forensic psychology* (pp. 440–473). New York: Wiley. (12)

Iggo, A., & Andres, K. H. (1982). Morphology of cutaneous receptors. *Annual Review of Neuroscience, 5*, 1–31. (4) doi: 10.1146/annurev.ne.05.030182.000245

Ikeda, K., Koga, A., & Minami, S. (2006). Evaluation of a cure process during alarm treatment for nocturnal enuresis. *Journal of Clinical Psychology, 62*, 1245–1257. (15) doi: 10.1002/jclp.20301

Ikonomidou, C., Bittigau, P., Ishimaru, M. J., Wozniak, D. F., Koch, C., Genz, K., Price, M. T., Stefovska, V., Horster, F., Tenkova, T., Dikranian, K. & Olney, J. W. (2000). Ethanol-induced apoptotic neurodegeneration and fetal alcohol syndrome. *Science, 287*, 1056–1060. (5) doi: 10.1126/science.287.5455.1056

Ilies, R., & Judge, T. A. (2003). On the heritability of job satisfaction: The mediating role of personality. *Journal of Applied Psychology, 88*, 750–759. (11) doi: 10.1037/0021-9010.88.4.750

Ilieva, I., Boland, J., & Farah, M. J. (2013). Objective and subjective cognitive enhancing effects of mixed amphetamine salts in healthy people. *Neuropharmacology, 64*, 496–505. (8) doi: 10.1016/j.neuropharm.2012.07.021

Imahori, T. T., & Cupach, W. R. (1994). A cross-cultural comparison of the interpretation and management of face: U.S. American and Japanese responses to embarrassing predicaments. *International Journal of Intercultural Relations, 18*, 193–219. (12) doi: 10.1016/0147-1767(94)90028-0

Imel, Z. E., Malterer, M. B., McKay, K. M., & Wampold, B. E. (2008). A meta-analysis of psychotherapy and medication in unipolar depression and dysthymia. *Journal of Affective Disorders, 110*, 197–206. (15) doi: 10.1016/j.jad.2008.03.018

Imhoff, M. C., & Baker-Ward, L. (1999). Preschoolers' suggestibility: Effects of developmentally appropriate language and interviewer supportiveness. *Journal of Applied Developmental Psychology, 20*, 407–429. (7) doi: 10.1016/S0193-3973(99)00022-2

Inglehart, R., Foa, R., Peterson, C., & Welzel, C. (2008). Development, freedom, and rising happiness. *Perspectives on Psychological Science, 3*, 264–285. (12) doi: 10.1111/j.1745-6924.2008.00078.x

Inouye, S. T., & Kawamura, H. (1979). Persistence of circadian rhythmicity in a mammalian hypothalamic "island" containing the suprachiasmatic nucleus. *Proceedings of the National Academy of Sciences, USA, 76*, 5962–5966. (10) doi: 10.1073/pnas.76.11.5962

International Schizophrenia Consortium. (2008). Rare chromosomal deletions and duplications increase risk of schizophrenia. *Nature, 455*, 237–241. (15) doi: 10.1038/nature07239

Inzlicht, M., & Schmeichel, B. J. (2012). What is ego depletion? Toward a mechanistic revision of the resource model of self-control. *Perspectives in Psychological Science, 7*, 450–463. (11) doi: 10.1177/1745691612454134

Iossifov, I., O'Roak, B. J., Sanders, S. J., Ronemus, M., Krumm, N., Levy, D., Stessman, H. A., Witherspoon, K. T., Vives, L., Patterson, K. E., Smith, J. D., Paeper, B., Nickerson, D. A., Dea, J., Dong, S., Gonzalez, L. E., Mandell, J. D., Mane, S. M., Murtha, M. T., ...Wigler, M. (2014). The contribution of *de novo* coding mutations to autism spectrum disorder. *Nature, 515*, 216–221. (15) doi: 10.1038/nature13908

Irwing, P. (2012). Sex differences in *g*: An analysis of the U.S. standardization sample of the

WAIS-III. *Personality and Individual Differences, 53*, 126–131. (9) doi: 10.1016/j.paid.2011.05.001

Isaacowitz, D. M., Toner, K., Goren, D., & Wilson, H. R. (2008). Looking while unhappy. *Psychological Science, 19*, 848–853. (12) doi: 10.1111/j.1467-9280.2008.02167.x

Ispas, D., Iliescu, D., Ilie, A., & Johnson, R. E. (2014). Exploring the cross-cultural generalizability of the five-factor model of personality: The Romanian NEO PI-R. *Journal of Cross-Cultural Psychology, 45*, 1074–1088. (14) doi: 10.1177/0022022114534769

Iverson, J. M., & Goldin-Meadow, S. (2005). Gesture paves the way for language development. *Psychological Science, 16*, 367–371. (8) doi: 10.1111/j.0956-7976.2005.01542.x

Ivry, R. B., & Diener, H. C. (1991). Impaired velocity perception in patients with lesions of the cerebellum. *Journal of Cognitive Neuroscience, 3*, 355–366. (3) doi: 10.1162/jocn.1991.3.4.355

Iyengar, S. S., & Lepper, M. R. (2000). When choice is demotivating. *Journal of Personality and Social Psychology, 79*, 995–1006. (8) doi: 10.1037//0022-3514.79.6.995

Iyengar, S. S., Wells, R. E., & Schwartz, B. (2006). Doing better but feeling worse. *Psychological Science, 17*, 143–150. (8) doi: 10.1111/j.1467-9280.2006.01677.x

Izazola-Licea, J. A., Gortmaker, S. L., Tolbert, K., De Gruttola, V., & Mann, J. (2000). Prevalence of same-gender sexual behavior and HIV in a probability household survey of Mexican men. *Journal of Sex Research, 37*, 37–43. (11) doi: 10.1080/00224490009552018

Jackson, D. C., Malmstadt, J. R., Larson, C. L., & Davidson, R. J. (2000). Suppression and enhancement of emotional responses to unpleasant pictures. *Psychophysiology, 37*, 515–522. (12) doi: 10.1111/1469-8986.3740515

Jacobs, B. L. (1987). How hallucinogenic drugs work. *American Scientist, 75*, 386–392. (3)

Jacobs, J., Weidemann, C. T., Miller, J. F., Solway, A., Burke, J. F., Wei, X.-X., Suthana, N., Sperling, M. R., Sharan, A. D., Fried, I., & Kahana, M. J. (2013). Direct recordings of grid-like neuronal activity in human spatial navigation. *Nature Neuroscience, 16*, 1188–1190. (7) doi: 10.1038/nn.3466

Jacobs, J. R., & Bovasso, G. B. (2009). Re-examining the long-term effects of experiencing parental death in childhood on adult psychopathology. *Journal of Nervous and Mental Disease, 197*, 24–27. (5) doi: 10.1097/NMD.0b013e3181927723

Jacobs, K. M., Mark, G. P., & Scott, T. R. (1988). Taste responses in the nucleus tractus solitarius of sodium-deprived rats. *Journal of Physiology, 406*, 393–410. (1) doi: 10.1113/jphysiol.1988.sp017387

Jacobson, N. C., & Newman, M. G. (2017). Anxiety and depression as bidirectional risk factors for one another: A meta-analysis of longitudinal studies. *Psychological Bulletin, 143*, 1155–1200. (15) doi: 10.1037/bul0000111

Jacobson, N. S., Dobson, K. S., Truax, P. A., Addis, M. E., Koerner, K., Gollan, J. K., Gortner, E., & Prince, S. E. (1996). A component analysis of cognitive-behavior therapy for depression. *Journal of Consulting and Clinical Psychology, 64*, 295–304. (15) doi: 10.1037/0022-006X.64.2.295

Jaeggi, S. M., Buschkuehl, M., Shah, P., & Jonides, J. (2014). The role of individual differences in cognitive training and transfer. *Memory*

& Cognition, 42, 464–480. (8) doi: 10.3758/s13421-013-0364-z

Jakubowski, K., Müllensiefen, D., & Stewart, L. (2017). A developmental study of latent absolute pitch memory. *Quarterly Journal of Experimental Psychology, 70*, 434–443. (4) doi: 10.1080/17470218.2015.1131726

James, E. L., Bonsall, M. B., Hoppitt, L., Tunbridge, E. M., Geddes, J. R., Milton, A. L., & Holmes, E. A. (2015). Computer game play reduces intrusive memories of experimental trauma via reconsolidation-update mechanisms. *Psychological Science, 26*, 1201–1215. (12) doi: 10.1177/0956797615583071

James, W. (1890). *The principles of psychology*. New York: Henry Holt. (1)

James, W. (1894). The physical basis of emotion. *Psychological Review, 1*, 516–529. (12) doi: 10.1037/0033-295X.101.2.205

James, W. (1961). *Psychology: The briefer course*. New York: Harper. (Original work published 1892) (10)

Janis, I. L. (1972). *Victims of groupthink*. Boston: Houghton Mifflin. (13)

Janis, I. L. (1985). Sources of error in strategic decision making. In J. M. Pennings & associates (Eds.), *Organizational strategy and change* (pp. 157–197). San Francisco: Jossey-Bass. (13)

Jaremko, M. E. (1983). Stress inoculation training for social anxiety, with emphasis on dating anxiety. In D. Meichenbaum & M. E. Jaremko (Eds.), *Stress reduction and prevention* (pp. 419–450). New York: Plenum Press. (12)

Jebb, A. T., Morrison, M., Tay, L., & Diener, E. (2020). Subjective well-being around the world: Trends and predictors across the life span. *Psychological Science, 31*, 293–305. (12) doi: 10.1177/0956797619898826

Jebb, A. T., Tay, L., Diener, E., & Oishi, S. (2018). Happiness, income satiation and turning points around the world. *Nature Human Behaviour, 2*, 33–38. (12) doi: 10.1038/s41562-017-0277-0

Jenkins, R., Dowsett, A. J., & Burton, A. M. (2018). How many faces do people know? *Proceedings of the Royal Society B, 285*, 20181319. (3) doi: 10.1098/rspb.2018.1319

Jensen, J. D., Bernat, J. K., Wilson, K. M., & Goonewardene, J. (2011). The delay hypothesis: The manifestation of media effects over time. *Human Communication Research, 37*, 509–528. (13) doi: 10.1111/j.1468-2958.2011.01415.x

Jensen, M. P., & Patterson, D. R. (2014). Hypnotic approaches for chronic pain management. *American Psychologist, 69*, 167–177. (10) doi: 10.1037/a0035644

Jensen, M. P., & Turk, D. C. (2014). Contributions of psychology to the understanding and treatment of people with chronic pain. *American Psychologist, 69*, 105–118. (6) doi: 10.1037/a0035641

Jeong, J. H., Lee, D. K., Liu, S.-M., Chua, S. C. Jr., Schwartz, G. J., & Jo, Y.-H. (2018). Activation of temperature-sensitive TRPV1-like receptors in ARC POMC neurons reduces food intake. *PLoS Biology, 16*, e2004399. (11) doi: 10.1371/journal.pbio.2004399

Ji, L-J., Nisbett, R. E., & Su, Y. (2001). Culture, change, and prediction. *Psychological Science, 12*, 450–456. (13) doi: 10.1111/1467-9280.00384

Jiang, Y., Costello, P., & He, S. (2007). Processing of invisible stimuli. *Psychological Science, 18*, 349–355. (10) doi: 10.1111/j.1467-9280.2007.01902.x

Joel, D., Berman, Z., Tavor, I., Wexler, N., Gaber, O., Stein, Y., Shefi, N., Pool, J., Urchs, S., Margulies, D. S., Liem, F., Hanggi, J., Jancke, L., & Assaf, Y. (2015). Sex beyond the genitalia: The human brain mosaic. *Proceedings of the National Academy of Sciences (U.S.A.), 112*, 15468–15473. (5) doi: 10.1073/pnas.1509654112

Johansson, P., Hall, L., Sikström, S., & Olsson, A. (2005). Failure to detect mismatches between intention and outcome in a simple decision task. *Science, 310*, 116–119. (8) doi: 10.1126/science.1111709

John, L. K., Donnelly, G. E., & Roberto, C. A. (2017). Psychologically informed implementations of sugary-drink portion limits. *Psychological Science, 28*, 620–629. (11) doi: 10.1177/0956797617692041

Johnson, D. D. P., & Fowler, J. H. (2011). The evolution of overconfidence. *Nature, 477*, 317–320. (8) doi: 10.1038/nature10384

Johnson, J. G., Cohen, P., Brown, J., Smailes, E. M., & Bernstein, D. P. (1999). Childhood maltreatment increases risk for personality disorders during early adulthood. *Archives of General Psychiatry, 56*, 600–606. (15) doi: 10.1001/archpsyc.56.7.600

Johnson, K. R., & Johnson, S. L. (2014). Cross-national prevalence and cultural correlates of bipolar I disorder. *Social Psychiatry and Psychiatric Epidemiology, 49*, 1111–1117. (15) doi: 10.1007/s00127-013-0797-5

Johnson, M. K., Hashtroudi, S., & Lindsay, D. S. (1993). Source monitoring. *Psychological Bulletin, 144*, 3–28. (7) doi: 10.1037/0033-2909.114.1.3

Johnson, W., & Bouchard, T. J., Jr. (2005). The structure of human intelligence: It is verbal, perceptual, and image rotation (VPR), not fluid and crystallized. *Intelligence, 33*, 393–416. (9) doi: 10.1016/j.intell.2004.12.002

Johnson, W., & Bouchard, T. J., Jr. (2007). Sex differences in mental abilities: g masks the dimensions on which they lie. *Intelligence, 35*, 23–39. (9) doi: 10.1016/j.intell.2006.03.012

Johnson, W., Bouchard, T. J., Jr., Krueger, R. F., McGue, M., & Gottesman, I. I. (2004). Just one g: Consistent results from three test batteries. *Intelligence, 32*, 95–107. (9) doi: 10.1016/S0160-2896(03)00062-X

Johnson, W., Carothers, A., & Deary, I. J. (2008). Sex differences in variability in general intelligence. *Perspectives on Psychological Science, 3*, 518–531. (9) doi: 10.1111/j.1745-6924.2008.00096.x

Johnson, W., te Nijenhuis, J., & Bouchard, T. J., Jr. (2008). Still just 1 g: Consistent results from five test batteries. *Intelligence, 36*, 81–95. (9) doi: 10.1016/j.intell.2007.06.001

Johnsrude, I. S., Mackey, A., Hakyemez, H., Alexander, E., Trang, H. P., & Carlyon, R. P. (2013). Swinging at a cocktail party: Voice familiarity aids speech perception in the presence of a competing voice. *Psychological Science, 24*, 1995–2004. (4) doi: 10.1177/0956797613482467

Johnston, J. C., & McClelland, J. L. (1974). Perception of letters in words: Seek not and ye shall find. *Science, 184*, 1192–1194. (8) doi: 10.1126/science.184.4142.1192

Johnston, J. J. (1975). Sticking with first responses on multiple-choice exams: For better or for worse? *Teaching of Psychology, 2*, 178–179. (8)

Johnstone, H. (1994, August 8). Prince of memory says victory was on the cards. *The Times* (London), p. 2. (7)

..., T. E., Jr. (1999). The clustering and contagion of suicide. *Current Directions in Psychological Science, 8,* 89–92. (15) doi: 10.1111/1467-8721.00021

Joint Committee on Standards for Educational and Psychological Testing of the American Educational Research Association, the American Psychological Association, and the National Council on Measurement in Education. (1999). *Standards for educational and psychological testing.* Washington, DC: American Educational Research Association. (9)

Jones, C. M., Braithwaite, V. A., & Healy, S. D. (2003). The evolution of sex differences in spatial ability. *Behavioral Neuroscience, 117,* 403–411. (5) doi: 10.1037/0735-7044.117.3.403

Jones, C. R., Huang, A. L., Ptácek, L. J., & Fu, Y.-H. (2013). Genetic basis of human circadian rhythm disorders. *Experimental Neurology, 243,* 28–33. (10) doi: 10.1016/j.expneurol.2012.07.012

Jones, C. R., Vilensky, M. R., Vasey, M. W., & Fazio, R. H. (2013). Approach behavior can mitigate predominantly univalent negative attitudes: Evidence regarding insects and spiders. *Emotion, 13,* 989–996. (15) doi: 10.1037/a0033164

Jones, E. E., & Goethals, G. R. (1972). Order effects in impression formation: Attribution context and the nature of the entity. In E. Jones, D. Kanouse, H. Kelley, R. Nisbett, S. Valins, & B. Wiener (Eds.), *Attribution: Perceiving the causes of behavior* (pp. 27–46). Morristown, NJ: General Learning Press. (13)

Jones, E. E., & Harris, V. A. (1967). The attribution of attitudes. *Journal of Experimental Social Psychology, 13,* 1–24. (13) doi: 10.1016/0022-1031(67)90034-0

Jones, E. E., & Nisbett, R. E. (1972). The actor and the observer: Divergent perception of the causes of behavior. In E. Jones, D. Kanouse, H. Kelley, R. Nisbett, S. Valins, & B. Wiener (Eds.), *Attribution: Perceiving the causes of behavior* (pp. 79–94). Morristown, NJ: General Learning Press. (13)

Jones, S. S., Collins, K., & Hong, H. W. (1991). An audience effect on smile production in 10-month-old infants. *Psychological Science, 2,* 45–49. (12) doi: 10.1111/j.1467-9280.1991.tb00095.x

Jordan, J. J., Hoffman, M., Bloom, P., & Rand, D. G. (2016). Third-party punishment as a costly signal of trustworthiness. *Nature, 530,* 473–476. (13) doi: 10.1038/nature16981

Joseph, R. (2000). Fetal brain behavior and cognitive development. *Developmental Review, 20,* 81–98. (5) doi: 10.1006/drev.1999.0486

Jost, J. T. (2019). The IAT is dead, long live the IAT: Context-sensitive measures of implicit attitudes are indispensable to social and political psychology. *Current Directions in Psychological Science, 28,* 10–19. (13) doi: 10.1177/0963721418797309

Jouvet, M., Michel, F., & Courjon, J. (1959). Sur un stade d'activité électrique cérébrale rapide au cours du sommeil physiologique [On a state of rapid electrical cerebral activity during physiological sleep]. *Comptes Rendus des Séances de la Société de Biologie, 153,* 1024–1028. (10)

Judge, T. A., & Ilies, R. (2002). Relationship of personality to performance motivation: A meta-analytic review. *Journal of Applied Psychology, 87,* 797–807. (14) doi: 10.1037//0021-9010.87.4.797

Judge, T. A., & Larsen, R. J. (2001). Dispositional affect and job satisfaction: A review and theoretical extension. *Organizational Behavior and Human Decision Processes, 86,* 67–98. (11) doi: 10.1006/obhd.2001.2973

Judge, T. A., Thoresen, C. J., Bono, J. E., & Patton, G. K. (2001). The job satisfaction–job performance relationship: A qualitative and quantitative review. *Psychological Bulletin, 127,* 376–407. (11) doi: 10.1037//0033-2909.127.3.376

Jueptner, M., & Weiller, C. (1998). A review of differences between basal ganglia and cerebellar control of movements as revealed by functional imaging studies. *Brain, 121,* 1437–1449. (10) doi: 10.1093/brain/121.8.1437

Juhasz, B. J. (2005). Age-of-acquisition effects in word and picture identification. *Psychological Bulletin, 131,* 684–712. (7) doi: 10.1037/0033-2909.131.5.684

Jung, C. G. (1965). *Memories, dreams, reflections* (A. Jaffe, Ed.). New York: Random House. (14)

Junginger, J., & Frame, C. L. (1985). Self-report of the frequency and phenomenology of verbal hallucinations. *Journal of Nervous and Mental Disease, 173,* 149–155. (15) doi: 10.1097/00005053-198503000-00003

Jürgensen, M., Kleinemeier, E., Lux, A., Steensma, T. D., Cohen-Kettenis, P. H., Hiort, O., Thyen, U., Kohler, B., & DSD Network Working Group. (2013). Psychosexual development in adolescents and adults with disorders of sexual development—Results from the German Clinical Evaluation Study. *Journal of Sexual Medicine, 10,* 2703–2714. (11) doi: 10.1111/j.1743-6109.2012.02751.x

Juslin, P., Winman, A., & Olsson, H. (2000). Naive empiricism and dogmatism in confidence research: A critical examination of the hard–easy effect. *Psychological Review, 107,* 384–396. (8) doi: 10.1037//0033-295X.107.2.384

Just, M. A., & Carpenter, P. A. (1987). *The psychology of reading and language comprehension.* Boston: Allyn & Bacon. (8)

Kable, J. W., Caulfield, M. K., Falcone, M., McConnell, M., Bernardo, L., Parthasarathi, T., Cooper, N., Ashare, R., Audrain-McGovern, J., Hornik, R., Diefenbach, P., Lee, F. J., & Lerman, D. (2017). No effect of commercial cognitive training on brain activity, choice behavior, or cognitive performance. *Journal of Neuroscieence, 37,* 7390–7402. (8) doi: 10.1523/JNEUROSCI.2832-16.2017

Kadosh, R. C., Henik, A., Catena, A., Walsh, V., & Fuentes, L. J. (2009). Induced cross-modal synaesthetic experience without abnormal neuronal connections. *Psychological Science, 20,* 258–265. (10) doi: 10.1111/j.1467-9280.2009.02286.x

Kagan, J., Reznick, J. S., & Snidman, N. (1988). Biological bases of childhood shyness. *Science, 240,* 167–171. (5) doi: 10.1126/science.3353713

Kagan, J., & Snidman, N. (1991). Infant predictors of inhibited and uninhibited profiles. *Psychological Science, 2,* 40–44. (5) doi: 10.1111/j.1467-9280.1991.tb00094.x

Kahn, A. S., Jackson, J., Kully, C., Badger, K., & Halvorsen, J. (2003). Calling it rape: Differences in experiences of women who do or do not label their sexual assault as rape. *Psychology of Women Quarterly, 27,* 233–242. (13) doi: 10.1111/1471-6402.00103

Kahneman, D. (2011). *Thinking, fast and slow.* New York: Farrar, Straus and Giraux. (8)

Kahneman, D., & Klein, G. (2009). Conditions for intuitive expertise: A failure to disagree. *American Psychologist, 64,* 515–526. (8) doi: 10.1037/a0016755

Kahneman, D., & Tversky, A. (1973). On the psychology of prediction. *Psychological Review, 80,* 237–251. (8) doi: 10.1037/h0034747

Kajonius, P., & Mac Giolla, E. (2017). Personality traits across countries: Support for similarities rather than differences. *PLoS One, 12,* article e0179646. (14) doi: 10.1371/journal.pone.0179646

Kamin, L. J. (1969). Predictability, surprise, attention, and conditioning. In B. A. Campbell & R. M. Church (Eds.), *Punishment and aversive behavior* (pp. 279–296). New York: Appleton-Century-Crofts. (6)

Kanaya, T., Scullin, M. H., & Ceci, S. J. (2003). The Flynn effect and U.S. policies. *American Psychologist, 58,* 778–790. (9) doi: 10.1037/0003-066X.58.10.778

Kanazawa, S. (2004). General intelligence as a domain-specific adaptation. *Psychological Review, 111,* 512–523. (9) doi: 10.1037/0033-295X.111.2.512

Kanazawa, S. (2012). Intelligence, birth order, and family size. *Personality and Social Psychology Bulletin, 38,* 1157–1164. (5) doi: 10.1177/0146167212445911

Kane, M. J., Brown, L. H., McVay, J. C., Silvia, P. J., Myin-Germeys, I., & Kwapil, T. R. (2007). For whom the mind wanders, and when. *Psychological Science, 18,* 614–621. (7) doi: 10.1111/j.1467-9280.2007.01948.x

Kane, M. J., Gross, G. M., Chun, C. A., Smeekens, B. A., Meier, M. E., Silvia, P. J., & Kwapil, T. R. (2017). For whom the mind wanders, and when, varies across laboratory and daily-life settings. *Psychological Science, 28,* 1271–1289. (8) doi: 10.1177/0956797617706086

Kanizsa, G. (1979). *Organization in vision.* New York: Praeger. (4)

Kanner, A. D., Coyne, J. C., Schaefer, C., & Lazarus, R. S. (1981). Comparison of two modes of stress measurement: Daily hassles and uplifts versus major life events. *Journal of Behavioral Medicine, 4,* 1–39. (12) doi: 10.1007/bf00844845

Kanwisher, N., & Yovel, G. (2006). The fusiform face area: A cortical region specialized for the perception of faces. *Philosophical Transactions of the Royal Society, B, 361,* 2109–2128. (3) doi: 10.1098/rstb.2006.1934

Kardas, M., & O'Brien, E. (2018). Easier seen than done: Merely watching others perform can foster an illusion of skill acquisition. *Psychological Science, 29,* 521–536. (8) doi: 10.1177/0956797617740646

Karg, K., Burmeister, M., Shedden, K., & Sen, S. (2011). The serotonin transporter promoter variant (5-HTTLPR), stress, and depression meta-analysis revisited. *Archives of General Psychiatry, 68,* 444–454. (15) doi: 10.1001/archgenpsychiatry.2010.189

Karim, J., & Weisz, R. (2010). Cross-cultural research on the reliability and validity of the Mayer-Salovey-Caaruso Emotional Intelligence Test (MSCEIT). *Cross-Cultural Research, 44,* 374–404. (12) doi: 10.1177/1069397110377603

Karno, M., Golding, J. M., Sorenson, S. B., & Burnam, A. (1988). The epidemiology of obsessive-compulsive disorder in five U.S. communities. *Archives of General Psychiatry, 45,* 1094–1099. (15) doi: 10.1001/archpsyc.1988.01800360042006

Karpicke, J. D., & Blunt, J. R. (2011). Retrieval practice produces more learning than elaborative studying with concept mapping. *Science, 331*, 772–775. (7) doi: 10.1126/science.1199327

Karpicke, J. D., & Roediger, H. L. III (2008). The critical importance of retrieval for learning. *Science, 319*, 966–968. (7) doi: 10.1126/science.1152408

Kassin, S. M. (2017). The killing of Kitty Genovese: What else does this case tell us? *Perspectives on Psychological Science, 12*, 374–381. (13) doi: 10.1177/1745691616679465

Kassin, S. M., Redlich, A. D., Alceste, F., & Luke, T. J. (2018). On the general acceptance of confessions research: Opinions of the scientific community. *American Psychologist, 73*, 63–80. (13) doi: 10.1037/amp0000141

Karatsoreos, I. N., Thaler, J. P., Borgland, S. L., Champagne, F. A., Hurd, Y. L., & Hill, M. N. (2013). Food for thought: Hormonal, experiential, and neural influences on feeding and obesity. *Journal of Neuroscience, 33*, 17610–17616. (11) doi: 10.1523/JNEUROSCI.3452-13.2013

Kärkkäinen, U., Mustelin, L., Raevuori, A., Kaprio, J., & Keski-Rahkonen, A. (2018). Successful weight maintainers among young adults—A ten-year prospective population study. *Eating Behaviors, 29*, 91–98. (11) doi: 10.1016/j.eatbeh.2018.03.004

Karra, E., O'Daly, O. G., Choudhury, A. I., Yousseif, A., Millership, S., Neary, M. T., Scott, W. R., Chandarana, K., Manning, S., Hess, M. E., Iwakura, H., Akamizu, T., Millet, Q., Gelegen, C., Drew, M. E., Rahman, S., Emmanuel, J. J., Williams, S. C. R., Ruther, U. U., ... Batterham, R. L. (2013). A link between FTO, ghrelin, and impaired brain food-cue responsivity. *Journal of Clinical Investigation, 123*, 3539–3551. (11) doi: 10.1172/JCI44403

Kasser, T., & Sheldon, K. M. (2000). Of wealth and death. Materialism, mortality salience, and consumption behavior. *Psychological Science, 11*, 348–351. (5) doi: 10.1111/1467-9280.00269

Kassin, S. M., Bogart, D., & Kerner, J. (2012). Confessions that corrupt: Evidence from the DNA exoneration case files. *Psychological Science, 23*, 41–45. (13) doi: 10.1177/0956797611422918

Kassin, S. M., & Gudjonsson, G. H. (2004). The psychology of confessions: A review of the literature and issues. *Psychological Science in the Public Interest, 5*, 33–67. (13) doi: 10.1111/j.1529-1006.2004.00016.x

Katz, S., Lautenschlager, G. J., Blackburn, A. B., & Harris, F. H. (1990). Answering reading comprehension items without passages on the SAT. *Psychological Science, 1*, 122–127. (9) doi: 10.1111/j.1467-9280.1990.tb00080.x

Kaufman, L., & Rock, I. (1989). The moon illusion thirty years later. In M. Hershenson (Ed.), *The moon illusion* (pp. 193–234). Hillsdale, NJ: Erlbaum. (4)

Kawa, A. B., Valenta, A. C., Kennedy, R. C., & Robinson, T. E. (2019). Incentive and dopamine sensitization produced by intermittent but not long access cocaine self-adminsitration. *European Journal of Neuroscience, 50*, 2663–2682. (15) doi: 10.1111/ejn.14418

Kayyal, M. H., & Russell, J. A. (2013). Americans and Palestinians judge spontaneous facial expressions of emotion. *Emotion, 13*, 891–904. (12) doi: 10.1037/a0033244

Kazdin, A. E., & Rabbitt, S. M. (2013). Novel models for delivering mental health services and reducing the burdens of mental illness.

Clinical Psychological Science, 1, 170–191. (15) doi: 10.1177/2167702612463566

Kee, N., Teixeira, C. M., Wang, A. H., & Frankland, P. W. (2007). Preferential incorporation of adult-generated granule cells into spatial memory networks in the dentate gyrus. *Nature Neuroscience, 10*, 355–362. (3, 7) doi: 10.1038/nn1847

Keel, P. K., & Klump, K. L. (2003). Are eating disorders culture-bound syndromes? Implications for conceptualizing their etiology. *Psychological Bulletin, 129*, 747–769. (11) doi: 10.1037/0033-2909.129.5.747

Keele, S. W., & Ivry, R. B. (1990). Does the cerebellum provide a common computation for diverse tasks? *Annals of the New York Academy of Sciences, 608*, 179–207. (3) doi: 10.1111/j.1749-6632.1990.tb48897.x

Keiser, H. N., Sackett, P. R., Kuncel, N. R., & Brothen, T. (2016). Why women perform better in college than admission scores would predict: Exploring the roles of conscientiousness and course-taking patterns. *Journal of Applied Psychology, 101*, 569–581. (9) doi: 10.1037/apl0000069

Kell, H. J., Lubinski, D., & Benbow, C. P. (2013). Who rises to the top? Early indicators. *Psychological Science, 24*, 648–659. (9) doi: 10.1177/0956797612457784

Keller, M. C., Fredrickson, B. L., Ybarra, O., Cote, S., Johnson, K., Mikels, J., Conway, A., & Wager, T. (2005). A warm heart and a clear head. *Psychological Science, 16*, 724–731. (2) doi: 10.1111/j.1467-9280.2005.01602.x

Keller, M. C., Thiessen, D., & Young, R. K. (1996). Mate assortment in dating and married couples. *Personality and Individual Differences, 21*, 217–221. (13) doi: 10.1016/0191-8869(96)00066-9

Kelley, H. H. (1967). Attribution theory in social psychology. In D. Levine (Ed.), *Nebraska Symposium on Motivation* (Vol. 15, pp. 192–238). Lincoln: University of Nebraska Press. (13)

Keltner, D., & Buswell, B. N. (1997). Embarrassment: Its distinct form and appeasement functions. *Psychological Bulletin, 122*, 250–270. (12) doi: 10.1037/0033-2909.122.3.250

Keltner, D., & Shiota, M. N. (2003). New displays and new emotions: A commentary on Rozin and Cohen (2003). *Emotion, 3*, 86–91. (12) doi: 10.1037/1528-3542.3.1.86

Kemeny, M. E., Foltz, C., Cavanagh, J. F., Cullen, M., Giese-Davis, J., Jennings, P., Rosenberg, E. L., Gillath, O., Shaver, P. R., Wallace, B. A., & Ekman, P. (2012). Contemplative/emotion training reduces negative emotional behavior and promotes prosocial responses. *Emotion, 12*, 338–350. (12) doi: 10.1037/a0026118

Kendler, K. S., Gardner, C. O., & Prescott, C. A. (1999). Clinical characteristics of major depression that predict risk of depression in relatives. *Archives of General Psychiatry, 56*, 322–327. (15) doi: 10.1001/archpsyc.56.4.322

Kendler, K. S., Maes, H. H., Sundquist, K., Ohlsson, H., & Sundquist, J. (2014). Genetic and family and community environmental effects on drug abuse in adolescence: A Swedish national twin and sibling study. *American Journal of Psychiatry, 171*, 209–217. (15) doi: 10.1176/appi.ajp.2013.12101300

Kendler, K. S., Walters, E. E., Neale, M. C., Kessler, R. C., Heath, A. C., & Eaves, L. J. (1995). The structure of the genetic and environmental risk factors for six major psychiatric disorders in women. *Archives of General*

Psychiatry, 52, 374–383. (15) doi: 10.1001/archpsyc.1995.03950170048007.

Kenrick, D. T., Griskevicius, V., Neuberg, S. L., & Schaller, M. (2010). Renovating the pyramid of needs: Contemporary extensions built upon ancient foundation. *Perspectives on Psychological Science, 5*, 292–314. (11) doi: 10.1177/1745691610369469

Kepes, S., Bushman, B. J., & Anderson, C. A. (2017). Violent video game effects remain a social concern: Reply to Hilgard, Engelhardt, and Rouder (2017). *Psychological Bulletin, 143*, 775–782. (2) doi: 10.1037/bul0000112

Kessler, R. C., Berglund, P., Demler, O., Jin, R., & Walters, E. E. (2005). Lifetime prevalence and age-of-onset distributions of *DSM-IV* disorders in the National Comorbidity Survey Replication. *Archives of General Psychiatry, 62*, 593–602. (15) doi: 10.1001/archpsyc.62.6.593

Kessler, R. C., Chiu, W. T., Demler, O., & Walters, E. E. (2005). Prevalence, severity, and comorbidity of 12-month *DSM-IV* disorders in the National Comorbidity Survey Replication. *Archives of General Psychiatry, 62*, 617–627. (15, 16) doi: 10.1001/archpsyc.62.6.617

Kety, S. S., Wendler, P. H., Jacobsen, B., Ingraham, L. J., Jansson, L., Faber, B., & Kinney, D. K. (1994). Mental illness in the biological and adoptive relatives of schizophrenic adoptees. *Archives of General Psychiatry, 51*, 442–455. (15) doi: 10.1001/archpsyc.1994.03950060006001

Keyes, K. M., Pratt, C., Galea, S., McLaughlin, K. A., Koenen, K. C., & Shear, M. K. (2014). The burden of loss: Unexpected death of a loved one and psychiatric disorders across the life course in a national study. *American Journal of Psychiatry, 171*, 864–871. (15) doi: 10.1176/appi.ajp.2014.13081132

Keysar, B., & Henly, A. S. (2002). Speakers' overestimation of their effectiveness. *Psychological Science, 13*, 207–212. (5) doi: 10.1111/1467-9280.00439

Keysar, B., Barr, D. J., & Horton, W. S. (1998). The egocentric basis of language use: Insights from a processing approach. *Current Directions in Psychological Science, 7*, 46–50. (5) doi: 10.1111/1467-8721.ep13175613

Kiatpongsan, S., & Norton, M. I. (2014). How much (more) should CEOs make? A universal desire for more equal pay. *Perspectives on Psychological Science, 9*, 587–593. (12) doi: 10.1177/1745691614549773

Kim, H., Di Domenico, S. I., & Connelly, B. S. (2019). Self-other agreement in personality reports: A meta-analytic comparison of self-and informant-report means. *Psychological Science, 30*, 129–138. (14) doi: 10.1177/0956797618810000

Kim, H. S., Sherman, D. K., & Taylor, S. E. (2008). Culture and social support. *American Psychologist, 63*, 518–526. (12) doi: 10.1037/0003-066X

Kim, J., & Hatfield, E. (2004). Love types and subjective well-being: A cross-cultural study. *Social Behavior and Personality, 32*, 173–182. (13) doi: 10.2224/sbp.2004.32.2.173

Kim, S. (1989). *Inversions.* San Francisco: W. H. Freeman. (4)

Kimble, G. A. (1961). *Hilgard and Marquis' conditioning and learning* (2nd ed.). New York: Appleton-Century-Crofts. (6)

Kimble, G. A. (1967). Attitudinal factors in eyelid conditioning. In G. A. Kimble (Ed.), *Foundations of Conditioning and Learning* (pp. 642–659). New York: Appleton-Century-Crofts (1)

e, G. A. (1993). A modest proposal for a minor revolution in the language of psychology. *Psychological Science, 4*, 253–255. (6) doi: 10.1111/j.1467-9280.1993.tb00269.x

Kimble, G. A., & Garmezy, N. (1968). *Principles of general psychology* (3rd ed.). New York: Ronald Press. (14)

Kinsey, A. C., Pomeroy, W. B., & Martin, C. E. (1948). *Sexual behavior in the human male.* Philadelphia: Saunders. (11)

Kinsey, A. C., Pomeroy, W. B., Martin, C. E., & Gebhard, P. H. (1953). *Sexual behavior in the human female.* Philadelphia: Saunders. (11)

Kirsch, I., Deacon, B. J., Huedo-Medina, T. B., Scoboria, A., Moore, T. J., & Johnson, B. T. (2008). Initial severity and antidepressant benefits: A meta-analysis of data submitted to the Food and Drug Administration. *PLoS Medicine, 5*(2), e45. (15) doi: 10.1371/journal. pmed.0050045

Kirsch, I., & Braffman, W. (2001). Imaginative suggestibility and hypnotizability. *Current Directions in Psychological Science, 10*, 57–61. (10) doi: 10.1111/1467-8721.00115

Kirsch, I., & Lynn, S. J. (1998). Dissociation theories of hypnosis. *Psychological Bulletin, 123*, 100–115. (10) doi: 10.1037/0033-2909.123.1.100

Kitayama, S., Park, J., Boylan, J. M., Miyamoto, Y., Levine, C. S., Markus, H. R., Karasawa, M., Coe, C. L., Kawakami, N., Love, G. D., & Ryff, C. D. (2015). Expression of anger and ill health in two cultures: An examination of inflammation and cardiovascular risk. *Psychological Science, 26*, 211–220. (5) doi: 10.1177/0956797614561268

Kivisalu, T. M., Lewey, J. H., Shaffer, T. W., & Canfield, M. L. (2017). An investigation of interrater reliability for the Rorschach Performance Assessment System (R-PAS) in a nonpatient U.S. sample. *Journal of Personality Assessment, 99*, 558–560. (14) doi: 10.1080/00223891.2017.1325244

Klahr, A. M., & Burt, S. A. (2014). Elucidating the etiology of individual differences in parenting: A meta-analysis of behavioral genetic research. *Psychological Bulletin, 140*, 544–586. (5) doi: 10.1037/a0034205

Kleen, J. K., Sitomer, M. T., Killeen, P. R., & Conrad, C. D. (2006). Chronic stress impairs spatial memory and motivation for reward without disrupting motor ability and motivation to explore. *Behavioral Neuroscience, 120*, 842–851. (12) doi: 10.1037/0735-7044.120.4.842

Klein, R. A., Ratliff, K. A., Vianello, M., Adams, R. B. Jr., Bahnik, S., Bernstein, M. J., Bocian, K., Brandt, M. J., Brooks, B., Brumbaugh, C. C., Cemalcilar, Z., Chandler, J., Cheong, W., Davis, W. E., Devos, T., Eisner, M., Frankowska, N., Furrow, D., Galliani, E. M., … Nosek, B. A. (2014). Investigating variability in replicability: A "many labs" replication project. *Social Psychology, 45*, 142–152. (2) doi: 10.1027/1864-9335/a000178

Klein, D. F. (1993). False suffocation alarms, spontaneous panics, and related conditions. *Archives of General Psychiatry, 50*, 306–317. (15) doi: 10.1001/archpsyc.1993.01820160076009

Kleinmuntz, B., & Szucko, J. J. (1984). A field study of the fallibility of polygraphic lie detection. *Nature, 308*, 449–450. (12) doi: 10.1038/308449a0

Klejnstrupl, N. R., Buhl-Wiggers, J., Jones, S., & Rand, J. (2018). Early life malaria exposure and academic performance. *PLoS One,*

13, e0199542. (9) doi: 10.1371/journal. pone.0199542

Knoll, J. L., IV, & Resnick, P. J. (2008). Insanity defense evaluations: Toward a model for evidence-based practice. *Brief Treatment and Crisis Intervention, 8*, 92–110. (15) doi: 10.1093/brief-treatment/mhm024

Ko, C.-H., Liu, G.-C., Hsiao, S., Yen, J.-Y., Yang, M.-J., Lin, W. C., Yen, C. F., & Chen, C.-S. (2009). Brain activities associated with gaming urge of online gaming addiction. *Journal of Psychiatric Research, 43*, 739–747. (15) doi: 10.1016/j. jpsychires.2008.09.012

Kobayashi, F. (2011). Japanese high school students' television viewing and fast food consumption. *Nutrition & Food Science, 41*, 242–248. (2) doi: 10.1108/00346651111151375

Kobayashi, F., Schallert, D. L., & Ogren, H. A. (2003). Japanese and American folk vocabularies for emotion. *Journal of Social Psychology, 143*, 451–478. (12) doi: 10.1080/00224540309598456

Kocsis, R. N. (2004). Psychological profiling of serial arson offenses: An assessment of skills and accuracy. *Criminal Justice and Behavior, 31*, 341–361. (14) doi: 10.1177/0093854803262586

Kocsis, R. N., Irwin, H. J., Hayes, A. F., & Nunn, R. (2000). Expertise in psychological profiling: A comparative assessment. *Journal of Interpersonal Violence, 15*, 311–331. (14) doi: 10.1177/088626000015003006

Koenigs, M., Huey, E. D., Raymont, V., Cheon, B., Solomon, J., Wassermann, E.M., & Grafman, J. (2008). Focal brain damage protects against post-traumatic stress disorder in combat veterans. *Nature Neuroscience, 11*, 232–237. (12) doi: 10.1038/nn2032

Koepp, M. J., Gunn, R. N., Lawrence, A. D., Cunningham, V. J., Dagher, A., Jones, T., Brooks, D. J., Bench, C. J., & Grasby, P. M. (1998). Evidence for striatal dopamine release during a video game. *Nature, 393*, 266–268. (3, 15) https://www.nature.com/articles/30498

Kohlberg, L. (1969). Stage and sequence: The cognitive-developmental approach to socialization. In D. A. Goslin (Ed.), *Handbook of socialization theory and research* (pp. 347–480). Chicago, IL: Rand McNally. (13)

Kohlberg, L., & Hersh, R. H. (1977). Moral development: A review of the theory. *Theory into Practice, 16*, 53–59. (13) doi: 10.1080/00405847709542675

Kolesinska, Z., Ahmed, S. F., Niedziela, M., Bryce, J., Molinska-Glura, M., Rodie, M., Jiang, J. P., Sinnott, R. O., Hughes, I. A., Darendeliler, F., Hiort, O., van der Zwan, Y., Cools, M., Guran, T., Holterhus, P. M., Bertelloni, S., Lisa, L., Arlt, W., Krone, N., Ellaithi, N., … Weintrob, N. (2014). Changes over time in sex assignment for disorders of sex development. *Pediatrics, 134*, e710–715. (11) doi: 10.1542/peds.2014-1088

Kong, D. T. (2014). Mayer-Salovey-Caruso Emotional Intelligence Test (MSCEIT/MEIS) and overall, verbal, and nonverbal intelligence: Meta-analytic evidence and critical contingencies. *Personality and Individual Differences, 66* 171–175. (12) doi: 10.1016/j. paid.2014.03.028

Konkle, T., Brady, T. F., Alvarez, G. A., & Oliva, A. (2010). Scene memory is more detailed than you think: The role of categories in visual long-term memory. *Psychological Science, 21*, 1551–1556. (8) doi: 10.1177/0956797610385359

Kontula, O., & Haavio-Mannila, E. (2009). The impact of aging on human sexual activity and

sexual desire. *Journal of Sex Research, 46*, 46–56. (11) doi: 10.1080/00224490802624414

Koob, G. F., & LeMoal, M. (1997). Drug abuse: Hedonic homeostatic dysregulation. *Science, 278*, 52–58. (15) doi: 10.1126/science.278.5335.52

Kopala-Sibley, D. C., Olino, T., Durbin, E., Dyson, M. W., & Klein, D. N. (2018). The stability of temperament from early childhood to early adolescence: A multi-method, multi-informant examination. *European Journal of Personality, 32*, 128–145. (5) doi: 10.1002/per.2151

Koppenaal, R. J. (1963). Time changes in the strengths of A-B, A-C lists: Spontaneous recovery? *Journal of Verbal Learning and Verbal Behavior, 2*, 310–319. (7) doi: 10.1016/S0022-5371(63)80099-7

Koriat, A., Bjork, R. A., Sheffer, L., & Bar, S. K. (2004). Predicting one's own forgetting: The role of experience-based and theory-based processes. *Journal of Experimental Psychology: General, 133*, 643–656. (7) doi: 10.1037/0096-3445.133.4.643

Korman, M., Doyon, J., Doljansky, J., Carrier, J., Dagan, Y., & Karni, A. (2007). Daytime sleep condenses the time course of motor memory consolidation. *Nature Neuroscience, 10*, 1206–1213. (10) doi: 10.1038/nn1959

Kornell, N., & Bjork, R. A. (2008). Learning concepts and categories. *Psychological Science, 19*, 585–592. (7) doi: 10.1111/j.1467-9280.2008.02127.x

Kornell, N., Castel, A. D., Eich, T. S., & Bjork, R. A. (2010). Spacing as the friend of both memory and induction in young and older adults. *Psychology and Aging, 25*, 498–503. (7) doi: 10.1037/a0017807

Kornell, N., Hays, M. J., & Bjork, R. A. (2009). Unsuccessful retrieval attempts enhance subsequent learning. *Journal of Experimental Psychology: Learning, Memory, and Cognition, 35*, 989–998. (7) doi: 10.1037/a0015729

Kotapati, V. P., Khan, A. M., Dar, S., Begum, G., Bachu, R., Adnan, M., Zubair, A., & Ahmed, R. A. (2019). The effectiveness of selective serotonin reuptake inhibitors for treatment of obsessive compulsive disorder: A systematic review and meta-analysis. *Frontiers in Psychiatry, 10*, article 523. (15) doi: 10.3389/fpsyt.2019.00523

Koten, J. W. Jr., Wood, G., Hagoort, P., Goebel, R., Propping, P., Willmes, K., & Boomsma, D. I. (2009). Genetic contribution to variation in cognitive function: An fMRI study in twins. *Science, 323*, 1737–1740. (9) doi: 10.1126/science.1167371

Kotowicz, Z. (2007). The strange case of Phineas Gage. *History of the Human Sciences, 20*, 115–131. (12) doi: 10.1177/0952695106075178

Kouchaki, M., Dobson, K. S. H., Waytz, A., & Kteily, N. S. (2018). The link between self-dehumanization and immoral behavior. *Psychological Science, 29*, 1234–1246. (13) doi: 10.1177/0956797618760784

Kouider, S., & Dehaene, S. (2007). Levels of processing during non-conscious perception: A critical review of visual masking. *Philosophical Transactions of the Royal Society B, 362*, 857–875. (4) doi: 10.1098/rstb.2007.2093

Kouider, S., Stahlhut, C., Gelskov, S. V., Barbosa, L. S., Dutat, M., de Gardelle, V., Christophe, A., Dehaene, S., & Dehaene-Lambertz, G. (2013). A neural marker of perceptual consciousness in infants. *Science, 340*, 376–380. (10) doi: 10.1126/science.1232509

Kountouris, Y., & Remoundou, K. (2014). About time: Daylight Savings Time transition and individual well-being. *Economics Letters, 122,* 100–103. (10) doi: 10.1016/j.econlet.2013.10.032

Kovacs, K., & Conway, A. R. A. (2016). Process overlap theory: A unified account of the general theory of intelligence. *Psychological Inquiry, 27,* 151–177. (9) doi: 10.1080/1047840X.2016.1153946

Kovas, Y., Haworth, C. M. A., Dale, P. S., & Plomin, R. (2007). The genetic and environmental origins of learning abilities and disabilities in the early preschool years. *Monographs of the Society for Research in Child Development, 72,* 1–144. (9) doi: 10.1111/j.1540-5834.2007.00439.x

Kozel, N. J., & Adams, E. H. (1986). Epidemiology of drug abuse: An overview. *Science, 234,* 970–974. (3) doi: 10.1126/science.3490691

Kraemer, D. L., & Hastrup, J. L. (1988). Crying in adults: Self-control and autonomic correlates. *Journal of Social and Clinical Psychology, 6,* 53–68. (14) doi: 10.1521/jscp.1988.6.1.53

Krähenbühl, S., & Blades, M. (2006). The effect of question repetition within interviews on young children's eyewitness recall. *Journal of Experimental Child Psychology, 94,* 57–67. (7) doi: 10.1016/j.jecp.2005.12.002

Kramer, P., & Bressan, P. (2018). Our (mother's) mitochondria and our mind. *Perspectives on Psychological Science, 13,* 88–100. (15) doi: 10.1177/1745691617718356

Kramer, P. D. (2006). *Freud: Inventor of the modern mind.* New York: Harper Collins. (14)

Kraschnewski, J. L., Boan, J., Esposito, J., Sherwood, N. E., Lehman, E. B., Kephart, D. K., & Sciamanna, C. N. (2010). Long-term weight loss maintenance in the United States. *International Journal of Obesity, 34,* 1644–1654. (11) doi: 10.1038/ijo.2010.94

Kraushaar, J. M., & Novak, D. C. (2010). Examining the affects of student multitasking with laptops during the lecture. *Journal of Information Systems Education, 21,* 241–251. (7) http://jise.org/Volume21/n2/JISEv21n2p241.pdf

Kredlow, M. A, Eichenbaum, H., & Otto, M. W. (2018). Memory creation and modification: Enhancing the treatment of psychological disorders. *American Psychologist, 73,* 269–285. (12) doi: 10.1037/amp0000185

Kreiman, G., Fried, I., & Koch, C. (2002). Single-neuron correlates of subjective vision in the human medial temporal lobe. *Proceedings of the National Academy of Sciences (U.S.A.), 99,* 8378–8383. (10) doi: 10.1073/pnas.072194099

Kreiner, D. S., Altis, N. A., & Voss, C. W. (2003). A test of the effect of reverse speech on priming. *Journal of Psychology, 137,* 224–232. (4) doi: 10.1080/00223980309600610

Kreitzer, A. C., & Regehr, W. G. (2001). Retrograde inhibition of presynaptic calcium influx by endogenous cannabinoids at excitatory synapses onto Purkinje cells. *Neuron, 29,* 717–727. (3) doi: 10.1016/S0896-6273(01)00246-X

Kreskin. (1991). *Secrets of The Amazing Kreskin.* Buffalo, NY: Prometheus. (2)

Kretch, K. S., & Adolph, K. E. (2013). Cliff or step? Posture-specific learning at the edge of a drop-off. *Child Development, 84,* 226–240. (5) doi: 10.1111/j.1467-8624.2012.01842.x

Kripke, D. F., Garfinkel, L., Wingard, D. L., Klauber, M. R., & Marler, M. R. (2002). Mortality associated with sleep duration and insomnia. *Archives of General Psychiatry, 59,* 131–136. (2) doi: 10.1001/archpsyc.59.2.131

Kropff, E., Carmichael, J. E., Moser, M.-B., & Moser, E. I. (2015). Speed cells in the medial entorhinal cortex. *Nature, 523,* 419–424. (7) doi: 10.1038/nature14622

Kross, E., Berman, M. G., Mischel, W., Smith, E. E., & Wager, T. D. (2011). Social rejection shares somatosensory representations with physical pain. *Proceedings of the National Academy of Sciences, 108,* 6270–6275. (4) doi: 10.1073/pnas.1102693108

Krueger, C., & Garvan, C. (2014). Emergence and retention of learning in early fetal development. *Infant Behavior and Development, 37,* 162–173. (5) doi: 10.1016/j.infbeh.2013.12.007

Krueger, D. W. (1978). The differential diagnosis of proverb interpretation. In W. E. Fann, I. Karacan, A. D. Pokorny, & R. L. Williams (Eds.), *Phenomenology and treatment of schizophrenia* (pp. 193–201). New York: Spectrum. (15)

Krueger, J. M., Rector, D. M., Roy, S., Van Dongen, H. P. A., Belenky, G., & Panksepp, J. (2008). Sleep as a fundamental property of neuronal assemblies. *Nature Reviews Neuroscience, 9,* 910–919. (10) doi: 10.1038/nrn2521

Krueger, R. F., Markon, K. E., & Bouchard, T. J., Jr. (2003). The extended genotype: The heritability of personality accounts for the heritability of recalled family environments in twins reared apart. *Journal of Personality, 71,* 809–833. (5) doi: 10.1111/1467-6494.7105005

Kruger, J., Wirtz, D., & Miller, D. T. (2005). Counterfactual thinking and the first instinct fallacy. *Journal of Personality and Social Psychology, 88,* 725–735. (8) doi: 10.1037/0022-3514.88.5.725

Krugers, H. J., Hoogenraad, C. C., & Groc. L. (2010). Stress hormones and AMPA receptor trafficking in synaptic plasticity and memory. *Nature Reviews Neuroscience, 11,* 675–681. (12) doi: 10.1038/nrn2913

Krupa, D. J., Thompson, J. K., & Thompson, R. F. (1993). Localization of a memory trace in the mammalian brain. *Science, 260,* 989–991. (3) doi: 10.1126/science.8493536

Kübler-Ross, E. (1975). *Death: The final stage of growth.* Englewood Cliffs, NJ: Prentice Hall. (5)

Kuhlmann, S., Piel, M., & Wolf, O. T. (2005). Impaired memory retrieval after psychosocial stress in healthy young men. *Journal of Neuroscience, 25,* 2977–2982. (12) doi: 10.1523/JNEUROSCI.5139-04.2005

Kuhn, G., Pickering, A., & Cole, G. G. (2016). "Rare" emotive faces and attentional orienting. *Emotion, 16,* 1–5. (12) doi: 10.1037/emo0000050

Kumar, A., Killingsworth, M. A., & Gilovich, T. (2014). Waiting for merlot: Anticipatory consumption of experiential and material purchases. *Psychological Science, 25,* 1924–1931. (12) doi: 10.1177/0956797614546556

Kumkale, G. T., & Abarracín, D. (2004). The sleeper effect in persuasion: A meta-analytic review. *Psychological Bulletin, 130,* 143–172. (13) doi: 10.1037/0033-2909.130.1.143

Kunar, M. A., Carter, R., Cohen, M., & Horowitz, T. S. (2008). Telephone conversation impairs sustained visual attention via a central bottleneck. *Psychonomic Bulletin and Review, 15,* 1135–1140. (8) doi: 10.3758/PBR.15.6.1135

Kunar, M. A., Rich, A. N., & Wolfe, J. M. (2010). Spatial and temporal separation fails to counteract the effects of low prevalence in visual search. *Visual Cognition, 18,* 881–897. (4) doi: 10.1080/13506280903361988

Kuncel, N. R., & Hezlett, S. A. (2010). Fact and fiction in cognitive ability testing for admissions and hiring decisions. *Current Directions in Psychological Science, 19,* 339–345. (9) doi: 10.1177/0963721410389459

Kuo, S. S., & Pogue-Geile, M. F. (2019). Variation in fourteen brain structure volumes in schizophrenia: A comprehensive meta-analysis of 246 studies. *Neuroscience and Biobehavioral Reviews, 98,* 85–94. (15) doi: 10.1016/jneubiorev.2018.12.030

Kupfer, D. J., First, M. B., & Regier, D. A. (2002). *A research agenda for DSM–V.* Washington, DC: American Psychiatric Association. (15)

Küpper-Tetzel, C. E. (2014). Understanding the distributed practice effect: Strong effects on weak theoretical grounds. *Zeitschrift für Psychologie, 222,* 71–81. (7) doi: 10.1027/2151-2604/a000168

Kurdi, B., Seitchik, A. E., Axt, J. R., Carroll, T. J., Karapetyan, A., Kaushik, N., Tomezsko, D., Greenwald, A. G., & Banaji, M. R. (2019). Relationship between the Implicit Association Test and intergroup behavior: A meta-analysis. *American Psychologist, 74,* 569–586. (13) doi: 10.1037/amp0000364

Kurdziel, L., Duclos, K., & Spencer, R. M. C. (2013). Sleep spindles in midday naps enhance learning in preschool children. *Proceedings of the National Academy of Sciences (U.S.A.), 110,* 17267–17272. (10) doi: 10.1073/pnas.1306418110

Kurihara, K., & Kashiwayanagi, M. (1998). Introductory remarks on umami taste. *Annals of the New York Academy of Sciences, 855,* 393–397. (4) doi: 10.1111/j.1749-6632.1998.tb10597.x

Kvavilashvili, L., Mirani, J., Schlagman, S., Foley, K., & Kornbrot, D. E. (2009). Consistency of flashbulb memories of September 11 over long delays: Implications for consolidation and wrong time slice hypotheses. *Journal of Memory and Language, 61,* 556–572. (7) doi: 10.1016/j.jml.2009.07.004

Kyllonen, P. C., & Christal, R. E. (1990). Reasoning ability is (little more than) working-memory capacity?! *Intelligence, 14,* 389–433. (9) doi: 10.1016/S0160-2896(05)80012-1

La Roche, M., & Christopher, M. S. (2008). Culture and empirically supported treatments: On the road to a collision? *Culture and Psychology, 14,* 333–356. (15) doi: 10.1177/1354067X08092637

Laborda, M. A., & Miller, R. R. (2013). Preventing return of fear in an animal model of anxiety: Additive effects of massive extinction and extinction in multiple contexts. *Behavior Therapy, 44,* 249–261. (15) doi: 10.1016/j.beth.2012.11.001

Labroo, A. A., Lambotte, S., & Zhang, Y. (2009). The "name-ease" effect and its dual impact on importance judgments. *Psychological Science, 20,* 1516–1522. (8) doi: 10.1111/j.1467-9280.2009.02477.x

Lackner, J. R. (1993). Orientation and movement in unusual force environments. *Psychological Science, 4,* 134–142. (4) doi: 10.1111/j.1467-9280.1993.tb00477.x

Laeng, B., Svartdal, F., & Oelmann, H. (2004). Does color synesthesia pose a paradox for early-selection theories of attention? *Psychological Science, 15,* 277–281. (4) doi: 10.1111/j.0956-7976.2004.00666.x

Laffaye, C., McKellar, J. D., Ilgen, M. A., & Moos, R. H. (2008). Predictors of 4-year outcome of community residential treatment for patients substance use disorders. *Addiction*, , 671–680. (15) doi: 10.1111/j.1360-0443.2008.02147.x

Lages, M., Boyle, S. C., & Jenkins, R. (2017). Illusory increases in font size improve letter recognition. *Psychological Science, 28*, 1180–1188. (4) doi: 10.1177/0956797617705391

Lahey, B. B. (2009). Public health significance of neuroticism. *American Psychologist, 64*, 241–256. (14) doi: 10.1037/a0015309

Lai, C. K., Skinner, A. L., Cooley, E., Murrar, S., Brauer, M., Devos, T., Calanchini, J., Xiao, Y. J., Pedram, C., Marshburn, C. K., Simon, S., Blanchar, J. C., Joy-Gaba, J. A., Conway, J., Redford, L, Klein, R. A., Roussos, G., Schellhaas, F. M. H., Burns, M., ... Nosek, B. A. (2016). Reducing implicit racial preferences: II. Intervention effectiveness across time. *Journal of Experimental Psychology: General, 145*, 1001–1016. (13) doi: 10.1037/xge0000179

Lai, C. S. L., Fisher, S. E., Hurst, J. A., Vargha-Khadem, F., & Monaco, A. P. (2001). A forkhead-domain gene is mutated in a severe speech and language disorder. *Nature, 413*, 519–523. (8) doi: 10.1038/35097076

Laird, J. D., & Lacasse, K. (2014). Bodily influences on emotional feelings: Accumulating evidence and extensions of William James's theory of emotions. *Emotion Review, 6*, 27–34. (12) doi: 10.1177/1754073913494899

Lake, R. I. E., Eaves, L. J., Maes, H. H. M., Heath, A. C., & Martin, N. G. (2000). Further evidence against the environmental transmission of individual differences in neuroticism from a collaborative study of 45,850 twins and relatives on two continents. *Behavior Genetics, 30*, 223–233. (3, 5, 14) doi: 10.1023/A:1001918408984

Lakens, D., & Evers, E. R. K. (2014). Sailing from the seas of chaos into the corridor of stability: Practical recommendations to increase the informational value of studies. *Perspectives on Psychological Science, 9*, 278–292. (2) doi: 10.1177/1745691614528520

Lally, J., Olesya, A., Brendon, S., Cullinane, M., Murphy, K. C., Gaughran, F., & Murray, R. M. (2017). Remission and recovery from first-episode psychosis in adults: Systematic review and meta-analysis of long-term outcome studies. *British Journal of Psychiatry, 211*, 350–358. (15) doi: 10.1192/bjp.bp.117.201475

Lamb, M. E., Orbach, Y., Hershkowitz, I., Horowitz, D., & Abbott, C. B. (2007). Does the type of prompt affect the accuracy of information provided by alleged victims of abuse in forensic interviews? *Applied Cognitive Psychology, 21*, 1117–1130. (7) doi: 10.1002/acp.1318

Lambie, J. A., & Marcel, A. J. (2002). Consciousness and the varieties of emotion experience: A theoretical framework. *Psychological Review, 109*, 219–259. (10) doi: 10.1037//0033-295X.109.2.219

Lamm, H., & Myers, D. G. (1978). Group-induced polarization of attitudes and behavior. *Advances in Experimental Social Psychology, 11*, 145–195. (13) doi: 10.1016/S0065-2601(08)60007-6

Lamminmäki, A., Hines, M., Kuiri-Hänninen, T., Kilpeläinen, L., Dunkel, L., & Sankilampi, U. (2012). Testosterone measured in infancy predicts subsequent sex-typed behavior in boys and girls. *Hormones and Behavior, 61*, 611–616. (5) doi: 10.1016/j.yhbeh.2012.02.013

Land, E. H., Hubel, D. H., Livingstone, M. S., Perry, S. H., & Burns, M. M. (1983). Colour-generating interactions across the corpus callosum. *Nature, 303*, 616–618. (4) doi: 10.1038/303616a0

Land, E. H., & McCann, J. J. (1971). Lightness and retinex theory. *Journal of the Optical Society of America, 61*, 1–11. (4) doi: 10.1364/JOSA.61.000001

Lang, J. W. B., & Lang, J. (2010). Priming competence diminishes the link between cognitive test anxiety and test performance: Implications for the interpretation of test scores. *Psychological Science, 21*, 811–819. (9) doi: 10.1177/0956797610369492

Langberg, J. M., & Becker, S. P. (2012). Does long-term medication use improve the academic outcomes of youth with attention-deficit/hyperactivity disorder? *Clinical Child and Family Psychology Review, 15*, 215–233. (8) doi: 10.1007/s10567-012-0117-8

Langlois, J. H., & Roggman, L. A. (1990). Attractive faces are only average. *Psychological Science, 1*, 115–121. (13) doi: 10.1111/j.1467-9280.1990.tb00079.x

Langlois, J. H., Roggman, L. A., & Musselman, L. (1994). What is average and what is not average about average faces? *Psychological Science, 5*, 214–220. (13) doi: 10.1111/j.1467-9280.1994.tb00503.x

Langworthy, R. A., & Jennings, J. W. (1972). Oddball, abstract olfactory learning in laboratory rats. *Psychological Record, 22*, 487–490. (1) doi: 10.1007/BF03394116

Lapate, R. C., Rokers, B., Li, T., & Davidson, R. J. (2014). Nonconscious emotional activation colors first impressions: A regulatory role for conscious awareness. *Psychological Science, 25*, 349–357. (10) doi: 10.1177/0956797613503175

Lara, T., Madrid, J. A., & Correa, Á. (2014). The vigilance decrement in executive function is attenuated when individual chronotypes perform at their optimal time of day. *PLoS One, 9*, e88820. (10) doi: 10.1371/journal.pone.0088820

Larkina, M., Güler, O. E., Kleinknecht, E., & Bauer, P. J. (2008). Maternal provision of structure in a deliberate memory task in relation to their preschool children's recall. *Journal of Experimental Child Psychology, 100*, 235–251. (5) doi: 10.1016/j.jecp.2008.03.002

Larsen, B., & Luna, B. (2015). *In vivo* evidence of neurophysiological maturation of the human adolescent striatum. *Developmental Cognitive Neuroscience, 12*, 74–85. (5) doi: 10.1016/j.dcn.2014.12.003

Larsen, L., Hartmann, P., & Nyborg, H. (2008). The stability of general intelligence from early adulthood to middle age. *Intelligence, 36*, 29–34. (9) doi: 10.1016/j.intell.2007.01.001

Larzelere, R. E., Cox, R. B. Jr., & Smith, G. L. (2010). Do nonphysical punishments reduce antisocial behavior more than spanking? A comparison using the strongest previous causal evidence against spanking. *BMC Pediatrics, 10*, article 10. (6) doi: 10.1186/1471-2431-10-10

Larzelere, R. E., Gunnoe, M. L., Ferguson, C. J., & Roberts, M. W. (2019). The insufficiency of the evidence used to categorically oppose spanking and its implications for families and psychological science: Comment on Gershoff et al. (2018). *American Psychologist, 74*, 497–499. (6) doi: 10.1037/amp0000461

Lashley, K. (1923a). The behavioristic interpretation of consciousness. *Psychological Review, 30*, 237–272, 329–353. (10) doi: 10.1037/h0073839

Lashley, K. S. (1923b). The behavioristic interpretation of consciousness II. *Psychological Review, 30*, 329–353. (10) doi: 10.1037/h0067016

Lashley, K. S., & McCarthy, D. S. (1926). The survival of the maze habit after cerebellar injuries. *Journal of Comparative Psychology, 6*, 423–433. (6) doi: 10.1037/h0073391

Lashley, K. S. (1951). The problem of serial order in behavior. In L. A. Jeffress (Ed.), *Cerebral mechanisms in behavior* (pp. 112–146). New York: Wiley. (8) http://languagelog.ldc.upenn.edu/myl/Lashley1951.pdf

Lassiter, G. D., Geers, A. L., Munhall, P. J., Ploutz-Snyder, R. J., & Breitenbecher, D. L. (2002). Illusory causation: Why it occurs. *Psychological Science, 13*, 299–305. (13) doi: 10.1111/1467-9280.00456

Latané, B., & Darley, J. M. (1968). Group inhibition of bystander intervention in emergencies. *Journal of Personality and Social Psychology, 10*, 215–221. (13) doi: 10.1037/h0026570

Latané, B., & Darley, J. M. (1969). Bystander "apathy." *American Scientist, 57*, 244–268. (13)

Latané, B., Williams, K., & Harkins, S. (1979). Many hands make light the work: The causes and consequences of social loafing. *Journal of Personality and Social Psychology, 37*, 822–832. (13) doi: 10.1037//0022-3514.37.6.822

Latner, J. D. (2003). Macronutrient effects on satiety and binge eating in bulimia nervosa and binge eating disorder. *Appetite, 40*, 309–311. (11) doi: 10.1016/S0195-6663(03)00028-X

Lau, H. C., Rogers, R. D., Haggard, P., & Passingham, R. E. (2004). Attention to intention. *Science, 303*, 1208–1210. (10) doi: 10.1126/science.1090973

Laumann, E. O. (1969). Friends of urban men: An assessment of accuracy in reporting their socio-economic attributes, mutual choice, and attitude development. *Sociometry, 32*, 54–69. (13) doi: 10.2307/2786634

Laumann, E. O., Gagnon, J. H., Michael, R. T., & Michaels, S. (1994). *The social organization of sexuality: Sexual practices in the United States.* Chicago, IL: University of Chicago Press. (11)

Launay, C., & Py, J. (2017). Capturing the scene: Efficacy test of the re-enactment investigation instruction. *Journal of Forensic Practice, 19*, 174–189. (7) doi: 10.1108/JFP-02-2015-0012

Laurin, K. (2018). Inaugurating rationalization: Three field studies find increased rationalization when anticipated realities become current. *Psychological Science, 29*, 483–495. (14) doi: 10.1177/0956797617738814

Laws, G., Byrne, A., & Buckley, S., (2000). Language and memory development in children with Down syndrome at mainstream schools and special schools: A comparison. *Educational Psychology, 20*, 447–457. (9) doi: 10.1080/713663758

Lawson, T. T. (2008). *Carl Jung, Darwin of the mind.* London: Karnac. (14)

Lazarus, R. S. (1977). Cognitive and coping processes in emotion. In A. Monat & R. S. Lazarus (Eds.), *Stress and coping* (pp. 145–158). New York: Columbia University Press. (12)

Leach, J. K., & Patall, E. A. (2013). Maximizing and counterfactual thinking in academic major decision making. *Journal of Career Assessment, 21*, 414–429. (8) doi: 10.1177/1069072712475178

Lee, A., Clancy, S., & Fleming, A. S. (1999). Mother rats bar-press for pups: Effects of lesions of the MPOA and limbic sites on maternal behavior and operant responding for pup-reinforcement. *Behavioural Brain Research, 100,* 15–31. (6) doi: 10.1016/S0166-4328(98)00109-0

Lee, J. C., Hall, D. L., & Wood, W. (2018). Experiential or material purchases? Social class determines purchase happiness. *Psychological Science, 29,* 1031–1039. (12) doi: 10.1177/0956797617736386

Lee, J. J., Mcgue, M., Iacono, W. G., Michael, A. M., & Chabris, C. F. (2019). The causal influence of brain size on human intelligence: Evidence from within-family phenotypic associations and GWAS modeling. *Intelligence, 75,* 48–58. (9) doi: 10.1016/j.intell.2019.01.011

Lee, K., Talwar, V., McCarthy, A., Ross, I., Evans, A., & Arruda, C. (2014). Can classic moral stories promote honesty in children? *Psychological Science, 25,* 1630–1636. (6) doi: 10.1177/0956797614536401

Lee, L., Loewenstein, G., Ariely, D., Hong, J., & Young, J. (2008). If I'm not hot, are you hot or not? *Psychological Science, 19,* 669–677. (13) doi: 10.1111/j.1467-9280.2008.02141.x

Lee, S.-H., Blake, R., & Heeger, D. J. (2005). Traveling waves of activity in primary visual cortex during binocular rivalry. *Nature Neuroscience, 8,* 22–23. (10) doi: 10.1038/nn1365

Lee, T., Thalamuthu, A., Henry, J. D., Trollor, J. N., Ames, D., Wright, M. J., Sachdev, P. S., & OATS Research Team. (2018). Genetic and environmental influences on the Older Australian Twins Study. *Behavior Genetics, 48,* 187–197. (3) doi: 10.1007/s10519-018-9897-z

Leff, J. (2002). The psychiatric revolution: Care in the community. *Nature Reviews Neuroscience, 3,* 821–824. (15) doi: 10.1038/nrn937

Legault, L., Gutsell, J. N., & Inzlicht, M. (2011). Ironic effects of antiprejudice messages: How motivational interventions can reduce (but also increase) prejudice. *Psychological Science, 22,* 1472–1477. (13) doi: 10.1177/0956797611427918

Legge, G. E., Ahn, S. J., Klitz, T. S., & Luebker, A. (1997). Psychophysics of reading: XVI. The visual span in normal and low vision. *Vision Research, 37,* 1999–2010. (8) doi: 10.1016/S0042-6989(97)00017-5

Lehtonen, M., Soveri, A., Laine, A., Järvenpää, J., de Bruin, A., & Antfolk, J. (2018). Is bilingualism associated with enhanced executive functioning in adults? A meta-analytic review. *Psychological Bulletin, 144,* 394–425. (8) doi: 10.1037/bul0000142

Leibniz, G. (1714). *The Principles of Nature and Grace, Based on Reason.* www.earlymoderntexts.com/pdfs /leibniz1714a.pdf (10)

Leising, D., Scharloth, J., Lohse, O., & Wood, D. (2014). What types of terms do people use when describing an individual's personality? *Psychological Science, 25,* 1787–1794. (14) doi: 10.1177/0956797614541285

Lekeu, F., Wojtasik, V., Van der Linden, M., & Salmon, E. (2002). Training early Alzheimer patients to use a mobile phone. *Acta Neurologica Belgica, 102,* 114–121. (7) https://www.actaneurologica.be/pdfs/2002-3/03-lekeu-salmon.pdf

Leloup, J.-C., & Goldbeter, A. (2013). Critical phase shifts slow down circadian clock recovery: Implications for jet lag. *Journal of Theoretical Biology, 333,* 47–57. (10) doi: 10.1016/j.jtbi.2013.04.039

Lemaitre, A.-L., Luyat, M., & Lafargue, G. (2016). Individuals with pronounced schizotypal traits are particularly successful at tickling themselves. *Consciousness and Cognition, 41,* 64–71. (4) doi: 10.1016/j.concog.2016.02.005

Lenneberg, E. H. (1967). *Biological foundations of language.* New York: Wiley. (8)

Lenneberg, E. H. (1969). On explaining language. *Science, 164,* 635–643. (8) doi: 10.1126/science.164.3880.635

Lenz, K. M., Nugent, B. M., Haliyur, r., & McCarthy, M. M. (2013). Microglia are essential to masculinization of brain and behavior. *Journal of Neuroscience, 33,* 2761–2772. (11) doi: 10.1523/JNEUROSCI.1268-12.2013

Lenzenweger, M. F., Johnson, M. D., & Willett, J. B. (2004). Individual growth curve analysis illuminates stability and change in personality disorder features. *Archives of General Psychiatry, 61,* 1015–1024. (15) doi: 10.1001/archpsyc.61.10.1015

Leonard, J. A., Lee, Y., & Schulz, L. E. (2017). Infants make more attempts to achieve a goal when they see adults persist. *Science, 357,* 1290–1294. (6) doi: 10.1126/science.aan2317

Leonard, L. B. (2007). Processing limitations and the grammatical profile of children with specific language impairment. In R. V. Kail (Ed.), *Advances in child development and behavior* (Vol. 35, pp. 139–171). Oxford, England: Elsevier. (8) doi: 10.1016/b978-0-12-009735-7.50009-8.

Leppänen, J. M., & Hietanen, J. K. (2003). Affect and face perception: Odors modulate the recognition advantage of happy faces. *Emotion, 3,* 315–326. (12) doi: 10.1037/1528-3542.3.4.315

Lerner, J. S., Li, Y., & Weber, E. U. (2013). The financial costs of sadness. *Psychological Science, 24,* 72–79. (12) doi: 10.1177/0956797612450302

Lerner, M. J. (1980). *The belief in a just world: A fundamental delusion.* New York: Plenum Press. (14)

Leuchtenburg, W. E. (1963). *Franklin D. Roosevelt and the New Deal 1932–1940.* New York: Harper & Row. (13)

Levari, D. E., Gilbert, D. T., Wilson, T. D., Sievers, B., Amodio, D. M., & Wheatley, T. (2018). Prevalence-induced concept change in human judgment. *Science, 360,* 1465–1467. (8) doi: 10.1126/science.aap8731

Levav, J., & Fitzsimons, G. J. (2006). When questions change behavior. *Psychological Science, 17,* 207–213. (11) doi: 10.1111/j.1467-9280.2006.01687.x

LeVay, S. (1991). A difference in hypothalamic structure between heterosexual and homosexual men. *Science, 253,* 1034–1037. (11) doi: 10.1126/science.1887219

Leventhal, A. M., Trujillo, M., Ameringer, K. J., Tidey, J. W., Sussman, S., & Kahler, C. W. (2014). Anhedonia and the relative reward value of drug and nondrug reinforcers in cigarette smokers. *Journal of Abnormal Psychology, 123,* 375–386. (15) doi: 10.1037/a0036384

Levine, J. A., Lanningham-Foster, L. M., McCrady, S. K., Krizan, A. C., Olson, L. R., Kane, P. H., Jensen, M. D., & Clark, M. M. (2005). Interindividual variation in posture allocation: Possible role in human obesity. *Science, 307,* 584–586. (11) doi: 10.1126/science.1106561

Levine, R. V. (1990). The pace of life. *American Scientist, 78,* 450–459. (12)

Levine, S. C., Vasilyeva, M., Lourenco, S. F., Newcombe, N. S., & Huttenlocher, J. (2005). Socioeconomic status modifies the sex difference in spatial skill. *Psychological Science, 16,* 841–845. (5) doi: 10.1111/j.1467-9280.2005.01623.x

Levinson, D. J. (1986). A conception of adult development. *American Psychologist, 41,* 3–13. (5) doi: 10.1037/0003-066X.41.1.3

Levy, B. J., McVeigh, N. D., Marful, A., & Anderson, M. C. (2007). Inhibiting your native language. *Psychological Science, 18,* 29–34. (8) doi: 10.1111/j.1467-9280.2007.01844.x

Lewandowsky, S., Stritzke, W. G. K., Freund, A. M., Oberauer, K., & Krueger, J. I. (2013). Misinformation, disinformation, and violent conflict: From Iraq and the "War on Terror" to future threats to peace. *American Psychologist, 68,* 487–501. (13) doi: 10.1037/a0034515

Leweke, F. M., Gerth, C. W., Koethe, D., Klosterkötter, J., Ruslanova, I., Krivogorsky, B., Torrey, E. F., & Yolken, R. H. (2004). Antibodies to infectious agents in individuals with recent onset schizophrenia. *European Archives of Psychiatry and Clinical Neuroscience, 254,* 4–8. (15) doi: 10.1007/s00406-004-0481-6

Lewis, D. A., & Gonzalez-Burgos, G. (2006). Pathophysiologically based treatment interventions in schizophrenia. *Nature Medicine, 12,* 1016–1022. (15) doi: 10.1038/nm1478

Lewis, D. O., Moy, E., Jackson, L. D., Aaronson, R., Restifo, N., Serra, S., & Simos, A. (1985). Biopsychosocial characteristics of children who later murder: A prospective study. *American Journal of Psychiatry, 142,* 1161–1167. (13) doi: 10.1176/ajp.142.10.1161.

Lewis, M., Sullivan, M. W., Stanger, C., & Weiss, M. (1991). Self development and self-conscious emotions. In S. Chess & M. E. Hertzig (Eds.), *Annual progress in child psychiatry and child development 1990* (pp. 34–51). New York: Brunner/Mazel. (5)

Leyland, A., Rowse, G., & Emerson, L.-M. (2019). Experimental effects of mindfulness inductions on self-regulatiion: Systematic review and meta-analysis. *Emotion, 19,* 108–122. (10) doi: 10.1037/emo0000425

Li, Q., Hill, Z., & He, B. J. (2014). Spatiotemporal dissociation of brain activity underlying subjective awareness, objective performance, and confidence. *Journal of Neuroscience, 34,* 4382–4395. (10) doi: 10.1523/JNEUROSCI.1820-13.2014

Li, W., Ma, L., Yang, G., & Gan, W.-B. (2017). REM sleep selectively prunes and maintains new synapses in development and learning. *Nature Neuroscience, 20,* 427–437. (10) doi: 10.1038/nn.4479

Li, W., Howard, J. D., Parrish, T. B., & Gottfried, J. A. (2008). Aversive learning enhances perceptual and cortical discrimination of indiscriminable odor cues. *Science, 319,* 1842–1845. (6) doi: 10.1126/science.1152937

Li, Z., Chang, S.-h., Zhang, L.-y., Gao, L., & Wang, J. (2014). Molecular genetic studies of ADHD and its candidate genes: A review. *Psychiatry Research, 219,* 10–24. (8) doi: 10.1016/j.psychres.2014.05.005

Libbrecht, N., Lievens, F., Carette, B., & Côté, S. (2014). Emotional intelligence predicts success in medical school. *Emotion, 14,* 64–73. (12) doi: 10.1037/a0034392

Libet, B., Gleason, C. A., Wright, E. W., & Pearl, D. K. (1983). Time of conscious intention to act in relation to onset of cerebral activities (readiness potential): The unconscious initiation of a freely voluntary act. *Brain, 106,* 623–642. (10) doi: 10.1093/brain/106.3.623

G. (2017). Infants' and children's salt taste perception and liking: A review. *Nutrients, 9.* (1) doi: 10.3390/nu9091011

Lim, C., & Putnam, R. D. (2010). Religion, social networks, and life satisfaction. *American Sociological Review, 75,* 914–933. (12) doi: 10.1177/0003122410386686

Lim, E. T., Uddin, M., De Rubeis, S., Chan, Y., Kamumbu, A. S., Zhang, X., D'Gama, A. M. Kim, S. N., Hill, R. S, Goldberg, A. P., Poultney, C., Minshew, N. J., Kushima, I., Aleksic, B., Ozaki, N., Parellada, M., Arango, C., Carracedo, A., Kolevzon, A.,... Walsh, C. A. (2017). Rates, distribution and implications of postzygotic mosaic mutations in autism spectrum disorder. *Nature Neuroscience, 20,* 1217–1224. (15) doi: 10.1038/nn.4598

Lindquist, K. A., Wager, T. D., Kober, H., Bliss-Moreau, E., & Barrett, L. F. (2012). The brain basis of emotion: A meta-analytic review. *Behavioral and Brain Sciences, 35,* 121–202. (12) doi: 10.1017/S0140525X11000446

Lilienfeld, S. O. (2007). Psychological treatments that cause harm. *Perspectives on Psychological Science, 2,* 53–70. (12, 15) doi: 10.1111/j.1745-6916.2007.00029.x

Lilienfeld, S. O., Ritschel, L. A., Lynn, S. J., Cautin, R. L., & Latzman, R. D. (2014). Why ineffective psychotherapies appear to work: A taxonomy of causes of spurious therapeutic effectiveness. *Perspectives on Psychological Science, 9,* 355–387. (15) doi: 10.1177/1745691614535216

Lilienfeld, S. O., Wood, J. M., & Garb, H. N. (2000). The scientific status of projective tests. *Psychological Science in the Public Interest, 1,* 27–66. (14) https://www.psychologicalscience.org/journals/pspi/pdf/pspi1_2.pdf

Lillberg, K., Verkasalo, P. K., Kaprio, J., Teppo, L., Helenius, H., & Koskenvuo, M. (2003). Stressful life events and risk of breast cancer in 10,808 women: A cohort study. *American Journal of Epidemiology, 157,* 415–423. (12) doi: 10.1093/aje/kwg002

Lim, S.-L., Penrod, M. T., Ha, O.-R., Bruce, J. M., & Bruce, A. S. (2018). Calorie labeling promotes dietary self-control by shifting the temporal dynamics of health- and taste-attribute integration in overweight individuals. *Psychological Science, 29,* 447–462. (11) doi: 10.1177/0956797617737871

Lin, C., Adolphs, R., & Alvarez, R. M. (2018). Inferring whether officials are corruptible from looking at their faces. *Psychological Science, 29,* 1807–1823. (13) doi: 10.1177/0956797618788882

Lin, J. Y., Franconeri, S., & Enns, J. T. (2008). Objects on a collision path with the observer demand attention. *Psychological Science, 19,* 686–692. (8) doi: 10.1111/j.1467-9280.2008.02143.x

Linck, J. A., Kroll, J. F., & Sunderman, G. (2009). Losing access to the native language while immersed in a second language. *Psychological Science, 20,* 1507–1515. (8) doi: 10.1111/j.1467-9280.2009.02480.x

Linck, J. A., Osthus, P., Koeth, J. T., & Bunting, M. F. (2013). Working memory and second language comprehension and production: A meta-analysis. *Psychonomic Bulletin & Review, 21,* 861–883. (7) doi: 10.3758/s13423-013-0565-2

Linden, W., Lenz, J. W., & Con, A. H. (2001). Individualized stress management for primary hypertension: A randomized trial. *Archives of Internal Medicine, 161,* 1071–1080. (12) doi: 10.1001/archinte.161.8.1071

Lindhiem, O., Bennett, C. B., Trentacosta, C. J., & McLear, C. (2014). Client preferences affect treatment satisfaction, completion, and clinical outcome: A meta-analysis. *Clinical Psychology Review, 34,* 506–517. (15) doi: 10.1016/j.cpr.2014.06.002

Lindsay, D. S., Hagen, L., Read, J. D., Wade, K. A., & Garry, M. (2004). True photographs and false memories. *Psychological Science, 15,* 149–154. (7) doi: 10.1111/j.0956-7976.2004.01503002.x

Lindsay, D. S., & Read, J. D. (1994). Psychotherapy and memories of childhood sexual abuse: A cognitive perspective. *Applied Cognitive Psychology, 8,* 281–338. (7) doi: 10.1002/acp.2350080403

Lipszyc, J., & Schachar, R. (2010). Inhibitory control and psychopathology: A meta-analysis of studies using the stop signal task. *Journal of the International Neuropsychological Society, 16,* 1064–1076. (8) doi: 10.1017/S1355617710000895

Lisanby, S. H., Maddox, J. H., Prudic, J., Devanand, D. P., & Sackeim, H. A. (2000). The effects of electroconvulsive therapy on memory of autobiographical and public events. *Archives of General Psychiatry, 57,* 581–590. (15) doi: 10.1001/archpsyc.57.6.581

Liu, F., Wollstein, A., Hysi, P. G., Ankra-Badu, G. A., Spector, T. D., Park, D, Zhu, G., Larsson, M., Duffy, D. L., Montgomery, G. W., Mackey, D. A., Walsh, S., Lao, O., Hofman, A., Rivadeneira, F., Vingerling, J. R., Uitterlinden, A. G., Martin, N. G., Hammond, C. J., & Kayser, M. (2010). Digital quantification of human eye color highlights genetic association of three new loci. *PLoS Genetics, 6,* e1000934. (3) doi: 10.1371/journal.pgen.1000934

Liu, I.-C., Blacker, D. L., Xu, R., Fitzmaurice, G., Lyons, M. J., & Tsuang, M. T. (2004). Genetic and environmental contributions to the development of alcohol dependence in male twins. *Archives of General Psychiatry, 61,* 897–903. (15) doi: 10.1001/archpsyc.61.9.897

Lo Vecchio, S., Andersen, H. H., & Arendt-Nielsen, L. (2018). The time course of brief and prolonged topical 8% capsaicin-induced desensitization in healthy volunteers evaluated by quantitative sensory testing and vasomotor imaging. *Experimental Brain Research, 236,* 2231–2244. (4) doi: 10.1007/s00221-018-5299-y

Locke, E. A., & Latham, G. P. (2002). Building a practically useful theory of goal setting and task motivation. *American Psychologist, 57,* 705–717. (11) doi: 10.1037//0003-066X.57.9.705

Locke, J. L. (1994). Phases in the child's development of language. *American Scientist, 82,* 436–445. (8)

Loeb, J. (1973). *Forced movements, tropisms, and animal conduct.* New York: Dover. (Original work published 1918) (6)

Loeber, S., Croissant, B., Heinz, A., Mann, K., & Flor, H. (2006). Cue exposure in the treatment of alcohol dependence: Effects on drinking outcome, craving and self-efficacy. *British Journal of Clinical Psychology, 45,* 515–529. (6) doi: 10.1348/014466505X82586

Loehlin, J. C. (1992). *Genes and environment in personality development.* Newbury Park, CA: Sage. (5, 14)

Loehlin, J. C., Horn, J. M., & Willerman, L. (1989). Modeling IQ change: Evidence from the Texas adoption project. *Child Development, 60,* 993–1004. (9) doi: 10.2307/1131039

Loehlin, J. C., & Martin, N. G. (2018). Personality types: A twin study. *Personality and Individual Differences, 122,* 99–103. (14) doi: 10.1016/j.paid.2017.10.012

Loewi, O. (1960). An autobiographic sketch. *Perspectives in Biology, 4,* 3–25. (3)

Loftus, E. (2003). Our changeable memories: Legal and practical implications. *Nature Reviews Neuroscience, 4,* 231–234. (7) doi: 10.1038/nrn1054

Loftus, E. F. (1975). Leading questions and the eyewitness report. *Cognitive Psychology, 7,* 560–572. (7) doi: 10.1016/0010-0285(75)90023-7

Loftus, E. F. (1993). The reality of repressed memories. *American Psychologist, 48,* 518–537. (7) doi: 10.1037/0003-066X.48.5.518

Loftus, E. F. (1997). Repressed memory accusations: Devastated families and devastated patients. *Applied Cognitive Psychology, 11,* 25–30. (7) doi: 10.1002/(SICI)1099-0720(199702)11:1<25::AID-ACP452>3.0.CO;2-J

Loftus, E. F., Feldman, J., & Dashiell, R. (1995). The reality of illusory memories. In D. L. Schacter (Ed.), *Memory distortion* (pp. 47–68). Cambridge, MA: Harvard University Press. (7)

Loftus, G. R. (1996). Psychology will be a much better science when we change the way we analyze data. *Current Directions in Psychological Science, 5,* 161–171. (2) doi: 10.1111/1467-8721.ep11512376

Long, G. M., & Toppine, T. C. (2004). Enduring interest in perceptual ambiguity: Alternating views of reversible figures. *Psychological Bulletin, 130,* 748–768. (4) doi: 10.1037/0033-2909.130.5.748

Longstreth, L. E. (1981). Revisiting Skeels' final study: A critique. *Developmental Psychology, 17,* 620–625. (9) doi: 10.1037/0012-1649.17.5.620

Lopes, P. N., Brackett, M. A., Nezlak, J. B., Schütz, A., Sellin, I., & Salovey, P. (2004). Emotional intelligence and social interaction. *Personality and Social Psychology Bulletin, 30,* 1018–1034. (12) doi: 10.1177/0146167204264762

Lopez, R. B., Hofmann, W., Wagner, D. D., Kelley, W. M., & Heatherton, T. F. (2014). Neural predictors of giving in to temptation in daily life. *Psychological Science, 25,* 1337–1344. (11) doi: 10.1177/0956797614531492

Lopez-Sola, C., Fontenelle, L. F., Alonso, P., Cuadras, D., Foley, D. L., Pantelis, C., Pujol, J., Yucel, M., Cardoner, N., Soriano-Mas, C., Menchon, J. M., & Harrison, B. J. (2014). Prevalence and heritability of obsessive-compulsive spectrum and anxiety disorder symptoms: A survey of the Australian twin registry. *American Journal of Medical Genetics Part B, 165,* 314–325. (15) doi: 10.1002/ajmg.b.32233

Lotto, R. B., & Purves, D. (2002). The empirical basis of color perception. *Consciousness and Cognition, 11,* 609–629. (4) doi: PII S1053-8100(02)00014-4

Lotze, M., Grodd, W., Birbaumer, N., Erb, M., Huse, E., & Flor, H. (1999). Does use of a myoelectric prosthesis prevent cortical reorganization and phantom limb pain? *Nature Neuroscience, 2,* 501–502. (4) doi: 10.1038/9145

Löw, A., Lang, P. J., Smith, J. C., & Bradley, M. M. (2008). Both predator and prey. *Psychological Science, 19,* 865–873. (12) doi: 10.1111/j.1467-9280.2008.02170.x

Lowe, K. B., Kroeck, K. G., & Sivasubramaniam, N. (1996). Effectiveness correlates of transformational and transactional leadership: A meta-analytic review of the MLQ literature.

Leadership Quarterly, 7, 385–425. (11) doi: 10.1016/S1048-9843(96)90027-2

Luan, M., & Li, H. (2017). Maximization paradox: Result of believing in an objective best. *Personality and Social Psychology Bulletin, 43,* 652–661. (8) doi: 10.1177/0146167217695552

Lubman, D. I., Yücel, M., Kettle, J. W. L., Scaffidi, A., Mackenzie, T., Simmons, J. G., & Allen, N. B. (2009). Responsiveness to drug cues and natural rewards in opiate addiction. *Archives of General Psychiatry, 66,* 205–212. (15) doi: 10.1001/archgenpsychiatry.2008.522

Lucas, R. E. (2005). Time does not heal all wounds. *Psychological Science, 16,* 945–950. (12) doi: 10.1111/j.1467-9280.2005.01642.x

Lucas, R. E., Clark, A. E., Georgellis, Y., & Diener, E. (2004). Unemployment alters the set point for life satisfaction. *Psychological Science, 15,* 8–13. (12) doi: 10.1111/j.0963-7214.2004.01501002.x

Lucas, R. E., Le, K., & Dyrenforth, P. S. (2008). Explaining the extraversion/positive affect relation: Sociability cannot account for extraverts' greater happiness. *Journal of Personality, 76,* 385–414. (14) doi: 10.1111/j.1467-6494.2008.00490.x

Lucas, R. E., & Schimmack, U. (2009). Income and well-being: How big is the gap between the rich and the poor? *Journal of Research in Personality, 43,* 75–78. (12) doi: 10.1016/j.jrp.2008.09.004

Luciano, M., Wainwright, M. A., Wright, M. J., & Martin, N. G. (2006). The heritability of conscientiousness facets and their relationship to IQ and academic achievement. *Personality and Individual Differences, 40,* 1189–1199. (14) doi: 10.1016/j.paid.2005.10.013

Luciano, M., Wright, M. J., Smith, G. A., Geffen, G. M., Geffen, L. B., & Martin, N. G. (2001). Genetic covariance among measures of information processing speed, working memory, and IQ. *Behavior Genetics, 31,* 581–592. (9) doi: 10.1023/A:1013397428612

Luczak, S. E., Yarnell, L. M., Prescott, C. A., Myers, M. G., Liang, T., & Wall, T. L. (2014). Effects of *ALDH2*2* on alcohol problem trajectories of Asian American college students. *Journal of Abnormal Psychology, 123,* 130–140. (15) doi: 10.1037/a0035486

Luders, E., Narr, K. I., Thompson, P. M., Rex, D. E., Jancke, L., Steinmetz, H., & Toga, A. W. (2004). Gender differences in cortical complexity. *Nature Neuroscience, 7,* 799–800. (9) doi: 10.1038/nn1277

Ludwig, J., Duncan, G. J., Gennetian, L. A., Katz, L. F., Kessler, R. C., Kling, J. R., & Sabonmatsu, L. (2012). Neighborhood effects on the long-term well-being of low-income adults. *Science, 337,* 1505–1510. (15) doi: 10.1126/science.1224648

Luescher, C., Robbins, T. W., & Everitt, B. J. (2020). The transition to compulsion in addiction. *Nature Reviews Neuroscience, 21,* 247–263. (15) doi: 10.1038/s41583-020-0289-z

Luk, G., Bialystok, E., Craik, F. I. M., & Grady, C. L. (2011). Lifelong bilingualism maintains white matter integrity in older adults. *Journal of Neuroscience, 31,* 16808–16813. (8) doi: 10.1523/JNEUROSCI.4563-11.2011

Lumian, D. S., & McRae, K. (2017). Preregistered replication of "affective flexibility": Evaluative processing goals shape amygdala activity. *Psychological Science, 28,* 1193–1200. (12) doi: 10.1177/0956797617719730

Luna, B., Padmanabhan, A., & O'Hearn, K. (2010). What has fMRI told us about the development of cognitive control through adolescence?

Brain and Cognition, 72, 101–113. (5) doi: 10.1016/j.bandc.2009.08.005

Luoto, S., Krams, I., & Rantala, M. J. (2019). A life history approach to the female sexual orientation spectrum: Evolution, development, causal mechanisms, and health. *Archives of Sexual Behavior, 48,* 1273–1308. (11) doi: 10.1007/s10508-018-1261-0

Luppino, F. S., de Wit, L. M., Bouvy, P. F., Stijnen, T., Cuijpers, P., Penninx, B. W. J. H., & Zitman, F. G. (2010). Overweight, obesity, and depression. *Archives of General Psychiatry, 67,* 220–229. (11) doi: 10.1001/archgenpsychiatry.2010.2

Luttrell, A., Petty, R. E., & Briñol, P. (2016). Ambivalence and certainty can interact to predict attitude stability over time. *Journal of Experimental Social Psychology, 63,* 56–68. (13) doi: 10.1016/j.jesp.2015.11.008

Lyamin, O. I., Mukhametov, L. M., Siegel, J. M., Nazarenko, E. A., Polyakova, I. G., & Shpak, O. V. (2002). Unihemispheric slow wave sleep and the state of the eyes in a white whale. *Behavioural Brain Research, 129,* 125–129. (10) doi: 10.1016/S0166-4328(01)00346-1

Lyamin, O. I., Kosenko, P. O., Lapierre, J. L., Mukhametov, L. M., & Siegel, J. M. (2008). Fur seals display a strong drive for bilateral slow-wave sleep while on land. *Journal of Neuroscience, 28,* 12614–12621. (10) doi: 10.1523/JNEUROSCI.2306-08.2008

Lyamin, O., Pryaslova, J., Lance, V., & Siegel, J. (2005). Continuous activity in cetaceans after birth. *Nature, 435,* 1177. (10) doi: 10.1038/4351177a

Lykken, D., & Tellegen, A. (1996). Happiness is a stochastic phenomenon. *Psychological Science, 7,* 186–189. (12) doi: 10.1111/j.1467-9280.1996.tb00355.x

Lykken, D. T. (1979). The detection of deception. *Psychological Bulletin, 86,* 47–53. (12) doi: 10.1037/0033-2909.86.1.47

Lykken, D. T., Bouchard, T. J., Jr., McGue, M., & Tellegen, A. (1993). Heritability of interests: A twin study. *Journal of Applied Psychology, 78,* 649–661. (3) doi: 10.1037/0021-9010.78.4.649

Lykken, D. T., McGue, M., Tellegen, A., & Bouchard, T. J. (1992). Emergenesis: Genetic traits that may not run in families. *American Psychologist, 47,* 1565–1577. (3) doi: 10.1037/0003-066X.47.12.1565

Lyn, H., Greenfield, P. M., Savage-Rumbaugh, S., Gillespie-Lynch, K., & Hopkins, W. D. (2011). Nonhuman primates do declare! A comparison of declarative symbol and gesture use in two children, two bonobos, and a chimpanzee. *Language & Communication, 31,* 63–74. (8) doi: 10.1016/j.langcom.2010.11.001

Lynam, D. R. (1996). Early identification of chronic offenders: Who is the fledgling psychopath? *Psychological Bulletin, 120,* 209–234. (13) doi: 10.1037/0033-2909.120.2.209

Lynn, R. (2009). What has caused the Flynn effect? Secular increases in the developmental quotients of infants. *Intelligence, 37,* 16–24. (9) doi: 10.1016/j.intell.2008.07.008

Lynn, R. (2013). Who discovered the Flynn effect? A review of early studies of the secular increase of intelligence. *Intelligence, 41,* 765–769. (9) doi: 10.1016/j.intell.2013.03.008

Lynn, S. J., Green, J. P., Kirsch, I., Capafons, A., Lilienfeld, S. O., Laurence, J.-R., & Montgomery, G. H. (2015). Grounding hypnosis in science: The "new" APA Division 30 definition of hypnosis as a step backward. *American Journal of Clinical Hypnosis, 57,* 390–401. (10) doi: 10.1080/00029157.2015.1011472

Lyons, M. J., Eisen, S. A., Goldberg, J., True, W., Lin, N., Meyer, J. M., Toomey, R., Faraone, S. V., Merla-Ramos, M., & Tsuang, M. T. (1998). A registry-based twin study of depression in men. *Archives of General Psychiatry, 55,* 468–472. (15) doi: 10.1001/archpsyc.55.5.468

Lyons, M. J., York, T. P., Franz, C. E., Grant, M. D., Eaves, L. J., Jacobson, K. C., Schaie, K. W., Panizzon, M. S., Boake, C., Xian, H., Toomey, R., Eisen, S. A., & Kremen, W. S. (2009). Genes determine stability and the environment determines change in cognitive ability during 35 years of adulthood. *Psychological Science, 20,* 1146–1152. (9) doi: 10.1111/j.1467-9280.2009.02425.x

Lyubomirsky, S., Dickerhoof, R., Boehm, J. K., & Sheldon, K. M. (2011). Becoming happier takes both a will and a proper way: An experimental longitudinal intervention to boost well-being. *Emotion, 11,* 391–402. (12) doi: 10.1037/a0022575

Ma, W. J., Husain, M., & Bays, P. M. (2014). Changing concepts of working memory. *Nature Neuroscience, 17,* 347–356. (7) doi: 10.1038/nn.3655

Ma-Kellams, C., & Blascovich, J. (2011). Culturally divergent responses to mortality salience. *Psychological Science, 22,* 1019–1024. (5) doi: 10.1177/0956797611413935

MacCallum, F., & Golombok, S. (2004). Children raised in fatherless families from infancy: A follow-up of children of lesbian and single heterosexual mothers at early adolescence. *Journal of Child Psychology and Psychiatry, 45,* 1407–1419. (5) doi: 10.1111/j.1469-7610.2004.00324.x

Macknik, S. L., King, M., Randi, J., Robbins, A., Teller, Thompson, J., & Martinez-Conde, S. (2008). Attention and awareness in stage magic: Turning tricks into research. *Nature Reviews Neuroscience, 9,* 871–879. (8) doi: 10.1038/nrn2473

MacLean, K. A., Ferrer, E., Aichele, S. R., Bridwell, D. A., Zanesco, A.P., Jacobs, T.L., King, B. G., Rosenberg, E. L., Sahdra, B. K., Shaver, P. R., Wallace, B. A., Mangun, G. R., & Saron, C.D. (2010). Intensive meditation training improves perceptual discrimination and sustained attention. *Psychological Science, 21,* 829–839. (10) doi: 10.1177/0956797610371339

Macmillan, M. (1997). *Freud evaluated.* Cambridge, MA: MIT Press. (14)

Macnamara, B. N., Hambrick, D. Z., & Oswald, F. L. (2014). Deliberate practice and performance in music, games, sports, education, and professions: A meta-analysis. *Psychological Science, 25,* 1608–1618. (8) doi: 10.1177/0956797614535810

Macnamara, B. N., Moreau, D., & Hambrick, D. Z. (2016). The relationship between deliberate practice and performance in sports: A. meta-analysis. *Perspectives on Psychological Science, 11,* 333–350. (8) doi: 10.1177/1745691616635591

MacQueen, D. A., Minassian, A., Henry, B. L., Geyer, M. A., Young, J. W., & Perry, W. (2018). Amphetamine modestly improves Conners' Continuous Performance Test performance in healthy adults. *Journal of the International Neuropsychological Society, 24,* 283–293. (8) doi: 10.1017/S135561771700090X

MacQuitty, J. (1996, August 1). Lily the stink loses its 33-year reputation by a nose. *The Times* (London), pp. 1–2. (11)

Madson, L. (2005). Demonstrating the importance of question wording on surveys. *Teaching*

...ychology, 32, 40–43. (2) doi: 10.1207/
...28023top3201_9

Maes, E., Boddez, Y., Alfei, J. M., Krypotos, A.-M., D'Hooge, R., De Houwer, J., & Beckers, T. (2016). The elusive nature of the blocking effect: 15 failures to replicate. *Journal of Experimental Psychology: General, 145,* e49–e71. (6) doi: 10.1037/xge0000200

Magnuson, K. A., & Duncan, G. J. (2006). The role of family socioeconomic resources in the Black–White test score gap among young children. *Developmental Review, 26,* 365–399. (9) doi: 10.1016/j.dr.2006.06.004

Mahoney, C. E., Cogswell, A., Koralnik, I. J., & Scammell, T. E. (2019). The neurobiological basis of narcolepsy. *Nature Reviews Neuroscience, 20,* 83–93. (10) doi: 10.1038/s41583-018-0097-x

Mahowald, M. W., & Schenck, C. H. (2005). Insights from studying human sleep disorders. *Nature, 437,* 1279–1285. (10) doi: 10.1038/nature04287

Maier, S. F., & Watkins, L. R. (1998). Cytokines for psychologists: Implications of bidirectional immune-to-brain communication for understanding behavior, mood, and cognition. *Psychological Review, 105,* 83–107. (12) doi: 10.1037/0033-295X.105.1.83

Mainland, J. D., Keller, A., Li, Y. R., Zhou, T., Trimmer, C., Snyder, L. L., Moberly, A. H., Adipietro, K. A., Liu, W. L. L., Zhuang, H. Y., Zhan, S. M., Lee, S. S., Lin, A., & Matsunami, H. (2014). The missense of smell: Functional variability in the human odorant receptor repertoire. *Nature Neuroscience, 17,* 114–120. (4) doi: 10.1038/nn.3598

Maki, R. H. (1990). Memory for script actions: Effects of relevance and detail expectancy. *Memory & Cognition, 18,* 5–14. (7) doi: 10.3758/BF03202640

Maldonado, R., Saiardi, A., Valverde, O., Samad, T. A., Roques, B. P., & Borrelli, E. (1997). Absence of opiate rewarding effects in mice lacking dopamine D2 receptors. *Nature, 388,* 586–589. (3) doi: 10.1038/41567

Malinowski, J., & Horton, C. L. (2014). Evidence for the preferential incorporation of emotional waking-life experiences into dreams. *Dreaming, 24,* 18–31. (10) doi: 10.1037/a0036017

Malmber, K. J., Raaijmakers, J. G. W., & Shiffrin, R. M. (2019). 50 years of research sparked by Atkinson and Shiffrin (1968). *Memory & Cognition, 47,* 561–574. (7) doi: 10.3758/s13421-019-00896-7

Malmquist, C. P. (1986). Children who witness parental murder: Posttraumatic aspects. *Journal of the American Academy of Child Psychiatry, 25,* 320–325. (7) doi: 10.1016/S0002-7138(09)60253-3

Malone, T., & Lusk, J. L. (2017). Th excessive choice effect meets the market: A field experiment on craft beer choice. *Journal of Behavioral and Experimental Economics, 67,* 8–13. (8) doi: 10.1016/j.socec.2017.01.008

Mameli, M., & Lüscher, C. (2011). Synaptic plasticity and addiction: Learning mechanisms gone awry. *Neuropharmacology, 61,* 1052–1059. (15) doi: 10.1016/j.neuropharm.2011.01.036

Mandler, G. (2013). The limit of mental structures. *Journal of General Psychology, 140,* 243–250. (7) doi: 10.1080/00221309.2013.807217

Mandy, W., & Lai, M.-C. (2016). Annual research review: The role of the environment in the developmental psychopathology of autism spectrum condition. *Journal of Child Psychology and Psychiatry, 57,* 271–292. (15) doi: 10.1111/jcpp.12501

Manfredini, R., Fabbian, F., Cappadona, R., & Modesti, P. A. (2018). Daylight saving time, circadian rhythms, and cardiovascular health. *Internal and Emergency Medicine, 13,* 641–646. (10) doi: 10.1007/s11739-018-1900-4

Mangan, M. A. (2004). A phenomenology of problematic sexual behavior. *Archives of Sexual Behavior, 33,* 287–293. (10) doi: 10.1023/B:ASEB.0000026628.95803.98

Mani, A., Mullainathan, S., Shafir, E., & Zhao, J. (2013). Poverty impedes cognitive function. *Science, 341,* 976–980. (9) doi: 10.1126/science.1238041

Mann, T., Nolen-Hoeksema, S., Huang, K., Burgard, D., Wright, A., & Hanson, K. (1997). Are two interventions worse than none? Joint primary and secondary prevention of eating disorders in college females. *Health Psychology, 16,* 215–225. (15) doi: 10.1037/0278-6133.16.3.215

Manning, R., Levine, M., & Collins, A. (2007). The Kitty Genovese murder and the social psychology of helping. *American Psychologist, 62,* 555–562. (13) doi: 10.1037/0003-066X.62.6.555

Manor, O., & Eisenbach, Z. (2003). Mortality after spousal loss: Are there socio-demographic differences? *Social Science and Medicine, 56,* 405–413. (12) doi: 10.1016/S0277-9536(02)00046-1

Maquet, P., Laureys, S., Peigneux, P., Fuchs, S., Petiau, C., Phillips, C., Aerts, J., Del Fiore, G., Degueldre, C., Meulemans, T., Luxen, A., Franck, G., Van der Linden, M., Smith, C., & Cleeremans, A. (2000). Experience-dependent changes in cerebral activation during human REM sleep. *Nature Neuroscience, 3,* 831–836. (10) doi: 10.1038/77744

Marchand, A., Coutu, M.-F., Dupuis, G., Fleet, R., Borgeat, F., Todorov, C., & Mainguy, N. (2008). Treatment of panic disorder with agoraphobia: Randomized placebo-controlled trial of four psychosocial treatments combined with imipramine or placebo. *Cognitive Behaviour Therapy, 37,* 146–159. (15) 10.1080/16506070701743120

Marcia, J. E. (1980). Identity in adolescence. In J. Adelson (Ed.), *Handbook of adolescent psychology* (pp. 159–187). New York: Wiley. (5)

Marcus, D. K., O'Connell, D., Norris, A. L., & Sawaqdeh, A. (2014). Is the dodo bird endangered in the 21st century? A meta-analysis of treatment comparison studies. *Clinical Psychology Review, 34,* 519–530. (15) doi: 10.1016/j.cpr.2014.08.001

Marian, V., & Neisser, U. (2000). Language-dependent recall of autobiographical memories. *Journal of Experimental Psychology: General, 129,* 361–368. (7) doi: 10.1037//0096-3445.129.3.361

Marks, D., & Kammann, R. (1980). *The psychology of the psychic.* Buffalo, NY: Prometheus. (2, 14)

Markström, U. (2014). Staying the course? Challenges in implementing evidence-based programs in community mental health services. *International Journal of Environmental Research and Public Health, 11,* 10752–10769. (15) doi: 10.3390/ijerph111010752

Marler, P. (1997). Three models of song learning: Evidence from behavior. *Journal of Neurobiology, 33,* 501–516. (6)

Marler, P., & Peters, S. (1981). Sparrows learn adult song and more from memory. *Science, 213,* 780–782. (6) doi: 10.1126/science.213.4509.780

Marler, P., & Peters, S. (1982). Long-term storage of learned birdsongs prior to production. *Animal Behaviour, 30,* 479–482. (6) doi: 10.1016/S0003-3472(82)80059-6

Marouli, E., Graff, M., Medina-Gomez, C., Lo, K. S., Wood, A. R., Kjaer, T. R., Fine, R. S., Lu, Y. C., Schurmann, C., Highland, H. M., Rueger, S., Thorleifsson, G., Justice, A. E., Lamparter, D., Stirrups, K. E., Turcot, V., Young, K. L., Winkler, T. W., Esko, T., ... Lettre, G. (2017). Rare and low-frequency coding variants alter human adult height. *Nature, 542,* 186–190. (3) doi: 10.1038/nature21039

Marriott, F. H. C. (1976). Abnormal colour vision. In H. Davson (Ed.), *The eye* (2nd ed., pp. 533–547). New York: Academic Press. (4)

Marsh, E. J., Meade, M. L., & Roediger, H. L., III. (2003). Learning facts from fiction. *Journal of Memory and Language, 49,* 519–536. (7) doi: 10.1016/S0749-596X(03)00092-5

Marshall, D. J., Vitacco, M. J., Read, J. B., & Harway, M. (2014). Predicting voluntary and involuntary readmissions to forensic hospitals by insanity acquittees in Maryland. *Behavioral Sciences and the Law, 32,* 627–640. (15) doi: 10.1002/bsl.2136

Martens, A., Johns, M., Greenberg, J., & Schimel, J. (2006). Combating stereotype threat: The effect of self-affirmation on women's intellectual performance. *Journal of Experimental Social Psychology, 42,* 236–243. (9) doi: 10.1016/j.jesp.2005.04.010

Martin, A., & Olson, K. R. (2015). Beyond good and evil: What motivations underlie children's prosocial behavior? *Perspectives on Psychological Science, 10,* 159–175. (13) doi: 10.1177/1745691615568998

Martin, D. J., & Lynn, S. J. (1996). The hypnotic simulation index: Successful discrimination of real versus simulating participants. *International Journal of Clinical and Experimental Hypnosis, 44,* 338–353. (10) doi: 10.1080/00207149608416097

Martin, J. M., Reimann, M., & Norton, M. I. (2016). Experience theory, or how desserts are like losses. *Journal of Experimental Psychology: General, 145,* 1460–1472. (8) doi: 10.1037/xge0000215

Martindale, C. (2001). Oscillations and analogies: Thomas Young, MD, FRS, genius. *American Psychologist, 56,* 342–345. (4) doi: 10.1037/0003-066X.56.4.342

Martsh, C. T., & Miller, W. R. (1997). Extraversion predicts heavy drinking in college students. *Personality and Individual Differences, 23,* 153–155. (14) doi: 10.1016/S0191-8869(97)00015-9

Marx, J. (2003). Cellular warriors at the battle of the bulge. *Science, 299,* 846–849. (11) doi: 10.1126/science.299.5608.846

Maslow, A. H. (1943). *A theory of human motivation. Psychological Review, 50,* 370–396. (11) doi: 10.1037/h0054346

Maslow, A. H. (1962). *Toward a psychology of being.* Princeton, NJ: Van Nostrand. (14)

Maslow, A. H. (1971). *The farther reaches of human nature.* New York: Viking Press. (14)

Mason, B. J., Goodman, A. M., Chabac, S., & Lehert, P. (2006). Effect of oral acamprosate on abstinence in patients with alcohol dependence in a double-blind, placebo-controlled trial: The role of patient motivation. *Journal of Psychiatric Research, 40,* 383–393. (15) doi: 10.1016/j.jpsychires.2006.02.002

Mason, D. A., & Frick, P. J. (1994). The heritability of antisocial behavior: A meta-analysis of twin and adoption studies. *Journal of Psychopathology and Behavioral Assessment, 16,* 301–323. (5) doi: 10.1007/BF02239409

Mason, M. F., Norton, M. I., Van Horn, J. D., Wegner, D. M., Grafton, S. T., & Macrae, C. N. (2007). Wandering minds: The default network and stimulus-independent thought. *Science, 315,* 393–395. (3) doi: 10.1126/science.1131295

Massimini, M., Ferrarelli, F., Huber, R., Esser, S. K., Singh, H., & Tononi, G. (2005). Breakdown of cortical effective connectivity during sleep. *Science, 309,* 2228–2232. (10) doi: 10.1126/science.1117256

Masson, J. M. (1984). *The assault on truth.* New York: Farrar, Straus and Giroux. (14)

Masters, W. H., & Johnson, V. E. (1966). *Human sexual response.* Boston: Little, Brown. (11)

Mastracci, S., & Adams, I. (2019). Is emotional labor easier in collectivist or individualist cultures? An East-West comparison. *Public Personnel Management, 48,* 325–344. (12) doi: 10.1177/0091026018814569

Matchock, R. L. (2018). Evening chronotype is associated with a more unrestricted sociosexuality in men and women. *Personality and Individual Differences, 135,* 56–59. (10) doi: 10.1016/j.paid.2018.06.054

Matson, J. L., Adams, H. L., Williams, L. W., & Rieske, R. D. (2013). Why are there so many unsubstantiated treatments in autism? *Research in Autism Spectrum Disorders, 7,* 466–474. (15) doi: 10.1016/j.rasd.2012.11.006

Matsunami, H., Montmayeur, J.-P., & Buck, L. B. (2000). A family of candidate taste receptors in human and mouse. *Nature, 404,* 601–604. (4) https://www.nature.com/articles/35007072/

Matthews, M. D. (2014). *Head strong: How psychology is revolutionizing war.* Oxford, UK: Oxford University Press. (1, 11)

Mattson, M. P., & Magnus, T. (2006). Ageing and neuronal variability. *Nature Reviews Neuroscience, 7,* 278–294. (5) doi: 10.1038/nrn1886

Mattson, S. N., Crocker, N., & Nguyen, T. T. (2011). Fetal alcoholism spectrum disorders: Neuropsychological and behavioral features. *Neuropsychology Review, 21,* 8–101. (5) doi: 10.1007/s11065-011-9167-9

May, C. P., Hasher, L., & Stoltzfus, E. R. (1993). Optimal time of day and the magnitude of age differences in memory. *Psychological Science, 4,* 326–330. (10) doi: 10.1111/j.1467-9280.1993.tb00573.x

May, L., Gervain, J., Carreiras, S., & Werker, J. F. (2018). The specificity of the neural response to speech at birth. *Developmental Science, 21,* e12564. (5) doi: 10.1111/desc.12564

May, P. A., Blankenship, J., Marais, A.-S., Gossage, J. P., Kalberg, W. O., Joubert, B., Cloete, M., Barnard, R., De Vries, M., Hasken, J., Robinson, L. K., Adnams, C. M., Buckley, D., Manning, M., Parry, C. D. H., Hoyme, H. E., Tabachnick, B., ... Seedat, S. (2013). Maternal alcohol consumption producing fetal alcohol spectrum disorders (FASD): Quantity, frequency, and timing of drinking. *Drug and Alcohol Dependence, 133,* 502–512. (5) doi: 10.1016/j.drugalcdep.2013.07.013

Mayberry, R. I., Lock, E., & Kazmi, H. (2002). Linguistic ability and early language exposure. *Nature, 417,* 38. (8) doi: 10.1038/417038a

Mayer, J. D., Caruso, D. R., & Salovey, P. (2000). Emotional intelligence meets traditional standards for an intelligence. *Intelligence,* 27, 267–298. (12) doi: 10.1016/S0160-2896(99)00016-1

Mayer, J. D., & Salovey, P. (1995). Emotional intelligence and the construction and regulation of feelings. *Applied and Preventive Psychology, 4,* 197–208. (12) doi: 10.1016/S0962-1849(05)80058-7

Mayer, J. D., & Salovey, P. (1997). What is emotional intelligence? In P. Salovey & D. J. Sluyter (Eds.). *Emotional development and emotional intelligence* (pp. 3–34). New York: Basic Books. (12)

Mayer, J. D., Salovey, P., Caruso, D. R., & Sitarenios, G. (2001). Emotional intelligence as a standard intelligence. *Emotion, 1,* 232–242. (12) doi: 10.1037//1528-3542.1.3.232

Mazandarani, A. A., Aguilar-Vafaie, M. E., & Domhoff, G. W. (2013). Content analysis of Iranian college students' dreams: Comparison with American data. *Dreaming, 23,* 163–174. (10) doi: 10.1037/a0032352

Mazar, N., Amir, O., & Ariely, D. (2008). The dishonesty of honest people: A theory of self-concept maintenance. *Journal of Marketing Research, 45,* 633–644. (11) doi: 10.1509/jmkr.45.6.633

Mazzoni, G., Laurence, J.-R., & Heap, M. (2014). Hypnosis and memory: Two hundred years of adventures and still going! *Psychology of Consciousness, 1,* 153–167. (10) doi: https://psycnet.apa.org/record/2014-25109-005

Mazzoni, G., & Memon, A. (2003). Imagination can create false autobiographical memories. *Psychological Science, 14,* 186–188. (7) doi: 10.1046/j.1432-1327.2000.01821.x

McCall, W. A. (1939). *Measurement.* New York: Macmillan. (9)

McCarthy, M. M., & Arnold, A. P. (2011). Reframing sexual differentiation of the brain. *Nature Neuroscience, 14,* 677–683. (11) doi: 10.1038/nn.2834

McClelland, J. L. (1988). Connectionist models and psychological evidence. *Journal of Memory and Language, 27,* 107–123. (8) doi: 10.1016/0749-596X(88)90069-1

McClelland, J. L., & Rumelhart, D. E. (1981). An interactive activation model of context effects in letter perception: Part 1. An account of basic findings. *Psychological Review, 88,* 375–407. (8) doi: 10.1037/0033-295X.88.5.375

McCormick, C., Rosenthal, C. R., Miller, T. D., & Maguire, E. A. (2018). Mind-wandering in people with hippocampal damage. *Journal of Neuroscience, 38,* 2745–2754. (7) doi: 10.1523/JNEUROSCI.1812-17.2018

McCornack, R. L. (1983). Bias in the validity of predicted college grades in four ethnic minority groups. *Educational and Psychological Measurement, 43,* 517–522. (9) doi: 10.1177/001316448304300220

McCourt, K., Bouchard, T. J., Jr., Lykken, D. T., Tellegen, A., & Keyes, M. (1999). Authoritarianism revisited: Genetic and environmental influences examined in twins reared apart and together. *Personality and Individual Differences, 27,* 985–1014. (5) doi: 10.1016/S0191-8869(99)00048-3

McCrae, R. R. (1996). Social consequences of experiential openness. *Psychological Bulletin, 120,* 323–337. (14) doi: 10.1037/0033-2909.120.3.323

McCrae, R. R., Chan, W., Jussim, L., De Fruyt, F., Löckenhoff, C. E., De Bolle, M., Costa, P. T. Jr., Hrebickova, M., Graf, S., Realo, A., Allik, J., Nakazato, K., Shimonaka, Y., Yik, M., Fickova, E., Brunner-Sciarra, M., Reatigui, N., de Figueora, N. L., Schmidt, V., ... Terracciano, A. (2013). The inaccuracy of national character stereotypes. *Journal of Research in Personality, 47,* 831–842. (14) doi: 10.1016/j.jrp.2013.08.006

McCrae, R. R., & Costa, P. T., Jr. (1987). Validation of the five-factor model of personality across instruments and observers. *Journal of Personality and Social Psychology, 52,* 81–90. (14) doi: 10.1037/0022-3514.52.1.81

McCrae, R. R., & Costa, P. T., Jr. (1997). Personality trait structure as a human universal. *American Psychologist, 52,* 509–516. (14) doi: 10.1037/0003-066X.52.5.509

McCrae, R. R., Costa, P. T., Jr., Ostendorf, F., Angleitner, A., Hrebícková, M., Avia, M. D., Sanz, J., Sanchez-Bernardos, M. L., Kusdil, M. E., Woodfield, R., Saunders, P. R. & Smith, P. B. (2000). Nature over nurture: Temperament, personality, and life span development. *Journal of Personality and Social Psychology, 78,* 173–186. (14) doi: 10.1037/0022-3514.78.1.173

McCrea, S. M., Liberman, N., Trope, Y., & Sherman, S. J. (2008). Construal level and procrastination. *Psychological Science, 19,* 1308–1314. (11) doi: 10.1111/j.1467-9280.2008.02240.x

McCrink, K., & Wynn, K. (2004). Large-number addition and subtraction by 9-month-old infants. *Psychological Science, 15,* 776–781. (5) doi: 10.1111/j.0956-7976.2004.00755.x

McDaniel, M. A., Fadler, C. L., & Pashler, H. (2013). Effects of spaced versus massed training in function learning. *Journal of Experimental Psychology: Learning, Memory and Cognition, 39,* 1417–1432. (7) doi: 10.1037/a0032184

McDaniel, M. A., Howard, D. C., & Einstein, G. O. (2009). The read-recite-review study strategy. *Psychological Science, 20,* 516–522. (7) doi: 10.1111/j.1467-9280.2009.02325.x

McDermid, C. D. (1960). How *money* motivates *men. Business Horizons, 3*(4), 93–100. (11) doi: 10.1016/S0007-6813(60)80034-1

McDougall, W. (1938). Fourth report on a Lamarckian experiment. *British Journal of Psychology, 28,* 321–345, 365–395. (2) doi: 10.1111/j.2044-8295.1938.tb00878.x and doi: 10.1111/j.2044-8295.1938.tb00882.x

McElheny, V. (2004). Three Nobelists ask: Are we ready for the next frontier? *Cerebrum, 5,* 69–81. (1)

McEwen, B. S. (2000). The neurobiology of stress: From serendipity to clinical relevance. *Brain Research, 886,* 172–189. (12) doi: 10.1016/S0006-8993(00)02950-4

McFerran, B., & Mukhopadhyay, A. (2013). Lay theories of obesity predict actual mass. *Psychological Science, 24,* 1428–1436. (11) doi: 10.1177/0956797612473121

McGovern, P. E., Glusker, D. L., Exner, L. J., & Voigt, M. M. (1996). Neolithic resinated wine. *Nature, 381,* 480–481. (3) doi: 10.1038/381480a0

McGrath, J. J., Féron, F. P., Burne, T. H. J., Mackay-Sim, A., & Eyles, D. W. (2003). The neurodevelopmental hypothesis of schizophrenia: A review of recent developments. *Annals of Medicine, 35,* 86–93. (15) doi: 10.1080/07853890310010005

McGue, M. (1999). The behavioral genetics of alcoholism. *Current Directions in Psychological Science, 8,* 109–115. (15) doi: 10.1111/1467-8721.00026

McGue, M., & Bouchard, T. J., Jr. (1998). Genetic and environmental influences on human behavioral differences. *Annual Review of oscience, 21,* 1-24. (9) doi: 10.1146/rev.neuro.21.1.1

McGuire, S., & Clifford, J. (2000). Genetic and environmental contributions to loneliness in children. *Psychological Science, 11,* 487–491. (3) doi: 10.1111/1467-9280.00293

McGuire, W. J., & Papageorgis, D. (1961). The relative efficacy of various types of prior belief-defense in producing immunity against persuasion. *Journal of Abnormal and Social Psychology, 62,* 327–337. (13) doi: 10.1037/h0042026

McGurk, H., & MacDonald, J. (1976). Hearing lips and seeing voices. *Nature, 264,* 746–748. (8) doi: 10.1038/264746a0

McIntyre, M., Gangestad, S. W., Gray, P. B., Chapman, J. F., Burnham, T. C., O'Rourke, M. T., & Thornhill, R. (2006). Romantic involvement often reduces men's testosterone levels—But not always: The moderating effect of extrapair sexual interest. *Journal of Personality and Social Psychology, 91,* 642–651. (11) doi: 10.1037/0022-3514.91.4.642

McIntyre, R. S., Konarski, J. Z., Wilkins, K., Soczynska, J. K., & Kennedy, S. H. (2006). Obesity in bipolar disorder and major depressive disorder: Results from a national community health survey on mental health and well-being. *Canadian Journal of Psychiatry, 51,* 274–280. (11) doi: 10.1177/070674370605100502

McKelvey, M. W., & McKenry, P. C. (2000). The psychosocial well-being of Black and White mothers following marital dissolution. *Psychology of Women Quarterly, 24,* 4–14. (5) doi: 10.1111/j.1471-6402.2000.tb01017.x

McKinnon, J. D., & Bennett, C. E. (2005). *We the people: Blacks in the United States.* Washington, DC: U.S. Census Bureau. (9)

McMillan, K. A., Asmundson, G. J. G., Zvolensky, M. J., & Carleton, R. N. (2012). Startle response and anxiety sensitivity: subcortical indices of physiologic arousal and fear responding. *Emotion, 12,* 1264–1272. (12) doi: 10.1037/a0029108

McMurtry, P. L., & Mershon, D. H. (1985). Auditory distance judgments in noise, with and without hearing protection. *Proceedings of the Human Factors Society* (Baltimore), pp. 811–813. (4) doi: 10.1177/154193128502900820

McNally, R. J. (1990). Psychological approaches to panic disorder: A review. *Psychological Bulletin, 108,* 403–419. (15) doi: 10.1037/0033-2909.108.3.403

McNally, R. J., Bryant, R. A., & Ehlers, A. (2003). Does early psychological intervention promote recovery from posttraumatic stress? *Psychological Science in the Public Interest, 4,* 45–77. (12) doi: 10.1111/1529-1006.01421

McNally, R. J., & Geraerts, E. (2009). A new solution to the recovered memory debate. *Perspectives on Psychological Science, 4,* 126–134. (7) doi: 10.1111/j.1745-6924.2009.01112.x

McNamara, J. M., Barta, Z., Fromhage, L., & Houston, A. I. (2008). The coevolution of choosiness and cooperation. *Nature, 451,* 189–192. (13) doi: 10.1038/nature06455

McNamara, P., McLaren, D., Smith, D., Brown, A., & Stickgold, R. (2005). A "Jekyll and Hyde" within: Aggressive versus friendly interactions in REM and non-REM dreams. *Psychological Science, 16,* 130–136. (10) doi: 10.1111/j.0956-7976.2005.00793.x

Mechelli, A., Crinion, J. T., Noppeney, U., O'Doherty, J., Ashburner, J., Frackowiak, R. S., & Price, C. J. (2004). Structural plasticity in the bilingual brain. *Nature, 431,* 757. (8) doi: 10.1038/431757a

Meddis, R., Pearson, A. J. D., & Langford, G. (1973). An extreme case of healthy insomnia. *EEG and Clinical Neurophysiology, 35,* 213–214. (10) doi: 10.1016/0013-4694(73)90180-6

Medvec, V. H., Madey, S. F., & Gilovich, T. (1995). When less is more: Counterfactual thinking and satisfaction among Olympic athletes. *Journal of Personality and Social Psychology, 69,* 603–610. (12) doi: 10.1037/0022-3514.69.4.603

Meeussen, L., Otten, S., & Phalet, K. (2014). Managing diversity: How leaders' multiculturalism and colorblindness affect work group functioning. *Group Processes & Intergroup Relations, 17,* 629–644. (13) doi: 10.1177/1368430214525809

Mégarbané, A., Noguier, F., Stora, S., Manchon, L., Mircher, C., Bruno, R., Dorison, N., Pierrat, F., Rethore, M. O., Trentin, B., Ravel, A., Morent, M., Lefranc, G., P. & Piquemal, D. (2013). The intellectual disability of trisomy 21: Differences in gene expression in a case series of patients with lower and higher IQ. *European Journal of Human Genetics, 21,* 1253–1259. (9) doi: 10.1038/ejhg.2013.24

Mehl, M. R., Vazire, S., Holleran, S. E., & Clark, C. S. (2010). Eavesdropping on happiness: Well-being is related to having less small talk and more substantive conversations. *Psychological Science, 21,* 539–541. (12) doi: 10.1177/0956797610362675

Mehr, S. A., Song, L. A., & Spelke, E. S. (2016). For 5-month-old infants, melodies are social. *Psychological Science, 27,* 486–501. (5) doi: 10.1177/0956797615626691

Meinz, E. J., & Hambrick, D. Z. (2010). Deliberate practice is necessary but not sufficient to explain individual differences in piano sight-reading skill: The role of working memory capacity. *Psychological Science, 21,* 914–919. (8) doi: 10.1177/0956797610373933

Melamed, S., Shirom, A., Toker, S., Berliner, S., & Shapira, I. (2006). Burnout and risk of cardiovascular disease: Evidence, possible causal paths, and promising research directions. *Psychological Bulletin, 132,* 327–353. (11) doi: 10.1037/0033-2909.132.3.327

Melamed, F., & Zaidel, E. (1993). Language and task effects on lateralized word recognition. *Brain and Language, 45,* 70–85. (8) doi: 10.1006/brln.1993.1034

Melby-Lervåg, M., Redick, T. S., & Hulme, C. (2016). Working memory training does not improve performance on measures of intelligence or other measures of "far transfer": Evidence from a meta-analytic review. *Perspectives on Psychological Science, 11,* 512–534. (8) doi: 10.1177/1745691616635612

Melchers, K. G., Ungor, M., & Lachnit, H. (2005). The experimental task influences cue competition in human causal learning. *Journal of Experimental Psychology: Animal Behavior Processes, 31,* 477–483. (6) doi: 10.1037/0097-7403.31.4.477

Melchers, M., Plieger, T., Montag, C., Reuter, M., & Spinath, F. M. (2018). The heritability of response styles and its impact on heritability estimates of personality: A twin study. *Personality and Individual Differences, 134,* 16–24. (14) doi: 10.1016/j.paid.2018.05.023

Mellers, B., Ungar, L., Baron, J., Ramos, J., Gurcay, B., Fincher, K., Scott, S. E., Moore, D., Atanasov, P., Swift, S. A., Murray, T., Stone, E., & Tetlock, P. E. (2014). Psychological strategies for winning a geopolitical forecasting tournament. *Psychological Sciece, 25,* 1106–1115. (8) doi: 10.1177/0956797614524255

Meltzoff, A. N., & Moore, M. K. (1977). Imitation of facial and manual gestures by human neonates. *Science, 198,* 75–78. (3) doi: 10.1126/science.198.4312.75

Meltzer, A. L., Makhanova, A., Hicks, L. L., French, J. E., McNulty, J. K., & Bradbury, T. N. (2017). Quantifying the sexual afterglow: The lingering benefits of sex and their implications for pair-bonded relationships. *Psychological Science, 28,* 587–598. (11) doi: 10.1177/0956797617691361

Melzack, R., & Wall, P. D. (1965). Pain mechanisms: A new theory. *Science, 150,* 971–979. (4) doi: 10.1126/science.150.3699.971

Melzack, R., Weisz, A. Z., & Sprague, L. T. (1963). Stratagems for controlling pain: Contributions of auditory stimulation and suggestion. *Experimental Neurology, 8,* 239–247. (12) doi: 10.1016/0014-4886(63)90034-7

"The Menace Within." (2011, July/August). *Stanford Alumni Magazine.* Downloaded December 19, 2014 from alumni.stanford.edu (13)

Mendieta-Zéron, H., López, M., & Diéguez, C. (2008). Gastrointestinal peptides controlling body weight homeostasis. *General and Comparative Endocrinology, 155,* 481–495. (11) doi: 10.1016/j.ygcen.2007.11.009

Menie, M. A. W. O., Penaherrera, M. A., Fernandes, H. B. F., Becker, D., & Flynn, J. R. (2016). It's getting bigger all the time: Estimating the Flynn effect from secular brain mass increases in Britain and Germany. *Learning and Individual Differences, 45,* 95–100. (9) doi: 10.1016/j.lindif.2015.11.004

Mennella, J. A., Spector, A. C., Reed, D. R., & Coldwell, S. E. (2013). The bad taste of medicines: Overview of basic research on bitter taste. *Clinical Therapeutics, 35,* 1225–1246. (11) doi: 10.1016/j.clinthera.2013.06.007

Merckelbach, H, Dekkers, T., Wessel, I., & Roefs, A. (2003). Dissociative symptoms and amnesia in Dutch concentration camp survivors. *Comprehensive Psychiatry, 44,* 65–69. (7) doi: 10.1053/comp.2003.50011

Mershon, D. H., & King, L. E. (1975). Intensity and reverberation as factors in the auditory perception of egocentric distance. *Perception and Psychophysics, 18,* 409–415. (4) doi: 10.3758/BF03204113

Messinger, D. S. (2002). Positive and negative: Infant facial expressions and emotions. *Current Directions in Psychological Science, 11,* 1–6. (12) doi: 10.1111/1467-8721.00156

Messner, C., & Wänke, M. (2011). Good weather for Schwarz and Clore. *Emotion, 11,* 436–437. (12) doi: 10.1037/a0022821

Metcalfe, J., Casal-Roscum, L., Radin, A., & Friedman, D. (2015). On teaching old dogs new tricks. *Psychological Science, 26,* 1833–1842. (9) doi: 10.1177/0956797615597912

Meule, A., van Rezori, V., & Blechert, J. (2014). Food addiction and bulimia nervosa. *European Eating Disorders, 22,* 331–337. (11) doi: 10.1002/erv.2306

Meuret, A. E., Rosenfield, D., Wilhelm, F. H., Zhou, E., Conrad, A., Ritz, T., & Roth, W. T. (2011). Do unexpected panic attacks occur spontaneously? *Biological Psychiatry, 70,* 985–991. (15) doi: 10.1016/j.biopsych.2011.05.027

Meyer-Lindenberg, A., Mervis, C. B., & Berman, K. F. (2006). Neural mechanisms in Williams syndrome: A unique window to genetic influences on cognition and behaviour. *Nature Reviews Neuroscience, 7*, 380–393. (8) doi: 10.1038/nrn1906

Meyer, J. P., Becker, T. E., & Vandenberghe, C. (2004). Employee commitment and motivation: A conceptual analysis and integrative model. *Journal of Applied Psychology, 89*, 991–1007. (11) doi: 10.1037/0021-9010.89.6.991

Mezuk, B., Rafferty, J. A., Kershaw, K. N., Hudson, D., Abdou, C. M., Lee, H., Eaton, W. W., & Jackson, J. S. (2010). Reconsidering the role of social disadvantage in physical and mental health: Stressful life events, health behaviors, race, and depression. *American Journal of Epidemiology, 172*, 1238–1249. (15) doi: 10.1093/aje/kwq283

Mezzanotte, W. S., Tangel, D. J., & White, D. P. (1992). Waking genioglossal electromyogram in sleep apnea patients versus normal controls (a neuromuscular compensatory mechanism). *Journal of Clinical Investigation, 89*, 1571–1579. (10) doi: 10.1172/JCI115751

Miellet, S., O'Donnell, P. J., & Sereno, S. C. (2009). Parafoveal magnification. *Psychological Science, 20*, 721–728. (8) doi: 10.1111/j.1467-9280.2009.02364.x

Mihalcescu, I., Hsing, W., & Leibler, S. (2004). Resilient circadian oscillator revealed in cyanobacteria. *Nature, 430*, 81–85. (10) doi: 10.1038/nature02533

Mihura, J. L., Meyer, G. J., Dumitrascu, N., & Bombel, G. (2013). The validity of individual Rorschach variables: Systematic reviews and meta-analyses of the comprehensive system. *Psychological Bulletin, 139*, 548–605. (14) doi: 10.1037/a0029406

Mikels, J. A., & Schuster, M. M. (2016). The interpretive lenses of older adults are not rose-colored—Just less dark: Aging and the interpretation of ambiguous scenarios. *Emotion, 16*, 94–100. (12) doi: 10.1037/emo0000104

Mikkelson, A. C., & Pauley, P. M. (2013). Maximizing relationship possibilities: Relational maximization in romantic relationships. *Journal of Social Psychology, 153*, 467–485. (8) doi: 10.1080/00224545.2013.767776

Milar, K. S. (2000). The first generation of women psychologists and the psychology of women. *American Psychologist, 55*, 616–619. (1) doi: 10.1037/0003-066X.55.6.616

Milek, A., Butler, E. A., Tackman, A. M., Kaplan, D. M., Raison, C. L., Sbarra, D. A., Vazire, S., & Mehl, M. R. (2018). Eavesdropping on happiness revisited: A pooled, multisample replication of the association between life satisfaction and observed daily conversation quantity and quality. *Psychological Science, 29*, 1451–1462. (12) doi: 10.1177/0956797618774252

Milgram, S. (1974). *Obedience to authority*. New York: Harper & Row. (13)

Milich, R., Wolraich, M., & Lindgren, S. (1986). Sugar and hyperactivity: A critical review of empirical findings. *Clinical Psychology Review, 6*, 493–513. (2) doi: 10.1016/0272-7358(86)90034-6

Miller, A. H., Maletic, V., & Raison, C. L. (2009). Inflammation and its discontents: The role of cytokines in the pathophysiology of major depression. *Biological Psychiatry, 65*, 732–741. (15) doi: 10.1016/j.biopsych.2008.11.029

Miller, C. T., Dibble, E., & Hauser, M. D. (2001). Amodal completion of acoustic signals by a nonhuman primate. *Nature Neuroscience, 4*, 783–784. (4) doi: 10.1038/90481

Miller, G. (2007a). Animal extremists get personal. *Science, 318*, 1856–1858. (2) doi: 10.1126/science.318.5858.1856

Miller, G. (2007b). The mystery of the missing smile. *Science, 316*, 826–827. (12) doi: 10.1126/science.316.5826.826

Miller, G. A. (1956). The magical number seven, plus or minus two: Some limits on our capacity for processing information. *Psychological Review, 63*, 81–97. (7) doi: 10.1037/0033-295X.101.2.343

Miller, J. F., Neufang, M., Solway, A., Brandt, A., Trippel, M., Mader, I., Hefft, S., Merkow, M., Polyn, S. M., Jacobs, J., Kahana, M. J. & Schulze-Bonhage, A. (2013). Neural activity in human hippocampal formation reveals the spatial context of retrieved memories. *Science, 342*, 1111–1114. (7) doi: 10.1126/science.1244056

Miller, J. G., Goyal, N., & Wice, M. (2017). A cultural psychology of agency: Morality, motivation, and reciprocity. *Perspectives on Psychological Science, 12*, 867–875. (13) doi: 10.1177/1745691617706099

Miller, L. C., & Fishkin, S. A. (1997). On the dynamics of human bonding and reproductive success: Seeking windows on the adapted-for human–environmental interface. In J. A. Simpson & D. T. Kenrick (Eds.), *Evolutionary social psychology* (pp. 197–235). Mahwah, NJ: Erlbaum. (2)

Miller, M. A., Hays, L. R., & Fillmore, M. T. (2012). Lack of tolerance to the disinhibiting effects of alcohol in heavy drinkers. *Psychopharmacology, 224*, 511–518. (15) doi: 10.1007/s00213-012-2786-x

Miller, R. M., Hannikainen, & Cushman, F. A. (2014). Bad actions or bad outcomes? Differentiating affective contributions to the moral condemnation of harm. *Emotion, 14*, 573–587. (12) doi: 10.1037/a0035361

Miller, S. L., & Maner, J. K. (2010). Scent of a woman: Men's testosterone responses to olfactory ovulation cues. *Psychological Science, 21*, 276–283. (4) doi: 10.1177/0956797609357733

Milne, S. E., Orbell, S., & Sheeran, P. (2002). Combining motivational and volitional interventions to promote exercise participation: Protection motivation theory and implementation intentions. *British Journal of Health Psychology, 7*, 163–184. (11) doi: 10.1348/135910702169420

Milner, B. (1959). The memory defect in bilateral hippocampal lesions. *Psychiatric Research Reports, 11*, 43–52. (7)

Milton, J., & Wiseman, R. (1999). Does psi exist? Lack of replication of an anomalous process of information. *Psychological Bulletin, 125*, 387–391. (2) doi: 10.1037/0033-2909.125.4.387

Milyavskaya, M., & Inzlicht, M. (2017). What's so great about self-control? Examining the importance of effortful self-control and temptation in predicting real-life depletion and goal attainment. *Social Psychological and Personality Science, 8*, 603–611. (11) doi: 10.1177/1948550616679237

Minde, K., Minde, R., & Vogel, W. (2006). Culturally sensitive assessment of attachment in children aged 18–40 months in a South African township. *Infant Mental Health Journal, 27*, 544–558. (5) doi: 10.1002/imhj.20106

Minder, F., Zuberer, A., Brandeis, D., & Drechsler, R. (2018). A review of the clinical utility of systematic behavioral observations in attention deficit hyperactivity disorder (ADHD). *Child Psychiatry & Human Development, 49*, 572–606. (8) doi: 10.1007/s10578-017-0776-2

Mineka, S. (1987). A primate model of phobic fears. In H. Eysenck & I. Martin (Eds.), *Theoretical foundations of behavior therapy* (pp. 81–111). New York: Plenum Press. (15)

Mineka, S., Davidson, M., Cook, M., & Keir, R. (1984). Observational conditioning of snake fear in rhesus monkeys. *Journal of Abnormal Psychology, 93*, 355–372. (15) doi: 10.1037/0021-843X.93.4.355

Mingroni, M. A. (2004). The secular rise in IQ: Giving heterosis a closer look. *Intelligence, 32*, 65–83. (9) doi: 10.1016/S0160-2896(03)00058-8

Minto, C. L., Liao, L.-M., Woodhouse, C. R. J., Ransley, P. G., & Creighton, S. M. (2003). The effect of clitoral surgery on sexual outcome in individuals who have intersex conditions with ambiguous genitalia: A cross-sectional study. *Lancet, 361*, 1252–1257. (11) doi: 10.1016/S0140-6736(03)12980-7

Mischel, W. (1973). Toward a cognitive social learning reconceptualization of personality. *Psychological Review, 80*, 252–283. (14) doi: 10.1037/h0035002

Mischel, W. (1981). Current issues and challenges in personality. In L. T. Benjamin, Jr. (Ed.), *The G. Stanley Hall Lecture Series* (Vol. 1, pp. 81–99). Washington, DC: American Psychological Association. (14)

Misrahi, M., Meduri, G., Pissard, S., Bouvattier, C., Beau, I., Loosfelt, H., Jolivet, A., Rapport, R., Milgrom, E., & Bougneres, P. (1997). Comparison of immunocytochemical and molecular features with the phenotype in a case of incomplete male pseudohermaphroditism associated with a mutation of the luteinizing hormone receptor. *Journal of Clinical Endocrinology and Metabolism, 82*, 2159–2165. (11) doi: 10.1210/jc.82.7.2159

Missotten, L. C., Luyckx, K., Branje, S. J. T., Hale, W. W. III, & Meeus, W. H. (2017). Examining the longitudinal relations among adolescents' conflict management with parents and conflict management with parents and conflict frequency. *Personality and Individual Differences, 117*, 37–41. (5) doi: 10.1016/j.paid.2017.05.037

Mitroff, S. R., & Biggs, A. T. (2014). The ultra-rare-item effect: Visual search for exceedingly rare items is highly susceptible to error. *Psychological Science, 25*, 284–289. (4) doi: 10.1177/0956797613504221

Miu, A. C., Vulturar, R., Chis, A., Ungureanu, L., & Gross, J. J. (2013). Reappraisal as a mediator in the link between 5-HTTLPR and social anxiety symptoms. *Emotion, 13*, 1012–1022. (12) doi: 10.1037/a0033383

Miyake, A., Kost-Smith, L. E., Finkelstein, N. D., Pollock, S. J., Cohen, G. L., & Ito, T. A. (2010). Reducing the gender achievement gap in college science: A classroom study of values affirmation. *Science, 330*, 1234–1237. (9) doi: 10.1126/science.1195996

Miyamoto, Y., Nisbett, R. E., & Masuda, T. (2006). Culture and the physical environment. *Psychological Science, 17*, 113–119. (13) doi: 10.1111/j.1467-9280.2006.01673.x

Mobbs, D., Yu, R., Meyer, M., Passamonti, L., Seymour, B., Calder, A. J., Schweizer, S., Frith, C. D., & Dalgleish, T. (2009). A key role for similarity in vicarious reward. *Science, 324*, 900. (6) doi: 10.1126/science.1170539

va, R. N., Murdock, M. H., Parekh, P. tcho, R. N., Huang, B. S., Huynh, T. N., ım, J., Shaver, D. C., Rosenthal, D. L., Alway, E. J., Lopez, K., Meng, Y., Nellissen, L., Grosenick, L., Milner, T. A., Deisseroth, K., Bito, H., Kasai, H., & Liston, C. (2019). Sustained rescue of prefrontal circuit dysfunction by antidepressant-induced spine formation. *Science, 364*, 147. (15) doi: 10.1126/science.aat8078

Moher, J., Lakshmanan, B. M., Egeth, H. E., & Ewen, J. B. (2014). Inhibition drives early feature-based attention. *Psychological Science, 25*, 315–324. (10) doi: 10.1177/0956797613511257

Moitra, E., Dyck, I., Beard, C., Bjornsson, A. S., Sibrava, N. J., Weisberg, R. B., Keller, M. B. (2011). Impact of stressful life events on the course of panic disorder in adults. *Journal of Affective Disorders, 134*, 373–376. (15) doi: 10.1016/j.jad.2011.05.029

Mojtabai, R., & Olfson, M. (2008). National trends in psychotherapy by office-based psychiatrists. *Archives of General Psychiatry, 65*, 962–970. (1) doi: 10.1001/archpsyc.65.8.962

Molina, B. S. G., Hinshaw, S. P., Swanson, J. M., Arnold, L. E., Vitiello, B., Jensen, P. S., Epstein, J. N., Hoza, B., Hechtman, L., Abikoff, H. B., Elliott, G. R., Greenhill, L. L., Newcorn, J. H., Wells, K. C., Wigal, T., Gibbons, R. D., Hur, K., Houck, P. R., & the MTA Cooperative Group. (2009). The MTA at 8 years: Prospective follow-up of children treated for combined-type ADHD in a multisite study. *Journal of the American Academy of Child and Adolescent Psychiatry, 48*, 484–500. (8) doi: 10.1097/CHI.0b013e31819c23d0

Moller, H. J. (1992). Attempted suicide: Efficacy of different aftercare strategies. *International Clinical Psychopharmacology, 6*(Suppl. 6), 58–59. (15) doi: 10.1097/00004850-199206006-00007

Mondloch, C. J., Leis, A., & Maurer, D. (2006). Recognizing the face of Johnny, Suzy, and me: Insensitivity to the spacing among features at 4 years of age. *Child Development, 77*, 234–243. (5) doi: 10.1111/j.1467-8624.2006.00867.x

Money, J., & Ehrhardt, A. A. (1972). *Man & woman, boy & girl*. Baltimore, MD: Johns Hopkins University Press. (11)

Mongrain, M., Chin, J. M., & Shapira, L. B. (2011). Practicing compassion increases happiness and self-esteem. *Journal of Happiness Studies, 12*, 963–981. (12) doi: 10.1007/s10902-010-9239-1

Montgomery, G., & Kirsch, I. (1996). Mechanisms of placebo pain reduction: An empirical investigation. *Psychological Science, 7*, 174–176. (4) doi: 10.1111/j.1467-9280.1996.tb00352.x

Montgomery, K. J., Seeherman, K. R., & Haxby, J. V. (2009). The well-tempered social brain. *Psychological Science, 20*, 1211–1213. (3) doi: 10.1111/j.1467-9280.2009.02428.x

Monti, M. M., Vanhaudenhuyse, A., Coleman, M. R., Boly, M., Pickard, J. D., Tshibanda, L., Owen, A. M., & Laureys, S. (2010). Willful modulation of brain activity in disorders of consciousness. *New England Journal of Medicine, 362*, 579–589. (10) doi: 10.1056/NEJMoa0905370

Montoya, R. M. (2008). I'm hot, so I'd say you're not: The influence of objective physical attractiveness on mate selection. *Personality and Social Psychology Bulletin, 34*, 1315–1331. (13) doi: 10.1177/0146167208320387

Montoya, R. M., Horton, R. S., & Kirchner, J. (2008). Is actual similarity necessary for attraction? A meta-analysis of actual and perceived similarity. *Journal of Social and Personal Relationships, 25*, 889–922. (13) doi: 10.1177/0265407508096700

Moon, J. R., Glymour, M. M., Vable, A. M., Liu, S. Y., & Subramanian, S. V. (2014). Short- and long-term associations between widowhood and mortality in the United States: Longitudinal analysis. *Journal of Public Health, 36*, 382–389. (12) doi: 10.1093/pubmed/fdt101

Moorcroft, W. (1993). *Sleep, dreaming, and sleep disorders: An introduction* (2nd ed.). Lanham, MD: University Press of America. (10)

Moorcroft, W. H. (2003). *Understanding sleep and dreaming*. New York: Kluwer. (10)

Moore, B. C. J. (1989). *An introduction to the psychology of hearing* (3rd ed.). London: Academic Press. (4)

Moore, D. S., & Johnson, S. P. (2008). Mental rotation in human infants. *Psychological Science, 19*, 1063–1066. (5) doi: 10.1111/j.1467-9280.2008.02200.x

Moors, A. (2009). Theories of emotion causation: A review. *Cognition & Emotion, 23*, 625–662. (12) doi: 10.1080/02699930802645739

Moran, E., & Kring, A. M. (2018). Anticipatory emotions in schizophrenia. *Cllinical Psychological Science, 6*, 63–75. (15) doi: 10.1177/2167702617730877

Moreira, J. F. G., & Telzer, E. H. (2018). Mother still knows best: Maternal influence uniquely modulates adolescent reward sensitivity during risk taking. *Developmental Science, 21*, e12484. (5) doi: 10.1111/desc.12484

Moreno-Jiménez, E. P., Glor-García, M., Tereros-Roncal, J., Rábano, A., Cafini, F., Palla-Bazarra, N., Avila, A., & Lorens-Martín, M. (2019). Adult hippocampal neurogenesis is abundant in neurologically healthy subjects and drops sharply in patients with Alzheimer's disease. *Nature Medicine, 25*, 554–560. (3) doi: 10.1038/s41591-019-0375-9

Morewedge, C. K., & Norton, M. I. (2009). When dreaming is believing: The (motivated) interpretation of dreams. *Journal of Personality and Social Psychology, 96*, 249–264. (10) doi: 10.1037/a0013264

Moriuchi, J. M., Klin, A., & Jones, W. (2017). Mechanisms of diminished attention to eyes in autism. *American Journal of Psychiatry, 174*, 26–35. (15) doi: 10.1176/appi.ajp.2016.15091222

Morris, G., Baker-Ward, L., & Bauer, P. J. (2010). What remains of that day: The survival of children's autobiographical memories across time. *Applied Cognitive Psychology, 24*, 527–544. (7) doi: 10.1002/acp.1567

Morris, M., Lack. L., & Dawson, D. (1990). Sleep-onset insomniacs have delayed temperature rhythms. *Sleep, 13*, 1–14. (10) doi: 10.1093/sleep/13.1.1

Morris, S. Z., & Gibson, C. L. (2011). Corporal punishments influence on children's aggressive and delinquent behavior. *Criminal Justice and Behavior, 38*, 818–839. (6) doi: 10.1177/0093854811406070

Morrison, A. P. (2019). Should people with psychosis be supported in choosing cognitive therapy as an alternative to antipsychotic medication: A commentary on current evidence. *Schizophrenia Research, 203*, 94–98. (15) doi: 10.1016/j.schres.2018.03.010

Mosing, M. A., Madison, G., Pederson, N. L., Kuja-Halkola, R., & Ullén, F. (2014). Practice does not make perfect: No causal effect of music practice on music ability. *Psychological Science, 25*, 1795–1803. (8) doi: 10.1177/0956797614541990

Moscovitch, M. (1985). Memory from infancy to old age: Implications for theories of normal and pathological memory. *Annals of the New York Academy of Sciences, 444*, 78–96. (7) doi: 10.1111/j.1749-6632.1985.tb37581.x

Moscovitch, M. (1989). Confabulation and the frontal systems: Strategic versus associative retrieval in neuropsychological theories of memory. In H. L. Roediger, III, & F. I. M. Craik (Eds.), *Varieties of memory and consciousness: Essays in honour of Endel Tulving* (pp. 133–160). Hillsdale, NJ: Erlbaum. (7)

Moscovitch, M. (1992). Memory and working-with-memory: A component process model based on modules and central systems. *Journal of Cognitive Neuroscience, 4*, 257–267. (7) doi: 10.1162/jocn.1992.4.3.257

Moskowitz, B. A. (1978). The acquisition of language. *Scientific American, 239*(5), 92–108. (8) doi: 10.1038/scientificamerican1178-92

Moss, E., Cyr, C., Bureau, J.-F., Tarabulsy, G. M., & Dubois-Comtois, K. (2005). Stability of attachment during the preschool period. *Developmental Psychology, 41*, 773–783. (5) doi: 10.1037/0012-1649.41.5.773

Mottus, R., Allik, J., Realo, A., Rossier, J., Zecca, G., Ah-Kion, J., Amoussou-Yeye, D., Backstrom, M., Barkauskiene, R., Barry, O., Bhowon, U., Bjorklund, F., Bochaver, A., Bochaver, K., de Bruin, G., Cabrera, H. F., Chen, S. X., Church, A. T., Cisse, D. D., ... Johnson, W. (2012). The effect of response style on self-reported conscientiousness across 20 countries. *Personality and Social Psychology Bulletin, 38*, 1423–1436. (14) doi: 10.1177/0146167212451275

Mottus, R., Realo, A., Vainik, U., Allik, J., & Esko, T. (2017). Educational attainment and personality are genetically intertwined. *Psychological Science, 28*, 1631–1639. (14) doi: 10.1177/0956797617719083

Mouzon, D. M., (2013). Can family relationships explain the race paradox in mental health? *Journal of Marriage and the Family, 75*, 470–485. (15) doi: 10.1111/jomf.12006

Mouzon, D. M. (2014). Relationships of choice: Can friendships or fictive kinships explain the race paradox in mental health? *Social Science Research, 44*, 32–44. (15) doi: 10.1016/j.ssresearch.2013.10.007

Mrazek, M. D., Franklin, M. S., Phillips, D. T., Baird, B., & Schooler, J. W. (2013). Mindfulness training improves working memory capacity and GRE performance while reducing mind wandering. *Psychological Science, 24*, 776–781. (10) doi: 10.1177/0956797612459659

Muchnik, L., Aral, S., & Taylor, S. J. (2013). Social influence bias: A randomized experiment. *Science, 341*, 647–651. (13) doi: 10.1126/science.1240466

Müller, M. M., Malinowski, P., Gruber, T., & Hillyard, S. A. (2003). Sustained division of the attentional spotlight. *Nature, 424*, 309–312. (8) doi: 10.1038/nature01812

Muñoz, R. F., Bunge, E. L., Chen, K., Schueller, S. M., Bravin, J. I., Shaughnessy, E. A., & Pérez-Stable, E. J. (2016). Massive open online interventions: A novel model for delivering behavioral-health services worldwide. *Clinical Psychological Science, 4*, 194–205. (15) doi: 10.1177/2167702615583840

Murali, M. S. (2001). Epidemiological study of prevalence of mental disorders in India. *Indian Journal of Community Medicine, 26*, 198. (15)

https://www.ncbi.nlm.nih.gov/pmc/articles/PMC2956997/

Muraskin, J., Sherwin, J., & Sajda, P. (2015). Knowing when not to swing: EEG evidence that enhanced perception-action coupling underlies baseball batter expertise. *NeuroImage, 123,* 1–10. (4) doi: 10.1016/j.neuroimage.2015.08.028

Muraven, M., & Baumeister, R. F. (2000). Self-regulation and depletion of limited resources: Does self-control resemble a muscle? *Psychological Bulletin, 126,* 247–259. (12) doi: 10.1037/0033-2909.126.2.247

Muris, P., Merckelbach, H., Otgaar, H., & Meijer, E. (2017). The malevolent side of human nature: A meta-analysis and critical review of the dark triad (narcissism, Machiavellianism, and psychopathy). *Perspectives on Psychological Science, 12,* 183–204. (13) doi: 10.1177/1745691616666070

Murphy, G. L., & Medin, D. L. (1985). The role of theories in conceptual coherence. *Psychological Review, 92,* 289–316. (8) doi: 10.1037/0033-295X.92.3.289

Murphy, M. L. M., Slavich, G. M., Chen, E., & Miller, G. E. (2015). Targeted rejection predicts decreased anti-inflammatory gene expression and increased symptom severity in youth with asthma. *Psychological Science, 26,* 111–121. (12) doi: 10.1177/0956797614556320

Murray, C., (2007). The magnitude and components of change in the black-white IQ difference from 1920 to 1991: A birth cohort analysis of the Woodcock-Johnson standardizations. *Intelligence, 35,* 305–318. (9) doi: 10.1016/j.intell.2007.02.001

Murray, C., Johnson, W., Wolf, M. S., & Deary, I. J. (2011). The association between cognitive ability across the lifespan and health literacy in old age: The Lothian birth cohort 1936. *Intelligence, 39,* 178–187. (9) doi: 10.1016/j.intell.2011.04.001

Murray, D. R., Murphy, S. C., von Hippel, W., Trivers, R., & Haselton, M. G. (2017). A preregistered study of competing predictions suggests that men *do* overestimate women's sexual interest. *Psychological Science, 28,* 253–255. (2) doi: 10.1177/0956797616675474

Murray, G., Nicholas, C. L., Kleiman, J., Dwyer, R., Carrington, M. J., Allen, N. B., & Trinder, J. (2009). Nature's clocks and human mood: The circadian system modulates reward motivation. *Emotion, 9,* 705–716. (10) doi: 10.1037/a0017080

Murray, H. A. (1943). *Thematic Apperception Test manual.* Cambridge, MA: Harvard University Press. (14)

Murrie, D. C., Boccaccini, M. T., Guarnera, L. A., & Rufino, K. A. (2013). Are forensic experts biased by the side that retained them? *Psychological Science, 24,* 1889–1897. (2) doi: 10.1177/0956797613481812

Myers, D. G. (2000). The funds, friends, and faith of happy people. *American Psychologist, 55,* 56–67. (12) doi: 10.1037/0003-066X.55.1.56

Nadig, A. S., & Sedivy, J. C. (2002). Evidence of perspective-taking constraints in children's on-line reference resolution. *Psychological Science, 13,* 329–336. (5) doi: 10.1111/j.0956-7976.2002.00460.x

Nagy, E. (2011). Sharing the moment: The duration of embraces in humans. *Journal of Ethology, 29,* 389–393. (5) doi: 10.1007/s10164-010-0260-y

Nahum, L., Bouzerda-Wahlen, A., Guggisberg, A., Ptak, R., & Schnider, A. (2012). Forms of confabulation: Dissociations and associations. *Neuropsychologia, 50,* 2524–2534. (7) doi: 10.1016/j.neuropsychologia.2012.06.026

Nairne, J. S., Pandeirada, J. N. S., Gregory, K. J., & Van Arsdall, J. E. (2009). Adaptive memory: Fitness relevance and the hunter-gatherer mind. *Psychological Science, 20,* 740–746. (7) doi: 10.1111/j.1467-9280.2009.02356.x

Nairne, J. S., Pandeirada, J. N. S., & Thompson, S. R. (2008). Adaptive memory: The comparative value of survival processing. *Psychological Science, 19,* 176–180. (7) doi: 10.1111/j.1467-9280.2008.02064.x

Nairne, J. S., Thompson, S. R., & Pandeirada, J. N. S. (2007). Adaptive memory: Survival processing enhances retention. *Journal of Experimental Psychology: Learning, Memory, and Cognition, 33,* 263–273. (7) doi: 10.1037/0278-7393.33.2.263

Nairne, J. S., VanArsdall, J. E., Pandeirada, J. N. S., Cogdill, M., & Le Breton, J. M. (2013). Adaptive memory: The mnemonic value of animacy. *Psychological Science, 24,* 2099–2105. (7) doi: 10.1177/0956797613480803

Nan, X., Zhao, X., Yang, B., & Iles, I. (2015). Effectiveness of cigarette warning labels: Examining the impact of graphics, message framing, and temporal framing. *Health Communication, 30,* 81–89. (13) doi: 10.1080/10410236.2013.841531

Napier, J. L., & Jost, J. T. (2008). Why are conservatives happier than liberals? *Psychological Science, 19,* 565–572. (2) doi: 10.1111/j.1467-9280.2008.02124.x

Nath, R. D., Bedbrook, C. N., Abrams, M. J., Basinger, T., Bois, J. S., Prober, D. A., Stemberg, P. W., Gradinaru, V., & Goentoro, L. (2017). The jellyfish *Cassiopea* exhibits a sleep-like state. *Current Biology, 27,* 2984–2990. (10) doi: 10.1016/j.cub.2017.08.014

National Institutes of Health. (2000). *The practical guide: Identification, evaluation, and treatment of overweight and obesity in adults* (NIH Publication No. 00–4084). Washington, DC: Author. (11)

National Science Foundation (2015). *Doctorate recipients from U.S. universities: 2014.* Retrieved from https://www.nsf.gov/statistics/2016/nsf16300/digest/nsf16300.pdf (1)

Nave, G., Camerer, C., & McCullough, M. (2015). Does oxytocin increase trust in humans? A critical review of research. *Perspectives on Psychological Science, 10,* 772–789. (3) doi: 10.1177/1745691615600138

Nave, G., Jung, W. H., Linner, R. K., Kable, J. W., & Koellinger, P. D. (2019). Are bigger brains smarter? Evidence from a large-scale preregistered study. *Psychological Science, 30,* 43–54. (9) doi: 10.1177/0956797618808470

Nay, W., Brown, R., & Roberson-Nay, R. (2013). Longitudinal course of panic disorder with and without agoraphobia using the national epidemiologic survey on alcohol and related conditions (NESARC). *Psychiatry Research, 208,* 54–61. (15) doi: 10.1016/j.psychres.2013.03.006

Neal, T. M. S., Slobogin, C., Saks, M. J., Faigman, D. L., & Geisinger, K. F. (2019). Psychological assessments in legal contexts: Are courts keeping "junk science" out of the courtroom? *Psychological Science in the Public Interest, 20,* 135–164. (14) doi:10.1177/1529100619888860

Nebes, R. D. (1974). Hemispheric specialization in commissurotomized man. *Psychological Bulletin, 81,* 1–14. (3) doi: 10.1037/h0035626

Nedelec, J. L., & Beaver, K. M. (2014). Physical attractiveness as a phenotypic marker of health: An assessment using a nationally representative sample of American adults. *Evolution and Human Behavior, 35,* 456–463. (13) doi: 10.1016/j.evolhumbehav.2014.06.004

Neher, A. (1991). Maslow's theory of motivation: A critique. *Journal of Humanistic Psychology, 31,* 89–112. (14) doi: 10.1177/0022167891313010

Nelson, C. A. III, Zeanah, C. H., Fox, N. A., Marshall, P. J., Smyke, A. T., & Guthrie, D. (2007). Cognitive recovery in socially deprived young children: The Bucharest Early Intervention Project. *Science, 318,* 1937–1940 (9) doi: 10.1126/science.1143921

Nelson, S. K., Kushlev, K., English, T., Dunn, E. W., & Lyubomirsky, S. (2013). In defense of parenthood: Children are associated with more joy than misery. *Psychological Science, 24,* 3–10. (12) doi: 10.1177/0956797612447798

Nelson, S. K., Layous, K., Cole, S. W., & Lyubomirsky, S. (2016). Do unto others or treat yourself? The effects of prosocial and self-focused behavior on psychological flourishing. *Emotion, 16,* 850–861. (12) doi: 10.1037/emo0000178

Nemeth, C. (1972). A critical analysis of research utilizing the prisoner's dilemma paradigm for the study of bargaining. In L. Berkowitz (Ed.), *Advances in experimental social psychology* (Vol. 6, pp. 203–234). New York: Academic Press. (13) doi: 10.1016/S0065-2601(08)60028-3

Nemeth, C. J. (1986). Differential contributions of majority and minority influence. *Psychological Review, 93,* 23–32. (13) doi: 10.1037/0033-295X.93.1.23

Neto, F., & Pinto, M. D. (2013). The satisfaction with life across the adult life span. *Social Indicators Research, 114,* 767–784. (11) doi: 10.1007/s11205-012-0181-y

Newall, C., Gonsalkorale, K., Walker, E., Forbes, G. A., Highfield, K., & Sweller, N. (2018). Science education Adult biases because of the child's gender and gender stereotypicality. *Contemporary Educational Psychology, 55,* 30–41. (5) doi: 10.1016/j.cedpsych.2018.08.003

Newman, B. (1988, September 9). Dressing for dinner remains an issue in the naked city. *The Wall Street Journal,* p. 1. (13)

Newman, E. J., Sanson, M., Miller, E. K., Quigley-McBride, A., Foster, J. L., Bernstein, D. M., & Garry, M. (2014). People with easier to pronounce names promote truthiness of claims. *PLoS One, 9,* Article 88671. (8) doi: 10.1371/journal.pone.0088671

Newman, E. J., & Schwarz, N. (2018). Good sound, good research: How audio quality influences perception of the research and the researcher. *Science Communication, 40,* 246–257. (8) doi: 10.1177/1075547018759345

"NextGen Speaks." (2014). *Science, 343,* 24–26. (10) https://www.researchgate.net/publication/278239780_NextGen_Speaks

Ng, S.-F., Lin, R. C. Y., Laybutt, R., Barres, R., Ownes, J. A., & Morris, M. J. (2010). Chronic high-fat diet in fathers programs beta-cell dysfunction in female rat offspring. *Nature, 467,* 963–966. (3) doi: 10.1038/nature09491

Nguyen, H.-H. D., & Ryan, A. M. (2008). Does stereotype threat affect test performance of minorities and women? A meta-analysis of experimental evidence. *Journal of Applied*

ology, 93, 1314–1334. (9) doi: 10.1037/
702

. S., Wild, C. J., Stojanoski, B., Battista, M.
E., & Owen, A. M. (2020). Bilingualism affords
no general cognitive advantages: A population
study of executive function in 11,000 people.
Psychological Science, 31, 548–567. Doi:
10.1177/0956797620903113 (8)

Nicholson, H., Foote, C., & Gigerick, S. (2009).
Deleterious effects of psychotherapy and
counseling in the schools. *Psychology in
the Schools, 46*, 232–237. (15) doi: 10.1002/
pits.20367

Nickerson, C., Schwarz, N., Diener, E., &
Kahneman, D. (2003). Zeroing in on the dark
side of the American Dream: A closer look
at the negative consequences of the goal for
financial success. *Psychological Science, 14*,
531–536. (12) doi: 10.1046/j.0956-7976.2003.
psci_1461.x

Nickerson, R. S., & Adams, M. J. (1979). Long-
term memory for a common object. *Cognitive
Psychology, 11*, 287–307. (7) doi: 10.1016/0010-
0285(79)90013-6

Nielsen, T. A., Zadra, A. L., Simard, V., Saucier, S.,
Stenstrom, P., Smith, C., & Kuiken, D. (2003).
The typical dreams of Canadian university
students. *Dreaming, 13*, 211–235. (10) doi:
10.1023/B:DREM.0000003144.40929.0b

Niessen, A. S. M., & Meijer, R. R. (2017). On
the use of broadened admission criteria
in higher education. *Perspectives on
Psychological Science, 12*, 436–448. (9) doi:
10.1177/1745691616683050

Nietzel, M. T., & Bernstein, D. A. (1987).
Introduction to clinical psychology. Upper
Saddle River, NJ: Prentice-Hall. (9)

Niiya, Y., Ellsworth, P. C., & Yamaguchi, S. (2006).
Amae in Japan and the United States: An
exploration of a "culturally unique" emotion.
Emotion, 6, 279–295. (12) doi: 10.1037/1528-
3542.6.2.279

Nikolova, Y. S., Koenen, K. C., Galea, S., Wang,
C.-M., Seney, M. L., Sibille, E., Williamson, D.
E., & Hariri, A. R. (2014). Beyond genotype:
Serotonin transporter epigenetic modification
predicts human brain function. *Nature
Neuroscience, 17*, 1153–1155. (12) doi: 10.1038/
nn.3778

Nir, Y., Andrillon, T., Marmelshtein, A., Suthana,
N., Cirelli, C., Tononi, G., & Fried, I. (2017).
Selective neuronal lapses precede human
cognitive lapses following sleep deprivation.
Nature Medicine, 23, 1474–1480. (10) doi:
10.1038/nm.4433

Nir, Y., & Tononi, G. (2010). Dreaming and
the brain: From phenomenology to
neurophysiology. *Trends in Cognitive Sciences,
14*, 88–100. (10)

Nisbet, E. K., & Zelenski, J. M. (2011).
Underestimating nearby nature: Affective
forecasting errors obscure the happy path to
sustainability. *Psychological Science, 22*, 1101–
1106. (12) doi: 10.1177/0956797611418527

Nisbett, R. E., Aronson, J., Blair, C., Dickens, W.,
Flynn, J., Halpern, D. F., & Turkheimer, E.
(2012). Intelligence. *American Psychologist, 67*,
130–159. (9) doi: 10.1037/a0026699

Nisbett, R. E., Peng, K., Choi, I., & Norenzayan,
A. (2001). Culture and systems of thought:
Holistic versus analytic cognition.
Psychological Review, 108, 291–310. (13) doi:
10.1037//0033-295X.108.2.291

Noguchi, K., Kamada, A., & Shrira, I. (2014).
Cultural differences in the primacy effect for
person perception. *International Journal of

Psychology, 49*, 208–210. (13) doi: 10.1002/
ijop.12019

Noice, H., & Noice, T. (2006). What studies of
actors and acting can tell us about memory
and cognitive functioning. *Current Directions
in Psychological Science, 15*, 14–18. (7) doi:
10.1111/j.0963-7214.2006.00398.x

Nolen-Hoeksema, S., & Watkins, E. R. (2011).
A heuristic for developing transdiagnostic
models of psychopathology: Explaining
multifinality and divergent trajectories.
Perspectives on Psychological Science, 6, 589–
609. (15) doi: 10.1177/1745691611419672

Norcross, J. C., Kohout, J. L., & Wicherski, M.
(2005). Graduate study in psychology: 1971 to
2004. *American Psychologist, 60*, 959–975. (1)
doi: 10.1037/0003-066X.60.9.959

Nordenström, A., Servin, A., Bohlin, G., Larsson,
A., & Wedell, A. (2002). Sex-typed toy play
behavior correlates with the degree of prenatal
androgen exposure assessed by CYP21
genotype in girls with congenital adrenal
hyperplasia. *Journal of Clinical Endocrinology
and Metabolism, 87*, 5119–5124. (5, 11) doi:
10.1210/jc.2001-011531

Nordgren, L. F., McDonnell, M.-H. M., &
Loewenstein, G. (2011). What constitutes
torture? Psychological impediments to an
objective evaluation of enhanced interrogation
tactics. *Psychological Science, 22*, 689–694. (13)
doi: 10.1177/0956797611405679

Nordgren, L. F., van Harreveld, F., & van
der Pligt, J. (2009). The restraint bias.
Psychological Science, 20, 1523–1528. (11) doi:
10.1111/j.1467-9280.2009.02468.x

Norman, R. A., Tataranni, P. A., Pratley, R.,
Thompson, D. B., Hanson, R. L., Prochazka,
M., Baier, L., Ehm, M. G., Sakul, H., Foroud,
T., Garvey, W. T., Burns, D., Knowler, W. C.,
Bennett, P. H., Bogardus, C., & Ravussin, E.
(1998). Autosomal genomic scan for loci linked
to obesity and energy metabolism in Pima
Indians. *American Journal of Human Genetics,
62*, 659–668. (11) doi: 10.1086/301758

Norman-Haignere, S. V., Albouy, P., Caclin,
A., McDermott, J. H., Kanwisher, N. G., &
Tillman, B. (2016). Pitch-responsive cortical
regions in congenital amusia. *Journal of
Neuroscience, 36*, 2986–2994. (4) doi: 10.1523/
JNEUROSCI.2705-15.2016

Norretranders, T. (1998). *The User Illusion.* New
York: Penguin books. (Original work published
1991) (10)

Norton, M. I., Frost, J. H., & Ariely, D. (2007).
Less is more: The lure of ambiguity, or why
familiarity breeds contempt. *Journal of
Personality and Social Psychology, 92*, 97–105.
(13) doi: 10.1037/0022-3514.92.1.97

Nosek, B. A., & Banaji, M. R. (2001). The go/no-go
association task. *Social Cognition, 19*, 625–664.
(13) doi: 10.1521/soco.19.6.625.20886

Nussbaum, A. D., & Dweck, C. S. (2008).
Defensiveness versus remediation:
Self-theories and modes of self-esteem
maintenance. *Personality and Social
Psychology Bulletin, 34*, 599–612. (14) doi:
10.1177/0146167207312960

Nutt, D. J., Lingford-Hughes, A., Erritzoe, D., &
Stokes, P. R. A. (2015). The dopamine theory of
addiction: 40 years of highs and lows. *Nature
Reviews Neuroscience, 16*, 305–312. (15) doi:
10.1038/nrn3939

Nye, C. D., Su, R., Rounds, J., & Drasgow,
F. (2012). Vocational interests and
performance: A quantitative summary of
over 60 years of research. *Perspectives on

Psychological Science, 7*, 384–403. (11) doi:
10.1177/1745691612449021

Oakley, D. A., & Halligan, P. W. (2013). Hypnotic
suggestion: Opportunities for cognitive
neuroscience. *Nature Reviews Neuroscience,
14*, 565–576. (10) doi: 10.1038/nrn3538

O'Brien, E., & Kassirer, S. (2019). People are
slow to adapt to the warm glow of giving.
Psychological Science, 30, 193–204. (12) doi:
10.1177/0956797618814145

O'Connell, K. A., Schwartz, J. E., & Shiffman,
S. (2008). Do resisted temptations during
smoking cessation deplete or augment self-
control resources? *Psychology of Addictive
Behaviors, 22*, 486–495. (11) doi: 10.1037/0893-
164X.22.4.486

O'Connor, A. R., & Moulin, C. J. A. (2008). The
persistence of erroneous familiarity in an
epileptic male: Challenging perceptual
theories of déjà vu activation. *Brain and
Cognition, 68*, 144–147. (10) doi: 10.1016/j.
bandc.2008.03.007

O'Kane, G., Kensinger, E. A., & Corkin, S. (2004).
Evidence for semantic learning in profound
amnesia: An investigation with patient H. M.
Hippocampus, 14, 417–425. (7) doi: 10.1002/
hipo.20005

O'Neill, T. A., & Hastings, S. E. (2011). Explaining
workplace deviance behavior with more than
just the "Big Five." *Personality and Individual
Differences, 50*, 268–273. (14) doi: 10.1016/j.
paid.2010.10.001

O'Toole, B. I. (1990). Intelligence and behaviour
and motor vehicle accident mortality. *Accident
Analysis and Prevention, 22*, 211–221. (9) doi:
10.1016/0001-4575(90)90013-B

Oei, N. Y. L., Both, S., van Heemst, D., & van der
Grond, J. (2014). Acute stress-induced cortisol
elevations mediate reward system activity
during subconscious precessing of sexual
stimuli. *Psychoneuroendocrinology, 39*, 111–
120. (4) doi: 10.1016/j.psyneuen.2013.10.005

Ogunniyi, A., Hall, K. S., Gureje, O., Baiyewu,
O., Gao, S., Unverzagt, F. W, Smith-Gamble,
V., Evans, R. E., Dickens, J., Musick, B. S., &
Hendrie, H. C. (2006). Risk factors for incident
Alzheimer's disease in African Americans and
Yoruba. *Metabolic Brain Disease, 21*, 224–229.
(7) doi: 10.1007/s11011-006-9017-2

Ohayon, M. M. (1997). Prevalence of *DSM–IV*
diagnostic criteria of insomnia: Distinguishing
insomnia related to mental disorders from
sleep disorders. *Journal of Psychiatric
Research, 31*, 333–346. (10) doi: 10.1016/S0022-
3956(97)00002-2

Ohi, K., Otowa, T., Shimada, M., Sasaki, T., & Tanii,
H. (2020). Shared genetic etiology between
anxiety disorders and psychiatric and related
phenotypes. *Psychological Medicine, 50*, 692–
704. (15) doi: 10.1017/S003329171900059X

Öhman, A., Eriksson, A., & Olofsson, C. (1975).
One-trial learning and superior resistance
to extinction of autonomic responses
conditioned to potentially phobic objects.
*Journal of Comparative and Physiological
Psychology, 88*, 619–627. (15) doi: 10.1037/
h0078388.

Öhman, A., & Mineka, S. (2003). The malicious
serpent: Snakes as a prototypical stimulus for
an evolved module of fear. *Current Directions
in Psychological Science, 12*, 5–9. (15) doi:
10.1111/1467-8721.01211

Oishi, S. (2010). The psychology of residential
mobility: Implications for the self, social
relationships, and well-being. *Perspectives

on *Psychological Science, 5*, 5–21. (5) doi: 10.1177/1745691609356781

Oishi, S., & Diener, E. (2014). Residents of poor nations have a greater sense of meaning in life than residents of wealthy nations. *Psychological Science, 25*, 422–430. (12) doi: 10.1177/0956797613507286

Oishi, S., & Kesebir, S. (2015). Income inequality explains why economic growth does not always translate to an increase in happiness. *Psychological Science, 26*, 1630–1638. (12) doi: 10.1177/0956797615596713

Oishi, S., & Schimmack, U. (2010). Culture and well-being: A new inquiry into the psychological wealth of nations. *Perspectives on Psychological Science, 5*, 463–471. (12) doi: 10.1177/1745691610375561

O'Keefe, P. A., Dweck, C. S., & Walton, G. M. (2018). Implicit theories of interest: Finding your passion or developing it? *Psychological Science, 29*, 1653–1664. (11) doi: 10.1177/0956797618780643

Olausson, H., Lamarre, Y., Backlund, H., Morin, C., Wallin, B. G., Starck, G., Ekholm, S., Strigo, I., Worsley, K., Vallbo, A. B., & Bushnell, M. C. (2002). Unmyelinated tactile afferents signal touch and project to insular cortex. *Nature Neuroscience, 5*, 900–904. (3) doi: 10.1038/nn896

O'Leary, K. D., Acevedo, B. P., Aron, A., Huddy, L., & Mashek, D. (2012). Is long-term love more than a rare phenomenon? If so, what are its correlates? *Social Psychological and Personality Science, 3*, 241–249. (13) doi: 10.1177/1948550611417015

Olff, M., Frijling, J. L., Kubzansky, L. D., Bradley, B., Ellenbogen, M. A., Cardoso, C., Bartz, J. A., Yee, J. R., & van Zuiden, M. (2013). The role of oxytocin in social bonding, stress regulation and mental health: An update on the moderating effects of context and individual differences. *Psychoneuroendocrinology, 38*, 1883–1894. (3) doi: 10.1016/j.psyneuen.2013.06.019

Oliet, S. H. R., Baimoukhametova, D. V., Piet, R., & Bains, J. S. (2007). Retrograde regulation of GABA transmission by the tonic release of oxytocin and endocannabinoids governs postsynaptic firing. *Journal of Neuroscience, 27*, 1325–1333. (3) doi: 10.1523/JNEUROSCI.2676-06.2007

Olivola, C. Y. (2018). The interpersonal sunk cost effect. *Psychological Science, 29*, 1072–1083. (8) doi: 10.1177/0956797617752641

Olney, J. W., & Farger, N. B. (1995). Glutamate receptor dysfunction and schizophrenia. *Archives of General Psychiatry, 52*, 998–1007. (15) doi: 10.1001/archpsyc.1995.03950240016004

Olsson, A., McMahon, K., Papenberg, G., Zaki, J., Bolger, N., & Ochsner, K. N. (2016). Vicarious fear learning depends on empathic appraisals and trait empathy. *Psychological Science, 27*, 25–33. (6) doi: 10.1177/0956797615604124

Olsson, M. J., Lundström, J. N., Kimball, B. A., Gordon, A. R., Karshikoff, B., Hosseini, N., Sorjonen, K., Hoglund, C. O., Solares, C., Soop, A., Axelsson, J., & Lekander, M. (2014). The scent of disease: Human body odor contains an early chemosensory cue of sickness. *Psychological Science, 25*, 817–823. (4) doi: 10.1177/0956797613515681

O'Mahony, M. (1978). Smell illusions and suggestion: Reports of smells contingent on tones played on television and radio.

Chemical Senses, 3, 183–189. (2) doi: 10.1093/chemse/3.2.183

Ong, D. C., Goodman, N. D., & Zaki, J. (2018). Happier than thou? A self-enhancement bias in emotion attribution. *Emotion, 18*, 116–126. (12) doi: 10.1037/emo0000309

Ono, F., & Watanabe, K. (2011). Attention can retrospectively distort visual space. *Psychological Science, 22*, 472–477. (10) doi: 10.1177/0956797611403319

Oostenbroek, J., Suddendorf, T., Nielsen, M., Redshaw, J., Kennedy-Costantini, S., Davis, J., Clark, S., & Slaughter, V. (2016). Comprehensive longitudinal study challenges the existence of neonatal imitation in humans. *Current Biology, 26*, 1334–1338. (3) doi: 10.1016/j.cub.2016.03.047

Open Science Collaboration. (2015). Estimating the reproducibility of psychological science. *Science, 349*, 943. (2) doi: 10.1126/science.aac4716

Orefice, L. L., Mosko, J. R., Morency, D. T., Wells, M. F., Tasnim, A., Mozeika, S. M., Ye, M. C., Chirila, A. M., Emanuel, A. J., Rankin, G., Fame, R. M., Lehtinen, M. K., Feng, G. P., & Ginty, D. D. (2019). Targeting peripheral somatosensory neurons to improve tactile-related phenotypes in ASD models. *Cell, 178*, 867–886. (15) doi: 10.1016/j.cell.2019.07.024

Oriña, M. M., Collins, W. A., Simpson, J. A., Salvatore, J. E., Haydon, K. C., & Kim, J. S. (2011). Developmental and dyadic perspectives on commitment in adult romantic relationships. *Psychological Science, 22*, 908–915. (5) doi: 10.1177/0956797611410573

Orne, M. T. (1959). The nature of hypnosis: Artifact and essence. *Journal of Abnormal and Social Psychology, 58*, 277–299. (10) doi: 10.1037/h0046128

Orne, M. T. (1969). Demand characteristics and the concept of quasi-controls. In R. Rosenthal & R. L. Rosnow (Eds.), *Artifact in behavioral research* (pp. 143–179). New York: Academic Press. (2) doi: 10.1093/acprof:oso/9780195385540.003.0005

Orne, M. T. (1979). On the simulating subject as a quasi-control group in hypnosis research: What, why, and how. In E. Fromm & R. E. Shor (Eds.), *Hypnosis: Developments in research and new perspectives* (2nd ed., pp. 519–565). New York: Aldine. (10)

Orne, M. T., & Evans, F. J. (1965). Social control in the psychological experiment: Antisocial behavior and hypnosis. *Journal of Personality and Social Psychology, 1*, 189–200. (10) doi: 10.1037/h0021933

Osimo, E. F., Beck, K., Marques, T. R., & Howes, D. D. (2019). Synaptic loss in schizophrenia: A meta-analysis and systematic review of synaptic protein and mRNA measures. *Molecular Psychiatry, 24*, 549–561. (15) doi: 10.1038/s41380-018-0041-5

Ostling, P. S., Davidson, K. S., Anyama, B. O., Helander, E. M., Wyche, M. Q., & Kaye, A. D. (2018). America's opioid epidemic: A comprehensive review and look into the rising crisis. *Current Pain and Headache Reports, 22*: 32. (3) doi: 10.1007/s11916-018-0685-5

Osofsky, J. D. (1995). The effects of exposure to violence on young children. *American Psychologist, 50*, 782–788. (13) doi: 10.1037/0003-066X.50.9.782

O'Suilleabhain, P. S., & Hughes, B. M. (2018). Neuroticism predicts all-cause mortality over 19 years: The moderating effects n functional status, and the angiotensin-

converting enzyme. *Journal of Psychosomatic Research, 110*, 32–37. (14) doi: 10.1016/j.jpsychores.2018.04.013

Otto, R. K., & Heilbrun, K. (2002). The practice of forensic psychology. *American Psychologist, 57*, 5–18. (1) doi: 10.1037//0003-066X.57.1.5

Owen, A. M., Coleman, M. R., Boly, M., Davis, M. H., Laureys, S., & Pickard, J. D. (2006). Detecting awareness in the vegetative state. *Science, 313*, 1402. (10) doi: 10.1126/science.1130197

Oxley, D. R., Smith, K. B., Alford, J. R., Hibbing, M. V., Miller, J. L., Scalora, M., Hatemi, P. K., & Hibbing, J. R. (2008). Political attitudes vary with physiological traits. *Science, 321*, 1667–1670. (3) doi: 10.1126/science.1157627

Oyserman, D., Coon, H. M., & Kemmelmeier, M. (2002). Rethinking individualism and collectivism: Evaluation of theoretical assumptions and meta-analyses. *Psychological Bulletin, 128*, 3–72. (13) doi: 10.1037/0033-2909.128.1.3

Packer, D. J. (2009). Avoiding groupthink: Whereas weakly identified members remain silent, strongly identified members dissent about collective problems. *Psychological Science, 20*, 546–548. (13) doi: 10.1111/j.1467-9280.2009.02333.x

Padgham, C. A. (1975). Colours experienced in dreams. *British Journal of Psychology, 66*, 25–28. (10) doi: 10.1111/j.2044-8295.1975.tb01436.x

Pagni, S. E., Bak, A. G., Eisen, S. E., Murphy, J. L., Finkelman, M. D., & Kugel, G. (2017). The benefits of a switch: Answer-changing on multiple-choice exams by first-year dental students. *Journal of Dental Education, 81*, 110–115. (8) doi: 10.1002/j.0022-0337.2017.81.1.tb06253.x

Paiva, V., Aranha, F., & Bastos, F. I. (2008). Opinions and attitudes regarding sexuality: Brazilian national research, 2005. *Revista de Saúde Pública, 42*(Suppl. 1). (11) doi: 10.1590/s0034-89102008000800008.

Paivandy, S., Bullock, E. E., Reardon, R. C., & Kelly, F. D. (2008). The effects of decision-making style and cognitive thought patterns on negative career thoughts. *Journal of Career Assessment, 16*, 474–488. (8) doi: 10.1177/1069072708318904

Palinkas, L. A. (2003). The psychology of isolated and confined environments. *American Psychologist, 58*, 353–363. (10, 15) doi: 10.1037/0003-066X.58.5.353

Pallini, S., Chirumbolo, A., Morelli, M., Baiocco, R., Laghi, F., & Eisenberg, N. (2018). The relation of attachment security status to effortful self-regulation: A meta-analysis. *Psychological Bulletin, 144*, 501–531. (5) doi: 10.1037/bul0000134

Palop, J. J., Chin, J., & Mucke, L. (2006). A network dysfunction perspective on neurodegenerative diseases. *Nature, 443*, 768–773. (7) doi: 10.1038/nature05289

Pan, S. C., & Rickard, T. C. (2018). Transfer of test-enhanced learning: Meta-analytic review and synthesis. *Psychological Bulletin, 144*, 710–756. (7) doi: 10.1037/bul0000151

Pan, W. W., & Myers, M. G. Jr. (2018). Leptin and the maintenance of elevated body weight. *Nature Reviews Neuroscience, 19*, 95–105. (11) doi: 10.1038/nrn.2017.168

Panikashvili, D., Simeonidou, C., Ben-Shabat, S., Hanus˘, L. Breuer, A., Mechoulam, E., & Shohami, E. (2001). An endogenous binoid (2-AG) is neuroprotective after njury. *Nature, 413,* 527–531. (3) doi: 8/35097089

Pardal, S., Alves, J. A., Mota, P. G., & Ramos, J. A. (2018). Dressed to impress: Breeding plumage as a reliable signal of innate immunity. *Journal of Avian Biology, 49,* e01579. (13) doi: 10.1111/jav.01579

Paris, J. (2012). The rise and fall of dissociative identity disorder. *Journal of Nervous and Mental Disease, 200,* 1076–1079. (15) doi: 10.1097/NMD.0b013e318275d285

Parish, W. L., Laumann, E. O., & Mojola, S. A. (2007). Sexual behavior in China: Trends and comparisons. *Population and Development Review, 33,* 729–756. (11) doi: 10.1111/j.1728-4457.2007.00195.x

Park, J., Kitayama, S., Markus, H. R., Coe, C. L., Miyamoto, Y., Karasawa, M., Curhan, K. B., Love, G. D., Kawakami, N., Boylan, J. M., & Ryff, C. D. (2013). Social status and anger expression: The cultural moderation hypothesis. *Emotion, 13,* 1122–1131. (2) doi: 10.1037/a0034273

Park, G., Lubinski, D., & Benbow, C. P. (2008). Ability differences among people who have commensurate degrees matter for scientific creativity. *Psychological Science, 19,* 957–961. (9) doi: 10.1111/j.1467-9280.2008.02182.x

Parker, E. S., Cahill, L., & McGaugh, J. L. (2006). A case of unusual autobiographical remembering. *Neurocase, 12,* 35–49. (7) doi: 10.1080/13554790500473680

Parker, J., Wales, G., Chalhoub, N., & Harper, V. (2013). The long-term outcomes of interventions for the management of attention-deficit hyperactivity disorder in children and adolescents: A systematic review of randomized controlled trials. *Psychology Research & Behavior Management, 6,* 87–99. (8) doi: 10.2147/PRBM.S49114

Parkinson, C., Walker, T. T., Memmi, S., & Wheatley, T. (2017). Emotions are understood from biological motion across remote cultures. *Emotion, 17,* 459–477. (12) doi: 10.1037/emo0000194

Parmeggiani, P. L. (1982). Regulation of physiological functions during sleep in mammals. *Experientia, 38,* 1405–1408. (10) doi: 10.1007/BF01955751

Parrott, A. C. (1999). Does cigarette smoking cause stress? *American Psychologist, 54,* 817–820. (3) doi: 10.1037/0003-066X.54.10.817

Pashler, H., & Harris, C. R. (2012). Is the replicability crisis overblown? Three arguments examined. *Perspectives on Psychological Science, 7,* 531–536. (2) doi: 10.1177/1745691612463401

Pashler, H., McDaniel, M., Rohrer, D., & Bjork, R. (2008). Learning styles: Concepts and evidence. *Psychological Science in the Public Interest, 9,* 105–119. (9) doi: 10.1111/j.1539-6053.2009.01038.x

Pasman, J. A., Verweij, K. J. H., Gerring, Z., Stringer, S., Sanchez-Roige, S., Treur, J. L., Abdellaoui, A., Nivard, M. G., Baselmans, B. M. L., Ong, J. S., Ip, H. F., van der Zee, M. D., Bartels, M., Day, F. R., Fontanillas, P., Elson, S. L., de Wit, H., Davis, L. K., MacKillop, J., & Vink, J. M. (2018). GWAS of lifetime cannabis use reveals new risk loci, genetic overlap with psychiatric traits, and a causal influence of schizophrenia. *Nature Neuroscience, 21,* 1161–1170. (15) doi: 10.1038/s41593-018-0206-1

Pasterski, V. L., Geffner, M. E., Brain, C., Hindmarsh, P., Brook, C., & Hines, M. (2005). Prenatal hormones and postnatal socialization by parents as determinants of male-typical toy play in girls with congenital adrenal hyperplasia. *Child Development, 76,* 264–278. (5) doi: 10.1111/j.1467-8624.2005.00843.x

Pate, J. L., & Rumbaugh, D. M. (1983). The language-like behavior of Lana chimpanzee: Is it merely discrimination and paired-associate learning? *Animal Learning and Behavior, 11,* 134–138. (8) doi: 10.3758/BF03212320

Patihis, L., & Pendergrast, M. H. (2019). Reports of recovered memories of abuse in therapy in a large age-representative U.S. national sample: Therapy type and decade comparisons. *Clinical Psychological Science, 7,* 3–21. (7) doi: 10.1177/2167702618773315

Patterson, D. R. (2004). Treating pain with hypnosis. *Current Directions in Psychological Science, 13,* 252–255. (10) doi: 10.1111/j.0963-7214.2004.00319.x

Patterson, T., & Hayne, H. (2011). Does drawing facilitate older children's reports of emotionally laden events? *Applied Cognitive Psychology, 25,* 119–126. (7) doi: 10.1002/acp.1650

Pauls, D. L., Abramovitch, A., Rauch, S. L., & Geller, D. A. (2014). Obsessive-compulsive disorder: An integrative genetic and neurobiological perspective. *Nature Reviews Neuroscience, 15,* 410–424. (15) doi: 10.1038/nrn3746

Paunonen, S. V., & Jackson, D. N. (2000). What is beyond the big five? Plenty! *Journal of Personality, 68,* 821–835. (14) doi: 10.1111/1467-6494.00117

Paus, T., Marrett, S., Worsley, K. J., & Evans, A. C. (1995). Extraretinal modulation of cerebral blood flow in the human visual cortex: Implications for saccadic suppression. *Journal of Neurophysiology, 74,* 2179–2183. (8) doi: 10.1152/jn.1995.74.5.2179

Pavlov, I. P. (1960). *Conditioned reflexes.* New York: Dover. (Original work published 1927) (6)

Pearce, J. M. (1994). Similarity and discrimination: A selective review and a connectionist model. *Psychological Review, 101,* 587–607. (6) doi: 10.1037/0033-295X.101.4.587

Pearl, P. L., Weiss, R. E., & Stein, M. A. (2001). Medical mimics. *Annals of the New York Academy of Sciences, 931,* 97–112. (8) https://pubmed.ncbi.nlm.nih.gov/11462759/

Pearlson, G. D., Petty, R. G., Ross, C. A., & Tien, A. Y. (1996). Schizophrenia—a disease of heteromodal association cortex? *Neuropsychopharmacology, 14,* 1–17. (15) doi: 10.1016/S0893-133X(96)80054-6

Peelle, J. E., Troiani, V., Grossman, M., & Wingfield, A. (2011). Hearing loss in older adults affects neural systems supporting speech comprehension. *Journal of Neuroscience, 31,* 12638–12643. (4) doi: 10.1523/JNEUROSCI.2559-11.2011

Pehlivanova, M., Wolf, D. H., Sotiras, A., Kaczkurkin, A. N., Moore, T. M., Ciric, R., Cook, P. A., de La Garza, A. G., Rosen, A. F. G., Ruparel, K., Sharma, A., Shinohara, R. T., Roalf, D. R., Gur, R. C., Davatzikos, C., Gur, R. E., Kable, J. W., & Satterthwaite, T. D. (2018). Diminished cortical thickness is associated with impulsive choice in adolescence. *Journal of Neuroscience, 38,* 2471–2481. (5) doi: 10.1523/JNEUROSCI.2200-17.2018

Peigneux, P., Laureys, S., Fuchs, S., Collette, F., Perrin, F., Reggers, J., Phillips, C., Degueldre, C., Del Fiore, G., Aerts, J., Luxen, A., & Maquet, P. (2004). Are spatial memories strengthened in the human hippocampus during slow wave sleep? *Neuron, 44,* 535–545. (10) doi: 10.1016/j.neuron.2004.10.007

Pembrey, M. E., Bygren, L. O., Kaati, G., Edvinsson, S., Northstone, K., Sjöström, M., Golding, J., & The ALSPAC Study Team. (2006) Sex-specific, male-line transgenerational responses in humans. *European Journal of Human Genetics, 14,* 159–166. (3) doi: 10.1038/sj.ejhg.5201538

Penfield, W., & Rasmussen, T. (1950). *The cerebral cortex of man.* New York: Macmillan. (3)

Peng, G., & Wang, W. S.-Y. (2011). Hemisphere lateralization is influenced by bilingual status and composition of words. *Neuropsychologia, 49,* 1981–1986. (8) doi: 10.1016/j.neuropsychologia.2011.03.027

Peng, K., & Nisbett, R. E. (1999). Culture dialectics, and reasoning about contradiction. *American Psychologist, 54,* 741–754. (13) doi: 10.1037/0003-066X.54.9.741

Pennycook, G., Cheyne, J. A., Barr, N., Koehler, D. J., & Fugelsang, S. A. (2015). On the reception and detection of pseudo-profound bullshit. *Judgment and Decision Making, 10,* 549–563. (8) doi: http://journal.sjdm.org/15/15923a/jdm15923a.pdf

Perani, D., & Abutalebi, J. (2005). The neural basis of first and second language processing. *Current Opinion in Neurobiology, 15,* 202–206. (8) doi: 10.1016/j.conb.2005.03.007

Pereira, S. M. P., Geoffroy, M.-C., & Power, C. (2014). Depressive symptoms and physical activity during 3 decades in adult life. *JAMA Psychiatry, 71,* 1373–1380. (15) doi: 10.1001/jamapsychiatry.2014.1240

Perez, E. A. (1995). Review of the preclinical pharmacology and comparative efficacy of 5-hydroxytryptamine-3 receptor antagonists for chemotherapy-induced emesis. *Journal of Clinical Oncology, 13,* 1036–1043. (3) doi: 10.1200/JCO.1995.13.4.1036

Perrin, P. B. (2016). Translating psychological science: Highlighting the media's contribution to contagion in mass shootings: Comment on Kaslow (2015). *American Psychologist, 71,* 71–72. (14) doi: 10.1037/a0039994

Perry, D. G., & Bussey, K. (1979). The social learning theory of sex differences: Imitation is alive and well. *Journal of Personality and Social Psychology, 37,* 1699–1712. (14) doi: 10.1037/0022-3514.37.10.1699

Perry, G. (2013). *Behind the shock machine: The untold story of the notorious Milgram psychology experiments.* New York: New Press. (13)

Perry, G. (2018). *The lost boys.* London: Scribe. (13)

Pert, C. B., & Snyder, S. H. (1973). The opiate receptor: Demonstration in nervous tissue. *Science, 179,* 1011–1014. (3, 4) doi: 10.1126/science.179.4077.1011

Pesta, B. J., & Poznanski, P. J. (2008). Black–White differences on IQ and grades: The mediating role of elementary cognitive tasks. *Intelligence, 36,* 323–329. (9) doi: 10.1016/j.intell.2007.07.004

Peterson, C. (2011). Children's memory reports over time: Getting both better and worse. *Journal of Experimental Child Psychology, 109,* 275–293. (7) doi: 10.1016/j.jecp.2011.01.009

Peterson, C., Warren, K. L., & Short, M. M. (2011). Infantile amnesia across the years: A 2-year follow-up of children's earliest memories. *Child Development, 82,* 1092–1105. (7) doi: 10.1111/j.1467-8624.2011.01597.x

Peterson, L. R., & Peterson, M. J. (1959). Short-term retention of individual verbal items.

Journal of Experimental Psychology, 58, 193–198. (7) doi: 10.1037/h0049234

Peterson, Z. D., Janssen, E., & Laan, E. (2010). Women's sexual responses to heterosexual and lesbian erotica: The role of stimulus intensity, affective reaction, and sexual history. *Archives of Sexual Behavior, 39,* 880–897. (11) doi: 10.1007/s10508-009-9546-y

Petrill, S. A., Luo, D., Thompson, L. A., & Detterman, D. K. (1996). The independent prediction of general intelligence by elementary cognitive tasks: Genetic and environmental influences. *Behavior Genetics, 26,* 135–147. (9) doi: 10.1007/BF02359891

Petrill, S. A., Plomin, R., Berg, S., Johansson, B., Pedersen, N. L., Ahern, F., & McClearn, G. E. (1998). The genetic and environmental relationship between general and specific cognitive abilities in twins age 80 and older. *Psychological Science, 9,* 183–189. (9) doi: 10.1111/1467-9280.00035

Petrova, P. K., Cialdini, R. B., & Sills, S. J. (2007). Consistency-based compliance across cultures. *Journal of Experimental Psychology, 43,* 104–111. (13) doi: 10.1016/j.jesp.2005.04.002

Petty, R. E., & Briñol, P. (2015). Emotion and persuasion: Cognitive and meta-cognitive processes impact attitudes. *Cognition & Emotion, 29,* 1–26. (13) doi: 10.1080/02699931.2014.967183

Petty, R. E., & Cacioppo, J. T. (1979). Effects of forewarning of persuasive intent and involvement on cognitive responses and persuasion. *Personality and Social Psychology Bulletin, 5,* 173–176. (13) doi: 10.1177/014616727900500209

Petty, R. E., & Cacioppo, J. T. (1981). *Attitudes and persuasion: Classic and contemporary approaches.* Dubuque, IA: William C. Brown. (13)

Pfungst, O. (1911). *Clever Hans.* New York: Holt. (2)

Phan, K. L., Wager, T., Taylor, S. F., & Liberzon, I. (2002). Functional neuroanatomy of emotion: A meta-analysis of emotion activation studies in PET and fMRI. *NeuroImage, 16,* 331–348. (12) doi: 10.1006/nimg.2002.1087

Phelps, E. A., & Hofmann, S. G. (2019). Memory editing from science fiction to clinical practice. *Nature, 572,* 43–50. (7) doi: 10.1038/s41586-019-1433-7

Phelps, E. A., O'Connor, K. J., Cunningham, W. A., Funayama, E. S., Gatenby, J. C., Gore, J. C., & Banaji, M. R. (2000). Performance on indirect measures of race evaluation predicts amygdala activation. *Journal of Cognitive Neuroscience, 12,* 729–738. (13) doi: 10.1162/089892900562552

Phelps, M. E., & Mazziotta, J. C. (1985). Positron emission tomography: Human brain function and biochemistry. *Science, 228,* 799–809. (1, 3) doi: 10.1126/science.2860723

Philippot, P., Chapelle, G., & Blairy, S. (2002). Respiratory feedback in the generation of emotions. *Cognition & Emotion, 16,* 605–627. (12) doi: 10.1080/02699930143000392

Phillips, A. J. K., Vidafar, P., Burns, A. C., McGlashan, E. M., Anderson, C., Rajaratnam, S. M. W., Lockley, S. W., & Cain, S. W. (2019). High sensitivity and interindividual variability in the response of the human circadian system to evening light. *Proceedings of the National Academy of Sciences (U.S.A.), 116,* 12019–12024. (10) doi: 10.1073/pnas.1901824116

Phillips, J. E., & Olson, M. A. (2014). When implicitly and explicitly measured racial attitudes align: The roles of social desirability and thoughtful responding. *Basic and Applied Social Psychology, 36,* 125–132. (13) doi: 10.1080/01973533.2014.881287

Phillips, T. M., & Pittman, J. F. (2007). Adolescent psychological well-being by identity style. *Journal of Adolescence, 30,* 1021–1034. (5) doi: 10.1016/j.adolescence.2007.03.002

Piaget, J. (1954). *The construction of reality in the child* (M. Cook, Trans.). New York: Basic Books. (Original work published 1937) (5)

Pichot, P. (1984). Centenary of the birth of Hermann Rorschach. *Journal of Personality Assessment, 48,* 591–596. (14) doi: 10.1207/s15327752jpa4806_3

Pierri, J. N., Volk, C. L. E., Auh, S., Sampson, A., & Lewis, D. A. (2001). Decreased somal size of deep layer 3 pyramidal neurons in the prefrontal cortex of subjects with schizophrenia. *Archives of General Psychiatry, 58,* 466–473. (15) doi: 10.1001/archpsyc.58.5.466

Pietschnig, J., Penke, L., Wicherts, J. M., Zeiler, M., & Voracek, M. (2015). Meta-analysis of associations between human brain volume and intelligence differences: How strong are they and what do they mean? *Neuroscience and Biobehavioral Reviews, 57,* 411–432. (9) doi: 10.1016/j.neubiorev.2015.09.017

Pietschnig, J., & Voracek, M. (2015). One century of global IQ gains: A formal meta-analysis of the Flynn effect (1909-2013). *Perspectives on Psychological Science, 10,* 282–306. (9) doi: 10.1177/1745691615577701

Pike, J. J., & Jennings, N. A. (2005). The effects of commercials on children's perceptions of gender appropriate toy use. *Sex Roles, 52,* 83–91. (5) doi: 10.1007/s11199-005-1195-6

Pinel, J. P. J., Assanand, S., & Lehman, D. R. (2000). Hunger, eating, and ill health. *American Psychologist, 55,* 1105–1116. (11) doi: 10.1037//0003-066X.55.10.1105

Pinker, S. (1994). *The language instinct.* New York: Morrow. (8)

Pinker, S. (2011). Taming the devil within us. *Nature, 478,* 309–311. (13) doi: 10.1038/478309a

Pinto, Y., Neville, D. A., Otten, M., Corballis, P. M., Lamme, V. A. F., de Haan, E. H. F., Foschi, N., & Fabri, M. (2017). Split brain: divided perception but undivided consciousness. *Brain, 140,* 1231–1237. (3) doi: 10.1093/brain/aww358

Planalp, E. M., Van Hulle, C., Lemery-Chalfant, K., & Goldsmith, H. H. (2017). Genetic and environmental contributions to the development of positive affect in infancy. *Emotion, 17,* 412–420. (5) doi: 10.1037/emo0000238

Plaut, V. C., Thomas, K. M., & Goren, M. J. (2009). Is multiculturalism or color blindness better for minorities? *Psychological Science, 20,* 444–446. (13) doi: 10.1111/j.1467-9280.2009.02318.x

Plaut, V. C., Thomas, K. M., Hurd, K., & Romano, C. A. (2018). Do color blindness and multiculturalism remedy or foster discrimination and racism? *Current Directions in Psychological Science, 27,* 200–206. (13) doi: 10.1177/0963721418766068

Plomin, R., Corley, R., DeFries, J. C., & Fulker, D. W. (1990). Individual differences in television viewing in early childhood: Nature as well as nurture. *Psychological Science, 1,* 371–377. (5) doi: 10.1111/j.1467-9280.1990.tb00244.x

Plomin, R., DeFries, J. C., McClearn, G. E., & McGuffin, P. (Eds.). (2001). *Behavioral genetics* (4th ed.) New York: Worth. (9)

Plomin, R., Fulker, D. W., Corley, R., & DeFries, J. C. (1997). Nature, nurture, and cognitive development from 1 to 16 years: A parent-offspring adoption study. *Psychological Science, 8,* 442–447. (9) doi: 10.1111/j.1467-9280.1997.tb00458.x

Plomin, R., & von Stumm, S. (2018). The new genetics of intelligence. *Nature Reviews Genetics, 19,* 148–159. (9) doi: 10.1038/nrg.2017.104

Plötner, M., Over, H., Carpenter, M., & Tomasello, M. (2015). Young children show the bystander effect in helping situations. *Psychological Science, 26,* 499–506. (13) doi: 10.1177/0956797615569579

Plous, S. (1993). *The psychology of judgment and decision making.* Philadelphia, PA: Temple University Press. (8)

Plous, S. (1996). Attitudes toward the use of animals in psychological research and education. *American Psychologist, 51,* 1167–1180. (2) doi: 10.1037/0003-066X.51.11.1167

Plutchik, R. (1982). A psychoevolutionary theory of emotions. *Social Science Information, 21,* 529–553. (12) doi: 10.1177/053901882021004003

Plutchik, R., & Ax, A. F. (1967). A critique of "determinants of emotional state" by Schachter and Singer (1962). *Psychophysiology, 4,* 79–82. (12) doi: 10.1111/j.1469-8986.1967.tb02740.x

Pochedly, J. T., Widen, S. C., & Russell, J. A. (2012). What emotion does the "facial expression of disgust" express? *Emotion, 12,* 1315–1319. (12) doi: 10.1037/a0027998

Pockett, S., & Miller, A. (2007). The rotating spot method of timing subjective events. *Consciousness and Cognition, 16,* 241–254. (10) doi: 10.1016/j.concog.2006.09.002

Poelman, M. P., de Vet, E., Velema, E., Seidell, J. C., & Steenhuis, I. H. M. (2014). Behavioural strategies to control the amount of food selected and consumed. *Appetite, 72,* 156–165. (11) doi: 10.1016/j.appet.2013.09.015

Polanczyk, G. V., Willcutt, E. G., Salum, G. A., Kieling, C., & Rohde, L. A. (2014). ADHD prevalence estimates across three decades: An updated systematic review and meta-regression analysis. *International Journal of Epidemiology, 43,* 434–442. (8) doi: 10.1093/ije/dyt261

Polczynska, M. M., Japardi, K., & Bookheimer, S. Y. (2017). Lateralizing language function with pre-operative functional magnetic resonance imaging in early proficient bilingual patients. *Brain and Language, 170,* 1–11. (8) doi: 10.1016/j.bandl.2017.03.002

Polivy, J., & Herman, C. P. (1985). Dieting and binging: A causal analysis. *American Psychologist, 40,* 193–201. (11) doi: 10.1037/0003-066X.40.2.193

Polk, T. A., Drake, R. M., Jonides, J. J., Smith, M. R., & Smith, E. E. (2008). Attention enhances the neural processing of relevant features and suppresses the processing of irrelevant features in humans: A functional magnetic resonance imaging study of the Stroop task. *Journal of Neuroscience, 28,* 13786–13792. (8) doi: 10.1523/JNEUROSCI.1026-08.2008

Pond, S. B., III, & Geyer, P. D. (1991). Differences in the relation between job satisfaction and perceived work alternatives among older and younger blue-collar workers. *Journal of Vocational Behavior, 39,* 251–262. (11) doi: 10.1016/0001-8791(91)90012-B

A., & White, L. T. (1993). Two years Effects of question repetition and tion interval on the eyewitness testimony of children and adults. *Developmental Psychology, 29,* 844–853. (7) doi: 10.1037/0012-1649.29.5.844

Popper, K. (1986). Predicting overt behavior versus predicting hidden states. *Behavioral and Brain Sciences, 9,* 254–255. (14) doi: 10.1017/S0140525X00022548

Porter, J., Craven, B., Khan, R. M., Chang, S.-J., Kang, I., Judkewitz, B., Volpe, J., & Sobel, N. (2007). Mechanisms of scent-tracking in humans. *Nature Neuroscience, 10,* 27–29. (4) doi: 10.1038/nn1819

Porter, S., Birt, A. R., Yuille, J. C., & Lehman, D. R. (2000). Negotiating false memories: Interviewer and rememberer characteristics relate to memory distortion. *Psychological Science, 11,* 507–510. (7) doi: 10.1111/1467-9280.00297

Post, R. M. (1992). Transduction of psychosocial stress into the neurobiology of recurrent affective disorder. *American Journal of Psychiatry, 149,* 999–1010. (15) doi: 10.1176/ajp.149.8.999.

Posthuma, D., De Geus, E. J. C., Baaré, W. F. C., Pol, H. E. H., Kahn, R. S., & Boomsma, D. I. (2002). The association between brain volume and intelligence is of genetic origin. *Nature Neuroscience, 5,* 83–84. (9) doi: 10.1038/nn0202-83

Poulin, M. J., Holman, E. A., & Buffone, A. (2012). The neurogenetics of nice: Oxytocin and vasopressin receptor genes and prosocial behavior. *Psychological Science, 23,* 446–452. (3) doi: 10.1177/0956797611428471

Powell, R. A., & Boer, D. P. (1994). Did Freud mislead patients to confabulate memories of abuse? *Psychological Reports, 74,* 1283–1298. (14) doi: 10.2466/pr0.1994.74.3c.1283

Powell, R. A., Digdon, N., Harris, B., & Smithson, C. (2014). Correcting the record on Watson, Rayner, and Little Albert. *American Psychologist, 69,* 600–611. (15) doi: 10.1037/a0036854

Pratkanis, A. R. (1992, Spring). The cargo-cult science of subliminal perception. *Skeptical Inquirer, 16,* 260–272. (4)

Pratt, J., Radulescu, P. V., Guo, R. M., & Abrams, R. A. (2010). It's alive! Animate motion captures visual attention. *Psychological Science, 21,* 1724–1730. (8) doi: 10.1177/0956797610387440

Pratte, M. S. (2018). Iconic memories die a sudden death. *Psychological Science, 29,* 877–887. (7) doi: 10.1177/0956797617747118

Preckel, F., Lipnevich, A. A., Boehme, K., Brandner, L., Georgi, K., Könen, T., Mursin, K., & Roberts, R. D. (2013). Morningness-eveningness and educational outcomes: The lark has an advantage over the owl at high school. *British Journal of Educational Psychology, 83,* 114–134. (10) https://pubmed.ncbi.nlm.nih.gov/23369178/

Prims, J. P., & Moore, D. A. (2017). Overconfidence over the lifespan. *Judgment and Decision Making, 12,* 29–41. (5) https://www.ncbi.nlm.nih.gov/pmc/articles/PMC5978695/

Principe, G. F., Kanaya, T., Ceci, S. J., & Singh, M. (2006). Believing is seeing. *Psychological Science, 17,* 243–248. (7) doi: 10.1111/j.1467-9280.2006.01692.x

Prochnow, D., Kossack, H., Brunheim, S., Muller, K., Wittsack, H. J., Markowitsch, H.-J., & Seitz, R. J. (2013). Processing of subliminal facial expressions of emotion: A behavioral and fMRI study. *Social Neuroscience, 8,* 448–461. (4) doi: 10.1080/17470919.2013.812536

Pronin, E., Berger, J., & Molouki, S. (2007). Alone in a crowd of sheep: Asymmetric perceptions of conformity and their roots in an introspection illusion. *Journal of Personality and Social Psychology, 92,* 585–595. (13) doi: 10.1037/0022-3514.92.4.585

Pronin, E., & Kugler, M. B. (2010). People believe they have more free will than others. *Proceedings of the National Academy of Sciences, 107,* 22469–22474. (1) doi: 10.1073/pnas.1012046108

Protzko, J., Aronson, J., & Blair, C. (2017). Raising IQ among school-aged children: Five meta-analyses and a review of randomized controlled trials. *Developmental Review, 46,* 81–101. (9) doi: 10.1016/j.dr.2017.05.001

Provine, R. (2000). *Laughter.* New York: Viking Press. (2, 12)

Provine, R. R. (2012). *Quirks: Yawning, laughing, crying, hiccupping, and beyond.* Boston: Harvard University Press. (5)

Provine, R. R., Cabrera, M. O., Brocato, N. W., & Krosnowski, K. A. (2011). When the whites of the eyes are red: A uniquely human cue. *Ethology, 117,* 1–5. (12) doi: 10.1111/j.1439-0310.2011.01888.x

Provine, R. R., Krosnowski, K. A., & Brocato, N. W. (2009). Tearing: Breakthrough in human emotional signaling. *Evolutionary Psychology, 7,* 52–56. (12) doi: 10.1177/147470490900700107

Provine, R. R., Nave-Blodgett, J., & Cabrera, M. O. (2013). The emotional eye: Red sclera as a uniquely human cue of emotion. *Ethology, 119,* 1–6. (12) doi: 10.1111/eth.12144

Public Agenda. (2001). *Medical research: Red flags.* Retrieved February 8, 2007, from www.publicagenda.org/charts/support-stem-cell-research-can-vary-dramatically-depending-question-wording-0. (2)

Purves, D., & Lotto, R. B. (2003). *Why we see what we do: An empirical theory of vision.* Sunderland, MA: Sinauer Associates. (4)

Purves, D., Williams, S. M., Nundy, S., & Lotto, R. B. (2004). Perceiving the intensity of light. *Psychological Review, 111,* 142–158. (4) doi: 10.1037/0033-295X.111.1.142

Purzycki, B. G., Apicella, C., Atkinson, Q. D., Cohen, E., McNamara, R. A., Willard, A. K., Xygalatas, D., Norenzayan, A., & Henrich, J. (2016). Moralistic gods, supernatural punishment and the expansion of human sociality. *Nature, 530,* 327–330. (13) doi: 10.1038/nature16980

Pyc, M. A., & Rawson, K. A. (2010). Why testing improves memory: Mediator effectiveness hypothesis. *Science, 330,* 335. (7) doi: 10.1126/science.1191465

Pyszczynski, T., Greenberg, J., & Solomon, S. (2000). Proximal and distal defense: A new perspective on unconscious motivation. *Current Directions in Psychological Science, 9,* 156–160. (5) doi: 10.1111/1467-8721.00083

Quadrel, M. J., Fischhoff, B., & Davis, W. (1993). Adolescent (in)vulnerability. *American Psychologist, 48,* 102–116. (5) doi: 10.1037/0003-066X.48.2.102

Quas, J. A., Malloy, L. C., Melinder, A., Goodman, G. S., D'Mello, M., & Schaaf, J. (2007). Developmental differences in the effects of repeated interviews and interview bias on young children's event memory and false reports. *Developmental Psychology, 43,* 823–837. (7) doi: 10.1037/0012-1649.43.4.823

Quattrocchi, M. R., & Schopp, R. F. (2005). Tarasaurus rex: A standard of care that could not adapt. *Psychology, Public Policy, and Law, 11,* 109–137. (15) doi: 10.1037/1076-8971.11.1.109

Quinn, P. C., & Liben, L. S. (2008). A sex difference in mental rotation in young infants. *Psychological Science, 19,* 1067–1070. (5) doi: 10.1111/j.1467-9280.2008.02201.x

Quinn, P. D., Chang, Z., Hur, K., Gibbons, R. D., Lahey, B. B., Rickert, M. E., Sjolander, A., Lichtenstein, P., Larsson, H., & D'Onofrio, B. M. (2017). ADHD medication and substance-related problems. *American Journal of Psychiatry, 174,* 877–885. (3) doi: 10.1176/appi.ajp.2017.16060686

Quoidbach, J., Dunn, E. W., Petrides, K. V., & Mikolajczak, M. (2010). Money giveth, money taketh away: The dual effect of wealth on happiness. *Psychological Science, 21,* 759–763. (12) doi: 10.1177/0956797610371963

Radomsky, A. S., Dugas, M. J., Alcolado, G. M., & Lavoie, S. L. (2014). When more is less: Doubt, repetition, memory, metamemory, and compulsive checking in OCD. *Behaviour Research and Therapy, 59,* 30–39. (15) doi: 10.1016/j.brat.2014.05.008

Rae, J. R., Gülgöz, S., Durwood, L., DeMeules, M., Lowe, R., Lindquist, G., & Olson, K. R. (2019). Predicting early-childhood gender transitions. *Psychological Science, 30,* 669–681. (11) doi: 10.1177/0956797619830649

Rahman, Q., Andersson, D., & Govier, E. (2005). A specific sexual orientation-related difference in navigation strategy. *Behavioral Neuroscience, 119,* 311–316. (5) doi: 10.1037/0735-7044.119.1.311

Raison, C. L., Klein, H. M., & Steckler, M. (1999). The moon and madness reconsidered. *Journal of Affective Disorders, 53,* 99–106. (2) doi: 10.1016/S0165-0327(99)00016-6

Rajecki, D. W., & Borden, V. M. H. (2011). Psychology degrees: Employment, wage, and career trajectory consequences. *Perspectives on Psychological Science, 6,* 321–335. (1) doi: 10.1177/1745691611412385

Ramachandran, V. S. (2003, May). Hearing colors, tasting shapes. *Scientific American, 288*(5), 52–59. (4) doi: 10.1038/scientificamerican0503-52

Ramachandran, V. S., & Blakeslee, S. (1998). *Phantoms in the brain.* New York: Morrow. (4)

Ramachandran, V. S., & Hirstein, W. (1998). The perception of phantom limbs: The D. O. Hebb lecture. *Brain, 121,* 1603–1630. (4) doi: 10.1093/brain/121.9.1603

Ramírez-Esparza, N., Mehl, M. R., Álvarez-Bermúdez, J., & Pennebaker, J. W. (2009). Are Mexicans more or less sociable than Americans? Insights from a naturalistic observation study. *Journal of Research in Personality, 43,* 1–7. (14) doi: 10.1016/j.jrp.2008.09.002

Ramirez, G., & Beilock, S. L. (2011). Writing about testing worries boosts exam performance in the classroom. *Science, 331,* 211–213. (9) doi: 10.1126/science.1199427

Ramirez, J. M., Santisteban, C., Fujihara, T., & Van Goozen, S. (2002). Differences between experience of anger and readiness to angry action: A study of Japanese and Spanish students. *Aggressive Behavior, 28,* 429–438. (12) doi: 10.1002/ab.80014

Ramsey, R., Darda, K. M., & Downing, P. E. (2019). Automatic imitation remains unaffected under cognitive load. *Journal of Experimental Psychology: Human Perception and Performance, 45,* 601–615. (6) doi: 10.1037/xhp0000632

Randler, C., Ebenhöh, N., Fischer, A., Höchel, S., Schroff, C., Stoll, J. C., Vollmer, C., & Piffer, D. (2012). Eveningness is related to men's mating success. *Personality and Individual Differences, 53,* 263–267. (10) doi: 10.1016/j.paid.2012.03.025

Ranganath, K. A., & Nosek, B. A. (2008). Implicit attitude generalization occurs immediately; explicit attitude generalization takes time. *Psychological Science, 19,* 249–254. (13) doi: 10.1111/j.1467-9280.2008.02076.x

Rasch, B., & Born, J. (2008). Reactivation and consolidation of memory during sleep. *Current Directions in Psychological Science, 17,* 188–192. (10) doi: 10.1111/j.1467-8721.2008.00572.x

Ratiu, P., & Talos, I.-F. (2004). The tale of Phineas Gage, digitally remastered. *New England Journal of Medicine, 351,* e21. (12) doi: 10.1056/NEJMicm031024

Rattenborg, N. C., Amlaner, C. J., & Lima, S. L. (2000). Behavioral, neurophysiological and evolutionary perspectives on unihemispherc sleep. *Neuroscience and Biobehavioral Reviews, 24,* 817–842. (10) doi: 10.1016/S0149-7634(00)00039-7

Rattenborg, N. C., Mandt, B. H., Obermeyer, W. H., Winsauer, P. J., Huber, R., Wikelski, M., & Benca, R. M. (2004). Migratory sleeplessness in the white-crowned sparrow (*Zonotrichia leucophrys gambelii*). *PLoS Biology, 2,* 924–936. (10) doi: 10.1371/journal.pbio.0020212

Rattenborg, N. C., Voirin, B., Cruz, S. M., Tisdale, R., Dell-Omo, G., Lipp, H.-P., ... Vyssotski, A. L. (2016). Evidence that birds sleep in mid-flight. *Nature Communications, 7,* article 12468. (10) doi: 10.1038/ncomms12468

Raven, J. (2000). The Raven's Progressive Matrices: Change and stability over culture and time. *Cognitive Psychology, 41,* 1–48. (9) doi: 10.1006/cogp.1999.0735

Ravizza, S. M., Uitvlugt, M. G., & Fenn, K. M. (2017). Logged in and zoned out: How laptop Internet use relates to classroom learning. *Psychological Science, 28,* 171–180. (7) doi: 10.1177/0956797616677314

Ravussin, Y., Leibel, R. L., & Ferrante, A. W. Jr. (2014). A missing link in body weight homeostasis: The catabolic signal of the overfed state. *Cell Metabolism, 20,* 565–572. (11) doi: 10.1016/j.cmet.2014.09.002

Rayner, K. (1998). Eye movements in reading and information processing: 20 years of research. *Psychological Bulletin, 124,* 372–422. (8) doi: 10.1037/0033-2909.124.3.372

Rayner, K., Schotter, E. R., Masson, M. E. J., Potter, M. C., & Treiman, R. (2016). So much to read, so little time: How do we read, and can speed reading help? *Psychological Science in the Public Interest, 17,* 4–34. (8) doi: 10.1177/1529100615623267

Rayner, K., White, S. J., Johnson, R. L., & Liversedge, S. P. (2006). Raeding wrods with jumbled lettres. *Psychological Science, 17,* 192–193. (8) doi: 10.1111/j.1467-9280.2006.01684.x

Raz, A., Kirsch, I., Pollard, J., & Nitkin-Kaner, Y. (2006). Suggestion reduces the Stroop effect. *Psychological Science, 17,* 91–95. (8) doi: 10.1111/j.1467-9280.2006.01669.x

Reardon, P. K., Seidlitz, J., Vandekar, S., Liu, S., Patel, R., Park, M. T. M., Alexander-Bloch, A.,

Clasen, L. S., Blumenthal, J. D., Lalonde, F. M., Giedd, J. N., Gur, R. C., Gur, R. E., Lerch, J. P., Chakravarty, M. M., Satterthwaite, T. D., Shinohara, R. T., & Raznahan, A. (2018). Normative brain size variation and brain shape diversity in humans. *Science, 360,* 1222–1227. (3) doi: 10.1126/science.aar2578

Reardon, S. (2016). Transgender youth study kicks off. *Nature, 531,* 560. (11) doi: 10.1038/531560a

Reber, T. P., Faber, J., Niediek, J., Boström, J., Elger, C. E., & Mormann, F. (2017). Single-neuron correlates of conscious perception in the human medial temporal lobe. *Current Biology, 27,* 2991–2998. (10) doi: 10.1016/j.cub.2017.08.025

Redding, R. E. (2001). Sociopolitical diversity in psychology. *American Psychologist, 56,* 205–215. (5) doi: 10.1037/0003-066X.56.3.205

Redick, T. S., Shipstead, Z., Meier, M. E., Montroy, J. J., Hicks, K. L., Unsworth, N., Kane, M. J., Hambrick, D. Z., & Engle, R. W. (2016). Cognitive predictors of a common multitasking ability: Contributions from working memory, attention control, and fluid intelligence. *Journal of Experimental Psychology: General, 145,* 1473–1492. (8) doi: 10.1037/xge0000219

Reed, J. M., & Squire, L. R. (1999). Impaired transverse patterning in human amnesia is a special case of impaired memory for two-choice discrimination tasks. *Behavioral Neuroscience, 113,* 3–9. (7) doi: 10.1037/0735-7044.113.1.3

Reed, M. D., Yim, Y. S., Wimmer, R. D., Kim, H., Ryu, C., Welch, G. M., Andina, M., King, H. O., Waisman, A., Halassa, M. H., Huh, J. R., & Choi, G. B. (2020). IL-17a promotes sociability in mouse models of neurodevelopmental disorders. *Nature, 577,* 249–253. (15) doi: 10.1038/s41586-019-1843-6

Reicher, G. M. (1969). Perceptual recognition as a function of meaningfulness of stimulus material. *Journal of Experimental Psychology, 81,* 275–280. (8) doi: 10.1037/h0027768

Reicher, S. D., Haslam, S. A., & Smith, J. R. (2012). Working toward the experimenter: Reconceptualizing obedience within the Milgram paradigm as identification-based followership. *Perspectives on Psychological Science, 7,* 315–324. (13) doi: 10.1177/1745691612448482

Reilly, D., Neumann, D. L., & Andrews, G. (2019). Investigating gender differences in mathematics and science: Results from the 2011 Trends in Mathematics and Science Survey. *Research in Science Education, 49,* 25–50. (5) doi: 10.1007/s11165-017-9630-6

Reinius, B., Saetre, P., Leonard, J. A., Blekhman, R., Merino-Martinez, R., Gilad, Y., & Jazin, E. (2008). An evolutionarily conserved sexual signature in the primate brain. *PLoS Genetics, 4,* e1000100. (5) doi: 10.1371/journal.pgen.1000100

Reisenzein, R. (1983). The Schachter theory of emotions: Two decades later. *Psychological Bulletin, 94,* 239–264. (12) doi: 10.1037/0033-2909.94.2.239

Remes, O., Brayne, C., van der Linde, R., & Lafortune, L. (2016). A systematic review of reviews on the prevalence of anxiety disorders in adult populations. *Brain and Behavior, 6,* e00497. (15) doi: 10.1002/brb3.497

Rensink, R. A., O'Regan, J. K., & Clark, J. J. (1997). To see or not to see: The need for attention to perceive changes in scenes. *Psychological Science, 8,* 368–373. (8) doi: 10.1111/j.1467-9280.1997.tb00427.x

Rentfrow, P. J., Gosling, S. D., & Potter, J. (2008). A theory of the emergence, persistence, and expression of geographic variation in psychological characteristics. *Perspectives on Psychological Science, 3,* 339–369. (14) doi: 10.1111/j.1745-6924.2008.00084.x

Repovš, G., & Baddeley, A. (2006). The multi-component model of working memory: Explorations in experimental cognitive psychology. *Neuroscience, 139,* 5–21. (7) doi: 10.1016/j.neuroscience.2005.12.061

Rescorla, R. A. (1968). Probability of shock in the presence and absence of CS in fear conditioning. *Journal of Comparative and Physiological Psychology, 66,* 1–5. (6) doi: 10.1037/h0025984

Rescorla, R. A. (1988). Pavlovian conditioning: It's not what you think it is. *American Psychologist, 43,* 151–160. (6) doi: 10.1037/0003-066X.43.3.151

Restle, F. (1970). Moon illusion explained on the basis of relative size. *Science, 167,* 1092–1096. (4) doi: 10.1126/science.167.3921.1092

Revusky, S. (2009). Chemical aversion treatment of alcoholism. In S. Reilly & T. R. Schachtman (Eds.), *Conditioned taste aversion* (pp. 445–472). New York: Oxford University Press. (6)

Reynolds, A. J., Temple, J. A., Ou, S.-R., Arteaga, I. A., & White, B. A. B. (2011). School-based early childhood education and age-28 well-being: Effects by timing, dosage, and subgroups. *Science, 333,* 360–364. (9) doi: 10.1126/science.1203618

Rhodes, G., Sumich, A., & Byatt, G. (1999). Are average facial configurations attractive only because of their symmetry? *Psychological Science, 10,* 52–58. (13) doi: 10.1111/1467-9280.00106

Rhodes, R. A., Murthy, N. V., Dresner, M. A., Selvaraj, S., Stavrakakis, N., Babar, S., Cowen, P. J., & Grasby, P. M. (2007). Human 5-HT transporter availability predicts amygdala reactivity *in vivo. Journal of Neuroscience, 27,* 9233–9237. (3) doi: 10.1523/JNEUROSCI.1175-07.2007

Riccio, D. C. (1994). Memory: When less is more. *American Psychologist, 49,* 917–926. (7) doi: 10.1037/0003-066X.49.11.917

Rice, W. R., Friberg, U., & Gavrilets, S. (2012). Homosexuality as a consequence of epigenetically canalized sexual development. *Quarterly Review of Biology, 87,* 343–368. (11) doi: 10.1086/668167

Rich, E. L., & Wallis, J. D. (2016). Decoding subjective decisions from orbitofrontal cortex. *Nature Neuroscience, 19,* 973–980. (3) doi: 10.1038/nn.4320

Richards, D. A., Ekers, D., McMillan, D., Taylor, R. S., Byford, S., Warren, F. C., Barrett, B., Farrand, P. A., Gilbody, S., Kuyken, W., O'Mahen, H., Wright, K. A., Hollon, S. H., Reed, N., Rhodes, S., Fletcher, E., & Finning, K. (2016). Cost outcome of behavioural activation versus Cognitive Behavioural Therapy for Depression (COBRA): A randomised, controlled, non-inferiority trial. *Lancet, 388,* 871–880. (15) doi: 10.1016/S0140-6736(16)31140-0

Richins, M. T., Barretto, M., Karl, A., & Lawrence, N. (2019). Empathic responses are reduced to competitive but not non-competitive outgroups. *Social Neuroscience, 14,* 345–358. (4) doi: 10.1080/17470919.2018.1463927

Richter, C. P. (1922). A behavioristic study of the activity of the rat. *Comparative Psychology Monographs, 1,* 1–55. (11)

. P. (1967). Psychopathology of periodic
ior in animals and man. In J. Zubin & H.
t (Eds.), *Comparative Psychopathology*
(pp. 205–227). New York: Grune & Stratton.
(10)

Richter, C. P. (1975). Deep hypothermia and
its effect on the 24-hour clock of rats and
hamsters. *Johns Hopkins Medical Journal, 136,*
1–10. (10)

Richters, J., Altman, D., Badcock, P. B., Smith, A.
M. A., de Visser, R. O., Grulich, A. E., Rissel, C.,
& Simpson, J. M. (2014). Sexual identity, sexual
attraction and sexual experience: The Second
Australian Study of Health and Relationships.
Sexual Health, 11, 451–460. (11) doi: 10.1071/
SH14117

Riddle, W. J. R., & Scott, A. I. F. (1995). Relapse
after successful electroconvulsive therapy: The
use and impact of continuation antidepressant
drug treatment. *Human Psychopharmacology,
10,* 201–205. (15) doi: 10.1002/hup.470100306

Rieger, G., Chivers, M. L., & Bailey, J. M. (2005).
Sexual arousal patterns of bisexual men.
Psychological Science, 16, 579–584. (11) doi:
10.1111/j.1467-9280.2005.01578.x

Rieger, G., Linsenmeier, J. A. W., Gygax, L., &
Bailey, J. M. (2008). Sexual orientation and
childhood gender nonconformity: Evidence
from home videos. *Developmental Psychology,
44,* 46–58. (11) doi: 10.1037/0012-1649.44.1.46

Rieger, G., Rosenthal, A. M., Cash, B. M.,
Linsenmeier, J. A. W., Bailey, J. M., &
Savin-Williams, R. C. (2013). Male bisexual
arousal: A matter of curiosity? *Biological
Psychology, 94,* 479–489. (11) doi: 10.1016/j.
biopsycho.2013.09.007

Riemer, H., Shavitt, S., Koo, M., & Markus, H. R.
(2014). Preferences don't have to be personal:
Expanding attitude theorizing with a cross-
cultural perspective. *Psychological Review, 121,*
619–648. (13) doi: 10.1037/a0037666

Rindermann, H., Becker, D., & Coyle, T. R. (2017).
Survey of expert opinion on intelligence: The
FLynn effect and the future of intelligence.
Personality and Individual Differences, 106,
242–247. (9) doi: 10.1016/j.paid.2016.10.061

Rindermann, H., & Thompson, J. (2013). Ability
rise in NAEP and narrowing ethnic gaps?
Intelligence, 41, 821–831. (9) doi: 10.1016/j.
intell.2013.06.016

Ritchie, S. J., Wiseman, R., & French, C. C. (2012).
Failing the future: Three unsuccessful attempts
to replicate Bem's 'retroactive facilitation of
recall' experiment. *PLoS One, 7,* e33423. (2)
doi: 10.1371/journal.pone.0033423

Ritvo, E. R. (2006). *Understanding the nature of
autism and Asperger's syndrome.* London:
Jessica Kingsley. (15)

Roane, B. M., & Taylor, D. J. (2008). Adolescent
insomnia as a risk factor for early adult
depression and substance abuse. *Sleep, 31,*
1351–1356. (15)

Roberts, B. W., & DelVecchio, W. F. (2000). The
rank-order consistency of personality traits
from childhood to old age: A quantitative
review of longitudinal studies. *Psychological
Bulletin, 126,* 3–25. (14) doi: 10.1037/0033-
2909.126.1.3

Roberts, B. W., Kuncel, N. R., Shiner, R., Caspi,
A., & Goldberg, L. R. (2007). The power of
personality. *Perspectives on Psychological
Science, 2,* 313–345. (14) doi: 10.1111/j.1745-
6916.2007.00047.x

Roberts, B. W., Walton, K. E., & Viechtbauer,
W. (2006). Patterns of mean-level change in
personality traits across the life course: A

meta-analysis of longitudinal studies.
Psychological Bulletin, 132, 1–25. (14) doi:
10.1037/0033-2909.132.1.1

Roberts, R. E., & Duong, H. T. (2014). The
prospective association between sleep
deprivation and depression among
adolescents. *Sleep, 37,* 239–244. (10, 15) doi:
10.5665/sleep.3388

Roberts, S., Henry, J. D., & Molenberghs, P. (2019).
Immoral behavior following brain damage: A
review. *Journal of Neuropsychology, 13,* 564–
588. (12) doi: 10.1111/jnp.12155

Roberts, S. B., Savage, J., Coward, W. A., Chew,
B., & Lucas, A. (1988). Energy expenditure
and intake in infants born to lean and
overweight mothers. *New England Journal
of Medicine, 318,* 461–466. (11) doi: 10.1056/
NEJM198802253180801

Roberts, S. C., Gosling, L. M., Carter, V., & Petrie,
M. (2008). MHC-correlated odour preferences
in humans and the use of oral contraceptives.
Proceedings of the Royal Society, B, 275, 2715–
2722. (4, 13) doi: 10.1098/rspb.2008.0825

Robertson, C. E., & Baron-Cohen, S. (2017).
Sensory perception in autism. *Nature Reviews
Neuroscience, 18,* 671–684. (15) doi: 10.1038/
nrn.2017.112

Robertson, I. H. (2005, Winter). The deceptive
world of subjective awareness. *Cerebrum, 7*(1),
74–83. (3)

Robertson, L. C. (2003). Binding, spatial attention
and perceptual awareness. *Nature Reviews
Neuroscience, 4,* 93–102. (3) doi: 10.1038/
nrn1030

Robin, J., Buchsbaum, B. R., & Moscovitch, M.
(2018). The primacy of spatial context in the
neural representation of events. *Journal of
Neuroscience, 38,* 2755–2765. (7) doi: 10.1523/
JNEUROSCI.1638-17.2018

Robinson, T. E., & Berridge, K. C. (2000). The
psychology and neurobiology of addiction:
An incentive-sensitization view. *Addiction,
95*(Suppl. 2), S91–S117. (15) doi: doi.
org/10.1046/j.1360-0443.95.8s2.19.x

Robinson, T. E., & Berridge, K. C. (2001).
Incentive-sensitization and addiction.
Addiction, 96, 103–114. (15) doi:
10.1046/j.1360-0443.2001.9611038.x

Rock, I., & Kaufman, L. (1962). The moon illusion,
II. *Science, 136,* 1023–1031. (4) doi: 10.1126/
science.136.3521.1023

Rodd, J., Gaskell, G., & Marslen-Wilson, W. (2002).
Making sense of semantic ambiguity: Semantic
competition in lexical access. *Journal of
Memory and Language, 46,* 245–266. (8) doi:
10.1006/jmla.2001.2810

Rodgers, J. L. (2001). What causes birth order-
intelligence patterns? *American Psychologist,
56,* 505–510. (5) doi: 10.1037/0003-066X.56.6-
7.505

Rodgers, J. L., Cleveland, H. H., van den Oord, E.,
& Rowe, D. C. (2000). Resolving the debate
over birth order, family size, and intelligence.
American Psychologist, 55, 599–612. (5) doi:
10.1037/0003-066X.55.6.599

Rodin, J. (1986). Aging and health: Effects of the
sense of control. *Science, 233,* 1271–1276. (5)
doi: 10.1126/science.3749877

Rodrigo, M. F., & Ato, M. (2002). Testing the group
polarization hypothesis by using logit models.
European Journal of Social Psychology, 32,
3–18. (13) doi: 10.1002/ejsp.86

Roediger, H. L., III, & Karpicke, J. D. (2006).
Test-enhanced learning. *Psychological
Science, 17,* 249–255. (7) doi: 10.1111/j.1467-
9280.2006.01693.x

Roediger, H. L., III, & McDermott, K. B. (1995).
Creating false memories: Remembering words
not presented in lists. *Journal of Experimental
Psychology: Learning, Memory, and
Cognition, 21,* 803–814. (7) doi: 10.1037/0278-
7393.21.4.803

Roenneberg, T., Kuehnle, T., Pramstaller, P. P.,
Ricken, J., Havel, M., Guth, A., & Merrow, M.
(2004). A marker for the end of adolescence.
Current Biology, 14, R1038–R1039. (10) doi:
10.1016/j.cub.2004.11.039

Roenneberg, T., Kumar, C. J., & Merrow, M. (2007).
The human circadian clock entrains to sun
time. *Current Biology, 17,* R44–R45. (10) doi:
10.1016/j.cub.2006.12.011

Roese, N. J., & Vohs, K. D. (2012). Hindsight bias.
Perspectives on Psychological Science, 7, 411–
426. (7) doi: 10.1177/1745691612454303

Rofé, Y. (2008). Does repression exist? Memory,
pathogenic, unconscious and clinical
evidence. *Review of General Psychology, 12,*
63–85. (14) doi: 10.1037/1089-2680.12.1.63

Rogers, C. R. (1961). *On becoming a person.*
Boston: Houghton Mifflin. (14)

Rogers, C. R. (1980). *A way of being.* Boston:
Houghton Mifflin. (14)

Rogers, T., & Feller, A. (2016). Discouraged by
peer excellence: Exposure to exemplary
peer performance causes quitting.
Psychological Science, 27, 365–374. (6) doi:
10.1177/0956797615623770

Rogers, T., & Milkman, K. L. (2016). Reminders
through association. *Psychological Science, 27,*
973–986. (11) doi: 10.1177/0956797616643071

Rogers, T., Moore, D. A., & Norton, M. I.
(2017). The belief in a favorable future.
Psychological Science, 28, 1290–1301. (8) doi:
10.1177/0956797617706706

Rogler, L. H. (2002). Historical generations and
psychology. *American Psychologist, 57,* 1013–
1023. (5) doi: 10.1037//0003-066X.57.12.1013

Rogoff, B., Morelli, G. A., & Chavajay, P. (2010).
Children's integration in communities and
segregation from people of different ages.
Perspectives on Psychological Science, 5, 431–
440. (5) doi: 10.1177/1745691610375558

Rohrer, D., & Pashler, H. (2007). Increasing
retention without increasing study time.
*Current Directions in Psychological Science,
16,* 183–186. (7) doi: 10.1111/j.1467-
8721.2007.00500.x

Rohrer, J. M., Egloff, B., & Schmukle, S. C.
(2015). Examining the effects of birth order
on personality. *Proceedings of the National
Academy of Sciences (U.S.A.), 112,* 14224–
14229. (5) doi: 10.1073/pnas.1506451112

Rohrer, J. M., Egloff, B., & Schmukle, S. S. (2017).
Probing birth-order effects on narrow
traits using specification-curve analysis.
Psychological Science, 28, 1821–1832. (5) doi:
10.1177/0956797617723726

Rohrer, J. M., Richter, D., Brümmer, M., Wagner,
G. G., & Schmulke, S. C. (2018). Successfully
striving for happiness: Socially engaged
pursuits predict increases in life satisfaction.
Psychological Science, 29, 1291–1298. (12) doi:
10.1177/0956797618761660

Rohrer, R., & Taylor, K. (2007). The shuffling of
mathematics problems improves learning.
Instructional Science, 35, 481–498. (7)

Roisman, G. I., Collins, W. A., Sroufe, L. A., &
Egeland, B. (2005). Predictors of young adults'
representations of and behavior in their
current romantic relationship: Prospective
tests of the prototype hypothesis. *Attachment*

and Human Development, 7, 105–121. (5) doi: 10.1080/14616730500134928

Rolls, E. T., & McCabe, C. (2007). Enhanced affective brain representations of chocolate in cravers vs. non-cravers. *European Journal of Neuroscience, 26,* 1067–1076. (3) doi: 10.1111/j.1460-9568.2007.05724.x

Romano, A., & Balliet, D. (2017). Reciprocity outperforms conformity to promote cooperation. *Psychological Science, 28,* 1490–1502. (13) doi: 10.1177/0956797617714828

Ronen, T., & Rosenbaum, M. (2001). Helping children to help themselves: A case study of enuresis and nail biting. *Research on Social Work Practice, 11,* 338–356. (6) doi: 10.1177/104973150101100304

Rooksby, M., Elouafkaoui, P., Humphris, G., Clarkson, J., & Freeman, R. (2015). Internet-assisted delivery of cognitive behavioural therapy (CBT) for childhood anxiety: Systematic review and meta-analysis. *Journal of Anxiety Disorders, 29,* 83–92. (15) doi: 10.1016/j.janxdis.2014.11.006

Rosa-Alcázar, A. I., Sánchez-Meca, J., Gómez-Conesa, A., & Marín-Martínez, F. (2008). Psychological treatment of obsessive-compulsive disorder: A meta-analysis. *Clinical Psychology Review, 28,* 1310–1325. (15) doi: 10.1016/j.cpr.2008.07.001

Rosch, E. (1978). Principles of categorization. In E. Rosch & B. B. Lloyd (Eds.), *Cognition and categorization* (pp. 27–48). Hillsdale, NJ: Erlbaum. (8)

Rosch, E., & Mervis, C. B. (1975). Family resemblances: Studies in the internal structure of categories. *Cognitive Psychology, 7,* 573–605. (8) doi: 10.1016/0010-0285(75)90024-9

Rose, J. E., Brugge, J. F., Anderson, D. J., & Hind, J. E. (1967). Phase-locked response to low-frequency tones in single auditory nerve fibers of the squirrel monkey. *Journal of Neurophysiology, 30,* 769–793. (4) doi: 10.1152/jn.1967.30.4.769.

Rose, N. S., Myerson, J., Roediger, H. L. III, & Hale, S. (2010). Similarities and differences between working memory and long-term memory: Evidence from the levels-of-processing span task. *Journal of Experimental Psychology: Learning, Memory, and Cognition, 36,* 471–483. (7) doi: 10.1037/a0018405

Rose, S. A., Feldman, J. F., & Jankowitz, J. J. (2011). Modeling a cascade of effects: The role of speed and executive functioning in preterm/full-term differences in academic achievement. *Developmental Science, 14,* 1161–1175. (7) doi: 10.1111/j.1467-7687.2011.01068.x

Rosenbaum, D. A., Fournier, L. R., Levy-Tzedek, S., McBride, D. M., Rosenthal, R., Sauerberger, K., VonderHaar, R. L., Wasserman, E. A., & Zentall, T. R. (2019). Sooner rather than later: Precrastination rather than procrastination. *Current Directions in Psychological Science, 28,* 229–233. (11) doi: 10.1177/0963721419833652

Rosenbaum, R. S., Köhler, S., Schacter, D. L., Moscovitch, M., Westmacott, R., Black, S. E., Gao, F. Q., & Tulving, E. (2005). The case of K. C.: Contributions of a memory-impaired person to memory theory. *Neuropsychologia, 43,* 989–1021. (7) doi: 10.1016/j.neuropsychologia.2004.10.007

Rosenfeld, M. J., Thomas, R. J., & Hausen, S. (2019). Disintermediating your friends: How online dating in the United States displaces other ways of meeting. *Proceedings of the National Academy of Sciences (U.S.A.), 116,* 17753–17758. (13) doi: 10.1073/pnas.1908630116

Rosenzweig, E. (2016). With eyes wide open: How and why awareness of the psychological immune is compatible with its efficacy. *Perspectives on Psychological Science, 11,* 222–238. (4, 13) doi: 10.1177/1745691615621280

Ross, L. (1977). The intuitive psychologist and his shortcomings: Distortions in the attribution process. In L. Berkowitz (Ed.), *Advances in experimental social psychology* (Vol. 10, pp. 173–220). New York: Academic Press. (13) doi: 10.1016/S0065-2601(08)60357-3

Ross, L. (2018). From the fundamental attribution error to the truly fundamental attribution error and beyond: My research journey. *Perspectives on Psychological Science, 13,* 750–769. (13) doi: 10.1177/1745691618769855

Ross, L. D., Amabile, T. M., & Steinmetz, J. L. (1977). Social roles, social control, and biases in social-perception processes. *Journal of Personality and Social Psychology, 35,* 485–494. (13) doi: 10.1037/0022-3514.35.7.485

Rothbaum, F., Weisz, J., Pott, M., Miyake, K., & Morelli, G. (2000). Attachment and culture: Security in the United States and Japan. *American Psychologist, 55,* 1093–1104. (5) doi: 10.1037//0003-066X.55.10.1093

Rottenberg, J., Devendorf, A. R., Kashdan, T. B., & Disabato, D. J. (2018). The curious neglect of high functioning after psychopathology: The case of depression. *Perspectives on Psychological Science, 13,* 549–566. (15) doi: 10.1177/1745691618769868

Rotton, J., & Kelly, I. W. (1985). Much ado about the full moon: A meta-analysis of lunar-lunacy research. *Psychological Bulletin, 97,* 286–306. (2) doi: 10.1037/0033-2909.97.2.286

Rouder, J. N., & Morey, R. D. (2011). A Bayes factor meta-analysis of Bem's ESP claim. *Psychonomic Bulletin & Review, 18,* 682–689. (2) doi: 10.3758/s13423-011-0088-7

Rounis, E., Maniscalco, B., Rothwell, J. C., Passingham, R., & Lau, H. (2010). Theta-burst transcranial magnetic stimulation to the prefrontal cortex impairs metacognitive visual awareness. *Cognitive Neuroscience, 1,* 165–175. (10) doi: 10.1080/17588921003632529

Rovee-Collier, C. (1997). Dissociations in infant memory: Rethinking the development of explicit and implicit memory. *Psychological Review, 104,* 467–498. (5) doi: 10.1037/0033-295X.104.3.467

Rovee-Collier, C. (1999). The development of infant memory. *Current Directions in Psychological Science, 8,* 80–85. (5) doi: 10.1111/1467-8721.00019

Rowe, J. W., & Kahn, R. L. (1987). Human aging: Usual and successful. *Science, 237,* 143–149. (5) doi: 10.1126/science.3299702

Rowe, M. L., & Goldin-Meadow, S. (2009). Early gesture selectively predicts later language learning. *Developmental Science, 12,* 182–187. (8) doi: 10.1111/j.1467-7687.2008.00764.x

Rozin, P. (1996). Sociocultural influences on human food selection. In E. D. Capaldi (Ed.), *Why we eat what we eat* (pp. 233–263). Washington, DC: American Psychological Association. (1)

Rozin, P., & Cohen, A. B. (2003). High frequency of facial expressions corresponding to confusion, concentration, and worry in an analysis of naturally occurring facial expressions of Americans. *Emotion, 3,* 68–75. (12) doi: 10.1037/1528-3542.3.1.68

Rozin, P., Fallon, A., & Augustoni-Ziskind, M. L. (1986). The child's conception of food: The development of categories of acceptable and rejected substances. *Journal of Nutrition Education, 18,* 75–81. (1) doi: 10.1016/S0022-3182(86)80235-7

Rozin, P., & Fallon, A. E. (1987). A perspective on disgust. *Psychological Review, 94,* 23–41. (1) doi: 10.1037/0033-295X.94.1.23

Rozin, P., Kabnick, K., Pete, E., Fischler, C., & Shields, C. (2003). The ecology of eating: Smaller portion sizes in France than in the United States help explain the French paradox. *Psychological Science, 14,* 450–454. (11) doi: 10.1111/1467-9280.02452

Rozin, P., & Kalat, J. W. (1971). Specific hungers and poison avoidance as adaptive specializations of learning. *Psychological Review, 78,* 459–486. (1, 6) doi: 10.1037/h0031878

Rozin, P., Lowery, L., Imada, S., & Haidt, J. (1999). The CAD triad hypothesis: A mapping between three moral emotions (contempt, anger, disgust) and three moral codes (community, autonomy, divinity). *Journal of Personality and Social Psychology, 76,* 574–586. (12) doi: 10.1037/0022-3514.76.4.574

Rozin, P., Markwith, M., & Ross, B. (1990). The sympathetic magical law of similarity, nominal realism and neglect of negatives in response to negative labels. *Psychological Science, 1,* 383–384. (8) doi: 10.1111/j.1467-9280.1990.tb00246.x

Rozin, P., Markwith, M., & Stoess, C. (1997). Moralization and becoming a vegetarian: The transformation of preferences into values and the recruitment of disgust. *Psychological Science, 8,* 67–73. (1) doi: 10.1111/j.1467-9280.1997.tb00685.x

Rozin, P., Millman, L., & Nemeroff, C. (1986). Operation of the laws of sympathetic magic in disgust and other domains. *Journal of Personality and Social Psychology, 50,* 703–712. (1) doi: 10.1037/0022-3514.50.4.703

Rozin, P., & Pelchat, M. L. (1988). Memories of mammaries: Adaptations to weaning from milk. *Progress in Psychobiology and Physiological Psychology, 13,* 1–29. (3)

Rubin, D. C., & Feeling, N. (2013). Measuring the severity of negative and traumatic events. *Clinical Psychological Science, 1,* 375–389. (12) doi: 10.1177/2167702613483112

Rubin, D. C., & Umanath, S. (2015). Event memory: A theory of memory for laboratory, autobiographical, and fictional events. *Psychological Review, 122,* 1–23. (7) doi: 10.1037/a0037907

Rubio-Fernández, P., & Geurts, B. (2013). How to pass the false-belief task before your fourth birthday. *Psychological Science, 24,* 27–33. (5) doi: 10.1177/0956797612447819

Ruch, J. (1984). *Psychology: The personal science.* Belmont, CA: Wadsworth. (3)

Rudman, L. A., & Goodwin, S. A. (2004). Gender differences in automatic in-group bias: Why do women like women more than men like men? *Journal of Personality and Social Psychology, 87,* 494–509. (13) doi: 10.1037/0022-3514.87.4.494

Rumelhart, D. E., & McClelland, J. L. (1982). An interactive activation model of context effects in letter perception: Part 2. The contextual enhancement effect and some tests and extensions of the model. *Psychological Review, 89,* 60–94. (8) doi: 10.1037/0033-295X.89.1.60

t, D. E., McClelland, J. L., & the PDP ch Group. (1986). *Parallel distributed ing*. Cambridge, MA: MIT Press. (8)

Rusak, B. (1977). The role of the suprachiasmatic nuclei in the generation of circadian rhythms in the golden hamster, *Mesocricetus auratus*. *Journal of Comparative Physiology A, 118*, 145–164. (10) doi: 10.1007/BF00611819

Rush, A. J., Trivedi, M. H., Wisniewski, S. R., Stewart, J. W., Nierenberg, A. A., Thase, M. E., Ritz, L., Biggs, M. M., Warden, D., Luther, J. F., Shores-Wilson, K., Niederehe, G., & Fava, M. (2006). Bupropion-SR, sertraline, or venlafaxine-XR after failure of SSRIs for depression. *New England Journal of Medicine, 354*, 1231–1242. (15) doi: 10.1056/NEJMoa052963

Rushton, J. P., & Bons, T. A. (2005). Mate choice and friendship in twins. *Psychological Science, 16*, 555–559. (13) doi: 10.1111/j.0956-7976.2005.01574.x

Russano, M. B., Meissner, C. A., Narchet, F. M., & Kassin, S. M. (2005). Investigating true and false confessions within a novel experimental paradigm. *Psychological Science, 16*, 481–486. (13) doi: 10.1111/j.0956-7976.2005.01560.x.

Russell, J. A. (1980). A circumplex model of affect. *Journal of Personality and Social Psychology, 39*, 1161–1178. (12) doi: 10.1037/h0077714

Russell, J. A. (1994). Is there universal recognition of emotion from facial expression? A review of the cross-cultural studies. *Psychological Bulletin, 115*, 102–141. (12) doi: 10.1037/0033-2909.115.1.102

Russo, J. E., Carlson, K. A., & Meloy, M. G. (2006). Choosing an inferior alternative. *Psychological Science, 17*, 899–904. (13) doi: 10.1111/j.1467-9280.2006.01800.x

Rutledge, T., & Hogan, B. E. (2002). A quantitative review of prospective evidence linking psychological factors with hypertension development. *Psychosomatic Medicine, 64*, 758–766. (12) doi: 10.1097/01.PSY.0000031578.42041.1C

Ryan, J. D., Althoff, R. R., Whitlow, S., & Cohen, N. J. (2000). Amnesia is a deficit in relational memory. *Psychological Science, 11*, 454–461. (7) doi: 10.1111/1467-9280.00288

Rydell, M., Lundström, S., Gillberg, C., Lichtenstein, P., & Larsson, H. (2018). Has the attention deficit hyperactivity disorder phenotype become more common in children between 2004 and 2014? Trends over 10 years from a Swedish general population sample. *Journal of Child Psychology and Psychiatry, 59*, 863–871. (8) doi: 10.1111/jcpp.12882

Sabini, J., Siepmann, M., Stein, J., & Meyerowitz, M. (2000). Who is embarrassed by what? *Cognition & Emotion, 14*, 213–240. (12) doi: 10.1080/026999300378941

Sacchi, D. L. M., Agnoli, F., & Loftus, E. F. (2007). Changing history: Doctored photographs affect memory for past public events. *Applied Cognitive Psychology, 21*, 1005–1022. (7) doi: 10.1002/acp.1394

Sackeim, H. A., Prudic, J., Devanand, D. P., Nobler, M. S., Lisanby, S. H., Peyser, S., Moody, B. J., & Clark, J. (2000). A prospective, randomized, double-blind comparison of bilateral and right unilateral electroconvulsive therapy at different stimulus intensities. *Archives of General Psychiatry, 57*, 425–434. (15) doi: 10.1001/archpsyc.57.5.425

Sackett, P. R., Borneman, M. J., & Connelly, B. S. (2008). High-stakes testing in higher education

and employment. *American Psychologist, 63*, 215–227. (9) doi: 10.1037/0003-066X.63.4.215

Sackett, P. R., & Walmsley, P. T. (2014). Which personality attributes are most important in the workplace? *Perspectives on Psychological Science, 9*, 538–551. (14) doi: 10.1177/1745691614543972

Sacks, D. W., Stevenson, B., & Wolfers, J. (2012). The new stylized facts about income and subjective well-being. *Emotion, 12*, 1181–1187. (12) doi: 10.1037/a0029873

Sacks, O. (2010, August 30). Face-blind. *The New Yorker, 86 (31)*, 36–43. (3)

Sadeh, T., Ozubko, J. D., Winocur, G., & Moscovitch, M. (2016). Forgetting patterns differentiate between two patterns of memory representation. *Psychological Science, 27*, 810–820. (7) doi: 10.1177/0956797616638307

Sadri-Vakili, G., Kumaresan, V., Schmidt, H. D., Famous, K. R., Chawla, P., Vassoler, F. M., Overland, R. P., Xia, E., Bass, C. E., Terwilliger, E. F., Pierce, R. C., & Cha, J. H. J. (2010). Cocaine-induced chromatin remodeling increases brain-derived neurotrophic factor transcription in the rat medial prefrontal cortex, which alters the reinforcing efficacy of cocaine. *Journal of Neuroscience, 30*, 11735–11744. (3) doi: 10.1523/JNEUROSCI.2328-10.2010

Saegert, S., Swap, W., & Zajonc, R. B. (1973). Exposure, context, and interpersonal attraction. *Journal of Personality and Social Psychology, 25*, 234–242. (13) doi: 10.1037/h0033965

Sagana, A., Sauerland, M., & Merckelbach, H. (2017). Witnesses' failure to detect covert manipulations in their written statements. *Journal of Investigative Psychology and Offender Profiling, 14*, 320–331. (8) doi: 10.1002/jip.1479

Sala, G., & Gobet, F. (2017). Does far transfer exist? Negative evidence from chess, music, and working memory training. *Current Directions in Psychological Science, 26*, 515–520. (8) doi: 10.1177/0963721417712760

Sales, B. D., & Folkman, S. (2000). *Ethics in research with human participants*. Washington, DC: American Psychological Association. (2)

Salimpoor, V. N., van den Bosch, I., Kovacevic, N., McIntosh, A. R., Dagher, A., & Zatorre, R. J. (2013). Interactions between the nucleus accumbens and auditory cortices predict music reward value. *Science, 340*, 216–219. (3) doi: 10.1126/science.1231059

Salmon, P. (2001). Effects of physical exercise on anxiety, depression, and sensitivity to stress: A unifying theory. *Clinical Psychology Review, 21*, 33–61. (12) doi: 10.1016/S0272-7358(99)00032-X

Salomons, T. V., Johnstone, T., Backonja, M.-M., & Davidson, R. J. (2004). Perceived controllability modulates the neural response to pain. *Journal of Neuroscience, 24*, 7199–7203. (12) doi: 10.1523/JNEUROSCI.1315-04.2004

Salthouse, T. A. (2006). Mental exercise and mental aging. *Perspectives on Psychological Science, 1*, 68–87. (8) doi: 10.1111/j.1745-6916.2006.00005.x

Salvatore, J. E., Kuo, S. I.-C., Steele, R. D., Simpson, J. A., & Collins, W. A. (2011). Recovering from conflict in romantic relationships: A developmental perspective. *Psychological Science, 22*, 376–383. (5) doi: 10.1177/0956797610397055

Salvatore, J. E., Lönn, S. L., Sundquist, J., Sundquist, K., & Kendler, K. S. (2018). Genetics, the rearing environment, and the intergenerational transmission of divorce: A Swedish national adoption study. *Psychological Science, 29*, 370–378. (3) doi: 10.1177/0956797617734864

Samuel, A. G. (2001). Knowing a word affects the fundamental perception of the sounds within it. *Psychological Science, 12*, 348–351. (8) doi: 10.1111/1467-9280.00364

Samuel, S., Roehr-Brackin, K., Pak, H., & Kim, H. (2018). Cultural effects rather than a bilingual advantage in cognition: A review and an empirical study. *Cognitive Science, 42*, 2313–2341. (8) doi: 10.1111/cogs.12672

Sanchez, L. M., & Turner, S. M. (2003). Practicing psychology in the era of managed care. *American Psychologist, 58*, 116–129. (15) doi: 10.1037/0003-066X.58.2.116

Sanders, A. R., Beecham, G. W., Guo, S., Dawood, K., Rieger, G., Badner, J. A., Martin, E. R. (2017). Genome-wide association study of male sexual orientation. *Scientific Reports, 7*, Article 16950. (11) doi: 10.1038/s41598-017-15736-4

Sanders, S. J., Xin, H., Willsey, A. J., Ercan-Sencicek, A. G., Samocha, K. E., Cicek, A. E., Murtha, M. T., Bal, V. H., Bishop, S. L., Shan, D., Goldberg, A. P., Cai, J. L., Keaney, J. F., Klei, L., Mandell, J. D., Moreno-DeLuca, D., Poultney, C. S., Robinson, E. B., Smith, L., ... State, M. W. (2015). Insights into autism spectrum disorder genomic architecture and biology from 71 risk loci. *Neuron, 87*, 1215–1233. (15) doi: 10.1016/j.neuron.2015.09.016

Sandfort, T. G. M., de Graaf, R., Bijl, R. V., & Schnabel, P. (2001). Same-sex sexual behavior and psychiatric disorders. *Archives of General Psychiatry, 58*, 85–91. (11) doi: 10.1001/archpsyc.58.1.85

Sandhya, S. (2009). The social context of marital happiness in urban Indian couples: Interplay of intimacy and conflict. *Journal of Marital and Family Conflict, 35*, 74–96. (11) doi: 10.1111/j.1752-0606.2008.00103.x

Santos, H. C., Varnum, M. E. W., & Grossman, I. (2017). Global increases in individualism. *Psychological Science, 28*, 1228–1239. (5) doi: 10.1177/0956797617700622

Sapolsky, R. M., & Share, L. J. (2004). A pacific culture among wild baboons: Its emergence and transmission. *PLoS Biology, 2*, 534–541. (13) doi: 10.1371/journal.pbio.0020106

Sapp, F., Lee, K., & Muir, D. (2000). Three-year-olds' difficulty with the appearance–reality distinction: Is it real or is it apparent? *Developmental Psychology, 36*, 547–560. (5) doi: 10.1037/0012-1649.36.5.547

Sasson, I., & Umberson, D. J. (2014). Widowhood and depression: New light on gender differences, selection, and psychological adjustment. *Journals of Gerontology, Series B: Psychological Sciences and Social Sciences, 69*, 135–145. (15) doi: 10.1093/geronb/gbt058

Sauce, B., & Matzel, L. D. (2018). The paradox of intelligence: Heritability and malleability coexist in hidden gene-environment interplay. *Psychological Bulletin, 144*, 26–47. (9) doi: 10.1037/bul0000131

Saucier, D. M., Green, S. M., Leason, J., MacFadden, A., Bell, S., & Elias, L. J. (2002). Are sex differences in navigation caused by sexually dimorphic strategies or by differences in the ability to use the strategies? *Behavioral Neuroscience, 116*, 403–410. (5) doi: 10.1037//0735-7044.116.3.403

Savage, J. E., Jansen, P. R., Stringer, S., Watanabe, K., Bryois, J., de Leeuw, C. A., Nagel, M., Awasthi, S., Barr, P. B., Coleman, J. R. I., Grasby, K. L., Hammerschlag, A. R., Kaminski, J. A., Karlsson, R., Krapohl, E., Lam, M., Nygaard, M., Reynolds, C. A., Trampush, J. W., ... Posthuman, D. (2018). Genome-wide association meta-analysis in 269,867 individuals identifies new genetic and functional links to intelligence. *Nature Genetics, 50*, 912–919. (9) doi: 10.1038/s41588-018-0152-6

Savage-McGlynn, E. (2012). Sex differences in intelligence in younger and older participants of the Raven's Standard Progressive Matrices Plus. *Personality and Individual Differences, 53*, 137–141. (9) doi: 10.1016/j.paid.2011.06.013

Savage-Rumbaugh, E. S. (1990). Language acquisition in a nonhuman species: Implications for the innateness debate. *Developmental Psychology, 23*, 599–620. (8) doi: 10.1002/dev.420230706

Savage-Rumbaugh, E. S., Murphy, J., Sevcik, R. A., Brakke, K. E., Williams, S. L., & Rumbaugh, D. M. (1993). Language comprehension in ape and child. *Monographs of the Society for Research in Child Development, 58*(Serial no. 233). (8) doi: 10.2307/1166068

Savage-Rumbaugh, E. S., Sevcik, R. A., Brakke, K. E., & Rumbaugh, D. M. (1992). Symbols: Their communicative use, communication, and combination by bonobos *(Pan paniscus).* In L. P. Lipsitt & C. Rovee-Collier (Eds.), *Advances in infancy research* (Vol. 7, pp. 221–278). Norwood, NJ: Ablex. (8)

Savic, I., Berglund, H., & Lindström, P. (2005). Brain response to putative pheromones in homosexual men. *Proceedings of the National Academy of Sciences (U.S.A.), 102*, 7356–7361. (4) doi: 10.1073/pnas.0407998102

Savin-Williams, R. C., & Vrangalova, Z. (2013). Mostly heterosexual as a distinct sexual orientation group: A systematic review of the empirical evidence. *Developmental Review, 33*, 58–88. (11) doi: 10.1016/j.dr.2013.01.001

Saxton, T. K., Nováková, L. M., Jash, R., Sandová, A., Plotená, D., & Havlíček, J. (2014). Sex differences in olfactory behavior in Namibian and Czech children. *Chemical Perception, 7*, 117–125. (4) https://link.springer.com/article/10.1007/s12078-014-9172-5

Sbarra, D. A., Law, R. W., & Portley, R. M. (2011). Divorce and death: A meta-analysis and research agenda for clinical, social, and health psychology. *Perspectives on Psychological Science, 6*, 454–474. (12) doi: 10.1177/1745691611414724

Scalera, G., & Bavieri, M. (2009). Role of conditioned taste aversion on the side effects of chemotherapy in cancer patients. In S. Reilly & T. R. Schachtman (Eds.), *Conditioned taste aversion* (pp. 513–541). New York: Oxford University Press. (6)

Scarborough, E., & Furomoto, L. (1987). *Untold lives: The first generation of American women psychologists.* New York: Columbia University Press. (1)

Schachter, S. (1982). Recidivism and self-cure of smoking and obesity. *American Psychologist, 37*, 436–444. (11) doi: 10.1037/0003-066X.37.4.436

Schachter, S., & Singer, J. (1962). Cognitive, social, and physiological determinants of emotional state. *Psychological Review, 69*, 379–399. (12) doi: 10.1037/h0046234

Schacter, D. L. (1987). Implicit memory: History and current status. *Journal of Experimental Psychology: Learning, Memory, and Cognition, 13*, 501–518. (7) doi: 10.1037/0278-7393.13.3.501

Schacter, D. L., Verfaellie, M., Anes, M. D., & Racine, C. (1998). When true recognition suppresses false recognition: Evidence from amnesic patients. *Journal of Cognitive Neuroscience, 10*, 668–679. (7) doi: 10.1162/089892998563086

Schaefer, J. D., Moffitt, T. E., Arsenault, L., Danese, A., Fisher, H. L., Houts, R., Sheridan, M. A., Wertz, J., & Caspit, A. (2018). Adolescent victimization and early-adult psychopathology: Approaching causal inference using a longitudinal twin study to rule out noncausal explanations. *Clinical Psychological Science, 6*, 352–371. (15) doi: 10.1177/2167702617741381

Schatzman, M. (1992, March 21). Freud: Who seduced whom? *New Scientist*, pp. 34–37. (14)

Scheele, D., Striepens, N., Güntürkün, O., Deutschländer, S., Maier, W., Kendrick, K. M., & Hurlemann, R. (2012). Oxytocin modulates social distance between males and females. *Journal of Neuroscience, 32*, 16074–16079. (3) doi: 10.1523/JNEUROSCI.2755-12.2012

Scheele, D., Wille, A., Kendrick, K. M., Stoffel-Wagner, B., Becker, B., Güntürkün, O., Maier, W., & Hurlemann, R. (2013). Oxytocin enhances brain reward system responses in men viewing the face of their female partner. *Proceedings of the National Academy of Sciences (U.S.A.), 110*, 20308–20313. (3) doi: 10.1073/pnas.1314190110

Scheiber, C., Chen, H. Y., Kaufman, A. S., & Weiss, L. G. (2017). How much does WAIS-IV perceptual reasoning decline across the 20 to 90-year lifespan when processing speed is controlled? *Applied Neuropsychology—Adult, 24*, 116–131. (9) doi: 10.1080/23279095.2015.1107564

Schellenberg, E. G., & Trehub, S. E. (2003). Good pitch memory is widespread. *Psychological Science, 14*, 262–266. (4) doi: 10.1111/1467-9280.03432

Schenk, T. (2006). An allocentric rather than perceptual deficit in patient D. F. *Nature Neuroscience, 9*, 1369–1370. (3) doi: 10.1038/nn1784

Schiebener, J., Wegmann, E., Pawlikowski, M., & Brand, M. (2014). Effects of goals on decisions under risk conditions: Goals can help to make better choices, but relatively high goals increase risk-taking. *Journal of Cognitive Psychology, 26*, 473–485. (11) doi: 10.1080/20445911.2014.903254

Schiffman, S. S., & Erickson, R. P. (1971). A psychophysical model for gustatory quality. *Physiology and Behavior, 7*, 617–633. (4) doi: 10.1016/0031-9384(71)90117-X

Schindler, S., Reinhard, M. A., Dobiosch, S., Steffan-Fauseweh, I., Özdemir, G., & Greenberg, J. (2019). The attenuating effect of mortality salience on dishonest behavior. *Motivation and Emotion, 43*, 52–62. (5) doi: 10.1007/s11031-018-9734-y

Schizophrenia Working Group of the Psychiatric Genomics Consortium. (2014). Biological insights from 108 schizophrenia-associated genetic loci. *Nature, 511*, 421–427. (15) doi: 10.1038/nature13595

Schkade, D. A., & Kahneman, D. (1998). Does living in California make people happy? *Psychological Science, 9*, 340–346. (12) doi: 10.1111/1467-9280.00066

Schlam, T. R., Wilson, N. L., Shoda, Y., Mischel, W., & Ayduk, O. (2013). Preschoolers' delay of gratification predicts their body mass 30 years later. *Journal of Pediatrics, 162*, 90–93. (11) doi: 10.1016/j.jpeds.2012.06.049

Schlesier-Stropp, B. (1984). Bulimia: A review of the literature. *Psychological Bulletin, 95*, 247–257. (11) doi: 10.1037/0033-2909.95.2.247

Schmelz, M., Grueneisen, S., Kabalak, A., Jost, J., & Tomasello, M. (2017). Chimpanzees return favors at a personal cost. *Proceedings of the National Academy of Sciences (U.S.A.), 114*, 7462–7467. (13) doi: 10.1073/pnas.1700351114

Schmid, M. C., Mrowka, S. W., Turchi, J., Saunders, R. C., Wilke, M., Peters, A. J., Ye, F. Q., & Leopold, D. A. (2010). Blindsight depends on the lateral geniculate nucleus. *Nature, 466*, 373–377. (3) doi: 10.1038/nature09179

Schmidt, M. F. H., Butler, L. P., Heinz, J., & Tomasello, M. (2016). Young children see a single action and infer a social norm: Promiscuous normativity in 3-year-olds. *Psychological Science, 27*, 1360–1370. (6) doi: 10.1177/0956797616661182

Schmidt-Daffy, M. (2011). Modeling automatic threat detection: Development of a face-in-the-crowd task. *Emotion, 11*, 153–168. (8) doi: 10.1037/a0022018

Schmidt, F. L., & Hunter, J. E. (1981). Employment testing: Old theories and new research findings. *American Psychologist, 36*, 1128–1137. (9) doi: 10.1037/0003-066X.36.10.1128

Schmidt, F. L., & Hunter, J. E. (1998). The validity and utility of selection methods in personnel psychology: Practical and theoretical implications of 85 years of research findings. *Psychological Bulletin, 124*, 262–274. (9) doi: 10.1037/0033-2909.124.2.262

Schmitt, A. P., & Dorans, N. J. (1990). Differential item functioning for minority examinees on the SAT. *Journal of Educational Measurement, 27*, 67–81. (9) doi: 10.1111/j.1745-3984.1990.tb00735.x

Schmitt, D. P., & 118 members of the International Sexuality Description Project. (2003). Universal sex differences in the desire for sexual variety: Tests from 52 nations, 6 continents, and 13 islands. *Journal of Personality and Social Psychology, 85*, 85–104. (3) doi: 10.1037/0022-3514.85.1.85

Schmolck, H., Buffalo, E. A., & Squire, L. R. (2000). Memory distortions develop over time. *Psychological Science, 11*, 39–45. (7) doi: 10.1111/1467-9280.00212

Schneider, M., Debbané, M., Bassett, A. S., Chow, E. W. C., Fung, W. L. A., van den Bree, M. B. M., Owen, M., Murphy, K. C., Niarchou, M., Kates, W. R., Antshel, K. M., Fremont, W., McDonald-McGinn, D. M., Gur, R. E., Zackai, E. H., Vorstman, J., Duijff, S. N., Klaassen, P. W. J., Swillen, A., ... Eliez, S. (2014). Psychiatric disorders from childhood to adulthood in 22q11.2 deletion syndrome: Results from the International Consortium on Brain and Behavior in 22q11.2 deletion syndrome. *American Journal of Psychiatry, 171*, 627–639. (15) doi: 10.1176/appi.ajp.2013.13070864

Schneider, P., Scherg, M., Dosch, H. G., Specht, H. J., Gutschalk, A., & Rupp, A. (2002). Morphology of Heschl's gyrus reflects enhanced activation in the auditory cortex of musicians. *Nature Neuroscience, 5*, 688–694. (3) doi: 10.1038/nn871

Schneider, W., Niklas, F., & Schmiedeler, S. (2014). Intellectual development from early childhood to early adulthood: The impact of early IQ differences on stability and change over time.

ng and Individual Differences, 32, 156–
) doi: 10.1016/j.lindif.2014.02.001

man, I., Zilberstein-Kra, Y., Leckman, J. F., & Feldman, R. (2011). Love alters autonomic reactivity to emotions. *Emotion, 11*, 1314–1321. (12) doi: 10.1037/a0024090

Schnider, A. (2003). Spontaneous confabulation and the adaptation of thought to ongoing reality. *Nature Reviews Neuroscience, 4*, 662–671. (7) doi: 10.1038/nrn1179

Schnider, A., Nahum, L., & Ptak, R. (2017). What does extinction have to do with confabulation? *Cortex, 87*, 5–15. (7) doi: 10.1016/j.cortex.2016.10.015

Schomacher, M., Müller, H. D., Sommer, C., Schwab, S., & Schäbitz, W.-R. (2008). Endocannabinoids mediate neuroprotection after transient focal cerebral ischemia. *Brain Research, 1240*, 213–220. (3) doi: 10.1016/j.brainres.2008.09.019

Schooler, C. (1972). Birth order effects: Not here, not now! *Psychological Bulletin, 78*, 161–175. (5) doi: 10.1037/h0033026

Schork, A. J., Won, H., Appadurai, V., Nudel, R., Gandal, M., Delaneau, O., Christiansen, M. R., Hougaard, D. M., Baekved-Hansen, M., Bybjerg-Grauholm, J., Pedersen, M. G., Agerbo, E., Pedersen, C. B., Neale, B. M., Daly, M. J., ... Werge, T. (2019). A genome-wide association study of shared risk across psychiatric disorders implicates gene regulation during fetal neurodevelopment. *Nature Neuroscience, 22*, 353–361. (15) doi: 10.1038/s41593-018-0320-0

Schotter, E. R., Tran, R., & Rayner, K. (2014). Don't believe what you read (only once): Comprehension is supported by regressions during reading. *Psychological Science, 25*, 1218–1226. (8) doi: 10.1177/0956797614531148

Schredl, M. (2000). Continuity between waking life and dreaming: Are all waking activities reflected equally often in dreams? *Perceptual and Motor Skills, 90*, 844–846. (10) doi: 10.2466/PMS.90.3.844-846

Schredl, M., Ciric, P., Götz, S., & Wittman, L. (2004). Typical dreams: Stability and gender differences. *Journal of Psychology, 138*, 485–494. (10) doi: 10.3200/JRLP.138.6.485-494

Schredl, M., & Goeritz, A. S. (2018). Nightmare themes: An online study of most recent nightmares and childhood nightmares. *Journal of Clinical Sleep Medicine, 14*, 465–471. (10) doi: 10.5664/jcsm.7002

Schubert, A.-L., Hagemann, D., & Frischkorn, G. T. (2017). Is general intelligence little more than the speed of higher-order processing? *Journal of Experimental Psychology—General, 146*, 1498–1512. (9) doi: 10.1037/xge0000325

Schuckit, M. A., & Smith, T. L. (1997). Assessing the risk for alcoholism among sons of alcoholics. *Journal of Studies on Alcohol, 58*, 141–145. (15)

Schuckit, M. A., & Smith, T. L. (2013). Stability of scores and correlations with drinking behaviors over 15 years for the self-report of the effects of alcohol questionnaire. *Drug and Alcohol Dependence, 128*, 194–199. (15) doi: 10.1016/j.drugalcdep.2012.08.022

Schuckit, M. A., Smith, T. L., Danko, G. P., Pierson, J., Hesselbrock, V., Bucholz, K. K., Kramer, J., Kuperman, S., Dietiker, C., Brandon, R., & Chan, G. (2007). The ability of the self-rating of the effects of alcohol (SRE) scale to predict alcohol-related outcomes five years later. *Journal of Studies of Alcohol, 68*, 371–378. (15) doi: 10.15288/jsad.2007.68.371

Schuermann, J., & Margraf, J. (2018). Age of anxiety and depression revisited: A meta-analysis of two European community samples (1964–2015). *International Journal of Clinical and Health Psychology, 18*, 102–112. (14) doi: 10.1016/j.ijchp.2018.02.002

Schulsinger, F., Knop, J., Goodwin, D. W., Teasdale, T. W., & Mikkelsen, U. (1986). A prospective study of young men at high risk for alcoholism. *Archives of General Psychiatry, 43*, 755–760. (15) doi: 10.1001/archpsyc.1986.01800080041006

Schultz, L. H., Connolly, J. J., Garrison, S. M., Leveille, M. M., & Jackson, J. J. (2017). Vocational interests across 20 years of adulthood: Stability, change, and the role of work experiences. *Journal of Research in Personality, 71*, 46–56. (5) doi: 10.1016/j.jrp.2017.08.010

Schumann, K., & Ross, M. (2010). Why women apologize more than men: Gender differences in thresholds for perceiving offensive behavior. *Psychological Science, 21*, 1649–1655. (5) doi: 10.1177/0956797610384150

Schumm, W. R. (2008). Re-evaluation of the "no differences" hypothesis concerning gay and lesbian parenting as assessed in eight early (1979–1986) and four later (1997–1998) dissertations. *Psychological Reports, 103*, 275–304. (5) doi: 10.2466/PR0.103.1.275-304

Schupp, H. T., Stockburger, J., Codispoti, M., Junghöfer, M., Weike, A. I., & Hamm, A. O. (2007). Selective visual attention to emotion. *Journal of Neuroscience, 27*, 1082–1089. (12) doi: 10.1523/JNEUROSCI.3223-06.2007

Schwartz, B. (2004). *The paradox of choice.* New York: HarperCollins. (8)

Schwartz, B., Ward, A., Monterosso, J., Lyubomirsky, S., White, K., & Lehman, D. R. (2002). Maximizing versus satisficing: Happiness is a matter of choice. *Journal of Personality and Social Psychology, 83*, 1178–1197. (8) doi: 10.1037//0022-3514.83.5.1178

Schwartz, C. E., Wright, C. I., Shin, L. M., Kagan, J., & Rauch, S. L. (2003). Inhibited and uninhibited infants "grown up": Adult amygdalar response to novelty. *Science, 300*, 1952–1953. (5) doi: 10.1126/science.1083703

Schwartz, G., Kim, R. M., Kolundzija, A. B., Rieger, G., & Sanders, A. R. (2010). Biodemographic and physical correlates of sexual orientation in men. *Archives of Sexual Behavior, 39*, 93–109. (11) doi: 10.1007/s10508-009-9499-1

Schwarz, K. A., & Pfister, R. (2016). Scientific psychology in the 18th century: A historical rediscovery. *Perspectives on Psychological Science, 11*, 399–407. (1) doi: 10.1177/1745691616635601

Schweinsberg, M., Madan, N., Vianello, M., Sommer, S. A., Jordan, J., Tierney, W., Awtrey, E., Zhu, L. L., Diermeier, D., Heinze, J. E., Srinivasan, M., Tannenbaum, D., Bivolaru, E., Dana, J., Davis-Stober, C. P., du Plessis, C., Gronau, Q. F., Hafenbrack, A. C., Liao, E. Y., ... Uhlmann, E. L. (2016). The pipeline project: Pre-publication independent replications of a single laboratory's research pipeline. *Journal of Experimental Social Psychology, 66*, 55–67. (2) doi: 10.1016/j.jesp.2015.10.001

Scott, N., Lakin, K. C., & Larson, S. A. (2008). The 40th anniversary of deinstitutionalization in the United States: Decreasing state institutional populations, 1967–2007. *Intellectual and Developmental Disabilities, 46*, 402–405. (15) doi: 10.1352/2008.46:402-405

Scott, T. R., & Verhagen, J. V. (2000). Taste as a factor in the management of nutrition. *Nutrition, 16*, 874–885. (1) doi: 10.1016/S0899-9007(00)00423-8

Scott, V. M., Mottarella, K. E., & Lavooy, M. J. (2006). Does virtual intimacy exist? A brief exploration into reported levels of intimacy in online relationships. *CyberPsychology and Behavior, 9*, 759–761. (13) doi: 10.1089/cpb.2006.9.759

Scovern, A. W., & Kilmann, P. R. (1980). Status of electroconvulsive therapy: Review of the outcome literature. *Psychological Bulletin, 87*, 260–303. (15) doi: 10.1037/0033-2909.87.2.260

Scripture, E. W. (1907). *Thinking, feeling, doing* (2nd ed.). New York: G. P. Putnam's Sons. (1)

Scullin, M. K., Krueger, M. L., Ballard, H. K., Pruett, N., & Bliwise, D. L. (2018). The effects of bedtime writing on difficulty falling asleep: A polysomnographic study comparing to-do lists and completed activity lists. *Journal of Experimental Psychology: General, 147*, 139–146. (10) doi: 10.1037/xge0000374

Sealey, L. A., Hughes, B. W., Sriskanda, A. N., Guest, J. R., Gibson, A. D., Johnson-Williams, L., Pace, D. G., & Bagasra, O. (2016). Environmental factors in the development of autism spectrum disorders. *Environment International, 88*, 288–298. (15) doi: 10.1016/j.envint.2015.12.021

Seamon, J. G., Lee, I. A., Toner, S. K., Wheeler, R. H., Goodkind, M. S., & Birch, A. D. (2002). Thinking of critical words during study is unnecessary for false memory in the Deese, Roediger, and McDermott procedure. *Psychological Science, 13*, 526–531. (7) doi: 10.1111/1467-9280.00492

Sebastián-Enesco, C., Hernández-Lloreda, M. V., & Colmenares, F. (2013). Two and a half-year-old children are prosocial even when their partners are not. *Journal of Experimental Child Psychology, 116*, 186–198. (13) doi: 10.1016/j.jecp.2013.05.007

Seeman, P., & Lee, T. (1975). Antipsychotic drugs: Direct correlation between clinical potency and presynaptic action on dopamine neurons. *Science, 188*, 1217–1219. (15) doi: 10.1126/science.1145194

Segal, N. L. (2000). Virtual twins: New findings on within-family environmental influences on intelligence. *Journal of Educational Psychology, 92*, 442–448. (9) doi: 10.1037/0022-0663.92.3.442

Segal, N. L., McGuire, S. A., & Stohs, J. H. (2012). What virtual twins reveal about general intelligence and other behaviors. *Personality and Individual Differences, 53*, 405–410. (9) doi: 10.1016/j.paid.2011.11.019

Segerstrom, S. C., & Nes, L. S. (2007). Heart rate variability reflects self-regulatory strength, effort, and fatigue. *Psychological Science, 18*, 275–281. (12) doi: 10.1111/j.1467-9280.2007.01888.x

Sekuler, A. B., & Bennett, P. J. (2001). Generalized common fate: Grouping by common luminance changes. *Psychological Science, 12*, 437–444. (4) doi: 10.1111/1467-9280.00382

Seligman, M. E. (1970). On the generality of the laws of learning. *Psychological Review, 77*, 406–418. (6) doi.org/10.1037/h0029790

Seligman, M. E. P. (1971). Phobias and preparedness. *Behavior Therapy, 2*, 307–320. (15) doi: 10.1016/S0005-7894(71)80064-3

Seligman, M. E. P., Allen, A. R., Vie, L. L., Ho, T. E., Scheier, L. M., Cornum, R., & Lester, P. B. (2019). PTSD: Catastrophizing in combat as risk and protection. *Clinical Psychological Science, 7,* 516–529. (12) doi: 10.1177/2167702618813532

Seligman, M. E. P., & Csikszentmihalyi, M. (2000). Positive psychology. *American Psychologist, 55,* 5–14. (12) doi: 10.1037/0003-066X.55.1.5

Seligman, M. E. P., Railton, P., Baumeister, R. F., & Sripada, C. (2013). Navigating into the future or driven by the past. *Perspectives on Psychological Science, 8,* 119–141. (6) doi: 10.1177/1745691612474317

Selye, H. (1979). Stress, cancer, and the mind. In J. Taché, H. Selye, & S. B. Day (Eds.), *Cancer, stress, and death* (pp. 11–27). New York: Plenum Press. (12)

Selzam, S., Krapohl, E., von Stumm, S., O'Reilly, P. F., Rimfeld, K., Kovas, Y., Dale, P. S., Lee, J. J., & Plomin, R. (2017). Predicting educational achievement from DNA. *Molecular Psychiatry, 22,* 267–272. (9) doi: 10.1038/mp.2016.107

Semenyna, S. W., Petterson, L. J., VanderLaan, D. P., & Vasey, P. L. (2017). A comparison of the reproductive output among the relatives of Samoan androphilic *Fa'afafine* and gynephilic men. *Archives of Sexual Behavior, 46,* 87–93. (11) doi: 10.1007/s10508-016-0765-8

Semmler, C., Brewer, N., & Wells, G. L. (2004). Effects of postidentification feedback on eyewitness identification and nonidentification confidence. *Journal of Applied Psychology, 89,* 334–346. (7) doi: 10.1037/0021-9010.89.2.334

Senghas, A., & Coppola, M. (2001). Children creating language: How Nicaraguan sign language acquired a spatial grammar. *Psychological Science, 12,* 323–328. (8) doi: 10.1111/1467-9280.00359

Senghas, A., Kita, S., & Özyürek, A. (2004). Children creating core properties of language: Evidence from an emerging sign language in Nicaragua. *Science, 305,* 1779–1782. (8) doi: 10.1126/science.1100199

Seo, M.-G., Barrett, L. F., & Bartunek, J. M. (2004). The role of affective experience in work motivation. *Academy of Management Review, 29,* 423–439. (11) doi: 10.2307/20159052

Seow, Y.-X., Ong, P. K. C., & Huang, D. (2016). Odor-specific loss of smell sensitivity with age as revealed by the specific sensitivity test. *Chemical Senses, 41,* 487–495. (4) doi: 10.1093/chemse/bjw051

Sergent, C., & Dehaene, S. (2004). Is consciousness a gradual phenomenon? *Psychological Science, 15,* 720–728. (10) doi: 10.1111/j.0956-7976.2004.00748.x

Seto, M. C., Lalumière, M. L., Harris, G. T., & Chivers, M. L. (2012). The sexual responses of sexual sadists. *Journal of Abnormal Psychology, 121,* 739–753. (11) doi: 10.1037/a0028714

Shafir, E. B., Smith, E. E., & Osherson, D. N. (1990). Typicality and reasoning fallacies. *Memory and Cognition, 18,* 229–239. (8) doi: 10.3758/BF03213877

Shafto, M., & MacKay, D. G. (2000). The Moses, mega-Moses, and Armstrong illusions: Integrating language comprehension and semantic memory. *Psychological Science, 11,* 372–378. (8) doi: 10.1111/1467-9280.00273

Shah, A. M., & Wolford, G. (2007). Buying behavior as a function of parametric variation of number of choices. *Psychological Science, 18,* 369–370. (8) doi: 10.1111/j.1467-9280.2007.01906.x

Shahar, D. R., Schultz, R., Shahar, A., & Wing, R. R. (2001). The effect of widowhood on weight change, dietary intake, and eating behavior in the elderly population. *Journal of Aging and Health, 13,* 186–199. (12) doi: 10.1177/089826430101300202

Shalev, I., Moffitt, T. E., Wong, T. Y., Meier, M. H., Houts, R. M., Ding, J., Cheung, C. Y., Ikram, M. K., Caspi, A., & Poulton, R. (2013). Retinal vessel caliber and lifelong neuropsychological functioning: Retinal imaging as an investigative tool for cognitive epidemiology. *Psychological Science, 24,* 1198–1207. (9) doi: 10.1177/0956797612470959

Shallice, T. (2019). The single case history of memory. In S. E. MacPherson & S. Della Sala (Eds.), *Cases of amnesia* (pp. 1–15). New York: Routledge. (2)

Shannon, D. A. (1955). *The Socialist Party of America.* New York: Macmillan. (13)

Shapiro, K. L., Caldwell, J., & Sorensen, R. E. (1997). Personal names and the attentional blink: A visual "cocktail party" effect. *Journal of Experimental Psychology: Human Perception and Performance, 23,* 504–514. (8) doi: 10.1037/0096-1523.23.2.504

Shaw, G. B. (1911). *The doctor's dilemma.* New York: Brentano's. (13)

Shaw, J., & Porter, S. (2015). Constructing rich false memories of committing crime. *Psychological Science, 26,* 291–301. (7) doi: 10.1177/0956797614562862

Shearn, D., Spellman, L., Straley, B., Meirick, J., & Stryker, K. (1999). Empathic blushing in friends and strangers. *Motivation and Emotion, 23,* 307–316. (12) doi: 10.1023/A:1021342910378

Sheldon, K., & Lyubomirsky, S. (2004). Achieving sustainable new happiness: Prospects, practices, and prescriptions. In P. A. Linley & S. Joseph (Eds.), *Positive psychology in practice* (pp. 127–145). Hoboken, NJ: Wiley. (12)

Sheldon, K. M., & Lyubomirsky, S. (2006). Achieving sustainable gains in happiness: Change your actions, not your circumstances. *Journal of Happiness Studies, 7,* 55–86. (12) doi: 10.1007/s10902-005-0868-8

Shenhav, A., & Buckner, R. L. (2014). Neural correlates of dueling affective reactions to win-win choices. *Proceedings of the National Academy of Sciences (U.S.A.), 111,* 10978–10983. (8) doi: 10.1073/pnas.1405725111

Shenhav, A., & Greene, J. D. (2014). Integrative moral judgment: Dissociating the roles of the amygdala and ventromedial prefrontal cortex. *Journal of Neuroscience, 34,* 4741–4749. (12) doi: 10.1523/JNEUROSCI.3390-13.2014

Shepard, R. N. (1990). *Mind sights.* New York: W. H. Freeman. (4)

Shepard, R. N., & Metzler, J. N. (1971). Mental rotation of three-dimensional objects. *Science, 171,* 701–703. (8) doi: 10.1126/science.171.3972.701

Shepherd, L., O'Carroll, R. E., & Ferguson, E. (2014). An international comparison of deceased and living organ donation/transplant rates in opt-in and opt-out systems: A panel study. *BMC Medicine, 12,* article 131. (13) doi: 10.1186/s12916-014-0131-4

Shepperd, J. A. (1993). Productivity loss in performance groups: A motivation analysis. *Psychological Bulletin, 113,* 67–81. (13) doi: 10.1037/0033-2909.113.1.67

Shergill, S. S., Brammer, M. J., Williams, S. C. R., Murray, R. M., & McGuire, P. K. (2000). Mapping auditory hallucinations in schizophrenia using functional magnetic resonance imaging. *Archives of General Psychiatry, 57,* 1033–1038. (15) doi: 10.1001/archpsyc.57.11.1033

Sherif, M. (1935). A study of some social factors in perception. *Archives of Psychology, 27,* 1–60. (13)

Sherif, M. (1966). *In common predicament.* Boston, MA: Houghton Mifflin. (13)

Sherwood, G. G. (1981). Self-serving biases in person perception: A reexamination of projection as a mechanism of defense. *Psychological Bulletin, 90,* 445–459. (14) doi: 10.1037/0033-2909.90.3.445

Shih, M., & Sanchez, D. T. (2005). Perspectives and research on the positive and negative implications of having multiple racial identities. *Psychological Bulletin, 131,* 569–591. (5) doi: 10.1037/0033-2909.131.4.569

Shimada-Sugimoto, M., Otowa, T., & Hettema, J. M. (2015). Genetics of anxiety disorders: Genetic epidemiological and molecular studies in humans. *Psychiatry and Clinical Sciences, 69,* 388–401. (15) doi: 10.1111/pcn.12291

Shimaya, A. (1997). Perception of complex line drawings. *Journal of Experimental Psychology: Human Perception and Performance, 23,* 25–50. (4) https://psycnet.apa.org/record/1997-02284-003

Shiota, M. N., & Levenson, R. W. (2007). Birds of a feather don't always fly farthest: Similarity in Big Five personality predicts more negative marital satisfaction trajectories in long-term marriages. *Psychology of Aging, 22,* 666–675. (13) doi: 10.1037/0882-7974.22.4.666

Shipstead, Z., & Engle, R. W. (2013). Interference within the focus of attention: Working memory tasks reflect more than temporary maintenance. *Journal of Experimental Psychology: Learning, Memory, and Cognition, 39,* 277–289. (7) doi: 10.1037/a0028467

Shipstead, Z., Harrison, T. L., & Engle, R. W. (2016). Working memory capacity and fluid intelligence: Maintenance and disengagement. *Perspectives on Psychological Science, 11,* 771–799. (7) doi: 10.1177/1745691616650647

Shoda, Y., Mischel, W., & Peake, P. K. (1990). Predicting adolescent cognitive and self-regulatory competencies from preschool delay of gratification. *Developmental Psychology, 26,* 978–986. (11) doi: 10.1037/0012-1649.26.6.978

Shogren, E. (1993, June 2). Survey finds 4 in 5 suffer sex harassment at school. *Los Angeles Times,* p. A10. (2)

Shohamy, D., Myers, C. E., Kalanithi, J., & Gluck, M. A. (2008). Basal ganglia and dopamine contributions to probabilistic category learning. *Neuroscience and Biobehavioral Reviews, 32,* 219–236. (7) doi: 10.1016/j.neubiorev.2007.07.008

Shook, N. J., & Fazio, R. H. (2008). Interracial roommate relationships. *Psychological Science, 19,* 717–723. (13) doi: 10.1111/j.1467-9280.2008.02147.x

Shrager, Y., Levy, D. A., Hopkins, R. O., & Squire, L. R. (2008). Working memory and the organization of brain systems. *Journal of Neuroscience, 28,* 4818–4822. (7) doi: 10.1523/JNEUROSCI.0710-08.2008

Shulman, E. P., & Cauffman, E. (2014). Deciding in the dark: Differences in intuitive risk judgment. *Developmental Psychology, 50,* 167–177. (5) doi: 10.1037/a0032778

Sibley, M. H., Kuriyan, A. B., Evans, S. W., Waxmonsky, J. G., & Smith, B. H. (2014). Pharmacological and psychosocial treatments for adolescents with ADHD: An updated systematic review of the literature. *Clinical*

...logy Review, 34, 218–232. (8) doi: ...6/j.cpr.2014.02.001

Baird, B., Perogamvros, L., Bernardi, G., LaRocque, J.J., Riedner, B., Boly, M., Postle, B. R., & Tononi, G. (2017). The neural correlates of dreaming. *Nature Neuroscience, 20,* 872–878. (10) doi: 10.1038/nn.4545

Sieber, J., & Ziegler, R. (2019). Group polarization revisited: A processing effort account. *Personality and Social Psychology Bulletin, 45,* 1482–1498. (13) doi: 10.1177/0146167219833389

Siegel, E. H., Sands, M. K., Van den Noortgate, W., Condon, P., Chang, Y., Dy, J., Quigley, K. S., & Barrett, L. F. (2018). Emotion fingerprints or emotion populations? A meta-analytic investigation of autonomic features of emotion categories. *Psychological Bulletin, 144,* 343–393. (12) doi: 10.1037/bul0000128

Siegel, J. M. (2005). Clues to the functions of mammalian sleep. *Nature, 437,* 1264–1271. (10) doi: 10.1038/nature04285

Siegel, J. M. (2009). Sleep viewed as a state of adaptive inactivity. *Nature Reviews Neuroscience, 10,* 747–753. (10) doi: 10.1038/nrn2697

Siegel, S. (1977). Morphine tolerance acquisition as an associative process. *Journal of Experimental Psychology: Animal Behavior Processes, 3,* 1–13. (6) doi: 10.1037/0097-7403.3.1.1

Siegel, S. (1983). Classical conditioning, drug tolerance, and drug dependence. *Research Advances in Alcohol and Drug Problems, 7,* 207–246. (6) https://link.springer.com/chapter/10.1007/978-1-4613-3626-6_6

Siegel, S. (2016). The heroin overdose mystery. *Current Directions in Psychological Science, 25,* 375–379. (6) doi: 10.1177/0963721416664404

Siegel, S., & Ramos, B. M. C. (2002). Applying laboratory research: Drug anticipation and the treatment of drug addiction. *Experimental and Clinical Psychopharmacology, 10,* 162–183. (6) doi: 10.1037//1064-1297.10.3.162

Sigman, M., & Whaley, S. E. (1998). The role of nutrition in the development of intelligence. In U. Neisser (Ed.), *The rising curve* (pp. 155–182). Washington, DC: American Psychological Association. (9)

Silva, E. J., & Duffy, J. F. (2008). Sleep inertia varies with circadian phase and sleep stage in older adults. *Behavioral Neuroscience, 122,* 929–935. (10) doi: 10.1037/0735-7044.122.4.928

Silver, E. (1995). Punishment or treatment? Comparing the lengths of confinement of successful and unsuccessful insanity defendants. *Law and Human Behavior, 19,* 375–388. (15) doi: 10.1007/BF01499138

Simmons, E. J. (1949). *Leo Tolstoy.* London: Lehmann. (15)

Simner, J., & Bain, A. E. (2013). A longitudinal study of grapheme-color synesthesia in childhood: 6/7 years to 10/11 years. *Frontiers in Human Neuroscience, 7,* Article 603. (4) doi: 10.3389/fnhum.2013.00603

Simner, J., & Ward, J. (2006). The taste of words on the tip of the tongue. *Nature, 444,* 438. (4) doi: 10.1038/444438a

Simon, B., Reichert, F., & Grabow, O. (2013). When dual identity becomes a liability: Identity and political radicalism among migrants. *Psychological Science, 24,* 251–257. (5) doi: 10.1177/0956797612450889

Simon, N. W., Mendez, I. A., & Setlow, B. (2007). Cocaine exposure causes long-term increases in impulsive choice. *Behavioral Neuroscience,*

121, 543–549. (3) doi: 10.1037/0735-7044.121.3.543

Simons, D. J., & Levin, D. T. (2003). What makes change blindness interesting? *The Psychology of Learning and Motivation, 42,* 295–322. (8) doi: 10.1016/S0079-7421(03)01009-0

Simons, T., & Roberson, Q. (2003). Why managers should care about fairness: The effects of aggregate justice perceptions on organizational outcomes. *Journal of Applied Psychology, 88,* 432–443. (11) doi: 10.1037/0021-9010.88.3.432

Simonsohn, U. (2015). Small telescopes: Detectability and the evaluation of replication results. *Psychological Science, 26,* 559–569. (2) doi: 10.1177/0956797614567341

Simpson, E. H., Kellendonk, C., & Kandel, E. (2010). A possible role for the striatum in the pathogenesis of the cognitive symptoms of schizophrenia. *Neuron, 65,* 585–596. (15) doi: 10.1016/j.neuron.2010.02.014

Singer, T., Seymour, B., O'Doherty, J., Kaube, H., Dolan, R. J., & Frith, C. D. (2004). Empathy for pain involves the affective but not sensory components of pain. *Science, 303,* 1157–1162. (4) doi: 10.1126/science.1093535

Singh, M., Hoffman, D. D., & Albert, M. K. (1999). Contour completion and relative depth: Petter's rule and support ratio. *Psychological Science, 10,* 423–428. (4) doi: 10.1111/1467-9280.00180

Singh, T., Neale, B., Daly, M., & Schizophrenia Exome Meta-analysis Consortium. (2019). Initial results from the meta-analysis of the whole-exomes of over 20,000 schizophrenia cases and 45,000 controls. *European Neuropsychopharmacology, 29,* Supplement 3, S813–S814. (15) doi: 10.1016/j.euroneuro.2017.08.057

Sirin, S. R., & Fine, M. (2007). Hyphenated selves: Muslim American youth negotiating identities on the fault lines of global conflict. *Applied Developmental Science, 11,* 151–163. (5) doi: 10.1080/10888690701454658

Sit, D. K., McGowan, J., Wiltrout, C., Diler, R. S., Dills, J., Luther, J., Yang, A., Ciolino, J. D., Seltman, H., Wisniewski, S. R., & Wisner, K. L. (2018). Adjunctive bright light therapy for bipolar depression: A randomized double-blind placebo-controlled trial. *American Journal of Psychiatry, 175,* 131–139. (15) doi: 10.1176/appi.ajp.2017.16101200

Skeels, H. M. (1966). Adult status of children with contrasting early life experiences. *Monographs of the Society for Research in Child Development, 31,* 1–65. (9) doi: 10.2307/1165791

Skinner, B. F. (1938). *The behavior of organisms.* New York: D. Appleton-Century. (6)

Skinner, B. F. (1990). Can psychology be a science of mind? *American Psychologist, 45,* 1206–1210. (6) doi: 10.1037/0003-066X.45.11.1206

Skinner, E. A., Edge, K., Altman, J., & Sherwood, H. (2003). Searching for the structure of coping: A review and critique of category systems for classifying ways of coping. *Psychological Bulletin, 129,* 216–269. (12) doi: 10.1037/0033-2909.129.2.216

Skoog, G., & Skoog, I. (1999). A 40-year follow-up of patients with obsessive-compulsive disorder. *Archives of General Psychiatry, 56,* 121–127. (15) doi: 10.1001/archpsyc.56.2.121

Slabbekoorn, H., & den Boer-Visser, A. (2006). Cities change the songs of birds. *Current Biology, 16,* 2326–2331. (6) doi: 10.1016/j.cub.2006.10.008

Slavich, G. M., & Cole, S. W. (2013). The emerging field of human social genomics. *Clinical Psychological Science, 1,* 331–348. (3) doi: 10.1177/2167702613478594

Sliwa, J., & Freiwald, W. A. (2017). A dedicated network for social interaction processing in the primate brain. *Science, 356,* 745–749. (3) doi: 10.1126/science.aam6383

Smith, A. M., Floerke, V. A., & Thomas, A. K. (2016). Retrieval practice protects memory against acute stress. *Science, 354,* 1046–1048. (7) doi: 10.1126/science.aah5067

Smith, D. E., Raswyck, G. E., & Davidson, L. D. (2014). From Hofmann to the Haight Ashbury and into the future: The past and potential of lysergic acid diethylamide. *Journal of Psychoactive Drugs, 46,* 3–10. (3) doi: 10.1080/02791072.2014.873684

Smith, D. M., Langa, K. M., Kabeto, M. U., & Ubel, P. A. (2005). Health, wealth, and happiness. *Psychological Science, 16,* 663–666. (12) doi: 10.1111/j.1467-9280.2005.01592.x

Smith, J. M., Bell, P. A., & Fusco, M. E. (1986). The influence of color and demand characteristics on muscle strength and affective ratings of the environment. *Journal of General Psychology, 113,* 289–297. (2) doi: 10.1080/00221309.1986.9711040

Smith, L. T. (1974). Interanimal transfer phenomenon: A review. *Psychological Bulletin, 81,* 1078–1095. (2) doi: 10.1037/h0037424

Smith, M. L. (1988). Recall of spatial location by the amnesic patient H. M. *Brain and Cognition, 7,* 178–183. (7) doi: 10.1016/0278-2626(88)90028-0

Smith, M. L., Glass, G. V., & Miller, T. I. (1980). *The benefits of psychotherapy.* Baltimore: Johns Hopkins University Press. (15)

Smith, T. O., Easton, V., Bacon, H., Jerman, E., Armon, K., Poland, F., & Macgregor, A. J. (2014). The relationship between benign joint hypermobility syndrome and psychological distress: A systematic review and meta-analysis. *Rheumatology, 53,* 114–122. (15) doi: 10.1093/rheumatology/ket317

Snook, B., Cullen, R. M., Bennell, C., Taylor, P. J., & Gendreau, P. (2008). The criminal profiling illusion: What's behind the smoke and mirrors? *Criminal Justice and Behavior, 35,* 1257–1276. (14) doi: 10.1177/0093854808321528

Snook, B., Eastwood, J., Gendreau, P., Goggin, C., & Cullen, R. M. (2007). Taking stock of criminal profiling: A narrative review and meta-analysis. *Criminal Justice and Behavior, 34,* 437–453. (14) doi: 10.1177/0093854806296925

Snyder, C. R. (2003). "Me conform? No way": Classroom demonstrations for sensitizing students to their conformity. *Teaching of Psychology, 30,* 59–61. (13)

Snyder, M., Tanke, E. D., & Bersheid, E. (1977). Social perception and interpersonal behavior: On the self-fulfilling nature of social stereotypes. *Journal of Personality and Social Psychology, 35,* 656–666. (13) doi: 10.1037/0022-3514.35.9.656

Society for Personality Assessment. (2005). The status of the Rorschach in clinical and forensic practice: An official statement by the Board of Trustees of the Society for Personality Assessment. *Journal of Personality Assessment, 85,* 219–237. (14) doi: 10.1207/s15327752jpa8502_16

Södersten, P., Brodin, U., Zandian, M., & Bergh, C. (2019). Eating behavior and the evolutionary perspective on anorexia nervosa. *Frontiers in*

Neuroscience, 13, article 596. (11) doi: 10.3389/fnins.2019.00596

Soderstrom, N. C., & Bjork, R. A. (2015). Learning versus performance: An integrative review. *Perspectives on Psychological Science, 10,* 176–199. (7) doi: 10.1177/1745691615569000

Solanto, M. V., Abikoff, H., Sonuga-Barke, E., Schachar, R., Logan, G. D., Wigal, T., Hechtman, L. Hinshaw, S., & Turkel, E. (2001). The ecological validity of delay aversion and response inhibition as measures of impulsivity in AD/HD: A supplement to the NIMH multimodal treatment study of AD/HD. *Journal of Abnormal Child Psychology, 29,* 215–228. (8) doi: 10.1023/A:1010329714819

Solinas, M., Belujon, P., Fernagut, P. O., Jaber, M., & Thiriet, N. (2019). Dopamine and addiction: What we have learned from 40 years of research. *Journal of Neural Transmission, 126,* 481–516. (15) doi: 10.1007/s00702-018-1957-2

Solinas, M., Thiriet, N., El Rawas, R., Lardeux, V., & Jaber, M. (2009). Environmental enrichment during early stages of life reduces the behavioral, neurochemical, and molecular effects of cocaine. *Neuropsychopharmacology, 34,* 1102–1111. (15) doi: 10.1038/npp.2008.51

Solms, M. (1997). *The neuropsychology of dreams.* Mahwah, NJ: Erlbaum. (10)

Solms, M. (2000). Dreaming and REM sleep are controlled by different brain mechanisms. *Behavioral and Brain Sciences, 23,* 843–850. (10) doi: 10.1017/S0140525X00003988

Solomon, D. A., Keller, M. B., Leon, A. C., Mueller, T. I., Shea, T., Warshaw, M., Maser, J. D., Coryell, W., & Endicott, J. (1997). Recovery from major depression. *Archives of General Psychiatry, 54,* 1001–1006. (15) doi: 10.1001/archpsyc.1997.01830230033005

Solter, A. (2008). A 2-year-old child's memory of hospitalization during early infancy. *Infant and Child Development, 17,* 593–605. (7) doi: 10.1002/icd.570

Song, H., & Schwarz, N. (2008). If it's hard to read, it's hard to do. *Psychological Science, 19,* 986–988. (8) doi: 10.1111/j.1467-9280.2008.02189.x

Song, H., & Schwarz, N. (2009). If it's difficult to pronounce, it must be risky. *Psychological Science, 20,* 135–138. (8) doi: 10.1111/j.1467-9280.2009.02267.x

Song, H., Stevens, C. F., & Gage, F. H. (2002). Neural stem cells from adult hippocampus develop essential properties of functional CNS neurons. *Nature Neuroscience, 5,* 438–445. (3) doi: 10.1038/nn844

Sonnentag, S., Arbeus, H., Mahn, C., & Fritz, C. (2014). Exhaustion and lack of psychological detachment from work during off-job time: Moderator effects of time pressure and leisure experiences. *Journal of Occupational Health Psychology, 19,* 206–216. (11) doi: 10.1037/a0035760

Sonuga-Barke, E. J. S. (2005). Causal models of attention-deficit/hyperactivity disorder: From common simple deficits to multiple developmental pathways. *Biological Psychiatry, 57,* 1231–1238. (8) doi: 10.1016/j.biopsych.2004.09.008

Soon, C. S., Brass, M., Heinze, H.-J., & Haynes, J.-D. (2008). Unconscious determinants of free decisions in the human brain. *Nature Neuroscience, 11,* 543–545. (10) doi: 10.1038/nn.2112

Sorge, R. E., Martin, L. J., Isbester, K. A., Sotocinal, S. G., Rosen, S., Tuttle, A. H., Wieskopf, J. S., Acland, E. L., Dokova, A., Kadoura, B., Leger, P., Mapplebeck, J. C. S., McPhail, M., Delaney, A., Wigerblad, G., Schumann, A. P., Quinn, T., Frasnelli, J., Svensson, C. I., ... Mogil, J. S. (2014). Olfactory exposure to males, including men, causes stress and related analgesia in rodents. *Nature Methods, 11,* 629–632. (2) doi: 10.1038/NMETH.2935

Sorrells, S. F., Paredes, M. F., Cebrian-Silla, A., Sandoval, K., Qi, D., Kelley, K. W., James, D., Mayer, S., Chang, J., Auguste, K. I., Hang, E. F. C., Gutierrez, A. J., Kriegstein, A. R., Mathern, G. W., Oldham, M. C., Huang, E. J., Garcia-Verdugo, J. M., Yang, Z. G., & Alvarez-Buylla, A. (2018). Human hippocampal neurogenesis drops sharply in children to undetectable levels in adults. *Nature, 555,* 377–381. (3) doi: 10.1038/nature25975

Soto, C. J. (2019). How replicable are links between personality traits and consequential life outcomes? The Life Outcomes of Personality Replication Project. *Psychological Science, 30,* 711–727. (14) doi: 10.1177/0956797619831612

Sowell, E. R., Thompson, P. M., Holmes, C. J., Jernigan, T. L., & Toga, A. W. (1999). *In vivo* evidence for post-adolescent brain maturation in frontal and striatal regions. *Nature Neuroscience, 2,* 859–861. (1) doi: 10.1038/13154

Spachtholz, P., Kuhbandner, C., & Pekrun, R. (2014). Negative affect improves the quality of memories: Trading capacity for precision in sensory and working memory. *Journal of Experimental Psychology: General, 143,* 1450–1456. (7) doi: 10.1037/xge0000012

Spanos, N. P. (1987-1988). Past-life hypnotic regression: A critical view. *Skeptical Inquirer, 12,* 174–180. (10)

Sparks, A. M., Fessler, D. M. T., Chan, K. Q., Ashokkumar, A., & Holbrook, C. (2018). Disgust as a mechanism for decision making under risk: Illuminating sex differences and individual risk-taking correlates of disgust propensity. *Emotion, 18,* 942–958. (12) doi: 10.1037/emo0000389

Sparrow, B., Liu, J., & Wegner, D. M. (2011). Google effects on memory: Cognitive consequences of having information at our fingertips. *Science, 333,* 776–778. (7) doi: 10.1126/science.1207745

Spearman, C. (1904). "General intelligence," objectively determined and measured. *American Journal of Psychology, 15,* 201–293. (9) doi: 10.2307/1412107

Sperling, G. (1960). The information available in brief visual presentations. *Psychological Monographs, 74,* whole number 498. (7) doi: 10.1037/h0093759

Sperry, R. W. (1967). Split-brain approach to learning problems. In G. C. Quarton, T. Melnechuk, & F. O. Schmitt (Eds.), *The neurosciences: A study program* (pp. 714–722). New York: Rockefeller University Press. (3)

Spira, A., & Bajos, N. (1993). *Les comportements sexuels en France* (Sexual behaviors in France). Paris: La documentation Française. (11)

Sproesser, G., Schupp, H. T., & Renner, B. (2014). The bright side of stress-induced eating. *Psychological Science, 25,* 58–65. (11) doi: 10.1177/0956797613494849

Squire, L. R., Haist, F., & Shimamura, A. P. (1989). The neurology of memory: Quantitative assessment of retrograde amnesia in two groups of amnesic patients. *Journal of Neuroscience, 9,* 828–839. (7) doi: 10.1523/JNEUROSCI.09-03-00828.1989

Sripada, C., Kessler, D., & Jonides, J. (2014). Methylphenidate blocks effort-induced depletion of regulatory control in healthy volunteers. *Psychological Science, 25,* 1227–1234. (11) doi: 10.1177/0956797614526415

Sritharan, R., Heilpern, K., Wilbur, C. J., & Gawronski, B. (2010). I think I like you: Spontaneous and deliberate evaluations of potential romantic partners in an online dating context. *European Journal of Social Psychology, 40,* 1062–1077. (13) doi: 10.1002/ejsp.703

Srna, S. Schrift, R. Y., & Zauberman, G. (2018). The illusion of multitasking and its positive effect on performance. *Psychological Science, 29,* 1942–1955. (8) doi: 10.1177/0956797618801013

Staddon, J. (1993). *Behaviorism.* London: Duckworth. (6)

Stahl, A. E., & Feigenson, L. (2015). Observing the unexpected enhances infants' learning and exploration. *Science, 348,* 91–94. (5) doi: 10.1126/science.aaa3799

Stallen, M., De Dreu, C. K. W., Shalvi, S., Smidts, A., & Sanfey, A. G. (2012). The herding hormone: Oxytocin stimulates in-group conformity. *Psychological Science, 23,* 1288–1292. (3) doi: 10.1177/0956797612446026

Stalnaker, T. A., Roesch, M. R., Franz, T. M., Calu, D. J., Singh, T., & Schoenbaum, G. (2007). Cocaine-induced decision-making deficits are mediated by miscoding in basolateral amygdala. *Nature Neuroscience, 10,* 949–951. (3) doi: 10.1038/nn1931

Stamm, K., Lin, L, & Christidis, P. (2017, November). Psychologists across the career span: Where do they practice? *Monitor on Psychology, 48*(10), p. 21. (1) https://www.apa.org/monitor/2017/11/datapoint

Stanley, D. J., & Spence, J. R. (2014). Expectations for replications: Are yours realistic? *Perspectives on Psychological Science, 9,* 305–318. (2) doi: 10.1177/1745691614528518

Stanovich, K. E. (2018). Cognitive unconscious and human rationality. *American Journal of Psychology, 131,* 231–237. (8) doi: 10.5406/amerjpsyc.131.2.0231

Starr, C., & Taggart, R. (1992). *Biology: The unity and diversity of life* (6th ed.). Belmont, CA: Wadsworth. (3)

Stavrova, O. (2019). Having a happy spouse is associated with lowered risk of mortality. *Psychological Science, 30,* 798–803. (12) doi: 10.1177/0956797619835147

Ste-Marie, D. M. (1999). Expert–novice differences in gymnastic judging: An information-processing perspective. *Applied Cognitive Psychology, 13,* 269–281. (8) doi: 10.1002/(SICI)1099-0720(199906)13:3<269::AID-ACP567>3.3.CO;2-P

Steel, Z., Marnane, C., Iranpour, C., Chey, T., Jackson, J. W., Patel, V., & Silove, D. (2014). The global prevalence of common mental disorders: A systematic review and meta-analysis 1980-2013. *International Journal of Epidemiology, 43,* 476–493. (15) doi: 10.1093/ije/dyu038

Steele, C. (2010). *Whistling Vivaldi.* New York: W. W. Norton. (9)

Steele, C. J., Bailey, J. A., Zatorre, R. J., & Penhune, V. B. (2013). Early musical training and white-matter plasticity in the corpus callosum: Evidence for a sensitive period. *Journal of Neuroscience, 33,* 1282–1290. (3) doi: 10.1523/JNEUROSCI.3578-12.2013

Steele, C. M., & Aronson, J. (1995). Stereotype threat and the intellectual test performance of African Americans. *Journal of Personality and Social Psychology, 69,* 797–811. (9) doi: 10.1037/0022-3514.69.5.797

n, H., Meyer-Lindenberg, A., Steinberg, gnusdottir, B., Morgen, K., Arnarsdottir, rnsdottir, G., BragiWalters, G., Jonsdottir, G. A., Doyle, O. M., Tost, H., Grimm, O., Kristjansdottir, S., Snorrason, H., Davidsdottir, S. R., Gudmundsson, L. J., Jonsson, G. F., Stefansdottir, B., Helgadottir, I., ... Stefansson, K. (2014). CNVs conferring risk of autism or schizophrenia affect cognition in controls. *Nature, 505*, 361-366. (15) doi: 10.1038/nature12818

Stefansson, H., Rujescu, D., Cichon, S., Pietiläinen, O. P. H., Ingason, A., Steinberg, S., Fossdal, R., Sigurdsson, E., Sigmundsson, T., Buizer-Voskamp, J. E., Hansen, T., Jakobsen, K. D., Muglia, P., Francks, C. Matthews, P. M., Gylfason, A., Halldorsson, B. V., Gudbjartsson, D., Thorgeirsson, T. E., ... Stefansson, K. (2008). Large recurrent microdeletions associated with schizophrenia. *Nature, 455*, 232-236. (15) doi: 10.1038/nature07229

Steffens, B. (2007). *Ibn al-Haytham: First scientist.* Greensboro, NC: Morgan Reynolds Publishing. (4)

Stein, M. B., Hanna, C., Koverola, C., Torchia, M., & McClarty, B. (1997). Structural brain changes in PTSD. *Annals of the New York Academy of Sciences, 821*, 76-82. (12) doi: 10.1111/j.1749-6632.1997.tb48270.x

Steinberg, L., Graham, S., O'Brien, L., Woolard, J., Cauffman, E., & Banich, M. (2009). Age differences in future orientation and delay discounting. *Child Development, 80*, 28-44. (11) doi: 10.1111/j.1467-8624.2008.01244.x

Steinhardt, P. (2014). Big Bang blunder bursts the multiverse bubble. *Nature, 510*, 9. (2) doi: 10.1038/510009a

Stella, N., Schweitzer, P., & Piomelli, D. (1997). A second endogenous cannabinoid that modulates long-term potentiation. *Nature, 382*, 773-778. (3) doi: 10.1038/42015

Stensola, H., Stensola, T., Solstad, T., Frøland, K., Moser, M.-B., & Moser, E. I. (2012). The entorhinal grid map is discretized. *Nature, 492*, 72-78. (7) doi: 10.1038/nature11649

Sterling, P. (2012). Allostasis: A model of predictive regulation. *Physiology & Behavior, 106*, 5-15. (11) doi: 10.1016/j.physbeh.2011.06.004

Sternberg, K. J., Baradaran, L. P., Abbott, C. B., Lamb, M. E., & Guterman, E. (2006). Type of violence, age, and gender differences in the effects of family violence on children's behavior problems: A mega-analysis. *Developmental Review, 26*, 89-112. (5) doi: 10.1016/j.dr.2005.12.001

Sternberg, R. J. (1997). The concept of intelligence and its role in lifelong learning and success. *American Psychologist, 52*, 1030-1037. (9) doi: 10.1037/0003-066X.52.10.1030

Sternberg, R. J., Nokes, C., Geissler, P. W., Prince, R., Okatcha, F., Bundy, D. A. & Grigorenko, E. L. (2001). The relationship between academic and practical intelligence: A case study in Kenya. *Intelligence, 29*, 401-418. (9) doi: 10.1016/S0160-2896(01)00065-4

Stevens, S. S. (1961). To honor Fechner and repeal his law. *Science, 133*, 80-86. (1) doi: 10.1126/science.133.3446.80

Stewart, B. D., von Hippel, W., & Radvansky, G. A. (2009). Age, race, and implicit prejudice. *Psychological Science, 20*, 164-168. (13) doi: 10.1111/j.1467-9280.2009.02274.x

Stewart, I. (1987). Are mathematicians logical? *Nature, 325*, 386-387. (9) doi: 10.1038/325386a0

Stice, E. (2002). Risk and maintenance factors for eating pathology: A meta-analytic review. *Psychological Bulletin, 128*, 825-848. (11) doi: 10.1037//0033-2909.128.5.825

Stice, E., & Shaw, H. (2004). Eating disorder prevention programs: A meta-analytic review. *Psychological Bulletin, 130*, 206-227. (15) doi: 10.1037/0033-2909.130.2.206

Stickgold, R., Malia, A., Maguire, D., Roddenberry, D., & O'Connor, M. (2000). Replaying the game: Hypnagogic images in normals and amnesics. *Science, 290*, 350-353. (7) doi: 10.1126/science.290.5490.350

Stille, L., Norin, E., & Sikstrom, S. (2017). Self-delivered misinformation: Merging the choice-blindness and misinformation effect paradigms. *PLoS One, 12*, e0173606. (8) doi: 10.1371/journal.pone.0173606

Stillman, P. E., Medvedev, D., & Ferguson, M. J. (2017). Resisting temptation: Tracking how self-control conflicts are successfully resolved in real time. *Psychological Science, 28*, 1240-1258. (11) doi: 10.1177/0956797617705386

Stone, A. A., Schwartz, J. E., Broderick, J. E., & Deaton, A. (2010). A snapshot of the age distribution of psychological well-being in the United States. *Proceedings of the National Academy of Sciences, U.S.A., 107*, 9985-9990. (12) doi: 10.1073/pnas.1003744107

Stone, V. E., Nisenson, L., Eliassen, J. C., & Gazzaniga, M. S. (1996). Left hemisphere representations of emotional facial expressions. *Neuropsychologia, 34*, 23-29. (3) doi: 10.1016/0028-3932(95)00060-7

Storms, M. D. (1973). Videotape and the attribution process: Reversing actors' and observers' points of view. *Journal of Personality and Social Psychology, 27*, 165-175. (13) doi: 10.1037/h0034782

Stoychev, K. R. (2019). Neuroimaging studies in patients with mental disorder and co-occurring substance abuse disorders: Summary of findings. *Frontiers in Psychiatry, 10*, article 702. (15) doi:10.3389/fpsyt.2019.00702

Strack, F., Martin, L. L., & Stepper, S. (1988). Inhibiting and facilitating conditions of the human smile: A nonobtrusive test of the facial feedback hypothesis. *Journal of Personality and Social Psychology, 54*, 768-777. (12) doi: 10.1037/0022-3514.54.5.768

Strange, D., Garry, M., Bernstein, D. M., & Lindsay, D. S. (2011). Photographs cause false memories for the news. *Acta Psychologica, 136*, 90-94. (7) doi: 10.1016/j.actpsy.2010.10.006

Strange, D., Sutherland, R., & Garry, M. (2004). A photographic memory for false autobiographical events: The role of plausibility in children's false memories. *Australian Journal of Psychology, 56*(Suppl. S), 137. (7)

Strauss, M., Ulke, C., Paucke, M., Huang, J., Mauche, N., Sander, C., Stark, T., & Hegerl, U. (2018). Brain arousal regulation in adults with attention-deficit/hyperactivity disorder (ADHD). *Psychiatry Research, 261*, 102-108. (8) doi: 10.1016/j.psychres.2017.12.043

Strauss, G. P., Visser, K. H., Lee, B. G., & Gold, J. M. (2017). The positivity offset theory of anhedonia in schizophrenia. *Clinical Psychological Science, 5*, 226-238. (15) doi: 10.1177/2167702616674989

Strenze, T. (2007). Intelligence and socioeconomic success: A meta-analytic review of longitudinal research. *Intelligence, 35*, 401-426. (9) doi: 10.1016/j.intell.2006.09.004

Striemer, C. L., Chapman, C. S., & Goodale, M. A. (2009). "Real-time" obstacle avoidance in the absence of primary visual cortex. *Proceedings of the National Academy of Sciences, 106*, 15996-16001. (3) doi: 10.1073/pnas.0905549106

Struckman-Johnson, C., Struckman-Johnson, D., & Anderson, P. B. (2003). Tactics of sexual coercion: When men and women won't take no for an answer. *Journal of Sex Research, 40*, 76-86. (13) doi: 10.1080/00224490309552168

Stulz, N., Lutz, W., Kopta, S. M., Minami, T., & Saunders, S. M. (2013). Dose-effect relationship in routine outpatient psychotherapy: Does treatment duration matter? *Journal of Counseling Psychology, 60*, 593-600. (15) doi: 10.1037/a0033589

Stuss, D. T., Alexander, M. P., Palumbo, C. L., Buckle, L., Sayer, L., & Pogue, J. (1994). Organizational strategies of patients with unilateral or bilateral frontal lobe injury in word list learning tasks. *Neuropsychology, 8*, 355-373. (7) http://dx.doi.org.prox.lib.ncsu.edu/10.1037/0894-4105.8.3.355

Suchak, M., Eppley, T. M., Campbell, M. W., Feldman, R. A., Quarles, L. F., & de Waal, F. B. M. (2016). How chimpanzees cooperate in a competitive world. *Proceedings of the National Academy of Sciences (U.S.A.), 113*, 10215-10220. (13) doi: 10.1073/pnas.1611826113

Sudre, G., Mangalmurti, A., & Shaw, P. (2018). Growing out of attention deficit hyperactivity disorder: Insights form the "remitted" brain. *Neuroscience & Biobehavioral Reviews, 94*, 198-209. (8) doi: 10.1016/j.neubiorev.2018.08.010

Sugden, N. A., & Marquis, A. R. (2017). Meta-analytic review of the development of face discrimination in infancy: Face race, face gender, infant age, and methodology modrate face discrimination. *Psychological Bulletin, 143*, 1201-1244. (5) doi: 10.1037/bul0000116

Sullivan, P. F., Kendler, K. S., & Neale, M. C. (2003). Schizophrenia as a complex trait: Evidence from a meta-analysis of twin studies. *Archives of General Psychiatry, 60*, 1187-1192. (15) doi: 10.1001/archpsyc.60.12.1187

Sullivan, R. C. (1980). Why do autistic children...? *Journal of Autism and Developmental Disorders, 10*, 231-241. (15) doi: 10.1007/BF02408474

Sun, Q., Townsend, M. K., Okereke, O. I., Rimm, E. B., Hu, F. B., Stampfer, M. J., & Grodstein, F. (2011). Alcohol consumption at midlife and successful ageing in women: A prospective cohort analysis in the Nurses' Health Study. *PLoS Medicine, 8*, e1001090. (2) doi: 10.1371/journal.pmed.1001090

Sun, Y.-G., Zhao, Z.-Q., Meng, X.-L., Yin, J., Liu, X.-Y., & Chen, Z.-F. (2009). Cellular basis of itch sensation. *Science, 325*, 1531-1534. (4) doi: 10.1126/science.1174868

Sundet, J. M., Eriksen, W., & Tambs, K. (2008). Intelligence correlations between brothers decrease with increasing age difference. *Psychological Science, 19*, 843-847. (9) doi: 10.1111/j.1467-9280.2008.02166.x

Suschinsky, K. D., & Lalumière, M. L. (2011). Prepared for anything? An investigation of female genital arousal in response to rape cues. *Psychological Science, 22*, 159-165. (11) doi: 10.1177/0956797610394660

Susskind, J. M., Lee, D. H., Cusi, A., Feiman, R., Grabski, W., & Anderson, A. K. (2008). Expressing fear enhances sensory acquisition. *Nature Neuroscience, 11*, 843-850. (12) doi: 10.1038/nn.2138

Sutin, A. R., Terracciano, A., Milaneschi, Y., An, Y., Ferrucci, L., & Zonderman, A. B. (2013). The effect of birth cohort on well-being: The legacy of economic hard times. *Psychological Science, 24*, 379–385. doi: 10.1177/0956797612459658

Suwabe, K., Hyodo, K., Byun, K., Ochi, G., Yassa, M. A., & Soya, H. (2017). Acute moderate exercise improves mnemonic discrimination in young adults. *Hippocampus, 27*, 229–234. (7) doi: 10.1002/hipo.22695

Swan, S. H., Liu, F., Hines, M., Kruse, R. L., Wang, C., Redmon, J. B., Spaarks, A., & Weiss, B. (2010). Prenatal phthalate exposure and reduced masculine play in boys. *International Journal of Andrology, 33*, 259–269. (5) doi: 10.1111/j.1365-2605.2009.01019.x

Swann, W. B., Jr., & Jetten, J. (2017). Restoring agency to the human actor. *Perspectives on Psychological Science, 12*, 382–399. (13) doi: 10.1177/1745691616679464

Swinton, S. S. (1987). *The predictive validity of the restructured GRE with particular attention to older students* (GRE Board Professional Rep. No. 83–25P. ETS Research Rep. 87–22). Princeton, NJ: Educational Testing Service. (9) http://dx.doi.org/10.1002/j.2330-8516.1987.tb00226.x

Szkudlarek, H. J., Desai, S. J., Renard, J., Pereira, B., Norris, C., Jobson, C. E. L., Rajakumar, N., Allman, B. L., & Laviolette, S. R. (2019). Delta-9-tetrahydrocannabinol and cannabidiol produce dissociable effects on prefrontal cortical executive function and regulation of affective behaviors. *Neuropsychopharmacology, 44*, 817–825. (3) doi: 10.1038/s41386-018-0282-7

Sznycer, D., Al-Shawaf, L., Bereby-Meyer, Y., Curry, O. S., De Smet, D., Ermer, E., Kim, S., Kim, S., Li, N. P., Seal, M. F. L., McClung, J., O, J. Q., Ohtsubo, Y., Quillien, T., Schaub, M., Sell, A., van Leeuwen, F., Cosmides, L., & Tooby, J. (2017). Cross-cultural regularities in the cognitive architecture of pride. *Proceedings of the National Academy of Sciences (U.S.A.), 114*, 1874–1879. (12) doi: 10.1073/pnas.1614389114

Szymanski, H. V., Simon, J. C., & Gutterman, N. (1983). Recovery from schizophrenic psychosis. *American Journal of Psychiatry, 140*, 335–338. (15)

Taber-Thomas, B. C., Asp, E. W., Koenigs, M., Sutterer, M., Anderson, S. W., & Tranel, D. (2014). Arrested development: early prefrontal lesions impair the maturation of moral judgment. *Brain, 137*, 1254–1261. (12) doi: 10.1093/brain/awt377

Tahiri, M., Mottillo, S., Joseph, L., Pilote, L., & Eisenberg, M. J. (2012). Alternative smoking cessation aids: A meta-analysis of randomized controlled trials. *American Journal of Medicine, 125*, 576–584. (10) doi: 10.1016/j.amjmed.2011.09.028

Takeda, Y., Kurita, T., Sakurai, K., Shiga, T., Tamaki, N., & Koyama, T. (2011). Persistent déjà vu associated with hyperperfusion in the entorhinal cortex. *Epilepsy & Behavior, 21*, 196–199. (10) doi: 10.1016/j.yebeh.2011.03.031

Takemura, K. (2014). Being different leads to being connected: On the adaptive function of uniqueness in "open" societies. *Journal of Cross-Cultural Psychology, 45*, 1579–1593. (13) doi: 10.1177/0022022114548684

Takeuchi, T., Duszkiewicz, A. J., Sonneborn, A., Spooner, P. A., Yamasaki, M., Watanabe, M., Smith, C. C., Fernandez, G., Deisseroth, K., Greene, R. W., & Morris, R. G. M. (2016). Locus coeruleus and dopaminergic consolidation of everyday memory. *Nature, 537*, 357–362. (7) doi: 10.1038/nature19325

Takizawa, R., Maughan, B., & Arseneault, L. (2014). Adult health outcomes of childhood bullying victimization: Evidence from a five-decade longitudinal British birth cohort. *American Journal of Psychiatry, 171*, 777–784. (15) doi: 10.1176/appi.ajp.2014.13101401

Talanow, T., & Ettinger, U. (2018). Effects of task repetition but no transfer of inhibitory control training in healthy adults. *Acta Psychologica, 187*, 37–53. (7) doi: 10.1016/j.actpsy.2018.04.016

Talhelm, T., Zhang, X., Oishi, S., Shimin, C., Duan, D., Lan, X., & Kitayama, S. (2014). Large-scale psychological differences within China explained by rice versus wheat agriculture. *Science, 344*, 603–608. (5) doi: 10.1126/science.1246850

Tamietto, M., Castelli, L., Vighetti, S., Perozzo, P., Geminiani, G., Weiskrantz, L., & de Gelder, B. (2009). Unseen facial and bodily expressions trigger fast emotional reactions. *Proceedings of the National Academy of Sciences, 106*, 17661–17666. (3) doi: 10.1073/pnas.0908994106

Tanaka, J. W., Curran, T., & Sheinberg, D. L. (2005). The training and transfer of real-world perceptual expertise. *Psychological Science, 16*, 145–151. (8) doi: 10.1111/j.0956-7976.2005.00795.x

Tannenbaum, D., Valasek, C. J., Knowles, E. D., & Ditto, P. H. (2013). Incentivizing wellness in the workplace: Sticks (not carrots) send stigmatizing signals. *Psychological Science, 24*, 1512–1522. (8) doi: 10.1177/0956797612474471

Tarr, M. J., & Gauthier, I. (2000). FFA: A flexible fusiform area for subordinate-level visual processing automatized by experience. *Nature Neuroscience, 3*, 764–769. (3) doi: 10.1038/77666

Taylor, C. B., Bryson, S., Luce, K. H., Cunning, D., Doyle, A. C., Abascal, L. B., Rockwell, R., Dev, P., Winzelberg, A. J., & Wilfley, D. E. (2006). Prevention of eating disorders in at-risk college-age women. *Archives of General Psychiatry, 63*, 881–888. (15) doi: 10.1001/archpsyc.63.8.881

Taylor, C. L. (2017). Creativity and mood disorders: A systematic review and meta-analysis. *Perspectives on Psychological Science, 12*, 1040–1076. (15) doi: 10.1177/1745691617699653

Teitelbaum, P., Pellis, V. C., & Pellis, S. M. (1991). Can allied reflexes promote the integration of a robot's behavior? In J. A. Meyer & S. W. Wilson (Eds.), *From animals to animats: Simulation of animal behavior* (pp. 97–104). Cambridge, MA: MIT Press/Bradford Books (10)

Telzer, E. H., Ichien, N. T., & Qu, Y. (2015). Mothers know best: Redirecting adolescent reward sensitivity toward safe behavior during risk taking. *Social Cognitive and Affective Neuroscience, 10*, 1383–1391. (5) doi: 10.1093/scan/nsv026

ten Brinke, L., Stimson, D., & Carney, D. R. (2014). Some evidence for unconscious lie detection. *Psychological Science, 25*, 1098–1105. (12) doi: 10.1177/0956797614524421

Terr, L. (1988). What happens to early memories of trauma? A study of twenty children under age five at the time of documented traumatic events. *Journal of the American Academy of Child and Adolescent Psychiatry, 27*, 96–104. (7) doi: 10.1097/00004583-198801000-00015

Terracciano, A., Abdel-Khalek, A. M., Ádám, N., Admaovová, L., Ahn, C., Ahn, H.-N., Alansari, B. M., Alcalay, L., Allik, J., Angleitner, A., Avia, M. D., Ayearst, L. E., Barbaranelli, C., Beer, A., Borg-Cunen, M. A., Bratko, D., Brunner-Sciarra, M., Budzinski, L., Camart, N., . . . McCrae, R. R. (2005). National character does not reflect mean personality levels in 49 cultures. *Science, 310*, 96–100. (14) doi: 10.1126/science.1117199

Terrace, H. S., Petitto, L. A., Sanders, R. J., & Bever, T. G. (1979). Can an ape create a sentence? *Science, 206*, 891–902. (8) doi: 10.1126/science.504995

Terzaghi, M., Sartori, I., Tassi, L., Rustioni, V., Proserpio, P., Lorusso, G., Manni, R., & Nobili, L. (2012). Dissociated local arousal states underlying essential features of non-rapid eye movement arousal parasomnia: An intracerebral stereo-electroencephalographic study. *Journal of Sleep Research, 21*, 502–506. (10) doi: 10.1111/j.1365-2869.2012.01003.x

Testa, M., Livingston, J. A., Vanzile-Tamsen, C., & Frone, M. R. (2003). The role of women's substance use in vulnerability to forcible and incapacitated rape. *Journal of Studies on Alcohol, 64*, 756–764. (13) doi: 10.15288/jsa.2003.64.756

Tetlock, P. E. (1992). Good judgment in international politics: Three psychological perspectives. *Political Psychology, 13*, 517–539. (8) doi: 10.2307/3791611

Tett, R. P., & Palmer, C. A. (1997). The validity of handwriting elements in relation to self-report personality trait measures. *Personality and Individual Differences, 22*, 11–18. (14) doi: 10.1016/S0191-8869(96)00180-3

Thal, S. B., & Lommen, M. J. J. (2018). Current perspective on MDMA-assisted psychotherapy for posttraumatic stress disorder. *Journal of Contemporary Psychotherapy, 48*, 99–108. (3) doi: 10.1007/s10879-017-9379-2

Thase, M. E. (2014). Combining cognitive therapy and pharmacotherapy for depressive disorders: A review of recent developments. *International Journal of Cognitive Therapy, 7*, 108–121. (15) doi: 10.1521/ijct.2014.7.2.108

"The medals and the damage done." (2004). *Nature, 430*, 604. (2) doi: https://www.nature.com/articles/430604a

Thibodeau, P. H., Hendricks, R. K., & Boroditsky, L. (2017). How linguistic metaphor scaffolds reasoning. *Trends in Cognitive Sciences, 21*, 852–863. (8) doi: 10.1016/j.tics.2017.07.001

Thierry, G., & Wu, Y. J. (2007). Brain potentials reveal unconscious translation during foreign-language comprehension. *Proceedings of the National Academy of Sciences, USA, 104*, 12530–12535. (8) doi: 10.1073/pnas.0609927104

Thomas, B. C., Croft, K. E., & Tranel, D. (2011). Harming kin to save strangers: Further evidence for abnormally utilitarian moral judgments after ventromedial prefrontal damage. *Journal of Cognitive Neuroscience, 23*, 2186–2196. (12) doi: 10.1162/jocn.2010.21591

Thomas, C., Avidan, G., Humphreys, K., Jung, K., Gao, F., & Behrmann, M. (2009). Reduced structural connectivity in ventral visual cortex in congenital prosopagnosia. *Nature Neuroscience, 12*, 29–31. (3) doi: 10.1038/nn.2224

Thomas, M. L., Patt, V. M., Bismark, A., Sprock, J., Tarasenko, M., Light, G. A., & Brown, G. G. (2017). Evidence of systematic attenuation in the measurement of cognitive deficits in schizophrenia. *Journal of Abnormal*

...ology, *126*, 312–324. (15) doi: 10.1037/...00256

...n, C. R., & Church, R. M. (1980). An explanation of the language of a chimpanzee. *Science, 208*, 313–314. (8) doi: 10.1126/science.7367862

Thomsen, L., Frankenhuis, W. E., Ingold-Smith, M., & Carey, S. (2011). Big and mighty: Preverbal infants mentally represent social dominance. *Science, 331*, 477–480. (5) doi: 10.1126/science.1199198

Thomson, D. R., Besner, D., & Smilek, D. (2015). A resource-control account of sustained attention: Evidence from mind-wandering and vigilance paradigms. *Perspectives on Psychological Science, 10*, 82–96. (8) doi: 10.1177/1745691614556681

Thoresen, C. J., Kaplan, S. A., Barsky, A. P., Warren, C. R., & de Chermont, K. (2003). The affective underpinnings of job perceptions and attitudes: A meta-analytic review and integration. *Psychological Bulletin, 129*, 914–945. (11) doi: 10.1037/0033-2909.129.6.914

Thorndike, E. L. (1918). The nature, purposes, and general methods of measurements of educational products. In E. J. Ashbaugh, W. A. Averill, L. P. Ayres, F. W. Ballou, E. Bryner, B. R. Buckingham, et al. (Eds.), *The seventeenth yearbook of the National Society for the Study of Education. Part II: The measurement of educational products* (pp. 16–24). Bloomington, IL: Public School Publishing Company. (9)

Thorndike, E. L. (1970). *Animal intelligence.* Darien, CT: Hafner. (Original work published 1911) (6)

Tillmann, B., Leveque, Y., Fornoni, L., Abouy, P., & Caclin, A. (2016). Impaired short-term memory for pitch in congenital amusia. *Brain Research, 1640*, 251–263. (4) doi: 10.1016/j.brainres.2015.10.035

Tilot, A. K., Kucera, K. S., Vino, A., Asher, J. E., Baron-Cohen, S., & Fisher, S. E. (2018). Rare variants in axonogenesis genes connect three familes with sound-color synesthesia. *Proceedings of the National Academy of Sciences (U.S.A.), 115*, 3168–3173. (4) doi: 10.1073/pnas.1715492115

Timberlake, W., & Farmer-Dougan, V. A. (1991). Reinforcement in applied settings: Figuring out ahead of time what will work. *Psychological Bulletin, 110*, 379–391. (6) doi: 10.1037/0033-2909.110.3.379

Tinbergen, N. (1958). *Curious Naturalists.* New York: Basic Books. (3)

Titchener, E. B. (1910). *A textbook of psychology.* New York: Macmillan. (1)

Todd, B. K., Fischer, R. A., Di Costa, S., Roestorf, A., Harbour, K., Hardiman, P., & Barry, J. A. (2018). Sex differences in children's toy preferences: A systematic review, meta-regression, and meta-analysis. *Infant and Child Development, 27*, e2064. (5) doi: 10.1002/icd.2064

Todorov, A., & Porter, J. M. (2014). Misleading first impressions: Different for different facial images of the same person. *Psychological Science, 25*, 1404–1417. (13) doi: 10.1177/0956797614532474

Tolman, E. C. (1938). The determinants of behavior at a choice point. *Psychological Review, 45*, 1–41. (1) doi: 10.1037/h0062733

Tolstoy, L. (1978). *Tolstoy's letters: Vol. I. 1828–1879.* New York: Charles Scribner's Sons. (Original works written 1828–1879) (5)

Tomasello, M. (2018). Great apes and human development: A personal history. *Child Development Perspectives, 12*, 189–193. (13) doi: 10.1111/cdep.12281

Tomasello, M., & Call, J. (2019). Thirty years of great ape gestures. *Animal Cognition, 22*, 461–469. (8) doi: 10.1007/s10071-018-1167-1

Tombaugh, C. W. (1980). *Out of the darkness, the planet Pluto.* Harrisburg, PA: Stackpole. (4)

Tonegawa, S., Morrissey, M. D., & Kitamura, T. (2018). The role of engram cells in the systems consolidation of memory. *Nature Reviews Neuroscience, 19*, 485–498. (7) doi: 10.1038/s41583-018-0031-2

Torrey, E. F., & Yolken, R. H. (2005). *Toxoplasma gondii* as a possible cause of schizophrenia. *Biological Psychiatry, 57*, 128S. (15)

Totonchi, D. A., Derlega, V. J., & Janda, L. H. (2019). Implicit sex guilt predicts sexual behaviors: Evidence for the validity of the sex-guilt implicit association test. *Journal of Sex & Marital Therapy, 45*, 50–59. (14) doi: 10.1080/0092623X.2018.1474409

Townshend, J. M., & Duka, T. (2003). Mixed emotions: Alcoholics' impairments in the recognition of specific emotional facial expressions. *Neuropsychologia, 41*, 773–782. (12) doi: 10.1016/S0028-3932(02)00284-1

Tracey, T. J. G., Wampold, B. E., Lichtenberg, J. W., & Goodyear, R. K. (2014). Expertise in psychotherapy: An elusive goal? *American Psychologist, 69*, 218–229. (8) doi: 10.1037/a0035099

Tracy, J. L., & Robins, R. W. (2004). Show your pride: Evidence for a discrete emotion expression. *Psychological Science, 15*, 194–197. (12) doi: 10.1111/j.0956-7976.2004.01503008.x

Tracy, J. L., Robins, R. W., & Lagattuta, K. H. (2005). Can children recognize pride? *Emotion, 5*, 251–257. (12) doi: 10.1037/1528-3542.5.3.251

Trahan, L. H., Stuebing, K. K., Fletcher, J. M., & Hiscock, M. (2014). The Flynn effect: A meta-analysis. *Psychological Bulletin, 140*, 1332–1360. (9) doi: 10.1037/a0037173

Trawalter, S., & Richeson, J. A. (2006). Regulatory focus and executive function after interracial interactions. *Journal of Experimental Social Psychology, 42*, 406–412. (13) doi: 10.1016/j.jesp.2005.05.008

Traxler, M. J., Foss, D. J., Podali, R., & Zirnstein, M. (2012). Feeling the past: The absence of experimental evidence for anomalous retroactive influences on text processing. *Memory & Cognition, 40*, 1366–1372. (2) doi: 10.3758/s13421-012-0232-2

Treanor, M., Brown, L. A., Rissman, J., & Craske, M. G. (2017). Can memories of traumatic experiences or addiction be erased or modified? A critical review of research on the disruption of memory consolidation and its applications. *Perspectives on Psychological Science, 12*, 290–305. (12) doi: 10.1177/1745691616664725

Treisman, A. (1999). Feature binding, attention and object perception. In G. W. Humphreys, J. Duncan, & A. Treisman (Eds.), *Attention, space and action* (pp. 91–111). Oxford, England: Oxford University Press. (3)

Treisman, A., & Souther, J. (1985). Search asymmetry: A diagnostic for preattentive processing of separable features. *Journal of Experimental Psychology: General, 114*, 285–310. (8) doi: 10.1037/0096-3445.114.3.285

Trevena, J. A., & Miller, J. (2002). Cortical movement preparation before and after a conscious decision to move. *Consciousness and Cognition, 11*, 162–190. (10) doi: 10.1006/ccog.2002.0548

Trickett, E. J. (2009). Community psychology: Individuals and interventions in community context. *Annual Review of Psychology, 60*, 395–419. (15) doi: 10.1146/annurev.psych.60.110707.163517

Trimmer, C. G., & Cuddy, L. L. (2008). Emotional intelligence, not music training, predicts recognition of emotional speech prosody. *Emotion, 8*, 838–849. (12) doi: 10.1037/a0014080

Trouche, E., Johansson, P., Hall, L., & Mercier, H. (2016). The selective laziness of reasoning. *Cognitive Science, 40*, 2122–2136. (8) doi: 10.1111/cogs.12303

Trueblood, J. S., Brown, S. D., Heathcote, A., & Busemeyer, J. R. (2013). Not just for consumers: Context effects are fundamental to decision making. *Psychological Science, 24*, 901–908. (8) doi: 10.1177/0956797612464241

Tsankova, N., Renthal, W., Kumar, A., & Nestler, E. J. (2007). Epigenetic regulation in psychiatric disorders. *Nature Reviews Neuroscience, 8*, 355–367. (3) doi: 10.1038/nrn2132

Tsay, C.-J. (2014). The vision heuristic: Judging music ensembles by sight alone. *Organizational Behavior and Human Decision Processes, 124*, 24–33. (13) doi: 10.1016/j.obhdp.2013.10.003

Tsilidis, K. K., Panagioutou, O. A., Sena, E. S., Aretouli, E., Evagelou, E., Howells, D. W., Salman, R. A. S., Macleod, M. R., & Ioannidis, J. P. A. (2013). Evaluation of excess significance bias in animal studies of neurological diseases. *PLoS Biology, 11*, e1001609. (2) doi: 10.1371/journal.pbio.1001609

Tugade, M. M., & Fredrickson, B. L. (2004). Resilient individuals use positive emotions to bounce back from negative emotional experiences. *Journal of Personality and Social Psychology, 86*, 320–333. (12) doi: 10.1037/0022-3514.86.2.320

Tuiten, A., Van Honk, J., Koppeschaar, H., Bernaards, C., Thijssen, J., & Verbaten, R. (2000). Time course of effects of testosterone administration on sexual arousal in women. *Archives of General Psychiatry, 57*, 149–153. (11) doi: 10.1001/archpsyc.57.2.149

Tulving, E. (1989). Remembering and knowing the past. *American Scientist, 77*, 361–367. (7)

Tulving, E., & Thomson, D. M. (1973). Encoding specificity and retrieval processes in episodic memory. *Psychological Review, 80*, 352–373. (7) doi: 10.1037/h0020071

Tuntiya, N. (2007). Free-air treatment for mental patients: The deinstitutionalization debate of the nineteenth century. *Sociological Perspectives, 50*, 469–488. (15) doi: 10.1525/sop.2007.50.3.469

Turner, B. L., Caruso, E. M., Dilich, M. A., & Roese, N. J. (2019). Body camera footage leads to lower judgments of intent than dash camera footage. *Proceedings of the National Academy of Sciences (U.S.A.), 116*, 1201–1206. (13) doi: 10.1073/pnas.1805928116

Turner, C. F., Villaroel, M. A., Chromy, J. R., Eggleston, E., & Rogers, S. M. (2005) Same-gender sex among U.S. adults: trends across the twentieth century and during the 1990s. *Public Opinion Quarterly, 69*, 439–462. (11) doi: 10.1093/poq/nfi025

Turner, R. S., & Anderson, M. E. (2005). Context-dependent modulation of movement-related discharge in the primate globus pallidus. *Journal of Neuroscience, 25*, 2965–2976. (10) doi: 10.1523/JNEUROSCI.4036-04.2005

Tuulari, J. J., Tuominen, L., de Boer, F. E., Hirvonen, J., Helin, S., & Nuutila, P. (2017). Feeding releases endogenous opioids in humans. *Journal of Neuroscience, 37*, 8284–8291. (3) doi: 10.1523/JNEUROSCI.0976-17.2017

Tversky, A., & Kahneman, D. (1981). The framing of decisions and the psychology of choice. *Science, 211*, 453–458. (8) doi: 10.1126/science.7455683

Tversky, A., & Kahneman, D. (1983). Extensional versus intuitive reasoning: The conjunctional fallacy in probability judgment. *Psychological Review, 90*, 293–315. (8) doi: 10.1037/0033-295X.90.4.293

Twenge, J. M. (2000). The age of anxiety? Birth cohort change in anxiety and neuroticism, 1952–1993. *Journal of Personality and Social Psychology, 79*, 1007–1021. (14) doi: 10.1037//0022-3514.79.6.1007

Twenge, J. M. (2006). *Generation me.* New York: Free Press. (5)

U.S. Department of Labor. (2008). *Occupational outlook handbook* (2008–2009 ed.). Retrieved November 9, 2008, from www.bls.gov. (1)

Uchino, B. N., Cacioppo, J. T., & Kiecolt-Glaser, J. K. (1996). The relationship between social support and physiological processes: A review with emphasis on underlying mechanisms and implications for health. *Psychological Bulletin, 119*, 488–531. (12) doi: 10.1037/0033-2909.119.3.488

Udolf, R. (1981). *Handbook of hypnosis for professionals.* New York: Van Nostrand Reinhold. (10)

Udry, J. R., & Chantala, K. (2006). Masculinity-femininity predicts sexual orientation in men but not in women. *Journal of Biosocial Science, 38*, 797–809. (11) doi: 10.1017/S002193200500101X

Ulrich, R. E., Stachnik, T. J., & Stainton, N. R. (1963). Student acceptance of generalized personality interpretations. *Psychological Reports, 13*, 831–834. (14) doi: 10.2466/pr0.1963.13.3.831

Ulrich, R. S. (1984). View through a window may influence recovery from surgery. *Science, 224*, 420–421. (4) doi: 10.1126/science.6143402

Umanath, S., & Marsh, E. J. (2014). Understanding how prior knowledge influences memory in older adults. *Perspectives on Psychological Science, 9*, 408–426. (5) doi: 10.1177/1745691614535933

Unkelbach, C., Koch, A., Silva, R. R., & Garcia-Marques, T. (2019). Truth by repetition: Explanations and implications. *Current Directions in Psychological Science, 28*, 247–253. (8) doi: 10.1177/0963721419827854

Vaillant, G. E., & Milofsky, E. S. (1982). The etiology of alcoholism: A prospective viewpoint. *American Psychologist, 37*, 494–503. (15) doi: 10.1037/0003-066X.37.5.494

Valentine, G., & Sofuoglu, M. (2018). Cognitive effects of nicotine: Recent progress. *Current Neuropharmacology, 16*, 403–414. (3) doi: 10.2174/1570159X15666171103152136

Valla, J. M., & Ceci, S. J. (2014). Breadth-based models of women's underrepresentation in STEM fields: An integrative commentary on Schmidt (2011) and Nye et al. (2012). *Perspectives on Psychological Science, 9*, 219–224. (5) doi: 10.1177/1745691614522067

Vallines, I., & Greenlee, M. W. (2006). Saccadic suppression of retinotopically localized blood oxygen level-dependent responses in human primary visual area V1. *Journal of Neuroscience, 26*, 5965–5969. (8) doi: 10.1523/JNEUROSCI.0817-06.2006

van Anders, S. M., Hamilton, L. D., & Watson, N. V. (2007). Multiple partners are associated with higher testosterone in North American men and women. *Hormones and Behavior, 51*, 454–459. (11) doi: 10.1016/j.yhbeh.2007.01.002

van Anders, S. M., & Watson, N. V. (2006). Relationship status and testosterone in North American heterosexual and non-heterosexual men and women: Cross-sectional and longitudinal data. *Psychoneuroendocrinology, 31*, 715–723. (11) doi: 10.1016/j.psyneuen.2006.01.008

Van Bavel, J. J., Mende-Siedlecki, P., Brady, W. J., & Reinero, D. A. (2016). Contextual sensitivity in scientific reproducibility. *Proceedings of the National Academy of Sciences (U.S.A.), 113*, 6454–6459. (2) doi: 10.1073/pnas.1521897113

van Bronswijk, S., Moopen, N., Beijers, L., Ruhe, H. G., & Peeters, F. (2019). Effectiveness of psychotherapy for treatment-resistant depression: A meta-analysis and meta-regression. *Psychological Medicine, 49*, 366–379. (15) doi: 10.1017/S003329171800199X

Van Cantfort, T. E., Gardner, B. T., & Gardner, R. A. (1989). Developmental trends in replies to Wh-questions by children and chimpanzees. In R. A. Gardner, B. T. Gardner, & T. E. Van Cantfort (Eds.), *Teaching sign language to chimpanzees* (pp. 198–239). Albany: State University of New York Press. (8)

Van Dam, N. T., van Vugt, M. K., Vago, D. R., Schmalzl, L., Saron, C. D., Olendzki, A., Meissner, T., Lazar, S. W., Kerr, C. E., Gorchov, J., Fox, K. C. R., Field, B. A., Britton, W. B., Brefczynski-Lewis, J. A., & Meyer, D. E. (2018). Mind the hype: A critical evaluation and prescriptive agenda for research on mindfulness and meditation. *Perspectives on Psychological Science, 13*, 36–61. (10) doi: 10.1177/1745691617709589

van den Hout, M., & Kindt, M. (2003). Repeated checking causes memory distrust. *Behaviour Research and Therapy, 41*, 301–316. (15) doi: 10.1016/S00005-7967(02)00012-8

van der Linden, D., Dunkel, C. S., & Figuerdo, A. J. (2018). How universal is the general factor of personality? An analysis of the Big Five in forager families of the Bolivian Amazon. *Journal of Cross-Cultural Psychology, 49*, 1081–1097. (14) doi: 10.1177/0022022118774925

van der Wal, R. C., & van Dillen, L. F. (2013). Leaving a flat taste in your mouth: Task load reduces taste perception. *Psychological Science, 24*, 1277–1284. (11) doi: 10.1177/0956797612471953

Van der Werf, Y. D., Altena, E., Schoonheim, M. M., Sanz-Arigita, E. J., Vis, J. C., De Rijke, W., & Van Someren, E. J. (2009). Sleep benefits subsequent hippocampal functioning. *Nature Neuroscience, 12*, 122–123. (10) doi: 10.1038/nn.2253

Van Der Zee, K. I., Huet, R. C. G., Cazemier, C., & Evers, K. (2002). The influence of the premedication consult and preparatory information about anesthesia on anxiety among patients undergoing cardiac surgery. *Anxiety, Stress, and Coping, 15*, 123–133. (12) doi: 10.1080/10615800290028431

van der Zwan, Y. G., Janssen, E. H. C. C., Callens, N., Wolffenbuttell, K. P., Cohen-Kettenis, P. T., van den Berg, M., Drop, S. L. S., Dessens, A. B., & Beerendonk, C. (2013). Severity of virilization is associated with cosmetic appearance and sexual function in women with congenital adrenal hyperplasia: A cross-sectional study. *Journal of Sexual Medicine, 10*, 866–875. (11) doi: 10.1111/jsm.12028

Van Dessel, P., Hughes, S., & De Houwer, J. (2018). Consequence-based approach-avoidance training: A new and improved method for changing behavior. *Psychological Science, 29*, 1899–1910. (11) doi: 10.1177/0956797618796478

van Duijl, M., Nijenhuis, E., Komproe, I. H., Gernaat, H. B. P. E., & de Jong, J. T. (2010). Dissociative symptoms and reported trauma among patients with spirit possession and matched healthy controls in Uganda. *Cultural Medicine and Psychiatry, 34*, 380–400. (15) doi: 10.1007/s11013-010-9171-1

van Egmond, M. C., Berges, A. N., Omarshah, T., & Benton, J. (2017). The role of intrinsic motivation and the satisfaction of basic psychological needs under conditions of severe resource scarcity. *Psychological Science, 28*, 822–828. (11) doi: 10.1177/0956797617698138

Vanhove, J. (2013). The critical period hypothesis in second language acquisition: A statistical critique and reanalysis. *PLoS One, 8*, e69172. (8) doi: 10.1371/journal.pone.0069172

Van Houtem, C. M. H. H., Laine, M. L., Boomsma, D. I., Ligthart, L., van Wijk, A. J., & De Jongh, A. (2013). A review and meta-analysis of the heritability of specific phobia subtypes and corresponding fears. *Journal of Anxiety Disorders, 27*, 379–388. (15) doi: 10.1016/j.janxdis.2013.04.007

Van Ijzendoorn, M. H., & Bakermans-Kranenburg, M. J. (2012). A sniff of trust: Meta-analysis of the effects of intranasal oxytocin administration on face recognition, trust to in-group, and trust to out-group. *Psychoneuroendocrinology, 37*, 438–443. (3) doi: 10.1016/j.psyneuen.2011.07.008

van IJzendoorn, M. H., Juffer, F., & Poelhuis, C. W. K. (2005). Adoption and cognitive development: A meta-analytic comparison of adopted and nonadopted children's IQ and school performance. *Psychological Bulletin, 131*, 301–316. (9) doi: 10.1037/0033-2909.131.2.301

van Prooijen, J.-W., & Acker, M. (2015). The influence of control on belief in conspiracy theories: Conceptual and applied extensions. *Applied Cognitive Psychology, 29*, 753–761. (8) doi: 10.1002/acp.3161

van Prooijen, J.-W., Staman, J., & Krouwel, A. P. M. (2018). Increased conspiracy beliefs among ethnic and Muslim minorities. *Applied Cognitive Psychology, 32*, 661–667. (8) doi: 10.1002/acp.3442

Vandello, J. A., Bosson, J. K., Cohen, D., Burnaford, R. M., & Weaver, J. R. (2008). Precarious manhood. *Journal of Personality and Social Psychology, 95*, 1325–1339. (5) doi: 10.1037/a0012453

Vasey, P. L., & VanderLaan, D. P. (2010). An adaptive cognitive dissociation between willingness to help kin and nonkin in Samoan *Fa'afafine. Psychological Science, 21*, 292–297. (11) doi: 10.1177/0956797609359623

Vasilenko, S. A. (2017). Age-varying associations between nonmarital sexual behavior and depressive symptoms across adolescence and young adulthood. *Developmental Psychology, 53*, 366–378. (11) doi: 10.1037/dev0000229

Vasilev, M. R., Kirkby, J. A., & Angele, B. (2018). Auditory distraction during g: A Bayesian meta-analysis of a ...uing controversy. *Perspectives on ...logical Science, 13,* 567–597. (8) doi: 10.1177/1745691617747398

Vasterling, J., Duke, L. M., Brailey, K., Constans, J. I., Allain, A. N., & Sutker, P. B. (2002). Attention, learning, and memory performances and intellectual resources in Vietnam veterans: PTSD and no disorder comparisons. *Neuropsychology, 16,* 5–14. (9) doi: 10.1037//0894-4105.16.1.5

Vazire, S., & Carlson, E. N. (2011). Others sometimes know us better than we know ourselves. *Current Directions in Psychological Science, 20,* 104–108. (14) doi: 10.1177/0963721411402478

Vega, V., & Malamuth, N. M. (2007). Predicting sexual aggression: The role of pornography in the context of general and specific risk factors. *Aggressive Behavior, 33,* 104–117. (13) doi: 10.1002/ab.20172

Verplanken, B., & Faes, S. (1999). Good intentions, bad habits, and effects of forming implementation intentions on healthy eating. *European Journal of Social Psychology, 29,* 591–604. (11) doi: 10.1002/(SICI)1099-0992(199908/09)29:5/6<591::AID-EJSP948>3.0.CO;2-H

Veselinovic, T., Schzrpenberg, M., Heinze, M., Cordes, J., Muhlbauer, B., Juckel, G., Habell, U., Ruther, E., Timm, J., Grunder, G., Bleich, S., Frieling, H., Borgman, M., Breunig-Lyriti, V., Schulz, C., Handschuh, D., Brune, M., Heller, J., Falkai, P., ... Naber, D. (2019). Disparate effects of first and second generation antipsychotics on cognition in schizophrenia—Findings from the randomized NeSSy trial. *European Neuropsychopharmacology, 29,* 720–739. (15) doi:10.1016/j.euroneuro.2019.03.014

Vevera, J., Zarrei, M., Hartmannova, H., Jedlickova, I., Musalkova, D., Pristoupilova, A., Oliveriusova, P., Treslova, H., Noskova, L., Hodanova, K., Stranecky, V., Jiricka, V., Preiss, N., Prihodova, K., Saligova, J., Wei, J., Woodbury-Smith, M., Bleyer, A. J., Scherer, S. W., & Kmoch, S. (2019). Rare copy number variation in extremely impulsively violent males. *Genes Brain and Behavior, 18,* article UNSP e12536. (13) doi:10.1111/gbb.12536

Viglione, D. J., & Taylor, N. (2003). Empirical support for interrater reliability of Rorschach Comprehensive System scoring. *Journal of Clinical Psychology, 59,* 111–121. (14) doi: 10.1002/jclp.10121

Viken, R. J., Rose, R. J., Kaprio, J., & Koskenvuo, M. (1994). A developmental genetic analysis of adult personality: Extraversion and neuroticism from 18 to 59 years of age. *Journal of Personality and Social Psychology, 66,* 722–730. (5, 14) doi: 10.1037/0022-3514.66.4.722

Visser, B. A., Ashton, M. C., & Vernon, P. A. (2006). Beyond *g:* Putting multiple intelligences theory to the test. *Intelligence, 34,* 487–502. (9) doi: 10.1016/j.intell.2006.02.004

Vittengl, J. R., Clark, L. A., Thase, M. E., & Jarrett, R. B. (2014). Are improvements in cognitive content and depressive symptoms correlates or mediators during acute-phase cognitive therapy for recurrent MDD. *International Journal of Cognitive Therapy, 7,* 251–271. (15) doi: 10.1521/ijct.2014.7.3.251

Vokey, J. R., & Read, J. D. (1985). Subliminal messages: Between the devil and the media. *American Psychologist, 40,* 1231–1239. (4) doi: 10.1037/0003-066X.40.11.1231

Volkow, N. D., & Boyle, M. (2018). Neuroscience of addiction: Relevance to prevention and treatment. *American Journal of Psychiatry, 175,* 729–740. (15) doi: 10.1176/appi.ajp.2018.17101174

Volkow, N. D., Fowler, J. S., Wang, G.-J., Hitzemann, R., Logan, J., Schyler, D. J., Dewey, S. L., & Wolf, A. P. (1993). Decreased dopamine D$_2$ receptor availability is associated with reduced frontal metabolism in cocaine abusers. *Synapse, 14,* 169–177. (15) doi: 10.1002/syn.890140210

Volkow, N. D., Wang, G.-J., & Fowler, J. S. (1997). Imaging studies of cocaine in the human brain and studies of the cocaine addict. *Annals of the New York Academy of Sciences, 820,* 41–55. (3) doi: 10.1111/j.1749-6632.1997.tb46188.x

Volkow, N. D., Wang, G.-J., Fowler, J., Gatley, S. J., Logan, J., Ding, Y.-S., Hitzemann, R., & Pappas. N. (1998). Dopamine transporter occupancies in the human brain induced by therapeutic doses of oral methylphenidate. *American Journal of Psychiatry, 155,* 1325–1331. (3) doi: 10.1176/ajp.155.10.1325

Volz, L. J., Hillyard, S. A., Miller, M. B., & Gazzaniga, M. S. (2018). Unifying control over the body: consciousness and cross-cuing in split-brain patients. *Brain, 241 (3),* e15. (3) doi: 10.1093/brain/awx359

von Bartheld, C. S., Bahney, J., & Heerculano-Houzel, S. (2016). The search for true numbers of neurons and glial cells in the human brain: A review of 150 years of cell counting. *Journal of Comparative Neurology, 524,* 3865–3895. (3) doi: 10.1002/cne.24040

von der Beck, I., Oeberst, A., Cress, U., & Nestler, S. (2017). Cultural interpretations of global information? Hindsight bias after reading Wikipedia articles across cultures. *Applied Cognitive Psychology, 31,* 315–325. (7) doi: 10.1002/acp.3329

von Stumm, S., Hell, B., & Chamorro-Premuzic, T. (2011). The hungry mind: Intellectual curiosity is the third pillar of academic performance. *Perspectives on Psychological Science, 6,* 574–588. (9) doi: 10.1177/1745691611421204

Vosoughi, S., Roy, D., & Aral, S. (2018). The spread of true and false news online. *Science, 359,* 1146–1151. (7) doi: 10.1126/science.aap9559

Voss, U., Holzmann, R., Hobson, A., Paulus, W., Koppehele-Gossel, J., Klimke, A., & Nitsche, M. A. (2014). Induction of self-awareness in dreams through frontal low current stimulation of gamma activity. *Nature Neuroscience, 17,* 810–812. (10) doi: 10.1038/nn.3719

Vroom, V. H., & Jago, A. G. (2007). The role of the situation in leadership. *American Psychologist, 62,* 17–24. (11) doi: 10.1037/0003-066X.62.1.17

Vyazovskiy, V. V., Cirelli, C., Pfister-Genskow, M., Faraguna, U., & Tononi, G. (2008). Molecular and electrophysiological evidence for net synaptic potentiation in wake and depression in sleep. *Nature Neuroscience, 11,* 200–208. (10) doi: 10.1038/nn2035

Vyazovskiy, V. V., Olcese, U., Hanlon, E. C., Nir, Y., Cirelli, C., & Tononi, G. (2011). Local sleep in awake rats. *Nature, 472,* 443–447. (10) doi: 10.1038/nature10009

Vygotsky, L. S. (1978). *Mind in society.* Cambridge, MA: Harvard University Press. (5)

Wade, K. A., Garry, M., Read, J. D., & Lindsay, D. S. (2002). A picture is worth a thousand lies: Using false photographs to create false childhood memories. *Psychonomic Bulletin and Review, 9,* 597–603. (7) doi: 10.3758/BF03196318

Wager, T. D., & Atlas, L. Y. (2013). How is pain influenced by cognition? Neuroimaging weighs in. *Perspectives on Psychological Science, 8,* 91–97. (3) doi: 10.1177/1745691612469631

Wager, T. D., Scott, D. J., & Zubieta, J.-K. (2007). Placebo effects on human μ-opioid activity during pain. *Proceedings of the National Academy of Sciences (U.S.A.), 104,* 11056–11061. (4) doi: 10.1073/pnas.0702413104

Wagner, A. D., Desmond, J. E., Demb, J. B., Glover, G. H., & Gabrieli, J. D. E. (1997). Semantic repetition priming for verbal and pictorial knowledge: A functional MRI study of left inferior prefrontal cortex. *Journal of Cognitive Neuroscience, 9,* 714–726. (3) doi: 10.1162/jocn.1997.9.6.714

Wai, J., & Putallaz, M. (2011). The Flynn effect puzzle: A 30-year examination from the right tail of the ability distribution provides some missing pieces. *Intelligence, 39,* 443–455. (9) doi: 10.1016/j.intell.2011.07.006

Wainright, J. L., Russell, S. T., & Patterson, C. J. (2004). Psychosocial adjustment, school outcomes, and romantic relationships of adolescents with same-sex parents. *Child Development, 75,* 1886–1898. (5) doi: 10.1111/j.1467-8624.2004.00823.x

Wald, G. (1968). Molecular basis of visual excitation. *Science, 162,* 230–239. (4) doi: 10.1126/science.162.3850.230

Waldinger, R. J., & Schulz, M. S. (2016). The long reach of nurturing family environments: Links with midlife emotion-regulatory styles and late-life security in intimate relationships. *Psychological Science, 27,* 1443–1450. (5) doi: 10.1177/0956797616661556

Waller, N. G., Kojetin, B. A., Bouchard, T. J., Jr., Lykken, D. T., & Tellegen, A. (1990). Genetic and environmental influences on religious interests, attitudes, and values: A study of twins reared apart and together. *Psychological Science, 1,* 138–142. (3) doi: 10.1111/j.1467-9280.1990.tb00083.x

Walsh, R., & Shapiro, S. L. (2006). The meeting of meditative disciplines and Western psychology. *American Psychologist, 61,* 227–239. (10) doi: 10.1037/0003-066X.61.3.227

Walster, E., Aronson, E., Abrahams, D., & Rottman, L. (1966). Importance of physical attractiveness in dating behavior. *Journal of Personality and Social Psychology, 4,* 508–516. (13) doi: 10.1037/h0021188

Walters, E. T. (2009). Chronic pain, memory, and injury: Evolutionary clues from snail and rat nociceptors. *International Journal of Comparative Psychology, 22,* 127–140. (4) https://escholarship.org/uc/item/9xz8q9r2

Walton, G. M., & Spencer, S. J. (2009). Latent ability. *Psychological Science, 20,* 1132–1139. (9) doi: 10.1111/j.1467-9280.2009.02417.x

Wampold, B. E., Mondin, G. W., Moody, M., Stich, F., Benson, K., & Ahn, H. (1997). A meta-analysis of outcome studies comparing bona fide psychotherapies: Empirically, "All must have prizes." *Psychological Bulletin, 122,* 203–215. (15) doi: 10.1037/0033-2909.122.3.203

Wan, L., Crookes, K., Dawel, A., Pidcock, M., Hall, A., & McKone, E. (2017). Face-blind for other-race faces: Individual differences in other-race recognition impairments. *Journal of Experimental Psychology: General, 146,* 102–122. (5) doi: 10.1037/xge0000249

Wandersman, A., & Florin, P. (2003). Community interventions and effective prevention.

American Psychologist, 58, 441–448. (15) doi: 10.1037/0003-066X.58.6-7.441

Wang, C., Jiang, Y., Ma, J., Wu, H., Wacker, D., Katritch, V., Han, G. W., Liu, W., Huang, X. P., Vardy, E., McCorvy, J. D., Gao, X., Zhou, X. E., Melcher, K., Zhang, C. H., Bai, F., Yang, H. Y., Yang, L. L., Jiang, H. L., … Xu, H. E. (2013). Structural basis for molecular recognition at serotonin receptors. *Science, 340,* 610–614. (3) doi: 10.1126/science.1232807

Wang, C.-H., Tsai, C. L., Tu, K.-C., Muggleton, N. G., Juan, C.-H., & Liang, W. K. (2015). Modulation of brain oscillations during fundamental visuo-spatial processing: A comparison between female collegiate badminton players and sedentary controls. *Psychology of Sport and Exercise, 16,* 121–129. (4) doi: 10.1016/j.psychsport.2014.10.003

Wang, D., Waldman, D. A., & Zhang, Z. (2014). A meta-analysis of shared leadership and team effectiveness. *Journal of Applied Psychology, 99,* 181–198. (11) doi: 10.1037/a0034531

Wang, M.-T., Eccles, J. S., & Kenny, S. (2013). Not lack of ability but more choice: Individual and gender differences in choice of careers in science, technology, engineering, and mathematics. *Psychological Science, 24,* 770–775. (5) doi: 10.1177/0956797612458937

Wang, X., Jiao, Y., & Li, L. (2017). Predicting clinical symptoms of attention deficit hyperactivity disorder based on temporal patterns between and within intrinsic connectivity networks. *Neuroscience, 362,* 60–69. (8) doi: 10.1016/j. neuroscience.2017.08.038

Wang, X., Jiao, Y., Tang, T., Wang, H., & Lu, Z. (2013). Altered regional homogeneity patterns in adults with attention-deficit hyperactivity disorder. *European Journal of Radiology, 82,* 1552–1557. (8) doi: 10.1016/j.ejrad.2013.04.009

Wardenaar, K. J., Lim, C. C. W., Al-Hamzawi, A. O., Alonso, J., Andrade, L. H., Benjet, C., Bunting, B., de Girolamo, G., Demyttenaere, K., Florescu, S. E., Gureje, O., Hisateru, T., Hu, C., Huang, Y., Karam, E., Kiejna, A., Lepine, J. P., Navarro-Mateu, F., Browne, M. O., & de Jonge, P. (2017). The cross-national epidemiology of specific phobia in the World Mental Health Surveys. *Psychological Medicine, 47,* 1744–1760. (15) doi: 10.1017/S0033291717000174

Warne, R. T., & Burningham, C. (2019). Spearman's *g* found in 31 non-Western nations: Strong evidence that *g* is a universal phenomenon. *Psychological Bulletin, 145,* 237–272. (9) doi: 10.1037/bul0000184

Warren, R. M. (1970). Perceptual restoration of missing speech sounds. *Science, 167,* 392–393. (4, 8) doi: 10.1126/science.167.3917.392

Warren, R. M. (1999). *Auditory perception.* Cambridge, England: Cambridge University Press. (4)

Washington, E. (2006). *Female socialization: How daughters affect their legislator fathers' voting on women's issues* (Working Paper No. 11924). Cambridge, MA: National Bureau of Economic Research. (2)

Wason, P. C. (1960). On the failure to eliminate hypotheses in a conceptual task. *Quarterly Journal of Experimental Psychology, 12,* 129–140. (8) doi: 10.1080/17470216008416717

Waterman, A. S. (2013). The humanistic psychology-positive psychology divide. *American Psychologist, 68,* 124–133. (14) doi: 10.1037/a0032168

Waters, E., Merrick, S., Treboux, D., Crowell, J., & Albersheim, L. (2000). Attachment security in infancy and early adulthood: A twenty-year

longitudinal study. *Child Development, 71,* 684–689. (5) doi: 10.1111/1467-8624.00176

Watrous, A. J., Tandon, N., Conner, C. R., Pieters, T., & Ekstrom, A. D. (2013). Frequency-specific network connectivity increases underlie accurate spatiotemporal memory retrieval. *Nature Neuroscience, 16,* 349–356. (7) doi: 10.1038/nn.3315

Watson, D., & Clark, L. A. (2006). Clinical diagnosis at the crossroads. *Clinical Psychology, 13,* 210–215. (15) doi: 10.1111/j.1468-2850.2006.00026.x

Watson, D., Wiese, D., Vaidya, J., & Tellegen, A. (1999). The two general activation systems of affect: Structural findings, evolutionary considerations, and psychobiological evidence. *Journal of Personality and Social Psychology, 76,* 820–838. (12) doi: 10.1037/0022-3514.76.5.820

Watson, J. B. (1913). Psychology as the behaviorist views it. *Psychological Review, 20,* 158–177. (6) doi: 10.1037/0033-295X.101.2.248

Watson, J. B. (1919). *Psychology from the standpoint of a behaviorist.* Philadelphia: Lippincott. (6)

Watson, J. B. (1925). *Behaviorism.* New York: W. W. Norton. (1, 6)

Watson, J. B., & Rayner, R. (1920). Conditioned emotional reactions. *Journal of Experimental Psychology, 3,* 1–14. (15) doi: 10.1037/h0069608

Watson, J. M., Balota, D. A., & Roediger, H. L., III (2003). Creating false memories with hybrid lists of semantic and phonological associates: Over-additive false memories produced by converging associative networks. *Journal of Memory and Language, 49,* 95–118. (7) doi: 10.1016/S0749-596X(03)00019-6

Watts, T. W., Duncan, G. J., & Quan, H. (2018). Revisiting the marshmallow test: A conceptual replication investigating links between early delay of gratification and later outcomes. *Psychological Science, 29,* 1159–1177. (11) doi: 10.1177/0956797618761661

Webster, A. A., & Carter, M. (2013). A descriptive examination of the types of relationships formed between children with developmental disability and their closest peers in inclusive school settings. *Journal of Intellectual & Developmental Disability, 38,* 1–11. (9) doi: 10.3109/13668250.2012.743650

Wegner, D. M. (2002). *The illusion of conscious will.* Cambridge, MA: MIT Press. (1, 10)

Wegner, D. M. (2009). How to think, say, or do precisely the worst thing for any occasion. *Science, 325,* 48–50. (13) doi: 10.1126/science.1167346

Wei, Y., Yang, C.-R., Wei, Y.-P., Zhao, Z.-A., Hou, Y., Schatten, H., & Sun, Q.-Y. (2014). Paternally induced transgenerational inheritance of susceptibility to diabetes in mammals. *Proceedings of the National Academy of Sciences, 111,* 1873–1878. (3) doi: 10.1073/pnas.1321195111

Weinberger, D. R. (1996). On the plausibility of "the neurodevelopmental hypothesis" of schizophrenia. *Neuropsychopharmacology, 14,* 1S–11S. (15) doi: 10.1016/0893-133X(95)00199-N

Weinberger, D. R. (1999). Cell biology of the hippocampal formation in schizophrenia. *Biological Psychiatry, 45,* 395–402. (15) doi: 10.1016/S0006-3223(98)00331-X

Weiskrantz, L., Warrington, E. K., Sanders, M. D., & Marshall, J. (1974). Visual capacity in the hemianopic field following a restricted occipital ablation. *Brain, 97,* 709–728. (3) doi: 10.1093/brain/97.1.709

Weissman, M. M., Leaf, P. J., & Bruce, M. L. (1987). Single parent women: A community study. *Social Psychiatry, 22,* 29–36. (5) doi: 10.1007/BF00583617

Weisz, J. R., Kuppens, S., Ng, M. Y., Vaugh-Coaxum, R. A., Ugueto, A. M., Eckshtain, D., & Corteselli, K. A. (2019). Are psychotherapies for young people growing stronger? Tracking trends over time for youth anxiety, depression, attention deficit/hyperactivity disorder, and conduct problems. *Perspectives on Psychological Science, 14,* 216–237. (15) doi: 10.1177/1745691618805436

Welchman, A. E., Stanley, J., Schomers, M. R., Miall, R. C., & Bülthoff, H. H. (2010). The quick and the dead: When reaction beats intention. *Proceedings of the Royal Society B, 277,* 1667–1674. (10) doi: 10.1098/rspb.2009.2123

Wellings, K., Field, J., Johnson, A., & Wadsworth, J. (1994). *Sexual behavior in Britain: The national survey of sexual attitudes and lifestyles.* New York: Penguin. (11)

Wellman, H. M., Cross, D., & Watson, J. (2001). Meta-analysis of theory-of-mind development: The truth about false beliefs. *Child Development, 72,* 655–684. (5) doi: 10.1111/1467-8624.00304

Wells, G. L., Malpass, R. S., Lindsay, R. C. L., Fisher, R. P., Turtle, J. W., & Fulero, S. M. (2000). From the lab to the police station. *American Psychologist, 55,* 581–598. (7) doi: 10.1037//0003-066X.55.6.581

Wells, G. L., Memon, A., & Penrod, S. D. (2006). Eyewitness evidence: Improving its probative value. *Psychological Science in the Public Interest, 7,* 45–75. (7) doi: 10.1111/j.1529-1006.2006.00027.x

Wells, G. L., Olson, E. A., & Charman, S. D. (2003). Distorted retrospective eyewitness reports as functions of feedback and delay. *Journal of Experimental Psychology: General, 9,* 42–52. (7) doi: 10.1037/1076-898X.9.1.42

Werker, J. F., & Tees, R. C. (2005). Speech perception as a window for understanding plasticity and commitment in language systems of the brain. *Developmental Psychobiology, 46,* 233–251. (8) doi: 10.1002/dev.20060

Wethington, E., Kessler, R. C., & Pixley, J. E. (2004). Turning points in adulthood. In O. G. Brim, C. D. Ryff, & R. C. Kessler (Eds.), *How healthy are we?* (pp. 586–613). Chicago, IL: University of Chicago Press. (5)

Wheeler, D. D. (1970). Processes in word recognition. *Cognitive Psychology, 1,* 59–85. (8) doi: 10.1016/0010-0285(70)90005-8

Wheeler, M. E., & Treisman, A. M. (2002). Binding in short-term visual memory. *Journal of Experimental Psychology: General, 131,* 48–64. (3) doi: 10.1037//0096-3445.131.1.48

Whisman, M. A., du Pont, A., & Butterworth, P. (2020). Longitudinal associations between rumination and depressive symptoms in a probability sample of adults. *Journal of Affective Disorders, 260,* 680–686. (14) doi: 10.1016/j.jad.2019.09.035

White, M. P., Alcock, I., Wheeler, B. W., & Depledge, M. H. (2013). Would you be happier living in a greener urban area? A fixed-effects analysis of panel data. *Psychological Science, 24,* 920–928. (12) doi: 10.1177/0956797612464659

White, S. J., Johnson, R. L., Liversedge, S. P., & Rayner, K. (2008). Eye movements when reading transposed text: The importance of word-beginning letters. *Journal of mental Psychology: Human Perception [Pe]rformance, 34*, 1261–1276. (8) doi: [1]7/0096-1523.34.5.1261

Whyte, S., Chan, H. F., & Torgler, B. (2018). Do men and women know what they want? Sex differences in online daters' educational preferences. *Psychological Science, 29*, 1370–1375. (13) doi: 10.1177/0956797618771081

Wichman, A. L., Rodgers, J. L., & MacCallum, R. C. (2006). A multilevel approach to the relationship between birth order and intelligence. *Personality and Social Psychology Bulletin, 32*, 117–127. (5) doi: 10.1177/0146167205279581

Widen, S. C., & Naab, P. (2012). Can an anger face also be scared? Malleability of facial expressions. *Emotion, 12*, 919–925. (12) doi: 10.1037/a0026119

Wilde, A., Chan, H.-N., Rahman, B., Meiser, B., Mitchell, P. B., Schofield, P. R., & Green, M. J. (2014). A meta-analysis of the risk of major affective disorder in relatives of individuals affected by major depressive disorder or bipolar disorder. *Journal of Affective Disorders, 158*, 37–47. (15) doi: 10.1016/j.jad.2014.01.014

Wilensky, A. E., Schafe, G. E., Kristensen, M. P., & LeDoux, J. E. (2006). Rethinking the fear circuit. *Journal of Neuroscience, 26*, 12387–12396. (12) doi: 10.1523/JNEUROSCI.4316-06.2006

Wilkins, L., & Richter, C. P. (1940). A great craving for salt by a child with corticoadrenal insufficiency. *Journal of the American Medical Association, 114*, 866–868. (1) doi: 10.1001/jama.1940.62810100001011

Wilkins, V. M., & Wenger, J. B. (2014). Belief in a just world and attitudes toward affirmative action. *Policy Studies Journal, 42*, 325–343. (14) doi: 10.1111/psj.12063

Wilkowski, B. M., Ferguson, E. L., Williamson, L. Z., & Lappi, S. K. (2018). (How) does initial self-control undermine later self-control in daily life? *Personality and Social Psychology Bulletin, 44*, 1315–1329. (11) doi: 10.1177/0146167218766857

Williams, C. L., Barnett, A. M., & Meck, W. H. (1990). Organizational effects of early gonadal secretions on sexual differentiation in spatial memory. *Behavioral Neuroscience, 104*, 84–97. (5) doi: 10.1037/0735-7044.104.1.84

Williams, K. D., & Karau, S. J. (1991). Social loafing and social compensation: The effects of expectations of coworker performance. *Journal of Personality and Social Psychology, 61*, 570–581. (13) doi: 10.1037/0022-3514.61.4.570

Williams, L. M. (1994). Recall of childhood trauma: A prospective study of women's memories of child sexual abuse. *Journal of Consulting and Clinical Psychology, 61*, 1167–1176. (7) doi: 10.1037/0022-006X.62.6.1167

Williams, R. L. (2013). Overview of the Flynn effect. *Intelligence, 41*, 753–764. (9) doi: 10.1016/j.intell.2013.04.010

Williams, R. W., & Herrup, K. (1988). The control of neuron number. *Annual Review of Neuroscience, 11*, 423–453. (3) doi: 10.1146/annurev.neuro.11.1.423

Williamson, D. A., Ravussin, E., Wong, M.-L., Wagner, A., DiPaoli, A., Caglayan, S., Ozata, M., Martin, C., Walden, H., Arnett, C., & Licinio, J. (2005). Microanalysis of eating behavior of three leptin deficient adults treated with leptin therapy. *Appetite, 45*, 75–80. (11) doi: 10.1016/j.appet.2005.01.002

Willuhn, I., Burgeno, L. M., Groblewski, P. A., & Phillips, P. E. M. (2014). Excessive cocaine

use results from decreased phasic dopamine signaling in the striatum. *Nature Neuroscience, 17*, 704–709. (15) doi: 10.1038/nn.3694

Wilson, T. D., Reinhard, D. A., Westgate, E. C., Gilbert, D. T., Ellerbeck, N., Hahn, C., Brown, C. L., & Shaked, A. (2014). Just think: The challenges of the disengaged mind. *Science, 345*, 75–77. (11) doi: 10.1126/science.1250830

Wilson, J. R., & the editors of *Life*. (1964). *The mind.* New York: Time. (4)

Wilson, R. I., & Nicoll, R. A. (2002). Endocannabinoid signaling in the brain. *Science, 296*, 678–682. (3) doi: 10.1126/science.1063545

Wilson-Mendenhall, C. D., Barrett, L. F., & Barsalou, L. W. (2013). Neural evidence that human emotions share core affective properties. *Psychological Science, 24*, 947–956. (12) doi: 10.1177/0956797612464242

Wimmer, H., & Perner, J. (1983). Beliefs about beliefs: Representation and constraining function of wrong beliefs in young children's understanding of deception. *Cognition, 13*, 103–128. (5) doi: 10.1016/0010-0277(83)90004-5

Winer, G. A., & Cottrell, J. E. (1996). Does anything leave the eye when we see? Extramission beliefs of children and adults. *Current Directions in Psychological Science, 5*, 137–142. (4) doi: 10.1111/1467-8721.ep11512346

Winer, G. A., Cottrell, J. E., Gregg, V., Fournier, J. S., & Bica, L. A. (2002). Fundamentally misunderstanding visual perception: Adults' belief in visual emissions. *American Psychologist, 57*, 417–424. (4) doi: 10.1037//0003-066X.57.6-7.417

Winkler, A., & Hermann, C. (2019). Placebo- and nocebo-effects in cognitive neuroenhancement: When expectation shapes perception. *Frontiers in Psychiatry, 10*, article 498. (8) doi: 10.3389/fpsyt.2019.00498

Winner, E. (1986, August). Where pelicans kiss seals. *Psychology Today*, 24–35. (5) http://my.ilstu.edu/~eostewa/ART309/ART309%20READINGS/Pelicans.pdf

Winner, E. (2000). Giftedness: Current theory and research. *Current Directions in Psychological Science, 9*, 153–156. (9) doi: 10.1111/1467-8721.00082

Winocur, G., & Hasher, L. (1999). Aging and time-of-day effects on cognition in rats. *Behavioral Neuroscience, 113*, 991–997. (10) doi: 10.1037/0735-7044.113.5.991

Winocur, G., & Hasher, L. (2004). Age and time-of-day effects on learning and memory in a non-matching-to-sample test. *Neurobiology of Aging, 25*, 1107–1115. (10) doi: 10.1016/j.neurobiolaging.2003.10.005

Winocur, G., Moscovitch, M., & Sekeres, M. (2007). Memory consolidation or transformation: Context manipulation and hippocampal representations of memory. *Nature Neuroscience, 10*, 555–557. (7) doi: 10.1038/nn1880

Wirz-Justice, A., Ajdacic, V., Rossler, W., Steinhausen, H. C., & Angst, J. (2019). Prevalence of seasonal depression in a prospective cohort study. *European Archives of Psychiatry and Clinical Neuroscience, 269*, 833–839. (15) doi: 10.1007/s00406-018-0921-3

Witkiewitz, K., & Marlatt, G. A. (2004). Relapse prevention for alcohol and drug problems: That was Zen, this is Tao. *American Psychologist, 59*, 224–235. (15) doi: 10.1037/0003-066X.59.4.224

Witt, J. K., Linkenauger, S. A., & Proffitt, D. R. (2012). Get me out of this slump! Visual

illusions improve sports performance. *Psychological Science, 23*, 397–399. (4) doi: 10.1177/0956797611428810

Witthoft, N., & Winawer, J. (2013). Learning, memory, and synesthesia. *Psychological Science, 24*, 258–263. (4) doi: 10.1177/0956797612452573

Woelfer, M., Kasties, V., Kahlfuss, S., & Walter, M. (2019). The role of depressive subtypes within the neuroinflammation hypothesis of major depressive disorder. *Neuroscience, 403*, 93–110. (15) doi: 10.1016/j.neuroscience.2018.03.034

Wojcik, S. P., Hovasapian, A., Graham, J., Motyl, M., & Ditto, P. H. (2015). Conservatives report, but liberals display, greater happiness. *Science, 347*, 1243–1246. (2) doi: 10.1126/science.1260817

Wolfe, J. M., Horowitz, T. S., & Kenner, N. M. (2005). Rare items often missed in visual searches. *Nature, 435*, 439–440. (4) doi: 10.1038/435439a

Wolman, B. B. (1989). *Dictionary of behavioral science* (2nd ed.). San Diego, CA: Academic Press. (9)

Wolpe, J. (1961). The systematic desensitization treatment of neuroses. *Journal of Nervous and Mental Disease, 132*, 189–203. (15) doi: 10.1097/00005053-196103000-00001

Wolraich, M. L., Lindgren, S. D., Stumbo, P. J., Stegink, L. D., Appelbaum, M. I., & Kiritsy, M. C. (1994). Effects of diets high in sucrose or aspartame on the behavior and cognitive performance of children. *New England Journal of Medicine, 330*, 301–307. (2) doi: 10.1056/NEJM199402033300501

Wong, Y. K., & Wong, A. C. N. (2014). Absolute pitch memory: Its prevalence among musicians and dependence on the testing context. *Psychonomic Bulletin & Review, 21*, 534–542. (4) doi: 10.3758/s13423-013-0487-z

Wood, J. M., Nezworski, T., Lilienfeld, S. O., & Garb, H. N. (2003). *What's wrong with the Rorschach?* San Francisco, CA: Jossey-Bass. (14)

Wood, M. J., Douglas, K. M., & Sutton, R. M. (2012). Dead and alive: Beliefs in contradictory conspiracy theories. *Social Psychological and Personality Science, 3*, 767–773. (8) doi: 10.1177/1948550611434786

Wood, S., Hanoch, Y., Barnes, A., Liu, P.-J., Cummings, J., Bhattacharya, C., & Rice, T. (2011). Numeracy and Medicare Part D: The importance of choice and literacy for numbers in optimizing decision making for Medicare's prescription drug program. *Psychology & Aging, 26*, 295–307. (8) doi: 10.1037/a0022028

Wood, W., & Eagly, A. H. (2002). A cross-cultural model of the behavior of women and men: Implications for the origins of sex differences. *Psychological Bulletin, 128*, 699–727. (5) doi: 10.1037//0033-2909.128.5.699

Wood, W., Lundgren, S., Ouellette, J. A., Busceme, S., & Blackstone, T. (1994). Minority influence: A meta-analytic review of social influence processes. *Psychological Bulletin, 115*, 323–345. (13) doi: 10.1037/0033-2909.115.3.323

Wood, W., & Quinn, J. M. (2003). Forewarned and forearmed? Two meta-analytic syntheses of forewarnings of influence appeals. *Psychological Bulletin, 129*, 119–138. (13) doi: 10.1037//0033-2909.129.1.119

Woods, J. H., & Winger, G. (1997). Abuse liability of flunitrazepam. *Journal of Clinical Psychopharmacology, 17*(Suppl. 3), S1–S57. (3) doi: 10.1097/00004714-199706001-00001

Woolley, A. W., Chabris, C. F., Pentland, A., Hashmi, N., & Malone, T. W. (2010). Evidence for a collective intelligence factor in the performance of human groups. *Science, 330*, 686–688. (13) doi: 10.1126/science.1193147

Worthington, E. L., Jr., Kurusu, T. A., McCullough, M. E., & Sandage, S. J. (1996). Empirical research on religion and psychotherapeutic processes and outcomes: A 10-year review and research prospectus. *Psychological Bulletin, 119*, 448–487. (15) doi: 10.1037/0033-2909.119.3.448

Worthman, C. M., & Trang, K. (2018). Dynamics of body time, social time and life history at adolescence. *Nature, 554*, 451–455. (5) doi: 10.1038/nature25750

Woychyshyn, C. A., McElheran, W. G., & Romney, D. M. (1992). MMPI validity measures: A comparative study of original with alternative indices. *Journal of Personality Assessment, 58*, 138–148. (14) doi: 10.1207/s15327752jpa5801_13

Wright, L. (1994). *Remembering Satan.* New York: Knopf. (7)

Writing Group for the Women's Health Initiative Investigators. (2002). Risks and benefits of estrogen plus progestin in healthy postmenopausal women. *Journal of the American Medical Association, 288*, 321–333. (2) doi: 10.1001/jama.288.3.321

Wu, K., Lindsted, K. D., Tsai, S.-Y., & Lee, J. W. (2008). Chinese NEO-PI-R in Taiwanese adolescents. *Personality and Individual Differences, 44*, 656–667. (14) doi: 10.1016/j.paid.2007.09.025

Wu, Y. Y., Stillwell, D., Schwartz, H. A., & Kosinski, M. (2017). Birds of a feather do flock together: Behavior-based personality-assessment method reveals personality similarity among couples and friends. *Psychological Science, 28*, 276–284. (13) doi: 10.1177/0956797616678187

Wulff, K., Gatti, S., Wettstein, J. G., & Foster, R. G. (2010). Sleep and circadian rhythm disruption in psychiatric and neurodegenerative disease. *Nature Reviews Neuroscience, 11*, 589–599. (10) doi: 10.1038/nrn2868

Wundt, W. (1896/1902). *Outlines of psychology* (C. H. Judd, Trans.). New York: Gustav Sechert. (Original work published 1896) (1)

Wundt, W. (1862/1961). Contributions to the theory of sensory perception. In T. Shipley (Ed.), *Classics in psychology* (pp. 51–78). New York: Philosophical Library. (Original work published 1862) (1)

Wyart, C., Webster, W. W., Chen, J. H., Wilson, S. R., McClary, A., Khan, R. M., & Sobel, N. (2007). Smelling a single component of male sweat alters levels of cortisol in women. *Journal of Neuroscience, 27*, 1261–1265. (4) doi: 10.1523/JNEUROSCI.4430-06.2007

Wynn, K., Bloom, P., Jordan, A., Marshall, J., & Sheskin, M. (2018). Not soble savages after all: Limits to early altruism. *Current Directions in Psychological Science, 27*, 3–8. (13) doi: 10.1177/0963721417734875

Xiang, C., Liu, S., Fan, Y., Wang, X., Jia, Y., Li, L., Cong, S. Y., & Han, F. (2019). Single nucleotide polymorphisms, variable number tandem repeats and allele influence on serotonergic enzyme modulation for aggressive and suicidal behavior. *Pharmacology Biochemistry and Behavior, 180*, 74–82. (13) doi: 10.1016/j.pbb.2019.03.008

Xie, J., & Padoa-Schioppa, C. (2016). Neuronal remapping and circuit persistence in economic decisions. *Nature Neuroscience, 19*, 855–861. (3) doi: 10.1038/nn.4300

Xu, A. J., & Wyer, R. S., Jr. (2008). The comparative mind set. *Psychological Science, 19*, 859–864. (11) doi: 10.1111/j.1467-9280.2008.02169.x

Yaakobi, E., Mikulincer, M., & Shaver, P. R. (2014). Parenthood as a terror management mechanism: The moderating role of attachment orientations. *Personality and Social Psychology Bulletin, 40*, 762–774. (5) doi: 10.1177/0146167214525473

Yamada, T., Yang, Y., Valnegri, P., Juric, I., Abnousi, A., Markwalter, K. H., … Bonni, A. (2019). Sensory experience remodels genome architecture in neural circuit to drive motor learning. *Nature, 569*, 708–713. (3) doi: 10.1038/s41586-019-1190-7

Yamagata, S., Suzuki, A., Ando, J., Ono, Y., Kijima, N., Yoshimura, K., Ostendorf, F., Angleitner, A., Riemann, R., Spinath, F. M., Livesley, W. J., & Jang, K. L. (2006). Is the genetic structure of human personality universal? A cross-cultural twin study from North America, Europe, and Asia. *Journal of Personality and Social Psychology, 90*, 987–998. (14) doi: 10.1037/0022-3514.90.6.987

Yang, K.-S. (2003). Beyond Maslow's culture-bound linear theory: A preliminary statement of the double-Y model of basic human needs. *Nebraska Symposium on Motivation, 49*, 175–255. (11)

Yeatts, P. E., Martin, S. B., & Petrie, T. A. (2017). Physical fitness as a moderator of neuroticism and depression in adolescent boys and girls. *Personality and Individual Differences, 114*, 30–35. (15) doi: 10.1016/j.paid.2017.03.040

Yeh, V. M., Schnur, J. B., & Montgomery, G. H. (2014). Disseminating hypnosis to health care settings: Applying the RE-AIM framework. *Psychology of Consciousness, 1*, 213–228. (10) https://pubmed.ncbi.nlm.nih.gov/25267941/

Yehuda, R. (1997). Sensitization of the hypothalamic-pituitary-adrenal axis in posttraumatic stress disorder. *Annals of the New York Academy of Sciences, 821*, 57–75. (12) doi: 10.1111/j.1749-6632.1997.tb48269.x

Yeomans, M. R., Tepper, B. J., Rietzschel, J., & Prescott, J. (2007). Human hedonic responses to sweetness: Role of taste genetics and anatomy. *Physiology & Behavior, 91*, 264–273. (1) doi: 10.1016/j.physbeh.2007.03.011

Yeonan-Kim, J., & Francis, G. (2019). Retinal spatiotemporal dynamics on emergence of visual persistence and afterimages. *Psychological Review, 126*, 374–394. (7) doi: 10.1037/rev0000141

Yik, M., Russell, J. A., & Steiger, J. H. (2011). A 12-point circumplex structure of core affect. *Emotion, 11*, 705–731. (12) doi: 10.1037/a0023980

Ying, Y.-W., Han, M., & Wong, S. L. (2008). Cultural orientation in Asian American adolescents: Variation by age and ethnic density. *Youth and Society, 39*, 507–523. (5) doi: 10.1177/0044118X06296683

Yoder, A. M., Widen, S. C., & Russell, J. A. (2016). The word *disgust* may refer to more than one emotion. *Emotion, 16*, 301–308. (12) doi: 10.1037/emo0000118

Yolken, R. H., Dickerson, F. B., & Torrey, E. F. (2009). Toxoplasma and schizophrenia. *Parasite Immunology, 31*, 706–715. (15) doi: 10.1111/j.1365-3024.2009.01131.x

Yoo, S.-S., Hu, P. T., Gujar, N., Jolesz, F. A., & Walker, M. P. (2007). A deficit in the ability to form new human memories without sleep. *Nature Neuroscience, 10*, 385–392. (10) doi: 10.1038/nn1851

Yoon, K. L., Hong, S. W., Joormann, J., & Kang, P. (2009). Perception of facial expressions of emotion during binocular rivalry. *Emotion, 9*, 172–182. (12) doi: 10.1037/a0014714

Yu, C. K.-C. (2008). Typical dreams experienced by Chinese people. *Dreaming, 18*, 1–10. (10) doi: 10.1037/1053-0797.18.1.1

Yu, X., Sonuga-Barke, E., & Liu, X. (2018). Preference for smaller sooner over larger later rewards in ADHD: Contribution of delay duration and paradigm type. *Journal of Attention Disorders, 22*, 984–993. (8) doi: 10.1177/1087054715570390

Yuen, R. K. C., Merico, D., Bookman, M., Howe, J. L., Thiruvahindrapuram, B., Patel, R. V., Whitney, J., Deflaux, N., Bingham, J., Wang, Z. Z., Pellecchia, G., Buchanan, J. A., Walker, S., Marshall, C. R., Uddin, M., Zarrei, M., Deneault, E., D'Abate, L., Chan, A. J. S., … Scherer, S. W. (2017). Whole genome sequencing resource identifies 18 new candidate genes for autism spectrum disorder. *Nature Neuroscience, 20*, 602–611. (15) doi: 10.1038/nn.4524

Yuval-Greenberg, S., & Heeger, D. J. (2013). Continuous flash suppression modulates cortical activity in early visual cortex. *Journal of Neuroscience, 33*, 9635–9643. (10) doi: 10.1523/JNEUROSCI.4612-12.2013

Zaccaro, S. J. (2007). Trait-based perspectives of leadership. *American Psychologist, 62*, 6–16. (11) doi: 10.1037/0003-066X.62.1.6

Zachar, P., First, M. B., & Kendler, K. S. (2017). The bereavement exclusion debate in the *DSM-5*: A history. *Clinical Psychological Science, 5*, 890–906. (15) doi: 10.1177/2167702617711284

Zadra, A., Desautels, A., Petit, D., & Montplaisir, J. (2013). Somnambulism: Clinical aspects and pathophysiological hypotheses. *Lancet Neurology, 12*, 285–294. (10) doi: 10.1016/S1474-4422(12)70322-8

Zahavi, A., & Zahavi, A. (1997). *The handicap principle.* New York: Oxford University Press. (13)

Zajonc, R. B. (1968). Attitudinal effects of mere exposure. *Journal of Personality and Social Psychology, 9* (Monograph Suppl. 2, Pt. 2). (13) doi: 10.1037/h0025848

Zaleskiewicz, T., Gasiorowska, A., & Kesebir, P. (2013). Saving can save from death anxiety: Mortality salience and financial decision-making. *PLoS One, 8*, e79407. (5) doi: 10.1371/journal.pone.0079407

Zaragoza, M. S., Payment, K. E., Ackil, J. K., Drivdahl, S. B., & Beck, M. (2001). Interviewing witnesses: Forced confabulation and confirmatory feedback increase false memories. *Psychological Science, 12*, 473–477. (7) doi: 10.1111/1467-9280.00388

Zarkadi, T., Wade, K. A., & Stewart, N. (2009). Creating fair lineups for suspects with distinctive features. *Psychological Science, 20*, 1448–1453. (7) doi: 10.1111/j.1467-9280.2009.02463.x

Zehr, D. (2000). Portrayals of Wundt and Titchener in introductory psychology texts: A content analysis. *Teaching of Psychology, 27*, 122–126. (1)

Zeigler-Hill, V., Enjaian, B., Holden, C. J., & Southard, A. C. (2014). Using self-esteem instability to disentangle the connection between self-esteem level and perceived

...ssion. *Journal of Research in Personality*, ...–51. (13) doi: 10.1016/j.jrp.2014.01.003

..., J. M., Santoro, M. S., & Whalen, D. C. (2012). Would introverts be better off if they acted more like extraverts? Exploring emotional and cognitive consequences of counterdispositional behavior. *Emotion, 12*, 290–303. (14) doi: 10.1037/a0025169

Zell, E., Krizan, Z., & Teeter, S. R. (2015). Evaluating gender similarities and differences using metasynthesis. *American Psychologist, 70*, 10–20. (5) doi: 10.1037/a0038208

Zentner, M., & Mitura, K. (2012). Stepping out of the caveman's shadow: Nations gender gap predicts degree of sex differentiation in mate preferences. *Psychological Science, 23*, 1176–1185. (3) doi: 10.1177/0956797612441004

Zepelin, H., & Rechtschaffen, A. (1974). Mammalian sleep, longevity, and energy metabolism. *Brain, Behavior, and Evolution, 10*, 425–470. (10) doi: 10.1159/000124330

Zerwas, S., Lund, B. C., Von Holle, A., Thornton, L. M., Berrettini, W. H., Brandt, H., Crawford, S., Fichter, M. M., Halmi, K. A., Johnson, C., Kaplan, A. S., La Via, M., Mitchell, J., Rotondo, A., Strober, M., Woodside, D. B., Kaye, W. H., & Bulik. C. M. (2013). Factors associated with recovery from anorexia nervosa. *Journal of Psychiatric Research, 47*, 972–979. (11) doi: 10.1016/j.jpsychires.2013.02.011

Zhang, N., Ji, L.-J., Bai, B., & Li, Y. (2018). Culturally divergent consequences of receiving thanks in close relationships. *Emotion, 18*, 46–57. (5) doi: 10.1037/emo0000385

Zhang, T., Kim, T., Brooks, A. W., Gino, F., & Norton, M. I. (2014). A "present" for the future: The unexpected value of rediscovery. *Psychological Science, 25*, 1851–1860. (12) doi: 10.1177/0956797614542274

Zhang, X., & Firestein, S. (2002). The olfactory receptor gene superfamily of the mouse. *Nature Neuroscience, 5*, 124–133. (4) doi: 10.1038/nn800

Zheng, Y., Plomin, R., & von Stumm, S. (2016). Heritability of intraindividual mean and variability of positive and negative affect: Genetic analysis of daily affect ratings over a month. *Psychological Science, 27*, 1611–1619. (12) doi: 10.1177/0956797616669994

Zhou, W., & Chen, D. (2009). Fear-related chemosignals modulate recognition of fear in ambiguous facial expressions. *Psychological Science, 20*, 177–183. (12) doi: 10.1111/j.1467-9280.2009.02263.x

Zhu, C., Zhang, X., Zhao, Q., & Chen, Q. (2018). Hybrid marriages and phenotypic heterosis in offspring: Evidence from China. *Economics & Human Biology, 29*, 102–114. (9) doi: 10.1016/j.ehb.2018.02.008

Zhu, D. H. (2014). Group polarization in board decisions about CEO compensation. *Organization Science, 25*, 552–571. (13) doi: 10.1287/orsc.2013.0848

Zhu, X., Dalal, D. K., & Hwang, T. (2017). Is maximizing a bad thing? *Journal of Individual Differences, 38*, 94–101. (8) doi: 10.1027/1614-0001/a000226

Zihl, J., von Cramon, D., & Mai, N. (1983). Selective disturbance of movement vision after bilateral brain damage. *Brain, 106*, 313–340. (3) doi: 10.1093/brain/106.2.313

Zimbardo, P. G. (2007). *The Lucifer effect: Understanding how good people turn evil.* New York, NY: Random House. (13)

Zimmerman, M. (2019). Severity and the treatment of depression: A review of two controversies. *Journal of Nervous and Mental Disease, 207*, 219–223. (15) doi: 10.1097/NMD.0000000000000960

Zocchi, D., Wennemuth, G., & Oka, Y. (2017). The cellular mechanism for water detection in the mammalian taste system. *Nature Neuroscience, 20*, 927–933. (4) doi: 10.1038/nn.4575

Zoëga, H., Valdimarsdóttir, U. A., & Hernández-Díaz, S. (2012). Age, academic performance, and stimulant prescribing for ADHD: A nationwide cohort study. *Pediatrics, 130*, 1012–1018. (8) doi: 10.1542/peds.2012-0689

Zolotor, A. J., & Puzia, M. E. (2010). Bans against corporal punishment: A systematic review of the laws, changes in attitudes and behaviours. *Child Abuse Review, 19*, 229–247. (6) doi: 10.1002/car.1131

Zuckerman, M., Li, C., & Hall, J. A. (2016). When men and women differ in self-esteem and when they don't: A meta-analysis. *Journal of Research in Personality, 64*, 34–51. (14) doi: 10.1016/j.jrp.2016.07.007

Zuriff, G. E. (1995). Continuity over change within the experimental analysis of behavior. In J. T. Todd & E. K. Morris (Eds.), *Modern perspectives on B. F. Skinner and contemporary behaviorism* (pp. 171–178). Westport, CT: Greenwood Press. (6)

structure that
is the nucleus of
, 55, *84*

Central nervous system
brain and spinal cord,
69, *69*

Central route to persuasion
attitude change that
requires investing
enough time and effort
to evaluate the evidence
and reason logically
about a decision, 424

Cerebellum (Latin for
"little brain") part of the
hindbrain, 69, 77

Cerebral cortex outer
covering of the forebrain
frontal lobe, 72–73
illustrations of, *69, 70*
occipital lobe, 70
parietal lobe, 72
temporal lobe, 71–72

Chaining reinforcing
one behavior with the
opportunity to engage
in the next one, *196,*
196–197

Change blindness failure to
detect changes in parts of
a scene, 249

Chemical senses
smell, 116–118
synesthesia, 118–119
taste, 115–116

Childhood. *See also*
Cognitive development
in infancy and
childhood; Infancy
amnesia, 240–241
exposure to no language
or two languages, 272
language in, 271–272
social development,
161–163

Children as eyewitnesses,
215

Chimpanzees, 269–270,
269–270

Chlorpromazine, 507

Choice blindness tendency
of people to act as if they
don't know what choice
they have made, 245, *245*

Choice-delay task
procedure offering a
choice between a small
reward now and a bigger
delayed reward later, 250

Chomsky, Noam, 268, 270

Chromosomes strands of
hereditary material, 84,
84, 85, 88

Chronic traumatic
encephalopathy (CTE),
478

Chunking storing
information in short-
term memory by
grouping items into
meaningful sequences or
clusters, 217

Cialdini, Robert, 424

Cigarette smoking, 64

Ciliary muscle, 98

Circadian rhythm rhythm
of activity and inactivity
lasting about a day,
315–318, *316*

Circumplex model theory
that emotions range

along a continuum
from pleasure to misery
and along another
continuum from arousal
to sleepiness, 379, *379*

Classical conditioning (or
Pavlovian conditioning)
process by which an
organism learns a new
association between
two stimuli—a neutral
stimulus and one that
already evokes a reflexive
response, 182–186
behaviorism, 179
definition of, 180
drug tolerance, 186–187
examples of, 182
explanations of, 184–186
operant conditioning
vs., 195
Pavlov and, 180–184

Clever Hans, 27–28

Climax, 359

Clinical psychologists those
who have an advanced
degree in psychology
with a specialty in
helping people with
psychological problems,
6, 7, *12*

Clinical social worker
specialist who does
work similar to a clinical
psychologist but with
different training, 7

Closure phenomenon that
we imagine the rest of
an interrupted familiar
figure, 127, *127*

Cocaine, 63, *67*

Cochlea fluid-filled canals
of the snail-shaped
organ that contains the
receptors for hearing,
108–109, *109*

Codeine, 65

Coercive persuasion, 428,
428

Cognition thinking and
using knowledge
attention, 246–249
attention and
categorization, 245–253
categorizing, 250–252
common errors in,
259–261
definition of, 9, 245
problem solving and
decision making, 255–
264
research in, 245–246

**Cognitive-behavior
therapy** treatment in
which therapists set
explicit behavioral goals,
but also try to change
people's interpretation of
situations, 515, *517*

Cognitive development in
infancy and childhood
concrete operations and
formal operations stages,
147–148, 154–156, *155*
fetus and newborns,
143–144
infancy, 144–147
Piaget's view of, 147–148
preoperational stage,
148, 150–154, *155*
research designs for

studying development,
141–142, *142*
sensorimotor stage,
148–149, *155*
summary of stages of
development, *155*

Cognitive dissonance state
of unpleasant tension
that people experience
when they hold
contradictory attitudes
or when their behavior
contradicts their stated
attitudes, *423,* 423–424

Cognitive psychologist
one who studies the
processes of thought and
knowledge, 9–10, *12*

Cognitive therapy treatment
that seeks to improve
psychological well-being
by changing people's
interpretation of events,
502, 514–515, 517, *517*

Cohort effects, 142, *143,* 358

Cohort group of people
born at a particular
time or who enter
an organization at a
particular time, 142

Collective unconscious
hypothesized residue
of the cumulative
experience of preceding
generations, 452

Collectivist cultures, 170, 438

Color-blindness. *See* Color
vision, deficiency

Color constancy tendency
of an object to appear
nearly the same color
under a variety of lighting
conditions, 104

Color vision
deficiency, 105, *105*
opponent-process
theory, 103
retinex theory, 104–105
trichromatic theory, *102,*
102–103

Coma condition caused by
traumatic brain damage,
in which the brain shows
a steady but low level of
activity and no response
to any stimulus, 310

Common fate tendency
to perceive objects as
part of the same group if
they change or move in
similar ways at the same
time, 128

Communist Manifesto
(Marx), 404

Community psychologist one
who tries to help people
change their environment,
both to prevent disorders
and to promote a positive
sense of mental well-
being, *12,* 518

Companionate love type of
love marked by sharing,
care, and protection, 435

Comparative psychologist
specialist who compares
different animal species,
18

Compulsion repetitive,
almost irresistible urge to
an action, 490–491

Conceptual networks,
251–252

Concrete operations. *See*
**Stage of concrete
operations**

Conditional positive regard,
455

Conditioned reflex, 180

Conditioned response (CR)
whatever response the
conditioned stimulus
elicits as a result of the
conditioning procedure,
180–181, *181,* 184–185

Conditioned stimulus (CS)
stimulus that elicits a
new response because of
the preceding conditions,
180–181, *181, 184,* 184–
185, *185,* 514, *514*

Conditioned taste aversion
type of learning that
associates a food with
illness, 201–203, *202, 203*

Condoms, *358*

Conduction deafness
hearing loss that
occurs when the bones
connected to the
eardrum fail to transmit
sound waves properly to
the cochlea, 109

Cones visual receptors
adapted for perceiving
color and detail in bright
light, *98,* 98–99, *99, 100*

Confabulations attempts of
patients with prefrontal
cortex damage to fill
in the gaps in their
memory, 239

Confidence intervals, 45

Confirmation bias tendency
to seek evidence to
support a favored
hypothesis instead
of considering other
possibilities, 259–260

Conformity altering one's
behavior to match other
people's behavior or
expectations, 436–438,
437

Conscientiousness
tendency to show
self-discipline, to be
dutiful, and to strive
for achievement and
competence, 461, *461*

Conscious processes,
307–313

Consciousness subjective
experience of perceiving
oneself and one's
surroundings
and action, 311–313
as a construction,
309–310
brain activity, 308–310
brain activity
measurement methods,
308
conscious and
unconscious processes,
307–313
definition of, 307
hypnosis, 328–333
measurement of, 307–308
measurement of the time
of a conscious decision,
312–313

mind-brain problem, 5
other states of, 343
purpose of, 313
sleep and dreams, 315–325
use of brain
measurements, 310–311

Consensus, 417

Consensus information
knowledge about how
someone's behavior
compares with other
people's behavior, 417

Conservation idea that
objects conserve such
properties as number,
length, volume, area, and
mass after changes in the
shape or arrangement of
the objects, 152–154,
153–154, 155

Consistency, 417

Consistency information
knowledge about how
someone's behavior
varies from one time to
the next, 417

Consolidation conversion of
short-term memory into
a long-term memory, 219

Conspiracy thinking,
261–262

Constancies, 129

Contempt reaction to a
violation of community
standards, 387

Context, *126*

Contingency management,
497

Continuation perceptual
filling in of the gaps when
lines are interrupted,
127, *127*

Continuous reinforcement
providing reinforcement
for every correct
response, 197, *197*

Contrast, 104

Contrast effects, 425

Control group individuals
treated in the same way
as the experimental
group except for the
procedure that the
experiment is designed
to test, 40, 42

Convenience sample group
chosen because of its
ease of study, 34, *35*

Convergence degree to
which the eyes turn in to
focus on a close object,
131

Cooperation, 406–407

Coping by reappraisal,
398–399

Copy number variant
deletion or duplication
of a small part of a
chromosome, 506

Corn, *90*

Cornea rigid transparent
structure on the surface
of the eyeball, *98, 98*

Corpus callosum axons
that connect the left and
right hemispheres of the
cerebral cortex, *69,* 74,
74, 85

Correlation measurement of
the relationship between
two variables

strategies for ...ying a problem ...nerating a ...satisfactory guess, 256

Hierarchy of needs system in which the most insistent needs take priority over less urgent ones, 339, *339*

Hindsight bias tendency to mold a recollection of the past to fit how events later turned out, 230

Hippocampus structure in the interior of the temporal lobe, 71, *238*, 238–239

Histamine, *61*

Histone tail, 85

Histones, 85, *86*

HIV (human immunodeficiency virus), 358

Hobbes, Thomas, *447*

Homeostasis maintenance of an optimum level of biological conditions within an organism, 338, *338*

Homosexuality. *See* Sexual orientation

Hormones chemicals released by glands and conveyed by the blood to alter activity in various organs throughout the body, 77, *79*

Horney, Karen, 452

Huichol tribe, *64*

Human factors specialist (or **ergonomist**) one who tries to facilitate the operation of machinery so that people can use it efficiently and safely, 8, *12*

Human-relations approach idea about job design, also known as *Theory Y*, that says employees like variety in their job, a sense of accomplishment, and a sense of responsibility, 344

Humanistic psychology field that deals with consciousness, values, and abstract beliefs, including spiritual experiences and beliefs that people live and die for, 454–456

Humanistic therapy, 515

Hume, David, *16*

Hunger motivation

brain mechanisms, 350

overeating and undereating, 351–354

physiology of hunger and satiety, 348–350

social influences on eating, 350–351

Hybrid vigor, 296

Hypermnesia gain of memory recall over time, 228

Hyperopia, *99*

Hypersomnolence disorder, 483

Hyperventilation rapid deep breathing, 486

Hypnosis condition of focused attention and increased suggestibility that occurs in the context of a special hypnotist-subject relationship, *16*

as an altered state of consciousness, 332–333

introduction to, 328

and memory, 330–331, *331*

and the brain, 329–330

uses and limitations of, 329–332

ways of inducing, 328–329

Hypoactive sexual desire disorder, 483

Hypochondria, *468*

Hypomania, *468, 504*

Hypothalamus brain structure just below the thalamus, important for hunger, thirst, temperature regulation, sex, and other motivated behaviors

definition of, 77

hormones, 77

hunger regulation, 349, *350*

illustrations of, *69, 71, 79*

sexual orientation, 365, *365*

Hypothesis clear predictive statement, 25, *25*

Hysteria, *468*

Hz (Hertz), 108

IAT (implicit association test) procedure of inferring prejudices or other attitudes by measuring reactions to combinations of categories, 414–415

Id according to Freud, the aspect of mental activity dominated by sexual and other biological drives, 450

Ideal self image people have of what they would like to be, 452, 455

Identity

and sexual development, 360–361

vs. role confusion, *159*

Identity achievement outcome of having explored various possible identities and then making one's own decisions, 163

Identity crisis adolescent's concerns with the future and the quest for self-understanding, 162

Identity development, 159, 162–163

Identity diffusion state of not having given serious thought to making decisions and having no clear sense of identity, 163

Identity foreclosure state of accepting decisions without much thought, 163

Identity moratorium state of considering the issues but not yet making decisions, 163

Idiographic approach intensive studies of individuals, 458

Illusory correlation an apparent relationship based on casual observations of unrelated or weakly related events, 38–39

Imitation, *205*, 454

Immune system, 500

Impaired hearing, 109–110

Implicit association test (IAT) procedure of inferring prejudices or other attitudes by measuring reactions to combinations of categories, 414–415

Implicit memory (or **indirect memory**) influence of an experience on what you say or do even though you might not be aware of the influence, 212–213, *213*

Implicit personality test procedure that measures personality based on changes in behavior, rather than a self-report, 471–472

Impossible events, 148, *149*

Incentive theories, 338, *338*

Incentives stimuli that pull us toward an action, 338

Independent variable item that an experimenter controls, 40

Indicated program, 518

Indifferent or uninvolved parents those who spend little time with their children and do little more than provide them with food and shelter, 172

Indirect influences, 88–89

Indirect memory (or **implicit memory**) influence of an experience on what you say or do even though you might not be aware of the influence, 212–213

Individual psychology study of the person as a whole rather than parts ("indivisible psychology"), 453–454

Individualistic cultures, 170, 438

Individuals with Disabilities Education Act (IDEA), 294

Induced movement incorrect perception that an object is moving, when in fact the background moves, 130

Industrial/organizational (I/O) psychology psychological study of people at work, 7–8, *12*

Industry vs. inferiority, *159*

Infancy

cognitive development, 144–147

hearing, 145–146

learning and memory, 146–147

social and emotional development in, 160–161

vision, *144*, 144–145

Infantile amnesia (or **childhood amnesia**) scarcity of early episodic memories, 240–241, *241*

Infectious diseases, and IQ, *290*

Inference, 229

Inferential statistics statements about large population based on an inferences from a smaller sample, 44–45

Inferiority complex exaggerated feeling of weakness, inadequacy, and helplessness, 453

Inflammation, 500

Information-processing model theory that information entering memory is processed, coded, and stored, 215–218, *216*

Informed consent statement by a participant that he or she has been told what to expect and now agrees to continue, 46, 440

Inhibitory messages, 59

Initiative vs. guilt, *159*

Inoculation effect tendency for people who reject a weak argument to then be disposed to resist a stronger argument suggesting the same conclusion, 428

Inoculation small-scale preview of an upcoming experience, 398

Insanity defense, 519–520

Insomnia consistently not getting enough sleep to feel rested the next day, 321–322

Institutional Review Board (IRB) group that reviews the ethics of an experimental procedure, 46

Instrumental conditioning, 191

Insulin hormone that helps glucose and several other nutrients enter the cells, 348–349, *349*

Intellectual abilities, and gender, 168, *169*

Intelligence

brain size and, 291

definition of, 283–286

evaluation of intelligence tests, 293–302

hierarchical models of, 285

individual differences in IQ scores, 288–291

measurement of, 19

multiple intelligences, 285–286

psychometric approach, 283–284

testing, 286–288

Intelligence quotient (IQ) tests procedures that try to predict people's performance in school and similar settings, 286–288

adopted children, 289–290

bias in, 299–302, *301*

distribution of scores, 293–294

environmental influences and interventions, 290

evaluation of, 293–302

family resemblances, 289

Flynn effect, 295–296

gene identification, 290

individual differences in, 288–291

intelligence quotient (IQ), 286

interpretation of fluctuations in scores, 298

reliability, 296, *296*

standardization, 293–296

Stanford-Binet IQ test, 286–287, *287*, 293

twins and single births, 289

validity, 297–298, 382

Wechsler tests, 287–288, 293

Interference, 233–234, *234*

Intermittent reinforcement (or **partial reinforcement**) procedure of reinforcing some responses and not others, 197

Internal attributions explanations of behaviors based on someone's attitudes, personality, abilities, or other characteristics, 417

International Statistical Classification of Diseases and Related Health Problems **tenth edition (ICD-10)** book that sets criteria for each psychiatric diagnosis, 482

Internet dating services, 433–434

Interpersonal attraction

dating and modern technology, 433–434

equity principle, 432

marriage and long-term commitments, 434–435

relationships, establishment of, 431–434

similarity, 431

Interpersonal influence

conformity, 436–438, *437*

group decision making, 442

obedience to authority, 438–441

Interposition, 131

Interpretation of Dreams, The (Freud), 16

e drug that can
red as a substitute
er opiates, 65,
7
Methamphetamine, 63
Method of loci mnemonic
device in which you first
memorize a series of
places, and then you use
a vivid image to associate
each location with
something you want to
remember, 227, *228*
Methyl groups, 85
Methylphenidate, 63–64,
67, 250
Metzler, Jacqueline, 245–246
Microexpressions sudden,
brief emotional
expressions, 371
Midlife transition period of
reassessing goals, setting
new ones, and preparing
for the rest of life,
163–164
Milgram, Stanley, 438–441
Milgram experiment,
438–441, *439, 440*
Military psychologist
specialist who provides
services to the military, 8
Miller, George, 217
Mind–brain problem
philosophical question of
how experience relates to
the brain, 5
Minimal stimuli, 121–124
Minimally conscious state
stage of emergence from
a coma in which people
have brief periods of
purposeful actions and
speech comprehension,
310
**Minnesota Multiphasic
Personality Inventory
(MMPI)** test consisting
of true–false questions
intended to measure
personality dimensions
that relate clinical
conditions, 468–469
Minority influence, 427, *427*
Mirror neurons cells
found in several brain
areas but especially
the frontal cortex that
are active when you
make a movement and
also when you watch
someone else make a
similar movement, 73
MMPI-2 second edition of
MMPI, *468*, 468–469
**MMPI (Minnesota
Multiphasic Personality
Inventory)** test
consisting of true–false
questions intended to
measure personality
dimensions that relate
clinical conditions,
468–469
M'Naghten rule principle
that, to be regarded
as insane in a court of
law, people must be so
disordered that they do
not understand what
they are doing, 519–520

Mnemonic device memory
aid based on encoding
items in a special way,
227, 227–228
Mode score that occurs most
frequently, 44
Modeling and imitation,
204–205
Molaison, Henry, *238*, 238–
239, 240
Monarchic theory of
intelligence, 283–284
Monism view that conscious
experience is inseparable
from the physical brain,
5, *69*
**Monoamine oxidase
inhibitors (MAOIs)**
drugs that block the
metabolic breakdown
of dopamine,
norepinephrine, and
serotonin, 501, *501*
Monocular cues
information about depth
that one can infer with
even one eye, 131, *131*
Monosodium glutamate
(MSG), 116
Monozygotic twins those
who develop from the
a single fertilized egg
(zygote) and therefore
have identical genes,
87, *88*
Moon illusion tendency to
perceive the moon at the
horizon as larger than
when it is higher in the
sky, 134–135
Moral reasoning, and
emotions, 380–381
Morality, logic vs. emotion,
405
Moray House Test, 297
Morgan, Christiana, 471
Morimura, Yasumasa,
461
Morning people, 316
Morpheme unit of meaning,
274–275, *275*
Morphine, 65, *67*, 114, *187*,
497
Moscovitch, Morris, 239
Motion blind, 71
Motion parallax tendency
for the images of close
objects to move faster
across the retina than
those of distant object do
as you travel, 131
Motion perception, 71
Motivation process
that determines the
reinforcement value of
an outcome
for addictive behavior,
494
conflicting, 338–340
hunger, 348–354
sexual motivation,
356–365
views of, 337–338, *338*
work motivation, 337–346
Motor nerves, 77
Motor neurons, *56*
Movement, perception of,
129–130
MSG (monosodium
glutamate), 116

Multiculturalism accepting,
recognizing, and
enjoying the differences
among groups and the
unique contributions
that each people can
offer, 416
Multiple intelligences
independent forms of
intelligence, 285–286
Multiple personality, 504
Multiplier effect tendency
for a small initial
advantage in some
behavior, possibly
genetic in origin, to
increase because the
environment recognizes
that advantage and
nurtures it, 89
Munch, Edvard, *479*
Murray, Henry, 471
Myelin insulating sheath
that speeds up the
transmission of impulses
along an axon, 55
**Myers–Briggs Type
Indicator (MBTI)** test
of normal personality,
loosely based on Carl
Jung's theories, 469–470
Myopia, *99*

n-back task procedure in
which someone hears a
list of letters or numbers
and responds not to the
current item but to the
one *n* items previously,
219
NA (Narcotics Anonymous),
496
Narcissistic personality
disorder, *483*
Narcolepsy condition
marked by sudden
attacks of sleepiness
during the day, 322
Narcotics Anonymous (NA),
496
Narcotics drugs that
produce drowsiness,
insensitivity to
pain, and decreased
responsiveness, 65, *67*
Native Americans, 351, *351*
Natural selection, 90
Naturalistic observation
careful examination of
what happens under
more or less natural
conditions, 35, *40*
Nature–nurture issue
question of how
differences in behavior
relate to differences
in heredity and
environment, 5–6
Near transfer benefit to a
skill from practicing a
similar skill, 263–264
Necker cube, 127, *127*
Negative afterimages
experiences of one color
after the removal of
another, 103
Negative reinforcement
increasing the probability
of a behavior by having
it avoid something; also

known as *escape learning*
or *avoidance learning*,
193, *194*
Negative symptoms
behaviors notable for
their absence instead of
their presence, 504
Neighborhood
improvement, 518
Neo-Freudians
psychologists who kept
parts of Freud's theory
while modifying others,
452
**NEO PI-R (NEO Personality
Inventory-Revised)**
test that designed to
measure neuroticism,
extraversion, openness,
agreeableness, and
conscientiousness, 469
Nerve deafness hearing
impairment resulting
from damage to the
cochlea, hair cells, or
auditory nerves, 109
Nervous system cells, 55
Neurocognitive theory, 325
**Neurodevelopmental
hypothesis** idea that
schizophrenia originates
with nervous system
impairments that
develop before birth
or in early childhood,
influenced by either
genetics or early
environment, especially
prenatal environment,
506–507
Neurons brain that receive
information and convey
it to other cells, *56*
action potential, 55–57,
57, 59, 125
nervous system cells, 55
synapses, *58*, 58–60
Neuroscience, 20
Neurotransmitter chemical
that activates receptors
on another cell
and antidepressants,
501, *501*
and behavior, 60
definition of, 58
overview of, *61*
Nicotine, 67
Night terror condition
that causes someone to
awaken screaming and
sweating with a racing
heart rate, sometimes
flailing with the arms and
pounding the walls, 323
Nightmares, 323
**95 percent confidence
interval** range within
which the true
population mean
probably lies, with 95
percent certainty, 45, *45*
Nitric oxide, *61*
Nobel Peace Prize, *17*, 180,
227, 257
Nomothetic approach
study that seeks general
principles of personality,
458
Nonhumans, ethical
concerns in research, 47

Nontraditional families,
173–174
Nonvisual senses
chemical senses, 115–118
cutaneous senses, 112–
114, *113*
hearing, 108–111
vestibular sense, 111–112
Norepinephrine, *61*, 501, *501*
Normal distribution
(or **normal curve**)
symmetrical frequency
of scores clustered
around the mean, 43–44,
293–294, *294*
Norms description of how
frequently various scores
occur, 293
Nostradamus, 29, *29*
Note taking, 226
Nucleus, *84*
Nucleus accumbens, 493–
494, *494*
Nudges acts intended to
encourage beneficial
actions, without using
significant rewards of
penalties, 426

Obedience to authority,
438–441
Obesity excessive
accumulation of body fat,
351, 351–352
Object permanence idea
that objects continue to
exist even when we do
not see or hear them,
148–149, *149*
Object size, 131
Objective personality test,
468–469
O'Brien, Dominic, 211
Observational research
designs
case history, 35, *40*
comparison of, *40*
correlational studies,
37–40, *40*
naturalistic observation,
35, *40*
surveys, 35–37, *40*
Obsession repetitive,
unwelcome stream of
thought, 490–491
**Obsessive-compulsive
disorder (OCD)**
disorder characterized
by repetitive unwelcome
stream of thought
and repetitive, almost
irresistible urges to an
action
and anorexia nervosa,
353
distrusting memory, 491
prevalence, 490
therapies, 491
Obsessive-compulsive
personality disorder, *483*
Occam, William of, 27
Occam's razor, 27
Occipital cortex, *125*
Occipital lobe area at
the rear of the head,
specialized for vision,
70, *70*
Odbert, H. S., 460
Oedipus complex according
to Freud, a period

when a boy develops a sexual interest in his mother and competitive aggression toward his father, 448

Offender profiling, 472–474, *474*

Old age, 165

Olfaction sense of smell, 116–118, *117*

Olfactory bulb, *71*, *117*

Olfactory nerve, *117*

Open-mindedness, 27

Openness to experience tendency to enjoy new intellectual experiences and new ideas, 461, *461*

Operant-conditioning chamber, 195, *195*

Operant conditioning (or instrumental conditioning) process of changing behavior by providing a reinforcer or punishment after a response, 195

applications of, 198–199

categories of reinforcement and punishment, 193–194, *194*

classical conditioning vs., *199*

definition of, 191

primary and secondary reinforcers, 192

punishment, 192–193, *193*–194

reinforcement, *192*, 192–194

schedules of reinforcement, *197*, 197–198

Skinner and shaping of responses, 195–198

Thorndike on, 190–191

Operational definition specification of the operations (or procedures) used to produce or measure something; if possible giving it a numerical value, 33

Operations reversible mental processes, 150

Opiate dependence, 497, *497*

Opiates either natural drugs derived from the opium poppy or synthetic drugs with a chemical structure resembling natural opiates, 65, *115*

Opponent-process theory idea that we perceive color in terms of paired opposites—red versus green, yellow versus blue, and white versus black, 103

Optic chiasm, 101, *101*

Optic nerve set of axons from the ganglion cells, which turns around and exits the eye, 98, 101, *101*

Optical illusions misinterpretation of a visual stimulus, *132–133*, 132–135

Oral stage psychosexual stage when infants derive intense pleasure from stimulation of the mouth, particularly while sucking at the mother's breast, 449, *449*

Orexin, 322

Orgasm. *See* Sexual motivation

Orne, Martin, 42

Otolith organs, 112, *112*

Otoliths, 112, *112*

Overconfidence, 259

Owls, 98, *99*

Oxytocin hormone released by women when nursing a baby and by both men and women during sexual activity, 79–80, 359

p < 0.05 statement that the probability that randomly generated results would resemble the observed results is less than 5 percent, 44

p-hacking analyzing the data one way after another to find a way that is statistically significant, 45

Pacinian corpuscle, *113*

Pain, 112–113

Pancreas, *79*

Panic disorder (PD) disorder characterized by frequent anxiety and occasional attacks of panic—rapid breathing, increased heart rate, chest pains, sweating, faintness, and trembling, 486

Paranoia, *468*

Parasympathetic nervous system neurons whose axons extend from the medulla and the lower part of the spinal cord to neuron clusters near the organs; it decreases the heart rate and promotes digestion and other nonemergency functions, *77*, *78*, 372

Parathyroid, *79*

Parental conflict, 174

Parenthood and happiness, 389

Parenting styles, 173

Parietal cortex, *330*

Parietal lobe area just anterior (forward) from the occipital lobe specialized for the body senses, including touch, pain, temperature, and awareness of the location of body parts in space, *70*, 72

Parkinson's disease condition marked by difficulty in initiating voluntary movement, slow movement, tremors, rigidity, and depressed mood, 60

Parsimony principle that we try to explain something

in the simplest possible way, avoiding new or unnecessary assumptions, 27–30

Passionate love type of love marked with sexual desire and excitement, 434

Pattern recognition, 263, *263–264*

Patterns, perceiving and recognizing, 124–128

Pavlov, Ivan P., *17*, 180–184, 184

Pavlovian conditioning, 180. *See also* **Classical conditioning**

Pay scale, 345

PCP (phencyclidine), *67*

PD (panic disorder), 486

Pearl Harbor attack, 442

Pearson, Lucy, *193*

Peptide transmitters, 59

Perceived intensity, *17*

Perception interpretation of sensory information, 96. *See also* **Sensation**

Periodic limb movement disorder prolonged "creepy-crawly" sensations in one's legs, accompanied by strong, repetitive leg movements, 323

Peripheral nervous system nerves connecting the spinal cord with the rest of the body, 69, *69*

Peripheral route to persuasion attitude change based mostly on emotions instead of information or logic, 424

Permissive parents those who are warm and loving but undemanding, 172

Perpetual motion machine, 27, *28*, 255

Persecution, delusion of, 505

Persistent vegetative state, 310, *310*

Person-centered therapy treatment in which the therapist listens to the client with total acceptance and unconditional positive regard, 515, *517*

Persona, 452

Personal fable conviction that "I am special—what is true for everyone else is not true for me.", 163

Personality set of ways in which people differ from one another in their interests, attitudes, and social behaviors, 467–474

definition of, 447

origins of, 462–464

psychodynamic theory, 447–452

structure of, 450

theories of, 447–456

traits, 458–464

Personality assessment

implicit personality tests, 471–472

introduction to, 467

Minnesota Multiphasic Personality Inventory (MMPI), 468–469

Myers-Briggs Type Indicator (MBTI), 469–470

NEO PI-R (NEO personality inventory-revised), 469

objective personality test, 468–469

offender profiling, 472–474, *474*

projective techniques, 470–471

standardized tests, 468

uses and misuses of, 472, *472*

Personality disorder maladaptive, inflexible way of dealing with the environment and other people, 481–482, *483*

Personality psychologist, *12*

Personality theories

collective unconscious, 452

humanistic psychology, 454–456

individual psychology, 453–454

learning approach, 454

neo-Freudians, 452

psychodynamic theory, 447–452

self-actualization, 455–456

unconditional positive regard, 455

Personality traits

Big Five model of personality, 460–461, *461*

issues in personality measurement, 459

origins of, 462–464

search for broad traits, 458–460

and states, 458

Persuasion, 198–199

attitude change and, 424–428

coercive persuasion, 428

resistance to, 427–428

Pessimistic explanatory style, 502

PET (positron-emission tomography) device that records radioactivity of various brain areas emitted from injected chemicals, 5, *5*, 75, 76, 376, *376*

Peterson, Lloyd, 218

Peterson, Margaret, 218

Peyote, 64

Pfungst, Oskar, 28

Phallic stage psychosexual stage during which children begin to play with their genitals, *449*, 449–450

Phantom limb continuing pain or sensations in a limb after it has been amputated, 114–115, *115*

Phencyclidine (PCP/angel dust), *67*, 508

Phenylalanine, 89

Phenylketonuria (PKU) inherited condition that,

if untreated, impairs brain development, 89

Phobia fear that interferes with normal living, 486

acquiring, 487–488

common phobias, 488–489

prevalence, 487

treatment for, 489–490

Phoneme unit of sound, such as *s* or *sh*, 274, *275*

Physical attractiveness, 432–433

Physical dependence condition characterized by withdrawal symptoms when one abstains from a drug, 494

Physical intensity, *17*

Physical punishment, and behavioral problems, 193

Physiological measures of emotion, 372

Physiological needs, *339*

PI3 kinase, 360

Piaget, Jean

on cognitive development in infancy, 147–148

preoperational stage, 148, 150–154, *155*

sensorimotor state, 148–149, *155*

stages of concrete operations and formal operations, 148, 154–156, *155*

summary of stages of development, *155*

vs. Vygotsky's views, 155–156

Pima people, 351, *351*

Pineal gland, *79*, 318

Pinker, Steven, 409

Pinna, 108

Pitch perception, 110–111

Pitch perception closely related to frequency of a sound, 108

Pituitary gland, *69*, 77, *79*

PKU (phenylketonuria) inherited condition that, if untreated, impairs brain development, 89

Place principle principle that the highest frequency sounds vibrate hair cells near the stirrup end, and lower frequency sounds vibrate hair cells at points farther along the membrane, 110

Placebo pill with no known pharmacological effects, 38, 40, 113, *502*

Plasticity change as a result of experience, 78–79

Plateau stage, 359

Pluralistic ignorance situation in which each person falsely assumes that others have a better-informed opinion, 408

Polarization, 442

Polgar, Judit, *262*

Polygraph machine that records sympathetic nervous system arousal as measured by blood pressure, heart rate,

Rationalization defense mechanisms in which people try to show that their actions are justifiable, 450–451

Raven, John C., 288, *288*, 295

Reaction formation defense mechanisms in which people present themselves as opposite of what they really are, 451

Readiness potential motor cortex activity prior to the start of a movement, 311, *311, 312*

Reading
eye movements, 277
and language, 274–277
word recognition, 275–276

Real self, 452

Realistic goals, 340–341

Reality vs. appearance, 152, *153*

Reappraisal reinterpreting a stressful situation to make it seem less threatening, 397, 398–399

Recall, *213*

Recency effect tendency to remember the final items in a list, 223–224

Receptors specialized cells that convert environmental energies into activities of the nervous system, 97, *115*, 117

Recessive gene whose effects appear only if the dominant gene is absent, 84

Reciprocation, 425

Recognition method of testing memory by asking someone to choose the correct item among options, 212, *213*, 214–215

Reconsolidation, 400

Reconstruction assembling an account of an event based partly on distinct memories and partly by inferring what else must have happened, 229

Recovered memories reports of long-lost memories, prompted by clinical techniques, 234–238

Red-green deficiency, 85, *86*

Reductionism, 454

Reference, delusion of, 505

Reflex rapid, automatic response to a stimulus, 77

Regeneration, 100

Regression return to a more immature level of functioning, 451

Reinforcement process of increasing the future probability of a response that is followed by a positive consequence, 190, *192*, 192–194, *197*, 197–198

Relationships, establishment of, 431–434

Relaxation, 399–400

Relearning method (or savings method) detecting of weak memories by comparing the speed of original learning to the speed of relearning, 212, *213*

Reliability repeatability of a test's scores, 296, *296*, 382

REM behavior disorder, 320

REM (rapid eye movement) sleep stage of sleep during which the sleeper's eyes move rapidly back and forth under the closed lids, 319–320, *322–323*, 499, *499*

Replicability, 26, 31, 45–46

Replicable results those that anyone can obtain, at least approximately, by following the same procedures, 26

Representative sample set of individuals that resembles the population, 34, *35*

Representativeness heuristic assumption that an item that resembles members of a category is probably also in that category, 256, 257–258

Repression process of moving an unacceptable memory or impulse from the conscious mind to the unconscious mind, 235, 240, 450

Research
cohort effects, 142, *143*, 358
cross-sectional study, 141–142, *142*
designs for studying development, 141–142, *142*
ethical considerations, 46–47
experiments, 40–43
general principles, 33–35
longitudinal study, 141–142, *142*
observational research designs, 35–40
replicability issues, 31, 45–46
results, evaluation of, 43–46
statistical calculations, 50–52

Resilience ability to handle difficult situations with a minimum of distress, 400

Resistance stage, 395

Resistance to persuasion, 427–428

Resolution stage, 359

Responsibility toward others, 407–408

Resting potential electrical polarization across the membrane of an axon, 57

Retina layer of visual receptors covering the back surface of the eyeball, 98, *98, 99, 101*

Retinal disparity difference in the apparent position of an object as seen by the left and right retinas, 131

Retinaldehydes, 100

Retinex theory idea that the cerebral cortex compares the patterns of light coming from different parts of the retina and synthesizes a color perception for each area, 104–105

Retrieval, 228–230, 233–234

Retrieval cues reminders to prompt one's memory, 225, *225*

Retroactive interference tendency for new memories to interfere with older memories, 234

Retrograde amnesia loss of memory for events that occurred before brain damage, 238, *238*

Reuptake, 60

Reversible figures items that can be perceived in more than one way, 127, *127*

Richter, Curt, 353

Risk-taking behavior, 162, *163*

Ritalin, 63–64, 67, 250

Rods visual receptors adapted for vision in dim light, 98, 98–99, *99*, 100

Rogers, Carl, 447, *447*, 455

Rohypnol (flunitrazepam), 65, *67*

Roosevelt, Franklin, 36

Rorschach, Hermann, 470

Rorschach inkblots technique based on people's interpretations of 10 ambiguous inkblots, 470, *470*

Rosch, Eleanor, 251

Ross, Dorothea, 205

Ross, Sheila, 205

Rousseau, Jean-Jacques, 447, *447*

Ruffini ending, *113*

Running amok, 480–481

s specific intellectual ability, *283*

Saccades quick eye movements from one fixation point to another, 71, 277

SAD (seasonal affective disorder) disorder in which someone repeatedly becomes depressed during a particular season of the year, 500

Sadness, 378, *378*, 380, 391

Safety needs, *339*

Sampling, *35*, 35–36

SAT (Scholastic Assessment Test), 51, 298, 300, *300*

Satiety, physiology of, 348–350

Satisficing searching choices only until you find something satisfactory, 256–257

Savings method (or relearning method) detecting of weak memories by comparing the speed of original learning to the speed of relearning, 212, *213*

Scaffolding, 156

Scatter plot representation in which each dot represents a given individual, with one measurement for that individual on the *x*-axis (horizontal) and another measurement on the *y*-axis (vertical), 38, *38*

Schachter, Stanley, 374–375

Schachter and Singer's theory of emotions proposal that the physiological state determines the intensity of the emotion, but a cognitive appraisal of the situation identifies the type of emotion, 374–375, *375*

Schedule of reinforcement rule for the delivery of reinforcement, *197*, 197–198

Schema organized way of interacting with objects, 147

Schizophrenia disorder characterized by prolonged deterioration of daily activities, and some combination of the following: hallucinations, delusions, disorganized speech and thought, movement disorder, and loss of normal emotional responses and social behaviors, 507
causes, 505–507
definition of, 504
delusions, 505
disordered speech and thought, 505
genetics and family background, *506*
hallucinations, 505
MMPI-2 clinical scales, 468
prevalence, 505
therapies, *507*, 507–508

Schizotypal personality disorder, *483*

Scholastic Assessment Test (SAT), 51

School psychologists specialists in the psychological condition of students, 8, *12*

Scientific-management approach (also known as **Theory X**) view that most employees are lazy, indifferent, and uncreative, and that the job should be made simple and foolproof, 344, *344*

Scientific method
critical thinking, 25–31, 259
evaluation of evidence, 25–31

gathering evidence, 25–26
hypothesis, 25, *25*
interpretation, 26
method, 25–26
replicability, 26, 31, 45–46
results, 26

Scientific theories
burden of proof, 26–27
evaluation of, 26–30
parsimony, 27–30

SCN (suprachiasmatic nucleus), 318, *318*

SD (standard deviation) a measurement of the amount of variation among scores in a distribution, 45, *50*, 50–51, *51*, 293, *293*

Season-of-birth effect tendency for people born in the winter or early spring to be slightly more likely than average to develop schizophrenia, 506

Seasonal affective disorder (SAD) disorder in which someone repeatedly becomes depressed during a particular season of the year, 500

Second-generation antipsychotic drugs medications that relieve schizophrenia while causing less risk of tardive dyskinesia, 508

Secondary reinforcers reinforcers that becoming reinforcing by association with something else, 192

Securely attached, 160

SEL (social and emotional learning programs), 518

Selective attrition tendency of certain kinds of people to drop out of a study, 141

Selective program, 518

Selective serotonin reuptake inhibitors (SSRIs) drugs that block reuptake of only serotonin, 501, *501*

Self-actualization becoming everything you are capable of being, to fulfill your potential, 339, 455–456

Self-concept image people have of what they really are, 455

Self-efficacy expectation of being able to perform a task successfully, 206

Self-esteem evaluation of one's own abilities, performance, and worth, 352, 409, 459–460

Self-fulfilling prophecies expectations that increase the probability of the predicted event, 413

Self-handicapping strategies acts to put oneself at a disadvantage to provide an excuse for a failure, 420

thereby supporting an unfavorable stereotype about their group, 300–302

Still-Face Paradigm procedure in which a parent plays with a child and then suddenly shifts to an unresponsive, expressionless face, 160

Stimulants drugs that increase energy, alertness, and activity, 63–64, *67*

Stimuli energies from the world that affect us in some way, 97

Stimulus control ability of a stimulus to encourage some responses and discourage others, 194

Stimulus generalization extension of a conditioned response from the training stimulus to similar stimuli, 183–184, *184*, 194, *195*

Stirrup, 109, *109*

Stop-signal task procedure in which a person responds as quickly as possible to a signal but inhibits the response if a second signal appears quickly after it, 250

Storage of memory, 228

Story reconstruction, 229

Strange Situation procedure in which a mother and her infant come into a room with many toys, and then both the mother and a stranger periodically come and go, 160

Stress nonspecific response of the body to any demand made upon it anxiety disorders, 486 coping with, 397–400 definition of, 394 depression, 500 effect of on health, 396–397 heart disease, 396–397 measurement of, 395 obesity, *351*, 352 overview of, 394–395 post-traumatic stress disorder (PTSD), 386, 397 resilience, 400 Selye's concept of, 394–395

Stressful experience, forgetting of, 400–401

Striving for superiority desire to seek personal excellence and fulfillment, 453

Stroboscopic movement illusion of movement created by a rapid succession of stationary images, 130

Stroop effect tendency to read a word instead of saying the color of ink in which it is printed, 248, *248*

Structuralism attempt to describe the structures that compose the mind, 16–17

Studying, organization of, 225–227

Subcortical areas, 77

Subjective well-being self-evaluation of one's life as pleasant, interesting, satisfying, and meaningful, 388

Sublimation transformation of sexual or aggressive energies into culturally acceptable, even admirable, behaviors, 451

Subliminal messages, 123

Subliminal perception influence by a stimulus presented so faintly or briefly that the observer does not consciously perceive it, 123–124

Substance dependence (addiction), 493–494

Substance-related disorders alcoholism, 202, 495–497 opiate dependence, 497, *497* substance dependence (addiction), 493–494

Substance use disorder inability to quit a self-destructive habit, 493

Suggestion, and memory, 235–237, *236*

Sunk cost effect willingness to do something because of money or effort already spent, 261

Superego memory of rules and prohibitions we learned from our parents and others, 450

Suppressed stimulus, 309

Suprachiasmatic nucleus (SCN), 318, *318*

Surface structure, *268*

Survey a study of the prevalence of certain beliefs, attitudes, or behaviors based on people's responses to questions overview of, *40* sampling, 35–36 seriousness of those responding, 36 surveyor biases, 37 wording the questions, 36, *37*

Surveyor biases, 37

Suspect lineups, 214–215

Sydney Opera House, 340–341, *341*

Sympathetic nervous system chains of neuron clusters just to the left and right of the spinal cord that arouse the body for vigorous action, 77, 78, 372

Synapse specialized junction between one neuron and another, 58, 58–60

Synaptic cleft, *59*

Synesthesia condition in which a stimulus of one type, such as sound, also elicits another experience, such as color, 118–119

Systematic desensitization method of gradually exposing people to the object of their fear, 489–490

Tablas, *64*

Tabletop illusion, 133, *134*

Tarasoff **case** California case that ruled that a therapist who has reason to believe that a client is dangerous to someone must warn the endangered person or take other steps to prevent harm, 519

Tardive dyskinesia condition characterized by tremors and involuntary movements, 508

Taste sense that detects chemicals on the tongue, 115–116

Taste buds receptors located in the folds on the surface of the tongue, 115–116, *116*

Taste preferences, 9–10

Taste receptors, 116

TAT (Thematic Apperception Test) projective personality technique in which a person is asked to make up a story for each picture, describing what events led up to this scene, what is happening now, and what will happen in the future, *471*

Technology, and dating, 433–434

Temperament child's tendency to be active or inactive, and to respond vigorously or quietly to new stimuli, 160

Temporal lobe area located toward the sides of the head; the main area for hearing and certain aspects of vision, *70*, 71–72

Temptation, 342–343

Teosinte, *90*

Terminal bouton presynaptic ending, 58, *58, 59*

Terror-management theory idea that we cope with our fear of death by avoiding thoughts about death and by affirming a worldview that provides self-esteem, hope, and value in life, 165

Test-retest reliability correlation between scores on a first test and a retest, 296

Test taking, 226–227

Testis, *79*

Testosterone hormone present in higher quantities in males than in females, 360, 364

Tetlock, Philip, 259

Texture gradient, 131

Thalamus, *69, 71*, 77

That's-not-all technique persuasive technique in which someone makes an offer and then improves the offer before you have a chance to reply, 425–426

THC (tetrahydrocannabinol), 66

Thematic Apperception Test (TAT) projective personality technique in which a person is asked to make up a story for each picture, describing what events led up to this scene, what is happening now, and what will happen in the future, *471*

Theory explanation or model that fits many observations and makes accurate predictions, 26

Theory of mind belief that other people have a mind, too, and that each person knows some things that other people don't know, 151–152, *152*

Thorndike, Edward L., *17*, 190–191

Threshold, 57

Thyroid gland, *79*

Tickle, 112

Timbre tone complexity, 108

Titchener, Edward, 16–17

Tobacco, 64

Toilet training, 514, *514*

Tolstoy, Leo, 490

Tombaugh, Clyde, 130

Tone-deaf, 111

Top-down process application of experience and expectations to interpret sensory experiences, 126, 246

Torture, 428

Touch perceptions, 57

Touch sensations, 72

Toxins, 518

Traditional Chinese philosophy, 479, *480*

Trait consistent tendency in behavior, such as shyness, hostility, or talkativeness, 458–464

Trait approach to personality belief that people have reasonably consistent behavioral characteristics, 458–460

Tranquilizers (or **anxiolytic drugs**) drugs that help people relax, 65

Transactional leader someone who tries to make an organization more efficient at doing what it is already doing by providing rewards (mainly pay) for effective work, 346

Transference applying to a therapist the behaviors and feelings a person originally established toward their father, mother, or other important person, 451, 513

Transformational grammar system for converting a deep structure into a surface structure, 268, *268*

Transformational leader someone who articulates a vision of the future, intellectually stimulates subordinates, and motivates them to use their imagination to advance the organization, 346

Traumatic memories, 235

Treatments abnormal behavior, 512–520 alcoholism, 496–497 depression, 501–503 major depression, 501–503 phobias, 489–490 psychotherapy, 512–517

Trichromatic theory (or **Young-Helmholtz theory**) theory that color vision depends on the relative rate of response of three types of cones, *102*, 102–103

Tricyclic drugs medications that interfere with axon's ability to reabsorb the neurotransmitters dopamine, norepinephrine, and serotonin after releasing them, 501, *501*

Trolley Dilemma, 380

Trust vs. mistrust, 159, *159*

Tubman, Harriet, *455*

Turing, Alan, 282

Tversky, D. Amos, *260*

Twin studies autism spectrum disorder, 508 estimating heritability, 86–88 happiness, 389 intelligence quotient (IQ), 289 obesity, 351 obsessive-compulsive disorder (OCD), 490 parenting styles, effects of, 172 personality origins, 462, *462* schizophrenia, 505–506, *507* sexual orientation, 363, *364*

2-AG, *61*, 66

Type 1 processing system used for tasks that are easy or that appear to be easy, 256

Type 2 processing system used for mathematical calculations and anything else that requires attention and effort, 256